WordPerfect® Bible

Susan Baake Kelly

SAMS

A Division of Macmillan Computer Publishing

11711 North College, Carmel, Indiana 46032 USA

FIRST EDITION
THIRD PRINTING—1991

International Standard Book Number: 0-672-22746-0
Library of Congress Catalog Card Number: 90-63274

Contributing Author: *Joe Kraynak*
Product Manager: *Marie Butler-Knight*
Acquisitions Editor: *Scott Arant*
Development Editor: *Stephen R. Poland*
Manuscript Editor: *Linda Hawkins*
Cover Design: *Tim Amrhein*
Book Design: *Scott Cook*
Illustrator: *Tami Hughes*
Production Assistance: *Jeff Baker, Claudia Bell, Scott Boucher, Brad Chinn , Martin Coleman, Scott Cook, Joelynn Gifford, Sandy Grieshop, Denny Hager, Betty Kish, Bob LaRoche, Michele Laseau, Sarah Leatherman, Kim Leslie, Matthew Morrill, Lisa Naddy, Howard Peirce, Cindy Phipps, Joe Ramon, Tad Ringo, Louise Shinault, Bruce Steed, Suzanne Tully, Johnna Van Hoose, Mary Beth Wakefield, Lisa Wilson, Christine Young*
Indexer: *Jill D. Bomaster*

To the best friends I've ever had: Mom and Jim, and my father, whose cherished memory is always with me.

"The newest computer can merely compound, at speed, the oldest problem in the relations between human beings, and in the end the communicator will be confronted with the old problem, of what to say and how to say it."

Edward R. Murrow, CBS News

Overview

Table of Contents

5   Search and Replace, *101*

6   The Speller and Thesaurus, *119*

12 Sort and Select, *341*

13 Printing and Fonts, *367*

III Command Reference, *609*

A Installation, *1095*

B Setup, *1113*

Contents by Feature

File Management

Formatting

Styles

Tables

Writer's Tools

Introduction

WordPerfect still amazes me. It seems as though the more I know, the less I know. And I feel as though I should have written an encyclopedia, not a bible. There is so much depth to this program, and so much more to come!

Despite the monumental nature of this project, I can assure you that *we*—so much combined effort was involved in this book that I cannot take all the credit—have tried our best to give you a comprehensive, practical, and readable book, which can serve many objectives: as a tutorial for the novice; as a step-by-step guide to important features such as merge, macros, tables, graphics, and styles; and as a comprehensive reference manual, arranged alphabetically by features and functions. You'll find *WordPerfect Bible* to be an invaluable adviser whether you

Have recently purchased WordPerfect and need to learn just enough to get by, perhaps intending to expand your knowledge as you become familiar with the program's capabilities;

or

Are already comfortable with WordPerfect but would like a reference guide, to help you refresh your memory about features you already know and quickly get up to speed on some of the features you haven't used yet;

or

Are already comfortable with WordPerfect's basics but need a guide to teach you how to use the program's advanced features.

WordPerfect Bible is organized into three major sections —"Refreshing the Basics," "Advanced Features," and "Command Reference"—and two appendixes, "Installation" and "Setup."

Part One, Refreshing the Basics

A tutorial designed to provide you with an overview of WordPerfect's basic features, "Refreshing the Basics" includes six chapters. Among other things, these chapters will teach you how to

- Start WordPerfect and use the menus, keyboard, and mouse.

- Create, edit, format, and print documents.

- Insert and delete text, and restore deleted text.

- Move and copy sentences, paragraphs, pages, or blocked sections of text.

- Format your documents using features such as bold and underline, left/right margins, centering, flush right, and justification.

- Save and retrieve documents.

- Work with the Reveal Codes screen to understand the hidden codes that control formatting.

- Spell check your documents.

- Use WordPerfect's Search features to locate text and codes, and Search/Replace to edit your documents.

- Use WordPerfect's Help menus, and run the on-line Tutorial.

- Exit WordPerfect.

If you are just learning WordPerfect, you will want to read all of the chapters in Part One, preferably in order. If you already know enough about WordPerfect to create, format, and save simple documents such as letters and memos, you can skim the first two chapters and concentrate on the others more carefully.

Part Two, Advanced Features

This section is designed to teach you WordPerfect's advanced features in thirteen chapters, which cover file management; newspaper and parallel columns; printing and fonts; graphics; macros; footnotes and endnotes; styles; outlining and paragraph numbering tools; lists, indexes, and tables of contents; and the Math, Tables, Merge, and Sort and Select features.

Each chapter covers a specific feature and teaches you how to use it step-by-step, with detailed and practical examples. You do not need to read these chapters in any particular order. Like the features themselves, each can stand on its own, and you can pick and choose the ones that suit your needs.

Part Three, Command Reference

The "Command Reference" section is an alphabetical reference guide that you can use to look up nearly any of WordPerfect's features and functions, and obtain enough information to help you understand and use them effectively. Boxed tips, cautions, and notes provide further information to help you use a feature more efficiently and avoid possible problems.

Each entry in this section includes a brief description of the feature or function, presents the keystrokes or menu selections that you'll need to use the feature, and provides a general, step-by-step description of how to use it. Brief examples are also included for many of the features in this section. Although it was not possible to include as much detail for these topics as in the other two sections of the book, you should find enough information here to use each feature effectively. Also, much of this information is supplemented by more comprehensive analysis in the other chapters.

Interim Releases of WordPerfect

WordPerfect Corporation is constantly improving the WordPerfect 5.1 program, and occasionally distributes new releases to those who need or request them. For this reason, you may find that a screen or menu shown in this book does not match yours in every detail. Occasionally, the book will discuss a menu item that was not available in earlier releases. While we have tried to call this to your attention whenever we were aware of it, it would be impossible to inform you of all such differences, especially for future releases. Two different releases of WordPerfect 5.1 were used while writing this book; the most recent version is dated 12/31/90.

If you don't know which release you are using, press the Help key (F3). The release date appears in the upper-right corner of the initial help screen. For more information about interim releases of the program, please contact WordPerfect Corporation in Orem, Utah.

Trademark Acknowledgments

All terms mentioned in this book that are known to be trademarks or service marks are listed below. In addition, terms suspected of being trademarks or service marks have been appropriately capitalized. SAMS cannot attest to the accuracy of this information. Use of a term in this book should not be regarded as affecting the validity of any trademark or service mark.

1-2-3 and Lotus are registered trademarks of Lotus Development Corporation.

AutoCAD is a registered trademark of Autodesk, Inc.

Dr. Halo is a registered trademark of Media Cybernetics, Inc.

Freelance Plus is a registered trademark of Lotus Development Corporation.

GEM Paint is a trademark of Digital Research Inc.

Harvard Graphics is a registered trademark of Software Publishing Corporation.

LaserJet is a trademark of Hewlett-Packard Co.

MacPaint and MacDraw are registered trademarks of Apple Computer, Inc.

Microsoft and Microsoft Windows Paint are registered trademarks of Microsoft Corporation.

Norton Utilities is a trademark of Peter Norton Computing.

PageMaker is a registered trademark of Aldus Corporation.

Quattro is a registered trademark of Borland International.

SuperCalc is a registered trademark of Computer Associates International, Inc.

Acknowledgments

I will always be grateful to Scott Arant for providing me with the initial opportunity to write this book, and to Brad Bunin for his assistance in smoothing the way.

Stephen Poland, my development editor at SAMS, has been nothing but patient, understanding, and knowledgeable. He also demonstrated an unlimited talent for providing encouragement when I thought I couldn't continue.

Linda Hawkins has been a delight to work with, and a valuable contributor to this "reeeeally big book" (as Ed Sullivan would have said). She has many fine qualities, like laughing at my silliest jokes and loving dogs.

Joe Kraynak did a wonderful job on the "Command Reference" section. He proved to be talented and, equally important, understanding and tolerant of my recalcitrant compulsion for perfection. And thanks to Eric Roach, who did the technical review of the Command Reference.

I'd also like to thank Tom Van Deusen for his help with this project. A WordPerfect Certified Instructor who runs a consulting firm specializing in WordPerfect instruction, programming, and consulting (based in the San Francisco Bay Area), Tom contributed invaluable technical advice and expertise.

My cousins Tom and Valerie Baake were inspirational for getting me out of the suburbs and up to the mountains of Siskiyou, and for the ideas, examples, and encouragement they both contributed toward this book.

As always, my husband, Jim, kept me going. He massaged my aching shoulders and neck whenever I asked, brought me pizzas, Chinese food, chocolate, frozen yoghurt, and various other delicacies whenever I was too busy to stop for a meal, and—best of all—inspired all this book's humor, which comes so instinctively to him.

This section would be incomplete without a word of thanks to the thousands of individuals at WordPerfect Corporation who create, develop, support, and continually improve a fine line of products, and who have proven that integrity is compatible with a highly profitable business.

PART ONE

REFRESHING THE BASICS

GETTING STARTED IN WORDPERFECT

Before you can use WordPerfect, you must install it on your computer system. This is a one-time process that copies the WordPerfect Program files from the original disks onto your computer's hard disk or to a set of floppy disks, and lets you set up your printer for use with WordPerfect. WordPerfect comes with an automatic Installation program, which is menu-driven and easy to follow. Since the original WordPerfect files are compressed and saved in a special format, it is actually the only method you can use to install WordPerfect. If you have not yet installed WordPerfect, please turn to Appendix A for complete instructions.

Starting WordPerfect

The method you use to start WordPerfect will vary according to whether or not you have a hard disk, and whether you are using a menu system such as the WordPerfect Shell. If you are using the Shell or another menu system, you start WordPerfect through a menu. If not, you type a DOS command to switch to the correct directory and then type the start-up command, WP. (Instructions are provided in this chapter for starting WordPerfect through the Shell, but there are so many other menu systems, including customized ones, that it would be impossible to include them all here.)

Starting WordPerfect on a Hard Disk

Begin by turning on the computer. After a few moments, you should see a C> prompt, similar to the one shown here:

```
C>
```

This tells you that the operating system, DOS, is running, so you can now start WordPerfect. If you see a menu instead (other than the Shell menu), follow your menu's instructions to start WordPerfect.

Starting WordPerfect from the DOS Prompt

You may be able to start WordPerfect by typing WP (if your AUTOEXEC.BAT file includes a path command that lists the directory containing your WordPerfect 5.1 files or if the WP.EXE file is in the current directory). To see if you can start it this way:

1. Type WP and press Enter.

   If a start-up screen appears briefly, followed by the WordPerfect Edit screen (as shown in Figure 1.1), you have succeeded in starting WordPerfect and can skip the rest of this section. If you see an error message instead, such as:

   ```
   Bad command or file name
   ```

   you must switch to the drive and subdirectory containing the WordPerfect files, as described below.

   If you installed WordPerfect on a drive other than C, such as D or E, switch to that drive now.

2. Type the drive name, followed by a colon, and then press the Enter key. For example, if the drive is D, type D: and press Enter.

   You should see a prompt indicating the current drive, such as:

   ```
   D>
   ```

   Your next step is to switch to the subdirectory containing the WordPerfect files. Usually the subdirectory name will be *WP* or *WP51*. Determine its name and then:

3. Type CD\ followed by the subdirectory name, and press Enter. For example, if your subdirectory is WP51, you'll type CD\WP51, and press Enter.

4. Type the start-up command, WP, and press Enter.

   In a few moments, you will see the WordPerfect Edit screen, as shown in Figure 1.1.

```
                                                    Doc 1 Pg 1 Ln 1" Pos 1"
```

Figure 1.1 *The WordPerfect Edit screen.*

> **Tip:** If you see a message when you start WordPerfect asking if other copies of WordPerfect are currently running, be careful. Unless you are using a network or running another copy of WordPerfect under an environment such as the WordPerfect Shell or Microsoft Windows, type N when you see this message. Otherwise, type Y. If you type Y, this prompt will appear: `Directory is in use. New WP Directory.` In response, you can either enter the name of a different directory or press Cancel (F1) to exit to DOS and then exit the other copy of WordPerfect correctly. You'll learn more about these prompts in the next chapter.

Starting WordPerfect Through the Shell Menu

If the WordPerfect Shell menu appears when you turn on the computer, as shown in Figure 1.2 (your menu options may differ), WordPerfect or WordPerfect 5.1 should be one of the options. To start WordPerfect, skip to step 4 in this section.

If you want to start WordPerfect through the Shell menu, but it did not appear when you started the computer, your next step is to start the Shell. You may be able to start it by typing `Shell` (if your AUTOEXEC.BAT file includes a path command that lists the directory containing your Shell files or if the SHELL.EXE file is in the current diurectory). To try it:

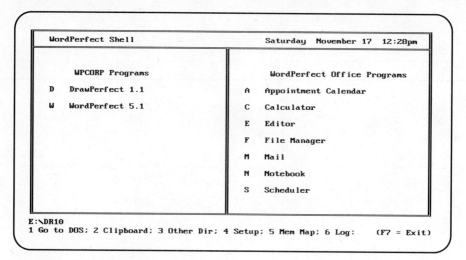

WordPerfect Shell	Saturday November 17 12:28pm

```
         WPCORP Programs                WordPerfect Office Programs

  D    DrawPerfect 1.1            A    Appointment Calendar

  W    WordPerfect 5.1            C    Calculator

                                  E    Editor

                                  F    File Manager

                                  M    Mail

                                  N    Notebook

                                  S    Scheduler


E:\DR10
1 Go to DOS; 2 Clipboard; 3 Other Dir; 4 Setup; 5 Mem Map; 6 Log:     (F7 = Exit)
```

Figure 1.2   *The Shell menu.*

1. Type Shell and press Enter.

   If the Shell menu appears, as shown in Figure 1.2, you can skip to step 4 to start WordPerfect. If you see an error message instead, such as:

   Bad command or file name

   you must switch to the subdirectory containing the Shell files, as described in step 2.

2. Determine the subdirectory name where you copied the Shell files, type CD\ followed by the subdirectory name, and then press Enter. For example, if your subdirectory containing the Shell files is WP51, type CD\WP51, and press Enter.

3. Start the Shell program by typing Shell and then pressing Enter.

   The Shell menu should appear, as shown in Figure 1.2.

4. To start WordPerfect, either press the highlighted letter next to the WordPerfect option on the Shell menu or use the arrow keys to move the cursor bar onto WordPerfect (or WordPerfect 5.1, whichever option is on your menu); then press Enter.

   A start-up screen will appear briefly, and then the WordPerfect Edit screen will appear, as shown in Figure 1.1.

Starting WordPerfect on Floppy Disks

If you don't have a hard disk, you should have followed the installation instructions to copy the WordPerfect Program files onto high-density 5¼-inch floppy diskettes, or 3½-inch disks. If you use 5¼-inch diskettes, you'll need the WordPerfect 1 and WordPerfect 2 diskettes to start WordPerfect. If you use 3½-inch disks, these will be combined on one disk.

The following instructions assume that you want to start WordPerfect from the B drive, so that you can automatically save and retrieve files from the data disk in drive B:

1. Start your computer using a disk containing the DOS system files, to load DOS into your computer's memory.

2. At the DOS A> prompt, insert the WordPerfect 1 diskette into drive A, and a formatted disk to store your files on into drive B.

3. Type B: and press Enter. The B> prompt should appear.

4. Type A:WP and press Enter.

   WordPerfect starts, and after a moment or two, a prompt will appear asking you to insert the WordPerfect 2 diskette.

5. When prompted to insert the WordPerfect 2 diskette, remove the WordPerfect 1 diskette from drive A, and replace it with the WordPerfect 2 diskette; then press Enter.

The start-up screen appears briefly, and then the WordPerfect Edit screen appears, as shown in Figure 1.1.

The WordPerfect Edit Screen

In WordPerfect, you can start typing a new document as soon as the Edit screen appears; unlike many other word processing programs, you don't have to open a file or follow any other steps to begin working on a document. The WordPerfect Edit screen is nearly blank, except for the cursor in the upper-left corner and a single line in the lower-right corner of the screen called the *status line*.

The cursor is a marker that indicates where the next character will appear as you type. On most screens, it appears as a small, blinking dash. In case you find the cursor difficult to see, WordPerfect has included a program called *CURSOR.COM*, which you can use to change its appearance; see *Cursor Appearance* in Part Three, "Command Reference," for more information.

The purpose of the status line is to tell you the current cursor position (its status), including:

Doc: The document number, 1 or 2. WordPerfect provides two separate screens so you can work with two different documents, copying information back and forth between them, using one as a scratch pad, or working from an outline while writing. To switch from one screen to the other, use the Switch key (Shift-F3), or select Switch Document from the pull-down Edit menu.

Pg: The page number, as determined by the size and type of paper you are using, and the top and bottom margins. By default, WordPerfect uses standard 8½" x 11" paper, with margins of 1" on all four sides. Once a page is full, WordPerfect creates a *soft page break*—represented by a dashed line across the screen— and the page number indicator changes to display the new page number. You can force a page to end on any line by pressing Ctrl-Enter; this is called a *hard page break*, and appears as two dashed lines.

Ln: The line number, as measured in inches from the top of the page. When you start WordPerfect or clear the screen to begin typing a new document, the cursor will initially appear on `Ln 1"` to leave an inch of blank space for the top margin in the printed document (although this blank space does not appear on the Edit screen). If you type enough text to reach the right margin, WordPerfect automatically wraps the cursor to the next line, and the line number changes. It also changes when you press Enter to end a paragraph or insert a blank line, or move the cursor up or down through the document.

Pos: The cursor position, in inches, as measured from the left side of the page. Since WordPerfect leaves 1" (each) left and right margins in the printed document, the cursor initially appears at the 1" position (although the blank space for the margin does not appear on the Edit screen). It changes each time you type a character or press the space bar, or move the cursor to the left or right through existing text. The Pos indicator has other functions. For example, it appears in uppercase (POS) when you press the Caps Lock key to type in uppercase, and it blinks on and off when you press the Num Lock key to use the numeric keypad to type numbers.

When you are working with newspaper or parallel columns, a column indicator, `Col`, will be added to the status line to tell you the column number where the cursor is currently located. If the cursor is in a table, the word `Cell` and the cell number where the cursor is located will be displayed. You'll learn more about these features in other chapters of this book.

WordPerfect also uses the status line to display prompts, menus, and error messages. For instance, if you select Exit to quit WordPerfect, a prompt will appear in the lower-left corner asking if you want to save the document on the Edit screen first. If you select Spell, a menu will appear on this line, providing several spell-checking options. If you make a mistake, such as trying to retrieve a file that is not in the current directory, an error message will appear on this line.

WordPerfect does not save your documents as you type them. However, once you do save the document on the Edit screen, WordPerfect displays its path and file name on the left side of the status line. Also, if you retrieve a file from disk, its name will appear there as you are working on the document.

The WordPerfect Keyboard

Figure 1.3 shows two different keyboard layouts, the PC/XT-style keyboard and the enhanced-style keyboard. Take a moment to become familiar with the keys described in this section, and locate them on your keyboard.

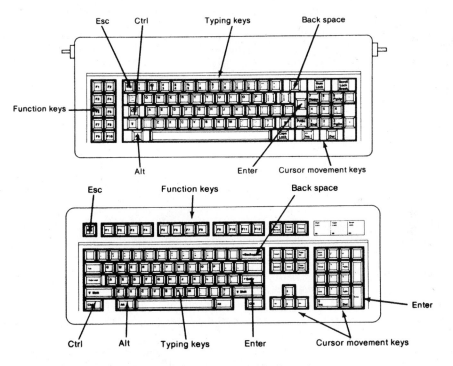

Figure 1.3   *The PC/XT keyboard and enhanced keyboard.*

In WordPerfect, keys such as letters, numbers, symbols, space bar, arrow keys, Enter, and Tab, work the same as in most other word processors. The Tab key moves the cursor to the next tab stop position. You can use it to indent the first line of a paragraph or to create tabular columns. The space bar inserts a blank space, which is considered a character in WordPerfect. You can use the Caps Lock key to type uppercase letters, but not symbols such as the dollar sign and question mark.

To type a symbol, press one of the two Shift keys first. To type numbers, use the number keys on the top row of the keyboard or, after pressing the Num Lock key, the number keys on the numeric keypad.

Unless you press Num Lock, most keys on the numeric keypad are used for cursor movement. For example, Up Arrow (8) moves the cursor up one line; Down Arrow (2), down one line; Right Arrow (6), to the right one character or space; and Left Arrow (4), to the left one character or space. The one exception is the key labeled 5; it has no function unless Num Lock is on. You'll learn about the other cursor movement keys in the next chapter, including Page Up and Page Down, Screen Up and Screen Down, and the Home and End keys. If you have an enhanced keyboard, it features an extra set of cursor movement, Insert, and Delete keys in the center section, so you can use them instead, and use the numeric keypad to type numbers only.

 Tip: Do not confuse the Left Arrow keys with the Backspace key. Left Arrow moves the cursor to the left, but Backspace deletes the space or character to the left of the cursor. The Delete key can also be used to erase a character. You'll learn more about Backspace and Delete in the next chapter.

The Insert, Caps Lock, and Num Lock keys are called *toggle keys*, because you press them once to turn them on, and then press them again when you are ready to turn them off. To tell you if they are on or off, WordPerfect provides on-screen indicators for each of these keys. For example, when you press Num Lock, the Pos indicator on the status line blinks until you type a character or press any key, indicating that the numeric keypad is in Numeric mode so the keys cannot be used for cursor movement. When Caps Lock is on, the Pos indicator appears in uppercase (POS), indicating that any letters you type will be capitalized. When you press the Insert key, a Typeover prompt appears in the lower-left corner of the screen, indicating that you are working in Typeover mode. This lets you type over and erase existing text. Unless you see this prompt, WordPerfect is in Insert mode, the default, and text you type will be inserted, pushing aside existing text to make room.

In WordPerfect's Typeover mode, a few keys operate differently. For instance, the Tab key moves the cursor to the next tab stop, but it does not insert a tab or move text, as it does in Insert mode. The space bar also changes, if you press it while the cursor is on a character. Instead of inserting a blank space, it erases the character and leaves a blank space in its place. The Backspace key still erases text to the left, but leaves a blank space for each character you erase.

The Enter key functions to end a paragraph or insert a blank line. You should not use it to end lines within a paragraph. Like other word processors, WordPerfect's *word wrap* feature automatically ends a line for you when the cursor reaches the right margin, and moves the cursor to the next line.

Tip: To reverse a key on the numeric keypad, you can press Shift before pressing the key. In other words, if Num Lock is off and you press Shift-4, instead of moving the cursor to the left, you type a 4. If Num Lock is on, pressing Shift-4 moves the cursor left one character or space.

Tip: Most keyboards have an auto-repeat feature. This means that if you press and continue to hold a key, it will be repeated until you release it. For instance, if you press Enter and hold it, you will insert several blank lines into your document. If you press a letter such as *t,* you'll type several *t*'s.

The Function Keys

The function keys are used extensively in WordPerfect, but you can also use the pull-down menus to duplicate most of their tasks. Each function key has four applications, depending on whether you press it alone or with the Alt, Shift, or Ctrl key. For example, when you press F3 alone, it brings up the main Help menu. When you press Shift-F3, it switches you to the other work area, Doc 1 or Doc 2. Alt-F3 displays the Reveal Codes screen, and Ctrl-F3 brings up the Screen menu. To use a function key in combination with one of the other three keys, press the Alt, Ctrl, or Shift key and hold it down while you press the function key once. Do not hold the function key itself down; in most cases, this just turns it on and off repeatedly.

WordPerfect has assigned a proper name to each of the 40 function key combinations. These key names appear on the keyboard template that comes with WordPerfect, and are represented by this color scheme: If the key name is printed in black on the template, you press the key alone. If it is green, you press it with Shift. If it is blue, you press it with Alt. If it is red, you press it with Ctrl.

Black: Press the key alone. F1 Cancel, F2 Search, F3 Help, F4 Indent, F5 List, F6 Bold, F7 Exit, F8 Underline, F9 End Field, F10 Save.

Red: Press Ctrl first, and hold it while pressing the function key. F1 Shell, F2 Spell, F3 Screen, F4 Move, F5 Text In/Out, F6 Tab Align, F7 Footnote, F8 Font, F9 Merge/Sort, and F10 Macro Define.

Green: Press Shift first, and hold it while pressing the function key. F1 Setup, F2 Backward Search, F3 Switch, F4 Left/Right Indent, F5 Date/Outline, F6 Center, F7 Print, F8 Format, F9 Merge Codes, and F10 Retrieve.

Blue: Press Alt and hold it while pressing the function key. F1 Thesaurus, F2 Replace, F3 Reveal Codes, F4 Block, F5 Mark Text, F6 Flush Right, F7 Columns/Table, F8 Style, F9 Graphics, and F10 Macro.

 Tip: The Help menus feature a copy of the keyboard template. To see it, press F3 twice. Notice the message on the second to last line: `Press 1 to view the PC/XT keyboard.` If your function keys are located on the left side of your keyboard instead of on the top row, you are using a PC/XT-style keyboard. If so, press 1 to see the template for your keyboard. When you finish, exit the Help menus by pressing the Enter key.

Enhanced keyboards include two extra function keys, F11 and F12. If you have one, you can use F11 for Reveal Codes, instead of Alt-F3, and F12 for Block, instead of Alt-F4.

Most of the function key applications are duplicated on the pull-down menus, which you can use with or without a mouse. If you are new to WordPerfect, you may find the pull-down menus easier to use.

Canceling Menus and Prompts

Whenever a menu or prompt is on the screen—such as the Block on prompt, which appears when you press Alt-F4 or F12 or select Block from the pull-down Edit menu—pressing Cancel (F1) removes the menu or prompt so that you can continue working in Edit mode. There are a few exceptions, including Reveal Codes, Help, Switch, and Macro Define. You'll learn more about these features later in this book. Also, certain keys perform a task as soon as you press them, and they cannot be revoked using the Cancel key. These include Tab, which moves the cursor to the next tab stop; Center (Shift-F6), which centers a line of text; and Underline (F8), which turns on Underline. To undo them, you have to delete the hidden codes they insert into your document. You'll learn more about these codes and how to erase them in Chapter 3.

If you are using a mouse, pressing the right and left buttons simultaneously is the equivalent of pressing the Cancel key (F1). If you have a three-button mouse, you can press the center button instead.

Escape

You can usually use the Esc key—like the Cancel key—to back out of a menu or prompt, except after pressing Help, Reveal Codes, Switch, or Macro Define. However, when you press Esc alone, it has a different function. The prompt `Repeat Value = 8` appears, and the next keystroke you press will be repeated eight times. For example, if you press the Down Arrow key, the cursor will move down eight lines (if there are eight lines below it inserted by typing text or pressing Enter). If you press Esc and then type a character such as *m*, WordPerfect will insert eight *m*'s at the cursor position. If you type a number after pressing Esc, it changes the number of times the next keystroke will be repeated. If you press Esc, type a number, and then press Enter, WordPerfect will use the number as the repeat value each time you press Esc, until you exit WordPerfect or change it again.

Using a Mouse

Some users feel that moving the cursor and selecting menu options with the mouse is much faster than using the keyboard. If you've installed your mouse correctly, you'll see a small block on the screen as you move the mouse. This is called the *mouse pointer,* and it moves on the screen as you move the mouse. You can move the cursor anywhere in a document by moving the mouse and pointer. When the mouse pointer is in the position you want, press the left button once; this is called *clicking.* As soon as you start typing, the pointer will disappear.

When positioning the cursor with the mouse, be careful to click and release the left button right away, without moving the mouse. If you press and hold a button, and then move the mouse, it's called *dragging.* When you press the left button and drag the pointer, a `Block on` prompt appears in the lower-left corner of the screen, indicating you have turned on WordPerfect's Block mode. Block is one of WordPerfect's most useful features; you can use Block to highlight a section of text and perform operations such as deleting, underlining, boldfacing, or moving it. You'll learn more about these and other Block operations in Chapter 4. Until then, if you accidentally turn on the Block feature with the mouse, just release the left button, and then click it again to turn Block off.

To scroll to another screen of text, you can press the right button and drag the mouse. First, make sure the mouse pointer is not on the status line or on the menu bar. Next, press the right mouse button and hold it down while you move the mouse up or down. If you drag it up, you'll move up through the previous screens. If you drag it down, you'll scroll down through the document. Release the right button to stop scrolling. Once you reach the top or bottom of the document, scrolling stops automatically. You can also use this dragging technique to move the cursor to the right or left edge of a line, if your lines are too wide to fit on the screen.

To select options from a menu or prompt, move the mouse pointer onto the option, and click the left button to select it. For example, when you select the Exit option from the pull-down File menu, this prompt will appear, asking if you want to save the document on the Edit screen:

```
Save document? Yes (No)
```

To select No with the mouse, you would move the pointer onto the word No, and click the left button once. In the next section, you'll learn how to use the mouse to display and select options from the pull-down menus.

Pressing a mouse button twice in succession is called *double-clicking*. Double-clicking the left button is the equivalent of pressing the Enter key in several menus and prompts. For example, if you select List Files from the pull-down File menu (as explained in the next section), a Dir prompt and the name of the current directory appear in the lower-left corner of the screen. Moving the mouse pointer onto the prompt and clicking the left button does not select it; instead, you can either move the pointer onto it and double-click the left button or click the right button.

If you have a three-button mouse, pressing the center button is the equivalent of pressing the Cancel key (F1), as explained earlier in the section "Canceling Menus and Prompts."

The Pull-Down Menus

WordPerfect 5.1 features pull-down menus as an alternative to the function keys. You can display them using either the mouse or the keyboard. The menu bar is shown in Figure 1.4. To activate it:

> **Keyboard:** Press Alt and then press the equal sign (=). (Some versions of WordPerfect may be set up so that the Alt key alone brings up the menu bar. To check your default, display the Setup menu, select the Display option, and then select Menu Options. In the Setup: Menu Options menu, look at the fourth option, **Alt Key Selects Pull-Down Menu**.)

> **Mouse:** Click the right mouse button once.

The nine menus are grouped according to major functions: File, Edit, Search, Layout, Mark, Tools, Font, Graphics, and Help. To pull down a menu and display its options:

Keyboard: Use the arrow keys to move the cursor onto the menu name, and then press Enter or Down Arrow to display it. Alternatively, you can type the highlighted letter in the name, such as E for **Edit** or S for **Search**. To close a menu, you can press Cancel (F1).

Mouse: Move the mouse pointer onto the menu name, and then click the left button to pull it down.

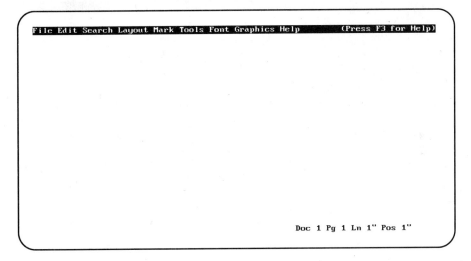

File Edit Search Layout Mark Tools Font Graphics Help   (Press F3 for Help)

Doc 1 Pg 1 Ln 1" Pos 1"

Figure 1.4   *The menu bar for the pull-down menus.*

Figure 1.5 shows how the File menu appears when you pull it down. Notice the triangular markers next to four of the options: Text In, Text Out, Password, and Setup. The markers indicate that these options lead to submenus, which pop out to the right when you move the cursor onto the option by using Down Arrow or dragging the mouse pointer onto the option. For example, Figure 1.6 shows the Setup menu that appears when the cursor is on the Setup option.

Several options on the pull-down menus appear in brackets, including Move, Copy, Append, Convert Case, and Protect Block on the Edit menu, and Table of Contents and List on the Mark menu. These features work in conjunction with the Block key, and you cannot select them until you turn on Block mode. When Block is on, options that do not work with the Block key will appear in brackets.

To select an option from one of the menus:

Keyboard: Highlight the option and press Enter, or type the highlighted letter in the name.

Mouse: Move the mouse cursor onto the option, then click the left mouse button once.

To exit from the menus without selecting an option:

Keyboard: Press the Cancel key (F1).

Mouse: Place the cursor anywhere in the Edit screen, outside of the menus, and click either button.

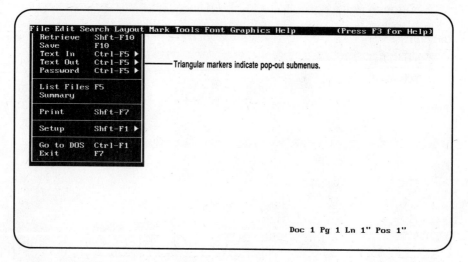

Figure 1.5 *The pull-down File menu.*

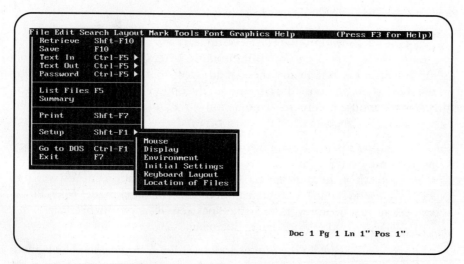

Figure 1.6 *When the cursor is on the Setup option, this submenu appears.*

Changing Menu Settings

If you use the pull-down menus extensively and want the menu bar to remain visible on your screen at all times, you can do this through the Setup: Menu Options menu. You can also use this menu to have a double line separate the menu from the Edit screen, or have the Alt key alone display the menu bar. To change any of these options:

1. Select Display from the Setup menu:

   Keyboard: Press the Setup key (Shift-F1), and select the second option, **Display**.

   Mouse: Display the pull-down **File** menu, select the Setup option, then **Display**.

   The Setup: Display menu appears.

2. Select the fourth option, **Menu Options**.

   The Setup: Menu Options screen appears, as shown in Figure 1.7.

```
Setup: Menu Options

        1 - Menu Letter Display            BOLD

Pull-Down Menu

        2 - Pull-Down Letter Display       REDLN

        3 - Pull-Down Text                 SHADW

        4 - Alt Key Selects Pull-Down Menu Yes

Menu Bar

        5 - Menu Bar Letter Display        REDLN

        6 - Menu Bar Text                  SHADW

        7 - Menu Bar Separator Line        No

        8 - Menu Bar Remains Visible       No


Selection: 0
```

Figure 1.7   *The Setup: Menu Options screen.*

If you want to select the menu bar using the Alt key alone, instead of Alt =, select the fourth option, Alt Key Selects Pull-Down Menu, and type Y to change it to Yes. If you want a double line under the menu bar, select the seventh option, Menu Bar Separator Line, and change it to Yes. To have the menu bar remain at the top of the screen at all times, select the eighth option, `Menu Bar Remains Visible`, and change it to Yes. When you finish changing the options, exit back to the Edit screen:

Keyboard: Press Exit (F7).

Mouse: Click the right button once.

WordPerfect's Defaults

WordPerfect makes many assumptions about how you want your documents formatted. These are called the *defaults,* and they include settings for the margins, tab stops, paper size and type, line spacing, and justification. Table 1.1 summarizes several of them. You can change these settings in individual documents, using one of the Format menus, or change the defaults themselves, using the Initial Codes option on the Setup: Initial Settings menu. You'll learn more about these defaults later in this book.

Table 1.1 *Formatting defaults.*

Format Option	Default Setting
Left and right margins:	1" each
Top and bottom margins:	1" each
Line spacing:	Single space
Tab stops:	Every ½", beginning at the left edge of the paper (position 0")
Paper:	8.5" x 11", Standard
Justification:	Full justification; both left and right margins are even
Page numbering:	None

 Tip: You can change WordPerfect's defaults using the Initial Codes option on the Setup: Initial Settings menu. Appendix B features a chart listing the settings in alphabetical order, and tells how to change each one.

Using the Tutorial

WordPerfect includes an on-screen Tutorial program, which you can use to familiarize yourself with WordPerfect. The entire tutorial takes two or three hours to complete, but you don't have to study all the lessons in one session. To run the tutorial on a computer with a hard disk:

1. Exit from WordPerfect so that you have a DOS prompt, such as C>. If you did not install the tutorial when you installed WordPerfect, you'll need to run the Installation program and install it now. (General instructions on how to use the Installation program are provided in Appendix A.)

2. Use the change directory command (CD) to switch to the directory containing your tutorial files. For example, if you copied them to the LEARN subdirectory of the WP51 directory, type: CD\WP51\LEARN.

3. Type tutor and press Enter. The tutorial's initial screen appears, as shown in Figure 1.8, and prompts you to type your name.

Type your first name and press Enter (←┘)

Figure 1.8 *When you start the WordPerfect tutorial, this screen appears. It prompts you to enter your name.*

4. Type your first name and press Enter.

The tutorial's main menu appears, as shown in Figure 1.9. It features six beginning lessons and an Advanced Lessons option, which leads to three lessons on two advanced subjects—mail merge and table of authorities. To select a lesson, move the cursor with the arrow keys to highlight it, and then press Enter. You can press F3 to exit from a lesson and return to this menu. To exit the tutorial and return to DOS, move the cursor onto the EXIT option, and press Enter.

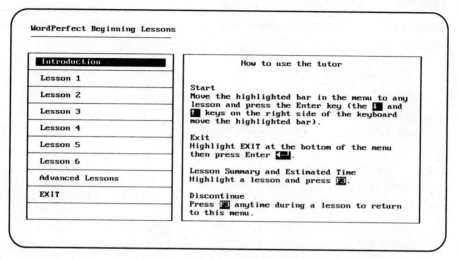

Figure 1.9   *The tutorial's main menu. Note the box on the right, which explains how to use the tutor. To select a lesson, use the arrow keys to move the cursor (a highlighted bar) onto the lesson, and press Enter. To exit, move the cursor onto the EXIT option, and press Enter.*

To run the tutorial on a computer that does not have a hard disk:

1. Place the WordPerfect 1 diskette in drive A, and the Learning diskette in drive B.

2. Type B: and press Enter.

3. Type tutor and press Enter.

    The tutorial's initial screen appears, as shown in Figure 1.8, and prompts you to type your name.

4. Type your first name and press Enter.

    The tutorial's main menu appears, as shown in Figure 1.9. It features six beginning lessons and an Advanced Lessons option, which leads to three more lessons on two advanced subjects: merge and table of authorities. To select a lesson, move the cursor with the arrow keys to highlight it, and then press Enter. You can press F3 to exit from a lesson and return to this menu. To exit from the tutorial back to DOS, move the cursor onto the EXIT option, and press Enter.

Exiting from WordPerfect

To exit WordPerfect correctly:

1. Either press the Exit key (F7) or select Exit from the **File** menu. A prompt appears asking if you want to save the document on the Edit screen:

   `Save document? Yes (No)`

2. Unless you have typed a document you want to save, type N. Next, you'll see this prompt, which asks if you want to exit WordPerfect:

   `Exit WP? No (Yes)`

   However, if you see this prompt instead:

   `Exit doc 1? No (Yes)`

   it means that you have opened up WordPerfect's other work area, Doc 2, and have not yet closed it. Before you can exit, WordPerfect always checks to see if you want to save the documents you were creating in Doc 1 and Doc 2. Your next step will be to select Yes, to exit from Doc 1. This will return you to Doc 2 (as evidenced by the Doc 2 indicator on the status line). You can then follow steps 1 through 3 in this section to exit from WordPerfect.

3. In response to the `Exit WP` prompt, and assuming you do want to exit WordPerfect, type Y. You will either return to DOS, as evidenced by a prompt such as C>, or to the menu that you used to start WordPerfect (such as the Shell).

   If you don't use this method to exit WordPerfect, you'll see an error message the next time you try to start the program. You'll learn more about this process in the next chapter.

BASIC WORDPERFECT SKILLS

In order to use WordPerfect effectively, there are some basic procedures you must learn. After you learn how to type a document, you'll need to know how to move the cursor around to edit it and how to insert and delete text. Next, you'll need to print the document, and then save it. After saving, you may want to clear the screen to begin typing another document. At the end of your work session, you'll need to exit from WordPerfect so that you can either turn off the computer or use a different program. This chapter will guide you through all of these operations. Since it's difficult to memorize them all the first time you use them, you'll also learn how to use WordPerfect's on-line help menus to refresh your memory.

Typing Your First Letter

So that you'll have some text to practice with as you learn about cursor movement, inserting and deleting text, and other topics in this chapter, type the letter shown in Figure 2.1. As you are typing, don't press the Enter key until after you've finished typing the last word in each paragraph. Instead, let word wrap end the lines for you automatically.

 Tip: The type of return that WordPerfect creates when you allow it to automatically wrap the cursor to the next line is called a *soft return*. When you press Enter yourself, you create a *hard return*. WordPerfect inserts invisible codes at the end of each line to indicate whether it ends in a soft return or a hard return. We'll explore these codes, and learn how to view them in Chapter 3.

```
July 24, 1990


Mr. Ralph Phatbuxs
120 Big Drive
Palm Beach, Florida

Dear Mr. Phatbuxs,

Thank you for your recent inquiry on the luxury motoryacht
"EXTRAVAGANCE".  You will find a comprehensive specification sheet
enclosed with a complete listing of inventory and equipment.
Please note that personal items such as tennis rackets and polo
ponies are not included in the sale.

This gracious vessel was built by the famous Fancischmanzi Boat
Yard in Italy and christened in 1985.  To date, she has been under
private  ownership  and  never  put  into  charter  service.
Nevertheless, she is well suited for charter, with an elaborate
master stateroom and accommodations for a small neighborhood.  All
staterooms have private baths with jacuzzi and the interior was
recently redecorated by Poodles of Paris.

The engines have been scrupulously maintained and allow cruising
speeds of ten knots while consuming a miserly 500 gallons per hour.
Granted, this will probably limit any long distance cruising but it
does allow you to motor around the harbor and show off.

Due to recent events in the stock market, the owner is most anxious
to sell. "EXTRAVAGANCE" is ready for inspection, so please contact
me for an appointment as soon as possible!


Kindest regards,



"Honest" Joe Smith


HJS/sbk
Enclosures

cc:IRS
```

Figure 2.1   Your first letter.

Saving Your Document

Since WordPerfect does not save files automatically, you must make the effort
yourself. While you're typing, the text on your Edit screen is contained only in the
computer's on-line memory (RAM). This memory is shut off when you turn your
computer off, and all its contents are lost forever.

WordPerfect has two different methods of saving. To save a document and continue working on it, you use the Save key (F10) or its equivalent, the Save option on the File menu. The other method is to save and then clear the screen, or exit from WordPerfect. To do this, you use the Exit option on the File menu, or the Exit key (F7). Since you'll want to continue working on your letter, we'll use the first method. The cursor can be anywhere in the document when you save it.

1. To select Save:

    Keyboard: Press the Save key (F10).

    Mouse: Display the File menu and select **Save**.

    This prompt appears:

    ```
    Document to be saved:
    ```

    At this point you need to type a file name for the document, following the rules imposed by DOS. You'll learn more about creating file names in Chapter 7, "File Management." You'll also learn how you can give WordPerfect files a descriptive file name containing up to 40 characters. Let's name this file LETTER.1.

2. Type `LETTER.1` and press Enter.

A message appears briefly, indicating that the file is being saved. After WordPerfect has saved your file, its name will appear in the lower-left corner of the screen. Notice that it includes the drive and subdirectory name where the file has been saved. It should be similar to this:

```
C:\WP\LETTER.1
```

Tip: You can type as many as 11 characters for a file name, split into two parts: a first part consisting of one to eight characters, and an optional second part, called a *file extension,* which can contain from one to three characters. You must separate the first part from the second by a period. WordPerfect 5.1 has a new feature, Long Document Names, which allows you to designate an additional document name of up to 68 characters for your WordPerfect files. You'll learn more about this feature in Chapter 7, "File Management."

Cursor Movement Using the Keyboard

The most basic method of moving the cursor is to use the four arrow keys: Up Arrow, Down Arrow, Left Arrow, and Right Arrow. Although the arrow keys are effective, they are slow. Fortunately, WordPerfect includes many speedier methods of moving the cursor. Read on to learn how to move the cursor word by word, to the left or right edge of the line, screen by screen, page by page, and more. Table 2.1 summarizes all of the important cursor movement techniques described in this section.

Moving the Cursor Word by Word

To practice moving the cursor word by word:

1. Move the cursor back to the beginning of the paragraph.

2. While watching the cursor, hold the Ctrl key and continue holding it while you press the Right Arrow key four times.

As you can see, the combination of Ctrl with the Right Arrow key moves the cursor word by word to the right. Ctrl and the Left Arrow key does the opposite: Moves the cursor word by word to the left.

Moving the Cursor to the Beginning or End of a Line

Another useful combination is the Home key with the Left or Right Arrow key. Use Home with the Right Arrow key to move the cursor to the right edge of the line, and Home with the Left Arrow key to move to the left edge. These combinations work a little differently than the Ctrl and arrow key combinations. Instead of holding down the Home key, you

1. Press the Home key once, and release it.

2. Press the Right or Left Arrow key.

Incidentally, the End key is identical to the Home, Right Arrow combination, and moves the cursor to the end of the line.

Moving the Cursor to the Top or Bottom of the Screen

A screen consists of 24 lines, single-spaced. Home with the Up Arrow key moves the cursor to the top of the screen, and Home with the Down Arrow key moves the cursor to the bottom of the screen. These keys are appropriately named Screen Up and Screen Down.

As long as you don't have the NumLock key engaged, you can use the plus and minus keys on the numeric keypad instead of Home, Up Arrow and Down Arrow. The plus key works the same as Home, Down Arrow, and the minus key works the same as Home, Up Arrow. However, if NumLock is on and you are using the numeric keypad to type numbers, you'll just type a plus or minus!

Screen Up and Screen Down are really useful when you want to scroll through a long document and review all of the text. Here's how Screen Down works:

1. Place the cursor at the top of the document.

2. Press Home, Down Arrow or the plus key (but be sure NumLock is off if you use the plus key). This moves the cursor to the bottom of the first screen.

3. Press Home, Down Arrow or the plus key again. This moves the cursor to the bottom of the next screen, pushing the previous screen up and out of the way.

4. Press Home, Down Arrow or the plus key once more. This moves the cursor to the third screen, pushing the previous one up and out of the way.

Moving the Cursor to the Beginning or End of the Document

You can also use the Home key to move the cursor to the beginning or end of the document, whether it consists of 1 page or 100 pages.

To move the cursor to the beginning of the document:

1. Press the Home key twice and release it.

2. Press the Up Arrow key once.

To move the cursor to the end of the document:

1. Press the Home key twice and release it.

2. Press the Down Arrow key once.

Moving the Cursor Page by Page

To move the cursor page by page, use the Page Up and Page Down keys. Page Down moves the cursor to the first line of the following page, if there is one. For instance, if the cursor is anywhere on page one of a two-page document, pressing Page Down will move it to the first line of page two. If there is only one page, Page Down will move the cursor to the last line that you've typed, or onto a blank line if you pressed Enter one or more times after typing the last line. Page Up moves the cursor to the first line of the previous page, if there is one. For example, if the cursor is anywhere on page three, pressing Page Up will move the cursor to the first line of page two. If there is only one page, Page Up will move the cursor to the first line of the single-page document.

 Tip: The Pg indicator on the status line tells you the page number where the cursor is currently located. Page breaks are represented on the Edit screen by a single line of dashes. You can force a page break by pressing Ctrl-Enter. The forced break is called a *hard page break* and is represented by a double line of dashes.

The Go To Key

To move the cursor to a specific page, you can use a combination called the *Go To* key. To use it:

1. Either press Ctrl-Home or select **Go to** from the pull-down **Search** menu. A Go to prompt appears in the lower-left corner of the screen.

2. Type the page number and then press Enter. The cursor will move to the first line on that page.

The Go To combination has several other applications. For example, to move the cursor to the top or bottom of the page the cursor is currently on:

1. Press Ctrl-Home, or select **G**o to from the **S**earch menu.

2. Press Up Arrow to go to the top, or Down Arrow to go to the bottom.

   To move the cursor to the beginning of the next paragraph:

1. Press Ctrl-Home, or select **G**o to from the **S**earch menu.

2. Press Enter.

   To move the cursor to the next occurrence of a specific character (except a number):

1. Press Ctrl-Home, or select **G**o to from the **S**earch menu.

2. Type the character.

   To return the cursor to the original position after pressing Page Up, Page Down, Screen Up, Screen Down, or Home with one of the arrow keys:

1. Press Ctrl-Home.

2. In response to the `Go to` prompt, press Ctrl-Home again.

Using Search to Move the Cursor

If you are not using a mouse, one of the fastest ways to move the cursor is to use WordPerfect's Search feature. For example, to search for the word *vessel* in your letter:

1. Move the cursor to the top of the document.

2. Select Search:

   Keyboard: Press the Forward Search key, F2.

   Mouse: Display the **S**earch menu and select **F**orward.

   You should see an arrow and a `Srch` prompt in the lower-left corner of the screen. The arrow indicates whether WordPerfect will search forward or backward through the document. Pressing the Up Arrow or Down Arrow key changes its direction, and changes the direction of your search.

3. Type the word you are searching for: `vessel`.

4. To start the search:

   Keyboard: Press F2 or Esc.

   Mouse: Click the right button.

The cursor should have moved to the second paragraph, in the blank space following the word vessel. The next time you select Search, the same word will appear next to the Srch prompt, and you could either press F2 to look for it again or type a different word or phrase. You'll learn much more about WordPerfect's Search key, as well as the Search and Replace feature, in Chapter 5.

 Tip: The word or phrase you type in response to the Srch prompt is called the *search string*. If you type it all in lowercase, WordPerfect will locate uppercase, lowercase, and mixed-case versions in your document. However, if you capitalize the entire search string, WordPerfect will locate only an uppercase version.

Table 2.1 *Basic cursor movement.*

Keys	Movement
Left Arrow	Left one character or space
Right Arrow	Right one character or space
Up Arrow	Up one line
Down Arrow	Down one line
Ctrl-Left Arrow	Word left
Ctrl-Right Arrow	Word right
Home,Left Arrow	Left edge of line
Home,Right Arrow	Right edge of line (or use End key)
Home,Up Arrow	Top of screen (or use the minus key on the numeric keypad)
Home,Down Arrow	Bottom of screen (or use the plus key on the numeric keypad)
Home,Home,Up Arrow	Top of document
Home,Home,Down Arrow	End of document
Page Up	First line of previous page
Page Down	First line of following page
Ctrl-Home,Up Arrow	Top of current page
Ctrl-Home,Down Arrow	Bottom of current page
Ctrl-Home,Enter	Beginning of next paragraph
F2	Search for any word or phrase

Cursor Movement Using the Mouse

Moving the cursor with the mouse is much faster than using the keyboard. If you've installed your mouse correctly, you'll see a small block on the screen (the mouse pointer) as you move the mouse. To move the cursor to another position, move the mouse pointer there, and then click the left mouse button. As soon as you start typing, the pointer disappears.

To move the cursor to another screen, drag the mouse by clicking the right button and holding it while you move the pointer. If you drag the pointer up, you'll scroll up through the previous screens. If you drag the pointer down, you'll scroll down through the document. If you reach the top or bottom of the document, scrolling will stop automatically.

You can also use this dragging technique to move the cursor to the right or left edge of a line, useful if your lines are too wide to fit on the screen.

> **Tip:** You can't drag the mouse pointer and scroll through your document if the mouse pointer is positioned on the status line at the bottom of the screen, or on the menu line at the top. Before trying to drag it, move it into the Edit screen and then click the right button.

Inserting Text

WordPerfect is automatically in Insert mode, so inserting text is easy: All you have to do is place the cursor in the position where you want to add the text, and start typing. As you type, existing text will be pushed to the right and, if necessary, down to the next line to make room for the new text. However, if you see a Typeover prompt in the lower-left corner of the screen, WordPerfect is not in Insert mode, and you must press the Insert key (or the key labeled Ins on the numeric keypad) once before you type. If you don't, you will type over and erase existing text. The exception is when the cursor is just left of a formatting code. You'll learn more about these codes in the next chapter.

To see how easy it is to insert text:

1. Move the cursor to the fourth paragraph in the body of the letter, and place it on the period following the word sell.

2. If you see the `Typeover` prompt in the lower-left corner of the screen, press the Insert key once.

3. Press the space bar once to insert a blank space.

4. Type the following phrase:

    `and his bank has instructed us to accept any generous offer`

If the text appears to go beyond the right margin after you've finished typing, just press the Down Arrow key once to help WordPerfect realign the margins. As you can see, the text you typed was inserted at the cursor position, pushing the period and the sentence that followed to the right and down, into their proper position.

Now try using Typeover:

1. Press the Insert key once, so that the `Typeover` prompt appears.

2. Move the cursor to the first letter in the closing, `Kindest regards`.

3. Type:

    `Sincerely yours`

This erases the original closing, `Kindest regards`, and replaces it with the new one, `Sincerely yours`.

If you want to insert a blank line, it doesn't matter if you are in Insert mode or Typeover mode. For example, try splitting the last paragraph in two, and then inserting a blank line to separate them:

1. Place the cursor on the first character in the second sentence (the quotation mark in front of `EXTRAVAGANCE`).

2. Press Enter twice. The first time you pressed Enter, WordPerfect split the paragraph in two. The second time you pressed it, WordPerfect inserted a blank line.

3. Press the Backspace key twice. This joins the paragraphs back together again.

4. Press the Insert key once. This turns off Typeover mode.

5. Press Enter twice to split the paragraphs again.

The paragraphs are split in two, with a blank line separating them.

The Insert key is an example of a toggle key. You press it once to turn Insert mode off and Typeover mode on. When you are finished using Typeover, you press Insert again to turn Typeover off and Insert on. Remember, WordPerfect is normally in Insert mode. Before continuing, make sure that Insert is on, since some of the keys you'll be studying in the next section work differently when you are using Typeover.

Deleting Text

WordPerfect includes many methods for deleting text. The most basic ones are the Delete and Backspace keys. The Delete key (and the one labeled *Del* on the numeric keypad) erases the character, blank space, or code that the cursor is on. The Backspace key erases the character, blank space, or code to the left of the cursor. Let's see how they work.

1. Place the cursor on the first character in the last line of the letter, the first *c* in `cc:IRS`.

2. Press the Delete key six times. This erases the entire line. Did you notice how the remaining characters in the line kept moving to the left as you deleted, filling in the blank space?

3. Now place the cursor on the first letter in the author's first name, the *J* in `Joe Smith`.

4. Press the Backspace key nine times, and watch as it erases text to the left of the cursor. Again, WordPerfect filled in the empty space as you deleted, by moving the remaining characters to the left. However, it works differently if you are in Typeover mode. Instead of filling in the empty space, WordPerfect leaves blank spaces where the characters were.

Deleting a Word

The combination of Ctrl-Backspace deletes the entire word the cursor is on, regardless of where the cursor is located in the word. If the cursor is on a blank space, Ctrl-Backspace deletes the entire word to the left. Home,Backspace deletes the characters to the left of the cursor, stopping at the beginning of the word. For instance, if the cursor is on the letter *h* in the word *comprehensive*, Home,Backspace will erase *compre* and leave *hensive*. If the cursor is on a blank space, it works just like the Ctrl-Backspace combination and erases the entire word to the left. Home,Delete is the opposite, deleting the character the cursor is on and those to the right of the cursor, until the end of the word. For example, if the cursor is on the letter *h* in the word *comprehensive*, Home,Delete will erase *hensive* and leave *compre*. If the cursor is on the first character in a word, Home,Delete erases the entire word. To use Home with Backspace or Delete, press Home, release it, then press Backspace or Delete.

Deleting from the Cursor to the End of a Line

The Ctrl-End combination deletes from the cursor to the end of the line. To try it:

1. Place the cursor on the word knots in the third paragraph of the body of the letter.

2. Press Ctrl-End.

Notice how WordPerfect moves up the lines below to fill in the empty space.

Deleting from the Cursor to the End of the Page

The Ctrl-Page Down combination deletes from the cursor to the end of the page. To try it:

1. Press Ctrl-Page Down. You'll see this prompt:

   Delete Remainder of page? No (Yes)

   Notice the assumption is No, so if you press any key except Y (uppercase or lowercase), your answer will be No.

2. Select Yes.

WordPerfect erases everything from the cursor position through the end of the page.

Deleting a Section of Text Using the Block Feature

To delete a continuous section of text, you can use WordPerfect's Block feature. To try it:

1. Move the cursor back to the beginning of the letter.

2. Turn on Block:

   Keyboard: Press the Block key, Alt-F4 (on some keyboards, you can press F12).

   Mouse: Display the Edit menu and select **Block**, or click the left button and hold it down while you move the mouse pointer.

Notice the `Block on` prompt in the lower-left corner of the screen. Your next step is to designate the block you want to erase. Let's erase everything through the salutation (`Dear Mr. Phatbuxs`).

3. Use the Down Arrow key or mouse to move the cursor and highlighting onto the blank line under the salutation.

4. To delete the highlighted block:

   Keyboard: Press the Delete or Backspace key.

   Mouse: Display the Edit menu and select **Delete**.

   You should see this prompt, asking if you want to delete the designated block:

   `Delete Block? No (Yes)`

5. Erase the block:

   Keyboard: Type Y.

   Mouse: Select Yes.

Deleting a Sentence, Paragraph, or Page Using the Move Feature

To delete a sentence, paragraph, or page, you can use WordPerfect's Move feature. Let's use it to erase the first paragraph of the letter (`Thank you for your recent inquiry ...`).

1. Place the cursor anywhere in the paragraph, and then:

   Keyboard: Press the Move key, Ctrl-F4.

   Mouse: Display the Edit menu and choose the Select option.

2. Select the **Paragraph** option. Notice that the entire paragraph is highlighted.

3. Select the third option, **Delete**.

WordPerfect erases the entire paragraph. You'll learn more about the Move and Block keys in Chapter 4.

Table 2.2 summarizes the many delete methods presented in this section.

Table 2.2 *Deleting text.*

Keys	Delete
Delete	Character that the cursor is on
Backspace	Character to the left of the cursor
Ctrl-Backspace	Word that the cursor is on
Home,Backspace	Characters to the left of the cursor, until the word boundary
Home,Delete	Characters to the right of the cursor, until the word boundary
Ctrl-End	From the cursor to the end of the line
Ctrl-Page Down	From the cursor to the end of the page
Ctrl-F4 S D	Sentence
Ctrl-F4 P D	Paragraph
Ctrl-F4 A D	Page
Alt-F4, move cursor, press Delete or Backspace	Blocked section

Undelete

As you've just seen, WordPerfect makes it quite easy to erase text. For those occasions where you find yourself wishing you hadn't deleted something, WordPerfect's Undelete feature makes it almost as easy to bring it back. Let's see how it works.

1. Move the cursor onto the word `gracious` and press Ctrl-Backspace to erase it.

2. Select Undelete:

   Keyboard: Press the Cancel key, F1.

   Mouse: Display the Edit menu and select the Undelete option.

   This prompt will appear at the bottom of the screen:

   `Undelete: 1 Restore; 2 Previous Deletion: 0`

   and `gracious` will appear in a highlighted block at the cursor position, as shown in Figure 2.2.

3. Select the **Restore** option.

This restores the word at the current cursor position. If you moved the cursor after pressing Ctrl-Backspace, the word won't be in its original position.

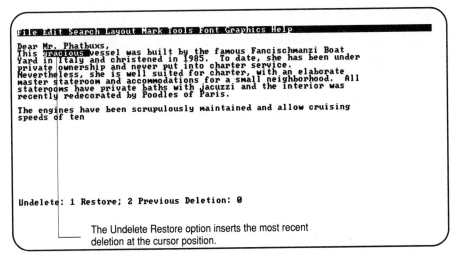

Figure 2.2 *Using Undelete to restore erased text.*

> **Tip:** Before selecting Cancel or pressing F1, be sure to place the cursor in the position where you want the text to be inserted when you bring it back.

WordPerfect remembers your last three deletions, so you can use the Previous Deletion option on the Undelete menu to bring any of them back. One deletion is anything you erase using Backspace, Delete, Ctrl-Backspace, Ctrl-End, or any of the other delete methods described in this chapter. If you use one of these methods several times in a row, such as pressing Backspace 10 times, WordPerfect considers it to be just one deletion. A deletion ends either when you move the cursor, or when you start typing. For example, if you press Ctrl-Backspace five times in a row to erase five words and then start typing, WordPerfect considers the five words to be one deletion. If you press the Backspace key once to erase an extra blank space, then move the cursor down a few lines, the blank space is one deletion. If you press the Insert key and turn on Typeover mode, then erase text as you type over it, that text can also be restored with Undelete.

To restore a previous deletion:

1. Place the cursor wherever you want the text, usually in its original position.

2. If there is a menu or prompt on your screen, press Cancel (F1) until it disappears.

3. Select Undelete:

> **Keyboard:** Press the Cancel key, F1.

> **Mouse:** Display the **Edit** menu and select **Undelete**.

4. Select **Previous Deletion**.

5. Next:

> *If the text you want to bring back appears,* select **Restore** from the menu.

> *If you don't see the text,* select **Previous Deletion** again, and select **Restore** if you see it.

If you still don't see it, it means you've made three other deletions since that one, and the text is no longer available to be restored. In that case, you can press Cancel (F1) or the space bar to remove the Undelete prompt.

As you've seen, the Cancel key operates differently if there is no menu or prompt on your screen: You can use it to undelete any of the last three deletions that you've made. It may be clearer if you think of it as canceling a deletion.

 Tip: Whenever you want to get rid of the Undelete prompt, press the space bar, the Enter key, or Cancel (F1). Remember, whenever a prompt or menu appears on the screen (even the Undelete menu), pressing Cancel will remove it. When the Undelete prompt appears, pressing the Up Arrow key has the same effect as selecting Previous Deletion. Pressing the Down Arrow key displays the third most recent deletion, then the second most recent.

Clearing the Screen

While learning how to insert and delete text, you've made many changes to the letter. Since you saved the letter before changing it, you can retrieve the original version. All you have to do is clear the one on your Edit screen without saving and retrieve the original file. Here's how:

1. Select Exit:

   Keyboard: Press the Exit key (F7).

   Mouse: Display the File menu and select Exit.

You'll see this prompt, asking if you wish to save the document:

`Save document? Yes (No)`

WordPerfect always asks if you want to save when you are exiting, just in case you've forgotten to save your work. Notice that the default is Yes. This means that if you press Enter or any other key except for N or n, you will be responding Yes to this question.

2. Select **No**.

 Warning: In response to the `Save document?` prompt, press N once and release it right away. Do not hold it down. Since the keys have an auto-repeat feature, if you hold the key down too long, WordPerfect assumes you mean to respond with No to the prompt that follows, `Exit WP? No (Yes)`.

The next prompt that appears asks if you want to exit from WordPerfect:

`Exit WP? No (Yes)`

Notice that it assumes No.

3. Select **No**.

If you were finished using WordPerfect, you would answer Yes in response to the `Exit WP?` prompt. In the next section, you'll learn how to retrieve the original letter.

Retrieving a Document

Retrieving your letter is easy.

1. Select Retrieve:

   Keyboard: Press the Retrieve key, Shift-F10.

   Mouse: Display the File menu and select **Retrieve**.

You should see this prompt:

```
Document to be retrieved:
```

2. Type the file name, Letter.1, and then press Enter. The original letter should appear on your screen almost immediately. If it does not, you probably misspelled the file name. If so, you'll see a prompt like this one:

```
ERROR: File not found
```

and it will include the file name you just typed. After a few seconds, the `Document to be retrieved` prompt will reappear. If this happens, just type the file name again and then press Enter.

> ▶ **Tip:** When you retrieve, you are actually only retrieving a *copy* of the file, and any changes that you make to it are not made to the disk version. When you save the file again after editing it, if you use the original file name, you erase the disk version and replace it with the screen version.

Printing

Printing your letter is easy, assuming you set up your printer correctly when you installed WordPerfect. Here's how you can tell:

1. Select Print:

   Keyboard: Press the Print key, Shift-F7.

   Mouse: Display the **File** menu and select **Print**.

   The main Print menu shown in Figure 2.3 will appear. Check the Options section of this menu for your printer's name; it should appear next to `Select Printer`.

2. If you don't see your printer's name, choose the Select Printer option. If you do see it, skip this step and step 3.

   The Print: Select Printer screen will appear. An example is shown in Figure 2.4. Notice that Figure 2.4 shows two printers, HP LaserJet Series II and QMS PS 810. An asterisk appears next to `QMS PS 810`, indicating that it is the currently selected printer.

```
Print
     1 - Full Document
     2 - Page
     3 - Document on Disk
     4 - Control Printer
     5 - Multiple Pages
     6 - View Document
     7 - Initialize Printer

Options
     S - Select Printer              QMS PS 810
     B - Binding Offset              0"
     N - Number of Copies            1
     U - Multiple Copies Generated by  Printer
     G - Graphics Quality            High
     T - Text Quality                High



Selection: 0
```

Figure 2.3   *The main Print menu.*

```
Print: Select Printer
   HP LaserJet Series II
 * QMS PS 810









 1 Select; 2 Additional Printers; 3 Edit; 4 Copy; 5 Delete; 6 Help; 7 Update: 1
```

Figure 2.4   *The Print: Select Printer screen.*

3. If you don't see your printer's name in this list, your printer is not installed. Turn to Appendix A and install it before trying to print. If you do see it, select it:

Keyboard: Move the cursor onto the printer name, and then type 1 or S.

Mouse: Place the mouse pointer on the printer name and click the left button; then place the pointer on the Select option and click the right button.

You should return to the main Print menu.

The four print options on the main Print menu appear at the top: **Full Document**, **Page**, **Document on Disk**, and **Multiple Pages**. Full Document, Page, and Multiple Pages pertain to the document on your Edit screen. If your document is longer than one page and you want to print the entire document, select Full Document. If it is only one page, you can use either Full Document or Page. If the document is longer than one page, selecting the Page option will print only the page the cursor is on. If you want to print several pages, but not the whole document, select Multiple Pages. The Document on Disk option allows you to print a document without retrieving it. In other words, you can print a document even though it is not currently on your Edit screen. A warning though: If you have changed the document on your Edit screen without saving it again, those changes will not appear in the printed version when you use the Document on Disk option. You'll learn more about this and other printing options in Chapter 13.

4. To print your letter, select **Full Document**.

The printer should start printing almost immediately. If it doesn't, do not select Full Document again because it won't work! When a printer refuses to start after you issue a print command such as this, it usually means there is a printer connection problem such as a loose cable, an on-line button that is currently switched off, or an incorrectly installed printer. Furthermore, WordPerfect remembers everything you ask it to print, regardless of whether or not the printer is actually functioning. Each time you select Full Document or one of the other print methods, the program assigns a job number to your request and places it in a *job list*, where it waits until the printer is ready. Once you do get the printer working, it will print the document once for each time you selected Full Document (or another print method). In Chapter 13 you will learn more about the job list and how to control it.

 Tip: If you hear a beep when you ask WordPerfect to print, your printer is probably set up for manual feed. In that case, insert the paper, select Print from the File menu or press the Print key (Shift-F7), and then select the Control Printer option and type G for Go.

Getting Help

If you forget how to use a WordPerfect feature, function key, or cursor movement key, you can use WordPerfect's on-line help to refresh your memory. If your computer does not have a hard disk, the WordPerfect help files won't be available until you insert the WordPerfect 1 disk into drive A, so do that before continuing.

1. To select Help:

   Keyboard: Press the Help key, F3.

   Mouse: Display the **Help** menu and select **Help**.

   The initial Help screen appears, as shown in Figure 2.5. The release date in the upper-right corner of the screen tells you which release of WordPerfect 5.1 you are using, and you will be asked for this date if you call the technical support line at WordPerfect Corporation. The screen describes the two ways you can get help: Press any letter for an alphabetical list, or press any function key for information about how to use it.

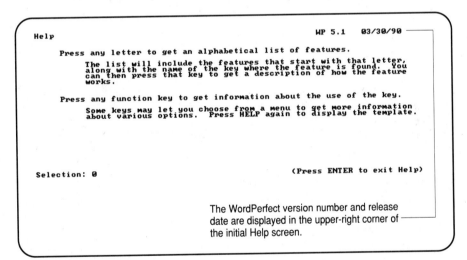

```
Help                                              WP 5.1   03/30/90

    Press any letter to get an alphabetical list of features.
         The list will include the features that start with that letter,
         along with the name of the key where the feature is found.  You
         can then press that key to get a description of how the feature
         works.

    Press any function key to get information about the use of the key.
         Some keys may let you choose from a menu to get more information
         about various options.  Press HELP again to display the template.




    Selection: 0                              (Press ENTER to exit Help)
```

The WordPerfect version number and release date are displayed in the upper-right corner of the initial Help screen.

Figure 2.5   The initial Help screen.

Perhaps you've forgotten how to save a document. To find out how:

2. Type the first letter of the feature: s for Save.

   Your screen should now resemble Figure 2.6. Look in the first column for the feature name, Save Text, which is listed in the third row. Now look across the row. In the middle column you will see the proper name of the key, Save. In the last column, you will see the actual keystroke(s) you must press to use this feature: F10. Notice the prompt More...Press s to continue. It indicates that there isn't enough room on this screen for all features beginning with the letter *s*.

3. To see the next screen, type s.

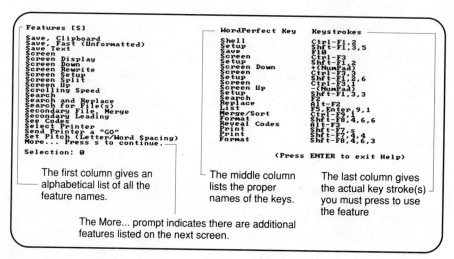

Figure 2.6   *The Help screen for the letter S.*

You can also use WordPerfect's Help feature to learn how to use a specific function key or cursor movement key. Let's try an example. Say you are confused by the Cancel key. You know that the key is F1, but don't understand why you sometimes see an Undelete prompt when you press it. If you were not already in Help mode, your first step would be to press F3, or display the Help menu and select Help. However, since you are already using help, you can just press the key you want to learn about.

4. Press the Cancel key, F1. Your screen should now resemble Figure 2.7.

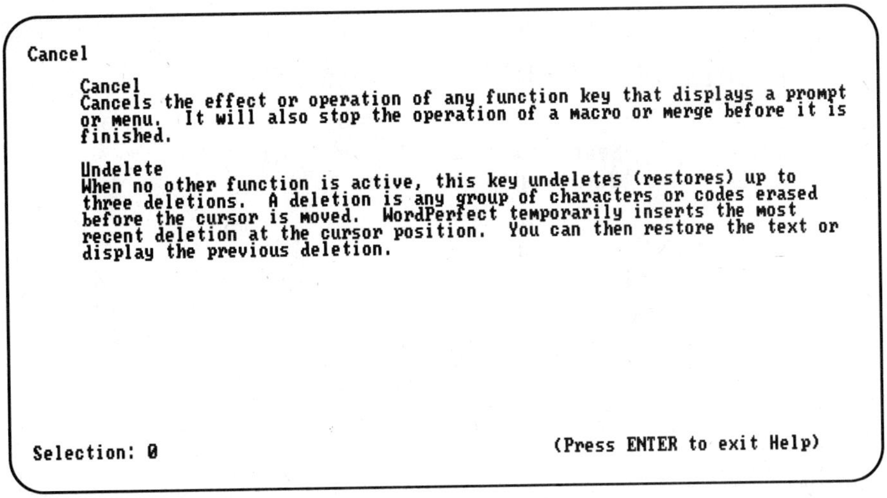

```
Cancel
     Cancel
     Cancels the effect or operation of any function key that displays a prompt
     or menu.  It will also stop the operation of a macro or merge before it is
     finished.

     Undelete
     When no other function is active, this key undeletes (restores) up to
     three deletions.  A deletion is any group of characters or codes erased
     before the cursor is moved.  WordPerfect temporarily inserts the most
     recent deletion at the cursor position.  You can then restore the text or
     display the previous deletion.




Selection: 0                                    (Press ENTER to exit Help)
```

Figure 2.7   *The Help screen for the Cancel key.*

Context-Sensitive Help

You can also access the help menus for specific keys by pressing those keys first, then pressing the Help key. This is called *context-sensitive help* because it applies to the task at hand. To try it:

1. Press the Enter key to exit from the Help menu.

2. Select Print:

     Keyboard: Press the Print key (Shift-F7).

     Mouse: Select **Print** from the **File** menu.

     The main Print menu appears, as shown in Figure 2.3.

3. Press the Help key, F3 (you cannot use the pull-down Help menu here).

     The Help screen for the main Print menu will appear, as shown in Figure 2.8. Notice that it branches to several other Help menus, one for each option on the Print menu. To view another one, you can type the letter or number next to it, such as S for Select Printer.

4. When you finish using help, press Enter to exit. You will return to the main Print menu, since WordPerfect assumes you still want to use it.

5. To back out of the Print menu, press Cancel (F1) or Enter.

```
Print
     1 - Full Document
     2 - Page
     3 - Document on Disk
     4 - Control Printer
     5 - Multiple Pages
     6 - View Document
     7 - Initialize Printer

Options
     S - Select Printer
     B - Binding Offset
     N - Number of Copies
     U - Multiple Copies Generated by
     G - Graphics Quality
     T - Text Quality

If you run WordPerfect on Novell NetWare, you have two additional options:

     A - Banners
     0 - Form Number

Selection: 0                              (Press ENTER to exit Help)
```

Figure 2.8   The Print key Help screen for context-sensitive help.

The Function Key Template

One of the help menus displays a copy of the function key template.

1. To view the function key template:

    Keyboard: Press F3 twice.

    Mouse: Display the **Help** menu and select **Template**.

    If you were already in Help mode, you could access the template by pressing F3 once. You should now see the function key template for the enhanced keyboard, as shown in Figure 2.9. Notice the message at the bottom: Press 1 to view the PC/XT keyboard template. If your function keys are located on the left side instead of on the top row, you are using a PC/XT style keyboard.

2. If you have a PC/XT style keyboard, press 1 to see the template for your keyboard.

    You may have noticed that most of the help screens include a message telling you how to exit from Help mode: (Press ENTER to exit help). You can also exit by pressing the space bar. As you've already seen, pressing the Cancel key does not get you out of Help mode. Instead, it provides a screen of information about how the Cancel key works. This is the one exception to the Cancel key's normal function, canceling a menu or prompt.

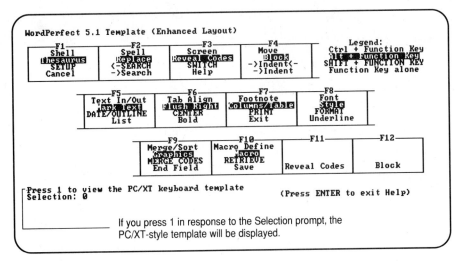

Figure 2.9   *The function key template.*

Exiting from WordPerfect

In this section, you'll learn how to exit WordPerfect correctly. A warning: You should never turn your computer off when WordPerfect is running. While you are using WordPerfect, the program creates several temporary files for data that can't fit in your computer's on-line memory (RAM), and moves data back and forth between them and the RAM. These temporary files are called *overflow files.* If you are using the Timed Backup feature, there may also be a backup file corresponding to the document on your Edit screen. If you shut off the computer while WordPerfect is still on, it does not have the opportunity to close these temporary files. The next time you start WordPerfect, you will see this error message:

```
Are other copies of WordPerfect currently running? (Y/N)
```

and unless you are using a network or running another copy of WordPerfect under an environment such as the WordPerfect Shell or Microsoft Windows, you will have to type N in order to erase the files and start the program. If you type Y, this prompt will appear:

```
Directory is in use. New WP Directory:
```

In response, you can either type a new directory or press Cancel (F1) to exit to DOS, then exit the other copy of WordPerfect correctly.

To exit WordPerfect:

1. Select Exit:

   Keyboard: Press the Exit key, F7.

   Mouse: Display the File menu and select Exit.

   A prompt appears asking if you want to save the document on the Edit screen. You may remember using this procedure earlier to clear the Edit screen. If you haven't made any changes to the letter since you retrieved it from the disk, you will also see this message in the lower-right corner of the screen:

   `(Text was not modified)`

   This means that the file on disk is identical to the one on your Edit screen (or there is nothing on the Edit screen), and you can answer No to the `Save document?` prompt.

2. Unless you want to save the file again, select No. Next, you'll see this prompt, which asks if you want to exit WordPerfect:

   `Exit WP? No (Yes)`

3. Assuming you do want to exit WordPerfect, answer Yes.

THE BASICS OF FORMATTING

WordPerfect is set up to use default formatting, such as 1" margins on all four sides of the page, single spacing, tab stop settings every $\frac{1}{2}$", standard-size paper (8.5" wide and 11" long), and full justification so that text is aligned against both the left and right margins (instead of ragged right). In this chapter, you'll learn how to change some of these features for the document on your Edit screen, and how to change the defaults for all new documents. You'll also study many of WordPerfect's other formatting options, such as indent, underline, and centering.

Many of these features have dedicated function keys, including bold and underline, center, flush right, indent, and tab align. Others are found on the Line Format and Page Format menus, including line spacing, margins, justification, page numbering, headers and footers, and paper size and type. Regardless of how you implement them, all these features have much in common. To begin with, they all insert hidden formatting codes into your document. Since the codes are saved along with the document, the new formatting only affects the document on your Edit screen. Some of these codes come in pairs and affect all the text they surround, while others are open codes and change everything that follows them in the document. The codes can only be seen in a special area called the *Reveal Codes screen,* which you'll study in this chapter.

Another common factor is that cursor position is crucial when you change the formatting. For instance, if you change the margins when the cursor is at the end of the document, it won't have any effect. Most open formatting codes, such as margins and line spacing, start affecting your document at the cursor position when you select them, and remain in effect until the end of the document, or until another formatting code is encountered that changes or cancels them. Formatting changes that come in pairs, such as bold and underline, stay on and affect all text you type until you turn the feature off.

Formatting a Letter

To study several of WordPerfect's most frequently used format options, including underline, left and right margins, flush right, and horizontal and vertical centering, use the following instructions to type the letter shown in Figure 3.1.

```
                                     1006 Manzanita Lane, Suite 4
                                      Cerritos, California 90701
                                          September 20, 1990

Natural Novelties
200 Mountain Avenue
Novato, California 94948


Dear Sirs:

I am writing in response to your advertisement in the San
Francisco Chronicle,  and  would  like  to  order  the
following:

        3 sets of Edible Greeting Cards (2 herbal mints, 1
        honey yoghurt).

        2  organic  pine  cone  bracelets  (1  medium,  1
        small),with matching earrings.


I have enclosed a cashiers check for $79.99, made out to
Natural Novelties. Please send the items by UPS, as I am
anxious to receive them as soon as possible.



                    Sincerely,

                    Maryanne Jones
```

Figure 3.1   *The order letter.*

Centering the Page Between the Top and Bottom Margins

Since this letter is short, you can center the page vertically, between the top and bottom margins. To do this, use the Center Page (top to bottom) option on the Format Page menu. This feature is useful for brief letters, title pages, table of contents, and other short pages. Although the letter won't appear centered on the Edit screen, it will be centered when you print it.

It doesn't matter whether you turn on Center Page before or after typing the letter. However, when you select the option, the cursor must be at the beginning of the first line of the page you want to center, before any text on the page. If it isn't, Center Page will have no effect.

Unlike most options on the Format Page menu, Center Page only affects the page the cursor is on, so you don't have to turn it off when you finish using it. This also means that if you want to center several pages in a row, you have to repeat the steps and select the option again at the top of each page.

To center the letter:

1. Display the Format Page menu:

   Keyboard: Press the Format key (Shift-F8), and select **P**age from the main Format menu shown in Figure 3.2.

   Mouse: Display the **L**ayout menu and select **P**age.

   The Format Page menu will appear, as shown in Figure 3.3. Notice that `Center Page (top to bottom)` is the first option.

2. Select the **C**enter Page option, and change it from No to Yes.

3. Return to the main Format menu.

   Keyboard: Press Enter.

   Mouse: Click both buttons (or the middle button, if you have one).

Changing the Left and Right Margins

You should be back in the main Format menu. Your next step is to change the left and right margins to 1.5" each. Like the Center Page feature, you can change margins before or after typing your letter, and cursor position is crucial. To change the margins for the entire document, the cursor must be on the first line. Also, it must be at the left margin. If not, WordPerfect will automatically insert a hard return, and force the margin change to start on the next line. Once you change the margins, the change remains in effect until the end of the document, or until you change them again.

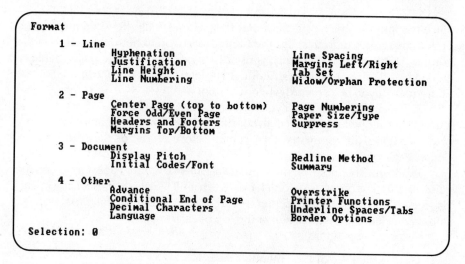

```
Format
     1 - Line
              Hyphenation                    Line Spacing
              Justification                  Margins Left/Right
              Line Height                    Tab Set
              Line Numbering                 Widow/Orphan Protection
     2 - Page
              Center Page (top to bottom)    Page Numbering
              Force Odd/Even Page            Paper Size/Type
              Headers and Footers            Suppress
              Margins Top/Bottom
     3 - Document
              Display Pitch                  Redline Method
              Initial Codes/Font             Summary
     4 - Other
              Advance                        Overstrike
              Conditional End of Page        Printer Functions
              Decimal Characters             Underline Spaces/Tabs
              Language                       Border Options
Selection: 0
```

Figure 3.2 *WordPerfect's main Format menu. Notice that it branches to four other menus: Line, Page, Document, and Other.*

```
Format: Page
     1 - Center Page (top to bottom)      No
     2 - Force Odd/Even Page
     3 - Headers
     4 - Footers
     5 - Margins - Top                    1"
                   Bottom                 1"
     6 - Page Numbering
     7 - Paper Size                       8.5" x 11"
               Type                       Standard
     8 - Suppress (this page only)


Selection: 0
```

Figure 3.3 *The Format Page menu. You can use the first option to center your letter between the top and bottom margins. When you select an option from this menu, the cursor should be at the beginning of the first line of the page, before any text.*

As you can see from the main Format menu, the option for left and right margins is on the Format Line menu.

1. Select the Line menu. The Format Line menu appears, as shown in Figure 3.4. The seventh option, Margins, can be used to change the left and right margins, which are set to 1" each by default. Let's change them to 1.5" each.

Tip: Notice that you can use the sixth option on the Format Line menu, Line Spacing, to switch from single spacing to another measurement, such as double, triple, or even a fraction like .5 or 1.5, if your printer supports them. You can use the eighth option, Tab Set, to change the tab stop settings, which are predefined for every ½". Later, you will be using the third option, Justification, to change from Full Justification to Left Justification to create a ragged right margin in the printed version of your document. All options on this menu are detailed in Part Three, "Command Reference."

2. Select **Margins**. Type 1.5 for the left margin, press Enter, type 1.5 for the right margin, and press Enter. You do not have to type the inch symbol.

3. Return to the Edit screen:

    Keyboard: Press the Exit key (F7).

    Mouse: Click the right mouse button.

You can tell that the left margin has been changed, because the position indicator (Pos) shows that the cursor is at position 1.5". As you type, you'll see that the right margin has been changed also. Vertical centering does not show up on the Edit screen, so you won't know until you print the page whether it is actually centered. However, if your monitor is capable of displaying graphics, you're in luck because WordPerfect will let you preview the printed version. After you finish typing the document, you'll learn how.

Using Flush Right

Notice that the first three lines of the letter are aligned against the right margin. To right-align single lines of text, you can use WordPerfect's Flush Right feature. When you select it, the cursor jumps immediately to the right margin. As you type, your text moves to the left. The last character on the line will be positioned exactly at the right margin. When you press the Enter key, Flush Right ends.

```
Format: Line
    1 - Hyphenation                        No
    2 - Hyphenation Zone -  Left           10%
                           Right           4%
    3 - Justification                      Full
    4 - Line Height                        Auto
    5 - Line Numbering                     No
    6 - Line Spacing                       1
    7 - Margins -  Left                    1"
               Right                       1"
    8 - Tab Set                            Rel; -1", every 0.5"
    9 - Widow/Orphan Protection            No

Selection: 0
```

Figure 3.4   *The Format Line menu. Use the Margins option on this menu to change the left and right margins to 1.5" each.*

To right-align and type the first three lines:

1. Select Flush Right:

    Keyboard: Press the Flush Right key, Alt-F6.

    Mouse: Display the pull-down Layout menu and select **Align**. The Align menu pops out to the right, as shown in Figure 3.5. Use it to select **Flush Right**.

2. Type the first line, the street address: `1006 Manzanita Lane, Suite 4` and press Enter.

3. Select **Flush Right** again and type the city, state, and ZIP code: `Cerritos, California 90701` and press Enter.

4. Select **Flush Right** again, type the date: `September 20, 1990` and press Enter.

5. Type the inside address and the salutation:

```
Natural Novelties
200 Mountain Avenue
Novato, California 94948

Dear Sirs:
```

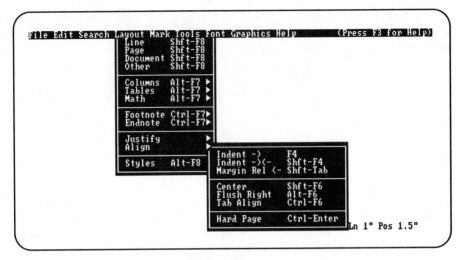

Figure 3.5   *When you select Align from the Layout menu, this menu pops out to the right. Use it to select one of WordPerfect's indent options; Margin Release; Center; Flush Right; or Tab Align; or to force a hard page break in your document.*

> ▶ **Tip:** To right-align a line of text after typing it, just place the cursor on the first character, select Flush Right, and then press the Down Arrow.

Underlining a Phrase

The first paragraph in the body of the letter includes an underlined phrase, <u>San Francisco Chronicle</u>. Underlining text is easy in WordPerfect: Just turn Underline on, type your text, and then turn it off. If you've already typed the text, block it first and then select Underline. If you use a monochrome monitor, you will see the text formatted in underline as you type it. If you use a color monitor, the underlined text usually appears in a different color from the regular text. Another indicator that you've turned on underline is the position number (Pos) in the lower-right corner of the screen, which will be underlined while you are typing underlined text. This is also the case if you move the cursor into a section of text that has been underlined.

Since Underline is used so often, WordPerfect has a dedicated function key for it: F8. Underline is also listed as an Appearance attribute on the Font menu, so you can select it using the Font key (Ctrl-F8) or the pull-down Font menu. If you select the pull-down Font menu and choose Appearance, the Appearance menu pops out to the right, as illustrated in Figure 3.6. You can use it to select Underline, Bold, or one of the other appearance attributes: Double Underline, Italics, Outline, Shadow, Small Cap, Redline, or Strikeout. You'll learn more about the appearance attributes in Chapter 13, "Printing and Fonts." If you press the Font key (Ctrl-F8) and select Appearance, the same options appear in this menu line at the bottom of the screen:

```
1 Bold 2 Undl 3 Dbl Und 4 Italc 5 Outln 6 Shadw 7 Sm Cap
8 Redln 9 Stkout: 0
```

Whichever method you use to turn on underline, the rest of the process is the same: You type the text, and then turn it off again.

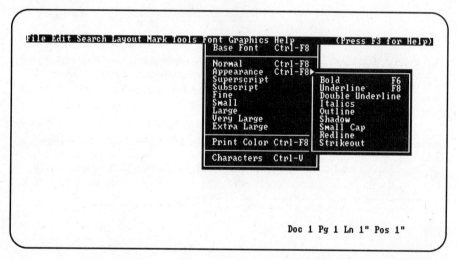

Figure 3.6 *When you display the Font menu and choose Appearance, this menu pops out to the right. Use it to turn on Underline or one of the other appearance attributes: Bold, Double Underline, Italics, Outline, Shadow, Small Cap, Redline, or Strikeout.*

Now type the first paragraph in the body of the letter. To underline the phrase San Francisco Chronicle:

1. Turn Underline on:

   Keyboard: Press the Underline key, F8.

   Mouse: Display the Font menu, select Appearance, and then select Underline.

2. Type: San Francisco Chronicle.

3. Turn Underline off and finish typing the paragraph:

> **Keyboard:** Press the Right Arrow key once. An alternative method is to press the Underline key (F8) again. A third but more laborious method is to select Normal from the pull-down Font menu or Font key (Ctrl-F8). If you use the Right Arrow key, watch the cursor as you press it. It will appear as though the cursor has not moved at all, and the position number on the status line will not change. Actually, pressing the Right Arrow key moves the cursor past the hidden formatting code that turns underline off. You'll learn more about these codes in the Reveal Codes section of this chapter. Regardless of which method you choose to turn off underline, they all do the same thing: move the cursor past the code that turns off underline.

> **Mouse:** Display the Font menu and select Normal.

 Tip: If your computer system includes an EGA or VGA monitor, you can use WordPerfect's Setup menu to change the screen font so that you'll see underline on the screen. However, this reduces the number of available foreground colors from 16 to 8. To select the underline font, press Setup (Shift-F1) or select Setup from the File menu. Next, select Display and then Colors/Fonts/Attributes. Select the third option from the Setup Colors/Fonts menu, Underline Font, 8 Foreground Colors. Press the Exit key (F7) or click the right mouse button to complete the process.

 Tip: The steps that you use to boldface text are nearly identical to the ones you use to underline text: Turn on Bold by pressing the Bold key (F6) or selecting Bold from the Font Appearance menu, type the text, and then turn Bold off.

Indenting Paragraphs

Notice that the next two paragraphs in the letter are indented. WordPerfect has two indent options: Left Indent and Left/Right Indent. The first one, Left Indent, indents the entire paragraph to the next tab stop position, $1/2$" from the left margin. You'll use it for the next two paragraphs in this letter. The second one, Left/Right Indent, indents a paragraph from both the left and right sides. You can use one of the indent options to format text as you type, or wait until after you've finished typing it. Whichever way you do it, always begin with the cursor at the left margin. Indent works on a paragraph-by-paragraph basis, and ends when you press Enter.

To indent the next two paragraphs from the left side:

1. Select Indent:

   Keyboard: Press the Left Indent key, F4.

   Mouse: Display the Layout menu and select **Align.** The Align menu pops out to the right, as shown in Figure 3.5. Select the first Indent option, with the single arrow (the second one is for Left/Right Indent).

2. Type the first indented paragraph:

   ```
   3 sets of Edible Greeting Cards (2 herbal mints, 1 honey
   yoghurt).
   ```

   As you type, the paragraph will automatically word wrap to the indented position. When you finish, press Enter. This will end indenting, and the cursor will move back to the left margin. Press Enter again to add a blank line.

3. Select Indent again, type the second indented paragraph, and press Enter twice:

   ```
   2 organic pine cone bracelets (1 medium, 1 small), with
   matching earrings.
   ```

4. Type the last paragraph in the body of the letter and press Enter:

   ```
   I have enclosed a cashiers check for $79.99, made out to
   Natural Novelties. Please send the items by UPS, as I am
   anxious to receive them as soon as possible.
   ```

Centering a Line of Text

Notice that the next two lines, the closing of the letter, are centered. You've already learned how to center text vertically, between the top and bottom margins. WordPerfect also lets you center text horizontally, between the left and right margins. This option is useful for short lines of text, such as the closing of this letter.

Like Indent and Flush Right, you can use Center to format text as you type, or wait until you've finished typing and then center it. In this case, you'll center the lines while typing. As soon as you press the Enter key, centering will end.

Turn on centering:

1. Select Center:

   Keyboard: Press the Center key (Shift-F6).

   Mouse: Display the pull-down Layout menu and select Align. A submenu displaying all the Align options pops out to the right, as illustrated in Figure 3.5. Select the fourth option, Center.

2. Type `Sincerely,` and press Enter twice.

3. Select **Center** again, type `Maryanne Jones`, and press Enter.

4. Now that you've completed the letter, save it using the name Order.ltr.

 Tip: To center a line of text that you've already typed, place the cursor at the left edge of the line and press the Center key, or select Center from the pull-down menu. The text may not be precisely centered until you realign it, by pressing a cursor movement key such as Down Arrow, Screen Down, or Page Down.

Using View Document to Preview the Printed Page

Although your letter will be centered between the top and bottom margins when printed, you cannot tell in the Edit screen. There are many other formatting features that WordPerfect cannot display on the Edit screen, including page numbering, headers and footers, footnotes and endnotes, margins, and full justification. However, when you use the View Document option on the Print menu, you'll see a preview in graphics mode that will include these features, and resemble the printed version as closely as possible. It will even display font attributes such as bold, underline, and italics. All this assumes your monitor is capable of displaying graphics.

To use WordPerfect's preview feature:

1. Display the main Print menu:

   Keyboard: Press the Print key (Shift-F7).

   Mouse: Display the **File** menu and select **Print**.

2. Select the sixth option, **View Document**.

You'll see a representation of the entire page, as shown in Figure 3.7, and you should be able to tell if your text is centered between the top and bottom margins.

Initially, the View Document screen displays the Full Document mode. This provides an overview of the entire page, but the text is too small to read. To enlarge it, you can select 100% or 200% from the menu line at the bottom. Use 100% to enlarge the page to actual size, or 200% to enlarge it to twice actual size. The Facing Pages option lets you view the layout of two facing pages, such as pages 2 and 3 or pages 4 and 5 (page 1 is always a right-hand page).

3. Select 100%, and see if you can observe a major difference in the appearance of the text in the preview mode and the Edit screen: Even though the text appears to have a ragged right margin in the Edit screen, View Document shows how it will actually print, with an even right margin. This default formatting option is called *Full Justification,* since it causes text to be aligned against both the right and left margins (in earlier versions of WordPerfect, it was called *Right Justification*). In the next section, you'll learn how to change it to ragged right.

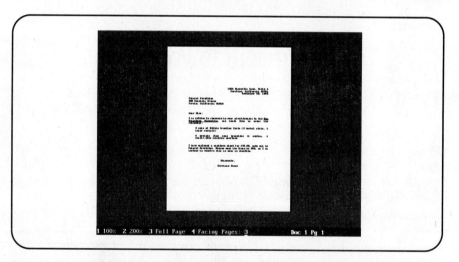

Figure 3.7 *When you select View Document from the main Print menu, you see a full-page layout of your letter. You can use it to verify that the page is centered between the top and bottom margins.*

While in View Document, you can use most of the regular cursor movement keys to scroll through the document, but you cannot do any editing. When you finish previewing the page, return to the Edit screen.

4. Return to the Edit screen:

> **Keyboard:** Press the Exit key (F7).

> **Mouse:** Click the right mouse button.

As you've just seen, View Document can be invaluable, especially when you produce complex documents such as newsletters that incorporate features like graphics, columns, and multiple fonts. You'll learn more about this useful option in Chapter 13.

> **Tip:** If your monitor cannot display graphics, your View Document screen will be similar to the Edit screen, except the status line will be different. You will be able to see features such as justification, margins, page numbers, headers, footers, and footnotes. However, you will not be able to enlarge the page to 200%, or display the full page or facing pages.

Justification

Although you cannot see Full Justification on the Edit screen, it is WordPerfect's default for the printed document. This means that both the left and right margin will be even, aligned against the margins. To create this effect, WordPerfect inserts extra blank spaces between words. Often these gaps are large and unsightly. If you prefer a ragged right margin, as on a typewriter, use the Format Line menu to change the Justification option to Left. Be sure to place the cursor at the top of the document before making this change, so that it will affect all text in the document.

To change the justification style for your letter from Full to Left, begin by moving the cursor to the top of the page.

1. Display the Format Line menu:

> **Keyboard:** Press the Format key (Shift-F8) and select Line.

> **Mouse:** Select Line from the pull-down Layout menu.

The Format Line menu appears, as shown in Figure 3.4.

2. Select the third option, Justification. This menu appears at the bottom of the screen:

```
Justification: 1 Left; 2 Center; 3 Right; 4 Full: 0
```

3. Select the first option, Left.

4. Return to the Edit screen:

> **Keyboard:** Press the Exit key (F7).

> **Mouse:** Click the right mouse button.

To verify that the letter now has a ragged right margin, you can either display the View Document screen or print the document.

Reveal Codes

You'll never be an expert at using WordPerfect until you understand Reveal Codes. Nearly all formatting changes that you make in WordPerfect insert hidden codes into your document. For example, when you underline text, WordPerfect inserts an Underline On code before the first character, and an Underline Off code after the last one. Figure 3.8 shows these codes in your letter: [UND] represents underline on, and [und] represents underline off. To prevent clutter, the codes are not visible in the Edit screen, but you'll often need to know where they are located. Displaying the Reveal Codes screen is the best way to find them.

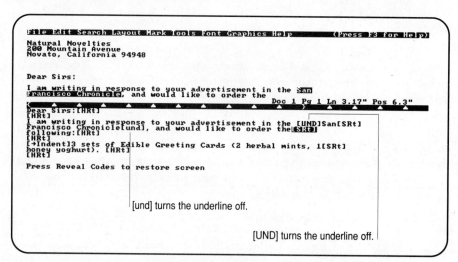

Figure 3.8 *The Reveal Codes screen showing underline codes surrounding the phrase* San Francisco Chronicle.

For example, if you decided to change the underlined phrase in your letter to italics, you'd have to erase the underlining and then format it with italics. The only way you can delete the underlining is to erase one of the underline codes. Although it's possible to find the code without looking into the Reveal Codes screen, it's much faster if you do use it. Also, say you decide to insert a few more words at the end of the underlined phrase. Unless you start with the cursor on the Underline Off code, [und], the text you type will not be underlined. Again, it's much faster to position the cursor correctly if you use Reveal Codes.

You'll also find Reveal Codes a valuable ally when you try to change a formatting feature such as margins or line spacing, and find that it doesn't work. This usually happens because the cursor was positioned before an existing code, so the existing code cancels the change you're trying to make. For example, suppose you decide to change the left and right margins in your letter from 1.5" to 1.25" each. You move the cursor back to the top of the page and follow the proper steps to change the left and right margins to 1.25". However, when you return to the Edit screen, you find your margins are still 1.5". You look in Reveal Codes and immediately discover the problem: The code that changes the margins to 1.5 is to the right of the code that changes them to 1.25, as shown in Figure 3.9. As a result, the first margin change code, for 1.25" margins, has no effect. The solution is easy: Place the cursor on the code you don't want, [L/R°Mar:1.5",1.5"] , and erase it by pressing the Delete key.

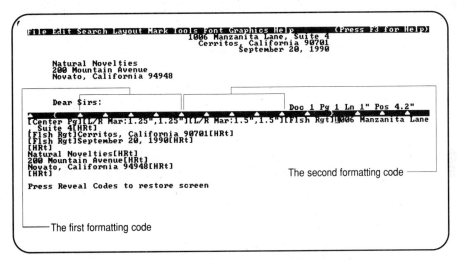

Figure 3.9 *Using Reveal Codes to discover why a formatting change is not working. In this example, the first formatting code has no effect, because no text appears between it and the second code. WordPerfect uses the second code to change the left/right margins for all subsequent text to 1.5" each.*

Reveal Codes can also help you by clarifying how some of the formatting options work. For example, if you turn on Reveal Codes, select Underline, and start typing, you'll see exactly how Underline works. When you turn on Underline, WordPerfect inserts a pair of formatting codes at the cursor position, which you can't see on the regular Edit screen. The first code, [UND], turns on underline. The second code, [und], turns it off. The cursor is positioned on the second code, [und]. As you type, your text is inserted between the two codes and formatted in underline. When you finish typing and press the Right Arrow key or Underline key, the cursor moves past the code that turns off underline, so it no longer affects your text.

Look at the Reveal Codes screen shown in Figure 3.8. As you can see, the screen is split in two horizontally. The top half is the regular Edit screen, and the lower half is the Reveal Codes screen. Between them is the tab ruler, a thick band with triangles and braces. The triangles represent the tab stop settings, pre-set for every half inch, and the braces represent the left and right margins. Since both margins are in the same position as a tab setting, they appear as braces. Otherwise, the left margin would be represented by a left bracket, and the right margin by a right bracket.

The text in the top half of the screen is the same as in the lower half, except that you can see more lines in the lower half. The main difference is that in the lower half, WordPerfect displays both the text and the formatting codes affecting the text. The codes include [HRt] for hard return, [SRt] for soft return, [UND] for underline on, and [und] for underline off. The cursor is in the same position in both screens, but in the Reveal Codes screen it is represented by a rectangular block. When you move it onto a code, the cursor expands to highlight the entire code. For example, in Figure 3.10 the cursor is highlighting the Underline On code, [UND]. This provides a clue about how to remove underlining from your text: With the cursor on the [UND] code, press the Delete key.

Tip: [HRt], the Hard Return code, appears wherever the Enter key was pressed to start a new paragraph or insert a blank line. [SRt] is the Soft Return code, appearing wherever the cursor automatically wrapped to the next line. All lines end in either a [SRt] code or a [HRt] code. You can join paragraphs together by erasing the [HRt] codes that separate them.

When Reveal Codes is on, you can do anything you can do when it's off: Move the cursor through the document, type, edit, and use any of WordPerfect's menus. You can even save a document and clear the Edit screen. In fact, you can keep it on the whole time you're using WordPerfect! While using it, watch for prompts and messages on the status line, just above the tab ruler. For instance, if you press the Font key (Ctrl-F8) while using Reveal Codes, the Font menu will appear above the tab ruler, as shown in Figure 3.11. If you use a full-screen menu, such as one of the Format menus, it will take over the screen while you're using it, but Reveal Codes will still be on when you return.

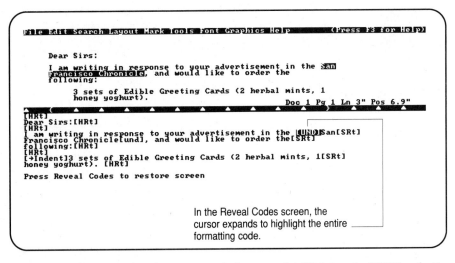

Figure 3.10　*The Reveal Codes screen with the cursor highlighting the [UND] code. To erase underlining from the phrase* San Francisco Chronicle, *press the Delete key while the cursor is highlighting either the [UND] code or the [und] code.*

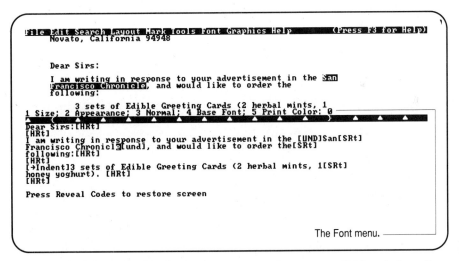

Figure 3.11　*When Reveal Codes is on, prompts and menus are displayed above the tab ruler. Here, the Font key was pressed (Ctrl-F8) and so the Font menu appears above the ruler.*

Deleting and Undeleting Codes in the Reveal Codes Screen

While displaying the Reveal Codes screen, you can erase a code and the formatting it represents by moving the cursor onto the code and then pressing the Delete key. If the cursor is to the right of a code, you can erase it by pressing the Backspace key. Be careful when you press Delete or Backspace in Reveal Codes, because you don't get any warning if you're about to erase a code. By contrast, if Reveal Codes is off and you press Backspace or Delete next to one of the hidden codes, WordPerfect shows you the code and asks if you want to delete it.

   If you accidentally erase a paired formatting code such as [UND] while using the Reveal Codes screen, you cannot get it back. However, if you erase an open formatting code such as left/right margins or line spacing, you can use WordPerfect's Undelete feature to restore it. You may remember studying Undelete in Chapter 2, as it applies to text. It also applies to codes, but it's hard to tell unless Reveal codes is turned on. Let's try it by deleting the left/right margin code. Begin by moving the cursor to the top of the letter.

1. Display the Reveal Codes screen:

   Keyboard: Press the Reveal Codes key, Alt-F3 (on most enhanced keyboards, you can press F11 instead).

   Mouse: Display the Edit menu and select the Reveal Codes option.

2. Place the cursor on the left/right margin code: `[L/R Mar:1.5",1.5"]`.

3. Press the Delete key to erase the code. Notice that your margins change immediately, reverting to the default settings of 1" each.

4. To restore the code that changes the margins to 1.5" each, use Undelete:

   Keyboard: Press Cancel (F1).

   Mouse: Display the Edit menu and select Undelete.

The margin code should appear to the left of your cursor in the Reveal Codes screen, and the `Undelete` prompt should appear above the tab ruler, as shown in Figure 3.12. Notice the [Block] code. It helps define the deletion that you can restore at this point: Anything that appears between `[Block]` and the cursor. In Figure 3.12, only the margin change code, `[L/R Mar:1.5",1.5"]`, is between `[Block]` and the cursor. Selecting Restore would undelete it.

5. If the left/right margin code appears, select the first option, **Restore**. If you don't see the code, select the **Previous Deletion** option once or twice, and select **Restore** when you see it.

After you select Restore to undelete the margin code, your margins should change again, back to 1.5" each.

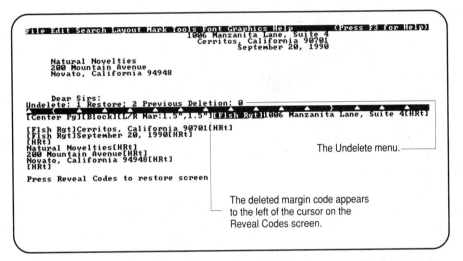

Figure 3.12 *Using Undelete in the Reveal Codes screen. Everything between [Block] and the cursor can be undeleted by selecting the Restore option. In this case, it applies to the left/right margin code.*

Now let's delete one of the underline codes and see what happens.

1. Place the cursor on the S at the beginning of the underlined phrase (San Francisco Chronicle).

The phrase should be surrounded by a pair of underline codes, with the cursor on or next to the [UND] code that turns on underlining. Notice that the text does not appear underlined (or in another color) in the Reveal Codes screen, as it does in the Edit screen.

2. Delete the [UND] code by placing the cursor on it and pressing the Delete key once.

The underlining disappears from the phrase in the Edit screen. Although the second code, [und], may still appear in Reveal Codes, as soon as you move the cursor past it and reformat the document, it will disappear.

If you try to use the Undelete feature to restore the underline code you just deleted, you'll find that WordPerfect does not offer it as one of the three deletions you can restore. Undelete cannot restore paired codes, such as bold and underline, because WordPerfect has no way of knowing where each member of the pair belongs! There is only one way to underline text after it has been typed. In the next section, you'll learn how. First, however, you should turn off Reveal Codes.

Reveal Codes is a toggle, so you turn it off the same way you turned it on:

Keyboard: Press the Reveal Codes key, Alt-F3 (or F11 on some keyboards).

Mouse: Display the Edit menu and select the Reveal Codes option.

Underlining Text After Typing It

To underline text that you've already typed, you have to designate the text as a block, and then select Underline. Let's use it to restore underlining to the phrase San Francisco Chronicle. Although you can start with the cursor at either end of the section, if you use the keyboard it's easier to start at the beginning. You'll understand why in a minute.

1. Place the cursor on the S in San Francisco Chronicle.

2. Turn on Block mode:

   Keyboard: Press Alt-F4 (the Block key). On some keyboards, you can press F12.

   Mouse: Display the Edit menu and select Block.

   A Block on prompt will appear in the lower-left corner of the screen. Your next task is to move the cursor and block highlighting to the opposite end of the section.

3. Highlight the entire phrase:

   Keyboard: Type e. As you will see, this moves the cursor and block highlighting to the next occurrence of the letter *e*, at the end of the phrase.

   Mouse: Drag the mouse to the end of the word Chronicle and release it.

4. Select Underline:

   Keyboard: Press the Underline key, F8.

   Mouse: Display the Font menu, select Appearance, and then select Underline.

The blocked text will be underlined immediately, and the Block on prompt will disappear.

Tip: When block is on, the fastest way to move the cursor is to type a letter, number, or other character that appears at the end of the section you are blocking. For example, if the last word you want to include is followed by a comma, just type a comma. This will move the cursor and block highlighting to the next comma. This trick only works if you turned on Block mode when the cursor was at the beginning of the section. If you started at the end, just use the regular cursor movement keys, such as Up Arrow.

Using Undelete to Copy Complex Formatting

Undelete is an easy way to copy codes and their formatting, and it can save you many keystrokes. For instance, if you frequently switch between left and right margins of 1" and 1.5" in a document, you can use this technique to duplicate the codes, instead of using the Format menu to insert new ones:

1. Highlight the [L/R Mar] code in Reveal Codes.

2. Press Delete to erase it, which also copies it into the special Undelete memory area.

3. Immediately restore the [L/R] code at the original position by pressing Cancel (F1) or by selecting Undelete from the pull-down Edit menu. Next, select the **Restore** option.

4. Now move the cursor to the position where you want to duplicate the margin change and make a copy of the [L/R] code by pressing Cancel (F1) and selecting the **Restore** option.

Changing the Size of the Reveal Codes Screen

When you select Reveal Codes, the screen is split nearly in half by the tab ruler. If you dislike this division, you can change the size of the Reveal Codes section through an option on WordPerfect's Setup menu. You can reduce it, enlarge it, or even modify it so that only the character or code under the cursor is displayed. To change it:

1. Display the main Setup menu:

   Keyboard: Press the Setup key (Shift-F1). The main Setup menu appears, as shown in Figure 3.13.

   Mouse: Select Setup from the File menu. A menu of Setup options pops out to the right.

2. Select **Display** and then **Edit-Screen Options.**

3. From the Setup Edit-Screen Options menu, select the sixth option, **Reveal Codes Window Size.**

4. Type the number of lines you want in the lower section; then press Enter and the Exit key (F7), or click the right mouse button.

   If you type 1, only the character or formatting code your cursor is currently on will appear in the Reveal Codes section.

```
Setup
      1  -  Mouse
      2  -  Display
      3  -  Environment
      4  -  Initial Settings
      5  -  Keyboard Layout              ENHANCED.WPK
      6  -  Location of Files




  Selection: 0
```

Figure 3.13 The main Setup menu.

Changing the Appearance of the Cursor in Reveal Codes

If you find it hard to see the cursor in the Reveal Codes screen, you can use the Setup menu to change its appearance. For instance, if you have a color monitor, you can select different colors, and if you have a monochrome monitor, you can select a different shading. However, if you have a CGA monitor, you cannot change the attributes, so this section does not apply to you.

To change the Reveal Codes cursor:

1. Display the main Setup menu:

   Keyboard: Press the Setup key (Shift-F1).

   Mouse: Select Setup from the File menu.

2. Select **D**isplay, then **C**olors/Fonts/Attributes, then **S**creen Colors.

   You should see the Setup Colors menu, as shown in Figure 3.14.

3. Move the cursor to the second line, `Blocked`. The blocked attribute is used for the Reveal Codes cursor, the tab ruler in Reveal Codes, text that you highlight in Block mode, and the cursor bar and header area of the List Files screen.

4. Choose a letter for the foreground color; then press the Right Arrow key and select one for the background. When you finish, press the Exit key (F7) twice or click the right mouse button.

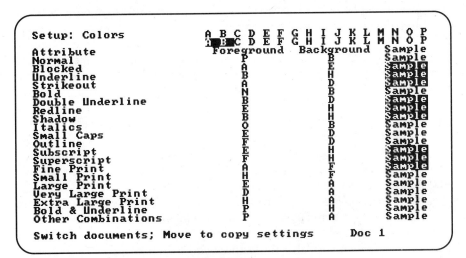

Figure 3.14   *The Setup: Colors menu for color monitors. It lets you change the foreground and background colors WordPerfect will use to represent text on the Edit screen that you have formatted with font attributes like bold, underline, italics, or small print. The last column, Sample, displays how each combination will appear in your text.*

   There is nothing mysterious about WordPerfect's Reveal Codes screen. The codes themselves are basically simple, and you can tell at a glance what most of them represent: [UND] means you've turned on underline; [Center] means you've turned on line centering; [Flsh Rgt] means you've selected Flush Right; [L/R Mar:1.5",1.5"] means you've changed the left and right margins to 1.5" each; and [Center Pg] means you've selected the Center Page (top to bottom) option.

> **Tip:** The Reveal Codes screen can be invaluable. To help you understand it, the codes are shown with each formatting feature in Part Three of this book, "Command Reference," and Appendix C of the WordPerfect manual lists them in alphabetical order.

Changing WordPerfect's Formatting Defaults

So far in this chapter you've learned how to change several formatting options for individual documents. What if you find yourself changing a feature nearly every time you type a document? For example, perhaps you prefer the look of a ragged right margin over WordPerfect's default of Full Justification, so you change it in every document you type. This involves many steps: display the Format or Layout menu, select Line, select Justification, select Left, and then exit back to the Edit screen. Since the document on the Edit screen appears to have a ragged right margin, you may not remember to change the justification style until after you print and review the document. Rather than going through all the work of changing the justification style each time you type a new document, consider changing the default for that option. Once you change the default, all new documents you create will be formatted with a ragged right margin.

To change default settings, you use the Initial Codes option on the Setup Initial Settings menu. You can use it to set new defaults for commonly used features such as margins, line spacing, base font, justification, page numbering, and paper size and type. Table 3.1 lists all of the features whose defaults you can change. Let's see how the Initial Codes option works by changing the justification to Left, and the left and right margins to 1.25" each.

Using Initial Codes to Change Default Settings

To select Initial Codes, begin by displaying the main Setup menu.

1. Display the main Setup menu:

    Keyboard: Press the Setup key, Shift-F1. The main Setup menu appears, as shown in Figure 3.13.

    Mouse: Display the File menu and select Setup.

2. Select the fourth option, **Initial Settings**. From the next menu, Setup Initial Settings, select the fifth option, **Initial Codes**. The Initial Codes screen appears, as shown in Figure 3.15. It resembles the Reveal Codes screen, except for this message above the status line, telling you what to do when you finish using Initial Codes:

`Initial Codes: Press Exit when done`

A more subtle difference is that the document and page indicators (`Doc 1 Pg 1`) do not appear on the status line.

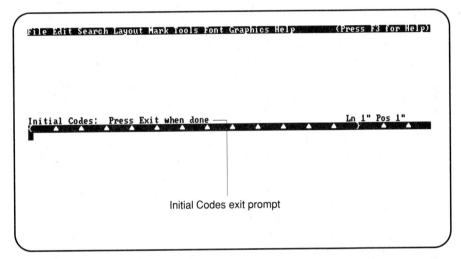

Initial Codes exit prompt

Figure 3.15 *When you select the Initial Codes option on the Setup Initial Settings menu, this screen appears. Although it resembles the Reveal Codes screen, notice this message on the status line:* Initial Codes: Press Exit when done.

You can use this screen to change the defaults for any of the formatting options listed in Table 3.1. Use the same procedure you would use to change them in a document. For example, to select Left Justification and change the right and left margins to 1.25":

1. Select the Format Line menu:

   Keyboard: Press the Format key (Shift-F8) and select **Line**.

   Mouse: Display the Layout menu and select **Line**.

2. Select **Margins**. Type 1.25 for the left margin and press Enter. Type 1.25 for the right margin and press Enter.

3. Select **Justification**, and then select the first option, **Left**.

4. Exit the Format menu:

Keyboard: Press the Exit key (F7).

Mouse: Click the right button.

You should be back in the Initial Codes menu. It now includes the codes for your new default margins, [L/R Mar:1.25",1.25"], and justification style, [Just:Left], as shown in Figure 3.16.

If you make a mistake or decide you don't want to change one of these defaults after all, erase it from the Initial Codes screen by highlighting the code and pressing the Delete key.

5. The last step is to exit back to the Edit screen:

Keyboard: Press the Exit key (F7) twice.

Mouse: Display the File menu and select Exit; then click the right button.

Since default settings do not insert codes into the Reveal Codes screen, if you select Reveal Codes now you will not see codes for the changes you just made.

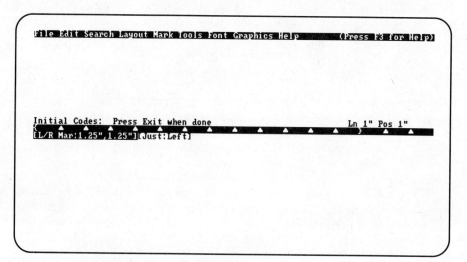

Figure 3.16 *The Initial Codes screen after changing the default margins to 1.25" each and selecting Left Justification. Each of these changes is represented by a formatting code in this screen. However, these codes do not appear in the document's Reveal Codes screen.*

Since you had a document on the Edit screen when you selected Initial Codes and changed the defaults, you won't notice the changes until you clear the screen, because changes you make in Initial Codes only affect new documents. Once you clear the screen, you can tell from the position indicator on the status line that the default margins are 1.25". However, since text on the Edit screen always appears ragged right, you can't determine if Left Justification is in effect. To verify that it is, display the Format Line menu, where you'll see that the word Left appears next to the Justification option, to signify that it is now the default. As you can see from Figure 3.4, it used to be Full.

You can always override your default settings. For instance, if you want to change the margins back to 1" each for the document currently on your Edit screen, just follow the usual steps: Display the Format Line menu, select Margins, and change them each to 1". This will insert a formatting code into your document at the cursor position, and change the margins from that point forward. Codes in the document (visible in Reveal Codes) always override changes you make in Document Initial Codes, which is discussed in a later section.

Table 3.1   *Formatting options that can be changed using the Setup Initial Codes option.*

Base Font	Line Spacing
Center Page	Margins, Left/Right
Column On	Margins, Top/Bottom
Column Definition	Math On
Decimal/Align Character	Math Column Definition
Endnote Options	New Page Number
Footnote Options	Page Number Style
Graphics Box Options	Page Number Position
Hyphenation On/Off	Paper Size/Type
Hyphenation Zone	Print Color
Justification	Tab Set
Kerning	Underline Spaces and Tabs
Language	Widow/Orphan On/Off
Line Height	Word and Letter Spacing
Line Numbering	

Inserting Your New Defaults into a Previously Saved Document

Since initial formatting is saved along with the document, previously saved documents will not include your new default formatting. To insert the new defaults into an existing document, you have to trick WordPerfect by retrieving the old document into a new document. WordPerfect creates a new document as soon as you type one character, even if it's a blank space. Here's how to do it.

1. Use Exit to clear the screen.

2. Press the space bar once.

3. Retrieve the document.

   If you use the List Files Retrieve option, WordPerfect will ask if you want to retrieve the file into the current document. If so, select **Yes**.

4. Save the document again.

   The file name will not appear next to the Document to be saved prompt, since WordPerfect considers this to be a new document. Instead, you'll have to type the file name yourself.

> **Tip:** There are certain formatting codes that you cannot include in Initial Codes, including indents, tabs, document comments, styles, and headers and footers. Sometimes WordPerfect lets you insert these codes, but disregards and removes them later. For instance, if you press the Indent key while using Initial Codes, an indent code will appear in the Initial Codes screen. However, it will not be used as default formatting in your new documents, and the next time you select Initial Codes it will be gone.

Document Initial Codes

As you know, formatting changes you make through the Initial Codes option on the Setup menu are permanent and affect any new documents you create. If you just want to change the defaults for the document currently on the Edit screen, you can use another option: Initial Codes on the Format Document menu. Like the defaults you change through the Setup menu's Initial Codes option, WordPerfect saves these defaults along with the file, in a special area called the *file prefix*. The prefix, which you do not have access to, also contains information about the default font and the printer currently in use. For this reason, changes to Initial Codes do not insert codes in the Reveal Codes screen. Changes that you make in Document Initial Codes override the defaults in Setup Initial Codes.

   Although it adds a few extra steps to the formatting process, there are many advantages to using Document Initial Codes instead of the regular formatting techniques for an individual document. For instance, if someone else edits your document, you won't have to worry about him or her accidentally erasing your codes and changing your formatting, since there are no codes to erase. Also, you don't have to worry about cursor position when you change the formatting. For example, if you use Document Initial Codes to change the left and right margins to 1.5" each, regardless of where the cursor is when you make the change, it will affect the entire document. You no longer have to worry about whether your cursor is positioned before or after the code when you start typing. Another advantage is that your Reveal Codes screen will be less cluttered, since the formatting changes don't appear in Reveal Codes.

Using Document Initial Codes

To select Document Initial Codes and change a document default, begin by displaying the main Format Document menu. The cursor can be anywhere in the document.

1. Display the Format Document menu:

    Keyboard: Press Format (Shift-F8) and select Document.

    Mouse: Display the Layout menu and select Document.

    The Format Document menu appears, as shown in Figure 3.17.

```
Format: Document
        1 - Display Pitch - Automatic Yes
                            Width        0.1"

        2 - Initial Codes
        3 - Initial Base Font             Courier 12pt
        4 - Redline Method                Printer Dependent
        5 - Summary




Selection: 0
```

Figure 3.17 *The Format Document menu. Use the second option, Initial Codes, to change the default formatting for the document currently on your Edit screen.*

2. Select the second option, Initial Codes.

The next screen is identical to the one you see when you select Initial Codes from the Setup menu, as shown in Figure 3.15. In fact, the steps you use are also identical. To change left and right margins, for example, display the Format Line menu, select Margins, and change them.

Any changes you make through this menu override WordPerfect's defaults and changes you make in the Setup menu's Initial Codes option. However, if you make a change that inserts a hidden code into your document, that change overrides both Initial Codes options.

MOVE, COPY, AND OTHER BLOCK OPERATIONS

WordPerfect's Move key (Ctrl-F4) and its pull-down menu equivalent, Select on the Edit menu, simplify the process of moving, copying, deleting, or appending a sentence, paragraph, or page. If a section of text does not fall into one of these convenient categories, you can block it first and then select Move, Copy, Delete, or Append. Here's what each of the options does:

- *Move* erases the text from its present position and prompts you to move the cursor and retrieve it at another location by pressing the Enter key.

- *Copy* leaves the text intact at the present position, copies it into memory, and prompts you to move the cursor and retrieve the copied text at another location.

- *Delete* erases the text. If you change your mind about deleting it, you can restore it again by pressing the Cancel key (F1) or by selecting Undelete from the pull-down Edit menu. This option was covered in Chapter 2.

- *Append* copies the text to another file. If you enter the name of an existing disk file, it will be added to the end of the file. If you enter a new file name, WordPerfect will create a new file for the copied text.

Using the Move and Copy Options to Edit Text

So that you'll have some text to work with while learning how to move, copy, and append, type the letter shown in Figure 4.1. Save it using this file name: MCBRIDE.LTR.

```
June 15, 1990


Ms. Leslie McBride
121 Vintage Place
Northridge, CA 91324


Dear Ms. McBride,

We are pleased to inform you that we have completed your holiday
reservations for your trip to New Zealand.  At your request, you
will be staying at the beautiful and luxurious Hyatt Regency.  We
think you will find it enchanting.

We received your deposit of $450.00 yesterday, and have credited
your account with that amount.

Your travel documents will arrive tomorrow via Federal Express.  If
they are not there by 10 a.m. tomorrow, please call.  We thank you
for your patronage.



Yours truly,


Sandy Morris
Travel Director
Exotic Excursions, Inc.
```

Figure 4.1   Letter to practice using Move, Copy, Delete, and Append.

Moving a Paragraph

Let's begin by selecting the second paragraph in the body of the letter and moving it to the first paragraph, before the second sentence.

1. Place the cursor anywhere in the paragraph.

2. **Keyboard:** Press the Move key (Ctrl-F4). This prompt appears:

   `Move: 1 Sentence; 2 Paragraph; 3 Page; 4 Retrieve: 0`

   Mouse: Display the **Edit** menu and choose the **Select** option. The Sentence, Paragraph, and Page options appear on a submenu that pops out to the right, as shown in Figure 4.2. Notice that the last two options, Tabular Column and Rectangle, appear in brackets; this is because they are unavailable unless you are using Block mode.

3. Select the second option, **Paragraph**. (Although there is only one sentence in this paragraph, if you select Sentence instead of Paragraph, the option will work differently.) Your screen should now resemble Figure 4.3. The entire paragraph is highlighted, and a menu appears at the bottom of the screen asking if you want to move, copy, delete, or append it.

4. Select **M**ove. The paragraph will disappear, and you'll see a message at the bottom of the screen prompting you to move the cursor and press Enter to retrieve the text. Your screen should now resemble Figure 4.4.

5. Move the cursor into the new position, placing it on the A at the beginning of the sentence At your request, you will be staying at the beautiful and luxurious Hyatt Regency.

6. Retrieve the paragraph by pressing the Enter key.

Your screen should now resemble Figure 4.5. Since you selected the Paragraph option, WordPerfect also included the blank line following it. As a result, the last two sentences were pushed down to form a new paragraph. If you had selected the Sentence option instead, the sentence would have been incorporated into the paragraph, as shown in Figure 4.6.

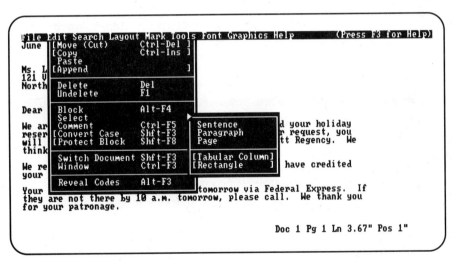

Figure 4.2   *This menu appears when you display the Edit menu and choose Select. You can use it to select a sentence, paragraph, or page to move, copy, delete, or append.*

Tip: If you change your mind after selecting Sentence, Paragraph, or Page, or discover you've selected the wrong text, press Cancel (F1) or click the left and right mouse buttons simultaneously (or middle button).

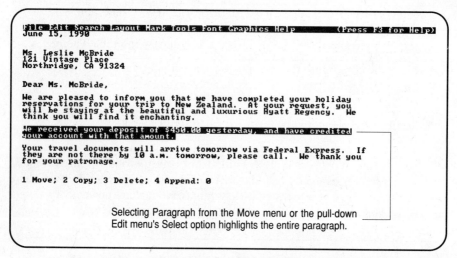

Selecting Paragraph from the Move menu or the pull-down Edit menu's Select option highlights the entire paragraph.

Figure 4.3   *After you select Paragraph, WordPerfect highlights the entire paragraph and asks if you want to move, copy, delete, or append it.*

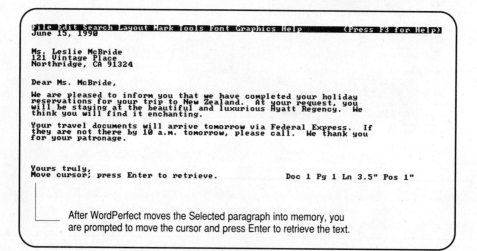

After WordPerfect moves the Selected paragraph into memory, you are prompted to move the cursor and press Enter to retrieve the text.

Figure 4.4   *After you select the Move option, the selected paragraph disappears and WordPerfect prompts you to move the cursor to the position where you want the text to appear when you select the Retrieve option.*

```
File Edit Search Layout Mark Tools Font Graphics Help        (Press F3 for Help)
June 15, 1990


Ms. Leslie McBride
121 Vintage Place
Northridge, CA 91324


Dear Ms. McBride,

We are pleased to inform you that we have completed your holiday
reservations for your trip to New Zealand.  We received your
deposit of $450.00 yesterday, and have credited your account with
that amount.

At your request, you will be staying at the beautiful  and luxurious
Hyatt Regency.  We think you will find it enchanting.

Your travel documents will arrive tomorrow via Federal Express.  If
they are not there by 10 a.m. tomorrow, please call.  We thank you
for your patronage.

                                    Doc 1 Pg 1 Ln 2.83" POS 5.4"
```

Figure 4.5   *This is how your letter should appear after you finish moving the second paragraph. Notice that the last two sentences of the original paragraph were moved down to form a new paragraph.*

```
File Edit Search Layout Mark Tools Font Graphics Help        (Press F3 for Help)
June 15, 1990


Ms. Leslie McBride
121 Vintage Place
Northridge, CA 91324


Dear Ms. McBride,

We are pleased to inform you that we have completed your holiday
reservations for your trip to New Zealand.  We received your
deposit of $450.00 yesterday, and have credited your account with
that amount.At your request, you will be staying at the beautiful
and luxurious Hyatt Regency.  We think you will find it enchanting.


Your travel documents will arrive tomorrow via Federal Express.  If
they are not there by 10 a.m. tomorrow, please call.  We thank you
for your patronage.

                                    Doc 1 Pg 1 Ln 2.83" POS 5.4"
```

Figure 4.6   *If you had selected the Sentence option instead of the Paragraph option to move the paragraph, this is how your letter would look.*

Moving a Sentence or Page

The steps that you use to move a sentence or page are almost identical to the ones you just used to move a paragraph, except that you select Sentence or Page in the third step. A warning: If you try to select a sentence that includes a word ending in a period, such as *Mrs.* or *etc.*, the Sentence option won't work correctly. Instead of selecting the entire sentence, it will only highlight text from the beginning of the sentence to the period following the abbreviation. For example, if you place the cursor at the beginning of the second sentence of the last paragraph in the body of the letter and select Sentence, WordPerfect only highlights this section:

```
If they are not there by 10 a.m.
```

When this happens, you have to block the text before selecting Move, Copy, or Delete. In the next section, you'll learn how.

Moving, Copying, or Deleting a Block of Text

If the section of text you want to move or copy does not fall into the category of sentence, paragraph, or page, you can move, copy, or delete it by marking it as a block first. Let's use Block to delete this sentence from the last paragraph in the body of the letter:

```
If they are not there by 10 a.m. tomorrow, please call.
```

When you use the block method to highlight text, you can begin with the cursor at either end. However, if you are using the keyboard, more cursor movement methods are available in Block mode if you start at the beginning.

1. Place the cursor on the first character in the sentence, I.

2. Turn Block on and move the cursor and highlighting to the end of the section:

    Keyboard: Press the Block key, Alt-F4 (or F12). Type 1. This will move the cursor and block highlighting to the next occurrence of the letter *l*. To highlight the rest of the sentence, type a period.

    Mouse: Click the left button to turn on Block mode, and hold it while you move the cursor to the end of the sentence. When you get there, release the button. If you make a mistake, click the left button again to turn off Block mode.

    A blinking Block on prompt appears in the lower-left corner of the screen.

3. Delete the block:

Keyboard: Press the Move key (Ctrl-F4). This prompt appears:

```
Move: 1 Block; 2 Tabular Column; 3 Rectangle: 0
```

Select Block. This prompt appears next:

```
1 Move; 2 Copy; 3 Delete; 4 Append: 0
```

Select **Delete**. Alternatively, you can press the Delete key, and type Y in response to the `Delete Block` prompt.

Mouse: Display the Edit menu and select **Delete**. In response to the `Delete Block` prompt, select **Yes**.

Tip: In addition to the regular cursor movement methods, there are many other techniques that you can use to move the cursor in Block mode. For example, if you press the space bar, the cursor and block highlighting moves to the next word. If you type a period, it moves to the end of the next sentence that ends in a period. If you press Enter, it moves to the end of the paragraph. If you type a character, it moves to the next occurrence of that character. Note that it is case-sensitive, so if you type *A*, it will move to the next *A*, not to the lowercase *a*. You can also use the Search feature in Block mode: Press the Forward Search key (F2), or display the Search menu and select Search Forward, type the text, then press Esc.

As you've probably figured out by now, the Move key or Select option on the Edit menu is just a shortcut that you can use to automatically block a sentence, paragraph, or page. When you press the Move key (Ctrl-F4) alone, this menu appears:

```
Move: 1 Sentence; 2 Paragraph; 3 Page; 4 Retrieve: 0
```

If you use the Select option on the Edit menu, only the Sentence, Paragraph, and Page options are listed, as shown in Figure 4.2. Regardless of which method you use, after you select sentence, paragraph, or page, this prompt appears:

```
1 Move; 2 Copy; 3 Delete; 4 Append: 0
```

Compare this to the way the Move key works if you press it after turning on Block mode and highlighting a section of text. First, this menu appears:

```
Move: 1 Block; 2 Tabular Column; 3 Rectangle: 0
```

After you select Block, this menu appears:

```
1 Move; 2 Copy; 3 Delete; 4 Append: 0
```

and it is identical to the prompt that appears after you press Move and select Sentence, Paragraph, or Page. As you can see, using Move or the Select option on the Edit menu to highlight a sentence, paragraph, or page just saves you a few steps: Turning on Block mode and moving the cursor to highlight the sentence, paragraph, or page.

Copying Blocked Text

Let's explore the difference between Move and Copy. Move literally means to pick up the highlighted text and move it to another position in the document. When you use it, it erases the blocked text, then waits for you to retrieve it somewhere else. Copy does not erase the highlighted text. Instead, it copies it into memory, and waits for you to move the cursor and retrieve it somewhere else. You don't have to copy it into the document currently on the Edit screen. You can clear the screen and retrieve it into a blank Edit screen, or switch to the Doc 2 work area and retrieve it into another document that you are working on there. You can even clear the screen, retrieve another file, and then copy the text into that file. As long as you don't press the Enter key (except if you use the Retrieve key method of retrieving a document, since you must press Enter to finish the command), WordPerfect will wait patiently with the Move cursor; press Enter to retrieve prompt, until you are ready to retrieve the copied text.

Let's use Block and Copy to copy the name and address in the letter for an envelope.

1. Place the cursor at the beginning of the name, on the M in Ms.

2. Turn Block on and move the cursor to the end of the section:

   Keyboard: Press the Block key, Alt-F4 (or F12). Type 4. This will move the cursor and block highlighting to the next occurrence of the number 4, at the end of the ZIP code.

   Mouse: Click the left button to turn on Block mode, and hold it while you drag the mouse and highlighting onto the 4 (the last number in the ZIP code). Release the button. If you make a mistake, click the left button again to turn off Block mode.

   The Block on prompt appears in the lower-left corner of the screen.

3. Select Copy:

   Keyboard: If you have an enhanced keyboard, press Ctrl-Insert. If not, press the Move key (Ctrl-F4). This prompt appears:

   Move: 1 Block; 2 Tabular Column; 3 Rectangle: 0

Select **Block**. This prompt appears next:

`1 Move; 2 Copy; 3 Delete; 4 Append: 0`

Select **Copy**.

Mouse: Display the **Edit** menu and select **Copy**.

The `Move cursor; press Enter to retrieve` prompt appears. This time, the text does not disappear from its current position. Instead, WordPerfect waits for you to move the cursor to the position where you want to retrieve another copy, and press Enter. In our hypothetical example, we will be using the copied name and address on an envelope, so we'll need to retrieve it into a clear screen. There are two ways to do this: Either use Exit to clear the letter from this screen or use Switch to switch to the Doc 2 Edit screen. Since the letter is already saved, let's clear the screen.

4. Clear the screen:

   Keyboard: Press the Exit key (F7).

   Mouse: Display the **File** menu and select **Exit**.

A `Save document` prompt appears. Select **No**. The next prompt asks if you want to exit from WordPerfect.

`Exit WP? No (Yes)`

Select **No**. This clears the screen.

5. Retrieve the name and address by pressing the Enter key.

   To complete the envelope, you would select Envelope as the Paper Size/Type option (on the Format: Page menu) and then change the margins. The steps are summarized below and assume that an Envelope Paper Definition is available for your printer under the Paper Size and Type option; WordPerfect includes one for most printers, including the laser printers. It also assumes that the return address is printed on your envelopes, or that you will be using a return address label. If this is not true, you'll have to use different margins. The procedure is covered in more detail in Part Three, "Command Reference," under *Paper Size and Type*.

   Start with the cursor on the first line of the document.

1. Select the Format: Page menu:

   Keyboard: Press Format (Shift-F8) and select the **Page** option.

   Mouse: Display the **Layout** menu and select **Page**.

2. Select the seventh option, Paper Size/Type. A list of paper types that have been defined for your printer appears.

3. Move the cursor onto the Envelope option, if there is one in your list, and choose the Select option. You will then return to the Format: Page menu. Your new Size/Type selection, Envelope, appears next to option 7 on the menu.

   If the envelope form has not yet been defined for your printer, you must use the Add option on the Format: Paper Size/Type menu to define it before continuing. See "Command Reference" (*Paper Size and Type*) for details.

4. Select Margins and change the top margin to 2" and the bottom margin to .5".

5. Press Enter and select Line. From the Format: Line menu, select Margins. Change the left margin to 4" and the right to .5".

6. Press Exit (F7) or click the right mouse button to return to the Edit screen.

Before printing, use the View Document option on the main Print menu to preview the envelope and make sure the margins are correct. After that, print it by inserting an envelope in your printer and selecting the Page option on the Print menu.

Table 4.1 summarizes the keystrokes for moving and copying text.

Table 4.1 *Moving and copying text.*

To Move a	Use These Keystrokes
Sentence	Ctrl-F4 1 1, move cursor to new location, press Enter
Paragraph	Ctrl-F4 2 1, move cursor to new location, press Enter
Page	Ctrl-F4 3 1, move cursor to new location, press Enter
Block	Alt-F4, move cursor to mark the block, press Ctrl-Delete (enhanced keyboard only) or Ctrl F4 1 1, move cursor to new location, press Enter

To Copy a	Use These Keystrokes
Sentence	Ctrl-F4 1 2, move cursor to new location, press Enter
Paragraph	Ctrl-F4 2 2, move cursor to new location, press Enter
Page	Ctrl-F4 3 2, move cursor to new location, press Enter
Block	Alt-F4, move cursor to mark the block, press Ctrl-Insert (enhanced keyboard only) or Ctrl F4 1 2, move cursor to new location, press Enter

Appending a Block of Text

WordPerfect's Append option, which can be a great help in writing and editing, has many uses. For example, before deleting a section from a document, you can use Append to add the section to a special file you might call *LEFTOUT*. If you change your mind later or decide to use the section somewhere else, you can easily retrieve it. You can also use Append in a merge operation, to add names and addresses to the end of a secondary file, for example. Or use Append to save the body of a letter to a separate file so that you can use it as a template for other letters in which only the recipient's name and address changes. Let's try this last technique with the MCBRIDE.LTR. Begin by clearing the name and address from your Edit screen.

1. Use Retrieve to retrieve the MCBRIDE.LTR file, or, if you did not type it earlier, clear your screen and type Figure 4.1.

2. Place the cursor at the beginning of the first paragraph (We are pleased to inform you ...).

3. Turn Block on and move the cursor to the end of the letter:

    Keyboard: Press the Block key, Alt-F4. Press Page Down.

    Mouse: Click the left button, hold it while you drag the mouse and highlighting to the end of the letter, then release it.

4. Select Append:

    Keyboard: Press the Move key (Ctrl-F4), select **Block**, then select **Append**.

    Mouse: Display the **Edit** menu, select **Append**, then select the first option, To File.

5. This prompt will appear:

    Append to:

Type the new file name, TRAVEL.LTR, and press Enter. If you type an existing file name, WordPerfect will add it to the end of the file. Once WordPerfect has saved the block, the prompt disappears. If you want to verify that the blocked section has been saved, clear the screen and retrieve the TRAVEL.LTR file.

If text falls into the category of sentence, paragraph, or page, you do not have to block it first in order to append it. Instead, press the Move key (Ctrl-F4), or display the Edit menu and choose the Select option. Next, select Sentence, Paragraph, or Page. The prompt will appear asking if you want to move, copy, delete, or append the blocked text. Select the Append option, and enter the file name.

Instead of appending a blocked section to a disk file, you can add it to a special memory area by pressing Enter instead of typing a file name in response to the `Append to` prompt. This is the same memory area where text is temporarily stored when you use the Copy or Move option. If you used one of these two options in the same edit session, the block you are appending will be added to the text that is already in this memory. As long as you don't use Copy or Move again, you can retrieve this text using the Retrieve option on the Move key, or the Paste option on the Edit key. You'll learn how in the next section.

Retrieving Previously Copied or Moved Text, or Text That You Appended to Memory

What happens if you highlight a sentence, paragraph, page, or other block of text, select Move or Copy, then decide you don't want to retrieve the text yet? Just press the Cancel key (F1) to get rid of the `Move cursor; press Enter to retrieve` prompt. The text you selected to move or copy will remain in memory until you're ready to use it, unless you move or copy another section. When you are ready to retrieve the text, use the Retrieve option on the Move key, or (for mouse users) the Paste option on the pull-down Edit menu.

You can also use this technique to retrieve previously moved or copied text, and make an extra copy of it somewhere else, or to retrieve text that you appended to memory (instead of to a file). In fact, you can make as many copies as you want, because the text will remain in memory until you move or copy another section of text, or exit WordPerfect. However, if you later use the Append option without a file name, the blocked text will be added to the text that you moved or copied, so you may get more than you expected when you retrieve!

The last text that you selected to Move or Copy was the name and address for the envelope. Clear the screen and then follow these instructions to retrieve another copy.

1. Select Retrieve or Paste:

    Keyboard: Press the Move key (Ctrl-F4) and select the fourth option, **Retrieve.**

    Mouse: Display the **Edit** menu and select **Paste.**

    This prompt appears:

    `Retrieve: 1 Block; 2 Tabular Column; 3 Rectangle: 0`

2. Select Block. The last text that you moved or copied, which should be the name and address, will appear at the cursor position.

An alternative method of retrieving the text is to press the Retrieve key (Shift-F10) or display the File menu and select Retrieve, and then press the Enter key instead of typing a file name. The effect is exactly the same as selecting Retrieve, Block from the Move key, or Paste and Block from the pull-down Edit menu.

The Difference Between Retrieve or Paste and Undelete

If you highlight text and select Delete instead of Move or Copy, it goes to the Undelete memory area, and you cannot use the Retrieve or Paste option to bring it back. Instead, you have to use the Restore option on the Cancel key (F1), or Undelete on the pull-down Edit menu, and then Restore from the `Undelete` prompt. In case this is confusing, let's take a moment to explore the difference between Retrieve or Paste, and the Undelete option on the Cancel key (F1) and Edit menu.

If you highlight text and select Move, Copy, or Append without a file name, it goes into a special memory area. You can retrieve this text, or make additional copies, by selecting Retrieve or Paste. However, you cannot restore it using Undelete. The converse is also true: If you erase text using the Delete option on the Move key, or any of the delete techniques that you studied in Chapter 2, including Backspace, Delete, Ctrl-Backspace, and Ctrl-End, Retrieve or Paste will not restore it. This text goes into a different memory area, and can only be restored using Undelete.

In fact, the best way to delete text if you aren't sure when you will restore it is to select the Move option, and then press Cancel. Since WordPerfect stores this text in a different area of memory from other deletions, the chances are greater that it will still be available when you want to restore it. Although the Undelete option restores the last three deletions, there are so many ways to erase text and send it to this memory area, that before you know it your text is gone for good! The Retrieve or Paste options can only restore the last section of text, but there are only three ways to get it there: Move, Copy, or Append without a file name.

The Delete Option

In Chapter 2 you learned how to delete a sentence, paragraph, page, or block with the Move option, so we'll just review the steps here.

To delete a sentence, paragraph, or page:

1. Begin by placing the cursor anywhere in the sentence, paragraph, or page that you want to erase.

2. Select the text:

    Keyboard: Press the Move key (Ctrl-F4).

    Mouse: Display the **Edit** menu and choose the **Select** option.

    Choose **Sentence**, **Paragraph**, or **Page**. The next menu asks if you want to Move, Copy, Delete, or Append the text.

3. Select the third option, **Delete**. The text disappears from your document.

To delete a block of text:

1. Place the cursor at the beginning of the section you want to erase.

2. Turn Block on, and move the cursor to the end of the section:

    Keyboard: Press the Block key, Alt-F4. Move the cursor to the end of the section.

    Mouse: Click the left button, and hold it while you move the cursor to the end of the section. Release the button.

3. Select Delete:

    Keyboard: Press the Delete or Backspace key.

    Mouse: Display the **Edit** menu, and select **Delete**.

4. In response to the `Delete Block` prompt that appears, type Y.

Working with Blocks of Text

WordPerfect's Block feature has a myriad of applications, and so far you've only scratched the surface. In this chapter, you've learned how to block text to move, copy, delete, or append it. In the last chapter, you learned how to use Block to underline text after typing it. Among the other operations that you can perform on a blocked section are

- Save.

- Print.

- Sort (alphabetize).

- Spell check.

- Convert the text from uppercase to lowercase or vice versa.

- Protect it so that the entire section remains on the same page.

- Search and replace inside a blocked section.

- Enhance a block with formatting such as centering or right alignment.

- Change the font size or appearance attributes, such as bold, italics, double underline, small, or large print.

- Format a block with a paired style.

- Designate entries for a list, index, or table of contents.

Many of WordPerfect's keys and menu options work differently when Block is on. For example, if you block a section and select Save, instead of asking you to save the entire document, WordPerfect asks for a block name and saves only the blocked section. If you press the Switch key (Shift-F3) when Block is on, instead of switching to Doc 2 (or Doc 1 if you're already in Doc 2), you'll be asked if you want to convert the highlighted text to uppercase or lowercase. You'll learn more about this and some of the other block operations in this section.

Using Block Mode to Right-Align Text That Has Already Been Typed

In the last chapter, you learned how to use WordPerfect's Flush Right feature to align text against the right margin. You used it to right-align the first three lines of your letter, selecting the option before typing each line. If you had typed the lines and later decided to right-align them, you could right-align all three lines at once by blocking them and then selecting Flush Right. Here's how:

1. Place the cursor anywhere on the first line you want to right-align.

2. Turn on Block mode and highlight the text:

   Keyboard: Press the Block key (Alt-F4). Move the cursor to highlight all the lines you want to include.

   Mouse: Click the left button to turn on Block mode, and hold it while you move the cursor to the end of the section. When you get there, release the button.

3. Select Flush Right:

   Keyboard: Press the Flush Right key, Alt-F6.

   Mouse: Display the pull-down **Layout** menu and select **Align**. From the Align menu that pops out to the right, select **Flush Right**.

   You will see this prompt:

```
[Just:Right]? No (Yes)
```

4. Select **Yes**.

When you use Block with Flush Right, WordPerfect uses the Justification option on the Line Format menu, selecting Right at the beginning of the section, then changing it to Full or Left at the end of the section (depending on which method you were using before the blocked section). The effect is exactly the same as selecting Flush Right at the beginning of each line. If you look into the Reveal Codes screen after right-aligning a section, you'll see these codes: [Just:Right] at the beginning, and [Just:Full] or [Just:Left] at the end.

The Block method of right-aligning can save you a lot of work, especially in a long section of text. If you don't use it, you have to place the cursor at the beginning of the section, display the Format Line menu, select Justification and change it to Right, move the cursor to the end of the section, display the Format Line menu again, and select Justification, then Left or Full.

Centering a Block of Text

Centering several consecutive lines of text is just like using Flush Right on a section: You block the text, then select Center. The steps are nearly identical.

1. Place the cursor anywhere on the first line you want to center.

2. Turn on Block mode and highlight the text:

   Keyboard: Press the Block key (Alt-F4). Move the cursor until you've highlighted all the lines you want to center.

   Mouse: Click the left button and hold it while you move the cursor to the end of the section. Release the button.

3. Select Center:

   Keyboard: Press the Center key, Shift-F6.

   Mouse: Display the Layout menu and select **Align**, then **Center**.

   You will see this prompt:

   [Just: Center]? No (Yes)

   because WordPerfect uses the Justification Center method from the Format Line menu to center a block of text. The effect is exactly the same as selecting Center at the beginning of each line.

4. Select **Yes**.

Boldfacing or Underlining Existing Text

In the last chapter, you learned how to use the Underline feature to underline text as you typed it, and you learned that the Bold feature is very similar. If you want to boldface or underline text that you've already typed, the procedure is different: You have to block it first and then select Bold or Underline. Here's how.

1. Turn on Block mode, and highlight the text:

   Keyboard: Press the Block key, Alt-F4. Move the cursor to the end of the section you want to underline or boldface.

   Mouse: Click the left button to turn on Block mode, and hold it while you move the cursor to the end of the section. Release the button.

   A `Block on` prompt appears in the lower-left corner of the screen.

2. Select underline or boldface for the blocked section:

   Keyboard: Press F6 for Bold, or F8 for Underline.

   Mouse: Display the Font menu, select Appearance, then select **Bold** or Underline.

The highlighted section is immediately formatted with bold or underline, and the `Block on` prompt disappears.

Saving a Block

To save a section of text, you can designate the text as a block first and then select Save. Instead of the familiar `Document to be saved` prompt, WordPerfect will ask you for a block name. After you type the name, WordPerfect will save the block just like any other file (using the name you typed). Let's use this technique to save the name and address from the McBride letter to a new file.

1. Place the cursor at the beginning of the name (on the `M` in `Ms.`).

2. Turn on Block mode and highlight the text:

   Keyboard: Press the Block key, Alt-F4. Move the cursor and highlighting to the end of the section (after the ZIP code).

   Mouse: Click the left button to turn on Block mode, and hold it while you move the cursor to the end of the section, after the ZIP code. Release the button.

3. Select Save:

> **Keyboard:** Press the Save key, F10.

> **Mouse:** Display the **File** menu and select the **Save** option.

This prompt will appear, asking for a file name for the block:

`Block name:`

4. Type a new file name, `MCBRIDE.ENV`, and press Enter. If you type the name of an existing file, you'll see another prompt asking if you want to replace it. Remember, replace means erase. If you don't want to erase the existing file, select **No** and type a different file name for the block.

That's all there is to it. If you want to verify that you saved it, clear the screen and then retrieve the MCBRIDE.ENV file.

Tip: If you don't want to save a blocked section permanently, instead of typing a file name in response to the `Block name` prompt, press the Enter key. You can retrieve this section using the Retrieve Block option on the Move key, or the Paste Block option on the Edit menu. However, once you exit WordPerfect, it will be deleted.

Printing a Block

As you know, you can use the Print menu to print a page, a range of pages, specific pages, or the entire document. However, it does not include an option to print a section of text, such as two paragraphs or half a page. To do this, you have to block the text and then select Print. Here's how:

1. Place the cursor at the beginning (or end) of the section you want to print.

2. Turn on Block mode and move the cursor to the opposite end of the section.

3. Select Print:

> **Keyboard:** Press the Print key, Shift-F7.

> **Mouse:** Display the **File** menu and select the **Print** option.

This prompt will appear:

`Print block? No (Yes)`

4. Select **Yes**. The printer should start right away, and the `Block on` prompt will disappear.

Case Conversion

You can convert a section of text from uppercase to lowercase, a wonderful feature for users who are oblivious to the Caps Lock key. To convert text, use Block with the Switch key, or the Convert Case option on the pull-down Edit menu. The Switch key usually works to move you into the Doc 2 Edit screen (or back to Doc 1 if you're already there). However, with Block on, it lets you switch the case of the blocked text. Let's use it to capitalize the company name at the end of the letter in **Figure** 4.1, `Exotic Excursions, Inc.`

1. Place the cursor on the first letter of the name, `E`.

2. Turn on Block mode.

3. Move the cursor to the end of the line, after the period.

4. Select Switch:

> **Keyboard:** Press the Switch key, Shift-F3.
>
> This prompt appears:
>
> `1 Uppercase; 2 Lowercase: 0`
>
> Select the first option, **Uppercase**.
>
> **Mouse:** Display the Edit menu and select Convert Case. Another menu pops out to the right, as shown in Figure 4.7. Select the first option, To Upper.

The prompt disappears, and the entire name is capitalized.

Block Protect

If you type tables, charts, or any section of text that you want to keep together on the same page, you'll find WordPerfect's Block Protect feature a handy tool. Its purpose is to prevent a block of text from being divided by a page break. Block Protect works by keeping the protected section together as one unit. If part of the block does not fit on the page, WordPerfect will move the entire block to the next page, not just the lines that don't fit. You can use this feature to ensure that your headings will always be printed with at least the first few lines of the paragraph that follows. That way, you don't end up with a heading all alone at the bottom of a page.

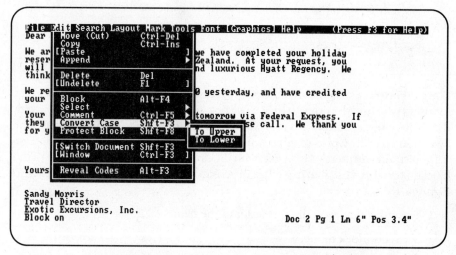

Figure 4.7   *When Block is on and you select Convert Case from the Edit menu, this menu pops out to the right. You can use it to convert all the highlighted text to uppercase or lowercase.*

To use Block Protect, start with the cursor at one end of the section.

1. Turn on Block mode, and highlight the text:

   Keyboard: Press the Block key, Alt-F4. Move the cursor and highlighting to the end of the section you want to protect.

   Mouse: Click the left button to turn on Block mode, and hold it while you move the cursor to the end of the section. Release the button.

2. Select Protect Block:

   Keyboard: Press the Format key (Shift-F8). This prompt will appear:

   `Protect block? No (Yes)`

   Type Y.

   Mouse: Display the Edit menu and select the Protect Block option.

WordPerfect inserts a Block Protect On code, [Block Pro:On], at the beginning of the section, and a Block Protect Off code, [Block Pro:Off], at the end (visible only in Reveal Codes). It considers everything in between these codes to be a whole unit, and will not divide it with a page break. Figure 4.8 shows an example. Block Protect keeps question 11 on the same page with the list of possible answers (a,b,c, and d). Before Block Protection was used, the question and answers were on different pages, as shown in Figure 4.9. In both figures, the page break is represented by the dashed line.

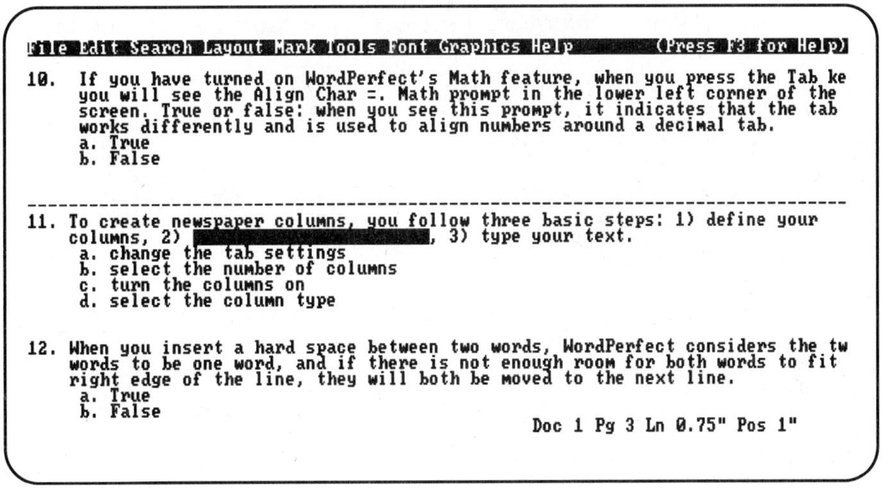

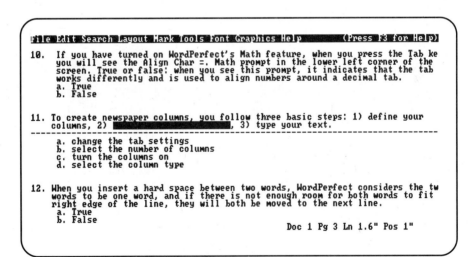

Figure 4.8   *Question 11 in this exam has been block protected so that it will always remain together as a unit on the same page.*

Figure 4.9   *Before Block Protect was used, the questions and answers were on different pages.*

Tip: WordPerfect has two other tools that you can use to help prevent undesirable page breaks: Conditional End of Page on the Format Other menu, and Widow/Orphan Protection on the Format Line menu. For more information, see Part Three, "Command Reference."

SEARCH AND REPLACE

WordPerfect's Search tools —Forward Search, Reverse Search, and Replace—are among WordPerfect's most useful features for regular editing tasks. As you learned in Chapter 2, Search is often the quickest method of moving the cursor to a specific word, especially in long documents. You can use Forward and Reverse Search to locate words, phrases, or formatting codes in your document, and Replace to find and change or erase them. If you have ever attempted to hunt through a lengthy report trying to find a name you misspelled several times, you'll really appreciate these tools.

Searching for Text

To practice using WordPerfect's Search and Search and Replace features, type the letter shown in Figure 5.1. Save it using the name *MIGGS*.

Let's begin by searching for the name *MIGGS*.

1. Move the cursor to the top of the page. Since WordPerfect searches all text from the cursor position forward (or backward if you reverse the search direction), moving the cursor to the top ensures that the entire letter will be searched.

2. Select Search:

   Keyboard: Press the Forward Search key, F2.

   Mouse: Display the pull-down Search menu. The Search menu shown in Figure 5.2 appears. Select the first option, Forward.

   Now you should see an arrow and a Srch prompt in the lower-left corner of the screen, as shown in Figure 5.3. The arrow tells you whether WordPerfect will search forward or backward through the document. When the arrow points to the right, WordPerfect will search forward, which will include all text to the right of and below the cursor. If you press the Up Arrow key, the arrow will change direction and point to the left. WordPerfect will then perform a reverse search, checking text to the left of and above the cursor. Notice that the cursor is next to the Srch prompt, where you will type the text that you want to locate.

August 28, 1990

Mr. James K. Hatfield
1500 Garden Court
Anchorage, Alaska 12345

Dear Mr. Hatfield,

This letter is to inform you that I have taken several precautionary steps to prevent your dog MIGGS from entering my garden again. Even after talking with you on several occasions and making you aware of the problem, I continue to find Miggs digging up my prize primroses on a regular basis. Therefore, I feel it is imperative to warn you that **a perimeter barb wire fence** has been installed around the garden, and **land mines** have been strategically placed within this area. Additionally, **a heat seeking laser gun** has been installed on a turret overlooking the garden.

I trust you will take care to see that your dog is kept under control. Otherwise, I feel it is safe to say that Miggs' only future gardening interests will be (under) daisies.

Cordially,

Martha McCoy

Figure 5.1   *Type this letter to practice using WordPerfect's Search, Reverse Search, and Replace features.*

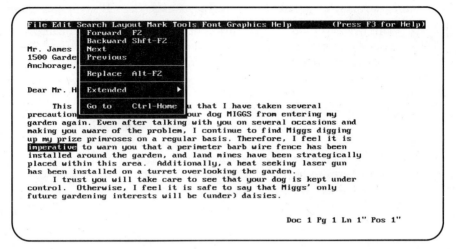

Figure 5.2   *The pull-down Search menu.*

```
August 28, 1990

Mr. James K. Hatfield
1500 Garden Court
Anchorage, Alaska 12345

Dear Mr. Hatfield,

     This letter is to inform you that I have taken several
precautionary steps to prevent your dog MIGGS from entering my
garden again. Even after talking with you on several occasions and
making you aware of the problem, I continue to find Miggs digging
up my prize primroses on a regular basis. Therefore, I feel it is
imperative to warn you that a perimeter barb wire fence has been
installed around the garden, and land mines have been strategically
placed within this area.  Additionally, a heat seeking laser gun
has been installed on a turret overlooking the garden.
     I trust you will take care to see that your dog is kept under
control.  Otherwise, I feel it is safe to say that Miggs' only
future gardening interests will be (under) daisies.


-> Srch:
       └──────────── Forward Search prompt
```

Figure 5.3   *The Forward Search prompt. This prompt appears when you select Forward from the pull-down Search menu or press the Forward Search key, F2. It indicates that WordPerfect will search to the right of and below the cursor.*

Tip: Whenever the `Srch` prompt appears, you can change the direction of your search. To search backward, press the Up Arrow key. To search forward, press the Down Arrow key.

The next step is to type the word or phrase that you want to locate. The text you type in response to the `Srch` prompt is called the *search string*, and it can contain up to 59 characters. If you type the search string all in lowercase letters, WordPerfect will locate uppercase, lowercase, and mixed-case versions in your document. If you type it all in uppercase, WordPerfect will only locate it in your document if it is all capitalized. If you capitalize only the first letter, as in *Miggs*, WordPerfect won't find it unless the first letter is capitalized (but the other letters can be in lowercase). For example, it will locate *Miggs* or *MIGGS*, but not *miggs* (because the *M* must be uppercase).

Let's search for the name *MIGGS*.

3. Type `MIGGS` all in uppercase characters.

4. To begin the search:

    Keyboard: Press F2 again.

    A common mistake in this step is to press the Enter key to start the search. Although this is usually the correct way to carry out a command, it doesn't work with the Search feature, because WordPerfect can search for codes as well as text. If you press Enter, it inserts a Hard Return code into your search string, and it appears as follows:

    `Srch: MIGGS[HRt]`

    If you leave it this way, WordPerfect will only locate *MIGGS* if it is followed by a hard return (if the word were at the end of a paragraph, for example). If you make this mistake, you can remove the [HRt] code by pressing the Backspace key.

    Mouse: With the cursor on the search string, double-click the left button (if you have three buttons, click the right button once).

The cursor will move to the blank space following the first occurrence of the word *MIGGS*. Note that WordPerfect has located the uppercase version of *MIGGS*.

Tip: After performing a search, you can return the cursor to its previous position by pressing the Go To combination twice: Ctrl-Home, Ctrl-Home.

Repeating a Search

1. Repeat the search to locate the next occurrence of *MIGGS*:

    Keyboard: Press F2.

    Mouse: Display the Search menu, and select the first option, Forward.

    The Srch prompt appears again, with the word MIGGS next to it. The first time you used Search, the prompt did not include a search string. It includes one now because WordPerfect assumes you want to repeat your previous search, and automatically suggests the word or phrase you last used. To complete the search, all you have to do is press F2 or move the mouse onto the search string and click the right button.

    If you did not want to search for the same word, you could either type a different search string or edit the existing one. To type a different one, you would not have to erase the word *MIGGS,* because as soon as you typed the first character of the new search string, *MIGGS* would disappear. If you wanted to edit the search string, you could press the Delete key, or the Right Arrow key, and edit it just like regular text.

2. To complete the search:

    Keyboard: Press F2.

    Mouse: With the cursor on the search string, click the right mouse button.

    The cursor will search for the next occurrence of *MIGGS.* Although *Miggs* appears twice more in the document, WordPerfect will not find it. Instead, this prompt appears at the bottom of the screen:

    * Not found *

    The prompt only appears for a few seconds, and then the cursor returns to MIGGS. This Not found prompt indicates that there are no more occurrences of the search string (MIGGS) in your document. Remember, if you type uppercase letters in the search string, WordPerfect will require an exact match in the document. Since you typed *MIGGS* all in uppercase in response to the Srch prompt, WordPerfect locates only *MIGGS* in the document, not *Miggs.*

    To find the other two occurrences of *Miggs,* you'll have to select Search again and edit the search string to change *MIGGS* to *Miggs* (you could also use *miggs*).

Tip: The Not found prompt indicates that there are no more occurrences of the search string in your document. If it appears the first time
you search for a word or phrase, it means WordPerfect did not find
the text at all. If so, check to see if you spelled it incorrectly, typed it
all in uppercase, or started at the end of the document and tried to
perform a forward search instead of a reverse search.

3. To edit the Srch prompt, begin by selecting **Search**. Next, press the Right
   Arrow key once to move the cursor onto the letter i. Now press the Insert
   key and type (in lowercase) iggs.

4. Press F2 or double-click the left mouse button to begin the search. The
   cursor should move to the second occurrence, in this phrase:

   Miggs digging up my primroses

5. To locate the last occurrence of *Miggs*, repeat the search again.

   Keyboard: Press F2 F2.

   Mouse: Display the **Search** menu and select the first option, **Forward**;
   then double-click the left button.

   The cursor will move to the last occurrence of *Miggs*, in this phrase:

   it is safe to say that Miggs' only future

   If you were to search for *Miggs* again, you would see the Not found
   prompt again, since there are no more occurrences.

Searching Backward

WordPerfect can also search backward through a document, which is helpful when
the cursor is at or near the end of the last page. Let's try searching for the word
garden. Since the cursor is now in the last paragraph of the body of the letter, we'll
use the Reverse Search feature.

1. Move the cursor to the end of the document.

2. Select Reverse Search:

   Keyboard: Press the Reverse Search key, Shift-F2. You could also press
   F2 and then reverse the direction by pressing the Up Arrow key. If you
   do, you should type the search string before pressing Up Arrow.
   Otherwise, WordPerfect will assume you want to edit the previous

search string, and will add garden to the word *miggs*. You'll end up with this search string: *gardenmiggs*. To fix it, you would have to press the Delete key five times to erase miggs.

Mouse: Display the **S**earch menu and select **B**ackward.

The Srch prompt will appear at the bottom of the screen, with the cursor pointing to the left.

3. Type garden in lowercase.

4. To begin the search, press F2 or double-click the left mouse button.

The cursor moves to the word *gardening*. Surprised? This illustrates an important point about WordPerfect's Search feature: The search is not restricted to whole words. Instead, WordPerfect will locate your search string regardless of where it is located, even if it is contained inside another word. In fact, searching for whole words isn't always possible. You can sometimes isolate a word by pressing the space bar before and after typing it in the search string, but if the word is at the end of a sentence or paragraph, WordPerfect won't find it because of the punctuation. For example, it would not find *garden* in this sentence, because it is followed by a period instead of a space:

```
Additionally, a heat seeking laser gun has been installed
on a turret overlooking the garden.
```

To continue searching in reverse, you could press Shift-F2 F2 or select Backward from the pull-down Search menu. Remember, it is not necessary to retype the word *garden*, because WordPerfect always remembers the previous search string.

> **Tip:** You can always change the direction of a search by pressing the Up Arrow key or the Down Arrow key, but it's best to do so only after you have typed the search string.

> **Tip:** WordPerfect's Search tools do not include an option to locate whole words. If you search for a common word such as *the*, the cursor will stop on any words containing it, such as *theater, breathe, ether, theirs,* and *feather.*

Beep on Search Failure

Whenever WordPerfect cannot locate your search string, a `Not found` prompt appears. Since it disappears after only a few seconds, you have to watch carefully to see it. If this is a problem, you can set your computer to make a beeping noise to alert you that the search has not been successful. To do this, press the Setup key (Shift-F1), or display the File menu and select Setup. From the main Setup menu, select Environment. From the Setup Environment menu, select Beep Options. Next, select the third option, Beep on Search Failure, and change it to Yes. To return to the Edit screen, press the Exit key (F7) or click the right mouse button.

Search and Replace

Whenever you want to locate a word or phrase and change it throughout the document, use WordPerfect's Replace feature. You can use Replace two ways: with or without Confirm. If you use Confirm, WordPerfect will pause at each occurrence of the search string and let you confirm whether or not you wish to replace it there. If you don't use it, WordPerfect will search through your document and make all the replacements automatically, without stopping to ask your permission.

If you are searching for a common word, or a word that could be contained inside another one, it's much safer to use the Confirm option. Figure 5.4 shows an example of what can happen if you don't use confirm. Imagine that Martha McCoy decided to add her husband's support to the letter, so she used Replace without Confirm to change all the occurrences of "I" to "we" (she typed both *i* and *w* in lowercase). As a result, she inadvertently changed many words that should have been left alone. In the first sentence alone, there are seven unwanted replacements, `Thwes`, `wes`, `wenform`, `precautweonary`, `MWeGGS`, `enterweng`, **and** `agawen`:

```
Thwes letter wes to wenform you that We have taken several
precautweonary steps to prevent your dog MWeGGS from
enterweng my garden agawen.
```

With that precaution in mind, let's use the Replace feature to change the dog's name from Miggs to Muggs.

1. Start with the cursor at the top or bottom of the document.

2. Select Replace:

   Keyboard: Press the Replace key (Alt-F2).

   Mouse: Display the Search menu and select Replace.

August 28, 1990

Mr. James K. Hatfweeld
1500 Garden Court
Anchorage, Alaska 12345

Dear Mr. Hatfweeld,

Thwes letter wes to wenform you that We have taken several precautweonary steps to prevent your dog MWeGGS from enterweng my garden agawen. Even after talkweng wweth you on several occasweons and makweng you aware of the problem, We contwenue to fwend Mweggs dweggweng up my prweze prwemroses on a regular baswes. Therefore, We feel wet wes wemperatweve to warn you that **a perwemeter barb wwere fence** has been wenstalled around the garden, and **land mwenes** have been strategwecally placed wwethwen thwes area. Addwetweonally, **a heat seekweng laser gun** has been wenstalled on a turret overlookweng the garden.

We trust you wwell take care to see that your dog wes kept under control. Otherwwese, We feel wet wes safe to say that Mweggs' only future gardenweng wenterests wwell be (under) daweswees.

Cordweally,

Martha McCoy

Figure 5.4   *When you select No for confirm, sometimes the results can be disas-
trous! Here, the letter i was changed to we throughout the document.*

This prompt will appear at the bottom of the screen:

```
w/Confirm? No (Yes)
```

3. Select **Yes** to use the Confirm option. The familiar `Srch` prompt appears.
   Your next step is to type the search string: `Miggs`.

   At this point, you could change the direction of the search by pressing the
   Up Arrow or the Down Arrow key. If you are at the end of the document,
   press Up Arrow to search backward.

4. Press F2 or double-click the left mouse button. You will now see the
   following prompt:

Replace with:

5. Type the new name: Muggs. Do not type the first character in lowercase. If you do, all the replacements will be made in lowercase (*muggs* instead of *Muggs*).

6. To begin the Search and Replace action, press F2 or double-click the left mouse button.

   If you started with the cursor at the top of the document, the cursor will stop at the first occurrence of *Miggs* (the uppercase version), as shown in Figure 5.5. Notice the Confirm prompt in the lower-left corner of the screen. It asks you to confirm whether or not you want to replace the word here. Since No is assumed, if you did not want to change *MIGGS* to *Muggs* here, you could select No by pressing Enter, N, or any other key except Y.

```
August 28, 1990


Mr. James K. Hatfield
1500 Garden Court
Anchorage, Alaska 12345          Cursor


Dear Mr. Hatfield,

     This letter is to inform you that I have taken several
precautionary steps to prevent your dog MIGGS from entering my
garden again. Even after talking with you on several occasions and
making you aware of the problem, I continue to find Miggs digging
up my prize primroses on a regular basis. Therefore, I feel it is
imperative to warn you that a perimeter barb wire fence has been
installed around the garden, and land mines have been strategically
placed within this area. Additionally, a heat seeking laser gun
has been installed on a turret overlooking the garden.
     I trust you will take care to see that your dog is kept under
control. Otherwise, I feel it is safe to say that Miggs' only
future gardening interests will be (under) daisies.


Confirm? No (Yes)                        Doc 1 Pg 1 Ln 2.83" Pos 5.1"
```

Figure 5.5   *When you use Replace with Confirm to change text, the cursor stops at each occurrence of the search string and asks you to confirm whether or not you want to change it at that point. Here, the cursor has stopped on* Miggs, *and WordPerfect is asking if you want to replace it with* Muggs.

7. Select **Yes** to replace *MIGGS* with *Muggs*.

   Whether you answer Yes or No, the cursor will then move to the next occurrence of *Miggs*, and the Confirm prompt will appear again. This process will continue until there are no more occurrences of the search string (*Miggs*).

8. The cursor highlights Miggs in the next sentence. Select **Yes** again to change it. The cursor will move to Miggs in the last sentence in the body of the letter, and the Confirm prompt will appear.

9. Select **Yes** again.

WordPerfect will search for another occurrence of *Miggs*. Since this is the last one, the Not found prompt will appear to indicate that the search has ended. The cursor will remain on the last position where you changed *Miggs* to *Muggs*.

 Tip: If you are using Replace with Confirm, you can stop the operation by pressing the Cancel key (F1) in response to the Confirm prompt.

Now repeat these steps and change *Muggs* back to *Miggs*. This time, use Replace without confirm so that you'll understand the difference.

1. Move the cursor to the top of the document.

2. Select Replace:

   Keyboard: Press the Replace key (Alt-F2).

   Mouse: Display the **Search** menu and select **Replace**.

3. In response to the w/Confirm prompt, select **No**.

4. In response to the Srch prompt, type Muggs and then press F2 or double-click the left mouse button.

5. In response to the Replace with prompt, type Miggs and then press F2 or double-click the left mouse button.

WordPerfect quickly searches through your letter, and automatically replaces *Muggs* with *Miggs* everywhere it is found. After the search is finished, the cursor will stop after the last occurrence of *Miggs,* in the last sentence. You can then move the cursor back to its original position (at the top of the document) by pressing the Go To key (Ctrl-Home) twice.

 Tip: To restrict Search and Replace to a specific section, instead of the entire document, use WordPerfect's Block and Replace features together. First, use Block to highlight the section. Next, select Replace, and then follow the steps outlined in this section to enter a search string and replacement text, and perform the action. WordPerfect will only replace your search string in the blocked section.

Searching for Hidden Codes

How many times have you tried to find a formatting code by turning on Reveal Codes and searching line by line through the document? Fortunately, there is an easier way: the Search feature. You can use Search to locate formatting codes or a combination of codes and text—one of this feature's most useful applications. In most cases, if you want to change a formatting feature, you have to position the cursor after the code. For example, if you select double spacing near the top of a document, and later decide to change it all back to single spacing, you won't be able to switch to single spacing unless you locate the Double Spacing code and place the cursor past it or erase it. If you just want to erase a code, the easiest way is to use Replace. Remember, you can't erase a formatting feature like bold or underline unless you delete the codes.

To insert a code into the search string, you usually press the same keys that you would press to use the formatting feature in Edit mode. For example, you would press F8 for Underline, F4 for Indent, or Shift-F8 L M for a left/right margin setting code. Unfortunately, you cannot use the mouse to insert formatting codes into the search string.

Try locating the Underline On code in the first paragraph. Begin with the cursor at the top of the page.

1. Select Search.

2. In response to the Srch prompt, press the Underline key, F8. The Underline On code appears in the search string: [UND].

3. To begin the search, press F2 or double-click the left mouse button. The cursor stops on the letter *i*. If you look in Reveal Codes, you'll see that the [UND] code is just left of the cursor, as shown in Figure 5.6. If you wanted to delete the underlining, you could press the Backspace key.

As you've just seen, to search for formatting codes, you usually press the same keys that you would press to use the formatting feature in Edit mode. However, sometimes the menus are different. For example, to search for line spacing, you'd select Search, and then press Format (Shift-F8). This menu line would appear:

```
1 Line; 2 Page; 3 Other: 0
```

You would select Line, and this menu line would appear:

```
1 Hyphen; 2 HZone; 3/; 4 Justification; 5 Line; 6 Margins;
7 Tab Set; 8 W/O: 0
```

Notice that Line Spacing is not on this menu. Select Line again, and this menu would appear:

```
1 Line Height; 2 Line Numbering; 3 Line Spacing: 0
```

```
1500 Garden Court
Anchorage, Alaska 12345


Dear Mr. Hatfield,

        This letter is to inform you that I have taken several
precautionary steps to prevent your dog Miggs from entering my
garden again. Even after talking with you on several occasions and
making you aware of the problem, I continue to find Miggs digging
up my prize primroses on a regular basis. Therefore, I feel it is
imperative to warn you that a perimeter barb wire fence has been
                                         Doc 1 Pg 1 Ln 3.5" Pos 1
▀▀▀▀▀▀▀▀▀▀▀▀▀▀▀▀▀▀▀▀▀▀▀▀▀▀▀▀▀▀▀▀▀▀▀▀▀▀▀▀▀▀▀▀▀▀▀▀▀▀▀▀▀▀▀▀▀▀▀▀▀▀
garden again. Even after talking with you on several occasions and[SRt]
making you aware of the problem, I continue to find Miggs digging[SRt]
up my prize primroses on a regular basis. Therefore, I feel it is[SRt]
[UND]Imperative[und] to warn you that [BOLD]a perimeter barb wire fence[bold] ha
s been[SRt]
installed around the garden, and [BOLD]land mines[bold] have been strategically[
SRt]
placed within this area.  Additionally, [BOLD]a heat seeking laser gun[bold][SRt
]

Press Reveal Codes to restore screen
```

 A search for an Underline On
formatting code moves the cursor
to the position just to the right of
the code.

Figure 5.6 *You can use Search to locate formatting codes. Here, the Underline On*
code was searched for, and the cursor stopped right after it.

Finally, you can select Line Spacing! When you do, this code appears next to the
Srch prompt: [Ln Spacing]. You can use it to locate all line spacing codes.
Unfortunately, WordPerfect does not allow you to be selective. You could not, for
example, locate only the Double Spacing codes: [Ln Spacing:2]. The same is true
for margins, tab settings, and many other formatting codes where variable
information is entered.

 Tip: To search for a Soft Return code, [SRt], select Search, press
Ctrl-V and then Ctrl-M. To search for a Soft Page code, [SPg], select
Search, press Ctrl-V and then Ctrl-K.

Note: One limitation of the Search feature is that you cannot use it to
search for specific codes such as double spacing, full justification, or
a particular margin setting.

Using Replace to Erase Text or Codes

As you've just learned, you can use WordPerfect's Search feature to locate a hidden formatting code such as [UND], and then delete it and the formatting it represents by pressing the Backspace key. An easier way to erase codes is with the Replace feature. Let's use it to erase all of the bold codes from the Miggs letter. Start with the cursor at the top of the document.

1. Move the cursor to the top of the letter.

2. Select Replace:

    Keyboard: Press the Replace key (Alt-F2).

    Mouse: Display the Search menu and select **R**eplace.

3. Select **No** in response to the w/Confirm? prompt. The Srch prompt appears.

4. To search for the Bold On code, press the Bold key (F6) once. This inserts the [BOLD] code into your search string.

5. Press Search (F2) or double-click the left mouse button. The Replace with prompt appears. If you leave it blank, WordPerfect will erase all occurrences of the search string.

6. Press F2 or double-click the left mouse button to leave it blank and start the action. WordPerfect removes all boldfacing. The cursor stops after the last Bold On code, which was at the beginning of this phrase:

```
heat seeking laser gun
```

Tip: You can use WordPerfect's Replace feature to erase text or codes. To do this, select Replace, type N for confirm, and enter the text or code in response to the Srch prompt. Leave the Replace with prompt blank by pressing F2 or the right mouse button. WordPerfect will then erase the search string everywhere it is found in your document.

Tip: You can use Replace to change underlined text to bold or vice versa. To do this, select Replace, and answer Yes for confirm. In response to the `Srch` prompt, press the Underline key (F8) once, type the text exactly as it appears in your document, then press the Underline key again. For example, if you were changing *imperative* in the Miggs letter, the search string would be: `[UND]imperative[und]`. In response to the `Replace with` prompt, press the Bold key (F6) once, type the text, then press the Bold key again. The replacement string should appear as follows: `[BOLD]imperative[bold]`.

Extended Search or Search and Replace

WordPerfect's Search tools will only look for the search string in the main text of a document. They do not search through headers, footers, footnotes, endnotes, graphic boxes, or graphic box captions. To do this, you have to extend the search by pressing the Home key first, and then selecting Search or Replace.

To use Extended Search:

1. Select Extended Search:

    Keyboard: Press the Home key and then press the Search key (F2) or Reverse Search key (Shift-F2).

    Mouse: Display the Search menu and select Extended. Another menu pops out to the right, as shown in Figure 5.7. Select Forward or Backward.

    The `Extended Srch` prompt appears, with a cursor pointing left or right, to indicate the direction you selected.

2. Type the search string or select the codes.

3. Start the search by pressing F2, or double-clicking the left mouse button. If WordPerfect locates the search string inside a header, footer, footnote, endnote, graphic box, or graphic box caption, the cursor will stop inside the appropriate screen and let you edit it. When you finish, you have two options: You can locate another occurrence of the search string by selecting Extended Search again and repeating the process. If you don't want to search further, or if you do and find that this is the last occurrence, press Exit to return to the Edit screen.

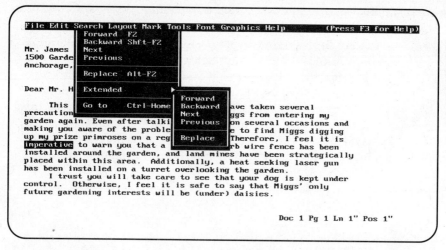

Figure 5.7   *When you use the mouse to select Extended Search, this menu pops out to the right. You can use it to search forward or backward through all text, including headers, footers, footnotes, endnotes, graphic boxes, and captions; to locate the next or previous occurrence of the search string; or to use the Extended Replace feature.*

To use Extended Replace:

1. Select Extended Replace:

   Keyboard: Press the Home key; then press the Replace key (Alt-F2).

   Mouse: Display the **S**earch menu, and select **E**xtended. From the menu that pops out to the right, select **R**eplace.

   The w/Confirm prompt appears.

2. Select **Y**es if you want to use confirm, or **N**o if you don't. The Extended srch prompt appears.

3. Type the search string, change the direction of the arrow if necessary, and then press F2 or double-click the left mouse button. The Replace with prompt appears.

4. Type the replacement text, and then start the search by pressing F2 or double-clicking the left mouse button.

   If you are using the Confirm option, the cursor will stop on the first occurrence of the search string and ask you to confirm that you want to replace it. If it's in a header, footer, footnote, endnote, graphic box, or graphic box caption, the cursor will stop in the corresponding screen (header, footer, etc.) and wait for your answer. After you type Y or N, it will automatically move to the next occurrence of the search string. If there are no more occurrences, the cursor will remain in the screen. To return to the Edit screen, press Exit (F7).

If you are not using Confirm, WordPerfect will automatically replace the text, regardless of where it is found. The cursor won't stop in one of the special screens (header, footer, footnote, endnote, graphic box, or graphic box caption) unless it is the last occurrence of the search string. At that point, you can press Exit (F7) to return to the Edit screen.

Search with Wild Cards

WordPerfect has a special character, ^X, that functions as a wild card. You can use it to substitute for any character on the keyboard. To enter it into the search string, press the Ctrl key and hold it down while pressing V, then X. You can't use this character to represent a code, and it can't be the first character in the search string.

For example, if you were writing a long report and used the notations (A), (B), and (C) for your headings, you could use the wild-card character to locate each heading in the document, even though the letters differ. This would be useful, for example, if you wanted to mark them for a table of contents.

1. Start with the cursor at the top of the document, and select Forward Search.

2. Type the first parenthesis: (

3. To insert the wild-card character as a substitute for A, B, or C, press Ctrl-V. You should see this prompt:

   ```
   Key =
   ```

4. Press Ctrl-X. The prompt should now appear as follows:

   ```
   (^X
   ```

5. Type the last parenthesis. The search string should appear as follows:

   ```
   (^X)
   ```

6. Start the search by pressing F2, or by double-clicking the left mouse button. The cursor will stop on the first heading, or anywhere a single letter or number appears between parentheses.

THE SPELLER AND THESAURUS

WordPerfect's Speller is an indispensable tool that you can use to correct spelling errors, typos, and other mistakes. The Speller's dictionary is comprehensive and includes over 125,000 words. If you've misspelled a word, the Speller will offer a list of possible corrections. You can then select one of these words, and WordPerfect will substitute it into your document, replacing the misspelled word in this position and anywhere else it appears. If the misspelled word was capitalized in your document, the substitution will also be capitalized. If you typed a word twice in a row, the Speller will stop and ask if you want to delete the second one. If you accidentally capitalized the first two letters of a word instead of just the first letter, the Speller will warn you that this is an irregular case and ask if you want it corrected. If the Speller does not find one of your words in its dictionary, such as a proper name, you can choose to skip it, add it to a supplementary dictionary, look it up, or edit it.

WordPerfect's Thesaurus is another helpful writer's tool; you can use it to find synonyms and antonyms for common words. When you look up a word in the Thesaurus, a list of synonyms and antonyms appears on the screen, arranged into groups of nouns, adjectives, and verbs. After you can select the most suitable word, WordPerfect will automatically replace the word in your document with the word you select from the Thesaurus.

Spell Checking a Document

To learn how to use WordPerfect's Speller, retrieve a document to the Edit screen. If you are spell checking a document that you just finished typing, it's a good idea to save it first. After you finish spell checking, be sure to save the document again. If you don't, you'll lose all the corrections!

If your computer does not have a hard disk, insert the Speller disk into drive B before proceeding.

1. To bring up the main Speller menu:

Keyboard: Press the Spell key, Ctrl-F2.

Mouse: Display the **Tools** menu and select the **Spell** option.

This menu line should appear at the bottom of your screen:

```
Check: 1 Word; 2 Page; 3 Document; 4 New Sup. Dictionary;
5 Look Up; 6 Count 0
```

f you see this menu instead:

```
WP{WP}US.LEX not found: 1 Enter Path; 2 Skip Language;
3 Exit Spell: 3
```

it means that WordPerfect cannot locate the main dictionary file, WP{WP}US.LEX. You may need to install the Speller or tell WordPerfect where the dictionary file is located. If you have not installed the Speller, turn to Appendix A and do so before you try to use the Speller again. If you did install it and know the directory it is in, select the first option, Enter Path, and enter the path and directory. To avoid doing this each time you use the Speller, you can use the Setup: Location of Files option to specify the path and directory name where your Speller files are located, as described later in the "Setup: Location of Files" section.

The first three options on the Speller menu, Word, Page, and Document, pertain to spell checking. You can check either the word the cursor is on, the page the cursor is on, or the entire document. If you select option 2, Page, or option 3, Document, WordPerfect will also check the spelling in any headers, footers, footnotes, or endnotes on the page or in the document. You can also use WordPerfect's Block feature to spell check a limited section of text, as described in "Spell Checking a Block of Text."

2. Select **Document**.

After you select it, you'll see a `* Please wait *` prompt as the Speller begins searching for words that are not in its dictionary. When it finds one, it will stop and display a screen like the one shown in Figure 6.1. This is called the *Not Found menu*. As the name implies, the Speller stops on any words that it cannot find in its dictionary. However, it doesn't necessarily mean that these words are misspelled. For instance, they may be proper nouns such as an individual's last name; terminology used in a particular industry, such as law or medicine; two words that you ran together by forgetting to press the space bar; or a double occurrence of a word, such as "the the time has come."

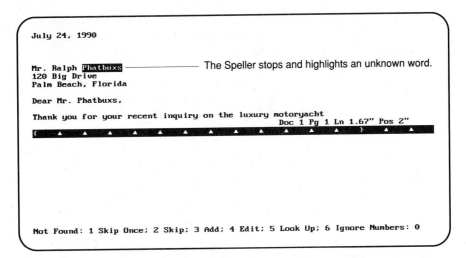

```
July 24, 1990


Mr. Ralph Phatbuxs ───────────── The Speller stops and highlights an unknown word.
120 Big Drive
Palm Beach, Florida

Dear Mr. Phatbuxs,

Thank you for your recent inquiry on the luxury motoryacht
                                    Doc 1 Pg 1 Ln 1.67" Pos 2"
{   ▲    ▲    ▲    ▲    ▲    ▲    ▲    ▲    ▲    ▲    ▲  }    ▲    ▲




Not Found: 1 Skip Once; 2 Skip; 3 Add; 4 Edit; 5 Look Up; 6 Ignore Numbers: 0
```

Figure 6.1   *When the Speller stops on a word that is not contained in the main dictionary, or in your supplementary dictionary, it stops on the word and displays the Not Found menu.*

As you can see from Figure 6.1, when the Speller stops on a word, the screen is split in half, with the tab ruler separating the two parts. The top half of this screen shows the unrecognized word, highlighted so it will stand out, and a line or two of the text surrounding it. Notice the status line above the tab ruler; it tells you exactly where the word is located in your document. For instance, the unrecognized word in Figure 6.1 is the letter recipient's name, Phatbuxs, and it is on line 1.67" and position 2". A menu line appears in the bottom half of the screen. If the Speller finds any alternative spellings for the word, they are listed under the tab ruler. For example, in Figure 6.2 the word *Thank* is misspelled, and the Speller suggests these words as possible replacements: *teak, thai, than, thank, that, thaw,* and *thick.*

When the cursor appears on the 0 in the menu line, the Speller has finished locating possible alternatives and is waiting for you to make a decision. You can select the correct spelling as soon as it appears, and you don't have to wait for the cursor to move onto the 0. If WordPerfect does not find the correct spelling for a highlighted word, try pressing Enter to see if there are any more words in the list. Since the screen size is limited, sometimes there isn't enough room to display them all.

In Figure 6.2 *thank* is the correct spelling. To substitute it into the document, you would type d. The Speller would then substitute it for the misspelled word in the document, here and anywhere else the particular misspelling were found, and then continue checking for other words that it couldn't find in the dictionary.

3. If the Speller stops on a word that is not found and its correct spelling appears in the list of suggested replacements, type the letter that appears next to it. If your version of WordPerfect is dated 1/19/90 or later, you can use a mouse to select the replacement by moving the mouse pointer onto it and clicking the left button (if you are unsure of the date, when you return to the Edit screen, press F3 once and look in the upper-right corner of the screen to find it).

4. If the Speller stops on a word that is misspelled or typed incorrectly but does not provide the correct replacement in the dictionary, you can select the Edit option to correct it. When you finish, press Exit (F7) or click the right mouse button to resume spell checking. (The Edit option is described in more detail in the next section.)

5. If the word is a proper noun, you can select *Skip Once, Skip,* or *Add.* The Speller will then move on to your next unrecognized or misspelled word, if there is one. The Skip Once, Skip, and Add options are described in more detail in the section entitled "Proper Nouns."

6. If the Speller cannot locate the correct replacement in its dictionary, and you are unsure how to spell it correctly so you can't use the Edit option, you can try locating the word in WordPerfect's dictionary, using the *Look Up* option. This option is explained in more detail in the section "Looking Up a Word."

7. To skip words that combine numbers and letters, you can select the sixth option, *Ignore Numbers.* The Speller will then ignore all such combinations during this session. This option is explained in more detail in the section "How the Speller Handles Words Containing Numbers."

 Tip: You can stop the Speller anytime by pressing the Cancel key (F1).

The Edit Option

Sometimes the Speller is unable to match the highlighted word with any words in its dictionary. When this happens, you can use the Edit option on the Not Found menu to correct it yourself. You can select the Edit option by pointing to it with the mouse pointer and clicking the left mouse button, by pressing the option number, 4, or by pressing the Left or Right Arrow key. When you select it, the cursor moves out of the Not Found menu and onto the first character in the highlighted word.

You can then correct it as you would any text on the Edit screen. For example, if you accidentally left out the space separating two words, you can select Edit, move the cursor to the first letter of the second word, and then press the space bar to insert a space between the two words.

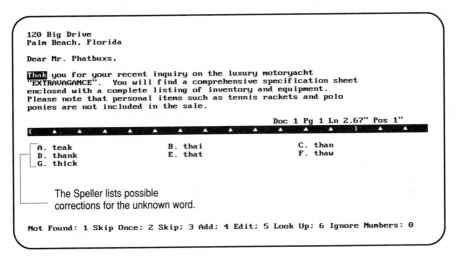

Figure 6.2 *Correcting a spelling error. To exchange the correct spelling,* thank, *for the misspelled version in the document, type the letter appearing next to it,* d.

While you are using the Edit option, a prompt appears at the bottom of the screen to remind you that you are using the Spell Edit option, as shown in Figure 6.3. It also tells you what to do when you finish editing: Press the Exit key (F7). You can also exit by moving the mouse pointer onto the word Exit in this prompt and clicking the right button. WordPerfect will then resume spell checking. After you use Edit, if the word is still not found in the dictionary, you'll see the Not Found prompt again and will either have to edit it again, select a skip option, look it up, or add it to the dictionary.

Proper Nouns

If the unrecognized word is a correctly spelled proper noun that isn't in the Speller's dictionary, as in Figure 6.1, you can select from among three of the options on the Not Found menu: *Skip Once, Skip,* and *Add.* If you select the first one, Skip Once, the Speller will skip this occurrence of the word and resume spell checking. However, if the Speller finds the same word later in this document (or on the page if you selected the Page option instead of Document), it will stop on it again and display the Not Found menu. If you select the second option, Skip, the Speller will skip it here and anywhere else it may find it in this document (or page).

```
does allow you to motor around the harbor and show off.

Due to recent events in the stock market, the owner is most anxious
to sell and his bank has instructed us to accept any generous
offer. "EXTRAVAGANCE" is ready for inspection, so please contact me
foran appointment as soon as possible!

Kindest regards,




The Speller's exit prompt



Spell Edit:  Press Exit when done                Doc 1 Pg 1 Ln 6.33" Pos 1"
```

Figure 6.3 *While you are using the Spell Edit option, a prompt reminds you that you're using it and indicates that you can press Exit when you finish, to return to the Speller.*

If the Speller stops on a word you will be using frequently in other documents, such as your company name, you may want to add it to the supplementary dictionary by selecting the Add option. Make sure the word is spelled correctly before you add it. Once you add a word to the dictionary, the Speller will recognize it as correctly spelled in the future, as long as it is spelled exactly the way it was when you selected Add. WordPerfect saves the words you add in a supplementary dictionary file, WP{WP}.US.SUP, which it creates in the current directory the first time you select the Add option. Unless you always use the same directory when working in WordPerfect, you should use the Setup: Location of Files menu to specify a directory for the WP{WP}.US.SUP. file. Otherwise, WordPerfect will create a different supplementary dictionary in each directory you are working in when you add a word during spell checking, and chances are none of them will contain all the words you thought you had added. This one-time task is described in the "Setup: Location of Files" section.

Tip: The supplementary dictionary file is a regular WordPerfect file, which you can retrieve and edit like any other file. You can even retrieve it and type your own list of words to add, and then alphabetize them using WordPerfect's Sort feature.

Tip: When you select the Add option from the Not Found menu, the words are not actually added to the supplementary dictionary until the Speller finishes checking your document. Instead, they are temporarily stored in RAM and added after the Speller is finished. If a message appears warning you that the dictionary is full, exit from the Speller by pressing Cancel (F1). The words you added will then be placed into the supplementary dictionary, and the memory (RAM) will be cleared. To spell check the rest of the document, you can Block it and select Spell, as described in the section "Spell Checking a Block of Text."

Looking Up a Word

When the Not Found menu appears but the Speller cannot locate the correct replacement in its dictionary, another option you may want to try (besides Edit) is the fifth one, Look Up. When you select it, this prompt appears:

```
Word or word pattern:
```

and you can try typing another spelling, or use wild cards to enter a pattern and look up words that are similar. For example, if you type

```
super*
```

and press Enter, the Speller will display a list of all words that begin with *super*, as shown in Figure 6.4. The asterisk in a word pattern represents any sequence of letters. You can also type a question mark in your word pattern, to represent one letter. For instance, if you type

```
super?
```

only three words will appear in the list: *super, superb,* and *supers* (although your version may vary slightly).

Notice the `Press Enter for more words` prompt in Figure 6.4. This indicates that there are too many words to fit on one screen. To view others, in alphabetical order, press Enter. There may be several screens. When the `Press Enter` prompt disappears, you've reached the last one.

The `Select Word` prompt at the bottom of the screen indicates that you can exchange the misspelled word in your document for one of the words in the list by typing the letter that appears next to it. If you don't find the correct word, press Enter until the `Word or word pattern` prompt appears. After that, you can either type another word or word pattern, or press Cancel to return to the Not Found menu.

```
ponies are not included in the sale.

This gracious vessel was built by the famous Fancischmanzi Boat
Yard in Italy and christened in 1985.  To date, she has been under
private ownership and never put into charter service.
Nevertheless, she is well suited for charter, with an elaborate
master stateroom and accommodations for a small neighborhood.  All
staterooms have private baths with jacuzzi and the interior was
recently redecorated by Poodles of Paris.

The engines have been scrupulously maintained and allow cruising
                                        Doc 1 Pg 1 Ln 4.17" Pos 6.4"
{    ▲    ▲    ▲    ▲    ▲    ▲    ▲    ▲    ▲    ▲    }    ▲

    A. super             B. superabduction     C. superabundance
    D. superabundant     E. superabundantly    F. superacute
    G. superalimentation H. superannuable      I. superannuate
    J. superannuated     K. superannuating     L. superannuation
    M. superannuitant    N. superannuities     O. superannuity
    P. superb            Q. superbly           R. supercargo
    S. supercargoes      T. supercargos        U. supercentral
    V. supercharge       W. supercharged       X. supercharger
Press Enter for more words

    Select Word: 0
```

Figure 6.4   *Using the Look Up option on the Not Found menu to look up all words that begin with* super.

How the Speller Handles Words Containing Numbers

If you type a word containing both letters and numbers, such as *B10, 4H,* or *F14,* the Speller will stop on the word and the Not Found prompt will appear. To skip words that combine numbers and letters, you can select the sixth option, Ignore Numbers. The Speller will then ignore all such combinations during this session. This option does not pertain to words consisting entirely of numbers, since the Speller never stops on them. Also, many common letter/number combinations, such as *1st* and *2nd,* are already in the main dictionary, so the Speller does not stop on them either.

Double-Word Occurrences

If you typed a word twice in a row, the Speller will stop and warn you that it has found a double-word occurrence, as shown in Figure 6.5. Both words will be highlighted. You then have several options: You can skip the words by selecting 1 or 2; delete the second occurrence of the word by selecting option 3, Delete 2nd; edit the words by selecting option 4, Edit; or select option 5 to have the Speller ignore double words for this session.

```
This gracious vessel was built by the famous Fancischmanzi Boat
Yard in Italy and christened in 1985.   To date, she has been under
private ownership and never put into charter service.
Nevertheless, she is well suited for charter, with an elaborate
master stateroom and accommodations for a small neighborhood.   All
staterooms have private baths with jacuzzi and ▊the▊ ▊the▊ interior was
recently redecorated by Poodles of Paris.

The engines have been scrupulously maintained and allow cruising
speeds of ten knots while consuming a miserly 500 gallons per hour.
Granted, this will probably limit any long distance cruising but it
                                              Doc 1 Pg 1 Ln 4.5" Pos 5.7"
```

```
Double Word: 1 2 Skip; 3 Delete 2nd; 4 Edit; 5 Disable Double Word Checking
```

Figure 6.5   *If you typed the same word twice in succession, the Speller will stop and give you the opportunity to delete the second occurrence, skip or edit the words, or disable the double-word checking.*

Irregular Case

The Speller stops on words containing irregular uppercase letters and displays the Irregular Case menu shown in Figure 6.6. Such a mistake usually occurs when you hold the shift key down too long and inadvertently capitalize both the first and second letters of a word. The Irregular Case menu provides five options. You can skip the word by selecting option 1 or 2, Skip; replace it by selecting option 3, Replace; edit it by selecting option 4, Edit; or disable this feature using option 5, Disable Case Checking.

In addition to the error of capitalizing the first two letters of a word, the Speller checks for several other types of mistakes. The Replace option corrects them as follows:

- If you capitalized the first two letters of a word containing three or more characters, selecting Replace will convert the second letter to lowercase. For example, *THe* would be converted to *The*. If you capitalized both letters in a two-letter word, as in *IT,* the Speller will not flag it as an irregular case.

- If you capitalized only the second letter in a word, selecting Replace will convert the second letter to lowercase and capitalize the first one. For example, *tHe* would be converted to *The*, and *iT* would be converted to *It*.

- If you capitalized all but the first letter of a word with three or more letters, selecting Replace will convert the first letter to uppercase, so that the entire word is in uppercase. For example, *tHE* would be converted to *THE*.

- If you capitalized the third letter only, selecting Replace will convert it to lowercase, so the entire word is in lowercase. For example, *thE* would be converted to *the*. The Speller only checks the first three letters of a word.

```
The engines have been scrupulously maintained and allow cruising
speeds of ten knots while consuming a miserly 500 gallons per hour.
Granted, this will probably limit any long distance cruising but it
does allow you to motor around the harbor and show off.

Due to recent events in the stock market, the owner is most anxious
to sell and his bank has instructed us to accept any generous
offer. "EXTRAVAGANCE" is ready for inspection, so please contact me
for an appointment as soon as possible!


                                        Doc 1 Pg 1 Ln 5.83" Pos 1"



Irregular Case: 1 2 Skip; 3 Replace; 4 Edit; 5 Disable Case Checking
```

Figure 6.6   *If you typed the first two letters of a word in uppercase, as in this example, WordPerfect stops to warn you and asks if you want to replace it. Selecting the Replace option (3) will change the word so that the second letter is no longer capitalized.*

Exiting the Speller

Once the Speller has finished checking your document, a prompt similar to this will appear:

```
Word count: 205                         Press any key to continue
```

The word count tells you how many words your document contains. The other part of the message, `Press any key to continue`, tells you what to do next. Assuming you selected the Document option to spell check the entire document, pressing any key or clicking the right mouse button will exit the Speller. However, if you used the Page option, the main Speller menu will appear. To exit from it, press Enter or Cancel (F1), or click the right mouse button.

If you don't have a hard disk in your computer, remove the Speller disk from drive B and replace it with your data disk before continuing.

Be sure to save the document to retain the corrections you've made through the Speller.

Setup: Location of Files

You can use the Setup: Location of Files option to specify the path and directory name for your main speller dictionary, supplementary dictionary, hyphenation dictionary, and thesaurus file. If you installed the main dictionary file (WP{WP}US.LEX) in a directory other than the one containing your WordPerfect program files, specifying the directory in this menu means you won't be asked to type the path and directory each time you use the Speller. By naming a directory for the supplementary dictionary file, you can ensure that all words you add while spell checking will be in the same file, instead of in separate supplementary files in each directory you use. If the Thesaurus file is not in the current directory or the one containing the WP.EXE file, you must specify the directory name in this menu, or you won't be able to use the Thesaurus.

Naming the directories in the Setup: Location of Files menu is a one-time procedure, and the information is saved in the WP{WP}.SET file. To use it:

1. Select Setup:

    Keyboard: Press Setup (Shift-F1).

    Mouse: Display the File menu and select Setup.

2. Select the Location of Files option. The Setup: Location of Files menu appears.

3. Select the third option: **Thesaurus/Spell/Hyphenation, Main, Supplementary.**

4. Type the path and directory name for the main Thesaurus, Speller, and Hyphenation files, and press Enter. Next, type one for the supplementary dictionary, and press Enter.

5. When you finish, exit back to the Edit screen:

    Keyboard: Press Exit (F7).

    Mouse: Click the right button.

Spell Checking a Block of Text

Sometimes it's useful to spell check a limited section of text, which you can do by blocking it first. For example, if you add a few paragraphs to a document you've already spell checked, you can speed up spell checking by limiting it to the new paragraphs. The process is simple. You use WordPerfect's Block feature to mark the section, and then select the Speller. The rest of the process is identical to using the Document option on the main Speller menu: WordPerfect searches the text, stopping on any unrecognized words to let you correct, skip, add, or edit them. When the Speller is finished, the Word count prompt appears, and you can press any key to exit the Speller.

1. Place the cursor at either end of the text you want to spell check.

2. Turn on Block:

    Keyboard: Press Alt-F4 (Block) or F12.

    Mouse: Display the **Edit** menu and select **Block**, or place the cursor at the beginning of the block, click the left button to turn on Block, and drag the mouse pointer to the end.

3. Move the cursor to the opposite end of the section you will be spell checking.

4. Select the Speller:

    Keyboard: Press the Spell key (Ctrl-F2).

    Mouse: Display the **Tools** menu and select Spell.

    The * Please wait * prompt will appear, as the Speller searches the blocked section for unrecognized words. If it stops on one, you can select a replacement or skip, add, or edit it. When the Speller is finished, or if it does not find any incorrectly spelled words, the Word count prompt appears.

5. When the Word count prompt appears, press any key or click the right mouse button to exit the Speller.

Using Other Options on the Main Speller Menu

So far in this chapter, you have studied only two of the six options on the main Speller menu: Page and Document. In this section, you'll learn how to use the other four: Word (1), New Sup. Dictionary (4), Look Up (5), and Count (6).

The Word Option

You can use the first option on the main Speller menu, Word, to check the spelling of any word in the document. To use it:

1. Place the cursor on the word you want to check.

2. Select Spell:

   Keyboard: Press Spell (Ctrl-F2).

   Mouse: Select Spell from the **T**ools menu.

3. From the main Speller menu, select **W**ord.

   If the cursor moves to the next word and the main Speller menu reappears, the word is correctly spelled. If it is not, another menu will appear, such as the Not Found menu or the Irregular Case menu, and you can use it to correct the word. After that, the cursor will move to the next word in the document, and the main Speller menu will appear again. You can then exit the Speller, look up the next word, or select one of the other spell-checking options, such as Page or Document.

4. To exit the Speller:

   Keyboard: Press Enter.

   Mouse: Click the right button.

New Sup. Dictionary

When you select the Add option from the Not Found menu while spell checking a document, WordPerfect adds the word to your supplementary dictionary. By default, the name of this supplementary dictionary file is WP{WP}US.SUP. If you want to use a different file as the supplementary dictionary, select the New Sup. Dictionary option from the main Speller menu, type the name of the file you want to use as the supplementary dictionary, and then proceed with spell checking.

Look Up

Whenever you are about to type a word, but aren't sure how to spell it, you can use the Look Up option on the main Speller menu to find the correct spelling in the dictionary. This option is nearly identical to the one on the Not Found menu, described earlier in the chapter, except that you use it to look up a word without typing it in the document. Also, you can't use the option to insert a word into your document.

If you want to look up a word and insert it into the document, use the Word option instead. Type the word in the correct position in your document, even though you may not be spelling it correctly, and then select the Word option on the main Speller menu. If the correct spelling isn't suggested on the Not Found menu, select Look Up from this menu, locate the correct spelling, and then type the letter that appears next to it. This will enable you to exchange the correct version for the misspelled word in your document.

Count

When you run the Speller to check the spelling on a page, highlighted block, or document, WordPerfect automatically counts the total number of words. If you just want to count the words in a document, without spell checking, use the Count option on the main Speller menu. This feature can only be used to count the words in the entire document; to count the words in a block or page, you have to check the spelling also.

To use the Count option:

1. Retrieve the document.

2. Select the main Speller menu:

   Keyboard: Press the Spell key (Ctrl-F2).

   Mouse: Display the **T**ools menu and select Spell.

3. Select option 6, Count.

   The Speller counts all the words in the document on your Edit screen. When it is finished, it displays the word count at the bottom of the screen, along with a prompt telling you to press any key to continue.

4. When the `Press any key to continue` prompt appears:

  Keyboard: Press any key.

  Mouse: Click the right mouse button.

  The main Speller menu will appear again.

5. To exit:

  Keyboard: Press Enter.

  Mouse: Click the right mouse button.

The cursor will be at the end of the document when the count is finished. To return it to the position it was in before you selected Count, you can use the GoTo option (press Ctrl-Home twice, or select Go to from the Search menu twice).

Note: The word count does not include words consisting entirely of numbers.

Tip: WordPerfect's Speller program, SPELL.EXE, provides several options that you can use to edit the dictionary. For example, you can add words, delete words, create a new dictionary, change the main dictionary, compress the dictionary to optimize disk space, combine dictionaries, and convert a dictionary from 4.2 to 5.1. For more information, see *Speller Utility* in Part Three, "Command Reference."

The Thesaurus

The Thesaurus provides a list of synonyms (words with similar meanings) and antonyms (words with opposite meanings) for commonly used words. You can look up any word in your document by placing the cursor on it and selecting the Thesaurus option. If the word is found in the Thesaurus, WordPerfect will display a list of synonyms and antonyms for it. If you find an appropriate substitute, you can select the Replace option and then type the letter appearing next to it in the list, and WordPerfect will exchange it for the one in your document.

  To use the Thesaurus:

1. Place the cursor anywhere on the word you want to look up in your document, or in the blank space following it.

2. If you don't have a hard disk, save your document, remove the data disk from drive B, and then insert the Thesaurus disk in drive B.

3. Select Thesaurus:

    Keyboard: Press the Thesaurus key, Alt-F1.

    Mouse: Display the Tools menu and select Thesaurus.

What happens next depends on whether synonyms for your word are found in the Thesaurus, or whether the Thesaurus file was found or not:

- If the word is found, a list of synonyms and antonyms for the word appears in a large box, as shown in Figure 6.7 for the word *catch*. Up to four lines of the document, including the word you are looking up, appear above the box. The word you are looking up is highlighted in the text.

- If the word is not in the Thesaurus, you'll see a `Word not found` message instead. It will soon change to this prompt, asking you to type a different word to look up:

`Word:`

If you don't want to look up another word, you can exit the Thesaurus by pressing the Cancel key (F1) twice or by clicking the right mouse button twice.

- If you did not install the Thesaurus when you installed WordPerfect, or if the Thesaurus file, WP{WP}US.THS, is not in one of the following directories:

    The directory specified on the Setup: Location of Files menu (as described in this chapter in the "Setup: Location of Files" section)

    The current directory (unless a different directory is named in the Setup: Location of Files menu)

    The directory containing your WP.EXE file

this prompt will appear:

`ERROR: File not found -- WP{WP}US.THS`

indicating that the Thesaurus file cannot be found. If you have not yet installed the Thesaurus, turn to Appendix A and do so before you try to use it again. Otherwise, use the Setup: Location of Files option to specify the path and directory name where the Thesaurus file is located, as described in the "Setup: Location of Files" section.

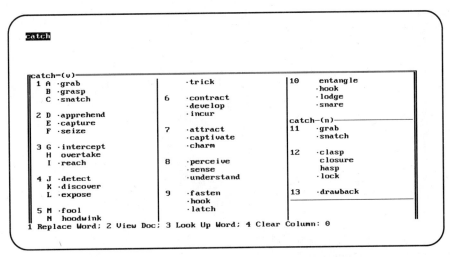

```
 catch

 catch=(v)
  1 A ·grab                      ·trick          10     entangle
    B ·grasp                                             ·hook
    C ·snatch           6        ·contract              ·lodge
                                 ·develop               ·snare
  2 D ·apprehend                 ·incur
    E ·capture                                   catch-(n)
    F ·seize            7        ·attract        11     ·grab
                                 ·captivate             ·snatch
  3 G ·intercept                 ·charm
    H  overtake                                  12     ·clasp
    I ·reach            8        ·perceive               closure
                                 ·sense                  hasp
  4 J ·detect                    ·understand             ·lock
    K ·discover
    L ·expose           9        ·fasten        13      ·drawback
                                 ·hook
  5 M ·fool                      ·latch
    N  hoodwink
 1 Replace Word; 2 View Doc; 3 Look Up Word; 4 Clear Column: 0
```

Figure 6.7   *When you look up a word that is included in WordPerfect's Thesaurus, a screen similar to this one appears, listing the synonyms in three columns. However, if the word is not found in the Thesaurus, the columns will be empty, and a Word prompt will appear so you can type a different word to look up.*

When WordPerfect locates a word in the Thesaurus, one or more columns of words are displayed, divided into groups of nouns, (n), verbs (v), adjectives (a), and antonyms (ant); these words are called *references*. Initially, a bolded letter appears next to each word in the first column. These letters are called the *reference menu*. If there are any words in the second and third columns, you can move the reference menu from column to column by pressing the Left and Right Arrow keys. The numbers indicate that a group of words is similar in meaning, such as the second group of verbs in Figure 6.7: *apprehend, capture,* and *seize;* these are called *subgroups*.

A word you can look up in the Thesaurus is called a *headword*. In addition to the word *catch*, there are several other headwords in Figure 6.7: Each is marked with a bullet. To look up one of these headwords, move the reference menu into the column and type the bolded letter next to it. For example, Figure 6.8 shows how the screen appears after *G* was typed to look up *intercept*. The headword (*intercept*) appears at the top of the second column, and seven synonyms appear below it: *abort, ambush, arrest, block, catch, seize,* and *thwart*. All but one (*ambush*) are themselves headwords, since they have bullets next to them. Typing the letter next to one of these words would display it and its synonyms and antonyms in the third column, as shown in Figure 6.9 for the headword *thwart*. At this point, it's still possible to look up another headword, such as *obstruct*, but it will replace *thwart* and its references in the third column, as shown in Figure 6.10.

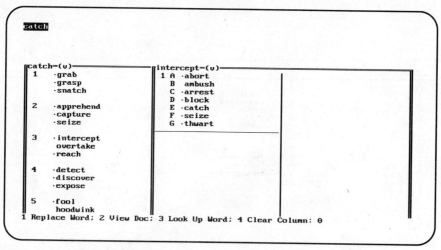

Figure 6.8 *After the letter G was typed to look up the headword* intercept, intercept *appeared at the top of the second column, with its synonyms and antonyms displayed below. The references for* catch *that were previously in the second and third columns were moved into the first column, and are not visible unless the reference menu is in that column and you scroll down through it.*

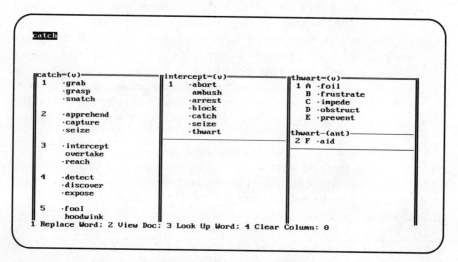

Figure 6.9 *After the letter G was typed to look up* thwart, thwart *appeared with its antonyms and synonyms in the third column.*

Each group of verbs, nouns, adjective, and antonyms in a column is separated by a solid line. If you don't see the solid line at the bottom of the column, as in the first column in Figure 6.8, there are more words in the column than can be displayed on one screen. To see the others, use the arrow keys to move the reference menu into the column, and then move the cursor down using the Down Arrow key (or any other cursor movement keys, such as Page Down, Home,Down Arrow, or Home,Home,Down Arrow). There are actually 38 words in the first column of Figure 6.8, although only 14 are visible. Initially, the other words were displayed in the second and third columns. However, after the headword *intercept* was looked up, WordPerfect placed it and its references in the second column, and moved the other references for *catch* into the first column.

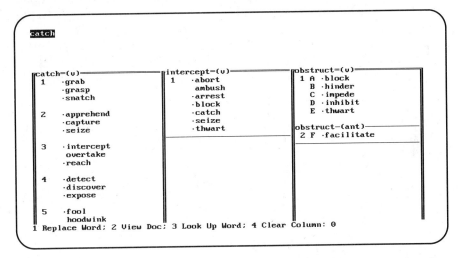

Figure 6.10   *When a headword appears at the top of each column, selecting another one to look up will replace the list in the last column. In this case, the cursor was in the third column, so* thwart *and its references (as shown in Figure 6.9) were replaced by* obstruct *and its references.*

 Tip: If a word is marked by a bullet, you can type the letter next to the word to see a list of synonyms for that word. If the second column is clear, the synonyms will appear there. If not, they will appear in the third column.

The Clear Column Option

To clear a headword and its references from a column, move the reference menu to the column you want to erase, and select the Clear Column option, or press Backspace or Delete. If the reference menu is in the last column and a headword appears at the top of each column, this will clear the last column. If the reference menu is in the second column and a headword appears at the top of the first and second column, this will clear the second column. However, this will not clear the column if there are too many words in the first column to fit on one screen. Instead, the references for the headword in column one that can't fit onto the first screen will be moved into the other columns, as in Figure 6.7.

If the reference menu is in the first column and a headword and its references appear in the second column, selecting the Clear Column option will move the words from the second column into the first. If the second column is empty or does not have a headword at the top, as in Figure 6.7, selecting Clear Column will clear all references, and the screen will contain only the empty box and the menu line. You can then use the Look Up Word option to look up another word, or exit the Thesaurus by pressing Cancel (F1) or Enter, or by clicking the right mouse button.

View Doc

To look up another word in your document and clear the Thesaurus screen of the other headwords, use the View Doc option on the Thesaurus menu. You can also use it to scroll through the document, and view the context of the word you are looking up, while keeping the Thesaurus on the screen.

To look up another word while using the Thesaurus:

1. Select the second option, View Doc.

   This moves the cursor into the Edit screen, placing it on the original word you looked up. This prompt appears above the Thesaurus box, to remind you that you are using this option:

   `View: Press Exit when done`

2. Use the regular cursor movement keys to position the cursor on the other word you want to look up. You cannot edit or type while using this option.

3. Press the Thesaurus key, Alt-F1.

   If the word is in the Thesaurus, WordPerfect will clear any headwords and references from the Thesaurus menu and replace them with the headword you just selected (and its references). If it is not found, the `Word not found` prompt will appear briefly, and the Thesaurus will be cleared of all headwords and references. Next, the `Word` prompt will appear, and you can enter another word to look up, or exit the Thesaurus by pressing Cancel (F1) twice, or by clicking the right mouse button twice.

   To scroll through the document without looking up another word:

1. Select option 2, View Doc.

This moves the cursor into the Edit screen, placing it on the original word you looked up. Use the regular cursor movement keys to move around in the document. You cannot type or edit while using this option. When you finish using it, return to the Thesaurus menu:

2. Press Exit (F7) or Enter, or click the right mouse button. This returns the cursor to the Thesaurus menu.

Look Up Word

The Look Up Word option lets you type a word to look up, which may be completely unrelated to the original word, or any other headwords in the Thesaurus screen. To use it:

1. Select option 3, Look Up Word.

   The Word prompt appears.

2. Type the word you want to look up, and then press Enter.

   If the word is a headword, it will appear along with its references in the first blank column, if there is one, or in the first column without a headword. If all three columns contain headwords at the top, it will replace the last column. If the word is not found in the Thesaurus, this prompt will appear:

   Word not found

and then the Thesaurus menu will reappear.

> **Tip:** If the screen is blank, or the cursor is on a blank line at the end of the document, you can still use the Thesaurus. Just select Thesaurus from the Tools menu or press Alt-F1, and then type the word you want to look up in response to the Word prompt. If you find a word you want inserted into the document, select the Replace Word option, and type the letter next to the word.

Replacing a Word

To replace the word you were looking up in your document with a word from the Thesaurus:

1. Move the reference menu to the column containing the word you want to use.

2. Select the first option, Replace Word, and type the letter next to the word you want to use.

WordPerfect will immediately substitute it for the word you were looking up in the document, and exit the Thesaurus.

Tip: If you change your mind after using the Thesaurus to replace a word in your document, press Cancel (F1) or select Undelete from the pull-down Edit menu. If the word appears in a highlighted block, select Restore. Otherwise, press Previous Deletion once or twice, and select Restore if it appears. After that, delete the word you substituted using the Thesaurus.

Exiting the Thesaurus

If you use the Replace Word option to replace the word you were looking up in your document, you will exit the Thesaurus menu as soon as the word is substituted into your document. To exit the Thesaurus without replacing a word, press Cancel (F1), Enter, or Exit (F7), or click the right mouse button.

Note: WordPerfect Corporation has thesaurus files for other languages, which can be purchased for use in WordPerfect 5.1. For more information, contact WordPerfect Corporation.

PART

TWO

ADVANCED FEATURES

FILE MANAGEMENT

All WordPerfect files have to be stored on a disk. Whether you use a hard disk or floppy disk for this purpose, you will eventually need help managing them. For instance, a hard disk has enough space for you to accumulate thousands of files. However, unless you divide it into separate areas called *directories,* you can only store a limited number of files on it. Also, at some point you may find that your hard disk is nearly full. If this happens, you will want to delete old files that you never use, or archive files that you aren't currently using, but may need in the future, to a floppy disk. Also, since hard disks are susceptible to failure in which files are destroyed, it is imperative that you make backup copies of all important files. WordPerfect can help you with all of these tasks through the List Files menu.

List Files is a remarkable collection of tools that you can use to perform important file management tasks, such as creating directories and subdirectories, changing the default directory, moving a group of files to another directory, copying several files from a hard disk to a floppy disk, and much more. You can also use it to retrieve, print, copy, rename, or delete files. Many of these tools can be used in place of the equivalent DOS (Disk Operating System) commands, which are harder to use since they are not menu options but commands you must type. Also, tools such as copy, move, and delete are not restricted to WordPerfect files, so you can use them to manage files from your other programs. As you find yourself creating more and more files on your disk, you'll soon find that List Files is indispensable!

The List Files Screen

Let's begin by displaying WordPerfect's List Files screen.

1. Select List Files:

    Keyboard: Press the List key (F5).

Mouse: Display the File menu and select the List Files option.

A `Dir` prompt will appear in the lower-left corner of the screen, followed by the name of the default drive and directory. It may be similar to this one:

`Dir C:\WP51\LETTERS\*.*`

Dir stands for Directory. Like the Dir command in DOS, as soon as you press Enter, WordPerfect's Dir command will list all files in the default directory and display each file's size and the date and time it was last saved.

2. Display all files in your default directory:

Keyboard: Press Enter.

Mouse: Click the right mouse button.

A screen resembling Figure 7.1 appears, except that your file names will be different. However, if you are using WordPerfect's Long Display feature, your screen will be more like the one shown in Figure 7.2. Notice the cursor, a highlight bar, initially appearing on `Current <Dir>` or, if you are using Long Display, on `Current Directory`. The Directory prompt appears on the first line, to remind you which directory you are viewing. In this case, it is your default directory. Let's take a moment to study it.

```
08-01-90  09:45a            Directory E:\WP\*.*
Document size:        0   Free:  4,870,144 Used:  2,966,186      Files:      52
.     Current    <Dir>                  ..     Parent     <Dir>
DOCUMENT.          <Dir>   01-04-90 09:55p  GRAPHICS.          <Dir>   01-04-90 09:55p
LEARN    .         <Dir>   01-04-90 09:55p  MACEDITO.          <Dir>   05-22-90 12:17p
MACROS   .         <Dir>   01-04-90 09:55p  PRINTER  .         <Dir>   01-04-90 09:55p
STYLES   .         <Dir>   01-04-90 09:55p  URSFILES .         <Dir>   06-20-90 10:40a
BOXES          22,964   05-10-90 02:34p  CHARACTR.DOC   47,099   03-30-90 12:00p
CONVERT .EXE  109,033   03-30-90 12:00p  CURSOR  .COM    1,452   03-30-90 12:00p
EGA512  .FRS    3,584   04-12-90 12:00p  EGAITAL .FRS    3,584   04-12-90 12:00p
EGASMC  .FRS    3,584   04-12-90 12:00p  EGAUND  .FRS    3,584   04-12-90 12:00p
FIXBIOS .COM       50   03-30-90 12:00p  GRAB    .COM   16,450   03-30-90 12:00p
GRAPHCNV.EXE  117,264   03-30-90 12:00p  HRF12   .FRS   49,152   04-12-90 12:00p
HRF6    .FRS   49,152   04-12-90 12:00p  INSTALL .EXE   69,376   03-30-90 12:00p
KEYS    .MRS    4,000   03-30-90 12:00p  MACROCNV.EXE   26,463   03-30-90 12:00p
NWPSETUP.EXE   28,672   03-30-90 12:00p  PRINTER .TST    8,665   03-30-90 12:00p
SPELL   .EXE   56,320   03-30-90 12:00p  STANDARD.CRS    2,555   03-30-90 12:00p
STANDARD.IRS    4,420   03-30-90 12:00p  STANDARD.PRS    1,942   03-30-90 12:00p
STANDARD.URS   30,275   03-30-90 12:00p  UGA512  .FRS    4,096   04-12-90 12:00p
UGAITAL .FRS    4,096   04-12-90 12:00p  UGASMC  .FRS    4,096   04-12-90 12:00p
UGAUND  .FRS    4,096   04-12-90 12:00p ▼ WP}WP{ .BV1        0   08-01-90 09:43a

1 Retrieve; 2 Delete; 3 Move/Rename; 4 Print; 5 Short/Long Display;
6 Look; 7 Other Directory; 8 Copy; 9 Find; N Name Search: 6
```

Figure 7.1 *The List Files screen (Short Display).*

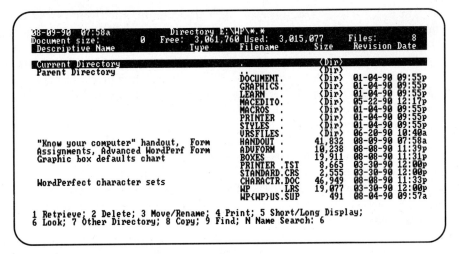

Figure 7.2   *The List Files screen with Long Display on.*

A directory is a subdivision of the disk. All disks, whether hard or floppy, have a root directory, which DOS automatically creates when you format the disk. You can divide the root directory into one or more divisions called *directories,* where you store a group of related files. You can further subdivide each directory into one or more divisions called *subdirectories.* The whole structure resembles an upside-down tree, and each directory or subdirectory is like a branch of the tree. Figure 7.3 illustrates this concept.

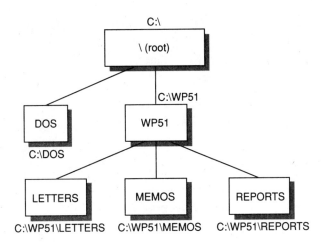

Figure 7.3   *Directories and subdirectories.*

The root directory is the top level, and is always represented by the backslash symbol (\). In Figure 7.3 there are two directories of the root directory: *WP51* and *DOS*. The WP51 directory has three subdirectories of its own, *LETTERS, MEMOS,* and *REPORTS*. The diagram also shows each subdirectory's path, the route from the root directory to the subdirectory. For instance, the path to LETTERS is C:\WP51\LETTERS. The drive and directory names in a path are always separated by backslashes. You must specify the path when performing operations such as copy and move.

The default directory is the one that is in use whenever you start WordPerfect. In other words, WordPerfect defaults to that directory. Whenever you save a new file, WordPerfect will automatically store it in the default directory, unless you type a different directory or drive along with the file name. Also, when you select List Files and press Enter, WordPerfect always displays the default directory, unless you type a different directory or drive before pressing Enter. The Directory prompt at the top of the List Files menu in Figures 7.1 and 7.2 tells you the name of the default drive and directory: `E:\WP`. The default directory is WP, and it is on drive E.

The asterisks at the end of the Directory prompt are called *wild cards*. Here, they represent all files in the directory. When you select List Files, you can use wild cards to restrict the directory listing to specific files, such as all those that begin with the letter *B* or all those with the extension *STY*. Remember, file names can contain from one to 11 characters, split into two parts. The first part can contain from one to eight characters. The second part, called the *file extension,* can contain from one to three characters, and is optional. The two parts of the file name are always separated by a period. The first asterisk in the Directory prompt represents the first one to eight characters in a file name, and the second asterisk represents the last one to three characters (the file extension). When you use the Directory command with the two asterisks, it shows all file names in the directory. There are many ways to restrict the listing when you select List Files. For example:

- To display only files that end in the extension *RPT,* you could select List Files and change the prompt to:

  `Dir E:\WP\*.RPT`

- You could restrict the list to include only file names that begin with the letter F, by typing:

  `Dir E:\WP\F*.*`

- To restrict the list to directory names and files without extensions, you could select List Files and change the prompt to:

  `Dir  E:\WP\*.`

To edit the `Dir` prompt, you can press the Left or Right Arrow key, Home, Left Arrow or Right Arrow, the End key, Delete, Backspace, or Ctrl-End:

- The Left and Right Arrow keys move the cursor one character to the left or right.

- Home,Left Arrow moves the cursor to the beginning of the prompt, on the drive name.

- Home,Right Arrow or the End key moves the cursor to the end of the prompt, after the last asterisk.

- The Delete key erases the character the cursor is on.

- The Backspace key erases the character left of the cursor.

- Ctrl-End erases from the cursor to the end of the prompt.

Let's move on and study the rest of the List Files screen, which is divided into three sections:

1. The header area.

2. The file list.

3. The List Files menu.

The Header Area

The *header area* is the first two lines at the top of the screen; if you use Long Display, it's the first three. The first line tells you

- The date and time, as stored in your computer.

- The name of the current drive and directory.

The second line tells you

- The Document size, which refers to the size of the document on your Edit screen, if there is one. If your Edit screen is clear, this Document size statistic will be 0.

- The amount of Free space available on the disk drive.

- The amount of space Used by the files in this list.

- The total number of Files in this list.

If you are using the Long Display, your screen will also include a third line that tells you the column names: Descriptive Name, Type, Filename, Size, and Revision Date. These column names describe the type of information appearing in each column of the file list. The first two items, Descriptive Name and Type, are unique to the Long Display. The last three, Filename, Size, and Revision Date, describe information that appears in both screens, even though it is not labeled in the Short Display screen. You'll learn more about the Descriptive Name and Type in the section entitled "The File List (Long Display)."

Let's study the header in Figure 7.1, shown again here.

```
08/01/90  09:45a        Directory E:\WP\*.*
Document size: 0  Free: 4,870,144 Used: 2,966,186  Files: 52
```

The first line tells you:

- The date is 8/01/90.

- The time is 9:45 a.m.

- The current directory is WP and it is on drive E. Since *.* appears after the directory name, all files in the directory were selected for display (although there may be too many to appear on one screen).

The second line tells you:

- The WordPerfect Edit screen is blank (since the Document size statistic is 0).

- 4,870,144 bytes of free space remain on drive E.

- The files in the WP directory use 2,966,186 bytes.

- There are 52 files in the WP directory.

The File List (Short Display)

The second part of the screen, the file list, displays files in the current directory, and any subdirectories it may have. If you are using Long Display, the list differs significantly, so you may want to skip this section and continue with the next one. As you can see from Figure 7.1, directory names always come first in the file list. The List Files screen in Figure 7.1 includes 10 directories:

```
Current <Dir>      Parent <Dir>
DOCUMENT <Dir>     GRAPHICS <Dir>
LEARN <Dir>        MACEDITO <Dir>
MACROS <Dir>       PRINTER <Dir>
STYLES <Dir>       VRSFILES <Dir>
```

The file names follow, in alphabetical order from left to right, separated by a line: BOXES on the left, then CHARACTR.DOC on the right, CONVERT.EXE on the left, CURSOR.COM on the right, and so on. If there were any file names that began with numbers, they would be first, just before BOXES.

In addition to the file names and extensions, the display includes each file's size, and the date and time it was last saved (revision date). For instance, the BOXES file in the list is 22,964 bytes in size and was saved on 5/10/90 at 2:34 p.m. Notice the small triangle at the bottom of the screen, under the line that separates the two sides. This tells you there are too many files to display on one screen. To view the next screenful, you can:

Keyboard: Press Page Down twice.

Mouse: Click the left mouse button and hold it while dragging the mouse down to the end.

There are many other ways to move the cursor with the keyboard:

- Pressing Home,Home,Down Arrow moves the cursor to the last file in the list.

- Pressing Home,Home,Up Arrow moves the cursor to the top, onto Current <Dir>.

- The Screen Down and Screen Up keys (Home,Down Arrow and Home,Up Arrow or the plus and minus keys on the numeric keypad) move the cursor to the top or bottom of the screen. If you press them twice, they move the cursor to the next screen (if there is one).

The File List (Long Display)

One of the options on the List Files menu is Short/Long Display. The Short Display is the default. If you change it to Long Display, your List Files screen will be virtually transformed! As you've already learned, the header area will include a third line with the column names: Descriptive Name, Type, Filename, Size, and Revision Date, as shown in Figure 7.2. More dramatically, instead of displaying the directory and file names in two columns, each directory and file name will appear alone in one row. As in the Short Display version of the List Files screen, directory names always come first in the file list, and the file names follow. If there are too many files to display on one screen, press Page Down,Home,Down Arrow, or Home,Home,Down Arrow. Cursor movement techniques are identical to those used with Short Display; see the previous section for more detailed information.

Like the Short Display version, for each file this screen displays

- The DOS file name and extension (under the heading Filename).

- The file Size.

- The date and time it was last saved (Revision Date).

The Long Display includes two additional items that are not in the Short Display:

- Descriptive Name.

- Type.

However, Descriptive Name and Type will not appear for an individual file if you didn't enter this information when saving it. This is special information you can enter for each file by turning on the Long Document Names feature or by creating a document summary. You'll learn how in the "Long Document Names and Default Document Type" section of this chapter. A more subtle difference is that this screen displays only WordPerfect files. If your directory includes any DOS files (ASCII files), macros, or program files such as WP.EXE, you won't see them at all.

There is one disadvantage to using the Long Display method: Displaying your List Files screen takes much longer. If your directory includes a large number of files, you'll really notice the difference.

> ► **Tip:** If you have saved a file with a password, you won't see its descriptive name in the Long Display version of the List Files screen. Instead, you'll see this prompt: `[Locked]`.

Current and Parent Directories

A common misunderstanding about the `Current <Dir>` and `Parent <Dir>` notation in the Short Display of the List Files screen is that all files on the right side of the List Files screen are in the parent directory, Parent <Dir>, and all the ones on the left side are in the current directory, Current <Dir>. This seems logical, given the way the screen is arranged, but it is not true. Actually, all files in the List Files screen are in the current directory.

When you are looking at a List Files screen, *current directory* simply means the directory you are viewing. Its name appears in the header at the top of the List Files screen, and it is always the last directory or subdirectory name. In Figure 7.1, the current directory is E:\WP. The parent directory is one level above the current directory. If there is one, its name appears to the left of the current directory name in the header. In Figure 7.1, the parent directory is E:\, the root directory. If the current directory shown in the header were E:\, there would be no parent directory, since E:\ is the top level.

If the current and parent directories are different, you can use the Look option on Parent <Dir> to view the List Files screen for that directory. In the next section, you'll learn how.

Using Look to View the Contents of a Directory

When the cursor is highlighting a directory name in the List Files screen, you can use the Look option to view the List Files screen for that directory. It then becomes the current directory, and you can use menu options such as Print, Delete, or Retrieve on the files. However, using Look does not change the default directory.

Let's digress for a minute to examine an important fact about the List Files menu. Notice in Figure 7.1 that the number 6 appears at the end of the menu line. This means that when you press Enter, you are selecting option 6. In most WordPerfect menus, this default selection is 0, so pressing Enter exits the menu. In List Files, pressing Enter selects the Look option, number 6.

To use the Look option to display your parent directory:

1. Place the cursor on `Parent <Dir>` (if you are using Long Display, move it onto `Parent Directory`).

2. Select the Look option:

    Keyboard: Type L or 6, or press Enter.

    Mouse: Drag the cursor onto the parent directory name, click the left button to highlight it, then drag the cursor onto `Look` in the menu line and click the left button again.

    A `Dir` prompt appears at the bottom of the screen, indicating the name of your parent directory. The prompt will be similar to:

    `Dir E:\*.*`

    (Your drive designator may be C or D, instead of E.) If your prompt shows only the root directory, such as Dir C:*.*, and is identical to the prompt on the first line in the header area, your current and parent directories are the same. If so, your file list won't change when you perform this exercise, and it will be meaningless. If your prompt differs from the one in the header area, then your parent and current directories are different, so you can proceed.

3. Complete the Look command:

    Keyboard: Press Enter.

    Mouse: Click the right button.

    The screen changes and displays the list of files in your parent directory. Figure 7.4 shows an example. Notice the Directory prompt in the header, indicating that the current directory is E:\.

The Directory prompt displays the
name of the current directory.

```
08-01-90  09:49a             Directory E:\*.*
Document size:  65,324   Free:  4,868,096 Used:          35     Files:        2

.       Current     <Dir>               ..    Parent    <Dir>
DR10      .         <Dir>  01-23-90 09:17a    HIJAAK     .       <Dir>  01-25-90 09:49a
WP        .         <Dir>  01-04-90 09:51p    H          .BAT       19  01-25-90 10:05a
W         .BAT         16  01-25-90 10:05a










1 Retrieve; 2 Delete; 3 Move/Rename; 4 Print; 5 Short/Long Display;
6 Look; 7 Other Directory; 8 Copy; 9 Find; N Name Search: 6
```

Figure 7.4   Using Look to view the parent directory.

Although you have changed the current directory, and can use menu
options like Retrieve or Delete on any of the files in the list, you have not
changed the default directory. To verify this, return to the Edit screen,
then use List Files again to display the default directory.

4. Return to the Edit screen:

    Keyboard: Press the space bar.

    Mouse: Click the right mouse button.

5. Display the default directory again:

    Keyboard: Press the List key (F5), Enter.

    Mouse: Display the File menu, select List Files, and then click the right
    button.

    This returns you to the original directory, not the one you displayed with
    the Look option.

    If you select the Look option and press Enter while the cursor is highlighting
    `Current <Dir>` (or `Current Directory`), you'll just display the same screen again.
    Many users do this by pressing Enter twice, since this action selects Look. In fact,
    you can get stuck in an endless loop by pressing Enter over and over again!
    However, the Look option with Current <Dir> is useful when you want to change
    the display of files in the current directory. For example, you could use it to view
    all files that begin with the letter *C.* Here's how:

1. Place the cursor on `Current <Dir>` and select **Look.**

2. In response to the `Dir` prompt, type c* and press Enter.

The screen changes, and only those files that begin with the letter *C* are included, as shown in Figure 7.5.

The Directory prompt tells you which files are being displayed.

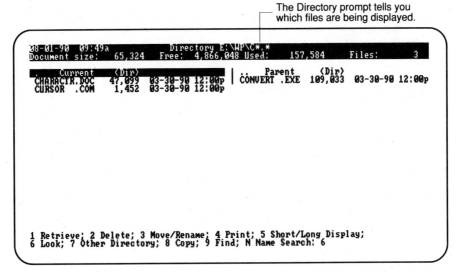

```
08-01-90  09:49a              Directory E:\WP\C*.*
Document size:    65,324  Free:   4,866,048 Used:      157,584      Files:        3
      Current       <Dir>                    ..   Parent      <Dir>
CHARACTR.DOC    47,099   03-30-90 12:00p    CONVERT .EXE  109,033   03-30-90 12:00p
CURSOR  .COM     1,452   03-30-90 12:00p





1 Retrieve; 2 Delete; 3 Move/Rename; 4 Print; 5 Short/Long Display;
6 Look; 7 Other Directory; 8 Copy; 9 Find; N Name Search: 6
```

Figure 7.5   *The List Files screen after using Look and Current <Dir> to restrict the file list to files whose names begin with the letter C.*

You can also use Look when the cursor is highlighting `Current <Dir>` to display the List Files screen for another directory. This is especially helpful if the directory is one or more levels above the current directory, since it doesn't appear in the current list. To do this:

1. Place the cursor on `Current <Dir>`, and select **Look**.

2. In response to the `Dir` prompt that appears in the lower-left corner, type the name and path of the new directory, and press Enter. For example, if the current directory is C:\WP\LETTERS, you can view the MACROS directory by changing the prompt to

`C:\WP\MACROS`

and pressing Enter.

To view the List Files screen for one of the subdirectories whose name appears in the current directory list, you don't need to use Current <Dir>. Instead, just:

1. Highlight the subdirectory name.

2. Select **Look**.

3. In response to the `Dir` prompt, press Enter.

 Tip: When you are in the List Files menu, pressing F5 always brings up the `DIR` prompt, regardless of whether the cursor is on a directory name or a file name when you press it.

Using Look to View the Contents of a File

Look has a different function when the cursor is highlighting a file: It lets you view the contents of a file without retrieving it from the disk. Imagine how useful this would be if you had saved hundreds of files, and had forgotten the name of a file you wanted to retrieve. Rather than retrieving them one by one, and clearing the screen after each one, you could use Look to view them in succession until you found the one you wanted and then retrieve it.

To use the Look option to view a file:

1. Place the cursor on the file.

2. Select Look:

> **Keyboard:** Type L or 6, or press Enter.

> **Mouse:** Click on the file name, then on the Look option.

Your screen should now resemble Figure 7.6 (except that the text of your file will differ). However, if your file was saved with a document summary, it will appear differently: Instead of the first screen of text, you'll see `Subject`, `Account`, `Keywords`, and other fields from the document summary, as shown in Figure 7.7. For more information about these fields, refer to the "Document Summary" section of this chapter.

Notice the header at the top of the screen. It displays the file name and path, the version of WordPerfect you were using when you created it (if you are looking at a WordPerfect file), and the date and time you last saved it. If your file includes a document summary, the header will include a second line with the Descriptive file name at the left, the document type in the middle, and the document summary creation date and time at the right. If your List Files screen is set to Long Display (as it would be if you changed the Long Document Names option to Yes), the header area will also differ. It will include a third line with these column headings: Descriptive Name, Type, Filename, Size, and Revision Date.

Unless your file has a summary, the cursor will be under the last line of text, and this menu will appear at the bottom of the screen:

```
Look: 1 Next Doc; 2 Prev Doc: 0
```

You can scroll through the document using the cursor movement keys, or select Next Doc or Prev Doc to use Look on the next or previous file in the order the files appear in the List Files screen.

Header line

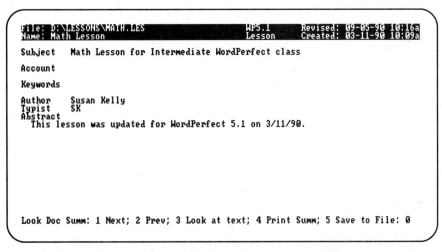

```
File: E:\WP\DOCUMENT\COLLEGE\HANDOUT        WP5.1      Revised: 01-21-90 10:07p

Know your computer:
hard disk vs. floppy disks


Are you working on a computer that has a hard disk drive, or one that
has two floppy disk drives but no hard disk? How do you know? Why
does it matter? It is important that you identify your computer because
the procedures for starting the WordPerfect program, exiting, saving
your documents, and displaying directories are different for the two
types of computers. None of the procedures are difficult. Use this
handout as a reference until you have them memorized (it will happen
sooner than you think!).

Identify your computer type. All of our computers have two external
floppy disk drives. You will find these drives labeled with "A" and "B"
stickers. The computers with hard disks also have "C" stickers on the
font, representing the internal hard drive. Therefore, if your computer
has all three stickers, A, B, and C, it has a hard disk. If your computer
has only two stickers, A and B, it does not have a hard disk.


Look: 1 Next Doc; 2 Prev Doc: 0
```

Figure 7.6   *When you use the Look option on the List Files menu to view the contents of the file without retrieving it, a header line appears at the top, displaying the file name and path, WordPerfect version, and revision date. This line does not appear when you retrieve a file.*

```
File: D:\LESSONS\MATH.LES              WP5.1     Revised: 09-05-90 10:16a
Name: Math Lesson                      Lesson    Created: 03-11-90 10:09a

Subject    Math Lesson for Intermediate WordPerfect class

Account

Keywords

Author     Susan Kelly
Typist     SK
Abstract
    This lesson was updated for WordPerfect 5.1 on 3/11/90.




Look Doc Summ: 1 Next; 2 Prev; 3 Look at text; 4 Print Summ; 5 Save to File: 0
```

Figure 7.7   *Using Look to view a file that includes a document summary.*

If your file has a summary, the first two options will function identically, but their names will be shortened to accommodate the additional menu options: Next Doc will be Next, and Prev Doc will be Prev. Also, the cursor will be under the 0 on the menu line, not under the last line of text. To view the text of the file, either select the third option, Look at Text, or press a cursor movement key such as Down Arrow. When you do, the menu line will change from:

```
Look Doc Sum: 1 Next; 2 Prev; 3 Look at Text; 4 Print Summ;
5 Save to File: 0
```

to:

```
Look: 1 Next Doc; 2 Prev Doc; 3 Look at Document Summary: 0
```

Select the third option, Look at Document Summary, when you are ready to return to the original menu, Look Doc Summ. You can use the fourth option on that menu, Print Summ, to print the document summary you are viewing. You can use the fifth one, Save to File, to save the summary to a separate file. For more information about these options, see "Saving and Printing a Document Summary" later in this chapter.

Cursor Movement in the Look Menu

There are many ways to move the cursor while using the Look option. For example, you can move it

- Line by line using the Up Arrow and Down Arrow keys.

- Up or down one screen at a time using the Screen Up and Screen Down keys (Home,Up Arrow or the minus key on the numeric keypad, and Home,Down Arrow or the plus key on the numeric keypad). They work the same as in Edit mode: Screen Up moves the cursor to the top of the screen. If you press Screen Up twice in a row, the cursor moves up to the next screen. Screen Down moves the cursor to the bottom of the screen. Pressing Screen Down twice moves the cursor down to the next screen.

- To the beginning or end of the file using Home,Home,Up Arrow and Home,Home,Down Arrow.

- To scroll forward through the document, type the letter s. To stop the scrolling, press s again (or any other key).

- You can also use the Search and Reverse Search keys, F2 and Shift-F2, but they work a little differently than they do in the Edit screen. Instead of moving the cursor onto the search string, they highlight it and move the cursor to the left edge of the line where it is found.

If the document is too wide for the screen:

- Use the End key to shift the text to the left and right. End is a toggle key. The first time you press it, the text moves to the left and you see the right edge; the second time, it moves to the right and you see the left edge.

- You can also press Right Arrow, which moves the cursor five characters at a time and shifts text to the left. It stops when all text at the right edge is displayed.

- The Left Arrow key is the opposite of the Right Arrow key. It moves the cursor five characters at a time, shifting text to the right, and stops when the cursor reaches the left margin.

- Home,Right Arrow shifts the entire screen to the left, so you only see text that was not displayed originally. Home,Left Arrow moves it back.

After you finish using Look, you can either return to the List Files screen, or use Look on the next or previous file in the list. To view the next file, select the first option, Next Doc (called *Next* if your file has a document summary). To view the previous file, select the second option, Prev Doc (or *Prev*). To return to the List Files screen, either press Enter, the space bar, or Cancel.

> ▶ **Tip:** You cannot edit or type any text while using the Look option.

Using the Clipboard to Copy Text

If you started WordPerfect from the Shell menu, you can copy text displayed through the Look option into the Clipboard. Once it's in the Clipboard, you can retrieve it into any WordPerfect document, or into a file created using DrawPerfect, PlanPerfect, DataPerfect, or any other WordPerfect Corporation software. Since you don't have to retrieve the files to copy the text, this trick is a quick-and-easy way to create a new document from text in several existing files.

To copy text into the Clipboard:

1. Move the cursor onto the file containing the text you want to copy.

2. Select the Look option from the List Files menu:

    Keyboard: Type L or 6, or press Enter.

    Mouse: Use the left button to click on the **Look** option.

3. Move the cursor to the beginning of the text you want to copy.

4. Block the text by pressing the Block key (Alt-F4), then moving the cursor to the end of the section.

5. Press Shell (Ctrl-F1). This prompt will appear:

   `Clipboard: 1 Save; 2 Append: 0`

6. If the Clipboard already contains text and you want to add this text to whatever is already there, select the second option, **Append**. If the Clipboard is currently empty, or if you want to erase it and replace it with this text, select the first option, **Save**.

Anytime you want to retrieve this text from the Clipboard, just press the Shell key (Ctrl-F1) and then select the fourth option, Retrieve.

> **Tip:** You can also save and append text from a document on your Edit screen into the Clipboard. Just block the text, press the Shell key (Ctrl-F1), and then select Save or Append. If you want to copy the entire document, you don't even need to block it. Just press Shell (Ctrl-F1), and then select Save or Append.

Name Search: Navigating Through the List Files Screen

Unless you are using a mouse, the Name Search option is the fastest way to move the cursor onto a file or directory name in the List Files screen. If your directory includes more than one screenful of files, it can be even faster than using a mouse. To use Name Search:

1. Type N. It doesn't matter where the cursor is located when you type it, because WordPerfect will search in both directions. The menu line at the bottom of the screen disappears, and this prompt appears in the lower-right corner of the screen:

   `(Name Search; Enter or arrows to Exit)`

2. If you are searching for a file, your next step is to type the first letter of the file name you want to highlight. If you are searching for a directory, type a backslash (\) before typing the first letter of the directory name.

   As soon as you type a letter, the cursor will move onto the first name that begins with that letter. If it isn't the file or directory you want, just type the second letter in the name. For instance, if you are searching for a file named *Johnson.ltr* and your directory includes a file named *James.ltr*, the cursor will highlight *James.ltr* first. To move it to *Johnson.ltr,* you'd have to type the letter *o.* If necessary, continue typing the third and fourth letters until the cursor highlights the file you want.

If there is no name in the list that matches the letters you type, the cursor will move to the one that is the closest in alphabetical order. Figure 7.8 shows an example. Name Search was selected and the letter *l* was typed. Since there were no file names that began with *l,* the cursor moved onto the first file that began with *m,* MACROCNV.EXE.

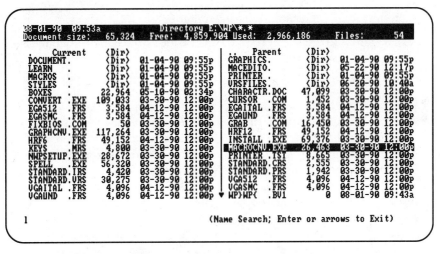

Figure 7.8   *In this example, the Name Search option from the List Files menu was used to locate file names beginning with the letter* l. *Since there were none in the list, WordPerfect searched for the next letter in alphabetical order, and the cursor moved onto the first file whose name began with the letter* m. *Notice that the menu line has disappeared from the bottom of the screen. You can bring it back by pressing Enter or one of the arrow keys.*

When you finish using Name Search, bring back the menu line.

3. Press Enter or an arrow key. If you press the Enter key, the cursor will remain on the file it is currently highlighting. If you press an arrow key, it will move the cursor in the direction of the arrow. For example, if the cursor is highlighting a file in the first column and you press the Right Arrow key, it will move to the adjacent file in column 2 (on the same line).

Using Search in the List Files Menu

You can also use the Search key or Reverse Search key to move the cursor onto a directory or file name in the List Files screen. If you are using the Long Display, the Search keys will also locate text in the Descriptive name or Type columns. Unlike Name Search, the Search keys only search in one direction, so you may want to move the cursor to the top of the list before you begin.

1. Press Search (F2) or Reverse Search (Shift-F2).

2. In response to the Srch prompt, type the file or directory name; this is called the *search string*.

3. The last step is to press Enter.

Since WordPerfect will stop if it finds the search string contained inside another word, you may not locate the file or directory you want the first time. If you don't, you'll have to repeat the search. For instance, if your screen were identical to the one shown in Figure 7.8, and the cursor were at the bottom of the file list, it would seem logical to search backward for MAC or MACRO if you wanted to move the cursor onto the subdirectory named *MACROS <Dir>*. However, this would move the cursor onto the first file with MAC or MACRO in the name: in this example, the MACROCNV.EXE file, not the subdirectory named *MACROS <Dir>*. To move it onto MACROS <Dir>, you would then have to repeat the search by pressing F2, Up Arrow, Enter.

Long Document Names and Default Document Type

As you know, DOS file names can contain a maximum of 11 characters. Until version 5.1, WordPerfect files had to conform to this rule also. If you can never remember what your file names mean and loathe whoever created that limit, you'll definitely want to take advantage of WordPerfect's Long Document Names feature. Even though you still have to assign a proper DOS name to each file, you can also create a second, more descriptive name, with as many as 68 characters. It can even include spaces! The first 30 characters will become the Descriptive name that you see in the Long Display version of the List Files screen, as shown in Figure 7.2.

A related feature is *Default Document Type,* which you can use to establish a standard document type. If the Long Document Names feature is on, the text you enter for the Default Document Type will always be suggested as the Long

Document Type when you save a document. Also, when you save the file, the first three characters will be suggested as the file extension. For instance, if you enter document as the Default Document Type, the suggested file extension will be *doc*.

 Tip: If you are using the Document Summary feature, WordPerfect will automatically copy the Long Document Name that you enter for the document, and the Default Document Type that you establish through Setup, into the second field of the summary, Document Name and Document Type.

To use Long Document Names and Default Document Type:

1. Select Setup:

   Keyboard: Press the Setup key (Shift-F1).

   Mouse: Display the File menu and select Setup.

2. Select Environment.

3. Select the fourth option, **Document Management/Summary**.

   The Setup Document Management/Summary screen appears, as shown in Figure 7.9. As you can see, Long Document Names is the third option in the menu. It is a toggle, so you can either select Yes to turn it on, or No to turn it off.

```
Setup: Document Management/Summary
      1 - Create Summary on Save/Exit     No
      2 - Subject Search Text             RE:
      3 - Long Document Names             No
      4 - Default Document Type




      Selection: 0
```

Figure 7.9   *The Setup Document Management/Summary menu.*

4. Select the third option, **Long Document Names**, and change it to **Yes**.

5. Select the fourth option, Default Document Type. Type up to 20 characters for the Default Document Type, and then press the Enter key.

6. To return to the Edit screen:

   Keyboard: Press the Exit key (F7) once.

   Mouse: Click the right button.

Now you've made two changes:

- From now on, your List Files screen will always display files using the Long Display method. To change it for the current editing session, you could use the Short/Long Display option (5) on the List Files menu. To change it permanently, you would have to use the Setup menu again, and change the Long Document Names option back to No.

- Whenever you select one of the two Save methods (Save or Exit) to save the document on your Edit screen, WordPerfect will ask for a long document name, then a long document type, and, finally, the DOS file name.

From now on, whenever you select one of the Save methods, the procedure will be different:

1. First, this prompt will appear:

   Long Document Name:

   Type a name, and then press Enter. You can type a maximum of 68 characters for the name, including spaces. You are not required to type a long document name, and can bypass it by pressing Enter.

2. This prompt will appear next:

   Long Document Type:

   If you set up a Default Document Type, WordPerfect will suggest it as the Type. If not, you can use this option to assign file types to your documents, grouping them together into categories that make sense to you. For example, you could classify them as forms, letters, memos, reports, and newsletters. The possibilities are endless! A document type can contain up to 20 characters, and is also optional. If you don't want one, press Enter to skip it. Otherwise, type the name and press Enter.

3. Next, you'll see the familiar prompt:

   Document to be saved:

   Here, WordPerfect expects a file name that conforms to DOS rules: eight characters, one period, three more characters, no spaces, and no reserved characters like:

```
* ? < > : ; = [ ] / \ " + = ,
```

If you've already saved the file, that name will appear. If you typed a Long Document Name, WordPerfect will supply a suggested name using characters from your Long Document Name, a period, and the first three characters of your Long Document Type (as the file extension). If you don't like the name, type another and press Enter.

 Tip: When using the Retrieve key or Retrieve option on the File menu to retrieve a file, you cannot type the Long Document Name. WordPerfect expects the DOS file name, and will assume the first eight characters you type are from that name. If such a file exists, it will be retrieved. If it does not, you will see an error message indicating the file was not found. To view Long Document Names and retrieve the files, use the Retrieve option on the List Files menu.

Directory Alias

Like file names, directory names must follow DOS rules, and can contain a maximum of 11 characters. However, WordPerfect 5.1 has a *Directory Alias* feature that you can use to assign a second, more descriptive name to a directory. Like Long Document names, a Directory Alias only appears in the Long Display version of the List Files screen.

To assign an alias for a directory, you create a special file using merge codes, and save it in the root directory. Say that you want to create an alias for your MACROS subdirectory, and that it is a subdirectory of the WP directory on drive C. The alias name will be MACRO AND KEYBOARD FILES. Begin with a clear Edit screen.

1. Type the name and full path of the directory:

   `C:\WP\MACROS`

2. Insert an End Field code:

   Keyboard: Press the End Field key (F9).

   Mouse: Select Merge Codes from the Tools menu, select More, and then select End Field from among the list of merge commands that pops out in a box on the right side of the screen.

   This inserts the {END FIELD} code, and moves the cursor to the next line. Your line should appear as follows:

```
C:\WP\MACROS{END FIELD}
```

3. Type the alias name on the second line:

```
MACRO AND KEYBOARD FILES
```

then insert another End Field code.

Note that only the first 30 characters you type for the alias name will be visible in the List Files screen, even though you can type a longer one. The second line should appear as follows:

```
MACRO AND KEYBOARD FILES{END FIELD}
```

4. Since this is the end of the record, insert an {END RECORD} code:

> **Keyboard:** Press the Merge Codes key (Shift-F9).

> **Mouse:** Select Merge Codes from the pull-down Tools menu.

5. Select the second option, End Record.

This inserts the {END RECORD} code and a hard page break, which is represented on the Edit screen by a dashed line.

6. Repeat this procedure for each alias you are creating.

Figure 7.10 shows an example of how the document should appear on the Edit screen when you finish. In it, alias names were created for three subdirectories of the WP directory (on drive E): MACROS, MACEDITO, and VRSFILES. Since case is irrelevant in this document, the names were typed in all uppercase letters.

7. When you finish, save the file in the root directory, using the name WP{WP}.DLN.

For instance, if your root directory is C:\, save it as C:\WP{WP}.DLN. After that, whenever you display the List Files screen with Long Display on, the alias will appear in the first column, as shown in Figure 7.11.

Redisplaying the Previous List Files Screen

From the Edit screen, you can press the List key (F5) twice to redisplay the previous List Files screen. For instance, say you select List Files, use the asterisks to restrict the display to those files ending in *LTR*, then retrieve one of the files and return to the Edit screen. After that, you could view the restricted list again (only the files ending in *LTR*) by pressing F5 twice. The cursor would be in the same position as the last time you looked at List Files, on the file name you retrieved.

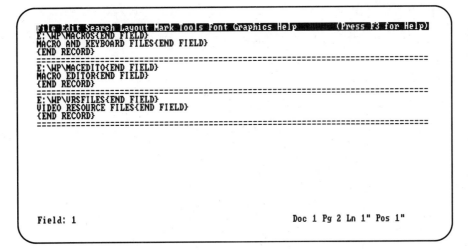

Figure 7.10 *To assign an alias name to a directory or subdirectory, you create a special file using merge codes, and save it in the root directory under the name WP{WP}.DLN. This is an example of how the file looks on the Edit screen.*

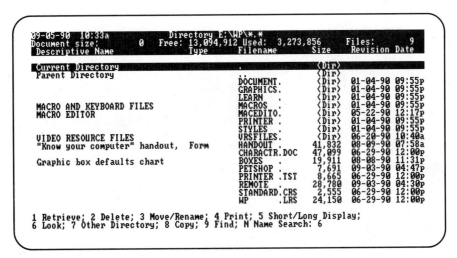

Figure 7.11 *When you use the Long Display option to view the List Files screen, the alias names you have assigned for each directory or subdirectory appear in the first column. Here, three of the subdirectories have alias names: MACROS, MACEDITO, and VRSFILES.*

WordPerfect saves the previous List Files screen in a special temporary file. As such, it's like a snapshot of the last List Files screen you were viewing before returning to the Edit screen. When you press List Files twice, you view this temporary file, not the directory as it currently exists. It is not updated when you make certain changes that affect List Files. Also, if you use List Files to retrieve a file, then edit it and save it again, the next time you press List Files twice, the statistics for file size and time saved will be incorrect (and possibly the date, if enough time has lapsed!).

If you use List Files to view the files on a different disk drive from the one where your default directory is located, the previous List Files screen is no longer available. After that, pressing F5 twice displays the entire default directory. For instance, say your default directory is C:\WP. You use List Files to display all the files on drive A. After deleting a file, you exit List Files. A few minutes later you press F5 twice. As a result, WordPerfect displays all the files in C:\WP, not in A:\. However, if you were to change the default directory to A, you would then be able to see the previous List Files screen if it was on drive C. Oddly enough, if the previous List Files screen were a subdirectory of drive A, or a restricted list of files on drive A, pressing F5 would not display it. Instead, you'd see all the files in A:\, the default directory.

Printing the List Files Screen

While you are viewing the List Files screen, you can print it by pressing the Print key, Shift-F7. This will print all subdirectories and files in the list, even if there are too many to fit on one screen. It also prints some of the header information: the directory name, the current date and time, and the amount of free disk space. Figure 7.12 shows the printout for the E:\WP directory. Compare it to the List Files display of the directory, shown in Figure 7.1, and you'll see 23 files that did not appear in the List Files version (all the files below VGAUND.FRS and WP}WP{.BV1).

 Tip: WordPerfect can print both the Long Display and Short Display versions of the List Files screen. Whichever version you are viewing when you press the Print key is the version that will be printed.

Using List Files to Retrieve a WordPerfect File

In Chapter 2 you learned how to retrieve a file using the Retrieve key or the File menu's Retrieve option. There is one major disadvantage to that method: If you spell the name incorrectly, you won't be able to retrieve it. Instead, you will see an error message saying that the file was not found. If this happens, you can retrieve through the List Files screen instead. Since the names of all files in the directory are listed in this screen, you don't have to type a file's name to retrieve it. All you have to do is

1. Locate the file in the list and move the cursor onto it.

2. Select **Retrieve**.

```
08-01-90  10:48a              Directory E:\WP\*.*
Free:  4,605,952

   .   Current   <Dir>              | ..    Parent    <Dir>
DOCUMENT.        <Dir>  01-04-90 09:55p | GRAPHICS.        <Dir>  01-04-90 09:55p
LEARN    .       <Dir>  01-04-90 09:55p | MACEDITO.        <Dir>  05-22-90 12:17p
MACROS   .       <Dir>  01-04-90 09:55p | PRINTER  .       <Dir>  01-04-90 09:55p
STYLES   .       <Dir>  01-04-90 09:55p | VRSFILES.        <Dir>  06-20-90 10:40a
BOXES    .      22,964  05-10-90 02:34p | CHARACTR.DOC    47,099  03-30-90 12:00p
CONVERT .EXE   109,033  03-30-90 12:00p | CURSOR   .COM    1,452  03-30-90 12:00p
EGA512   .FRS    3,584  04-12-90 12:00p | EGAITAL  .FRS    3,584  04-12-90 12:00p
EGASMC   .FRS    3,584  04-12-90 12:00p | EGAUND   .FRS    3,584  04-12-90 12:00p
FIXBIOS  .COM       50  03-30-90 12:00p | GRAB     .COM   16,450  03-30-90 12:00p
GRAPHCNV.EXE   117,264  03-30-90 12:00p | HRF12    .FRS   49,152  04-12-90 12:00p
HRF6     .FRS   49,152  04-12-90 12:00p | INSTALL  .EXE   69,376  03-30-90 12:00p
KEYS     .MRS    4,800  03-30-90 12:00p | MACROCNV.EXE    26,463  03-30-90 12:00p
NWPSETUP.EXE    28,672  03-30-90 12:00p | PRINTER  .TST    8,665  03-30-90 12:00p
SPELL    .EXE   56,320  03-30-90 12:00p | STANDARD.CRS     2,555  03-30-90 12:00p
STANDARD.IRS     4,420  03-30-90 12:00p | STANDARD.PRS     1,942  03-30-90 12:00p
STANDARD.VRS    30,275  03-30-90 12:00p | VGA512   .FRS    4,096  04-12-90 12:00p
VGAITAL  .FRS    4,096  04-12-90 12:00p | VGASMC   .FRS    4,096  04-12-90 12:00p
VGAUND   .FRS    4,096  04-12-90 12:00p | WP}WP{   .BV1        0  08-01-90 10:28a
WP}WP{   .CHK        0  08-01-90 10:28a | WP}WP{   .GF1        0  08-01-90 10:44a
WP{WP}   .SET    2,476  08-01-90 10:30a | WP}WP{   .SPC    4,096  08-01-90 10:28a
WP{WP}   .SPW   13,122  04-27-90 12:00p | WP}WP{   .TV1        0  08-01-90 10:28a
WP{WP}US.HYC     9,676  04-27-90 12:00p | WP{WP}US.LCN       16  01-04-90 10:02p
WP{WP}US.LEX   363,260  04-27-90 12:00p | WP{WP}US.SUP      473  07-31-90 06:31p
WP{WP}US.THS   357,528  04-27-90 12:00p | WP       .DRS  473,897  04-12-90 12:00p
WP       .EXE  222,720  03-30-90 12:00p | WP       .FIL  596,622  03-30-90 12:00p
WP       .LRS   19,077  03-30-90 12:00p | WP       .MRS    5,928  03-30-90 12:00p
WP       .QRS   16,959  03-30-90 12:00p | WP-PIF   .DVP      416  03-30-90 12:00p
WP51     .INS    2,307  07-16-90 08:54a | WP51-286.PIF      369  03-30-90 12:00p
WP51-386.PIF       369  03-30-90 12:00p | WPHELP   .FIL  191,347  03-30-90 12:00p
WPINFO   .EXE    8,704  03-30-90 12:00p |
```

Figure 7.12 A directory printout.

If you retrieve a DOS text file or a file that was created with WordPerfect 5.0 or 4.2, WordPerfect will convert the copy (of that file) as it retrieves it into WordPerfect 5.1. While this is happening, you'll see a prompt indicating that the conversion is in progress. If you save this document after retrieving it, the original disk version (in WordPerfect 4.2 or 5.0 format, or DOS text format) will be erased and replaced with the WordPerfect 5.1 version. You cannot retrieve program files such as WP.EXE (the main WordPerfect program file), WPHELP.FIL (the main Help file), or WP{WP}US.LEX (one of the Speller files). If you try, you'll see this prompt:

```
ERROR: Incompatible file format
```

and the menu will reappear.

When using List Files to retrieve, be careful not to press Enter instead of typing R or 1. Instead of selecting the Retrieve option, pressing Enter selects the Look option. You can always tell when you are in Look because the file name, path, WordPerfect version, and date and time of the last revision appear in a header at the top of the screen, as shown in Figure 7.6. Also, a menu line appears in the lower-left corner of the screen, with two options: Next Doc and Prev Doc. When you retrieve a file, you never see this information at the top of the screen. If you accidentally select Look, just press the space bar to return to the List Files screen and then select Retrieve.

A common misconception is that by displaying the List Files screen, you clear the Edit screen. Wrong! If you display the List Files screen while another document is on the Edit screen, the Document size statistic in the header area will be a number other than 0, because it corresponds to the size of the document on the Edit screen. For example, the Document size shown in Figure 7.4 is 65,324. If the Document size is not 0 and you try to retrieve a file, this warning will appear:

```
Retrieve into current document? No (Yes)
```

because WordPerfect will think you want to add this file to the document currently in the Edit screen. If this happens and you do not want to combine the files, select No, then exit from List Files and use Exit to clear the Edit screen. After clearing it, you can safely retrieve the other file. If you select Yes and inadvertently add the two files together, be sure to use Exit to clear the screen without saving, so you don't save the two files as one. Remember, when the Edit screen is clear, the Document size shown on line two of the List Files screen will always be 0. If it isn't, do not use the Retrieve option, unless you intend to combine the file you are retrieving with the document already on your Edit screen, or you want to insert the current default formatting or printer name into an existing file (see the following tip).

 Tip: Every WordPerfect file is saved with a prefix that includes information about the printer and default formatting. If the Edit screen is clear and you press the space bar once, WordPerfect will insert this prefix, as though you were starting to type a new document. If you then look at the Document Size statistic in the List Files screen, you'll see a number representing the prefix.

Marking a Group of Files

In the List Files screen, there are five options that you can use on a group of files:

- Copy.
- Move.
- Print.
- Delete.
- Find.

To use them this way, you have to mark each file with an asterisk.

1. Place the cursor on the first file name and type an asterisk.

2. Repeat for each file that you want to mark. The asterisks appear at the beginning of each file name, as shown in Figure 7.13, and the Marked statistic in the second line of the header shows how many files you've marked. If you change your mind and want to unmark a file, just highlight it again and type an asterisk.

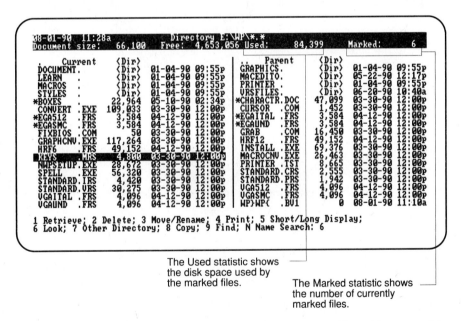

The Used statistic shows the disk space used by the marked files.

The Marked statistic shows the number of currently marked files.

Figure 7.13 *In the List Files menu, you can mark one or more files with an asterisk, and then print, delete, find, copy, or move them all. An asterisk appears at the beginning of each file name that you mark.*

Marking All Files in the List

There are two ways to simultaneously mark all files in the directory. You can

- Press Home and type an asterisk.

or

- Press the Mark Text key, Alt-F5.

If one or more files is already marked, pressing Home,Asterisk or Alt-F5 unmarks them all. Since this is a toggle, you can mark them all again by pressing Home,Asterisk or Alt-F5 once more.

After you mark one or more files, the second line of the List Files header will change. Where WordPerfect usually indicates the total number of files in the directory, you'll see the total number that have been marked. For instance, in Figure 7.13, the Marked statistic shows that six files have been marked. Also, the Used statistic will change to reflect only the disk space used by the marked files.

Making Backup Copies

One of the most important options on the List Files menu is the Copy option, which you can use to copy one or more files to another directory or disk drive, or to the same directory under a different name. Because both hard disks and floppy diskettes are susceptible to failure, it's important that you make backup copies of your documents. WordPerfect makes it easy.

Copying One File to Another Drive or Directory

To copy a file:

1. Display the List Files menu.

2. Move the cursor onto the file that you want to copy.

3. Select the Copy option. This prompt will appear:

   Copy this file to:

4. You can then copy the file to another disk drive, or to another directory.

- To copy the file to another disk drive, type the name of the drive and press Enter. For instance, to copy the highlighted file from drive C to drive A, type `A:` and press Enter. This copies the file to drive A, under the same file name.

- To copy a file to another directory, type the whole path. For instance, to copy a file from C:\WP51 to the subdirectory C:\WP51\DOCUMENT, select Copy and type `\WP51\DOCUMENT` and then press Enter. If the file is located in the DOCUMENT subdirectory and you want to copy it into the WP51 subdirectory one level above, select Copy and type `\WP51` and then press Enter.

Each of these examples assumes that you want to use the same file name for the copy. If not, just type a different name after the drive or path name. For instance, to copy a file named *JOHNSON.LTR* from drive C to a file named *JOHNSON.1* on drive A, select Copy and type `A:JOHNSON.1` and then press Enter.

One of the many advantages of using WordPerfect's Copy option, instead of the DOS equivalent, is that you'll be warned if you try to make a copy of a file using an existing file name. Two files in the same directory can't have the same name, so if you see a `Replace` prompt when you try to copy a file, be careful! It means WordPerfect has found another file with the same name on the drive or directory you are trying to copy to, and if you select Yes you will erase that file. If you aren't sure what's in that file and want to be safe, don't replace it. Instead, follow these steps:

1. Type N in response to the `Replace` prompt.

2. Select the Copy option again.

3. Type a different file name and press Enter.

You can also use the Copy option to make an extra copy of a file in the same directory. To do this:

1. Highlight the file.

2. Select Copy.

3. Type a different file name and press Enter.

Since you are copying into the same directory, you don't have to type the directory name.

Selecting a Group of Files to Copy Simultaneously

In the last section, you learned how to copy an individual file. To copy a group of files, the procedure is different.

1. Begin by marking each file you want to copy with an asterisk. (If you've forgotten how, see the section "Marking a Group of Files.")

2. Select Copy from the List Files menu. This prompt will appear:

   `Copy marked files? No (Yes)`

3. Select **Yes** to copy them. This prompt will appear:

   `Copy all marked files to:`

The same rules that apply to copying individual files, outlined in the previous section, apply to copying a group of files. For instance:

- To copy all the files in a directory on drive C to drive A, just type A: and press Enter.

- To copy all marked files to another directory, type the directory name and path, such as \WP\LETTERS, and press Enter.

The files will be copied to the drive or directory you've specified, and all will have the same names.

If you select No in response to the `Copy marked files?` prompt and the cursor is highlighting a file name, WordPerfect will assume you want to copy only the file that the cursor is highlighting. You'll see this prompt: `Copy this file to.` However, if the cursor is on a directory name, the copy operation will be canceled and the List Files menu will reappear.

 Warning: When copying a group of files to a floppy disk, be sure you have enough formatted disks before you begin! If there isn't enough room for all of the files on the first disk, when it is full, WordPerfect will prompt you to replace it with another one. This will continue until all of the files have been copied.

Deleting Files

After using WordPerfect for a while, you may find that you're cluttering up your hard disk with files you never use, and you want to delete them. If so, you can use the Delete option on the List Files menu. Once you delete a file in WordPerfect, you can't get it back, unless you have a special utility program. (WordPerfect Corporation does not offer such a program, but you can probably purchase one, such as the Norton Utilities, from your software dealer.) If you think there is even a remote possibility that you'll want to use a file again, consider using the Move option instead of Delete. That way, you can move it onto a floppy disk, file it away in a safe place, and erase it from your hard disk—all in one command! You'll learn how to use Move in the next section; for now, let's study Delete.

Deleting One File

To erase one file:

1. Display the List Files menu.

2. Move the cursor onto the file name.

3. Select **D**elete.

   WordPerfect then gives you a chance to change your mind, displaying a prompt that asks if you want to delete the file. For instance, if you highlight a file named *SALES90.RPT* in the WP directory on drive C, and select Delete, you'll see this prompt:

   ```
   Delete C:\WP\SALES90.RPT? No (Yes)
   ```

   Notice that the assumption is No.

4. To erase the file:

   Keyboard: Type Y or y. Pressing any other key selects No.

   Mouse: Select Yes.

   After WordPerfect deletes the file, it updates the List Files screen, and the file name disappears from the list.

Deleting a Group of Files

To erase a group of files:

1. Mark each file you want to delete with an asterisk. (If you've forgotten how, see the section "Marking a Group of Files.")

2. Select Delete. You should see this prompt:

   ```
   Delete marked files? No (Yes)
   ```

   Notice that the assumption is No.

3. Select **Y**es. This prompt appears:

   ```
   Marked files will be deleted. Continue? No (Yes)
   ```

When you delete a group of files, WordPerfect gives you two chances to change your mind!

4. Select **Yes** if you want to delete them.

You will see a `* Please wait *` prompt as the files are erased. After finishing, WordPerfect updates the screen and the file names disappear from the list.

Moving Files

The Move/Rename command is one of the most useful tools on the List Files menu. You can use it to

- Move one or more files to another disk drive.

- Rename a file.

- Simultaneously rename a file and move it to another directory or disk drive.

In this section, you'll learn how to use it to move files. Remember, this is a great way to clean up your hard disk. If yours includes hundreds of files you never use, just move them to floppy disks, and store the disks in a safe place in case you ever need them again.

Moving One File

To move a file to another directory or disk drive:

1. Display the List Files menu.

2. Move the cursor onto the file name.

3. Select the **Move/Rename** option.

   A prompt will appear asking for the new file name. For example, if you highlight a file named *PROFIT90.RPT* in the WP51 directory of drive C and select Move/Rename, this prompt will appear:

   `New name: C:\WP51\PROFIT90.RPT`

4. You can then move the file to another disk, or to another directory.

   - To move this file onto another disk and simultaneously erase it from this directory, type the drive designator and press Enter. For instance, to move it from C to the disk in drive A, type `A:` and press Enter.

- To move it to another subdirectory, edit the prompt to include the subdirectory name and press Enter. For instance, to move the PROFIT90.RPT file to the REPORTS subdirectory of WP51, press the Right Arrow key until the cursor is on the letter *P* in PROFIT and then type REPORTS\. The prompt should appear as follows:

```
New name: C:\WP51\REPORTS\PROFIT90.RPT
```

If the file is in the REPORTS subdirectory and you want to move it up one level to the WP51 subdirectory, erase REPORTS\ from the prompt, so that it appears as follows:

```
New name: C:\WP51\PROFIT90.RPT
```

After WordPerfect has moved the file, the screen will be updated and the old name will no longer appear in your file list.

Moving a Group of Files

To move a group of files:

1. Mark each one with an asterisk. (If you've forgotten how, see the section "Marking a Group of Files.")

2. Select the **Move/Rename** option. You should see this prompt:

```
Move marked files? No (Yes)
```

3. Select **Yes**. Next, this prompt will appear asking where you want to move them:

```
Move marked files to:
```

4. You can move the files to another disk, or subdirectory:

   - To move the files to another disk, type the drive name and press Enter.

   - To move them to another subdirectory, type the full path to the subdirectory, such as \WP51\DOCUMENT, and press Enter.

After WordPerfect has moved the files, their names will disappear from your screen.
If you select No in response to the Move marked files? prompt and the cursor is highlighting a file name, WordPerfect will assume you want to move or rename that file. The New name prompt will appear, waiting for you to move or rename the file the cursor is highlighting. If the cursor is on a directory name, Move will be canceled and the List Files menu will reappear.

Renaming a File

To change a file name, use the Move/Rename option. You can either rename a file and leave it in the same directory, or simultaneously move and rename it. To rename a file:

1. Move the cursor onto the file.

2. Select **Move/Rename**.

   The `New name` prompt appears, showing the file name and directory. For example, if you were renaming the SALES90.RPT file in the WP51 directory of drive C, this prompt would appear:

   `New name: C:\WP51\SALES90.RPT`

3. Type a new name or edit the existing one, and press Enter.

   - To rename the file but leave it in the same directory, just type the new name (or edit the old one) and press Enter. You will see the effect almost immediately, as the screen is updated to place the file in the correct alphabetical order.

   - To rename the file and simultaneously move it to another directory or disk drive, type the drive name or directory name followed by the new file name and press Enter. For example, to rename it PROFIT90.RPT and move it to the DOCUMENT subdirectory of WP51, type `\WP51\DOCUMENT\PROFIT90.RPT` and press Enter.

Since two files in a directory cannot have the same name, if you ask WordPerfect to rename a file, and another one with the same name already exists in the directory you are renaming it to, you will see a prompt asking if you want to replace the other file. Replace means erase, so if you select Yes you will erase the other file. To be safe, select No, select the option again, and think of another name!

Printing Disk Files

The Print option on the List Files menu lets you print one or more files without retrieving them to the Edit screen. You can use it to print the entire file, a specific page, a range of pages, non-consecutive pages, or the document summary.

To print a file:

1. Highlight it with the cursor bar.

2. Select the **P**rint option.

This prompt will appear in the lower-left corner of the screen:

```
Page(s) : (All)
```

3. Select the pages you want to print according to Table 7.1.

Table 7.1   Selecting the pages to be printed.

To Print	*Use These Keystrokes*
Entire document	Press Enter
Specific page	Type the page number; press Enter
Range of pages	Type the first and last numbers, separated by a hyphen; press Enter
Non-consecutive pages	Type the page numbers, separated by commas; press Enter
Range & specific pages	Type the specific page numbers, separated by a comma, and the range numbers, separated by a hyphen; press Enter
The first through a specific page	Type a hyphen, then the last page number; press Enter
All odd pages	Type O and press Enter
All even pages	Type E and press Enter
Document summary	Type S and press Enter
Document summary and entire document	Type S- and press Enter

Once you enter the page numbers, your printer should start printing almost immediately. If it doesn't, do not return to List Files and select Print again, because it won't work! When a printer refuses to start after you issue a print command, it is usually related to a printer connection problem, such as a loose cable, an on-line button that is currently switched off, or an incorrectly installed printer. Furthermore, WordPerfect remembers everything you ask it to print, regardless of whether or not the printer is actually functioning. Each time you ask it to print a document, WordPerfect assigns a job number to your request and places it in a job list where it waits until the printer is ready. Once you do get the printer working, it will print the document once for each time you selected Print. The job list is covered in more detail in the "Printer Control" section of Chapter 13.

Be careful if you use the List Files Print option to print a file while it is on your Edit screen. Remember, when you retrieve a document and edit it, the document on screen differs from the one on disk until you save it again. The List Files Print option prints the disk version, not the one on your Edit screen! To avoid an unwanted discrepancy, save the document before selecting Print from the List Files screen.

Printing a Group of Files

To print a group of files:

1. Mark each file that you want to print with an asterisk. (If you've forgotten how, see the section "Marking a Group of Files.")

2. Select the **Print** option. This prompt will appear:

   `Print marked files? No (Yes)`

3. Select **Yes**.

The `Page(s): (All)` prompt will appear, asking which page numbers you want to print. If you limit the page numbers, the limit will apply to all marked documents. For instance, if you enter 1-3 in response to this prompt, only pages one through three of each file will be printed. To print all pages of all marked files, press Enter.

 Tip: If you see this message: `Document not formatted for current printer. Continue? No (Yes)`, it means that when you last saved the file, you were using a different printer definition, and the document is still formatted for that printer. If you select Yes in response to this prompt, WordPerfect will print the file and try to substitute the closest available fonts. This will have no effect on the document on disk, and it will remain formatted for the other printer. However, the printed version may not be exactly what you had expected.

Creating and Changing Directories

In this section, you'll learn how to use the List Files' Other Directory option, which has two functions: You can use it to create a new directory or change the default directory.

By dividing your hard disk into subdirectories, you can organize your files more logically, and make it easier to locate them. Think of the disk as a file cabinet, and each directory as a file folder where you place related information, your files.

Creating a New Directory

To create a new directory:

1. Display the List Files screen.

2. Select **Other** Directory.

   The cursor can be anywhere when you do this (either on a file name or on a directory name). If it is on a file name, you will see this prompt:

   `New directory =`

   followed by the current directory's name and path. If the cursor is on a directory name, the prompt will also include that directory's name. This happens because WordPerfect assumes that when you highlight a directory name and select the Other Directory option, your intention is to make it the default directory, not to create a new directory.

   Either way, your next step is to:

3. Type the new directory name:

   - If you want the directory to be a subdirectory of the current one (one level below it), you don't need to type a path. For instance, if your current directory is WP51 and you want to create a subdirectory named *DOCUMENT* one level below WP51, you would type `DOCUMENT`.

   - If you want the directory to be on the same level, you would have to type the path, or edit the existing one. For instance, if your current directory is C:\WP51\REPORTS and you want to create C:\WP51\LETTERS, you would change the prompt to `\WP51\LETTERS`.

4. Press Enter.

A prompt will appear asking if you want to create the new directory. For instance, if your current directory is WP51 and you are creating a subdirectory named *LETTERS,* this prompt appears: `Create LETTERS? No (Yes)`. If the directory already exists, you won't see the prompt asking if you want to create it. Instead, the command just makes it the new default directory. You'll learn more about this in the next section.

5. Select **Yes.**

WordPerfect will create the directory and update the screen. If it is a subdirectory of the current directory, the new directory name will appear at the top with the other subdirectory names.

Creating a new directory does not mean it has become the default directory or the current directory. One more step is required: using Other Directory again to change the default directory.

Changing the Default Directory

To change the default directory to a directory whose name appears in your List Files screen:

1. Move the cursor onto the directory name.

2. Select **Other Directory.** A `New directory` prompt will appear, indicating that the highlighted directory will become the new default directory. For example, if the default directory is WP51 and you highlight DOCUMENT <Dir> and select Other Directory, the prompt will appear as follows:

   `New directory = C:\WP51\DOCUMENT`

3. Press Enter to implement the option and change the default directory. Next, WordPerfect will give you a chance to view the directory list. A `Dir` prompt will appear, such as:

   `Dir C:\WP51\DOCUMENT`

4. You then have two options:

   • To view the list of files in the new default directory, press Enter.

   • If you don't want to see the list, just press Cancel (F1).

If the directory you want to change to does not appear in the List Files screen, you can still make it the default directory:

1. Select **Other Directory.**

2. Type the directory name and path.

3. Press Enter.

4. Next, either press Enter to view the list of files in the new default directory, or press Cancel (F1).

Another Method of Creating or Changing the Directory

You don't have to be in the List Files screen to change the default directory, or create a new one. When you press F5 or select List Files from the File menu, this prompt appears in the lower-right corner of the screen:

```
(Type = to change default Dir)
```

As soon as you type the equal sign (=), the New directory prompt appears. The remaining steps are similar to using the Other Directory option in List Files.

To create a new directory using this method:

1. Select List Files:

   Keyboard: Press F5.

   Mouse: Display the File menu and select List Files.

   The Dir prompt appears.

2. Type the equal sign. The New directory prompt appears.

3. Type the new directory name, and press Enter. The next prompt asks if you want to create the new directory.

4. Select Yes.

   WordPerfect will create the directory. To see it, display the List Files screen.

   If you want to change to an existing directory, instead of creating a new one, follow steps 1 and 2 above. When you get to step 3, just type the existing directory name and press Enter. Next, the Dir prompt appears. If you want to view the directory file list, press Enter. If not, press Cancel (F1) to remove the Dir prompt.

Changing the Default Directory Permanently

When you change the default directory through the Other Directory option on the List Files menu, it remains in effect only until you exit WordPerfect. The next time you start the program, the default directory will revert back to the default documents directory specified in the Setup: Location of Files menu. To permanently change the default directory, you have to change it through the Setup menu.

To change the default directory permanently:

1. Select Setup:

    Keyboard: Press the Setup key (Shift-F1).

    Mouse: Display the File menu and select Setup.

2. Select the sixth option, Location of Files. The Location of Files menu will appear, as shown in Figure 7.14. In earlier versions of WordPerfect 5.1, this menu only included seven options, so don't panic if your screen doesn't include the last one, Spreadsheet Files.

3. Select the seventh option, **Documents.**

4. Type the directory name and path for the new default directory, and press Enter three times to return to the Edit screen. Do not try to type the name of a directory that does not yet exist. If you do, you'll see this error message:

```
ERROR: Invalid drive/path specification
```

If this happens, you have two options. The first is to type the name of an existing directory. The second is to exit from this menu, use the Other Directory option on the List Files menu to create the directory, then repeat these steps to make it the default directory.

Deleting a Directory

If you want to delete a directory, it must be empty. WordPerfect will not let you delete a directory if it contains one or more files. Your first step, then, is to erase all files, or move them to a different directory. Once you've finished that task, you can delete the directory:

1. Move the cursor onto the directory name in the List Files menu.

2. Select the Delete option. A prompt will appear asking if you want to delete, and it will specify the directory and path name. For instance, if you are erasing the LETTERS subdirectory one level below WP51 it will appear as follows:

```
Delete C:\WP51\LETTERS? No (Yes)
```

```
Setup: Location of Files
     1 - Backup Files                    E:\WP\DOCUMENT

     2 - Keyboard/Macro Files            E:\WP\MACROS

     3 - Thesaurus/Spell/Hyphenation
                          Main           E:\WP
                          Supplementary  E:\WP

     4 - Printer Files                   E:\WP\PRINTER

     5 - Style Files                     E:\WP\STYLES
             Library Filename            FONT.STY

     6 - Graphic Files                   E:\WP\GRAPHICS

     7 - Documents                       E:\WP\DOCUMENT

     8 - Spreadsheet Files


Selection: 0
```

Figure 7.14 *The Setup: Location of Files menu. You can use the seventh option,
Documents, to change the default directory permanently. In earlier
versions of WordPerfect 5.1, this menu did not include the last option,
Spreadsheet Files.*

3. Select **Yes** to delete it. The screen will be updated, and the directory
   name will be erased. However, if the directory you are trying to delete is
   not empty, you will see a different prompt:

   `ERROR: Directory not empty`

   and the menu line will reappear at the bottom of the screen. If this
   happens, use the Look option to display the directory, as described
   previously, and erase or move all the files. After that, you can delete the
   directory.

Tip: You cannot delete a directory from inside the directory. Instead,
you must be in the parent directory, or any other directory that is
above it.

Using Find to Locate a File

If your directories include a large number of files, and you have trouble remembering your file names, the Find option on the List Files menu can help you locate

a specific file very quickly, by searching all the displayed files for a word or phrase. The word or phrase, called the *search text,* can contain up to 39 characters, and you can search for it on the first page, in the entire document, in the document summary, or in any of the summary's fields. Find can also search for all or part of the file name, or for files created on a specific date, or between a range of dates. If you want to get really complex, you can combine three conditions and locate files by specifying different criteria for the document summary, first page, and entire document. However, if you can remember that much about a document, you can probably remember its file name!

To use Find:

1. Display the List Files screen for the directory where you think the file is located. If you've marked one or more files with an asterisk, WordPerfect will only search through the marked files, not the entire directory. You can unmark them by pressing Home,Asterisk.

2. Select the Find option. This menu will appear:

```
Find: 1 Name; 2 Doc Summary; 3 First Pg; 4 Entire Doc;
5 Conditions; 6 Undo: 0
```

3. Select one of the first four options:

   - To search for a file name, select the first option, **Name**. This prompt appears:

     ```
     Word pattern
     ```

     Type all or part of the name, and press Enter. For instance, to locate a file named *JOHNSTON.LTR*, you could type *JOHN*, *LTR*, *STON*, or the entire file name.

   - To search for text inside a document summary, select the second option, **Doc Summary**. In response to the `Word pattern` prompt, type a word that you know is in the summary. You can also search for a phrase, but you must surround it with quotation marks. To find an exact match, leave one blank space between the last character and the end quotation mark. To locate text in a specific field of the document summary, such as Subject or Keywords, you must select Conditions first. You'll learn how in the section "The Conditions Option."

   - To search for a word or phrase in the document itself, you can use either the First **Pg** option or the **Entire Doc** option. When you select First **Pg**, WordPerfect searches through the first 4,000 characters or the first page, whichever comes first. If your documents tend to be lengthy, searching the first page of each file will be much faster than searching the entire file, so try that option first. If it doesn't work, repeat the search using the Entire Doc option. Either way, after selecting one of these two options, you'll see the `Word pattern` prompt. Type the word or phrase, then press Enter.

Regardless of which of the first four options you select, after you type the word pattern and press Enter, WordPerfect will begin searching through all the displayed files for your search text. After it is finished, the screen will be updated to display only files that contain the word or phrase. If it isn't found in any of the files, you'll see this prompt:

```
* Not found *
```

and the List Files screen will be cleared of all files, since there are no matching ones. If this happens, you can redisplay the previous file list by selecting the Undo option from the Find menu.

Undo works differently if you've performed more than one search; instead of restoring the entire directory, it restores the last list of files you were viewing. For instance, say you use Find to search your entire LETTERS subdirectory for a certain letter to Mike Johnson (using *Mike Johnson* as the search text). WordPerfect finds 10 matching files, but since you gave them all names like *JOHNSON.LTR* and *JOHNSON2.LTR*, you still don't know which document to retrieve. You think it may have his company name in it also, so you use Find again to search for the company name in the 10 listed files. However, no matching files are found this time, and WordPerfect clears all files from the List Files screen. What do you do? Select the Undo option, and the 10 JOHNSON letters reappear instantly! You can use Undo to restore the file lists displayed by the three previous searches.

 Tip: When you select one of the first four options on the Find menu and type a file name, word, or phrase in response to the `Word pattern` prompt, case is irrelevant. You can type it all in uppercase, all in lowercase, or in a combination.

Using Search Patterns

Remember the asterisk wild cards, which you studied earlier in the chapter? You can use these and other symbols in your word pattern to restrict the search. An asterisk can represent zero or more characters. The question mark (?) is another wild card, and it represents one character. For example, if you type `p?ge` in response to the `Word pattern` prompt, WordPerfect will locate files containing any of these words: *page, pageboy, pageant, paged.*

If you type `Inter*nal`, for example, WordPerfect will locate files containing any of these words: *interregional, internal, interpersonal, international, interdenominational, Internal Affairs Tribunal.*

You can also use several logical operators with the Find option, including a semicolon, a space, a comma, and a hyphen:

- If you use a semicolon (;) or blank space to join two words, the search will locate only files containing both of them. For example, if you type `Mike;Franklin` or `Mike Franklin` in response to the `Word pattern` prompt, WordPerfect will display only files containing both *Mike* and *Franklin*. The names do not have to be next to each other in the document.

- To locate files containing either of the words, join them with a comma. For example, if you type `Mike Franklin,` WordPerfect will display a file if it contains either the name *Mike* or *Franklin,* or both *Mike* and *Franklin.*

- You can use a hyphen to specify words or phrases that you do not want to locate. If you type `Mike-Franklin,` WordPerfect will locate files containing *Mike,* but not if they contain the word *Franklin.*

- You can also combine the operators. For instance, if you type `Mary,Janice;Ann` WordPerfect will locate files containing either *Mary* and *Ann,* or *Janice* and *Ann.*

The Conditions Option

If you select the fifth option on the Find menu, Conditions, the Find Conditions menu shown in Figure 7.15 appears. You can use it to restrict the search to

- A specific revision date or range of dates.

- Text in the document summary, first page, and/or entire document.

- Specific fields in the document summaries.

Better yet, you can use a combination of these conditions to restrict the search. For example, you can find all files created in August 1990 that contain a certain client name on the first page.

The first option on the Find Conditions menu is Perform Search. Notice that it is the default, automatically selected when you press the Enter key, since the number 1 appears next to `Selection` at the bottom of the menu. When you finish typing your search text, use this option to begin the search. As in the Find menu, WordPerfect will search all the files in the List Files screen, then update the list to display only those that meet your criteria. If there are none, the file list will be empty.

You can use the second option, Reset Conditions, to clear all previous search conditions from the menu. When you use one or more of the Conditions options to restrict your search, these restrictions remain in effect until you select and change them for another search (or exit WordPerfect).

```
Find: Conditions                          Files Selected:   70

    1 - Perform Search
    2 - Reset Conditions

    3 - Revision Date - From
                        To

    4 - Text - Document Summary
               First Page
               Entire Document

    5 - Document Summary
        Creation Date - From
                        To

        Document Name
        Document Type
        Author
        Typist
        Subject
        Account
        Keywords
        Abstract

Selection: 1
```

Figure 7.15 *The Find Conditions menu.*

To search for all files saved on a specific date, between two dates, or before
or after a certain date, select the third option, Revision Date. Revision Date refers
to the last time you saved the file. To search for all files created between two dates,
enter the starting date next to the From field, and the ending date next to the To
field. For example, to search for all files created between January 1, 1990, and
March 30, 1990, type 1/1/90 for From, and 3/30/90 for To. You can type the dates
with or without leading zeroes, using either slashes or hyphens to separate the day,
month, and year. Each of these dates is valid:

```
01-04-90
1-4-90
01/04/90
1/4/90
```

There are many other ways to limit the date search:

- To search for all files created since a certain date, enter the date next to the
From field, and leave the To field blank. For example, to search for all files
created from August 1, 1990, up to the present, enter 8-1-90 next to the
From field, then press Enter to leave the To field blank.

- To search for all files created up to a specific date, enter the date next to the
To field, and leave From blank. For example, to search for all files in the
directory that were created before March 1, 1990, leave the From field blank,
and enter 3/1/90 for the To field.

- To search for all files created on one specific day, enter that day next to both
the From and To fields.

After you enter the date or dates, select Perform Search to start the search.

The fourth option on the Find Conditions menu, Text, lets you search for text in the document summary, first page, or entire document. How do these differ from the options of the same name in the previous menu (Find)? They don't, unless you combine them. Instead of performing three separate searches—the first to exclude files whose document summaries don't include a certain word or phrase, the second to further narrow the list to files whose first page meet another criterion, and the last to find some other search text in the entire document— WordPerfect can perform all three of these searches in one pass. There is only one caveat: All three conditions must be true for a file to be found. To use one or more of the Text conditions, just select Text and then type separate search text for the document summary, First Page, and/or Entire Document. To begin the search, select Perform Search.

To search for text in one or more Document Summary fields, select the fifth option, Document Summary. This moves the cursor into the first field, Creation Date. If you don't want to type text for this field, use the Enter key or Down Arrow key to move to the field you want to type search text for and then type it. You can type search text in more than one field, such as in Author Name and Subject. If you do, both criteria must be met for the file to be found. Also, you can enter partial information in a field, and it will still be found. For example, if you enter *Jones* as the author name, WordPerfect will locate files containing *Jones, M.Jones,* or *Mary Jones.*

Password Protection

If you are concerned about others using your files, you can lock them up with a password so nobody else can retrieve, print, or even look at them. Be careful with this option. If you forget a password, you'll never again be able to access the file. You will, however, be able to delete it.

To assign a password to a file:

1. Retrieve the document to your Edit screen.

2. Select Password:

    Keyboard: Press the Text In/Out key (Ctrl-F5) and select **Password**.

    Mouse: Display the **File** menu and select Password.

3. Select **Add/Change**. This prompt will appear:

    `Enter Password:`

    A password can contain up to 23 characters, including spaces.

4. Type your password and then press Enter. This prompt will appear, asking you to type the password a second time:

```
Re-Enter Password
```

5. Type the password again. If you don't type it exactly as you did the first time, the `Enter Password` prompt will reappear, and you'll have to type the password two more times.

6. Your last step is to save the file, using the Save or Exit method. If you don't save it after assigning a password, it won't include the password protection.

When you ask WordPerfect to retrieve a document that you saved with a password, you'll see a prompt asking you to Enter the password. Type the password and press Enter. If you type it incorrectly, you'll see this message:

```
ERROR: File is locked
```

If you are using the List Files Retrieve option, the main List Files menu will reappear (if you are using one of the early versions of WordPerfect 5.1, you'll return to the Edit screen). If you are using the Retrieve key or Retrieve option on the File menu, WordPerfect will give you another chance to type the password.

Go to DOS or Shell

Although WordPerfect's List Files menu gives you the ability to perform most file management tasks, occasionally you may want to return to DOS to format a floppy disk, change the date, or run another program, such as DrawPerfect. If your computer has enough memory, you don't have to exit WordPerfect to perform such tasks. Instead, you can keep WordPerfect running while you temporarily exit to DOS. When you finish using it, you can return to WordPerfect with just a few keystrokes and, if you had a document on your Edit screen when you exited, the cursor will be right where you left it.

The option varies slightly, depending on whether you started WordPerfect from the Shell menu or from DOS. If you started WordPerfect from DOS, you'll go directly to the DOS prompt. If you started WordPerfect from the Shell menu, you'll return to the Shell first.

Exiting to DOS If You Started WordPerfect from DOS

If you started WordPerfect from DOS, follow these steps to temporarily exit to DOS.

1. Select Go to DOS:

   Keyboard: Press the Shell key (Ctrl-F1).

   Mouse: Display the **F**ile menu and select **G**o to DOS. This prompt will appear:

   `1 Go to DOS; 2 DOS Command: 0`

   The first option, Go to DOS, lets you exit to DOS and perform as many tasks as you want, including running another program if you have enough memory. The second option, DOS Command, lets you run only one DOS command, then return to WordPerfect.

2. Select the first option, **G**o to DOS. The WordPerfect Edit screen will disappear, and you'll go directly to DOS. Your screen will resemble Figure 7.16, and include

   • A few lines of information about your version of DOS.

   • A message telling you to use Exit to return to WordPerfect.

   • The DOS prompt.

   When you finish using DOS and are ready to return to WordPerfect, the prompt `Enter 'EXIT' to return to WordPerfect` tells you what to do: Type the word `Exit`. This prompt reappears after each DOS command you issue. If you run another program, it appears as soon as you exit from it.

3. To return to WordPerfect, type `Exit` (uppercase or lowercase) and press the Enter key.

```
Microsoft(R) MS-DOS(R)  Version 3.30
            (C)Copyright Microsoft Corp 1981-1987

Enter 'EXIT' to return to WordPerfect
E:\WP\DOCUMENT\ADVBOOK\CHA8>
```

Figure 7.16 *Using the Go to DOS option if you started WordPerfect from DOS.*

Exiting to DOS If You Are Running the Shell

If you started DOS through WordPerfect's Shell menu, follow these steps to temporarily exit to DOS:

1. Select Go to Shell:

   Keyboard: Press the Shell key (Ctrl-F1).

   Mouse: Select **G**o to Shell from the **F**ile menu. This menu will appear:

   ```
   1 Go to Shell; 2 Clipboard: 2 Save; 3 Append; 4 Retrieve;
   5 DOS Command: 0
   ```

2. Select the first option, **G**o to Shell. You'll return to the Shell menu, where an asterisk will appear next to the WordPerfect option to show that WordPerfect is still running. Incidentally, you can bypass the Go to Shell menu and go directly to the Shell by pressing Alt-Shift-Space bar.

3. Select the first option from the Shell menu, **G**o to DOS. The screen will change to resemble Figure 7.17. Notice the message at the top, telling you how to return to the Shell menu:

   ```
   Enter the DOS command 'EXIT' (or press F7) to return
   to the shell
   ```

   After you finish using a DOS command or running another program, the word (shell) will always appear next to the DOS prompt, as a reminder that you're using the Shell. For example, if your Shell files are in the WP directory of drive C, the prompt will appear as follows:

   ```
   (shell) C:\WP
   ```

   When you see it, do not try to start WordPerfect again by typing WP. Instead, you must press the Exit key (F7), or type exit.

4. When you are ready to return to WordPerfect, press F7. You can also type exit and press the Enter key. You'll return to the Shell menu, with the cursor highlighting the WordPerfect option.

5. Press Enter to return to WordPerfect.

Dos Command

DOS Command is the second option on the Go to Dos menu, and the fifth one on the Go to Shell menu. You can use it to run one DOS command, such as FORMAT or CHKDSK, and then return directly to WordPerfect. To use it,

1. Select DOS Command. This prompt will appear:

    ```
    DOS  Command:
    ```

    ```
    Enter the DOS command 'EXIT' (or Press F7) to return to the shell.

    Microsoft(R) MS-DOS(R)  Version 3.30
                (C)Copyright Microsoft Corp 1981-1987

    (shell) E:\DR10>
    ```

Figure 7.17 Using the Go to DOS option if you started WordPerfect from the Shell.

2. Type the command you want to use and press Enter. After the command is executed, you'll see this prompt at the bottom of the screen:

    ```
    Press any key to continue
    ```

3. To return to WordPerfect, press a key like Enter or the space bar. If you were editing a document when you selected the DOS Command option, the cursor will be right where you left it. If you make a mistake typing the command, you'll see the prompt Bad command or file name at the top of the screen, and the Press any key to continue prompt at the bottom. If this happens, press any key to return to WordPerfect.

 Tip: When you exit to DOS temporarily, there are a few commands you should not use. Do not run the CHKDSK/F command or delete any of WordPerfect's program files. Also, do not start a memory-resident program.

Timed Document Backup and Original Document Backup

WordPerfect includes two automatic backup methods, *Timed Document Backup* and *Original Document Backup*. You should understand that these methods are meant only as a supplement to, not a substitute for, your regular backup procedure. If a file is important to you, be sure to make regular backup copies on separate disks. It doesn't matter which method you use—the List Files Copy option, the DOS Copy option, a special disk backup program such as Fast Save or Fastback, or whatever—just do it, and do it frequently!

The Timed Document Backup option saves the document on your Edit screen at regular intervals that you've specified, such as every five or 10 minutes. Its purpose is to provide a recent copy of your work in progress, in case the power fails and the computer is turned off before you can save your work. The backup file is saved under the name {WP}WP.BK1 if you're working on the Edit screen in Doc 1 when the backup interval is reached, or {WP}WP.BK2 if you're working in Doc 2. If you exit WordPerfect correctly (by selecting Exit and responding Yes to the Exit WP prompt), the timed backup file will be erased and you can forget about it. If you don't exit correctly, whether it's because of a power failure or because you just forgot and turned off the computer while WordPerfect was still running, the next time you start the program you'll see this prompt:

```
Old backup file exists. 1 Rename; 2 Delete: 1
```

Before you can use WordPerfect, you'll have to decide whether to rename or delete the {WP}WP.BK1 or {WP}WP.BK2 file. Renaming it is much safer, because you can later retrieve the file and decide whether you really want to keep it. If you're anxious to get on with your work and you select the Delete option, you may regret it later.

The purpose of the Original Document Backup option is to prevent you from accidentally erasing a file on disk. This is easy to do if you ask WordPerfect to save a document under a file name that's already being used. If you answer Yes to the Replace prompt that appears as a warning, WordPerfect erases the original file. However, if Original Document Backup is on when you do this, WordPerfect will rename the existing version instead of erasing it. The renamed file will retain its original first name (the first one to eight characters in the file name), but have a special extension to distinguish it: BK!. For instance, if you ask WordPerfect to save a document under the name PARTONE, but a file of the same name already exists, WordPerfect will rename the existing version to PARTONE.BK! before saving the new one under the name PARTONE.

The disadvantage to using the Original Document Backup option is that you'll accumulate many extra files on your disk. Each time you retrieve a file, edit, and then save it again, WordPerfect will make the backup copy from the one you are replacing as you save. Since you won't need most of these files, you'll have to erase them at regular intervals, or you'll soon run out of room on your disk. Another problem is that if you are in the habit of saving files with the same first name and different extensions, such as *JONES.LT1, JONES.LT2,* and *JONES.LT3,* the Original Document Backup method won't work for you. Each of these files would be backed up under the same name, JONES.BK!. This backup file would contain only the one you saved most recently.

Before retrieving a backup file created with the Original Document Backup feature, you should rename it and remove the BK! extension. If you don't, when you save it again you'll receive an error message warning you that WordPerfect can't rename the file, and the `Document to be Saved` prompt will reappear. You should then type a different name for the document on your Edit screen, since WordPerfect can't create the backup file while you are using the BK! file name.

To turn on one or both of WordPerfect's automatic backup features:

1. Select Setup:

   Keyboard: Press the Setup key (Shift-F1).

   Mouse: Display the File menu and select Setup.

2. Select Environment.

3. Select Backup Options. The menu shown in Figure 7.18 will appear.

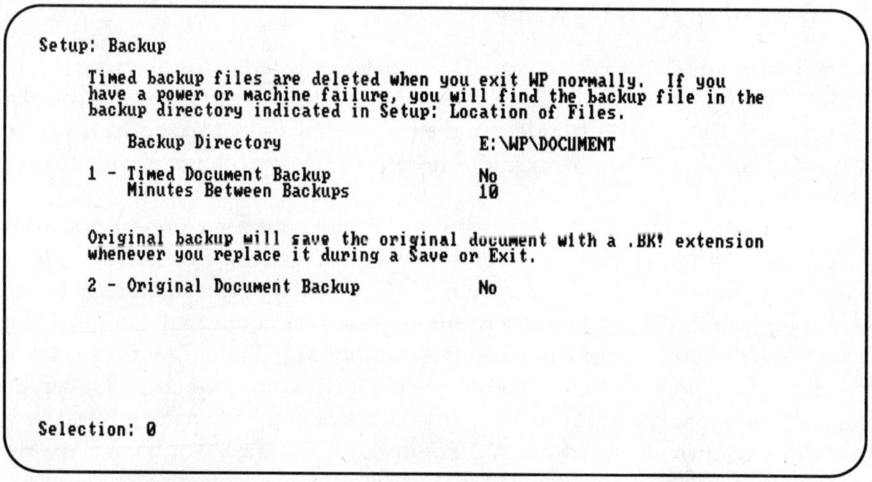

```
Setup: Backup
        Timed backup files are deleted when you exit WP normally.  If you
        have a power or machine failure, you will find the backup file in the
        backup directory indicated in Setup: Location of Files.

        Backup Directory                        E:\WP\DOCUMENT

    1 - Timed Document Backup                   No
        Minutes Between Backups                 10

        Original backup will save the original document with a .BK! extension
        whenever you replace it during a Save or Exit.

    2 - Original Document Backup                No




Selection: 0
```

Figure 7.18 *Using the Setup Backup menu.*

4. Turn on one or both of the backup options:

- To use Timed Document Backup, select the option, select Yes (if it isn't already selected), and enter the number of minutes you want to use for the backup interval.

- To use Original Document Backup, select the option, and change it from No to Yes.

Each backup file created with the Original Document Backup option will be saved in the same directory as its original file. For example, if you save a file named *JONESLTR* in a subdirectory whose path is C:\WP\LETTERS, the backup file will be saved as:

```
C:\WP\LETTERS\JONESLTR.BK!
```

Backup files created with the Timed Document Backup option will be saved in the directory specified in the Setup: Location of Files menu. Although this Backup Directory name appears in the Setup Backup menu, as shown in Figure 7.18, you cannot change it there. To select a different directory:

1. Press Enter twice to return to the main Setup menu.

2. Select **L**ocation of Files.

3. Select the first option, **B**ackup Files.

4. Type the name and full path of the directory that you want to use, then press Enter and Exit (F7). If you don't use this option to name a directory for your timed backup files, they will be saved in the directory containing the WordPerfect program file WP.EXE.

Document Summary

WordPerfect's Document Summary feature lets you save identifying information about a file, separate from the actual text. The summary can include

- A long document name.

- A document type.

- The names of the author and typist.

- A brief description of the subject.

- An account number, such as a client identification number or Social Security number.

- Keywords to help identify the file.

- An abstract of up to 780 characters that you can use to summarize the document.

In addition, WordPerfect automatically supplies the date and time you first created the summary. If you've saved it more than once (after editing), it will also include the date and time of the most recent revision.

The purpose of the document summary is to help you locate a file more easily. Earlier in this chapter you learned how to use the Find option on the List key to search through your document summaries, and quickly locate a document containing specific information in one or more of the fields (subject, account, keywords, and so on). Also, when you use the Look option, the document summary will appear at the top, as shown in Figure 7.7. If you've used it correctly, the document summary should provide a good overview of the file, so you won't have to scroll through it.

Creating a Document Summary

To create a document summary for the document on your Edit screen:

1. Display the Format Document menu:

   Keyboard: Press the Format key (Shift-F8) and select **Document**.

   Mouse: Select **Document** from the **Layout** menu.

2. Select the fifth option, **Summary**. The Document Summary screen shown in Figure 7.19 will appear. Let's examine each of the options.

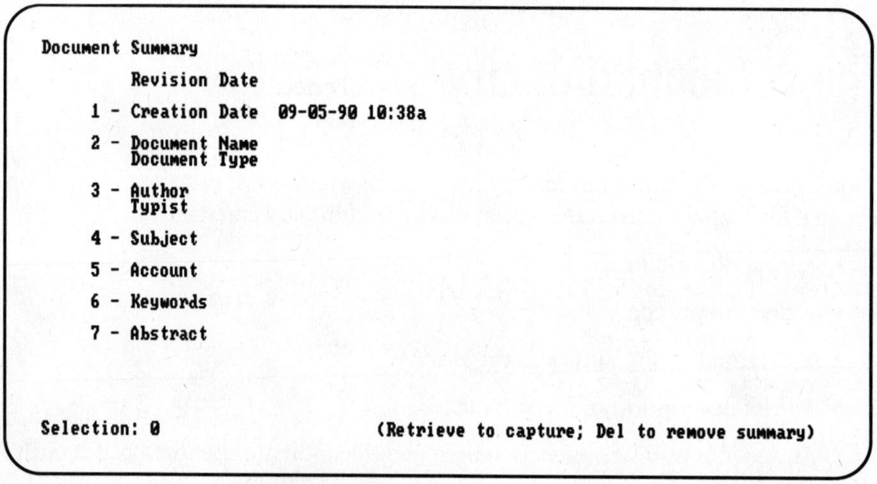

```
Document Summary
          Revision Date
     1 - Creation Date  09-05-90 10:38a
     2 - Document Name
         Document Type
     3 - Author
         Typist
     4 - Subject
     5 - Account
     6 - Keywords
     7 - Abstract


 Selection: 0                   (Retrieve to capture; Del to remove summary)
```

Figure 7.19 The Document Summary screen.

Revision Date: If you've edited and saved the file more than once, the date and time of the most recent revision appears at the top of the screen, next to Revision Date. **You cannot change the Revision Date.**

Creation Date: The current date and time will appear next to the first option, Creation Date. If you have saved this document previously, without a document summary, the creation date that you see here will not correspond to the first time you saved it. However, you can change it by selecting the option, and typing the actual creation date (if you can remember it!).

 Tip: If you want the Creation Date in your document summary to reflect the date that you first saved the file, you should always create a document summary the first time you save the file.

Document Name and Document Type: If you are using WordPerfect's Long Document Names feature and have already supplied a Long Document Name and Type for this file, WordPerfect will automatically enter them in the Document Name and Document Type option. If not, you can type them yourself. The Name can contain a maximum of 68 characters, and the Type can contain up to 20. These will appear as the Descriptive Name and Type in the List Files menu, if you are using the Long Display version.

Author and Typist: You can use this field to type the names of the author and typist with up to 60 characters. Alternatively, you can use the Retrieve option to have WordPerfect insert the Author and Typist names that you last entered into a document summary, as explained in the next section.

Subject: Type up to 152 characters to describe the subject. If your document includes the heading *RE:* followed by a brief description of the subject, you can use the Retrieve option to have WordPerfect insert the subject automatically. This is explained in the next section.

Account: Use this field to type account information, such as a social security number or customer identification number. It can contain up to 152 characters.

Keywords: You can use this field to type words that will help you identify the document. It can contain up to 152 characters.

Abstract: You can use this field to type a summary of the document, containing up to 780 characters. If you use the Retrieve option, as described in the next section, WordPerfect will automatically insert the first 400 characters of your document.

When you finish typing all the information for your document summary, press Enter to return to the Edit screen. After that, be sure to save the document using the Save or Exit method, so that the summary will be saved along with it. You can also save the document summary as a separate file, as you'll learn in the "Saving and Printing a Document Summary" section.

The Retrieve Option

Notice this prompt in the lower-right corner of the Document Summary screen:

```
(Retrieve to capture; Del to remove summary)
```

You can use the Retrieve option to retrieve information for three of the other fields in the summary: *Subject, Author and Typist,* and *Abstract.* For example, if your document includes the heading *RE:* followed by a brief description of the subject, a convention often used in memos and letters, WordPerfect can search for this description and copy it into the Subject field of the Summary. The heading *RE:* is called the *Subject Search Text.* WordPerfect will copy either the first 39 characters that follow *RE:,* or all the text after *RE:* and before the first [HRt] code, whichever comes first. The Retrieve feature will also insert the first 400 characters of your document into the Abstract field, and the Author and Typist names that you last entered into a document summary, if you did it in the current editing session. Unfortunately, you cannot be selective about which fields to retrieve; it's either all three or nothing!

To use the Retrieve feature, start with the cursor next to Selection at the bottom of the menu, as it is when you first display the menu.

1. Select Retrieve:

   Keyboard: Press the Retrieve key (Shift-F10).

   Mouse: Select Retrieve.

   This prompt will appear:

   ```
   Capture Document Summary Fields? No (Yes)
   ```

2. Select **Yes.**

   WordPerfect will copy the data into the three Document Summary fields.

   If you are in the habit of using a heading other than *RE:* in your documents, you can use the Setup menu to change this Subject Search Text to the one you use. To do this:

1. Select Setup:

   Keyboard: Press the Setup key (Shift-F1).

   Mouse: Select Setup from the File menu.

2. Select **E**nvironment.

3. Select **D**ocument Management/Summary.

4. Select the second option on the Document Management/Summary menu, **S**ubject Search Text.

5. Type the text you want to use and press Enter.

Saving and Printing a Document Summary

Earlier in this chapter (in the section entitled "Using Look to View the Contents of a File"), you learned how to save a document summary as a separate file, and how to print it. Neither Save nor Print appears as an option in the Document Summary menu, but you can still use them.

To print a summary (assuming you are in the Document Summary menu), press the Print key (Shift-F7). An example of a printed document summary is shown in Figure 7.20.

To save a summary:

1. Press the Save key (F10).

   This prompt appears:

   `Enter filename`

2. Type a file name and press Enter.

   If you ask WordPerfect to save the summary under an existing file name, you'll see this prompt:

   `File Already Exists: 1 Replace; 2 Append: 2`

You must decide if you want to replace the existing file, or append the summary to the end of it. If you select Append, WordPerfect will create a page break at the end of the document, and copy the summary there.

You can also print a document summary using the Print option on the List Files menu, or the Document on Disk option on the Print menu. When you use one of these options, WordPerfect prompts you for the pages that you want to print.

Type S to print the document summary. You can print both the document summary and page numbers, but be sure to type the *S* before you enter the page numbers. To print the document summary and the entire document, type S-.

```
System Name:   D:\LESSONS\MATH.LES
System Filetype:   WP5.1
Document Name:   Math Lesson
Document Type:   Lesson

Creation Date:   03-11-90 10:09a
Revision Date:   09-05-90 10:23a

Author:   Susan Kelly
Typist:   SK
Subject:   Math Lesson for Intermediate WordPerfect class
Account:
Keywords:

Abstract:   This lesson was updated for WordPerfect 5.1 on
3/11/90.
```

Figure 7.20 *The printed version of a document summary.*

Both the printed and saved versions of your document summary will include two additional items, *System Name* and *System Filetype*. System Name is the DOS file name and path. In Figure 7.20, it is D:\LESSONS\MATH.LES. System Filetype refers to the version of WordPerfect you were using when you typed the document. In Figure 7.20, it is WP5.1 (WordPerfect 5.1).

Deleting a Document Summary

Document Summary is one of the few format menu options that do not insert a code into your document. If you ever want to delete one, display the Document Summary menu, press the Delete key, and answer Yes to the Delete Document Summary prompt that appears. After that, be sure to save it again (if you don't, it will still include the summary).

Tip: If you copy text from a file that includes a document summary and place it into a new document, the new document will contain the same document summary. For instance, say you retrieve a file into Doc 1 that has been saved with a document summary. You then use the Move key and Switch keys to copy a paragraph from this file into the blank editing screen in Doc 2. When you display the Document Summary menu, you'll find that the paragraph in Doc 2 contains the same document summary as the file in Doc 1! You then have two options: Either delete the summary or edit it.

Mandatory Document Summary

If you want to create a document summary for every file you save, you can use the Setup menu to make it mandatory. Here's how.

1. Select Setup:

    Keyboard: Press the Setup key (Shift-F1).

    Mouse: Select Setup from the File menu.

2. Select the third option, **Environment.**

3. Select the fourth option, **Document Management/Summary.** The Document Management/Summary menu appears, as shown in Figure 7.9.

4. Select the first option, **Create Summary on Save/Exit,** and change it to Yes.

5. Press the Exit key (F7).

From then on, whenever you use Exit or Save to save a new file, WordPerfect will take you directly to the Document Summary menu so you can create the summary.

If you don't want to type a summary for a particular document, just press Enter when the Document Summary menu appears. The Document to be saved prompt will appear, and you can proceed to type your file name and save it. However, the next time you select Save or Exit with this file on the Edit screen, WordPerfect will again prompt you for the document summary. It will do this until you finally break down and type one!

NEWSPAPER AND PARALLEL COLUMNS

WordPerfect features two basic types of columns for text: *newspaper* and *parallel*. Newspaper columns are used for snaking text that flows up and down from one column to another, as in a newsletter. The newsletter shown in Figure 8.1 is an example. Parallel columns are used to keep related blocks of text next to each other on the same page, as in a side-by-side language translation or a movie script. An example is shown in Figure 8.2. You read parallel columns across the page, from left to right. You read text in newspaper columns vertically, up and down the page. In both types, WordPerfect treats each column as a separate page of text, and any editing changes you make only affect the column where the cursor is currently located. You can create up to 24 columns per page, and you can mix standard text with columnar text on the same page. The columns appear side by side on screen and in the printed document.

 Tip: Another way to create parallel text columns is with the Tables feature. You'll learn how in Chapter 10.

To define columns and to turn them on and off, use the Columns/Tables key (Alt-F7), or the Columns option on the pull-down Layout menu. You can define your columns at any point in the document, but you don't have to turn them on until you are ready to use them. However, it's usually easier to define them right before turning them on. The basic steps are the same for newspaper and parallel columns: Define the type, number, and size of the columns, turn them on, and start typing. Since newspaper columns are easier to work with, let's begin by creating the newsletter shown in Figure 8.1.

Remote Controllers of America

The Journal for Contemporary Couch Potatoes   *March 18, 1991*

LATEST HEALTH REPORT:
A newly released medical report raves about the health advantages of having a remote control for your television. In their latest research, professors at the University of Zenith have found conclusive evidence that a remote control greatly reduces the odds of developing heel spurs, back strains and arthritis of the index finger. According to Dr. Tube of the university medical school; "a significant amount of heel and foot injuries are greatly diminished with the use of a TV zotter. Research has shown that after hours of lying in the horizontal position, a severe amount of strain is suddenly thrust upon the foot by getting up to change the channel".

Dr. Tube goes on to state that the use of a handheld control allows the use of other digits in the hand, thereby encouraging dexterity of the fingers and enhanced muscle tone. "Most controls on the television unit force one to place repetitious pressure on the first two joints of the index finger, which results in potential calcification of joints in later years."

NEW MODEL ANNOUNCED:
Controllomatic Corporation unveiled its newest and latest model for the upcoming TV season. This super hi-tech model, dubbed the ZR144, is the most powerful zotter on the market. It has full VCR and Stereo compatibility, and is capable of functioning up to 2400 feet away. Additionally, the new ZR144 allows rapid channel change with little or no chance of overheating, at the staggering pace of 20 channels per second. That should really drive your co-viewers crazy! Designed by the famous Italian studio of Statique, this sleek zotter has a deluxe pistol grip handle, quick release and black anodized finish. Look for a road test of this baby in an upcoming newsletter!

HELPFUL HINTS: Barbi Jean from South Fork writes: " When I'm lying on the couch watching TV for hours, I find many ways to be productive. My favorite is to carefully search, by hand, underneath all the cushions and feel for spare change that may have fallen in the cracks. It's profitable and a great way to pass the time during those bad commercials. The only real hazards are the occasional crumbs and other debris that may collect under fingernails!"

Figure 8.1   Newspaper columns.

CUDDLY'S USED PET SHOP

WEEKLY SPECIALS

FREDDIE
Three year old boa
constrictor.

Freddie is house trained. Great for the person on
the go, with rodent problem or neighbor with small,
obnoxious dog.

ANGEL
Five year old Siberian
Husky male.

Angel also answers to "MUSH". He prefers air
conditioning or colder climates. Steady worker, low
mileage and never raced, must be seen to be
appreciated.

DOODLEDO
One year old banti
rooster.

Doodledo answers to any name. Known to be an
early riser, excellent with kids and would make
ideal dinner guest. PRICE REDUCTION!

SQUEEK
A rare 6 month old
Hungarian mouse.

Squeek is rust colored, with a medium length coat.
He was raised from championship blood lines. A
real show stopper! Must be sold separately from
Freddie.

YANG
Fifteen year old male
Siamese cat.

Yang eats little, quiet and hardly moves. Speaks
some Chinese (MOW). Excellent choice for mauve
interiors. CLOSEOUT! CALL FOR PRICE QUOTE

THUD
Adorable male Indian
elephant.

Thud weighs slightly over 4,000 lbs, needs loving
family with large yard or small forest. Cheap to
Keep! (fluctuates with peanut prices)

BOING
Exotic Australian
Kangaroo.

Boing is a great novelty item. Comes complete with
unique nondetachable storage pouch. Slightly
temperamental (has a mean dropkick), vaulted
ceilings are highly recommended.

Figure 8.2   Parallel columns.

Newspaper Columns

The newsletter you will be creating has two columns of equal width, separated by
$1/2$". In fact, these are WordPerfect's column defaults, so your task will be easy.
Before you define and turn on the columns, center and type the heading, and
change the Justification style to Left.

1. Select Center:

     Keyboard: Press the Center key, Shift-F6.

     Mouse: Display the Layout menu, select **Align**, then select **Center**.

2. Type the heading: Remote Controllers of America. The example uses
   a large italic font for the heading. You may wish to change it also before
   typing the text.

3. Press Enter twice to create some blank space between the heading and
   the shaded box.

4. Change the Justification style to Left:

     Keyboard: Press the Format key, Shift-F8, and select the first option,
     Line.

     Mouse: Display the Layout menu and select **Line**.

5. Select the third option, **Justification**, and change it to Left. Return to the
   Edit menu:

     Keyboard: Press the Exit key, F7.

     Mouse: Click the right button.

   Next, create the shaded box containing the journal description and date.

Creating the Shaded Box

In this section, you'll learn how to create the shaded box at the top of the page. As
you'll see, WordPerfect's Text Box option on the Graphics menu makes it easy.
Since you'll study this feature in Chapter 14, the steps will be described here but
not in great detail. Think of this section as a sneak preview of all the wonderful
things you can do with the Graphics menu!

1. Select the Text Box option:

     Keyboard: Press the Graphics key (Alt-F9). This menu line appears:

```
1 Figure; 2 Table Box; 3 Text Box; 4 User Box; 5 Line;
6 Equation: 0
```

Select the third option, Text Box. This menu line appears next:

```
Text Box: 1 Create; 2 Edit; 3 New Number; 4 Options: 0
```

Select the first option, **Create**.

Mouse: Display the **Graphics** menu and select Text Box. A submenu pops out to the right, as shown in Figure 8.3. Select the first option, **Create**.

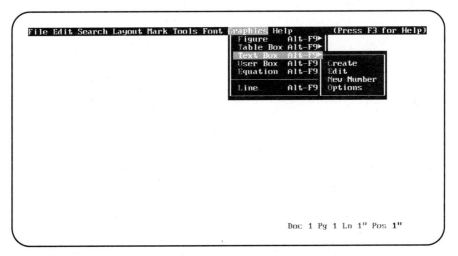

Figure 8.3 *When you display the Graphics menu and select Text Box, this menu pops out to the right.*

The Definition Text Box menu appears, as shown in Figure 8.4. Notice that most of the options have defaults, including Horizontal Position and Size. If you were to press Enter now, WordPerfect would create a small box, 3.25" wide and .625" high, and align it against the right margin. To change the position of the box and widen it, use the Horizontal Position option.

2. Select the sixth option, **Horizontal Position**. This menu appears:

```
Horizontal Position: 1 Left; 2 Right; 3 Center; 4 Full: 0
```

Select the fourth option, **Full**. This immediately alters the width of the box, changing it from 3.25" to 6.5" (leaving 1" each for the left and right margins).

3. The next step is to type the text inside the box. To do this, select the last option on the Definition Text Box menu, **Edit**. This places the cursor into

a special screen where you can type your text. Notice the prompt at the bottom, reminding you that this is not the regular Edit screen:

`Box: Press Exit when done, Graphics to rotate text`

4. Type the journal description: `The Journal for Contemporary Couch Potatoes`. Before typing it, you could change the font to a bold italic font, as in the example.

```
Definition: Text Box
      1 - Filename
      2 - Contents            Text
      3 - Caption
      4 - Anchor Type         Paragraph
      5 - Vertical Position   0"
      6 - Horizontal Position Right
      7 - Size                3.25" wide x 0.625" (high)
      8 - Wrap Text Around Box Yes
      9 - Edit


Selection: 0
```

Figure 8.4   The Definition Text Box menu.

5. Use WordPerfect's Flush Right feature to right-align the date:

    Keyboard: Press the Flush Right key, Alt-F6.

    Mouse: Display the pull-down **Layout** menu and select **Align**; then select **Flush Right**. Type the date: `March 18, 1991`.

6. To exit back to the Definition Text Box menu:

    Keyboard: Press the Exit key (F7).

    Mouse: Display the **File** menu and select **Exit**.

    The box is now complete, and you can return to the Edit screen.

7. Exit back to the Edit screen, and insert a blank line:

    Keyboard: Press Enter twice.

    Mouse: Click the right mouse button and then press Enter.

    You will see an outline of the box (the top border) on the Edit screen, but you won't be able to see its contents. To preview it, use WordPerfect's View Document option.

8. Select View Document:

>   **Keyboard:** Press the Print key (Shift-F7).

>   **Mouse:** Display the File menu and select **Print**.

9. Select the sixth option, View Document. Unless you've already used View Document in this edit session, you should see the entire page, including the shaded box. Although this provides an overview of the entire page, the text is too small to read. Select 100% to enlarge the page to actual size, as shown in Figure 8.5.

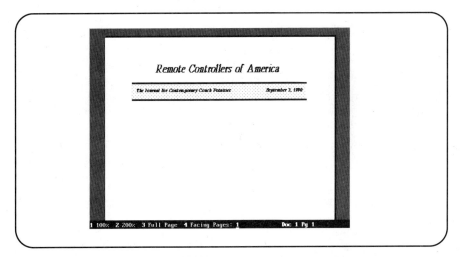

Remote Controllers of America

The Journal for Contemporary Couch Potatoes   September 3, 1990

1 100%   2 200%   3 Full Page   4 Facing Pages: **1**   Doc: 1 Pg 1

Figure 8.5   *The newsletter with text box and heading, as seen in the View Document screen. The dots represent the gray shading, which is set to 10% by default.*

When you finish using View Document, return to the Edit screen by pressing the Exit key (F7). Now, at last, you are ready to define the columns.

1. Select Columns:

>   **Keyboard:** Press the Columns/Tables key (Alt-F7). This prompt appears:

```
1 Columns; 2 Tables; 3 Math: 0
```

>   Select the first option, **Columns**. The next prompt asks if you want to define the columns or turn them on or off:

```
Columns: 1 On; 2 Off; 3 Define: 0
```

>   **Mouse:** Display the Layout menu and select Columns. A submenu pops out to the right, as shown in Figure 8.6. You can use it to define the columns or turn them on or off.

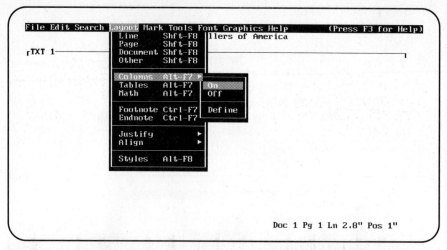

Figure 8.6 *When you display the Layout menu and select Columns, this submenu pops out to the right. You can use it to define columns, turn them on, or turn them off.*

2. Select **Define**. The Text Column Definition screen appears, as shown in Figure 8.7.

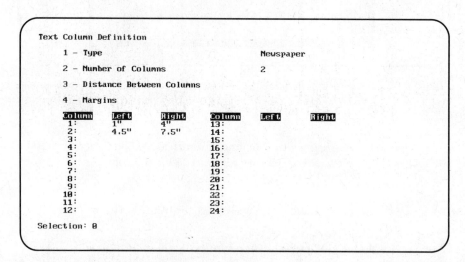

Figure 8.7 *The Text Column Definition screen. Use this menu to select the type and number of columns, the distance separating the columns, and the column margins.*

Although you won't be changing any of the options on the Text Column Definition menu, take a moment to study them.

The first option is *Type.* You can use it to select the type of column you want to use: Newspaper, Parallel, or Parallel with Block Protect. As you can see, Newspaper is the default type.

The second option is *Number of Columns,* and the default is two. You can define from two to 24 columns per page.

The third option is *Distance Between Columns.* Unless you change it, WordPerfect will separate your columns by ½". Unlike the other three options on this menu, WordPerfect does not display the distance unless you select the option.

The last option is *Margins.* WordPerfect automatically calculates the column margins, based on the left and right margins currently in use for the document, and your selections for the number of columns and distance between columns. Notice that it assumes you want your columns to be even in width, 3" each in this case. You can override these margins by selecting the Margins option and typing different ones. The columns do not have to be even in width. You can even override the document margins. For instance, even though the document margins are 1" each, you can change the left margin of the first column to ½", and the right margin of the second column to 8".

Since you won't be changing any of the column defaults, the next step is to exit from this menu and turn on the columns.

 Tip: If you receive this message after defining your columns: `Error: text columns can't overlap`, you have to change the column margins before continuing, because they overlap. For example, if the margins in the first column are 1" and 4", and the margins in the second columns are 3.8" and 7.5", the right margin of column 1 overlaps the left margin of column 2. WordPerfect won't let you define the columns until you change the margins.

---

3. Exit from this menu:

   Keyboard: Press Enter.

   Mouse: Click the right mouse button.

   This menu line appears again:

   `Columns: 1 On; 2 Off; 3 Define: 0`

4. Turn on Column mode by selecting **On**. A `Col 1` indicator appears on the status line to indicate that you are now working in Column mode.

> **Warning:** If you select On from the Columns menu and see the error message `ERROR: No text columns defined`, you have not yet defined columns. You cannot turn on columns if you haven't gone through the steps of defining them, as described in this section.

Since you used all the defaults, defining and turning on the newspaper columns only required four quick steps: Select the Columns option from the Columns/Table key or Layout menu, select Define, exit from the menu, and select On.

Now type the text shown in Figure 8.1. As you type, WordPerfect will automatically format it into the columns you have defined, and the text will flow up and down through the columns. If you were to type enough text to fill up the second column, WordPerfect would create a page break. Any text you typed after that would flow into the first column on the second page. Once you finish typing the text, you could turn the columns off. However, you won't be typing any more text, so it really isn't necessary.

When you finish typing the document, save it using this name: REMOTE.

Forcing a Column to End Early

In Chapter 2 you learned that you could force a page break by pressing Ctrl-Enter. In Column mode, this combination works differently: You press it to end a column, and force the cursor into a new one. If the cursor is in the last column on the page when you press Ctrl-Enter, WordPerfect will create a new page and move the cursor to the first column on the new page. A warning: Do not use Ctrl-Enter for cursor movement. Use it only to create a new column, or to force existing text into the next column.

Let's use Ctrl-Enter to force the "NEW MODEL ANNOUNCED" section into the second column. This will improve the appearance of your document by making the two columns more even in length.

1. Move the cursor onto the N in `NEW`.

2. Force the column to end at this position by pressing Ctrl-Enter.

As you can see from the printed version in Figure 8.8, this forces the heading and paragraph that follows it to the top of the second column, and makes the columns more even in length.

Remote Controllers of America

The Journal for Contemporary Couch Potatoes   *March 18, 1991*

LATEST HEALTH REPORT:

A newly released medical report raves about the health advantages of having a remote control for your television. In their latest research, professors at the University of Zenith have found conclusive evidence that a remote control greatly reduces the odds of developing heel spurs, back strains and arthritis of the index finger. According to Dr. Tube of the university medical school; "a significant amount of heel and foot injuries are greatly diminished with the use of a TV zotter. Research has shown that after hours of lying in the horizontal position, a severe amount of strain is suddenly thrust upon the foot by getting up to change the channel".

Dr. Tube goes on to state that the use of a handheld control allows the use of other digits in the hand, thereby encouraging dexterity of the fingers and enhanced muscle tone. "Most controls on the television unit force one to place repetitious pressure on the first two joints of the index finger, which results in potential calcification of joints in later years."

NEW MODEL ANNOUNCED:

Controllomatic Corporation unveiled its newest and latest model for the upcoming TV season. This super hi-tech model, dubbed the ZR144, is the most powerful zotter on the market. It has full VCR and Stereo compatibility, and is capable of functioning up to 2400 feet away. Additionally, the new ZR144 allows rapid channel change with little or no chance of overheating, at the staggering pace of 20 channels per second. That should really drive your co-viewers crazy! Designed by the famous Italian studio of Statique, this sleek zotter has a deluxe pistol grip handle, quick release and black anodized finish. Look for a road test of this baby in an upcoming newsletter!

HELPFUL HINTS: Barbi Jean from South Fork writes: " When I'm lying on the couch watching TV for hours, I find many ways to be productive. My favorite is to carefully search, by hand, underneath all the cushions and feel for spare change that may have fallen in the cracks. It's profitable and a great way to pass the time during those bad commercials. The only real hazards are the occasional crumbs and other debris that may collect under fingernails!"

Figure 8.8 *You can use Ctrl-Enter to force a column to end before the bottom of the page. In this version of the newsletter, Ctrl-Enter was used to move the "NEW MODEL ANNOUNCED" section into the second column.*

Removing Column Formatting

You can remove column formatting and reformat the text so that it spans the entire page by locating and deleting the Column Definition code or the Column On code. If you erase the Column Definition code, WordPerfect will also erase the Column On code. Let's use that method.

If you don't know where the Column Definition code is, and it's not at the beginning of the document, the easiest way to locate it is to use WordPerfect's Search feature. Start with the cursor at the top of the document.

 Tip: If you had defined your columns at the top of the document, you could locate the Column Definition code by pressing Home, Home, Up Arrow. This would place the cursor on the first line of the first page, before any formatting codes. By looking in the Reveal Codes screen, you could then locate the Column Definition code. In fact, if it were the first code in the document, the cursor would already be highlighting it.

1. Move the cursor to the top of the document.

2. Select Search:

    Keyboard: Press the Forward Search key, F2.

    Mouse: Display the Search menu and select Forward.

    The Srch prompt appears at the bottom of the screen.

3. Insert the Column Definition code into the search string by pressing the Columns/Table key (Alt-F7). This menu appears:

    `1 Columns; 2 Tables; 3 Math: 0`

    Select the first option, **Columns.** This menu appears:

    `Column: 1 On; 2 Off; 3 Def: 0`

    Select the third option, **Def.** The [Col Def] code should now appear in the Srch prompt.

4. Start the search:

    Keyboard: Press F2.

    Mouse: Click the right button.

5. Turn on Reveal Codes so you'll be able to see the code:

Keyboard: Press Alt-F3 (if you have an extended keyboard, you can press F11).

Mouse: Display the **Edit** menu and select **Reveal Codes**.

6. If the search is successful, the cursor will be just to the right of the Column Definition code:

```
[Col Def:Newspaper;2;1",4";4.5",7.5"]
```

as shown in Figure 8.9. If the search is not successful, you'll see a Not found prompt. Reverse the search direction and try the search again by pressing Shift-F2 F2. You'll probably find that the code was above or to the left of the cursor.

Take a moment to study the Column Definition code. It defines

- The type of columns: newspaper.

- The number of columns: 2.

- The margins for the first column: 1" and 4".

- The margins for the second column: 4.5" and 7.5".

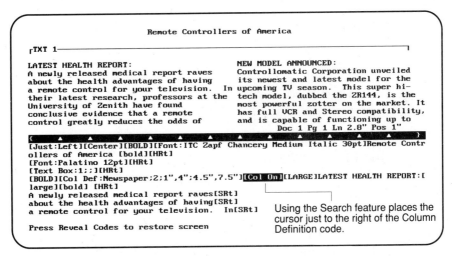

Figure 8.9 *If you use WordPerfect's Search feature to locate the Column Definition code, the cursor will stop on the right side of the code. You can erase it by pressing the Backspace key or by moving the cursor onto the code and pressing the Delete key.*

7. Erase the [Col Def] code by pressing the Backspace key once, or by pressing the Left Arrow key to move the cursor onto the code and then pressing the Delete key.

Tip: If you accidentally erase a Column On code, you can use Undelete to restore the code and format the document back into columns. However, if you erase the Column Definition code, Undelete will restore the definition code, but not the Column On code. Your text will not be reformatted into columns until you select Column On.

8. Exit from Reveal Codes:

   Keyboard: Press Alt-F3 (or F11 if you have an extended keyboard).

   Mouse: Display the Edit menu and select **Reveal Codes.**

The text should now be realigned and span the width of the entire page. If you move the cursor to the end of the page, you'll see that what used to be the second column has now become the second page. Do you remember pressing Ctrl-Enter to force the column to end early? At that point WordPerfect inserted a Hard Page code, [HPg]. Since you've removed the column formatting, the Hard Page break code now forces WordPerfect to start a new page.

Redefining Columns

If you decide that you'd prefer the newsletter in three columns instead of two, just change the column definition and reformat the text into the new columns. If you followed the instructions in the last section to remove column formatting, your document is no longer in columns, so start by clearing the screen and retrieving the original newsletter.

1. Use Exit to clear the screen without saving:

   Keyboard: Press the Exit key (F7) and type N N.

   Mouse: Select Exit from the File menu and select **No** in response to the Save document and Exit WP prompts.

2. Retrieve the original document:

   Keyboard: Press the Retrieve key (Shift-F10), type the file name (Remote), and press Enter.

   Mouse: Select **Retrieve** from the File menu, type the file name (Remote), and press Enter.

To redefine your columns, cursor position is crucial. Your new definition won't have any effect if the cursor is positioned above or to the left of the existing Column Definition code, because the new definition code will be inserted before the old one. As with all formatting codes, if WordPerfect encounters two Column Definition codes next to each other, it will ignore the first one and use the second one. Also, WordPerfect won't allow you to redefine the columns if the cursor is in a column. You can tell if this is the case because Col 1 will appear on the status line. Since the columns start just past the Column On code, the cursor must be on or before it. To place the cursor directly on it, you can use the Search feature.

3. Move the cursor onto the [Col On] code. If you use Search to locate the [Col Def] code, as described in the previous section, WordPerfect will place the cursor directly on the [Col On] code, since it immediately follows the [Col Def] code.

4. Display the Text Column Definition screen again:

    Keyboard: Press the Columns/Tables key (Alt-F7). Select **Columns**, then **Define**.

    Mouse: Display the **Layout** menu and select **Columns**, then **Define**.

5. Select the Number of Columns option, and type 3. Press Enter.

6. Exit back to the Edit screen:

    Keyboard: Press Enter twice.

    Mouse: Click the right button twice.

    Notice that there are now two Column Definition codes, the original one that defined two newspaper columns, and the one representing the three columns you just defined. Since you don't need the original one anymore, it's a good idea to delete it.

7. Move the cursor onto the original Column Definition code [Col Def:Newspaper;2;1",4";4.5",7.5"] and press the Delete key. WordPerfect then reformats the text into the three columns. To see how it will look when printed, preview it in the View Document screen. Figure 8.10 shows the printed version of this newsletter with three columns.

Remote Controllers of America

The Journal for Contemporary Couch Potatoes　　　March 18, 1991

LATEST HEALTH REPORT:

A newly released medical report raves about the health advantages of having a remote control for your television. In their latest research, professors at the University of Zenith have found conclusive evidence that a remote control greatly reduces the odds of developing heel spurs, back strains and arthritis of the index finger.

According to Dr. Tube of the university medical school; "a significant amount of heel and foot injuries are greatly diminished with the use of a TV zotter. Research has shown that after hours of lying in the horizontal position, a severe amount of strain is suddenly thrust upon the foot by getting up to change the channel".

Dr. Tube goes on to state that the use of a handheld control allows the use of other digits in the hand, thereby encouraging dexterity of the fingers and enhanced muscle tone. "Most controls on the television unit force one to place repetitious pressure on the first two joints of the index finger, which results in potential calcification of joints in later years."

NEW MODEL ANNOUNCED:

Controllomatic Corporation unveiled its newest and latest model for the upcoming TV season. This super hi-tech model, dubbed the ZR144, is the most powerful zotter on the market. It has full VCR and Stereo compatibility, and is capable of functioning up to 2400 feet away. Additionally, the new ZR144 allows rapid channel change with little or no chance of overheating, at the staggering pace of 20 channels per second. That should really drive your co-viewers crazy! Designed by the famous Italian studio of Statique, this sleek zotter has a deluxe pistol grip handle, quick release and black anodized finish. Look for a road test of this baby in an upcoming newsletter!

HELPFUL HINTS:

Barbi Jean from South Fork writes: " When I'm lying on the couch watching TV for hours, I find many ways to be productive. My favorite is to carefully search, by hand, underneath all the cushions and feel for spare change that may have fallen in the cracks. It's profitable and a great way to pass the time during those bad commercials. The only real hazards are the occasional crumbs and other debris that may collect under fingernails!"

Figure 8.10 *This is how the newsletter appears after you increase the number of columns to three. To change the number of columns, column margins, or distance between columns, you have to change the column definition. When you do this, cursor position is crucial.*

Tip: You can define your columns at any point in the document, but you don't have to turn them on until you are ready to use them. If you define your columns at the top of the document, you'll always know where the Column Definition code is located—in case you want to change the definition. You can turn your columns on and off throughout the document, or turn them off and define a new set of columns.

Cursor Movement in Columns

Cursor movement within both newspaper and parallel columns is essentially the same as in a non-columnar document. For instance, you can use the arrow keys to move character by character, Ctrl with the arrow keys to move word by word, Home with the arrow keys to move to the beginning or end of a line, or to the top or bottom of the screen. However, these keys act within a column, not across to other columns on the page. For example, if the cursor is at the left margin on the page, and you press Home, Right Arrow (or the End key), the cursor will move to the end of the line in the first column, not to the right margin of the page. If you move the cursor to the end of a line within a column and then press Right Arrow, it wraps down to the next line in the same column, not across to the next one.

To move the cursor between columns, use these combinations:

Go To with the Left or Right Arrow key: The combination of Ctrl-Home is called the *Go To* key. For mouse users, the pull-down menu equivalent is Go To on the Search menu. When you use it, this prompt appears in the lower-left corner of the screen: Go to. In response, you can press the Right Arrow key to move the cursor to the next column on the right, or the Left Arrow key to move to the next column on the left.

Go To with Home and the Left or Right Arrow key: If your document includes more than two columns on the page, you can move the cursor from the first to the last column or vice versa by pressing Ctrl-Home, then Home-Right or Home-Left Arrow. Here's how to use it: Press Ctrl-Home, release both keys, then press Home and the Right or Left Arrow key.

Alt with the arrow keys: If you have an enhanced keyboard (with dedicated cursor movement keys between the letter keys and numeric keypad), you can move between columns by pressing the Alt key followed by the Left or Right Arrow.

Editing Text in Columns

Editing text in columns is no different from editing text that is not in columns. Like cursor movement, editing changes such as insertions and deletions only affect the column where the cursor is currently located. For example, if the cursor is at the left margin of the first column and you press Ctrl-End to delete the line, it will not delete text in the second column. However, text from the second column may be moved into the first column to fill in the empty space, especially if you delete a large section in the first column. WordPerfect considers each column to be a separate page. If you keep this in mind, it makes perfect sense: If you were to delete a paragraph from page one, text from page two would move up to fill in the space on page one.

Let's try some deletions. Start with the cursor at the top of the document.

1. Place the cursor in the blank space following the word television, at the end of the first sentence (under the heading LATEST HEALTH REPORT).

   Keyboard: If you don't have a mouse, the quickest way to move the cursor is to use the Search feature. Press F2, type a period, and then press F2 again.

   Mouse: Drag the cursor to the blank space following the word television, and click the left button once.

2. Delete from the cursor to the end of the line by pressing Ctrl-End. WordPerfect only deletes text from the first column. To verify this, you can use Undelete.

3. Select Undelete:

   Keyboard: Press Cancel (F1).

   Mouse: Display the Edit menu and select Undelete.

   The text that you just erased by pressing Ctrl-End appears in a highlighted block, as shown in Figure 8.11. As you can see, WordPerfect only erased the two words at the end of the line in the first column: In their. Your Undelete prompt may differ slightly, but the block will not include text from the second column.

4. Restore the text by selecting the first option on the menu, **Restore**.

Let's try deleting the whole paragraph and see how it affects the second column.

1. Delete the paragraph:

   Keyboard: Press the Move key (Ctrl-F4), and select the **Paragraph** option.

   Mouse: Display the **Edit** menu, and choose the **Select** option, then the **Paragraph** option.

   The entire paragraph is now highlighted, and this prompt appears:

   `1 Move; 2 Copy; 3 Delete; 4 Append: 0`

   Select **Delete**, and the paragraph will disappear.

2. Move the cursor to the end of the document to reformat the columns. Text that was previously at the top of column 2 should move to the bottom of column 1 to fill in the blank space. To get an overview, you may want to use the View Document option on the Print menu.

3. Use the Undelete option again to restore the paragraph to its original location (under the heading LATEST HEALTH REPORT).

   WordPerfect inserts the paragraph, and immediately moves text from the bottom of the first column back to column 2.

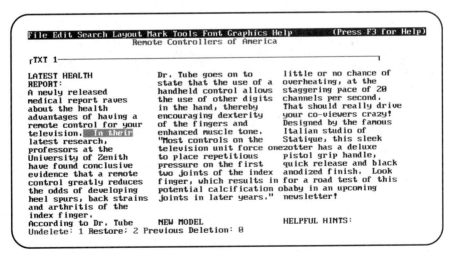

Figure 8.11 *When you delete text from the first column, it has no effect at all on the second column. Here, Undelete was selected to restore the text erased when Ctrl-End was pressed. This action only erased text from the first column.*

Formatting an Existing Document into Newspaper Columns

You can convert an existing document into newspaper or parallel columns by retrieving it to the Edit screen, defining the columns, then turning them on. As you move the cursor down through the document to reformat it, the text will automatically flow into the columns.

> **Tip:** WordPerfect does not allow you to use footnotes inside newspaper or parallel columns, but you can use endnotes. If you retrieve an existing document that contains footnotes and change it into columns, WordPerfect will automatically convert the footnotes into endnotes.

Parallel Columns

Parallel columns are used to type related blocks of text across from each other in side-by-side columns, as shown in Figure 8.2. Although they look like tabular columns, parallel columns offer a significant advantage: You can use word wrap within each column. This means that when you insert or delete text within a column, it has no effect on the adjacent column.

As you'll see when you define parallel columns, WordPerfect offers two types: *Parallel* and *Parallel with Block Protect.* Parallel columns can span a page break, so that the text from each column flows into the corresponding column on the next page. In the other type, Parallel with Block Protect, text in columns is automatically surrounded by block protection, and cannot extend across a page break. The latter type is useful for small sections of text that are short enough to remain on one page, or when you want to prevent WordPerfect from splitting a side-by-side section between two pages.

Defining parallel columns is very similar to defining newspaper columns. The real difference is in how you enter the text. After typing the first section of text in column 1, you press Ctrl-Enter to force the cursor into the next column. After typing the text in column 2, you press Ctrl-Enter again. WordPerfect then turns the columns off, moves the cursor back to the first column, inserts a blank line, and turns the columns on again so you can type the next block of text.

To practice, let's define and type the document shown in Figure 8.2. Start with a clear screen.

1. Center and type the two lines in the heading:

```
Cuddly's Used Pet Shop
     Weekly Specials
```

Press Enter three times to leave a few blank lines between the heading and the columns.

2. Select Columns:

Keyboard: Press the Columns/Tables key (Alt-F7) and select the first option, **Columns**, then the third option, **Define**.

Mouse: Display the **Layout** menu and select **Columns**, then **Define**.

The Text Column Definition menu appears, as shown in Figure 8.7.

3. Select **Type**. This menu line appears:

```
Column Type: 1 Newspaper; 2 Parallel; 3 Parallel with
Block Protect: 0
```

Select the second option, **Parallel**.

4. Select the fourth option, **Margins**. As you can see from Figure 8.2, you'll define two columns that are uneven in width. The first starts at the left margin and is 2" wide, and the second is 4" wide and ends at the right margin. One-half inch separates them. Enter these margins:

	Left	**Right**
Column 1:	1"	3"
Column 2:	3.5"	7.5"

5. You've completed the column definition, and your screen should now resemble Figure 8.12.

6. Turn on Column mode:

Keyboard: Press Enter and select On.

Mouse: Click the right mouse button and then select On.

The `Col 1` indicator appears on the status line.

7. Type the first paragraph in column 1:

```
FREDDIE
Three year old boa constrictor.
```

8. Press Ctrl-Enter to move to column 2. Type Freddie's description (Freddie is house trained...).

```
Text Column Definition

    1 - Type                            Parallel

    2 - Number of Columns               2

    3 - Distance Between Columns

    4 - Margins
    Column   Left     Right    Column   Left      Right
      1:     1"       3"         13:
      2:     3.5"     7.5"       14:
      3:                         15:
      4:                         16:
      5:                         17:
      6:                         18:
      7:                         19:
      8:                         20:
      9:                         21:
     10:                         22:
     11:                         23:
     12:                         24:

    Selection: 0
```

Figure 8.12 *This is how your Text Column Definition screen should look after you finish defining the parallel columns.*

9. Press Ctrl-Enter to move back to column 1. Notice that WordPerfect has automatically inserted a blank line to separate the columns. Type the second paragraph in column 1 (ANGEL, Five year old...). When you finish, press Ctrl-Enter.

10. Continue typing the paragraphs in this manner, typing the text and then pressing Ctrl-Enter to move into the next column, until you finish the last one.

11. Save the document using the name *PETSHOP*.

A Warning About Cursor Movement in Parallel Columns

Once you have created a column and typed text in it, do not use Ctrl-Enter to move the cursor to the next column. This combination not only moves the cursor, but it also forces the text into the next column and ruins the alignment of your columns. Figure 8.13 shows what can happen. The cursor was placed on the word DOODLEDO in the first column and Ctrl-Enter was pressed, forcing the entire paragraph into the second column and leaving a large blank gap in column 1. It's difficult to recover from such a mistake.

Instead of using Ctrl-Enter to move the cursor, use Go To with the arrow keys. If you have an enhanced keyboard, use Alt with the arrow keys. These techniques are described in a previous section, and they apply to both newspaper and parallel columns.

If you accidentally press Ctrl-Enter and make a mess of your columns, you can fix them by locating and deleting the extra code that WordPerfect inserted when you pressed these keys. To help you understand the codes surrounding parallel columns, study the Reveal Codes screen shown in Figure 8.14. It shows the two columns describing Thud the elephant. The cursor is on the first word in the second column. You can see that there are two columns in the top half of the screen, but in the Reveal Codes section it appears as though all text is on the left side. Don't let this confuse you. Because WordPerfect considers each column as a separate page, text in the Reveal Codes screen always appears on the left side, regardless of which column it is actually in.

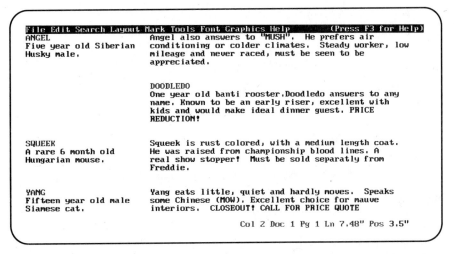

Figure 8.13   *If you use Ctrl-Enter after you've already created columns and typed text in them, you'll ruin the alignment. In this example, Ctrl-Enter was pressed when the cursor was on the D in the word DOODLEDO (in the first column). It moved the entire paragraph into column 2 and left a large gap in column 1.*

Each block of text in the first column begins with a Column On code, [Col On]. You can see one at the beginning of the line, next to the [BOLD] code:

```
[Col On][BOLD]THUD[bold][HRt]
```

At the end of the block, where Ctrl-Enter was pressed to move to column 2, there is a Hard Page code, [HPg]. This ended the column and forced the cursor into the second one. You can see the [HPg] code next to the word elephant. After the text was typed in the second column and Enter was pressed twice, Ctrl-Enter was pressed again. This ended the column, and moved the cursor back to the first one. WordPerfect then inserted three codes:

1. A Column Off code, [Col Off], which follows the two [HRt] codes.

2. A [HRt] code to create a blank line between the blocks.

3. A Column On code, [Col On], to start the next block of text in the first column. You can see it next to the [BOLD] code and the name BOING.

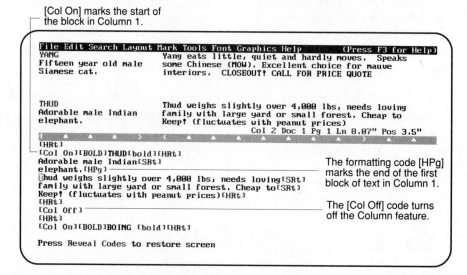

Figure 8.14 *To understand the codes surrounding parallel columns, it helps to study the Reveal Codes screen.*

Now that you understand the codes, it shouldn't be hard to fix the columns. Figure 8.15 shows the Reveal Codes screen for the Doodledo section. As you can see, the [HPg] code is in the wrong position. It belongs at the end of the first block, after the word rooster. Instead, it is next to the Column On and Bold codes at the beginning of the block:

```
[Col On][BOLD][HPg]
```

To fix the columns, delete the [HPg] code and insert another at the correct position. To erase the code, highlight it with the cursor and press Delete. Next, move the cursor to the position where the second column should begin, at the beginning of the sentence Doodledo answers to any name. Press Ctrl-Enter to insert a [HPg] code. After that, the columns will be aligned correctly.

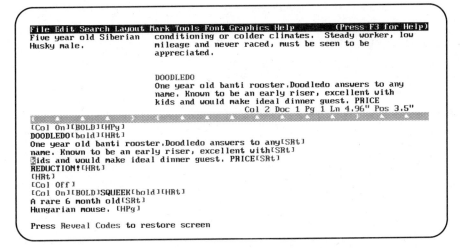

Figure 8.15 *The Reveal Codes screen for the "Doodledo" section. The [HPg] code is next to the Column On and Bold codes at the beginning of the block, so it forced the text that should have been in column 1 into column 2.*

 Tip: If you insert text after you finish typing your columns, be careful of the cursor position. If you inadvertently start with the cursor in between the Column Off and Column On codes, the text won't be formatted into columns. Instead, it will span the width of the page.

Parallel Columns with Block Protection

In the last section, you learned how to use regular parallel columns. What if you reached the end of the page while typing, and WordPerfect placed a page break in the middle of one of your side-by-side blocks, as shown in Figure 8.16? You could force the BOING paragraph to the next page by inserting a few extra blank lines above it, or by forcing a hard page break. However, if you later inserted or deleted text above these lines, you might have to delete the lines or hard page break. If you had used WordPerfect's other type of parallel columns, Parallel with Block Protect, you wouldn't have to worry about this situation because WordPerfect surrounds each parallel group with Block Protection codes. Rather than split a protected group between two pages, WordPerfect automatically moves the entire section to the next page.

```
File Edit Search Layout Mark Tools Font Graphics Help          (Press F3 for Help)


YANG                      Yang eats little, quiet and hardly moves.  Speaks
Fifteen year old male     some Chinese (MOW). Excellent choice for mauve
Siamese cat.              interiors.  CLOSEOUT! CALL FOR PRICE QUOTE


THUD                      Thud weighs slightly over 4,000 lbs, needs loving
Adorable male Indian      family with large yard or small forest. Cheap to
elephant.                 Keep! (fluctuates with peanut prices)


BOING                     Boing is a great novelty item. Comes complete with
Exotic Australian         unique nondetachable storage pouch. Slightly
---------------------------------------------------------------------------
Kangaroo.                 temperamental (has a mean dropkick), vaulted
                          ceilings are highly recommended.



                                    Col 2 Doc 1 Pg 2 Ln 1.58" Pos 3.5"
```

Figure 8.16 *To prevent WordPerfect from inserting a page break in the middle of a parallel group, as illustrated here, use WordPerfect's second type of parallel columns, Parallel with Block Protect.*

To define and use these columns, follow the same steps that you used to define Parallel columns, with one difference: For the column type, select Parallel with Block Protect instead of Parallel. The other steps are identical: Type the text in the first column, press Ctrl-Enter, type the related text in the second column, press Ctrl-Enter, and start again in the first column.

When you press Ctrl-Enter in this type of parallel column, WordPerfect inserts Column On and Off codes surrounding the side-by-side groups of text, just as in regular parallel columns. In addition, it inserts two block protection codes:

1. [Block Pro:On] at the beginning of the section, just before the Column On code.

2. [Block Pro:Off] at the end, just before the Column Off code.

You can see these codes in Figure 8.17, surrounding the section about Freddie the boa constrictor. The cursor is highlighting the [Block Pro:On] code at the beginning of the first column. The [Block Pro:Off] code is located at the end of the section, after the word dog.

If you insert text after you finish typing the columns, make sure that you type it inside the block protect codes. For example, to add a sentence at the end of the second column, begin with the cursor on the [Block Pro:Off] code. This will guarantee that the text you type is inserted to the left of the code and included in the protected section. It helps to use Reveal Codes before you start typing. If you don't, you may accidentally place the cursor on the [Col Off] code instead, and your text will be inserted between the Block Protection Off code and the Column Off code. If so, it won't be protected along with the rest of the group and can be split between two pages.

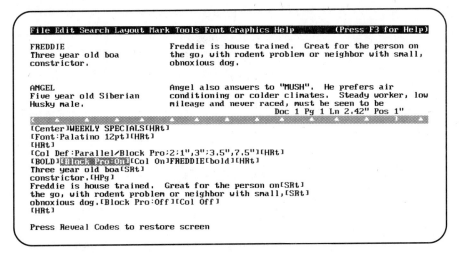

Figure 8.17 *The Reveal Codes screen for a group of parallel columns with block protection. The cursor is highlighting the [Block Pro:On] code at the beginning of the first column. At the end of the section is the [Block Pro:Off] code. The text between these two codes will always remain together on the same page.*

If you remove column formatting from parallel columns, by deleting the Column Definition or Column On code, the results will be similar to Figure 8.18. The [HPg] codes that WordPerfect used to separate text in the first column from text in the second column are converted into hard page breaks. The fastest way to remove these page breaks is to use the Replace feature. Here's how:

1. Move the cursor to the top of the document and select Replace:

   Keyboard: Press Alt-F2.

   Mouse: Display the **S**earch menu and select **R**eplace.

2. In response to the w/Confirm prompt, select **No**.

3. In response to the Srch prompt, insert the Hard Page code by pressing Ctrl-Enter. Press F2.

4. In response to the Replace with prompt, press Enter to insert a [HRt] code. This code will prevent the sections that are separated by a hard page break from running together.

5. Press F2 to start the replace action. WordPerfect will then remove all the hard page breaks and replace them with [HRt] codes.

```
File Edit Search Layout Mark Tools Font Graphics Help        (Press F3 for Help)
                       CUDDLY'S USED PET SHOP

                          WEEKLY SPECIALS


FREDDIE
Three year old boa constrictor.
=================================================================================
Freddie is house trained.  Great for the person on the go, with rodent problem o
neighbor with small, obnoxious dog.

ANGEL
Five year old Siberian Husky male.
=================================================================================

Angel also answers to "MUSH".  He prefers air conditioning or colder climates.
Steady worker, low mileage and never raced, must be seen to be appreciated.

DOODLEDO
One year old banti rooster.
=================================================================================

                                    Doc 1 Pg 1 Ln 1" Pos 1"
```

Figure 8.18 *When you remove column formatting from parallel columns, the [HPg] codes turn into hard page breaks, represented by dashed lines. The best way to remove them is to use WordPerfect's Replace feature.*

Turning Off Column Display to Speed Up Formatting

You may have noticed that when you make editing changes and scroll through text in columns, it takes a little longer to reformat than in standard text. The Setup menu includes an option that you can use to change the way columns are displayed, to speed up reformatting. Instead of displaying the columns side by side, it lets you display them on separate pages, in the correct column position. This option has no effect on the printed version of the document. Your columns will still be printed side by side, and appear that way in View Document.

To use this option:

1. Select the Setup Display menu:

    Keyboard: Press the Setup key (Shift-F1) and select the second option, **Display.**

    Mouse: Display the **File** menu and select Se**t**up, then **D**isplay.

2. Select the sixth option, **Edit-Screen Options.**

3. Select the seventh option, **Side-by-Side Columns Display**, and change it to No, then exit back to the Edit screen.

Newspaper columns will now appear on separate pages, each in the correct column position. On the first page, column 1 will appear in its normal position at the left side of the page, but column 2 will be empty. On the second page, column 1 will be empty, and column 2 will include text. For example, the Remote Controllers Newsletter is shown this way in Figure 8.19. The cursor is on the first line of column 2. Although the cursor appears to be on a separate page from the first column, and a page break appears above it, the status line indicates that it is actually on the first page, in the second column:

```
Col 2 Doc 1 Pg 1 Ln 2.8" Pos 4.5"
```

```
which results in potential calcification
of joints in later years."


NEW MODEL ANNOUNCED:
Controllomatic Corporation unveiled
its newest and latest model for the
---------------------------------------------------------------
                              upcoming TV season.  This super hi-
                              tech model, dubbed the ZR144, is the
                              most powerful zotter on the market. It
                              has full VCR and Stereo compatibility,
                              and is capable of functioning up to
                              2400 feet away.  Additionally, the new
                              ZR144 allows rapid channel change
                              with little or no chance of overheatin
                              at the staggering pace of 20 channels
                              per second. That should really drive
                              your co-viewers crazy!  Designed by
                              the famous Italian studio of Statique,
                              this sleek zotter has a deluxe pistol
                              grip handle, quick release and black
                              anodized finish.  Look for a road test
                              of this baby in an upcoming
                                 Col 2 Doc 1 Pg 1 Ln 2.8" Pos 4.5"
```

Figure 8.19 *Using the Setup menu, you can change the way newspaper columns are displayed. Instead of being side by side on the screen, they will appear to be on separate pages but in their correct column positions.*

When you change Side-by-Side Columns Display to No, parallel columns will appear, as shown in Figure 8.20. Note the dashed lines representing the hard page breaks. (The first one is just after the words boa constrictor.) These are the positions where you pressed Ctrl-Enter to move the cursor into the second column, after typing related text in the first column. After you typed the block in the second column, you pressed Ctrl-Enter again. Remember, WordPerfect turned columns off at that point, and then turned them on again right away so you could type the next column. For this reason, the paragraph that begins with Freddie is house trained appears to be on the same page as the first paragraph about Angel.

```
File Edit Search Layout Mark Tools Font Graphics Help      (Press F3 for Help)
                  CUDDLY'S USED PET SHOP

                  WEEKLY SPECIALS


FREDDIE
Three year old boa
constrictor.
=================================================================================
                  Freddie is house trained.  Great for the person on
                  the go, with rodent problem or neighbor with small,
                  obnoxious dog.


ANGEL
Five year old Siberian
Husky male.
=================================================================================
                  Angel also answers to "MUSH".  He prefers air
                  conditioning or colder climates.  Steady worker, low
                  mileage and never raced, must be seen to be
                                    Col 2 Doc 1 Pg 1 Ln 3.6" Pos 3.5"
```

Figure 8.20 *Because parallel columns include page breaks at the end of each block of text in the first column, they appear differently than newspaper columns when you change the Side-by-Side Columns Display option to No.*

MATH

WordPerfect's Math feature lets you incorporate calculations into your documents, so that you can add, subtract, multiply, and divide, and calculate subtotals, totals, grand totals, and averages. Adding and subtracting down a column of numbers is the easiest way to use Math. For example, Figure 9.1 displays a column of weekly advertising expenses. The author of this memo did not type the Total statistic (77,725.86) at the bottom of the column. In fact, all she had to type was a plus sign. After she selected the Calculate option from the Math menu, WordPerfect calculated the sum and automatically inserted it next to the plus sign. The plus sign does not appear in the printed version of the memo, shown in Figure 9.1, but is always visible on the Edit screen, as shown in Figure 9.3.

Figure 9.8 illustrates another way you can use WordPerfect's Math feature. In this example, formulas were set up to calculate the sales tax (in the second numeric column), and then add it to the price (in the first numeric column) to obtain the total cost for each item (in the last column). The only numbers typed were the prices; the Tax and Total columns are calculations. Later in this chapter, you will learn how to set up these formulas, using WordPerfect's Math Definition menu. You can define calculation formulas in four columns, and use up to 20 other columns to enter numbers to be included in your calculations or in text such as labels.

Whichever method you use for your calculations, you must turn on Math and press the Tab key before typing any numbers that you want WordPerfect to calculate, since this is how you designate mathematical columns. You cannot calculate numbers typed at the left margin.

WordPerfect's Six Math Functions

WordPerfect provides six math functions that you can use to calculate numeric columns. If you want to add a column, use the plus sign (+) to subtotal all numbers above it. If your column includes two subtotals, you can add them using the totals function, represented by the equal sign (=). You can use an asterisk (*) to obtain a grand total, the sum of two or more totals. To designate a number as a negative one and subtract it from the others, type a minus sign in front of it, or place parentheses around it. You can also designate a negative number by typing an N in front of it. Unlike the minus sign and parentheses, the N is not printed, so there will be no indication in the printed document that the number is negative. Use the extra subtotal character (t) next to a number when you want WordPerfect to consider the number as a subtotal and include it in a total calculation, even though it is actually not a subtotal of other numbers above it. The uppercase T represents an extra total. It works like the extra subtotal, except that you use it to include a number in a grand total. These functions are summarized in Table 9.1.

Table 9.1 *Math functions.*

Operator	Symbol	Function
Subtotal	+	Use a subtotal to add all numbers above it in the same column. If there is a subtotal or total above it, WordPerfect only subtotals the numbers up to the previous function.
Extra Subtotal	t	Use an extra subtotal to designate a single number as a subtotal so that WordPerfect will include it in the next total calculation.
Total	=	Use a total to add all subtotals and extra subtotals above it in the column. If there is a total above, WordPerfect will add the numbers up only to the previous total.
Extra Total	T	Use an extra total to designate a single number as a total, so WordPerfect will include it in the next grand total calculation.
Grand Total	*	Use a grand total to add all totals and extra totals above it in the column. If there is a grand total above it, WordPerfect will add the numbers up only to the previous function.
Negative	N – ( )	Use N to designate a negative number so that WordPerfect will subtract it in any calculation that follows. You can also use a minus sign or parentheses. The minus sign and parentheses appear in the printed document, but the N does not.

Adding and Subtracting Numbers in Columns

Adding a column of numbers, like the one shown in the memo in Figure 9.1, is an easy task. Here are the basic steps:

1. Change the tab stops.

2. Turn on the Math feature.

3. Press Tab and then type the first number. Press Enter, tab to the column, and type the next number. Repeat until you've typed all numbers. To subtract, type minus signs before the numbers, or surround them with parentheses.

4. Type a plus sign at the bottom of the column.

5. Select the Calculate option from the Math menu.

Turning on Math enables you to calculate the numbers at the bottom of the column, and automatically converts all tab settings into decimal tabs. When you use decimal tabs for your numbers, WordPerfect aligns the numbers so that each decimal point is positioned at the tab stop. Regardless of the number of digits, all numbers in the column will be aligned around the decimal point, as shown in Figure 9.1.

To add the numeric column shown in Figure 9.1, the first step is to erase all the tab stops and insert a single tab stop 4" from the left margin; the actual tab stop position will be at 5", since relative tabs are WordPerfect's default.

1. To change the tab stop settings:

   Keyboard: Press Format (Shift-F8) and select Line.

   Mouse: Display the Layout menu and select Line.

Select Tab Set. Press Ctrl-End to erase all the tab stops. Type 4 and press Enter. Press the Exit key (F7) twice to return to the Edit screen. You just set a single tab stop at the 5" position (4" from the left margin).

 Tip: When using math columns, be sure to set the tab stops so that each column is wide enough to contain the largest number you will be typing. If not, WordPerfect won't be able to calculate the numbers correctly.

```
                          MEMORANDUM


DATE:       October 6, 1990

TO:         Jane Ketchum

FROM:       Angela Smithfield

SUBJECT:    Advertising expenses


As you requested, I have compiled this list of our weekly
advertising expenses for the month of October.


October 1-6                      $ 17,440.21
October 8-13                       13,900.88
October 15-20                       9,654.55
October 22-27                      14,510.33
October 29-November 3              22,219.89

Total:                           $ 77,725.86
```

Figure 9.1 *By turning on WordPerfect's Math feature, you can easily total numeric columns such as this one.*

2. To turn on Math:

> **Keyboard:** Press the Columns/Tables key, Alt-F7.
>
> This prompt will appear:
>
> `1 Columns; 2 Table; 3 Math: 0`
>
> Select the third option, **Math**. This prompt appears:
>
> `Math: 1 On; 2 Off; 3 Define; 4 Calculate: 0`
>
> Select the first option, **On**.
>
> **Mouse:** Display the **Layout** menu and select **Math**. Another menu will pop out to the right, as shown in Figure 9.2. Select the first option, **On**.

This prompt appears in the lower-left corner of the screen, indicating that the Math feature is on:

`Math`

and WordPerfect inserts a [Math On] code at the cursor position, visible only in Reveal Codes. If you turn Math off later in the document, a [Math Off] code will be inserted, and the `Math` prompt will disappear. If you move the cursor out of the area where Math is on, you won't be able to calculate numbers. Do *not* type any numbers that you want to include in a calculation unless the Math prompt appears in the lower-left corner of the screen.

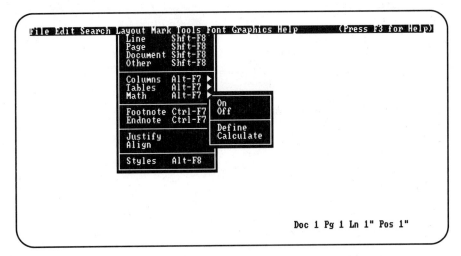

Figure 9.2 *When you select the Math option from the pull-down Layout menu, this menu appears. Use it to turn Math on or off, to define math columns, or to calculate.*

3. Type the first heading, October 1-6, and press the Tab key. This prompt appears:

Align char = . Math

indicating that the alignment character is a decimal point, and the Math feature is on. Notice that the cursor is now at Pos 5". As you type, the cursor will remain on the tab stop setting, and the numbers will be inserted to the left. After you type the decimal point, the remaining characters will be inserted to the right of the tab stop. When you finish typing, the decimal point will be positioned at the tab stop position, 5".

4. Type the dollar sign, insert a space, and type the first expense figure: $ 17,440.21.

 Tip: You cannot calculate a column of numbers if it begins at the left margin. Always press Tab before typing in a numeric column so that the Align char prompt appears.

5. Repeat steps 3 and 4 to type the other four headings and numbers in the column (see Figure 9.1).

In the next step, you will type a plus sign at the bottom of the column to designate where the subtotal should be calculated. After you select the Calculate option, WordPerfect will automatically add all the numbers above the plus sign and display the resulting sum to the left of it. You must press Tab before typing the plus sign and the `Align char` prompt must be visible, or WordPerfect will not perform the calculation. The plus sign does not appear in the printed document. You can verify this by using the View Document option on the Print menu.

 Warning: Never enter numbers that are to be calculated unless Math is on and you see the `Align char` prompt.

 Tip: When Math is turned on, the Tab key inserts decimal tabs. WordPerfect automatically aligns columns of numbers around the tab, regardless of the number of digits they contain, because the decimal points are always positioned at the tab stop.

6. Type `Total`, press Tab and type a dollar sign, insert a space, and then type a plus sign. Your screen should now resemble Figure 9.3.

7. To calculate the subtotal:

Keyboard: Press the Columns/Tables key, Alt-F7, select **Math**, and then select Calculate.

Mouse: Display the Layout menu, select **Math**, and then select Calculate.

The subtotal, $ 77,725.86, appears almost instantly.

Notice the comma after the second 7. By default, WordPerfect includes a comma as the thousands' separator in numbers that it calculates. Also, the results of calculations always include two digits after the decimal point, even if the numbers being added are whole numbers. For example, if you were to type and calculate this column:

```
1,000
2,000
3,000
```

```
October 1-6                    $ 17,440.21
October 8-13                     13,900.88
October 15-20                     9,654.55
October 22-27                    14,510.33
October 29-November 3            22,219.89

Total:                            $ +




Math                                    Doc 1 Pg 1 Ln 2.33" Pos 5"
```

Figure 9.3   *This is how your screen should look after you finish typing the labels, numbers, and the plus sign for the subtotal calculation.*

WordPerfect would display the resulting sum as 6,000.00. If the results of a calculation are negative, WordPerfect surrounds the number in parentheses. For example, if you were to type and calculate this column:

```
-200
1,000
-900
```

the resulting sum would be displayed as (100.00). You can change the parentheses to a minus sign, or change the number of digits, using the Define option on the Math menu. This process is described in the section entitled "Using Math Columns."

You can also change the thousands' separator from a comma to another character, such as a period, or change the alignment character from a decimal point to a different character, such as a blank space. To do this, use the third option on the Format Other menu, **Decimal/Align Character—Thousands' Separator.** Because WordPerfect will insert a formatting code at the cursor position, be sure that the cursor is at the top of the document before you change this option.

If you were going to continue typing in the document, your next step would be to turn Math off and change the tab stop settings again so you could use the Tab key for text. If you don't type any more text, it is not necessary to turn Math off. By turning Math on and off, you can create several math areas in a document.

> **Tip:** Even if Math is not turned on, you can use the Tab Align feature to align numbers around their decimal points (Ctrl-F6 or Layout menu, Align, Tab Align), but you can't total the numbers.

Editing Numbers in a Numeric Column

If you were to change any of the numbers in the column, WordPerfect would not update the subtotal automatically. Instead, you would have to select the Calculate option from the Math menu again. Try changing the expense figure in the last row, and calculating the subtotal again:

1. Change the expense figure for the last week in the list, from 22,219.89 to 18,450.00. Edit the number just like regular text, which it is. You can even use Search and Replace to locate and replace it.

2. Select the Calculate option to update the subtotal:

    Keyboard: Press the Columns/Tables key, Alt-F7, select **Math**, and then select **Calculate**.

    Mouse: Display the **Layout** menu, select **Math**, and then select **Calculate**.

    WordPerfect should have changed the subtotal to $ 73,955.97.

Adding Subtotals

If your memo included weekly expense figures for each month in the quarter, as shown in Figure 9.4, you could have WordPerfect subtotal each month's expenses and then add the three subtotals together to obtain a total for the entire quarter. Use a subtotal operator (plus sign) to add each month's figures. To add the three subtotals, type an equal sign (=) at the bottom of the column, representing the total function. After calculating, your screen would resemble Figure 9.5.

> **Tip:** To subtract down a column, designate numbers as negative so that WordPerfect adds the negative numbers to the positive ones.

MEMORANDUM

DATE: October 6, 1990

TO: Jane Ketchum

FROM: Angela Smithfield

SUBJECT: Advertising expenses

As you requested, I have compiled this list of our weekly advertising expenses for the fourth quarter.

October 1-6	$ 17,440.21
October 8-13	13,900.88
October 15-20	9,654.55
October 22-27	14,510.33
October 29-November 3	22,219.89
October total:	**$ 77,725.86**
November 5-10	$ 12,365.00
November 12-17	8,377.80
November 19-24	12,100.02
November 26-December 1	18,944.33
November total:	**51,787.15**
December 3-8	$ 13,559.35
December 10-15	17,455.00
December 17-22	19,478.00
December 24-29	21,721.45
December total:	**72,213.80**
4TH QUARTER TOTAL:	**201,726.81**

Figure 9.4 *You can add two or more subtotals in a numeric column, such as the three monthly expense subtotals shown here.*

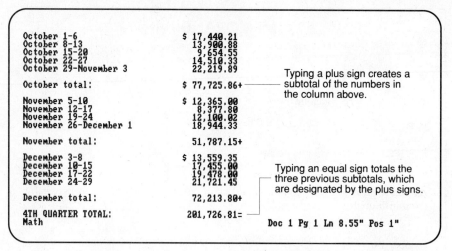

```
October 1-6                        $ 17,440.21
October 8-13                         13,900.88
October 15-20                         9,654.55
October 22-27                        14,510.33
October 29-November 3                22,219.89    Typing a plus sign creates a
                                                  subtotal of the numbers in
October total:                     $ 77,725.86+   the column above.

November 5-10                      $ 12,365.00
November 12-17                        8,377.80
November 19-24                       12,100.02
November 26-December 1               18,944.33

November total:                      51,787.15+

December 3-8                       $ 13,559.35
December 10-15                       17,455.00    Typing an equal sign totals the
December 17-22                       19,478.00    three previous subtotals, which
December 24-29                       21,721.45    are designated by the plus signs.

December total:                      72,213.80+

4TH QUARTER TOTAL:                  201,726.81=
Math                                              Doc 1 Pg 1 Ln 8.55" Pos 1"
```

Figure 9.5   *To calculate a total for the quarter, type an equal sign at the bottom of the column. When you select Calculate, WordPerfect will use it to add the three monthly expense subtotals.*

The Extra Subtotal and Extra Total Functions

Two other functions that you can use in numeric columns are the extra subtotal, t, and the extra total, T. Figure 9.6 shows an example of when you would need to use one. The Total Expenses figure ($4,500) is designated as an extra subtotal by the lowercase t. As a result, WordPerfect treats the number as a subtotal and includes it in the total calculation for INCOME (subtracting it because of the N operator). Without it, WordPerfect would have completely disregarded the $4,500 when calculating the INCOME figure, as shown in Figure 9.7.

The uppercase T represents the extra total function. It works just like the extra subtotal, except that you use it to include a single number in a grand total calculation, as designated by an asterisk.

Using Math Columns

To perform more complex mathematical operations, such as calculating the sales tax and adding it to the price in Figure 9.8, you can define math columns. Up to four of your columns can contain formulas. The formulas can add, subtract, divide, multiply, or average. They can include fixed numbers, such as 6% sales tax, numbers you've typed in the same row in other columns, such as the prices in Figure 9.8, or numbers in the same row that WordPerfect has calculated using a formula. You can also create total columns and use them to sum numbers in the column to the left.

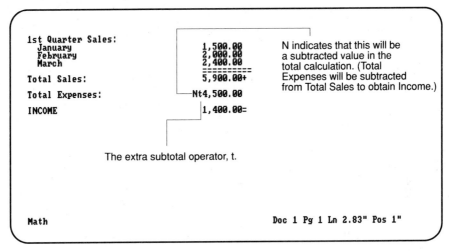

Figure 9.6   *If you want to designate a single number as a subtotal and include it in a total calculation, use the extra subtotal operator, t. In this example, t has been typed next to the Total Expenses figure, so the figure will be included in the INCOME calculation.*

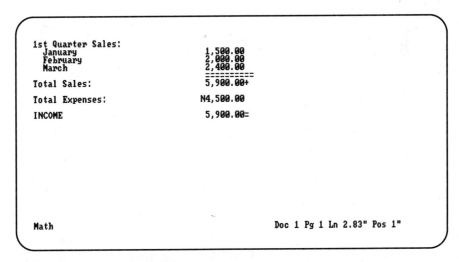

Figure 9.7   *Without the extra subtotal operator, WordPerfect does not include Total Expenses in the calculation for INCOME.*

In the next chapter, you'll learn how to use WordPerfect's Table feature. Since tables can also be used for mathematical operations and have some advantages, you may want to skim through that chapter before studying this section. You may find that tables are easier to use.

```
                    Invoice

                 Price        Tax         Total
Copy paper        7.99       0.52!         8.51!
Toner            99.99       6.50!       106.49!
Diskettes        22.99       1.49!        24.48!

                                         139.48+




Math                            Doc 1 Pg 1 Ln 3.5" Pos 1"
```

Figure 9.8   *WordPerfect can compute formulas across columns. Here, the program determines the sales tax for each item and adds it to the sales price.*

Defining Math Columns

To define the three columns shown in Figure 9.8, use the Define option on the Math menu.

1. Select Define:

   Keyboard: Press the Columns/Tables key, Alt-F7, and select Math.

   Mouse: Display the Layout menu and select Math.

   Select the third option, **Define.** The Math Definition screen appears, as shown in Figure 9.9.

   The cursor is highlighting the first 2 in the Type row. The row above it, Columns, displays the column letters. The cursor is currently in column A. When typing, you designate each column by pressing the Tab key, and WordPerfect labels your columns A through X. For example, in Figure 9.8, column A is Price, and it is located at the first tab stop. Column B, Tax, is at the second tab stop. Column C, `Total`, is at the third tab stop. The labels at the left margin, `Copy paper`, `Toner`, and `Diskettes`, are not columns and can't be used in calculations.

```
Math Definition            Use arrow keys to position cursor

Columns                    A B C D E F G H I J K L M N O P Q R S T U V W X

Type                       2 2 2 2 2 2 2 2 2 2 2 2 2 2 2 2 2 2 2 2 2 2 2 2

Negative Numbers           ( ( ( ( ( ( ( ( ( ( ( ( ( ( ( ( ( ( ( ( ( ( ( (

Number of Digits to        2 2 2 2 2 2 2 2 2 2 2 2 2 2 2 2 2 2 2 2 2 2 2 2
   the Right (0-4)

Calculation    1
   Formulas    2
               3
               4

Type of Column:
   0 = Calculation    1 = Text     2 = Numeric    3 = Total

Negative Numbers
   ( = Parentheses (50.00)         - = Minus Sign  -50.00


Press Exit when done
```

Figure 9.9   *The Math Definition screen.*

The second row in the Math Definition screen, where the cursor is positioned, is `Type`. Use it to designate whether you want to type numbers or text in the column, or have WordPerfect calculate a formula, or use it for totals. WordPerfect's default column type is numeric. The options for column type are:

0 for a calculation formula

1 for a text column

2 for numbers that will be used in a calculation

3 for a totals column

These are defined under the heading `Type of Column`:

`0 = Calculation    1 = Text    2 = Numeric    3 = Total`

In the example shown in Figure 9.8, column A will be numeric, and columns B and C will be calculations. In numeric, calculation, and total columns, WordPerfect converts the tab stops into decimal tabs. In text columns, the tab stops remain left tabs so that text will be aligned in the usual way: The first character will be at the tab stop, and all others will be inserted to the right of it. Total columns are used to add figures from the column to the left. You won't be defining a total column in this example, but will learn more about it later.

The `Negative Numbers` row shows how WordPerfect will display the results of a calculation or total if the number is negative. By default, calculated numbers are enclosed in parentheses, but you can change this to a minus sign. This is depicted under the heading `Negative Numbers`:

`( = Parenthesis (50.00)`   `- = Minus Sign -50.00`

The last option is `Number of Digits to the Right`. The default selection is 2, so WordPerfect always displays the results of calculations or totals with two digits after the decimal point. You can change this option to any number between 0 and 4. Numbers with more than four digits are rounded up.

To move the cursor and select options in the Math Definition screen, use the arrow keys.

WordPerfect uses the middle section of the screen, `Calculation Formulas`, to display the formulas you create for your calculation columns. It includes only four rows because you are limited to four calculation columns. As soon as you select 0 to define the formula for column B, the cursor will move to the first row in the section.

Tip: By default, WordPerfect displays numbers that it calculates with two digits after the decimal point, and encloses negative numbers in parentheses. These defaults have no effect on numbers that you type, only on the ones that WordPerfect calculates.

2. Since column A is numeric and you don't need to make any changes to the other two options for the column, `Negative Numbers` and `Number of Digits to the Right`, press the Right Arrow key to move the cursor to the `Type` row under column B. This will be your first calculation column.

3. Type 0 to designate column B as a calculation column.

WordPerfect moves the cursor to the Calculation Formulas area and inserts a B between the cursor and the row number (1), indicating that the first calculation will be in column B. To calculate a sales tax of 6 $\frac{1}{2}$%, multiply the number in column A by .065. To represent multiplication, type an asterisk. The other operators you can use in calculation formulas are a plus sign to add, a minus sign to subtract, and a slash to divide. These are summarized in Table 9.2. To use fractions in a formula, either type them in parentheses, such as (1/5), or use the decimal equivalent, such as .2 for $\frac{1}{5}$.

Table 9.2 *Operators used in calculation formulas.*

To Represent:	Operator	Example
Addition	+	A+B
Subtraction	–	B–C
Multiplication	*	A*100
Division	/	C/100

You can also use four special functions by themselves, as the entire calculation formula: a plus sign (+) to add all the numbers across a row; a plus sign and slash (+/) to average numbers across a row; an equal sign (=) to add numbers across total columns; and an equal sign and slash (=/) to average numbers across total columns. You'll learn more about these functions later.

4. Type the formula:

   .065*A

   and then press Enter. You can use uppercase or lowercase to type the column letter (A) in your formula. The cursor moves back to the Columns row, under column C. This column will also contain a formula, to add the numbers in column A and column B.

5. Type 0, and then type this formula:

   a+b

   and press Enter.

   The cursor moves back to the first row, under column D. You've finished defining the three columns, and your Math Definition screen should now resemble Figure 9.10. The prompt in the lower-left corner of the screen tells you what to do next: Press Exit when done.

6. To complete the math definition, press the Exit key, F7. The main Math menu appears again. Use it to turn on Math.

7. Select **On**. The Math indicator appears in the lower-left corner of your screen. Before typing the numbers, define the tab stops.

8. Use the Format Line menu to erase the old tab stops, and define them at 3", 4.5", and 6".

   Now you are ready to type the numbers in column A.

```
Math Definition            Use arrow keys to position cursor

Columns                    A B C D E F G H I J K L M N O P Q R S T U V W X

Type                       2 0 0 2 2 2 2 2 2 2 2 2 2 2 2 2 2 2 2 2 2 2 2 2

Negative Numbers           ( ( ( ( ( ( ( ( ( ( ( ( ( ( ( ( ( ( ( ( ( ( ( (

Number of Digits to        2 2 2 2 2 2 2 2 2 2 2 2 2 2 2 2 2 2 2 2 2 2 2 2
  the Right (0-4)

Calculation    1    B      .065*A
  Formulas     2    C      a+b
               3
               4

Type of Column:
    0 = Calculation     1 = Text      2 = Numeric    3 = Total

Negative Numbers
    ( = Parentheses (50.00)        - = Minus Sign  -50.00


Press Exit when done
```

Figure 9.10 *The Math Definition screen after defining the three columns and typing the formulas for Tax and Total.*

Typing in Math Columns

The only text you type will be the labels at the left margin and the prices in column A. However, you must create columns B and C by tabbing over to them. WordPerfect will then insert an exclamation point in each column to signify that you want the formula calculated at this position.

1. Enter the first row title, Copy paper, then press the Tab key and type the price, 7.99.

2. Press the Tab key twice to move the cursor into columns B and C.

    WordPerfect displays exclamation points (!) in the two calculation columns, indicating that they contain formulas that you want to calculate for this row. After you select the Calculate option, the results of your formulas will be displayed to the left of the exclamation points. Like the plus sign that you used earlier to represent subtotals, the exclamation points will not appear in the printed version of your document. If you want to type a symbol such as the dollar sign in one of the calculation columns, insert it to the left of the exclamation point. Do not type any numbers. To prevent WordPerfect from calculating a formula in a specific position, you can erase the exclamation point.

3. Repeat steps 1 and 2 for the next two rows. The last calculation will be a subtotal that adds the three figures in column C, so you'll type a plus sign to represent it.

4. Move the cursor down two lines and then press the Tab key three times.

   WordPerfect inserts exclamation points under the headings Tax and Total in the last row. If you were to use the Calculate option now, the results of both calculations would be 0, since the first column does not have a price to use in the calculation. To add the three figures in the Totals column, you have to erase the exclamation points and type a plus sign.

5. Erase both exclamation points in the last row, but be careful not to erase the decimal tabs you created by pressing the Tab key to move the cursor there. If you do, your subtotal calculation won't work. The easiest way to do this is to use Replace, as follows:

   a) Move the cursor up one line.

   b) Select **Replace** (Alt-F2 or Replace on the pull-down Search menu) and enter N for Confirm.

   c) In response to the Srch prompt, press the Columns/Tables key, Alt-F7, and select **Math**. This menu appears:

   ```
   Math: 1 On; 2 Off; 3 Def; 4 +; 5 =; 6 *; 7 t; 8 T; 9 !;
   A N: 0
   ```

   d) Select the ninth option to insert the exclamation point code into the Srch prompt.

   e) Press F2 twice.

6. Type a plus sign in column C. If you need to move the cursor to get to column C, use the arrow keys, not the Tab key. The Tab key will only insert exclamation points again. The last step is to calculate.

7. Calculate the formulas:

   Keyboard: Press the Columns/Tables key, Alt-F7, select **Math**, and then select **Calculate**.

   Mouse: Display the **Layout** menu, select **Math**, and then select **Calculate**.

   Your document should now resemble Figure 9.8. If you print the document, the exclamation points and plus sign will not appear.

Redefining Math Columns

If you need to change a formula, the type of column, the method used to display negative numbers, or the number of digits to the right of the decimal point for any of your columns, just place the cursor after the [Math Def] code, select Define from the Math menu, and make any necessary changes in the Math Definition screen. For example, if the sales tax were increased to 7%, you could follow these steps to redefine the formula in column B and calculate the correct figures.

1. Place the cursor anywhere after the [Math Def] code, but before the first Price figure in column A.

2. Select Define:

   Keyboard: Press the Columns/Tables key, Alt-F7, and select **Math**.

   Mouse: Display the Layout menu and select **Math**.

   Select the third option, **Define**.

3. Move the cursor to column B, type 0, change the formula to .07*A, and press Enter.

4. Press Exit (F7) and select the **Calculate** option.

The calculated numbers should all change to reflect the increased sales tax, and your screen should resemble Figure 9.11.

Your last step should be to locate and delete the original Math Definition code from your document, since WordPerfect is no longer using it.

```
                        Invoice

                   Price        Tax        Total
   Copy paper       7.99       0.56!        8.55!
   Toner           99.99       7.00!      106.99!
   Diskettes       22.99       1.61!       24.60!

                                          140.14+




   Math                          Doc 1 Pg 1 Ln 3.5" Pos 1"
```

Figure 9.11 The invoice after changing the sales tax formula in column B to 7% and recalculating.

Tip: To change a math definition, the ideal cursor position is right after the original Math Definition code so that you can delete the original after making the change. To locate it, you can use WordPerfect's Search feature.

Order of Precedence in Mathematical Formulas

WordPerfect calculates all formulas from left to right, regardless of the operators used, and does not multiply and divide first. For example, the results of this formula:

    3+2*2

would be 10. WordPerfect would add 3+2 first, then multiply the result, 5, by 2. In this formula:

    10+1/4

WordPerfect would add 10+1 to get 11, then divide 11 by 4. The result would be 2.75.

You can change the calculation order by typing parentheses. The results of the first example would be different if you entered the formula this way:

    3+(2*2)

WordPerfect would multiply 2*2 first, then add it to 3, and the result would be 7. If you typed the second formula this way:

    10+(1/4)

WordPerfect would add 10 to 1/4, and the result would be 10.25.

If you define a formula incorrectly, after you select the Calculate option, two question marks will appear next to the exclamation point, as shown below:

    ??!

For example, if you defined a formula that divided column A by column B, then typed 12 in column A and 0 in column B, as shown below, the two questions marks would appear after you select Calculate.

    12   0   ??!

Since WordPerfect can't divide by 0, it warns you with the question marks.

Calculating Averages

To calculate averages for a row of numbers, define a calculation column and enter these symbols for the formula:

+/

For example, to obtain the average weekly sales for four types of vehicles, as shown in Figure 9.12, follow these instructions:

```
                  Monthly Sales: June 1991

             Week 1    Week 2    Week 3    Week 4    Average

Sedans        3,142     2,811     1,901     3,459     2,828!
Sports cars     826       900       945       875       887!
Station wagons  319       255       287       322       296!
Trucks          900     1,012     1,131     1,345     1,097!

              5,188+    4,980+    4,267+    6,005+    5,110!




Math                                     Doc 1 Pg 1 Ln 3" Pos 1"
```

Figure 9.12 WordPerfect can calculate averages, as shown in this example.

1. Set tab stops at 2.5", 3.5", 4.5", 5.5", and 6.5".

2. Use the Math Definition screen to define columns A, B, C, and D as numeric, and column E as a calculation column. Enter this formula for column E: +/

   If you wanted to obtain a total in column E instead of an average, you would type only the plus sign.

3. Change the Number of Digits to the Right in each column to 0.

4. Exit the Math Definition screen and turn on Math.

5. Type the labels at the left margin and the numbers in columns A through D. Press Tab to insert exclamation points in the last column so that WordPerfect will calculate the averages.

6. In the bottom row, type a plus sign in columns A, B, C, and D. Press Tab to insert an exclamation point in the last column.

   In the last row, columns A through D will display total vehicle sales for the week. Column E will represent the average weekly sale of all vehicle types.

7. Select the Calculate option.

   When you finish, your document should resemble Figure 9.12.

    Tip: You can move or copy a numeric column by using Block to designate the column and then selecting the Tabular Column option from the Move key (Ctrl-F4).

Total Columns

Instead of totaling numbers at the bottom of a column, you can define a total column to the right, where WordPerfect will calculate your subtotals, totals, and grand totals. Figure 9.13 shows an example. Column B was designated as a total column, so the subtotal and total operators add numbers in the column to the left. The two subtotal operators (+) were used to sum Total Sales and Total Expenses, and the equals operator (=) was used to subtract Total Expenses from Total Sales.

   To duplicate this example, follow these instructions:

1. Erase the old tab stops, and set one at 5" and one at 6.5".

2. Use the Math Definition screen to define column A as numeric, and B as a total column (type 3). Change the *Number of Digits to the Right* in each column to 0.

3. Exit the Math Definition screen and turn on Math.

4. Type the labels at the left margin and the numbers in column A. In column B of the Total Sales and Total Expenses rows, type plus signs. Type an equal sign in column B of the INCOME row.

   The operator must be on the line below the last number to be included in the calculation. For example, if you typed 300, 400, and 500 in column A and asked WordPerfect to subtotal these figures in a total column to the right, as shown below:

```
300
400
500   +
```

the result would be 700. WordPerfect would not include 500 in the calculation, because it appears on the same line as the subtotal operator. To obtain the correct result, the subtotal operator must be below the last number, as shown below:

```
300
400
500
      +1,200
```

5. Select the Calculate option. When you finish, your document should resemble Figure 9.13.

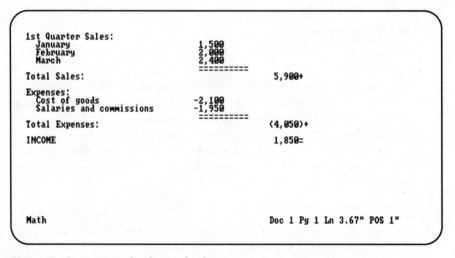

Figure 9.13 An example of a total column.

TABLES

WordPerfect Corporation introduced the Tables feature in version 5.1, and it has proven to be an important and useful improvement. A table is a series of horizontal rows and vertical columns that intersect to form a matrix of boxes called *cells*. If you've ever worked with a spreadsheet such as PlanPerfect, Excel, or Lotus, the concept will be familiar. In fact, you can use tables just like a spreadsheet, setting up mathematical formulas that WordPerfect will calculate automatically.

Tables have many other applications besides mathematical ones. You can create elaborate forms, such as invoices, order forms, sign-up sheets, charts, calendars, and lists. Chapter 14 includes an example of one such form, an appointment and "To Do" list (Figure 14.5). You can even set up a table as a merge application, to be used over and over again.

Anything you would normally type in tabular columns or parallel text columns is a good candidate for a table. When you first define a table, it appears as shown in Figure 10.1, with the cells separated by horizontal and vertical lines. By enlarging individual cells and removing all the lines in and around the table, the text will appear the same as text formatted in parallel or tabular columns, as shown in Figure 10.14. In fact, in the printed version you won't be able to tell the difference. Among other advantages, tables are much easier to use than tabular or parallel columns. WordPerfect Corporation recognized that many users would want to convert existing tabular or parallel columns into tables, so they have provided an option to convert text in parallel or tabular columns into table format.

As in a spreadsheet, WordPerfect identifies columns by letters, and rows by numbers, and the intersection of a row and column is called a *cell*. The rows are numbered from top to bottom, so the first row is 1, the second is 2, etc. The column letters are assigned from left to right, so the first is A, the second is B, etc. WordPerfect assigns a letter-number combination to each cell, indicating its position in the matrix. As you can see from Figure 10.1, the first cell in the upper-left corner is A1, and the one in the row below it is A2. The cell to the right of A1 is B1. This figure also shows the default style for the lines in and around a table: Double lines around the outside borders, and single lines inside the table. You can change any of the lines to single, double, dashed, dotted, thick, or extra thick, or remove them altogether.

	Column A	Column B	Column C	Column D	Column E
Row 1	Cell A1	Cell B1	Cell C1	Cell D1	Cell E1
Row 2	Cell A2	Cell B2	Cell C2	Cell D2	Cell E2
Row 3	Cell A3	Cell B3	Cell C3	Cell D3	Cell E3
Row 4	Cell A4	Cell B4	Cell C4	Cell D4	Cell E4
Row 5	Cell A5	Cell B5	Cell C5	Cell D5	Cell E5

Figure 10.1 *A table is a matrix of columns and rows. The columns are labeled with letters from left to right, and the rows are numbered from top to bottom. The intersection of a row and column is called a cell, which is identified by a letter-number combination representing its position, such as A1, B1, A2, or B2.*

Creating a Table

To create a new table, you select the option, designate the number of columns and rows you want it to include, and press Enter. WordPerfect then generates the table structure and places you in the table editor.

To learn how to create a table, follow these instructions to define the Ship Traffic table shown in Figure 10.2. Start with a blank Edit screen.

```
                          SHIP TRAFFIC

            ┌──────────────────────────────────────────────┐
            │          Due to arrive Friday, February 8     │
            ├──────────────────┬─────────────────┬──────────┤
            │Ship              │Arriving From    │Port/Berth│
            │Busted Bilge      │Long Beach       │Oakland/67│
            │Wake Watcher      │Vancouver BC     │Oakland/68│
            │Diesel Demon      │Los Angeles      │SFO/38    │
            │Tidal Tramp       │Long Beach       │Oakland/24│
            │Big Bertha        │Long Beach       │SFO/96    │
            └──────────────────┴─────────────────┴──────────┘


                   Cell A2 Doc 1 Pg 1 Ln 2.34" Pos 1.62"
```

Figure 10.2 *Ship Traffic table.*

1. Select Table:

> **Keyboard:** Press the Columns/Tables key (Alt-F7) and select the second option, **Tables**, from the menu line:
>
> ```
> 1 Columns; 2 Tables; 3 Math: 0
> ```
>
> **Mouse:** Display the **Layout** menu and select **Tables**, as shown in Figure 10.3.

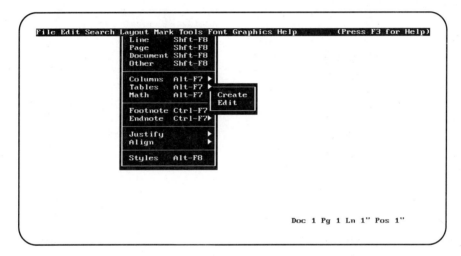

Figure 10.3   Selecting the Tables option from the Layout menu.

2. Select the first option, **Create**.

> This prompt appears, asking how many columns you want the table to include, and assumes 3:
>
> ```
> Number of Columns: 3
> ```
>
> The maximum is 32. You can always add more columns later, if needed.

3. Enter 3 for the number of columns.

> The next prompt asks how many rows you want, and assumes 1:
>
> ```
> Number of Rows: 1
> ```
>
> The maximum is 32,765. Like columns, you can add more rows later if you need to.

4. Enter 7 for the number of rows.

> After you press Enter, the table structure and table editor will appear, as shown in Figure 10.4. The cursor is in the upper-left corner, inside cell A1, and the cursor is expanded to highlight the entire cell. Notice that a

new item has been added to the status line: the name of the cell the cursor is currently in, A1. The Table Edit menu at the bottom of the screen includes options to change the structure and appearance of the table, or of individual cells, columns, or rows. Later, you will use it to join all the cells in the first row together, boldface and center the heading (*Due to arrive Friday, February 8*), create the gray-shading effect, and remove the vertical lines, as shown in the printed version in Figure 10.6. However, since you cannot enter text in your table until you return to the Edit screen, that will be your next step.

```
Table Edit:  Press Exit when done          Cell A1 Doc 1 Pg 1 Ln 1.14" Pos 1.12"

Ctrl-Arrows Column Widths; Ins Insert; Del Delete; Move Move/Copy;
1 Size; 2 Format; 3 Lines; 4 Header; 5 Math; 6 Options; 7 Join; 8 Split: 0
```

Figure 10.4 *The table structure.*

Notice the prompt above the double line at the bottom of the screen, telling you what to do when you are finished using the table editor:

Table Edit: Press Exit when done.

5. To return to the Edit screen:

Keyboard: Press Exit (F7).

Mouse: Click the right button.

The Table Edit menu disappears, and you return to the Edit screen. If you look in Reveal Codes, you'll see that WordPerfect has inserted several codes into your document. The first is a Table Definition code:

[Tbl Def:I;3,2.17",2.17",2.17"]

The Roman numeral I indicates that this is the first table in the document. The next number, 3, represents the number of columns in the table. The remaining three numbers, 2.17" each, refer to the width of each of the three columns. WordPerfect initially creates columns of the same width, but provides two methods that you can use to widen or compress one or more of the columns (you'll learn how later). Below that are seven lines of [Row] and [Cell] codes:

```
[Row][Cell][Cell][Cell]
```

Each row in the table is represented by a [Row] code, and each column is represented by a [Cell] code. At the end of the table, there is a [Tbl Off] code. WordPerfect won't allow you to delete the [Row], [Cell], or [Tbl Off] codes. However, you can delete the Table Definition code. This would erase the table structure, converting the [Cell] codes into tabs, and the [Row] codes into hard returns, but leave any text that you had typed. You'll learn more about this later in the chapter.

> ▶ **Tip:** When you are working in a table, the `Cell` notation on the status line indicates the name of the current cell.

Typing Text in the Table

Begin by typing the headings in the second row. You'll type the text in the first row later, after using the table editor to change the formatting.

1. Move the cursor down to cell A2, and type this heading:

    ```
    Ship
    ```

    To move the cursor:

    Keyboard: Press Down Arrow.

    Mouse: Use the mouse pointer to move the cursor into A2.

    Do not press Enter to move the cursor. As shown in Figure 10.5, this just expands the current cell and row to another line (in Figure 10.5, it was pressed five times, to exaggerate the effect). If you did press Enter, press Backspace to delete the hard return and move the cursor back up. WordPerfect will also create another line and expand the cell (and row) if you type enough text to fill the first line.

    Within a cell, keys such as Enter, End, and the arrow keys function as if the cell were an entire page. When a cell is empty you can use the four arrow keys to move from cell to cell, such as Down Arrow to move down one cell, or Right Arrow to move right one cell. However, once you've typed text in a cell, these keys will only move the cursor character by character. For example, if you move the cursor back to the first character in the cell (the S in Ship) and press Right Arrow, you'll see that you have to press it five times to get to the next cell.

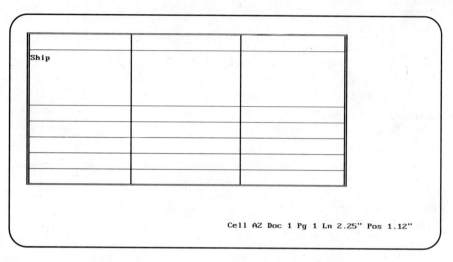

Cell A2 Doc 1 Pg 1 Ln 2.25" Pos 1.12"

Figure 10.5 *Individual cells can contain multiple lines. Pressing Enter after typing an entry expands the cell and all others in the row to another line. Here, it was pressed five times to exaggerate the effect. WordPerfect will also create another line and expand the cell (and row) if you type enough text to fill the first line.*

To move the cursor from cell to cell after you've typed text in the cells, use the Tab key. Pressing Tab once moves the cursor right one cell. If the cursor is in the last column in a row, it moves to the first cell in the next row. Shift-Tab does the opposite, moving the cursor to the left one cell, or, if it is in the first cell in a row, to the last cell in the row above. If you have an enhanced keyboard, you can also use Alt with any of the four arrow keys to move from cell to cell (the arrow keys in the middle section of the keyboard, not those on the numeric keypad). Cursor movement within a table is summarized in Table 10.1.

Since the Tab key is used for cursor movement in a table, if you want to use the Tab feature to indent a line inside a cell, you have to press Home-Tab instead.

2. Move the cursor to the right one column to cell B2, and type:

   Arriving From

3. Move the cursor to the right one column to cell C2, and type:

   Port/Berth

4. Type the remaining entries shown in Figure 10.2 for the three columns:

Ship	Arriving From	Port/Berth
Busted Bilge	Long Beach	Oakland/67
Wake Watcher	Vancouver BC	Oakland/68
Diesel Demon	Los Angeles	SFO/38
Tidal Tramp	Long Beach	Oakland/24
Big Bertha	Long Beach	SFO/96

5. Save the table using this name: *SHIPS.TBL*

Always save a table before using the table editor to modify it, in case you make an undesirable modification and can't figure out how to undo it.

Table 10.1 *Cursor movement within a table.*

Keystroke	Cursor Movement
Tab Ctrl-Home, → Alt-→ (enhanced)	One cell right
Shift-Tab Ctrl-Home, ← Alt-← (enhanced)	One cell left
↑ (from first line in cell) Alt-↑	One cell up
↓ (from last line in cell) Alt-↓	One cell down
Ctrl-Home, Home, ← Alt-Home, ←(enhanced)	First cell in row
Ctrl-Home, Home, → Alt-Home, → (enhanced)	Last cell in row
Ctrl-Home, Home, ↑ Alt-Home, Home, ↑ (enhanced)	First cell in column
Ctrl-Home, Home, ↓ Alt-Home, Home, ↓ (enhanced)	Last cell in column
Ctrl-Home, ↑	Beginning of first line in current cell
Ctrl-Home, ↓	Beginning of last line in current cell
Ctrl-Home, Home, Home, ↑ Alt-Home, Home, ↑ (enhanced)	First cell in table
Ctrl-Home, Home, Home, ↓ Alt-Home, Home, ↓ (enhanced)	Last cell in table

continued

Table 10.1 *(continued)*

From inside the editor, Ctrl-Home followed by the cell designator (such as C5) moves the cursor into that cell.

Using the Table Editor

In the printed version of the Ship Traffic table, shown in Figure 10.6, the first row in the table has been joined together to form one large cell, the text inside it has been centered and boldfaced, and it has been formatted with gray shading. Also, the vertical lines in all of the rows have been removed, and the line under the second row (the column headings Ship, Arriving From, and Port/Berth) has been changed to a double line. In this section, you'll learn how to use the table editor to create these effects.

SHIP TRAFFIC

Due to arrive Friday, February 8		
Ship	**Arriving From**	**Port/Berth**
Busted Bilge	Long Beach	Oakland/67
Wake Watcher	Vancouver BC	Oakland/68
Diesel Demon	Los Angeles	SFO/38
Tidal Tramp	Long Beach	Oakland/24
Big Bertha	Long Beach	SFO/96

Figure 10.6 *For headings, you can join cells at the top of the table together to form one large cell, as shown here. Notice the gray shading effect.*

Begin by placing the cursor anywhere inside the table and then:

Keyboard: Press Columns/Tables (Alt-F7).

You should be back in the table editor. However, if the cursor was outside of table when you pressed Alt-F7, you'll see this prompt instead:

`1 Columns; 2 Tables; 3 Math: 0`

Select **Tables**, and this prompt will appear:

`Table: 1 Create;  2 Edit: 0`

Select **Edit**.

Mouse: Display the Layout menu and select **Tables**. Notice that the Create option appears in brackets. Since the cursor is already inside a table, WordPerfect does not let you use Create, as indicated by the brackets. Select **Edit**.

You should now be back in the table editor.

Using the Join Option

To combine the three cells in the top row into one large cell, block the cells and then use the Join option on the Table Edit menu:

1. With the cursor in cell A1, turn on Block by pressing Alt-F4.

   Although you can select options on the Table Edit menu with the mouse, you cannot display the pull-down menu bar while working in the table editor.

2. Move the cursor to cell C1, extending the block highlighting to the end of the row.

3. Select the Join option (7). This prompt appears:

   ```
   Join cells? No (Yes)
   ```

4. Select **Yes**.

The three cells are joined into one, and the vertical lines that separated them disappear. Next, you can use the Format option to select Center, so that when you type the text in this cell, WordPerfect will automatically center it.

> **Tip:** The Split option (8) on the main Table Edit menu is the opposite of Join. If you wanted to split cell A1 back into three cells, you could select Split, choose Columns to split it back into columns (as opposed to splitting a cell vertically into rows), and then enter the number of columns you want to split it into: 3.

Using the Format Option

There are two ways to center text in a cell: You can use the Format option on the Table Edit menu, or you can return to the Edit screen and format it in the usual way, by pressing the Center key or selecting Align Center from the pull-down Layout menu. The advantage to using the Center option inside the editor is that if you use the Insert option to create a new row from this cell, as described later, the formatting will also be transferred to the new row.

When you select Format on the Table Edit menu, you'll see that it provides many options, including some that may be familiar, such as the Font Size and Appearance menus. Table 10.2 describes all the Format options. Unlike the equivalent formatting options on the Format and Font menus, formatting text from inside the Table Edit menu does not insert hidden codes into your document. Also, you cannot use them to format a portion of the text inside a cell, such as boldfacing only one of the six words in cell A1. Any formatting that you define outside of the table editor takes priority over formatting defined in the editor, and the Format Cell options in the Table Edit menu override the Format Column options.

To center and boldface the text in cell A1:

1. Select the Format option (2) from the Table Edit menu.

   This prompt appears:

   ```
   Format: 1 Cell; 2 Column; 3 Row Height: 0
   ```

   Notice this line of information just above the menu line:

   ```
   Cell: Top;Left;Normal          Col: 6.5";Left;Normal
   ```

   Top is the cell's vertical alignment and means that if you had changed the row height to Single-line fixed or Multi-line fixed, text in this cell would be aligned against the top of the cell. Left refers to the Justification currently in use; after you select Center, this item will change to Center. Since the cell is not yet formatted with any of the Font attributes such as bold, italics, or large, the last item indicates the font is Normal. After you select Bold, this will change to Bold. The items on the right refer to the entire column (A). Since you joined the three cells together, the column width in cell A1 matches the table width: 6.5". If the cursor were in A2, B2, or C2, the column width would be 2.17". Left and Normal are the Justification type and Font attributes for the column.

 Tip: While in the table editor, you can widen a cell from inside the table editor by pressing Ctrl-Right Arrow, and reduce it by pressing Ctrl-Left Arrow.

Since you will only be centering text in the cell the cursor is currently in, use the Cell option. If you were to use Column, all columns in the table would be centered.

2. Select the first option, **Cell.**

   This menu appears:

   ```
   Cell: 1 Type; 2 Attributes; 3 Justify; 4 Vertical
   Alignment; 5 Lock: 0
   ```

3. Select the third option, **Justify.** The Justification options appear:

   ```
   Justification: 1 Left; 2 Center; 3 Right; 4 Full;
   5 Decimal Align; 6 Reset: 1
   ```

4. Select the second option, **Center.**

Table 10.2   *The Format options on the Table Edit menu.*

For an individual cell, use Format to:

Cell Type:	Select Numeric or Text for the cell type. By default, WordPerfect assumes you want all cells to be numeric, so you can use them in calculations.
Attributes:	Select Size and Appearance options for the cell: superscript, subscript, fine, small, large, very large, extra large, bold, underline, double underline, italics, outline, shadow, small caps, redline, and strikeout. You can also select Normal to turn off all attributes in the cell, so it will be formatted with the Base Font in the document, or Reset so that the cell will have the same attributes as the column.
Justification:	Change the Justification to left, center, right, full, or decimal align, or reset the justification to match the column's justification setting. The default is Left.
Vertical Alignment:	If you have changed the row height to Single-line fixed or Multi-line fixed, you can use this option to align text against the Top, Bottom, or Center of the cell. However, it only appears in the printed version and in View Document. Top is the default. WordPerfect leaves a small amount of space between the text and the top, left, and right lines in the cell. You can adjust this spacing using the Spacing Between Text and Lines option on the Table Options menu,

continued

Table 10.2   *(continued)*

	shown in Figure 10.7. To access this menu, select Options (6) on the main Table Edit menu.
Lock:	Turn the Lock feature on. This locks the contents of a cell, and prevents you from typing in it, or editing existing text. Use it to lock cells containing text such as headings or math formulas, especially in forms that someone else will be filling in, so they can't accidentally erase them. In the Edit screen, WordPerfect won't allow you to move the cursor into a locked cell (but you can still move the cursor into it and use options on the Table Edit menu). To lock a group of cells, block them first. You cannot move or copy a locked cell.

For a column, these formatting options are available:

Width:	Use this option to enter a number for the column width. Another way to change the width of a column is by pressing Ctrl-Right Arrow to widen it, or Ctrl-Left Arrow to decrease it. As you widen a column, WordPerfect may need to decrease the width of other columns to the right to accommodate the change.
Attributes:	Select Size and Appearance options for the column: superscript, subscript, fine, small, large, very large, extra large, bold, underline, double underline, italics, outline, shadow, small caps, redline, and strikeout. You can also select Normal to turn off all attributes in the cell, so it will be formatted with the Base Font in the document.
Justify:	Change the Justification for the column to left, center, right, full, or decimal align. The default is Left.
Number of Digits:	Use this option to change the number of digits that WordPerfect will display in a number that has been calculated using a math formula. The default is 2.

Row Height, the third option on the Format menu, provides four options:

Single-line fixed:	This option lets you enter a fixed number for the row height, but only lets you type one line of text in each cell in the row, regardless of the height you select. A cell formatted with this option will not expand if you type more text than can fit on a line. If you change the height to a fixed number, the row does not appear different on the Edit screen, but does in the printed version and in View Document.
Single-line automatic:	This option permits only one line of text in each cell in the row, and calculates the row height automatically, according to the font in use. Like the Single Line Fixed option, a cell formatted with this option will not expand if you type more text than can fit on a line, and actual row height can only be seen in the printed version or View Document.
Multi-line fixed:	Use this option to select a fixed row height, but type more than one line of text in each cell in the row. A warning: If you type too much text in a cell to fit within the fixed row height you've selected, it will not appear in the printed version, even though you can see it on the Edit screen. Check View Document before printing to see if you need to expand the row height.
Multi-line automatic:	This is the default for row height. If allows you to type multiple lines in a cell, and prints all of them. The row height expands to accommodate the largest cell in the row.
	To change the height for several rows, block them first, then select Row Height.

Notice that all the cells in the first two rows are formatted in bold. Although you can format the cells individually, the fastest method is to block them first, and then select Bold. Start with the cursor in cell A1:

1. Turn on Block by pressing Alt-F4.

2. Move the cursor down to extend the block highlighting to cells A2, B2, and C2.

3. Select the Format option, and then select **Cell**.

4. Select the second option, **Attributes**. This menu appears:

   `1 Size; 2 Appearance; 3 Normal; 4 Reset; 0`

5. Select the second option, **Appearance**.

   This menu appears, with nine Appearance options:

   `1 Bold 2 Undln 3 Dbl Und 4 Italc 5 Outln 6 Shadw 7 Sm Cap`
   `8 Redln 9 Stkout: 0`

   When you format a cell using one of these options, all text in the cell will be affected. If you only wanted to format a portion of the text in a cell, such as one word, you would have to exit the Table Edit menu and use the regular method of boldfacing text: the Bold key or the Appearance option on the Font menu.

6. Select the first option, **Bold**.

   The highlighting disappears, and the text in row 2 now appears in bold.

Gray Shading

To create the shading effect in cell A1, as shown in Figure 10.6, use the Shade option on the Lines menu. The gray shading will only show up in the printed version.

1. Move the cursor to A1, and select the third option, **Lines**.

   This menu appears, providing options that you can use to change the lines that border this cell (A1):

   `Lines: 1 Left; 2 Right; 3 Top; 4 Bottom; 5 Inside;`
   `6 Outside; 7 All; 8 Shade: 0`

   The line just above the menu indicates which type of line is being used to form the border of each side of this cell (A1):

   `Top=Double; Left=Double; Bottom=None; Right=Double`

   The lines on the top, left, and right are Double, and there is no line on the bottom. You may be wondering about the Bottom border. Although there is a line below cell A1, it is considered the top line for cells A2, B2, and C2. If you were to place the cursor in cell A2 and select Lines, you would see that it does not have a bottom line either, because the line below it is considered the top line for cell A3. Also, cell A2 does not have a line on the right, because the line separating it from cell B2 is considered the left line of B2.

2. Select the eighth option, **Shade**. This menu appears:

   `Shading: 1 On; 2 Off: 0`

3. Select the first option, **On**.

   The cell number on the status line (A1) changes to reverse video. However, gray shading will only show up in the printed version of the document and in View Document, where it usually appears as a series of dots. Initially gray shading is set to 10%. If you find after printing the document that this is too light or dark, you can change the percentage of black using the Options selection (6) on the Table Edit menu. This leads to the Table Options menu, shown in Figure 10.7; Gray Shading is the fourth option.

   You are now ready to return to the Edit screen, and enter the text in cell A1.

```
Table Options

        1 - Spacing Between Text and Lines
                  Left                    0.083"
                  Right                   0.083"
                  Top                     0.1"
                  Bottom                  0"

        2 - Display Negative Results      1
                  1 = with minus signs
                  2 = with parentheses

        3 - Position of Table             Left

        4 - Gray Shading (% of black)     10




    Selection: g
```

Figure 10.7   *To change the percentage of gray shading, select option 6 (Options) on the Table Edit menu, and then select the Gray Shading option (4). To darken it, enter a larger number such as 25%. To lighten it, use a smaller number such as 5%.*

4. To return to the Edit screen,

   Keyboard: Press Exit (F7).

   Mouse: Click the right button.

5. Press Enter to insert a blank line, and then type the heading in cell A1:

   `Due to arrive Friday, February 8.`

Notice that WordPerfect centers and boldfaces the text automatically, as you type it.

6. Press Enter to insert another blank line below the heading.

Removing the Vertical Lines

To remove the vertical lines separating the three columns, use the Lines option on the Table Edit menu. The vertical lines separating column A (Ship) from column B (Arriving From) are actually the left lines in column B, and the ones separating column B from column C are the left lines in column C.

1. Place the cursor in cell B2 and select the table editor:

    Keyboard: Press Columns/Tables (Alt-F7).

    Mouse: Display the **L**ayout menu and select **T**ables, then **E**dit.

2. Block the entire column by pressing Block (Alt-F4), then moving the cursor and highlighting down to cell B7.

3. Select the third option on the Table Edit menu, **L**ines.

4. Select the first option, **L**eft.

5. Select the first option from the next menu, **N**one.

    Now repeat these steps to remove the lines that represent the left border of column C.

6. Start with the cursor in C2, and block the entire column by pressing Block (Alt-F4), then moving the cursor and highlighting down to cell C7.

7. Select the third option on the Table Edit menu, **L**ines.

8. Select the first option, **L**eft; then select **N**one from the next menu.

This removes all the vertical lines from inside the table. Next, use the Lines option to change the line under the second row to a double line.

Tip: To remove all horizontal and vertical lines inside the table, leaving only the box around it: Bring up the table editor, place the cursor in the first cell, turn on Block and highlight all the rest of the cells, and then select Lines, Inside, and None.

Changing the Type of Line

Since the second row contains the column headings, you may want to differentiate it from the data in the rows below with a double line. Since what appears to be the line below row 2 is actually the top line of row 3, start with the cursor in A3.

1. With the cursor in cell A3, turn on Block and move the cursor and block highlighting to C3.

   You can use Go To to move to cell C3, by pressing Ctrl-Home and entering C3.

2. Select the Lines option (3) from the menu.

3. Select Top (3), and then select Double (3).

Expanding the Table to Include Additional Rows

To increase the number of rows or columns in a table, you can use the table editor's Size option. In this section, you'll learn how to add more rows to the table, as shown in Figure 10.8, and then use the Move key to copy the two rows of headings. Two steps are involved:

1. Increase the size of the table to 12 rows.

2. Copy the first row, Cell A1, and insert it above row 8, and copy the second row and insert it above row 9. You can later return to the Edit screen and edit the text in the copied cells.

Using the Size Option in the Table Editor

To expand the table, begin with the cursor anywhere in the table and bring up the Table Edit menu.

1. Select the first option on the Table Edit menu, Size.

This prompt appears:

```
Table Size: 1 Rows; 2 Columns: 0
```

SHIP TRAFFIC

Due to arrive Friday, February 8		
Ship	**Arriving From**	**Port/Berth**
Busted Bilge	Long Beach	Oakland/67
Wake Watcher	Vancouver BC	Oakland/68
Diesel Demon	Los Angeles	SFO/38
Tidal Tramp	Long Beach	Oakland/24
Big Bertha	Long Beach	SFO/96
Due to depart Friday, February 8		
Ship	**Destination**	**Port/Berth**
Itsgone Valdez	Tokyo	Oak/22
Pacific Slug	Mexico	SFO/P8OE
Alaskan Queen	Tacoma	Oak/23
Kon Tiki	Panama	Oak/34
Bow First	Japan	SFO/P8OB

Figure 10.8 To create more rows in the table, you can use the Size option on the Table Edit menu.

2. Select the first option, **R**ows. This prompt appears:

```
Number of Rows: 7
```

It shows the current number of rows in the table. Since you will be using copy to create the two rows of headings later, you only need to expand it to 12 rows.

3. Type 12 and press Enter.

WordPerfect adds the extra rows above the cursor, as shown in Figure 10.9. The cursor should be in the last row.

```
┌─────────────────────────────────────────────────────────────────────────┐
│ Ship                 Arriving From       Port/Berth                       ║
│                                                                           ║
│ Busted Bilge         Long Beach          Oakland/67                       ║
│                                                                           ║
│ Wake Watcher         Vancouver BC        Oakland/68                       ║
│                                                                           ║
│ Diesel Demon         Los Angeles         SFO/38                           ║
│                                                                           ║
│ Tidal Tramp          Long Beach          Oakland/24                       ║
│                                                                           ║
│ Big Bertha           Long Beach          SFO/96                           ║
│                                                                           ║
│                                                                           ║
│                                                                           ║
│                                                                           ║
│                                                                           ║
│                                                                           ║
│ ▄▄▄▄▄▄▄▄▄▄▄▄                                                               ║
│ Table Edit:  Press Exit when done         Cell A12 Doc 1 Pg 1 Ln 5.24" Pos 1.12"│
└─────────────────────────────────────────────────────────────────────────┘
 Ctrl-Arrows Column Widths; Ins Insert; Del Delete; Move Move/Copy;
 1 Size; 2 Format; 3 Lines; 4 Header; 5 Math; 6 Options; 7 Join; 8 Split: 0
```

Figure 10.9 *After you use the Size option to increase the number of rows in the table, it should appear as shown here.*

Using the Move Key to Copy a Row

When you use the Copy option, it will copy both the cell, its formatting and other options (lines), and text.

To copy the first row and its heading and insert it above row 8:

1. Move the cursor into A1; then press the Move key (Ctrl-F4).

   This prompt appears:

   `Move: 1 Block; 2 Row; 3 Column; 4 Retrieve: 0`

2. Select the second option, **Row**. This prompt appears next:

   `1 Move: 2 Copy; 3 Delete: 0`

3. Select the second option, Copy.

   The `Updating table` prompt appears briefly. After that, this prompt appears above the double line, telling you what to do next:

   `Move cursor; press Enter to retrieve.`

4. Move the cursor down to cell A8, and press Enter.

   WordPerfect copies the cell to the new location. Your screen should now resemble Figure 10.10.

```
                  Due to arrive Friday, February 8

 Ship                   Arriving From         Port/Berth

 Busted Bilge           Long Beach            Oakland/67

 Wake Watcher           Vancouver BC          Oakland/68

 Diesel Demon           Los Angeles           SFO/38

 Tidal Tramp            Long Beach            Oakland/24

 Big Bertha             Long Beach            SFO/96

              Due to arrive Friday, February 8


 Table Edit:  Press Exit when done          Cell ▓▓ Doc 1 Pg 1 Ln 4.04" Pos 4.25"

 Ctrl-Arrows Column Widths; Ins Insert; Del Delete; Move Move/Copy;
 1 Size; 2 Format; 3 Lines; 4 Header; 5 Math; 6 Options; 7 Join; 8 Split: 0
```

Figure 10.10   *After you use the Move key to copy cell A1, WordPerfect copies the text, formatting, and other options that you used in the original cell, such as the type of lines that formed the borders.*

Repeat these steps to copy the second row. Since the text is nearly identical, it will save you some formatting steps (the text will already be boldfaced).

1. Move the cursor into A2, then press the Move key (Ctrl-F4).

2. Select **R**ow and then **C**opy.

   The Move cursor; press Enter to retrieve prompt appears.

3. Move the cursor to A9, and then press Enter.

   WordPerfect copies the cells and their text, inserting it above row 9 (so it becomes row 9). Notice that WordPerfect did not copy the double line below the headings, since it was actually the top line of the next row. To create the double line:

4. Move the cursor into A10, press Block (Alt F4), and move the cursor and block highlighting into C10.

5. Select **L**ines (3), then **T**op (3), then **D**ouble (3).

6. Press Exit to return to the Edit menu, and then modify the text in these cells:

   In A8, change *arrive* to *depart.*

   In B9, change *Arriving From* to *Destination.*

7. Type the remaining data in cells A10 through C15, as shown in Figure 10.8; then save the document again under the same name, *SHIPS.TBL.*

Using the Move Key to Move a Row

Now that you've saved the final version of the table, you may want to experiment with some of the other options on the Table Edit menu. For example, if you found out that the Alaskan Queen was actually arriving, not departing, you could use the Move key to move it up into the Arriving section of the table.

1. Place the cursor anywhere in row 12, bring up the Table Edit menu, and press the Move key (Ctrl-F4).

2. Select the second option, **R**ow.

3. Select the first option, **M**ove.

    An `Updating table` prompt appears, and then the text from the row appears to be erased. The `Move cursor; press Enter to retrieve` prompt appears just above the double line, telling you what to do next.

4. Move the cursor up to row 7.

5. To complete the move, press Enter.

    The row is inserted above what was row 7 (Big Bertha), and now becomes row 7.

Inserting and Deleting Rows and Columns in the Table Editor

You may have noticed this prompt above the menu line in the table editor:

```
Ctrl-Arrows Column Widths; Ins Insert; Del Delete;
Move Move/Copy;
```

It serves to remind you that these keys function differently when you are using the table editor: The Ctrl-Arrow keys widen or contract a column, Ins (Insert) inserts rows or columns, Del (Delete) deletes rows or columns, and Move moves or copies rows or columns. In the previous section, you learned how to use the Move key to copy rows. In this section, you'll explore two of the other options, Insert and Delete.

Inserting Rows and Columns

In a previous section, you added several rows in your table using the Size option, and learned that this option inserts rows at the bottom of the table. If you wanted to insert an additional row into the first section of the table, for an arriving ship, it would be easier to use the Insert option on the Table Edit menu. This method inserts rows above the cursor, and inserts columns to the left of the cursor.

When creating the new rows or columns, WordPerfect copies the structure and formatting from the current cell (if you selected the formatting through the Table Edit menu). For instance, if you were to insert a row above the first one in the Ships table, the cell would fill the entire row, as A1 does, and would include gray shading. If you were to exit the table editor and type text in the new cell, it would be formatted with bold and center.

To insert one or more rows above the cursor, begin with the cursor in row 2.

1. From inside the table editor, press the Ins key (Insert) once. This prompt appears:

   ```
   Insert: 1 Rows; 2 Columns: 0
   ```

2. Select the first option, **Rows**. This prompt appears:

   ```
   Number of Rows: 1
   ```

   WordPerfect assumes you only want to insert one row above the cursor, suggesting 1 as the default.

3. Enter the number of rows you want to insert, or press Enter to insert 1.

   WordPerfect immediately inserts the blank row (or rows) above the cursor.

To insert one or more columns to the left of the cursor, begin with the cursor in B2.

1. Press the Ins key (Insert) once.

2. Select the second option, **Columns**. This prompt appears:

   ```
   Number of columns: 1
   ```

   WordPerfect suggests 1 as the default.

3. Enter the number of columns you want to insert, or press Enter to insert only 1.

WordPerfect immediately inserts the blank column (or columns) left of the cursor. Since it is a copy of the column the cursor was in, if you were to insert a column while the cursor was in A1 of the Ship Traffic table, it would copy the entire table. A1 contains all three columns: A, B, and C.

 Tip: To insert one or more rows or columns into a table, bring up the Table Edit menu and press Insert. Select 1 for Rows or 2 for Columns; then enter the number of rows or columns you want to insert. Rows are inserted above the cursor, and columns are inserted to the left of the cursor.

Deleting Rows and Columns

To delete a row or column, use the Delete (Del) key in the table editor. It is similar to the Insert option.

To delete a row or column from inside the table editor:

1. Place the cursor anywhere in the row or column.

2. Press the Delete (Del) key. This prompt appears:

   `Delete: 1 Rows; 2 Columns: 0`

3. Select **Rows** to erase one or more rows, or **Columns** to erase one or more columns.

   This prompt appears if you selected Rows:

   `Number of Rows: 1`

   If you selected Columns, this prompt appears:

   `Number of Columns: 1`

   In both cases, WordPerfect suggests 1 as the default, assuming you only want to delete the row or column where the cursor is currently located.

4. Enter the number of rows or columns you want to delete, or press Enter to delete only the current one.

If you are deleting rows and enter 2 or more, WordPerfect deletes the current row and the rows below. If you are deleting columns and enter 2 or more, WordPerfect deletes the current column and the columns to the right.

If you have an enhanced keyboard, you can also insert or delete rows from the Edit screen, without bringing up the table editor. To delete a row, place the cursor anywhere in the row, and press Ctrl-Del (Delete). This prompt will appear:

```
Delete Row? No (Yes)
```

Select **Yes**, and WordPerfect will erase the row. To insert a row, place the cursor anywhere in the row, and press Ctrl-Ins (Insert). WordPerfect will automatically insert a row above the cursor, without further prompting.

Tip: To restore rows or columns right after you delete them in the Table Edit menu, press the Cancel key (F1) and type Y in response to the Undelete Row(s)? or Undelete Column(s)? prompt.

Tip: To delete a row or column, place the cursor anywhere in the row or column, bring up the Table Edit menu, and press the Delete key. Select 1 for rows or 2 for columns; then enter the number of rows or columns you want to delete.

Deleting the Table Structure, Text, or Both

WordPerfect provides several options for deleting your table. You can delete the entire table and all text in it, delete only the text and leave the structure, or delete the structure and leave the text. It all depends on where the cursor is positioned when you use the Delete option.

To delete an entire table, including the text it contains:

1. Use Reveal Codes to locate the Table Definition code that WordPerfect created when you defined the table, and place the cursor on the code:

   ```
   [Tbl Def:I;3,2.17",2.17",2.17"]
   ```

   If you don't include the Table Definition code in this block, WordPerfect will delete the text inside the table and leave the table structure, as shown in Figure 10.11.

2. Turn on Block and then extend the block highlighting below the last cell in the table.

3. Press the Delete or Backspace key, and select **Yes** in response to the Delete Block prompt.

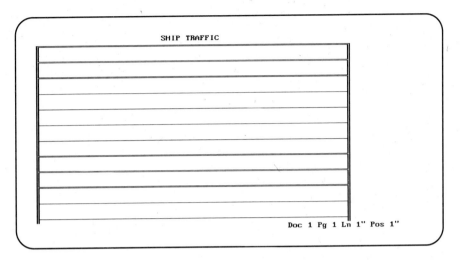

Figure 10.11   *To delete an entire table, you must block it all and include the Table Definition code in the block. If you don't include the code, WordPerfect will delete the text inside the table, but leave the table structure, as shown here.*

This should delete the entire table. If you change your mind, you can bring it back using the Undelete option (F1, R, or Undelete Restore on the pull-down Edit menu).

To delete the text from your table, but leave the table structure intact, as shown in Figure 10.11:

1. Place the cursor one position past the Table Definition code.

2. Turn on Block, and then extend the block highlighting below the last cell in the table.

3. Press the Delete or Backspace key, and select **Yes** in response to the `Delete Block` prompt.

Another method you can use to delete all the text is to place the cursor in the first cell, press Ctrl-PgDn, and type Y in response to the `Delete Remainder of page?` prompt. (But this also deletes any other text on the page that may not be in the table.)

To delete the table structure, but leave the text:

1. Place the cursor on the Table Definition code in Reveal Codes.

2. Press Delete.

This removes the table structure, including all the lines, and leaves only the text. It also converts the [Row] codes into [HRt] codes (hard returns), and the [Cell] codes into [Tab] codes. For example, if you delete the Table Definition code from the Ship Traffic table, the three columns (`Ship`, `Arriving From`, and `Port/Berth`) will be separated by one tab stop each, as shown in the Reveal Codes section of Figure 10.12. To spread the columns out, you can change the tab stop settings. Figure 10.13 shows how the columns will appear if you erase the old tab stop settings and set new ones every 2", starting at 2".

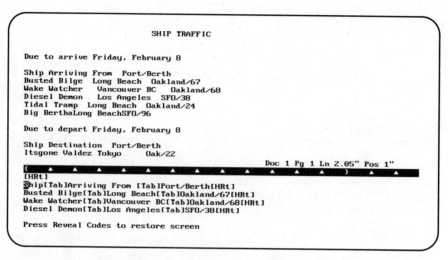

Figure 10.12   *If you delete the Table Definition code from a document, WordPerfect leaves the text, separating it with tabs. You may need to change the tab stops to spread the columns out. In Figure 10.13, they were changed to every 2".*

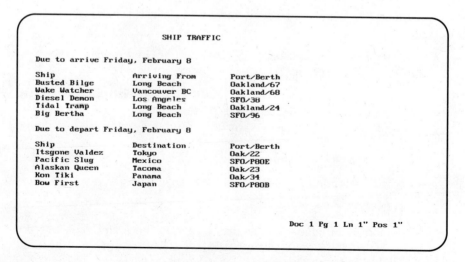

Figure 10.13   *The Ship Traffic table after erasing the Table Definition code and changing the tab stop settings to every 2".*

Simulating Parallel Text Columns

If you studied Chapter 8, you learned how to use the Columns feature to create parallel columns like the ones shown in Figure 8.2. You can use the Tables feature to create the same effect as parallel text columns, by removing all the lines inside and outside the cells, and tables are easier to use. In fact, while Figure 10.14 appears identical to Figure 8.2, it was created using Tables instead of Parallel Columns. To learn how, follow the instructions in the upcoming steps.

If you've already typed the example in Figure 8.2, you don't have to retype all the text, because WordPerfect lets you create a table from existing parallel columns, or from columns created with tabs. A later section, "Creating a Table from Text in Parallel Columns," explains this procedure.

1. Clear the screen, and center and type the two-line heading:

    CUDDLY'S USED PET SHOP
    WEEKLY SPECIALS

2. Create a table:

    Keyboard: Press the Columns/Tables key (Alt-F7) and select the second option, **Tables**; then select the first option, **Create**.

    Mouse: Display the Layout menu and select **Tables**, then **Create**.

3. Enter 2 for the number of columns, and 7 for the number of rows.

    Once you press Enter, the table structure appears, with the cursor in A1. WordPerfect creates columns of equal width, but the ones in Figure 10.14 are uneven. To change the column widths:

4. Decrease the width of the first column by pressing Ctrl-Left Arrow five times.

 Tip: One advantage of converting parallel columns into tables is that you can then move or copy entire columns, by using the Move key inside the Table Edit menu. Another advantage is that you can use footnotes inside a table, but not in parallel columns.

5. Move the cursor into cell A2, and widen the column by pressing Ctrl-Right Arrow five times.

6. Exit from the table editor to the Edit screen:

Keyboard: Press Exit (F7).

Mouse: Click the right button.

CUDDLY'S USED PET SHOP

WEEKLY SPECIALS

FREDDIE
Three year old boa
constrictor.

Freddie is house trained. Great for the person on the go, with rodent problem or neighbor with small, obnoxious dog.

ANGEL
Five year old Siberian
Husky male.

Angel also answers to "MUSH". He prefers air conditioning or colder climates. Steady worker, low mileage and never raced, must be seen to be appreciated.

DOODLEDO
One year old banti
rooster.

Doodledo answers to any name. Known to be an early riser, excellent with kids and would make ideal dinner guest. PRICE REDUCTION!

SQUEEK
A rare 6 month old
Hungarian mouse.

Squeek is rust colored, with a medium length coat. He was raised from championship blood lines. A real show stopper! Must be sold separately from Freddie.

YANG
Fifteen year old male
Siamese cat.

Yang eats little, quiet and hardly moves. Speaks some Chinese (MOW). Excellent choice for mauve interiors. CLOSEOUT! CALL FOR PRICE QUOTE

THUD
Adorable male Indian
elephant.

Thud weighs slightly over 4,000 lbs, needs loving family with large yard or small forest. Cheap to Keep! (fluctuates with peanut prices)

Figure 10.14   Parallel columns created with WordPerfect's Tables feature. They appear to be identical to the columns in Figure 8.2, which were created using the Columns feature.

7. Select Bold using the Bold key or Bold option on the Font Appearance menu, and type the first line in cell A1:

   ```
   FREDDIE
   ```

8. Turn off Bold, press Enter, and then type the rest of the paragraph:

   ```
   Three year old boa constrictor.
   ```

9. Move the cursor to cell B1 and type this paragraph:

   ```
   Freddie is house trained.  Great for the person on the go,
   with rodent problem or neighbor with small, obnoxious dog.
   ```

10. Move the cursor to cell A2, and enter the next paragraph:

    ```
    ANGEL
    Five year old Siberian Husky male.
    ```

11. Repeat these steps until you have entered all of the data shown in Figure 10.14; then save the table using this name: *PETS.TBL.*

Removing All Grid Lines from the Table

Since parallel columns usually don't have lines around them, you can use the Lines option on the Table Edit menu to remove all the grid lines.

1. Bring up the Table Edit menu:

   Keyboard: Place the cursor anywhere in the table, and press Columns/Tables (Alt-F7).

   Mouse: Display the Layout menu and select **Tables**, then **Edit**.

2. Place the cursor in cell A1, and turn on Block by pressing Alt-F4.

3. Use PgDn to move the cursor to the last cell in the table.

4. Select the Lines option (3), and then select the seventh option, **All**.

   The next menu displays the options for line type: None, Single, Double, Dashed, Dotted, Thick, and Extra Thick.

5. Select the first option, **None**.

   All the lines disappear from your table. Once you exit back to the Edit screen, it should be indistinguishable from the parallel columns in Figure 8.2.

6. Exit back to the Edit menu, and save the table again using the same name, *PETS.TBL.*

Creating a Table from Text in Parallel Columns

If you've already created the Pet Shop columns shown in Figure 8.2, clear the screen and retrieve it, and then follow these steps to convert it into a table:

1. Place the cursor in the line below WEEKLY SPECIALS.

2. Turn on Block mode, and move the cursor to the end of the document, extending the block highlighting to the last line.

3. Create a table:

    Keyboard: Press Columns/Tables (Alt-F7), and select **Tables**, then **Create**.

    Mouse: Display the **Layout** menu, select **Tables**, and then select **Create**.

    This prompt appears:

    Create Table from: 1 Tabular Column: 2 Parallel Column: 0

4. Select the second option, **Parallel Column**.

    WordPerfect creates the table, and places you in the table editor. Next, erase the lines from your new table.

5. Place the cursor in cell A1, turn on Block by pressing Alt-F4, and move the cursor to the last cell in the second column of the table.

6. Select the **Lines** option (3), and then select the seventh option, **All**.

    The next menu displays the options for line type: None, Single, Double, Dashed, Dotted, Thick, and Extra Thick.

7. Select the first option, **None**.

    All the lines disappear from your table. Once you return to the Edit screen, it should look like the parallel columns in Figure 8.2.

8. Exit to the Edit screen, and save the table.

    You could use a similar procedure to create a table from data that is formatted using one of the tab options, such as the tab key, the Tab Align key, or decimal tabs created through the Math feature. The only difference is in the fourth step, where you select Tabular Column instead of Parallel Column. Also, before turning on Block, be careful to position the cursor on or past the Tab Set code, if there is one in the document.

Tip: If you want to place a table into newspaper or parallel columns, place two or more tables next to each other, or wrap text around a table, you can create a table inside of a graphics box. Use any of the box types on the Graphics menu, such as a Figure box, Table box, or Text box. See Chapter 14 for more information about graphics.

Creating Header Rows for Multiple-Page Tables

WordPerfect's tables can span a page break and are split at a row border, never in the middle of a row. If your table will be one or more pages long, you can create a header for it from one or more of the rows in your table. For instance, if you select one row for the header, the first row in the table will become the header on all subsequent pages. If you select two, the first two rows will appear as the header. These header rows are not visible in the Edit screen (except the original rows that they were created from), but they will print at the top of every page in the table, and you can use View Document to preview them. Header rows are designated by an asterisk next to the cell number on the status line, such as: A1*.

To create a header for a table that spans more than one page:

1. Place the cursor anywhere in the table, and bring up the Table Edit menu.

2. Select the fourth option on the menu, **Header**. This prompt appears:

    ```
    Number of header rows: 0
    ```

3. Enter the number of rows you want to use as the header.

WordPerfect will count rows from the top of the table. For example, if you enter 2 for the number of rows, the first two rows will be used. If you enter 1, only the first row will be used.

To see the header rows, either print the document or use View Document.

Spreadsheet Import

If you use Lotus, PlanPerfect, Microsoft Excel, Quattro, or Quattro Pro, you can import data from any of your spreadsheet files, and WordPerfect will automatically format it into a table.

There are some limitations to this feature. WordPerfect tables can contain a maximum of 32 columns; If you try to import more from the spreadsheet file, you'll receive an error message, and the extra cells will be omitted from the new table. Although you can import a spreadsheet into an existing table, it will erase any text in the table, so it should have enough blank cells to contain the ones you are importing. You may find it easier to let WordPerfect create the table automatically, when importing the spreadsheet.

To import data from a spreadsheet and create a new table:

1. To select Spreadsheet Import, begin by:

    Keyboard: Pressing the Text In/Out key (Ctrl-F5).

    Mouse: Displaying the File menu and selecting Text In.

2. Next, select the Spreadsheet option.

3. From the next menu, select the first option, **Import**. The Spreadsheet: Import menu appears, as shown in Figure 10.15.

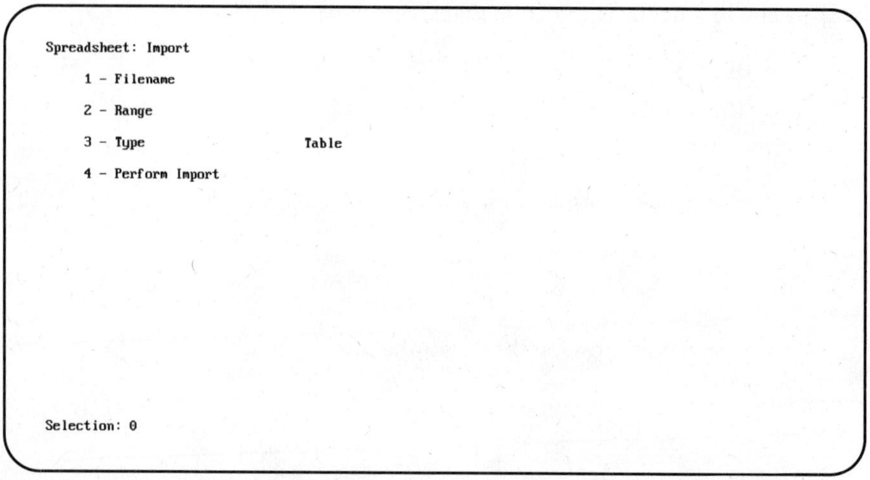

```
Spreadsheet: Import

    1 - Filename

    2 - Range

    3 - Type              Table

    4 - Perform Import








Selection: 0
```

Figure 10.15   *The Spreadsheet: Import menu. You can use this menu to retrieve a spreadsheet file, or a range of cells from a file, and WordPerfect will format it into a table.*

4. Select the first option, **Filename**, and then enter the name of the file you want to import. You can press List (F5) to retrieve it from the List Files menu.

5. If you want to import a range instead of the entire spreadsheet, select the **Range** option (2), and enter the range of cells to import. If you used named ranges in the spreadsheet, press List (F5). A list of named ranges will appear in a box, as shown in Figure 10.16, and you can move the cursor bar onto one and press Enter to select it.

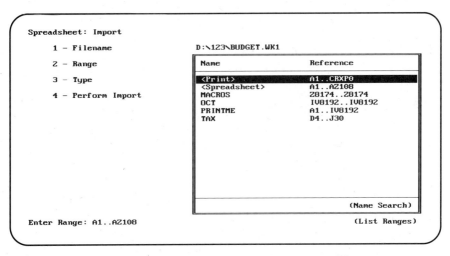

Figure 10.16 *Selecting a range of cells to import from a spreadsheet.*

6. Select the fourth option, **Perform Import**.

An `Importing Spreadsheet` prompt will appear, and then WordPerfect retrieves the spreadsheet data, converting the cells into table format. Once it is in table format, you can use it like any other WordPerfect table.

If you will be making changes to the spreadsheet and want to be able to update the WordPerfect table to reflect the latest changes, you can use the Create Link option on the Spreadsheet menu, instead of the Import option. This method treats the spreadsheet as a dynamic element, and lets you update the WordPerfect table after making changes to the linked spreadsheet through your spreadsheet program. For more information, see *Spreadsheet* in Part Three, "Command Reference."

Using Math in Tables

You have probably noticed the Math option on the main Table Edit menu, which is the key to incorporating mathematical formulas into your tables. It lets you use the same math operators that you studied in Chapter 9: + for addition, – for subtraction, * for multiplication, / for division, + for subtotals, = for totals, and * for grand totals. In tables, WordPerfect can calculate values using numbers in other cells in the table, alone or in combination with fixed numbers, or calculate subtotals, totals, and grand totals.

For example, Figure 10.17 shows a table of key interest rates such as the Prime Rate and Discount Rate, showing how much each has changed since a year earlier. The last column, Percent Change, is a formula that subtracts the Year Earlier column from the Annual % Rate column, divides by the Year Earlier column, and then multiplies by 100 to convert the result to a percent. The resulting calculation indicates that the Prime Rate has decreased 13.04%, the Discount Rate has remained the same, the Federal Funds Rate has decreased 17.71%, etc.

The columns in this table are as follows:

Column A is the name of the interest rate.

Column B is the Annual % rate statistic.

Column C is the Year Earlier statistic.

Column D is the formula for Percent Change.

and the formula in column D is (for row 4):

```
B4-C4/C4*100
```

Notice that WordPerfect calculates the formula from left to right, and does not multiply and divide first as you might have expected. Instead, the first operation is B4 – C4, and that result is divided by C4, then multiplied by 100. You can change the calculation order by typing parentheses, so WordPerfect will perform the operations in the parentheses first. If you define a formula incorrectly, two question marks will appear in the cell. This may mean that the formula refers to a cell that does not exist.

Incidentally, the graphic image in Figure 10.17 was created in DrawPerfect and placed at the top of the table for visual interest. See Chapter 14, "Graphics," to learn how it was done.

If you've read this far in the chapter, you already have all the skills needed to create this table, and enter the data in columns A, B, and C. Note that the first row contains the headings, Annual % rate, Year Earlier, and Percent Change. The lines bordering the cells in the first row were all set to None. The last row has a Single line for the Top setting, and a Double line for the Bottom setting. The remaining rows inside the table have a Single line at the Top, and the other border lines are all set to None. The Format Cell menu in the table editor was used to set Justification to Decimal Alignment in the numeric columns, B, C, and D.

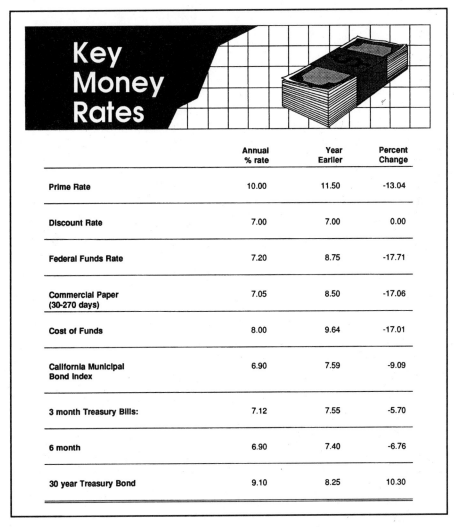

	Annual % rate	Year Earlier	Percent Change
Prime Rate	10.00	11.50	-13.04
Discount Rate	7.00	7.00	0.00
Federal Funds Rate	7.20	8.75	-17.71
Commercial Paper (30-270 days)	7.05	8.50	-17.06
Cost of Funds	8.00	9.64	-17.01
California Municipal Bond Index	6.90	7.59	-9.09
3 month Treasury Bills:	7.12	7.55	-5.70
6 month	6.90	7.40	-6.76
30 year Treasury Bond	9.10	8.25	10.30

Figure 10.17   *In this table, a math formula was used to calculate the last column, Percent Change.*

To enter the formula in column D:

1. Bring up the Table Edit menu, and place the cursor in the *Prime Rate* row of column D.

2. Select the fifth option, **Math**.

This prompt will appear at the bottom of the screen:

```
Math: 1 Calculate; 2 Formula; 3 Copy Formula; 4 +; 5 =;
6 *: 0
```

3. Select the second option, Formula. This prompt appears:

```
Enter formula:
```

4. Type this formula, and then press Enter (assuming you are in row 2; otherwise, change the cell numbers to match the row, such as B3 or B4):

```
B2-C2/C2*100
```

WordPerfect should calculate the number as soon as you press Enter. Instead of typing the formula in each of the remaining rows, you can use the Copy Formula option to copy it.

5. Select the Math option again; then select the Copy Formula option (3).

This prompt will appear:

```
Copy Formula To: 1 Cell; 2 Down; 3 Right: 0
```

You will be copying the formula down, to the next eight rows.

6. Select the second option, Down.

This prompt will appear:

```
Number of times to copy formula: 1
```

7. Type 8 and press Enter.

WordPerfect then copies your formula, and calculates it in each cell.

As you move the cursor into these cells, the formula will appear above the double line on the left side of the screen, preceded by an equal sign (=). Also, when you exit the table editor, you'll see that when the cursor is in a cell with a formula, the formula appears on the left side of the status line.

Note that the negative numbers are displayed with a minus sign. If you prefer, you can change the display so that they are surrounded by parentheses. To do this, select Options on the Table Edit menu (6), and the menu in Figure 10.7 appears. Select the Display Negative Results option (2), and change it to 2, With Parentheses.

You may wish to use the Lock option on the Format Cell menu to prevent anyone from changing the formulas in these cells. To do this:

1. Start with the cursor in the first cell containing a formula, turn on Block, and highlight the entire column.

2. Select the Format option (2).

3. Select Cell (1).

4. Select Lock (5), and then select On (1).

Updating the Formulas

If you change any of the numbers in columns B or C, you must enter the Table Edit menu and recalculate the formulas. To do this:

1. Bring up the Table Edit menu.

2. Select **Math (5)**.

3. Select the first option, Calculate.

   WordPerfect will recalculate all the formulas and display the new numbers.

MERGE

Everyone receives form letters. Although the concept has a negative connotation, and we throw most of the form letters we get in the trash without even opening them, they can be both useful and necessary. In fact, you probably read them without even thinking about the fact that they are form letters. For example, you might receive a letter informing you that your adjustable-rate mortgage has been changed and your monthly payments will be lower; that you have received a full scholarship and been accepted into a prestigious university; that your credit card limit has been increased because you are such a responsible consumer; or that you are receiving an extra dividend from one of your stocks. All happy news that you would not dream of tossing out!

WordPerfect's merge feature makes it easy to create form letters, combining information from two or more sources to create a series of documents that appear to be personalized for each recipient. For example, you can merge a standard form letter with a list of names, addresses, and other variable information, and WordPerfect will produce a personalized letter for each individual. You can then create labels or envelopes from the list, without retyping the names and addresses. For documents such as memos, where you just want to fill out a form, print it, and then clear the screen, you don't even need to maintain the variable information in a file. Instead, you can use merge to bring up the form, and WordPerfect will automatically move the cursor to the blank positions where you need to fill out the information.

Using Merge to Create Form Letters

In this section, you will learn how to use WordPerfect's merge feature to create the form letters shown in Figure 11.1. It involves creating two related files, a primary file and a secondary file. The *primary* file is a template for the form, whether it be a letter, envelope, mailing label, invoice, memo, or phone list. The *secondary* file contains the actual names, addresses, phone numbers, and any other variable information you want to maintain, and can be compared to a Rolodex file. Both files include special merge codes to represent and distinguish information such as name and address. When you merge the primary and secondary files, WordPerfect will create a letter for each set of data, inserting information from the secondary file in positions designated by codes in the primary file.

March 1, 1991

Joe Brown
25 Cabrillo Blvd.
Larkspur, CA 93212

Dear Joe,

Our records indicate that Striker is due for his rabies shot.

For your convenience, we have scheduled an appointment for Striker on March 10, at 10 a.m.. If this is not convenient for you, please call us as soon as possible to schedule another appointment.

We look forward to seeing you and Striker again.

Sincerely,

The Marin K-9 Clinic

March 1, 1991

Maryanne Schwartz
1201 Grand Ave
Novato, CA 94947

Dear Maryanne,

Our records indicate that Muffin is due for her distemper shot.

For your convenience, we have scheduled an appointment for Muffin on March 11, at 4:30 p.m.. If this is not convenient for you, please call us as soon as possible to schedule another appointment.

We look forward to seeing you and Muffin again.

Sincerely,

The Marin K-9 Clinic

March 1, 1991

Alan Raymond
55 Calvin Ave.
Petaluma, CA 94965

Dear Alan,

Our records indicate that Diesel is due for his corona shot.

For your convenience, we have scheduled an appointment for Diesel on March 18, at 5 p.m.. If this is not convenient for you, please call us as soon as possible to schedule another appointment.

We look forward to seeing you and Diesel again.

Sincerely,

The Marin K-9 Clinic

March 1, 1991

Annie Larkin
310 Green St.
Mill Valley, CA 93211

Dear Annie,

Our records indicate that Boswell is due for his parvo shot.

For your convenience, we have scheduled an appointment for Boswell on March 15, at 11 a.m.. If this is not convenient for you, please call us as soon as possible to schedule another appointment.

We look forward to seeing you and Boswell again.

Sincerely,

The Marin K-9 Clinic

Figure 11.1 *You can use WordPerfect's Merge feature to create these form letters without typing each one individually. Instead, you type the standard text in a form called a primary file, and insert codes where you want the variable information, such as name and address, to appear. You type the actual names, addresses, and other information in a special file called the secondary file. WordPerfect can then merge the two files and create a letter for each set of data, inserting each item in its designated position in the primary file.*

In the primary file, you use the *FIELD* merge code to represent distinct pieces of information that will vary from letter to letter, such as owner's name, street, city, ZIP code, and the dog's name. These codes tell WordPerfect where to insert the actual data when you combine the primary and secondary files in the merge operation. You can assign numbers to the fields or make up names to help you identify them, such as OWNER, STREET, and CITY. For example, the primary file for the veterinarian's letters is shown in Figure 11.2. Notice the many {FIELD} codes, including {FIELD}OWNER~, {FIELD}STREET~, and {FIELD}DOG~. A primary file can include standard text and codes, as in the veterinarian's appointment letter, or it can consist entirely of {FIELD} codes, such as a primary file for an envelope or label.

In the secondary file, you use {*END FIELD*} codes to define and separate each field, such as owner, street, and city. Each complete set of fields is called a *record*, and you use {END RECORD} codes to distinguish them. For example, in the secondary file for the veterinarian's letter, shown in Figure 11.3, a record is all the information for one individual's letter. This includes the owner's name, street address, city, ZIP code, salutation, dog name, whether the dog is a male or female, type of shot, appointment date and time, and owner's phone number. The first two lines of this secondary file, beginning with the {FIELD NAMES} code and ending with the {END RECORD} code, are a special record that you'll learn about shortly.

```
{DATE}

{FIELD}OWNER~
{FIELD}STREET~
{FIELD}CITY~, CA {FIELD}ZIP~


Dear {FIELD}SALUTATION~,

Our records indicate that {FIELD}DOG~ is due for {FIELD}HIS OR HER~
{FIELD}SHOT~ shot.

For your convenience, we have scheduled an appointment for {FIELD}DOG~ on
{FIELD}DATE~, at {FIELD}TIME~. If this is not convenient for you, please call
us as soon as possible to schedule another appointment.

We look forward to seeing you and {FIELD}DOG~ again.



Sincerely,



The Marin K-9 Clinic
```

Figure 11.2 The primary file for the veterinarian's appointment letter.

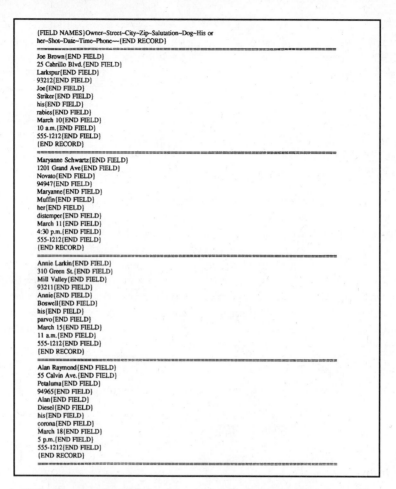

Figure 11.3 *The secondary file for the veterinarian's appointment letter. The*
{END FIELD} codes separate each field of information, and the
{END RECORD} codes define a complete record, which in this
case is all the information for one individual's letter.

You may have noticed that the secondary file in Figure 11.3 includes one field that does not appear in the primary file shown in Figure 11.2: the phone number. In fact, you can include many additional fields in the secondary file, because WordPerfect does not require that you use every one of them in your primary file. This allows you to maintain information in the secondary file that you may need for other purposes, such as printing a weekly appointment list with the owners' phone numbers. A primary file to produce envelopes for these letters would contain even fewer fields than the one in Figure 11.2: Owner, street, city, and ZIP, as shown in Figure 11.4.

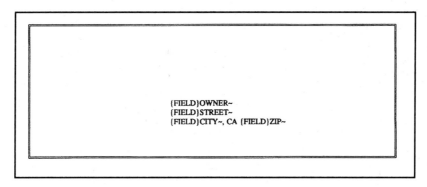

{FIELD}OWNER~
{FIELD}STREET~
{FIELD}CITY~, CA {FIELD}ZIP~

Figure 11.4 *You could use this primary file to create envelopes for the veterinarian's letters. Notice that it only uses four fields from the secondary file: owner, street, city, and ZIP.*

If you are storing your secondary file on a hard disk, you should be able to maintain thousands of records in the file; the only limit is the storage capacity of your disk. Within individual records, WordPerfect also permits you to create an unlimited number of fields. However, there are a few important rules you must follow when setting up your secondary file:

- Each record must end in an {END RECORD} code.

- All records in the secondary file must contain the same number of fields.

- Each field in each record must contain the same type of information. If the information is unavailable for a field, it must be left empty with an {END FIELD} code at the end.

- Individual fields can include as many lines as necessary, but each field must end in an {END FIELD} code. The one exception is the last field, which can end with {END RECORD}.

A primary file is required for all merge operations, but a secondary file is not. Later in this chapter, you'll learn how to set up such a merge operation, and type the names and addresses into the form as you run the merge. This type of merge is recommended for forms such as memos, or any standard letter where you don't need to save the variable data.

Creating the Primary File

In this section, you'll learn how to create the primary file shown in Figure 11.2. You'll type the standard text and use the Merge Codes menu to insert the {FIELD} and {DATE} codes in the appropriate positions. If you type merge codes like regular text, your merge won't work. Since you are creating a new file, start with a blank Edit screen.

The Date Code

The {DATE} code at the top of the letter will be converted into the current date when you merge the file. Don't use it unless your computer maintains the date accurately.

To insert the {DATE} merge code:

1. Bring up the Merge Codes menu:

   Keyboard: Press the Merge Codes key (Shift-F9).

   This menu appears:

   ```
   1 Field; 2 End Record; 3 Input; 4 Page Off;
   5 Next Record; 6 More: 0
   ```

   Mouse: Display the Tools menu and select Merge Codes.

   The Merge Codes menu pops out to the right, as shown in Figure 11.5.

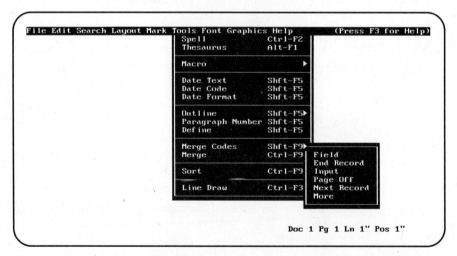

Figure 11.5 *When you select Merge Codes from the Tools menu, six options pop out to the right. Use the last one, More, to display additional codes.*

2. Select the last option, **More.**

   A list of additional merge codes appears in a box on the upper-right side of the screen, as shown in Figure 11.6. Although WordPerfect offers 68 merge codes, you can only select five from the main Merge menu: Field, End Record, Input, Page Off, and Next Record. The others are displayed in this list. If you are familiar with WordPerfect's macro language, many will be familiar to you. You can move through this menu using the regular cursor movement keys, or use Name Search. In this case, Name Search will be faster.

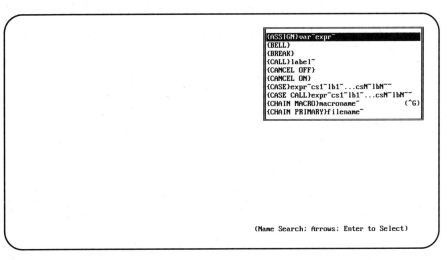

```
{ASSIGN}var~expr~
{BELL}
{BREAK}
{CALL}label~
{CANCEL OFF}
{CANCEL ON}
{CASE}expr~cs1~lb1~...csN~lbN~~
{CASE CALL}expr~cs1~lb1~...csN~lbN~~
{CHAIN MACRO}macroname~                    (^G)
{CHAIN PRIMARY}filename~
```

(Name Search; Arrows; Enter to Select)

Figure 11.6 *When you select the More option from the main Merge Codes menu, this list of additional codes appears in a pop-up box. To select the merge {DATE} code, you can use Name Search to locate it.*

3. Type D. This places the cursor on the {DATE} code in the Merge Codes menu.

4. Press Enter. This inserts the {DATE} code in your document. If you look in Reveal Codes, it will appear differently:

   [Mrg:DATE]

Warning: You must use the Merge Codes menu to insert merge codes such as {FIELD} and {END RECORD} in your primary and secondary files. If you type them like regular text, your merge will not work. In Reveal Codes, the merge codes always appear differently. For example, {FIELD} codes appear as [Mrg:FIELD], and {DATE} codes appear as [Mrg:DATE].

The Field Codes

To insert the {FIELD} codes in the primary file, as shown in Figure 11.2, you'll select the {FIELD} merge code from the main Merge Codes menu. Notice that the state was not entered as a {FIELD} code. Since all the veterinarian's patients reside in the same state, California, the state is not a variable piece of information, and it is not necessary to use a {FIELD} code to represent it in the primary file. This would not be the case if the veterinarian's office was near the border of two states, and she had clients from both states.

Instead of making up names for each of your fields, you can use numbers, as shown in Figure 11.7. Using numbers will save you an extra step when you type the secondary file. However, it's much easier to understand how the merge works if you create descriptive names for your fields. Compare the primary file in Figure 11.7 with the one in Figure 11.2. Although they will produce identical results when you merge them with the same secondary file, the version shown in Figure 11.2 is much easier to understand. Imagine that someone else had created this application, and then left the company without training a successor. If you were hired to replace her, you would probably prefer the version shown in Figure 11.2.

> **Tip:** The names you assign to your fields can include several words, separated by spaces. For example, the seventh field in the primary file for the veterinarian's letter contains three words: {FIELD}HIS OR HER.

You'll see another significant advantage when you type the data in your secondary file: WordPerfect will always prompt you with the name of the field you are supposed to be entering. For example, if you are typing information about the owner, this prompt will appear in the lower-left corner of the screen:

```
Field: Owner
```

If you don't use field names, the prompt will only show the field number, such as:

```
Field: 1
```

If you use numbers instead of names, you should print a list of what type of data belongs in each field number, or you may forget and enter the wrong data. The results can be amusing, such as when the salutation in a merged letter is *Dear Muffin* instead of *Dear Maryanne*, but trying to fix these mistakes is not!

Insert the {FIELD} codes:

1. Press Enter twice to move the cursor down a few lines; then select Merge Codes:

Keyboard: Press the Merge Codes key (Shift-F9).

Mouse: Display the Tools menu and select Merge Codes.

```
{DATE}


{FIELD}1~
{FIELD}2~
{FIELD}3~, CA {FIELD}4~


Dear {FIELD}5~,

Our records indicate that {FIELD}6~ is due for {FIELD}7~ {FIELD}8~ shot.

For your convenience, we have scheduled an appointment for {FIELD}6~ on {FIELD}9~, at
{FIELD}10~. If this is not convenient for you, please call us as soon as possible to schedule
another appointment.

We look forward to seeing you and {FIELD}6~ again.



Sincerely,


The Marin·K-9 Clinic
```

Figure 11.7 *Instead of using names for your fields, WordPerfect lets you number them, as shown here. However, it's much easier to work with names, especially when entering data into the secondary file.*

2. Select the first option, **Field**.

    An `Enter Field:` prompt appears in the lower-left corner of the screen. The first field you'll enter is the owner. Since case is irrelevant when you type field names, you can type *owner* or *OWNER*.

3. Type the first field, `OWNER`, and press Enter. To use a number instead, type 1. Press Enter again to move the cursor down a line.

    The field should appear as follows on your screen:

    `{FIELD}OWNER~`

    (unless you typed it in lowercase). In Reveal codes, your {FIELD} code should appear as `[Mrg:FIELD]`.

    Notice the tilde character at the end of the field name (~). WordPerfect automatically inserts a tilde after each field to indicate where it ends. If you make a mistake while typing a field name, you can delete it and retype it, but be careful not to delete the {FIELD} code or the tilde character. If you do, the merge won't work correctly. For instance, if you erase the tilde from the first field, OWNER, WordPerfect will exclude both the owner information and the two address lines when you run the merge. If you erase the tilde, you can type it again. On most keyboards, it is the first key on the top row of numbers, left of the 1, and you have to press the Shift key first to enter it. However, if you erase the {FIELD} code, you must use the Merge Codes menu to insert it again.

The cursor should now be on the line below your first field, since that is where the street address belongs.

> **Tip:** Many of WordPerfect's merge commands are followed by the tilde character (~), which designates the end of the command. Be careful not to erase it.

4. Use Merge Codes, as described in steps 1 and 2, to enter the second field: STREET. To use a number instead, type 2.

5. Move the cursor to the next line, and use Merge Codes to enter the third field: CITY (or 3).

6. Type a comma, press the space bar once and type CA, and then press the space bar again. Use Merge Codes to enter the fourth field: ZIP (or 4).

   If you forget the comma and blank spaces separating the city, state, and ZIP, your address lines will appear as follows after you merge the files:

   ```
   LarkspurCA93212
   NovatoCA94947
   ```

   It may help to visualize how you would type the city, state, and ZIP code in a letter. If you want it to appear like this:

   ```
   Larkspur, CA 93212
   ```

   enter the codes like this:

   ```
   {FIELD}City~, CA {FIELD}Zip~
   ```

7. Press Enter three times and type Dear and then press the space bar once to separate it from the SALUTATION field. Use Merge Codes to enter the fifth field, SALUTATION (or 5). Type a comma after the {FIELD} code, and press Enter twice.

8. Type

   ```
   Our records indicate that
   ```

   press the space bar, and use Merge Codes to enter the sixth field, DOG (or 6).

9. Press the space bar, type

    `is due for`

    press the space bar, and then use Merge Codes to enter the seventh field, `HIS OR HER`. Although you could leave this field out and substitute text, such as "a" (so it will read "is due for a ____ shot"), it makes the letter seem more personal to include "his" or "her" (or 7).

10. Press the space bar, then use Merge Codes to Enter the eighth field, `SHOT` (or 8).

11. Press the space bar and type `shot`, followed by a period. Then press Enter twice and type

    `For your convenience, we have scheduled an appointment for`

    press the space bar, and then use Merge Codes to enter the DOG field again (or 6).

    As you can see, you can use the same field more than once in a primary file, even though you only type it once in the secondary file.

Tip: Be sure to include spaces in your primary file to separate items such as city, state, and ZIP code. Think about how the line would look if you were typing the actual items, not entering merge codes to represent them. And don't forget punctuation marks, such as the comma after the SALUTATION and DATE fields, and the period that follows the SHOT and TIME fields.

---

12. Press the space bar, type

    `on`

    and then use Merge Codes to enter the ninth field, `DATE` (or 9).

13. Press the space bar, type

    `,at`

    press the space bar, and then use Merge Codes to enter the tenth field, `TIME` (or 10).

14. Type a period, press the space bar, and then type:

    `If this is not convenient for you, please call us as soon as possible to schedule another appointment.`

    `We look forward to seeing you and`

15. Press the space bar, use Merge Codes to enter the sixth field again, DOG (or 6).

16. Press the space bar and then type the rest of the letter:

```
again.

Sincerely,

The Marin K-9 Clinic
```

When you finish, your primary file should resemble Figure 11.2.

 Tip: To make formatting changes in a primary file, such as margins, tab setting, or line spacing, you should use the Initial Codes option on the Format Document menu. Likewise, to change the Base Font for the entire document, use the Initial Base Font option on the same menu. Otherwise, the codes will be included in every form generated by the merge, and the merge will run slower and require more disk space.

17. Save the primary file under this name: *Dogs.pf.*

Although it is optional, you may want to use a recognizable extension, such as *PF*, to identify your primary files. You can then use the same first name with the *SF* extension to identify your secondary file, as in *DOGS.SF.* If you use the same first name for both the primary and secondary files, varying only the extension, you can tell at a glance (when looking at the List Files screen) that they work together.

18. Use Exit to clear the screen.

If you print your primary file to proofread it, be forewarned that WordPerfect does not print the merge codes, and they are not visible in the View Document screen. Although field names (or numbers if you used them) will appear, the codes such as {FIELD} and {DATE} will not.

The next step is to type the secondary file.

Creating the Secondary File

The secondary file for this merge, shown in Figure 11.3, is where you will store the names, addresses, phone numbers, and other variable data. As you'll see, you can use the information in this file repeatedly to create other forms such as letters, envelopes, mailing labels, and lists.

Follow these instructions to type the four records in the secondary file. As you type the secondary file, remember that all records must have the same number of fields, each containing the same type of information, and each field must end in an {END FIELD} code. The most common mistake beginners make is forgetting to type one of the fields. Unless it's the last field in the record, this always results in misplaced fields in the merged documents.

The {FIELD NAMES} Record

If you want to use field names instead of numbers, WordPerfect has a special merge command that you must use to establish them: {FIELD NAMES}. This command creates a separate record at the top of the file, naming each field. If you used numbers instead of names in the primary file, you can skip this section and continue with the next one.

Be sure to clear the Edit screen before you begin.

1. Select Merge Codes:

   Keyboard: Press the Merge Codes key (Shift-F9).

   Mouse: Display the Tools menu and select Merge Codes.

2. Select the **M**ore option. The box with additional merge codes appears, as shown in Figure 11.6.

3. Type F to move the cursor onto the {FIELD} command, and then press Down Arrow once, so the cursor is highlighting the {FIELD NAMES} command. Press Enter to insert it in your document.

   This prompt will appear in the lower-left corner of your screen, asking for the name you want to assign to your first field:

   `Enter Field 1:`

4. Type `OWNER` and then press Enter.

5. The prompt will reappear, asking you to enter Field 2. Type `Street` and press Enter.

6. Repeat until you have typed these names for each of the 11 fields in your secondary file:

   ```
   3       City
   4       Zip
   5       Salutation
   6       Dog
   7       His or her
   8       Shot
   9       Date
   10      Time
   11      Phone
   ```

   You must spell the field names exactly the same way in the primary and secondary files. Do not, for example, type *Zip* in the secondary file and

Zipcode in the primary file, or *Shot* in the primary file and *Shots* in the secondary file. Unless the fields are identical, WordPerfect will not be able to match them when you perform the merge. However, case is not relevant, so you can use uppercase in one file and lowercase in the other.

After you enter Phone for the last field name, this prompt will appear:

```
Enter Field 12
```

and you can press Enter to signal that you have finished entering the field names.

7. Press the Enter key to leave Field 12 blank.

As you can see from Figure 11.8, WordPerfect has created a special record at the top of your secondary file, with an {END RECORD} code at the end. The {FIELD NAMES} merge code appears at the beginning, followed by your 11 field names, separated from each other by a tilde character (~). An extra tilde and an {END RECORD} code appear last to show that this is the end of the record.

 Tip: If you forget to enter a field name in the {FIELD NAMES} record or want to insert an additional one, just type it in the correct position, and then type a tilde to separate it from the next field (or, if it is the last field, to separate it from the {END RECORD} code).

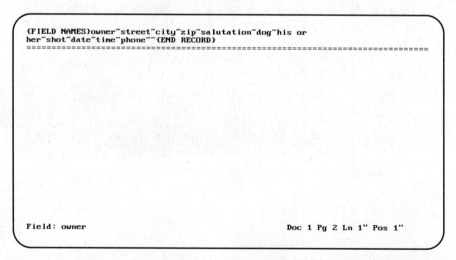

```
{FIELD NAMES}owner~street~city~zip~salutation~dog~his or
her~shot~date~time~phone~~{END RECORD}
==============================================================================
```

```
Field: owner                                    Doc 1 Pg 2 Ln 1" Pos 1"
```

Figure 11.8 After you finish entering your field names, WordPerfect creates this record at the top of the secondary file. This step is not necessary if you are using numbers instead of names for your fields, but it makes data entry easier. As you are typing, WordPerfect will prompt you with the field names, so you'll know what type of information you are supposed to be entering at each position.

Now that you have entered the {FIELD NAMES} record, you are ready to type the names, addresses, and other variable information in your secondary file.

 ## Entering the Data for Each Field and Record

Typing the actual data should be easy, especially if you used field names, because WordPerfect prompts you with the field name at each position. For example, in Figure 11.8 the prompt indicates that you are to type data for the OWNER field.

1. With the cursor on the first line below the page break, enter the first owner: Joe Brown.

> ▶ **Tip:** A field can contain as many lines as necessary and does not end until you insert the {END FIELD} code. To include another line, either press Enter and type it, or continue typing until WordPerfect automatically inserts a soft return and wraps the cursor to the next line.

2. To insert the {END FIELD} code:

   Keyboard: Press the End Field key, F9.

   Mouse: Display the Tools menu, select Merge Codes, select More, and then select {END FIELD}.

   This inserts both the {END FIELD} code and a [HRt] code, and moves the cursor to the next line. Notice that the prompt in the lower-left corner of the screen has changed to:

   Field: Street

3. Type the street:

   25 Cabrillo Blvd.

   and repeat step 2 to insert an {END FIELD} code.

4. Repeat these steps until you have finished entering all the remaining data for Joe Brown's record, separating each field with an {END FIELD} code:

   Larkspur{END FIELD}
   93212{END FIELD}
   Joe{END FIELD}
   Striker{END FIELD}
   his{END FIELD}
   rabies{END FIELD}
   March 10{END FIELD}

```
10 a.m.{END FIELD}
555-1212{END FIELD}
```

After you finish typing the phone number and inserting the {END FIELD} code, notice that the prompt in the lower-left corner displays field 12, even if you used field names. Since there are only 11 fields per record, this indicates that you have entered all of the fields for the first record. To complete it, the next step is to insert an {END RECORD} code and a page break.

5. To select {END RECORD}:

> **Keyboard:** Press Merge Codes (Shift-F9) and select the second option, End Record.

> **Mouse:** Display the **Tools** menu, select Merge Codes, and then select End Record.

This inserts the {END RECORD} code, and WordPerfect creates a hard page break to separate it from the next record, as shown in Figure 11.9. When WordPerfect merges the primary and secondary files, the next customer's letter will begin on a new page, if there is any more data in the secondary file.

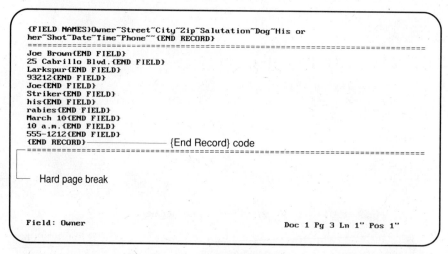

Figure 11.9 *After you finish typing the first record in the secondary file and insert an {END RECORD} code, WordPerfect creates a hard page break, represented on screen by a double line of dashes. When you produce the letters in the merge operation, this will separate it from the next customer's letter.*

6. Repeat steps 1 through 5 to enter the data for the next three records.

7. Save the file under the name *DOGS.SF,* and then use Exit to clear the screen.

 Tip: WordPerfect does not require that you use all fields from the secondary file in a primary file. The only limit to the number of fields you can maintain in the secondary file is your disk's storage capacity.

Merging the Primary and Secondary Files to Generate the Form Letters

The last step in the process of creating the form letters is performing the merge, and it is the easiest one. All you have to do is select Merge, enter the names of your primary and secondary files, and sit back and watch WordPerfect do the work. Start with a clear screen, since the completed letters will appear on the Edit screen after WordPerfect merges the two files.

1. Select Merge:

   Keyboard: Press the Merge/Sort key (Ctrl-F9) and select **Merge (1)**.

   Mouse: Display the **Tools** menu and select **Merge**.

   This prompt appears at the bottom of the screen:

   `Primary file:`   `(List Files)`

   The prompt on the right is a reminder that you can use the List Files menu (Retrieve option) to select the primary file.

2. Type the name of your primary file, `DOGS.PF`, and then press Enter. WordPerfect then prompts you for the secondary file name:

   `Secondary file:`   `(List Files)`

   again reminding you that you can use List Files.

3. Type the name of your secondary file, `DOGS.SF`, and then press Enter.

   A `* Merging *` message will appear while WordPerfect is creating the letters, and then they will appear on screen, separated by hard page breaks. The cursor should be at the end of the last one, on page 4. To view the others, press Page Up, or drag the mouse up to the previous pages.

Now that the letters have been merged to the Edit screen, you can print them, save them to a new file, or clear them. In fact, they are no different from letters you type yourself in WordPerfect, without using merge.

 Tip: If necessary, you can press the Cancel key (F1) to stop a merge.

Merging Directly to the Printer

If your secondary file is enormous, and your computer's memory is limited, WordPerfect may not be able to produce a letter from each record in your secondary file. To test this, I duplicated the veterinarian's secondary file until it contained over 4,000 records. When I ran this merge on my 286 laptop computer, which has 640K of RAM (random access memory) and a 20 megabyte hard disk, it produced 3,653 pages and then stopped. What finally halted the merge was the fact that I ran out of space on the hard disk, and I received this message:

```
ERROR: WP disk full — Press any key to continue
```

In the unlikely event that this happens to you, there are two possible solutions:

1. Use the More option on the Merge Codes menu to insert these codes in your primary file: {PAGE OFF} at the top of the file, and {PRINT} at the end. When you run the merge, the letters will be sent directly to the printer, instead of to the Edit screen. However, you won't be able to proofread and edit them before printing, and the letters that result from the merge won't be saved.

2. Use WordPerfect's Block Save feature to split the secondary file into two or more files, and then perform separate merge operations using the same primary file. Make an extra copy of the original file before you begin. Also, you may want to sort the file before splitting it. For example, you could sort the DOGS file by owner's last name, and move all those whose names begin with M through Z into a new file.

Missing Data

If you don't have the information for a particular field in the secondary file, leave a blank field with an {END FIELD} code in its place. For example, if the Zip code were missing from Joe Brown's record, you would have to type it like this:

```
Joe Brown{END FIELD}
25 Cabrillo Blvd.{END FIELD}
Larkspur{END FIELD}
{END FIELD}
Joe{END FIELD}
Striker{END FIELD}
his{END FIELD}
rabies{END FIELD}
March 10{END FIELD}
10 a.m.{END FIELD}
555-1212{END FIELD}
{END RECORD}
```

If you do not leave the blank field and {END FIELD} code where the Zip code belongs, WordPerfect will place the salutation data in the ZIP code position in the primary file, since SALUTATION is the next field in the secondary file. After you've performed the merge, the letter will appear as shown in Figure 11.10. As you can see, it then moves up the data for all fields that follow in the record: The dog's name is inserted where the salutation belongs, "his" is inserted where the dog's name belongs, "rabies" is inserted where "his" belongs, and the date is inserted where the shot belongs. In the next paragraph, the time is inserted where the date belongs, and the phone number is inserted where the time belongs. The phone number does not belong in the letter at all. Quite a mess!

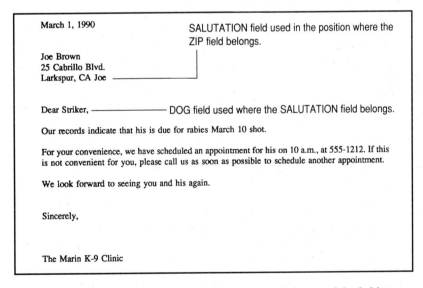

Figure 11.10   *This is what happens if you forget to include one of the fields in your secondary file. Here, the ZIP code data was left out. If the information is unavailable for a field, leave a blank line with an {END FIELD} code to prevent results like these.*

Creating a List from Your Secondary File

Suppose that you wanted to create a list that included the owner's name, dog's name, type of shot, and time and date of the appointment. To do this, you could create the primary file shown in Figure 11.11. After you merge it with DOGS.SF, the list would appear as shown in Figure 11.12. The {PAGE OFF} code is the key to creating a list, for it prevents each record from starting on a separate page. You should also change your tab stop settings in the primary file, or you could end up with results like these:

```
Joe Brown Striker    rabies     March 10  10 a.m.
Maryanne Schwartz    Muffin     distemper March 11  4:30 p.m.
Annie Larkin    Boswell    parvo      March 15  11 a.m.
Alan Raymond    Diesel     corona     March 18  5 p.m.
```

This happens when the text in one or more fields varies significantly in length. For example, in the second row, the owner's name (Maryanne Schwartz) is too long to fit between the left margin and the first tab stop. As a result, the next field (dog) started at a different tab stop position from the two records that follow, and all the other fields in the row were misaligned. Another way to prevent this is to place the merge {FIELD} codes in a table, so that individual fields can wrap to the next line, while remaining in the same column.

```
{FIELD}owner~      {FIELD}dog~       {FIELD}shot~       {FIELD}date~, {FIELD}time~
{PAGE OFF}
```

Figure 11.11 *The primary file for the list. When you merge it with DOGS.SF, WordPerfect will create the list shown in Figure 11.12.*

Joe Brown	Striker	rabies	March 10, 10 a.m.
Maryanne Schwartz	Muffin	distemper	March 11, 4:30 p.m.
Annie Larkin	Boswell	parvo	March 15, 11 a.m.
Alan Raymond	Diesel	corona	March 18, 5 p.m.

Figure 11.12 *By creating a new primary file and merging it with the secondary file, you can create a list like this one.*

Follow these instructions to create the list shown in Figure 11.12. Start with a blank editing screen.

1. Change the tab stop settings to 2, 3.5, and 4.5" from the left margin.

2. Use the Field option on the Merge Codes menu to enter the first field, {FIELD}Owner~. (It should be at the left margin.)

3. Press tab and enter the next field, {FIELD}Dog~.

4. Press tab and enter the next field, {FIELD}Shot~.

5. Press tab and enter the last two fields, separated only by a comma and a space: {FIELD}Date~, {FIELD}Time~.

6. Press Enter to move the cursor to the next line. After you run the merge, this will separate each record by one blank line.

7. Use the More option on the Merge Codes menu to insert the {PAGE OFF} command on the last line.

8. Save the file as *DOGLIST.PF* and clear the screen.

9. Run a merge using DOGLIST.PF as the primary file, and DOGS.SF as the secondary file. When you finish, your list should resemble Figure 11.12.

> **Tip:** If you do not want to see merge commands such as {FIELD} and {END FIELD} on the Edit screen, you can change the Merge Codes Display option on the Setup: Edit-Screen Options menu to No (Setup, Display, Edit-Screen Options, Merge Codes Display). This will show you how your text will look without the merge commands.

Column Titles

The easiest way to include a row of column titles in your list, as shown in Figure 11.13, is to type them after merging the files. If you were to type them in the primary file, WordPerfect would create a title row for each record in the secondary file when you run the merge. There is a way around this, but it requires some extra work: You have to use three more merge commands in your primary file, {LABEL}label~, {GO}label~, and {NEXT RECORD}. Essentially, you use the three commands to create a loop. When you run the merge, everything inside the loop is repeated until there are no more records in the secondary file. Since the column titles are outside of the loop, WordPerfect only prints them once.

The {LABEL}label~ and {GO}label~ commands differ from the other merge codes you've studied in this chapter, because they are followed by arguments. An *argument* is an additional item that WordPerfect requires to carry out the command. For instance, the argument for the {GO}label~ command is a label that you will define using the {LABEL}label~ command, assigning it the name *List*. The {GO}label~ command will direct WordPerfect to go to your List label and perform the instructions that follow it.

Here's how the loop works. The {LABEL}List~ command identifies this section of the primary file as a label named *List*. Since the column titles are above the {LABEL} command, they are not included. You can make up a different label name, if it seems more descriptive. The instructions that are included in the List label section are as follows:

1. The {FIELD} commands: Get the first record in the secondary file, and enter the data for the *Owner's name*, *Dog*, *Shot*, and *Appointment date* in the appropriate columns.

2. {NEXT RECORD}: Go to the next record in the secondary file.

3. {GO}list~: Go to the *List* label, and repeat its instructions. This creates the loop, which ends when there are no more records in the secondary file.

To modify your primary file to include column titles, as shown in Figure 11.14, follow these instructions. Be careful to enter the merge commands exactly as described.

1. Retrieve the DOGLIST.PF, and type the column titles above each column: Owner's name, Dog, Shot, and Appointment date. Insert a blank line below it.

2. Select the **More** option from the Merge Codes menu, and type L to move the cursor onto the {LABEL} command. Press Enter to insert it in your document. In response to the Enter Label prompt, type the label name, List. After you press Enter, a tilde will appear at the end.

3. Move the cursor to the end of the document, and use the **More** option on the Merge Codes menu to insert the {NEXT RECORD} command.

4. Use the **More** option on the Merge Codes menu to insert the {GO} command. In response to the Enter label prompt, type the label name: List. After you press Enter, a tilde will appear at the end.

Save the file again, and then clear the screen and run the merge. The results should be identical to Figure 11.13.

Merging Without a Secondary File

Instead of typing variable data such as names and addresses in a secondary file, you can create a form letter that allows you to enter this information during the merge process. Imagine a personnel office in a large corporation that sends hundreds of letters a day to acknowledge resumes that have been received. It would not be practical, or even desirable, to create a secondary file with all the names and addresses. Instead, the staff could set up a form letter thanking each individual, save it as a primary file, and use merge to fill it out each time they receive a resume.

Owner's name:	Dog:	Shot:	Appointment date:
Joe Brown	Striker	rabies	March 10, 10 a.m.
Maryanne Schwartz	Muffin	distemper	March 11, 4:30 p.m.
Annie Larkin	Boswell	parvo	March 15, 11 a.m.
Alan Raymond	Diesel	corona	March 18, 5 p.m.

Figure 11.13   *The appointment list with column titles. The line under the titles was created using the Line option on the Graphics menu.*

Owner's name:	Dog:	Shot:	Appointment date:
{LABEL}List~			
{FIELD}owner~	{FIELD}dog~		{FIELD}shot~{FIELD}date~,
{FIELD}time~			
{NEXT RECORD}{GO}list~			

Figure 11.14   *To include a row of column titles in your list, as shown in Figure 11.13, set up a loop using the {LABEL}, {GO}, and {NEXT RECORD} merge commands in the primary file, as shown here.*

Use this method only if you do not anticipate using the variable information (names and addresses) again, since it will not be saved. Later, you'll learn how to insert selected paragraphs into the sample form letter at the time of the merge, so you can use the same primary file to generate a variety of responses to the job seekers' resumes. For instance, you might want to inform certain applicants that the position was filled, arrange interviews for others, and tell some that the company is experiencing a hiring freeze.

The primary file for this application appears in Figure 11.15. Notice that the variable information is represented by {INPUT} codes, instead of {FIELD} codes. When you use the merge, these codes force the cursor to stop at that position, display the message that appears between the code and the tilde, and pause for you to type the data. For example, the first time it stops, you will type the name and address. After you finish typing it, you press End Field (F9) and the cursor moves to the position of the next {INPUT} code, where you will type the salutation.

```
{DATE}


{INPUT}Enter name and address, press F9~

Dear {INPUT}Type the salutation, press F9~


We have received your letter and resume, and wish to take this opportunity to thank you for
your interest in employment opportunities with PCX Corporation.

Although your credentials and experience are most impressive, we regret to say that we do
not have any openings in your area at this time. However, we will keep your resume on file
for six months, and will contact you as soon as a suitable position becomes available.



Sincerely,


Marjorie Jackson
Personnel Administrator
```

Figure 11.15   *The primary file with INPUT commands.*

To type the primary file shown in Figure 11.15, follow these instructions. Begin by clearing the Edit screen:

1. Use Merge Codes to enter the {DATE} code.

2. To enter the first {INPUT} code:

   Keyboard: Press Merge Codes (Shift-F9) and select the third option, Input.

   Mouse: Display the Tools menu, select Merge Codes, and then select Input.

This prompt will appear, asking you to type a message:

`Enter Message:`

When the cursor stops at this position during the merge operation, the message you create in this step will appear in the lower-left corner of the screen. If the person using this primary file was not very proficient in WordPerfect, reminding them to type the name and address and then press F9 to continue to the next position, would be helpful. Incidentally, if you don't want to use messages, you could use WordPerfect's

{KEYBOARD} merge code instead of {INPUT}. It works the same way, but does not provide a message.

3. Type this message:

   `Enter name and address, press F9~`

4. Press Enter twice, type `Dear`, then repeat step 2 to insert the second {INPUT} code. Type this message:

   `Type the salutation, press F9~`

   and press Enter.

5. Type the rest of the letter.

6. Save the file under the name *RESUMES.PF*, and then use Exit to clear the screen.

   To run the merge:

1. Select **Merge** from the Merge/Sort key or the **Tools** menu, and enter the name of the primary file, `RESUMES.PF`.

   The next prompt asks for the name of the secondary file. Since there is none for this type of merge, you can press Enter to leave it blank.

2. Press Enter in response to the `Secondary file` prompt.

   The first {INPUT} code disappears, and the cursor is positioned there for you to type the data, as shown in Figure 11.16. The prompt that you typed next to the {INPUT} code in the primary file now appears in the lower-left corner of the screen, to remind you what to do:

   `Enter name and address, press F9`

3. Type the name and address, pressing Enter after each line:

   ```
   Mr. Joseph Blacker
   2009 Hilltop Avenue
   Inverness, CA 95060
   ```

   To signal that you've finished entering all the text for this field, use End Field.

4. Press the End Field key, F9. (You cannot use the pull-down menus.) This moves the cursor to the next field, and the rest of the letter suddenly appears. The {INPUT} code has disappeared, and your prompt appears at the bottom of the screen, reminding you to:

   `Type the salutation, press F9`

5. Type the salutation:

   `Mr. Blacker`

6. Press F9 again. This moves the cursor to the end of the document.

It is important to press F9 in the last step, even though you can see that there are no more {INPUT} codes. This allows WordPerfect to search the rest of the letter to see if there are any remaining codes. If you forget to press F9 after typing the data for the last field, the last prompt will remain on your screen even after you clear it using Exit (if you did not create prompts for your {INPUT} codes, the `* Merging *` message will remain).

> **Tip:** When you finish running a merge that uses {INPUT} codes, the cursor should be at the end of the document. If it is not, press F9. If you clear the screen and a merge prompt still appears, you forgot to press F9.

After that, you can print the merged letter. If you save it, be sure to use the same name as the primary file.

You can include both {FIELD} and {INPUT} codes in a primary file, using the {INPUT} codes for information you don't need to save in the secondary file. For instance, in the primary file for the veterinarian's letter, you could use {INPUT} codes for shot type, whether the dog should be addressed as "his" or "her," and the date and time. When you run such a merge, WordPerfect will stop and let you fill out each field in each record that is represented by an {INPUT} code, and use the variable data from the secondary file for the ones represented by a {FIELD} code.

```
December 17, 1990




Dear ──────────        WordPerfect pauses the merge operation,
                       waiting for the name and address to be typed.










Enter name and address, press F9                    Doc 2 Pg 1 Ln 1.5" Pos 1"
```

Figure 11.16 *When you merge the RESUMES primary file, WordPerfect retrieves the letter, erases the first {INPUT} code and pauses there, waiting for you to type the name and address. As soon as you press F9, it searches for the next {INPUT} code, erases it, and waits for you to type the salutation.*

Using Other Advanced Merge Commands to Automate the Production of the Letters and Envelopes

Recall the hypothetical situation of Marjorie Jackson, the personnel administrator for PCX Corporation. Marjorie receives about 100 resumes and job applications each day. Up until now, her administrative assistant has answered most of them by using WordPerfect's merge feature to fill out and send the form letter shown in Figure 11.15. However, Ms. Jackson has recently obtained the results of an efficiency study conducted for her department, which indicated that this form letter is only suitable for about 70% of the applicants' letters. The other 30% represent 25 to 35 letters a day. The administrative assistant answers most of these letters with one of the four reply letters shown in Figure 11.17 (also in WordPerfect primary file format). Since he has many other duties and can only devote two hours a day to this task, the company wants to automate the production of these letters to the fullest extent possible. This includes giving him the ability to print envelopes using the names and addresses in a secondary merge file, instead of using a typewriter. Since Ms. Jackson is well-acquainted with WordPerfect, she decides to spend a little of her own time tackling this problem.

To implement this goal, Ms. Jackson will set up two primary files—one for the envelopes and one for the form letters—and a secondary file for the actual data. Because WordPerfect's merge language includes commands that can select text for the primary file based on specific information in the secondary file (during the merge process), only one primary file will be needed for the reply letter.

The procedure will be as follows:

1. Ms. Jackson will review each resume and assign an application status to each individual, as shown in Table 11.1.

2. The administrative assistant will enter each applicant's data, including the status that Ms. Jackson has assigned him or her, into a record in the secondary file. The information the assistant enters in the STATUS field is the crux of the operation; when the primary and secondary files are merged, WordPerfect will use the information in the STATUS field to select one of four paragraphs to include in the reply letter: the "Hiring Freeze" paragraph, the "No Openings" paragraph, the "Position Filled" paragraph, or the "Interview" paragraph. These paragraphs are shown in Table 11.2.

3. The administrative assistant will run the two merges: the merge that produces the reply letters and the merge that produces the envelopes.

Once these procedures have been implemented, Ms. Jackson will create menu-driven macros that will further automate the second and third steps, so that when the administrative assistant is out sick or on vacation, another employee can perform the tasks easily, by selecting options from a menu.

Figure 11.17   *The four reply letters, in WordPerfect primary file format.*

Table 11.1   *Applicant statuses and descriptions.*

Status	Description
Filled	Position Filled
Freeze	Hiring Freeze
Recontact	Recontact for Interview If Opening in Next Six Months
Interview	Interview for Current Opening

Table 11.2   *The four reply paragraphs: Hiring Freeze, No Openings, Position Filled, and Interview.*

Hiring Freeze:	We are currently experiencing a hiring freeze. It is anticipated that the hiring freeze will be in effect for at least ___ months. We will advertise in local newspapers when hiring is resumed. Until then, we wish you the best of luck in your employment search.
No Openings:	Although your credentials and experience are most impressive, we regret to say that we do not have any openings for _____ in the _____ department at this time. However, we will keep your resume on file for six months, and will contact you for an interview as soon as a suitable position becomes available.
Position Filled:	The position you have applied for, _____, has been filled. However we are most impressed by your credentials and experience, and will keep your resume in the active file for six months. If, during that time, a similar position becomes available, we will contact you for an interview.
Interview:	We are most impressed by your credentials and experience and are very interested in having you on our team. We anticipate a suitable opening in the _____ department soon and have scheduled an interview for _____, at _____with _____. Please let me know as soon as possible if this is convenient.

Designing the Secondary File

The secondary file will contain the names, addresses, position applied for, and other relevant information, as shown in Table 11.3.

Table 11.3 *The fields in the secondary file.*

1. Mr/Ms	11. Work Phone
2. First Name	12. Home Phone
3. Middle Name	13. Status
4. Last Name	14. Department
5. Title	15. Position
6. Company	16. Freeze Months
7. Address	17. Interview Date
8. City	18. Interview Time
9. State	19. Interviewer
10. Zip	20. Notes

As you can see, the secondary file contains 20 fields, a relatively large number. This provides flexibility, as Ms. Jackson anticipates she will eventually want her assistant to print daily reports from some of the data. For example, he could print a report sorted by applicant's status, last name, date and time of the interview, or the interviewer.

Not all of the records in the secondary file will contain data for all of these fields. For example, if an applicant does not currently have a job, he or she won't have a title or company name for the currently held position. Some applicants won't include middle names or initials on their resumes. Applicants for whom an interview has not been scheduled will not have an interview date, time, or interviewer.

The secondary file follows. Notice that it includes a file header and six data records. To create this secondary file, follow the general instructions in the section "Creating the Secondary File," earlier in this chapter. Save it using this name: *APPLICAN.SF.*

The secondary file: APPLICAN.SF:

```
{FIELD NAMES}Mr/Ms~
First Name~
Middle Name~
Last Name~
Title~
Company~
```

```
Address~
City~
State~
Zip~
Work Phone~
Home Phone~
Status~
Department~
Position~ ·
Freeze Months~
Interview Date~
Interview Time~
Interviewer~
Notes~~{END RECORD}
=============================================
Ms.{END FIELD}
Doretha{END FIELD}
{END FIELD}
Fuller{END FIELD}
{END FIELD}
GTC Security Services{END FIELD}
80 Swan Way
Suite 200{END FIELD}
Los Angeles{END FIELD}
CA{END FIELD}
98233{END FIELD}
(310) 555-1212{END FIELD}
(310) 555-0000{END FIELD}
Filled{END FIELD}
Security{END FIELD}
Director{END FIELD}
{END FIELD}
{END FIELD}
{END FIELD}
{END FIELD}
Excellent credentials{END FIELD}
{END RECORD}
=============================================
Mr.{END FIELD}
Ralph{END FIELD}
C.{END FIELD}
McCarthy{END FIELD}
Certified Public Accountant{END FIELD}
{END FIELD}
```

```
2375 Stuart Avenue{END FIELD}
Rockaway{END FIELD}
NJ{END FIELD}
09772{END FIELD}
(609) 555-1212{END FIELD}
(609) 555-0000{END FIELD}
Interview{END FIELD}
Finance{END FIELD}
Accountant{END FIELD}
{END FIELD}
March 12, 1992{END FIELD}
3:00 pm{END FIELD}
Mary Shaw{END FIELD}
{END FIELD}
{END RECORD}
==================================================
Mr.{END FIELD}
Larry{END FIELD}
{END FIELD}
Friedman{END FIELD}
Chef{END FIELD}
Freels Hotel{END FIELD}
805 Highland Avenue{END FIELD}
San Francisco{END FIELD}
CA{END FIELD}
94133{END FIELD}
{END FIELD}
{END FIELD}
Frozen{END FIELD}
Food Preparation{END FIELD}
Baker{END FIELD}
2{END FIELD}
{END FIELD}
{FND FIELD}
{END FIELD}
{END FIELD}
{END RECORD}
==================================================
{END FIELD}
Terry{END FIELD}
R.{END FIELD}
Gillespie{END FIELD}
{END FIELD}
{END FIELD}
```

```
366 Pierce Street{END FIELD}
Albany{END FIELD}
CA{END FIELD}
94707{END FIELD}
{END FIELD}
(415) 555-1883{END FIELD}
Recontact{END FIELD}
Engineering{END FIELD}
Mechanical Engineer{END FIELD}
{END FIELD}
{END FIELD}
{END FIELD}
{END FIELD}
Engineering degree Purdue University, 1988{END FIELD}
{END RECORD}
=============================================
Ms.{END FIELD}
Bernice{END FIELD}
B.{END FIELD}
Burke{END FIELD}
Attorney at Law{END FIELD}
Schlinder, Burke, Weitzman, & Stewart{END FIELD}
4225 Cola Ballena{END FIELD}
Berkeley{END FIELD}
CA{END FIELD}
94705{END FIELD}
(415) 555-7000 ext 22{END FIELD}
(415) 555-7223{END FIELD}
Interview{END FIELD}
Legal{END FIELD}
Attorney{END FIELD}
{END FIELD}
March 17, 1992{END FIELD}
2:30 pm{END FIELD}
Bill Weingart, chief legal counsel for our firm. Because
Mr. Weingart's primary office is at our New York headquar-
ters, he only comes to California twice a year to inter-
view prospective attorneys. We hope therefore that it will
be possible for you to meet with Mr. Weingart at the
proposed date and time{END FIELD}
{END FIELD}
{END RECORD}
=============================================
```

```
Mr.{END FIELD}
A.{END FIELD}
M.{END FIELD}
Deschenes{END FIELD}
{END FIELD}
{END FIELD}
3688 Lake Shore Avenue{END FIELD}
Oakland{END FIELD}
CA{END FIELD}
94705{END FIELD}
(510) 555-1993{END FIELD}
(510) 555-8221{END FIELD}
Filled{END FIELD}
Maintenance{END FIELD}
Gardener{END FIELD}
{END FIELD}
{END FIELD}
{END FIELD}
{END FIELD}
{END FIELD}
{END RECORD}
================================================
```

Since the envelope primary file is the least complex of the two primary files, and will serve as the basis for the name and address section of the letter primary file, you'll create it first (in the next section). After that, you'll develop the primary file for the conditional form letters.

Creating the Envelope Primary File

Follow these steps to create the primary file for envelopes. When you merge it with the secondary file containing the job applicant information, WordPerfect will produce an envelope for each applicant.

1. Use the Initial Codes option on the Format: Document menu to set up the formatting for your envelope primary file (Shift-F8 D C, or Layout Document C). You'll need to change the paper size and type, and all four margins.

   Since all printers are different, it's impossible to provide precise margins for your envelope form. As an example, the following measurements would be used on a Hewlett-Packard LaserJet II printer:

   Paper Size and Type: 9.5" x 4", Envelope (Format: Page menu)

Top and Bottom Margins: 2", .5" (Format: Page menu)

Left and right margins: 4.75", .25" (Format: Line menu)

2. Return to the Edit screen and use the **Field** option on the Merge Codes menu to insert the following fields into the envelope primary file (Shift-F9 **F** or Tools Merge Codes, Field). Note that extra spaces in the first line were added here to help you distinguish the fields; in your file, only one space should separate each field on the first line.

```
Mr/Ms        First Name      Middle Name      Last Name
Title
Company
Address
City, State Zip
```

When you finish, your primary file should resemble Figure 11.18.

```
{FIELD}Mr/Ms~ {FIELD}First Name~ {FIELD}Middle Name~ {FIELD}Last Name~
{FIELD}Title~
{FIELD}Company~
{FIELD}Address~
{FIELD}City~, {FIELD}State~ {FIELD}Zip~
```

Figure 11.18   *The envelope primary file.*

3. Save the envelope using this name: *ENV.PF*.

Missing Information

As you learned earlier in this chapter, even if the actual data is missing from any of the fields in a record in your secondary file, you are still required to leave an {END FIELD} code to designate the field's position. However, sometimes the results of such a merge are unacceptable. For example, if data for the COMPANY field is missing from one of the records in your secondary file, and you leave a blank field with an {End Field} code in its position, the merged envelope will appear as follows:

```
Terry R. Gillespie
Accounting Supervisor

366 Pierce Street
Albany, CA  94707
```

As you can see, WordPerfect leaves a blank line where the company information would normally be inserted during the merge process. Similarly, if the middle name or initial were missing from one of the records in the secondary file, WordPerfect would leave an extra space between the first and last name.

Since Ms. Jackson's company receives many applications from candidates whose applications:

Don't include a company name or title, because they are unemployed or self-employed.

Don't include a middle name or initial.

Don't provide enough information to determine if their title should be Mr. or Ms., as in foreign names that are unfamiliar.

she decides to provide for these contingencies by using the {IF NOT BLANK} command. This command simply tells WordPerfect what to do if a field in the secondary file is not blank (that is, if it *does* contain data). The syntax of the {IF NOT BLANK} command is as follows:

```
{IF NOT BLANK}field~
{END IF}
```

Note that the {IF NOT BLANK} command must be followed by an {END IF} command. This signals the end of the statement and tells WordPerfect where to go in the event that the statement is false. In other words, if the field is blank, the merge will skip this section and resume with the commands that follow the {END IF} command. For example, to prevent WordPerfect from leaving a blank line where the COMPANY field belongs (if it contains no data), the COMPANY field should appear as follows in the primary file:

```
{FIELD}Company~{IF NOT BLANK}Company~[HRt]
{END IF}{FIELD}Address~
```

Note that there should *not* be a space separating the {END IF} and {FIELD} commands on the second line, or the resulting envelope will include a blank space before the address. Also, the [HRt] at the end of the first line is the code that represents a hard return (inserted by pressing Enter) and is only visible in the Reveal Codes screen. Do not type it!

The results of using this command will be:

- If the COMPANY field is not blank—that is, if the individual record in the secondary file contains a company name (in the COMPANY field)— WordPerfect will insert the Company name, followed by a hard return [HRt] code, and then insert the address data on the next line.

- If the COMPANY field is blank, WordPerfect will ignore that section of the primary file, which includes the [HRt] code, and continue the merge with the next field, ADDRESS. In other words, it will skip the hard return that would otherwise create a blank line after the company name (since there is none) and resume with the instructions that follow the {END IF} command. Since the [HRt] code is included between the {IF NOT BLANK} and the {END IF} codes, this prevents WordPerfect from inserting a blank line at this position (when *COMPANY* is blank).

Tip: An {END IF} command is required for each use of the {IF NOT BLANK} command in a primary file.

You will need to use the {IF NOT BLANK} and {END IF} commands for each field in the primary file where data may be unavailable. In this example, you should use them for four of the fields:

Mr/Ms	To prevent a blank space if the field is blank
Middle Name	To prevent a blank space if the field is blank
Title	To prevent a blank line if the field is blank
Company	To prevent a blank line if the field is blank

Follow these instructions to insert the {IF NOT BLANK} and {END IF} commands into the envelope primary file:

1. If you cleared the screen after step 3 of the last section, retrieve the envelope primary file you saved earlier: *ENV.PF.*

2. To insert the first set of {IF NOT BLANK} and {END IF} codes, position the cursor in the blank space after the tilde character (~) that follows {FIELD}MR/MS.

3. Insert the {IF NOT BLANK} command:

    Keyboard: Press Merge Codes (Shift-F9) and select **More** (an alternative method is to press Shift-F9 twice).

    Mouse: Display the **T**ools menu, select Me**r**ge Codes, and then select **M**ore.

    A box listing additional merge commands appears on the right side of the screen.

Tip: To display the box of merge commands that are not on the main Merge Codes menu, you can either press the Merge Codes key (Shift-F9) and select More, or press the Merge Codes key twice.

4. Highlight the **{IF NOT BLANK}field~** command, and press Enter. This prompt appears in the lower-left corner of the screen:

   `Enter Field`

5. In response, type the field name: MR/MS and press Enter.

6. Press the space bar once.

   This inserts the blank space that will separate Mr. or Ms. from the first name data if the Mr/Ms field contains data in the secondary file. The next step will be to insert the {END IF} command.

7. To insert the {END IF} command:

   Keyboard: Press Merge Codes (Shift-F9) and select **More**.

   Mouse: Display the Tools menu, select **Merge** Codes, and then select **More**.

   Highlight the {END IF} command and press Enter.

8. Delete the blank space that separates the {END IF} command from the {FIELD}First Name~ command.

9. Repeat these steps to insert an **{IF NOT BLANK}field~** command for the MIDDLE NAME, TITLE, and COMPANY fields. Each line is shown below. Note that the fields you are supposed to add are shown in bold and italics, to help you differentiate them. Be careful not to insert extra blank spaces.

   Line 1:

   {FIELD}Mr/Ms~*{IF NOT BLANK}Mr/Ms~* {*END IF*}{FIELD}First Name~ {FIELD}Middle Name~*{IF NOT BLANK}Middle Name~* {*END IF*}{FIELD}Last Name~

   (Note that there is no blank space separating the {END IF} command from the {FIELD} commands that follow. The space is inserted before the {END IF} command.)

   Line 2:

   {FIELD}Title~*{IF NOT BLANK}Title~[HRt]*

   Line 3:

   {*END IF*}{FIELD}Company~*{IF NOT BLANK}Company~[HRt]*

   Line 4:

   {*END IF*}{FIELD}Address~

   Line 5: (no changes)

   {FIELD}City~, {FIELD}State~ {FIELD}Zip~

When you finish inserting the {IF NOT BLANK} AND {END IF} commands, your primary file should appear similar to Figure 11.19. However, the first and second lines in Figure 11.19, which include the Mr./Ms., First Name, Middle Name, and Last Name fields, should be a single line in your document, and it will extend way past the right margin on your screen. Since this line was too wide for the printed page, it had to be split between two lines in the figure, so you see it all.

10. The last step is to save the file again, using the same name: ENV.PF.

```
{FIELD}Mr/Ms~{IF NOT BLANK}Mr/Ms~ {END IF}{FIELD}First Name~
{FIELD}Middle Name~{IF NOT BLANK}Middle Name~ {END IF}{FIELD}Last Name~
{FIELD}Title~{IF NOT BLANK}Title~
{END IF}{FIELD}Company~{IF NOT BLANK}Company~
{END IF}{FIELD}Address~
{FIELD}City~, {FIELD}State~  {FIELD}Zip~
```

Figure 11.19 *The envelope primary file after inserting {IF NOT BLANK} and {END IF} merge commands for four of the fields.*

Merging and Printing the Envelopes

To merge the primary envelope file with the list of applicants in your secondary file, start by clearing the Edit screen and then:.

1. Select Merge:

    Keyboard: Press Merge/Sort (Ctrl-F9) and select the first option, **Merge**.

    Mouse: Display the **Tools** menu and select **Merge**.

    This prompt appears:

    ```
    Primary file      (List Files)
    ```

    Note that the List Files message on the right side indicates that you can press the List key (F5), and then use the Retrieve option on the List Files menu to retrieve the primary file. This is helpful if you've forgotten the exact file name.

2. In response, enter the name of the primary file: ENV.PF. Next, this prompt appears:

    ```
    Secondary file     (List Files)
    ```

3. Enter the name of the secondary file: `APPLICAN.SF`. Again, note the prompt indicating that you can use the List key (F5) to retrieve it.

A `* Merging *` prompt will appear while WordPerfect is performing the merge. After the envelopes appear on the screen, you can proofread them, edit as necessary, and then print the envelopes.

The Form Letter Primary File

The primary file that will be used to produce the four different reply letters is shown in Figure 11.20. Although it may appear impossibly complex at first glance, it is actually very logical. This section will explain it step by step. After applying a bit of analysis to the structure, you should have no trouble understanding it.

The name and address section of the letter primary file is identical to the envelope primary file that you created earlier, except that it will not use the same formatting (such as Envelope for the Paper Size/Type). Because of this, you can save some work: Just retrieve the ENV.PF file, modify the formatting, and then complete the rest of the reply letter primary file. Follow these steps:

1. Clear the screen and retrieve the ENV.PF file.

2. Use the Initial Codes option on the Format: Document menu to delete the formatting codes for the margins, and the Paper Size/Type (Shift-F8 D C or **Layout Document** C).

   The document will then return to the default formatting for your version of WordPerfect (unless you've changed it, it should be 8.5" x 11" Standard Paper Size/Type, and 1" margins on all four sides of the page). If you will be using letterhead, you may want to change the top margin setting to accommodate it before exiting from the Initial Codes menu.

3. Save the file using this name: *APPLICAN.PF*.

   A warning: Be careful not to press Enter in response to the `Document to be saved` prompt until you've typed the new file name; otherwise, you may inadvertently save it under the same name as the envelope file, ENV.PF, erasing the original envelope primary file in the process (but you'd have to press Enter and then type Y in response to the `Replace` prompt).

4. Position the cursor at the end of the last line, after `{FIELD}Zip~`, press Enter twice, and then type `Dear`.

5. Use the merge Field option to insert the *Mr/Ms* and *Last Name* fields on the salutation line, separated by one space (Shift-F9 **F** or **Tools, Merge**

Codes, Field). At the end of the salutation, type a colon. It should appear as follows:

```
{FIELD}Mr/Ms~ {FIELD}Last Name~:
```

6. Press Enter twice, and then type the first paragraph in the body of the letter:

```
We have received your letter and resume and wish to take
this opportunity to thank you for your interest in employ-
ment opportunities with PCX Corporation.
```

{FIELD}Mr/Ms~{IF NOT BLANK}Mr/Ms~ {END IF}{FIELD}First Name~
{FIELD}Middle Name~{IF NOT BLANK}Middle Name~ {END IF}{FIELD}Last Name~
{FIELD}Title~{IF NOT BLANK}Title~
{END IF}{FIELD}Company~{IF NOT BLANK}Company~
{END IF}{FIELD}Address~
{FIELD}City~, {FIELD}State~ {FIELD}Zip~

Dear {FIELD}Mr/Ms~ {FIELD}Last Name~,

We have received your letter and resume and wish to take this opportunity to thank you for
your interest in employment opportunities with PCX Corporation.

{IF}"{FIELD}Status~"="Filled"~{COMMENT}
~The position you have applied for, {FIELD}Position~, has been filled. However we are most
impressed by your credentials and experience, and will keep your resume in the active file for
six months. If, during that time, a similar position becomes available, we will contact you for
an interview.{END IF}{COMMENT}

~{IF}"{FIELD}Status~"="Frozen"~{COMMENT}
~We are currently experiencing a hiring freeze. It is anticipated that the hiring freeze will be
in effect for at least {FIELD}Freeze Months~ months. We will advertise in local newspapers
when hiring is resumed. Until then, we wish you the best of luck in your employment
search.{END IF}{COMMENT}

~{IF}"{FIELD}Status~"="Recontact"~{COMMENT}
~Although your credentials and experience are most impressive, we regret to say that we do
not have any openings for {FIELD}Position~ in the {FIELD}Department~ department at this
time. However, we will keep your resume on file for six months, and will contact you for an
interview as soon as a suitable position becomes available.{END IF}{COMMENT}

~{IF}"{FIELD}Status~"="Interview"~{COMMENT}
~We are most impressed by your credentials and experience and are very interested in having
you on our team. We anticipate a suitable opening in the {FIELD}Department~ department
soon and have scheduled an interview for {FIELD}Interview Date~, at {FIELD}Interview
Time~ with {FIELD}Interviewer~. Please let me know as soon as possible if this is
convenient.{END IF}

Please feel free to write to me at the address above if you have any questions. Thank you.

Yours truly,

Marjorie Jackson
Personnel Administrator

Figure 11.20 The primary file for the four reply letters.

Using the {IF}expr~ and {END IF} Merge Codes

The next paragraph that will be inserted into the body of the reply letter will be determined during the merge, and depends on the contents of the STATUS field in the secondary file: *Interview, Filled, Freeze,* or *Recontact.* Notice that four sets of **{IF}**expr~ **{END IF}** codes appear in the primary file. These codes are used to instruct WordPerfect how to handle each of the four possible statuses.

For the moment, ignore the {COMMENT} codes in these paragraphs and concentrate on the **{IF}**expr~ **{END IF}** codes. The {COMMENT} codes will be explained in the next section.

Here's how the {IF}expr~ {END IF} codes will work in this primary file:

- A pair of {IF}expr~ and {END IF} codes surrounds each of the four paragraphs, as shown in Figure 11.20. (Note that *expr* in the {IF} code means *expression.*)

- The {IF}expr~ code sets up a test. Its purpose is to determine the contents of the STATUS field, and perform a specific action if the status is found to match the condition being tested.

In WordPerfect's merge language, this test is expressed as follows in the first paragraph:

```
{IF}"{FIELD}Status~"="Filled"~
```

where the expression (expr~) being tested is (without the quote marks):

{FIELD}Status~ = Filled

Translated into English, WordPerfect interprets this test to mean that if the contents of the field named *Status* (in the secondary file) are found to be the word "Filled" (that is, are "equal to" filled), then continue with the instructions that follow immediately after the test. To return to the merge language, these instructions include everything that follows the tilde character (~) after "Filled" (the tilde signifies the end of the IF expression) and precedes the {END IF} code at the end of the paragraph. In English, the instructions are the text of the "Position Filled" paragraph, which will be inserted into the letter if the STATUS field contains the word "filled."

Notice that the two parts of the test, *{FIELD}Status~* and *Filled,* are enclosed in quotation marks. This is required, because these two parts represent text that is being compared: the contents of the STATUS field—Interview, Filled, Freeze, or Recontact—and the word "filled."

If the test proves false, and the contents of the STATUS field are *not* the word "Filled," WordPerfect will ignore everything between this line and the next {END IF} code, and then continue the merge. Since three other sets of {IF}expr~ and {END IF} codes follow, the merge will perform the other tests and determine which paragraph to insert. However, if the STATUS field in the secondary file is blank or is spelled differently, such as *Filed* instead of *Filled*, none of these paragraphs will be included in the merged letter.

The {IF}expr~ and {END IF} codes surrounding the other three paragraphs work just like the ones in the first paragraph. The logic is as follows:

- If the STATUS field contains the word "Filled," WordPerfect will insert the "Position Filled" paragraph (shown in Table 11.2).

- If the STATUS field contains the word "Interview," WordPerfect will insert the "Interview" paragraph (shown in Table 11.2).

- If the STATUS field contains the word "Recontact," WordPerfect will insert the "No Openings" paragraph (shown in Table 11.2).

- If the STATUS field contains the word "Frozen," WordPerfect will insert the "Hiring Freeze" paragraph (shown in Table 11.2).

Warning: In a primary merge file, every {IF}expr~ code must be followed at some point by an {END IF} code. If you forget one or more, the merge application will not work correctly (or, more likely, it won't work at all).

Using the {COMMENT}comment~ Merge Code

The {COMMENT}comment~ code allows you to position merge codes and text in a more organized way, so that sections of a primary file which contain other merge codes will be easier to read and understand. Anything that you place between the {COMMENT} code and the tilde used to end the comment will not appear in the documents that WordPerfect creates when you run the merge.

The {COMMENT} codes are optional in our example, but helpful. They are used to exclude the [HRt] codes that follow the first and last line of each paragraph, so that WordPerfect won't insert extra blank lines into the merged letters. For example, if you don't use them, you'll have to type the first paragraph as follows:

```
{IF}"{FIELD}Status~"="Filled"~The position you have ap-
plied for, {FIELD}Position~, has been filled. However we
are most impressed by your credentials and experience, and
will keep your resume in the active file for six months.
If, during that time, a similar position becomes avail-
able, we will contact you for an interview.{END IF}
```

and type the second one immediately after it. You cannot, for example, just press Enter and insert a [HRt] code after the tilde that follows "Filled," as shown below:

```
{IF}"{FIELD}Status~"="Filled"~
The position you have applied for, {FIELD}Position~, has
been filled.....
```

If you do, one or more extra blank lines will be inserted into the merged letter. Use of the COMMENT codes, as instructed in the next section, will prevent this problem.

Entering the Four Conditional Paragraphs

In this section, you'll type the four conditional paragraphs and their codes. The first step will be to insert the {IF}expr~ code.

1. To insert the first {IF}expr~ code:

    Keyboard: Press Merge Codes (Shift-F9) and select **More** (or press Shift-F9 twice).

    Mouse: Display the **Tools** menu, select **Merge Codes**, and then select **More**.

    A box of merge codes pops out to the right.

2. Move the cursor onto the {IF}expr~ code, and press Enter to select it. This prompt will appear:

    ```
    Enter Expression:
    ```

    The expression that you are supposed to insert at this position is:

    ```
    "{FIELD}Status~"="Filled"~
    ```

    Notice that it requires the use of the {FIELD} code. However, you cannot use the Merge Codes menu to enter the {FIELD} code at this point. Instead, you have to press Enter to implement the {IF}expr~ command, then move the cursor back and insert the rest of the expression so that it precedes the tilde which ends the expr~ part of the {IF}expr~ code. At this point, you can insert the first quotation mark before pressing Enter. Remember, the contents of the STATUS field will be compared to the word "Filled" during the merge, so it must be enclosed in quotation marks.

3. Type a quotation mark and then press Enter. This inserts the {IF} code, followed by a quotation mark and a tilde: {IF}"~.

4. Next, press Left Arrow to move the cursor left one position, placing it on the tilde, and then use the Field option on the Merge Codes menu to insert the {FIELD}Status~ code:

Keyboard: Press Shift-F9 and select **Field.**

Mouse: Display the **Tools** menu, select **Merge** Codes, and then select **Field.**

In response to the `Enter Field` prompt, type:

`Status`

and press Enter. The prompt should now appear as follows:

`{IF}"{FIELD}status~~`

(with two tildes at the end).

5. Type a quotation mark, an equal sign, and another quotation mark, as follows:

   `"="`

6. Type:

   `Filled`

   followed by another quotation mark.

7. Press Right Arrow once to move the cursor past the tilde character. Next, insert the {COMMENT} merge code:

   Keyboard: Press Merge Codes (Shift-F9) and select **More** (or press Shift-F9 twice).

   Mouse: Display the **Tools** menu, select **Merge** Codes, and then select **More.**

8. Move the cursor onto the {COMMENT}comment~ code in the box, and press Enter to select it. In response to the `Enter Comment:` prompt, press Enter (to leave it blank).

   This line should now appear as follows:

   `{IF}"{FIELD}Status~"="Filled"~{COMMENT}~`

9. Press Left Arrow once to place the cursor on the last tilde, and then press Enter.

   This moves the tilde down to the next line, and is needed to prevent WordPerfect from inserting a [HRt] code and blank line if this paragraph is not used in the letter.

10. Press the Right Arrow to move the cursor past the tilde, and then type the following "Position Filled" paragraph. Be sure to use the Field option on the Merge Codes menu to insert the {FIELD}Position~ code on the first line (step 4 provides general instructions).

```
The position you have applied for, {FIELD}Position~, has
been filled. However we are most impressed by your creden-
tials and experience, and will keep your resume in the
active file for six months. If, during that time, a simi-
lar position becomes available, we will contact you for an
interview.
```

11. At the end of the paragraph, insert the {END IF} code:

Keyboard: Press Merge Codes (Shift-F9) and select **More** (or press Shift-F9 twice).

Mouse: Display the Tools menu, select **Merge** Codes, and then select **More**.

Highlight the {END IF} code inside the box, and press Enter. This inserts the {END IF} code.

12. Insert the second {COMMENT} code, at the end of the paragraph. Press Left Arrow once to move the cursor back onto the tilde, and then press Enter twice to move it down two lines. This tilde belongs at the beginning of the next paragraph, so WordPerfect can use it to exclude the two [HRt] codes you just created by pressing Enter.

Tip: The {IF}expr~ and {END IF} codes can be used to set up a test that WordPerfect will use during the merge to determine which text to insert into a merged letter. In this example, these codes instruct WordPerfect to check the contents of the STATUS field in the secondary file, and use it to determine which of the four paragraphs to insert into the merged letter.

13. Follow the instructions in steps 1 through 12 of this section to enter the next three paragraphs and their codes. Note that the last paragraph does not require a {COMMENT} code at the end (in fact, if you accidentally insert it, the merge will stop after the first record).

14. Type the last paragraph in the body of the letter and the letter closing, as follows:

```
Please feel free to write to me at the address above if
you have any questions. Thank you.

Yours truly,

Marjorie Jackson
Personnel Administrator
```

15. Save the file again, using the same name, APPLICAN.PF, and then clear the Edit screen.

Merging and Printing the Conditional Form Letters

To merge the primary letter file with the list of applicants, follow the instructions in the section, "Merging and Printing the Envelopes." The only difference is that in step 2, you'll enter the name of the letter primary file, *APPLICAN.PF*. Be sure to clear the screen before you begin.

A * Merging * prompt will appear while WordPerfect is performing the merge. Once the letters appear on the Edit screen, they are just like any other document. You can now proofread and edit them, print them, and even save them as a new file.

SORT AND SELECT

Sort and select are powerful features that you can use to rearrange information in your files. You can use WordPerfect's Sort feature to alphabetize data or sort it in numeric order, using ascending or descending sort order. The data can be arranged in lines, paragraphs, tables, or in merge format. You can use a line sort to rearrange lists of information typed in tabular columns. For instance, you could use it to alphabetize a list of names and phone numbers. If your data is in a secondary merge file, you rearrange it with the merge sort, using any of the fields as the sort order. If your data is arranged in paragraphs, so that one or more items exceeds one line in length, you use the paragraph sort. The Select feature lets you extract information from a list. For example, if you had a merge file with hundreds of names and addresses from all over the country, and you wanted to send a form letter only to the California residents, you could use Select to create a new secondary file containing only the records of those in California.

Line Sort

Line sorts are the easiest type of sort. For example, if you were to type a list like the following one, only a few short steps would be needed to alphabetize it by first or last name.

John Smith
Mike Jones
Maryanne Rome
Michael Sanchez
Arlene Lee
Kathy Carpenter

This list contains only one column of information, typed at the left margin. If your list includes two or more columns, you must use the tab key to separate the columns, and each line must end in a hard or soft return. For instance, if you were to include each individual's salary, as shown below, you would type the name, then press tab once and type the salary (you might have to change the tab stop settings so you'd only have to press tab once to get to the second column).

Name	Salary
John Smith	20,000
Mike Jones	17,000
Maryanne Rome	33,000
Michael Sanchez	29,500
Arlene Lee	45,000
Kathy Carpenter	19,500

In a line sort, each row of information is called a *record,* and it consists of one complete set of data. In the example above, there are six records. The first record is:

John Smith   20,000

and the last record is:

Kathy Carpenter   19,500

Records are divided into *fields*, which are separated by tab stops. Each record in the sample list above has two fields: name and salary. Each field can have one or more words, separated by a blank space. The Name field in this example contains two words. The type of information in each field must be the same. For example, WordPerfect could not sort a list such as this using the information in the second column, salary or title (although it could be sorted by name, since the first column contains only names), since it is not set up correctly:

John Smith	20,000
Mike Jones	Secretary
Maryanne Rome	33,000
Michael Sanchez	Manager
Arlene Lee	45,000
Kathy Carpenter	Accountant

To learn how to perform a line sort, set tab stops at 3", 4", 5", and 6", and type the list shown in Figure 12.1. Save the file using the name HOUSES. It is important that you change the tab stop settings and separate each column by a single tab stop, because this is how WordPerfect determines the field numbers that you will use to specify the sort order. The first field is at the left margin, the second field is at the first tab position, the third field is at the second tab position, etc. In the example shown in Figure 12.1, the fields are:

Field 1: Street	Left margin, 1"
Field 2: City	First tab stop, 3"
Field 3: Size	Second tab stop, 4"
Field 4: Price	Third tab stop, 5"
Field 5: Agent	Fourth tab stop, 6"

Street	City	Size	Price	Agent
100 Bella Vista	Fairfax	3br 2ba	129,000	Andrea Smith
2000 Cielo Ave	Novato	4br 3ba	132,800	Janet Court
5 Sandpiper Lane	Larkspur	2br 1ba	147,500	Mike Milland
199 Riviera	Inverness	3br 2ba	119,300	Andrea Smith
77 Corte Eliseo	Novato	5br 3ba	187,000	Andrea Smith
399 Redwood St	Kentfield	2br 2ba	201,600	Mike Milland
100 Cascade Ave	Belvedere	4br 2ba	209,000	Andrea Smith
4 Chester Lane	Novato	2br 1ba	112,300	Mike Milland
212 Francis St	Larkspur	3br 1ba	139,900	Mike Milland
22 Woodland	Ignacio	5br 4ba	149,300	Janet Court
901 Goodhill St	Novato	5br 3ba	189,000	Janet Court
499 Redwood St	Kentfield	4br 2ba	235,500	Mike Milland
308 Valley Fair Rd	Larkspur	3br 1ba	112,900	Janet Court
2010 Stetson	Tiburon	3br 3ba	234,000	Mike Milland
451 Carrera Drive	Fairfax	2br 2ba	149,000	Andrea Smith
99 Ardmore	Novato	3br 2ba	113,000	Janet Court
129 Main St	Belvedere	4br 3ba	266,000	Mike Milland
1018 Ocean View Rd	Belvedere	2br 1ba	219,000	Janet Court

Figure 12.1 *Type this list to practice using Line Sort.*

If you were to type the list without changing the tab stop settings, you could not sort the list correctly. Because some of the street addresses are short, such as 99 Ardmore, you would have to press the tab key twice to move the cursor to the 3" position to type the city. In such a case, City would be the third field. After typing a longer street address, such as 5 Sandpiper Lane, you would press the tab key only once to move the cursor into the next column, so City would be the second field. As a result, you would not be able to sort by City or any of the fields that follow it.

 Tip: Always save a file before you sort it in case you make a mistake in the sort definition and the results are not what you wanted.

To begin the line sort of the list you just typed:

1. Select Sort:

    Keyboard: Press the Merge/Sort key, Ctrl-F9. This menu line appears:

    `1 Merge; 2 Sort; 3 Convert Old Merge Codes: 0`

    Select the second option, **Sort**.

    Mouse: Display the **Tools** menu and select **Sort**.

    This prompt appears, asking for the name of the file that you want to sort:

```
Input file to sort: (Screen)
```

WordPerfect assumes that the file is already on the Edit screen. If it weren't, you would not have to retrieve the file in order to sort it. Instead, you could type its name in response to this prompt.

2. Since the input file is on the Edit screen, press Enter or click the right mouse button.

The next prompt asks where you want to place the output file, which will contain the results of the sort action:

```
Output file for sort: (Screen)
```

Again, WordPerfect assumes you want it to appear on the Edit screen. If not, you could type a file name.

3. To send the sorted list to the Edit screen, press Enter or click the right mouse button.

The Sort by Line screen will appear, as shown in Figure 12.2. As you'll see later in this chapter, when you change the type of sort to Merge or Paragraph, the Sort by Line heading at the top (under the tab ruler) also will change.

Defining the Sort Order

Below the heading in the Sort by Line screen is the section where you'll define your sort order, by specifying criteria for up to nine keys. The line below that is where you can enter selection criteria to restrict your list, which you'll learn more about later. Below that is a section that shows you the defaults for Action, sort Order, and the Type of sort.

The menu line at the bottom lists seven options. Perform Action is the first option, but you don't use it until you have defined your sort and are ready to carry it out. You can use the second option, View, to temporarily leave the Sort menu and scroll through your document. While using View, you cannot edit the text. When you finish looking at it, return to the Sort menu by pressing Exit (F7).

You use the third option, Keys, to define the sort order. In other words, this is where you specify whether you want to sort by street, city, size, price, or agent, or a combination. You can actually define up to nine keys. For example, to sort the list shown in Figure 12.1 by city, and within each city in ascending price order, you would define two keys: City and Price. The results of such a sort appear in Figure 12.3. The list has been rearranged alphabetically according to city, so the first three houses are in Belvedere, the next two are in Fairfax, then Ignacio, and so on. Within each city, the houses are listed in ascending price order. For example, the first house in Novato is priced at $112,300, the next is $113,000, then $132,800, and so on.

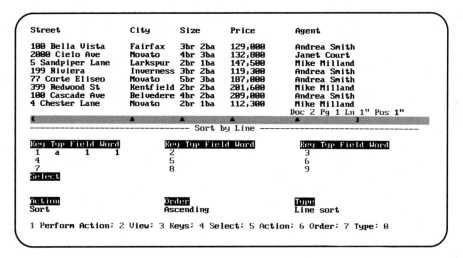

```
 Street             City      Size    Price     Agent

 100 Bella Vista    Fairfax   3br 2ba  129,000  Andrea Smith
 2000 Cielo Ave     Novato    4br 3ba  132,000  Janet Court
 5 Sandpiper Lane   Larkspur  2br 1ba  147,500  Mike Milland
 199 Riviera        Inverness 3br 2ba  119,300  Andrea Smith
 77 Corte Eliseo    Novato    5br 3ba  187,000  Andrea Smith
 399 Redwood St     Kentfield 2br 2ba  201,600  Mike Milland
 100 Cascade Ave    Belvedere 4br 2ba  209,000  Andrea Smith
 4 Chester Lane     Novato    2br 1ba  112,300  Mike Milland
                                                 Doc 2 Pg 1 Ln 1" Pos 1"

------------------------------ Sort by Line ------------------------------

 Key Typ Field Word          Key Typ Field Word          Key Typ Field Word
  1   a    1    1              2                           3
  4                           5                           6
  7                           8                           9
 Select

 Action                      Order                       Type
 Sort                        Ascending                   Line sort

 1 Perform Action; 2 View; 3 Keys; 4 Select; 5 Action; 6 Order; 7 Type: 0
```

Figure 12.2 *The Sort by Line screen.*

```
 Street               City      Size    Price     Agent

 100 Cascade Ave      Belvedere 4br 2ba  209,000  Andrea Smith
 1010 Ocean View Rd   Belvedere 2br 1ba  219,000  Janet Court
 129 Main St          Belvedere 4br 2ba  266,000  Mike Milland
 100 Bella Vista      Fairfax   3br 2ba  129,000  Andrea Smith
 451 Carrera Drive    Fairfax   2br 2ba  149,000  Andrea Smith
 22 Woodland          Ignacio   5br 4ba  149,300  Janet Court
 199 Riviera          Inverness 3br 2ba  119,300  Andrea Smith
 399 Redwood St       Kentfield 2br 2ba  201,600  Mike Milland
 499 Redwood St       Kentfield 4br 2ba  235,500  Mike Milland
 300 Valley Fair Rd   Larkspur  3br 1ba  112,900  Janet Court
 212 Francis St       Larkspur  3br 1ba  139,900  Mike Milland
 5 Sandpiper Lane     Larkspur  2br 1ba  147,500  Mike Milland
 4 Chester Lane       Novato    2br 1ba  112,300  Mike Milland
 99 Ardmore           Novato    3br 2ba  113,000  Janet Court
 2000 Cielo Ave       Novato    4br 3ba  132,000  Janet Court
 77 Corte Eliseo      Novato    5br 3ba  187,000  Andrea Smith
 901 Goodhill St      Novato    5br 3ba  189,000  Janet Court
 2010 Stetson         Tiburon   3br 3ba  234,000  Mike Milland




                                                  Doc 1 Pg 1 Ln 1" Pos 1"
```

Figure 12.3 *The results of sorting the HOUSES list using two keys: City and Price.*

In a line sort, you can use three criteria to define each key: Type, Field, and Word. Notice that WordPerfect has already supplied defaults for the first key:

Key	Typ	Field	Word
1	a	1	1

Unless you change these defaults, WordPerfect will use an alphanumeric sort type, and the sort order will be the first word in the first field (at the left margin). For example, this would sort the HOUSES file by the first word in the street address, and the results would be virtually meaningless.

Let's explore the three criteria.

Type: Use Type to specify whether the information is numeric or alpha-numeric. Alphanumeric data can be letters, a combination of letters and numbers, or numbers if they contain exactly the same number of digits. In the HOUSES list, all the figures in the Price field have the same number of digits, so you could use an alphanumeric type to sort by price. How-ever, you would have to use the numeric type if any of the prices had more than or fewer than six digits. For example, if one of the prices were 95,000, it would end up at the bottom of the list after sorting, as shown in Figure 12.4. In an alphanumeric sort, WordPerfect sorts from left to right by the first character, then the second, and so forth. As a result, any number beginning with 1 or 2 appears before 9 in the sorted list, regard-less of the number of digits it contains. In such a case, you would have to use the numeric sort type. You also would have to use a numeric type to sort a list such as this one:

7.85
$100.00
$2,000.88
100.02
2,220,000.11
4,500.12

As you can see, numeric data can include dollar signs, commas, and decimal points.

Field: Use Field to specify which column contains the information for your sort key. The first field is the column that begins at the left margin, the second field is the first tab stop, and each of the remaining fields is separated by one tab stop.

Word: If a field includes more than one word, use this option to specify which word to use for the sort order. For example, to sort the HOUSES list by the agents' last names, you would select field five, word two. However, this wouldn't work if any of the names in the Agent column included middle initials, such as Mike A. Milland. Since *A* would be the second word, Mike A. Milland would be first in the resulting list. In such a case, you could use negative numbers to count the words from right to left instead of left to right. To sort by last name in this example, you would enter -1 as the word. If a name includes a third word, such as *Jr.* or *Sr.*, you could use a hard space instead of a regular space to separate it from the last name. This tricks WordPerfect into treating the two words as one word, even though they appear to be separated by a blank space. To type a hard space, press Home first, and then press the space bar.

The fourth option on the main Sort by Line menu, Select, lets you set up selection conditions. For instance, you could use it to restrict the list to houses in the city of Novato, or to houses in a certain price range. You'll learn more about Select later in this chapter. The next option, Action, is related. If you've set up a selection condition, you can use Action to specify whether you want to sort and select, or just select. Until you use the fourth option to establish a selection condition, the Action option is unavailable, and you cannot choose it from the menu.

Sorting the Price field using the alphanumeric type moved 95,000 to the bottom of the list, out of order.

```
 Street                City        Size    Price       Agent

 4 Chester Lane        Novato      2br 1ba  112,300     Mike Milland
 308 Valley Fair Rd    Larkspur    3br 1ba  112,900     Janet Court
 99 Ardmore            Novato      3br 2ba  113,000     Janet Court
 199 Riviera           Inverness   3br 2ba  119,300     Andrea Smith
 100 Bella Vista       Fairfax     3br 2ba  129,000     Andrea Smith
 2000 Cielo Ave        Novato      4br 3ba  132,800     Janet Court
 212 Francis St        Larkspur    3br 1ba  139,900     Mike Milland
 5 Sandpiper Lane      Larkspur    2br 1ba  147,500     Mike Milland
 451 Carrera Drive     Fairfax     2br 2ba  149,000     Andrea Smith
 Court22 Woodland      Ignacio     5br 4ba  149,300     Janet Court
 77 Corte Eliseo       Novato      5br 3ba  187,000     Andrea Smith
 901 Goodhill St       Novato      5br 3ba  189,000     Janet Court
 399 Redwood St        Kentfield   2br 2ba  201,600     Mike Milland
 100 Cascade Ave       Belvedere   4br 2ba  209,000     Andrea Smith
 1010 Ocean View Rd    Belvedere   2br 1ba  219,000     Janet Court
 2010 Stetson          Tiburon     3br 3ba  234,000     Mike Milland
 499 Redwood St        Kentfield   4br 2ba  235,500     Mike Milland
 129 Main St           Belvedere   4br 3ba  266,000     Mike Milland
 118 Smith Ranch Rd    Novato      3br 3ba  95,000      Janet Court



 Typeover                                    Doc 2 Pg 1 Ln 1" Pos 1"
```

Figure 12.4 *If one of the prices in the HOUSES list had fewer than six digits, you would have to use a numeric sort instead of an alphanumeric one. If you used an alphanumeric sort, WordPerfect would not place the price in the correct numeric order, as shown in this example.*

The sixth option, Order, lets you change the sort order from ascending to descending. If you are sorting numbers, ascending order lists the smallest number first, and the largest one last. For example, Table 12.1 shows the Price column sorted in ascending and descending order. If you are sorting alphanumeric data in ascending order, the *A*'s come first and the *Z*'s last. Descending order is the opposite. For example, if you sorted the HOUSES list in descending order by city, the rows would be in this order:

Tiburon
Novato
Larkspur
Kentfield
Inverness
Ignacio
Fairfax
Belvedere

However, numbers come before letters, and lowercase letters come before uppercase ones. For example, if you were to sort this list in ascending order:

Northridge Lane
5th Avenue
Park Avenue
de Long Ave
Mt. Shasta Blvd
Stage Road
1st Street
Delany Place
South St
n. Freemont Ave

the results would be as follows:

1st Street
5th Avenue
de Long Ave
Delany Place
Mt. Shasta Blvd
n. Freemont Ave
Northridge Lane
Park Avenue
South St
Stage Road

Table 12.1   *The Price column sorted in ascending and descending numeric order.*

Ascending	Descending
112,300	266,000
112,900	235,500
113,000	234,000
119,300	219,000
129,000	209,000
132,800	201,600
139,900	189,000
147,500	187,000
149,000	149,300
149,300	149,000
187,000	147,500
189,000	139,900
201,600	132,800
209,000	129,000
219,000	119,300

Ascending	Descending
234,000	113,000
235,500	112,900
266,000	112,300

The last option on the Sort menu is Type. You can use Type to change the type of sort to Paragraph or Merge. You'll learn how to use these other sort types later in this chapter.

Now, let's proceed with the line sort of our HOUSES list. We'll use the Keys option to define the sort order. City will be the first key, and Price the second.

1. Select the **Keys** option from the Sort by Line screen.

   The cursor moves to the Key 1 definition area, as shown in Figure 12.5. Notice the message at the bottom of the screen, prompting you to select Alphanumeric or Numeric as the key type. Since Alphanumeric is the default, you can leave it and press the Right Arrow key to move to the next option, Field. If you type *a*, the cursor will automatically move to Field.

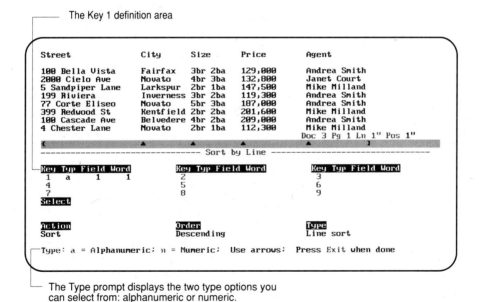

Figure 12.5 *After you select the Keys option from the main Sort menu, the cursor moves to the Key 1 definition area. Since the first option is Type, the message at the bottom of the screen prompts you to select either an alphanumeric or a numeric sort.*

2. Type a or press the Right Arrow key.

   Since City is the second field in the HOUSES list, your next step will be to change Field from 1 to 2. There is only one word in the City column, so you can leave the default of 1 for Word.

3. Type 2, and then press the Right Arrow key twice.

   The next step is to define the second key, which will be price. Price is the fourth field, and has one word. Remember, you can use either the alphanumeric or the numeric sort type, since each price contains the same number of digits.

4. Type a for the sort type, type 4 for the field, and 1 for the word. Press the Exit key (F7) when you finish.

   The menu line reappears at the bottom of the screen. The keys should appear as shown below:

Key	Typ	Field	Word	Key	Typ	Field	Word
1	a	2	1	2	a	4	1

   Your last step will be to sort the list, using Perform Action.

5. Select option 1, Perform Action.

   The results of your first sort should be similar to Figure 12.3, with the list in alphabetical order by city, and within each city group, in ascending price order. However, there is one important difference: WordPerfect sorted every line in your file, including the line of headings and the blank line separating it from the data. Blank lines always end up at the top, so that was not a problem. However, WordPerfect interpreted the heading City as being the name of a city, and placed it in the correct alphabetical order after Belvedere. As shown below, the line of headings are now in the fourth row:

```
100 Cascade Ave      Belvedere 4br 2ba  209,000 Andrea Smith
1018 Ocean View Rd   Belvedere 2br 1ba  219,000 Janet Court
129 Main St          Belvedere 4br 3ba  266,000 Mike Milland
 Street              City      Size     Price   Agent
100 Bella Vista      Fairfax   3br 2ba  129,000 Andrea Smith
```

   To prevent WordPerfect from sorting data such as the headings, you can limit the sort to a specific section by blocking it before sorting. In the next section, you'll learn how. Since you saved the original file before performing this sort, you can clear this version from the screen and retrieve the unsorted one.

Block Sort

When you want to limit the sort action to a specific section in a document, use WordPerfect's Block feature to define the area. To try it, clear the screen without saving the sorted list, and then retrieve the original HOUSES file. This time, you'll sort the file by the agents' last names, and then by size.

1. Move the cursor to the beginning of the list, and place it on the 1 (in 100 Bella Vista).

2. Turn on Block mode, and then move the cursor to the end of the list:

    Keyboard: Press Alt-F4 (or F12) and then Page Down.

    Mouse: Click the left button and hold it while dragging the mouse to the end of the list.

    The cursor should be in the blank line under the last row (1018 Ocean View Rd).

3. Select Sort:

    Keyboard: Press the Merge/Sort key, Ctrl-F9.

    Mouse: Display the **Tools** menu and select **S**ort.

    This time, WordPerfect goes directly to the Sort by Line screen, without asking for the input and output file names. As you learned in Chapter 4, many of WordPerfect's features work differently when Block is on. When you turn on Block mode and select Sort, WordPerfect assumes you want to sort the highlighted section on the Edit screen, and send the results to the Edit screen.

    Notice that WordPerfect has retained the keys that you defined in the last sort. Until you exit WordPerfect or change them, these keys will always appear when you select Sort.

4. Select option 3, Keys, and erase the existing key definitions by pressing Ctrl-End.

5. Enter the following information for the three keys:

Key	Typ	Field	Word	Key	Typ	Field	Word	Key	Typ	Field	Word
1	a	5	2	2	a	3	1	3	a	3	2

    Key 1 will be the last name, which is in field 5, word 2. Key 2 will be the number of bedrooms, which is word 1 in field 3. Key 3 will be the number of bathrooms, word 2 in field 3. The third key can break a tie. For example, if one agent has several houses containing the same number of bedrooms, WordPerfect will sort those houses according to the number of bathrooms. For example, a two-bedroom, one- bath house listed with Mike Milland would appear before a two-bedroom, two-bath house.

6. Press the Exit key (F7) and then select option 1, **P**erform Action.

The results of your block sort appear in Figure 12.6. This time, the heading line has not been included in the sort.

```
Street              City       Size      Price      Agent

1018 Ocean View Rd  Belvedere  2br 1ba   219,000    Janet Court
308 Valley Fair Rd  Larkspur   3br 1ba   112,900    Janet Court
99 Ardmore          Novato     3br 2ba   113,000    Janet Court
2000 Cielo Ave      Novato     4br 3ba   132,800    Janet Court
901 Goodhill St     Novato     5br 3ba   189,000    Janet Court
22 Woodland         Ignacio    5br 4ba   149,300    Janet Court
4 Chester Lane      Novato     2br 1ba   112,300    Mike Milland
5 Sandpiper Lane    Larkspur   2br 1ba   147,500    Mike Milland
399 Redwood St      Kentfield  2br 2ba   201,600    Mike Milland
212 Francis St      Larkspur   3br 1ba   139,900    Mike Milland
2010 Stetson        Tiburon    3br 3ba   234,000    Mike Milland
499 Redwood St      Kentfield  4br 2ba   235,500    Mike Milland
129 Main St         Belvedere  4br 3ba   266,000    Mike Milland
451 Carrera Drive   Fairfax    2br 2ba   149,000    Andrea Smith
199 Riviera         Inverness  3br 2ba   119,300    Andrea Smith
100 Bella Vista     Fairfax    3br 2ba   129,000    Andrea Smith
100 Cascade Ave     Belvedere  4br 2ba   209,000    Andrea Smith
77 Corte Eliseo     Novato     5br 3ba   187,000    Andrea Smith



                                            Doc 2 Pg 1 Ln 1" Pos 1"
```

Figure 12.6 *After you perform the block sort, the rows are in order by the agents' last names and then by size.*

Using Select

What if your list contained 300 houses, and you wanted to narrow it down to those in a particular city, or those listed with one agent? Use the Select option on the Sort menu. Let's try it. Begin by clearing the screen, and retrieving the original HOUSES file. After you finish using Select, the records that did not meet your conditions will be erased from the screen, so always be sure you have an original on disk, containing all the records.

1. Block the list and select Sort, as described in the previous section.

The Sort menu appears. It should still include the three keys that you defined in the last section. Say that you want to restrict the list to Janet Court's houses. Since key 1 is already defined as the agents' last names, it will be easy to set up the selection condition. Basically, you will instruct WordPerfect to select only the rows where Agent, which is key 1, equals Janet Court. It is expressed as follows: key1=Court.

2. Choose the fourth option on the Sort menu, Select. This prompt line appears at the bottom of the screen:

```
+(OR), *(AND), =, <>, >, <, >=, <=; Press Exit when done
```

The symbols are called *operators,* and you use them to define the records you want to select by typing the Key, the operator, and the condition. In this example, you'll use the equal sign as the operator, to specify that key 1, Agent, must match this condition: Janet Court. Table 12.2 explains the operators and how to use them.

3. For the selection condition, type:

```
key1 = Court
```

You do not have to capitalize the *C,* and the spaces are optional. Your screen should now appear as shown in Figure 12.7.

 Tip: When you enter selection conditions, case is not relevant. For example, WordPerfect will select all houses with Court as the agent whether you type key1=court, key1=Court, or even key1=COURT.

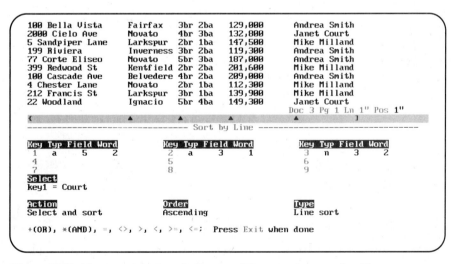

Figure 12.7 After you set up a selection condition, your screen should appear as shown here.

4. Press Enter to return to the menu, and then select the first option, **P**erform Action.

The resulting list will include only six records, those with Janet Court as the sales agent:

```
1018 Ocean View Rd  Belvedere  2br 1ba  219,000  Janet Court
308 Valley Fair Rd  Larkspur   3br 1ba  112,900  Janet Court
99 Ardmore          Novato     3br 2ba  113,000  Janet Court
2000 Cielo Ave      Novato     4br 3ba  132,800  Janet Court
901 Goodhill St     Novato     5br 3ba  189,000  Janet Court
22 Woodland         Ignacio    5br 4ba  149,300  Janet Court
```

Notice that they are in order by Size. Remember, the three sort keys that you defined in the last section are still in use: agent's last name is key 1, number of bedrooms is key 2, and number of bathrooms is key 3. You could have restricted the action to *Select Only* if you wanted to select Janet Court's houses, but not sort them. To try it, clear the screen and retrieve the original HOUSES file again.

1. Block the list and select **S**ort. The main Sort menu appears. Notice that the three keys are still defined.

2. Choose the fifth option, **A**ction. This prompt appears at the bottom of the screen:

```
Action: 1 Select and Sort; 2 Select Only: 0
```

3. Choose the second option, Select Only. Under the Action heading, the type of action changes from *Select and Sort* to *Select*.

4. Select the first option, **P**erform Action.

The resulting list appears as follows:

```
2000 Cielo Ave      Novato     4br 3ba  132,800  Janet Court
22 Woodland         Ignacio    5br 4ba  149,300  Janet Court
901 Goodhill St     Novato     5br 3ba  189,000  Janet Court
308 Valley Fair Rd  Larkspur   3br 1ba  112,900  Janet Court
99 Ardmore          Novato     3br 2ba  113,000  Janet Court
1018 Ocean View Rd  Belvedere  2br 1ba  219,000  Janet Court
```

This time, the houses are not sorted according to size. Instead, they appear in their original order.

 Tip: After you use Select, the selection condition will remain in the Sort screen. If you later want to perform a Sort Only action, you must erase the condition. To erase it, choose the Select option and press Ctrl-End.

Table 12.2   *Operators used to create selection conditions.*

+ Or: *The record will be selected if it meets either of two conditions. For example, assuming key 1 is Agent, you could use it as follows to select records where Janet Court or Mike Milland is the Agent: key1=Court + key1=Milland. The results would be:*

2000 Cielo Ave	Novato	4br 3ba	132,800	Janet Court
308 Valley Fair Rd	Larkspur	3br 1ba	112,900	Janet Court
99 Ardmore	Novato	3br 2ba	113,000	Janet Court
1018 Ocean View Rd	Belvedere	2br 1ba	219,000	Janet Court
22 Woodland	Ignacio	5br 4ba	149,300	Janet Court
901 Goodhill St	Novato	5br 3ba	189,000	Janet Court
129 Main St	Belvedere	4br 3ba	266,000	Mike Milland
5 Sandpiper Lane	Larkspur	2br 1ba	147,500	Mike Milland
399 Redwood St	Kentfield	2br 2ba	201,600	Mike Milland
2010 Stetson	Tiburon	3br 3ba	234,000	Mike Milland
499 Redwood St	Kentfield	4br 2ba	235,500	Mike Milland
4 Chester Lane	Novato	2br 1ba	112,300	Mike Milland
212 Francis St	Larkspur	3br 1ba	139,900	Mike Milland

* And: *The record will be selected only if it meets both conditions. Assuming key 1 is Agent and key 2 is City, you could use it as follows to select houses that match these two conditions: they are located in Novato, and Janet Court is the agent: key1=Court * key2=novato. The results would be:*

99 Ardmore	Novato	3br 2ba	113,000	Janet Court
901 Goodhill St	Novato	5br 3ba	189,000	Janet Court
2000 Cielo Ave	Novato	4br 3ba	132,800	Janet Court

= Equals: *The record will be selected only if it matches the condition exactly. For example, assuming key 1 is City, you can use the equal sign as follows to select all houses in Novato: key1=Novato. The results would be:*

99 Ardmore	Novato	3br 2ba	113,000	Janet Court
901 Goodhill St	Novato	5br 3ba	189,000	Janet Court
4 Chester Lane	Novato	2br 1ba	112,300	Mike Milland
77 Corte Eliseo	Novato	5br 3ba	187,000	Andrea Smith
2000 Cielo Ave	Novato	4br 3ba	132,800	Janet Court

continued

Table 12.2   (continued)

< > Not equal to: *Only records that do not match the selection condition will be chosen. Assuming key 1 is City, you could use it as follows to select all houses except those in the city of Novato: key1< >Novato. The results would be:*

129 Main St	Belvedere	4br 3ba	266,000	Mike Milland
1018 Ocean View Rd	Belvedere	2br 1ba	219,000	Janet Court
100 Cascade Ave	Belvedere	4br 2ba	209,000	Andrea Smith
451 Carrera Drive	Fairfax	2br 2ba	149,000	Andrea Smith
100 Bella Vista	Fairfax	3br 2ba	129,000	Andrea Smith
22 Woodland	Ignacio	5br 4ba	149,300	Janet Court
199 Riviera	Inverness	3br 2ba	119,300	Andrea Smith
499 Redwood St	Kentfield	4br 2ba	235,500	Mike Milland
399 Redwood St	Kentfield	2br 2ba	201,600	Mike Milland
5 Sandpiper Lane	Larkspur	2br 1ba	147,500	Mike Milland
308 Valley Fair Rd	Larkspur	3br 1ba	112,900	Janet Court
212 Francis St	Larkspur	3br 1ba	139,900	Mike Milland
2010 Stetson	Tiburon	3br 3ba	234,000	Mike Milland

> Greater than: *Only records that are greater than the value expressed by the selection condition will be chosen. Assuming key 1 is Price, you could use it to select all houses priced at greater than $200,000: key1>200000. The results would be:*

399 Redwood St	Kentfield	2br 2ba	201,600	Mike Milland
100 Cascade Ave	Belvedere	4br 2ba	209,000	Andrea Smith
1018 Ocean View Rd	Belvedere	2br 1ba	219,000	Janet Court
2010 Stetson	Tiburon	3br 3ba	234,000	Mike Milland
499 Redwood St	Kentfield	4br 2ba	235,500	Mike Milland
129 Main St	Belvedere	4br 3ba	266,000	Mike Milland

< Less than: *Only records that are less than the value expressed by the selection condition will be chosen. Assuming key 1 is the first word in the Size field, you could use it as follows to select all homes with three or fewer bedrooms: key1<4br. The results would be:*

451 Carrera Drive	Fairfax	2br 2ba	149,000	Andrea Smith
4 Chester Lane	Novato	2br 1ba	112,300	Mike Milland
399 Redwood St	Kentfield	2br 2ba	201,600	Mike Milland
5 Sandpiper Lane	Larkspur	2br 1ba	147,500	Mike Milland
1018 Ocean View Rd	Belvedere	2br 1ba	219,000	Janet Court
2010 Stetson	Tiburon	3br 3ba	234,000	Mike Milland
99 Ardmore	Novato	3br 2ba	113,000	Janet Court
212 Francis St	Larkspur	3br 1ba	139,900	Mike Milland
199 Riviera	Inverness	3br 2ba	119,300	Andrea Smith

100 Bella Vista	Fairfax	3br 2ba	129,000	Andrea Smith
308 Valley Fair Rd	Larkspur	3br 1ba	112,900	Janet Court

> = Greater than or equal to: *Only records that are greater than or equal to the value expressed by the selection condition will be chosen. Assuming key 1 is the first word in the Size field, you could use it to select all homes with four or more bedrooms: key1>=4br. The results would be:*

2000 Cielo Ave	Novato	4br 3ba	132,800	Janet Court
499 Redwood St	Kentfield	4br 2ba	235,500	Mike Milland
129 Main St	Belvedere	4br 3ba	266,000	Mike Milland
100 Cascade Ave	Belvedere	4br 2ba	209,000	Andrea Smith
77 Corte Eliseo	Novato	5br 3ba	187,000	Andrea Smith
901 Goodhill St	Novato	5br 3ba	189,000	Janet Court
22 Woodland	Ignacio	5br 4ba	149,300	Janet Court

< = Less than or equal to: *Only records that are less than or equal to the value expressed by the selection condition will be chosen. Assuming key 1 is Price, you could use it to select all homes priced at less than $129,000: key1<=129000. The results would be:*

4 Chester Lane	Novato	2br 1ba	112,300	Mike Milland
308 Valley Fair Rd	Larkspur	3br 1ba	112,900	Janet Court
99 Ardmore	Novato	3br 2ba	113,000	Janet Court
199 Riviera	Inverness	3br 2ba	119,300	Andrea Smith
100 Bella Vista	Fairfax	3br 2ba	129,000	Andrea Smith

( ) *You can use parentheses to group conditions, so WordPerfect will evaluate them as a unit. For example, assuming key 2 is Size and key 1 is Price, this selection condition produces different results when you place parentheses around the key 1 section:*

Key2>3br + key1>=150000 * key1<=200000

As shown above, the condition means a house must have more than three bedrooms, **or** a price of $150,000 or more, **and**, in all cases, a price of less than or equal to $200,000. WordPerfect evaluates size first, and restricts the list to houses with more than three bedrooms. Next, WordPerfect checks for prices. If a house is priced at under $150,000, it can only be included if it has more than three bedrooms. Because of the AND condition, WordPerfect rejects anything over $200,000. The first house in the list meets the first of the two OR conditions, more than three bedrooms, so the fact that its price is less than $150,000 is not relevant.

2000 Cielo Ave	Novato	4br 3ba	132,800	Janet Court
22 Woodland	Ignacio	5br 4ba	149,300	Janet Court

continued

Table 12.2 *(continued)*

77 Corte Eliseo	Novato	5br 3ba	187,000	Andrea Smith
901 Goodhill St	Novato	5br 3ba	189,000	Janet Court

Key2>3br + (key1>=150000 * key1<=200000)

With the parentheses around the key 1 section, the condition means that the price must be between $150,000 and $200,000, **or** the house must have more than three bedrooms, regardless of price. Since price is in parentheses, WordPerfect evaluates it first, and selects houses priced between $150,000 and $200,000. Next, the OR condition is evaluated, and WordPerfect adds to the list any houses with more than three bedrooms, regardless of their price. Even though they don't meet the price condition, the first house and the last three houses are selected because they meet the first OR condition, more than three bedrooms. If the original list had included a 2br, 2ba house that cost $159,000, it would have been included in the results because it meets the second OR condition, price between $150,000 and $200,000.

2000 Cielo Ave	Novato	4br 3ba	132,800	Janet Court
22 Woodland	Ignacio	5br 4ba	149,300	Janet Court
77 Corte Eliseo	Novato	5br 3ba	187,000	Andrea Smith
901 Goodhill St	Novato	5br 3ba	189,000	Janet Court
100 Cascade Ave	Belvedere	4br 2ba	209,000	Andrea Smith
499 Redwood St	Kentfield	4br 2ba	235,500	Mike Milland
129 Main St	Belvedere	4br 3ba	266,000	Mike Milland

Global Selection

WordPerfect includes a global key that you can use to search all fields for any word, and select all records that contain it. The global key is represented by *keyg*. You can use this option even if you haven't defined any keys. For example, in the HOUSES list, you could use it to find all houses with Andrea Smith as the agent, even though none of your keys is defined as Agent. To do this, you would choose the Select option from the main Sort menu, then type:

```
keyg=smith
```

as shown in Figure 12.8. Notice that key 1 is the default (field 1, word 1), not Agent. When you use a global condition, WordPerfect searches every field in the document, so you don't need to define the key.

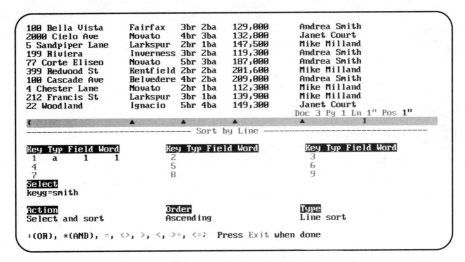

```
100 Bella Vista      Fairfax   3br 2ba    129,000    Andrea Smith
2000 Cielo Ave       Novato    4br 3ba    132,800    Janet Court
5 Sandpiper Lane     Larkspur  2br 1ba    147,500    Mike Milland
199 Riviera          Inverness 3br 2ba    119,300    Andrea Smith
77 Corte Eliseo      Novato    5br 3ba    187,000    Andrea Smith
399 Redwood St       Kentfield 2br 2ba    201,600    Mike Milland
100 Cascade Ave      Belvedere 4br 2ba    209,000    Andrea Smith
4 Chester Lane       Novato    2br 1ba    112,300    Mike Milland
212 Francis St       Larkspur  3br 1ba    139,900    Mike Milland
22 Woodland          Ignacio   5br 4ba    149,300    Janet Court
                                           Doc 3 Pg 1 Ln 1" Pos 1"
[    ▲         ▲         ▲              ▲        ]
------------------------------ Sort by Line ------------------------------
Key Typ Field Word      Key Typ Field Word      Key Typ Field Word
  1   a   1    1           2                       3
  4                        5                       6
  7                        8                       9
Select
keyg=smith

Action                  Order                   Type
Select and sort         Ascending               Line sort

+(OR), *(AND), =, <>, >, <, >=, <=:  Press Exit when done
```

Figure 12.8   *Here is how you would define a global key to search all data in the document for the word* smith. *It is not necessary to define key 1 as Agent.*

If the HOUSES list included descriptive paragraphs, as shown in Figure 12.9, you could still use the global key to select houses with Andrea Smith as the agent. You would have to change the sort type to Paragraph, and type the same selection condition: keyg=smith. The results appear in Figure 12.10.

 Tip: You can only include one word in the global key, so you could not type: *keyg=Andrea Smith.*

Paragraph Sort

When information is arranged in paragraphs, as shown in Figure 12.9, you can still use Sort or Select, but you must change the sort type to Paragraph. A paragraph is defined as ending in two or more hard returns, or a page break. To change the sort type, use option 7 on the main Sort menu: Type. Since paragraphs can include more than one line per record, when you change the sort type to Paragraph, Line is added to the key definition, as shown in Figure 12.11. Also, the screen heading changes to Sort by Paragraph.

100 Bella Vista, Fairfax
$129,000. This beautiful 3br, 2 ba house is priced right. Contact Andrea Smith for more information.

199 Riviera, Inverness
$119,000. Stunning 3br, 2ba home with fabulous ocean views. All this plus 2 acres? Unbelievable! For details and a video, call Andrea Smith in our San Rafael office.

212 Francis St, Larkspur
$139,000. 3br, 1ba fixer upper in fabulous location. Low price includes remodeling credit. To find out more, ask Mike Milland.

5 Sandpiper Lane, Larkspur
$147,500. Starter home for a small family. This 2br, 1ba house is in impeccable condition, with professional landscaping and lovely pool. Contact Mike Milland for details.

2000 Cielo Ave, Novato
$132,000. This huge 4br, 3ba house needs some TLC, but at this price you can afford it! Price just reduced $10,000. To see it, contact Janet Court in our Novato office. Hurry, it won't last long!

99 Ardmore, Novato
$113,000. Family home. 3br, 2ba, great neighborhood for kids, best schools. Priced for quick sale. Contact Janet Court.

Figure 12.9 *You can use the global key to restrict this list to the two houses with Andrea Smith as the agent. Use a paragraph sort, and enter the Select condition as keyg=smith.*

```
100 Bella Vista, Fairfax
$129,000. This beautiful 3br, 2 ba house is priced right. Contact
Andrea Smith for more information.

199 Riviera, Inverness
$119,000. Stunning 3br, 2ba home with fabulous ocean views. All
this plus 2 acres? Unbelievable! For details and a video, call
Andrea Smith in our San Rafael office.




                                         Doc 2 Pg 1 Ln 1" Pos 1"
```

Figure 12.10 *The results of using a global key to select Andrea Smith's houses.*

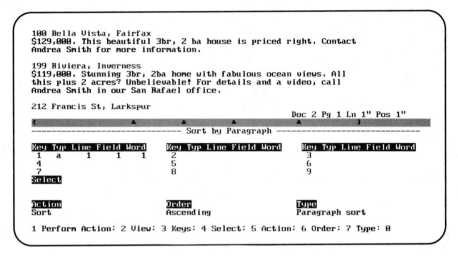

```
100 Bella Vista, Fairfax
$129,000. This beautiful 3br, 2 ba house is priced right. Contact
Andrea Smith for more information.

199 Riviera, Inverness
$119,000. Stunning 3br, 2ba home with fabulous ocean views. All
this plus 2 acres? Unbelievable! For details and a video, call
Andrea Smith in our San Rafael office.

212 Francis St, Larkspur
                                                  Doc 2 Pg 1 Ln 1" Pos 1"

------------------------------ Sort by Paragraph -------------------------
Key Typ Line Field Word   Key Typ Line Field Word   Key Typ Line Field Word
 1   a    1    1    1       2                         3
 4                          5                         6
 7                          8                         9
Select

Action                    Order                     Type
Sort                      Ascending                 Paragraph sort

 1 Perform Action; 2 View; 3 Keys; 4 Select; 5 Action; 6 Order; 7 Type; 0
```

Figure 12.11 *The Sort by Paragraph screen. This menu resembles the Sort by Line screen, except for the heading,* Sort by Paragraph, *and the additional item that you can use to define the keys:* Line.

In a paragraph sort, you use four criteria to define each key: Type, Line, Field, and Word. For example, to sort the data in Figure 12.9 by city, you would enter this information for key 1:

Key	Typ	Line	Field	Word
1	a	1	1	−1

Since the data on line 1 is not separated by tabs, it is all considered field 1. City is the fourth word in four of the records, and the third word in two of them, so you must count backward by using −1 for the word. This will force WordPerfect to sort by the last word on line 1, which is always the city.

To sort the same records by price, you would change key 1 to price by entering:

Key	Typ	Line	Field	Word
1	a	2	1	1

All data on line 2 is in the same field, and price is always the first word.

You also can use selection conditions on paragraph data. For example, to restrict the list to houses with prices greater than $120,000, you would choose the Select option and type:

```
key1>$120000
```

You must include the dollar sign, because it is considered a part of each word. If there were a blank space separating it from the price, you would not include the dollar sign. However, you would have to change the key word to 2, since the dollar sign would become the first word, and price the second.

Merge Sort

Say that your HOUSES data was in a secondary merge file, as shown in Figure 12.12. To use Sort or Select on this file, begin by changing the sort type to Merge, using the Type option on the main Sort menu. The remaining steps are similar to the ones you've already learned: define your keys, then select Perform Action. If you read the previous chapter about WordPerfect's merge operations, it should be easy to define your keys. As you learned, each field ends with the {END FIELD} code, and each record ends with the {END RECORD} code. Individual records in the HOUSES file would contain five fields each, as shown below:

Field 1:	100 Bella Vista{END FIELD}
Field 2:	Fairfax{END FIELD}
Field 3:	3br 2ba{END FIELD}
Field 4:	129,000{END FIELD}
Field 5:	Andrea Smith{END FIELD}
	{END RECORD}

Like the paragraph sort, in a merge sort you use four criteria to define each key: Type, Field, Line, and Word. For example, to sort by city, you would define key 1 as field 2:

Key	Typ	Field	Line	Word
1	a	2	1	1

Since the City field contains only one line and one word in each record, you would leave the defaults for the line and word criteria, line 1 and word 1.

To sort by agent's last name, you would define key 1 as field 5, word 2:

Key	Typ	Field	Line	Word
1	a	5	1	2

Since agent's last name is the last word in the field, you could also use –1 as the key word.

You can also use selection conditions with a secondary merge file. For example, to select only those records belonging to a particular agent, such as Janet Court, you would enter this selection condition:

```
key1=court
```

assuming key 1 is defined as the Agent, field 5, word 2 (or –1).

```
{FIELD NAMES}Street~City~Size~Price~Agent~~{END RECORD}
===============================================================================
100 Bella Vista{END FIELD}
Fairfax{END FIELD}
3br 2ba{END FIELD}
129,000{END FIELD}
Andrea Smith{END FIELD}
{END RECORD}
===============================================================================
2000 Cielo Ave{END FIELD}
Novato{END FIELD}
4br 3ba{END FIELD}
132,000{END FIELD}
Janet Court{END FIELD}
{END RECORD}
===============================================================================
5 Sandpiper Lane{END FIELD}
Larkspur{END FIELD}
2br 1ba{END FIELD}
147,500{END FIELD}
Mike Milland{END FIELD}
{END RECORD}
===============================================================================
199 Riviera{END FIELD}
Typeover                                            Doc 1 Pg 1 Ln 1" Pos 1"
```

Figure 12.12   *The HOUSES data in secondary merge file format.*

Table Sort

When data is arranged in a table, as shown in Figure 12.13, you can sort it by using the Table Sort feature. In a table sort, you can use four criteria to define the keys: Type, Cell, Line, and Word. Each row in the table is a record, and each cell is the equivalent of a field. For example, to sort by city, you would use Cell 2, Line 1, Word 1 as the key. To sort by agent's last name, you would use Cell 5, Line 1, Word 2 (or –1). Aside from the terminology, Table Sort is similar to the Line Sort and Paragraph Sort features you've already studied. As long as the cursor is positioned inside the table when you select Sort, the Sort Table menu will appear automatically.

Tip: WordPerfect can automatically convert the data shown in Figure 12.1 into a table. To convert it, place the cursor on the first word in the first row, press Alt-F4 to turn on Block, and move the cursor to the end of the last row. Press the Math/Columns key (Alt-F7), select Tables, select Create, and then select Tabular Column.

To sort the table shown in Figure 12.13 by city, begin with the cursor on the first street address: `1018 Ocean View Rd`. It's essential that you begin with the cursor inside the table. To prevent the titles from being sorted and appearing in the middle of the list, you should block the data before selecting Sort.

Street	City	Size	Price	Agent
1018 Ocean View Rd	Belvedere	2br 1ba	219,000	Janet Court
22 Woodland	Ignacio	5br 4ba	149,300	Janet Court
308 Valley Fair Rd	Larkspur	3br 1ba	112,900	Janet Court
2000 Cielo Ave	Novato	4br 3ba	132,800	Janet Court
99 Ardmore	Novato	3br 2ba	113,000	Janet Court
901 Goodhill St	Novato	5br 3ba	189,000	Janet Court
129 Main St	Belvedere	4br 3ba	266,000	Mike Milland
399 Redwood St	Kentfield	2br 2ba	201,600	Mike Milland
499 Redwood St	Kentfield	4br 2ba	235,500	Mike Milland
212 Francis St	Larkspur	3br 1ba	139,900	Mike Milland
5 Sandpiper Lane	Larkspur	2br 1ba	147,500	Mike Milland
4 Chester Lane	Novato	2br 1ba	112,300	Mike Milland
2010 Stetson	Tiburon	3br 3ba	234,000	Mike Milland
100 Cascade Ave	Belvedere	4br 2ba	209,000	Andrea Smith
100 Bella Vista	Fairfax	3br 2ba	129,000	Andrea Smith
451 Carrera Drive	Fairfax	2br 2ba	149,000	Andrea Smith
199 Riviera	Inverness	3br 2ba	119,300	Andrea Smith
77 Corte Eliseo	Novato	5br 3ba	187,000	Andrea Smith

Figure 12.13   The HOUSES data in table format.

1. Turn on Block mode:

    Keyboard: Press Alt-F4.

    Mouse: Display the **Edit** menu and select **Block**.

2. Move the cursor to the end of the table, and place it in the last cell, highlighting all text in the table. **Important: Do not move the cursor outside of the table.**

3. Select Sort:

    Keyboard: Press the Merge/Sort key (Ctrl-F9).

    Mouse: Display the **Tools** menu and select **Sort**.

    This takes you directly to the Sort Table menu, as shown in Figure 12.14.

4. Select the third option, **Keys**, and define the key as follows:

<u>Key Typ Cell Line Word</u>
1   a   2   1   1

Press Exit when you finish, to return to the main menu.

5. Select **P**erform Action.

The records should now be in city order, as shown in Figure 12.15.

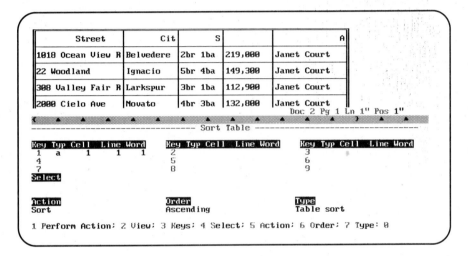

Figure 12.14   *The Sort Table menu. This menu only appears after you place the cursor inside a table and select Sort.*

Street	City	Size	Price	Agent
100 Cascade Ave	Belvedere	4br 2ba	209,000	Andrea Smith
129 Main St	Belvedere	4br 3ba	266,000	Mike Milland
1018 Ocean View Rd	Belvedere	2br 1ba	219,000	Janet Court
100 Bella Vista	Fairfax	3br 2ba	129,000	Andrea Smith
451 Carrera Drive	Fairfax	2br 2ba	149,000	Andrea Smith
22 Woodland	Ignacio	5br 4ba	149,300	Janet Court
199 Riviera	Inverness	3br 2ba	119,300	Andrea Smith
499 Redwood St	Kentfield	4br 2ba	235,500	Mike Milland
399 Redwood St	Kentfield	2br 2ba	201,600	Mike Milland
308 Valley Fair Rd	Larkspur	3br 1ba	112,900	Janet Court
5 Sandpiper Lane	Larkspur	2br 1ba	147,500	Mike Milland
212 Francis St	Larkspur	3br 1ba	139,900	Mike Milland
2000 Cielo Ave	Novato	4br 3ba	132,800	Janet Court
77 Corte Eliseo	Novato	5br 3ba	187,000	Andrea Smith
901 Goodhill St	Novato	5br 3ba	189,000	Janet Court
99 Ardmore	Novato	3br 2ba	113,000	Janet Court
4 Chester Lane	Novato	2br 1ba	112,300	Mike Milland
2010 Stetson	Tiburon	3br 3ba	234,000	Mike Milland

Figure 12.15   *The results of sorting the table by city.*

Printing and Fonts

WordPerfect provides many printing methods and gives you great control over your printer. You can print a page, an entire document, a blocked section of text, a range of pages, all odd pages or all even pages, several non-consecutive pages, or a document on disk that you have not retrieved to the Edit screen. You can even mark a group of disk files for printing and continue working on the document on the Edit screen. WordPerfect places each print request that you issue into a printer *job list*, assigning sequential numbers to the requests and printing them in that order. You can use the Printer Control screen to view the list of print jobs, stop the printer temporarily, rush a print job, or cancel one or all of them.

WordPerfect supports hundreds of different printers, including laser printers, dot-matrix printers, and letter-quality printers.

Print Methods

WordPerfect has several printing methods. In Chapter 2, you learned that you can use the Full Document option from the main Print menu to print the entire document on your Edit screen, or the Page option to print just the page that the cursor is on. You can use two methods to print a document that is not currently on the Edit screen: the Print option on the List Files menu or the Document on Disk option on the Print menu. If you want to print a range of pages, such as 5-9, or one or more specific pages, such as 1, 5, and 9, you can use the Multiple Pages or Document on Disk option on the Print menu, or the List Files Print option. To print a section of a document on the Edit screen, you can use WordPerfect's Block feature to highlight it and then select Print. These techniques are summarized in Table 13.1.

Table 13.1   *Printing techniques.*

To Print:	Use:
Single page on the Edit screen	Page option on the main Print menu
Entire document on the Edit screen	Full Document option on the main Print menu
Several pages or range of pages on the Edit screen	Multiple Pages option on the main Print menu
Document on disk	Print option on the List Files menu *or* Document on Disk option on the main Print menu
Blocked section on the Edit screen	Use the Block feature to highlight the section, press the Print key or select Print from the File menu, and type Y

The Full Document and Page Options on the Print Menu

To print the document on the Edit screen:

1. Display the main Print menu:

    Keyboard: Press the Print key (Shift-F7).

    Mouse: Select **Print** from the File menu.

    The main Print menu shown in Figure 13.1 will appear. The four print options on this menu appear near the top: Full Document (1), Page (2), Document on Disk (3), and Multiple Pages (5). Full Document, Page, and Multiple Pages print the document on your Edit screen. The Document on Disk option prints a file on disk, and you do not need to retrieve it.

    Before you select one of the print methods, check the Options section of this menu for your printer's name, which is next to `Select Printer`. If it does not appear, you'll need to select it first. You may be able to select it using the Select Printer option, if the printer is installed.

2. If your printer's name does not appear next to `Select Printer` on the main Print menu, choose the Select Printer option (S). The Print: Select Printer screen will appear, as shown in Figure 13.2. If your printer appears in the list, highlight it and choose the Select option (1). After you select the printer, you'll return to the main Print menu, and you can then print your document.

```
Print

     1 - Full Document
     2 - Page
     3 - Document on Disk
     4 - Control Printer
     5 - Multiple Pages
     6 - View Document
     7 - Initialize Printer


Options

     S - Select Printer                    QMS PS 810
     B - Binding Offset                    0"
     N - Number of Copies                  1
     U - Multiple Copies Generated by      Printer
     G - Graphics Quality                  High
     T - Text Quality                      High




Selection: 0
```

Figure 13.1   The main Print menu.

If your printer is not in the list, choose the Additional Printers option (2) to see the available printer definitions in any .ALL files you may have copied when you installed WordPerfect. (Each printer resource file (PRS) contains the specific information WordPerfect needs to communicate with a single printer. WordPerfect gets this information from the corresponding .ALL file, which contains data for a related group of printers. When you installed WordPerfect, the Installation program copied the necessary .ALL files from the Printer diskette to your printer directory, and used the .ALL file to create an individual .PRS file for the printer you selected.)

If your printer appears in the Additional Printers list, move the cursor onto it and choose the Select option (1). WordPerfect will then copy the necessary information from the .ALL file and create a .PRS file for your printer.

If you don't see your printer's name in the Additional Printers list, the .ALL file was not copied during installation. Turn to Appendix A for installation instructions.

If you selected a printer from the Additional Printers list, after WordPerfect has finished creating the .PRS file, press Exit (F7) twice or click the right mouse button twice to return to the Print: Select Printer menu. Your printer will now appear in the Select Printer list, and you can use the Select option (1) to choose it.

3. From the main Print menu, select **Page** or **Full Document**:

Page: Select this option if the document is only one page long, or if you only want to print the page the cursor is on.

Full Document: Select this option to print the entire document on the Edit screen, regardless of its length.

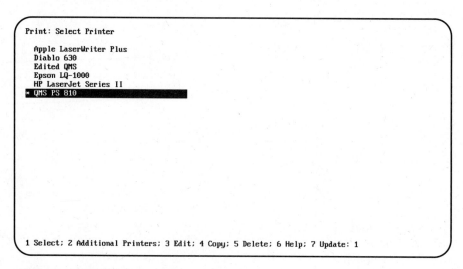

```
Print: Select Printer

   Apple LaserWriter Plus
   Diablo 630
   Edited QMS
   Epson LQ-1000
   HP LaserJet Series II
 ► QMS PS 810




 1 Select; 2 Additional Printers; 3 Edit; 4 Copy; 5 Delete; 6 Help; 7 Update: 1
```

Figure 13.2 *The Print: Select Printer screen.*

Once you select one of these options, the printer should start printing almost immediately, provided that it is turned on and correctly installed. If it doesn't print, check for a loose cable or an on-line button that is currently switched off, or check to see if your printer is correctly installed. Do not select the print option again, because nothing will happen. WordPerfect remembers everything you ask it to print, regardless of whether or not the printer is actually functioning. Each time you select Full Document, Page, or one of the other print options, WordPerfect assigns a job number to your request and places it in a *job list,* where it waits until the printer is ready. Once you do get the printer working, it will print all the jobs in the list, even if they are duplicates. The job list is explained in "Printer Control" later in this chapter.

If you hear a beep after you issue a print command, check the Printer Control screen. From the main Print menu, select the Control Printer option (4). If a message such as Press "G" to continue appears in the Current Job Information section of the screen, you are probably using a form that is defined for manual feed. If so, you'll need to type G to let WordPerfect know you have inserted the paper into the printer.

Printing Disk Files

To print a file without retrieving it to the Edit screen, you can use either the Print option on the List Files menu or the Document on Disk option on the main Print menu. You can use either of these options to print the entire file, a specific page, a range of pages, non-consecutive pages, or the document summary. The List Files Print option lets you mark and print a group of files in the same directory.

A warning: If you use one of these options to print a file while it is on your Edit screen, be careful! When you retrieve a document and make changes to it, the document on screen differs from the one on disk, until you save it again. The List Files and Document on Disk print options print the disk version, not the one on your Edit screen. To be certain that the document on your Edit screen matches the one on disk before you print it using one of these options, save the document before selecting it.

The List Files Print Option

To print one or more files through the List Files menu:

1. Display the List Files menu:

   Keyboard: Press List (F5).

   Mouse: Display the File menu and select List Files.

   A `Dir` prompt appears, followed by the current directory name and path.

2. In response to the `Dir` prompt, type the path to the directory containing the file or files you want to print, or accept the current directory by:

   Keyboard: Pressing Enter.

   Mouse: Clicking the right button.

3. Move the cursor onto the file you want to print. To print more than one file, highlight each one and mark it by typing an asterisk. To mark all the files in the directory, press Home asterisk or Alt-F5 (after marking all the files, you can unmark an individual file by highlighting it and pressing the asterisk key).

4. Select the Print option. If you marked one or more files, a prompt will appear asking if you want to print the marked files. Select **Yes**.

5. This prompt will appear in the lower-left corner of the screen, asking which page numbers you want to print:

```
Page(s) : (All)
```

6. Select the pages you want to print, using one of the methods described below. If you have marked a group of files to print, your selection will apply to all documents. If you are only printing one file, it will apply to the individual document.

- To print the entire document, select All.

- To limit printing to a specific page, enter the page number.

- To print a range of pages, type the first and last numbers, separated by a hyphen. For instance, to print pages 4 through 10, you would type 4-10.

- To print several non-consecutive pages, type the page numbers, separated by commas. For instance, to print pages 1, 3, 5, and 12, you would type 1,3,5,12. Always type the page numbers in numerical order.

- You can combine these techniques and print both a range and specific pages. For example, to type pages 1-5 and pages 9, 12, and 14, you would type 1-5,9,12,14.

- To print from the first through a specific page, type a hyphen followed by the last page number you want to print. For instance, to print pages 1 through 10, you would type -10.

- To print all odd pages, enter O.

- To print all even pages, enter E.

- To print the document summary, type S.

- To print the entire document and its summary, type S-.

These methods are summarized in Table 13.2.

Table 13.2 *Selecting the pages to be printed.*

To Print:	Keystrokes:
Entire document	Select All
Specific page	Type the page number; press Enter
Range of pages	Type the first and last numbers, separated by a hyphen; press Enter
Non-consecutive pages	Type the page numbers, separated by commas; press Enter
Range and specific pages	Type the specific page numbers, separated by a comma, and the range numbers, separated by a hyphen; press Enter

To Print:	Keystrokes:
The first through a specific page	Type a hyphen, then the last page number; press Enter
All odd pages	Type O and press Enter
All even pages	Type E and press Enter
Document summary	Type S and press Enter
Document summary and entire document	Type S- and press Enter

Once you enter the page numbers, your printer should start printing almost immediately. If you see this message:

```
Document not formatted for current printer. Continue? No (Yes)
```

you were using a different printer definition when you saved the file, and the document is still formatted for that printer. If you select Yes to continue, WordPerfect will print the file and try to substitute the closest available fonts. Although this will have no effect on the document on disk, the printed version may not be exactly what you had expected.

The Document on Disk Option

The Document on Disk option is similar to the List Files Print option in that it prints a disk file, except you cannot use it to mark a group of files for printing. To use it:

1. Display the main Print menu:

    Keyboard: Press the Print key (Shift-F7).

    Mouse: Select **P**rint from the **F**ile menu.

2. Select Document on Disk. This prompt will appear, asking for the name of the document you want to print:

    ```
    Document name:
    ```

3. Enter the document name. Be sure to include the path if it is not in the current directory.

The next prompt asks which pages you want to print. Follow the rules outlined in the previous section to select the entire document, individual pages, a range of pages, non-consecutive pages, all odd or even pages, or the document summary.

The Multiple Pages Option

You can use the Multiple Pages option to print selected pages of the document on your Edit screen. Like the Document on Disk option, you can use it to print the entire document, a specific page, a range of pages, non-consecutive pages, or the document summary. To use it:

1. Retrieve the document.

2. Display the main Print menu:

   Keyboard: Press the Print key (Shift-F7).

   Mouse: Select Print from the File menu.

3. Select the Multiple Pages option (5). This prompt will appear, asking which page numbers you want to print:

   `Page(s):`

4. Enter the pages you want to print, using one of the methods described in "The List Files Print Option" section.

Printing a Block

To print a consecutive section of text on the Edit screen, such as two paragraphs or a table that spans half a page, use WordPerfect's Block feature to designate the text and select Print. To print a block:

1. Place the cursor at the beginning (or end) of the section you want to print.

2. Turn on Block mode:

   Keyboard: Press Alt-F4 or F12.

   Mouse: Display the Edit menu and select **Block**.

3. Move the cursor to the opposite end of the section.

4. Select Print:

   Keyboard: Press the Print key, Shift-F7.

   Mouse: Display the File menu and select the **Print** option.

This prompt will appear:

```
Print block? No (Yes)
```

5. Select **Yes**.

Printing to a Disk File

WordPerfect lets you print a document to a disk file, instead of to a printer. This is useful if you want to print the file on a computer that does not have WordPerfect, because the file will include all the printer and formatting information needed to print the document using the DOS COPY command (*COPY FILENAME LPT1*).

To print a disk file, change the port on the Select Printer: Edit menu, naming a file instead of an interface, and then print the document.

1. Display the main Print menu:

    Keyboard: Press the Print key (Shift-F7).

    Mouse: Select **P**rint from the **F**ile menu.

2. Choose the **S**elect Printer option (S).

    The Print: Select Printer menu appears, listing the printers you have installed. Select the printer you will be using when you actually print this document (on the other computer, for example).

3. Highlight the printer you want to use, and select the **E**dit option (3). The Select Printer: Edit menu appears.

4. Select the **P**ort option (2). This menu line appears:

    ```
    Port: 1 LPT 1; 2 LPT 2; 3 LPT 3; 4 COM 1; 5 COM 2;
    6 COM 3; 7 COM 4; 8 OTHER: 0
    ```

    The LPT and COM options represent hardware interfaces. LPT designates a parallel connection, and COM is a serial connection. Make note of which interface you were using to connect your printer, since you'll want to change it back again after printing the file to disk. Printers are usually connected to one of the parallel interfaces. You can use the last option, Other, to designate a file or other device.

5. Select **O**ther (8). This prompt appears:

    ```
    Device or Filename:
    ```

6. Type a file name, including the path and directory if it is not the current one, and press Enter.

The file name will appear after the Port option. If a prompt appears asking if you are using a network printer, select **No**.

7. Return to the main Print menu:

 Keyboard: Press Exit (F7) twice.

 Mouse: Click the right button twice.

8. Select the **Full Document** option.

WordPerfect then prints the document to the disk file you named in step 6.

If you want to print a different document to a disk file, repeat these steps and assign a different name to the port. If you don't, you will override the file you last printed to disk, since the same file name will be used. Alternatively, you can rename the disk file you just printed, and continue to use the same name for the printer port. Once you have finished printing disk files, change the port setting back to the original one, so you can use the printer again.

If this is a procedure you will be using frequently, you may want to make a copy of the printer file, and permanently change the port setting on the copied version to a disk file. To copy the printer file, display the main Print menu, choose Select Printer, highlight the printer, and select the Copy option. In response to the `Printer filename` prompt, change the first part of the name, but retain the extension *.PRS*. Next, change the Port to Other and enter a file name, as described in this section. After that, whenever you want to print to a disk file, use Select Printer to choose this "printer."

Printer Control

Each time you select a print option such as Full Document, Page, or Document on Disk, WordPerfect assigns a sequential number to your print command and places it in a print job list. If you issue several print requests, WordPerfect prints them in the order you issued the commands. You can issue up to 99 print requests. To view the list of documents waiting to be printed, or to control the printer, you can use the Control Printer option on the main Print menu. From this menu you can select *Stop* to stop a print job temporarily, *Go* to start it again, *Cancel Job(s)* to cancel one or more print jobs completely, or *Rush Job* if you have issued several print requests and want to move one job to the top of the list so it will be the next one printed.

To use the Control Printer menu:

1. Display the main Print menu:

 Keyboard: Press the Print key (Shift-F7).

 Mouse: Display the File menu and select **Print**.

2. Select Control Printer (4).

The Print: Control Printer menu appears, as shown in Figure 13.3.

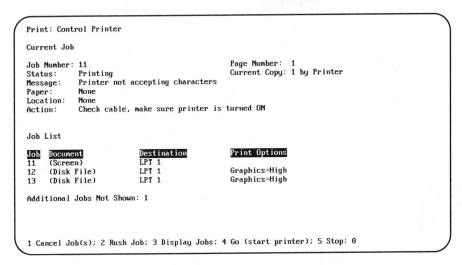

```
Print: Control Printer

Current Job

Job Number: 11                              Page Number:  1
Status:      Printing                       Current Copy: 1 by Printer
Message:     Printer not accepting characters
Paper:       None
Location:    None
Action:      Check cable, make sure printer is turned ON


Job List

Job  Document          Destination        Print Options
11   (Screen)          LPT 1
12   (Disk File)       LPT 1              Graphics=High
13   (Disk File)       LPT 1              Graphics=High

Additional Jobs Not Shown: 1




 1 Cancel Job(s); 2 Rush Job; 3 Display Jobs; 4 Go (start printer); 5 Stop: 0
```

Figure 13.3 *The Print: Control Printer menu.*

If there is a current print job, information about it is displayed near the top of the screen: Job Number, Status, Message, Paper, Location, and Action. The Job List area near the middle of the screen indicates how many print requests are waiting to be printed, if there are any. The first column, Job, displays each print job number. The Document column indicates whether you used one of the print options that prints a disk file, such as Document on Disk, or the text currently on the Edit screen, such as Full Document. The Destination column indicates which printer interface is being used for the print job, helpful if you are using more than one printer simultaneously. The Print Options column indicates whether you had changed any of the print options on the main Print menu before issuing the print command, such as changing the number of copies or the Text Quality.

Since there is only enough room to display three print jobs on this screen, the Additional Jobs Not Shown line directly below the job list indicates how many others are waiting. If there are any, you can select the Display Jobs option (3) to see the others. Figure 13.4 shows an example of the Job List screen that appears when you select Display Jobs. Notice that this screen displays all print jobs, not just the ones that couldn't fit on the first screen.

To stop a print job temporarily, without canceling it, use the Stop option (5). This is useful if the printer is jammed, or if you need to change a print wheel or insert manual-feed paper. Once you are ready to start it again, type G to use the Go option. If you hear a beep after you issue a print command, check this screen to see if a message such as Press "G" to continue appears in the Current Job section of the screen.

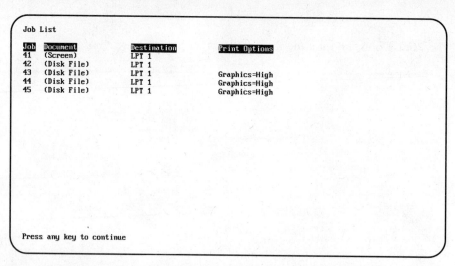

Figure 13.4 *The Job List screen. If a number (other than 0) appears next to the Additional Jobs Not Shown line on the Print: Control Printer screen, you can see the additional print jobs on this screen by selecting the Display Jobs option.*

To cancel one or more print jobs, select the Cancel Job(s) option (1). Cancel an individual print job by entering its job number, or cancel all print jobs by typing an asterisk and selecting Yes in response to the `Cancel all print jobs` prompt that appears. The printer may not stop immediately, since some of the information may have already been sent to the printer's memory. If you are working on a network, the Cancel Job(s) option may have no effect at all, since print job information is stored in the network's print spooler while waiting to be printed.

If you have asked WordPerfect to print several documents, and then find you need one printed immediately, you can use the Rush Job option (2) to move it to the top of the list. You can choose to print the job immediately, or wait until the current job is finished. When you select Rush Job, WordPerfect asks for the job number. After you enter it, you will be asked if you want to interrupt the current print job. If you select No, WordPerfect will complete the current print job and then print the rushed one. If you select Yes, WordPerfect will finish printing the current page, if possible, and then print the job that you have selected to rush. After that, WordPerfect will finish printing the interrupted print job.

Previewing the Printed Document: View Document

In Chapter 3 you learned that the screen version of a document is usually not an exact representation of the printed version, since many features cannot be seen on the Edit screen. These include full justification, headers and footers, footnotes, endnotes, graphics, margins, page numbering, and for most monitors, font sizes and appearance attributes such as small, large, very large, italics, and double underlining (except for monitors equipped with a Hercules interface card with *RamFont* mode, which can display font attributes). WordPerfect's View Document option lets you preview the printed version to see the overall page layout, font sizes, and much more. This feature is invaluable—especially when you produce complex documents, such as newsletters that incorporate features like graphics, columns, and multiple fonts—and it can save you a lot of paper.

To use View Document:

1. Display the main Print menu:

   Keyboard: Press the Print key (Shift-F7).

   Mouse: Display the **F**ile menu and select **P**rint.

   The main Print menu appears.

2. Select the sixth option, **V**iew Document.

   Depending on how you last used it, the screen may appear in *Full Page* mode, providing an overview of the page layout; in *100%* mode, which enlarges it to actual size; in *200%* mode, which enlarges it to twice actual size; or in *Facing Pages* mode, which lets you view two facing pages simultaneously, such as pages 2 and 3 or pages 4 and 5. To change the view, select one of these options by typing the number next to it (1,2,3, or 4). Figure 13.5 shows the Full Page mode.

   When you use the Facing Pages option in the View Document screen, odd-numbered pages always appear on the right side, including page 1. This can be confusing if you change the starting page number on a page so that a page that would normally be odd-numbered becomes even-numbered. For example, say you were typing a book, maintaining each chapter in a separate file, and that Chapter 1 ended on page 21. Since the next page number in sequence is 22, you would change the first page in the Chapter 2 file to page 22. Since page 22 is even, WordPerfect would display it on the left side of the View Document screen when you select Facing Pages, even though it is actually the first physical page in the file (and would be the first printed page if you were to print the file).

When in doubt about which side of the screen a page will appear on in View Document when you use Facing Pages, just check the status line: If the Pg indicator shows the page to be odd-numbered, it will appear on the right side, and if the Pg indicator shows the page to be even-numbered, it will appear on the left side.

In View Document, you can use most of the regular cursor movement keys to scroll through the document, but you cannot type or edit. When you finish using View Document, you can return either to the Edit screen or to the main Print menu.

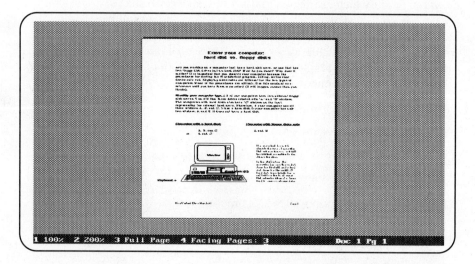

Figure 13.5 *Use the Full Page option on the View Document menu to see the overall layout of the page. To read the text, use 100% or 200%.*

3. Exit View Document:

    To exit to the Edit screen:

    Keyboard: Press Exit (F7).

    Mouse: Click the right mouse button.

    To return to the Print menu:

    Keyboard: Press the space bar or Cancel (F1).

    Mouse: Press the two buttons simultaneously, or the center button if you have one.

Print Options

The Options section of the main Print menu includes options that you can use to select another printer and specify the binding offset, the number of copies, the method of generating extra copies, and the graphics and text quality.

 Tip: If you want to change Binding Offset, Number of Copies, Graphics Quality, or Text Quality permanently, use the Setup: Print Options menu. From the main Setup menu, select Initial Settings (4) and then Print Options (8).

Printing Multiple Copies

To print several copies of a document, you can use the Number of Copies option (N) on the main Print menu. Select it and change the number just before you issue the print command. Once you change this option, it remains in effect until you clear the document from the Edit screen, change the option again, or exit WordPerfect.

The Multiple Copies Generated By option lets you have the printer generate the extra copies, instead of WordPerfect. If your printer is capable of generating them, the copies should be printed more quickly, especially if the document includes graphics or several different fonts. If it is not capable, only one copy will be printed. The disadvantage to having the printer generate the copies is that if the document has more than one page, the copies will not be collated.

Selecting Another Printer

If you have installed more than one printer, switching between them is easy:

1. Display the main Print menu:

   Keyboard: Press the Print key (Shift-F7).

   Mouse: Display the File menu and select Print.

2. Choose the Select Printer option. A list of installed printers appears.

3. Move the cursor onto the name of the printer you wish to use; then select it using the first option, Select.

This places an asterisk next to the printer name and returns you to the main Print menu, where the name of the printer you just selected should appear next to `Select Printer`. WordPerfect will use this printer definition for all subsequent print jobs, until you repeat the steps and select a new printer from the list, even if you exit WordPerfect. However, if you retrieve a file that was saved when a different printer was selected, that printer will become the currently selected printer until you clear the screen again. This happens because WordPerfect stores information about the printer, fonts, and formatting along with each file.

If your printer is not listed on the Print: Select Printer screen, try using the Additional Printers option to select it, as described earlier in "The Full Document and Page Options on the Print Menu" section. If that doesn't work, you will have to use WordPerfect's Installation program to install it.

Graphics and Text Quality

The Graphics Quality and Text Quality options on the main Print menu let you change the print quality for text or graphics, or print text separately from graphics—useful if your printer has trouble printing a document that includes a large graphics file. If you use a dot-matrix printer, you may want to change the Text Quality to Draft when printing rough drafts, to speed up printing and save unnecessary wear and tear on your printer. On certain printers, increasing the print quality decreases printing speed. WordPerfect saves the Graphics Quality and Text Quality settings when you save the document.

To change the Graphics quality and/or Text Quality:

1. Display the main Print menu.

   Keyboard: Press the Print key (Shift-F7).

   Mouse: Select **P**rint from the **F**ile menu.

2. If you want to change the Graphics Quality, select Graphics Quality, (G). This prompt appears:

   `Graphics Quality: 1 Do Not Print; 2 Draft; 3 Medium; 4 High:`

3. Select the graphics quality you want to use.

4. If you want to change the Text Quality, select Text Quality (T). This prompt appears:

   `Text Quality: 1 Do Not Print; 2 Draft; 3 Medium; 4 High:`

5. Select the text quality you want to use.

These settings remain in effect until you change them or clear the screen. Once you clear the screen, they revert to the default settings, as established through the Setup: Print Options menu.

If a graphics file that you retrieve into a WordPerfect graphics box is very large, it will use a lot of memory. When you try to print the document, WordPerfect may print incomplete pages, or not print it at all. In such a case, you can print the document in two passes. The first time, set the Text Quality option to *Do Not Print*, and then issue the print command. After printing, put the paper back into your printer, set the Graphics Quality option to *Do Not Print* and the Text Quality option to *High*, and print the document again. For more information about using graphics files in your WordPerfect documents, see Chapter 14.

Fonts

A font is a set of characters, including letters, numbers, punctuation, and symbols, in a certain typeface, size, and weight. For example, Helvetica 12-point Bold is a font; Helvetica is the typeface, Bold is the weight, and 12-point is the size. You are probably familiar with typefaces such as Courier, Times Roman, and Helvetica, since their use is widespread. For example, in Figure 13.6, Group A is printed in Helvetica, Group B in Times Roman, and Group C in Courier.

Font sizes are measured either by point size or by pitch. A *point* is a vertical measurement that equals about $^1/_{72}$". Common point sizes are 10 and 12 for regular text, and 14 for headings; in Figure 13.6, the Times Roman font (Group B) is 10-point, and the Helvetica font (Group A) is 14-point. Point size is the measurement from the tip of an *ascender* to the tip of a *descender*. *Descenders* are the tails that extend under the baseline in several lowercase letters, as in the letters *g, j, p, q,* and *y*. *Ascenders* are the lines extending above the main part of many lowercase letters, such as *b, d, f,* and *h*. You can think of the *baseline* as an invisible line that serves as the base underneath most of the letters, excluding letters like *p* and *g* that have descenders. The *x-height* is literally the height of the letter *x*, and it is used to measure the distance from the baseline to the top of lowercase letters like *x* and *e* that do not have ascenders.

Pitch is a horizontal measurement representing the number of characters per inch. It applies only to monospaced fonts such as Courier and Elite, that were created for use on typewriters. In Figure 13.6, the Courier font (Group C) is 10 pitch. In monospaced fonts, the number of characters per inch is always the same, since each character uses the same amount of horizontal space (hence the name *monospaced*). In contrast, proportionally spaced fonts, such as Times Roman and Helvetica, feature variable character spacing, so an inch of type may include 10, 15, or even 22 characters, depending upon which characters you type in that inch. For example, an uppercase *W* or *M* would use more space than a lowercase *l* or *i*. Most published material is printed in proportionally spaced fonts, including this book.

The last component that defines a font is its *weight* (or style), such as regular (sometimes called upright), italic, bold, and bold italic. Each of the following are separate fonts: Helvetica 12-point Italic, Helvetica 12-point Bold, and Helvetica 14-point Italic.

Another important characteristic of a font is whether it has *serifs,* the horizontal cross-strokes at the end of the letters that look like arms and tails. A typeface that does not have these cross-strokes, such as Helvetica, is called *sans serif,* while one that does have them, such as Times Roman, is called a *serif* typeface. In the Times Roman typeface (Group B) in Figure 13.6, notice the distinctive serifs in the *F* in *February*, and compare them with the *F* in the Helvetica type (Group A). Sans serif fonts are generally used for headings, subheads, drop caps, and other display type, while serif fonts are used for body copy (the main text). Serif fonts are considered more legible than sans serif fonts, since the cross-strokes help guide your eye through the text and differentiate between letters.

```
              ABC Baby Supplies - Monthly Net profits

                          Group A

January   .................................  $ 7,788.50
February  .................................    5,496.25
March     .................................    6,589.20
April     .................................    5,569.57
May       .................................    4,434.55
June      .................................    3,457.75
July      .................................    3,456.90
August    .................................    4,932.23
September .................................    5,819.45
October   .................................    6,725.66
November  .................................    5,637.55
December  .................................    4,549.24


                          Group B

January   .................................  $ 2,258.10
February  .................................    2,195.33
March     .................................    3,289.92
April     .................................    1,859.65
May       .................................    3,736.89
June      .................................    4,787.05
July      .................................    3,676.32
August    .................................    5,941.33
September .................................    4,412.26
October   .................................    6,733.43
November  .................................    3,237.76
December  .................................    4,149.41


                          Group C

January   . . . . . . . . . . . . .  $ 9,358.00
February  . . . . . . . . . . . . .    6,557.12
March     . . . . . . . . . . . . .    7,866.43
April     . . . . . . . . . . . . .    6,458.98
May       . . . . . . . . . . . . .    5,323.80
June      . . . . . . . . . . . . .    5,565.75
July      . . . . . . . . . . . . .    4,677.22
August    . . . . . . . . . . . . .    5,021.51
September . . . . . . . . . . . . .    7,121.78
October   . . . . . . . . . . . . .    7,737.84
November  . . . . . . . . . . . . .    6,522.25
December  . . . . . . . . . . . . .    5,465.13
```

Figure 13.6 Helvetica, Times Roman, and Courier typefaces.

The fonts that will be available for your use depend on the type of printer you have. All printers come with at least one internal (built-in) font. PostScript laser printers, such as the Apple LaserWriter Plus, feature the largest selection of internal fonts, and usually include Times Roman, Helvetica, ITC Bookman, ITC Avant Garde, Palatino, New Century Schoolbook, ITC Zapf Chancery, and Helvetica Narrow. For many printers, additional fonts are available on cartridges that plug into a slot on the printer, or on disks. Fonts on disk are called *soft fonts*. When you use them to format a document, WordPerfect sends the font information from the computer's memory into the printer's memory. A wide variety of soft fonts is available for laser printers. For example, Bitstream Corporation offers a vast selection of typefaces. Their Charter, Dutch (Times Roman), and Swiss (Helvetica) typefaces and installation kit are offered for a nominal fee to registered WordPerfect users.

Aside from the amount of money that you wish to spend to purchase fonts, the only real limitation to their use is your printer and the amount of memory that it contains. For example, a Hewlett-Packard LaserJet II printer is only capable of printing up to 16 fonts per page, and a maximum of 32 can be contained simultaneously in the printer's memory. However, it is unlikely that you'd ever want to print a page containing that many fonts.

PostScript fonts are outline fonts, which means that there is only one file for each typeface, and this file can be used to generate fonts of many different sizes. When you use PostScript fonts in WordPerfect, you select the typeface and weight first and then choose the size that you want for the particular application. In bit-mapped fonts, each character is essentially a picture made up of a pattern of tiny dots called *bits,* and each font is a separate file. To use a bit-mapped font, you select the typeface, weight, and size all at once.

Cartridge fonts are easier to use than soft fonts because all you have to do is plug them in and turn on the printer, and they do not require printer memory. Also, they can help assure font standardization in an organization, and are more convenient to use on networks. Although soft fonts are usually less expensive than cartridge fonts and are available in a wider variety of typefaces and point sizes, their major disadvantage is that they can take up a great deal of storage space and printer memory, especially the larger sizes.

 Note: The software instructions that control a laser printer are called its *page description language*. Adobe System's PostScript is the language used by printers such as the Apple Laserwriter Plus and many other laser printers. Printers like the Hewlett-Packard LaserJet II and compatibles use a language called HP PCL (printer command language). The Hewlett-Packard LaserJet III uses the PCL-5 language, which provides scalable fonts like the ones on PostScript printers.

Installing Fonts

Once you have installed your printer, you can find out which of its internal fonts WordPerfect supports through the Base Font option on the main Font menu.

1. Select the main Font menu:

    Keyboard: Press the Font key (Ctrl-F8).

    Mouse: Display the pull-down Font menu.

2. Select **Base Font**.

A list of available fonts will appear (but if your printer is not installed, an error message will appear instead, indicating that the printer has not yet been installed). For example, Figure 13.7 shows the Base Font screen that appears for a Hewlett-Packard LaserJet II printer. Notice that only four fonts appear on the list: Courier 10cpi, Courier 10cpi Bold, Line Draw 10cpi (Full), and Line Draw 16.67cpi. These are the only internal fonts that come with this printer. Although WordPerfect supports many of the soft fonts and cartridge fonts that you can buy for it, you must install them through the Print menu before you can use them. This is also true for the additional fonts available for other laser printers.

```
Base Font

* Courier 10cpi
  Courier 10cpi Bold
  Line Draw 10cpi (Full)
  Line Printer 16.67cpi












1 Select; N Name search: 1
```

Figure 13.7 The Base Font screen showing internal fonts for the Hewlett-Packard LaserJet II printer.

To install your font cartridges or soft fonts, exit back to the Edit screen and follow these steps:

1. Display the main Print menu:

   Keyboard: Press the Print key (Shift-F7).

   Mouse: Display the **File** menu and select **Print**.

2. Choose **Select Printer** (S).

   The Print: Select Printer menu appears, displaying the printers that have been installed on your system.

3. Highlight the printer you want to install fonts for, and select the **Edit** option.

   The Select Printer: Edit menu appears.

4. Select the **Cartridges and Fonts** option (4).

The Select Printer: Cartridges and Fonts screen appears. It should be similar to the one shown in Figure 13.8 for the Hewlett-Packard LaserJet II printer. If WordPerfect cannot locate the printer .ALL file, you'll see a different screen instead, as shown in Figure 13.9. If you installed the printer .ALL file in a different directory, enter the path and name. Otherwise, you won't be able to continue until you use WordPerfect's Installation program to copy it.

Note: Each printer resource file (PRS) contains the specific information WordPerfect needs to communicate with a single printer. WordPerfect gets this information from the corresponding .ALL file, which contains data for a related group of printers. When you installed WordPerfect, the Installation program copied the necessary .ALL files from the Printer diskette to your printer directory, and used the .ALL file to create an individual .PRS file for the printer you selected.

```
Select Printer: Cartridges and Fonts

Font Category                        Quantity        Available

Built-In
Cartridges                              2               2
Soft Fonts                            350 K           350 K




NOTE: Most fonts listed under the Font Category (with the exception of Built-In)
are optional and must be purchased separately from your dealer or manufacturer.
If you have fonts not listed, they may be supported on an additional printer
diskette.  For more information call WP at (801) 225-5000.

If soft fonts are marked '*', you must run the Initialize Printer option in WP
each time you turn on your printer.  Doing so deletes all soft fonts in printer
memory and downloads those marked with '*'.

If soft fonts are not located in the same directory as your printer files, you
must specify a Path for Downloadable Fonts in the Select Printer: Edit menu.

1 Select; 2 Change Quantity; N Name search: 1
```

Figure 13.8 *The Select Printer: Cartridges and Fonts screen for the Hewlett-Packard LaserJet II printer.*

Notice the message near the middle of the Select Printer: Cartridge and Fonts screen, indicating that most of these fonts are optional and must be purchased separately. When you select a font category other than Built-In, WordPerfect lists all the cartridges or soft fonts that it supports for your printer. However, the fonts in these categories are not built into the printer, so you must purchase them separately. If you don't, you won't be able to use them, even though they appear in these menus and you can select them. If you format a document using a font that you don't have, you will usually get an error message when you try to print it, and will have to cancel the print job and start over after changing the font.

```
Printer file not found

     The printer file (.ALL) which was used to create this printer
     selection cannot be found.

     Please specify the directory where the printer files can be found.
     If you do not know which printer disk contains the printer file, try
     each disk until one succeeds.
```



```
Directory for printer files: \
```

Figure 13.9 *If the printer .All file is not found when you try to select the Cartridges and Fonts option from the Select Printer: Edit menu, this screen appears instead of the Select Printer: Cartridges and Fonts screen.*

Installing Cartridge Fonts

If your printer supports fonts on cartridges, a Cartridges line will appear in the Select Printer: Cartridges and Fonts menu. To install your cartridges:

1. Move the cursor onto the `Cartridges` line; then choose the **Select** option.

    The Select Printer: Cartridges menu will appear, with a list of the font cartridges that WordPerfect supports for your printer. Figure 13.10 shows an example.

2. Move the cursor onto your cartridge name, and type an asterisk (*) to select it. If you change your mind, you can deselect it by pressing the asterisk key again.

    WordPerfect won't allow you to select more cartridges than the number shown next to `Total` in the upper-right corner of the screen, because this represents the total number of slots available for cartridges in your printer (although you can change this number by returning to the previous menu and using the Change Quantity option).

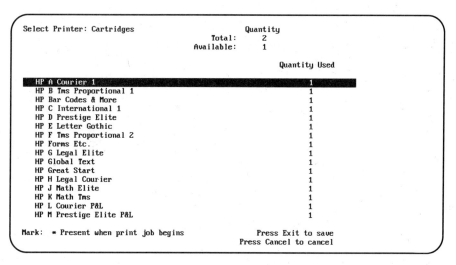

Figure 13.10   *The Select Printer: Cartridges menu for the Hewlett-Packard LaserJet II printer.*

3. After you finish selecting your cartridges, exit back to the Select Printer: Edit menu:

   Keyboard: Press the Exit key (F7) twice.

   Mouse: Click the right button twice.

   WordPerfect will then update your printer file with the font selections you have just made. While this is happening, you will see an `Updating font` prompt in the lower-left corner of the screen. After you return to the Select Printer: Edit menu, you can press Exit or click the right mouse button three more times to return to the Edit screen. The newly installed fonts will now appear whenever you select the Base Font option from the Font menu.

Installing Soft Fonts

To install soft fonts (be sure that you're in the Select: Printer Cartridges Fonts Print Wheels menu; if you are in the Select Printer: Edit menu, you can get there by selecting the fourth option, **Cartridges/Fonts/Print Wheels**):

1. If you have added extra memory to your laser printer, your first step should be to use the Change Quantity option (2) to specify the new amount. Move the cursor onto the `Soft Fonts` line in the Select Printer: Cartridges and Fonts screen, select Change **Q**uantity, and enter the quantity.

2. With the cursor on the Soft Fonts line, choose Select.

   What happens next depends on the printer type. For some printers, you'll go directly to the Select Printer: Soft Fonts menu, and a list of the soft fonts that WordPerfect suppports will appear. For others, such as the Hewlett-Packard LaserJet II, you will be asked to select a Font Group, such as HP AC TmsRmn/Helv US, or HP AD TmsRmn/Helv R8. If you aren't sure which group to select, check the package that came with the fonts. After you select a group, the Select Printer: Soft Fonts menu will appear; an example is shown in Figure 13.11, for the Hewlett-Packard LaserJet II printer.

```
Select Printer: Soft Fonts                         Quantity    * Fonts
                                         Total:      350 K        32
                                     Available:      350 K        32

HP AC TmsRmn/Helv US                                     Quantity Used

  + (AC) Helv  6pt                                              8 K
  + (AC) Helv  6pt (Land)                                       8 K
  + (AC) Helv  6pt Bold                                         8 K
  + (AC) Helv  6pt Bold (Land)                                  8 K
  + (AC) Helv  6pt Italic                                       8 K
  + (AC) Helv  6pt Italic (Land)                                8 K
  + (AC) Helv  8pt                                              9 K
  + (AC) Helv  8pt (Land)                                       9 K
  + (AC) Helv  8pt Bold                                        11 K
  + (AC) Helv  8pt Bold (Land)                                 11 K
  + (AC) Helv  8pt Italic                                      10 K
  + (AC) Helv  8pt Italic (Land)                               10 K
  + (AC) Helv  10pt                                            13 K
  + (AC) Helv  10pt (Land)                                     13 K
  + (AC) Helv  10pt Bold                                       13 K
  + (AC) Helv  10pt Bold (Land)                                13 K

Mark:  * Present when print job begins          Press Exit to save
       + Can be loaded/unloaded during job    Press Cancel to cancel
```

Figure 13.11 *The Select Printer: Soft Fonts menu for the Hewlett-Packard LaserJet II printer.*

If you see the Printer File Not Found screen instead of the font list, WordPerfect cannot find the font information it needs, probably because you did not copy your printer's .ALL file onto the hard disk when you installed it.

The fonts are listed in alphabetical order, and there may be too many to fit on one screen. You can use the regular cursor movement keys such as Down Arrow, Screen Down (Home,Down Arrow), or Page Down to scroll down and see the others. You can also use Name Search to go directly to a specific font name, by pressing the Search key (F2) and typing the first letter of the font name.

As the last two lines on the screen imply, there are two methods of marking soft fonts: with an asterisk or a plus sign. Fonts that you mark with an asterisk will be present when you start the print job, after you use the Initialize Printer command on the main Print menu to send them into the printer's memory. Once you have issued this command, the fonts will remain in your printer's memory until you turn off the printer, even if you exit WordPerfect. Use an asterisk to mark soft fonts that you will be using frequently. It may take several minutes for WordPerfect to send all of your fonts to the printer's memory, a process referred to as *downloading*, but you only have to do this once, when you first turn on your printer for the day.

Use the other method, the plus sign, to mark soft fonts that you will be using infrequently, such as landscape fonts or extra large fonts. Individual fonts marked with a plus sign are downloaded when you print a document that uses them. It usually takes longer than the other method, because each time you print a document formatted with one or more of these fonts, WordPerfect must download the font information to the printer's memory, print the document, and then erase the font(s) from the printer's memory.

Notice the `Total` and `Available` statistics at the top of the screen. In the `Quantity` column, they indicate the total amount of printer memory for soft fonts, and how much is still available. In the `Fonts` column, they indicate how many fonts can be marked, and how many have already been marked. The statistic in the `Quantity Used` column next to each individual font indicates how much printer memory it will use. As you mark fonts with an asterisk, this number will be reduced until you cannot select any more. Only the fonts marked with an asterisk are included in this calculation, since they are all downloaded to the printer at once when you use the Initialize Printer option. Certain printers have limits on the total number of fonts that they can hold in their memory. For example, the Hewlett-Packard LaserJet Series II can hold a maximum of 32 fonts at once, regardless of how much of the printer's memory is available. Also, it cannot print more than 16 fonts per page.

3. To mark a font for selection with an asterisk, move the cursor onto the font name and type an asterisk; an asterisk (*) will appear to the left of the font name. To mark a font with the plus sign, move the cursor onto the font name and type a plus sign (+). To deselect a font, highlight it and type * or +. You can mark fonts with both an asterisk and a plus sign.

4. After you have marked all the soft fonts you want to use, exit back to the Select Printer: Edit screen:

   Keyboard: Press the Exit key (F7) twice.

   Mouse: Click the right button twice.

WordPerfect will then update your printer file with the font selections you have just made. While this is happening, you will see an Updating font prompt in the lower-left corner of the screen. When it finishes, you'll return to the Select Printer: Edit screen.

Once you have marked all your soft fonts, you have one last step to complete: designating the drive and subdirectory where your soft font files are located. If you don't, WordPerfect won't be able to find your fonts, and you'll get an error message when you try to print a document formatted with one or more of them.

5. From the Select Printer: Edit menu, select the Path for Downloadable Fonts and Printer Command Files option (6).

6. Enter the path and name of the directory where your soft font files are located.

7. To return to the Edit screen:

   Keyboard: Press Exit (F7) three times.

   Mouse: Click the right button three times.

The newly installed fonts will now appear whenever you select the Base Font option from the Font menu.

Using Fonts in Your Documents

When you install your printer, WordPerfect defines one font as the *Initial Base Font;* this font is the default and will be used to format all new documents, unless you override it using one of the other two font options: *Initial Base Font* on the Format Document menu or *Base Font* on the Font menu. The Initial Base Font is often a Courier font, since Courier is built into nearly all printers. You can change this default font for all text in an individual document using the Initial Base Font option on the Format Document menu. To change the font at a certain position in a document, use the Base Font option on the Font menu. You can also use the Font menu to change the *size* or *appearance* of the Initial Font or Base Font currently in use.

 Tip: Before printing a document that includes fonts marked as present when the print job begins, be sure to use the Initialize Printer option on the main Print menu to download the font information to your printer.

Initial Base Font

The Initial Base Font is the default font, just as single spacing is the default line spacing, and the default margin settings are 1" each. WordPerfect uses the Initial Base Font to format all text, including headers, footers, endnotes, footnotes, page numbers, and figure captions, unless you override it using one of the two other options, Document Initial Base Font or Base Font. Like these other defaults, the Initial Base Font setting does not appear as a code in your document. However, when you save a document, information about the Initial Base Font and all other default formatting is stored along with the file, in the file *header*.

Once you change the Initial Base Font, all new documents will be affected, but previously saved documents will remain unaltered. For example, if you change the Initial Base Font to Times Roman 12-point, then retrieve a file that you had saved when Courier 10 pitch was the Initial Base Font, that document will still be formatted with Courier 10 as the Initial Base Font. However, when you clear the screen and type a new document, its Initial Base Font will be Times Roman 12-point.

Since the Initial Base Font is part of the printer definition, you change it through the Select Printer:Edit menu, and cursor position is irrelevant. To change it:

1. Display the main Print menu:

    Keyboard: Press the Print key (Shift-F7).

    Mouse: Display the File menu and select **Print**.

2. Choose **Select Printer**. The Print: Select Printer menu appears, displaying the printers that have been installed on your system.

3. Highlight the printer you want to select a new Initial Base Font for, and select the **Edit** option.

    The Select Printer: Edit screen appears. Your current Initial Base Font appears next to option 5, Initial Base Font.

4. Select Initial Base Font (5).

    A list of all the fonts that you have installed for use with this printer will appear, as shown in Figure 13.12 for the Hewlett-Packard LaserJet Series II printer.

    If there are too many fonts to fit on one screen, you can scroll through the list using the regular cursor movement keys, or use the Name Search option to go directly to a font name.

```
Select Printer: Initial Font

  CG Times  6pt (WP)
  CG Times  8pt (WP)
  CG Times  8pt Bold (WP)
  CG Times  8pt Italic (WP)
  CG Times 10pt (WP)
  CG Times 10pt Bold (WP)
  CG Times 10pt Italic (WP)
  CG Times 12pt (WP)
  CG Times 12pt Bold (WP)
  CG Times 12pt Italic (WP)
  CG Times 14pt (WP)
  CG Times 14pt Bold (WP)
  CG Times 14pt Italic (WP)
  CG Times 18pt Bold (WP)
  CG Times 24pt Bold (WP)
* Courier 10cpi
  Courier 10cpi Bold
  Helv  6pt (AC)
  Helv  6pt Bold (AC)
  Helv  6pt Italic (AC)
  Helv  8pt (AC)

1 Select; N Name search: 1
```

Figure 13.12   *Changing the Initial Base Font.*

5. Move the cursor onto the font that you wish to use, and then choose the **Select** option. If you are using a PostScript printer, you will have an additional step: Enter the point size. You will then return to the Select Printer: Edit screen, where you'll see the font name you just selected next to the Initial Base Font option.

6. To return to the Edit screen:

    Keyboard: Press the Exit key (F7) three times.

    Mouse: Click the right button three times.

Document Initial Base Font

The Initial Base Font option on the Format: Document menu changes only the document on the Edit screen. The font is initially the same as the Initial Base Font on the Select Printer: Edit menu. Once you change it, it will override the font on the Select Printer: Edit menu. Neither of these options inserts a code into your document; instead, the font information is saved in the file header.

The cursor can be anywhere in the document when you change the Document Initial Base Font, since it does not insert a code. To change it:

1. Display the Format: Document menu:

    Keyboard: Press Format (Shift-F8) and select **Document.**

    Mouse: Display the **Layout** menu and select **Document.**

2. Select Initial Base Font (3).

3. Move the cursor onto the font you want to use and then select it by:

    Keyboard: Pressing Enter.

    Mouse: Clicking the left mouse button on the font and then clicking it on Select.

    If you have a PostScript printer, you'll be asked to enter the point size.

4. To return to the Edit menu:

    Keyboard: Press Exit (F7).

    Mouse: Click the right button.

If you use footnotes or endnotes in a document and wish to print them in a different font than the rest of the text, changing the Document Initial Base Font saves you the trouble of changing the Base Font each time you type a footnote or endnote. For example, say you want to use Times Roman 10-point for your footnotes and Times Roman 12-point for the rest of the text. Your first step would be to change the Document Initial Base Font to Times Roman 10-point, which can be done from any position in the document. Next, move the cursor to the first line of the document and change the Base Font to Times Roman 12-point. Changing the Base Font inserts a code into the document that affects all body text from that point forward, but it will not change footnotes or endnotes (except if a Footnote or Endnote Option code follows a Base Font code).

Base Font

You can use the Base Font option on the Font menu to change the font as often as you want within a document. Unlike the two Initial Base Font options, this one inserts a code that you can see in the Reveal Codes screen, such as [Font:Times Roman 12 pt]. Changing the Base Font is similar to many other formatting changes that insert codes, such as line spacing and margin changes made through the Format: Line menu, in that it alters text from the cursor position forward, unless another font code is encountered later in the document.

The Base Font option overrides both Initial Base Font methods. However, it will only change headers, footers, and automatic page numbers if the Base Font code precedes the codes for these options. For example, if the first code in your document is a Header A code, and the second code is a font code that changes the Base Font to Times Roman 12-point, the header will not be formatted using the Times Roman 12-point font. Instead, it will use the Initial Base Font on the Select Printer: Edit menu, or, if it differs, the Initial Base Font on the Format: Document menu.

To change the Base Font, begin by placing the cursor in the position where you want the change to start. Next:

1. Display the main Font menu:

   Keyboard: Press the Font key (Ctrl-F8).

   Mouse: Display the pull-down Font menu.

2. Select Base Font.

3. Move the cursor onto the font that you wish to use, and select it. If you are using a PostScript printer, enter the point size.

After that, you are returned to the Edit screen. If you look in Reveal Codes, you'll see the Base Font code left of the cursor.

Automatic Font Changes

The Base Font option is useful when you want to switch to a font with a different typeface, such as from Times Roman to Helvetica. However, if you just want to change the size or weight of the typeface that you are currently using, such as from 12-point to 14-point, or from regular to italic, it's more convenient to use the Size and Appearance options on the Font menu. Bold and Underline are two of the Appearance options; aside from the fact that the others do not have dedicated function keys, they work the same way.

When you use an attribute such as Bold, WordPerfect makes an *automatic font change,* selecting a bold font in the same typeface that you are currently using, if it is available. For instance, if your Base Font is Times Roman 12-point, and you select Bold for headings, WordPerfect will print the headings in a Times Roman 12-point Bold font (assuming it is available). If you later change the Base Font in the document, replacing the Times Roman 12-point font with Palatino 12-point, WordPerfect will change the bold headings to a Palatino 12-point Bold font. The Size and Appearance options on the Font menu are called font *attributes.* When you select one, WordPerfect makes an *automatic font change,* switching to a font with the selected attribute in the same typeface, if available.

The font appearance attributes are bold, underline, double underline, italics, outline, shadow, small caps, redline, and strikeout. The font size attributes are fine, small, large, very large, extra large, subscript, and superscript. Figure 13.13 shows how they appear when printed on a PostScript printer, using Times Roman 12-point as the Base Font.

WordPerfect bases the size and appearance changes on the font that you are currently using in the document, whether it is the Base Font, Document Initial Base Font, or Initial Base Font on the Select Printer: Edit menu. The change is a variation of the Base Font or Initial Font currently in use, and WordPerfect substitutes the most appropriate font it can find from the list of available fonts for this printer. It selects Size attributes using the following percentages of the Base font or Initial Font:

Fine 60%

Small 80%

Large 120%

Very Large 150%

Extra Large 200%

Superscript and Subscript 60%

This is Times Roman 12 point, the *Base Font* for this document. Here is what happens when you use the Font key's *Size* option to select:

Fine: this size is 60% of the Base Font's size.

Small: this size is 80% of the Base Font's size.

Large: this size is 120% of the Base Font's size.

Very Large: this size is 150% of the Base Font's size.

Extra Large: this size is 200% of the Base Font's size.

Subscript is used for the 2 in this number: H_2O

Superscript is used for the 3 in this number: 6^3

Here is what happens when you use the Font key's *Appearance* options:

This is in bold.

This is underlined.

This is double underlined.

This is italicized.

This is outline.

This is shadow.

THIS IS SMALL CAPS.

This is redlined

~~This is strikeout~~

Figure 13.13 *Size and Appearance attributes.*

For example, if your Base Font is set to Times Roman 12-point and you format a section of text using the Large attribute, WordPerfect will use a Times Roman 14.4-point font or the closest available font, such as 14-point. Very Large text would be printed in Times Roman 18-point. You can change the percentages for the Size attributes using the Size Attribute Ratios option on the Setup: Print Options menu (as described in Part Three, "Command Reference"). If you print a document formatted with any of the attributes and are dissatisfied with the substitutions that WordPerfect has made, you can use the Printer program (PTR.EXE) to modify the selections. You probably won't need to do this if you use the built-in fonts on a PostScript printer, but for other printers, it can provide you with precise control over the automatic font changes.

Tip: The Size and Appearance attributes are printer-dependent. To see how your printer interprets them for a specific Base Font, retrieve the PRINTER.TST file, change the font at the top of the document, and then print it. If you are dissatisfied with the results, you can use the Printer program (PTR.EXE) to change them, as described in Part Three under *Automatic Font Changes*.

If you already know how to use the Bold and Underline keys, you'll find the Size and Appearance options easy to understand because they work essentially the same way. If you haven't typed the text yet, turn the attribute on, type the text, and then turn it off.

To format text with an attribute as you type it:

1. Select the Font menu:

   Keyboard: Press the Font key (Ctrl-F8).

   Mouse: Display the Font menu.

2. Select Size or Appearance:

   Keyboard: Select Size (**1**) or Appearance (**2**).

   If you select Size, this menu will appear at the bottom of the screen:

   ```
   1 Suprscpt; 2 Subscpt; 3 Fine; 4 Small; 5 Large; 6 Vry
   Large; 7 Ext Large: 0
   ```

   If you select Appearance, this menu will appear:

   ```
   1 Bold 2 Undrln 3 Dbl Und 4 Italc 5 Outln 6 Shadw
   7 SmCap  8 Redln 9 Stkout: 0
   ```

Mouse: Select one of the Size options—Superscript, Subscript, Fine, Small, Large, Very Large, or Extra Large—or select Appearance. If you select Appearance, the options pop out to the right, as shown in Figure 13.14: Bold, Underline, Double Underline, Italics, Outline, Shadow, Small Cap, Redline, and Strikeout.

Figure 13.14 *The pull-down Font menu, with Appearance options displayed to the right.*

3. Select the attribute.

4. After you finish typing the text that you want to format with the attribute, press the Right Arrow key once to move the cursor past the code that turns off the attribute.

To format text that has already been typed with a Size or Appearance attribute, you must block it first:

1. Highlight the text with the Block feature.

2. Select the Size or Appearance attribute from the Font menu, as described in the preceding steps.

This turns the attribute on and off, inserting codes around the blocked text.

Tip: The Bold and Underline options on the Font menu duplicate the Bold and Underline keys, F6 and F8. Unless you use a mouse, it is easier to use the dedicated function keys for bold and underline.

Style and Design

There are a few mistakes to avoid in selecting fonts. The first is the temptation to include too many different fonts on a page, which can greatly detract from the message you are trying to convey and give your document a cluttered, disorderly appearance. Always remember that you want your reader to grasp a message, not be impressed by a document full of fonts that shout out for attention. You should usually limit the number of typefaces on a page to two or three.

Another mistake is to mix two serif typefaces, such as Times Roman for headings and Palatino for body text, or two sans serif typefaces. If you are ever in doubt, don't mix typefaces at all. Instead, use one typeface in several sizes and weights, such as Times Roman 12-point for body text, Times Roman 14-point Bold for headings, and Times Roman 10-point Italic for footers. Other errors include mixing different typefaces or point sizes for body text. Don't, for example, use different typefaces for text in side-by-side columns.

The judicious use of italic and bold fonts can increase the contrast on a page, and heighten reader interest by emphasizing important words or phrases. You should also use an italic font when naming the title of a publication. However, you should generally avoid using these attributes for long sections of text. An abundance of bold text darkens a page, while excessive use of italics lightens it. Ideally, a page should have enough contrast to help the reader locate important information, but not so much that it overwhelms.

Finally, avoid the overuse of uppercase letters in headings, especially if they are longer than one line. Unless a heading is very short—one or two words at the most—this technique tends to reduce legibility and slow down the reader. Instead, use a slightly larger font, or a bold font.

Paper Size and Type

Unless you are printing on the default paper size and type, which is standard 8.5" x 11" paper, you must specify the size and type of the form you will be using. For instance, to print on envelopes, you would have to specify an envelope form, with dimensions such as 9.5" x 4". To select a form, use the Paper Size and Type option on the Format Page menu. If the form is not yet defined for your printer, you will have to create a definition for it.

To select a form, begin with the cursor at the top of the page. Like most formatting options, this one inserts a code in your document, so the cursor must be at the top of the page. (If you want to format the entire document with this form, the cursor should be at the top of the document.)

1. Display the Format: Page menu:

    Keyboard: Press Format (Shift-F8) and select **Page** (**2**).

    Mouse: Display the **Layout** menu and select the **Page** option.

2. Select Paper **Size**/Type (7).

    A list of paper sizes and types that have already been defined for your printer appears; an example is shown in Figure 13.15. If the form you want to use is not listed, follow the instructions in the next section to define it.

```
Format: Paper Size/Type
                                              Font  Double
Paper type and Orientation   Paper Size   Prompt Loc   Type  Sided  Labels

(1 x 2 5/8) inch Avery label 8.5" x 11"     No   Contin  Port  No      3 x 10
1" x 4"                      8.5" x 11"     No   Contin  Port  No      2 x 10
Envelope - Wide              9.5" x 4"      Yes  Manual  Land  No
LONG                         8.5" x 11.8"   No   Contin  Port  No
Standard                     8.5" x 11"     No   Contin  Port  No
Standard - Wide              11" x 8.5"     No   Contin  Land  No
[ALL OTHERS]                 Width ≤ 8.5"   Yes  Manual        No














1 Select; 2 Add; 3 Copy; 4 Delete; 5 Edit; N Name Search: 1
```

Figure 13.15   *The Format: Paper Size/Type menu, displaying the forms that have been defined for this printer.*

3. Place the cursor on the form you want to use, and choose the **Select** option (1).

    You return to the Format: Page menu, and the form you just selected appears next to the Paper Size/Type option.

4. To return to the Edit screen:

    Keyboard: Press Exit (F7).

    Mouse: Click the right button.

Defining a Form

To create a definition, use the Format: Edit Paper Definition menu.

1. Display the Format:Page menu:

   Keyboard: Press Format (Shift-F8) and select **Page** (**2**).

   Mouse: Display the **L**ayout menu and select the **P**age option.

2. Select Paper Size/Type (7).

3. Select the **A**dd option (2). The Format: Paper Type screen appears, as shown in Figure 13.16.

   You may find it easier to modify an existing paper definition than to create a new one. Instead of selecting Add, you can highlight a definition that resembles the one you want to create, select the Copy option (3), and then select the Edit option (5) to modify it as necessary. If you use this method, skip to step 5.

```
Format: Paper Type

    1 - Standard

    2 - Bond

    3 - Letterhead

    4 - Labels

    5 - Envelope

    6 - Transparency

    7 - Cardstock

    8 - [ALL OTHERS]

    9 - Other




Selection: 1
```

Figure 13.16 The Format: Paper Type menu appears when you choose the Add option to create a new form. Use it to specify the form type.

4. Select the paper type, or use the Other option (9) to enter a name for the form.

   Next, the Format: Edit Paper Definition menu appears, as shown in Figure 13.17. Use it to specify the Paper Size and other features such as Location, which can be continuous, manual, or a bin; Font Type, which lets you select a landscape font for a form such as an envelope; and Labels, if you are creating a form for labels, to define the individual label size, number of labels per page, top and left corners of the form, distance between labels, and label margins.

 Tip: You can use the Labels macro to have WordPerfect automatically define the forms for commonly used labels, including the Avery and 3M labels listed in Figure 13.18. For more information about how to use this macro, see *Labels* in Part Three, "Command Reference."

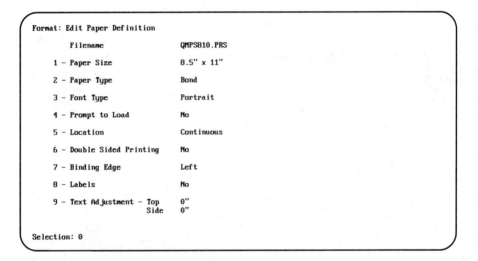

```
Format: Edit Paper Definition

        Filename            QMPS810.PRS

    1 - Paper Size          8.5" x 11"

    2 - Paper Type          Bond

    3 - Font Type           Portrait

    4 - Prompt to Load      No

    5 - Location            Continuous

    6 - Double Sided Printing   No

    7 - Binding Edge        Left

    8 - Labels              No

    9 - Text Adjustment - Top   0"
                     Side   0"

Selection: 0
```

Figure 13.17 *The Format: Edit Paper Definition menu.*

5. Make any necessary changes on the Format: Edit Paper Definition menu. For more details, see *Paper Size and Type* and *Labels*, *Printing* in Part Three, "Command Reference."

6. To return to the Format: Paper Size/Type menu:

   Keyboard: Press Enter.

   Mouse: Click the right button.

7. To use the new form, choose the **S**elect option (1).

```
                    Label Page/Size Definitions
Labels      Sizes            Labels per.  Labels     Sizes           Labels per.
            H x W       Sheet RowxCol                H x W      Sheet RowxCol

5160 Avery  1" x 2 5/8"      30 10 x 3    5161 Avery  1" x 4"         20 10 x 2
5162 Avery  1 1/3" x 4"      14  7 x 2    5163 Avery  2" x 4"         10  5 x 2
5164 Avery  3 1/3" x 4"       6  3 x 2    5165 Avery  8 1/2" x 11"     1  1 x 1
5196 Avery  2 3/4" x 2 3/4"   9  3 x 3    5197 Avery  1 1/2" x 4"     12  6 x 2
5260 Avery  1" x 2 5/8"      30 10 x 3    5261 Avery  1" x 4"         20 10 x 2
5262 Avery  1 1/3" x 4"      14  7 x 2    5266 Avery  2/3" x 3 7/16"  30 15 x 2
5267 Avery  1/2" x 1 3/4"    80 20 x 4    5293 Avery  1 2/3" round    12  4 x 3
5294 Avery  2 1/2" round      9  3 x 3    5295 Avery  3 1/3" round     6  3 x 2
7701 3M     11" x 8 7/16"     1  1 x 1    7709 3M     3 1/3" x 2 5/6"   9  3 x 3
7712 3M     2 1/2" x 2 5/6"  12  4 x 3    7721 3M     1 1/2" x 2 5/6"  21  7 x 3
7730 3M     1" x 2 5/8"      30 10 x 3    7733 3M     1" x 2 5/6"      33 11 x 3




1 Select; 2 Name Search; 3 Mark (*): 1
```

Figure 13.18 *You can use the Labels macro to have WordPerfect define the forms for the Avery and 3M labels listed in this menu.*

Graphics

WordPerfect's graphics and desktop publishing features have opened up a whole new world for WordPerfect users. Armed with these tools, you can design interesting and attractive documents that were once unthinkable in a word processing program: newsletters, flyers, reports, advertisements, brochures, letterhead stationery, fax forms, training manuals, catalogs, inserts, and just about any document whose appearance you want to improve. If you've read this far in the book, you have already studied many of the tools. After reading this chapter, you will be able to:

- Create horizontal and vertical lines using the Graphics menu.

- Design Text boxes for applications such as pull quotes and tables. Pull quotes are quotations that have been taken from the body of an article and set off in a display format such as a shaded box with thick horizontal lines for the top and bottom borders.

- Create Figure boxes so that you can integrate graphics files into your WordPerfect text documents, such as:

  Clip-art from a wide variety of sources;

  Illustrations from a paint or drawing program such as DrawPerfect, Harvard Graphics, or Adobe Illustrator;

  Business graphics from a spreadsheet program like PlanPerfect, Quattro Pro, Excel, or Lotus 1-2-3;

  Scanned illustrations such as manual artwork, your company logo, or a signature.

To some extent, this chapter is about desktop publishing. Although it is an overused term, it can be thought of as the application of personal computers to the publishing process to create the appearance of a professionally published document. Once this process involved numerous manual steps and was labor-intensive. Now, all you need is the right software and hardware.

WordPerfect Graphics: An Overview

Although WordPerfect does not claim to offer the full range of page makeup/layout features provided by a dedicated desktop publishing program, such as Ventura Publisher or Aldus PageMaker, it does provide many features that will help you design professional-looking documents. And using them does not have to be complicated or difficult. It can be as simple as placing a box around a table of contents, as shown in Figure 14.1; separating newspaper columns with vertical lines, as shown in Figure 14.2; or underscoring a heading with a horizontal line, as shown in Figure 14.3. Another relatively simple example appears in Chapter 8, where Figure 8.1 features a shaded Text box above newspaper columns.

Table of Contents

Lesson 1: Printing and Fonts

Installing your printer	1
Installing fonts	3
Initializing the printer	5
Initial Font, Base Font, Document Initial Font	5
Changing size and appearance attributes	8
Print options	12

Lesson 2: Newspaper Columns

Setting margins	15
Creating the header	18
Creating the footer	19
Defining columns	21
Typing in columns	24
Cursor movement in columns	25
Creating the vertical rules	26
Hyphenation	28
Shaded boxes	32

Lesson 3: Using the Graphics key

The horizontal rule	35
Creating a figure and retrieving a graphic	37
Removing the border around the figure	39
Creating a text box	44
Changing the text box options	45
Changing the line height	47

Lesson 4: Styles

Using styles	49
Editing styles	52
Saving styles	55
Supplemental exercise: Using styles	56
Creating and applying styles	56
Using a Style Library	61

Figure 14.1 Table of contents surrounded by a box.

WordPerfect also makes it easy to integrate graphics into your documents. For example, Figures 14.4, 14.5, and 14.6 incorporate clip-art illustrations from DrawPerfect: the globe in 14.4, the businessman in 14.5, and the gas pump in 14.6. In Chapter 10, a modified DrawPerfect graphic (a stack of dollar bills on a grid) was used to enhance the table in Figure 10.17. To help you experiment with graphics, WordPerfect includes 30 clip-art files that were created in DrawPerfect. Appendix B of the WordPerfect manual illustrates them and provides their file names.

Susan B. Kelly

Software Training: Why bother?

Software training is one of the most important investments that your company can make. Unfortunately, many firms do not understand why, and are unwilling to make the financial commitment.

I can relate stories about corporations who have invested thousands of dollars in the most modern hardware, and in powerful software packages like WordPerfect and Lotus 1-2-3, yet whose administrative and clerical workers refuse to turn on their computers. Why? Because they have absolutely no idea how they work, and resent not being provided with a modicum of guidance.

I have seen companies stuck in a bind who had no choice but to hire a $100 per hour (or more) consultant. Why? To solve problems that anyone who had taken a four-hour *Introduction to DOS* class could have figured out in sixty seconds.

Imagine investing a few thousand dollars to purchase ten copies of WordPerfect, a multi-featured program that not only provides complete word processing capabilities, but also has significant power for applications such as form letters and mailing list management, file management, newsletters, desktop publishing, and math. Next, picture ten secretaries who must start using it right away, with no training, and who either quit and find another job, or learn just enough to print simple letters and memos. Those who do learn just enough to get by waste countless hours of company time trying to figure out mysteries such as why the letter they typed yesterday and need to print today seemingly disappeared from the disk, or why the editing changes they just finished making to a twenty-page report do not appear in the printed version. And

they never learn shortcuts such as how to move the cursor word by word, to the beginning or end of the line, or to the top or bottom of a page; how to cut and paste blocks of text; or how to print a selected range of pages instead of the entire document. They may as well be using typewriters, since they are not taking advantage of the many unique benefits of their word processor. In fact, many revert to using typewriters for tasks that they think can be handled more efficiently, such as labels and envelopes. Can a price be put on such wasted resources?

In my experience, lack of training is often resented by employees. They come to view the company as cheap, and wonder why they are working there. In an era where administrative and secretarial skills are becoming scarce, this is not good business practice.

Another serious problem is the potential damage that can be done by workers who are unfamiliar with commands such as *FORMAT*. Some of you may have experienced the trauma of a hard disk that has been erased by improper use of the *FORMAT* command. If you were really unlucky, the blow was compounded many times over because the disk was not backed up properly.

In companies that provide inadequate software training, there is a desperate need for advice. In response, an unofficial computer "guru" usually emerges, who enjoys computers and has been able to teach herself or himself a little more than the average employee. The guru helps her fellow

employees with minor questions that she can answer by reading the manual, and everyone thinks she is a genius. Before long, word of her talent spreads throughout the company, and then everyone relies on her for help with all of their computer problems. The individual is rarely able to answer all these questions right away, and ends up spending so much time figuring them out that he or she is unable to perform well in his or her actual capacity (which is never officially one of a computer support person). This represents another wasted resource, but can also provide the company with a flimsy excuse for insufficient training.

I keep asking myself why companies are so unwilling to invest in training. The best companies I know care about their employees, have invested a great deal of money to hire, promote, and maintain them, and try to keep them satisfied. They do this not out of the milk of human kindness, but for sound economic reasons. Software training may be expensive, and often costs more than the software itself, but the benefits far outweigh the costs.

My advice? Find yourself an instructor or training firm whose expertise can be verified, whose references rave about how much they were helped by the training, and who is willing to provide additional support after the class ends. And don't worry about the price. If you do this, I promise that you won't have to become one of my horror stories.

Figure 14.2 Separating newspaper columns with vertical lines.

Susan B. Kelly

Software Training: Why bother?

Software training is one of the most important investments that your company can make. Unfortunately, many firms do not understand why, and are unwilling to make the financial commitment.

I can relate stories about corporations who have invested thousands of dollars in the most modern hardware, and in powerful software packages like WordPerfect and Lotus 1-2-3, yet whose administrative and clerical workers refuse to turn on their computers. Why? Because they have absolutely no idea how they work, and resent not being provided with a modicum of guidance.

I have seen companies stuck in a bind who had no choice but to hire a $100 per hour (or more) consultant. Why? To solve problems that anyone who had taken a four-hour *Introduction to DOS* class could have figured out in sixty seconds.

Imagine investing a few thousand dollars to purchase ten copies of WordPerfect, a multi-featured program that not only provides complete word processing capabilities, but also has significant power for applications such as form letters and mailing list management, file management, newsletters, desktop publishing, and math. Next, picture ten secretaries who must start using it right away, with no training, and who either quit and find another job, or learn just enough to print simple letters and memos. Those who do learn just enough to get by waste countless hours of company time trying to figure out mysteries such as why the letter they typed yesterday and need to print today seemingly disappeared from the disk, or why the editing changes they just finished making to a twenty-page report do not appear in the printed version. And they never learn shortcuts such as how to move the cursor word by word, to the beginning or end of the line, or to the top or bottom of a page; how to cut and paste blocks of text; or how to print a selected range of pages instead of the entire document. They may as well be using typewriters, since they are not taking advantage of the many unique benefits of their word processor. In fact, many revert to using typewriters for tasks that they think can be handled more efficiently, such as labels and envelopes. Can a price be put on such wasted resources?

In my experience, lack of training is often resented by employees. They come to view the company as cheap, and wonder why they are working there. In an era where administrative and secretarial skills are becoming scarce, this is not good business practice.

Another serious problem is the potential damage that can be done by workers who are unfamiliar with commands such as *FORMAT*. Some of you may have experienced the trauma of a hard disk that has been erased by improper use of the *FORMAT* command. If you were really unlucky, the blow was compounded many times over because the disk was not backed up properly.

In companies that provide inadequate software training, there is a desperate need for advice. In response, an unofficial computer "guru" usually emerges, who enjoys computers and has been able to teach herself or himself a little more than the average employee. The guru helps her fellow employees with minor questions that she can answer by reading the manual, and everyone thinks she is a genius. Before long, word of her talent spreads throughout the company, and then everyone relies on her for help with all of their computer problems. The individual is rarely able to answer all these questions right away, and ends up spending so much time figuring them out that he or she is unable to perform well in his or her actual capacity (which is never officially one of a computer support person). This represents another wasted resource, but can also provide the company with a flimsy excuse for insufficient training.

I keep asking myself why companies are so unwilling to invest in training. The best companies I know care about their employees, have invested a great deal of money to hire, promote, and maintain them, and try to keep them satisfied. They do this not out of the milk of human kindness, but for sound economic reasons. Software training may be expensive, and often costs more than the software itself, but the benefits far outweigh the costs.

My advice? Find yourself an instructor or training firm whose expertise can be verified, whose references rave about how much they were helped by the training, and who is willing to provide additional support after the class ends. And don't worry about the price. If you do this, I promise that you won't have to become one of my horror stories.

Figure 14.3 Underscoring a heading with a horizontal line.

STOP UNWANTED JUNK MAIL

The junk mail Americans receive in one day could produce enough energy to heat 250,000 homes.

B ACKGROUND. The "junk mail" issue is a tough one to sort through. After all, many of us rely on mail from non-profit groups for credible information about important environmental and social issues. Plus, direct mail is a fundraising lifeline for environmental grass-roots groups and a key means of mobilizing grass-roots action to protect the earth.

But *unwanted* junk mail is more than just a nuisance——it's an environmental hazard. If you saved up all the unwanted paper you'll receive in the mail this year, you could have the equivalent of 1-1/2 trees. And so could each of your neighbors. And that adds up to about 100 million trees every year.

DID YOU KNOW

• Americans receive almost *4 million tons* of junk mail every year.

• About 44% of the junk mail is never even opened or read.

• According to recent research, the average American still spends 8 full months of his or her life just opening junk mail.

• If only 100,000 people stopped their junk mail, we could save up to 150,000 trees every year. If a million people did, we could save up to 1.5 million trees.

SIMPLE THINGS TO DO

• **Write to: Mail Preference Service, Direct Marketing Association,** 6 East 43rd St., New York, NY 10017. They'll stop your name from being sold to most large mailing list companies. This will reduce your junk mail up to 75%.

• **Recycle the junk mail you already get:** If it's printed on newsprint, toss it in with the newspapers. If it's quality paper, make a separate pile for it——many recycling centers accept both white and colored paper.

Figure 14.4 *WordPerfect makes it easy to include graphic figures in your documents. This example replicates a page from a popular book,* 50 Simple Things You Can Do to Save the Earth. *The globe is a DrawPerfect clip-art figure, Globe-1.wpg. The border was also created in DrawPerfect, to produce the rounded edges.*

Date: _____

Scheduled appointments		To do
9:00		1
9:30		
10:00		2
10:30		
11:00		3
11:30		
12:00		4
12:30		
1:00		5
1:30		
2:00		6
2:30		
3:00		7
3:30		
4:00		8
4:30		
5:00		9
5:30		

Notes:

Figure 14.5 *Another document that incorporates DrawPerfect clip art, the business-man sitting on a table (Sittin-1.wpg). The appointment and "To Do" list below the figure is a WordPerfect table (see Chapter 10 to learn how to create tables).*

Employment Opportunities

Petroleum Dispensing Engineer

Application Closing Date: Salary:
December 13, 1991 $915 - $950

**You're Invited
to Apply!**

Tom's has an opening for a petroleum dispensing engineer. This is a full time position at one of the more prestigious interstate locations.

The petroleum dispensing engineer functions as part of the management team at the service dispensing island, and is part of a staff of five. The PDE will be responsible for dealing directly with the public and maintaining the general appearance of the grounds on a daily basis.

Duties

Duties may include but are not limited to:

Dispensing petroleum to individual clients' vehicles, while ignoring questions pertaining to daily escalating petroleum prices and the confiscation of oil fields in Iraq and Kuwait.

Being able to cleverly evade client requests for checking tire inflation pressures and removing dirt and windshield obstructions (previous experience dealing with senior citizens is desirable).

Assisting in departmental sales of unnecessary replacement items such as air filters, batteries, windshield wipers, & spare tires (with special commission incentives).

Maintaining the general appearance of the service island, which requires hands to be covered with grease as much as possible for an even distribution of oil on pumps, walls, and clients' vehicles.

**Basic
Requirements**

At least two years of progressively responsible experience in a similar position, or equivalent retail experience in the automotive industry. A completed supplemental application is required as part of the application process.

*Figure 14.6 Job announcement with DrawPerfect clip-art, the gasoline pump
(Gaspump.wpg).*

You can also incorporate scanned images into your WordPerfect documents. As an example, Figure 14.7 features a graphite drawing of a deer that was scanned using a full-page scanner. Once it was scanned and sized and then saved in TIFF (Tagged Image File Format), WordPerfect could import this image directly into a Figure box. It was then used to embellish the cover of a hypothetical brochure. Incidentally, to create a brochure of this size in WordPerfect, it was necessary to define the form using the Paper Size and Type option on the Format: Page menu.

Wildlife Management Seminar

May 23rd, 1991

L.W. Conner Hall • Arcata University • Arcata, California

Figure 14.7 *A brochure that incorporates scanned artwork, an original drawing of a deer. (© 1991, by Jim Kelly)*

Once you master WordPerfect, you can even use it to produce camera-ready pages to take to a printer. For example, Figure 14.8 displays the cover of a recent issue of *The WordPerfectionist*, a newsletter produced by the WordPerfect Support Group. The shaded box at the top of the page, which includes the masthead and the words *The WordPerfectionist*, is actually printed in a shade of light blue.

The layout of this newsletter is fairly complicated and requires a thorough knowledge of WordPerfect and the related technology; nonetheless, it can and has been done! The staff write the entire newsletter in WordPerfect 5.1, print the page proofs on their HP LaserJet Series II printer, using PostScript fonts (the printer is equipped with a QMS JetScript PostScript board), and then use WordPerfect to print the camera-ready copy on their Linotronic L100P typesetter. This provides better resolution for the final product: 1270 dpi (dots per inch), compared with the 300 dpi produced by most laser printers (including the HP LaserJet Series II and III printers). For more information about the WordPerfect Support Group's newsletter and other services and products, including typesetting from WordPerfect on a Linotronic L100P typesetter, call them at (301) 387-4500, or write to them at Lake Technology Park, P.O. Box 130, McHenry, Maryland 21541.

Another example of a camera-ready page is Figure 14.4, which replicates a page from a popular and practical book, *50 Simple Things You Can Do to Save the Earth*. In the version in Figure 14.4, the globe is a DrawPerfect clip-art figure, *Globe-1.wpg*, and the border was also created in DrawPerfect, to produce the rounded edges. In the original version (reproduced here with permission from the Earthworks Group, in Berkeley, California), a slightly smaller globe appears at the top of each page, serving as a logo for the book's environmental theme. *(50 Simple Things You Can Do to Save the Earth* is available in many bookstores. If you cannot find it, contact the publishers for more information: EarthWorks Press, Box 25, 1400 Shattuck Avenue, Berkeley, California 94709, (415) 841-5866.)

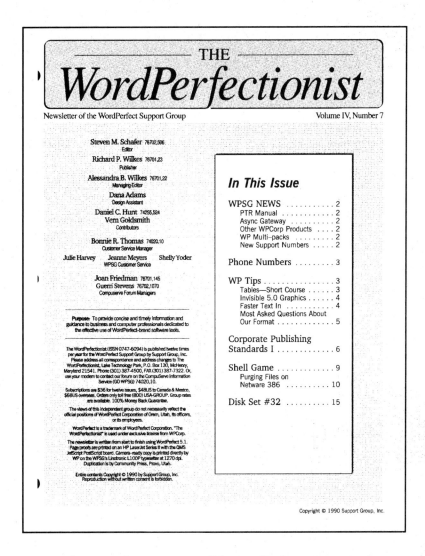

Figure 14.8 *The cover of a recent issue of* The WordPerfectionist, *a newsletter produced by the WordPerfect Support Group. This newsletter is produced entirely in WordPerfect and printed directly from the WordPerfect program on a typesetting machine.*

While documents with complex layouts, such as the newsletter shown in Figure 14.9, can be created in WordPerfect, you may find it time-consuming and laborious. In fact, to provide a step-by-step explanation of how this newsletter was created would probably require about 10 pages in this book, since the newsletter uses so many of WordPerfect's advanced features. If such applications are your primary reason for using WordPerfect and you plan to produce such documents on a daily basis, you might want to consider using dedicated page layout software instead. However, less complicated documents, such as flyers, training manuals, two- or three-column newsletters, fax forms, and letterhead stationery, are not hard to produce, once you understand the techniques. The real advantage to using WordPerfect for such documents is that you won't need to purchase and learn another software program. Considering the money you'll spend and the time it takes to master such a program, you may not be able to justify such a purchase, unless you use the program constantly. Also, programs like Ventura Publisher and PageMaker include basic text editors, but lack most of the sophisticated word processing features that WordPerfect users take for granted.

Eastridge Estates

Homeowner's Association Newsletter

August 1990

1989 - 1990 Officers

President	John Kelly
Vice President	Andrew David
Treasurer	Sony Anderson
Secretary	Michael Potter

Board Members

Susan Murphy	Joan Davis
Scott Carper	Martha Campbell

Committees & Board Liaisons

Financial	Frank Henderson
Architectural	Richard Hammer
Landscape	Susan Heller
Parking	Ken Mabel
Hospitality	Cynthia Ramirez
Recreation	William Chan
Newsletter	Kelly Duffy
Maintenance	Ray Hamilton

Resident Manager

Robert Earle	555-1212

Attention!

Robert Earle, our resident manager, has an answering machine and welcomes your calls. He promises to respond to all messages within eight hours, but can only do so if you leave one!

A Word From the President

Our last board meeting was July 14th. Haven't the weeks just flown by this summer? At the last meeting we reviewed several proposals for concrete repair work needed on the driveways and streets throughout the complex, and settled on the lowest one. As you have probably noticed, work is currently in progress. We expect this job to be completed by the end of October.

The new landscaping looks great. However, we are concerned about the current drought conditions and excess water usage. At the next meeting, the Board will be exploring some modifications that should help conserve water.

An insurance claim is pending for roof damage caused by the painters. Anyone with additional information is welcome to speak at our next meeting.

Doesn't our complex look beautiful? While it is true that much repair work has been required lately, this is an integral part of maintaining our property values. We apologize for the inconveniences caused by some of the work, but know all our homeowners share in our pride of our community.

Complaint Department:

As usual, the suggestion box contained many letters this month about dogs, noisy teenagers, and speeding cars. Here are the most frequent complaints:

1. Dog owners not cleaning up after their pets.

2. Dog owners not keeping their pets on leashes when walking them in the complex.

3. Cars speeding through the complex and ignoring stop signs.

4. Teenagers in the pool and clubhouse with loud radios and cassette players.

Figure 14.9 *While you can use WordPerfect to create documents with complex layouts, such as this newsletter, doing so can be laborious and time-consuming.*

If you are serious about creating attractive documents, you'll need a laser printer. If you are using a daisywheel printer, you will not be able to print graphics at all. Although you can print graphics on a dot-matrix printer, the quality will not compare. Laser printers have declined significantly in price in the past few years. (As of this writing, the least expensive ones cost around $1,000.)

If you don't have a laser printer, consider using a desktop publishing service center. These services are flourishing all over the country. In the San Francisco Bay Area, for example, there are literally hundreds, many having evolved from traditional copy centers that offered photocopying and related services. Most offer self-service laser printing: You follow their instructions to format your document for their equipment, bring it in on a disk, insert it into their computer, and then print it directly on their laser printer. If that's too complicated, most service centers can do the work for you. The fees are based on an hourly or per page rate. Expect to pay 25¢ to $1 per page, or $5 to $10 per hour. Most offer additional services, such as full-page scanning, printing on a color laser printer, and typesetting directly from WordPerfect on a typesetting machine such as the Linotronic 300. Many of these service centers can print documents sent by modem or on disk, convenient if you live in a small town or in the country.

Tip: All the documents in this chapter were printed on a QMS PS 810 printer, using the internal PostScript fonts. Companies such as Adobe and Bitstream offer a wide variety of excellent fonts for this and other laser printers, including the popular Hewlett-Packard LaserJet printers, and those that emulate them.

WordPerfect's Edit screen cannot display the contents of graphics boxes, nor the horizontal and vertical lines that you can create using the Graphics menu. However, you can use WordPerfect's special Print Preview mode, View Document, to see them as they will appear when printed. You can use this special screen to view a document in 100% mode; zoom in and view it in 200% mode; see the entire page layout; or view facing pages such as pages 2 and 3.

WordPerfect includes many other important features that you'll need for desktop-publishing applications. Typographic controls such as line height (leading), kerning, word spacing, hyphenation, and letter spacing are available. You can mix a large variety of fonts, selecting typefaces like Times Roman and Helvetica in various sizes, such as 10-point, 12-point, and 14-point, and weights such as light, regular, medium, bold, and italic.

Although WordPerfect does not supply any fonts, since this is a function of the printer you are using, an extensive selection of fonts is available for laser printers, and even for some of the dot-matrix printers. Your computer does not have to be physically connected to a particular printer in order to choose fonts for that printer, or to use View Document to see approximately how that document will look. This is useful if you want to print your final copy on a laser printer attached to another computer in your office, or at a service bureau. Even though your computer is not attached to the printer, you can install the appropriate printer driver from the Installation disk, as described in Appendix A, select that printer, and then edit the printer definition to indicate what combination of font cartridges and soft fonts will be available. If your printer is capable, you can even print in color.

The use of styles allows you to name and save sets of formatting codes that you use frequently, so that you can standardize your formatting and easily change formatting characteristics throughout the document. In desktop-publishing applications, styles are indispensable. WordPerfect also includes tools that can help you manage longer documents, including automatic pagination, headers and footers; the ability to generate lists, an index, and a table of contents; and the ability to link several files together via a Master Document in order to print them as one document, or generate a single index, list, or table of contents for all of the files. All of these features are covered in other chapters of this book, or in Part Three, "Command Reference."

Horizontal and Vertical Lines

In the jargon of desktop publishing, horizontal and vertical lines are referred to as *rules*. Used judiciously, they can enhance many of your documents. Creating them in WordPerfect is straightforward and logical, once you acquaint yourself with the five options on the Graphics Horizontal Line and Graphics Vertical Line menus. Consider how few steps are required to create the horizontal rule shown in Figure 14.3:

1. Position the cursor in the blank line under the heading.

2. Display the main **Graphics** menu (press Alt-F9 or use the pull-down **Graphics** menu) and select the Line option.

3. Select the first option:

    Keyboard: (Create Line) Horizontal.

    Mouse: Create Horizontal.

4. The Graphics: Horizontal Line menu appears, as shown in Figure 14.10. Leave all the default settings, and then return to the Edit screen by pressing Enter or clicking the right mouse button.

This procedure creates a horizontal line at the current cursor position, filling all the space between the left and right margins. Since you cannot see the line on the Edit screen, you have to depend on the View Document screen to make sure it is correctly positioned between your heading and the text that follows (the preferable alternative to wasting large quantities of paper printing revisions).

Normally, you should separate the horizontal line from the text that follows by one blank line (one hard return).

If you look in the Reveal Codes screen, you'll see the code for the horizontal line you just created, which should be similar to this code:

```
[HLine:Full,Baseline,6.5",0.013",100%]
```

HLine indicates that the code represents a horizontal line. Full is the default for the horizontal position of your line, and it indicates that the line will span the width of the page between the left and right margins. Baseline is the default for the Vertical Position option (on the Graphics: Horizontal Line menu), and means that the line will be positioned on the baseline of the current line; you can change this option so that your line will be printed at a different horizontal position on the page. For example, if you wanted it 1.5" from the top of the page, you could change the Vertical Position option to *Set Position*, and then type 1.5. The first number, 6.5", represents the length of the line. Note that it corresponds to the page width, 8.5", minus 2" for the (1" each) left and right margins. The next number in the code, 0.013", represents the width of the line. The last one, 100%, represents the degree of gray shading. By default, both horizontal and vertical lines are completely black, but you can decrease the gray shading to lighten it, especially useful for a thick line if you want to position text inside it.

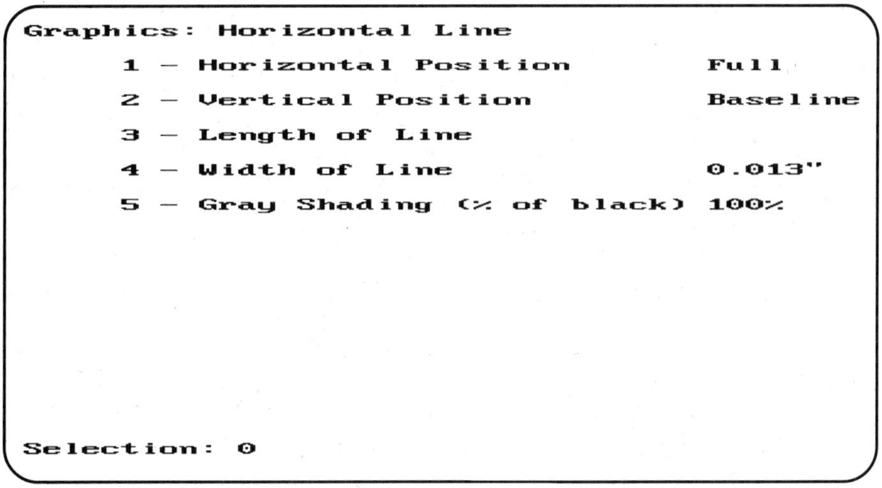

```
Graphics:  Horizontal  Line
      1  —  Horizontal  Position          Full
      2  —  Vertical  Position            Baseline
      3  —  Length  of  Line
      4  —  Width  of  Line               0.013"
      5  —  Gray  Shading  (% of  black)  100%




Selection:  0
```

Figure 14.10 *The Graphics: Horizontal Line menu.*

Tip: By default, horizontal and vertical lines are completely black. In other words, the Gray Shading option on both the Graphics Horizontal Line menu and the Graphics: Vertical Line menu is set to 100%. To create a thick line with text inside of it, resembling a Text box without borders, you could change the width of the line, change the gray shading to 10%, press Enter and type the text, and then use the Advance option on the Format: Other menu to move the text up so it will be printed inside the thick line.

Tip: Although you can create a horizontal line across a page using WordPerfect's Underline feature (F8 or Appearance and then Underline on the Font menu), this type of line will not change if you change the left or right margin, or switch to a larger or smaller font. In contrast, a horizontal line created through the Graphics: Horizontal Line menu, as described in this section, will adjust as you change the margins or the font, and still span the width of the page.

Changing the Length of a Horizontal Line

Figure 14.11 shows a shorter version of the horizontal line in Figure 14.3. If you prefer this version, changing the existing line is not difficult. Assuming you created the horizontal line described in the previous section, all you need to do is display the Graphics: Horizontal Line menu again, and then modify two options: *Horizontal Position* and *Length of Line*.

The first step is to calculate the line length of the heading ("Software Training: Why bother?") before editing the line. Yours will probably differ from the one used in this example, especially if you are using a different font and margin settings in your document.

1. Determine the length of your heading by placing the cursor at the end of the line. On the Edit screen, the cursor will appear to be on a blank space, but if you look in Reveal Codes, you'll see that it is actually on the [HRt] code at the end of the line. Next, write down the cursor position indicated by the Pos statistic on the status line (in this example, it was 5.44"). Subtract the left margin setting (.75 in this example), and you have the line length.

5.44" (First position following text of the heading)
−.75" (Left margin)
4.69" (Line length of the heading)

Susan B. Kelly

Software Training: Why bother?

Software training is one of the most important investments that your company can make. Unfortunately, many firms do not understand why, and are unwilling to make the financial commitment.

I can relate stories about corporations who have invested thousands of dollars in the most modern hardware, and in powerful software packages like WordPerfect and Lotus 1-2-3, yet whose administrative and clerical workers refuse to turn on their computers. Why? Because they have absolutely no idea how they work, and resent not being provided with a modicum of guidance.

I have seen companies stuck in a bind who had no choice but to hire a $100 per hour (or more) consultant. Why? To solve problems that anyone who had taken a four-hour *Introduction to DOS* class could have figured out in sixty seconds.

Imagine investing a few thousand dollars to purchase ten copies of WordPerfect, a multi-featured program that not only provides complete word processing capabilities, but also has significant power for applications such as form letters and mailing list management, file management, newsletters, desktop publishing, and math. Next, picture ten secretaries who must start using it right away, with no training, and who either quit and find another job, or learn just enough to print simple letters and memos. Those who do learn just enough to get by waste countless hours of company time trying to figure out mysteries such as why the letter they typed yesterday and need to print today seemingly disappeared from the disk, or why the editing changes they just finished making to a twenty-page report do not appear in the printed version. And they never learn shortcuts such as how to move the cursor word by word, to the beginning or

end of the line, or to the top or bottom of a page; how to cut and paste blocks of text; or how to print a selected range of pages instead of the entire document. They may as well be using typewriters, since they are not taking advantage of the many unique benefits of their word processor. In fact, many revert to using typewriters for tasks that they think can be handled more efficiently, such as labels and envelopes. Can a price be put on such wasted resources?

In my experience, lack of training is often resented by employees. They come to view the company as cheap, and wonder why they are working there. In an era where administrative and secretarial skills are becoming scarce, this is not good business practice.

Another serious problem is the potential damage that can be done by workers who are unfamiliar with commands such as *FORMAT*. Some of you may have experienced the trauma of a hard disk that has been erased by improper use of the *FORMAT* command. If you were really unlucky, the blow was compounded many times over because the disk was not backed up properly.

In companies that provide inadequate software training, there is a desperate need for advice. In response, an unofficial computer "guru" usually emerges, who enjoys computers and has been able to teach herself or himself a little more than the average employee. The guru helps her fellow employees with minor questions that she can answer by reading the manual, and everyone thinks she is a genius. Before long,

word of her talent spreads throughout the company, and then everyone relies on her for help with all of their computer problems. The individual is rarely able to answer all these questions right away, and ends up spending so much time figuring them out that he or she is unable to perform well in his or her actual capacity (which is never officially one of a computer support person). This represents another wasted resource, but can also provide the company with a flimsy excuse for insufficient training.

I keep asking myself why companies are so unwilling to invest in training. The best companies I know care about their employees, have invested a great deal of money to hire, promote, and maintain them, and try to keep them satisfied. They do this not out of the milk of human kindness, but for sound economic reasons. Software training may be expensive, and often costs more than the software itself, but the benefits far outweigh the costs.

My advice? Find yourself an instructor or training firm whose expertise can be verified, whose references rave about how much they were helped by the training, and who is willing to provide additional support after the class ends. And don't worry about the price. If you do this, I promise that you won't have to become one of my horror stories.

Figure 14.11 *In this version of the article that appeared in Figure 14.3, the horizontal line has been shortened.*

Now edit the line and change the line length:

2. Display the main Graphics menu (press Alt-F9 or use the pull-down Graphics menu), and select the Line option.

3. Select the third option:

> **Keyboard:** (Edit Line) Horizontal.

> **Mouse:** Edit Horizontal.

If you did not create the original line, as described in the previous section, select the (Create Line) Horizontal option instead, called Create Horizontal on the pull-down menu.

4. Select the first option on the Graphics: Horizontal Line menu (Figure 14.10), Horizontal Position.

As you can see from the prompt that appears at the bottom of the screen, WordPerfect provides five choices for the horizontal position of your line. Table 14.1 describes them briefly. Since the default setting, Full, was used in Figure 14.3, the line fills the horizontal space between the left and right margins (at the cursor position), and the Length of Line option on this menu is blank. You cannot shorten your line unless you change the Horizontal Position from Full to one of the other four options. In fact, WordPerfect won't even let you select the Length of Line option from the menu. As soon as you change Horizontal Position to Left, you'll see 0" next to the Length of Line option.

Table 14.1 *The five choices for Horizontal Position on the Graphics: Horizontal Line menu.*

Left	Choose this option if you want the line to start at the left margin position.
Right	Choose this option if you want the line to be flush right (ending at the right margin position).
Center	Choose this option if you want the line to be centered between the left and right margins.
Full	The default option. Use Full if you want the line to span the width of the page between the left and right margins.
Set Position	Begin the line at a specific position, as measured from the left margin. For example, if the heading were indented 1", you could use this method to start the horizontal line at the indented position. You don't even need to calculate it: If you place the cursor at the position where you want the line to start before you bring up the Graphics: Horizontal Line menu, WordPerfect will supply the correct position automatically (when you select Set Position).

5. Select the Left option for Horizontal Position.

6. Select the third option on the Graphics: Horizontal Line menu, Length of Line.

7. Enter the number that you determined in step 1 for the line length.

8. Return to the Edit scrren by pressing Enter or clicking the right mouse button.

You can use View Document to see the new line, which should now resemble Figure 14.11.

Tip: The Width of Line option on the Graphics: Horizontal Line and Graphics: Vertical Line menus lets you change the width of your horizontal and vertical lines. Although you can enter a number in inches, you may find it more convenient to enter it in points by typing the number followed by a *p*, as in *2p* for 2 points. Note that a setting of 2 points will make the line approximately twice as wide as the current one.

Tip: You can create horizontal or vertical lines in headers, footers, and styles.

Creating Vertical Lines

Vertical lines are no more difficult to create than horizontal lines. For example, to create a vertical line from the top to the bottom margin, positioned at the left margin:

1. Start with the cursor at the top of the page (on the first line).

2. Display the main Graphics menu (press Alt-F9 or use the pull-down Graphics menu), and select the Line option.

3. Select the second option:

   Keyboard: (Create Line) Vertical.

   Mouse: Create Vertical.

4. The Graphics: Vertical Line menu appears, as shown in Figure 14.12. Leave all the default settings, and then return to the Edit screen by pressing Enter or clicking the right mouse button.

```
Graphics: Vertical Line
     1 - Horizontal Position        Left Margin
     2 - Vertical Position          Full Page
     3 - Length of Line
     4 - Width of Line              0.013"
     5 - Gray Shading (% of black) 100%




Selection: 0
```

Figure 14.12   *The Graphics: Vertical Line menu.*

To see the line, use the View Document option (on the main Print menu) in Full Page mode. If you look in the Reveal Codes screen, you'll see the code for the line you just created:

```
[VLine:Left Margin,Full Page,9",0.013",100%]
```

It indicates that this is a vertical line (VLine), positioned at the left margin (Left Margin), and that it fills the entire page (Full Page). 9" refers to the length of the line and represents the 11" standard page length minus 2" for the top and bottom margins. The next statistic, 0.013", represents the width of the line, and 100% represents the degree of gray shading.

Before you can change the length of the line, you must change the Vertical Position option. The default, *Full Page*, does not permit you to access the Length of Line option (just as the *Full* setting for the Horizontal Position option on the Graphics: Horizontal Line menu did not permit you to change the line length of a horizontal line). You can edit the line and change the Vertical Position to:

Top: Begin at the top margin. You can then change the Length of Line option to the position where you want the line to end, as measured from the top margin.

Bottom: End at the bottom margin. You can then change the Length of Line option to the position where you want it to begin, as measured from the bottom margin.

Centered: The line will always be centered between the top and bottom margins. You can then change the Length of Line option and reposition the line to another centered position between the top and bottom margins.

Set Position: Start at a specific position from the top of the page. You can then change the Length of Line option to a specific length, as measured from the position you just entered to the position where you want the line to end.

In the next section, you'll learn how to use the Horizontal Position option on the Graphics: Vertical Line menu to place vertical lines between columns.

Vertical Lines in Text Columns

Figure 14.2 illustrates a popular use of WordPerfect's Vertical Line feature. As you can see, the three newspaper columns are separated by vertical lines that span the length of the columns. Although it might appear complicated, the Vertical Line option on the Graphics menu allows you to create this effect easily. To practice, retrieve one of your files that is in parallel or newspaper columns, or type the example shown in Figure 14.2. If you forget how to create text columns, refer to Chapter 8.

Neither horizontal nor vertical lines appear on the Edit screen. To see them, you must print the document, or preview them in the View Document option on the main Print menu.

Tip: To create three newspaper columns, press Columns/Table (Alt-F7) or display the Layout menu, select Columns, select Define, change Number of Columns to 3, exit the Text Column Definition menu, and then select On.

Start with the cursor in the first line of text in the first column. This will make it easy to begin the vertical line at the top of the text column, because WordPerfect will automatically supply the position where the cursor is currently located. As you will see, on the Graphics: Vertical Line menu, this starting position for the vertical line is called the *Horizontal Position*.

1. Place the cursor in the first column, on the first line of text.

   Make sure it is past the [Col Def] code, or your vertical line will be positioned near the right margin, instead of after the first column. Col 1 should appear on the status line.

2. Select the Graphics Line menu:

   Keyboard: Press Graphics (Alt-F9) and select the Line option (5).

   Mouse: Display the Graphics menu and select Line.

3. Select the Create Vertical Line option:

> **Keyboard:** Select the second option, (Create Line) Vertical.

> **Mouse:** Select the Create Vertical option.

The Graphics: Vertical Line menu appears, as shown in Figure 14.12.

4. Select the first option, **Horizontal Position.** This menu appears at the bottom of the screen:

```
Horizontal Position: 1: Left; 2 Right; 3 Between Columns;
4 Set Position: 0
```

You can use the Left option to place the vertical line just left of the left margin, or the Right option to place it just right of the right margin. If you want the line to start at a specific position, you can use the Set Position option. In text columns, you can use Between Columns to position it between any of the columns.

5. Select the third option, **Between Columns.** The prompt changes to:

```
Place line to right of column: 1
```

> **Tip:** If you make a mistake and inadvertently return to the Edit screen before you complete these steps, you can edit the vertical line by repeating steps 1 and 2, and then selecting the Edit Vertical Line option in step 3.

6. To place your first vertical line between the first and second columns, type 1 and press Enter once (so you remain in the Graphics: Vertical Line menu).

Since the line is supposed to begin at the top of the text columns, your next step is to change the Vertical Position option, and shorten it. Notice that the default for this option is Full Page. If you leave it, the line will start just below the top margin, and end just above the bottom margin.

7. Select the Vertical Position option. This menu appears:

```
Vertical Position: 1 Full Page; 2 Top; 3 Center; 4 Bottom;
5 Set Position: 0
```

As explained earlier in this section, the default is Full Page.

8. Select the Set Position option, and press Enter to accept the suggested position, which will be the position where the cursor is currently located. If your cursor was on the first line of columnar text when you began, the line will begin at the top of the text column, as shown in Figure 14.2.

When you changed the Vertical Position, WordPerfect also changed the Length of Line statistic. When Vertical Position was Full Page, the line length was assumed to be the entire page, so it was left blank. The number that appears there now reflects the amount of space between the Vertical Position (which was set at the top of the text column) and the bottom margin.

9. Press Enter or click the right mouse button to exit from the Graphics: Vertical Line menu.

10. Repeat steps 1-8 to create the vertical line between the second and third columns. You do not need to move the cursor into the second column before creating the second vertical line, since you will be using the Set Position option to determine the Vertical Position, and the Between Columns option to determine the Horizontal Position. The only difference in the procedure will be that in step 6, you must enter 2 instead of 1. This places the second line to the right of column 2 (instead of column 1).

Use the View Document option on the main Print menu if you want to preview how the lines will appear in the printed version of your document.

 Tip: Vertical and horizontal lines do not appear on the Edit screen. Use the View Document option on the main Print menu to preview them before printing.

When you separate newspaper columns with vertical lines, you may wish to follow the example in Figure 14.2 and change the Justification option on the Format Line menu to Left, and then use WordPerfect's automatic hyphenation feature to help even the line lengths. Full Justification, WordPerfect's default, creates an appearance that many graphic designers consider too harsh. As you can see from the version in Figure 14.13, this is due to the extra blank space that the printer must insert between words to create the effect of an even right margin. In narrow columns, it usually results in distracting "rivers" of blank space running down the columns. The principles of layout and typography for desktop publishing are complex and beyond the scope of this book. However, several excellent books are available to introduce you to this intricate subject, including:

Design for Desktop Publishing by John Miles (Chronicle Books, San Francisco, California)

Desktop Publishing with Style by Daniel Will-Harris (And Books, South Bend, Indiana)

Design Principles for Desktop Publishers by Tom Lichty (Scott, Foresman Computer Books, Glenview, Illinois)

Basic Desktop Design and Layout by David Collier and Bob Cotton (North Light Books, an imprint of F & W Publications, Inc., Cincinnati, Ohio)

Graphic Design For The Electronic Age by Jan V. White (a Xerox Press Book published by Watson-Guptill Publications, New York)

Susan B. Kelly

Software Training: Why bother?

Software training is one of the most important investments that your company can make. Unfortunately, many firms do not understand why, and are unwilling to make the financial commitment.

I can relate stories about corporations who have invested thousands of dollars in the most modern hardware, and in powerful software packages like WordPerfect and Lotus 1-2-3, yet whose administrative and clerical workers refuse to turn on their computers. Why? Because they have absolutely no idea how they work, and resent not being provided with a modicum of guidance.

I have seen companies stuck in a bind who had no choice but to hire a $100 per hour (or more) consultant. Why? To solve problems that anyone who had taken a four-hour *Introduction to DOS* class could have figured out in sixty seconds.

Imagine investing a few thousand dollars to purchase ten copies of WordPerfect, a multi-featured program that not only provides complete word processing capabilities, but also has significant power for applications such as form letters and mailing list management, file management, newsletters, desktop publishing, and math. Next, picture ten secretaries who must start using it right away, with no training, and who either quit and find another job, or learn just enough to print simple letters and memos. Those who do learn just enough to get by waste countless hours of company time trying to figure out mysteries such as why the letter they typed yesterday and need to print today seemingly disappeared from the disk, or why the editing changes they just finished making to a twenty-page report do not appear in the printed version. And they never learn shortcuts such as how to move the

cursor word by word, to the beginning or end of the line, or to the top or bottom of a page; how to cut and paste blocks of text; or how to print a selected range of pages instead of the entire document. They may as well be using typewriters, since they are not taking advantage of the many unique benefits of their word processor. In fact, many revert to using typewriters for tasks that they think can be handled more efficiently, such as labels and envelopes. Can a price be put on such wasted resources?

In my experience, lack of training is often resented by employees. They come to view the company as cheap, and wonder why they are working there. In an era where administrative and secretarial skills are becoming scarce, this is not good business practice.

Another serious problem is the potential damage that can be done by workers who are unfamiliar with commands such as *FORMAT*. Some of you may have experienced the trauma of a hard disk that has been erased by improper use of the *FORMAT* command. If you were really unlucky, the blow was compounded many times over because the disk was not backed up properly.

In companies that provide inadequate software training, there is a desperate need for advice. In response, an unofficial computer "guru" usually emerges, who enjoys computers and has been able to teach herself or himself a little more than the average employee. The guru helps her fellow employees with minor questions that she can answer

by reading the manual, and everyone thinks she is a genius. Before long, word of her talent spreads throughout the company, and then everyone relies on her for help with all of their computer problems. The individual is rarely able to answer all these questions right away, and ends up spending so much time figuring them out that he or she is unable to perform well in his or her actual capacity (which is never officially one of a computer support person). This represents another wasted resource, but can also provide the company with a flimsy excuse for insufficient training.

I keep asking myself why companies are so unwilling to invest in training. The best companies I know care about their employees, have invested a great deal of money to hire, promote, and maintain them, and try to keep them satisfied. They do this not out of the milk of human kindness, but for sound economic reasons. Software training may be expensive, and often costs more than the software itself, but the benefits far outweigh the costs.

My advice? Find yourself an instructor or training firm whose expertise can be verified, whose references rave about how much they were helped by the training, and who is willing to provide additional support after the class ends. And don't worry about the price. If you do this, I promise that you won't have to become one of my horror stories.

Figure 14.13   *Newspaper columns with an even right margin, created by setting the Justification option on the Format: Line menu to Full. To exaggerate the effect, most of the hyphens were removed. To decide which version you prefer, compare this with Figure 14.2, which uses Left Justification.*

Tip: To take full advantage of WordPerfect's automatic hyphenation feature, keep a hyphenation dictionary handy, such as the *Word Division Manual*, by Devern J. Perry and J.E. Silverthorn (South-Western Publishing Co.). That way, whenever you are unsure if WordPerfect is suggesting the correct position for a hyphen, you can quickly look it up in your dictionary (instead of canceling the hyphenation in that word). In narrow columns, such as the ones in Figure 14.2, hyphenation is essential to maintain a polished appearance.

Integrating Graphics into Your WordPerfect Documents

WordPerfect's Graphics menu allows you to integrate graphics files into your documents to incorporate them into newsletters, flyers, brochures, and other text documents. Graphics files that you can use in WordPerfect include (but are not limited to):

- The 30 graphic images that are provided with WordPerfect. These figures are displayed, along with their file names, in Appendix B of the WordPerfect manual.

- Clip art in any of the following file formats:

  CGM Computer Graphics Metafile

  DHP Dr. Halo PIC

  EPS Encapsulated PostScript (Files in EPS format must conform to specific rules to be used in WordPerfect. For more information, see *Graphics, Formats and Programs* in the WordPerfect manual.

  GEM GEM Draw

  HPGL Hewlett-Packard Graphics Language Plotter file

  IMG GEM Paint

  MSP Microsoft Windows Paint

  PCX PC Paintbrush

  PIC Lotus 1-2-3 PIC

PNTG Macintosh Paint

PPIC PC Paint Plus

TIFF Tagged Image File

WPG WordPerfect Graphics

DXF AutoCAD (after conversion using WordPerfect's Graphic Conversion program).

- Illustrations that you create yourself using one of the many painting, drawing, or other graphics programs whose formats are compatible with WordPerfect. These include DrawPerfect, AutoCAD, Adobe Illustrator, CorelDraw, Freelance Plus, Dr. Halo, GEM Paint, GEM SCAN, Macintosh Paint, Micrografx Designer, PC Paint Plus, PC Paintbrush, Arts and Letters, PicturePak, Symphony, Microsoft Windows Paint, and Harvard Graphics (if you save Harvard Graphics file in EPS, HPGL, or CGM format).

- Picture files (with the extension *PIC*) from spreadsheet programs such as Lotus 1-2-3, Quattro, Excel, SuperCalc, and Symphony.

- Graphic images on the screen that you capture using the GRAB.COM utility included with WordPerfect. This utility can only be used if the screen display is in Graphics mode. For example, you can use it to capture WordPerfect's View Document screen, but not the WordPerfect Edit screen. See Part Three, "Command Reference," for more information about GRAB.COM, under *Graphics, Screen Capture (GRAB.COM)*.

- Scanned images in TIFF format, such as your company logo, a drawing, or even a photograph (although retouching and resizing in another program may be necessary before you retrieve it into WordPerfect).

- Text or graphic images from your computer screen. For example, if you were writing a computer training manual, you could use a program like Hijaak (from Inset Systems) to capture the screens and menus, and then convert them into WPG or TIFF format, which WordPerfect can retrieve into a graphics box without any modification. Hijaak can also convert images from Macintosh programs such as MacPaint, MacDraw, or SuperPaint.

For more information about graphics file formats that have been tested with WordPerfect 5.1, see the *Graphics, Formats and Programs* section of the WordPerfect manual. However, since WordPerfect Corporation is constantly updating their program, you may also want to contact the technical support department at WordPerfect Corporation (still toll-free) to see if they now support the format you want to use.

If you want to use a graphic image that is not saved in one of the file formats that WordPerfect can retrieve directly into a graphics box, you may be able to convert it into WPG (WordPerfect Graphics) format using WordPerfect's Graphics

Conversion program, *GRAPHCNV.EXE*. This creates a copy of the file and saves it in the WPG format. If you installed the Utility files when you installed WordPerfect, GRAPHCNV.EXE should already be in your WordPerfect directory. If not, just run the Installation program (see Appendix A) and install only the Utility files (on the Install/Learn/Utilities disks). For more information about using GRAPHCNV.EXE, see *Graphics, Conversion* in Part Three, "Command Reference," and the *Graphics, Conversion Program* section in the WordPerfect manual.

Once you have incorporated a graphic image into a WordPerfect document, you can manipulate it in many ways, changing the height and/or width of the box that contains the graphic; altering its horizontal and vertical position on the page; changing or removing the border that surrounds the box; changing the gray shading or amount of blank space inside or outside the box; inserting a caption above or below the box; or scaling, rotating, moving, or inverting the graphic image inside the box.

Warning: Bit-mapped graphics, such as TIFF files, often require relatively large amounts of disk space (in fact, it is not unusual for them to use 1 megabyte). Vector graphics, such as those created with DrawPerfect, are not usually as big. In any case, if a graphic file that you retrieve into a WordPerfect graphics box is very large, WordPerfect may print an incomplete page, or may not print the document at all.

If you have a laser printer, you may be able to solve this problem by installing additional memory into the printer. For example, the Hewlett-Packard LaserJet Series II printer comes with 512K memory, usually enough to print a bit-mapped graphic that is about half a page in size (assuming you set the Graphic Quality option on the main Print menu to High). The Hewlett-Packard LaserJet Series III printer includes 1 megabyte (1,024K) of memory. You can purchase additional memory for these printers, increasing the memory to 1, 2, or 4 megabytes.

If WordPerfect is printing only part of a page that includes a graphic image, a possible solution is to print the page in two passes. The first step is to change the Graphics Quality option on the main Print menu to *Do Not Print,* and print the page. This prints the text, and omits the graphics box. Next, change the Graphics Quality option to *High*, change the Text Quality option to *Do Not Print,* reinsert the paper, and print the page a second time. This prints the graphics box and omits the text. If the document is formatted with downloadable soft fonts, it may also help if you edit your printer definition file (Shift-F7 S E C), and mark your soft fonts with a plus (+) symbol instead of an asterisk (*). If you do, WordPerfect can remove them from printer memory when they are not being used (such as when you are printing graphics only). See Chapter 13 for more information about soft fonts. Also, try removing any TSR programs (terminate and stay resident), which require extra computer memory (RAM), or changing the Contents option to Graphic on Disk, as described later (in the section entitled "The Contents Option on the Definition: Figure Menu").

Creating a Figure and Retrieving a Graphic into It

In this section, you will learn how to create a Figure box and place a computer picture into it, as shown in Figure 14.14. The computer illustration is actually a separate file, PC-1.WPG, and it is one of 30 clip-art files that are provided with WordPerfect, on the PTR/Program/Graphics disk. To retrieve it into the box, you will use an option on the Definition: Figure menu. If you did not install the graphics files when you installed WordPerfect, you'll have to do this before continuing. Appendix A provides general installation instructions.

You can use the same procedure to retrieve a different graphic image to practice with, as long as the image was created in one of the formats supported by WordPerfect. (Most of these formats were listed earlier.)

> **Tip:** The 30 clip-art images provided with WordPerfect were created in DrawPerfect. Appendix B of your WordPerfect manual displays the others. Note that their file names end in the extension *WPG* (WordPerfect Graphics).

Follow these steps to retrieve the computer illustration into the article. You'll begin by creating a Figure box.

1. Create a Figure box:

   Keyboard: Press Graphics (Alt-F9). This menu appears:

   ```
   1 Figure; 2 Table Box; 3 Text Box; 4 User Box; 5 Line;
   6 Equation: 0
   ```

   Mouse: Display the **Graphics** menu, as shown in Figure 14.15.

   As you can see, WordPerfect features five different types of boxes into which you can retrieve text, equations, or graphic images: Figure, Table, Text, User, and Equation. When you create one of these boxes, a Definition menu appears for the specific type you've selected. Each of these menus contains the same nine options. To a certain extent, you can use them interchangeably. In other words, you could place a text file inside a Figure box, a graphic inside an Equation box or Text box, or an equation inside a Table box. The main differences between the five types are outlined in Table 14.2.

**Software Training:
Why bother?**

*Software training is one of the most important
investments that your company can make. Unfortunately, many firms do not understand why, and
are unwilling to make the financial commitment.*

I can relate stories about corporations who have invested thousands of dollars in the most modern hardware, and in powerful software packages like WordPerfect and Lotus 1-2-3, yet whose administrative and clerical workers refuse to turn on their computers. Why? Because they have absolutely no idea how they work, and resent not being provided with a modicum of guidance.

I have seen companies stuck in a bind who had no choice but to hire a $100 per hour (or more) consultant. Why? To solve problems that anyone who had taken a four-hour *Introduction to DOS* class could have figured out in sixty seconds.

Imagine investing a few thousand dollars to purchase ten copies of WordPerfect, a multi-featured program that not only provides complete word processing capabilities, but also has significant power for applications such as form letters and mailing list management, file management, newsletters, desktop publishing, and math. Next, picture ten secretaries who must start using it right away, with no training, and who either quit and find another job, or learn just enough to print simple letters and memos.

Those who do learn just enough to get by waste countless hours of company time trying to figure out mysteries such as why the letter they typed yesterday and need to print today seemingly disappeared from the disk, or why the editing changes they just finished making to a twenty-page report do not appear in the printed version. And they never learn shortcuts such as how to move the cursor word by word, to the beginning or end of the line, or to the top or bottom of a page; How to cut and paste blocks of text; Or how to print a selected range of pages instead of the entire document. They may as well be using typewriters, since they are not taking advantage of the many unique benefits of their word processor. In fact, many revert to using typewriters for tasks that they think can be handled more efficiently, such as labels and envelopes. Can a price be put on such wasted resources?

In my experience, lack of training is often resented by employees. They come to view the company as cheap, and wonder why they are working there. In an era where administrative and secretarial skills are becoming scarce, this is not good business practice.

Another serious problem is the potential damage that can be done by workers who are unfamiliar with commands such as *FORMAT*. Some of you may have experienced the trauma of a hard disk that has been erased by improper use of the *FORMAT* command. If you were really unlucky, the blow was compounded many times over because the disk was not backed up properly.

In companies that provide inadequate software training, there is a desperate need for advice. In response, an unofficial computer "guru" usually emerges, who enjoys computers and has been able to teach herself or himself a little more than the average employee. The guru helps her fellow employees with minor questions that she can answer by reading the manual, and everyone thinks she is a genius. Before long, word of her talent spreads throughout the company, and then everyone relies on her for help with all of their computer problems. The individual is rarely able to answer all these questions right away, and ends up spending so much time figuring them out that he or she is unable to perform well in his or her actual capacity (which is never officially one of a computer support person).

Figure 14.14   *Another variation of the "Software Training" article, which incorporates an illustration (the PC-1.WPG file) into a Figure box at the top of
the page.*

Table 14.2   *Differences between the five graphics box types, Figure, Table,
Text, User, and Equation.*

- The borders that surround them:

    For example, a Figure box has single-line borders on all four sides, while a Text box features thick lines for the top and bottom border, but has no borders on the left and right sides. A User box has no borders. These and eight other features can be changed through the Options menus for each type of box; you'll learn how shortly. Also, Table 14.3 compares the default options for the five box types.

continued

Table 14.2 *(continued)*

- The amount of blank space inside and outside the borders:

    While a Figure box has no inside border space, a Table box or Text box has .167" by default. If you were to type text inside a Figure box, it would be aligned right against the lines that form the border, an undesirable effect. Like the border styles, the blank space inside and outside the borders can be changed through the Options menus.

- The lists of captions that WordPerfect maintains for each type of box:

    You can create a caption for an individual box using the third option on the Definition menu (for each type), Caption. If you do type captions, you can have WordPerfect automatically produce a separate list of captions for each type of box and include the page number where the box is located. See Chapter 18, "Lists, Indexes, and Tables of Contents, for more details about this procedure.

- The position of the caption, as defined on the Options menus:

    If you create an Equation box, you can position the caption below it, above it, on the left side, or on the right side, but never inside the box. For the other four box types—Figure, Text, Table, and User—you can only position the caption above or below the box, but you can place it inside or outside the border.

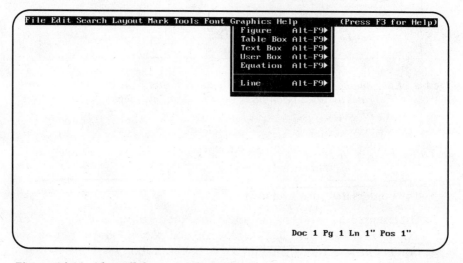

Figure 14.15 *The pull-down Graphics menu.*

Tip: For more information about using WordPerfect's Equation Editor, see *Equation Editor* in Part Three, "Command Reference."

2. Select **Figure** and then **Create**.

The Definition: Figure menu will appear, as shown in Figure 14.16. It features nine options, including ones to change the size of the box, its horizontal and vertical position on the page, and the contents. While creating this example, you will use five of them: Vertical Position, Horizontal Position, Size, Edit, and Contents. All nine options are described in the next section. Note that each graphics box Definition menu (Figure, Table Box, Text Box, User Box, and Equation) includes the same nine options, although their applications may vary.

Your next step is to retrieve the graphics file, PC-1.WPG, using the Filename option on this menu.

Tip: You can renumber graphics boxes at any point in your document, which is useful if this file is a continuation of another one (such as another chapter in a book where each chapter is kept in a separate file). For more information, see *Graphics, New Numbers* in Part Three, "Command Reference."

Note: If you make a mistake and accidentally exit to the Edit screen before completing these steps, you can return to the Definition: Figure menu by pressing Graphics (Alt-F9) or displaying the Graphics menu, selecting Figure, then Edit. WordPerfect will ask which figure you want to edit; unless you have created more than one Figure box, type 1 and press Enter. Otherwise, enter the number of the Figure box containing the figure you are editing.

3. Select the first option, **Filename**.

The `Enter filename` prompt appears in the lower-left corner of your screen. Notice the message at the right: (`List Files`). This is a reminder that you can use the List key (F5) to locate and retrieve the file (if you have forgotten how, refer to Chapter 7, "File Management"). F5 works as long as this prompt is visible. If it is not, press Cancel (F1), and then select the Filename option again.

```
Definition: Figure
      1 - Filename
      2 - Contents              Empty
      3 - Caption
      4 - Anchor Type           Paragraph
      5 - Vertical Position     0"
      6 - Horizontal Position   Right
      7 - Size                  3.25" wide x 3.25" (high)
      8 - Wrap Text Around Box  Yes
      9 - Edit



Selection: 0
```

Figure 14.16 *The Definition: Figure menu.*

4. Enter the file name: PC-1.WPG. Note that you do not have to type the extension, *wpg* (although you would if you were retrieving a graphics file with a different extension, such as *TIF* or *PIC*). Also, unless the PC-1.WPG file is in the current directory, or in the one named for Graphic Files in the Setup: Location of Files menu, you must include the complete path, such as:

\WP\GRAPHICS\PC-1

If WordPerfect locates your file, it retrieves it and displays its name next to the Filename option on the Definition: Figure menu. If you see an error message instead, indicating that the file was not found, either the file is in a different directory or you did not install it. Try using List Files to locate it. Make sure that the (List Files) prompt still appears in the lower-right corner of the screen; if it does not, press Cancel (F1) and select the Filename option again. Next, press List (F5) Enter, and then search through your directories. If you find it, highlight it and select the Retrieve option (1) on the List Files menu.

Once you save this document, the PC-1.WPG file and Figure box will be saved along with it, and you won't need access to the PC-1.WPG file anymore. This can be undesirable, especially if the graphics file is large, because the WordPerfect document will be even larger. In extreme cases, you won't be able to print your document. To overcome this limitation, WordPerfect has included a Graphic on Disk option, available by selecting the Contents option on the Definition: Figure menu. If you find that your file size swells drastically after you retrieve a graphics file, consider using this option to reduce it.

The Nine Options on the Graphic Box Definition Menus

The nine options on the graphics box Definition menus are the same for each of the graphics boxes: Figure, Text, Table, User, and Equation, although their use varies.

Filename: You can use this option to retrieve a graphics or text file into the box or, if you change the Contents option on the Definition menu to *Equation*, an equation file (created using the Equation Editor). You can also leave it blank. After selecting this option, you can use the List Files menu to retrieve a file.

Contents: You can use this option to change the contents of the box to *Graphic*, *Graphic on Disk*, *Text*, or *Equation*. In order to use WordPerfect's Equation Editor, you must select Equation for this option. However, as long as you are creating an Equation box, this option will automatically be set to Equation. Likewise, if you select a Text box, the default setting will be Text. For the other three graphics box types (Figure, Table, and User), the default is *Empty*. If you select Filename and retrieve a graphics file, Contents will automatically change to Graphic. If you retrieve text, it will change to Text.

Caption: Use this option if you want to include a caption above or below a box. If you are creating an equation, you can also choose to position the caption on the left or right side (using the Options menu, as explained later in this chapter). When you select the Caption option, WordPerfect automatically supplies a caption. This suggested caption will vary according to the type of graphics box you are creating and its number in your document. For instance, for the first Figure box in your document, WordPerfect will suggest *Figure 1* as the caption. If you create an Equation, WordPerfect will supply (1) for the first Equation box. In any case, you can include text with the suggested caption, or you can press Backspace to erase the suggested caption, and then type a different one.

Anchor Type: By default, the Anchor Type is always set to *Paragraph*, so the graphics box is anchored to a paragraph and moves around with it as you add or delete text or move the paragraph while editing the document. WordPerfect automatically positions the Graphics Box code at the beginning of the paragraph. However, if there isn't enough room at the bottom of the page for the box, it will move (and not necessarily with the text of the paragraph) to the next page. You can change Anchor Type to *Page* or *Character*. The Page Type remains at a fixed position on a page. You can position a page-anchored graphics box anywhere on the page. However, to position one at the top of the current page, the cursor must be at the beginning of the first line of the page when you define the graphics box. If it is not on the first line, the graphics box will be bumped to the top of the next page. You can also put such a graphics box code on an earlier page, because when you select this Anchor Type, WordPerfect will ask how many pages to skip (and suggest 0 for the current page). If you change the Anchor Type to Character, WordPerfect will treat the graphics box just like any character on a line (assuming you anchor it to a line of text), and it will move around with the line as you edit the document. This type of box is represented on screen by a small character box on the line, which has no relation to the size it will actually have in the printed version.

Vertical Position: The available selections for Vertical Position are determined by the Anchor Type you are using for the graphics box: *Paragraph, Page,* or *Character.* If you select Paragraph, WordPerfect asks you to enter an offset position, which will be used to determine where to place the box in relation to the paragraph it is in. The default is 0, meaning the top of the box will be aligned with the top of the first line in the paragraph. If you are using Page, you can select Full Page to have the box fill the entire page between the margins; **T**op to align the box against the top of the page; **B**ottom to align it against the bottom; **C**enter to center it; or Set Position to specify a specific position where you want the box to begin, as measured from the top of the page. If you are using Character, you can position the graphics box so that the current line of text is even with the **T**op, **C**enter, or **B**ottom of the graphics box. You can also align the text with the **B**aseline of the box, useful if you want the last line of an equation to be aligned with (and actually on) the baseline of the text line.

Horizontal Position: As with the Vertical Position option, the available selections for Horizontal Position are determined by the Anchor Type that you are using. If you are using *Character,* you cannot change the Horizontal Position. If you are using *Paragraph,* the default, you can change the Horizontal Position to **L**eft, **R**ight, **C**enter, or **F**ull. Left aligns the graphics box against the left margin; Right aligns it against the right margin; Center centers it between the left and right margins; and Full causes the box to fill all the space between the left and right margins. Exceptions to all four occur when the paragraph is indented, or in columns, or if another graphics box is included. If you are using Page as the Anchor Type, you can set the Horizontal Position to Margins, Columns, or Set Position. The first method, Margins, lets you position the box against the left or right margin (**L**eft, **R**ight), center it between the left and right margins (**C**enter), or fill all the space between the left and right margins (**F**ull). Columns lets you position the box in relation to text columns (newspaper or parallel): At the left or right side of one or more columns (**Left, Right**), centered between one or more columns (**Center**), or filling all the space between one or more columns (**Full**). The **Set Position** method lets you specify a specific position where you want the box to begin, as measured from the left side of the page.

Size: You can use this option to change the size of the graphics box. You can choose to change the width alone, leaving WordPerfect to calculate a new height in accordance with the original scale (Set Width/Automatic Height); change the height alone, letting WordPerfect calculate the width to maintain the original scale (Set Height/Auto Width); set both height and width yourself (Set **Both**); or have WordPerfect automatically determine both dimensions (Auto Both). Be careful if you use the Both option after retrieving a graphics file into the box, because you can easily distort the image inside the box. If you use the Auto Both option, WordPerfect will restore the original dimensions of the graphic: in other words, the measurements it had when it was originally created (whether in a graphics program or by being scanned).

Wrap Text Around Box: By default, this is set to *Yes* for all five box types. This means that WordPerfect will not position text in the same space as a graphics box; instead, text will be wrapped around the box. If you change this option to *No*, text (or another graphic) can be positioned inside the box borders. You can use this feature to superimpose graphics boxes or to create the appearance of text typed inside a box, as shown in Figure 14.1.

Edit: You can use the Edit option to edit the contents of the box. If the box contains a graphic, the Graphics Editor appears. You can use it to view the graphic image inside the box, and move, scale, rotate, invert, and make other changes, as described later in this chapter. If the box contains a text file, the Text Editor appears and you can use it to edit the text. If the box is blank, you can type text in it. If the Contents option is set to Equation, selecting Edit brings up WordPerfect's Equation Editor, which you can use to type scientific and mathematical equations (although WordPerfect cannot calculate them).

 Tip: If you retrieve a scanned image into a graphics box, print the document and find that the resolution has deteriorated, edit the graphics box and change the Size option to Auto Both. This will restore the original dimensions of the graphic, and can improve the resolution.

Tip: If your printer is capable of printing rotated text, you can use a graphics box to produce this effect. To do this, create a graphics box, select the Edit option (on the graphics box Definition menu), and type the text. Next, press Graphics (Alt-F9) and select 90°, 180°, or 270° (degrees) for the amount of (counterclockwise) rotation.

The Contents Option on the Definition: Figure Menu

Graphics files tend to be large, especially scanned files in the TIFF format (it is not uncommon for these files to exceed 100K). Fortunately, WordPerfect provides an alternative to saving the graphic image along with the document: Graphic on Disk. When you use it, WordPerfect maintains the graphic files independently of the document file. The disadvantage is that the graphics file must be in the current directory when you print the document or use View Document to preview it. Also, if you plan to print the document on another computer, you must copy both the document and graphics file to the other disk.

If you want to change Contents to Graphic on Disk:

1. Select the second option, Contents.

2. Select the second option, Graphic on Disk.

3. In response to the `Graphics file to be saved` prompt, press the Cancel key, F1 (since the PC-1.WPG file is already saved on disk).

 Tip: If you use the Graphic on Disk option, as described in the section "The Contents Option on the Definition: Figure Menu," you can include a graphics box (which references a graphic file such as PC-1.WPG) in a Style. For more information about WordPerfect's Style feature, see Chapter 15.

The Edit Option on the Definition: Figure Menu

Assuming your monitor is capable of displaying graphics, the Edit option lets you view the graphic image and make certain changes to it. For instance, you can move, scale, rotate, and invert the graphic and cause it to print and display in black and white. To examine this menu:

1. Select the Edit option on the Definition: Figure menu. Your screen should now resemble Figure 14.17.

   As you can see, WordPerfect lets you:

   - Move the computer around inside the box using the Move option or the arrow keys.

   - Change the size of the graphic within the box using the Scale option or the PgUp and PgDn keys.

   - Rotate it around or create a mirror image using Rotate or, if you just want to rotate it, the plus and minus keys on the numeric keypad.

   - Print and display it in black and white (instead of using shading or a fill pattern to represent colors) using the Black and White option.

   - If the image is a bit-mapped one (which the computer picture is not, but scanned files and graphics created in most paint programs are), you can use the Invert On option to reverse the colors so that the blacks turn white and the whites turn black. For most other types of images (vectorgraphics), the Invert option just reverses the background color. In such a case, a white background will turn black, usually obliterating the graphic image itself!

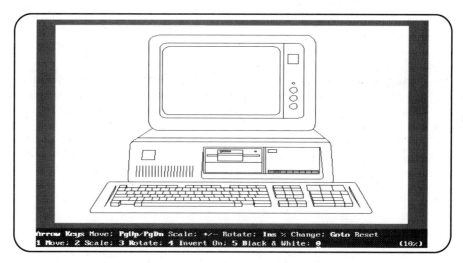

Figure 14.17   *Using the Edit option on the Definition: Figure menu to edit the PC-1.WPG graphic.*

Note the percentage figure in the lower-right corner of the screen, which should be 10%. This number represents the degree to which WordPerfect will move, scale, or rotate the graphic inside the box when you use the keys. By pressing the Ins (Insert) key, you can change the percentage to

5% or 1% for smaller increments, or 25% for larger ones. For instance, if you select 25% and then press the plus key twice (on the numeric keypad) to rotate the figure 50%, the computer will be upside down in the box.

While experimenting with these features, if you end up distorting the graphic image (of the computer) beyond your ability to repair it, just press the Go To combination: Ctrl-Home. This will reset the figure, so it will be identical to the original version.

The next step will be to exit back to the Edit screen and use the Print menu's View Document option to see the graphic as it will appear in the printed version of your document.

2. To return to the Edit screen:

   Keyboard: Press Exit (F7) twice.

   Mouse: Click the left mouse button twice.

The Figure box you just created is represented on the Edit screen by the top line of a border, with the words Fig 1 at the top left side. If you press Enter about 12 times, this border will turn into a complete box. However, the PC illustration inside the box cannot be displayed on the Edit screen. To see it, you use the View Document option on the Print menu, or print the document. If you look into the Reveal Codes screen, you'll see that WordPerfect has created a hidden code for your new Figure box:

```
[Fig Box:1;PC-1.WPG;]
```

Notice that it includes the name of the graphics file you retrieved into the Figure box, PC-1.WPG. Next, use the View Document option to see how this graphic will appear in the printed version of your document.

3. To use View Document:

   Keyboard: Press Print (Shift-F7) and select View Document.

   Mouse: Select Print from the File menu, and then select View Document.

Observe the border (box) around the computer, as displayed in the View Document screen. By default, all four sides of the border are single lines. Later, you will learn how to remove them. Also, notice how large the figure is compared to Figure 14.14. In the next section, you will learn how to change the size of the Figure box, so it will take up less space on the page.

4. To return to the Edit screen:

   Keyboard: Press Exit (F7).

   Mouse: Click the left mouse button.

Editing the Figure

To edit the Figure box and change its size:

1. Select the Figure Edit option:

   Keyboard: Press Graphics (Alt-F9) and select **Figure**, and then select **Edit**.

   Mouse: Select **Figure** from the **Graphics** menu, and then select **Edit**.

   In response to the Figure number prompt, type 1 and press Enter. This returns you to the Definition: Figure menu (for the Figure box you've already defined). In the next step, you will use the Size option to reduce the height of the box from 3.25" to 2".

2. Select **Size**, and then select the second option, **Height/Auto Width**.

3. Type 2 for the Height. Press Enter. The Height changes to 2". Notice that WordPerfect has automatically changed the width as well, from 3.25" to 2.76". This maintains the original scale of the Figure box.

4. Return to the Edit screen:

   Keyboard: Press Exit (F7).

   Mouse: Click the right button.

   You may wish to use View Document on the Print menu again, displaying the document in Full Page mode to see the new size in relation to the entire page.

Removing the Border Around the Figure

In this section you will learn how to use the Figure Options command to change the single-line border that was visible in the View Document screen. As you'll see momentarily, you can change the border style for any or all of the four borders to a thick line, extra-thick line, double line, dotted line, dashed line, or no line (which removes the border altogether).

Like most formatting changes, changing the border will insert a formatting code into your document, visible only in Reveal Codes. It is imperative that the cursor be on or to the left of the Figure Box code before you change the border style, so that the option code will precede the Figure Box code. If it is not, the change will have no effect on this box (but it would affect subsequent Figure boxes in the document, if there were any). Your next step, then, must be to place the cursor on or before the Figure Box code.

1. Display the Reveal Codes screen:

   Keyboard: Press Alt-F3 .

   Mouse: Select **R**eveal Codes from the **E**dit menu.

2. Place the cursor on the [Fig Box:1;PC-1.WPG;] code.This will guarantee that the Figure Option code is inserted to the left of the Figure Box code.

3. Display the Options: Figure menu:

   Keyboard: Press Graphics (Alt-F9) and select **F**igure and then **O**ptions.

   Mouse: Select **F**igure from the **G**raphics menu and then **O**ptions.

   The Options: Figure menu appears, as shown in Figure 14.18. It includes options to change the style of each of the four borders, the space inside and outside the border, the gray shading, and the position of your caption. When you change one of these options, WordPerfect places a formatting code in your document and alters any other figures you create from the current cursor position to the end of the document (unless another Figure Options change is made later in the document). The nine selections on the Options: Figure menu are the same for Text boxes, Table boxes, User boxes, and Equation boxes, except that the defaults differ. These options are described briefly in Part Three, "Command Reference, under the heading *Graphics, Options*. Also, Table 14.3 compares the defaults for the five graphics box types.

4. Select **B**order Style.

   Notice that the default style for each of the four borders is single lines. If you had created a Text box or Table box instead of a Figure box, the defaults would have been *None* for the left and right borders, and *Thick* for the top and bottom. If you had created a User Box, the defaults for all four borders would have been *None.* Table 14.3 lists other differences between the five box types (on their Options menus).

5. Type N four times. This removes the single lines from all four borders.

6. Press Exit (F7) or the right mouse button to return to the Edit screen; then use the View Document option again to verify that WordPerfect has removed the borders from your figure.

Table 14.3   *Comparing the defaults on the Options menus for the five graphic boxes: Figure, Table, Text, User, and Equation.*

Options:	Figure	Table Box	Text Box	User Box	Equation
1. Border Style:					
Left	Single	None	None	None	None
Right	Single	None	None	None	None
Top	Single	Thick	Thick	None	None
Bottom	Single	Thick	Thick	None	None
2. Outside Border Space:					
Left	0.167"	0.167"	0.167"	0.167"	0.083"
Right	0.167"	0.167"	0.167"	0.167"	0.083"
Top	0.167"	0.167"	0.167"	0.167"	0.083"
Bottom	0.167"	0.167"	0.167"	0.167"	0.083"
3. Inside Border Space:					
Left	0"	0.167"	0.167"	0"	0.083"
Right	0"	0.167"	0.167"	0"	0.083"
Top	0"	0.167"	0.167"	0"	0.083"
Bottom	0"	0.167"	0.167"	0"	0.083"
4. First Level Numbering Method:	Numbers	Roman	Numbers	Numbers	Numbers
5. Second Level Numbering Method:	Off	Off	Off	Off	Off
6. Caption Number Style:	[BOLD] Figure 1 [bold]	[BOLD] Table1 [bold]	[BOLD] 1 [bold]	[BOLD] 1 [bold]	[BOLD] (1) [bold]
7. Position of Caption:	Below box, Outside borders	Above box, Outside borders	Below box, Outside borders	Below box, Outside borders	Right side
8. Minimum Offset from paragraph:	0"	0"	0"	0"	0"
9. Gray Shading (% of black):	0%	0%	10%	0%	0%

```
Options: Figure

    1 - Border Style
            Left                            Single
            Right                           Single
            Top                             Single
            Bottom                          Single
    2 - Outside Border Space
            Left                            0.167"
            Right                           0.167"
            Top                             0.167"
            Bottom                          0.167"
    3 - Inside Border Space
            Left                            0"
            Right                           0"
            Top                             0"
            Bottom                          0"
    4 - First Level Numbering Method        Numbers
    5 - Second Level Numbering Method       Off
    6 - Caption Number Style                [BOLD]Figure 1[bold]
    7 - Position of Caption                 Below box, Outside borders
    8 - Minimum Offset from Paragraph       0"
    9 - Gray Shading (% of black)           0%

Selection: 0
```

Figure 14.18   *The Options: Figure menu.*

 Tip: If you want to do any of the following: 1) place a table into newspaper or parallel columns, 2) place two or more tables next to each other, or 3) wrap text around a table, you should create a table inside of a graphics box. Use any of the box types on the Graphics menu, such as a Figure box, Table box, or Text box.

Retrieving or Typing Text in a Graphics Box

WordPerfect provides two methods for creating the appearance of text inside a box. For both methods, the first step is to create a graphics box such as a Figure or Text box. The Definition menu for the box type appears (such as the Definition: Figure menu). Use it to select one of the two methods:

- The first method: Either select the Filename option and retrieve a text file into the box, or select the Edit option and type your text inside the box.

- The second method: Select the Wrap Text Around Box option on the Definition menu and change it to No, so that the text can share the space with the box.

You've already studied the first method in Chapter 8, where instructions were provided to create a newsletter (Figure 8.1) with a shaded Text box above the newspaper columns. The second method is illustrated in Figure 14.1, at the beginning of this chapter. Here, a graphics box with double-line borders on all four sides surrounds a table of contents. To create it, the following steps were used:

On the first line of the document:

1. Change the top and bottom margins to 1.5" each.

2. Change the figure options so that the **B**order Style for each of the four borders is double lines.

3. Use the Graphics menu to create a figure with these specifications:

   a) Anchor **T**ype   **Page**

   b) **V**ertical Position   **Full Page**

   c) **H**orizontal Position   **Margin, Full**

   d) **W**rap Text Around Box   **No**

4. Change the left and right margins to 1.5" each so that the text that follows does not run against the borders of the box.

5. Press Enter three times (before you type the text, the cursor should be on a line below the [Fig Box:1;;] code).

6. Type the text (in this case, the text was a table of contents that WordPerfect automatically generated for a document).

The text will appear inside the box when you print the document or view it using the View Document option on the Print menu.

In Conclusion: Keep It Simple

WordPerfect's graphics features are powerful tools. Used carefully, they can dramatically improve the appearance of your documents. However, the opposite can also be true. When used improperly, they can clutter up your documents and detract from the message you are trying to convey. Since much has been written about this subject—layout and typography in desktop publishing—including many books and magazine articles, you should have no trouble finding good information about it. It is also helpful to study every piece of professionally produced literature you receive (including the junk mail!). If you do this, you will soon develop a sense of design and be confident in your choices as you use WordPerfect's graphics features. When in doubt, keep your designs simple!

STYLES

A *style* is a name that you assign to a set of formatting codes and/or text. Think of styles as customized formatting codes, since you decide what formatting to include. The well-planned use of WordPerfect's styles will make your formatting infinitely easier; they are especially helpful for changing rough drafts of your documents into their final form for printing. Don't think that styles are an esoteric and difficult feature, reserved for desktop publishing and other advanced applications, because this just isn't true: They are an essential tool that you can use to simplify all your work.

Styles are the best way to format long documents, such as instruction manuals, where you change features such as fonts and line spacing frequently. If you use styles for all your formatting, you are free to play "what if" with your documents, changing their appearance as much as you want, without wasting countless hours finding and erasing unwanted formatting codes, then inserting new ones. Instead, you just change the formatting codes in the styles. The new formatting will be applied everywhere in the document that you have used the styles.

You can also use styles as templates to insert complex formatting into a document after typing the text. For example, Figure 15.1 shows the text from the second page of a newsletter. After typing the text, the operator used three keystrokes to turn on the newsletter's style, and the results appear in Figure 15.2. The style changes the Base Font and all four margins, establishes newspaper columns and turns them on, inserts a header with a thick horizontal line, a footer with two thick lines and the page number, and the two vertical lines separating the columns. The company produces this newsletter monthly, and it is always at least 12 pages long. Using the style to format the newsletter saves time, standardizes the formatting, and allows it to be changed more easily.

A much simpler but equally worthwhile example is the use of styles to help alleviate a problem many users have. As you probably know, when you switch from a font such as Courier to a font whose line length is longer than the screen, such as Times Roman 12-point, individual lines of text become longer, both on screen and in the printed version of your document. Many users are troubled by the on-screen display of these longer lines, because the screen is not wide enough to display them in their entirety. Instead, as the cursor moves back and forth between the extreme left and right margins as you are typing and editing, the screen shifts left and right. You can never see the entire line at once.

FACULTY UPDATE

CCDS will begin the next school year with some new teachers on campus. Some committees are still completing the interviewing process, yet there are several announcements for the fall.

Barbara Smith, a librarian at school for the last 13 years, will retire to her Marinhome to spend more time in her avocational pursuits. Barbara is profiled in this issue of THE PIPER. Ann Brown will return to her native Vermont after a single year at school. While we respect Ann's decision to return to the East, we shall miss her wisdom and skill in the classroom. Mike Novak will reduce his classroom load, but will be on campus to direct the 5th grade and Upper School recorder and instrumental ensembles.

Several veteran teachers will be absent for the first semester: Mike Jones will take a medical leave, replaced by Irene Layton, while Bart Connair will travel abroad during the fall semester. Barry's sabbatical replacement will be Don Cameron, a musician and director who served as a substitute teacher earlier in the year. Angela James will return from her leave to continue on the 5th grade classroom team.

Jackie Younger, 2nd grade teacher, has received a teaching assignment in the Peace Corps as a volunteer assigned to the Philippines. She will work in a teacher-training program there for two years. Anne Curtain will move from the 3rd grade to Jackie's 2nd grade assignment, and Sue Duerr will move from 5th grade to the 3rd grade team.

Annie Jones will retire from the Spanish department, to be succeeded by Lois Kelly. Lois is Irish, educated in Mexico and Spain. She recently received undergraduate and graduate degrees from Michigan State University. Jeff Zimmerman will return to teach 6th grade science, having spent the present year in a 5th grade classroom.

We are delighted that Mark Conner will be at CCDS full time next year as our Director of Learning Services, a position she has held on a part-time basis for several years.

As previously announced, Mary Davis will divide her time between the new position of Director of Admissions and Associate Teacher in the Lower School, supporting classroom teachers by providing additional enrichment and remedial support. Hilda Lee, an experienced teacher and administrator, has been appointed Head of the Lower School. Ms. Lee is presently the Director of the Lower School at Town School in New York City.

BARBARA SMITH

After tending the library, and especially the audio-visual section, for 13 years at Marin Country Day School, Barbara Smith will be leaving this year for a life of relaxation and travel.

She arrived at our campus when the office stopped where the copy machines now are, the Lower School circle was a parking lot, and the Music Building sat next to the Art Building. (It's now the "gallery" art building.) The library, too, was much smaller, and the AV department consisted of some record players, a couple of tape recorders, two slide projectors, and two movie projectors (one of which was broken). Movies and slides were usually shown to classes in the library since most rooms didn't have a screen and couldn't get dark enough. You can still see where the curtain and the screen were fastened back then in the reading area where the large circular table is located. Barbara helped that library grow with CCDS into the quality resource that it is today, with a large collection of AV materials, from videotapes and VCR's to computer software.

She moved from Belgium to the U.S. in 1947, living in Salt Lake City and getting an MA degree in French and history from the University of Utah. Moving to the Bay Area in 1949, she worked towards a PhD, and was a TA in French at Berkeley until she married and had her first son. She returned to school to receive a teaching credential from Stanford and worked as a high school French teacher in Los Altos, having her second son in the process. Moving back to Berkeley, she returned to UC to get a Masters degree in library science rather than a PhD in French.

"I liked books and I thought it was a good thing to bring books and people together."

Barbara looks forward to a life of reading and travel, and time to spend with her grandchild (with anther on the way). Her only regret, as the library installs a microfiche machine, is that she will not be around to see her work and planning finally pay off as the library gets computerized. She will, however try to get her mind off if by cruising the Nile in NOvember. She plans to work with the Marin Literacy Council, and volunteer at the library of the Marin World Affairs Council.

We all wish Barbara Smith good luck and we invite her back any time to the library and school she helped build. I'm sure the parent library volunteer coordinator will let her know when she could help.

- Bill Been

Figure 15.1 *A page from a newsletter.*

FACULTY UPDATE

CCDS will begin the next school year with some new teachers on campus. Some committees are still completing the interviewing process, yet there are several announcements for the fall.

Barbara Smith, a librarian at school for the last 13 years, will retire to her Marinhome to spend more time in her avocational pursuits. Barbara is profiled in this issue of THE PIPER. Ann Brown will return to her native Vermont after a single year at school. While we respect Ann's decision to return to the East, we shall miss her wisdom and skill in the classroom. Mike Novak will reduce his classroom load, but will be on campus to direct the 5th grade and Upper School recorder and instrumental ensembles.

Several veteran teachers will be absent for the first semester: Mike Jones will take a medical leave, replaced by Irene Layton, while Bart Connair will travel abroad during the fall semester. Barry's sabbatical replacement will be Don Cameron, a musician and director who served as a substitute teacher earlier in the year. Angela James will return from her leave to continue on the 5th grade classroom team.

Jackie Younger, 2nd grade teacher, has received a teaching assignment in the Peace Corps as a volunteer assigned to the Philippines. She will work in a teacher-training program there for two years. Anne Curtain will move from the 3rd grade to Jackie's 2nd grade assignment, and Sue Duerr will move from 5th grade to the 3rd grade team.

Annie Jones will retire from the Spanish department, to be succeeded by Lois Kelly. Lois is Irish, educated in Mexico and Spain. She recently received undergraduate and graduate degrees from Michigan State University. Jeff Zimmerman will return to teach 6th grade science, having

spent the present year in a 5th grade classroom.

We are delighted that Mark Conner will be at CCDS full time next year as our Director of Learning Services, a position she has held on a part-time basis for several years.

As previously announced, Mary Davis will divide her time between the new position of Director of Admissions and Associate Teacher in the Lower School, supporting classroom teachers by providing additional enrichment and remedial support. Hilda Lee, an experienced teacher and administrator, has been appointed Head of the Lower School. Ms. Lee is presently the Director of the Lower School at Town School in New York City.

BARBARA SMITH

After tending the library, and especially the audio-visual section, for 13 years at Marin Country Day School, Barbara Smith will be leaving this year for a life of relaxation and travel.

She arrived at our campus when the office stopped where the copy machines now are, the Lower School circle was a parking lot, and the Music Building sat next to the Art Building. (It's now the "gallery" art building.) The library, too, was much smaller, and the AV department consisted of some record players, a couple of tape recorders, two slide projectors, and two movie projectors (one of which was broken.) Movies and slides were usually shown to classes in the library since most rooms didn't have a screen and couldn't get dark enough. You can still see where the curtain and the screen were fastened back then in the reading area where the large circular table is located. Barbara helped that library grow with CCDS into the quality resource that it is today, with a large collection of AV materials, from

videotapes and VCR's to computer software.

She moved from Belgium to the U.S. in 1947, living in Salt Lake City and getting an MA degree in French and history from the University of Utah. Moving to the Bay Area in 1949, she worked towards a PhD, and was a TA in French at Berkeley until she married and had her first son. She returned to school to receive a teaching credential from Stanford and worked as a high school French teacher in Los Altos, having her second son in the process. Moving back to Berkeley, she returned to UC to get a Masters degree in library science rather than a PhD in French.

"I liked books and I thought it was a good thing to bring books and people together."

Barbara looks forward to a life of reading and travel, and time to spend with her grandchild (with anther on the way). Her only regret, as the library installs a microfiche machine, is that she will not be around to see her work and planning finally pay off as the library gets computerized. She will, however try to get her mind off if by cruising the Nile in NOvember. She plans to work with the Marin Literacy Council, and volunteer at the library of the Marin World Affairs Council.

We all wish Barbara Smith good luck and we invite her back any time to the library and school she helped build. I'm sure the parent library volunteer coordinator will let her know when she could help.

- Bill Been

BEST BETS FOR SUMMER

San Francisco Giants Baseball Camp, for 8-13 year olds. Week-long camps in the EAst Bay led by former major leaguers, college and high school coaches. For brochure, call 935-3505.

1

Figure 15.2 The newsletter page after turning on a style.

Figures 15.3 and 15.4 illustrate this problem with two screen versions of the same letter. Figure 15.3 was formatted using a Courier 10-pitch font, while Figure 15.4 was formatted using Times Roman 12-point. The cursor is in the same position in both documents, at the end of the first line in the first paragraph. In Figure 15.4, several words are missing from the left side, but in Figure 15.3 you can see all of the text at once, including the words that are missing from 15.4. If the documents you produce tend to be lengthy and you switch font size and appearance attributes frequently for headings, subheadings, italics, etc., you are probably in the habit of making these font changes while typing, even though the on-screen display is annoying. In this chapter, you will learn an effective way to deal with this dilemma: using styles to switch from Courier to the other fonts just prior to the final printing.

```
File Edit Search Layout Mark Tools Font Graphics Help
July 24, 1990


Mr. Ralph Phatbuxs
120 Big Drive
Palm Beach, Florida

Dear Mr. Phatbuxs,

Thank you for your recent inquiry on the luxury motoryacht
"EXTRAVAGANCE".  You will find a specification sheet enclosed with
a complete listing of inventory and equipment.  Please note that
personal items such as tennis rackets and polo ponies are not
included in the sale.

This gracious vessel was built by the famous Fancischmanzi Boat
Yard in Italy and christened in 1985.  To date, she has been under
private ownership and never put into charter service.
Nevertheless, she is well suited for charter, with an elaborate
master stateroom and accommodations for a small neighborhood.  All
staterooms have private baths with jacuzzi and the interior was
recently redecorated by Poodles of Paris.
                                    Doc 1 Pg 1 Ln 2.67" Pos 6.8"
```

Figure 15.3 Sample letter on the Edit screen formatted with Courier 10 pitch.

```
File Edit Search Layout Mark Tools Font Graphics Help




t inquiry on the luxury motoryacht "EXTRAVAGANCE".  You will
et enclosed with a complete listing of inventory and equipment.  Please
 such as tennis rackets and polo ponies are not included in the sale.

 built by the famous Fancischmanzi Boat Yard in Italy and christened
as been under private ownership and never put into charter service.
l suited for charter, with an elaborate master stateroom and
ll neighborhood.  All staterooms have private baths with jacuzzi and
y redecorated by Poodles of Paris.

rupulously maintained and allow cruising speeds of ten knots while
gallons per hour.  Granted, this will probably limit any long distance
ow you to motor around the harbor and show off.
                                    Doc 1 Pg 1 Ln 2.94" Pos 7.45"
```

Figure 15.4 Sample letter on the Edit screen formatted with Times Roman 12-point.

You can extend this application to include a switch from double spacing to single spacing. Although double-spaced text is much easier to read on the Edit screen, most applications require the final printed version to be single-spaced. This is also useful when you are typing a document that must be edited or proofread before the final printing.

What Are Styles?

Essentially, a style is a name that you assign to a set of instructions; these instructions can include formatting, text, and graphics. Styles come in three types: open, paired, and outline. Use Open styles to turn on features such as headers or page numbering, and leave them on throughout the document. Use Paired styles to format one or more sections of the document, turning the style codes on and off throughout the text as you do when formatting text with bold or underline. Outline styles are only used with WordPerfect's Outline and Paragraph Numbering features, so you'll study them in Chapter 17.

WordPerfect automatically saves your styles along with the document you were typing when you created them. You can also save a group of styles as a separate file, and retrieve them into other documents. You can even set up a Style Library, a file of frequently used styles that is automatically available for use in all new documents that you create.

Let's take a closer look at paired and Open styles. As the name implies, codes for *Paired* styles come in pairs, like underline and boldface codes. You turn them on and off as you use them, placing [Style On] and [Style Off] codes around the text. Figure 15.5 shows the Reveal Codes screen for a paragraph that has been formatted using a Paired style. Notice the [Style On] and [Style Off] codes surrounding the paragraph. Applying a Paired style is like using the Bold or Underline key. To apply a style to a section of text before typing it, turn the style on, type the text, then turn the style off. If the text has already been typed, you apply a style by blocking the text and selecting the style from the Styles menu.

Unlike Paired styles, *Open* styles can only be turned on. Turning one on inserts an [Open Style] code into your document. Its formatting affects all text from that point forward, unless WordPerfect encounters a subsequent formatting code or style that changes it. As such, Open Style codes are similar to formatting codes like line spacing, margins, and tab settings, for they can only be altered by another code that appears later in the document. To apply an Open style, you just select it from the Styles menu.

Styles have innumerable applications, and are especially helpful in standardizing a company's formatting. For example, say your company policy states that all sales reports must include a footer formatted in a Helvetica 10-point Italic font, with the date at the left margin, a centered page number surrounded by dashes, and the word *Confidential* at the right margin. This task requires quite a few keystrokes: You press the Format key, select Page, select Footers, select Footer A, select Every Page, press the Font key, select Base Font, move the cursor bar onto the desired font and press Enter, press the Date key, select Date Code, press the Center key, type the dash, press Ctrl-B for the Page Number code, type the second dash, press the Flush Right key, type *Confidential*, then press Exit twice. That's a lot of work!

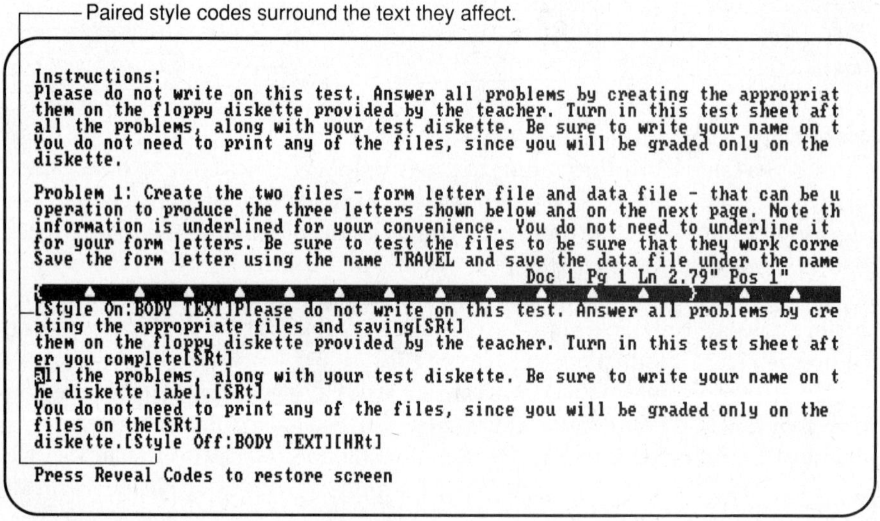

Paired style codes surround the text they affect.

```
Instructions:
Please do not write on this test. Answer all problems by creating the appropriat
them on the floppy diskette provided by the teacher. Turn in this test sheet aft
all the problems, along with your test diskette. Be sure to write your name on t
You do not need to print any of the files, since you will be graded only on the
diskette.

Problem 1: Create the two files - form letter file and data file - that can be u
operation to produce the three letters shown below and on the next page. Note th
information is underlined for your convenience. You do not need to underline it
for your form letters. Be sure to test the files to be sure that they work corre
Save the form letter using the name TRAVEL and save the data file under the name
                                               Doc 1 Pg 1 Ln 2.79" Pos 1"
[Style On:BODY TEXT]Please do not write on this test. Answer all problems by cre
ating the appropriate files and saving[SRt]
them on the floppy diskette provided by the teacher. Turn in this test sheet aft
er you complete[SRt]
all the problems, along with your test diskette. Be sure to write your name on t
he diskette label.[SRt]
You do not need to print any of the files, since you will be graded only on the
files on the[SRt]
diskette.[Style Off:BODY TEXT][HRt]

Press Reveal Codes to restore screen
```

Figure 15.5 The Reveal Codes screen showing a Paired style applied to a paragraph.

Having studied this book, you realize that you can save some time by creating a style that would produce just such a footer. You set up each worker's computer so that your footer can be inserted into every new sales report with only three keystrokes: Alt-F8, Enter. The next thing you know, you're a company hero! Since over 1,000 of these sales reports are created every day in your company, you are soon rewarded with a handsome bonus for all the time you have saved them, and you receive a promotion.

Incidentally, in case you are wondering why you should use a style instead of a macro for the footer, here's the explanation. When you use a macro for formatting, it inserts embedded codes into your document. If you ever want to change the formatting, you have to locate and erase each code, then insert new ones. When you use a style, you only change the formatting once, inside the style, and it changes all the text that has been formatted with that style.

Imagine that the week after you receive your big bonus, the president leaves the company, and a new one arrives who hates Helvetica fonts, has a thing about italics, and believes that the report dates are always inaccurate and misleading because so many of the computer's clocks don't work properly. She immediately changes the company policy so that all footers must be printed in Times Roman

10-point, with the company name instead of the date at the left margin. Worse, she makes it retroactive to the beginning of the year. You calmly proceed to assure everyone that it won't be a problem, then modify the style, and copy it onto all of the company's computers. After that, all new documents will include the modified footer style. For those who need to change the footer in existing documents, you provide written instructions explaining how easy it is: Just retrieve the document and select Update from the Styles menu. If you had used a macro for the footer, you would have to edit the old footer code in each document, a task that would require at least eight keystrokes in addition to the ones you would use to change the text and font in the footer.

Creating an Open Style

Let's create the footer style described earlier.

1. Begin by clearing the Edit screen.

2. Display the main Styles menu:

   Keyboard: Press the Style key (Alt-F8).

   Mouse: Select Styles from the Layout menu.

   The initial Styles menu will appear, as shown in Figure 15.6. You should see the headings Name, Type, and Description, but no style information should appear under them.

   If you see a list of styles, as shown in Figure 15.7, you are using a default set of styles called a *Style Library*, and these are the styles in your library. Incidentally, the ones shown in Figure 15.7 are from *Library.sty*, a Style Library included with the WordPerfect program. You'll learn more about the Library option later.

   In the meantime, you can either ignore the other styles, or use the Delete option to erase them from this document. Deleting them won't harm any other document or erase the styles permanently from your disk.

   To delete a style, highlight it, select **Delete** or press the Delete key, and then select the **Including Codes** option from the menu.

   To create your first style, FOOTER:

3. Select the **Create** option from the main Styles menu. The Styles: Edit menu will appear, as shown in Figure 15.8. It features five options. You can use them to:

   Name your style.

Change the style type from paired to open (or change an outline style into a regular style).

Enter a brief description of what the style does.

Enter the formatting codes and/or the text.

Change the meaning of the Enter key in a Paired style.

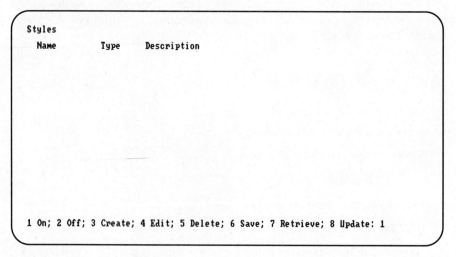

Figure 15.6 An empty Styles screen.

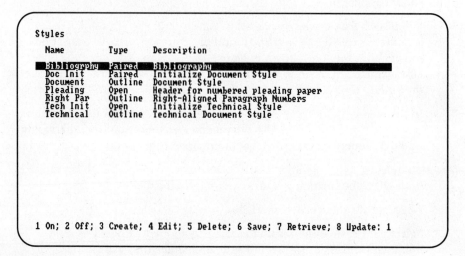

Figure 15.7 A Styles screen with seven styles.

Like many of WordPerfect's menus, the Styles: Edit menu has defaults for some of the options. WordPerfect assumes you want the Style Type to be Paired, and the Enter key to function as it normally does, inserting a [HRt] code into your document when you use a Paired style.

```
Styles: Edit
     1 - Name
     2 - Type          Paired
     3 - Description
     4 - Codes
     5 - Enter          HRt




Selection: 0
```

Figure 15.8 *The Styles: Edit menu, which you can use to create a new style or edit an existing one.*

The first option on the menu is Name, which you use to name your styles. If you don't name them, WordPerfect will number them consecutively (1,2,3,4, etc.). A style name can contain up to 12 characters. Unlike file names, style names can also include spaces, as in *HEADING 4*. A space counts as one of the 12 characters allowed in the style name. In the next step, let's name this style *FOOTER*.

4. To name your style, select the **Name** option, and then type FOOTER and press Enter.

   The next step is to specify what type of style you want this one to be: paired or open. Since footers are usually turned on and remain on throughout the document, let's make it an Open style.

5. Select **Type** and then **Open**.

   Did you notice a change in the screen? Since the fifth option, Enter, is only available for Paired styles, it disappeared from the menu as soon as you selected Open.

The last step before selecting the formatting is to type a brief description of what it does. The maximum length of the description is 54 characters. Since this information will appear in the initial Styles menu, to help remind you of the purpose of this style, you should always type a description. Try to make it as explicit as possible.

6. Select **Description**, and type:

   Footer with page number, date, Confidential

   and then press Enter.

   Now you are ready to define the formatting for this style. You'll do this (in the next step) by selecting the Codes option and then following the same steps to select the formatting feature that you would use in the Edit screen.

7. Select **Codes**.

   The Style Editor screen will appear, as shown in Figure 15.9. Notice that Reveal Codes is on. As you select the formatting for this style, the corresponding codes will appear in the Reveal Codes section (below the tab ruler). If you include text in the style, it will appear in both the Reveal Codes section and the editing section at the top. The prompt Style: Press Exit when done appears above the tab ruler, to remind you that you're using the Style Editor.

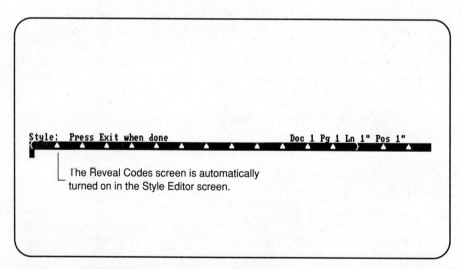

Style: Press Exit when done   Doc 1 Pg 1 Ln 1" Pos 1"

The Reveal Codes screen is automatically turned on in the Style Editor screen.

Figure 15.9 The Style Editor screen used to select the formatting for an Open style.

Entering Codes and Text in the FOOTER Style

Now comes the real work, defining the formatting, and entering the text for your FOOTER style. The one-line footer will include:

- The date at the left margin.

- A page number surrounded by dashes (actually hyphens) in the center of the line.

- The word *Confidential* at the right margin.

The entire footer will be formatted in a Helvetica 10-point Italic font; if you don't have Helvetica 10-point Italic, try to use another small italic font.

1. Display the Format: Page menu:

   Keyboard: Begin by pressing the Format key (Shift-F8) and selecting **Page**.

   Mouse: Select **Page** from the **Layout** menu.

2. From the Format: Page menu, select **Footers**, **Footer A**, and then **Every Page**.

3. Change the font for the footer:

   Keyboard: Press the Font key (Ctrl-F8) and select **Base Font**.

   Mouse: Select **Base Font** from the pull-down **Font** menu.

   Select a base font by moving the cursor bar onto it and pressing Enter.

4. To insert the date:

   Keyboard: Press the Date key (Shift-F5) and select **Date Code**.

   Mouse: Select **Date Code** from the **Tools** menu.

5. Center and type the page number code:

   Keyboard: Press the Center key (Shift-F6) and type a hyphen.

   Mouse: Select **Align** from the **Layout** menu, select **Center**, and then type a hyphen.

6. For the page number code, press Ctrl-B (this inserts the page number code, ^B). Finish by typing another hyphen.

7. Select Flush Right:

   Keyboard: Press the Flush Right key (Alt-F6).

Mouse: Select Align from the Layout menu and then Flush Right.

8. Type Confidential.

When you finish, the screen should resemble Figure 15.10. Notice the date, page number code (^B), and the word Confidential in the top half of the screen, and the formatting codes in the Reveal Codes section.

9. To complete the footer, press Exit (F7) twice.

Since you're still defining a style, you return to the Style Editor. Your screen should resemble Figure 15.11, showing the Footer A code inside the Reveal Codes menu.

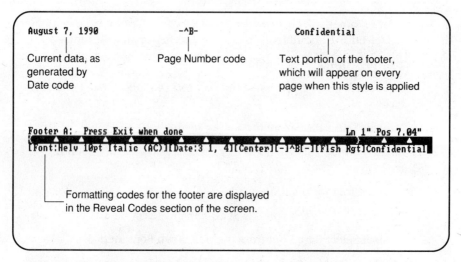

Figure 15.10 *Creating the footer.*

10. To return to the main Styles menu, press the Exit key (F7) twice.

You should see the Name, Type, and Description for your new Footer style, in a single line under the column headings (Name, Type, and Description). If you were ready to apply this style, you would now select On from the menu. Since this is an Open style, this action would insert an [Open Style:FOOTER] code.

Creating a Paired Style

Now let's try creating a Paired style that will turn on boldfacing and centering in headings. You should still be in the Styles menu.

1. Select Create.

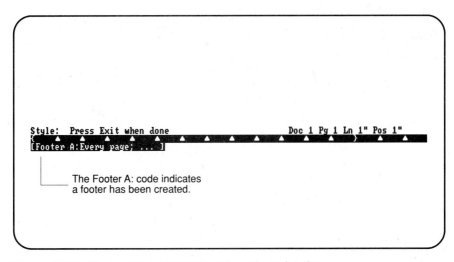

Figure 15.11 *The completed FOOTER style in the Style Editor screen.*

2. Select **Name** and type this style name:

   HEADINGS

   and then press Enter.

   Since the default for Type is paired, you don't have to change the second option. However, you should always enter a description for your styles, so that will be your next step.

3. Select **Description** and type:

   Boldfaces and centers headings

   and press Enter.

   In the next step, use the Codes option to select the formatting for your style.

4. Select **Codes.**

   The screen shown in Figure 15.12 will appear. Like the screen you saw when creating the Open style (Figure 15.9), Reveal Codes is on, and the screen is split by the tab ruler. However, because this is a Paired style, it has something extra: the Comment box with the message Place Style On Codes above, and Style Off Codes below, and the corresponding [Comment] code in the Reveal Codes section.

   WordPerfect never prints a comment, and the Comment box appears here to symbolize the text that you will format with this style. Any formatting codes to the left of the [Comment] code will be turned on by this style; these are the *Style On* codes. If you type any text in this style, it will appear to the left of the comment in the Reveal Codes section of the screen. It will also appear above the Comment box in the edit section. If you want to change the formatting after the Style Off code in your document, place the formatting codes to the right of the [Comment] code. There are specific restrictions pertaining to the use of codes that follow the [Comment] code, and you'll learn them shortly.

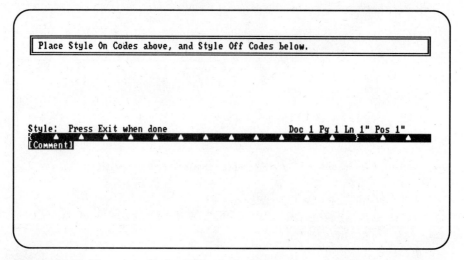

Figure 15.12 *The screen used to select the formatting for a Paired style.*

Entering Codes and Text in the HEADINGS Style

To insert the bold and center formatting in the HEADINGS style:

1. Select Bold:

    Keyboard: Press the Bold key (F6).

    Mouse: Display the Font menu and select **Appearance**, then **Bold**.

2. Select Center:

    Keyboard: Press the Center key (Shift-F6).

    Mouse: Display the **Layout** menu, select **Align**, and then **Center**.

    As you can see, WordPerfect has inserted [BOLD] and [Center] codes on the left side of the [Comment] code. These codes will turn on boldfacing and centering whenever you apply this style. However, you don't need to insert the codes that turn them off at the end of the style. When you turn off a Paired style, WordPerfect cancels its formatting and returns to the formatting that was in effect before the style was turned on. In fact, after you apply this code in the document, you can move your cursor onto the [Style Off] code and see that it includes the code to turn off boldfacing, [bold] (but WordPerfect 5.1 has no Center Off code).

In a Paired style, even if you do place a formatting code after the [Comment] code, in many cases WordPerfect will ignore it! This happens when you try to change the same formatting feature in both the Style On and Style Off sections. For instance, say you design a Paired style that changes the left/right margin settings to 1.5" each, and you place a second left/right margin setting code after the [Comment] code to change them to 1.25" each. You then apply the style to two paragraphs. As a result, the left and right margins in the two paragraphs change to 1.5" each. However, after the Style Off code, WordPerfect completely disregards the 1.25" left/right margin code that you placed after the [Comment] code in the style, and reverts back to the margins that were in effect before the style was turned on, the default setting of 1" each. If you are ever in doubt about how WordPerfect is interpreting the Style Off formatting, just turn on Reveal Codes and place the cursor on the Style Off code. It will expand to display the actual formatting codes that are being used, as shown in Figure 15.13 for the example described in this paragraph.

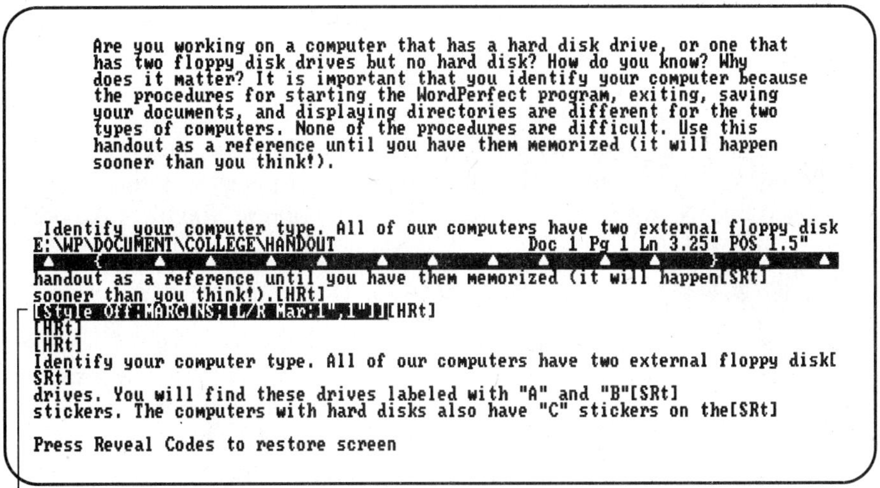

Placing the cursor on the Style Off code expands the code to show the formatting codes that will affect text formatted with this style code.

Figure 15.13 *An expanded Style Off code as seen in the Reveal Codes screen.*

The only exceptions to this rule are these options on the Format Page menu: Headers and Footers, Page Numbering, Top and Bottom margins, and Paper Size and Type. Since these features are generally meant to be turned on and left on, they are not canceled after a Paired style, regardless of whether you place them before or after the [Comment] code. If you place them after the [Comment] code, they won't take effect until after the style is turned off. Also, you can change one of these options both before and after the [Comment] code. However, if you include one of these page formatting codes in a Style On code, the cursor must be on the first line of the page when you turn on the style, or the Style On code will have no effect. The Style Off code will affect all subsequent pages, regardless of where the cursor is when you turn on the style.

For instance, if you create a Paired style to change the top margin to 2.5" in the style and 1.5" after it, the Style On code must be on the first line of the page you want it to affect. If not, it will not change the page at all. The Style Off code will format all subsequent pages with a top margin of 1.5".

 Tip: While selecting the formatting for a Paired style, if you accidentally erase the [Comment] code, you can restore it by pressing Exit (F7) to back out of the menu and then selecting Codes again from the Styles Edit menu.

Since you are finished defining the formatting for the HEADINGS style, return to the Styles Edit menu:

3. Press the Exit key (F7).

The last option on this menu is Enter, and it is currently set to the default, [HRt]. If you leave this default, the Enter key will function normally, inserting a Hard Return code. If you select the option, you'll see the other choices:

`Enter: 1 Hrt; 2 Off; 3 Off/On: 0`

The second one, Off, means pressing Enter will turn the style off, leaving the cursor in place. This would be useful in the HEADINGS style, since you'll be using it to format single-line headings. However, after typing a heading you would also want to press Enter to move the cursor to the next line. Rather than pressing Enter twice, once to turn the style off and once to move to the next line, you could place a [HRt] code in the Style Off section of the style, after the [Comment] code. That way, pressing Enter would do both: Turn the style off, and move the cursor to the next line.

The Off/On option turns the style off, and then turns it back on again. Use it when you want to format several paragraphs in a row with the style, especially if you want to include formatting that affects the first line of each paragraph, like a tab or margin release. Since it does not move the cursor to the next line, you should include one or more [HRt] codes after the [Comment] code in the style (use two if you want a blank line separating the paragraphs). If you don't, you won't be able to start a new paragraph or insert a blank line until you turn the style off.

Let's leave the Enter key set to [HRt], and move along. Since you won't be creating any more styles now, return to the main Styles screen.

4. Press Exit (F7) once to return to the main Styles screen. From there, you'll apply your first style.

Applying Your Two Styles

Now comes the easy part! To apply the FOOTER style, all you have to do is:

1. Highlight it with the cursor bar.

2. Select **On**. (Since the On option is the default choice, you can press Enter to select it.)

   This places you back in the Edit screen. Look in Reveal Codes (Alt-F3), and you'll see the [Open Style:FOOTER] code.

3. Press the Left Arrow key to place the cursor onto the code. As shown in Figure 15.14, the code expands, displaying the Footer A code in the style.

> **Tip:** When you apply the FOOTER style, the cursor must be on the first line of the first page where you want the footer to appear. If it isn't, your footer won't begin printing until the following page.

To verify that the style is actually working, you can either print the page or use View Document (Shift-F7 **V** or **File Print** View Document). If you use View Document, press Home,Down Arrow to see the footer at the bottom of the page.

Before continuing, return to the Edit screen, and then press the Right Arrow key to move the cursor past the Open Style code. You may also wish to exit the Reveal Codes screen.

Next, use the Paired style to format a short heading.

4. Select style:

   Keyboard: Press Style (Alt-F8).

   Mouse: Select **Layout** and then **Styles**.

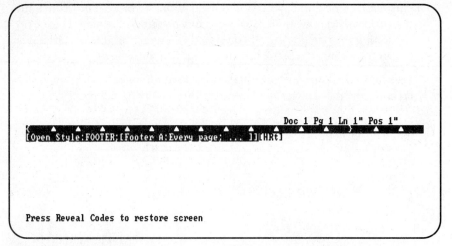

```
                                                    Doc 1 Pg 1 Ln 1" Pos 1"
[Open Style:FOOTER;[Footer A:Every page; ... ]][HRt]




Press Reveal Codes to restore screen
```

Figure 15.14 *The Expanded FOOTER Style code as seen in Reveal Codes.*

5. Highlight the *HEADINGS* style, and then select **On**.

 Tip: To move the cursor onto a style name in the main Styles menu, you can use the Name Search option. It works exactly as it does in the List Files menu. Type N to select Name Search (or press F2). The Style menu disappears. Next, type the first one or two letters of the style name (or more if necessary). When the cursor is highlighting the style you want, press Enter so the Styles menu reappears.

6. Type this heading:

```
1st Quarter Preliminary Sales Report
```

7. Press the Right Arrow key once, and then press Enter.

Pressing Right Arrow moved the cursor past the Style Off code and turned off the HEADINGS style. You could have pressed the Style key and selected the Off option to do this, but it is not necessary and requires several extra keystrokes. Both methods do the same thing: Move the cursor to the right of the Style Off code, and turn the style off (if you don't understand, you may want turn on Reveal Codes and repeat these steps, watching the cursor in the Reveal Codes screen).

The heading that you just typed should now be boldfaced and centered. Let's look at the style in Reveal Codes.

8. Press Alt-F3, or select **R**eveal Codes from the **E**dit menu. Place the cursor onto the [Style On:HEADINGS] code, and it will expand to show you the formatting codes it contains: [BOLD] and [Center].

If you move the cursor onto the [Style Off:HEADINGS] code, you'll see the [bold] code that WordPerfect uses to turn off boldfacing at this point.

Tip: To locate a Style On, Style Off, or Open Style code in your document, you can use WordPerfect's Search feature. Select **F**orward or **B**ackward Search by pressing F2 or Shift-F2, or by selecting the **F**orward or **B**ackward option from the Search menu. In response to the Srch prompt, press the Style key (Alt-F8). A menu appears with these three options: Style **O**n, Style O**f**f, and Open **S**tyle. Select the one you want to search for, and WordPerfect will insert the corresponding code into the search string. Press F2 or click the right mouse button to begin the search. If the cursor locates the code, it will stop just past it; use Reveal Codes to see it. For more information about using WordPerfect's Search feature, see Chapter 5.

Editing Styles

Editing a style is easy: You just highlight the style in the Styles menu, and select the **E**dit option. You can then change the style name, type, description, formatting codes, or (for Paired styles only) use of the Enter key. In this section, you'll learn how to change the HEADINGS style so that all headings are printed in a Helvetica 14-point Bold font, begin at the left margin, and include a horizontal line underneath. You'll also edit the FOOTER style to remove the word *Confidential*, and replace it with the report title, *1st Quarter Preliminary Sales Report*.

Tip: If you edit a style and change the Type (open, paired) after applying it in the document, the styles in the document will not be affected and will remain set to the original type.

1. Select Style:

Keyboard: Press Style (Alt-F8).

Mouse: Select **L**ayout and then **S**tyles.

2. Highlight the HEADINGS style with the cursor, select **Edit**, and then select **Codes**.

3. Erase the [BOLD] and [Center] codes by pressing Delete twice.

4. Change the font:

    Keyboard: Press the Font key (Ctrl-F8) and select Base **Font**.

    Mouse: Select Base **Font** from the pull-down **Font** menu.

5. Highlight the Helvetica 14-point Bold font (if you don't have it, try to select another large and bold font), and press Enter.

6. Press the Right Arrow key to move the cursor past the [Comment] code.

7. Press Enter again to insert a [HRt] code in the style.

    When you use this style to format a heading, the [HRt] code will create a blank line, separating the text of your heading from the horizontal line.

8. Create a horizontal line:

    Keyboard: Press the Graphics key (Alt-F9), select **Line**, and then select **Horizontal** (the first option, create a horizontal line).

    Mouse: Select **Line** from the **Graphics** menu and then select **Create Horizontal**.

    Press Enter to accept the defaults on the Graphics: Horizontal Line menu for horizontal and vertical position, length and width of line, and gray shading.

9. Press Exit twice to return to the main Styles menu.

    Next, change the FOOTER style.

10. Highlight the FOOTER style, and select **Edit**.

11. Select **Codes**.

12. Edit the footer:

    Keyboard: Press Format (Shift-F8) and select **Page**.

    Mouse: Select **Page** from the **Layout** menu.

    Select **Footer**, **Footer A**, then **Edit**.

13. Erase the word *Confidential* and type:

    `1st Quarter Preliminary Sales Report`

14. To complete the changes, press Exit until you are back in the Edit screen.

Tip: If you are working in the Edit screen, you can edit a footer contained inside a style without going through the Styles menu. Just use the Format key to edit it, as though it were a regular embedded code.

Next, let's use View Document to see the changes.

15. Select View Document:

> **Keyboard:** Press the Print key (Shift-F7) and select **View Document.**

> **Mouse:** Select **Print** from the File menu, and then Select **View Document.**

As you can see from the printed version in Figure 15.15, the FOOTER style includes the report title, and the HEADINGS style is now flush left, is in a larger font, and has a horizontal line underneath it. In our imaginary report where the HEADINGS style was applied 12 times, these easy steps would have changed the appearance of all 12 of those headings. Thanks to styles, what was formerly a time-consuming and complex task has become nearly effortless.

 Tip: Here's a trick you can use to copy a style. If you edit a style and change its name, WordPerfect will ask if you want to rename it wherever you have applied it in the document. You'll see this prompt: `Rename Styles in Document? No (Yes)`. If you've already used this style in your document, you should select Yes. If you select No, the new style name will replace the old one in the Styles menu, but not in the document. If you exit to the Edit screen and then return to the Styles menu, you'll see both styles, because WordPerfect will recreate the original definition when it encounters the style code in your document. The new style will not yet be applied in your document.

Saving and Retrieving Your Styles

When you save a document using the Save or Exit key or menu options, any styles that you created for it are automatically saved along with the document. You can also save your styles as a separate file: Just select the Save option on the main Styles menu, and type a file name for your styles. It's a good idea to use a three-character extension such as *STY* to clearly identify the file as one containing only styles. Style files are saved in the current directory, unless you have used the Setup Location of Files menu to designate a directory for your style files. You'll learn more about this later in the chapter, in the "Using a Style Library" section.

Figure 15.15 *The revised HEADINGS and FOOTER styles used in a document.*

Whenever you want to retrieve a style file into another document or a blank editing screen, just select the Retrieve option from the main Styles menu. If you know the file name, just type it and press Enter. Since the (List Files) prompt appears in the lower-right corner of the screen when you select Retrieve, if you aren't sure of the exact file name, you can press List Files (F5) and Enter, and then retrieve the file from the list.

It is not necessary to save your styles as a separate file in order to copy them from one document into another. Instead, you can select the Retrieve option on the main Styles menu, type the file name of the document containing the styles that you want to use (or use the List Files menu to retrieve the file), then sit back and watch WordPerfect retrieve the styles into the Styles menu of the document currently on your Edit screen. This will retrieve only the styles from the other document, not the text.

You can retrieve as many style files as you want into a document. However, if one of the styles in your current Styles menu has the same name as a style in the document or style file you are retrieving styles from, you could end up erasing the formatting in your new style and replacing it with the formatting from the retrieved style. WordPerfect does provide a warning if this is about to happen. If you select the Retrieve option on the main Styles menu and this prompt appears:

```
Style(s) already exist. Replace? No (Yes)
```

it means WordPerfect has found one or more styles with the same name. The prompt asks for your permission to erase the matching styles in your document, and replace them with the ones from the other file. Unfortunately, it does not allow you to be selective about which styles to replace and which to leave alone. All duplicate styles are replaced when you answer Yes. If you select No in response to the Replace prompt, WordPerfect will not retrieve styles with the same name as existing ones. Instead, only the styles with unique names will be retrieved.

There is an advantage to replacing existing styles. You'll learn all about it in the next section.

Exchanging Style Files

The fastest and most efficient method of turning a rough draft into a polished product is to maintain two separate files containing identically named styles, but with different formatting codes. Just before the final printing, switch the styles and reformat the document everywhere that you applied your styles. For instance, say you were to type the form shown in Figure 15.16, using styles from a file named *DRAFT.STY.*

After printing, proofreading, and editing the document, you could use the Retrieve option on the main Styles menu to switch to the FINAL style file, a change that would only require a few keystrokes: You would select Retrieve from the main

Styles menu, type the file name (FINAL.STY) and press Enter, and then type Y in response to the `Replace` prompt. After you return to your document, the Courier font would be replaced by the Helvetica and Times Roman fonts, as shown in Figure 15.17.

```
                                           Class: _____

                                           Date:  _____


Course Evaluation

It has been our pleasure having you in this class. Please take a
few moments to evaluate the course that you have just completed.
Your feedback will help in our efforts to continually improve both
the course content and our teaching methods.
```

| Please *circle* the most appropriate response. |

Course materials	Excellent	Good	Average	Fair	Poor
Quality of exercises	Excellent	Good	Average	Fair	Poor
Instructor's knowledge	Excellent	Good	Average	Fair	Poor
Instructor's delivery	Excellent	Good	Average	Fair	Poor
Class pace	Excellent	Good	Average	Fair	Poor
Learning environment	Excellent	Good	Average	Fair	Poor

| **Overall class rating** | **Excellent** | **Good** | **Average** | **Fair** | **Poor** |

```
I wish I had learned more about:


I wish I had learned less about:


Comments:
```

Figure 15.16   The draft version of an evaluation form, in Courier font.

Such an exchange of style files would alleviate the problem created by the on-screen display of the Times Roman and Helvetica fonts. Since you wouldn't have to switch styles until just before printing the final document, you could type and edit it in Courier, so the screen would be wide enough to show all characters on a line. Another advantage to using styles for this task is that it would make it easier for you to experiment with the fonts. Imagine if you wanted to change the font for the response options in the table (Excellent, Good, etc.). If you weren't using styles, you would have to change the font in 11 places: after Course materials, before and after Quality of the exercises, before and after Instructor's knowledge, etc.! With styles, you would only change it once, inside the style that is being used to format the response options.

Here's how it works. When creating the document, you apply the DRAFT styles to your text. After you finish typing and proofreading, you use the Retrieve option on the main Styles menu to retrieve the file containing the FINAL styles, and this replaces the DRAFT styles. The document then changes to conform to the formatting codes contained in the FINAL styles.

Both the DRAFT and FINAL style files contain four styles, with the same names: *Headings*, *Large*, *Setup*, and *Small*. However, the DRAFT styles contain no formatting at all. In Figure 15.16, which is formatted with the DRAFT styles, the entire document uses the default margins and font (the Initial Base Font that was in use, Courier). The styles in the FINAL file make these changes, as shown in Figure 15.17:

- The Base Font for the document becomes Times Roman 12-point.

- The top and bottom margins become .5" each.

- Justification is changed to Left.

- The response section (Excellent, Good, etc.) is formatted with a Times Roman 10-point Italic font.

- Text in the sections the user of this form is supposed to fill in—*Class* and *Date* at the top of the page, and these three lines at the bottom: *I wish I had learned more about*, *I wish I had learned less about*, and *Comments*—is formatted in Small Caps and in a Large version of the Base Font (Times Roman).

- This text— *Course Evaluation* and *Please circle the most appropriate response*—is formatted with Helvetica 14-point Bold.

Note that WordPerfect's Table feature was used to create the response section in the middle (everything between the *Please circle* and *Overall class rating* lines). For more information about the Table feature, see Chapter 10.

The following chart explains what happens when you switch from the Draft to the Finals style:

CLASS: _____

DATE: _____

Course Evaluation

It has been our pleasure having you in this class. Please take a few moments to evaluate the course that you have just completed. Your feedback will help in our efforts to continually improve both the course content and our teaching methods.

Please *circle* the most appropriate response.

Course materials	*Excellent*	*Good*	*Average*	*Fair*	*Poor*
Quality of exercises	*Excellent*	*Good*	*Average*	*Fair*	*Poor*
Instructor's knowledge	*Excellent*	*Good*	*Average*	*Fair*	*Poor*
Instructor's delivery	*Excellent*	*Good*	*Average*	*Fair*	*Poor*
Class pace	*Excellent*	*Good*	*Average*	*Fair*	*Poor*
Learning environment	*Excellent*	*Good*	*Average*	*Fair*	*Poor*
Overall class rating	*Excellent*	*Good*	*Average*	*Fair*	*Poor*

I WISH I HAD LEARNED MORE ABOUT:

I WISH I HAD LEARNED LESS ABOUT:

COMMENTS:

Figure 15.17 *The final version of an evaluation form, with Helvetica and Times Roman fonts.*

Style Name:	Application:
HEADINGS	A Paired style, it surrounds the text in sections the user of this form is supposed to fill in: *Class* and *Date* at the top of the page, and these three lines at the bottom: *I wish I had learned more about*, *I wish I had learned less about*, and *Comments*. When the FINAL HEADINGS style is applied, it turns on two font attributes: *Large* on the Font Size menu, and *Small Cap* on the Font Appearance menu.
LARGE	A Paired style, it surrounds this text: *Course Evaluation* and *Please circle the most appropriate response.* When the FINAL LARGE style is applied, it changes the font to Helvetica Bold 14-point.
SETUP	An Open style, it is turned on at the top of the page, and stays on through the entire document. When the FINAL SETUP style is applied, it changes the top and bottom margins to .5" each, establishes a Base Font of Times Roman 12-point, and changes Justification to Left.
SMALL	A Paired style, it surrounds the response options: Excellent, Good, Average, Fair, and Poor. When the FINAL SMALL style is applied, it changes the font to Times Roman 10-point Italic. The SMALL style codes were applied separately on each line in the response section, so the headings such as *Course materials* and *Quality of exercises* would be formatted using the Base Font of Times Roman 12-point (although the bold was applied in the document, not through a style).

Creating a Paired Style from Codes in a Document

An alternative method of creating a Paired style is to block the section of the document that contains the codes you want in the style, and copy them. Use these steps:

1. Turn Reveal Codes on so you can see the codes.

   Keyboard: Press Reveal Codes (Alt-F3 or F11).

   Mouse: Display the Edit menu and select **R**eveal Codes.

2. Place the cursor at the beginning of the section you want to block, and then block the section by:

> **Keyboard:** Pressing the Block key (Alt-F4 or F12).

> **Mouse:** Selecting the **B**lock option on the **E**dit menu.

Next, move the cursor to the end of the section containing the codes. Note that the text inside your block won't become part of the style.

3. Display the main Styles menu:

> **Keyboard:** Press Styles (Alt-F8).

> **Mouse:** Select Styles from the **L**ayout menu.

4. Select Create. This copies the codes from the highlighted block into the style you are creating.

5. To verify that you've copied all the ones you wanted, or to further modify the formatting in the new style, select the Codes option. When you finish, use exit to return to the Styles: Edit menu.

6. Before exiting the Styles: Edit menu, be sure to name your new style and add a description for it.

To include both text and codes in a style, you have to use Block with the Copy option. Follow these steps:

1. Place the cursor at the beginning of the section, turn on Block mode, and block the section containing the codes (see step 2 of the previous steps for details).

2. Select Copy:

> **Keyboard:** Press Move (Ctrl-F4) and select **B**lock, then **C**opy (or press Ctrl-Insert).

> **Mouse:** Select **C**opy from the **E**dit menu.

3. Select the Create option from the Styles menu:

> **Keyboard:** Press the Style key (Alt-F8) and select Create.

> **Mouse:** Select Styles from the **L**ayout menu and select Create.

4. Select Codes; then press Enter to retrieve the text and codes that you copied.

5. The last step is to exit back to the main Styles menu, name your new style, and enter a description.

Using a Style Library

You already know that you can save a set of styles as a separate file, and retrieve it for use in any other document that you create. As a matter of fact, if you find yourself retrieving a particular style file on a regular basis, you may wish to carry this one step further and establish it as a Style Library. It then becomes the default set of styles, automatically available for use in any new document that you create. Styles that you may wish to keep in a Style Library include an envelope style to set up all the formatting for envelopes, a letterhead style that types your name and address at the top of the page, and a setup style that establishes your Base Font, margins, justification, and other formatting you use on a regular basis.

To establish a Style Library from an existing style file:

1. Display the main Setup menu.

    Keyboard: Press the Setup key (Shift-F1).

    Mouse: Select Setup from the File menu.

2. Select the Location of Files option. The Setup: Location of Files menu shown in Figure 15.18 appears.

3. Select the fifth option, Style Files and Library Filename.

You can use the first part of this option, *Style Files*, to name a directory for your style files. If you do, style files that you save through the Styles menu will automatically be placed in that directory. Be sure to create the directory before typing its name here. If you enter a directory that doesn't exist or type the name or path incorrectly, you'll receive an error message. If you don't want to name a directory, just press Enter.

Use the second part of this option, *Library Filename*, to name the style file that you want to use as a Style Library. Just type the file name, press Enter, and then press Exit (F7).

Once you set up a Style Library, the default styles will automatically be available in any new document you create. You'll see them whenever you press the Style key or select Styles from the Layout menu. This will also be the case if you retrieve an existing document that was saved without any styles. It will not be true for an existing document that you saved before establishing the Style Library, if it included styles of its own. However, you can add the Style Library's styles into such a document by selecting the Update option from the main Styles menu.

You've already learned a little about the Update option. You can use it in any document to retrieve all the styles from the Style Library. However, if any of the styles in your current document have the same names as styles from your Style Library, they will be erased and replaced with the Library versions. You will not receive a warning, as you do when you select the Retrieve option. As you learned earlier, Update is also useful when you have made a change to a style in the Library, and want to implement that change in an existing document.

```
Setup: Location of Files
      1 - Backup Files                    E:\WP
      2 - Keyboard/Macro Files            E:\WP\MACROS
      3 - Thesaurus/Spell/Hyphenation
                      Main                E:\WP
                      Supplementary       E:\WP
      4 - Printer Files                   E:\WP\PRINTER
      5 - Style Files                     E:\WP\STYLES
              Library Filename            FONT.STY
      6 - Graphic Files
      7 - Documents                       E:\WP\DOCUMENT




Selection: 0
```

Figure 15.18 *The Setup: Location of Files menu.*

There is one drawback to using a Style Library, especially if it contains a large number of styles. All styles in the library are automatically saved with each new document you create, regardless of whether or not you are actually using them in that document. Even if they are not applied, styles use a lot of disk space. In the next section, you'll learn a fool-proof method of deleting all the styles you aren't using in a document.

Deleting Styles

To save disk space and eliminate clutter in your Styles menu, you can delete styles that you aren't using in your document. Here's how.

1. Display the main Styles menu, and highlight the first style in the list that you want to delete.

2. Either select the Delete option, or press the Delete key. This prompt will appear:

```
Delete Styles: 1 Leaving Codes; 2 Including Codes; 3
Definition Only: 0
```

If you select the first option, *Leaving Codes*, WordPerfect will erase this style from the Styles menu, and also erase its Style On and Style Off, or Open Style code(s) in your document. However, the formatting codes that the style inserted will remain in the text. For example, if you were to delete the FOOTER style (which you created earlier in this chapter) after applying it, your document would still contain a footer code, but it would not be inside a style.

If you select the second option, *Including Codes*, WordPerfect will delete all occurrences of both the style codes and formatting, wherever they are found in your document, and the style will disappear from the menu.

As you've probably guessed by now, you can use the last option, *Definition Only*, to erase the styles that you aren't actually using in your document. When you use Definition Only on a style, WordPerfect erases the style from the menu, but not from the document. When you return to the Edit screen and move the cursor to the end of the document, WordPerfect will find any style codes that you've applied, and use them to recreate their style definitions. To see them again, just return to the Styles menu. Since this helps reduce the file size of your document, you should use it after you've finished typing and editing each file that contains style codes. The only disadvantage is that WordPerfect cannot recreate the style descriptions in the menu.

Using Search and Replace to Delete Style Codes

Another way to delete style codes from your document is to use WordPerfect's Replace feature. In one Replace action, you can erase all Paired styles in a document, or all Open styles. Unlike the Delete options in the Styles menu, Replace will not erase the styles from the Styles menu.

To use the Replace feature:

1. Move the cursor to the top of the document.

2. Select Replace:

   Keyboard: Press the Replace key (Alt-F2).

   Mouse: Select **R**eplace from the **S**earch menu.

   This prompt appears:

   ```
   w/Confirm No (Yes)
   ```

   Select **N**o.

3. Press the Style key (Alt-F8). This prompt appears:

   ```
   1 Style On; 2 Style Off; 3 Open Style: 0
   ```

To delete all Paired styles, you can select either of the first two options, *Style On* or *Style Off*. Since they come in pairs, deleting one member of the pair automatically deletes the other. To erase all Open styles, use the *Open Style* option.

4. Select one of the options: Style On, Style Off, or Open Style. The corresponding code will appear in the Srch prompt:

```
[Style On]
[Style Off]
[Open Style]
```

5. Press Search (F2) again. This prompt will appear:

```
Replace with:
```

To erase all the codes, you'll leave it blank.

6. Leave the prompt blank and begin the replace action by pressing Search (F2) again.

WordPerfect will search through your entire document and automatically erase all the [Style On], [Style Off], or [Open Style] codes. The cursor will stop right after the position where the last style code was located (before you erased it).

Unfortunately, when you use Replace you cannot be selective about which Paired or Open styles to erase! However, if you turn Reveal Codes on first, and set the Confirm option to Yes in step 2, WordPerfect will stop on each style code and let you decide if you want to erase it or not.

Using Graphics in Styles

You've already learned that you can use the Horizontal Line option on the Graphics key in a style. With WordPerfect 5.1, you can also include graphic images in your styles, such as the graphics files included with WordPerfect (BUTTERFLY.WPG, PC-1.WPG, TELEPHONE.WPG, etc.), DrawPerfect files, or even a scanned file such as your logo or signature. WordPerfect will automatically designate the graphic in your style as a Graphic on Disk, so the graphics file you want to use must be in the current directory, or in the default graphics directory established through the Setup: Location of Files option. If not, you won't be able to print it, or see it in View Document or in the graphics editor.

To include a graphic image in a style, follow these steps:

1. Use the Styles menu to create a Paired style. The exact steps are described in this chapter in the section "Creating a Paired Style."

2. Select the Codes option on the Styles: Edit menu.

3. Use the Graphics key (Alt-F9) or **Graphics** option on the pull-down menu to create the type of box you want to use: **Figure**, **Table Box**, **Text Box**, **User Box**, or **Equation**. See Chapter 14 if you have forgotten how to create a graphics box.

   A Definition menu will appear, corresponding to the box type you selected. For instance, if you are creating a Figure box, the Definition: Figure menu will appear.

4. Select **Filename**, and type the name of the graphics file you want to use. If you are unsure of the name, press List (F5) Enter, locate the file name and highlight it with the cursor, and then select **Retrieve**.

   After selecting the graphics file, you will return to the Definition menu and can edit the graphics box, if necessary.

5. When you finish, you can return to the Style Editor by pressing Enter or clicking the right mouse button.

   You should see the code for the graphic in the Style Off area following the [Comment] code. For example, if you had created a Figure box and used the CLOCK.WPG file, you would see this code:

   ```
   [Fig Box:1;CLOCK.WPG;UBUB]
   ```

   The remaining steps are the same as for other styles. Use this screen to select any other formatting that you want to use in your style, or to type text in it; then press Exit (F7) to return to the Styles: Edit menu.

6. When you finish using the Styles: Edit menu, press Enter or the right mouse button to return to the main Styles menu. From there, you can turn the graphics style on by highlighting it and pressing Enter, or selecting **On**.

   This will place the style and the graphics box it contains into your document.

Editing a Graphic in a Style

If you ever need to edit a graphics file that is inside a style, be sure to do it through the Styles menu. If you try to use the Edit option on the Graphics key or Graphics pull-down menu, you'll receive this error message:

```
ERROR: Box is defined in style; Edit style to edit box.
```

To edit a graphics box contained inside a style:

1. Display the main Styles menu, and highlight the style with the cursor.

2. Select **Edit**.

3. Select **Codes**.

Use the Graphics menu or key to edit your graphic in the usual way. For more information about how to edit a graphics box, see Chapter 14.

Style Shortcuts Using Macros

Macros can be indispensable and can be especially useful to help you apply your styles in a document. In this section, you'll learn how to create a macro that applies an Italics style to existing text. You could name it ALTI. Here's how it will work: You press Alt-I, and the macro turns on Block mode, then pauses while you move the cursor and block highlighting to the end of the section that you want to format with the Italics style. After you finish moving the cursor, you press Enter. The macro then brings up the Styles menu, uses the Name Search feature to locate the style, and selects it.

To create a macro like this, follow these steps. (If you don't know much about macros, you may want to read Chapter 19 before continuing.)

1. Press Macro Define (Ctrl-F10), or select **Macro** from the **Tools** menu, and then **Define** from the submenu. In response to the `Define macro` prompt, type your macro name and press Enter (if you use an Alt name, just press Alt and the letter—you won't need to press Enter).

2. In response to the `Description` prompt, type a brief description, and press Enter.

3. Press Block (Alt-F4).

4. Press Ctrl-Page Up, and then select the Pause option from the menu.

5. Press Enter (to end the pause when the macro is used).

6. Press Style (Alt-F8).

7. Press Search (F2) or N to use the Name Search option.

8. Type the style name (to move the cursor bar onto the style in the menu), and then press Enter.

9. Select On.

10. Press Macro Define (Ctrl-F10) to end the macro definition.

That's all there is to it! If you named your macro ALT-I, here's how you can use it to format a section of text: Press Alt-I, move the cursor to the end of the section that you want formatted with the style, then press Enter. Wasn't that easy? The best macros are the ones that expedite a task you perform frequently, however unpretentious they may be.

FOOTNOTES AND ENDNOTES

Among the many valuable tools that WordPerfect provides for writers are automatic footnotes and endnotes. Footnotes and endnotes are used in documents such as theses, articles, and research papers to document the source of quotations, information, and opinions; to include supplemental material; to define terminology; and to cross-reference other parts of the document. Footnotes are printed at the bottom of the page where the reference is made, and endnotes are printed at the end of the document.

WordPerfect greatly simplifies the task of creating, editing, and printing footnotes and endnotes. When you create an endnote or footnote by placing the cursor next to the text you want to reference and selecting Footnote or Endnote from the menu, the program automatically inserts a superscripted note number in your document and moves the cursor into a special screen where you type the text. You don't have to worry about leaving space for your footnotes at the bottom of each page, because WordPerfect automatically calculates the space for you. If you insert or delete a footnote or endnote, WordPerfect automatically renumbers the ones that follow, maintaining the correct numerical order. Footnote text is subtracted from the total number of lines available for regular text, so if you insert, delete, or edit a footnote, WordPerfect adjusts the page, shifting text as necessary to accommodate the change. If a footnote is too long to fit on the page, WordPerfect will print the rest of it on the next page. Since WordPerfect numbers footnotes and endnotes separately, you can use both types in one document. They are both identified in the text by superscripted numbers, but you can distinguish them by changing the numbering method for one type to letters or characters.

While entering the text for a Footnote or Endnote, you can use WordPerfect's regular formatting and editing features, such as the spell checker, the Move and Copy options, Format menu options like margins and line spacing, and Font menu options like bold, underline, and italics. After you finish typing the text, exit back to the Edit screen and continue typing or editing your document. Footnotes and endnotes do not appear in the Edit screen, but you can use View Document to check them.

Creating Footnotes

To practice creating footnotes, type the document shown in Figure 16.1 and follow these steps to create the two footnotes shown at the bottom of the page in Figure 16.2. You can create the footnotes as you type the document, or wait until you've finished and then go back and insert them.

To create the footnotes:

1. Move the cursor to the end of the first paragraph (after the quotation mark that follows `los Angeles`). This is where the first footnote number will appear.

2. Select Footnote:

   Keyboard: Press the Footnote key (Ctrl-F7). This prompt will appear:

   `1 Footnote; 2 Endnote; 3 Endnote Placement: 0`

   Select the first option, **Footnote**. This prompt will appear:

   `Footnote: 1 Create; 2 Edit; 3 New Number; 4 Options: 0`

   Mouse: Display the **Layout** menu and select **Footnote**. Another menu will pop out to the right, as shown in Figure 16.3.

3. Select the first option, **Create**.

   You should see a screen that resembles the Edit screen, except for the footnote number on the first line and the message `Footnote: Press Exit when done` at the bottom, as shown in Figure 16.4. Although WordPerfect formats the footnote number in this screen with superscript, most monitors can't display superscripted characters. Your number may appear in a different color, or highlighted with bold. Notice that the number is indented ½".

 Tip: If you erase the footnote number while using the Footnote screen, you can get it back by pressing the Footnote key (Ctrl-F7) or by pressing Cancel (F1) and selecting Restore.

The Europeans Arrive

When the Spanish explorer, Manuel de Ayala, first scouted San Francisco Bay in 1775, he spent several weeks anchored in a secluded cove on the north side of Angel Island. After abandoning his other anchorages near Sausalito due to poor conditions, he chose what later came to be known as Ayala Cove because it was sheltered from the wind, and because there was plenty of fresh water and firewood available on the island. In his mapping of the Bay, he named the island "Isla de Nuestra Señora de los Angeles".

Over the next few decades, other explorers and sailors used the island for a source of firewood, so that it was often referred to as "Wood Island". It is mentioned in Richard Henry Dana's <u>Two Years Before the Mast</u> as "a small island,...covered with trees to the water's edge,...which, in a week's time, gave us enough wood to last us a year."

Meanwhile, the Russian fur traders, who had established a permanent settlement up at Fort Ross, built a small storage building on Angel Island to hold the sea otter furs they were hunting from San Francisco Bay. It is said that they made an agreement with John Sutter to sell him their equipment when they left.

Figure 16.1 Type this document to practice creating footnotes.

4. Type the text of the first footnote, using underline for the book title:

    Claus, Francis J., <u>Angel Island: Jewel of San Fransisco Bay</u>, Menlo Park, CA, Baircliff Press, 1982.

    Although footnotes are usually brief, WordPerfect allows up to 65,000 bytes for each footnote. This translates into approximately 65,000 characters, probably more than you'll ever need. You can format footnote text like regular text, using features such as line spacing, margins, bold, underline, italics, tab, Base Font, or indent. After typing the footnote text, you can check the spelling by pressing the Spell key (Ctrl-F2) or by selecting Spell from the pulll-down Tools menu.

The Europeans Arrive

When the Spanish explorer, Manuel de Ayala, first scouted San Francisco Bay in 1775, he spent several weeks anchored in a secluded cove on the north side of Angel Island. After abandoning his other anchorages near Sausalito due to poor conditions, he chose what later came to be known as Ayala Cove because it was sheltered from the wind, and because there was plenty of fresh water and firewood available on the island. In his mapping of the Bay, he named the island "Isla de Nuestra Señora de los Angeles".[1]

Over the next few decades, other explorers and sailors used the island for a source of firewood, so that it was often referred to as "Wood Island". It is mentioned in Richard Henry Dana's <u>Two Years Before the Mast</u> as "a small island,...covered with trees to the water's edge,...which, in a week's time, gave us enough wood to last us a year."[2]

Meanwhile, the Russian fur traders, who had established a permanent settlement up at Fort Ross, built a small storage building on Angel Island to hold the sea otter furs they were hunting from San Francisco Bay. It is said that they made an agreement with John Sutter to sell him their equipment when they left.

---

[1] Clauss, Francis J., <u>Angel Island: Jewel of San Francisco Bay</u>, Menlo Park, CA, Baircliff Press, 1982.

[2] Dana, Richard Henry. <u>Two Years Before the Mast</u>, Cleveland, Ohio: World Publishing Company, 1946.

Figure 16.2 *The sample document with two footnotes.*

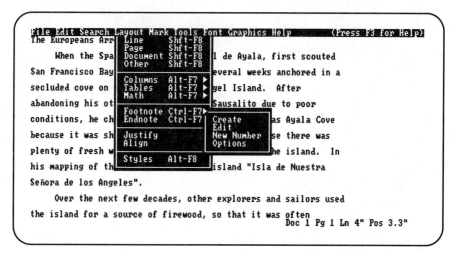

Figure 16.3   *When you select the Footnote option from the Layout menu, this menu appears. Select the first option to create a footnote number, and type the text of the footnote.*

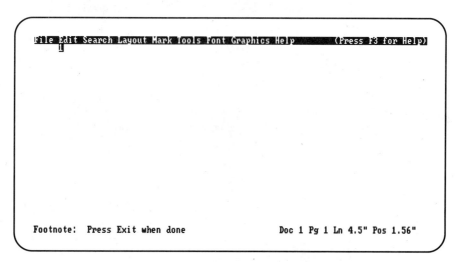

Figure 16.4   *When you ask WordPerfect to create a footnote, this screen appears. Use it to format and type the text of the footnote, which will be printed at the bottom of the page where the number is located.*

5. When you're finished typing and formatting the text of your footnote, return to the Edit screen by pressing the Exit key (F7).

A number will appear as a reference to the footnote, as shown in Figure 16.5. It will be printed in superscript if your printer is capable, but probably won't appear that way on the screen, since most monitors cannot display superscripting.

You cannot see the footnote text at the bottom of the page in the Edit screen. However, the first 50 characters are visible in the Reveal Codes screen, as part of the footnote code, and you can see all of the footnote text in View Document.

6. To see the footnote code:

   Keyboard: Press the Reveal Codes key, Alt-F3.

   Mouse: Display the **E**dit menu and select **R**eveal Codes.

As shown in Figure 16.6, Reveal Codes displays the footnote code, the note number, and some of the text. Since you underlined the book title, you should also see the Underline On code, [UND].

```
File Edit Search Layout Mark Tools Font Graphics Help      (Press F3 for Help)
The Europeans Arrive
     When the Spanish explorer, Manuel de Ayala, first scouted
San Francisco Bay in 1775, he spent several weeks anchored in a
secluded cove on the north side of Angel Island.  After
abandoning his other anchorages near Sausalito due to poor
conditions, he chose what later came to be known as Ayala Cove
because it was sheltered from the wind, and because there was
plenty of fresh water and firewood available on the island.  In
his mapping of the Bay, he named the island "Isla de Nuestra
Señora de los Angeles". ─────────────────────────── Footnote number
     Over the next few decades, other explorers and sailors used
the island for a source of firewood, so that it was often
                                        Doc 1 Pg 1 Ln 4" Pos 3.36"
```

Figure 16.5 When you create a footnote and type the text in the Footnote screen, WordPerfect automatically inserts a footnote number in the document.

To view all of the text of your footnote and see exactly where it will be positioned when printed, you can use the View Document option on the Print menu.

7. Select View Document:

   Keyboard: Press the Print key, Shift-F7.

   Mouse: Display the **F**ile menu and select **P**rint.

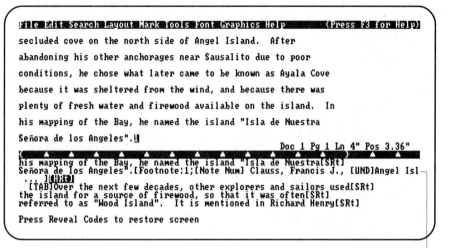

The footnote code, containing the note number, some of its text, and an Underline On code.

Figure 16.6   *The footnote code and part of the footnote text, as seen in the Reveal Codes screen.*

From the main Print menu, select the sixth option, **View Document.** If the Full Page option is in effect, enlarge the page to actual size with the 100% option, so you'll be able to read the text. To move the cursor to the bottom of the page and view the footnote, press Screen Down (Home,Down Arrow or the plus key on the numeric keypad). The footnote will be separated from the rest of the text by one blank line and a 2" horizontal line, and should resemble Figure 16.7. If you use a monochrome monitor that is not equipped with a graphics card, your screen will appear differently but you can still scroll to the bottom of the page and view the footnote.

Tip: Footnotes do not print in the area reserved for the bottom margin. Instead, they reduce the number of text lines on the page.

8. When you finish viewing the footnote, press Exit (F7) to return to the Edit screen.

9. To create the second footnote, move the cursor to the end of the second paragraph and repeat steps 2 through 5.

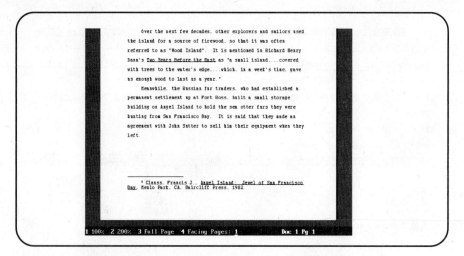

Figure 16.7 The footnote as seen in the View Document screen, using the 100% option.

 Tip: If you have an enhanced keyboard, you can install a special keyboard layout called *SHORTCUT* and use these keystrokes to create footnotes and endnotes: Ctrl-F to create a footnote and Ctrl-E to create an endnote. To install the keyboard, press Setup (Shift-F1) and select the fifth option, Keyboard Layout. A list of keyboards appears (assuming you chose to install them when you installed WordPerfect). Select SHORTCUT and then press Exit.

Creating Endnotes

Endnotes are reference material placed at the end of documents, such as research papers, articles, and theses. Like footnotes, endnotes are referenced in the text with numbers or letters; however, WordPerfect prints endnotes at the end of the document, without a page break. Since WordPerfect numbers endnotes separately from footnotes, you can have both types in a document. However, you should change the numbering scheme for endnotes so that the reader is not confused by two sets of numbers. You'll learn how in the section "Changing Footnote and Endnote Options." Like footnotes, individual endnotes can contain up to 65,000 bytes, roughly 65,000 characters.

Creating and editing an endnote is similar to creating a footnote. Follow these steps to create an endnote:

1. Select Endnote:

   Keyboard: Press the Footnote key (Ctrl-F7) and select the second option, **Endnote.**

   Mouse: Display the **Layout** menu and select **Endnote.** Another menu will pop out to the right, as shown in Figure 16.8.

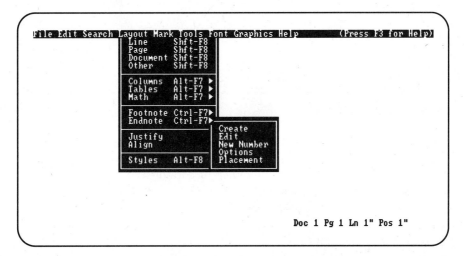

Figure 16.8 *This menu appears when you select the Endnote option from the Layout menu. To create an endnote, select the Create option, type the text, and press Exit.*

2. Select the **Create** option.

   You should now be in the Endnote screen, as shown in Figure 16.9. It is similar to the Footnote screen, except that the note number is not indented or superscripted and is followed by a period.

3. Format and type the text of your endnote.

4. Press Exit (F7) to return to the document.

   The endnote will be referenced by a highlighted number on your screen, which will be superscript in the printed text. Like footnotes, endnotes are not visible in the Edit screen. To view the endnote you just created, you can move the cursor to the end of the document and use the View Document option on the Print menu. Your endnote will appear after the last line of regular text. You can also use the Reveal Codes screen to see the endnote code and up to 50 characters of the text.

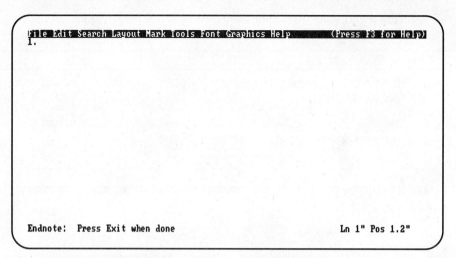

Figure 16.9 *The Endnote screen.*

WordPerfect prints endnotes immediately after the last text in a document. To force WordPerfect to print the endnotes on a new page, you can create a hard page break at the end of a document containing endnotes. You should type a title at the top of the new page, identifying it as the first page of endnotes.

Editing Footnotes or Endnotes

To edit the text of a footnote or endnote, to change the formatting, or just to look at it, use the Edit option on the Footnote or Endnote menu. These options return you to the same Footnote or Endnote screen that you used to create the notes, so you can make any necessary changes.

When you select the Edit option from the Footnote menu, WordPerfect searches to the right of the cursor until it finds the next footnote number, and asks if this is the note you want to edit. If it is, just press Enter. If not, type the number and then press Enter. If the cursor is at the top of the document, WordPerfect will suggest 1 as the number. If there are no footnotes following the cursor position and you press Enter to accept the suggested number, WordPerfect will inform you with a Not found prompt. The Endnote Edit option works identically, except that you select Endnote first, then Edit.

To edit the first footnote in your practice document, begin with the cursor at the top of the document. Next:

1. Select Footnote/Edit:

> **Keyboard:** Press the Footnote key, Ctrl-F7, select **F**ootnote, and then select the second option, **E**dit.

Mouse: Display the Layout menu and select Footnote, then Edit.

This prompt will appear:

```
Footnote number? 1
```

2. Press Enter. This takes you to the Footnote screen, which you used earlier to create the footnote. Use it to remove the underlining and italicize the book title.

3. Turn on Reveal Codes and delete one of the underline codes. Use WordPerfect's Block feature to highlight the book title, *Angel Island: Jewel of San Francisco Bay*, then select italics from the Font Appearance menu.

4. To return to the Edit screen, press Exit (F7).

The cursor should be next to the number of the footnote you just finished editing. If the cursor was somewhere else in the document when you selected the Edit option, you can return to that position by pressing the Go To key (Ctrl-Home) twice.

Deleting a Footnote or Endnote

To erase a footnote or endnote, just delete the code that represents it. This will erase both the number and the footnote or endnote text. WordPerfect will automatically renumber any footnote or endnote numbers that follow it. If you accidentally erase a footnote or endnote, you can use Undelete to restore it.

Practice by deleting the first footnote:

1. Place the cursor on the footnote number, at the end of the first paragraph.

 Tip: You can use WordPerfect's Search feature to locate a footnote or endnote number in your document. To do this, press Search (F2), press the Footnote key (Ctrl-F7), select Footnote or Endnote, and then select Note. A [Footnote] or [Endnote] code will appear in the search string. If you want to change the search direction, press the Up Arrow key. To begin the search, press F2 or Esc. The cursor will stop right after the note, and you can press Backspace to erase it. The Search procedure cannot locate a specific footnote or endnote number, so if you don't find the one you want, repeat the search until you find it.

2. Press the Delete key. This prompt will appear:

   ```
   Delete [Footnote:1]? No (Yes)
   ```

3. Select **Yes**.

   Both the number and footnote text will be deleted. If you can see the paragraph containing the second footnote number, it will immediately change to 1. If not, move the cursor past it, and you should see the number change from 2 to 1. To verify that the text of the first footnote has also been deleted, you may want to check the View Document screen.

4. To restore the deleted footnote and its number, move the cursor back to the end of the first paragraph and use Undelete:

   > **Keyboard:** Press Cancel (F1).

   > **Mouse:** Display the **Edit** menu and select **Undelete**.

   Provided that you haven't deleted anything since the footnote number, you should see this prompt at the bottom of the screen:

   ```
   Undelete: 1 Restore; 2 Previous Deletion:
   ```

   and the footnote number at the cursor position.

5. If the footnote number appears at the cursor position, select **Restore**. If not, select **Previous Deletion** until you see it, and then select **Restore**.

Moving a Footnote or Endnote

In the previous section, you learned how to use Undelete to restore a footnote after erasing it. This is also an easy method of moving a footnote or endnote number to another position in the document—just move the cursor into the new position before selecting Restore. Whenever you move a footnote or endnote number, or a section of text that contains one, WordPerfect will automatically renumber the other notes so that they remain in correct numerical sequence.

Use these steps to move a footnote or endnote number:

1. Place the cursor on the number, press the Delete key, and type Y in response to the prompt asking if you want to delete it.

2. Move the cursor to the new position.

3. Press Cancel (F1). If the number appears at the cursor position, select **Restore**. If not, select **Previous Deletion** until you see it and then select **Restore**.

The deleted note number will reappear in the new position. If any notes follow, WordPerfect will renumber them.

To move a section of text containing a footnote or endnote, use Move, or Block and Move, as described in Chapter 4. The notes will be moved along with the text and correctly renumbered in their new position.

Inserting a Footnote or Endnote

To insert a footnote or endnote, place the cursor in the position where you want to add it, and follow the same procedure that you would use to create a new footnote or endnote. WordPerfect will automatically renumber any note numbers that follow in the document, but it doesn't happen immediately. Instead, each number is changed after you move the cursor past it. You can reformat all the numbers at once by moving the cursor to the end of the document, or by using the Rewrite option on the Screen key, Ctrl-F3 (there is no mouse equivalent).

Renumbering Footnotes or Endnotes

Both the Footnote and Endnote menus include a New Number option that you can use to renumber your footnotes and endnotes. If you split a lengthy document into two or more files, you can use this option to continue the numbering sequence from the first file. Instead of starting with 1 in the second file, you can select the next number in sequence, and WordPerfect will automatically renumber all the notes that follow. For instance, if you use this option to change the first footnote in your practice document to 10, the second footnote will become 11. If there were additional footnotes, they would be renumbered consecutively starting with 12.

To renumber a footnote or endnote, begin with the cursor at the top of the page, or to the left of the first note you want to renumber.

1. Select Footnote or Endnote:

    Keyboard: Press the Footnote key (Ctrl-F7) and select **F**ootnote or **E**ndnote.

    Mouse: Display the **L**ayout menu and select **F**ootnote or **E**ndnote.

2. Select the third option, **N**ew Number.

    If you select Footnote, this prompt will appear:

    `Footnote number?`

If you select Endnote, you'll see this prompt:

`Endnote number?`

3. Type the new number for your next footnote or endnote, and then press Enter.

If the document contains any other footnotes and endnotes, WordPerfect will automatically renumber them after you move the cursor past them. To speed up the process, move the cursor to the end of the document, or use the Rewrite option on the Screen key (Ctrl-F3).

Changing Footnote Options

As with most WordPerfect features, there are many ways that you can customize footnote attributes. For example, you can change the spacing within or between footnotes; remove the line separating text from footnotes, or have it stretch horizontally across the width of the page; change the footnote numbering scheme; or use different formatting for the footnote number. When changing one or more of these attributes, be aware of your cursor position. Like most formatting features, changing footnote options inserts a formatting code in your document. Unless the cursor is at the top of the page, you can't be sure that the changes will affect all footnotes in your document. You won't have this problem if you change your footnote options in Document Initial Codes, because the changes will affect the entire document, regardless of the cursor position.

To change one or more of the footnote options:

1. Begin by placing the cursor at the top of the page or by selecting Initial Codes from the Format Document menu.

2. Select Footnote Options:

    Keyboard: Press the Footnote key (Ctrl-F7), select **Footnote**, and then select the fourth option, **Options**.

    Mouse: Display the Layout menu and choose **Footnote**, then **Options**.

The Footnote Options menu appears, as shown in Figure 16.10.

The first menu selection, Spacing Within Footnotes and Between Footnotes, actually contains two options. The first, Spacing Within Footnotes, is set to single spacing, since this is the most commonly used format for research papers. You can change it by typing any line-spacing increment that your printer is capable of printing, such as 2 for double-spacing, 3 for triple-spacing, .5 for $\frac{1}{2}$", or 1.5 for 1 $\frac{1}{2}$". Since this option affects all footnotes, you can't use it to change the spacing of individual footnotes. Instead, you would have to edit the footnotes one by one and use the Line Spacing option on the Format Line menu. The second part, Spacing Between Footnotes, refers to the amount of blank space between individual footnotes. The default setting is .167", the line height used for a 10-pitch font such as Courier. You can increase or decrease it by any value your printer can handle. Increasing either of these options will reduce the number of lines available for text on each page.

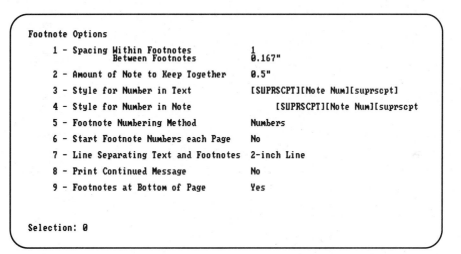

```
Footnote Options
       1 - Spacing Within Footnotes            1
                   Between Footnotes           0.167"
       2 - Amount of Note to Keep Together     0.5"
       3 - Style for Number in Text            [SUPRSCPT][Note Num][suprscpt]
       4 - Style for Number in Note                     [SUPRSCPT][Note Num][suprscpt
       5 - Footnote Numbering Method           Numbers
       6 - Start Footnote Numbers each Page     No
       7 - Line Separating Text and Footnotes  2-inch Line
       8 - Print Continued Message             No
       9 - Footnotes at Bottom of Page          Yes


   Selection: 0
```

Figure 16.10   *The Footnote Options menu.*

 Tip: If you change your footnote options in Document Initial Codes, the changes will affect the entire document, regardless of the cursor position.

You can use the second option on the Footnote Options menu, Amount of Note to Keep Together, to adjust the number of lines that WordPerfect will keep together in a footnote if it must be split between two pages. This option only affects a footnote if it is near the end of the page. The default setting is $\frac{1}{2}$", so WordPerfect tries to keep at least $\frac{1}{2}$" of the footnote on the same page as the text that it references. If it can't, both the footnote and the text containing the reference number will be moved to the next page. If the footnote text is too long to fit on one page, you'll know while typing it, because a page break will appear in the Footnote screen. Everything below the line representing the page break will be printed on the next page in the document.

The third and fourth options on the Footnote Options menu affect the appearance of the footnote numbers in the printed text. The program is set up to print the numbers in superscript, but you can change the formatting to bold, underline, italics, or any other font attributes your printer can handle, or identify them using characters such as brackets. You can use the third option to change the appearance of the footnote number in the text, and the fourth to change it in the footnote itself. For example, if your printer can't print superscript and you want to change both numbers to bold, follow these steps:

1. Select the third option, Style for Number in Text. This prompt appears:

   ```
   Replace with: [SUPRSCPT][Note Num][suprscpt]
   ```

   The first and last code represent superscript on and off, and [Note Num] represents the footnote number. If you accidentally erase the [Note Num] code, press Footnote (Ctrl-F7) and select Footnote, then Number Code.

2. Press Delete once to erase the Superscript On code, [SUPRSCPT]. Press the Bold key (F6) once to insert a Bold On code, [BOLD].

3. Move the cursor onto the Superscript Off code, [suprscpt], and press Delete to erase it. Press the Bold key to insert the Bold Off code, [bold]. When you finish, the prompt should appear as follows:

   ```
   Replace with: [BOLD][Note Num][bold]
   ```

4. Press Enter to implement the change.

5. Select the fourth option, Style for Number in Note.

6. In the footnote itself, the number is indented five spaces, so your first step is to move the cursor onto the [SUPRSCPT] code. After that, just repeat steps 2 through 4 to change the style to bold.

7. When you finish using the Footnote Options screen, press Enter to implement the changes.

You can use the fifth option, Footnote Numbering Method, to change the footnote numbering style. This is useful if you type both footnotes and endnotes in the same document. Instead of using numbers to identify the footnotes or endnotes, you can use letters or other characters such as asterisks. An identical option is available in the Endnote Options menu. If you select letters, WordPerfect uses lowercase letters in sequential order: a, b, c, d, etc. If you select characters, WordPerfect lets you enter one to five characters. If you type one character, such as an asterisk, one asterisk will represent the first footnote, two asterisks will represent the second, three will represent the third, etc. If you select several characters, such as an asterisk, pound sign (#), and tilde (~), the first footnote will be represented by one asterisk, the second by one pound sign, and the third by one tilde. The fourth will be two asterisks, the fifth two pound signs, etc. The scheme is as follows:

```
Footnote 1: *    Footnote 4: **    Footnote 7: ***
Footnote 2: #    Footnote 5: ##    Footnote 8: ###
Footnote 3: ~    Footnote 6: ~~    Footnote 9: ~~~
```

Tip: If you don't wish to use one of the characters on the regular keyboard for the Footnote Numbering Method, you can use the Compose key, Ctrl-2, to select a character from one of WordPerfect's 12 character sets. See *Compose Key* in Part Three, "Command Reference," for more information.

If you're using characters to represent footnotes, you may want to change the next option, Start Footnote Numbers each Page, to Yes. By default, WordPerfect numbers footnotes sequentially throughout the document. If you change this option to Yes, WordPerfect will start the numbering sequence over on each page, so that the first footnote on each page will always be 1, a, or the first character you've selected for the numbering method.

If you don't like the line that WordPerfect prints at the bottom of the page to separate text from footnotes, use the seventh option, Line Separating Text and Footnotes, to remove or change it. By default, WordPerfect prints a 2" line above the footnote text, as shown in Figure 16.2. You can select No line to remove it, or Margin to Margin to extend the line all the way to the right margin.

If any of your footnotes have to be split between pages, you can use the eighth option, Print Continued Message, to have WordPerfect print a continued notice on both pages. By default, the option is set to No. If you change it to Yes, WordPerfect will print this message below the last line of the footnote being split:

```
(continued...)
```

and this message above the first footnote line on the next page:

```
(...continued)
```

The last option on the Footnote Options menu is Footnotes at Bottom of Page. By default, WordPerfect prints footnotes at the bottom of the page, regardless of how much text is on the page. If the page isn't full, WordPerfect will leave several blank lines between the last line of text and the first footnote, as shown in Figure 16.11. If you select this option and change it to No, WordPerfect will leave only two blank lines after the text and then print the footnotes. Figure 16.12 shows the difference.

 Tip: Once you insert a Footnote Option code in a document, WordPerfect will reformat any footnotes that follow, to include any formatting changes you've made in the document up to that point. For instance, if you change the left and right margins to 1.5" each at the top of the document, then insert a Footnote Option code, all footnotes will have 1.5" margins.

The Europeans Arrive

When the Spanish explorer, Manuel de Ayala, first scouted San Francisco Bay in 1775, he spent several weeks anchored in a secluded cove on the north side of Angel Island. After abandoning his other anchorages near Sausalito due to poor conditions, he chose what later came to be known as Ayala Cove because it was sheltered from the wind, and because there was plenty of fresh water and firewood available on the island. In his mapping of the Bay, he named the island "Isla de Nuestra Señora de los Angeles".[1]

Over the next few decades, other explorers and sailors used the island for a source of firewood, so that it was often referred to as "Wood Island". It is mentioned in Richard Henry Dana's <u>Two Years Before the Mast</u> as "a small island,...covered with trees to the water's edge,...which, in a week's time, gave us enough wood to last us a year."[2]

---

[1] Clauss, Francis J., <u>Angel Island: Jewel of San Francisco Bay</u>, Menlo Park, CA, Baircliff Press, 1982.

[2] Dana, Richard Henry. <u>Two Years Before the Mast</u>, Cleveland, Ohio: World Publishing Company, 1946.

Figure 16.11 *WordPerfect prints footnotes at the bottom of the page, regardless of how much text is on the page. You can change this using the Footnote Options menu. Figure 16.12 shows the difference.*

The Europeans Arrive

   When the Spanish explorer, Manuel de Ayala, first scouted San Francisco Bay in 1775, he spent several weeks anchored in a secluded cove on the north side of Angel Island. After abandoning his other anchorages near Sausalito due to poor conditions, he chose what later came to be known as Ayala Cove because it was sheltered from the wind, and because there was plenty of fresh water and firewood available on the island. In his mapping of the Bay, he named the island "Isla de Nuestra Señora de los Angeles".[1]

   Over the next few decades, other explorers and sailors used the island for a source of firewood, so that it was often referred to as "Wood Island". It is mentioned in Richard Henry Dana's <u>Two Years Before the Mast</u> as "a small island,...covered with trees to the water's edge,...which, in a week's time, gave us enough wood to last us a year."[2]

---

   [1] Clauss, Francis J., <u>Angel Island: Jewel of San Francisco Bay</u>, Menlo Park, CA, Baircliff Press, 1982.

   [2] Dana, Richard Henry. <u>Two Years Before the Mast</u>, Cleveland, Ohio: World Publishing Company, 1946.

Figure 16.12   *If you use the Footnote Options menu to change the Footnotes at Bottom of Page option to No, WordPerfect will separate footnote text from the document by only two blank lines. Contrast this with Figure 16.11.*

Changing Endnote Options

WordPerfect provides five options on the Endnote Options screen, as shown in Figure 16.13. As you can see, they are identical to the first five options on the Footnote Options menu. The first option controls the spacing within and between endnotes. Unless you change the defaults, endnotes will be printed single-spaced and separated from each other by .167". The second option controls the amount of an endnote that WordPerfect will keep at the bottom of the page, if it is the last one on the page and is too long to fit on the page. The third and fourth options control the way endnotes are printed. Unless you change the defaults, endnote numbers in the text are printed in superscript, but the numbers in the endnotes themselves are not superscripted and are followed by a period. The last option determines the way endnotes are identified. By default, endnotes are identified by numbers. As described in the previous section, you can change them to letters or characters.

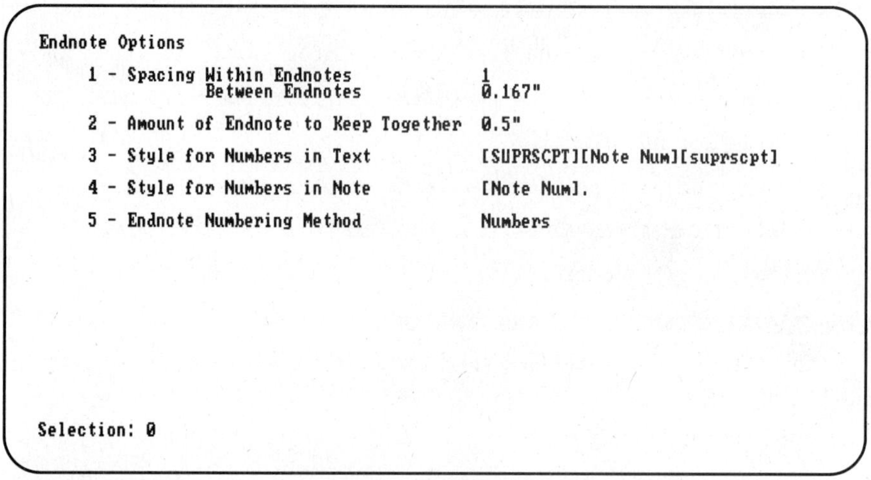

```
Endnote Options
    1 - Spacing Within Endnotes          1
              Between Endnotes           0.167"
    2 - Amount of Endnote to Keep Together   0.5"
    3 - Style for Numbers in Text        [SUPRSCPT][Note Num][suprscpt]
    4 - Style for Numbers in Note        [Note Num].
    5 - Endnote Numbering Method         Numbers




Selection: 0
```

Figure 16.13   *The Endnote Options menu.*

How Formatting Changes in a Document Affect Footnotes and Endnotes

Unless you change the formatting in individual footnotes or endnotes, WordPerfect follows the default formatting specified in Initial Codes and prints the notes using the document's Initial Base Font. Changing the font or other formatting in the document will not change the footnote or endnote text unless the formatting code is followed by a Footnote or Endnote Options code. For example, changing margins using the Format Line menu or changing the font using the Base Font option on the Font menu will not affect your footnotes or endnotes. To extend the formatting changes to your footnotes or endnotes, place the cursor after the format code (or codes), select Footnote Options or Endnote Options and press Enter. It is not necessary to make any changes in the Options menu, because WordPerfect will insert a [Ftn Opt] or [End Opt] code in your document, regardless of whether you change anything.

Changing Endnote Placement

By default, WordPerfect prints all endnotes at the end of the document, immediately following the last text, but you can change this using the Endnote Placement option. For example, you could use it to print endnotes at the end of each section, or after each chapter. The option inserts an Endnote Placement code at the cursor position, and forces a hard page break so the endnotes will be printed on a separate page from the text that follows. All notes between the Endnote Placement code and the beginning of the document are printed at the code position. If there is a previous Endnote Placement code above it, only the endnotes between the two codes will be printed. When you use the option, WordPerfect also asks if you want to renumber the endnotes that follow, or continue with the next number in sequence.

To change endnote placement, begin by moving the cursor to the position where you want the first group of endnotes printed.

1. Select Endnote Placement:

   Keyboard: Press the Footnote key, Ctrl-F7. Select the third option, Endnote **Placement.**

   Mouse: Display the **L**ayout menu, select **E**ndnote, and then select the last option, **P**lacement.

   This prompt will appear:

   `Restart endnote numbering? Yes (No)`

   If you select Yes, the numbering scheme will start over, and the next endnote after the code will be 1. If you select No, the numbers will continue in the same sequence.

2. Select **Y**es or **N**o.

   WordPerfect inserts an Endnote Placement code and a hard page break, which is represented by a line of dashes. A boxed message that represents the Endnote Placement code appears above the hard page break, as shown in Figure 16.14. The message warns you that WordPerfect has not yet allocated any space for your endnotes, in case you want to edit, move, insert, or delete any before printing. When you are ready to determine their placement in the printed document, and see how it affects the other text on the page, you can generate the endnotes.

```
┌─────────────────────────────────────────────────────────────────┐
│ File Edit Search Layout Mark Tools Font Graphics Help   (Press F3 for Help) │
│ Señora de los Angeles".▌                                          │
│                                                                   │
│     Over the next few decades, other explorers and sailors used   │
│ the island for a source of firewood, so that it was often         │
│ referred to as "Wood Island".  It is mentioned in Richard Henry   │
│ Dana's Two Years Before the Mast as "a small island,...covered    │
│ with trees to the water's edge,...which, in a week's time, gave   │
│ us enough wood to last us a year."▌                               │
│ ┌───────────────────────────────────────────────────────────────┐ │
│ │ Endnote Placement                                             │ │
│ │ It is not known how much space endnotes will occupy here.     │ │
│ │ Generate to determine.                                        │ │
│ │                                                               │ │
│ └───────────────────────────────────────────────────────────────┘ │
│ ================================================================  │
│                                    Doc 1 Pg 2 Ln 1" Pos 1"        │
└─────────────────────────────────────────────────────────────────┘
```

Figure 16.14   *When you use the Endnote Placement option, WordPerfect inserts a hard page break and this boxed message (representing the Endnote Placement code), which reminds you that the endnotes may require more space on the page. To determine exactly how much they will need, you can use the Generate option on the Mark Text menu.*

To generate the endnotes:

1. Select Generate:

   Keyboard: Press the Mark Text key, Alt-F5. Select the sixth option, **Generate.**

   Mouse: Display the **Mark** menu and select **Generate.**

   The Mark Text Generate menu appears.

2. Select the fifth option, **Generate Tables, Indexes, Cross References, etc.** A prompt appears asking if you want to continue.

3. Select **Yes.** After WordPerfect generates the space for the endnotes, the boxed message reappears, reduced to this prompt:

   Endnote Placement

The text of the endnotes does not appear on the Edit screen, but you can tell how many lines they will use by placing the cursor under the box and observing the line number indicator (Ln) on the status line. If the notes are too long to fit on this page, the page number will also change.

If you want to continue typing text right after the endnotes, you can delete the hard page break. However, unless you locate the Endnote Placement code and enter a hard return after it, the text will be printed above the endnotes, not below them.

Converting Footnotes into Endnotes or Endnotes into Footnotes

WordPerfect comes with two macros that you can use to change your footnotes into endnotes, or endnotes into footnotes. To convert all footnotes into endnotes, press the Macro key (Alt-F10) and type FOOTEND. To change all endnotes into footnotes, press the Macro key (Alt-F10) and type ENDFOOT. It doesn't matter where the cursor is located when you use these macros, because the cursor will move to the top of the document before searching for notes to convert. If you see a File not found message when you try to use one of these macros, you probably didn't install them when you installed WordPerfect. Turn to Appendix A for information on installation.

Another method you can use to convert footnotes into endnotes is to define newspaper columns at the top of the document, turn them on, and move the cursor to the end of the document to reformat all the text into columns. Since WordPerfect doesn't allow footnotes in text columns, it will automatically convert all your footnotes into endnotes. Once this has been done, you can delete the Column Definition code at the top and reformat the document again.

OUTLINING AND PARAGRAPH NUMBERING TOOLS

Composing a document such as a report, thesis, article, or book is rarely easy. Even professional writers are known to experience so-called writer's block, and many writers procrastinate until someone imposes a deadline on them. As an antidote, it really helps to be organized and prepared, as our high-school English teachers were so fond of drilling into us. Because outlines are indispensable tools for organizing your ideas and preparing yourself for a writing project, WordPerfect offers two methods for creating and managing outlines: outlining and paragraph numbering.

WordPerfect's outlining tools provide an automatic numbering system that you can use to insert automatic paragraph numbers at different levels, such as I, II, and III for Level 1, and A, B, and C for Level 2. These numbers will automatically change as you edit the outline, and move, copy, delete, or insert sections of text that include automatic paragraph numbers. For instance, in the sample outline shown in Figure 17.1, if the three paragraphs under IC ("Most efficient harvest method," "Provides maximum employment potential," and "Activity is concentrated") were moved and inserted above section A, WordPerfect would renumber it and all the automatic paragraph numbers in section I, as shown in Figure 17.2. You would not have to scroll through the document and change them yourself. If you are in the habit of writing from an outline, you'll appreciate this feature immediately, because you know that an outline is rarely static.

Clearcutting Old Growth Forests

I. Economic Advantages
    A. Highest yield per acre
    B. Best quality of wood
    C. Most efficient harvest method
        1. Provides maximum employment potential
        2. Activity is concentrated
    D. Easiest to replant and manage -- old growth canopy has limited underbrush growth

II. Environmental Impact
    A. Initial site disturbance
        1. Wildlife displaced, including endangered species
        2. Recreational/aesthetic value destroyed
    B. Topsoil exposed and eroded
        1. Siltation of riverbeds
            a. Impact on fisheries
            b. Degradation of water quality
        2. Greater susceptibility to disease
        3. Replanting creates mono-culture forest

III. Solutions
    A. Eliminate clearcutting
        1. Cut selectively to develop sustained yield
    B. Logging closures
        1. In sensitive wildlife areas
        2. On steep terrain/watersheds
    C. Economic mitigation
        1. Stress sustained yield = sustained employment
        2. Increased recreational/tourism potential
        3. Restructure U.S. Forest Service receipts
        4. Fisheries economy rejuvenated

Figure 17.1   *An outline that uses the default formatting style for the automatic paragraph numbers: Roman numerals for the first level, uppercase letters for the second level, and Arabic numbers for the third. This paragraph numbering format is called Outline.*

Using WordPerfect's Paragraph Numbering Feature

WordPerfect's Paragraph Numbering feature is useful and time-saving, and it is not an exaggeration to say that it is easy to use. In fact, to insert an automatic paragraph number at the left margin, all you have to do is position the cursor there and:

1. Select the Paragraph Number option:

    Keyboard: Press Date/Outline (Shift-F5) and select the **Para Num** option.

    Mouse: Display the **T**ools menu and select **P**aragraph Number.

Clearcutting Old Growth Forests

I. Economic Advantages
   A. Most efficient harvest method
         1. Provides maximum employment potential
         2. Activity is concentrated
   B. Highest yield per acre
   C. Best quality of wood
   D. Easiest to replant and manage -- old growth canopy has limited underbrush growth

II. Environmental Impact
   A. Initial site disturbance
         1. Wildlife displaced, including endangered species
         2. Recreational/aesthetic value destroyed
   B. Topsoil exposed and eroded
         1. Siltation of riverbeds
               a. Impact on fisheries
               b. Degradation of water quality
         2. Greater susceptibility to disease
         3. Replanting creates mono-culture forest

III. Solutions
   A. Eliminate clearcutting
         1. Cut selectively to develop sustained yield
   B. Logging closures
         1. In sensitive wildlife areas
         2. On steep terrain/watersheds
   C. Economic mitigation
         1. Stress sustained yield = sustained employment
         2. Increased recreational/tourism potential
         3. Restructure U.S. Forest Service receipts
         4. Fisheries economy rejuvenated

Figure 17.2   *In this version of the outline shown in Figure 17.1, the three paragraphs under heading IC were moved and inserted above section IA, and WordPerfect automatically renumbered them and the other letters (A, B, and C) in the section, to reflect their new position in the outline.*

This prompt will appear:

```
Paragraph Level (Press Enter for Automatic):
```

2. **Press Enter or click the right mouse button. This inserts a Roman numeral I, followed by a period:**

```
I.
```

to represent a Level 1 paragraph number.

When you create an outline, regardless of which of the two methods you use (the Paragraph Number option or the Outline option), WordPerfect uses a default numbering style for each level; this scheme is called the *Outline* format. The first level is defined as any automatic paragraph number that you insert at the left margin position; in WordPerfect's default paragraph numbering scheme, Roman numerals are used for this level, as you have just seen. These numbers are inserted in ascending numeric order: I, II, III, etc., as shown in Figure 17.1. The second level, any automatic paragraph number that you insert after pressing the Tab, Indent, or Left/Right Indent key, is represented by uppercase letters: A, B, C, etc. The third level is an automatic paragraph number that you insert at the second tab stop position, after indenting twice using any combination of the Tab, Indent, or Left/Right Indent keys. Level 3 is represented by Arabic numbers: 1, 2, 3, etc. This scheme continues for up to eight levels of automatic paragraph numbers, each designated by a different style of letters and numbers. Table 17.1 illustrates the formatting scheme.

***Table 17.1** The Outline format.*

Level 1:	Uppercase Roman numerals followed by a period	I. II. III. IV. V. VI. VII. VIII. IX. X. ad infinitum
Level 2:	Uppercase letters followed by a period	A. B. C. D. E. F. G. H. I. J. ad infinitum
Level 3:	Arabic numbers followed by a period	1. 2. 3. 4. 5. 6. 7. 8. 9. 10. ad infinitum
Level 4:	Lowercase letters followed by a period	a. b. c. d. e. f. g. h. i. j. ad infinitum
Level 5:	Parenthesized numbers	(1) (2) (3) (4) (5) (6) (7) (8) (9) (10) ad infinitum
Level 6:	Parenthesized lowercase letters	(a) (b) (c) (d) (e) (f) (g) (h) (i) (j) ad infinitum
Level 7:	Lowercase Roman numerals followed by a closing parenthesis	i) ii) iii) iv) v) vi) vii) viii) ix) x) ad infinitum
Level 8:	Lowercase letters followed by a closing parenthesis	a) b) c) d) e) f) g) h) i) j) ad infinitum

Later in this chapter you'll learn how to change this default numbering format. As you'll see, you can make up your own numbering scheme, representing the different levels by any letter, number, bullet, or other symbol that you want to use (as long as your printer is capable of printing it).

An outline with four levels is illustrated in Figure 17.1. As you can see, the Level 1 headings are:

    I.   Economic Advantages

    II. Environmental Impact

    III. Solutions

Level 2 headings include the following, under heading I:

A. Highest yield per acre

B. Best quality of wood

C. Most efficient harvest method

D. Easiest to replant and manage

Level 3 headings include the following, under heading IC:

   1. Provides maximum employment potential

   2. Activity is concentrated

Level 4 headings include the following, under IIB1:

a. Impact on fisheries

b. Degradation of water quality

    Use the following instructions to create the outline shown in Figure 17.1, using the Paragraph Numbering option. This method is easier to work with than the Outline option, and will provide an introduction to many of the concepts that are common to both tools.

    Begin with a blank Edit screen. Turn on center and boldface, and type the title: `Clearcutting Old Growth Forests`. Next:

  1. Insert an automatic paragraph number at the first level:

> **Keyboard:** Press Date/Outline (Shift-F5) and select the **Para Num** option. In response to the `Paragraph Level` prompt, press Enter.

> **Mouse:** Display the **Tools** menu and select **Paragraph Number**. In response to the `Paragraph Level` prompt, click the right mouse button.

> This should have inserted I. at the cursor position. In the Reveal Codes screen, you'll see that it is actually a code:

`[Par Num:Auto]`

 Tip: Instead of pressing Enter in step 1, you can create your own paragraph level by typing your own number, such as 1, 2, or 3. This procedure is not advisable though, because if you move such a number to another tab stop position, WordPerfect will not be able to convert it to represent the new level. In other words, if you type a 2 in response to the `Paragraph Level (Press Enter for Automatic)` prompt (creating a Level 2 paragraph number) and then press Tab twice, the number will remain as a Level 2 entry (such as A, B, or C).

2. Press the space bar once, and type the first heading:

```
Economic Advantages
```

Press Enter to end the paragraph, and move the cursor to the next line.

3. Press Indent (F4) or Tab to indent to the second level; then follow the instructions in step 1 to insert another automatic paragraph number. Next, press the space bar and type:

```
Highest yield per acre
```

and press Enter.

4. Press Indent (F4) or Tab, and then follow the instructions in step 1 to insert another automatic paragraph number at Level 2. Press the space bar and type:

```
Best quality of wood
```

and press Enter.

5. Press Indent (F4) or Tab, and then follow the instructions in step 1 to insert another automatic paragraph number. Next, press the space bar and type:

```
Most efficient harvest method
```

and press Enter.

6. Press Indent (F4) or Tab twice, and then follow the instructions in step 1 to insert an automatic paragraph number at Level 3. Press the space bar and type:

```
Provides maximum employment potential
```

and press Enter.

7. Repeat step 6 to insert another paragraph number at Level 3. Press the space bar and type:

```
Activity is concentrated
```

and press Enter.

In the next entry (D), the entire paragraph should wrap to the indented position. To achieve this, use the Indent key instead of the Tab key:

8. Press Indent (F4) and follow the instructions in step 1 to insert another automatic paragraph number. Type:

```
Easiest to replant and manage—old growth canopy has lim-
ited underbrush growth
```

and press Enter.

Tip: To insert an automatic paragraph number at a level other than Level 1, begin by pressing Tab, Indent (F4), or Left/Right Indent (Shift-F4) to move the cursor to the appropriate level; then have WordPerfect insert the automatic paragraph number. The Tab key indents only the first line, while the Indent key indents the entire paragraph from the left margin. The Left/Right Indent key also indents the entire paragraph, but indents it from both the left and right margins.

That completes the first section of the outline, under Roman numeral I. You should now be able to insert automatic paragraph numbers and type the second and third sections, "Environmental Impact" and "Solutions," following the guidelines just given. Table 17.2 summarizes the instructions to insert automatic paragraph numbers:

Table 17.2   *Instructions for inserting automatic paragraph numbers.*

Level 1:	**Keyboard:** Press Date/Outline (Shift-F5) and select the **Para Num** option. In response to the `Paragraph Level` prompt, press Enter.
	Mouse: Display the **T**ools menu and select **P**aragraph Number. In response to the Paragraph Level prompt, click the right mouse button.
Level 2:	Press Tab, Indent, or Left/Right Indent so that the cursor is at the first tab stop from the left margin; then follow the Level 1 instructions to insert an automatic paragraph number.
Level 3:	Press Tab, Indent, or Left/Right Indent twice, so that the cursor is at the second tab stop from the left margin; then follow the Level 1 instructions to insert an automatic paragraph number.
Level 4:	Press Tab, Indent, or Left/Right Indent three times, so that the cursor is at the third tab stop from the left margin; then follow the Level 1 instructions to insert an automatic paragraph number.
Level 5:	Press Tab, Indent, or Left/Right Indent four times, so that the cursor is at the fourth tab stop from the left margin; then follow the Level 1 instructions to insert an automatic paragraph number.

continued

Table 17.2 *(continued)*

Level 6: Press Tab, Indent, or Left/Right Indent five times, so that the cursor is at the fifth tab stop from the left margin; then follow the Level 1 instructions to insert an automatic paragraph number.

Level 7: Press Tab, Indent, or Left/Right Indent six times, so that the cursor is at the sixth tab stop from the left margin; then follow the Level 1 instructions to insert an automatic paragraph number.

Level 8: Press Tab, Indent, or Left/Right Indent seven times, so that the cursor is at the seventh tab stop from the left margin; then follow the Level 1 instructions to insert an automatic paragraph number.

When you finish typing the outline, save it under the name: *CLEARCUT.OUT*. After saving it, you can experiment with your sample outline, inserting, deleting, and moving paragraph numbers and their text, as instructed in the following section. Only then will you understand how useful WordPerfect's Outline and Paragraph Numbering features really are, because in the real world, an outline is rarely static.

Editing an Outline

Begin by adding another Level 1 paragraph number between the existing ones. After you rewrite the screen, you'll see the paragraph numbers that follow it change automatically.

1. Place the cursor in the blank line above the heading II. Environmental Impact and follow the instructions in the previous section to insert another automatic paragraph number.

2. To rewrite the screen, either move the cursor to the end of the document or press the Screen key (Ctrl-F3), and select **Rewrite** (there is no mouse equivalent of the Rewrite option).

This allows WordPerfect to rewrite the Edit screen and update the other Level 1 automatic paragraph numbers. The automatic paragraph number next to Environmental Impact should have changed to III, and the one next to Solutions should have changed to IV.

Deleting a paragraph from the outline will also change the automatic paragraph numbers that follow. To try it:

1. Place the cursor at the left margin of the first Level 2 paragraph (A. Highest yield per acre) and press Ctrl-End to delete it.

Notice that WordPerfect has changed the letters next to the other three paragraphs in section I. These automatic paragraph numbers used to be B, C, and D; now they are A, B, and C.

If you move a paragraph or section of the outline, WordPerfect will also renumber the ones that follow. Follow these instructions to move the "Environmental Impact" section and position it after the "Solutions" section:

1. Place the cursor in the blank line above Environmental Impact. **Press** the Backspace key to delete the II you created earlier (if you did create it).

2. To move the section:

    Keyboard: Press Block (Alt-F4), move the cursor down to the blank line under the last paragraph (Replanting creates mono-culture forest), and then press Move (Ctrl-F4). Select the **Block** option and then the **Move** option.

    Mouse: Click the left button to turn on Block mode, and hold it while you move the cursor to the end of the section; then release the button. Display the **Edit** menu and select **Move**.

3. To reinsert the section below the "Solutions" section: Move the cursor to the blank line under the "Solutions" section, and press Enter.

Notice that this only changes the Level 1 automatic paragraph numbers: the II that was next to Environmental Impact has changed to a III, and the III that was next to Solutions has become a II. The automatic paragraph numbers at other levels, such as A, B, 1, 2, a, and b, remain the same in both sections.

Using WordPerfect's Outline Feature

WordPerfect's Outline feature is similar to its Paragraph Numbering feature in that both techniques insert Paragraph Number codes, which WordPerfect will change as you move, copy, delete, and insert other automatic paragraph numbers. The real difference in the two options is the keystrokes that you use to insert the numbers, and change them to other levels. Once you turn on the Outline feature, WordPerfect changes the function of three keys: Enter, Tab, and Margin Release. As you'll see:

*   Pressing Enter inserts an automatic paragraph number. Pressing Enter twice in succession inserts an automatic paragraph number, and then moves it and the cursor to the next line.

*   Pressing Tab immediately after inserting an automatic paragraph number (by pressing Enter) moves the number to the next level.

- Pressing Shift-Tab (the Margin Release combination) immediately after inserting an automatic paragraph number moves the number back to the previous level.

To familiarize yourself with WordPerfect's Outline feature, follow these instructions to type the outline shown in Figure 17.1 (the same one you used earlier, while studying the Paragraph Number option). Begin by clearing the Edit screen and typing the title.

To turn on WordPerfect's Outline feature:

1. Select Outline:

    Keyboard: Press the Date/Outline key, Shift-F5. Select the fourth option, **Outline.**

    The following menu will appear:

    ```
    Outline: 1 On; 2 Off, 3 Move Family; 4 Copy Family;
    5 Delete Family: 0
    ```

    Mouse: Access the **Tools** pull-down menu and choose **Outline.** The Outline menu will pop out to the right, as shown in Figure 17.3.

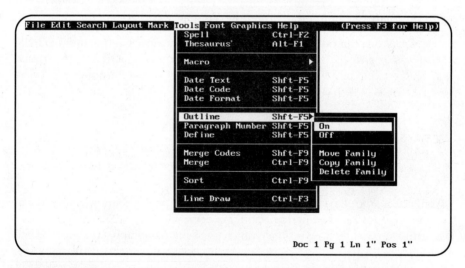

Figure 17.3 *When you select Outline from the pull-down Tools menu, this menu pops out to the right.*

2. Select the first option, **On.**

An Outline prompt will appear in the lower-left corner of the screen, to indicate that you have turned on Outline mode. Remember, pressing Enter when Outline is on will insert an automatic paragraph number at the cursor position. This can be disconcerting, especially if you are trying to use the Enter key to insert a blank line. There is a solution to this dilemma: If you press the Ctrl-V combination before pressing Enter, WordPerfect will insert a blank line, instead of an automatic paragraph number.

 Tip: When the Outline feature is on, pressing Enter inserts an automatic paragraph number. You can press Enter without inserting an automatic paragraph number by pressing the Ctrl-V combination first and then pressing Enter. If you really dislike this feature, you can turn it off by changing the seventh option on the Paragraph Number Definition menu, *Enter Inserts Paragraph Number*, to No (Shift-F5 D E N).

To create the first section of the outline, under the heading "Economic Advantages," follow these steps:

1. Press the Enter key. This inserts a [Para Num:Auto] code, visible in Reveal Codes, and represented on the Edit screen by an *I*. The fact that it is an automatic paragraph number, represented by *Auto* in the code, means that:

   WordPerfect will automatically renumber it as necessary, to accommodate editing changes such as inserting, deleting, or moving other paragraphs that contain automatic paragraph numbers.

   If you move the number to another tab stop position, it will change to represent the new level. For instance, if you were to press Tab now, the I would be converted into an A. (If you do try this, press Shift-Tab to return it to the previous level.)

2. Press the space bar and then type this heading: `Economic Advantages`.

 Tip: When Outline is on, pressing Enter inserts an automatic paragraph number. Before typing, either press the space bar, Home-Tab, Indent (F4), or Left/Right Indent (Shift-F4). If you press Enter immediately after inserting an automatic paragraph number, without typing or pressing any other keys, both the number and the cursor will move to the next line.

3. Press the Enter key.

   A Roman numeral II will appear. In the next step, you'll move it to the next level, and convert it into an A.

4. Press the Tab key.

Both the cursor and the automatic paragraph number move to the right one tab stop position. Notice that the II has been converted into an A, the numbering style used to represent a Level 2 paragraph number.

As you have just seen, when Outline is on, the Tab key works differently. If you press Tab immediately after pressing Enter to insert an automatic paragraph number, WordPerfect moves both the cursor and the automatic paragraph number to the next tab stop position and automatically converts the number to the next level. If you want to move the cursor one or more tab stops to the right without moving and converting the automatic paragraph number, use the Indent (F4) key, the Left/Right Indent (Shift-F4) key, or press the space bar once and then press the Tab key. You can also press the Home-Tab combination after the paragraph number, which creates a *hard tab code*. This will move the cursor to the next tab stop position, without changing the level of the automatic paragraph number.

5. Press the space bar once, and then type the next paragraph: Highest Yield Per Acre.

Tip: If you press the Tab key too many times while using the Outline feature, you can move the cursor and automatic paragraph number back to the previous tab stop by pressing the Margin Release combination, Shift-Tab.

6. Press the Enter key.

   Another Level 2 automatic paragraph number (B) appears at the cursor position, because WordPerfect assumes you want to continue inserting paragraph numbers on the same level as the previous entry.

7. Press the space bar and type the next paragraph: Best quality of wood.

8. Press the Enter key, to insert the next automatic paragraph number: C. Press the space bar, and type the next paragraph: Most efficient harvest method.

9. Press Enter and then press Tab.

   WordPerfect inserts another automatic paragraph number and moves it to the next level. This level is represented by Arabic numbers, 1 in this case.

10. Press the space bar once, and then type the next paragraph: Provides maximum employment potential.

11. Press the Enter key to insert a 2. Press the space bar and type: `Activity is concentrated.`

12. Press the Enter key.

    Since WordPerfect assumes you want to continue inserting automatic paragraph numbers on the same level, a 3 is inserted. However, the next automatic paragraph number is supposed to be on the second level (D). To move it back:

13. Press the Margin Release combination: Shift-Tab. This moves the automatic paragraph number to the previous tab stop, and converts it to Level 2. It should now appear as a D on the Edit screen.

14. Press the space bar and type the next paragraph:

    `Easiest to replant and manage—old growth canopy has limited underbrush growth`

    Notice that instead of wrapping to the indented position under the D, as in Figure 17.1, the second line of the paragraph returns to the left margin. To change it, you can erase the tab before the D, and replace it with an Indent (by pressing F4). Tip: If you turn on Reveal Codes, this task will be easy.

    To continue, place the cursor in the blank space after the period following the word growth, and then:

15. Press the Enter key.

    This inserts an E. However, the outline in Figure 17.1 does not include an E in the first section. Instead, this should be a blank line, and the line below it should begin with a II (the first automatic paragraph number of the next section).

16. Press the Margin Release combination, Shift-Tab. This moves the automatic paragraph number back to the left margin and converts it to a II.

17. Press the Enter key to insert a blank line above the II. The automatic paragraph number will move with the cursor.

18. Press the space bar, and type the next paragraph: `Environmental Impact.`

    Step 18 completes the first section of the outline. You should now be able to complete the rest yourself, following the same general instructions to insert the automatic paragraph numbers. Table 17.3 summarizes these instructions.

Table 17.3 *Using WordPerfect's Outline feature to insert automatic paragraph numbers.*

Level 1:	Press Enter. Before typing any text, press one of the following: The space bar Home-Tab Indent (F4) Left/Right Indent (Shift-F4) The Home-Tab combination indents only the first line, while the Indent key indents the entire paragraph from the left margin. The Left/Right Indent key also indents the entire paragraph, but indents it from both the left and right margins. You cannot use Tab, because it moves the automatic paragraph number to another level. If you press Enter immediately after inserting an automatic paragraph number, without typing or pressing any other keys, both the number and the cursor will move to the next line. You can press Enter without inserting an automatic paragraph number by pressing the Ctrl-V combination first and then pressing Enter.
Levels 2 through 8:	Press Enter and then press the Tab key as many times as necessary to indent the cursor, and change the automatic paragraph number to the desired level.
To back up one level:	Moving both the cursor and automatic paragraph number back to the previous level, press the Margin Release combination, Shift-Tab.

Turning Off the Outline Feature

When you finish, you can turn off the Outline function. However, unless you will be typing more text below the outline, this step is entirely optional.

To turn Outline off:

1. Select Outline:

    Keyboard: Press Date/Outline (Shift-F5) and select **Outline**.

Mouse: Display the **Tools** pull-down menu and select **Outline**.

2. Select Off.

The `Outline` prompt in the lower-left corner will disappear, to indicate that you are no longer in Outline mode, and the Enter, Tab and Shift keys will revert to their regular functions. Look in the Reveal Codes screen, and you'll see that WordPerfect has inserted an [Outline Off] code. If you move the cursor back into the section where Outline is on—between the Outline On and Off codes— the `Outline` prompt will reappear, and the Enter, Tab and Shift keys will again be converted to their Outline functions.

If you accidentally erase the [Outline On] code in a document, it will not erase the automatic paragraph numbers. In fact, it can be advantageous to do so after you complete the outline, because the Enter, Tab, and Margin Release keys will revert to their regular functions.

Tip: You can use WordPerfect's Outline feature to create an outline anywhere in a document and turn Outline on and off as often as you want within a document. When you turn it on, an [Outline On] code is inserted at the cursor position. Turning it off inserts an [Outline Off] code. If you do turn Outline off and then turn it on again in the same document, the numbering scheme will start over when you turn Outline on again. You can change the starting number using the *Starting Paragraph Number* option on the Paragraph Number Definition menu (Shift-F5 D S).

The Paragraph Numbering Formats

WordPerfect offers four pre-defined paragraph numbering formats that you can use for your outlines—Paragraph, Outline, Legal, and Bullets—as well as an option that lets you design your own format. These formats specify how the automatic paragraph numbers at each level of an outline will appear on the Edit screen: as Roman numerals, uppercase letters, lowercase letters, numbers, etc. You can change the format regardless of whether you created the outline with the Paragraph Numbering feature or with the Outline feature.

WordPerfect's default paragraph numbering format is called *Outline*, and it was used to format the outline in Figure 17.1, "Clearcutting Old Growth Forests." Figure 17.4 shows how this outline appears if you convert it to the *Paragraph* format. As you can see:

- The Roman numerals that represented the first level of automatic paragraph numbers—I, II, and III—have been replaced by Arabic numbers—1, 2, and 3.

- The uppercase letters that represented the second level—A, B, C, and D—have been converted to lowercase letters—a, b, c, and d.

- The Arabic numbers that represented the third level—1, 2, 3, and 4—have been converted to lowercase Roman numerals—i, ii, iii, and iv.

- The lowercase letters that represented the fourth level—a and b—have been converted to Arabic numbers in parentheses—(1) and (2).

Table 17.4 explains the numbering scheme used for the Paragraph format. Contrast it with the Outline format displayed in Table 17.1.

Table 17.4   The Paragraph format.

Level 1:	Arabic numbers followed by a period	1. 2. 3. 4. 5. 6. 7. 8. 9. 10. ad infinitum
Level 2:	Lowercase letters followed by a period	a. b. c. d. e. f. g. h. i. j. ad infinitum
Level 3:	Lowercase Roman numerals followed by a period	i. ii. iii. iv. v. vi. vii. viii. ix. x. ad infinitum
Level 4:	Parenthesized Arabic numbers	(1) (2) (3) (4) (5) (6) (7) (8) (9) (10) ad infinitum
Level 5:	Parenthesized lowercase letters	(a) (b) (c) (d) (e) (f) (g) (h) (i) (j) ad infinitum
Level 6:	Parenthesized lowercase Roman numerals	(i) (ii) (iii) (iv) (v) (vi) (vii) (viii) (ix) (x) ad infinitum
Level 7:	Arabic numbers followed by a closing parenthesis	1) 2) 3) 4) 5) 6) 7) 8) 9) 10) ad infinitum
Level 8:	Lowercase letters followed by a closing parenthesis	a) b) c) d) e) f) g) h) i) j) ad infinitum

Changing the Paragraph Numbering Format

To convert an outline to one of the other numbering formats, all you have to do is place the cursor at the top of the page and select the format from WordPerfect's Paragraph Number Definition menu. Follow these steps to change your outline to the Paragraph numbering format.

Clearcutting Old Growth Forests

1. Economic Advantages
    a. Highest yield per acre
    b. Best quality of wood
    c. Most efficient harvest method
        i. Provides maximum employment potential
        ii. Activity is concentrated
    d. Easiest to replant and manage -- old growth canopy has limited underbrush growth

2. Environmental Impact
    a. Initial site disturbance
        i. Wildlife displaced, including endangered species
        ii. Recreational/aesthetic value destroyed
    b. Topsoil exposed and eroded
        i. Siltation of riverbeds
            (1) Impact on fisheries
            (2) Degradation of water quality
        ii. Greater susceptibility to disease
        iii. Replanting creates mono-culture forest

3. Solutions
    a. Eliminate clearcutting
        i. Cut selectively to develop sustained yield
    b. Logging closures
        i. In sensitive wildlife areas
        ii. On steep terrain/watersheds
    c. Economic mitigation
        i. Stress sustained yield = sustained employment
        ii. Increased recreational/tourism potential
        iii. Restructure U.S. Forest Service receipts
        iv. Fisheries economy rejuvenated

Figure 17.4 You can easily convert an outline to another paragraph numbering format. In this version of the "Clearcutting Old Growth Forests" outline, the Paragraph format was used.

Begin with the cursor at the top of the first page of your outline, since this procedure inserts a code into your document. Incidentally, you can change the numbering format anytime, even before you begin typing an outline.

  1. Display the Paragraph Number Definition menu:

    Keyboard: Press the Date/Outline key (Shift-F5) and select the **Define** option.

    Mouse: Display the Tools menu and select **Define**.

    The Paragraph Number Definition menu will appear, as shown in Figure 17.5. As you can see, the numbering format options are:

    2—**Paragraph**

    3—**Outline**

    4—**Legal** (1.1.1)

5—Bullets

6—User-defined

The other four options on this menu, 1, 7, 8, and 9, are explained briefly in Table 17.5.

```
Paragraph Number Definition

    1 - Starting Paragraph Number              1
          (in legal style)
                                           Levels
                          ┌─1─┐ ┌─2─┐ ┌─3─┐ ┌─4─┐ ┌─5─┐ ┌─6─┐ ┌─7─┐ ┌─8─┐
    2 - Paragraph           1.    a.    i.   (1)   (a)   (i)   1)    a)
    3 - Outline             I.    A.    1.    a.   (1)   (a)   i)    a)
    4 - Legal (1.1.1)       1    .1    .1    .1    .1    .1    .1    .1
    5 - Bullets             •     o     -     ■     *     +     .     x
    6 - User-defined

    Current Definition      I.    A.    1.    a.   (1)   (a)   i)    a)
    Attach Previous Level         No    No    No    No    No    No    No

    7 - Enter Inserts Paragraph Number         Yes

    8 - Automatically Adjust to Current Level  Yes

    9 - Outline Style Name


Selection: 0
```

Figure 17.5 The Paragraph Number Definition menu.

 Warning: Changing any of the options on the Paragraph Number Definition menu inserts a [Par Num Def] code into your document. If you want the changes to affect the entire document, the cursor should be at the top of the first page before you select this option.

The format that is currently in effect, Outline, is identified in the center of the menu, under the heading `Current Definition`. Instead of naming the format style, it displays a row of letters and numbers indicating what the first paragraph in that numbering scheme will look like for each of the eight levels:

```
I.   A.   1.   a.   (1)   (a)   i)   a)
```

If you look next to option 3, `Outline`, you'll see the same row of letters and numbers.

2. Select the second option, **Paragraph**. The change is immediately reflected under the `Current Definition` heading:

```
1.   a.   i.   (1)   (a)   (i)   1)   a)
```

3. Return to the Edit screen by pressing Exit (F7) twice, or clicking the right mouse button twice.

WordPerfect should change the numbering style for all automatic paragraph numbers. If the numbers have not changed, you may need to rewrite the screen, as explained in the next step.

4. If the numbers have not yet changed and you need to rewrite the screen, either move the cursor to the end of the document, or press the Screen key (Ctrl-F3) and select **R**ewrite (there is no mouse equivalent of the Rewrite option).

Your outline should now resemble Figure 17.4. If you look in Reveal Codes, you will see that WordPerfect has inserted a [Par Num Def] code to represent the change you just made (i.e., selecting the Paragraph numbering format). If you want to experiment with the other two numbering formats, either erase this [Par Num Def] code or position the cursor anywhere after it (to the right of or below the code) before changing the format again. Figure 17.6 shows the "Clearcutting Old Growth Forests" outline formatted with the *Legal* numbering format, and Figure 17.7 shows it formatted with the *Bullet* format. Legal is the fourth option on the Paragraph Number Definition menu, and Bullets is the fifth.

Clearcutting Old Growth Forests

1 Economic Advantages
    1.1 Highest yield per acre
    1.2 Best quality of wood
    1.3 Most efficient harvest method
        1.3.1 Provides maximum employment potential
        1.3.2 Activity is concentrated
    1.4 Easiest to replant and manage -- old growth canopy has limited underbrush growth

2 Environmental Impact
    2.1 Initial site disturbance
        2.1.1 Wildlife displaced, including endangered species
        2.1.2 Recreational/aesthetic value destroyed
    2.2 Topsoil exposed and eroded
        2.2.1 Siltation of riverbeds
            2.2.1.1 Impact on fisheries
            2.2.1.2 Degradation of water quality
        2.2.2 Greater susceptibility to disease
        2.2.3 Replanting creates mono-culture forest

3 Solutions
    3.1 Eliminate clearcutting
        3.1.1 Cut selectively to develop sustained yield
    3.2 Logging closures
        3.2.1 In sensitive wildlife areas
        3.2.2 On steep terrain/watersheds
    3.3 Economic mitigation
        3.3.1 Stress sustained yield = sustained employment
        3.3.2 Increased recreational/tourism potential
        3.3.3 Restructure U.S. Forest Service receipts
        3.3.4 Fisheries economy rejuvenated

Figure 17.6 *In this version of the "Clearcutting Old Growth Forests" outline, the Legal format was used.*

Clearcutting Old Growth Forests

- **Economic Advantages**
  - o Highest yield per acre
  - o Best quality of wood
  - o Most efficient harvest method
    - - Provides maximum employment potential
    - - Activity is concentrated
  - o Easiest to replant and manage -- old growth canopy has limited underbrush growth

- **Environmental Impact**
  - o Initial site disturbance
    - - Wildlife displaced, including endangered species
    - - Recreational/aesthetic value destroyed
  - o Topsoil exposed and eroded
    - - Siltation of riverbeds
      - ■ Impact on fisheries
      - ■ Degradation of water quality
    - - Greater susceptibility to disease
    - - Replanting creates mono-culture forest

- **Solutions**
  - o Eliminate clearcutting
    - - Cut selectively to develop sustained yield
  - o Logging closures
    - - In sensitive wildlife areas
    - - On steep terrain/watersheds
  - o Economic mitigation
    - - Stress sustained yield = sustained employment
    - - Increased recreational/tourism potential
    - - Restructure U.S. Forest Service receipts
    - - Fisheries economy rejuvenated

Figure 17.7 *In this version of the "Clearcutting Old Growth Forests" outline, the Bullet format was used.*

You may want to test your printer on a short sample outline to determine if it is capable of printing the bullet characters used for the Bullets numbering format. Most laser and dot-matrix printers are capable of printing them, because WordPerfect can instruct these printers to use a graphical method of printing special characters such as these. If your printer has a daisywheel or thimble, you probably won't be able to print the bullets.

Table 17.5 *Options 1, 7, 8, and 9 on the Paragraph Number Definition screen.*

Option 1: Starting Paragraph Number (in legal style)	If you want the first automatic paragraph number in an outline to be something other than 1, you can use the *Starting Paragraph Number* option to change it. For instance, if you select this option and type 5, then select the Paragraph numbering format, the first number that WordPerfect will insert

---

when you turn on Outline and press Enter will be a 5 (instead of a 1). If you leave the default numbering format, Outline, WordPerfect will insert a (Roman numeral) V, instead of an I.

Option 7: Enter Inserts Paragraph Number

When the Outline feature is on, pressing Enter inserts an automatic paragraph number. You can disable this feature by changing the *Enter Inserts Paragraph Number* option to No. Once you do, (change it to No) the only way you can insert an automatic paragraph number is to use the Paragraph Number option: Press Date/Outline (Shift-F5) and select **P**ara Num, or use the **P**aragraph Number option on the pull-down Tools menu. However, you will still be able to use important outline tools, such as Outline Styles and Move Family, Copy Family, and Delete Family.

Option 8: Automatically Adjust to Current Level

In Outline mode, pressing Enter inserts an automatic paragraph number at the same level as the previous entry, if there was one (otherwise it inserts a Level 1 paragraph number). In other words, if you type a Level 2 entry and press Enter, WordPerfect will insert an automatic paragraph number on the next line, indented to the Level 2 position. Also, it will be formatted with the same numbering style as the previous level (such as an uppercase letter if you are using the default numbering format, Outline). If you change the *Automatically Adjust to Current Level* option to No, pressing Enter will always insert a first-level paragraph number at the left margin. You can still change the level of this paragraph number, by pressing Tab.

Option 9: Outline Style Name

You can use this option to create and use customized styles for your outlines. Unlike regular styles, an outline style

continued

Table 17.5 *(continued)*

contains a group of styles, one for each level of paragraph numbers (1 through 8). For more information, see *Outline Style* in Part Three, "Command Reference." For a detailed overview of styles, see Chapter 15.

Tip: Any automatic paragraph number that you insert at a tab stop position following the seventh one will be formatted with the Level 8 numbering style.

Warning: Pay attention to the cursor position when you change an option on the Paragraph Number Definition menu, because this always inserts a [Par Num Def] code into your document at the cursor position. If you insert a [Par Num Def] code in the middle of an outline, WordPerfect will start the numbering scheme all over again with the first number: 1., I, 1 or the Level 1 style bullet, depending on the paragraph numbering format you are using. Even if you just bring up the Paragraph Number Definition menu and then press Enter to return to the Edit screen without making any changes, WordPerfect will still insert this code, and restart the numbering scheme from that point forward.

Defining Your Own Numbering Format

If none of the four pre-defined formats meets your needs for an outline numbering style, you can create your own, using the *User-defined* option on the Paragraph Number Definition menu. This permits you to select your own formatting style for each level, using any combination of numbers, letters, bullets, or other symbols. In fact, you can use a character from any of WordPerfect's character sets, if your printer is capable of printing them. If you want to use special characters that aren't part of normal keyboard, such as bullets, you can use the Compose feature (but use Ctrl-2, not Ctrl-V. For more information about how to do this, see *Compose Key* in Part Three, "Command Reference").

To create your own numbering scheme:

1. Display the Paragraph Number Definition menu:

   Keyboard: Press the Date/Outline key (Shift-F5) and select the **Define** option.

   Mouse: Display the **Tools** menu and select **Define**.

   The Paragraph Number Definition menu will appear, as shown in Figure 17.5.

2. Select the sixth option, **User-defined**.

   The cursor will move to the `Current Definition` line, as shown in Figure 17.8. Notice that the lower-left corner of the screen has changed, and now includes several lines of information about the characters you can use for your format. It indicates, for example, that you can use Arabic numerals for this level by typing a *1;* uppercase letters by typing an uppercase *A;* or lowercase letters by typing a lowercase *a.*

```
Paragraph Number Definition

    1 - Starting Paragraph Number                    1
          (in legal style)
                                                   Levels
                               1     2     3     4     5     6     7     8
    2 - Paragraph             1.    a.    i.    (1)   (a)   (i)   1)    a)
    3 - Outline               I.    A.    1.    a.    (1)   (a)   i)    a)
    4 - Legal (1.1.1)         1     .1    .1    .1    .1    .1    .1    .1
    5 - Bullets               •     o     —     ■     *     +     .     x
    6 - User-defined

    Current Definition        I.    A.    1.    a.    (1)   (a)   i)    a)
    Attach Previous Level           No    No    No    No    No    No    No

    7 - Enter Inserts Paragraph Number             Yes

    8 - Automatically Adjust to Current Level      Yes

    9 - Outline Style Name

1 - Digits, A - Uppercase Letters, a - Lowercase Letters
I - Uppercase Roman, i - Lowercase Roman
X - Uppercase Roman/Digits if Attached, x - Lowercase Roman/Digits if Attached
Other character - Bullet or Punctuation
```

The cursor moves to the Current Definition line.

Figure 17.8 *When you select the User-defined option on the Paragraph Number Definition menu, the cursor moves to the Current Definition line, and four lines of information appear in the lower-left corner of the screen.*

3. Type the letter, number, or symbol in the format you want to use for Level 1, and press Enter or Tab. If you want to leave the suggested style, just press Enter.

   The cursor will move to the right, so you can select the style for the second level.

4. Continue typing the characters you want to use for each level, pressing Enter or Tab to move to the next level. If you make a mistake, you can move the cursor to the left by pressing Shift-Tab.

5. When you finish, press Exit (F7) or the right mouse button three times.

You return to the Edit screen, and your User-defined numbering format is in effect.

 Tip: If you want to define a paragraph numbering format that is similar to one of WordPerfect's pre-defined formats (such as Outline or Paragraph), select that format first and then select the User-defined option. WordPerfect will display the selected format in the User-defined row, and you will have less editing to do to customize it.

The Attach Previous Level Option

You may have noticed the *Attach Previous Level* option on the Paragraph Number Definition menu. It is set to Yes for the Legal format, and set to No for all the others. However, you can still use this feature with any of the other formats, by selecting the User-defined numbering format, and then changing Attach Previous Level to Yes. This creates a numbering format in which levels below the first are displayed along with the numbers and letters from the previous level. Here, a picture really is worth a thousand words, so Figure 17.9 shows how the "Clearcutting Old Growth Forests" outline from Figure 17.1 appears after changing this option to Yes for Levels 2, 3, and 4. The changes are summarized here:

- In the first section ("Economic Advantages") the Level 2 entries—"Highest yield per acre," "Best quality of wood," "Most efficient harvest method," and "Easiest to replant and manage"—have been converted from A, B, C, and D to I.A, I.B, I.C, and I.D.

- The Level 3 entries in the first section—"Provides maximum employment potential" and "Activity is concentrated"—have been converted from 1 and 2 to I.C.1 and I.C.2. In the second section ("Environmental Impact"), the Level 4 entries—"Impact on fisheries" and "Degradation of water quality"—have been converted from a and b into II.B.1.a and II.B.1.b.

To use this option, begin by displaying the Paragraph Number Definition menu (Figure 17.5). Next:

1. Select **Paragraph** or **Outline** as the numbering format (the Legal format uses this method by default).

2. Select **User-defined**. Next, press the Down Arrow key to place the cursor on Attach Previous Level.

3. Select **Yes** for each level you want to attach to the previous one.

4. Exit back to the Edit screen.

Clearcutting Old Growth Forests

I. Economic Advantages
    I.A. Highest yield per acre
    I.B. Best quality of wood
    I.C. Most efficient harvest method
        I.C.1. Provides maximum employment potential
        I.C.2. Activity is concentrated
    I.D. Easiest to replant and manage -- old growth canopy has limited underbrush growth

II. Environmental Impact
    II.A. Initial site disturbance
        II.A.1. Wildlife displaced, including endangered species
        II.A.2. Recreational/aesthetic value destroyed
    II.B. Topsoil exposed and eroded
        II.B.1. Siltation of riverbeds
            II.B.1.a. Impact on fisheries
            II.B.1.b. Degradation of water quality
        II.B.2. Greater susceptibility to disease
        II.B.3. Replanting creates mono-culture forest

III. Solutions
    III.A. Eliminate clearcutting
        III.A.1. Cut selectively to develop sustained yield
    III.B. Logging closures
        III.B.1. In sensitive wildlife areas
        III.B.2. On steep terrain/watersheds
    III.C. Economic mitigation
        III.C.1. Stress sustained yield = sustained employment
        III.C.2. Increased recreational/tourism potential
        III.C.3. Restructure U.S. Forest Service receipts
        III.C.4. Fisheries economy rejuvenated

Figure 17.9 *In this version of the "Clearcutting Old Growth Forests" outline, the Attach Previous Level option has been changed to Yes for Levels 2, 3, and 4. As a result, the letters and numbers representing these levels are displayed along with the numbers and letters from the previous level.*

The Move Family, Copy Family, and Delete Family Options on the Outline Menu

The Outline menu provides options that you can use to move, copy, and delete groups of outline entries called *families*. Essentially, a family consists of an automatic paragraph number, the paragraph of text that follows it, plus any automatic paragraph numbers and text that follow it and are at a level below it. For example, if you were to select Move Family when the cursor was on the first paragraph in the outline displayed in Figure 17.1 ("I. Economic Advantages"), WordPerfect would highlight everything in section I, as shown in Figure 17.10.

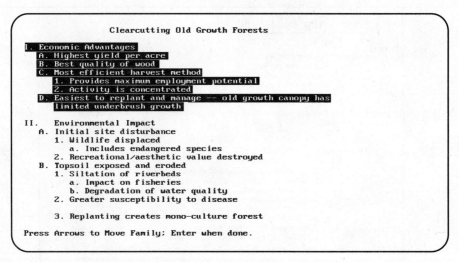

Figure 17.10   *When the cursor is on the first paragraph in this outline, represented by the Roman Numeral I, and the Move Family option is selected, WordPerfect highlights all the automatic paragraph numbers and text in the section, stopping before the next automatic paragraph number on the same level (II).*

If the cursor were on the fourth paragraph, Most efficient harvest method, and you selected one of these options, the family would consist of these paragraphs:

C. Most efficient harvest method

1. Provides maximum employment potential

2. Activity is concentrated

If the cursor were on the third paragraph, Best quality of wood, the family would be limited to that line only, because the paragraph on the line below it is on the same level (Level 2).

To move, copy, or delete a family:

1. Position the cursor on the first line of the family that you want to move, copy, or delete.

2. Display the main Outline menu:

   Keyboard: Press Date/Outline (Shift-F5).

   Mouse: Display the **T**ools menu.

3. Select **Outline.**

   If you used the mouse, the menu displayed in Figure 17.3 appears. If you used the Date/Outline key, this menu appears:

   ```
   Outline: 1 On; 2 Off; 3 Move Family; 4 Copy Family;
   5 Delete Family: 0
   ```

4. Your next step depends on which of the three options you select: Move Family, Copy Family, or Delete Family. The following explanation details each procedure:

Move Family:

If you select Move Family, WordPerfect will highlight the family, and this prompt will appear (visible in Figure 17.10):

```
Press Arrows to Move Family; Enter when done.
```

Use the Up, Down, Left, or Right Arrow keys to move the highlighted family to the new position. Pressing Right or Left Arrow changes the level of the family: Right Arrow moves it down one level, such as from I to A. Left Arrow moves it to the previous level, such as from A to I (but you can't move a family more than one level past the level of the line that precedes it). To move to the top of the outline, use Home,Up Arrow; to move to the bottom, use Home,Down Arrow. When the cursor and family are in the position you want, press Enter to insert it there. As you move the family, the numbers will change to reflect the new position, even before you press Enter.

Copy Family:

The Copy Family option works like the Move Family option, except that the family is not erased from the original position. Instead, an extra copy is inserted when you press Enter in response to the prompt (`Press Arrows to Move Family; Enter when done`).

Delete Family:

If you select Delete Family, WordPerfect will highlight the family, and this prompt will appear asking if you want to delete it:

```
Delete Outline Family? No (Yes)
```

Select **Yes** if you want to erase it. If you change your mind, you can use Cancel to bring it back after deleting it (F1, or Undelete on the Edit menu).

If you change your mind while using one of these options, and decide not to move, copy, or delete the highlighted family, press Cancel (F1).

The Move Family, Copy Family, and Delete Family options only work when Outline is on. In other words, you won't be able to use them unless the cursor is inside a section where Outline is on, and the Outline prompt appears in the lower-left corner of the Edit screen.

Tips and Tricks

The following sections introduce a few simple tips that can facilitate your use of WordPerfect's Outline and Paragraph Numbering features. First, you'll learn how you can insert an automatic paragraph number using only two keystrokes: Alt-N. This will save you a few steps each time you insert an automatic paragraph number, and, if you use this feature often, it will also save you a lot of time. Next, you'll learn how to keep your outline on the Edit screen in Doc 2 while composing the manuscript in Doc 1, so that you can switch back and forth between the outline and the document as needed.

A Macro for Automatic Paragraph Numbering

If you use WordPerfect's Paragraph Number option frequently, you can save time by creating a macro that will automatically insert an automatic paragraph number into your document. A macro is basically a file containing a sequence of keystrokes that you use frequently. It serves as a shortcut. When you use such a macro, it replays the keystrokes exactly as you typed them when you created the macro file, inserting them into your document at the cursor position. If you are unfamiliar with the concept of macros, you may want to skim through Chapter 19. However, it will not be necessary to create the macro described below.

The name of this macro will be Alt-N. To create it, begin by clearing the Edit screen (since the keystrokes will actually be used and insert an automatic paragraph number). Next:

1. Turn on macro definition by pressing Ctrl-F10, or by displaying the Tools menu, selecting **Macro**, then **Define**.

2. In response to the Define macro prompt, enter the macro name by pressing the Alt key and holding it down while typing N.

3. In response to the Description prompt, type a brief description, such as Inserts paragraph number. Press Enter when you finish.

4. Press Date/Outline (Shift-F5) or use the mouse to display the **Tools** menu.

5. Select the Para Num option: Type P or select **Paragraph Number**.

6. In response to the `Paragraph Level` prompt, press Enter or click the right mouse button, so WordPerfect inserts an automatic paragraph number.

7. Turn off macro definition by pressing Ctrl-F10, or by displaying the **Tools** menu, selecting **Macro**, then **Define**.

8. Clear the Edit screen again.

   Once the macro is defined, whenever you want to use it to insert an automatic paragraph number at the cursor position, just press the keystrokes you named it under: Alt-N.

9. Test the macro by pressing Alt-N.

   This should insert an automatic paragraph number at the cursor position.

Using Doc 2 and Doc 1

While writing an original document, such as a report, take advantage of the fact that WordPerfect provides two separate work areas, Doc 1 and Doc 2, and use them to keep your outline available in one work area, while composing the manuscript in the other one. You can switch to Doc 2 whenever you want to review the outline, copy headings, or, if you are suffering from writer's block, just get away from the blank screen in Doc 1.

The following instructions assume that you are starting with the cursor in Doc 1. If you are unsure, just look at the status line, where you should see `Doc 1`. To use the Switch feature:

1. Switch to the other work area:

   Keyboard: Press the Switch key (Shift-F3).

   Mouse: Select the **Switch Document** option from the **Edit** menu.

   If you were working in Doc 1, this moves you to Doc 2. If you were in Doc 2, this moves you to Doc 1.

2. Type your outline or, if you have already typed and saved it, retrieve it.

3. Follow the instructions in step 1 to use the Switch option again, and return to the other document area (presumably Doc 1).

   This returns you to Doc 1, where you can write your manuscript. Whenever you want to return to Doc 2 to view the outline, follow the instructions in step 1.

LISTS, INDEXES, AND TABLES OF CONTENTS

Compiling an index, a table of contents, or a list of items such as illustrations or charts for a lengthy document like a proposal, thesis, or book used to be a tedious procedure, and revisions were time-consuming. WordPerfect has changed all that, providing tools that can help you automate the process.

To create a list, index, or table of contents, you follow a three-step process. First, you go through the document and use a special procedure to mark each word or phrase that you want to include; WordPerfect inserts a pair of codes around the text, marking it for your list, index, or table. Although this is the most laborious part of the process, you can use macros and/or styles to help. If you are creating an index, this step is optional. Next, you use a special menu to define the list, index, or table of contents, and select a page numbering style for the entries. The last step is the simplest: You ask WordPerfect to generate any list, index, or table that you've defined (all are generated simultaneously). WordPerfect then searches the document, locates all the items you've marked, and produces your list, index, or table of contents, complete with page numbers for each entry, using the format you've specified.

Creating Lists

WordPerfect lets you create up to 10 separate lists in each document, so you can produce lists for exhibits, graphs, tables, charts, headings, illustrations, and any other important items. After you mark the text in your document, define the list, and generate it, WordPerfect will create a list from each item you've marked. If you choose to have WordPerfect include page numbers when you define the list, the items will be arranged by page number, as in Figure 18.1. If not, they will be arranged in the order they were found in the document.

DrawPerfect Graphics

Figure 1: Butterfly	2
Figure 2: Diploma	4
Figure 3: Balloons	8
Figure 4: Computer	16
Figure 5: Globe	28
Figure 6: Calendar	29
Figure 7: Bicycle	34

Figure 18.1 *A list of Figure boxes from a document about DrawPerfect's graphic images, showing the page number where each figure appears in the document. This list was automatically generated by WordPerfect, using the captions in each Figure box.*

Of the 10 lists you can define, lists 6 through 10 are reserved for the five types of graphic boxes: Figure boxes, Table boxes, Text boxes, Equation boxes, and User-defined boxes. Since these are among the most common items to be included in a list, you do not have to mark the items individually in the document. WordPerfect will automatically generate lists from these items, if you have entered captions for them. All you have to do is define the list and select a numbering style. The list numbers that WordPerfect reserves for graphics boxes are as follows:

List number:	Includes the captions for:
6	Figure boxes
7	Table boxes
8	Text boxes
9	User boxes
10	Equation boxes

 Tip: A word or phrase in your document can only be marked for one list. If you want to include it in several lists, the only way to do it is to use another copy of the document, marking the word or phrase for a different list in each document.

Marking Items for a List

The first step in creating a list is to mark the items you want to appear on it. Whether you are marking entries for your list as you type them, or waiting until you complete the document, the procedure is the same: You block the word or phrase, select List from the Mark Text menu, and then type the list number for the entry. If you are marking entries after typing the document, you can use WordPerfect's Search feature to locate individual items, as described in the next section. Remember, you do not have to mark Graphic boxes or Equation boxes because WordPerfect can automatically generate lists from their captions. To create one of these lists, skip to the section "Defining the List Style."

Follow these steps to mark each item that you want to include in one of your lists. If you are creating more than one list for a document, keep a written record of the type of items you are including in each list, to avoid confusion.

1. Place the cursor at the beginning of the word or phrase.

    You may want to check Reveal Codes to determine the actual cursor position, and make sure you aren't about to include a formatting code, such as [BOLD], when you block the text. If you do, it will appear in the generated list, along with the item you are marking.

2. Turn on Block mode:

    Keyboard: Press the Block key (Alt-F4 or F12).

    Mouse: Display the **Edit** menu and select **Block**, or click the left button and hold it while dragging the pointer to the end of the block.

3. Move the cursor to the end of the word or phrase, extending the block highlighting.

4. Select Mark Text:

    Keyboard: Press Mark Text (Alt-F5).

    This menu appears at the bottom of the screen:

    `Mark for 1 ToC; 2 List; 3 Index; 4 ToA: 0`

    Mouse: Display the **Mark** menu, as shown in Figure 18.2.

5. Select the **List** option:

    This prompt will appear at the bottom of the screen:

    `List Number:`

    Use any number between 1 and 5 for the list. Remember, lists 6 through 10 are reserved for graphics boxes.

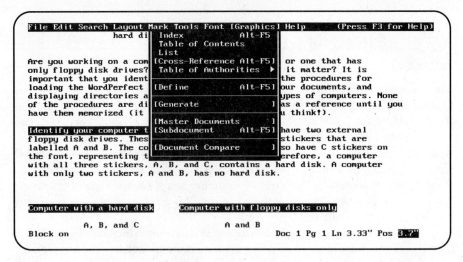

Figure 18.2 *The pull-down Mark menu after blocking a word or phrase. Notice that several of the selections are bracketed, including Cross-Reference, Define, and Generate, to indicate that they cannot be used in Block mode.*

6. Type the number of the list in which you want this word or phrase to be included, and press Enter.

The block highlighting disappears. If you look in Reveal Codes, you'll see that WordPerfect has inserted a pair of codes around the word or phrase you just marked. For instance, if you marked the heading *Drift net fishing* for list 1, it will appear as follows:

```
[Mark:List,1]Drift net fishing[End Mark:List,1]
```

The first code, [Mark:List,1], indicates that this is the beginning of the text you have marked for inclusion in list 1, and the second code, [End Mark:List,1], denotes the end. If you accidentally erase one of these codes, WordPerfect will erase the other as well, and you'll have to mark the entry again.

Repeat these six steps to mark each item in the document that you want to include in a list.

Using Search to Locate Items

To locate text that you want to mark for a list, index, or table of contents, you can use WordPerfect's Search feature.

1. Select Forward or Backward search:

   Keyboard: Press Forward Search (F2) or Backward Search (Shift-F2).

Mouse: Display the Search menu and select Forward or Backward.

2. Type the word or phrase you want to search for; this is called the *search string*.

3. To start the search:

   Keyboard: Press F2.

   Mouse: Click the right mouse button.

The cursor will stop just past the next occurrence of the word or phrase. If it is not the one you want to mark, select Search again and repeat the process; since WordPerfect retains the last search string, you won't have to retype it.

> **Tip:** To speed up the process of marking entries for a list, create and use a macro. The macro will turn on Block mode, pause while you move the cursor to the end of the word or phrase you want to mark, and wait until you press Enter. It will then select List from the Mark Text menu, and stop to let you type the list number (if you always use the same list number, have the macro enter it automatically). Assign a name such as Alt-L to this macro, and you'll only have to press two keystrokes to start it. For more information about macros, see Chapter 19.

Defining the List Style

The second step in creating a list is to decide where you want WordPerfect to generate your list(s), and then define and select a page numbering style for each list. You can place a list anywhere in a document, but lists usually appear on a separate page at the end of the document, preceded by a hard page break. You must repeat the definition process for each list you want WordPerfect to generate, including graphic boxes.

1. Move the cursor to the position in the document where you want the list to appear after WordPerfect generates it. If you want the list at the end, move the cursor to the end of the document.

2. Create a hard page break so that the list will begin on a new page:

   Keyboard: Press Ctrl-Enter.

   Mouse: Display the Layout menu and select Align, then Hard Page.

A double dashed line will appear on the screen, representing the forced page break.

3. If you want a title for your list, type it now, so it will precede the code that WordPerfect inserts when you define the list. Be sure to insert a few blank lines after the title to separate it from the list entries that WordPerfect will generate.

4. Define a list:

Keyboard: Press the Mark Text key (Alt-F5).

This menu will appear:

```
1 Cross-Ref; 2 Subdoc; 3 Index; 4 ToA Short Form;
5 Define; 6 Generate: 0
```

Select the fifth option, **Define**.

Next, you'll see the Mark Text: Define menu shown in Figure 18.3. Select the second option, Define List.

Mouse: Display the **Mark** menu and select the **Define** option.

Another menu will pop out to the right, as shown in Figure 18.4. It includes options to define an index, table of contents, list, or table of authorities. Select the List option.

```
Mark Text: Define

      1 - Define Table of Contents

      2 - Define List

      3 - Define Index

      4 - Define Table of Authorities

      5 - Edit Table of Authorities Full Form







  Selection: 0
```

Figure 18.3 The Mark Text: Define menu. To define a list, use the second option, Define List.

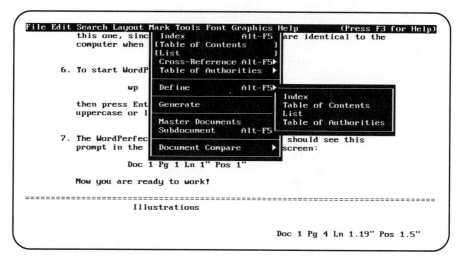

Figure 18.4 *When you select Define from the Mark menu, this menu appears, providing options to define an index, table of contents, list, or table of authorities.*

5. In response to the `List Number (1-10)` prompt, type the list number you are defining and press Enter. This number should correspond to the number you used when you marked the entries, as described previously. If you want WordPerfect to generate a list for your graphics boxes, enter the number corresponding to the type of box: 6 for Figure boxes, 7 for Table boxes, 8 for Text boxes, 9 for User boxes, or 10 for Equation boxes.

The List Definition menu for the list number you have selected appears, as shown in Figure 18.5. It provides five numbering styles. The first, *No Page Numbers*, will compile a list of entries without any page number references. The second, *Page Numbers Follow Entries*, will create a list with the page numbers a few spaces to the right of the entry. The third, *(Page Numbers) Follow Entries*, also creates a list with the page numbers a few spaces to the right of the entry, but the page numbers are in parentheses. The fourth, *Flush Right Page Numbers*, will place the page numbers flush right, at the right margin. The fifth option, *Flush Right Page Numbers with Leaders*, also places the page numbers at the right margin but separates each entry from its page number by a row of dots, called *dot leaders*. The last method is the default, which was used in the table of contents shown in Figure 18.7. Figure 18.1 uses the fourth style, Flush Right Page Numbers, which does not have the dot leaders.

6. Select one of the page numbering styles.

```
List 1  Definition

    1 - No Page Numbers

    2 - Page Numbers Follow Entries

    3 - (Page Numbers) Follow Entries

    4 - Flush Right Page Numbers

    5 - Flush Right Page Numbers with Leaders




Selection: 5
```

Figure 18.5 *The List Definition menu for List 1. Use this menu to select one of the four numbering styles for your list, or to create a list of entries alone, without page numbers (option 1).*

After you select a style, you return to the Edit screen. If you look in Reveal Codes, you'll see that WordPerfect has inserted a definition code for your list. For example, if you defined list 1 and selected 5 for the page numbering style, it will appear as follows: **[Def Mark:List,1:5]**. The position of this code corresponds to the position where the list will appear when it is generated.

If you have marked entries in your document for more than one list, or want to define another list for your graphics boxes, create a hard page break and repeat the preceding steps to define your next list.

The last step in the three-step process of creating a list is to have WordPerfect generate the list(s) from the entries you have marked in the document.

Generating a List

Generating means having WordPerfect compile the list from the items you have marked, using the page numbering style you have selected. If you have also defined and marked items for a table of contents, index, table of authorities, or cross-references, WordPerfect will also generate these as it scans your document. It is always a good idea to save your document just before following this procedure, so do that first.

1. Save the document.

2. Select Generate:

Keyboard: Press the Mark Text key (Alt-F5) and select the sixth option, Generate.

Mouse: Display the **Mark** pull-down menu and select **Generate**.

The Mark Text: Generate menu shown in Figure 18.6 will appear.

```
Mark Text: Generate

    1 - Remove Redline Markings and Strikeout Text from Document

    2 - Compare Screen and Disk Documents and Add Redline and Strikeout

    3 - Expand Master Document

    4 - Condense Master Document

    5 - Generate Tables, Indexes, Cross-References, etc.








Selection: 0
```

Figure 18.6   *The Mark Text: Generate menu. Use the fifth option on this menu, Generate Tables, Indexes, Cross-References, etc., to generate a list after you have marked all entries and defined the list and selected a page numbering style.*

3. Select the fifth option, **Generate Tables, Indexes, Cross-References, etc.**

   This message will appear at the bottom of the screen:

   ```
   Existing tables, lists, and indexes will be replaced.
   Continue? Yes (No)
   ```

   This is a warning that if you have already defined and generated an index, table of contents, list, or table of authorities, WordPerfect will erase it and then create it again. If you did, but the entries are still marked and you did not erase the definition code, you can safely select **Yes**. Your regenerated index, table of contents, list, or table of authorities will have the same page numbering style and appear in the same location as the old one. If you have not defined any of these items, the message is irrelevant.

4. Select **Yes** to generate the list.

   While WordPerfect is scanning the document for entries that you've marked for your list, this message will appear:

   ```
   Generation in progress. Pass: n, Page n
   ```

After WordPerfect finishes, the completed list will appear on the Edit screen, in the position where you defined it. If you look in Reveal Codes, you'll see a new code that WordPerfect has inserted at the end of your list: [End Def]. Be careful not to erase this code. If you later edit the document and want WordPerfect to update the list to include new or revised entries, you can use the Generate option again to replace the original list. However, if the [End Def] code is missing, WordPerfect won't be able to completely erase the original list, and you may end up with two lists, both the original and the revised one.

If you want to retain the list that WordPerfect has generated, be sure to save the document again.

 Tip: To change the page numbering style after you've generated a list, delete the original [Def Mark] code at the beginning of the list, and then use the Define option on the Mark Text menu to redefine the list and select a new page numbering style. After you have WordPerfect generate the list again, it will appear with the new page numbering style.

Updating a List

If you change any of the words or phrases you've marked for a list, or if you mark new items to include, you can update your list by using the Generate option again. WordPerfect will then erase the original list and create a new one.

To change an entry that is already marked, locate and erase the [Mark:List] code next to it, and then mark it again. The easiest way to find the [Mark:List] code is to use the Search feature:

1. Start at the top of the document, and select Forward Search:

   Keyboard: Press Forward Search (F2).

   Mouse: Select Forward from the pull-down Search menu.

   The Srch prompt appears, with an arrow pointing to the right to signify that this will be a forward search.

2. Press Mark Text (Alt-F5). (You cannot use the mouse to select Mark Text when using the Search feature.)

   The following menu will appear at the bottom of the screen:

   ```
   1 ToC/List; 2 EndMark; 3 Index; 4 ToA; 5 Defs and Refs;
   6 Subdocs: 0
   ```

Notice that the Mark Text options are different when you are using Search because they represent codes that you can search for in the document, not options to mark text.

3. Select the first option, ToC/List.

   This code will appear in the Srch prompt, indicating that you have selected it as the search string:

   → Srch: [Mark]

4. To start the search:

   Keyboard: Press Esc or F2.

   Mouse: Click the right mouse button.

   The cursor will stop just past the first occurrence of the code. Note that if your document also includes codes to mark text for a table of contents, such as [Mark: ToC,1], WordPerfect will also stop on these codes as you use the Search feature. This happens because the code you selected to search for in step 2, ToC/List, represents both the Mark Text List code and the Mark Text Table of Contents code.

5. If this is the entry you want to change, delete the code by pressing the Backspace key and selecting **Yes** in response to the prompt that asks if you want to delete the code. For example, if you marked this item for inclusion in list 1, you'll see this prompt:

   Delete [Mark:List,1]? No (Yes)

   Erasing this code also erases the other part of the pair, the [End Mark:List] code. After that, you can follow the steps outlined in the "Marking Items for a List" section to mark the entry again.

6. If this is not the entry you want to change, search for the next one by:

   Keyboard: Pressing Search (F2) twice.

   Mouse: Selecting **Forward** from the **S**earch menu, and then clicking the right button.

   WordPerfect always retains the last search string, so you don't have to repeat the steps to enter the [Mark] code again.

7. After you finish marking your changes, follow the instructions in the "Generating a List" section to have WordPerfect generate the list again. Remember, every time you generate a list, table or index, you replace (not erase) all those generated previously, so any revisions you've made to the list will appear in this new, updated version.

Creating a Table of Contents

Creating a table of contents is very similar to creating a list, although WordPerfect only permits one table of contents in a document. First, you designate each word or phrase you want to include in the table by blocking and marking it. Next, you define the table and select a page numbering style. The last step is to have WordPerfect generate it.

A table of contents can include up to five levels of headings and subheadings, as illustrated in Figure 18.7. You select the level for each entry while marking it. Use the first level to represent a main heading. For example, if you were creating a table of contents for a book, the title of each chapter would probably be a level 1 heading. When WordPerfect generates your table of contents, level 1 headings always start at the left margin. Level 2 entries are first-level subheadings, such as the major topics in each chapter of a book. WordPerfect indents level 2 headings to the first tab stop, $1/2$" from the level 1 headings (unless you change the default tab settings). Level 3 entries are indented to the second tab stop, Level 4 entries to the third tab stop, and Level 5 entries to the fourth tab stop. As you'll see when you define the page numbering style for your table of contents, WordPerfect will let you select a different numbering style for each level.

Marking Items for a Table of Contents

As with a list, the first step in creating a table of contents is to go through the document and mark each word or phrase that you want to include. Follow these steps to mark your entries:

1. Place the cursor at the beginning of the word or phrase.

   You may want to check Reveal Codes to determine the actual cursor position and whether any formatting codes are between the cursor and text you are about to block, so you won't include them in the block.

2. Turn on Block mode, and then move the cursor to the end of the word or phrase, extending the block highlighting.

3. Select Table of Contents from the Mark Text menu:

   Keyboard: Press Mark Text (Alt-F5).

   This menu appears at the bottom of the screen:

   `Mark for 1 ToC; 2 List; 3 Index; 4 ToA: 0`

   Select the first option, ToC.

Table of Contents

Issue definition: Drift net fishing	2
Advantages	3
Efficiency of method	3
Social gains	5
Recent dietary improvement in Asia	9
Disadvantages	11
Short-term seabound losses	13
Coastal rockfish fisheries	15
Impact on existing demand	17
Anadromous fisheries	18
Marine mammals	22
Potential solutions	23
Advantages	23
Restored oceanic balance	24
Sustained yield	24
Disadvantages	25
Short-term production setback	25
Solutions	27
Drift-net ban	27
Improved management	28
Aquaculture	29
Enlightened use of overlooked species	31

Figure 18.7 *A table of contents. Notice that it uses the Flush Right with Leader page numbering style.*

Mouse: Display the **M**ark menu, as shown in Figure 18.2, and select Table of **C**ontents.

Next, this prompt will appear:

```
ToC Level:
```

asking for the level number for this entry.

4. Enter the level number, from 1 to 5. As soon as you press Enter, the procedure is completed, and the block highlighting disappears.

If you look in Reveal Codes, you'll see that WordPerfect has inserted a pair of codes around the word or phrase you just marked. For instance, if you marked a phrase as a level 1 heading, this code will appear just before it:

```
[Mark:ToC,1]
```

and this code after it:

```
[End Mark:ToC,1].
```

The number that follows `ToC` indicates the level you have selected for this entry.

If you accidentally erase one of these codes, WordPerfect will erase the other member of the pair, and you'll have to mark the entry again.

Repeat these steps to mark each item in the document that you want to include in the table of contents. Once you have finished, you can define the style and generate the table.

Defining the Table of Contents Style

The next step in creating a table of contents is to decide where you want WordPerfect to generate it, then define it and select a page numbering style for each level. The table of contents usually appears at the beginning of a document, or right after the title page, if you're using one. Wherever you decide to place it, you'll probably want to separate it from the rest of the text with hard page breaks.

1. Move the cursor to the position in the document where you want the table to appear after WordPerfect generates it, and create a hard page break.

2. Select the Define option from the Mark Text menu:

   Keyboard: Press the Mark Text key (Alt-F5).

   This menu will appear:

   ```
   1 Cross-Ref; 2 Subdoc; 3 Index; 4 ToA Short Form;
   5 Define; 6 Generate: 0
   ```

   Select the fifth option, **Define**. The Mark Text: Define menu will appear, as shown in Figure 18.3. Select the first option, Define Table of Contents.

   Mouse: Display the **Mark** menu and select **Define**, as shown in Figure 18.4; then select Table of Contents.

   The Table of Contents Definition menu will appear, as shown in Figure 18.8. The next step is to define the number of levels you will be using. The table of contents shown in Figure 18.7 has five levels, the maximum. Level 1 entries start at the left margin, level 2 entries are indented 1/2", and each level below is indented one additional tab stop.

3. Select the first option, **Number of Levels**, and enter the number of levels you want in your table.

   As soon as you type a number, Flush right with leader appears next to the Page Numbering option for each level you have selected, since it is the default page numbering style. This style is illustrated in Figure 18.7. Unless you want to use this style for each level in your table of contents, your next step is to change it.

```
Table of Contents Definition

    1 - Number of Levels          1

    2 - Display Last Level in     No
        Wrapped Format

    3 - Page Numbering - Level 1  Flush right with leader
                         Level 2
                         Level 3
                         Level 4
                         Level 5










Selection: 0
```

Figure 18.8 *The Table of Contents Definition menu.*

4. If you want to change the page numbering style for one or more levels,
    select the third option, **P**age Numbering.

    This menu will appear at the bottom of the screen:

    ```
    1 None; 2 Pg # Follows; 3 (Pg #) Follows; 4 Flush Rt;
    5 Flush Rt with Leader: 0
    ```

    You can select a different method for the entire table, or for any of the
    levels. Use the first option, *None,* if you do not want page numbers to
    appear next to the entries. The second, *Pg # Follows*, positions the page
    numbers a few spaces after the entry. The third, *(Pg #) Follows*, also
    positions the page numbers a few spaces after the entry, but they appear
    in parentheses. The fourth, *Flush Rt*, places the page numbers at the right
    margin. The fifth option, *Flush Rt with Leader*, also places the page
    numbers at the right margin but separates each entry from its page
    number by a row of dots, called *dot leaders.* The two flush right options
    are not available if you've chosen to display the last level in wrapped
    format, as discussed in the following paragraph.

    The second option on the Table of Contents Definition menu, Display
    Last Level in Wrapped Format, determines how entries on your last level
    will be displayed. The default setting is No, meaning they will be dis-
    played on a separate line, as illustrated in the table of contents shown in
    Figure 18.7. If you change this option to Yes, entries in the last level of
    your table will be displayed next to each other, separated by a semicolon,
    as shown in Figure 18.9. As you can see, if there are too many entries to
    fit on one line, the others are wrapped to the next one. When you use the
    wrapped format, WordPerfect won't let you select *Flush Rt* or *Flush Rt*

with Leader for the page numbering style on the last level, since the entries must follow each other on the same line.

```
October in the Railroad Earth . . . . . . . . . . . . . . . .   5
    Extended prelude to further work . . . . . . . . . . . .   7
            Workaday experience (7); Heroic aspect of job (9);
            Romance overlooked by others (12); implied promise
            (13)
```

Figure 18.9 A partial table of contents with the last level in wrapped format.

5. Select a page numbering style for each level in your table of contents, and press Enter when you finish. You have to type a number for each level, because if you press Enter instead, you'll return to the Selection prompt at the bottom of the screen.

   This completes the table of contents definition; you can return to the Edit screen by pressing Enter or clicking the right mouse button. If you look in Reveal Codes, you'll see the definition code that WordPerfect has inserted for your table. For example, if you defined a table with four levels and used the fifth page numbering style for each level, it will appear as follows:

   `[Def Mark:ToC,4:5,5,5,5]`.

The first number, 4, is the number of levels in the table. The other numbers refer to the page numbering style you have selected for each of the four levels.

 Tip: If your table of contents is at the beginning of a document, and you are including page numbers in the printed version, you can force WordPerfect to start numbering after the table of contents. Place the cursor at the top of the first document page after the table of contents, and use the New Page Number option on the Format: Page Numbering menu to change the page number to 1.

The next step is the easiest: Select the Generate option, and sit back and relax while WordPerfect compiles the table for you.

Generating a Table of Contents

If you read the section about creating lists, you may recall that WordPerfect generates all lists, tables, indexes, and cross-references in a document in a single process, replacing any previous lists or tables. This does not imply that you must have them all ready at the same time. For example, if you've already defined and generated a list, when you generate the table of contents, WordPerfect will just replace it with an identical one.

Before generating the table of contents, be sure to save your document. Next, follow these steps:

1. Select Generate from the Mark Text menu:

    Keyboard: Press the Mark Text key (Alt-F5) and select the sixth option, **Generate.**

    Mouse: Display the **Mark** pull-down menu and select **Generate.**

    The Mark Text: Generate menu shown in Figure 18.6 will appear.

2. Select the fifth option, **Generate Tables, Indexes, Cross-References,** etc.

    This message will appear at the bottom of the screen:

    ```
    Existing tables, lists, and indexes will be replaced.
    Continue? Yes (No)
    ```

    Remember, this is only a warning that if you have already defined and generated an index, table of contents, list, or table of authorities, WordPerfect will erase it and then create it again. If you have not defined any of these items, the message is irrelevant.

3. Select **Yes.**

    While WordPerfect is scanning the document for entries that you've marked for your table of contents, this message will appear:

    ```
    Generation in progress. Pass: n, Page n
    ```

When the process is completed, the table of contents will appear on the Edit screen, in the position where you placed the table definition code. If you want to retain the table, be sure to save the document.

Tip: Rather than saving the table with the document, you can block the table of contents and save it as a separate document. To do this, start with the cursor at the beginning of the table, turn on Block mode, move the cursor to the end of the table, then select Save (press F10 or display the File menu and select Save). In response to the `Block name` prompt, type a name for the new file. As soon as you press Enter, WordPerfect will save it.

Updating a Table of Contents

Making changes in a table of contents is similar to changing text that you've marked for a list. If you change any of the words or phrases you've marked for your table of contents, if a marked item is moved to a new page because you have added or deleted a paragraph or two above it, or if you mark new items, just update your table by using the Generate option again. WordPerfect will then erase the old table, and create a new one.

If you have changed a table of contents entry and need to mark it again, locate the [Mark:ToC] code next to it, erase it, and then mark the entry again. You can use the Search feature to help you locate the codes. Since the codes and procedure are identical, refer to the "Updating a List" section, earlier in this chapter.

Creating an Index

Of the three reference tools discussed in this chapter, the index can be the most time-consuming to create—if you mark each occurrence of each entry in your document. However, WordPerfect offers a shortcut: Instead of marking each item in the document that you want to include in the index, you can type a list of all the words and phrases that you want indexed, save it as a separate file called a *concordance file,* and then have WordPerfect use this file to compile the index. When you select the Generate option, WordPerfect will search your document for each entry in the concordance file, and produce an index containing all matching entries in the document. Entries from the concordance file that do not match text in the document will not appear in the index. Since this procedure is much easier than going through a document and marking each item individually, you'll study it first.

An index can have two levels of headings. The subheadings are listed directly below the headings and are indented one tab stop. For example, in Figure 18.10, the heading *Driftnet fishing* has two subheadings, *domestic market* and *foreign fleet*. Notice that WordPerfect capitalizes the first word in each heading, and uses lowercase for the subheadings. The page numbering styles available for your index will be familiar, since they are the same as the ones for lists and table of contents. For example, Figure 18.10 shows an index formatted using the *Page Numbers Follow Entries* style.

Index

Congressional testimony 7, 12, 15
Driftnet fishing 2, 5, 8, 11
            domestic market 6
            foreign fleet 3, 6
Future implications 2, 12, 15
Potential solutions 16, 20, 23
            aquaculture 4, 8, 19
            elimination of driftnets 9
            restrictions on catch 12
Short-term implications 16, 19, 21

Figure 18.10   *An index formatted using the Page Numbers Follow Entries page numbering style.*

Creating a Concordance File

To create a concordance file, you type each word or phrase on a separate line, pressing Enter after each one. Although an individual entry can exceed one line, it must be followed by a [HRt] code. If you want to include subheadings for any of the entries, you must mark them. After you type all the entries, you should use the Sort feature to alphabetize them, since this will speed up the index generation. Next, you save the file, clear the Edit screen, retrieve the document you want to index, and define the index. As you'll see, WordPerfect will ask if you want to use a concordance file and give you the opportunity to name it. Since a concordance file is independent of the document, you can use the same one to index all similar documents.

Clear the Edit screen, and follow these steps:

1. Type each word or phrase, pressing Enter after each entry. If you want to designate any of them as subheadings, follow the instructions in the next section to mark them.

2. When you finish, be sure to save the concordance file, using a distinct name from the document you will be indexing. After that, you should alphabetize the concordance file, as described below.

Defining Subheadings in a Concordance File

Follow these steps if you want to include subheadings in your concordance file:

1. Place the cursor on the word or phrase you want to use as a subheading. If it includes more than one word, use Block to highlight the entire phrase.

2. Select Index:

   Keyboard: Press Mark Text (Alt-F5) and choose the third option, Index.

   Mouse: Display the **Mark** pull-down menu and select **Index**.

   An `Index heading` prompt will appear at the bottom of the screen, followed by the word or phrase you are marking. For example, if you had blocked *foreign fleet*, the prompt would appear as follows:

   `Index heading: foreign fleet`

3. Since this will be a subheading, type the name of the index heading under which you want this item to appear, and press Enter.

   As soon as you start typing, the suggested heading will disappear. After you press Enter, WordPerfect will display the word or phrase your cursor is on, and suggest it as the subheading. For example, if you had changed the index heading to *Driftnet fishing* in step 3 and then pressed Enter, the prompt would appear as follows:

   `Subheading: foreign fleet`

4. To accept this as the subheading, press Enter. If you look in Reveal Codes, you'll see that WordPerfect has placed an index code next to the item, naming the heading and subheading. For the example described above, the code would appear as follows:

   `[Index:Driftnet fishing;foreign fleet]`

5. Repeat the procedure for each item you want to use as a subheading, and then save the concordance file.

Sorting the Concordance File

Once you've typed and saved your concordance file, alphabetize it following these steps:

1. Select Sort:

   Keyboard: Press Merge/Sort (Ctrl-F9) and select the Sort option.

   Mouse: Display the **Tools** menu and select **Sort**.

   WordPerfect will ask for the name of an input file, suggesting the document on the Edit screen with this prompt: (Screen). After you press Enter to accept (Screen) as the input file, you will be asked to name the output file. Again, (Screen) will be suggested, meaning the results of the sort you are about to perform will be placed on the Edit screen.

2. Press Enter twice to accept *Screen* for the input and output file.

   Next, the Sort by Line screen should appear. If you see a different screen, such as the Sort Secondary Merge File or Sort by Paragraph screen, use the **Type** option (7) to change it to the **Line** option (2).

3. Select the first option on the Sort by Line menu, **Perform Action**.

   WordPerfect sorts the document by the first character in each word and places the results on the Edit screen.

4. Save the document again, to retain the alphabetized list, and then clear the screen.

   If you want to mark individual items in the document, continue on to the next section. If not, you are ready to define and generate the index, so skip to the "Defining the Index" section.

 Tip: You can mark individual items in a document for the index and still use a concordance file. WordPerfect will generate the index using both: indexing both entries from the concordance file, and the words or phrases you've marked individually.

 Warning: If your concordance file is large and your computer's memory (RAM) is limited, you may run out of memory when generating the index, and a warning will appear. If so, try to limit the concordance file to the most important words and phrases.

Marking Text in the Document to Be Included in an Index

If you want to mark individual items in your document so WordPerfect will include them in the index, retrieve the document and follow these steps. You may want to use the Search feature to help you locate them, as described in the section "Making Changes in an Index" (later in this chapter). Marking items for an index is similar to creating a list or table of contents, but you don't have to block the text unless the entry is longer than one word.

1. To select a word or phrase as an entry in your index:

    To mark a single word, place the cursor anywhere in the word you want to mark.

    To mark a phrase, start with the cursor at the beginning of the phrase, turn on Block mode, and move the cursor to the last character you want to include.

2. Select Index:

    Keyboard: Press the Mark Text (Alt-F5) key. Although the menu that you see if you are marking a single word will be slightly different from the one you see if you are blocking a phrase, in both cases you'll select the third option, Index.

    Mouse: Display the **Mark** menu and select **Index**.

    A prompt will appear at the bottom of the screen, asking for the index heading. It will be followed by the word or phrase the cursor was on when you selected the Index option. WordPerfect assumes that you want to use this text as the heading, although you can type something else as the heading and use this as the subheading instead.

3. Your next step depends on whether you want this item to be a heading or a subheading:

    If you want the text to be a heading, press Enter to accept it.

    If you want it to be a subheading, type the heading you want it to appear under, and then press Enter.

    Next, this prompt appears: Subheading. If you typed a different heading in step 3, it will be followed by the word the cursor was on, or the phrase you blocked.

4. Your next step depends on the action you took in step 3:

If you pressed Enter to index the item as a heading, you have two options: 1) If you want a subheading, type it and then press Enter; 2) If you don't want a subheading, press Enter to leave it blank.

If you typed a different heading in step 3, WordPerfect assumes you want the word your cursor was on when you selected this option or the blocked text to be a subheading, so it appears after the `Subheading` prompt. You have a few options: You can 1) Press Enter to accept it as the subheading; 2) Type a different subheading; 3) If you don't want a subheading, press Ctrl-End to delete the text, and then press Enter.

5. Repeat each step to mark all the items for your index, and save the document.

Each word or phrase you designate as an entry will be marked with an [Index] code, visible in Reveal Codes. If the item only includes a heading, it will appear as follows:

```
[Index:Heading]
```

where "Heading" will actually be the word or blocked phrase, or text you selected in step 3. If it includes a heading and subheading, it will appear as follows:

```
[Index:Heading;subheading]
```

where "subheading" is the text you selected in step 4.

 Tip: To avoid duplicating entries, you may want to make a list of all the words or phrases you want to designate as headings and subheadings in your index, and make sure that they are spelled the same when you mark them. If you mark a word or phrase that varies by even one character, it will appear as a new entry in your index, not as another page number reference. To make it even easier, run the spell checker before generating the index.

Defining an Index

The next step in creating an index for your document is defining it, and deciding which page numbering style to use. Although an index can be placed anywhere in a document, it usually appears on a separate page at the end. Assuming that's where you want to place the index, follow these steps:

1. Move the cursor to the end of the document you are indexing, and create a hard page break.

2. Select the Define option from the Mark Text menu:

   Keyboard: Press the Mark Text key (Alt-F5) and select the fifth option, **Define.**

   Mouse: Display the **Mark** pull-down menu and select **Define.**

3. Select the Index option.

   You'll see the following prompt at the bottom of the screen:

   ```
   Concordance Filename (Enter=none):
   ```

4. If you are using a concordance file, type its name and then press Enter. If you're not using a concordance file, just press Enter to leave the prompt blank. The Index Definition menu appears, as shown in Figure 18.11.

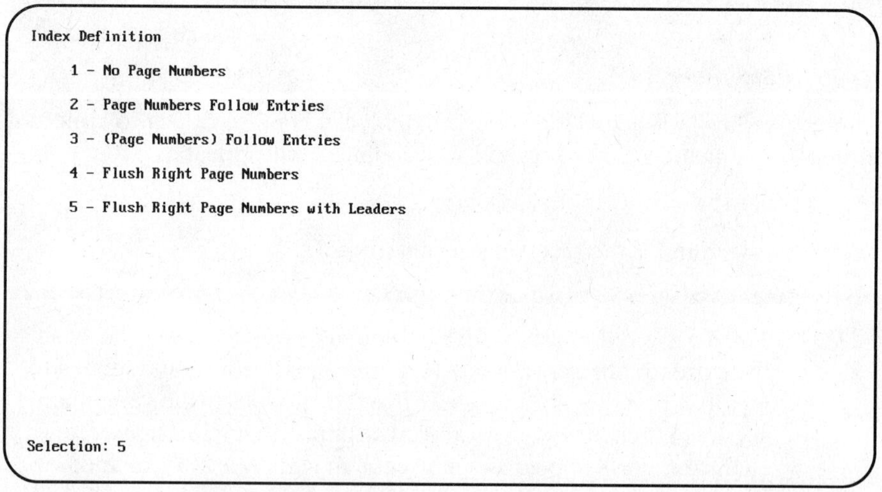

```
Index Definition

    1 - No Page Numbers

    2 - Page Numbers Follow Entries

    3 - (Page Numbers) Follow Entries

    4 - Flush Right Page Numbers

    5 - Flush Right Page Numbers with Leaders




Selection: 5
```

Figure 18.11   *The Index Definition menu.*

5. Select one of the five page numbering options. The options are the same as those for lists and tables, and are explained in detail in the section entitled "Defining the List Style."

   This completes the index definition process. If you use Reveal Codes, you'll see an index definition code, such as:

   ```
   [Def Mark:Index,3]
   ```

The number following the word Index represents the page numbering style you've selected; in this example, the third style was used. If you named a concordance file, its name will also appear in the code, after the number. For example, if you named the concordance file *concord.txt*, it will appear as follows:

```
[Def Mark:Index,3;concord.txt]
```

Generating an Index

The last step in creating an index is to have WordPerfect generate it. The process is identical to generating a list or table of contents. Remember, if you've already defined and generated a list, table of contents, or another index, WordPerfect will replace it with an identical one. Begin by saving the document, and then follow these steps:

1. Select the Generate option:

    Keyboard: Press the Mark Text key (Alt-F5) and select the sixth option, **Generate**.

    Mouse: Display the **Mark** pull-down menu and select **Generate**.

    The Mark Text: Generate menu shown in Figure 18.6 will appear.

2. Select the fifth option, **Generate Tables, Indexes, Cross-References, etc.**

    This message will appear at the bottom of the screen:

    ```
    Existing tables, lists, and indexes will be replaced.
    Continue? Yes (No)
    ```

3. Select **Yes**. This prompt will appear at the bottom of the screen while WordPerfect is creating the index:

    ```
    Generation in progress. Pass: n, Page n
    ```

    When the process is completed, the index will appear on the Edit screen, in the position where you placed the definition code. If you want to retain the index along with the document, save it again.

    If a prompt such as this one appears at the bottom of the screen while WordPerfect is generating the index:

    ```
    Not enough memory to use entire concordance file.
    Continue? No (Yes)
    ```

it is a warning that your computer does not have enough memory (RAM) available to complete the indexing process. This usually happens if you are using a large concordance file, and your computer's memory is limited. If you select Y, the program will match as many entries from the concordance file as it can with items in your document, but the resulting index probably won't contain all the entries. It's safer to select N, since this will stop the index generation process. You can then try to free up some memory, or reduce the size of the concordance file.

If you need to free up memory, start by checking to see if the Doc 2 Edit screen is open. If so, you should close it. To do this:

1. Switch to Doc 2:

    Keyboard: Press Switch (Shift-F3).

    Mouse: Display the Edit menu and select the **S**witch Document option.

2. To close the Doc 2 Edit screen and return to the Doc 1 Edit screen:

    Keyboard: Press Exit (F7).

    Mouse: Select E**x**it from the **F**ile menu.

    The `Save document?` prompt appears.

3. Your next action depends on whether or not there is text in Doc 2, and whether you want to save it:

    If the Doc 2 Edit screen is clear, or if you do not want to save the document it contains, type N in response to the `Save document?` prompt, and then type Y in response to the `Exit doc 2?` prompt.

    If you want to save the document in the Doc 2 Edit screen, type Y in response to the `Save document?` prompt, enter a file name and save it; then type Y in response to the `Exit doc 2?` prompt.

    Either way, this closes the Doc 2 Edit screen and returns you to Doc 1. It may free up enough memory for you to generate the index.

    If you are running WordPerfect under the Shell or another menu program, or concurrently running another program, you can free up some memory by closing those programs. Another possible solution is to reduce the size of the concordance file and then regenerate it.

Making Changes in an Index

You make changes in an index in much the same way as you make changes in lists and tables. If you have changed any of the words or phrases you marked, just erase the old codes, mark them again, and update your index by using the Generate option. WordPerfect will then erase the old index and create a new one.

To locate the index codes with the Search key:

1. Start with the cursor at the top of the document, and select Forward Search:

    Keyboard: Press Forward Search (F2).

    Mouse: Display the Search menu and select **Forward**.

2.   Press Mark Text (Alt-F5). (You cannot use the mouse.)

3. Select the third option from the menu, **Index**. The search prompt will appear as follows:

    → `Srch: [Index]`

4. To start the search:

    Keyboard: Press F2.

    Mouse: Click the right button.

The cursor will stop just past the first occurrence of the index code, and you can erase it by pressing Backspace and typing Y in response to the prompt asking if you want to delete it.

 Tip: Whenever you ask WordPerfect to print a document containing a [Def Mark] code that defines a list, index, or table of contents, you'll see this warning: `Document may need to be generated. Print? No (Yes)` and you must type Y if you want to print it. Unless you've made changes to the marked entries in your list, index, or table since you last generated it, you should go ahead and print it. Otherwise, select No, use the Generate option again, and then print it.

M ACROS

As you perform tasks in WordPerfect, you may notice that you are repeating certain keystrokes or typing standard text frequently. Whenever you notice such a pattern developing, you should consider creating a macro to perform the task automatically. There are basically two types of macros in WordPerfect: macros that you create by recording keystrokes as you use them on the Edit screen and macros that consist primarily of commands from the macro programming language, which you create through the Macro Editor. You can also combine these techniques, recording keystrokes in a macro and then editing it to include commands from the macro language. WordPerfect saves all macros in a special type of file, with the extension *WPM*.

The first type of macro is a sequence of keystrokes that you record while using them so that you can repeat them anytime by pressing a few keys to start the macro. For example, if you wanted a macro to type your name and address, you would turn on the macro definition feature, type your name and address, and then turn off macro definition. After that, you could have WordPerfect type your name and address by pressing just two keys, such as Alt-N. This kind of macro can serve as a shortcut for repetitive tasks such as typing boilerplate text, formatting with bold or italics, formatting and printing on an envelope or label, or blocking and moving text. It can include text and WordPerfect commands like formatting or font changes. When you use such a macro, WordPerfect replays the keystrokes exactly as you typed them originally.

After you become familiar with some basic programming concepts, you can design more complex macros using WordPerfect's macro command language. For instance, you can create macros that display prompts or menus on the screen, ask for input from the keyboard, prompt the user with a beep or message, make decisions based on user input, enter the path and name of the current document, and check for conditions such as whether there is a document on the Edit screen, whether Reveal Codes is active, or whether Block is on.

Creating Keystroke Macros

Creating a simple macro, such as one that types a paragraph of boilerplate text, is easy: Select Macro Define, type a file name for the macro, type a brief description of what the macro will do, and then enter the keystrokes for the macro. At this point it's as though a tape recorder is keeping track of every key you press. When you finish, you select Macro Define again, and WordPerfect automatically saves your new macro. Although you can move, copy, rename, and delete a macro file, you cannot retrieve one like a regular WordPerfect file (by using the Retrieve key, the Retrieve option on the List Files menu, or Retrieve on the pull-down File menu). If you need to change a macro or view its contents, you must use the Macro Editor.

WordPerfect lets you use two types of file names for your macros. The first is like any other file name and can include one to eight characters (letters and/or numbers). For example, you could name a macro LIST, PRINT, or MOVE. The second type includes Alt combined with one of the letter keys, A through Z. WordPerfect automatically supplies the three-character extension WPM to both types of macros when you create them. For example, if you type LIST when prompted for a name during macro definition, the actual name will be *LIST.WPM*. If you type ALTB (or press Alt-B), the file name will be *ALTB.WPM*. The difference in the two types of macro names is how you use them. To use a macro such as LIST, you have to select Macro Execute and enter the macro name. To use an Alt macro, you just press the Alt key along with the letter key, such as Alt-B.

If you press Enter instead of typing a name while defining a macro, WordPerfect saves the macro under the name WP{WP}WPM. You use this macro by pressing Alt-F10 and then pressing Enter. Unlike other macros, you cannot edit or change it.

Tip: Because you can create an Alt key macro for each letter of the alphabet, you are limited to 26 of these shortcut macros. If this is not enough, you can use WordPerfect's Keyboard Layout feature to assign macros to the 26 Ctrl and letter key combinations, such as Ctrl-A. See Part Three, "Command Reference," for more information about Keyboard Layout.

Macros are saved in the current directory, unless you type a path and directory as part of the macro name when defining it, or if you have designated a separate directory for your macros and keyboard layout files through the Setup: Location of Files menu (as explained in the section "Setup").

> **Warning:** Never try to retrieve a macro like a regular WordPerfect file. You can use List Files to move, copy, rename, and delete macros, but not to retrieve them. To edit or view them, you must use the Macro Editor.

Creating a Macro to Type Text

If you've never used macros, you can learn the basics by creating and using a simple macro that types frequently used text for you. Follow these steps to create a macro named *CC* that will type a memo distribution list such as this one:

```
cc: A. McDowell
    M. Jensen
    H. Hampkin
  C. Lassiter
```

As you create a macro and enter the keystrokes you want it to contain, WordPerfect will use them on the Edit screen. For example, when you type the names for your memo distribution list, WordPerfect will enter them as text. For this reason, if you are working on a document, save it before you begin defining a macro in case you make a mistake. In most cases, you should also clear the Edit screen.

To create the macro:

1. Select Macro Define:

   Keyboard: Press the Macro Define key, Ctrl-F10.

   Mouse: Display the **Tools** menu and select **Macro**. The Macro menu pops out to the right, as shown in Figure 19.1. Select the Define option.

> **Warning:** If you are working on a document on the Edit screen, save it before you define a macro because the keystrokes that you record in the macro perform their task on the Edit screen as you record them.

This prompt appears, asking for the new macro's name:

```
Define macro:
```

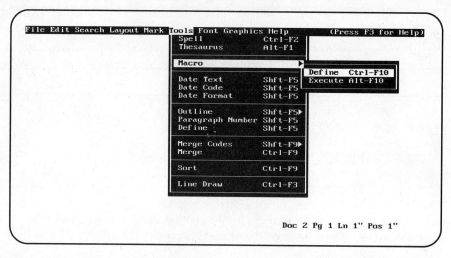

Figure 19.1 *When you display the Tools menu and select Macro, this menu pops out to the right. Use it to define or execute a macro.*

2. Type the macro name:

    CC

    and press Enter.

    If this prompt appears:

    CC.WPM Already Exists: 1 Replace; 2 Edit; 3 Description: 0

    WordPerfect is warning you that a macro named *CC* already exists. If you are positive you don't need the macro, you can select the Replace option to erase it and replace it with the new macro you are defining. However, if you are unsure or think the macro may have been created by one of your co-workers, it is safer to cancel the operation and then start again, using a different name for this macro, such as *CC1* or *Memolist*. If you choose to cancel it, press Cancel (F1) and return to step 1.

    The next prompt asks for a description of the macro. This is an optional step. You'll see the description when you use the Macro Editor, and it can be a useful reminder of what the macro does. Also, if you use the List File menu's Look option to view a macro, the description is all you will see. A description can contain up to 39 characters.

3. For the description, type

    Memo distribution list

    and then press Enter. If you don't want to enter a description, you can skip this step by pressing Enter.

The blinking `Macro Def` prompt in the lower-left corner of the screen indicates that WordPerfect is now recording all your keystrokes into the macro. This includes every character you type and all cursor movement and editing keystrokes, such as Backspace, Left Arrow, and Enter.

4. Type this list (or substitute your own list of names). You may want to press Tab before each name to align them in a column.

```
cc: A. McDowell
    M. Jensen
    H. Hampkin
    C. Lassiter
```

Press Enter after typing each name, including the last one.

5. When you finish typing the names, end macro definition the same way you started it:

Keyboard: Press Ctrl-F10 again.

Mouse: Display the **T**ools menu, select **M**acro, and then select the **D**efine option.

The `Macro Def` prompt disappears, and your macro file is now saved under the name *CC.WPM*. To clear the names from your Edit screen, use the Exit key (F7) or select **E**xit from the **F**ile menu.

Using the Macro

From now on, whenever you want WordPerfect to type the distribution list for you, use these two steps:

1. Select Macro Execute:

Keyboard: Press the Macro key, Alt-F10.

Mouse: Display the **T**ools menu and select **M**acro, then **E**xecute.

This prompt will appear in the lower-left corner of the screen, asking for the macro name:

`Macro:`

2. Type the macro name, `CC`, and press Enter. The macro completes its work almost instantly.

> **Tip:** While defining a macro, you can use the mouse to select options from the pull-down menus, but it is not advisable because there are too many inconsistencies. Do not use the mouse to move the cursor, or the macro may not function properly.

Editing the Macro

If you want to add another name to the distribution list, it's not necessary to redefine your macro; instead, just select the Macro Editor, move the cursor into position, and type the name. There are two ways to reach the Macro Editor. The first is to press Home Ctrl-F10, type the macro name, and press Enter twice. The second is to select Macro Define, type the macro name, and choose Edit in response to the prompt that asks if you want to replace the macro, edit it, or change the description. Since the latter method works both with the keyboard and the mouse, that method will be explained first.

1. Select Macro Define:

   Keyboard: Press the Macro Define key (Ctrl-F10).

   Mouse: Display the **Tools** menu, select **Macro**, and then select the **Define** option.

2. In response to the Define macro prompt, type the macro name, CC, and press Enter. Since you've already created a macro named *CC,* this prompt will appear:

   CC.WPM Already Exists: 1 Replace; 2 Edit; 3 Description: 0

3. Select the second option, **Edit.**

   This brings up the Macro Editor, as shown in Figure 19.2. The file name (CC.WPM) appears on the second line, and the macro description on the third (if you typed it). Below is a box containing codes and text that represent the keystrokes you pressed while defining your macro. The cursor is at the beginning. The centered dots between words represent the blank spaces you inserted by pressing the space bar. Keystroke commands and macro commands are shown in braces. For instance, the {Enter} command is a keystroke command and represents the positions where you pressed the Enter key while recording the macro. If you used the tab key, it is represented by {Tab}.

   Notice {DISPLAY OFF} at the beginning of the macro. This is a macro command, which WordPerfect automatically inserted when you created the macro. WordPerfect usually inserts {DISPLAY OFF} in a new macro to prevent the keystrokes from being displayed as you use it. There are a few exceptions, such as when you use the {PAUSE} command, as described later in the chapter, or when the macro stops inside a WordPerfect menu. Macros run faster with Display off, but it must be turned on in some macros or they won't work. For example, later in this chapter you'll learn how to create a macro that pauses in the Format Line menu to let you enter a number for the line spacing. Unless Display is on, you won't be able to see the menu, and the macro will be useless. Macro commands appear in all uppercase inside the curly braces, which distinguishes them from the keystroke commands such as {Enter}, where only the first letter is capitalized.

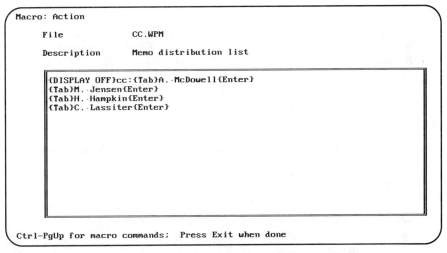

```
Macro: Action

    File          CC.WPM

    Description   Memo distribution list

   ┌─────────────────────────────────────────────────────────┐
   │{DISPLAY OFF}cc:{Tab}A. McDowell{Enter}                    │
   │{Tab}M. Jensen{Enter}                                      │
   │{Tab}H. Hampkin{Enter}                                     │
   │{Tab}C. Lassiter{Enter}                                    │
   │                                                           │
   │                                                           │
   │                                                           │
   │                                                           │
   │                                                           │
   │                                                           │
   │                                                           │
   └─────────────────────────────────────────────────────────┘

Ctrl-PgUp for macro commands;   Press Exit when done
```

Figure 19.2 The Macro Editor, with keystrokes for the memo distribution list macro.

To add a name to the list, place the cursor wherever you want the name, and type it as you normally would. To move the cursor, use regular cursor movement keys such as Down Arrow or Page Down, or use the mouse.

4. Place the cursor on the blank line below the last name in the list.

If you want to include a {Tab} command before the name, you cannot simply press the Tab key. So that you can use keys such as Tab, Enter, Cancel, and Exit while editing, WordPerfect provides a separate method of entering them as keystroke commands in the Macro Editor: Command Insert mode. If you want to insert only one command, as in this case, press Ctrl-V first. To insert several commands, press Ctrl-F10, press the keys, and then press Ctrl-F10 again.

5. If you want to insert the {Tab} command into the macro, press Ctrl-V, and then press Tab.

6. Type this name (or substitute another for your list):

   M. Cunningham

   If you want WordPerfect to insert a blank line below M.Cunningham and move the cursor there, as in the previous lines, the {Enter} command must appear at the end of the line. Use Ctrl-V to insert it into your macro. Pressing the Enter key alone only moves the cursor to the next line in the Macro Editor itself, and has no effect on macro execution.

7. To insert the {Enter} command into the macro, press Ctrl-V, and then press Enter.

   Now your macro is complete, and you can exit back to the Edit screen. If you make a mistake during macro editing, press Cancel (F1) and type Y in response to the Cancel changes? prompt that appears.

8. Press Exit (F7) to end macro editing.

From now on, the macro should include the name *M. Cunningham* at the bottom of the list. Try using it again to make sure that it works correctly.

 Tip: While using the Macro Editor, you can insert commands for many function keys just by pressing the key. However, so that you can use keys such as Cancel, Exit, Enter, Delete, Backspace, Tab, and the cursor movement keys while editing your macro, you must use Command Insert mode by pressing Ctrl-V or Ctrl-F10 to insert them as commands. If you use Ctrl-V, only the next keystroke becomes a command in the macro. If you use Ctrl-F10, all keystrokes become commands, until you press Ctrl-F10 again.

Using the Pause Command in a Macro

WordPerfect includes a powerful set of commands that you can use in your macros. For instance, the {PAUSE} command temporarily stops a macro, allowing you to perform an action such as selecting a menu option or responding to a prompt. In this section, you will learn how to use {PAUSE} in a macro that lets you designate a section of text and then select a font attribute, such as bold, underline, or italics, to format it. Here's how it works: {PAUSE} turns on Block mode, pauses to let you move the cursor and highlight the text, selects the Font Appearance menu, pauses while you select an attribute such as italics, then carries out the command. In the next section, you'll use {PAUSE} in a macro that selects the Line Spacing option on the Format Line menu and waits while you enter the spacing.

Follow these steps to create the font attribute macro, using the name ALTA:

1. Select Macro Define:

    Keyboard: Press Ctrl-F10.

    Mouse: Display the **Tools** menu, select **Macro**, and then select **Define**.

    The `Define macro` prompt appears.

2. Press Alt-A, or type `ALTA` and press Enter.

3. For the description, type

    `Blocks and selects Font Appearance`

    and then press Enter.

4. Turn on Block mode:

    Keyboard: Press Block (Alt-F4).

    Mouse: Display the **Edit** menu and select **Block**.

    `Block on` appears next to the `Macro Def` prompt in the lower-left corner of the screen. The next step is to select the {PAUSE} command. When you use the macro, it will pause here to let you move the cursor and designate the end of the block. You insert the command with the Macro Commands key, Ctrl-PgUp.

5. Press the Macro Commands key, Ctrl-PgUp. This prompt appears at the bottom of the screen:

    `1 Pause; 2 Display; 3 Assign; 4 Comment: 0`

6. Type 1 to select the Pause option, and press Enter.

7. Press the Font key, Ctrl-F8, and select the second option, Appearance. The Font Appearance menu is displayed, as shown below:

    `1 Bold 2 Undrln 3 Dbl Und 4 Italc 5 Outln 6 Shadw 7 Sm Cap`
    `8 Redln 9 Stkout: 0`

    When you use this macro, WordPerfect will pause here and let you select the one you want to use.

8. Insert another {PAUSE} command by pressing the Macro Commands key, Ctrl-PgUp, and selecting Pause. To complete the command, press Enter.

9. End macro definition by pressing Ctrl-F10 again.

Notice that the Font Appearance menu is still visible. Block mode is also on, as you'll see after you cancel the Font Appearance menu (in the next step).

10.   Press Cancel (F1) twice to exit the Font Appearance menu, and turn off Block mode.

Using the Font Attribute Macro

To use this macro to block a section of text and select a font appearance attribute, such as italics:

1.   Place the cursor at the beginning of the section you want to format, and press Alt-A. The macro pauses to let you designate the block.

2.   Move the cursor to the end of the section you want to include in the block, and press Enter. The Font Appearance menu is displayed.

3.   Select one of the options.

This turns off the macro and formats the blocked section with the appearance option you selected. For example, if you selected Bold, the text will be boldfaced and surrounded by Bold On and Bold Off codes.

Creating a Macro in the Macro Editor

In addition to the {PAUSE} command you used in the Alt-A macro, WordPerfect's macro language includes over 65 other commands. Only four of them can be inserted into a macro while you are defining it: PAUSE, DISPLAY, ASSIGN, and COMMENT. These appeared on the menu that you saw when you pressed Ctrl-PgUp while creating the Alt-A macro:

```
1 Pause; 2 Display; 3 Assign; 4 Comment: 0
```

To insert any of the other 65 commands, or to insert a PAUSE, DISPLAY, ASSIGN, or COMMENT command into an existing macro, use the Macro Editor.

You can go directly to the editor to create a macro with commands, or you can create the macro, leaving the commands out, then edit it and insert the commands. To learn how to create a macro from inside the editor, in this section you will define a macro for line spacing. It works by selecting the Format Line menu, pausing while you enter a number for line spacing, and then returning to the Edit screen.

1. To go to the Macro Editor:

   Keyboard: Press Home and then Ctrl-F10 (Macro Define).

   Mouse: Display the **Tools** menu, select **Macro**, select the **Define** option, and then select **Edit**.

   You cannot use the pull-down menu to go directly to the Macro Editor.

2. In response to the `Define macro` prompt, enter the macro name: ALTS.

3. Type this description:

   `Line spacing macro, with pause`

   and press Enter.

   This takes you directly to the Macro Editor. This macro contains nothing but the {DISPLAY OFF} command, which WordPerfect has automatically inserted. Since you need to be able to see the Format menus while using the macro, the next step is to erase the {DISPLAY OFF} command.

4. Press the Delete key once to erase the {DISPLAY OFF} command.

5. Enter these keystrokes to access the Line Spacing option on the Format Line menu:

   `Shift-F8 L S`

   Shift-F8 inserted the {Format} command. When you use the macro, it will bring up the Format menu. The next keystroke, L, will select the Line menu, and S will select the Line Spacing option. Your next step is to insert the {PAUSE} command, so that when you use this macro you can type the number for line spacing. The prompt at the bottom of the screen provides a clue about how to do this: Press the Macro Commands key, Ctrl-PgUp.

   `Ctrl-PgUp for macro commands`

6. Press Ctrl-PgUp.

   The Macro Commands menu appears in a box on the right side of the screen, as shown in Figure 19.3. Although you can only see the first five commands, there are actually 69 in the list. You can scroll through the list and see the other commands by pressing regular cursor movement keys like Down Arrow or Page Down. To move the cursor directly onto a command, you can use Name Search by typing the first letter of the command.

7. Type P. This moves the cursor onto the {Para Down} command. To move to the {PAUSE} command, either press Down Arrow twice or type au.

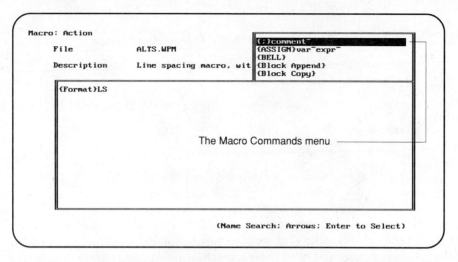

```
Macro: Action

    File          ALTS.WPM           {;)comment~
                                     {ASSIGN}var~expr~
    Description   Line spacing macro, wit {BELL}
                                     {Block Append}
                                     {Block Copy}

    {Format}LS




                        The Macro Commands menu




                        (Name Search; Arrows; Enter to Select)
```

Figure 19.3 *When you press Ctrl-PgUp from inside the Macro Editor, a box appears containing macro commands.*

8. Press Enter to insert the {PAUSE} command into your macro.

   The next step is to insert {Enter} and {Exit} commands. In a previous section, you pressed Ctrl-V to insert the {Enter} command into the macro. This time, try using the Ctrl-F10 method.

 Warning: You cannot enter a macro command such as {PAUSE} by typing it as text in the Macro Editor. Instead, you must press Ctrl-PgUp and select it from the Macro Commands menu.

9. Press the Macro Define key, Ctrl-F10.

   This prompt appears:

   Press Macro Define to enable editing

   Until you press Ctrl-F10 again, any keys you press will become commands in your macro, so be careful. For instance, if you press the Left Arrow key to try moving the cursor, WordPerfect will insert the {Left} command. Also, you won't be able to use the Backspace key to erase these commands. Instead, you'll add a {Backspace} command into your macro. If you do enter any commands accidentally, you can erase them after pressing Ctrl-F10 to turn off Macro Define.

10. Press Enter; then press Exit (F7).

    Your screen should now resemble Figure 19.4

```
Macro: Action                                    {Para Up}
                                                 {PAUSE}
    File             ALTS.WPM                    {PAUSE KEY}key~
                                                 {PROMPT}message~
    Description      Line spacing macro, wit     {QUIT}

    {Format}LS{PAUSE}{Enter}{Exit}








    Press Macro Define to enable editing
```

Figure 19.4 *The completed macro, with {PAUSE} command.*

11. Press Ctrl-F10 to turn off Command mode so that you can press the Exit key to leave the Macro Editor. This prompt reappears at the bottom of the screen:

    `Ctrl-PgUp for macro commands;  Press Exit when done`

12. Press Exit (F7) to end macro editing, and return to the Edit screen.

    Now you can test the macro. When you press ALTS, the Format Line menu should appear, with the cursor on the Line Spacing option. It pauses there, waiting for you to enter a number such as 2 for double spacing. Type the number for the line spacing you wish to use, then press Enter. You then return to the Edit screen. If you look in Reveal Codes, you should see the line spacing code.

    As you have seen, there are many other macro commands available for you to explore. The various commands are categorized by function in Table 19.1. Some of the commands appear in more than one category. In the next section, you'll study some of the others.

Table 19.1 *WordPerfect's macro commands, categorized by function.*

User Interface Commands

BELL
CHAR
INPUT
LOOK
ORIGINAL KEY

continued

Table 19.1 (continued)

PAUSE
PAUSE KEY
PROMPT
STATUS PROMPT
TEXT

Flow Control Commands

BREAK
CALL
CASE
CASE CALL
CHAIN
ELSE
END FOR
END IF
END WHILE
FOR
FOR EACH
GO
IF
IF EXISTS
LABEL
NEST
NEXT
ON CANCEL
ON ERROR
ON NOT FOUND
QUIT
RESTART
RETURN
RETURN CANCEL
RETURN ERROR
RETURN NOT FOUND
SHELL MACRO
WHILE

Macro Termination Commands

BREAK
QUIT
RESTART

RETURN
RETURN CANCEL
RETURN ERROR
RETURN NOT FOUND

Handling External Conditions

CANCEL OFF
CANCEL ON
ON CANCEL
ON ERROR
ON NOT FOUND
RETURN CANCEL
RETURN ERROR
RETURN NOT FOUND

Macro Execution

CHAIN
NEST
SHELL MACRO

Assign a Value to a Variable

ASSIGN
CHAR
IF EXISTS
LEN
LOOK
MID
NEXT
SYSTEM
TEXT
VAR n
VARIABLE

System Variables

KTON
NTOK
STATE
SYSTEM
ORIGINAL KEY

continued

Table 19.1 *(continued)*

Execution Control

DISPLAY OFF
DISPLAY ON
MENU OFF
MENU ON
SPEED
WAIT

Programming Tools

{;} (Comment)
BELL
DISPLAY OFF
DISPLAY ON
SPEED
STEP OFF
STEP ON

Tip: You can repeat a macro as many times as you like using the Esc key. Press Esc, and in response to the `Repeat Value =` prompt, type the number of times you want the macro to repeat (but don't press Enter). Next, run the macro by pressing Alt-F10 and entering the macro name or, for Alt-key macros, by pressing the Alt-letter combination.

Setup

WordPerfect saves each macro in the current directory you are using when you create it. If you switch directories frequently, this means you could have macros scattered all over your disk. You could even have two different macros with the same name in different directories. To avoid this, specify one specific directory for your macros through the Setup: Location of Files menu; WordPerfect will automatically save all macros there.

The first step is to define the directory for your macro files. To do this, use the Other Directory option on the List Files menu, as described in Chapter 7, "File Management." Next, use the Setup: Location of Files menu to designate the directory:

1. Display the main Setup menu:

   Keyboard: Press Setup (Shift-F1).

   Mouse: Display the File menu and select Setup.

2. Select the Location of Files option.

3. Select the **Keyboard/Macro Files option (2)**.

4. Enter the name of the disk drive and the path to the subdirectory, if necessary.

5. To return to the Edit screen:

   Keyboard: Press Exit (F7).

   Mouse: Click the right button.

> **Tip:** You can have WordPerfect run a macro when you start the program, by typing this command to start it: Wp/m-*macroname*. To simplify the procedure, create a batch file to start WordPerfect with the macro.

Designing a Custom Menu

One of the most useful applications for WordPerfect's macro command language is creating customized menus. They can resemble the ones that appear at the bottom of the screen, like the Alt-P macro shown in Figure 19.5, or they can be full-screen menus, such as the Alt-F macro shown in Figure 19.8. Like most of WordPerfect's menus, you can set up your custom menus so the user can press a letter or number to select an option, and you can display these characters in bold or another attribute.

The best way to learn about the macro language is to use it. In this section, you'll create a macro that brings up the customized menu shown in Figure 19.5. It provides three print options: View Document, Print, and Cancel Printing. The *View Document* option displays the View Document screen, waits for the user to press Enter, and then returns to the Edit screen. The *Print* option selects the Full

Document option from the main Print menu, and prints the entire document on the Edit screen. The *Cancel Printing* option selects the Cancel Jobs option from the Print: Control Printer menu, cancels all print jobs and then returns to the Edit screen.

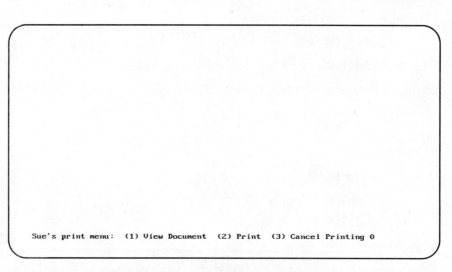

Sue's print menu: (1) View Document   (2) Print   (3) Cancel Printing 0

Figure 19.5   *Sue's Print menu (Alt-P macro). You can use WordPerfect's macro programming language to create a customized menu like this one. You can easily modify the macro to include different options.*

The entire macro listing is shown in Figure 19.6. It includes several commands that will probably be new to you, including {CHAR}, {CASE}, {VARIABLE}, {ELSE}, {LABEL}, {GO}, and {QUIT}. In the step-by-step instructions that follow, you'll learn how to enter each keystroke. Feel free to use different options in your version, instead of View Document, Print, and Cancel Printing.

Before you create the Alt-P macro, you should understand a few basics about WordPerfect's macro command language . In many macros, you will want the user to enter information at the keyboard so that the macro can use it to make a decision. For example, when using the Alt-P macro, the user will select an option from the menu by typing 1, 2, or 3. Once the information is obtained from the user, it must be stored so the macro can act on it. To store it, you use a variable in the macro.

A variable is essentially a storage location in memory (RAM) that you create and name through a macro command such as *ASSIGN*, *TEXT*, or *CHAR*. The contents of the variable can be obtained from the user, or you can establish it inside the macro. For example, in the Alt-P macro, you will use the {CHAR} command to set up a variable and ask the user to type 1, 2, or 3 for its contents. The {ASSIGN} command lets you establish a variable and its contents from inside the macro, without the intervention of the user. For instance, to create a variable named *LIMIT* with the number 10 as its contents, you would insert the ASSIGN command into the macro and type the variable name and contents after it, so it would appear as follows:

```
{ASSIGN}Limit~10~
```

```
{CHAR}Option~ Sue's print menu:   (1) View Document;
(2) Print;   (3) Cancel printing: 0 {Left}~

{CASE}{VARIABLE}Option~~
1~View~
2~Print~
3~Cancel~
{ELSE}
{GO}Exit~~

{LABEL}View~
{Print}v
{PAUSE}{Enter}{Exit}
{QUIT}

{LABEL}Print~
{Print}1
{QUIT}

{LABEL}Cancel~
{Print}cc*Y{Exit}
{QUIT}

{LABEL}Exit~
{QUIT}
```

Figure 19.6 *The listing for the Alt-P macro.*

Macro variable names can contain up to seven characters, including letters, numbers, and characters from any of WordPerfect's character sets (but one character from the extended character sets equals three standard characters), and you can create up to 256 of them. You can actually type a longer name for a variable, but WordPerfect disregards any characters after the first seven. Since case is ignored, *LIMIT* would be considered the same variable as *Limit* or *limit*. If your macro included these two commands, in the order shown here:

```
{ASSIGN}Limit~10~
{ASSIGN}LIMIT~30~
```

only one variable would exist, and it would contain the number 30. Although the variable would initially contain 10, as soon as the second {ASSIGN} command was executed, 10 would be replaced with 30.

Many of WordPerfect's macro commands are followed by parameters or arguments and require that you use a precise syntax when typing them, including a tilde character (~) to show where the argument ends. An argument is an additional item that is needed to carry out the command, such as a message, a variable, the command for a WordPerfect key such as {Print}, or a time period. For example, the syntax for the {SPEED} command is

```
{SPEED}100ths second~
```

The argument is the time, expressed in 100ths of a second (so 100 is the equivalent of 1 second). In the macro, the {SPEED} command must end in a tilde, such as:

```
{SPEED}100~
```

If you forget to type the tilde character when it is required in a macro command, the command will not work. In some cases, your entire macro may fail. On most keyboards, the tilde is the first key on the top row of numbers, left of the 1, and you have to press the Shift key first to enter it.

If a command requires an argument and/or a tilde, you'll know when you select it from the Macro Commands menu (in the Macro Editor) because each command's syntax is displayed there. For example, in Figure 19.3 the cursor is highlighting the first command in this menu, {;}comment~. A tilde appears at the end of the command to indicate that it is required. The comment command lets you annotate your macros with comments, which have no effect on the macro's performance. However, if you enter a comment into a macro and forget to type a tilde at the end, all commands that follow will be considered part of the comment (unless another tilde is encountered later in the macro), and your macro probably won't work. In Figure 19.4, two commands in the Macro Commands menu require both arguments and tildes: {PAUSE KEY}key~ and {PROMPT}message~.

Creating the Print Menu Macro

The Alt-P macro can be broken down into three parts. The first part is the first two lines, beginning with the {CHAR} command and ending with the {Left} command. {CHAR} is followed by a variable named *Option,* a tilde, a message, and another tilde. The message is the information describing the options on Sue's print menu. When you use the macro, the message line appears at the bottom of the screen, as shown in Figure 19.5. This part of the macro prompts the user to choose a number, and then enters that number into a variable, *Option.*

The second part of the macro is the six lines beginning with the {CASE}{VARIABLE} command and ending with the {GO}Exit command. The {CASE} command evaluates the character typed by the user, which has been placed into the variable named *Option,* and specifies what to do in each case. Depending on whether the user presses 1, 2, or 3, it directs the macro to the corresponding {LABEL} command. Because the section includes an {ELSE} command, it specifies what to do if the user types something other than 1, 2, or 3: Go to the EXIT label.

The third section consists of the four {LABEL} commands. These contain the actual keystrokes that WordPerfect will perform when the user selects that option. For example, if the user types 1, the macro will select View Document from the Print menu, then pause and wait until the user presses the Enter key to return to the Edit screen.

To create this macro, you should go directly to the Macro Editor. Let's name it ALTP.

1. Press Home and then Macro Define (Ctrl-F10).

   The `Define macro` prompt appears.

2. Enter the macro name: `ALTP`.

   The `Description` prompt appears.

3. Enter this description:

   `Print menu`

   As soon as you press Enter, you'll go directly to the Macro Editor. Your next step is to erase the {DISPLAY OFF} command, so the keystrokes will appear as you use the macro.

4. Press the Delete key once.

   Next, enter the first part of the macro, beginning with the {CHAR} command.

The {CHAR} Command

The syntax for the first command in the macro, {CHAR}, is: {CHAR} Variable~ Message~. It appears as follows in this macro:

```
{CHAR}Option~ Sue's print menu: (1) View Document; (2)
Print;  (3) Cancel printing: 0 {Left}~
```

Here, {CHAR} establishes a variable named *Option*, and prompts the user with the message to enter 1, 2, or 3 for the variable. The message is the line describing the three options on Sue's print menu; when you use the macro, it appears as shown in Figure 19.5. After the user types a character, the macro stores it in the variable Option. For instance, if the user types 1 to select the View Document option, 1 will be stored in the variable. You must include a tilde (~) after the variable name (Option), and at the end of the message section. The {Left} command before the last tilde moves the cursor left one character, so that in the menu line it will be positioned on the 0, as it appears in most WordPerfect menus. {CHAR} accepts only one character, so as soon as the user types a number or letter, the macro moves on to the next command.

To enter the {CHAR} command:

1. Press Ctrl-PgUp, type char to move the cursor onto the {CHAR} command in the box, and then press Enter to insert it into the macro.

   Notice that the command's syntax is shown in the box:
   `{CHAR}var~message~.`

2. Type the variable name, Option, followed by a tilde.

 Warning: If you forget to type a tilde character when it is required in a command, the command won't work, and your entire macro may fail.

3. Type the message:

   ```
   Sue's print menu: (1) View Document; (2) Print;  (3)
   Cancel printing: 0
   ```

   If the text extends off the screen, you can press Enter to move it to the next line, without affecting the macro.

4. To insert the {Left} command, press Ctrl-V, and then press Left Arrow.

   To end the message, you must type a tilde.

5. Type a tilde, and then press Enter twice, to move the cursor to the next line and insert a blank one.

   Next, enter the section beginning with the {CASE} command.

The {CASE} Command

The syntax for the {CASE} command is: {CASE} expression~, case 1~ label 1~, case 2~ label 2~, case 3~ label 3~~. It appears as follows in the macro:

```
{CASE}{VARIABLE}Option~~
1~View~
2~Print~
3~Cancel~
{ELSE}
{GO}Exit~~
```

Here, {CASE} evaluates the expression, which is a variable named *Option*. It then selects the corresponding label, where the macro will go for further instructions. Translated into English, this means in the case where the variable named *Option* contains the number 1, go to the label that appears next to 1 in the list, View. If the Option variable is 2, go to the Print label. If the Option variable is 3, go to the Cancel label. If the Option variable is something other than 1, 2, or 3, go to the Exit label.

The {VARIABLE} Command

The syntax for the {VARIABLE} command is: {VARIABLE} var~. It appears as follows in this macro:

```
{VARIABLE}Option~
```

Here, the {VARIABLE} command lets the macro use the variable named *Option*. The entire command is the expression that the {CASE} command will use to make a decision. For example, if the user types 1, it translates into: In the case where the variable named *Option* is 1, use the label that appears next to 1 (View). A tilde must follow the variable name.

The {ELSE} Command

The syntax for the {ELSE} command is: {ELSE}. Here, it tells the macro what to do if the user does not type 1, 2, or 3: Use the {GO}Exit command.

The {GO} Command

The syntax of the {GO} command is: {GO}label~. It appears as follows in this macro:

```
{GO}Exit~
```

Here, it tells the macro to go to the label named *Exit*. The label name must be followed by a tilde.

To enter this section:

1. Press Ctrl-PgUp, type CAS, and press Enter. This places the {CASE} command in the macro.

2. Press Ctrl-PgUp again, type V, and press Enter. This places the {VARI-ABLE} command in the macro.

3. Type the variable name, Option.

4. Type two tildes; then press Enter.

   The tildes are necessary to end the expression and the {VARIABLE} command.

5. Type the case numbers and label names, as follows:

   ```
   1~View~
   2~Print~
   3~Cancel~
   ```

   Be sure to type a tilde after each number, and after each name. The next step is to insert the {ELSE} command.

6. Press Ctrl-PgUp, type E, and press Enter twice. Now insert the {GO} command.

7. Press Ctrl-PgUp, type G, and press Enter.

8. Type the label: Exit.

9. End the section by typing two tildes, and pressing Enter three times.

   The first tilde ends the {GO}label command, and the second ends the entire {CASE} command.
   Next, enter the third part of the macro, the {LABEL} commands.

The {LABEL} Command

The syntax of the {LABEL} command is: {LABEL}Label~. The four {LABEL} commands appear as follows in this macro:

```
{LABEL}View~
{Print}v
{PAUSE}{Enter}{Exit}
{QUIT}

{LABEL}Print~
{Print}1
{QUIT}

{LABEL}Cancel~
{Print}cc*Y{Exit}
{QUIT}

{LABEL}Exit~
{QUIT}
```

Specific WordPerfect instructions follow each {LABEL} command. For example, the View label selects the main Print menu, then the View Document option. It pauses until the user presses Enter, and then exits to the Edit screen. The Print label selects 1 on the main Print menu, the Full Document option. The Cancel label selects c, the Control Printer option on the main Print menu, then selects c, the Cancel Jobs option, on the Print: Control Printer menu. The asterisk selects the option to cancel all print jobs, and the Y confirms it. The last command, {Exit}, returns the user to the Edit screen. The Exit label uses the {QUIT} command to exit the macro. Notice that the {QUIT} command is used after each label, since it stops the macro after it has performed the instructions.

 Tip: If you want to use different options on your menu, change the message after the {CHAR} command, so the menu describes your options. Also, create different names for your labels in the {CASE} and {LABEL} sections, and enter the necessary keystrokes in the {LABEL} section to perform your tasks.

The {QUIT} Command

The syntax of the {QUIT} command is: {QUIT}. It is used after each label in this macro to end the macro after it has performed the label's instructions. In the case of the EXIT label, it is the only instruction, so all EXIT does is stop the macro.

1. Press Ctrl-PgUp, type L, and press Enter. This inserts the first {LABEL} command into the macro.

2. Type the label name, View; then type a tilde and press Enter.

3. Enter the Print command by pressing Print (Shift-F7). Type V (or 6) for the View Document option. Press Enter.

4. Enter the {PAUSE} command by pressing Ctrl-PgUp, typing PAU, then pressing Enter.

5. Press Ctrl-V and then press Enter. To insert the Exit command, press Ctrl-V again, and then press Exit (F7). Press Enter to move to the next line.

6. To enter the {QUIT} command, press Ctrl-PgUp, type Q, then press Enter. Press Enter twice.

7. Press Ctrl-PgUp, type L, and press Enter.

8. Type the second label's name, Print, then type a tilde and press Enter.

9. Enter the Print command by pressing Print (Shift-F7). Type 1 (or F) for the Full Document option. Press Enter twice.

10. To enter the {QUIT} command, press Ctrl-PgUp, type Q, then press Enter. Press Enter to move to the next line.

11. Press Ctrl-PgUp, type L, and press Enter.

12. Type the third label's name, Cancel, then type a tilde and press Enter.

13. Enter the Print command by pressing Print (Shift-F7). Type C (or 4) for the Control Printer option, C for Cancel Jobs, then an asterisk and Y to cancel all print jobs. Press Ctrl-V, then press Exit (F7) to insert an {Exit} command so that the macro will return to the Edit screen after you use this option.

14. Press Enter to move to the next line, then enter the {QUIT} command by pressing Ctrl-PgUp, type Q, then press Enter. Press Enter twice.

15. Press Ctrl-PgUp, type L, and press Enter. Type the last label's name, Exit, then type a tilde and press Enter.

16. To enter the {QUIT} command, press Ctrl-PgUp, type Q, then press Enter.

    That completes the macro. If your macro keystrokes are identical to Figure 19.6, you can exit the Macro Editor.

17. Press Exit (F7).

Testing the Alt-P Macro

To test the View Document, Print, and Cancel functions of your macro, you may want to type a few lines on the screen, or retrieve a document. Turn the printer off, so that after you select Print, you'll have a print job to cancel.

1. Press Alt-P, and select the first option, View Document. After you finish using it, press Enter to return to the Edit screen.

2. Press Alt-P and select the second option, Print.

    Since your printer is not turned on, if you were to look in the Print: Control Printer screen, you would see an error message, indicating that the printer is not accepting characters.

3. Press Alt-P and select the third option, Cancel printing.

The macro cancels the print job, and you return to the Edit screen. However, it happens so fast, you may not be able to see it. If you want to be able to see the Control Printer screen as the macro cancels your print job, edit the macro and insert a {SPEED} command in the Cancel label, as described in the section "The {SPEED} Command."

The {STEP ON} and {STEP OFF} Commands

If the macro does not work correctly, edit it and make sure all your keystrokes are the same as the ones shown in Figure 19.6. If it still doesn't work, WordPerfect provides {STEP ON} and {STEP OFF} commands that may help you find the problem. {STEP ON} works by running the macro one step at a time, so you can see each keystroke or command as you run your macro. Macro commands such as {QUIT} and keystroke commands such as {Print} are represented by the codes shown in Table 19.2.

If you only want to test a certain section of the macro, edit it and place a {STEP ON} command at the beginning and a {STEP OFF} command at the end. For example, if the Cancel option in your Alt-P macro weren't working correctly, you could place the {STEP ON} and {STEP OFF} commands as shown below:

```
{LABEL}Cancel~
{STEP ON}
{Print}cc*Y{Exit}
{STEP OFF}
{QUIT}
```

To insert the {STEP ON} and {STEP OFF} commands into your macro, press Ctrl-PgUp from inside the Macro Editor and select them from the list of macro commands that appears inside the box on the right side of the screen.

Table 19.2 *Macro and keystroke command codes. These codes appear when you use the {STEP ON} and {STEP OFF} commands to debug a macro.*

Macro Command Codes	
1	{ASSIGN}
2	{BELL}
3	{BREAK}
4	{CALL}
5	{CANCEL OFF}

continued

Table 19.2 *(continued)*

6	{CANCEL ON}
7	{CASE}
8	{CASE CALL}
9	{CHAIN}
10	{CHAR}
11	{;} (comment)
12	{DISPLAY OFF}
13	{DISPLAY ON}
14	{ELSE}
15	{END FOR}
16	{END IF}
17	{END WHILE}
18	{FOR}
19	{FOR EACH}
20	{GO}
21	{IF}
22	{LABEL}
23	{LOOK}
24	{NEST}
25	{NEXT}
26	{SHELL MACRO}
27	{ON CANCEL}
28	{ON ERROR}
29	{ON NOT FOUND}
30	{PAUSE}
31	{PROMPT}
32	{QUIT}
33	{RESTART}
34	{RETURN}
35	{RETURN CANCEL}
36	{RETURN ERROR}
37	{RETURN NOT FOUND}
38	{SPEED}
39	{STEP ON}
40	{TEXT}
41	{STATE}
42	{WAIT}
43	{WHILE}
44	{Macro Commands}
45	{STEP OFF}
46	{ORIGINAL KEY}

47	{IF EXISTS}
48	{MENU OFF}
49	{MENU ON}
50	{STATUS PROMPT}
51	{INPUT}
52	{VARIABLE}
53	{SYSTEM}
54	{MID}
55	{NTOK}
56	{KTON}
57	{LEN}
58	{~}
59	{PAUSE KEY}

Keystroke Command Codes

1	^A	
2	^B	Page Number
3	^C	Merge from Console
4	^D	Merge Date Code
5	^E	Merge End Record
6	^F	Merge Field
7	^G	Merge Macro
8	^H	Home
9	^I	Tab
10	^J	Enter
11	^K	Delete to End of Line
12	^L	Delete to End of Page
13	^M	Search Value for [SRt]
14	^N	Merge Next Record
15	^O	Merge Output Prompt
16	^P	Merge Primary File
17	^Q	Merge Quit
18	^R	Merge End Field Code
19	^S	Merge Secondary File
20	^T	Merge Text to Printer
21	^U	Update Screen Merge Code
22	^V	Ignore Meaning of Following Merge Code
23	^W	Up
24	^X	Right and Search Wild Card
25	^Y	Left

continued

Table 19.2   *(continued)*

26	^Z	Down
27	^[	Escape
28	^\	
29	^]	
30	^^	Reset Keyboard Map
31	^_	
32	Cancel	
33	Forward Search	
34	Help	
35	Indent	
36	List	
37	Bold	
38	Exit	
39	Underline	
40	Merge End Field	
41	Save	
44	Setup	
45	Backwards Search	
46	Switch	
47	Left/Right Indent	
48	Date/Outline	
49	Center	
50	Print	
51	Format	
52	Merge Commands	
53	Retrieve	
56	Thesaurus	
57	Replace	
58	Reveal Codes	
59	Block	
60	Mark Text	
61	Flush Right	
62	Columns/Table	
63	Style	
64	Graphics	
65	Macro	
68	Shell	
69	Spell	
70	Screen	
71	Move	
72	Text In/Out	

73	Tab Align
74	Footnote
75	Font
76	Merge/Sort
77	Macro Define
80	Backspace
81	Delete Right
82	Delete Word
83	Word Right
84	Word Left
85	Home,Home,Right (End key)
86	Home,Home,Left (Begin key on Victor computer)
88	GoTo (Ctrl-Home)
89	PgUp
90	PgDn
91	Screen Down (+ on numeric keypad)
92	Screen Up (– on numeric keypad)
93	Typeover
94	Left Margin Release (reverse tab)
95	Hard Page (Ctrl-Enter)
96	Soft Hyphen (Ctrl,Hyphen)
97	Required (Hard) Hyphen (Home,Hyphen)
98	Required (Hard) Space (Home,Spacebar)
99	Para Up
100	Para Down
101	Item Left
102	Item Right
103	Item Up
104	Item Down
105	Alt-Home
106	Delete Row (Ctrl-Delete)
107	Menu Bar (Alt=)
108	Block Append
109	Block Move
110	Block Copy

After editing the Alt-P macro, follow these steps to debug your macro:

1. Turn off the printer, run the macro, and select the Print option (so the Cancel option will try to cancel the print job).

2. Select the Cancel option. If this prompt appears on your status line:

```
Key Cmd 50
```

your first step is correct. As you can see from Table 19.2, this code represents the Print key. If another prompt, letter, or number appears, make a note of it so you can change it later through the Macro Editor.

3. To move to the next step, press Enter.

The Print menu should appear. If a c or 4 appears in the lower-left corner of the screen, your macro's next step is correct: It selects the Control Printer option. Write it down if it is incorrect.

4. Press Enter to move to the next step.

The Print: Control Printer menu is displayed. If a c or 1 appears in the lower-left corner in this screen, the macro has selected the correct option, Cancel Job(s).

5. Press Enter.

An asterisk should appear in the lower-left corner of the screen to indicate that the macro has selected all print jobs to cancel.

6. Press Enter.

A Y should appear in the lower-left corner of the screen. It selects Yes in response to the prompt asking if you want to cancel all print jobs.

7. Press Enter. This prompt should appear:

```
Key Cmd 38
```

As you can see from Table 19.2, this code represents the Exit key. In the macro, it exits from the Print menu back to the Edit screen.

8. Press Enter. This prompt should appear next:

```
MACRO CMD 45
```

Table 19.2 indicates that it represents the {STEP OFF} command. After you press Enter at this point, the macro will resume normal operation and finish its task without your intervention.

9. Press Enter.

If your macro displayed different prompts, letters, or numbers in any of the steps, use the Macro Editor to erase them and insert the correct commands. When you finish testing your macro, edit it again and erase the {STEP ON} and {STEP OFF} commands, so you can use the macro without pressing Enter after each step.

The {SPEED} Command

The {SPEED} command slows down a macro, so you can watch it perform its task. The syntax is {SPEED}100ths second~, where 100 is one second. To insert it into your Alt-P macro, edit it, move the cursor to the position where you want the {SPEED} command, press Ctrl-PgUp, type SP, press Enter, type a number representing the speed, and then type a tilde. (Display must be on for the {SPEED} command to work.) For example, to delay the Cancel option for one second, enter the command before the {Print} label, using 100 as the number. After you finish, the {LABEL}Cancel command should appear as follows:

```
{LABEL}Cancel~
{SPEED}100~
{Print}cc*Y{Exit}
{QUIT}
```

Menu Display Commands

Most WordPerfect menus let you select an option by pressing either a number or a letter corresponding to the option name, such as 1 or F for Full Document on the Print menu. These numbers and letters usually appear in bold. You can easily change the display of your Alt-P menu so it resembles a WordPerfect menu and permits the user to type 1 or V for View Document, 2 or P for Print, and 3 or C for Cancel Printing. You can even have these numbers and letters appear in bold on the Edit screen, similar to WordPerfect menus.

To display the menu this way, edit the macro and make two changes. First, modify the message section to indicate with bold that the user can press either a number or a letter. WordPerfect features special control characters to signify where you want bold turned on and off in the menu line:

{^]} means turn bold on.
{^\} means turn bold off.

To turn bold on before the 1, 2, 3, and 0 in the message:

1. Press Ctrl-V.

2. Press Ctrl-].

This character appears: {^]}.

Turn bold off after the V, P, and C in the message:

1. Press Ctrl-V.

2. Press Ctrl-\.

This character appears: {^\}.

When you finish, the {CHAR} statement should appear as follows:

```
{CHAR}Option~ Sue's print menu: {^]}1 V{^\}iew Document;
{^]}2 P{^\}rint; {^]}3 C{^\}ancel printing: {^]}0 {Left}~
```

Next, modify the {CASE}{VARIABLE} section, to add a Case Label statement for each uppercase and lowercase letter that the user can type to select an option. If you want to use both uppercase and lowercase letters, you'll need a label for V, v, P, p, C, and c. When you finish, this section should appear as follows:

```
{CASE}{VARIABLE}Option~~
1~View~
V~View~
v~View~
2~Print~
P~Print~
p~Print~
3~Cancel~
C~Cancel~
c~Cancel~
{ELSE}
{GO}Exit~~
```

Be sure to type a tilde after each letter, and after each label. The macro user will now be able to type any of the following numbers or letters to select an option:

1, v, or V for the View Document option
2, p, or P for the Print option
3, c, or C for Cancel printing

There are several other attribute on/off characters besides the bold on and off that you can use in your macros, including:

{^R}	Reverse video on
{^S}	Reverse video off
{^T}	Underline on
{^U}	Underline off
{^V}	Mnemonic attribute on; this is the attribute selected for Menu Letter Display in the Setup: Menu options menu (Shift F1, D, M, M)
{^Q}	Turn off all attributes, including Mnemonic

To insert {^V} while using the Macro Editor, press Ctrl-V and then type V. To insert any of the others, press Ctrl and type the letter (R, S, T, U, or Q). If WordPerfect enters other commands into your macro unexpectedly when you press a combination such as Ctrl-R, you are probably using a keyboard layout that has assigned another function to that Ctrl-letter combination. If so, you can erase the extra commands, return to the original keyboard definition by pressing Ctrl-6, and then press Ctrl and the letter to enter the attribute character. For more information about keyboard layouts, see Part Three, "Command Reference."

The WordPerfect manual provides information about other attribute characters, including blink, outline, italics, and shadow, and about cursor positioning characters that you can use to place your messages at any position on the screen.

Using the {TEXT} Command to Obtain Information from the User

WordPerfect provides another command that you can use to obtain information from a user while a macro is running, {TEXT}. In the last section, you learned how to use the {CHAR} command to obtain a number or letter from the user and place it in a variable. While {CHAR} accepts only one character, the {TEXT} command accepts up to 120. The only other difference is that the user must press Enter after typing an entry in response to this command. With the {CHAR} command, the macro continues as soon as a single character is typed.

The syntax for the two commands is nearly identical:

```
{TEXT} Variable~ Message~
```

In the envelope macro shown in Figure 19.7, the {TEXT} command is used as follows to obtain the envelope recipient's name:

```
{TEXT}name~
{Del to EOP} ENVELOPE MACRO {Enter}{Enter}
Type the recipient's name, then press Enter {Enter}
or stop the macro by pressing F1 Enter {Enter}{Enter}~
```

The {Del to EOP} command inside the {TEXT} command clears the screen so that the message will appear in the upper-left corner, instead of in the lower-left corner. To enter it in a macro, press Ctrl-L. After the user types a name in response to the prompt, it is placed in the *name* variable. In the next line:

```
{VARIABLE}name~
```

the macro uses the {VARIABLE} command to enter the envelope recipient's name on the Edit screen.

The next section begins with a COMMENT command:

```
{;}This section sets up the formatting for an envelope~
```

The COMMENT command lets you annotate your macro with descriptions like this one to help you remember how the macro works. The comments do not affect the macro's performance.

The other commands in this section of the macro move the cursor to the top of the document, sets up these formatting options for the envelope: Left margin 4", Center Page, Paper Size/Type 9.5" x 4", Envelope, and then moves the cursor to the end of the document.

In the last section, the user is prompted to type the address. After he or she presses F7, the macro displays the envelope in the View Document screen and stops. The {PROMPT} and {PAUSE KEY} commands are explained in the next section.

```
{TEXT}name~
{Del to EOP}{^]}ENVELOPE MACRO{^\}{Enter}{Enter}
Type the recipient's name, then press Enter{Enter}
or stop the macro by pressing F1 Enter{Enter}{Enter}~
{VARIABLE}name~

{;}This section sets up the formatting for an envelope~
{Home}{Home}{Home}{Up}
{Format}LM4{Enter}{Enter}{Enter}PCYSNE{Enter}{Enter}{Exit}
{Home}{Home}{Home}{Down}{End}{Enter}

{PROMPT}Type the address.
When you finish, preview the envelope{Enter}
by pressing F7~
{PAUSE KEY}{Exit}~

{Print}V
```

Figure 19.7 In this macro, the {TEXT} command is used to obtain a name for the envelope recipient, since it accepts up to 120 characters.

Conveying Messages to the Macro User

You can use several macro commands to convey a message to the user during macro execution, without prompting for information, or to stop a macro for user input in one of WordPerfect's menus. For example, you used the {PAUSE} command in the Alt-S macro to pause the macro in the Format Line menu and let the user enter a number for line spacing. The other commands include {PAUSE KEY}, {INPUT}, {PROMPT}, {STATUS PROMPT}, and {WAIT}.

The {PAUSE KEY} Command

The {PAUSE KEY} command is like the {PAUSE} command, except that it lets you designate a key other than Enter to end the pause. Use it whenever you want the user to do something that requires the normal use of the Enter key, such as typing several paragraphs. The syntax of this command is: {PAUSE KEY}key~. In the envelope macro shown in Figure 19.7, the command is used at the end of the macro:

```
{PAUSE KEY}{Exit}~
```

Here, the user must press Exit (F7) to indicate that he or she has finished typing the address and is ready to go to the View Document screen.

The {PROMPT} Command

The {PROMPT} command displays a message at the bottom of the screen but disappears almost immediately unless a command such as {WAIT} or {PAUSE KEY} follows to slow down or pause the macro. The command's syntax is: {PROMPT}message~. It is used in the envelope macro shown in Figure 19.7 to ask the user to type an address and press F7:

```
{PROMPT}Type the address.
When you finish, preview the envelope{Enter} by pressing F7~
{PAUSE KEY}{Exit}~
```

Since the {PAUSE KEY} command follows the {PROMPT} command in this macro, the message remains on the screen until the user starts typing the address.

The {STATUS PROMPT} Command

The {STATUS PROMPT} command is like the {PROMPT} command, except that the message remains on screen while the user is typing the address until he or she presses Exit (F7). The syntax is nearly identical: {STATUS PROMPT}message~. However, at the point in the macro where you want the message to disappear, you must include an empty {STATUS PROMPT} command:

```
{STATUS PROMPT}~
```

If your macro does not have an empty {STATUS PROMPT} command, the message will remain on the Edit screen after the user finishes using the macro, even if the user clears the Edit screen.

If you use {STATUS PROMPT} instead of {STATUS}, this section of the macro should appear as follows:

```
{STATUS PROMPT}Type the address.
When you finish, preview the envelope{Enter} by pressing F7~
{PAUSE KEY}{Exit}~
{STATUS PROMPT}~
```

The {INPUT} Command

The {INPUT} command displays a message during macro execution and pauses the macro until the user presses the Enter key. Use it to communicate to the user that he or she must take a particular action, such as moving the cursor to a certain position. As soon as the user presses Enter, the macro moves on to the next command. The syntax for the command is: {INPUT}message~.

The {WAIT} Command

The {WAIT} command lets you pause a macro for a certain period of time, as measured in seconds. The syntax is: {WAIT}10ths second~. For instance, if you wanted the macro to pause for 5 seconds while the user read an explanation of the macro, you would type: {WAIT}500~. You could then have the macro clear the explanations from the screen and perform its other tasks.

Other Commands That Make Decisions

The Alt-F macro displayed in Figure 19.8 brings up a full-screen menu and lets the user view the List Files screen for any directory shown in the list. If you use many different directories and subdirectories, this is a convenient method of listing the directories you use most and displaying the List Files screen for any of them. Once you have used the macro to view the List Files screen for a particular directory, you can make it the default by highlighting Current <Dir>, selecting the Other Directory option (7) on the List Files menu, and pressing Enter.

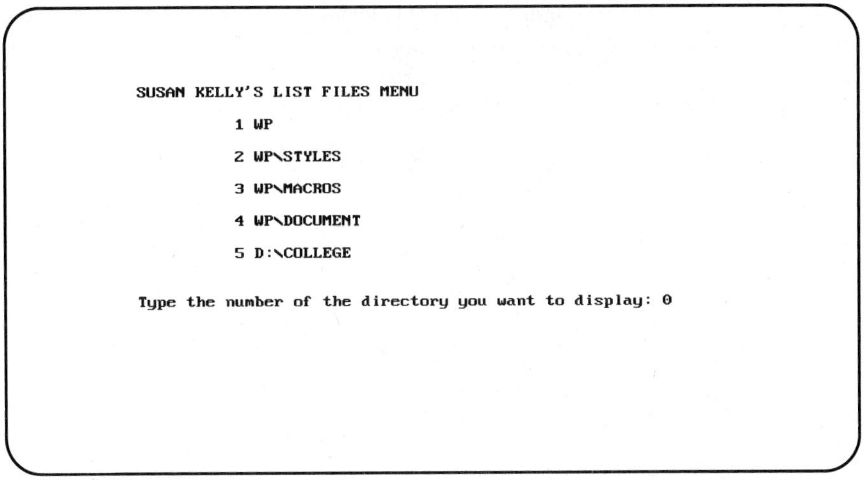

```
                SUSAN KELLY'S LIST FILES MENU
                    1 WP

                    2 WP\STYLES

                    3 WP\MACROS

                    4 WP\DOCUMENT

                    5 D:\COLLEGE

        Type the number of the directory you want to display: 0
```

Figure 19.8 *The Alt-F macro brings up this full-screen menu, which can be used to view the List Files screen for any directory shown in the list. {IF} AND {ENDIF} commands are used to check the number typed by the user and instruct the macro to display the appropriate directory. If you are working on a document when you use the macro, it will not be affected (unless you retrieve a file).*

Like the Alt-P macro, the Alt-F macro uses a {CHAR} command to obtain a number from the user and place it in a variable. However, instead of using the **{CASE}** command to make a decision, it uses another method: A series of {IF} and {ENDIF} statements. For example, if the user types 3 to view the WP\MACROS subdirectory, the macro is directed to this statement:

```
{IF}{VAR 1}=3~
{List}\WP\MACROS{Enter}
{QUIT}
{END IF}
```

Translated into English, it means that if variable 1 contains the number 3, the macro displays the List Files menu for the \WP\MACROS subdirectory. Since the {QUIT} command follows, the macro ends at that point, leaving the user in the List Files menu. Each {IF} statement must be followed by an {END IF} statement.

The {VAR n} command used in this macro is like the {VARIABLE}var~ command, except that you can only use it when your variable name is a number between 0 and 9. Instead of using {VARIABLE}1~ to access the data in variable 1, you can use the shortcut, {VAR 1}. This command:

```
{IF}{VAR 1}=3~
```

functions identically to:

```
{IF}{VARIABLE}1~=3~
```

To enter the {VAR n} command in a macro, press Ctrl-V; then press Alt and the number, such as Alt-1 for {VAR 1}.

This macro also uses the {BELL} command to have the computer beep when the prompt appears asking the user to type a number:

```
Type the number of the directory you want to display:
{BELL}0{Left}~
```

You can use this command anywhere in a macro where you want to grab the user's attention.

Learning More About Macros

Part Three of this book, "Command Reference," provides additional information about macros, including how to chain two macros so the first macro will include a command to run the second immediately after it has completed its actions; how to nest two macros so the first macro starts a second macro at any point, completes the second macro's action, then continues where it (the first macro) left off; and how to convert WordPerfect 4.1, 4.2, and 5.0 macros to WordPerfect 5.1. The WordPerfect manual includes four appendixes about the macro language, and several books are available that are devoted entirely to WordPerfect's macros. With these resources, you can continue to expand your knowledge and use of this wonderful feature.

PART
THREE

COMMAND
REFERENCE

INTRODUCTION TO THE COMMAND REFERENCE SECTION

The following Command Reference section offers an alphabetical list of WordPerfect's features, allowing you to quickly find information about the feature you want to use. Although the description of each feature is not comprehensive, it offers enough information to help you understand the feature and use it effectively. Tips, cautions, and notes are included to save you time and help you avoid trouble. The information about each feature is handled in the following format:

Name of Feature (see also *Other References to the Feature*)

Function: Explains the purpose and use of the feature.

Keystrokes: *Keyboard*

This section provides a list of keyboard keystrokes you need to press to use the feature. This section is helpful for users who have already used the feature but cannot recall the specific keystrokes required.

Mouse

This section tells how to use the mouse instead of the keyboard. It provides a list of menu selections and mouse "keystrokes" you need to press to use the feature.

Codes: Whenever you use a feature that inserts hidden formatting codes, such as [BOLD] and [bold], the codes are listed here.

Example:

```
Included with many of the features is an example of the feature or
of the menu you use to access the feature. These examples are
usually brief, giving you a general idea of the use of the feature
or of a setting you can enter for the feature.
```

One or more paragraphs follow the example, providing general information about the feature. This section may also include a list of options for the feature. Following this section is a step-by-step description of how to use the feature:

Using the Feature

1. Perform the steps as described in the left column of this list to use the feature.

   Look to this column for more information about the step you are about to perform and for information about what happens after you perform the step.

2. Perform the next step as described.

   The list continues until you complete the specific task.

Tip: Tips are included for some of the features. These tips tell you how to use the feature to save time and effort, or how to use the feature in a unique way.

Note: Notes are included to provide information about a feature that may apply to your computer or to a specific situation. These notes also supply general information, such as DOS naming conventions and information about warning messages that you may encounter.

Caution: Caution boxes provide warnings that will help you avoid trouble.

A

Absolute Tab Settings (see *Tab, Set*)

Addition (see *Math* and *Tables, Math*)

Advance

Function: Offsets printed text up, down, left, or right from the cusor position, or to a specific line or position on the page.

Keystrokes:

Keyboard	*Mouse*
Shift-F8 (Format)	Layout
4 (Other)	Other
1 (Advance)	Advance
1 (Up), **2** (Down), **3** (Line), **4** (Left), **5** (Right), or **6** (Position) *distance*	Up, Down, Line, Left, Right, or Position *distance*
F7 (Exit)	Right mouse button

Codes: [AdvUp]
[AdvDn]
[AdvLft]
[AdvRgt]
[AdvToLn]
[AdvToPos]

Example:

Advanced to position, from margin to position 2"
This line is normal (not indented)!
Advanced Left 1"
This line is normal (not advanced left)!
Advanced right 4"
This line right below it is normal!

The Advance feature inserts one of the hidden codes listed above to tell the printer how far to offset the text in the specified direction from the cursor, or to advance it to a specific line or position. This feature is useful for printing information on pre-printed forms, to advance text into a graphics box, or to kern loose character pairs if your printer does not.

 Advancing Printed Text

1. Move the cursor where you want the Advance to start.

2. Press Shift-F8 (Format) or display the **Layout** menu.   A list of formatting options appears.

3. Select **Other** (4).   The Format: Other menu appears.

4. Select **1** (**Advance**).   A list of Advance options appears.

5. Select the direction in which you want to advance the text, or select **Position** or **Line** to advance the text to a specific position on the page.   A message appears, prompting you to enter a distance. This distance is relative to the cursor position if you advance the text up, down, left, or right. If you use Advance to Line or Position, this distance is an absolute position set from the edge of the page.

6. Enter a distance (in inches) or a line number (followed by ∨) or a position number.   The ∨ tells WordPerfect to advance the following text the number of lines specified.

7. Press F7 (Exit) or click the right mouse button.   This returns you to the Edit screen.

8. Type the text you want to advance.   The text does not appear shifted on screen, but it will advance to the specified position when printed. When the cursor is on the advanced text, the status line displays the line and position number. You can see how the advanced text will look in print by using View Document.

Note: Advance to Position, Advance Left, and Advance Right affect only the current line. Advance Down, Advance Up, and Advance to Line affect the current line and all lines that follow. If you used Advance to Line or Advance Up or Advance Down, repeat the steps, entering an opposite code at the place where you want the advance to stop. Text from this point on will not be shifted.

 Note: If you advance to a position that is not physically possible, WordPerfect ignores the entry and does not insert an Advance code.

Align/Decimal Character (see *Decimal/Align Character*)

Align Text (see *Tab Align*)

Alphabetize (see *Sort and Select*)

Appearance Attributes

Function: Changes the appearance of the printed text to a different style, such as bold, italic, or outline.

Keystrokes:

Keyboard	*Mouse*
Ctrl-F8 (Font)	Font
2 (Appearance)	Appearance
1 (Bold), **2** (Underline), **3** (Double Underline), **4** (Italic), **5** (Outline), **6** (Shadow), **7** (Small Caps), **8** (Redline), or **9** (Strikeout)	**Bold**, **Underline**, **Double Underline**, **Italic**, **Outline**, **Shadow**, **Small Caps**, **Redline**, or **Strikeout**

Codes: [BOLD][bold]
[UND][und]
[DBL UND][dbl und]
[ITALC][italc]
[OUTLN][outln]
[SHADW][shadw]
[SM CAP][sm cap]
[REDLN][redln]
[STKOUT][stkout]

Example:

> **Bold** <u>Underline</u> <u>Double Underline</u> *Italic* Outline
>
> **Shadow** SMALL CAPS Redline ~~Strikeout~~

When you begin typing a document, an *initial* font is always in use for the text you type, such as Courier 12-point or Roman 10-point. This font specifies the type size and typeface for your characters. You can modify this default font by using an appearance attribute, such as bold, italic, or shadow. The default typeface and size remain the same, but the text *appears* differently on screen and when printed. In other words, if you are using Times Roman 12-point as the initial font, and you select italics, the printed text will use Times Roman 12-point italic—a variation of the default.

You can add attributes in either of two ways: by changing the attribute before typing text or by blocking a section of text and then changing it. Either way, WordPerfect inserts two hidden codes: one that turns the attribute on and one that turns it off.

Typing Text with an Appearance Attribute

1. Move the cursor to the place where you want to insert the text.

2. Press Ctrl-F8 (Font) or display the Font menu.

   A list of Font options appears.

3. Select Appearance (2).

   The Appearance menu appears, giving you a choice of bold, underline, double underline, italic, outline, shadow, small caps, redline, or strikeout.

4. Select one of the options listed.	WordPerfect inserts a pair of hidden codes that turns the attribute on and off, and then positions the cursor between them.
5. Type the text as you normally would.	On screen, the text may appear in another color or in a different degree of intensity. Certain monitors can display attributes like underline, bold, and italics. Refer to *Colors/Fonts/Attributes*.
6. Press Right Arrow or Down Arrow to move the cursor past the Attribute Off code.	Any text you type outside the Attribute On/Off codes is normal. Any text you type between the codes appears in the selected attribute.

 ## Modifying an Existing Character's Appearance Attribute

1. Move the cursor to the beginning or end of the block you want to affect.	
2. Press Alt-F4 (Block) or select **B**lock from the **E**dit menu.	This turns on Block mode and anchors the cursor, letting you stretch the highlight over the block.
3. Move the cursor to stretch the highlighting over the text you want to change.	You can use the cursor keys or the Search feature, or type the character or punctuation mark you want to stretch to.
4. Press Ctrl-F8 (Font) or display the **F**ont menu.	The Font menu appears.
5. Select **A**ppearance (**2**).	The Appearance menu appears, giving you a choice of bold, underline, double underline, italic, outline, shadow, small caps, redline, or strikeout.

6.   Select one of the options listed.   This inserts the on and off codes around the block for the appearance attribute you selected. The highlighted text may change to represent the new appearance attribute.

Tip: To change to bold and underline, the process is even easier. To type bold or underlined text, press F6 (Bold) or F8 (Underline) before you type the string of text. WordPerfect inserts the Attribute On and Off codes and positions the cursor between them. Type the string of text, and then press the Right Arrow key to move the cursor past the Attribute Off code. To modify existing text, highlight the block and then press F6 for bold or F8 for underline; WordPerfect will insert both the beginning and end codes. For other attributes, you must use the Font/Appearance menu as explained earlier.

Note: The easiest way to remove an attribute is to delete either one of the attribute's paired codes in the Reveal Codes screen. Both codes will be deleted, and the text will return to normal.

Tip: Appearance attributes are defined in the Printer Resource File (PRS). If you are not getting the results you want when you select an appearance attribute, you may want to modify it using the Printer program. Refer to *Automatic Font Changes*.

Append

Function: Copies a block of text from one file and adds it to the end of another.

Keystrokes:

Keyboard	*Mouse*
Alt-F4 (Block)	Edit
Ctrl-F4 (Move)	Block
1 (Block)	Edit
4 (Append)	Append
filename (of target)	To File
OR	*filename* (of target)
Ctrl-F4 (Move)	OR
1 (Sentence), **2**	Edit
(Paragraph), or **3**	Select
(Page)	Sentence, **P**aragraph, or **P**age
4 (Append)	Append
filename (of target)	*filename* (of target)

Example:

```
Installing hard-disk protection¶
Mace Utilities is a collection of software utilities
designed to protect your data from damage and help you
recover from whatever damage they can't prevent. The package
includes a wide variety of tools, some to be used daily and
others to be used only occasionally.

Append to: f:\norton\ch7.wp5
```

The Append feature offers a convenient way to transfer text from one document to another. Instead of working on two documents simultaneously and using Shift-F3 to switch from one to the other, you can use Append to copy the text you want to move from the source document to the target document. The text is added to the end of the target document. If the specified target file does not exist, WordPerfect creates it.

You can append a sentence, a paragraph, a page, a rectangle, columns created with tabs or indents, or a marked block. When you append a tabular column or rectangle, the marked block is stored in a temporary file. To retrieve the block, press Ctrl-F4 (Move), select **4** (Retrieve), then **2** (Tabular Column) or **3** (Rectangle).

Appending a Block

1. Move the cursor to the beginning or end of the block you want to append.

    If the text is a sentence, paragraph, or page, you don't have to block it first. If that's the case, skip the next step.

2. Press Alt-F4 (Block) or select **Block** from the **Edit** menu, and then move the cursor to stretch the highlight over the text you want to append.

    You can use the cursor keys or the Search feature, or type the character or punctuation mark you want to stretch to.

3. Press Ctrl-F4 (Move) or choose **Select** from the **Edit** menu.

    The Move menu appears.

4. Select the type of block you want to move: a block of text, a tabular column, a rectangle, or a sentence, paragraph, or page.

5. Select 4 (Append).

    `Append to:` appears on screen, prompting you to enter a file name.

6. Type a file name and press Enter.

    If the named file exists, the block is appended to that file. If the file does not exist, WordPerfect creates it.

 Tip: You can use the Append feature as a safety net during the editing process. Create a file called JUNK. Whenever you want to delete a chunk of text, append the block to your JUNK file first and then delete the block from your document. If you decide later that you want that original block, you can retrieve it from the JUNK file.

 Tip: You can use the mouse to highlight a block of text without using the pull-down menus. Move the mouse cursor to the beginning of the block you want to highlight, hold down the left mouse button, and drag the cursor to the end of the block. When you release the left mouse button, the block is highlighted.

Append to Clipboard (see *Clipboard*)

ASCII Files (see *DOS Text Files*)

Attributes (see *Appearance Attributes* and *Size Attributes*)

Automatic Font Changes

Function: Lets you use the PTR program to change the fonts that WordPerfect has assigned to each size and appearance attribute for a particular font, such as small, large, bold, underline, and italics for the Times Roman 12-point font.

Keystrokes: From DOS prompt, type `ptr/afc`
Shift-F10 (Retrieve)
F5 (List)
Type name of subdirectory where *.PRS files are located, Enter
Cursor to printer file name, Enter, Enter
Cursor to printer name, Enter
Cursor to font name, Enter
Cursor to attribute, Enter
Cursor to desired font for this attribute
Type *
F7 (Exit)
Repeat for each attribute for this font; then repeat for each font you want to change
Alt-F7 (Quit), Y (Save)
Enter, Y, Y

Whenever you use the Ctrl-F8 (Font) key or Font pull-down menu to format text using a size attribute such as Fine, Small, or Large, or an appearance attribute such as italics, shadow, or double underline, WordPerfect makes an *automatic font change*. The change is a variation of the Base Font or Initial Font currently in use. WordPerfect substitutes the most appropriate font it can find from the list of available fonts for this printer. It selects Size attributes using the following percentages of the Base Font or Initial Font:

Fine 60%
Small 80%
Large 120%
Very Large 150%
Extra Large 200%
Superscript and Subscript 60%

For example, if your Base Font is set to Times Roman 12-point and you format a section of text using the Large attribute, WordPerfect will use a Times Roman 14.4-point font, if available. Very Large would be Times Roman 18-point. You can change the percentages for the size attributes using an option on the Setup: Print Options menu. For an appearance attribute such as bold or italic, WordPerfect will try to use a font of that style in the same point size, such as Times Roman 12-point bold. If the most appropriate font for a size or appearance attribute is unavailable, it will find the best substitute.

If you print a document formatted with any of the attributes and are dissatisfied with the substitutions that WordPerfect has made, you can use the Printer program to modify the selections. You probably won't need to do this if you use the built-in fonts on a PostScript printer, but for most other printers, it can provide you with precise control over the automatic font changes.

Running the Printer Program to Modify the Automatic Font Changes

1. Change to the directory containing the Printer program file (PTR.EXE) and your Printer program files (PRS).

   PTR.EXE should have been copied when you installed WordPerfect. It is on the PTR program disk, but you cannot copy it directly from the disk. If you need to install it, use the WordPerfect Installation program.

2. Type `ptr/afc` and press Enter. If you know the name of your printer's PRS file, type `ptr/afc filename.prs`, press Enter, and skip to step 6.

   The Printer program starts, and the screen features a large empty box. `Printers` appears at the top of the box, prompting you for a printer file name.

3. Press Shift-F10 (Retrieve).	WordPerfect prompts you to enter the name of the printer file you wish to modify.
4. Press F5 (List), type the path where the *.PRS files are located, and press Enter.	A list of the installed printer files appears. Each file ends in the extension .PRS.
5. Use the cursor keys to highlight the printer file you want to modify, and press Enter twice to retrieve it.	The printer's name appears inside the box.
6. Highlight the printer name and press Enter.	A list of available fonts for this printer appears.
7. Highlight the font whose attributes you want to change, and press Enter.	The Automatic Font Changes menu appears. The left column, Feature, lists each size and appearance attribute. The right column, Font Name, shows the font currently assigned for each attribute.
8. Move the cursor onto the attribute you want to assign a different font for, and press Enter.	A list of available fonts appears.
9. Highlight the font you want to assign to this attribute, and type an asterisk (*).	This selects the font, so whenever you format text with this attribute, WordPerfect will print it using this font.
10. Press F7 (Exit).	This returns you to the Automatic Font Changes menu. If you want to modify another attribute, highlight it and repeat steps 8-10. When you finish, continue to step 11.
11. Press F7 (Exit).	This returns you to the list of available fonts for this printer. If you want to modify the attributes for any of the other fonts, repeat steps 7-11. When you finish, continue to step 12 to exit the Printer program and save your changes.

12. Press Alt-F7 (Quit) and type Y (Save).

This tells WordPerfect to save the changes you have made to the printer file.

13. Press Enter and type Y to replace the old PRS file with the new one, or type a new file name for the printer file.

14. Press Y to exit the Printer program.

You return to the DOS prompt.

 ## Changing the Size Attribute Ratios

1. Press Shift-F1 (Setup) or select Setup from the File menu.

The Setup options appear.

2. Select Initial Settings (4).

The Setup: Initial Settings menu appears.

3. Select 8 (Print Options).

The Setup: Print Options menu appears.

4. Select 6 (Size Attribute Ratios), and enter the percentages you want for each size attribute.

5. Press F7 (Exit) or click the right mouse button.

WordPerfect saves the changes in the WP{WP}.SET file, and returns you to the Edit screen. Unless you are using a PostScript printer or have not yet installed your cartridges and fonts for the printer you are using, you must follow steps 7-10 to update the information in the PRS file for your printer. If you have a PostScript printer, the changes are made automatically. If you haven't installed the cartridges and fonts yet, you can skip steps 7-10 because the new percentages will be installed when you install the cartridges and fonts.

6. Press Shift-F7 (Print), or select **Print** from the **File** menu.

The main Print menu appears.

7. Choose **S** (Select Printer).

A list of installed printers appears.

8. Move the cursor onto the printer you want to update, and select **7** (**Update**).

9. Press F7 (Exit) until you return to the Edit screen.

Automatic Format and Rewrite

Function: Reformats your document as you edit it.

Keystrokes:

Keystrokes	*Mouse*
Shift-F1 (Setup)	File
2 (Display)	Setup
6 (Edit-Screen Options)	Display
1 (Automatically Format and Rewrite)	Edit-Screen Options Automatically Format and Rewrite
Y (Yes) or N (No)	Y (Yes) or N (No)
F7 (Exit)	Right mouse button

Automatic Format and Rewrite gives you immediate feedback concerning how your editing changes affect the appearance of your document. If you insert text, the text automatically rewraps to accommodate the change. If you change tabs or margins, the text is automatically shifted. By default, this option is set to Yes. If you change it to No, text will be rewritten as you move the cursor through the document.

 Turning On Automatic Format and Rewrite

1. Press Shift-F1 (Setup) or select **Setup** from the **File** menu.

The main Setup menu appears.

2. Select **Display** (**2**).

The Setup:Display menu appears.

3. Select **6** (**Edit-Screen Options**).

The Setup: Edit-Screen Options menu appears.

4. Select **1** (**Automatically Format and Rewrite**).

The cursor moves to the selected option.

5.   Press Y to turn the option on or   Your selection is displayed on
     N to turn it off.   screen.

6.   Press F7 (Exit) or click the right   WordPerfect returns you to your
     mouse button.   document.

 Note: If you set the Automatic Format and Rewrite option
to No, you can reformat your document manually in either
of two ways. The first method is to move the cursor to the
end of your document; press Home,Home,Down Arrow or
Page Down or Screen Down. The second way is to press
Ctrl-F3 (Screen) and select **3** (**Rewrite**).

B

Backspace

Function: Deletes characters, codes, or words.

Keystrokes: *Keyboard*
Backspace
Ctrl-Backspace

You can use the Backspace key alone to delete the character, code, or space to the left of the cursor, or with the Ctrl key to delete a word. If you bump into a formatting code on the Edit screen while pressing the Backspace key, WordPerfect will tell you which code it is and ask if you want to delete it. If you highlight the code in Reveal Codes, however, WordPerfect will delete the code without warning you.

Backspace (alone)	Deletes the character, space, or formatting code to the left of the cursor.
Ctrl-Backspace	Deletes the word the cursor is on or the word to the left of the cursor if the cursor is on a blank space.

 Note: You can restore text erased with Backspace or Ctrl-Backspace by using the Undelete feature, F1 (Cancel). Refer to *Undelete*. If you press Ctrl-Backspace repeatedly, without typing anything or moving the cursor, it's exactly the same as using Block Delete—whatever you delete is considered a single deletion, and you can get it all back with F1 (Cancel).

Backup, Timed and Original

Function: Automatically creates backup files to protect files from power outages and accidental erasure.

Keystrokes: *Keyboard*   *Mouse*
Shift-F1 (Setup)   **File**
3 (Environment)   **Setup**
1 (Backup Options)   **Environment**
1 (Timed Document   **Backup Options**
Backup) or **2** (Original   **Timed Document Backup or**
Document Backup)   **Original Document Backup**
F7 (Exit)   **Right mouse button**

Example:

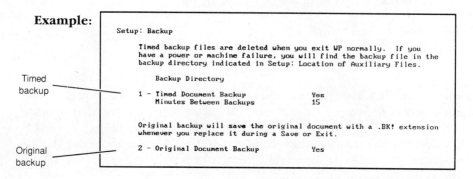

Timed backup

Original backup

```
Setup: Backup

     Timed backup files are deleted when you exit WP normally.  If you
     have a power or machine failure, you will find the backup file in the
     backup directory indicated in Setup: Location of Auxiliary Files.

          Backup Directory

     1 - Timed Document Backup              Yes
          Minutes Between Backups           15


     Original backup will save the original document with a .BK! extension
     whenever you replace it during a Save or Exit.

     2 - Original Document Backup           Yes
```

WordPerfect's Backup feature offers two automatic backup options. Timed Backup automatically saves the document that's displayed on screen to disk at specified intervals. For example, you can choose to save your working copy to disk every 10 minutes. If you experience a power outage, you can retrieve a file called WP{WP}.BK1 (for Doc 1) or WP{WP}.BK2 (for Doc 2) from disk. This file contains the version of your document that the Timed Backup feature most recently saved to disk. If you exit WordPerfect correctly, using the F7 (Exit) key, WordPerfect erases the Timed Backup file. Timed Backup files are saved in the Backup Directory specified in the Setup Location of Files menu, or if you don't name a directory there, in the directory containing the WordPerfect program file WP.EXE.

The second option, Original Backup, creates a permanent backup file. Whenever you save an edited file to disk, WordPerfect renames the original file using the file's original first name, and adding a special extension: BK!. WordPerfect then stores the edited version under the file's original name. For instance, if you retrieve and edit a file named *REPORT1*, then save it, the original version (on disk) is renamed *REPORT1.BK!* Each time you retrieve and edit the file, the previous version is saved to the BK! file. Original Backup files are saved in the same directory as the original file.

You can use this option to turn on either or both of the backup methods. However, they are not a substitute for your regular backup procedure.

Setting Backup Options

1. Press Shift-F1 (Setup) or select Setup from the **File** menu.	The main Setup menu appears.
2. Select **Environment (3)**.	The Setup: Environment menu appears.
3. Select **1** (Backup Options).	
4. Select **1** (Timed Document Backup).	The cursor moves up to the Timed Backup options.
5. Press Y to set the backup option.	WordPerfect prompts you to enter the amount of time between backups.
6. Enter the number of minutes between backups.	Ten to 15 minutes is a safe range. The default is 30 minutes. If you are a fast typist, you should back up more frequently.
7. Press **2** (Original) to move the cursor to the Original Backup option.	
8. Press Y, turning the option on.	
9. Press F7 (Exit) or click the right mouse button.	This exits the Backup Options screen and returns you to your document.

If you select the Timed Backup option and you experience a power outage while working on a document, you may be able to retrieve some of your changes. When you restart WordPerfect, you'll see a message telling you that a backup file exists and asking if you want to rename or delete it. Choose option **1** (Rename), type a name for the file, and press Enter. (You must rename the file to remove the BK! extension. If you don't, WordPerfect won't let you save the file again.) You can then retrieve the file to see if it is a more recent version than the last one you saved in the regular way.

Backward Search (see *Search*)

Base Font (see *Fonts*)

Baseline Placement for Typesetters (see also *Line Height*)

Function: Anchors the first baseline at the top margin, if line height is set to fixed.

Keystrokes:

Keyboard	*Mouse*
Shift-F8 (Format)	Layout
4 (Other)	Other
6 (Printer Functions)	Printer Functions
5 (Baseline Placement for Typesetters)	Baseline Placement for Typesetters
Y (Yes)	Y (Yes)
F7 (Exit)	Right mouse button

Codes: [Bline:On]
[Bline:Off]

By default, WordPerfect prints the top of the first line of text even with the top margin. The baseline itself (the imaginary line that text sits on) is below the top margin, so that nothing is printed in the space reserved for the top margin. For example, the top of the uppercase *W* is printed right at the top margin. If you change the font in the first line, it will change the position of the baseline. If you select Yes for the Baseline Placement for Typesetters option, the baseline of the first line of text will always be printed at the top margin, and the characters will extend up into the margin. For example, the bottom of the uppercase *W* would be printed at the top margin. Also, font changes will have no effect on baseline placement, since it will always be at the top margin.

Setting the Baseline

1. Position the cursor where you want to turn Baseline Placement on.

   This is usually at the beginning of the document.

2. Press Shift-F8 (Format) or display the **Layout** menu.

   A list of formatting options appears.

3. Select **Other** (4).

   The Format: Other menu appears.

4. Select **6** (Printer Functions).

   The Format: Printer Functions menu appears.

5. Select **5** (**B**aseline Placement for Typesetters). | You have the option to turn Baseline Placement on or off.

6. Press Y to turn Baseline Placement on.

7. Press Enter twice.

8. Select Line (**1**). | The Format: Line menu appears.

9. Select **4** (Line **H**eight), change the line height setting to fixed, and enter a measurement. | You can leave the setting WordPerfect has chosen for your font or enter another measurement.

10. Press F7 (Exit). | WordPerfect inserts the [Bline:On] and [Ln Height] codes at the cursor position.

Now, whenever you use a feature that places the text in a specific position on the page, such as Advance, the baseline of that text will be positioned in the precise spot you indicate.

 Tip: If you place the [Bline:On] and [Ln Height] codes in the Document Initial Settings, they will affect the entire document. Refer to *Initial Settings*.

Batch Files (see *DOS Text Files*)

Beep Options

Function: Lets you turn the beep function on or off when certain prompts appear on the status line.

Keystrokes:

Keyboard	*Mouse*
Shift-F1 (Setup)	File
3 (Environment)	Setup
2 (Beep Options)	Environment
1 (Beep on Error), 2 (Beep on Hyphenation), or 3 (Beep on Search Failure)	Beep Options Beep on Error, Beep on Hyphenation, or Beep on Search Failure

Keystrokes: *Keyboard*   *Mouse*
                  Y (Yes) or N (No)   Yes or No
                  F7 (Exit)   Right mouse button

Example:

```
Setup: Beep options

  1 - Beep on Error                    No

  2 - Beep on Hyphenation             Yes

  3 - Beep on Search Failure           No
```

Three Beep options are available. You can have WordPerfect beep when an error message appears, when you are asked to select a position for hyphenation, or when you are using Search or Replace and WordPerfect fails to find the search string you specified.

Setting the Beep Options

1. Press Shift-F1 (Setup) or select Setup from the File menu.

   The main Setup menu appears.

2. Select Environment (3).

   The Setup: Environment menu appears.

3. Select 2 (Beep Options).

   The three Beep options appear.

4. Select the Beep option you want to change.

5. Press Y to turn the option on or N to turn it off.

6. Repeat steps 4 and 5 for either of the other two options you want to change.

7. Press F7 (Exit) or click the right mouse button.

   The Beep Options screen disappears, and your settings are saved.

Binding

Function: Shifts text on two-sided pages to allow for binding.

Keystrokes:

Keyboard	*Mouse*
Shift-F7 (Print)	**File**
B (Binding Offset)	**Print**
distance	**Binding Offset**
F7 (Exit)	*distance*
	Right mouse button

Example:

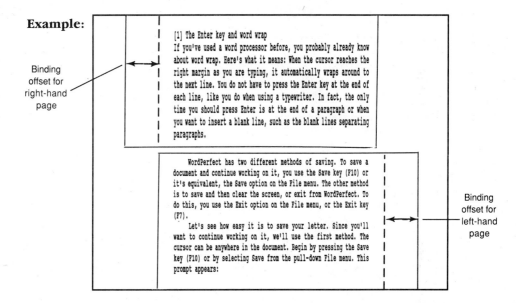

Binding offset for right-hand page

[1] The Enter key and word wrap
If you've used a word processor before, you probably already know about word wrap. Here's what it means: When the cursor reaches the right margin as you are typing, it automatically wraps around to the next line. You do not have to press the Enter key at the end of each line, like you do when using a typewriter. In fact, the only time you should press Enter is at the end of a paragraph or when you want to insert a blank line, such as the blank lines separating paragraphs.

WordPerfect has two different methods of saving. To save a document and continue working on it, you use the Save key (F10) or it's equivalent, the Save option on the File menu. The other method is to save and then clear the screen, or exit from WordPerfect. To do this, you use the Exit option on the File menu, or the Exit key (F7).

Let's see how easy it is to save your letter. Since you'll want to continue working on it, we'll use the first method. The cursor can be anywhere in the document. Begin by pressing the Save key (F10) or by selecting Save from the pull-down File menu. This prompt appears:

Binding offset for left-hand page

The Binding feature lets you insert extra space in the inside margin (or gutter) of a two-sided page so pages can be bound or inserted into a binder. Text on odd-numbered (right-hand) pages is shifted to the right, and text on even-numbered (left-hand) pages is shifted to the left. Although this feature does not insert a code into the document, WordPerfect does save the binding offset information with the document.

Setting a Binding Width

1. Press Shift-F7 (Print) or select **Print** from the **File** menu.	The main Print menu appears.
2. Select **B** (Binding Offset).	WordPerfect prompts you to enter a binding width.

3. Type a binding width and press Enter.

The default unit of measure is inches; if you want to change the unit of measure, refer to *Units of Measure*. You can enter a fraction, such as 2/3, and WordPerfect will convert it to its decimal equivalent.

4. Press F7 (Exit) or click the right mouse button.

WordPerfect returns you to your document. When you print the document, it will include the extra space you've specified.

Note: Use this option only when you plan on printing two-sided copies. For one-sided printing, use the margin settings to insert the extra space needed for binding.

Note: You can change the Binding Offset so it will affect the top or bottom margin of the page instead of the left or right margin. To do this, use the Format Page menu's Paper Size/Type options. Select the paper type you want to change, or create a new one, and then select the Edit option. The seventh option on the next menu lets you change the binding edge from Left to Top for that form.

Block

Function: Lets you mark a block of text so you can perform an operation on that block, such as move, copy, delete, print, save, or italicize.

Keystrokes: *Keyboard*
Alt-F4 or F12 (Block)

Mouse
Edit
Block
OR
Hold down left mouse button
Drag mouse cursor to end of block

Code: [Block]

Example:

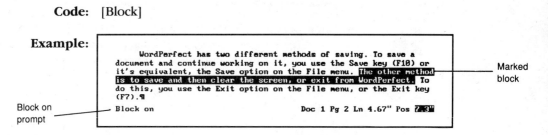

WordPerfect has two different methods of saving. To save a
document and continue working on it, you use the Save key (F10) or
it's equivalent, the Save option on the File menu. The other method
is to save and then clear the screen, or exit from WordPerfect. To
do this, you use the Exit option on the File menu, or the Exit key
(F7).¶

Block on   Doc 1 Pg 2 Ln 4.67" Pos 7.3"

Marked
block

Block on
prompt

The Block feature has no function by itself. Instead, you use it to designate a section of the document. You must then enter another command to tell WordPerfect what to do with the block.

 ## Marking a Block

1. Move the cursor to the beginning or end of the block you want to mark.	This position will become your pivot point, letting you *stretch* the highlight up, down, left, or right of this position.
2. Press Alt-F4 (Block) or select **B**lock from the **E**dit menu.	A Block on prompt starts flashing in the lower-left corner of your screen.
3. Move the cursor to the opposite end of the block you want to mark.	As you move the cursor, the block highlighting stretches with it.
4. Select the operation you want to perform on the block.	The available operations are listed below. If you change your mind, you can cancel the Block feature by pressing F1 (Cancel) or Alt-F4 (Block).

 Tip: You can use the mouse to highlight a block of text without using the pull-down menus. Move the mouse cursor to the beginning of the block you want to highlight, hold down the left mouse button, and drag the cursor to the end of the block. When you release the left mouse button, the block is highlighted.

Tip: After pressing Alt-F4 to mark the beginning of the block, you can move the cursor in a number of ways. Using the arrow keys is the slowest method. You can also use the Search feature to stretch the highlight to a character or word. You can press a character key or punctuation key (such as a period) to stretch the highlight to the next occurrence of that character or punctuation mark. You can even press Enter to stretch the highlight to the end of the paragraph, at the hard return.

When you're done marking the block, you can choose one of the following features to tell WordPerfect what to do with it. For more information about one of the following features, refer to that feature in this reference section.

F6 (Bold)	Alt-F2 (Replace)
Shift-F6 (Center)	F10 (Save)
Del or Backspace (Delete)	F2 (→Search)
Alt-F6 (Flush Right)	Ctrl-F1 (Shell)
Ctrl-F8 (Font)	Ctrl-F9 (Sort)
Shift-F8 (Protect Block)	Ctrl-F2 (Spell)
Ctrl-F5 (Comment)	Alt-F8 (Style)
Alt-F5 (Mark Text)	Shift-F3 (Switch)
Ctrl-F4 (Move Block)	Ctrl-F5 (Text In/Out)
Shift-F7 (Print)	F8 (Underline)
Shift-F2 (←Search)	Alt-F7, **2** (**T**able)
Ctrl-F4 (Append)	

Block Append (see *Append*)

Block Comments (see *Comments*)

Block Copy (see *Copy Block*)

Block Protect

Function: Prevents a block from being split by a soft page break.

Keystrokes:
Keyboard	*Mouse*
Alt-F4 (Block)	Edit
Highlight block	**Block**
Shift-F8 (Format)	Highlight block
Y (**Yes**) or N (**No**)	Edit
	Protect Block

Codes: [Block Pro:On]
[Block Pro:Off]

Example:

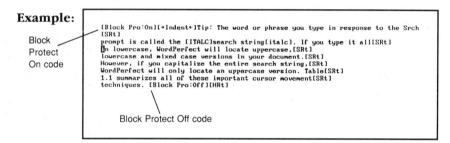

Block
Protect
On code

```
[Block Pro:On][+Indent+]Tip: The word or phrase you type in response to the Srch
[SRt]
prompt is called the [ITALC]search string[italc]. If you type it all[SRt]
in lowercase, WordPerfect will locate uppercase,[SRt]
lowercase and mixed case versions in your document.[SRt]
However, if you capitalize the entire search string,[SRt]
WordPerfect will only locate an uppercase version. Table[SRt]
1.1 summarizes all of these important cursor movement[SRt]
techniques. [Block Pro:Off][HRt]
```

Block Protect Off code

Block protection is useful for keeping tables, charts, and other blocks of text from being split between two pages as you edit the document. With Block Protect on, if part of the block can't fit on the page, WordPerfect moves the entire block to the next page, not just the lines that don't fit. You can then add lines to your table or chart without worrying where the page break is going to fall.

 Protecting a Block

1. Move the cursor to the beginning of the block you want to protect.

2. Press Alt-F4 (Block) or select **Block** from the Edit menu to start highlighting the block.

   `Block on` starts flashing in the lower-left corner of the screen.

3. Move the cursor to the end of the block you want to protect, but stop short of the hard return.

   This stretches the highlight over the entire block.

4. Press Shift-F8 (Format) and press Y, or select Protect Block from the Edit menu.

WordPerfect inserts a [Block Pro:On] code at the beginning of the block and a [Block Pro:Off] code at the end.

 Tip: You can also use the Block Protect feature to keep a heading together with the first paragraph under that heading. Just highlight the heading and one or more lines of the following paragraph before protecting the block.

Bold

Function: Formats text with the Bold attribute.

Keystrokes: *Keyboard*
F6 (Bold)

Mouse
Font
Appearance
Bold

Codes: [BOLD]
[bold]

Example:

The Bold feature adds emphasis to text by printing it darker or heavier. You can add the bold attribute in either of two ways: by entering a bold command and then typing your text, or by highlighting existing text with the Block feature and then entering the Bold command. In either case, WordPerfect inserts two codes—[BOLD] to turn bold on and [bold] to turn it off.

Typing Bolded Text

1. Position the cursor where you want to type the bolded text.

2. Press F6 (Bold), or display the Font menu and select **A**ppearance and then **B**old.

   You can also select Bold from the Font/Appearance menu: Ctrl-F8, A. WordPerfect inserts the hidden [BOLD] and [bold] codes and positions the cursor between them. The Pos number on the status line appears bold.

3. Type the text you want to appear boldface.

   Text appears in a different color or brighter, depending on your monitor.

4. Press Right Arrow or Down Arrow to move the cursor past the Bold Off code.

   You can also move the cursor past the Bold Off code by pressing F6 (Bold) again.

 Bolding Existing Text

1. Move the cursor to the beginning of the text you want to bold.

2. Press Alt-F4 (Block) or select **B**lock from the Edit menu.

   This anchors the cursor so you can stretch the highlight over your text.

3. Move the cursor to the end of the block you want to bold.

4. Press F6 (Bold).

   WordPerfect inserts a [BOLD] code at the beginning of the block and a [bold] code at the end of the block and turns the Block feature off.

 Unbolding Text

1. Press Alt-F3 or F11 (Reveal Codes) or select **R**eveal Codes from the Edit menu.

   This splits the screen. In the bottom half of the screen are the [BOLD] and [bold] codes.

2. Move the cursor so it is highlighting either the [BOLD] or [bold] code, and press the Del key.

Both Bold codes are deleted, and the text returns to normal.

 Note: If bolded text does not appear different from other text on screen, refer to the *Colors/Fonts/Attributes* feature described in this reference section. You shouldn't have to turn on Reveal Codes every time you want to find out if something is bold.

Borders (see *Graphics, Options*)

Box (see *Graphics, Create*)

Bullets (see also *Outline*)

Function: Lets you type bullets.

Keystrokes: *Keyboard*
Ctrl-V or Ctrl-2
Number from character
set, such as 4,0
Enter
OR
Alt and ASCII code on
numeric keypad

There are several methods you can use to type bullets. You can use the Compose key, the Alt key with the numeric keypad, or WordPerfect's Outline or Paragraph Number feature. For more information about Outline or Paragraph Number, see those sections. (See also *Compose Key*.) These are some of the bullets you can create:

Character Set and Number	Type of Bullet
4,0	● Bullet
4,1	○ Hollow Bullet
4,2	■ Square Bullet
4,3	• Small Bullet
4,37	○ Large Hollow Bullet
4,44	● Large Bullet
4,45	○ Small Hollow Bullet
4,46	■ Large Square Bullet
4,47	■ Small Square Bullet
4,49	□ Small Hollow Square Bullet
5,18	▣ Inverse Bullet

Creating Bullets with the Compose Key

1. Position the cursor where you want the bullet to appear in the document.

2. Press Ctrl-V (Compose), or select Characters from the Font menu, or press Ctrl-2 (use the 2 on the top of the keyboard, not on the numeric keypad).

    If you press Ctrl-V, a Key = prompt appears.

3. Type the number of the character set you want to use, a comma, and the number of the character you want to use for the bullet and press Enter.

    The bullet appears on the Edit screen. If you place the cursor on it in Reveal Codes, the code will expand to show the two numbers.

Tip: If the bullets don't appear in the printed version of your document, change the Graphic Quality option on the main Print menu (Shift-F7,G) to Medium. As long as your printer has graphics capability (most laser printers and dot-matrix printers do), WordPerfect should be able to print the characters graphically.

Creating Bullets with the Alt Key

To create bullets with the Alt key, press Alt and then type the decimal value on the numeric keypad:

Alt-254 ■   Produces a small, solid box, the equivalent of pressing the Compose key and typing 4,2.

Alt-7 •   Produces a solid circle, same as Compose key and 4,0.

Alt-16 ➤   Produces a solid arrow tip, same as Compose key and 6,27.

Cancel

Function: Cancels a menu or prompt and returns you to the previous screen. If there is no menu or prompt, undeletes previously erased text.

Keystrokes:

Keyboard	*Mouse*
F1 (Cancel)	Middle button on a three-button mouse
	Both buttons on a two-button mouse

You can use the Cancel feature to exit a WordPerfect menu or status line message without saving any changes you've made, cancel a hyphenation request, stop a search or macro in progress, or even recover up to three deletions (refer to *Undelete*).

 Note: F1 does not cancel the Help menu. You must press Enter instead. Also, F1 does not let you cancel a macro definition. To cancel the definition, you must press Ctrl-F10. To cancel a pull-down menu, press F7 (Exit) or click the right mouse button.

 Canceling a Menu or Prompt

1. Press F1 (Cancel), or click the middle button on a three-button mouse or both buttons on a two-button mouse.

   The operation ceases and you are returned to the previous screen.

 Note: If you've worked your way through two or more menus, you may have to press F1 (Cancel) more than once to return to your document.

Cancel Print Job (see *Control Printer*)

Capitalization, Converting Text

Function: Changes characters from lower- to uppercase and vice versa.

Keystrokes: *Keyboard*   *Mouse*
Alt-F4 (Block)   **Edit**
Highlight block   **Block**
Shift-F3 (Switch)   **Highlight block**
1 (Uppercase) or   **Edit**
2 (Lowercase)   **Convert Case**
                        Uppercase or Lowercase

Example:

Case Conversion options ———

```
[1]Typing your first letter ¶
     So that you'll have some text to practice with as you learn
about cursor movement, inserting and deleting text, and other
topics in this chapter, go ahead and type the letter shown in
1 Uppercase; 2 Lowercase: 0
```

You can type text in all uppercase characters by pressing the Caps Lock key or holding down the Shift key and then typing the text as usual. If the text is already typed, you can convert it from lower- to uppercase and back. WordPerfect is sensitive to case. If you change from upper- to lowercase, the program can keep the first character of the sentence uppercase, as well as words like *I* or *I'm*.

Switching Capitalization for a Block of Text

1. Move the cursor to the beginning or end of the block you want to affect.

2. Press Alt-F4 (Block) or select **Block** from the **Edit** menu.

   This anchors the cursor, letting you stretch the highlight over the block.

3. Move the cursor to highlight all the text you want to change.

   You can use the cursor keys or the Search feature, or type the character or punctuation mark you want to stretch to.

4. Press Shift-F3 (Switch) or select Convert Case from the **Edit** menu.

   The Case menu appears.

5. Choose **1** (Uppercase) or **2** (Lowercase).

   The highlighted text changes case.

 Tip: To make sure WordPerfect keeps the first character of a sentence uppercase, highlight the period in the previous sentence.

Caption (see *Graphics, Create* and *Graphics, Options*)

Cartridges and Fonts (see also *Fonts* and *Initialize Printer*)

Function: Lets you install the interchangeable print cartridges, print wheels, or downloadable soft font files that you will be using with your printer.

Keystrokes: | *Keyboard* | *Mouse* |
| --- | --- |
| Shift-F7 (Print) | **File** |
| **S** (Select Printer) | **Print** |
| Cursor key (to highlight printer) | **Select Printer** |
| | Click on selected printer |
| **3** (Edit) | **Edit** |
| **4** (Cartridges and Fonts) | **Cartridges and Fonts** |
| | Click on selected printer |
| Cursor key (to selection) | **Select Fonts** |
| **1** (Select Fonts) | *** (Present) and/or + (Can Be Loaded)** |
| *** (Present) and/or +** (Can Be Loaded) | **Right mouse button** |
| F7 (Exit) | |

Example:

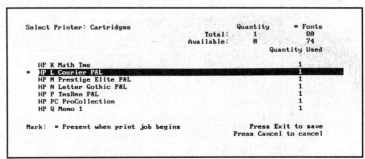

```
Select Printer: Cartridges                          Quantity    * Fonts
                                        Total:         1           80
                                        Available:     0           74
                                                        Quantity Used

      HP K Math Tms                                        1
   *  HP L Courier P&L                                     1
      HP M Prestige Elite P&L                              1
      HP N Letter Gothic P&L                               1
      HP P TmsRmn P&L                                      1
      HP PC ProCollection                                 1
      HP Q Memo 1                                          1

   Mark:  * Present when print job begins          Press Exit to save
                                                    Press Cancel to cancel
```

Most printers support a very limited number of fonts, requiring you to work within their limitations. Some printers, such as laser printers, support the use of additional fonts on cartridges or in files (called soft fonts), or on print wheels. WordPerfect's Cartridges and Fonts feature lets you install these additional fonts and take advantage of the increased capabilities.

Fonts that have already been installed appear on the Base Font menu. Whenever you want to change fonts in a document, simply display this menu, by pressing Ctrl-F8 (Font), and select the base font you want to use. (Refer to *Fonts*.)

 ## Installing Fonts

1. Press Shift-F7 (Print) or select **Print** from the **File** menu.	The main Print menu appears.

2. Choose **S** (Select Printer).

A list of defined printers appears. The currently active printer is highlighted and marked with an asterisk.

3. Move the cursor to the printer of your choice.

4. Select **3** (Edit).

The Select Printer: Edit menu appears.

5. Select **4** (Cartridges and Fonts).

The Select Printer: Cartridges and Fonts menu appears. It displays available types of fonts: soft fonts, cartridges, built-in fonts, slot fonts, and/or print wheels.

6. Highlight the type of font you want to install, and choose **1** (Select Fonts).

If you select soft fonts, you may be asked to select a font group before you can select individual fonts. A list of available fonts, cartridges, or print wheels appears.

7. Highlight the cartridge or font you want to install.

Don't mark any soft fonts, cartridges, or print wheels you don't have. Most fonts must be purchased separately.

8. Type * to mark the cartridge or font as Present When Print Job Begins, or + (for soft fonts and print wheels) to mark it as Can Be Loaded/Unloaded During Print Job. Some fonts can be marked with both symbols and swapped in and out of printer memory if necessary.

For a soft font, * indicates that you must initialize to download it, and the font stays in memory even after the print job. Marking a cartridge or print wheel with an asterisk means you will insert the wheel or cartridge before asking WordPerfect to print. + indicates that WordPerfect will load the font into memory or ask you to insert the print wheel during the print job. Soft fonts are unloaded after the print job ends, reducing the possibility of running out of memory.

9. Repeat steps 7 and 8 for all the fonts you want to use.

10. Press F7 (Exit) or click the right mouse button five times.

WordPerfect returns you to the Edit screen.

 Note: Marking the fonts you want to use does not make those fonts immediately available to your printer. You may have to initialize your printer first. Refer to *Initialize Printer*.

 Note: When you bring up a list of cartridges or fonts, three options appear at the bottom of the screen: **1** (Select Fonts), **2** (Change Quantity), and **3** (Name Search). You selected the first option in the previous steps. The second option lets you enter the number of slots available on your printer for cartridges, the number of print wheels you can install, or the amount of memory available for soft font files. WordPerfect has set the numbers according to manufacturer specifications, but if your system has been modified, you can change these numbers.

Case Conversion (see *Capitalization, Converting Text*)

Center Page, Top to Bottom

Function: Centers single-page document between top and bottom margins on printed page.

Keystrokes: *Keyboard*

Cursor to top of page
Shift-F8 (Format)
2 (Page)
1 (Center Page), Y
F7 (Exit)

Mouse

Cursor to top of page
Layout
Page
Center Page, Y
Right mouse button

Code: [Center Pg]

Example:

```
                                    SAMS
                                    11711 North College Avenue
                                    Carmel, IN  46032
                                    August 16, 1990


         Ms. Linda Hawkins
         5407 South Carpathia Avenue
         Beardstown, IL  60248

         Dear Linda,

         We just received your order dated July 1, 1990 and are presently
         processing it. You should be receiving your merchandise by the end
         of the week.

         Please realize that the delay in shipment is no fault of ours. We
         process orders as soon as we receive them, and we have no control
         over postal delays.

         Thanks again for sending us your business, and please let us know
         if we can be of any further assistance.

         Sincerely,


         Mitzi La Rouche
```

The Center Page feature is especially useful for centering short pages, such as letters, title pages, and tables of contents.

Centering a Page

1. Move the cursor to the top of the page.

   Make sure the cursor is before any codes.

2. Press Shift-F8 (Format) or display the **Layout** menu.

   A list of formatting options appears.

3. Select **Page** (**2**).

   The Format: Page menu appears.

4. Select **1** (Center Page) and press Y to confirm.

5. Press F7 (Exit) or click the right mouse button.

   This returns you to your document.

Center Tab (see *Tab, Set*)

Center Text

Function: Centers text between left and right margins or over a column.

Keystrokes: *Keyboard*   *Mouse*
Shift-F6 (Center)   Layout
                     Align
                     Center

Code: [Center]

Example:

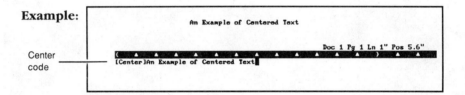

Center
code

The Center feature lets you center text as you type it, or center an existing block of text. You can center a line of text between the margins, center text over tabular or text columns, or center each line of text in a highlighted block. You can also use it to create dot leaders in front of centered text.

 Centering as You Type

1. Position the cursor at the left margin.

2. Press Shift-F6 (Center), or display the Layout menu and select **Align** and then **Center**.

   The cursor moves to the center of the line. If you want to create dot leaders, perform this step for a second time.

3. Type the text.

   The text appears centered.

4. Press Enter.

   This inserts a hard return and begins a new paragraph.

Centering Existing Text

1. Move the cursor to the beginning of the line you want to center.

   The line must end with a Hard Return, Flush Right, or Tab code.

2. Press Shift-F6 (Center), or display the **Layout** menu and select **Align** and then **Center**.

   WordPerfect centers the text. If you want to create dot leaders, perform this step a second time.

3. Press Down Arrow.

   This moves the cursor to the next line of text and rewrites the screen.

 Centering a Column Heading

Over newspaper or parallel columns:

1. Position the cursor at the left column margin.

2. Press Shift-F6 (Center), or display the **Layout** menu and select **Align** and then **Center**.

   The cursor moves to the center of the column.

3. Type the text.

   The text appears centered over the column.

4. Press Enter.

   This inserts a hard return and begins a new paragraph.

Over columns created with tabs or indents:

1. Center the cursor over the column using the Tab key.

2. Press Shift-F6 (Center), or display the Layout menu and select **Align** and then **Center**.

3. Type the text.

   The column head appears centered.

 Centering a Block of Lines

1. Highlight the block of text you want to center.

   Use the Block feature (Alt-F4) to highlight the text.

2. Press Shift-F6 (Center), or display the Layout menu and select **Align** and then **Center**.

[Just Center]? No (Yes) appears.

3. Press Y to center the text.

A [Just Center] code is placed at the beginning of the section. At the end of the section, another Justify code is inserted, returning you to the justification style you were using.

 Tip: You can center a block of lines to create your own letterhead. Experiment with fonts, type styles, and various graphics, to make it as attractive and unique as possible.

Centimeters (see *Units of Measure*)

Character Sets, WordPerfect's (see *Compose Key*)

Clear Screen (see *Exit*)

Clipboard (see also *Shell*)

Function: Lets you transfer data between various WordPerfect Corporation programs, such as WordPerfect, DrawPerfect, PlanPerfect, and DataPerfect.

Keystrokes:

Keyboard	*Mouse*
Ctrl-F1 (Shell)	File
2 (Save) or 3 (Append)	Goto Shell
Ctrl-F1 (Shell)	Save or Append
1 (Go to Shell)	File

Select program letter	Goto Shell
Retrieve file	Select program letter
Cursor to position of insertion	Retrieve file
	Cursor to position of insertion
Ctrl-F1 (Shell)	File
4 (Retrieve)	Goto Shell
	Retrieve

Example:

```
June 15, 1990


Ms. Leslie McBride
121 Vintage Place
Northridge, CA 91324


Dear Ms. McBride,

We are pleased to inform you that we have completed your holiday
reservations for your trip to New Zealand.  At your request, you
will be staying at the beautiful and luxurious Hyatt Regency.  We
think you will find it enchanting.
```

Clipboard options ——— `1 Go to Shell; Clipboard: 2 Save; 3 Append; 4 Retrieve; 5 DOS Command: 0`

The Clipboard is a temporary storage location for data. If you start WordPerfect from the Shell menu, you can use it to transfer data between WordPerfect and other WordPerfect Corporation programs, such as DrawPerfect, PlanPerfect, and DataPerfect. WordPerfect includes three Clipboard options: Save, Append, and Retrieve. Use the Save option to save the entire document on the Edit screen to the Clipboard, or a block that you've highlighted with WordPerfect's Block feature. Use the Append option to add the document or block to the Clipboard's current contents. Use the Retrieve option to retrieve the Clipboard's contents anywhere on the Edit screen. You can also retrieve the contents of the Clipboard into another WordPerfect Corporation program, using the Go to Shell option on WordPerfect's Shell Clipboard menu. Once you exit the Shell, the contents of the Clipboard are deleted.

 ## Copying to the Clipboard

1. If you want to copy a block instead of the entire document, use the Block feature to highlight the block of text you want to copy. Otherwise, skip to step 2.

2. \ Press Ctrl-F1 (Shell) or select Goto Shell from the **File** menu. | The Shell Clipboard options appear at the bottom of the screen.

3. Select **2** (**Save**) or **3** (**Append**). | The Save option replaces whatever is presently in the Clipboard. Append adds the data to the end of the Clipboard.

After you've copied data into the Clipboard, you can retrieve the data in WordPerfect or in another WordPerfect Corporation program.

 ## Copying from the Clipboard into WordPerfect

1. Press Ctrl-F1 (Shell) or select Goto Shell from the **File** menu. | The Shell Clipboard options appear.

2. Select **4** (**Retrieve**). | WordPerfect retrieves the entire contents of the Clipboard at the cursor position.

 ## Copying from the Clipboard to Another Program

1. Press Ctrl-F1 (Shell) or select Goto Shell from the **File** menu. | The Shell Clipboard options appear.

2. Select **1** (**Go to Shell**). | The Shell menu appears, listing the programs available.

3. Select the program you will be copying the contents of the Clipboard into and retrieve the file, if necessary. | The Shell starts the program.

4. Position the cursor where you want to insert the text.

5. Press Ctrl-F1 (Shell). | The Shell Clipboard menu appears at the bottom of the screen.

6. Select **4** (**Retrieve**). | The text from the Clipboard is inserted at the cursor position.

7. Save your work.

Note: When you select Retrieve from the Clipboard menu, the entire contents of the Clipboard is inserted at the cursor location. You cannot copy only a section of the Clipboard's contents into a document.

 Managing the Clipboard

1. Press Ctrl-F1 (Shell) or select **Goto Shell** from the **File** menu.

The Shell Clipboard options appear.

2. Select **1** (**Go to Shell**)

The Shell menu appears, listing the programs available.

3. Select **2** (Clipboard).

The contents of the Clipboard appear on screen. A menu at the bottom provides three options: Clear the Clipboard, Save the contents as a DOS text (ASCII) file, or Retrieve a DOS text file.

4. Select **1** (**Clear**), **2** (**Save as text file**), or **3** (**Retrieve text file**).

If you choose to clear the contents, the text is cleared from the screen and from the Clipboard. If you choose to save the contents of the Clipboard into an ASCII file, you are prompted to enter a file name.

5. Enter a file name for the file you want to save or retrieve, and press Enter.

Include a drive and directory, if necessary. If you choose to retrieve a file, the DOS text file appears on screen.

 Caution: Before you clear the Clipboard, you may want to save the contents to disk, just in case. However, the Save as Text File option saves the Clipboard contents as an ASCII file, not as a WordPerfect file. Know what's on the Clipboard at all times, so you won't overwrite the contents by mistake.

Codes (see *Reveal Codes*)

Colors/Fonts/Attributes

Function: Controls the on-screen appearance of normal text and text formatted with attributes such as bold, italics, and large print.

Keystrokes:

Keyboard	*Mouse*
Shift-F1 (Setup)	File
2 (Display)	Setup
1 (Colors/Fonts/ Attributes)	Display Colors/Fonts/Attributes
1 (Screen Attributes) or 1 (Screen Colors)	Screen Attributes or Screen Colors
Assign screen color or font to attributes	Assign screen color or font to attributes
F7 (Exit)	Right mouse button

Example:

```
Setup: Attributes

Attribute        Blink  Bold  Blocked  Underline  Normal  Sample
Normal             N      N      N         N         Y     Sample
Blocked            N      N      Y         N         N     Sample
Underline          N      N      N         Y         N     Sample
Strikeout          N      N      N         N         Y     Sample
Bold               N      Y      N         N         Y     Sample
```

— Monochrome screen

The Colors/Fonts/Attributes feature lets you control how text formatted with various font attributes will appear *on screen*. This does not affect the printed version of the attributes. Your options are limited by the type of monitor and graphics adapter in your computer system. If you have a monochrome monitor, you can't change screen colors, but you may be able to change the shading of the foreground or background.

Modifying Colors/Fonts/Attributes

1. Press Shift-F1 (Setup) or select Setup from the File menu.

   The main Setup menu appears.

2. Select **Display** (2).	The Setup: Display menu appears.

3. Select **1** (Colors/Fonts/Attributes).

The menu that appears next depends on the type of monitor and graphics interface card in your computer. If you have a monochrome monitor without graphics capability, you'll go directly to the Setup:Attributes screen. If you have a color monitor, you'll go to the Setup:Colors/Fonts screen.

Monochrome Monitor:

If you have a monochrome monitor without graphics capability, the Setup:Attributes screen appears. For each of the attributes listed in the left column, such as Normal, Blocked, and Underline, you can select from among five monitor capabilities: Blink, Bold, Blocked, Underline, and Normal. The last column displays a sample of how the combination will appear on screen.

1. Move the cursor to the attribute you want to change; then move to the desired capability column and press Y to turn it on, or N to turn it off.	Use the arrow keys to move the cursor.
2. Repeat for each attribute you want to change.	Assuming you were using Doc 1, this changes the attributes for the Doc 1 work area. You can switch to Doc 2 and repeat the steps, or copy the attributes from Doc 1.
3. If you want to change the attributes in Document 2, press Shift-F3 (Switch). To copy the attributes from Doc 1 to Doc 2, press Ctrl-F4 (Move).	When you finish, press F7 (Exit) to return to the Edit screen.
4. Press F7 (Exit) twice.	WordPerfect returns you to the Edit screen.

Color Monitor:

If you have a color monitor with a VGA or EGA interface card, the next menu provides options to change the screen font. You can choose to display italics, underline, small caps, or 512 characters from the WordPerfect character sets, instead of 256. Each of these options reduces the number of available foreground colors to eight. The default is Normal Font, which provides 16 colors for the foreground and 8 for the background.

If you have a color monitor with a CGA, PC3270, or MGCA card, or if your EGA or VGA card doesn't have enough memory to take advantage of the screen fonts, a menu with two options will appear: Fast Text Display and Screen Colors. If you select Yes for Fast Text Display, WordPerfect reformats the screen faster, but it could cause snow or static. On a CGA monitor, 16 foreground colors and 8 background colors are available.

1. Select **1** (**Screen Colors**). Move the cursor to the attribute you want to change; then type the letter representing the color you want to use.

    The Setup Colors screen appears. For each of the attributes listed in the left column, such as Normal, Blocked, Underline, and Strikeout, you can select a background and foreground (text) color. The last column on the right shows how the color combinations will appear on screen. Use the arrow keys to move the cursor.

2. Repeat for each attribute you want to change.

    Assuming you were using Doc 1, this changes the attributes for the Doc 1 work area. You can switch to Doc 2 and repeat the steps, or copy the attributes from Doc 1.

3. If you want to change the attributes in Document 2, press Shift-F3 (Switch). To copy the attributes from Doc 1 to Doc 2, press Ctrl-F4 (Move).

    When you finish, press F7 (Exit) to return to the Edit screen.

4. Press F7 (Exit) twice.

    WordPerfect returns you to the Edit screen.

Monitor with Hercules Interface:
If your computer system includes a Hercules Graphics Card Plus or a Hercules InColor Card with RamFont, a different menu appears, with options for 12 fonts and 256 characters, 6 fonts and 512 characters, or the default Normal Font. If you leave it set to Normal Font, selecting screen attributes is identical to selecting them on monochrome monitors. If you select 12 or 6 fonts, your screen will display appearance attributes like underline, italics, double underlining, superscript, and subscript, and different font size attributes such as small, large, and very large.

Colors, Print (see *Print Color*)

Column Definition

Function: Lets you define the type of columns, the number of columns, the distance separating them, and the left and right margins for each column.

Keystrokes:

Keyboard	*Mouse*
Alt-F7 (Columns/Table)	Layout
1 (Columns)	Columns
3 (Define)	Define
Enter the type and number of columns, the distance between them, and the column margins	Enter the type and number of columns, the distance between them, and the column margins

Codes: [Col Def:]
[Col On]
[Col Off]

Example:

> In order to use WordPerfect effectively, there are some basic procedures you must learn. After you learn how to type a document, you'll need to know how to move the cursor around and edit it; how to insert and delete text; and how the returns within each paragraph, you can later insert and delete text anywhere within a paragraph, and WordPerfect will automatically readjust the margins for you. If you don't, you'll create a lot of extra work for yourself, and you'll

WordPerfect lets you create two types of columns for text: newspaper and parallel. Newspaper columns are just like those in a newspaper; text automatically wraps from the bottom of one column to the top of the next. Parallel columns are used to keep related blocks of text side by side, as in a movie script or language translation.

The basic steps for defining columns are the same for newspaper and parallel columns: define the type of columns, the number of columns, the distance separating them, and the left and right margins for each column. To use the default settings of two evenly spaced newspaper columns, separated by 1/2 inch, just select the Define option and leave all the settings by pressing Enter.

Defining Columns

1. Position the cursor at the point where you want the columns to begin.

2. Press Alt-F7 (Columns/Table) or display the **Layout** menu.

   The column options appear.

3. Select **Columns** (**1**).

4. Select **Define** (**3**).

   The Text Column Definition menu appears.

5. Select **1** (**Type**) and press 1, 2, or 3 to select the type of column you want to create.

   WordPerfect provides three types: **1** (**Newspaper**), **2** (**Parallel**), and **3** (**Parallel with Block Protect**).

6. Select **2** (**Number of Columns**), type the number of columns you want across the page, and press Enter.

   WordPerfect assumes you want columns of equal width and performs the calculations. A Column list appears in the lower half of the screen, showing you the margins for each column.

7. Choose **3** (**Distance Between Columns**) and enter the number of inches you want to separate the columns.

   WordPerfect uses .05" as the default.

8. Select **4** (**Margins**) if you want to customize the margin settings.

   Use the Enter key or Up Arrow and Down Arrow to move from setting to setting, and type the desired settings.

9. Press F7 (Exit) until you return to the Columns menu.

   This menu appears:
   `Columns: 1 On; 2 Off; 3 Define: 0`

10. Select **1** (**On**).

    This enters the [Col On] code, turning the Column feature on. `Col 1` appears on the status line.

After defining the columns, you can start typing the text that you want to appear in the columns. How you type the text varies, depending on whether you defined newspaper columns or parallel columns.

Typing in Newspaper Columns

1. Type the text you want to appear in the first column. When you fill the first column, the cursor automatically wraps to the second column.

   You can end a column before the cursor reaches the bottom of the page by pressing Ctrl-Enter.

2. Continue typing.

   WordPerfect automatically formats the text into newspaper columns.

 ### Typing in Parallel Columns

1. Type the text you want to appear in the first column; then press Ctrl-Enter.

   This creates the second column and places the cursor at the top.

2. Type the text in the second column and then press Ctrl-Enter.

   The cursor moves to the first column.

3. Continue typing the side-by-side columns this way, creating new ones by pressing Ctrl-Enter.

   Do not use Ctrl-Enter after you've finished typing the text. To move the cursor to the next column, press Ctrl-Home,Left Arrow or Right Arrow. On an enhanced keyboard, press Alt-Left Arrow or Alt-Right Arrow.

When you finish typing text in columns, you can turn off the columns. If you won't be typing any more text in the document, this step is optional.

 ### Turning Off Columns

1. Press Alt-F7 (Columns/Tables) or display the **L**ayout menu.

   The Column options appear.

2. Select **C**olumns (**1**).

   The Columns menu appears.

3. Select **O**ff (**2**).

   This inserts the [Col Off] code, turning the Column feature off.

Column Display

Function: Changes column display from side-by-side to staggered, to increase the display refresh speed.

Keystrokes:

Keyboard	*Mouse*
Shift-F1 (Setup)	File
2 (Display)	Setup
6 (Edit-Screen Options)	Display
7 (Side-by-Side Column Display)	Edit-Screen Options
	Side-by-Side Column Display
Y or N	Y or N
F7 (Exit)	Right mouse button

Example:

```
                              paragraph. Instead, let word
                              wrap end the lines for you
                              automatically. If you
                              accidentally press Enter at the
                              end of a line, just press the
                              gray backspace key once, then
------------------------------------------------------------------  Page
continue typing. Also, don't                                        break
worry about your spelling
mistakes. Later in this
chapter, you'll learn how to
use WordPerfect's built-in
spelling checker to correct
them.
```

By default, WordPerfect displays your columns side by side, so you can see how they'll appear when printed. Although this view of your columns is helpful when you're creating them, it can slow you down when you're entering and editing text. You can change the default so that the columns will appear staggered on screen. In this mode, the cursor moves more quickly, and you can scroll around the screen more easily.

 ## Changing the Column Display

1. Press Shift-F1 (Setup) or select Setup from the File menu.

   The main Setup menu appears.

2. Select Display (2).

   The Setup: Display menu appears.

3. Select 6 (Edit-Screen Options).

   The Edit-Screen Options menu appears.

4. Select **7** (Side-by-Side Column Display).

You are prompted to turn the option on or off.

5. Press N to turn the option off or Y to turn it on.

6. Press F7 (Exit) or click the right mouse button to return to your document.

The columns appear staggered on screen and separated by page breaks. This has no effect on the printed document. If you print it or use the View Document feature, WordPerfect displays the columns side by side.

Columns, Move (see *Move Block*)

Columns, Side-by-Side (see *Column Display*)

Columns, Tabular (see *Tab Key*)

Comments

Function: Lets you add non-printing comments to your document.

Keystrokes:

Keyboard	*Mouse*
Ctrl-F5 (Text In/Out)	**Edit**
4 (Comment)	**Comment**
1 (Create), **2** (Edit), or **3** (Convert to Text)	**Create, Edit, or Convert to Text**
Enter text to create or edit a comment	Enter text to create or edit a comment
F7 (Exit)	Right mouse button

Code: [Comment]

Example:

```
the first line of page two. If there is only one page, Page Up will
move the cursor to the first line of the single-page document.

┌──────────────────────────────────────────────────────────┐
│ Don't forget to insert quarterly sales figures.          │─────── Comment
└──────────────────────────────────────────────────────────┘        box

     If your letter is only one page and you want to try using Page
Up and Page Down to move to a new page, just insert several blank
```

The Comment feature lets you add comments to your document that appear in a box on screen but are not printed. Each comment can be up to 1 kilobyte (about 1,024 characters) in length. Inserting a comment within a line of text will break up the displayed line but will not affect the printed text or the View Document display. However, you may want to insert comments on a separate line, after a hard return, so they won't appear to split your text on screen.

 ## Creating a Comment

1. Position the cursor where you want the comment to appear.

2. Press Ctrl-F5 (Text In/Out) or open the Edit menu.

3. Select 4 (Comment) or Comment from the Edit menu. — The Comment menu appears.

4. Select Create (1). — A box appears prompting you to enter your comment.

5. Type the comment. It can include approximately 1,024 characters.

6. Press F7 (Exit) or click the right mouse button. — The comment appears on screen, in a double-lined box. A [Comment] code appears on the Reveal Codes screen.

 ## Editing a Comment

1. Position the cursor anywhere after the comment you want to edit but before any subsequent comment. — WordPerfect will search backward for the first comment it can find. If it doesn't find one, it then searches forward.

2. Press Ctrl-F5 (Text In/Out) or display the Edit menu.

3. Select 4 (Comment) or Comment form the Edit menu.

The Comment menu appears.

4. Select Edit (2).

The cursor appears inside the box of the specified comment.

5. Edit the comment.

Most editing features are available, except for Search, Speller, and Thesaurus.

6. Press F7 (Exit) or click the right mouse button.

The edited comment appears on screen, in a double-lined box.

 ## Deleting a Comment

1. Position the cursor on top of or just after the comment.

You can do this either in the normal display or on the Reveal Codes screen.

2. Press Backspace if the cursor is after the comment, or Del if the cursor is on the comment.

A message appears asking if you want to delete the comment. If you are in the Reveal Codes screen, WordPerfect deletes the comment without asking you to confirm.

3. Press Y to delete the comment or N to keep it.

If you press Y, the comment and its code disappear.

If you decide that you want to use the comment as a part of your document, you can convert it into regular text. When you print the document, the comment will be printed.

 ## Converting a Comment into Text

1. Position the cursor anywhere after the comment you want to edit but before any subsequent comment.

WordPerfect will search backward for the first comment it can find. If it doesn't find one, it then searches forward.

2. Press Ctrl-F5 (Text In/Out) or display the Edit menu.

3. Select 4 (Comment) or Comment from the Edit menu.	The Comment menu appears.
4. Select Convert to Text (3).	The Comment box disappears, and the comment is transformed into text.

You can also convert a block of text into a comment, using WordPerfect's Block feature.

 ## Converting Text into a Comment

1. Move the cursor to the beginning or end of the block you want to affect.	
2. Press Alt-F4 (Block) or select Block from the Edit menu.	
3. Move the cursor to stretch the highlighting over the text you want to change.	
4. Press Ctrl-F5 (Text In/Out) or display the Edit menu and select Comment.	WordPerfect asks if you want to create a comment.
5. Press Y.	WordPerfect converts the blocked text into a comment.

If the on-screen comments start to get in the way of your editing, you can hide the comments.

 ## Hiding Comments

1. Press Shift-F1 (Setup) or select Setup from the File menu.	The main Setup menu appears.
2. Select Display (2).	The Setup: Display menu appears.
3. Select 6 (Edit-Screen Options).	The Setup: Edit Screen Options menu appears.
4. Select 2 (Comments Display).	The cursor moves to option 2.
5. Press N for No.	This turns the option off.

6.	Press F7 (Exit) or click the right mouse button.	The cursor returns to the Edit screen. The comments no longer appear on screen, but the codes are visible on the Reveal Codes screen.

Compare Documents (see also *Redline*)

Function: Compares two versions of a document and marks the differences.

Keystrokes:

Keyboard	*Mouse*
Alt-F5 (Mark Text)	Mark
6 (Generate)	Generate
2 (Compare Screen and Disk Documents and Add Redline and Strikeout)	Compare Screen and Disk Documents
filename of file on disk	*filename* of file on disk
Enter	Enter

The Compare Documents feature compares two documents and marks the changes. WordPerfect compares the on-screen document to its disk version, to see what has been added, erased, or moved. Text that has been added and appears in the screen version but not in the disk version is surrounded by redline codes, and text that has been deleted from the screen version is surrounded by strikeout codes. If text was moved, prompts appear before and after the section that has been moved. The comparison is done on a phrase-by-phrase basis, so the entire phrase is formatted in redline or strikeout, not just a word or character. A phrase is a section of text between two phrase markers: a comma, period, colon, semicolon, question mark, exclamation point, Hard Return code, Hard Page code, Footnote code, Endnote code, or the end of the document.

Comparing the On-Screen Version of Document to the Version on Disk

1.	Save the edited on-screen document under a different name from the disk version you are comparing it with.	This gives you the option of referring to the edited version after the comparison.

2. Press Alt-F5 (Mark Text) or display the **M**ark menu.	The Mark Text menu appears.
3. Select **G**enerate (6).	The Mark Text Generate menu appears.
4. Select **2** (Compare Screen and Disk Documents and Add Redline and Strikeout).	WordPerfect prompts you to enter a file name or suggests one.
5. Type the name of the disk file you want to compare and press Enter.	WordPerfect compares the documents and marks the on-screen version with redline and strikeout codes. If text was moved, prompts appear before and after the moved section.

To restore the on-screen version to its appearance before you used Compare Documents, you can use the Remove Redline Markings and Strikeout Text option.

Removing Redline Marks and Erasing Strikeout Text

1. Press Alt-F5 (Mark Text) or display the **M**ark menu.	The Mark Text menu appears.
2. Select **G**enerate.(6).	The Mark Text: Generate menu appears.
3. Select **1** (Remove Redline Markings and Strikeout Text from Document).	A warning message appears. If you confirm your request, WordPerfect will erase all redlining and strikeout codes and text, and will remove the prompts that show where text has been moved. WordPerfect will even remove the codes that existed before you performed the comparison.
4. Press Y to remove the redlining codes and strikeout text or N to keep them.	

Tip: If deleted or inserted text appears as normal text on your screen, you can use the Setup menu to change the appearance attribute for strikeout and redline text. Refer to *Colors/Fonts/Attributes*.

Compose Key (see also *Character Sets, WordPerfect's*)

Function: Lets you type characters that are not on the keyboard, including characters from any of WordPerfect's 12 character sets.

Keystrokes:

Keyboard	*Mouse*
Ctrl-V or Ctrl-2	Font
(Compose)	Characters
n,nn (where *n* is the number of the WordPerfect character set, and *nn* is the number of the character in that set)	*n,nn* (where *n* is the number of the WordPerfect character set, and *nn* is the number of the character in that set)
OR	OR
A character and a diacritical mark	A character and a diacritical mark
OR	OR
Two characters to create a digraph	Two characters to create a digraph
Enter	Enter

Example:

```
Typographic Symbols
Charset: 4
Contains: Common typographic symbols not found in
          ASCII.

4,0 • Bullet                        4,10 » Right Double Guillemet
4,1 o Hollow Bullet                 4,11 £ Pound/Sterling
4,2 ▪ Square Bullet                 4,12 ¥ Yen
4,3 · Small Bullet                  4,13 ₧ Pesetas
4,4 ▪ Base Asterisk                 4,14 ƒ Florin/Guilder
4,5 ¶ Paragraph Sign                4,15 ª Feminine Spanish Ordinal
4,6 § Section Sign                  4,16 º Masculine Spanish Ordinal
4,7 ¡ Inverted Exclamation Point    4,17 ½ 1/2
4,8 ¿ Inverted Question Mark        4,18 ¼ 1/4
4,9 « Left Double Guillemet
```

WordPerfect lets you print many characters that are not on the keyboard, such as bullets, the paragraph and section symbols, fractions such as 2/3 and 5/8, math symbols such as the summation and plus or minus symbols, and characters with accents, circumflexes, and tildes. To insert one of these characters into your document, use the Compose key.

 Typing a WordPerfect Character

1. Move the cursor where you want the character to appear.

2. Press Ctrl-V or Ctrl-2 (Compose) or select **Characters** from the **Font** menu.

   Unless you pressed Ctrl-2, Key= appears at the bottom of the screen, prompting you to type the necessary characters. If you press Ctrl-2, the Key= does not appear, but it works the same as pressing Ctrl-V.

3. Type the number of the character set; then type a comma and the character number.

   To determine the code for a specific character, print the file named CHARACTR.DOC or turn to Appendix P of the WordPerfect documentation. (CHARACTR.DOC should be located in the directory that contains your WordPerfect program files.) For example, to type → from the math character set, type 6,21.

4. Press Enter to insert the character.

   If WordPerfect cannot display the character, it will display a box in place of the character. You can see characters in View Document. Press Shift-F7 (Print) or select **Print** from the **File** menu and select **6** (View Document).

> **Note:** If you have a graphics-based printer (laser or dot-matrix), WordPerfect will create a bit-mapped character during printing even if your current font does not include that character. You should be able to print all the characters in WordPerfect's character sets. If you have a printer that is not graphics-based, you can print only those characters that your printer supports. If your printer does not support the character, it may appear on screen, but it won't be printed.

Diacriticals are accent marks used to represent phonetic values. Digraphs are characters that are joined together, such as Æ and ™ (trademark). You can type some of the common digraphs and diacriticals, as listed in Table C.1, without using the numbers from the character set. Instead, you use characters on the keyboard such as tilde, circumflex, and underscore. More are shown in the reference section of the WordPerfect manual, under *Compose.*

Typing a Diacritical or Digraph

1. Position the cursor where you want the character to appear in the document.

2. Press Ctrl-V (Compose), or select Characters from the Font menu, or press Ctrl-2.

3. Type a character and a diacritical mark, or type the two characters in the digraph.

   For instance, to type ñ, you would type the tilde character and the letter n. To type a digraph, you would type the two letters or symbols, such as AE for Æ. You can type the characters for a diacritical or digraph in either order.

Table C.1 *Common digraphs and diacriticals.*

Common Digraphs

Character	Result
ae	æ
ss	ß
P|	¶
ao	å
a=	a̠
??	¿
rx	℞
co	©

Common Diacriticals

Name	Character	Result
Acute	'	á
Caron	v	ž
Cedilla	,	ç
Centered dot	:	l·
Circumflex	^	â
Crossbar	- (hyphen)	ŧ
Dot above	. (period)	ċ
Grave	`	è
Macron	‾ (underline)	ū
Ogonek	;	ą
Ring above	@	å
Slash	/	ø
Stroke	\	ł
Tilde	~	ñ
Umlaut	"	ü

Concordance (see *Index, Concordance*)

Condense Master Document (see *Master Document*)

Conditional End of Page

Function: Keeps a specified number of lines together on a page.

Keystrokes:

Keyboard	*Mouse*
Shift-F8 (Format)	Layout
4 (Other)	Other
2 (Conditional End of Page)	Conditional End of Page
n (where *n* is the number of lines you want kept together)	*n* (where *n* is the number of lines you want kept together)
Enter	Enter
F7 (Exit)	Right mouse button

Code: [Cndl EOP:#]

Example:

Conditional End of Page code

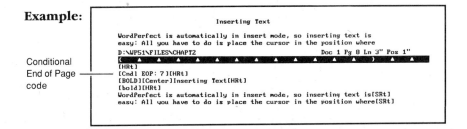

```
                              Inserting Text

   WordPerfect is automatically in insert mode, so inserting text is
   easy: All you have to do is place the cursor in the position where
   D:\WP51\FILES\CHAPT2                         Doc 1 Pg 8 Ln 3" Pos 1"
   [HRt]
   [Cndl EOP: 7][HRt]
   [BOLD][Center]Inserting Text[HRt]
   [bold][HRt]
   WordPerfect is automatically in insert mode, so inserting text is[SRt]
   easy: All you have to do is place the cursor in the position where[SRt]
```

The Conditional End of Page feature protects lines from being separated by a page break. You can use it to keep a heading or title on the same page as the text that follows it, preventing an awkward page break. You can still separate protected lines by using a hard page break (Ctrl-Enter).

 ## Inserting a Conditional End of Page

1. Move the cursor to the line just above the lines you want to keep together.

   The line may contain text or be blank.

2. Press Shift-F8 (Format) or display the Layout menu.

   A list of formatting options appears.

3. Select **Other** (4).

The Format: Other menu appears.

4. Select **2** (Conditional End of Page).

WordPerfect prompts you to enter the number of lines you want to keep together.

5. Type the number of lines you want to keep together and press Enter.

If your document is double-spaced, every line counts for two lines of text.

6. Press F7 (Exit) or click the right mouse button twice.

WordPerfect returns you to your document and inserts the [Cndl EOP:nn] code at the cursor position.

Control Printer (see *Printer Control*)

Convert Comment to Text (see *Comments*)

Convert Old Merge Codes (see *Merge, Convert Old Codes*)

Convert Program (CONVERT.EXE) (see also *WordPerfect File Conversion*)

Function: Converts WordPerfect files into formats compatible with other word-processing documents and converts files created in other programs into WordPerfect's format.

Keystrokes: *Keyboard*
Exit WordPerfect
Change to the drive and directory containing the CONVERT.EXE file
convert
d:\path\filename.ext (for input file)
d:\path\filename.ext (for output file)
Select conversion option

Example:

```
Name of Input File? d:\wp51\files\chapt2
Name of Output File? d:\wp51\files\chapt2.doc


0 EXIT
1 WordPerfect to another format
2 Revisable-Form-Text (IBM DCA Format) to WordPerfect
3 Final-Form-Text (IBM DCA Format) to WordPerfect
4 Navy DIF Standard to WordPerfect
5 WordStar 3.3 to WordPerfect

Enter number of Conversion desired
```

If you share data files with others who do not use WordPerfect, you can use the Convert program to convert the files you send and receive into a useable format.

Note: To use the Convert feature, you must have installed the WordPerfect Utility programs. If you did not install them, start the installation program now, and install the Utility programs.

   Converting Files

1. Exit WordPerfect.

2. Change to the drive and directory that contains the CONVERT.EXE program.

   This is usually the c:\WP51 directory unless you specified otherwise during installation.

3. Type `convert` at the DOS prompt and press Enter.

   The Convert program starts and prompts you to enter the name of the file you want to convert. This is called the input file.

4. Type the path name and file name of the file you want to convert and press Enter.

   WordPerfect prompts you to enter the name of the output file where you want to save the converted file.

5. Type a path name and file name of where you want the converted file stored and press Enter.

   This tells the Convert feature where to save the converted file. A list of conversion options appears.

6. Select option 1 to convert from WordPerfect to another format, or select the format of the file you want to convert.

If you select option 1, another menu appears asking which format you want to convert the file to; select a format. WordPerfect performs the conversion. You can find the converted file in the directory where you told Convert to store it.

Copy Block

Function: Keeps a block of text in its original location and copies the block to another location.

Keystrokes:

Keyboard	*Mouse*
Alt-F4 (Block)	**Edit**
Highlight block	**Block**
Ctrl-F4 (Move)	Highlight block
1 (Block)	OR
2 (Copy)	**Edit**
Move cursor to new location	**Select**
Enter	**Sentence**, **Paragraph**, or **Page**
	Edit
	Copy
	Move cursor to new location
	Double-click left mouse button

When you choose to copy a block of text, the original block is not affected. A copy of the block is written to a special memory buffer, and this copy can be inserted anywhere in the document. You can use this feature with the Switch feature to copy blocks of text from one document to another.

 Copying a Block

1. Press Alt-F4 (Block) and highlight the block of text you want to copy, or choose **Select** from the **Edit** menu and select **Sentence**, **Paragraph**, or **Page**.

Refer to *Block*.

2. If you highlighted a block using Alt-F4, press Ctrl-F4 (Move).

The Move menu appears. If you highlighted a sentence, paragraph, or page, the Copy option is already displayed; skip to step 4.

3. Select **1** (**Block**) or if you have an enhanced keyboard, press Ctrl-Ins and skip step 4.

Four options appear: Move, Copy, Delete, and Append.

4. Select **2** (Copy).

A message appears at the bottom of the screen telling you to move the cursor and press Enter to insert the block.

5. Move the cursor to the place where you want to copy the block and press Enter.

You can press Shift-F3 (Switch) to switch to the other document editing screen and copy the block to create a new document or add it any existing text. The block is inserted at the cursor location.

 Tip: You can use the mouse to highlight a block of text without using the pull-down menus. Move the mouse cursor to the beginning of the block you want to highlight, hold down the left mouse button, and drag the cursor to the end of the block. When you release the left mouse button, the block is highlighted.

Copy Files

Function: Copies files from one disk or directory to another.

Keystrokes:

Keyboard	*Mouse*
F5 (List)	File
Enter	List Files
Cursor to file name	Enter
8 (Copy)	Cursor to file name
d:\directory\filename.ext	Copy
Enter	*d:\directory\filename.ext*
	Enter

Example:

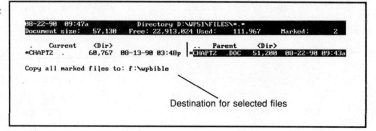

Destination for selected files

The Copy Files feature lets you copy one or more files by selecting the files from a list.

 ## Copying Files

1.	Press F5 (List) or select List Files from the File menu.	The `Dir` prompt appears, asking you to type the drive and directory that contains the files you want to list.
2.	Press Enter to view all the files in the current directory, or enter the drive and directory whose files you want to view.	A list of files in the selected directory appears.
3.	Highlight the name of the file you want to copy. If you want to copy more than one file, type * next to each file. To mark all files in the current directory, press Alt-F5 or Home,*.	This selects the file(s) to be copied. If you change your mind and do not want to mark all files, press Alt-F5 or Home,* again.
4.	Select **8** (Copy), and press Y if asked to confirm your request.	If you marked one file, WordPerfect asks where you want to copy it. If you marked more than one file, WordPerfect asks for confirmation. After you press Y to confirm, WordPerfect prompts you to enter the drive and directory where you want the files copied.
5.	Type the drive and directory to which you want the files copied.	If you are copying one file to the same directory, type a different name for the file.

6. Press Enter.   WordPerfect copies the selected
                                    file(s) to the specified directory.

Copy Text (see *Copy Block* and *Move Sentence, Paragraph, or Page*)

Count Words (see *Word Count*)

Cross-Reference

Function: Automatically updates cross-references to page numbers, graphics box numbers, footnotes or endnotes, or paragraph outline numbers.

Keystrokes:

Keyboard
Cursor to position where you want reference number
Alt-F5 (Mark Text)
1 (Cross-Ref)
1 (Mark **R**eference), 2 (Mark **T**arget), or 3 (Mark **B**oth Reference and Target)
1 (Page Number), 2 (Paragraph/Outline Number), 3 (Footnote Number), 4 (Endnote Number), or 5 (Graphics Box Number)
Enter
target name

Mouse
Cursor to position where you want reference number
Mark
Cross-Reference
Mark **R**eference, Mark **T**arget, or Mark **B**oth Reference and Target
Page Number, Paragraph/Outline Number, **F**ootnote Number, **E**ndnote Number, or **G**raphics Box Number
Enter
target name

Codes: [Ref]
[Target]

Example:

```
For more information about New York City's driver safety program,[SRt]
refer to page [Ref(DRIVER SAFETY):Pg 7].[HRt]
```

```
The Driver Safety Program[Target(DRIVER SAFETY)][HRt]
```

You can use WordPerfect's Cross-Reference feature to refer to any of five elements: text on a specific page number, a footnote number, an endnote number, an automatic paragraph number created with the outline feature or the paragraph number feature, or a graphics box number. The cross-reference always includes both a reference and a target. For instance, you could type See the example in at the position where you want to reference it in the document, mark it as the reference, and then mark the Figure 1 code as the target. The phrase would then change to *See the example in Figure 1*. If you later edit the document, and the figure number changes, you can update the cross-reference. For example, if you insert another figure before Figure 1, so that Figure 1 is renumbered to Figure 2, you can update the reference so it will change to *See the example in Figure 2*.

The Cross-Reference feature lets you enter two codes to keep your references up to date: a reference code where you refer to the item and a target code where the reference item appears. If, during the editing process, the reference item moves to a different page, or the footnote, endnote, paragraph, or outline number changes, you can generate the references again, and the numbers will be updated automatically.

This feature offers three options. If you're only referring to a single target item and it's already somewhere in the text, you can mark both reference and target. If the target does not yet exist, you can mark the reference, but you'll have to mark the target later. If your reference refers to two or more targeted items, you can mark the reference once, and then mark each target individually. If you have several targets for a single reference, WordPerfect will list all the numbers separated by a comma and a space.

Marking Reference and Target

1. Position the cursor where you want to insert the reference.

2. Type a lead-in phrase, such as See figure, and press the space bar.

3. Press Alt-F5 (Mark Text) or display the **M**ark menu.

    The Mark Text menu appears.

4. Select Cross-**R**eference (**1**).

    The Mark Text: Cross-Reference menu appears, providing options to mark the reference, the target, or both.

5. Select **3** (Mark **B**oth Reference and Target).

    The Tie Reference To menu appears, asking you to choose the type of reference you want to use: page number, paragraph/outline number, footnote or endnote number, or graphics box number.

6. Select the type of reference you want to use.

    The prompt that appears depends on the reference you selected. WordPerfect may tell you to move the cursor to the page, paragraph, footnote, or endnote you want to mark and press Enter. If you selected Graphics Box, WordPerfect will prompt you to select a type of box and then mark it.

7. Move the cursor right after the code for the paragraph number, footnote or endnote, or graphics box, or to the page you want to mark and press Enter.

    If the target is a graphics box, a footnote or endnote, or an outline number, you can use the Search feature to move the cursor there quickly. A prompt appears, such as Cross-Ref: Move to Page; Press Enter.

8. Type a target name and press Enter.

Caution: If you choose to mark the reference and target separately, make sure you use the same target name for both codes. If the target name differs in any way, the Cross-Reference feature won't be able to match them and automatically update them.

Marking Reference Only

1. Position the cursor where you want to insert the reference.

2. Type a lead-in phrase, such as See page, and press the space bar.

3. Press Alt-F5 (Mark Text) or display the **Mark** menu.

   The Mark Text menu appears.

4. Select Cross-**Reference** (**1**).

   The Mark Text: Cross-Reference menu appears, with options to mark the reference, the target, or both.

5. Select **1** (Mark **Reference**).

   The Tie Reference To menu appears, asking you to choose the type of reference you want to use.

6. Select the type of reference you want to use.

   Target name: appears at the bottom of the screen.

7. Type a target name and press Enter.

   You return to your document. A question mark marks your reference in the Edit screen, and a [Ref] code with the target name appears in the Reveal Codes screen. After you mark the target and generate the cross-references, the ? will be converted into the number, letter, or graphics box number that refers to the target item.

Marking Target Only

1. Position the cursor in the space
   after the target.

2. Press Alt-F5 (Mark Text) or   The Mark Text menu appears.
   display the **Mark** menu.

3. Select Cross-**R**eference (**1**).   The Mark Text: Cross-Reference
                                         menu appears, providing options
                                         to mark the reference, the target,
                                         or both.

4. Select **2** (Mark **T**arget).   `Target name:` appears at the
                                         bottom of the screen.

5. Type a target name and press   You return to your document.
   Enter.   The target is marked with a code
                                         that includes its target name,
                                         visible only in Reveal Codes.

Once the reference and target codes are inserted in your text, you can update your references whenever you need to, such as after making changes that may have moved a target to another page. Refer to *Generate*.

 Note: The Cross-Reference feature is normally confined to a single document. That is, you can't have a reference in one document that refers to a targeted item in another document. If you wish to do this, you must create a master document. Refer to *Master Document*.

Ctrl/Alt Key Mapping (see *Keyboard Layout, Map*)

Cursor Appearance

Function: Changes the appearance of the cursor.

Keystrokes: *Keyboard*
Exit WordPerfect
Change to the drive and directory that contains the
CURSOR.COM file
cursor, Enter
Cursor keys to set size and shape
Enter

Example:

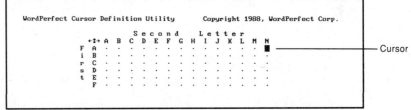

```
WordPerfect Cursor Definition Utility      Copyright 1988, WordPerfect Corp.

                          S e c o n d    L e t t e r
                  ←↕→ A  B  C  D  E  F  G  H  I  J  K  L  M  N
              F    A    ·  ·  ·  ·  ·  ·  ·  ·  ·  ·  ·  ·  ·  ■ ——————————————— Cursor
              i    B    ·  ·  ·  ·  ·  ·  ·  ·  ·  ·  ·  ·  ·  ·
              r    C    ·  ·  ·  ·  ·  ·  ·  ·  ·  ·  ·  ·  ·  ·
              s    D    ·  ·  ·  ·  ·  ·  ·  ·  ·  ·  ·  ·  ·  ·
              t    E    ·  ·  ·  ·  ·  ·  ·  ·  ·  ·  ·  ·  ·  ·
                   F    ·  ·  ·  ·  ·  ·  ·  ·  ·  ·  ·  ·  ·  ·
```

The Cursor program (CURSOR.COM) lets you change the size and shape of
your cursor. Before you can use this program, you must have it installed.
You cannot copy the program directly from your program disks to your
WP51 directory. If you did not install the utility programs, you must do so
now.

 ## Adjusting the Cursor

1. Exit WordPerfect and go to DOS.

2. Change to the drive and directory
   that contains the CURSOR.COM
   program.

   This is usually the C:\WP51
   directory unless you specified
   otherwise during installation.

3. Type cursor and press Enter.

   A cursor grid appears. The
   location of the cursor on the grid
   is represented with a two-letter
   coordinate (for example, DE).
   The first letter indicates the row;
   the second letter indicates the
   column. You can use these
   coordinates later to change the
   cursor's appearance more easily.
   For example, you can type
   cursor:DE at the DOS prompt to
   bypass the grid.

4. Use the cursor keys to move the cursor on the grid until it is the size and shape you want.

To see how the cursor will look in a document, press the space bar. Press it again to return to the grid.

5. Press Enter.

This selects the cursor and returns you to the DOS prompt.

Cursor Movement (see also *Cursor Speed*)

Function: Lets you move the cursor through the document.

Keystrokes: *Keyboard*
Left Arrow
Right Arrow
Up Arrow
Down Arrow
PgUp
PgDn
Home
End
Home,Up Arrow or (–) on numeric keypad
Home,Down Arrow or (+) on numeric keypad
Tab
Shift-Tab

The cursor movement keys let you move the cursor through your document. Table C.2 summarizes the cursor movement options.

Table C.2 *Cursor movement.*

Key	*Movement*
Left Arrow	Left one character
Right Arrow	Right one character
Up Arrow	Up one line
Down Arrow	Down one line
Ctrl-Left Arrow	Left one word
Ctrl-Right Arrow	Right one word
Home,Left Arrow	Left side of screen
Home,Right Arrow	Right side of screen
Home,Home,Left Arrow	Beginning of line after formatting codes

continued

Table C.2 *(continued)*

Key	*Movement*
Home,Home,Right Arrow or End	End of line
Home,Up Arrow or (−) on the numeric keypad	Top of screen, then up one screen at a time
Home,Down Arrow or (+) on the numeric keypad	Bottom of screen, then down one screen at a time
PgUp	First line on previous page
PgDn	First line on next page
Ctrl-Up Arrow	Up one paragraph (on keyboard with enhanced BIOS)
Ctrl-Down Arrow	Down one paragraph (on keyboard with enhanced BIOS)
Home,Home,Up Arrow	Beginning of document (after formatting codes)
Home,Home,Home,Up Arrow	Beginning of document (before formatting codes)
Home,Home,Down Arrow	End of document
Tab	In Typeover mode, moves cursor to next tab stop. In a table, moves cursor to next cell.
Shift-Tab	In Typeover mode, moves cursor to previous tab stop. In a table, moves cursor to previous cell.

Note: If the cursor doesn't appear to move when you press one of the arrow keys, it's probably moving over a hidden code. Just keep pressing the arrow key until the cursor does move. Also, if you choose to view a document from the List Files screen, you can only use the cursor to scroll through the document. You cannot move the cursor left or right, and you cannot edit the document in this view.

Cursor Speed (see also *Cursor Movement*)

Function: Changes the speed at which the cursor moves or other keys repeat.

Keystrokes: *Keyboard*   *Mouse*
             Shift-F1 (Setup)   File
             3 (Environment)   Setup
             3 (Cursor Speed)   Environment
             Select repeat speed   Cursor Speed
             F7 (Exit)   Select repeat speed
                                         Right mouse button

Example:

```
Setup: Environment

      1 - Backup Options

      2 - Beep Options

      3 - Cursor Speed                    50 cps

Characters Per Second: 1 15; 2 20; 3 30; 4 40; 5 50; 6 Normal: 0
```
Cursor
speed
settings

If you hold down a keyboard key instead of releasing it immediately, the key's function will be repeated. If you hold down the Right Arrow key, for example, the cursor will move from character to character, left to right, across the screen. If you hold down a letter key, such as M, it will be typed repeatedly. You can change this repeat speed through the Setup: Environment menu. (The default speed is 50 characters per second.)

Changing the Key Repeat Speed

1. Press Shift-F1 (Setup) or select Setup from the File menu.

   The Setup menu appears.

2. Select Environment (3).

   The Setup: Environment menu appears.

3. Select 3 (Cursor Speed).

   Six cursor speed options appear. The last one, Normal, returns your computer to its normal setting.

4. Select the setting you wish to use.

   The value appears on screen.

5. Press F7 (Exit) or click the right mouse button.

   Your setting is saved, and you are returned to the Edit screen.

D

Date and Time, Format

Function: Lets you change the format for the Date and Time feature.

Keystrokes:

Keyboard	*Mouse*
Shift-F5 (Date/Outline)	Tools
3 (Date Format)	Date Format
Type a format	Type a format
F7 (Exit)	Right mouse button

Example:

```
3 1, 4         = December 25, 1984
%6 %3 1, 4     = Tue Dec 25, 1984
%2/%1/5 (6)    = 01/01/85 (Tuesday)
$2/$1/5 ($6) =   1/ 1/85 (Tue)
8:90           = 10:55am
```

The default format for the date and/or time is to spell out the month and enter the numbers for the day and then the year in four digits. WordPerfect also assumes you want to insert only the date. If you want to change the format, or include the day of the week or the time, you can make those changes by using the Date Format screen. Changes you make work only in the current editing session, so (after you exit WordPerfect) the date format reverts to the default the next time you use it. To change it permanently, change the setting on the Setup/Initial Settings menu. Refer to *Initial Settings*.

 Changing the Date Format

1. Press Shift-F5 (Date/Outline) or display the **Tools** menu.

2. Select Date Format (**3**).

   The Date Format menu appears, listing various format options.

3. Type the format you want to use.

   For example, 2/1/5 will produce this format: 2/25/91 or 4/25/90. To insert the time in this format, 10:55 am, type 8:90.

4. Press F7 Exit twice, or click the right mouse button twice.	WordPerfect returns you to the Edit screen.

Date and Time, Inserting

Function: Inserts the system date and/or time at the cursor location.

Keystrokes:

Keyboard	*Mouse*
Shift-F5 (Date/Outline)	**Tools**
1 (Date Text) or **2** (Date Code)	Date Text or Date Code

Code: [Date:]

Example:

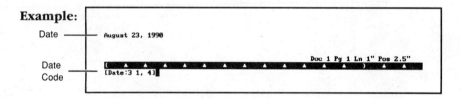

Date ———— August 23, 1998

Date Code ———— [Date:3 1, 4]

Doc 1 Pg 1 Ln 1" Pos 2.5"

If your computer has an internal clock, or if you enter a date and time when you start up your computer, WordPerfect can insert that information directly from your system into your document. You can insert the date and/or time in either of two ways: as text or as a code. If you enter the date and time as a code, WordPerfect inserts the current date and time whenever you retrieve or print the document. If you enter the date and time as text, they are treated just like regular text and are not updated.

 Inserting the Date Code

1. Position the cursor where you want to insert the date.

2. Press Shift-F5 (Date/Outline) or display the **Tools** menu.

3. Select Date Code (**2**).

Today's date is inserted at the cursor location. It appears as text in the Edit screen, but in Reveal Codes, you can see the actual date code.

> **Tip:** Create a template or boilerplate for business letters, and insert a Date code in the heading. Whenever you use the boilerplate, the correct date will be inserted at the code. You can also include the Date/Time code in the header or footer of a document to indicate the date and/or time a document was created or edited.

 Inserting Date Text

1. Position the cursor where you want to insert the date.

2. Press Shift-F5 (Date/Outline) or display the **Tools** menu.

3. Select Date **Text** (**1**).

Today's date is inserted at the cursor location, just as if you had typed it. No Date code is used, so the date you just inserted will be the same whenever you retrieve or print the file.

Decimal/Align Character (see also *Decimal Tabs*, *Tab Align*, and *Thousands' Separator*)

Function: Lets you choose the character to use as the decimal character for Tab Align, for decimal tabs, and in math operations.

Keystrokes:

Keyboard	*Mouse*
Shift-F8 (Format)	Layout
4 (Other)	Other
3 (Decimal/Align Character)	Decimal/Align Character
character	*character*
F7 (Exit)	Right mouse button

Code: [Decml/Algn Char:]

By default, WordPerfect uses a period as the decimal/align character, because when you align columns of numbers, you usually want the numbers to be aligned around the decimal points. However, you may wish to use Tab Align to align text around a different character. For example, if you're writing a memo, you may want to align text around the colons. The Decimal/Align Character feature lets you choose whatever character you wish to use for the Tab Align feature.

Changing the Decimal/Align Character

1. Press Shift-F8 (Format) or display the Layout menu.

   A list of formatting options appears.

2. Select **Other (4)**.

   The Format: Other menu appears.

3. Select **3** (Decimal/Align Character).

   WordPerfect prompts you to enter the character of your choice.

4. Type the character you want to use for decimal tabs.

   You can use a space by pressing the space bar, or you can enter a character such as a colon.

5. Press F7 (Exit) or click the right mouse button.

   WordPerfect returns you to the Edit screen and inserts a [Decml/Algn Char] code at the cursor location.

Decimal Tabs (see also *Decimal/Align Character, Tab Align,* and *Tab, Set*)

Function: Aligns columns of numbers around a decimal tab.

Keystrokes: *Keyboard*   *Mouse*
                  Shift-F8 (Format)   Layout
                  1 (Line)   Line
                  8 (Tab Set)   Tab Set
                  Ctrl-End (Delete Tabs)   Ctrl-End (Delete Tabs)
                  D at each tab position   D at each tab position
                  F7 (Exit) twice   Right mouse button twice

Codes: [Tab Set:Rel;n,n,n...]
             [Dec Tab]

Example:

```
1st Quarter Sales:  $1300.50
                      $458.47
                   $75,466.32
```

By setting Decimal Tabs, you can convert the regular Tab key into a Decimal Tab key and use it to align columns of numbers around their decimal points.

 Setting and Using Decimal Tabs

1. Press Shift-F8 (Format) or display the Layout menu.	A list of formatting options appears.
2. Select **Line (1)**.	The Format: Line menu appears.
3. Select **8 (Tab Set)**.	The Tab Set menu appears.
4. Press Ctrl-End if you want to delete all the tab settings.	This erases all tab stop settings.
5. Move the cursor to each position where you want to create a decimal tab, and type D.	This inserts decimal tabs. The numbers are relative, so if you type D at the +4" setting, you insert a decimal tab 4" from the left margin. If your left margin is 1", the tab stop is 5" from the left edge of the page.
6. Press F7 (Exit) or click the right mouse button twice.	You return to the Edit screen. The Tab key will now act as a Decimal Tab key at each position where you set a decimal tab.
7. Press Tab.	The Align char = . message appears.
8. Type all the digits in one number that are to appear left of the decimal point.	The digits are inserted to the left of the cursor, and the cursor remains at the tab stop position.
9. Type a decimal point; then type the remaining digits.	The decimal point stays at the tab stop position, and the remaining numbers are inserted to the right of it. The cursor moves normally.

Default Settings (see *Initial Settings*)

Define Macro (see *Macro, Recording Keystrokes* and *Macros, Macro Editor*)

Delete Block (see *Delete Text*)

Delete Codes (see also *Reveal Codes*)

Function: Lets you delete hidden codes.

Keystrokes:

Keyboard	*Mouse*
Alt-F3 or F11 (Reveal Codes)	Edit
	Reveal Codes
Cursor to code, Del or cursor to right of code, Backspace	Cursor to code, Del or cursor to right of code, Backspace
Alt-F3 or F11 (Reveal Codes)	Edit
	Reveal Codes

Example:

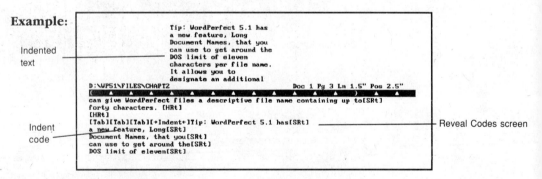

Indented text

Indent code

Reveal Codes screen

Sometimes, it is necessary to delete formatting codes. For example, you may decide that you don't want a section indented, or you may want to change text that's boldfaced back to normal. You can delete codes just as easily as you can delete text. Simply highlight the code and press the Del key or move the cursor to the right of the code and press Backspace. The only problem with deleting codes is finding them, and it's much easier to find codes in the Reveal Codes screen.

Deleting a Hidden Code

1. Press Alt-F3 or F11 (Reveal Codes) or select **R**eveal Codes from the **E**dit menu.

    Your screen is split in two by the tab ruler. The top part is the normal screen. In the lower part, the same text appears, but you can see the codes that affect the text.

2. Highlight the code you want to delete in the lower part of the screen.

    The entire code is highlighted and the Del key will delete it. If the cursor is just to the right of the code, you can use the Backspace key to delete it.

3. Press Del.

    The code is removed.

4. Press Alt-F3 or F11 (Reveal Codes) or select **R**eveal Codes from the **E**dit menu.

    The screen returns to normal.

 Note: You don't have to use the Reveal Codes screen to delete a code. If you know where a code is located, you can delete it in the Edit screen using the Backspace or Del key. Codes such as bold and underline are easy to locate, since the text appears different near them. If you try to delete a code and you are not in Reveal Codes, WordPerfect will prompt you to confirm the deletion.

Tip: You can use Search to locate codes and Replace to locate and erase them. To use Search, press F2 (→Search) or Shift-F2 (←Search). When asked what you want to search for, press the same keys you used to insert the code; for example, if you're searching for [BOLD], press F6 (Bold). Press F2 or Shift-F2 again to begin the search. If WordPerfect finds the code, the cursor moves to the right of the code. You can use the Backspace key to remove it. If you see a Not Found prompt, WordPerfect could not find the code; try searching in the opposite direction. To use Replace, press Alt-F2, select Y or N for confirm, insert the code by pressing the same keys you pressed to insert the code, then press F2 twice.

Delete Files and Directories (see also *List Files*)

Function: Deletes selected files from disk.

Keystrokes: *Keyboard*   *Mouse*
F5 (List)   File
Enter   List Files
Select the files to delete   Enter
2 (Delete), Y   Select the files to delete
                                     Delete, Y

Caution: The Delete Files feature lets you delete a file or a group of files from disk using the List Files screen. Once you delete these files, you cannot use WordPerfect to recover them. If you used the Original Backup option (discussed in *Backup, Timed and Original*), you may be able to recover an earlier version of the file. You should be absolutely sure of which files you want to delete before you begin using this feature.

Deleting Files

1. Press F5 (List) or select List **Files** from the File menu.	WordPerfect prompts you to enter the drive and directory that contains the files you want to list.
2. Press Enter to view the files in the current directory, or type the drive and directory whose files you want to view and press Enter.	A list of files appears.
3. Highlight the name of the file you want to delete. If you want to delete more than one file, type * next to each one.	This selects the file(s) to be deleted. You can select or unselect all the files by pressing Alt-F5 (Mark Text) or Home,*.
4. Select **2** (Delete).	If you selected only one file by moving the cursor onto it, WordPerfect asks if you want to delete it. If you marked one or more files, WordPerfect asks if you want to delete the marked files.
5. If you are erasing only one file and are absolutely certain you want to delete it, press Y. If you are not sure, press N. If you marked one or more files, press Y twice to delete them, or press N if you are unsure.	WordPerfect erases the file(s) from the List Files screen and from your disk. If you marked one or more files and then selected No in response to either of the two prompts, WordPerfect will ask if you want to delete the highlighted file.

Once you have deleted all the files in a directory, you can then delete the directory. To do this, display the List Files screen and place the cursor on the directory name you want to delete. Select **2** (Delete) and press Y.

Delete Text (see also *Undelete*)

Function: Deletes text from document.

Keystrokes: See Table D.1.

You can delete text from a document in any of several ways. For example, you can press the Del key to erase a character or Ctrl-Backspace to delete a word, or you can mark a block of text and then press the Del key and type Y. WordPerfect stores the deleted text in a temporary buffer. If you decide that you want it back, you can then restore the text by pressing F1 (Cancel) and choosing **1** (**Restore**). You can restore up to the last three deletions. Table D.1 lists some of the most commonly used methods for deleting text.

Table D.1 *Keystrokes for deleting text.*

Keystroke	*What You Delete*
Backspace	Character to left of cursor
Del	Character the cursor is highlighting
Ctrl-Backspace	Word the cursor is on or, if the cursor is in a blank space, the word to the left of the cursor
Ctrl-End	Cursor to end of line
Ctrl-PgDn,Y	Cursor to end of page
Alt-F4, highlight text, Backspace,Y or Del,Y	Highlighted block of text
Home,Backspace	Cursor to beginning of word
Home,Del	Cursor to end of word

 Deleting a Block

1. Move the cursor to the beginning or end of the block you want to delete.

2. Press Alt-F4 (Block) or select **B**lock from the **E**dit menu.

   A Block on prompt starts flashing in the lower-left corner of your screen.

3. Move the cursor to the opposite end of the block you want to delete.

   As you move the cursor, the block highlighting stretches with it.

4. Press Backspace or Del.

   WordPerfect asks if you want to delete the block.

5. Press Y to delete the block or N to cancel the operation.

If you press Y, the block disappears. If you press N, the highlighting and `Block on` prompt remain. Press F1 (Cancel) or Alt-F4 to turn the Block feature off.

Tip: You can use the mouse to highlight a block of text without using the pull-down menus. Move the mouse cursor to the beginning of the block you want to highlight, hold down the left mouse button, and drag the cursor to the end of the block. When you release the left mouse button, the block is highlighted.

Note: When you delete a block of text, you may inadvertently delete codes included in or surrounding the block. Before you mark the block, you may want to turn on the Reveal Codes screen to see exactly what you're including as you mark the block.

Diacriticals, Digraphs (see *Compose Key*)

Directory, Alias

Function: Lets you assign a descriptive name to your directory.

Keystrokes:

Keyboard	Mouse
On a blank	*On a blank WordPerfect Edit*
WordPerfect Edit screen	*screen*
d:\path\directory	*d:\path\directory*
F9 (End Field)	**Tools**
descriptive name	**Merge Codes**
F9 (End Field)	**More**

Shift-F9 (Merge Codes)	{END FIELD}
2 (End Record)	*descriptive name*
F7 (Exit), **Y**	**Tools**
d:\wp{wp}.dln (where	**Merge Codes**
d is the name of the	**More**
drive that holds your	{END FIELD}
WordPerfect files)	**Tools**
Enter, **N**	**Merge Codes**
	End Record
	Right mouse button, **Y**
	d:\wp{wp}.dln (where *d* is the
	name of the drive that holds your
	WordPerfect files)
	Enter, **N**

Example:

```
d:\wp51\files{END FIELD}
Document files for WordPerfect Bible Command Reference Section{END FIELD}
{END RECORD}
=================================================================================
```
———— DOS directory name

———— Descriptive name

Because of the limitations of DOS, directories' names can include a maximum of eight characters and an optional three-character extension. In WordPerfect, you can go beyond the DOS limitations and enter more descriptive names (aliases) for your directories. When you use the Long Display option on the List Files screen, up to 30 characters of this descriptive name appear under the Descriptive Name heading. To assign aliases to your directories, you must create a special file using merge codes and save the file in the root directory.

Assigning an Alias to Your Directory

1. Start with a blank Edit screen.

2. Type the complete path to the directory, including the directory's DOS name.

   The path and directory name appear on screen as you type.

3. Press F9 (End Field) or display the **T**ools menu, select **M**erge Codes and then **M**ore, and select {END FIELD}.

   The {END FIELD} code is inserted at the cursor position, and the cursor moves to the next line.

4. Type a descriptive name for the directory.

5. Press F9 (End Field) or display the **Tools** menu, select **Merge Codes** and then **More**, and select {END FIELD}.

The {END FIELD} code is inserted at the cursor position, and the cursor moves to the next line.

6. Press Shift-F9 (Merge Codes) or select **Merge** Codes from the **Tools** menu.

The Merge menu line appears.

7. Select **End Record** (**2**).

A double-dashed line appears under your entry, representing a hard page break, and the cursor moves to the next line.

8. Repeat steps 2-7 for each directory you want to assign an alias to.

9. Press F7 (Exit) and then Y.

WordPerfect asks if you want to save the document.

10. Type *d:*\wp{wp}.dln and press Enter.

d stands for the disk that contains your WordPerfect files, probably C. The file must be saved to the root directory, *not* to the WordPerfect directory. This names your alias file.

11. Press N to keep working in WordPerfect, or press Y to exit.

To see the aliases in the List Files screen, you must turn on the Long Display. To do that, press F5 (List) or select List Files from the File menu and press Enter. Select **5** (Short/Long Display), then **2** (Long Display), and press Enter. Now, whenever you view the List Files screen for this or any other directory, you'll see the aliases under the heading Descriptive Name. However, after you exit and restart WordPerfect, WordPerfect will revert to the Short Display. To change the default, you must use the Setup: Environment menu. (Refer to *Environment Setup*.)

Directory, Create (see also *List Files*)

Function: Lets you create a directory without leaving WordPerfect.

Keystrokes: *Keyboard* *Mouse*
F5 (List) File
Enter List Files
7 (Other Directory) Enter
d:\path\directory Other Directory
Enter, Y *d:\path\directory*
Enter, Y

Example:

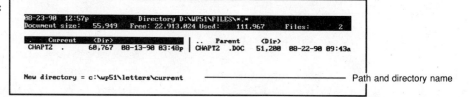

```
08-23-90  12:57p             Directory D:\WP51\FILES\*.*
Document size:    55,949   Free: 22,913,024 Used:    111,967     Files:        2

.      Current    <Dir>         ..     Parent     <Dir>
CHAPT2  .          60,767  08-13-90 03:48p │ CHAPT2  .DOC   51,200  08-22-90 09:43a


New directory = c:\wp51\letters\current  ────────────────────── Path and directory name
```

To better organize your files, you can subdivide your disk into directories. For example, if you've saved a large number of files in the WP51 subdirectory, your List Files screen may become cluttered. If so, you may want to create a new directory and move some of the files into it. In many programs, you cannot create a directory. Instead, you must exit to DOS to perform this task. In WordPerfect, however, you can create a new directory and move files into it, using the List Files menu.

Creating a New Directory

1. Press F5 (List) or select List Files from the File menu and press Enter.

   A list of files in the current directory appears.

2. Select 7 (Other Directory).

   WordPerfect prompts you to enter a name for the new directory.

3. Type the complete path, if necessary, and a new name for the directory.

To create a directory on another disk drive, the path should include the drive designator, such as C: or D:. If the directory is on the same level or one level above the current directory, it must include any directory names leading to the new directory, separated by a backslash, such as: `c:\wp51\letters\current`. However, to create a subdirectory of the current directory, you only need to type the directory name.

4. Press Enter and then Y to create the new directory.

You can now use the directory to hold files.

 Tip: With four List Files options, Delete, Copy, Other Directory, and Rename/Move, you can perform most of your file management from within WordPerfect. For example, you can create a new directory and then move a group of files from the current directory to the new one. (Refer to *Move File*.)

Directory, Default (see also *Location of Files*)

Function: Lets you change the default directory for your files.

Keystrokes:

Keyboard	*Mouse*
F5 (List)	File
Enter	List Files
7 (Other Directory)	Enter
d:\path\directory	Other Directory
Enter twice	*d:\path\directory*
OR	Enter twice
	OR

Keystrokes: *Keyboard*   *Mouse*
Cursor on directory   Cursor on directory name
name   Other Directory
7 (**Other Directory**)   Enter twice
Enter twice

Unless you change it, WordPerfect assumes you want the default directory to be the one containing your WordPerfect program files. This means that WordPerfect will automatically save new files there, unless you tell WordPerfect to save the file to a different directory. Also, whenever you select List Files and press Enter, WordPerfect will display the files in the default directory. This directory will include all of the WordPerfect program files and any files you have saved. You can change the default directory permanently, using the Location of Files option on the Setup menu (refer to *Location of Files*), or you can change it for the current editing session using List Files. There are two ways to change the default directory for the current editing session: Press F5 (List) and type an equal sign (=) followed by the directory name, or select the Other Directory option on the List Files menu.

Changing the Default Directory Temporarily

1. Press F5 (List) or select List Files from the **File** menu and press Enter.

   A list of files in the current directory appears.

2. If the directory you want to use as the default directory is displayed, move the cursor to it.

   This will save you from having to type the name of the directory.

3. Select 7 (**Other Directory**).

   If you highlighted a directory before selecting **Other Directory**, WordPerfect asks for confirmation. If you did not highlight a directory, WordPerfect prompts you to type a name for the new default directory.

4. If necessary, type a complete path to the new default directory, including the directory's name.

The path may include the letter of the drive (if the directory is on another drive) and any directory names leading to the new default directory—for example, *c:\wp51\letters\current*. If you are creating a directory on the current drive at a level below the current directory, simply type the directory name.

5. Press Enter to make this directory the new default.

If the new directory does not exist, WordPerfect prompts you to confirm its creation. If the directory does exist, WordPerfect displays a prompt showing a complete path to the directory and indicating which files will be listed (*.*). You can edit the *.* entry at this point to view a select list of files. For example, type *.WPF to see a list of all files with the WPF extension.

6. Press Enter again if you want to see a list of files in the new default directory. If you don't, press F1 (Cancel) twice.

The new directory appears on screen. This directory remains the default until you exit WordPerfect or change the default. If you press F1 (Cancel), you return to the Edit screen.

 ## Changing the Default Directory Using the Equal Sign

1. Press F5 (List) or select List Files from the File menu.

The Dir prompt appears in the lower-left side of the screen, and the Type = to change default Dir prompt appears on the right side.

2. Type = and then type the path
   and name of the directory you
   want to change to, or edit the
   Dir prompt to include it.

3. Press Enter.   This changes the default
                                         directory.

4. To display the file list, press Enter
   again. Otherwise, press F1
   (Cancel) to return to the Edit
   screen.

Directory, Deleting (see *Delete Files*)

Disk Space (see *List Files*)

Display Comments (see *Comments*)

Display Pitch

Function: Sets the amount of space used by one character on the Edit
screen.

Keystrokes:

Keyboard	*Mouse*
Shift-F8 (Format)	Layout
3 (Document)	Document
1 (Display Pitch)	Display Pitch
Y (Automatic) or **N** (No)	**Y** (Automatic) or **N** (No)
pitch width	*pitch width*
F7 (Exit)	Right mouse button

Examples:

```
Environment Variable¶            If you do, it means that the MACE environment
Finally, you'll be asked whethe  will not appear properly in the environment sp
variable, as Figure 7.13 shows.  addition, your search path or your prompt may
environment variables, see Chap  truncated. If this happens, see the section ca
Figure 7.13[em]Choosing whether  Your Environment Space Is Too Small" in Chapte
environment variable.¶           instructions on how to proceed.¶
The Mace Utilities need a varia  (c)Manual Installation¶
The value assigned to this vari  The only part of the Mace Utilities you really
path to the directory in which   the Installation program for is installing pas
you accepted the default, this   You can do the rest without it.¶
any case, the Installation prog  As noted, if you want to install the Mace Util
of the directory in which you i  an existing directory that contains files, you
```

Columns overlap after font change.

```
Environment Variable¶            installed, but you're not
Finally, you'll be asked         quite finished. You'll
whether to set an                learn the few steps
environment variable, as         required to complete the
Figure 7.13 shows. For an        process in the section
explanation of environment       called "Completing the
variables, see Chapter 3.¶       Configuration." Note that
Figure 7.13[em]Choosing          none of the changes you
whether to install the           have made will take effect
environment variable.¶           until you reboot your
The Mace Utilities need a        computer.¶
variable whose name is           [ic:CAU]Caution: When you
```

Change in Display Pitch setting corrects overlap.

WordPerfect normally displays text on the screen the same way it will appear when printed, even if you change the font size. The amount of space used by each character on the screen is regulated by the Display Pitch feature. WordPerfect automatically sets the Display Pitch, to accurately portray the number of characters that will fit on a line for the font size you have selected. In some circumstances, you may want to change it. For instance, text in newspaper or parallel columns sometimes appears to overlap on screen when you change the font, as shown in the first example. Also, formatting features that use absolute measurements, such as tabs, may appear to be using too much space. You can use Display Pitch to change the way text appears on the Edit screen, but the option has no effect on the way the text is printed.

Note: Keep in mind that *points* differ from *pitch,* which represents *characters per inch*. 18-point print is fairly large; 18 characters per inch is a small type size. Points measure the vertical size, with one point equaling 1/72 inch, whereas pitch is a horizontal measurement of the number of characters per inch.

Displaying Pitch

1. Press Shift-F8 (Format) or display the Layout menu.	A list of formatting options appears.
2. Select **Document (3)**.	The Format: Document menu appears.
3. Select **1** (Display Pitch).	WordPerfect asks if you want it to automatically determine the display pitch for the font you're using or if you want to enter a display pitch manually.
4. Press Y for automatic or N for manual.	If you pressed N, you are prompted to enter a width.
5. Enter a pitch width.	.1" is the default for a font like Courier 10, so 10 characters per inch are displayed if you are using it.
6. Press F7 (Exit) or click the right mouse button.	WordPerfect returns you to the Edit screen.

Display Setup

Function: Lets you change the way text and menus appear on screen.

Keystrokes:

Keyboard	*Mouse*
Shift-F1 (Setup)	Setup
2 (Display)	Display
Select option	Select option
Enter change	Enter change
F7 (Exit)	Right mouse button

Example:

```
Setup: Display

    1 - Colors/Fonts/Attributes

    2 - Graphics Screen Type        Hercules 720x348 Mono

    3 - Text Screen Type            Auto Selected

    4 - Menu Options

    5 - View Document Options

    6 - Edit-Screen Options
```

The Setup: Display menu offers the following options for customizing your display:

Colors/Fonts/Attributes: Controls the way text formatted with attributes such as bold and italic appears on screen. Refer to *Colors/Fonts /Attributes*.

Graphic Screen Type: Lets you select a graphics driver corresponding to your monitor and display card. This driver is used to display screens in the Graphics Editor, the Equation Editor, and the View Document display. Refer to *Graphics Screen Type*.

Text Screen Type: Lets you select a text driver for use in the Edit screen. This is helpful if you are using a monitor with special features like extended text mode or special fonts. Refer to *Text Screen Type*.

Menu Options: Controls the way the mnemonic selection letters in menu options appear. Lets you change the appearance of your pull-down menus and menu bar and select whether or not you want the menu bar to remain visible or if you want it separated from the Edit screen by a line. Refer to *Menu Options, Setup*.

View Document Options: Controls the appearance of the View Document screen. Refer to *View Document*.

Edit-Screen Options: Lets you change several elements that affect the appearance of the Edit screen, including whether or not you will see document comments, the file name on the status line, side-by-side columns, or merge codes. This option also lets you change the size of the Reveal Codes window. Refer to *Edit-Screen Options*.

Changing Your Display Setup

1. Press Shift-F1 (Setup) or select Setup from the **File** menu. — The main Setup menu appears.

2. Select **Display (2)**. — The Setup: Display menu appears, listing six options for customizing the display.

3. Select the item you want to change as described above.

4. Select each option you want to change, and enter the change for that option. — When you select the option, the cursor moves up to that option, and you can enter your change.

5. Press F7 (Exit) or click the right mouse button. — WordPerfect returns you to your document.

Doc 1 and Doc 2 (see *Switch* and *Windows*)

Document Comments (see *Comments*)

Document Compare (see *Compare Documents*)

Document Conversion (see *Convert Program (CONVERT.EXE)*)

Document Format (see *Format Document*)

Document Management/Summary
(see also *List Files*)

Function: Lets you attach a summary to each document, with information that's separate from the actual text, to help you organize and locate your documents.

Keystrokes:

Keyboard	*Mouse*
Shift-F8 (Format)	Layout
3 (Document)	Document
5 (Summary)	Summary
Select options	Select options
Enter information	Enter information
F7 (Exit)	Right mouse button

Example:

```
Document Summary
        Revision Date  08-23-90 02:24p
    1 - Creation Date  08-23-90 02:03p
    2 - Document Name  Herman Melville's Epistemology
        Document Type  American Literature
    3 - Author         Nicholas Kraynak
        Typist         Alexandra Kraynak
    4 - Subject        Melville's epistemology and how it relates to
                       Spinoza's metaphysics.
    5 - Account        Attacks current theory that this is an adventure
                       novel.
    6 - Keywords       Melville Epistemology Spinoza Metaphysics American
                       Literature
    7 - Abstract       In the sense that one can understand Being (essence)
                       through a single being (an attribute of that
                       essence), Melville's epistemology agrees with
                       Spinoza's metaphysic, but Melville goes far beyond
                       that.
    Selection: 0                    (Retrieve to capture; Del to remove summary)
```

The Document Summary feature can help you organize and locate files by providing an overview of the contents. You can create a document summary from anywhere in a document. You simply access the Document Summary screen and enter information such as the author name, typist, subject, and long document name and type. These summaries make document management much easier. If you use them correctly, when you choose 6 (Look) on the List Files screen, you won't have to scroll through a document to find out what's in it, because you'll see the Document Summary screen first. Also, you can search for text inside all document summaries in the current List Files menu using the Find option. You can print a document summary and even save it separately from the document.

Creating a Document Summary

1. Press Shift-F8 (Format) or display the Layout menu.

   A list of formatting options appears.

2. Select **Document (3)**.

   The Format: Document menu appears.

3. Select **5 (Summary)**.

   The Document Summary screen appears. You can enter information for any item listed; none are mandatory.

4. Select **2 (Document Name)** and enter a descriptive name for the document and a document type.

   The long document name and document type will appear in the List Files menu if you use the Long Display.

5. Select **3 (Author/Typist)** and enter an author name and a typist's name, if it applies.

   You can type up to 60 characters for each entry. You can press Shift-F10 (Retrieve) to use the author and typist names from the previous summary.

6. Select **4 (Subject)** and enter the subject of the document.

   You can enter up to 160 characters. WordPerfect can search for and retrieve this information from your document—press Shift-F10 (Retrieve).

7. Select **5 (Account)** and enter account information, if it applies.

   You can enter up to 160 characters.

8. Select **6 (Keywords)** and enter keywords that will help identify the document.

   You can enter up to 160 characters. If you enter keywords, you can use the Find command in the List Files screen to locate a document.

9. Select **7 (Abstract)** and type an abstract summarizing the document.

   Your abstract can be up to 780 characters. If you press Shift-F10 (Retrieve), WordPerfect will retrieve the first 400 characters of the document.

10. Press F7 (Exit) or click the right mouse button.

    This returns you to the Edit screen.

Note: If you have a RE: comment in the document, you can copy up to 39 characters of that information directly from the document and insert it in the Subject field. With the cursor to the right of `Selection:` press Shift-F10 (Retrieve) and type Y. This will also copy the first 400 words from the document and insert them into the Abstract field. Follow the same procedure to copy the author and typist name from the last document summary you created, if you created it in the same editing session.

 Tip: If you want to copy the subject entry from your documents, but you typed something other than RE: (for example, Subject: or Topic:) in your document to mark the subject, you can tell WordPerfect to look for that text instead. Press Shift-F1 (Setup) or select Setup from the File menu; select Environment (3), **4** (**Document Management/ Summary**), **2** (**Subject Search Text**); and then enter the heading you use (for example, `Topic:`). From then on, WordPerfect will look for that heading to find the text for the subject entry.

 Tip: If you want to save a document summary with each document you create, you can make it mandatory upon saving. Press Shift-F1 (Setup) or select Setup from the File menu; select Environment (3), **4** (**Document Management/ Summary**), **1** (**Create Summary on Save/Exit**); press Y and then F7 (Exit). Now, whenever you try to save a document that does not already have a summary, WordPerfect will display the Document Summary screen, prompting you to create one.

Document on Disk (see *Print Document on Disk*)

Document Size (see *List Files*)

DOS Command (see *Go to DOS* or *Go to Shell*)

DOS Text Files (see also *Text Out*)

Function: Lets you use WordPerfect to create and edit DOS Text files, such as CONFIG.SYS and AUTOEXEC.BAT. You can also use this option to convert a WordPerfect file into a DOS Text file (ASCII file), so it can be used with other programs.

Keystrokes:

Keyboard	*Mouse*
Ctrl-F5 (Text In/Out)	File
1 (DOS Text)	Text Out
1 (Save)	DOS Text
d:\path\filename.ext	Save
Enter	*d:\path\filename.ext*
	Enter

Example:

```
@ECHO OFF
PATH C:\DOS;C:\PCTOOLS;F:\WORD5;C:\NC;
MIRROR C: /TC
PROMPT $P$G
6710\mouse
VER
d:
cd\wp51
wp
```

You can use the DOS Text option to create DOS Text files (also called ASCII files), or to convert WordPerfect files into DOS Text files. The procedure removes all formatting codes. Some codes, such as tab, indent, flush right, and center, are converted into spaces.

One of the most common uses for this feature is to create batch files. Batch files act as mini programs, with commands directing DOS to perform one or more tasks. For example, the AUTOEXEC.BAT file shown in the example performs several functions, such as setting up a path, displaying the current directory name in the DOS prompt, changing to the D drive, and starting WordPerfect. AUTOEXEC.BAT is a special file that is run as soon as the computer is started, so the computer will automatically start WordPerfect when it is turned on. With WordPerfect's DOS Text feature, you can create batch files the same way you create a WordPerfect document. The only difference is the method you use to save the files.

Saving a DOS Text File

1. Retrieve the WordPerfect file you are converting, or start with a blank screen and type the commands for the DOS Text file. If you want to edit an existing DOS Text file, such as your AUTOEXEC.BAT file, retrieve it by pressing Ctrl-F5 (Text In/Out), selecting **1** (DOS Text) and **2** (Retrieve), and then entering the file name.

   Formatting commands like margin changes, line spacing, headers and footers, and footnotes and endnotes will be removed when you save the DOS Text file, and codes like tab and indent will be converted into spaces.

2. Enter any changes you wish to make to the document.

3. Press Ctrl-F5 (Text In/Out) or select Text **O**ut from the **F**ile menu.

   A list of Text Out options appears.

4. Select **1** (DOS Text) and then **1** (Save), or select DOS **T**ext from the pull-down menu.

   WordPerfect prompts you to type a name for the DOS Text file. If you are converting a WordPerfect file and want to use the same name, you can press Shift-F10 to retrieve the file name.

5. Type the drive and directory where you want the file saved, if it differs from the current one; then type the file name and press Enter.

    If you are creating a batch file, be sure to include the extension .BAT. Since the file will remain on the screen after you save it as a DOS Text file, the last step is to clear the screen. If a file already exists under the same name, WordPerfect displays a prompt asking if you want to replace the file.

6. If WordPerfect displays the Replace? prompt, press Y to replace the file on disk or N to cancel.

7. Press F7 (Exit) or select Exit from the File menu.

    WordPerfect asks if you want to save the document as a WordPerfect file.

8. Press N in response to the Save document prompt.

    WordPerfect asks if you want to exit the program.

9. Type Y if you want to exit WordPerfect, or N if you don't.

If you edited your AUTOEXEC.BAT file and want to use it right away, exit WordPerfect, and restart the computer by pressing Ctrl-Alt-Del or by pressing your computer's reset button. To use any other type of batch file, exit WordPerfect, change to the drive and directory where it is saved, and then type the first part of the file name (you don't need to type the BAT extension).

Dot Leaders (see *Tab, Set*)

Double Spacing (see *Line Spacing*)

Double Underline (see *Appearance Attributes*)

Downloadable Fonts (see *Cartridges and Fonts*)

Draw (see *Line Draw*)

Dual Document Editing (see *Switch* and *Windows*)

Edit-Screen Options

Function: Lets you customize the way WordPerfect displays and updates the document on screen.

Keystrokes:

Keyboard	*Mouse*
Shift-F1 (Setup)	File
2 (Display)	Setup
6 (Edit-Screen Options)	Display
Select option	Edit-Screen Options
Enter change	Select option
F7 (Exit)	Enter change
	F7 (Exit)

Example:

```
Setup: Edit-Screen Options

    1 - Automatically Format and Rewrite    Yes

    2 - Comments Display                     Yes

    3 - Filename on the Status Line          Yes

    4 - Hard Return Display Character        ¶

    5 - Merge Codes Display                  Yes

    6 - Reveal Codes Window Size             10

    7 - Side-by-side Columns Display         Yes
```

You can use the Edit-Screen options to control the display of several WordPerfect features on the Edit screen, including the display of document comments, the file name, hard return character, merge codes, and newspaper and parallel columns. They also let you change the size of the Reveal Codes screen and the method of reformatting as you edit text. The following options are available:

Automatically Format and Rewrite: Determines whether or not WordPerfect updates your screen as you edit, rather than as you move the cursor through the document. The Default is Yes, so the screen is reformatted as you edit. Selecting No increases your editing speed. For more information, see *Automatic Format and Rewrite.*

Comments Display: Lets you turn off the display of document comments so they will not be visible on the Edit screen. The default is Yes, so comments are displayed. Refer to *Comments* for more information.

Filename on the Status Line: If you have saved the document on the Edit screen, or if you retrieve a file from the disk, its file name appears in the lower-left corner of the screen. You can use this option to prevent the file name from being displayed. The default is Yes.

Hard Return Display Character: You can use this option to display a character on the Edit screen wherever a Hard Return code is located. This will tell you whether a line ends in a hard return or soft return. For instance, to display the paragraph symbol, ¶, select the option, press the Alt key, and type the number's decimal value on the numeric keypad: 20. You can also use a character from any of WordPerfect's 12 character sets, as listed in the file CHARACTR.DOC (refer to *Compose Key*). Even though the hard return display character appears on the Edit screen, it will not be printed. To change it back to the default, select the option and press the space bar once.

Merge Codes Display: You can use this option to turn off the display of merge codes such as {END FIELD}. The default is Yes, so merge codes are displayed. If you select No, the codes won't be displayed but the text, such as field names and numbers, will be. For more information, see *Merge.*

Reveal Codes Window Size: You can use this option to change the size of the Reveal Codes screen. Enter 2 or more for the number of lines you want to use for the Reveal Codes window. If you select 1 line, Reveal Codes will show only the character or code that the cursor is on. The default size is 10.

Side-by-side Columns Display: This option lets you change the on-screen display of newspaper or parallel columns, to speed up editing and reformatting. The default is Yes, so columns are displayed next to each other. If you select No, columns appear on separate pages, but in the correct column position. Regardless of how they appear on the Edit screen, WordPerfect always prints columns side-by-side.

 ## Changing the Edit-Screen Options

1. Press Shift-F1 (Setup) or select Setup from the **File** menu.	The main Setup menu appears.

2. Select **Display (2)**.   The Setup: Display menu
                                                                        appears.

3. Select **6** (Edit-Screen Options).   The options listed above appear.

4. Select the number or letter of the   When you select an option, the
    option you want to change, and   cursor moves up to that option
    make the change.   so you can change it. For the
                                                                        five Yes/No options, the cursor
                                                                        returns to the Selection area after
                                                                        you press Y or N. For the two
                                                                        others, you have to press Enter
                                                                        after making the change.

5. Press F7 (Exit) or click the right   This returns you to the Edit
    mouse button.   screen and the document you
                                                                        were working on.

End Key (see *Cursor Movement*)

Endnotes/Footnotes, Creating and Deleting

Function: Lets you create footnotes or endnotes, which WordPerfect
               will automatically number and renumber if you insert or
               delete a footnote or endnote.

Keystrokes: *Keyboard*   *Mouse*
                 Ctrl-F7 (Footnote)   Layout
                 1 (Footnote) or   Footnote or Endnote
                 2 (Endnote)   Create
                 1 (Create)   Type text
                 Type text   F7 (Exit)
                 F7 (Exit)

Code: [Footnote:n;[Note Num]...]

Example:

```
        1 Herman Melville, Moby Dick, ed. Harrison Hayford and Hershel
    Parker (New 1967), p. 208


    Footnote: Press Exit when done                    Doc 1 Pg 1 Ln 1.67" Pos 3.5"
```

The Endnotes/Footnotes feature lets you create footnotes or endnotes, which WordPerfect will automatically number and renumber if you insert or delete one or more. You type the text for the footnotes and endnotes in a special screen, and WordPerfect automatically prints them in the correct position: Footnotes are printed at the bottom of the page where they are referenced, and endnotes are printed at the end of the document.

 ## Creating an Endnote or Footnote

1. Move the cursor to the place where you want to insert the number for the note.

   This is usually after you first mention the note or where you end a quote.

2. Press Ctrl-F7 (Footnote) or display the Layout menu.

   A menu appears offering three options: footnote, endnote, and endnote placement.

3. Select Footnote (**1**) or Endnote (**2**).

   The Footnote or Endnote menu appears.

4. Select Create (**1**).

   A note screen appears. The number of the note is in the upper-left corner of the screen.

5. Type the text for your note.

   As you type, the text appears on screen. You can enter over 60,000 characters.

6. Press F7 (Exit) or click the right mouse button.

   The note number is inserted at the cursor position. If you display the Reveal Codes screen, you can see the [Footnote:n;[Note Num]...] code that WordPerfect inserts.

 Tip: In most books and articles, you'll notice that footnotes and endnotes are printed in a smaller font. If your printer supports smaller fonts, you can use one of these fonts for your notes. Before you begin typing, Press Ctrl-F8 (Font), select 4 (Base Font), and select the font you wish to use. The note will be printed in that font. You can also vary the type by using an attribute, such as bold or italic.

Deleting an Endnote or Footnote

1. Place the cursor on the number
   of the note you want to delete.

2. Press Del.   WordPerfect asks if you want to
                                                 delete the note reference.

3. Press Y to continue or N to cancel   If you press Y, WordPerfect
   the delete.   erases the note number and the
                                                 text.

 Note: If you accidently delete a note, you can restore the
note number and the text. Press F1 (Cancel) and select **1**
(**R**estore). You can also search for a note. Press F2
(→Search) or Shift-F2 (←Search). When asked what you
want to search for, press Ctrl-F7 (Footnote). Select
Footnote or Endnote; then select **1** (Note) and press F2 to
start the search.

Endnotes/Footnotes, Editing

Function: Lets you edit an existing endnote or footnote.

Keystrokes: *Keyboard*   *Mouse*
          Ctrl-F7 (Footnote)   Layout
          1 (Footnote) or   Footnote or Endnote
          2 (Endnote)   Edit
          2 (Edit)   Edit text
          Edit text   F7 (Exit)
          F7 (Exit)

You can edit an existing endnote or footnote from anywhere in the
document. Just tell WordPerfect which note you want to edit and edit the
text as you normally would.

Editing an Endnote or Footnote

1. Press Ctrl-F7 (Footnote) or display the Layout menu.

   A menu appears letting you choose to work with an endnote or footnote.

2. Select Footnote (**1**) or Endnote (**2**).

   The Footnote or Endnote menu appears.

3. Select Edit (**2**).

   WordPerfect prompts you to enter the number or character of the note you want to edit.

4. Type the number or character of the note you want to edit, and press Enter.

   The text of the note appears on screen.

5. Edit the note as you normally would.

   The changes appear on screen.

6. Press F7 (Exit) or click the right mouse button.

   Your changes are saved, and you return to your document.

Endnotes/Footnotes, New Numbers

Function: Renumbers subsequent notes starting at any point in the document.

Keystrokes:

Keyboard
Ctrl-F7 (Footnote)
1 (Footnote) or **2** (Endnote)
3 (New Number)
n (where *n* is the number you want to start with)
Ctrl-F3 (Screen)
1 (Rewrite)

Mouse
Layout
Footnote or Endnote
New Number
n (where *n* is the number you want to start with)
Ctrl-F3 (Screen)
Rewrite

Codes: [New End Num:n]
[New Ftn Num:n]

Example:

```
D:\WP51\FILES\MOBY.WP5                           Doc 1 Pg 1 Ln 8" Pos 5.4"
[                                                                        ]
soul. Ahab comprehends this in the Chapter "The Sphynx," when he[SRt]
says, "O Nature, and O soul of man! how far beyond all utterance[SRt]
are your linked analogies! not the smallest atom stirs or lives in[SRt]
matter but has is cunning duplicate in mind.[New Ftn Num:5]█[Footnote:5;[Note Nu
m] Melville, page 264.]
                                                    |
                                        New Footnote Number code
```

The New Number option lets you start a new numbering sequence for your footnotes or endnotes at any point in the document. You enter a [New Num:n] code, and tell WordPerfect which number you want to start with. Notes from that point on will be numbered consecutively starting with the new number.

Entering a New Number

1. Position the cursor to the left of the number where you want to start the new numbering.

   You may need to display the Reveal Codes screen to check the position of your cursor.

2. Press Ctrl-F7 (Footnote) or display the Layout menu.

   You can choose to change the numbers for footnotes or endnotes.

3. Select Footnote (1) or Endnote (2).

   The Footnote or Endnote menu appears.

4. Select New Number (3).

   WordPerfect prompts you to enter the number you want to start with.

5. Type the number with which you want to start the consecutive numbering and press Enter.

   You are returned to your document.

6. Press Ctrl-F3 (Screen).

   The Screen menu appears.

7. Select 1 (Rewrite).

   The screen is updated to show the changes.

Endnotes/Footnotes, Options

Function: Lets you enter settings to customize the appearance of your endnotes and/or footnotes.

Keystrokes: *Keyboard*   *Mouse*
Ctrl-F7 (Footnote)   **Layout**
1 (Footnote) or   **Footnote or Endnote**
2 (Endnote)   **Options**
4 (Options)   Choose option
Choose option   Enter change
Enter change   **Right mouse button**
F7 (Exit)

Codes: [End Opt]
[Ftn Opt]

Example:

```
Footnote Options
    1 - Spacing Within Footnotes              1
            Between Footnotes                 0.167"
    2 - Amount of Note to Keep Together       0.5"
    3 - Style for Number in Text              [SUPRSCPT][Note Num][suprscpt]
    4 - Style for Number in Note                      [SUPRSCPT][Note Num][suprscpt
    5 - Footnote Numbering Method             Numbers
    6 - Start Footnote Numbers each Page      No
    7 - Line Separating Text and Footnotes    2-inch Line
    8 - Print Continued Message               No
    9 - Footnotes at Bottom of Page           Yes
```

The Endnote/Footnote options let you enter various settings that control the layout of your endnotes and/or footnotes. The following five options are available for both endnotes and footnotes:

Spacing (Within and Between Notes): By default, notes are single-spaced with an extra .16" between notes.

Amount of Note to Keep Together: By default, .5" of a note is kept on a page to prevent an awkward split.

Style for Number in Text: The number that refers to the note appears slightly above the baseline (superscript). This is the standard way of doing things, but you can change the attribute to bold, italic, or something else.

Style for Number in Note: The number in the note is normally indented. In an endnote, the number is followed by a period. In a footnote, the number is a superscript. You can change these options or even modify the appearance of the number with Ctrl-F8 (Font).

Numbering Method: If you don't like using numbers to refer to your notes, you can choose to use letters (a, b, c, etc.) or characters (*, #, etc.). If you choose to use characters, you can use up to five characters. WordPerfect will run through the characters, then use double characters, triple characters, etc.

In addition to these five options, the Footnote Options screen provides the following four options:

Start Footnote Numbers Each Page: You can number footnotes separately on each page instead of keeping a running count.

Line Separating Text and Footnotes: By default, WordPerfect prints a line between where the document text ends on a page and where the footnotes start. You can choose to have the line go completely across the page or get rid of it altogether.

Print Continued Message: If you have a footnote that starts on one page and continues on the next, you can have WordPerfect print a "Continued" message at the end of the footnote on the first page and the beginning of the footnote on the next page.

Footnotes at Bottom of Page: By default, footnotes are printed at the bottom of the page. By setting this option to No, you can have the footnotes printed immediately after the reference.

 ## Setting Endnote/Footnote Options

1.	Press Ctrl-F7 (Footnote) or display the Layout menu.	You can set the options for either endnotes or footnotes.
2.	Select Footnote (**1**) or Endnote (**2**), or choose Footnote or Endnote from the Layout menu.	The Footnote or Endnote menu appears.
3.	Select Options (**4**).	The Options menu appears.
4.	Select the option you want to change and enter the change.	When you select an option, the cursor moves up to that option. You can then enter the change. When you press Enter, the cursor moves back down to Selection: and you can choose another option to change.
5.	Press F7 (Exit) or click the right mouse button.	This returns you to the Edit screen.

Endnotes, Placement

Function: Lets you select where you want to print endnotes.

Keystrokes:

Keyboard	*Mouse*
Ctrl-F7 (Footnote)	Layout
3 (Endnote **P**lacement)	**P**lacement
Y (Restart Numbering) or **N** (Continue Numbering)	**Y** (Restart Numbering) or **N** (Continue Numbering)
Generate endnotes (refer to *Generate*)	Generate endnotes (refer to *Generate*)

Codes: [Endnote Placement]
[New End Num:]

Example:

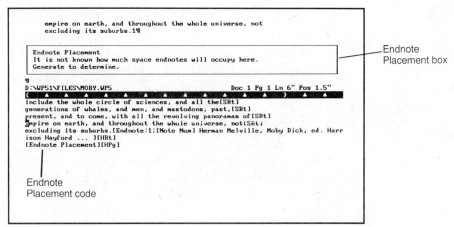

Endnote
Placement box

Endnote
Placement code

By default, WordPerfect prints your endnotes at the end of the document or master document. You may, however, want the endnotes printed somewhere else. For example, you may be printing a master document that consists of several chapters, and you want the endnotes printed at the end of each chapter rather than at the end of the manuscript. You can tell WordPerfect where you want the endnotes printed.

 ## Placing Endnotes

1. Position the cursor where you want the endnotes printed.

For example, you may position the cursor at the end of a chapter or immediately after the endnote is referred to.

2. Press Ctrl-F7 (Footnote) or display the **Layout** menu.

A menu appears, giving you the option to position your endnotes.

3. Select **3** (Endnote **P**lacement) or select **P**lacement from the pull-down menu.

WordPerfect asks if you want to restart endnote numbering. If you choose to restart numbering, the first endnote after this code will be 1 or a. If you choose not to restart, numbering will continue from the last number used.

4. Press Y to start renumbering or N to continue from where you left off.

The Endnote Placement box appears with a hard return after it.

5. If you want the endnotes to appear on a separate page, move the cursor before the Placement box and press Ctrl-Enter.

This inserts a Hard Page code before the Placement box.

If you want to see how much space the endnotes will occupy in the printed document, you must generate the endnotes. You don't have to generate the endnotes to have them print. This just gives you some idea of how much space they'll take up.

 Generating Endnotes

1. Press Alt-F5 (Mark Text) or display the **Mark** menu.

The Mark Text menu appears.

2. Select **G**enerate (6).

The Mark Text: Generate menu appears.

3. Select **5** (Generate Tables, Indexes, Cross-References, etc.)

A warning message appears, telling you that old tables and indexes will be replaced.

4. Type Y, telling WordPerfect to continue.

WordPerfect generates the endnotes and changes the message in the Endnote Placement box, telling you that the notes have been generated.

End of Field (see *Merge*)

End of Record (see *Merge*)

Enhanced Keyboard Definition (see *Keyboard Layout, Select*)

Environment Setup

Function: Lets you customize nine features that affect WordPerfect's operating environment.

Keystrokes: *Keyboard*   *Mouse*
Shift-F1 (Setup)   **File**
3 (Environment)   Setup
Choose option   Environment
Enter change   Choose option
F7 (Exit)   Enter change
                           Right mouse button

Example:

```
Setup: Environment
     1 - Backup Options
     2 - Beep Options
     3 - Cursor Speed                    50 cps
     4 - Document Management/Summary
     5 - Fast Save (unformatted)         Yes
     6 - Hyphenation                     External Dictionary/Rules
     7 - Prompt for Hyphenation          When Required
     8 - Units of Measure
     9 - Alternate Keyboard              No
```

You can customize WordPerfect's operating environment through the Setup: Environment menu. This menu lets you modify the following features:

Backup Options: Original Backup performs an automatic backup of your original file whenever you save an edited version of it. The backup file has the same base name as the original file, but has the BK! extension.

Timed Backup saves the on-screen version of a document every few minutes to a file called WP{WP}.BK1 or WP{WP}.BK2. If there is a power failure, or if you turn off the computer without exiting WordPerfect, the backup file remains on disk and you can rename it and retrieve it. For more information, refer to *Backup, Timed and Original*.

Beep Options: This leads to a menu with three options: Beep on Error, Beep on Hyphenation, Beep on Search Failure. If you don't want your computer to beep at you, you can turn off the beep function for these features. For more information, refer to *Beep Options*.

Cursor Speed: When you hold down a key, the key repeats at a certain number of characters per second. You can use this option to decrease the key repeat speed, which is 50 characters per second by default, or to return to your keyboard's original speed. It affects both cursor movement keys and character keys. For more information, see *Cursor Speed*.

Document Management/Summary: This leads to a menu with four options. The first two options are covered in *Document Management/ Summary*. The third option, Long Document Names, is set to No. If you change it to Yes, it forces WordPerfect to prompt you for a long document name when you save a document and changes the List Files screen to Long Display, so that the long document names will appear. The fourth, Default Document Type, lets you establish a standard document type that WordPerfect will suggest as the file extension when you save a new file. For more information, see Chapter 7, "File Management."

Fast Save: By default, this option is set to Yes. WordPerfect saves documents without formatting them for the printer. If you set the option to No, it takes longer to save a file, but if you print the file from disk, it will print more quickly because it's already formatted. For more information, refer to *Fast Save*.

Hyphenation: You can use this option to choose the hyphenation method that WordPerfect will use when you turn the automatic hyphenation feature on: External Dictionary/Rules or Internal Rules. The default is External Dictionary/Rules method, and it is more accurate. For more information, refer to *Hyphenation*.

Prompt for Hyphenation: When you turn on WordPerfect's hyphenation feature, WordPerfect automatically hyphenates words according to the dictionary rules. It will only ask for your input about a hyphen when it cannot determine the correct position for the hyphen, or when the hyphen could be correctly placed in more than one position. The Prompt for Hyphenation option brings up a menu with three choices: Never, When Required, and Always. When Required is the default. If you change it to Never, WordPerfect will automatically hyphenate words without stopping to ask for your approval, using the rules from the dictionary you selected (internal or external). If WordPerfect cannot determine how to hyphenate a word, it will wrap it to the next line. If you select Always, WordPerfect will ask you to confirm all hyphens.

Units of Measure: This option leads to another menu with two options. You can use the first, Display and Entry of Numbers, to change the display of measurements such as margins, tabs, line height, and other features that require a measurement. You can use the second, Status Line Display, to change the unit of measure for the Ln and Pos number displayed on the status line. The default for both options is inches, as represented by the inch mark. For more information, see *Units of Measure*.

Alternate Keyboard: You can use this option to select a keyboard layout that redefines three keys: F1, Esc, and F3. F1 becomes the Help key, Esc becomes the Cancel key, and F3 becomes the repeat value key. The default is No. This option was not available in early versions of WordPerfect 5.1.

 Selecting Environment Options

1. Press Shift-F1 (Setup) or choose Setup from the File menu.	The main Setup menu appears.
2. Select Environment (3).	The Setup: Environment menu appears.
3. Select the option you want to change, and enter the change.	When the cursor moves back to the Selection area, you can select another option to change.
4. Press F7 (Exit) or click the right mouse button.	This returns you to the Edit screen.

Equation Editor, Creating Equations

Function: Lets you create, edit, and print mathematical or scientific equations in your documents. (The Equation Editor cannot calculate equations.)

Keystrokes: *Keyboard*   *Mouse*

Alt-F9 (Graphics)   **Graphics**

6 Equation   **Equation**

1 (Create)   **Create**

9 (Edit)   **Edit**

Create equation   Create equation

Ctrl-F3 (Screen) or F9   Ctrl-F3 (Screen) or F9

F7 (Exit)   Right mouse button

Example:

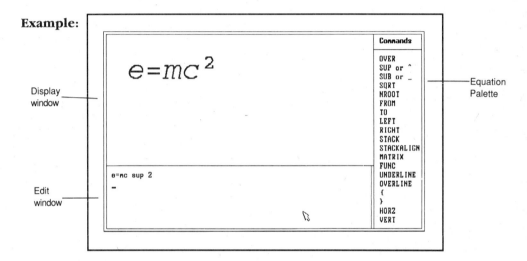

The Equation Editor consists of three windows: the Edit window, the Equation Palette, and the Display window. You will use the Edit window to create and edit the equation. The Equation Palette contains several equation commands and hundreds of symbols you may need for assembling your equations. Instead of typing the commands you need, you can select them from the palette. The Display window lets you see how your equation will look when printed. Whenever you want to view the formula, press Ctrl-F3 (Screen) or F9. (This is a good way to check whether your mathematical operations are written in the order in which you intended.)

 Accessing the Equation Editor

1. Position the cursor where you
   want the equation to appear.

2. Press Alt-F9 (Graphics) or display   The Graphics Box menu appears,
   the **Graphics** menu.   asking you to define a graphics
                                           box.

3. · Select **Equation** (6).   This tells WordPerfect that you want to work with equations.

4. Select **Create** (1).   The Definition: Equation screen appears.

5. Select **9** (Edit).   The Equation Editor appears on screen.

When the Equation Editor is displayed, you can create your equation. To create the equation, simply type it in the editing screen. For example, to create the equation x = y [x] z, type x = y times z. You can use any characters on the keyboard and any characters from WordPerfect's character sets (refer to *Compose Key*). To determine what you must type for a given equation command, refer to the commands listed in the Equation Palette.

Instead of typing the equation commands (such as "times"), you can choose the commands from the Equation Palette. Press F5 (List) to activate the Palette or click in the Palette window. Highlight the command you want to insert. An example for the proper syntax for the command appears on the status line. Press Enter or Ctrl-Enter to insert the command. If the command offers both a keyword (such as "times") and a symbol (such as [x]), Enter inserts the keyword, and Ctrl-Enter inserts the symbol. This affects only the way the command appears in the Edit window. The symbol will appear in the Display window no matter what option you choose. To leave the Palette without entering a command, press F1 (Cancel) or F7 (Exit).

 Note: Any spaces you type in an equation are not treated as spaces you type in normal text. To insert a bona fide space, type a tilde (~). To insert a 1/4 space, type a backward accent (`).

Erase (see *Delete Text*)

Esc Key

Function: Used alone, the Esc key lets you repeat the next keystroke any number of times. If a menu or prompt appears, pressing Esc usually cancels it.

Keystrokes: Esc

Unless there is a menu or prompt on the screen, when you press Esc, this prompt appears: Repeat Value = 8. The next key you press (except a number) will be repeated eight times. For example, if you press Esc and then press the Delete key, WordPerfect will erase the next eight characters. If you press Esc, and then press the Down Arrow key, the cursor will move down eight lines. You can change the repeat value (the number of times that a keystroke will be repeated) for the next keystroke, for the rest of the editing session, or permanently; refer to *Repeat Value, Change.*

If there is a menu or prompt on the screen, you can usually press Esc to back out of it. For example, you can use it to cancel the Print menu, Format menu, Speller menu, Setup menu, Graphics menu, and the Font menu. You cannot use it to back out of the List Files menu, the Help menu, or the Exit menu. To exit those menus, you may need to press some other key, such as the space bar or the Enter key.

Execute Macro (see *Macros*)

Exit (F7)

Function: Takes you out of an option, menu, or special screen while saving the changes, or exits WordPerfect with or without saving changes to the document.

Keystrokes: *Keyboard*   *Mouse*
                 F7 (Exit)   File
                                    Exit

The Exit key has several functions. You can use it to perform any of the following tasks:

- Save the document on the Edit screen, and then exit from WordPerfect.

- Exit WordPerfect without saving the document on the Edit screen.

- Save the document on the Edit screen and then clear the Edit screen to work on another document.

- Clear the Edit screen without saving the document you were working on.

- Exit a menu and save the changes you have made to one or more options.

- Exit back to the Edit screen from a special screen such as the Header or Footer Edit screen, the Footnote Edit screen, or the Tab Set menu.

Do not use the Exit key to back out of a menu or prompt if you have made changes but do not want to save them. Instead, press F1 (Cancel). You cannot use Exit to exit from the Help menu; only the Enter key or the space bar will work.

 ## Save Document on Screen and Exit WordPerfect

1. Press F7 (Exit) or select Exit from the File menu.

   The Save document prompt appears, asking if you want to save the document. If you see the Text was not modified prompt in the lower-right corner of the screen, you do not have to save the file because you haven't changed it since last saving it. If this is the case, press N and skip to step 5.

2. Press Y.

   The Document to be saved prompt appears, asking for a file name for the document.

3. Type the file name and then press Enter.

   If the Replace prompt appears, go to step 4. Otherwise, WordPerfect saves the file. After it finishes saving, the Exit WP prompt appears, asking if you want to exit WordPerfect. If the other document work area is open (Doc 1 or Doc 2), you'll be asked if you want to exit Doc 1 (or Doc 2) instead of WordPerfect.

4. If the Replace prompt appears, press Y if you want to replace the file on disk with the one on the Edit screen, or N if you do not want to. If you press N, the next step is to type a different file name and then press Enter.

   Next, the Exit WP prompt appears, asking if you want to exit WordPerfect. If the other document work area is open (Doc 1 or Doc 2), you'll be asked if you want to exit Doc 1 (or Doc 2) instead of WordPerfect.

5. Press Y.

This exits WordPerfect, unless the other document work area (Doc 1 or Doc 2) was open.

6. If you exit to Doc 1 or Doc 2, press F7 (Exit) or select Exit from the File menu again. If you want to save the document in this work area, repeat steps 1 through 4; then press Y in response to the `Exit WP` prompt. If you don't want to save it, type N and then Y.

This exits WordPerfect.

 ### Exit WordPerfect Without Saving Document

1. Press F7 (Exit) or select Exit from the File menu.

The `Save document` prompt appears, asking if you want to save the document.

2. Press N.

The `Exit WP` prompt appears, asking if you want to exit WordPerfect. If the other document work area is open (Doc 1 or Doc 2), you'll be asked if you want to exit Doc 1 (or Doc 2) instead of WordPerfect.

3. Press Y.

This exits WordPerfect or the other document work area.

4. If you exit to Doc 1 or Doc 2, press F7 (Exit) or select Exit from the File menu. If the screen contains a document you want to save, perform steps 1 through 4 in the previous section; then press Y in response to the `Exit WP` prompt. If you don't want to save it, press N and then Y.

This exits WordPerfect.

Save Document and Clear Screen

1. Press F7 (Exit) or select Exit from the File menu.	The Save document prompt appears, asking if you want to save the document. If you see the Text was not modified prompt in the lower-right corner of the screen, you do not have to save the file, because you haven't changed it since last saving it. If this is the case, press N and skip to step 5.
2. Press Y.	The Document to be saved prompt appears, asking for a file name for the document.
3. Type the file name and then press Enter.	If the Replace prompt appears, go to step 4. Otherwise, WordPerfect saves the file. The next prompt asks if you want to exit WordPerfect, or exit Doc 1 or Doc 2.
4. If the Replace prompt appears, press Y if you want to replace the file on disk with the one on the Edit screen, or N if you do not want to. If you press N, the next step is to type a different file name and then press Enter.	The next prompt asks if you want to exit WordPerfect, or exit Doc 1 or Doc 2.
5. Press N.	This clears the screen so you can begin typing a new document, or retrieve and edit one.

 Clear Screen Without Saving Document

1. Press F7 (Exit) or select Exit from the File menu.	The Save document prompt appears, asking if you want to save the document.
2. Press N.	The next prompt asks if you want to exit WordPerfect, or exit Doc 1 or Doc 2.

3. Press N.   This clears the screen so you can begin typing a new document, or retrieve and edit one.

Exit WordPerfect (see *Exit*)

Expand Master Document (see *Master Document*)

Extended Search/Replace (see *Search and Replace*)

Extra Large Print (see *Size Attributes*)

F

Fast Save (see also *Print Document on Disk*)

Function: Saves document without formatting it for printing, so it takes less time to save.

Keystrokes:

Keyboard	*Mouse*
Shift-F1 (Setup)	File
3 (Environment)	Setup
5 (Fast Save)	Environment
Y (On) or N (Off)	Fast Save
F7 (Exit)	Yes or No
	Right mouse button

By default, Fast Save is set to Yes, so WordPerfect saves your documents without formatting them for printing. Instead, it saves only the name of the printer resource file. If you print the file from disk, WordPerfect makes a copy of it and then reformats it before printing. The advantage of Fast Save is that it takes less time to save a file. The only disadvantage is that it may take a little longer to print the document.

If you edit them, fast-saved documents may take up *more* disk space than formatted documents. When you fast-save an edited document, the file prefix is not updated, and old settings remain in the file, increasing the size of the file. If you retrieve the file again, the old settings are deleted. If Fast Save is off, the prefix is updated and old settings are removed when you save the file. Also, whenever you save or print a fast-saved file from disk, WordPerfect makes a temporary copy of that file on disk, which requires adequate disk space.

 Changing the Fast Save Option

1. Press Shift-F1 (Setup) or choose Setup from the **File** menu.

   The main Setup menu appears.

2. Select Environment (**3**).

   The Setup: Environment menu appears.

3. Select **5** (Fast Save).	The cursor moves up to the Fast Save option.
4. Press Y to turn Fast Save on or N to turn it off.	The cursor moves back down to `Selection:`.
5. Press F7 (Exit) or click the right mouse button.	You return to your document.

Figure Box (see *Graphics*)

Figures (see *Graphics*)

File, Retrieve (see *Retrieve File*)

File, Save (see *Save File*)

File Directory (see *Location of Files*)

File List (see *List Files*)

File Management (see *List Files*)

Filename on Status Line (see *Edit-Screen Options*)

Find

Function: Searches for a word or phrase in the document or document summary, for a file name, or for files created between a range of dates.

Keystrokes:

Keyboard	*Mouse*
F5 (List), Enter	**File**
9 (Find)	**List Files, Enter**
Select item to search	**Find**
Enter character string	Select item to search
	Enter character string

Example:

```
08-30-90  02:06p              Directory F:\GAME\*.*
Document size:        0   Free: 26,685,440 Used:     524,800    Files:      168

    . Current       <Dir>          ..   Parent      <Dir>
  AC_AIRWO.BAK   3,072  08-09-90 08:18a    AC_AIRWO.DOC   3,072  08-09-90 08:18a
  AC_ARKIS.DOC   3,072  07-23-90 12:51p    AC_ASTYA.BAK   3,072  08-08-90 01:20p
  AC_ASTYA.DOC   3,072  08-08-90 01:43p    AC_BASEB.BAK   3,072  08-29-90 09:25a
  AC_BASEB.DOC   3,072  08-29-90 09:27a    AC_BOYAN.DOC   3,072  07-20-90 09:46a
  AC_CAVEM.BAK   3,072  08-08-90 03:12p    AC_CRYST.DOC   3,072  07-23-90 09:29a
  AC_DOUBL.BAK   3,072  08-14-90 11:59a    AC_DOUBL.DOC   3,072  08-14-90 04:14p
  AC_JACKN.BAK   3,584  08-28-90 04:56p    AC_JACKN.DOC   3,072  08-28-90 04:58p
  AC_LITTL.BAK   3,072  08-29-90 10:52a    AC_LITTL.DOC   3,072  08-29-90 10:54a

  Word pattern: ac *.*
```

List of files found

Search phrase

The List Files screen displays a list of files in the current directory. If the list is short, you may have no problem locating the file you want to work with. With longer lists, however, you may need some help. The Find feature offers such help, letting you search for files by name or date or by a word or phrase that appears in the document or document summary. You can narrow the scope of your search by filtering out some of the files, and you can even use wild-card characters to substitute for characters you can't recall.

When you choose **9 (Find)** from the List Files screen, a menu line appears at the bottom of the screen, listing the following six choices:

Name lets you search for a file by name. You can use wild-card characters to replace characters or to find groups of characters. For example, `ch?.doc` will find CH1.DOC, CH2.DOC, etc. `ch*.doc` will find CHAPTER1.DOC, CHOSEN.DOC, etc. You can also type a partial name. For example, `co` will locate files named COMPARE.DOC, COMMENT.WPF, and COLUMN.TYP. Refer to Table F.1.

Doc Summary allows you to search for text that appears only in your document summary.

First Page tells WordPerfect to search only the first page or first 4,000 words of each document for a word or phrase.

Entire Document tells WordPerfect to search through the entire document to find the search text.

Conditions displays the Conditions options menu, which you can use to narrow the scope of your search to a date or range of dates, or to a specific field in the document summary. Refer to *Find, Conditions*.

Undo lets you back up one step in the search and remove the existing search conditions. Say you search for all files with .DOC as the extension and end up with a list of 40 files. You then search the resulting list for all files that mention roses, for example, and you end up with two files. If you decide that this list is too narrow, you can choose Undo to return to the previous list.

 Searching for a File

1. Press F5 (List) or choose List **Files** from the **File** menu.	WordPerfect displays the path to the current directory. You can enter a path to a different directory, if you wish.
2. Press Enter or enter the path to the directory you want to search.	WordPerfect displays a list of all files in the selected directory.
3. Select **9** (Find).	A menu line appears, listing the six options described above.
4. Select an option to specify which part of the file you want to search: Name, Doc Summary, First Page, or Entire Doc.	WordPerfect asks you to type a search phrase. This phrase can contain up to 39 characters. Case is not relevant.
5. Type the search phrase and press Enter.	To search for a pattern of words, enclose the phrase in quotation marks. See Table F.1 for examples. When you press Enter, WordPerfect searches the files and displays only the files that match your entry.
6. Repeat the steps as needed to restrict the list even further.	If you go too far, select **9** (Find) and **6** (Undo) to back up one step.

Table F.1 *Examples of search phrases.*

Search Phrase	Will Find
To search for file names	
oo	BOOK.DOC, LOOK.DOC, ROOK.BK!
ch*.bk!	CHAPTER1.BK!, CH3.BK!, CHOSEN.BK!
-.bk!	All files except those with the .BK! extension.
To search for text in documents	
Melville	Files that contain the word "Melville."
"general info"	Files that contain character strings like "general info" and "general information."
" general info "	Files that contain the exact phrase "general info."
sales;figures or sales figures	Files that contain both "sales" *and* "figures."
sales,figures	Files that contain "sales" *or* "figures."
-figures	Files that do not contain "figures."

Find, Conditions

Function: Lets you narrow the search performed with Find by entering specific conditions.

Keystrokes: *Keyboard*   *Mouse*
                  F5 (List)   **File**
                  Enter   Enter
                  9 (Find)   **List Files**
                  5 (Conditions)   **Find**
                  Enter conditions   **Conditions**
                  1 (Perform Search) Enter conditions
                                          Perform Search

Example:

```
Find: Conditions                                    Files Selected:   13
      1 - Perform Search
      2 - Reset Conditions
      3 - Revision Date - From    8/18/91
                     To    8/28/91
      4 - Text - Document Summary  Phoenix
                 First Page        Sales info
                 Entire Document   early warning
      5 - Document Summary
          Creation Date - From
                        To
          Document Name
          Document Type
          Author
          Typist
          Subject
          Account
          Keywords
          Abstract
Selection: 1
```

When you select **5** (Conditions) from the Find menu, WordPerfect displays the following list of conditions you can specify for your search:

Reset Conditions lets you clear all previous search conditions from the menu. (Search conditions remain in effect after you use them until you select and change them.)

Revision Date searches for only those files that have been edited and saved between the two dates you enter. To search for files on one specific date, type that date for both the From and To entry. (Be sure to enter the date in the proper format, for example, 8-9-91.)

Text lets you search the document summary, the first page of the document, and the entire document all at once. You can enter different search phrases for each.

Document Summary lets you specify search criteria for one or more items in the document summary, such as the summary's creation date and the author, account, and subject.

If you enter information for more than one item, the file must meet all conditions. For example, if you enter a revision date on the Conditions screen and then perform a search for all files with the .DOC extension, WordPerfect will display only those files that have the .DOC extension *and* have been revised on the given date. The conditions you enter stay in effect until you change the conditions, exit WordPerfect, or reset (clear) the conditions.

Setting Conditions for Find

1. Press F5 (List) or select List Files from the **File** menu.	WordPerfect displays the path to the current directory. You can enter a path to a different directory, if you wish.
2. Press Enter or enter a path to the directory you want to search.	WordPerfect displays a list of files in the selected directory.
3. Select **9** (**Find**).	The Find menu appears.
4. Select **5** (**Conditions**).	The Find Conditions screen appears. Three of the options can be used to restrict the search conditions: Revision Date, Text, and Document Summary.
5. Select an option and enter a search phrase or date.	When you select an option, the cursor moves up to that option. You can then type your search phrase or date. When you press Enter, the cursor moves back down to `Selection:` and you can choose another option.
6. Select **1** (**Perform Search**).	WordPerfect performs the search and displays a list of files that meet the specified conditions.

Tip: The Revision Date condition is useful for backing up the files you edited during the day. Select **2** (**Revision Date**) and type today's date for both the From and To entry. When you perform the search, only those files you edited today will be listed. You can select all the files on the List Files screen by marking them with an asterisk (Home,*) and then copy them to a floppy disk by selecting Copy.

Fine Print (see *Size Attributes*)

Flush Right

Function: Aligns text flush against the right margin.

Keystrokes: *Keyboard*   *Mouse*
Alt-F6 (Flush Right)   Layout
Type text   **Align**
Enter   **Flush Right**
                           Type text
                           Enter

Example:

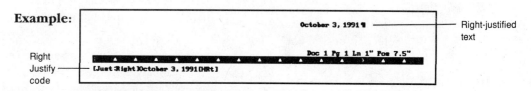

Right-justified text

Right Justify code

The Flush Right feature lets you align a line of text flush against the right margin. You can use it either as you type or after you type to right align an existing line of text. You can also use Flush Right together with the Alt-F4 (Block) feature to right align a block of text.

Typing a Line of Text Flush Right

1. Press Alt-F6 (Flush Right), or display the Layout menu and select **Align** and then **Flush Right**.

WordPerfect inserts the [Flsh Rgt] code to the left of the cursor and moves the cursor to the right margin.

2. Type your text.

As you type, the characters are inserted to the left of the cursor and the cursor remains at the right margin.

3. Press Enter.

WordPerfect inserts the [HRt] code and moves the cursor to the next line. This ends flush right.

Note: To right align several lines in a row as you type, use the Justification Right option on the Format: Line menu instead. Refer to *Format Line*.

 Making an Existing Line Flush Right

1. Make sure the line you want to move flush right ends with a Hard Return code, [HRt].

   The Flush Right code will affect all text up to the first hard return it encounters, but it will right-align only one line of text.

2. Press Alt-F6 (Flush Right), or display the **Layout** menu and select **Align** and then **Flush Right**.

   WordPerfect inserts the [Flsh Rgt] code at the beginning of the line, and pushes the entire line to the right.

3. Press the Down Arrow key.

   This moves the cursor outside of the right-justified line and reformats it, if necessary.

Flush Right with Dot Leaders

Function: Aligns text flush against the right margin and inserts dot leaders before the text.

Keystrokes:

Keyboard	*Mouse*
Alt-F6 (Flush Right)	Layout
Alt-F6 (Flush Right)	**Align**
	Flush Right
	Layout
	Align
	Flush Right

Code: [Flsh Rgt]

Example:

```
File Edit Search Layout Mark Tools Font Graphics Help

Bonsai . . . . . . . . . . . . . . . . . . . . . . . . . . . . . . . . . . . . 25¶
Cypress. . . . . . . . . . . . . . . . . . . . . . . . . . . . . . . . . . . . 45¶
Elm. . . . . . . . . . . . . . . . . . . . . . . . . . . . . . . . . . . . . . 49¶
Fruit Trees. . . . . . . . . . . . . . . . . . . . . . . . . . . . . . . . . . 55¶
¶
```

Sometimes, it is useful to insert dot leaders before text that is right aligned. For example, in a table of contents, like the one show in the example, it might be difficult for the reader to determine which page numbers correspond to which headings; the dot leaders can help significantly.

 Typing Text Flush Right with Dot Leaders

1. Type the text that you want to appear on the left, if any.

For example, if you're typing a table of contents, you can type the headings on the left.

2. Press Alt-F6 (Flush Right) twice, or display the Layout menu and select **Align** and then **Flush Right** twice.

WordPerfect inserts the [Flsh Rgt] code to the left of the cursor and moves the cursor to the right margin, inserting dot leaders between the text on the left and the cursor.

3. Type the text that you want to appear flush right.

For example, you might type the page number on which the heading appears.

4. Press Enter.

WordPerfect inserts a [HRt] code and moves the cursor to the next line.

Font Directory (see *Path for Downloadable Fonts and Printer Files*)

Fonts (see also *Cartridges and Fonts*)

Function: Lets you change the default font for new documents, or the default font for the document on the Edit screen, or the font for the document on the Edit screen.

Keystrokes:

Keyboard	*Mouse*
Font Change for All New Documents:	Font Change for All New Documents:
Shift-F7 (Print)	File
S (Select Printer)	Print

3 (Edit)   Select Printer
5 (Initial Base Font)   Edit
Highlight font   Initial Base Font
Select font   Highlight font
F7 (Exit)   Select font
                                   Right mouse button

Font Change for Entire   Font Change for Entire Document
Document on Screen: on Screen:
Shift-F8 (Format)   Layout
3 (Document)   Document
3 (Initial Base Font)   Initial Base Font
Highlight font   Double-click font
1 (Select)   Right mouse button
F7 (Exit)

Font Change Within   Font Change Within Document:
Document: Font
Ctrl-F8 (Font)   Base Font
4 (Base Font)   Highlight font
Highlight font   Select font
Select font

Code: [Font:]

Example:

```
Document: Initial Font

   Roman  5cpi
   Roman  5cpi Italic
   Roman  6cpi
   Roman 10cpi Italic
   Roman 12cpi
   Roman 12cpi Italic
 * Roman 15cpi

 1 Select; N Name search: 1
```

In WordPerfect, a font represents a set of characters in a particular typeface, size, and weight (bold or italic). For example, Helvetica 12-point Bold is a font; Helvetica is the typeface, Bold is the weight, and 12-point is the size. Point size is a vertical measurement, and there are approximately 72 points in one inch. The fonts that will be available for your use depend on the printer. Laser printers and dot-matrix printers usually include several built-in fonts; for laser printers and certain dot-matrix printers, you can purchase additional fonts on disks (called *soft fonts*) or on cartridges.

When you install your printer, WordPerfect defines one font as the *Initial Base Font*; this font will be used to format all new documents unless you override it using one of the other font options, *Initial Base Font* on the Format Document menu, or *Base Font* on the Font menu. You can change the Initial Base Font for all new documents by using the Initial Base Font option on the Select Printer: Edit menu, but it will not change previously saved documents that were created when a different Initial Base Font was in use. Like all default format settings, such as margins and line spacing, changing the Initial Base Font does not insert a code into your document. Instead, the font information is saved in the document prefix when you save the file.

You can use the Initial Base Font option on the Format Document menu to change the Initial Base font for the document currently on the Edit screen. This action does not insert a code into your document, but saves the information in the document prefix. It only alters the document that is currently on the Edit screen.

Within a document, you can use the Font key (Ctrl-F8) or pull-down Font menu to change the font itself, or to change the *size* or *appearance* of the font currently in use. For instance, you can change the Base Font from Courier to Times Roman; change the appearance of the base font currently in use to bold, underline, double underline, italics, or small caps; or change the size of the base font in use to fine, small, large, very large, or extra large. These size and appearance changes are called *attributes,* and they are printer-dependent. For this reason, you should see how your printer interprets them before using them extensively in your documents. If you are dissatisfied, you can use the printer program (PTR.EXE) to change them (refer to *Automatic Font Changes*). Any change that you make using the Base Font option on the Font menu inserts a code into your document, so it affects only the document on the Edit screen, beginning at the cursor position.

 Changing the Default Font for New Documents

1.	Press Shift-F7 (Print) or select **Print** from the **File** menu.	The main Print menu appears.
2.	Choose **S** (**Select Printer**).	A list of installed printers appears on the Print: Select Printer menu.
3.	Highlight the printer for which you want to change the default for the Initial Base Font.	
4.	Select **3** (**Edit**).	The Select Printer: Edit menu appears.

5. Select **5** (Initial Base Font).	A list of installed fonts appears.
6. Highlight the font of your choice and press Enter or double-click on the font. If you are using a Postscript printer, select the point size.	This returns you to the Select Printer: Edit menu.
7. Press F7 (Exit) or click the right mouse button three times.	This saves the font change.

All new documents will use this as the Initial Base Font. Files previously saved will retain the initial font that was in use when you saved them. Both Document Initial Base Font and Base Font on the Font menu override this setting.

 ## Changing Initial Font for the Document on the Edit Screen

1. Press Shift-F8 (Format) or display the Layout menu.	A list of format options appears.
2. Select **Document (3)**.	The Format: Document menu appears.
3. Select **3** (Initial Base Font).	A list of installed fonts appears on the Document: Initial Font screen.
4. Highlight the font you want to use and press Enter or double-click on the font. If you have a Postscript printer, enter the point size.	This returns you to the Format: Document menu. The font you selected is shown next to option 3.
5. Press F7 (Exit) or click the right mouse button.	This returns you to the Edit screen.

This setting now overrides the Initial Base Font setting on the Printer menu, for this document only. Only a change to the Base Font on the Font key or Font menu will override it.

Changing the Document Initial Font changes the font for all headers, footers, endnotes, equations, and graphics box captions, unless you changed the Base Font and the feature includes a Base Font code in the special screen in which you created it. However, if the document also includes a Graphics Box Option code, Footnote Options code, or Endnotes Options code, any footnotes, endnotes, equations, or graphic box captions will use the font that is in effect at the position of the options code pertaining to the feature.

Changing Fonts Within a Document

1. Position the cursor where you want to change the base font.

2. Press Ctrl-F8 (Font) or display the Font menu.   A list of font options appears.

3. Select 4 (Base Font) or Base Font from the menu.   A list of installed fonts appears.

4. Highlight the font you want to use and press Enter or double-click on the font. If you have a Postscript printer, enter the point size.   This returns you to your document. WordPerfect inserts a font code at the cursor position. This font is in effect from this point to the point at which you change it again, or until the end of the document. It overrides both the Document Initial Font and the Printer Initial Font.

 Tip: Base Font codes do not change headers or footers, unless the font code appears before the header or footer code. Base Font codes do not change footnotes or endnotes, unless you include a Footnote or Endnote Options code after the font code.

 Tip: You can use different fonts for graphic figure captions, headers and footers, and footnotes and endnotes by inserting a Base Font code when you create or edit one. The change affects only that specific feature, not the text within the document itself.

Fonts, Download to Printer (see *Initialize Printer*)

Footers (see *Headers and Footers*)

Footnotes (see *Endnotes and Footnotes*)

Force Odd/Even Page (see also *Page Numbering*)

Function: Forces a page number to be odd or even, inserting a soft page break if necessary.

Keystrokes:

Keyboard	*Mouse*
Shift-F8 (Format)	Layout
2 (Page)	Page
2 (Force Odd/Even Page)	Force Odd/Even Page
1 (Odd) or 2 (Even)	Odd or Even
F7 (Exit)	Right mouse button

Codes: [Force:Odd]
[Force:Even]

Occasionally, you may want to force a page to be numbered as an odd or even page. For example, you may want the first page of a manual to be an odd page so that it appears as a right-hand page. The Force Odd/Even Page feature lets you do just that.

 Forcing an Odd/Even Page

1. Move the cursor to the top of the page where you want to force the Odd/Even page.

The cursor must be at the top of the page so that if WordPerfect has to insert a page break, it will be *before* the page instead of in the middle of it.

2.	Press Shift-F8 (Format) or display the Layout menu.	A list of formatting options appears.
3.	Select **Page** (**2**).	The Format: Page menu appears.
4.	Select **2** (**Force Odd/Even Page**).	WordPerfect prompts you to choose odd or even.
5.	Select **1** (**Odd**) or **2** (**Even**).	The first option, Odd, forces the text following the cursor to start printing on an odd-numbered page. The second option, Even, forces it to print on an even-numbered page.
6.	Press F7 (Exit) or click the right mouse button.	WordPerfect inserts a [Force:Odd] or [Force:Even] code at the cursor position.

If the page number must be changed, WordPerfect inserts a Soft Page code [SPg], and the pages that follow are renumbered accordingly. Also, the page number on the status line will change if the page has been forced to become another number.

Forced Insert/Typeover

Function: Ensures you are in Insert or Typeover mode when you are using a macro.

Keystrokes: *Keyboard (Forced Insert)*
Home,Home,Ins

Keyboard (Forced Typeover)
Home,Ins

If you're creating a macro that inserts text in your document, and you want to be sure that Insert mode is on before text is typed, use Forced Insert instead of the Ins key when defining the macro. Otherwise, the macro might type over and erase existing text. If you have the macro press the Ins key, and you're already in Insert mode, the toggle command will put the macro in Typeover mode. Instead of toggling Insert mode on or off, Forced Insert always sets the mode to Insert.

Forcing Insert Mode

1. Begin creating your macro until you get to the point where you want to be in Insert mode.

2. Press Home,Home,Ins.   This will force WordPerfect into Insert mode when you run the macro.

3. Continue creating your macro.

If you're creating a macro that types over text in your document, and you want to be sure that Typeover mode is on before text is typed, use Forced Typeover. Otherwise, the macro may insert text without typing over and removing the unwanted text. If you have the macro press the Ins key and you're already in Typeover mode, the toggle command will put the macro in Insert mode. Instead of toggling Insert mode on or off, Forced Typeover always sets the mode to Typeover.

 Forcing Typeover Mode

1. Begin creating your macro until you get to the point where you want to be in Typeover mode.

2. Press Home,Ins.   This will force WordPerfect into Typeover mode when you run the macro.

3. Continue creating your macro.

Forced Page Break (see *New Page*)

Foreign Characters (see *Compose Key*)

Foreign Languages

Function: Lets you insert a foreign language code so that WordPerfect will use the speller, thesaurus, and hyphenation dictionaries for that language—provided you have purchased and installed them—and use the language for the sort order and date format.

Keystrokes:

Keyboard	*Mouse*
Shift-F8 (Format)	Layout
4 (Other)	Other
4 (Language)	Language
language code	*language code*
F7 (Exit)	Right mouse button

Code: [Lang:xx]

Example:

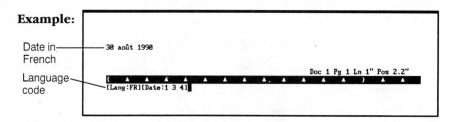

Date in French → 30 août 1990

Doc 1 Pg 1 Ln 1" Pos 2.2"

Language code → [Lang:FR][Date:1 3 4]

If you write or edit in a foreign language, you can use the Foreign Languages feature to insert a language code for any of the languages shown in Table F.2. Whenever you use this feature, it affects several options. If you insert a date in the document, WordPerfect formats the date for that language. If you sort that section of the document, it will be sorted according to the alphabet of the selected language. If you purchased and installed special Foreign Language dictionaries from WordPerfect Corporation for the speller, thesaurus, and hyphenation feature, WordPerfect will use the appropriate dictionary whenever you spell check or hyphenate the document or ask for a list of synonyms. This feature does not change the language of WordPerfect's menu options.

> **Tip:** If you place the language code into Document Initial Codes, it will affect the entire document. In addition, the code will change the `Continued...` message that appears when a footnote is too long to fit on a page, and the graphics box captions "Figure" and "Table." Refer to *Initial Codes*.

 ## Changing the Reference Language

1.	Press Shift-F8 (Format) or display the **Layout** menu.	A list of formatting options appears.
2.	Select **Other** (4).	The Format: Other menu appears.
3.	Select 4 (**Language**).	You are prompted to enter a two-character code for the language you want to use. See Table F.2 or press F3 (Help) to see a list.
4.	Type a two-character code for the language you want to use, and press Enter.	The cursor moves down to `Selection:`.
5.	Press F7 (Exit) or click the right mouse button.	WordPerfect inserts the [Lang:xx] code at the cursor position. From this point till you change the option, WordPerfect will use this language for reference.

Table F.2 *Language codes.*

Language	Code
Afrikaans	AF
Catalan	CA
Croatian	HR
Czechoslovakian	CZ
Danish	DK

continued

Table F.2 *(continued)*

Language	Code
Dutch	NL
English (Australian)	OZ
English (United Kingdom)	UK
English (United States)	US
Finnish	SU
French (Canada)	CF
French (France)	FR
German (Germany)	DE
German (Switzerland)	SD
Greek	GR
Hungarian	HU
Icelandic	IS
Italian	IT
Norwegian	NO
Portuguese (Brazil)	BR
Portuguese (Portugal)	PO
Russian	RU
Slovak	SL
Spanish	ES
Swedish	SV
Ukrainian	YK

 Note: The Foreign Languages feature stays in effect only in the current document, and only up to the point at which you insert another such code.

Format (see also *Initial Codes* and *Initial Settings*)

Function: Offers various formatting options for the current document.

Keystrokes:

Keyboard	*Mouse*
Shift-F8 (Format)	Layout
1 (Line), 2 (Page) 3 (Document), or 4 (Other)	Line, Page, Document, or Other
Select option	Select option
Enter change	Enter change
F7 (Exit)	Right mouse button

Example:

```
Format
    1 - Line
                Hyphenation                    Line Spacing
                Justification                  Margins Left/Right
                Line Height                    Tab Set
                Line Numbering                 Widow/Orphan Protection
    2 - Page
                Center Page (top to bottom)    Page Numbering
                Force Odd/Even Page            Paper Size/Type
                Headers and Footers            Suppress
                Margins Top/Bottom
    3 - Document
                Display Pitch                  Redline Method
                Initial Codes/Font             Summary
    4 - Other
                Advance                        Overstrike
                Conditional End of Page        Printer Functions
                Decimal Characters             Underline Spaces/Tabs
                Language                       Border Options
    Selection: 0
```

The Format menu leads to the following four menus, which you can use to change various formatting features for the current document:

Line lets you change several settings that control the way lines are formatted across the page, including hyphenation, justification, line spacing, line height, left and right margins, and tabs. Make sure the cursor is before or at the beginning of the line you want to affect before choosing one of these options. Refer to *Format Line*.

Page features options that let you control the layout of your pages. For example, you can enter the paper size and type on which you intend to print, center the page between the top and bottom margins, add a header or footer, or change the top and bottom margin settings. Before you choose one of these options, make sure the cursor is at the top of the page you want to affect. Some options affect only one page; others affect all pages that follow. Refer to *Format Page*.

Document lets you change several format settings for the entire document. For example, you can change the initial base font, initial codes, and redline method, and attach a summary to the document. You can change these options from anywhere in the document; they affect the entire document. Refer to *Format Document*.

Other includes several advanced formatting options. For example, you can use overstrike to print two or more characters in one position, change the decimal/align character and/or thousands' separator, and use Conditional End of Page to keep a specific number of lines from being divided by a page break.

Changing Format Settings

1. Press Shift-F8 (Format) or display the Layout menu.	The four Format submenus are listed.
2. Select one of the four Format submenus: **Line**, **Page**, **Document**, or **Other**.	A menu appears, displaying a list of formatting options, along with the current setting for each option.
3. Select the option whose setting you want to change, and enter the new setting.	When you select an option, the cursor moves up to that option, so you can type a new setting. For certain items, you must press Enter after typing your change to move the cursor back down to Selection:. From there, you can select another option.
4. Press F7 (Exit) or click the right mouse button.	This returns you to the Edit screen and saves the settings you just entered. The changes affect only the current document. To change the default settings for new documents, use the Setup Initial Codes option. (See *Initial Settings*.)

Format Document

Function: Lets you enter certain format settings for the entire document on the Edit screen.

Keystrokes:

Keyboard	*Mouse*
Shift-F8 (Format)	Layout
3 (Document)	Document
Select option	Select option
Enter change	Enter change
F7 (Exit)	Right mouse button

Example:

```
Format: Document
        1 - Display Pitch - Automatic  Yes
                            Width       0.1"

        2 - Initial Codes

        3 - Initial Base Font           Roman 10cpi

        4 - Redline Method              Printer Dependent

        5 - Summary
Selection: 0
```

The Format: Document menu lets you set formatting options for the document currently on the Edit screen. Any settings you enter here do not enter a code. When you display the Format: Document menu, the following five options appear:

Display Pitch lets you change the amount of space used by each character on screen. It can be useful when columnar text overlaps or when features such as tabs appear to be using too much space on screen. Refer to *Display Pitch*.

Initial Codes lets you view and change any initial codes that were set through the Setup Initial Codes option. Changes you make in Document Initial Codes override the initial codes for this document only. These codes do not appear in the Reveal Codes screen of your document, but they do control the overall format for the document. These codes are useful for formatting that must affect the entire document, or in primary merge files. Refer to *Initial Codes*.

Initial Base Font allows you to choose the default font for this document, and overrides the Initial Base Font set through the Select Printer: Edit menu. Like Document Initial Codes, it does not insert a formatting code. You can override this setting for a block of text by pressing Ctrl-F8 (Font) or by displaying the Font menu and choosing the Base Font option.

Redline Method allows you to change how redlined text will be printed. Refer to *Redline Method*.

Summary lets you create or edit a document summary for the current document on the Edit screen, including information such as date, author, subject, and account. This summary can help you locate the file later. Refer to *Document Management/Summary*.

Changing a Document's Format Settings

1. Press Shift-F8 (Format) or display the Layout menu.

   The list of formatting options appears.

2. Select **Document** (3).

   The Format: Document menu appears.

3. Select an option and enter your change.

   When you select an option, the cursor moves up to that option. For certain items, you must press Enter to move the cursor back down to Selection:. From there, you can choose another option.

4. Press F7 (Exit) or click the right mouse button.

   WordPerfect saves your settings and returns you to your document.

Format Line

Function: Provides several formatting options that affect lines.

Keystrokes: *Keyboard*   *Mouse*
Shift-F8 (Format)   Layout
1 (Line)   Line
Select option   Select option
Enter change   Enter change
F7 (Exit)   Right mouse button

Example:

```
Format: Line
    1 - Hyphenation                          No
    2 - Hyphenation Zone - Left              10%
                           Right             4%
    3 - Justification                        Full
    4 - Line Height                          Auto
    5 - Line Numbering                       No
    6 - Line Spacing                         1
    7 - Margins - Left                       1.5"
                  Right                      0.5"
    8 - Tab Set                              Rel: -1", every 0.5"
    9 - Widow/Orphan Protection              No
Selection: 0
```

The Format: Line menu lets you set formatting options that affect lines of text, such as justification and left and right margins. Any settings you enter here override the settings you may have entered on the Setup: Initial Codes screen (refer to *Initial Settings*). Whenever you change a format setting using this menu, WordPerfect inserts a code in the text, and it takes affect at that position. You can use this menu to change the following options:

Hyphenation turns WordPerfect's automatic hyphenation on or off, or lets you change the *zone* in which a word must fall in order to be subject to hyphenation. Refer to *Hyphenation* and *Hyphenation Zone*.

Justification lets you select the method of justification: left, right, center, or full. Full is the default. Refer to *Justification*.

Line Height specifies how much vertical space is allotted each line from the bottom of one line to the bottom of the next (baseline to baseline). This option is set to automatic, but you can change the setting to fixed and specify a different number. Refer to *Line Height*.

Line Numbering turns the line numbering feature on or off. You can turn line numbering on to print numbers next to each line of text, as in a legal document. Refer to *Line Numbering*.

Line Spacing controls the spacing between lines. It is set to single spaced, but you can change it to double, triple, or even a fraction, such as .5. Refer to *Line Spacing*.

Margins lets you set the left and right margins for your document or a section of your document. Refer to *Margins, Left/Right*.

Tab Set lets you change your tab stop settings; insert right, decimal, or center tabs; use dot leaders; or change to absolute tabs. Refer to *Tab, Set*.

Widow/Orphan Protection ensures that at least two lines of a paragraph appear on the same page. The default is No, so the first line of a paragraph may appear alone at the end of a page, or the last line of a paragraph may appear at the top of the following page. Refer to *Widow/Orphan Protection*.

 ## Changing Line Format Settings

1. Position the cursor at the place where you want the change to take effect.

2. Press Shift-F8 (Format) or display the Layout menu.   A list of format options appears.

3. Select Line (1).

The Format: Line menu appears.

4. Select an option and enter your change.

When you select an option, the cursor moves up to that option. In some options, you must press Enter to move the cursor back down to `Selection:`. From there, you can choose another option.

5. Press F7 (Exit) or click the right mouse button.

WordPerfect returns you to your document and inserts a Line Format code at the cursor location.

Format Other

Function: Lets you change settings for several advanced features, including Conditional End of Page, Advance, Language, and Border options for tables and graphic boxes.

Keystrokes:

Keyboard	*Mouse*
Shift-F8 (Format)	Layout
4 (Other)	Other
Select option	Select option
Enter change	Enter change
F7 (Exit)	F7 (Exit)

Example:

```
Format: Other
        1 — Advance
        2 — Conditional End of Page
        3 — Decimal/Align Character      .
              Thousands' Separator       ,
        4 — Language                     US
        5 — Overstrike
        6 — Printer Functions
        7 — Underline — Spaces           Yes
                        Tabs             No
        8 — Border Options
Selection: 0
```

The Format: Other menu lets you set formatting options for the following special formatting and printing options:

Advance offsets printed text in the direction and distance you specify. Refer to *Advance*.

Conditional End of Page protects a specified number of lines from being split by a page break. See *Conditional End of Page*.

Decimal/Align Character and Thousands' Separator lets you change the alignment character used with Tab Align, Math, and Decimal Tabs and the character separating thousands from hundreds. See *Decimal/Align Character* and *Thousands' Separator*.

Language changes the language that WordPerfect uses to format the date and time and to sort text alphabetically. If you purchased spelling, thesaurus, and hyphenation dictionaries in another language, this option instructs WordPerfect to use the specified dictionary. Refer to *Foreign Languages*.

Overstrike lets you print one character on top of another. Refer to *Overstrike*.

Printer Functions offers several options useful in desktop publishing applications, including kerning, leading, word and letter spacing, and baseline placement. Refer to *Baseline Placement for Typesetters*, *Kerning*, and *Leading Adjustment*.

Underline Spaces/Tabs tells WordPerfect whether or not to underline spaces and tabs when text is underlined or double-underlined. Refer to *Underline Spaces and Tabs*.

Border Options lets you change settings for the border options for tables and graphics boxes.

 Entering Settings for Special Formatting Options

1. Position the cursor where you want the format change to take effect.	
2. Press Shift-F8 (Format) or display the **Layout** menu.	A list of formatting options appears.
3. Select Other (4).	The Format: Other menu appears.
4. Select an option and enter your change.	When you select an option, the cursor moves up to that option. For some options, you must press Enter to move the cursor back down to Selection:. From there, you can choose another option.

5. Press F7 (Exit) or click the right mouse button.

WordPerfect returns you to the Edit screen.

Format Page

Function: Controls the layout of the page.

Keystrokes:

Keyboard	*Mouse*
Shift-F8 (Format)	Layout
2 (Page)	Page
Select option	Select option
Enter change	Enter change
F7 (Exit)	Right mouse button

Example:

```
Format: Page
     1 - Center Page (top to bottom)      No
     2 - Force Odd/Even Page
     3 - Headers
     4 - Footers
     5 - Margins - Top                    1"
                   Bottom                 1"
     6 - Page Numbering
     7 - Paper Size                       8.5" x 11"
               Type                       Standard
     8 - Suppress (this page only)
Selection: 0
```

The Format: Page menu provides formatting options that affect the layout of your page or pages. Before you choose one of these options, make sure the cursor is at the top of the first page or the page you want the change to affect:

Center Page Top to Bottom centers the text between the top and bottom margins on the current page only, and only when printed. Refer to *Center Page, Top to Bottom.*

Force Odd/Even Page forces the current page to be an odd- or even-numbered page and, if necessary, creates a page break, numbers the page, and renumbers the following pages. Refer to *Force Odd/Even Page.*

Headers and *Footers* let you enter standard text, such as a heading, that you want printed at the top or bottom of every page. Refer to *Headers and Footers.*

Margins, Top and Bottom allows you to change the setting for the top and bottom margins for current page and all subsequent pages. Refer to *Margins, Top/Bottom.*

Page Numbering lets you have WordPerfect automatically number pages. You can select a numbering style and a position where the number should appear. You can also choose to start numbering with a new number. Refer to *Page Numbering*.

Paper Size/Type lets you copy, edit, create, or delete a paper size and type, or select one for the document on the Edit screen. Refer to *Paper Size and Type*.

Suppress lets you turn off page numbering and all the headers and footers or individual headers or footers for a given page. Also lets you turn off only page numbering or change the page number position to bottom center. Refer to *Suppress*.

 Entering Page Format Settings

1. Position the cursor at the top of the page on which you want the format change to take effect.

2. Press Shift-F8 (Format) or display the **Layout** menu.

   A list of formatting options appears.

3. Select **Page (2)**.

   The Format: Page menu appears.

4. Select an option and enter your change.

   When you select an option, the cursor moves up to that option or it displays another screen with more options.

5. Press F7 (Exit) or click the right mouse button.

   WordPerfect returns you to the Edit screen.

 Tip: When you change one of the formatting options on the **Line**, **Page**, or **Other** menu, WordPerfect inserts a code in the text. You can view the codes by pressing Alt-F3 or F11 (Reveal Codes) or by selecting **Reveal Codes** from the Edit menu. However, the codes may not give you a clear idea of how the formatting change will affect the document. To see how the document will look in print, use View Document: Press Shift-F7 (Print) or select **Print** from the **File** menu and select **6** (View Document).

Forms (see *Paper Size and Type*)

Forward Search (see *Search*)

Function Key Template (see *Function Keys*)

Function Keys

Function: Give you access to WordPerfect's features.

Keystrokes: *Refer to Table F.3.*

Table F.3 Function keys.

Key	Alone	Shift	Alt	Ctrl
F1	Cancel	Setup	Thesaurus	Shell
F2	→Search	←Search	Replace	Spell
F3	Help	Switch	Reveal Codes	Screen
F4	→Indent	→Indent←	Block	Move
F5	List	Date/Outline	Mark Text	Text In/Out
F6	Bold	Center	Flush Right	Tab Align
F7	Exit	Print	Columns/Table	Footnote
F8	Underline	Format	Style	Font
F9	End Field	Merge Codes	Graphics	Merge/Sort
F10	Save	Retrieve	Macro	Macro Define
F11	Reveal Codes			
F12	Block			

G

Generate (see also *Cross-Reference*; *Index, Mark Text*; *Table of Authorities*; *Table of Contents*; and *Lists*)

Function: Generates lists, indexes, tables of contents, tables of authorities, and indexes, and updates cross-references.

Keystrokes:

Keyboard	*Mouse*
Alt-F5 (Mark Text)	Mark
6 (Generate)	Generate
5 (Generate Tables, Indexes, Cross-References, etc.)	Generate Tables, Indexes, Cross-References, etc.
Y (Replace) or N (Cancel)	Y (Replace) or N (Cancel)

Code: [End Def]

Example:

```
Mark Text: Generate
    1 - Remove Redline Markings and Strikeout Text from Document
    2 - Compare Screen and Disk Documents and Add Redline and Strikeout
    3 - Expand Master Document
    4 - Condense Master Document
    5 - Generate Tables, Indexes, Cross-References, etc.

Existing tables, lists, and indexes will be replaced.  Continue? Yes (No)
```

The Generate Tables, Indexes, Cross-References, etc., option on the Mark Text menu performs the last step in producing lists, indexes, tables, and cross-references. Once you have marked your text, inserted Endnote Placement codes, and defined your tables, lists, and indexes, you must use the Generate option to create the tables, lists, and indexes, and to update your cross-references. If you have any previous tables, lists, or indexes in the document, they are replaced with newer, up-to-date versions.

Generating Tables, Lists, Indexes, and Cross-References

1. Press Alt-F5 (Mark Text) or display the **Mark** menu.

   The Mark Text menu appears.

2. Select **Generate** (6).

   The Mark Text: Generate menu appears.

3. Select **5** (Generate Tables, Indexes, Cross-References, etc.).

   A message appears, warning you that you are about to replace any existing tables, indexes, or cross-references.

4. Press Y or Enter to continue or N to cancel the operation.

   If you press Y or Enter, the generation begins. A counter at the bottom of the screen shows the progress of the generation. When WordPerfect has finished, the lists, tables, indexes, etc., appear, and WordPerfect inserts an [End Def] code at the end of each one.

 Caution: If you edit your document later, make sure you perform this operation again to update your tables, lists, indexes, and cross-references. Also, be careful not to delete any [Def Mark] or [End: Def] codes. If you delete an [End: Def] code, WordPerfect will regenerate the table or list but will not replace it. You'll still have the old lists, index, table, and so forth in your document as well as the new ones. If you erase the [Def Mark] code, leaving the [End: Def] code, WordPerfect won't be able to generate and will warn you that there is an [End: Def] without a matching [Def Mark] code.

Go *(see Printer Control)*

Go to DOS (see also *Go to Shell*)

Function: Lets you go to DOS without exiting WordPerfect.

Keystrokes: *Keyboard* *Mouse*
Ctrl-F1 (Shell) **File**
1 (Go to DOS) or **Go to DOS**
2 (DOS Command) **Go to DOS or DOS Command**
Perform DOS function Perform DOS function
Type exit Type exit
Enter Enter

Example:

```
        Microsoft(R) MS-DOS(R)  Version 3.30
                  (C)Copyright Microsoft Corp 1981-1987


        Enter 'EXIT' to return to WordPerfect
        D:\WP51\FILES>
```

DOS
command
prompt

You can run a DOS command in either of two ways without exiting WordPerfect: If your computer has enough memory, you can go to the regular DOS screen without leaving WordPerfect and perform one or more DOS commands or run another program, or you can enter a single DOS command and then return to WordPerfect. Before you begin, you need to be aware of a few precautions:

- Do not type wp to return to WordPerfect when you're done. Instead, press F7 (Exit) or type exit and press Enter. Otherwise, you'll load another copy of WordPerfect into memory.

- Do not use CHKDSK/F, DELETE, RENAME, or any other commands that may affect WordPerfect or WordPerfect's program files.

- You can run another program from the DOS prompt without exiting WordPerfect, but be aware of your memory limitations. If you try to enter a command that goes beyond the limitations of RAM, DOS will display an error message and return you to your document.

Going to DOS

1. Press Ctrl-F1 (Shell) or display the File menu and select **Go to DOS**.

   If you are running WordPerfect under the Shell, Go to DOS won't be an option. Refer to *Go to Shell*. If you use the File menu, you must select **Go to DOS** once and then select it from the next menu.

2. Select **1** (Go to DOS) or **2** (DOS Command).

   Select Go to DOS if you want to run another program or execute more than one command. Select DOS Command if you want to run only one command. If you select **Go** to DOS, the WordPerfect Edit screen disappears, and the DOS prompt appears. If you choose DOS Command, a DOS command prompt appears on the status line, asking you to type the command.

3. Enter your DOS command, perform an operation in DOS, or run another program.

   DOS executes the command. If you chose DOS **Command**, DOS executes the command and then prompts you to press any key to continue. When you press a key, you are automatically returned to the Edit screen.

4. If you chose Go to DOS and you are now ready to return to WordPerfect, type `exit` and press Enter.

   You are returned to the Edit screen.

Go To Key

Function: Move cursor quickly to specified location.

Keystrokes: *Keyboard*   *Mouse*
                       Ctrl-Home   Search
                                         Goto

The Go To key lets you jump from one location to another within the document in a variety of ways. For example, you can move to the next occurrence of a letter or punctuation mark, to the top or bottom of a page, or to a specific page number. To use the Go To feature, press Ctrl-Home and then enter one of the keystrokes listed in Table G.1 in response to the Go to prompt.

Table G.1 *Go To keystrokes.*

Keystroke	Cursor Goes to
character	Specified character (case sensitive), if the character appears within the next 20,000 characters
Enter	Hard return
Up Arrow	Top of current page
Down Arrow	Bottom of current page
page number	Top of specified page number
Alt-F4 (Block)	Beginning of marked block
Left Arrow or Right Arrow in columns or tables	Other column or cell (in tables)
Home,Left Arrow or Right Arrow in columns or tables	First column or cell at the left or right side of the page
Up Arrow or Down Arrow in columns or tables	First or last line in the column or cell

If you used any of the following keys, press Ctrl-Home twice to return the cursor to its previous location:

Alt-F4 (Block): To rehighlight the last block used, press Alt-F4; then press Ctrl-Home twice
Esc (Escape)
Ctrl-Home (Go To)
Home,arrow key
PgUp or PgDn
Alt-F2 (Replace)
– or + on numeric keypad or Home,Up Arrow or Home,Down Arrow (Screen Up or Down)
F2 (→Search) or Shift-F2 (←Search)

Go to Shell *(see also* Go to DOS *and* Clipboard*)*

Function: If you started WordPerfect from the Library or Office Shell menu, lets you go to the Shell without exiting WordPerfect.

Keystrokes:
Keyboard	*Mouse*
Ctrl-F1 (Shell)	**File**
1 (Go to Shell)	**G**oto Shell
Perform Shell function	Go to Shell
Select WordPerfect	Perform Shell function
program letter	Select WordPerfect program letter
Shortcut	
Alt-Shift-space bar	

Example:

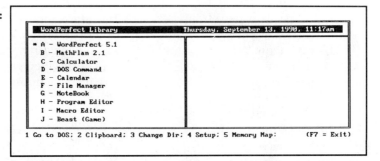

```
┌──────────────────────────────────────────────────────────────────┐
│ WordPerfect Library              Thursday, September 13, 1990, 11:17am │
│                                                                    │
│ * A - WordPerfect 5.1                                              │
│   B - MathPlan 2.1                                                 │
│   C - Calculator                                                   │
│   D - DOS Command                                                  │
│   E - Calendar                                                     │
│   F - File Manager                                                 │
│   G - NoteBook                                                     │
│   H - Program Editor                                               │
│   I - Macro Editor                                                 │
│   J - Beast (Game)                                                 │
│                                                                    │
│ 1 Go to DOS; 2 Clipboard; 3 Change Dir; 4 Setup; 5 Memory Map;    (F7 = Exit) │
└──────────────────────────────────────────────────────────────────┘
```

If you are running WordPerfect under the WordPerfect Office or WordPerfect Library Shell, you can use a Shell feature, start another program, or run a DOS command without exiting WordPerfect. Before you begin, you need to be aware of a few precautions:

- If you are using the WordPerfect Library, you should use version 2.0 dated 6/30/88 or later with WordPerfect 5.1. If you use an earlier version, you may have trouble with some of the features.

- If you're running a DOS command from Shell, do not type wp to return to WordPerfect when you're done. Instead, press F7 (Exit) or type exit and press Enter. Otherwise, you'll load another copy of WordPerfect into memory.

- If you're in DOS, do not use CHKDSK/F, DELETE, RENAME, or any other commands that may affect WordPerfect or WordPerfect's program files.

- You can run another program from the Shell without exiting WordPerfect, but be aware of your memory limitations. If you try to enter a command that goes beyond the limitations of RAM, Shell will display an error message.

 Going to Shell

1. Press Ctrl-F1 (Shell) or display the File menu and select Goto Shell.

   If you use the File menu, you must select Goto Shell once and then select it from the next menu. A list of Shell and Clipboard options appears.

2. Select **1** (Go to Shell).

   The Shell menu appears. Since WordPerfect is still in memory, an asterisk appears next to the WordPerfect option in the Shell menu.

3. Start another program, use a Shell feature, or go to DOS to run a DOS command.

   The Shell offers several features, including a calculator, clipboard, and notebook.

4. When you are finished, select the WordPerfect program letter from the Shell menu or highlight the WordPerfect option and press Enter.

   This returns you to the WordPerfect Edit screen. If you were working on a document, it should still be there.

Graphics, Conversion (GRAPHCNV.EXE)

Function: Converts graphics files that were created in other formats into WordPerfect (.WPG) format.

Keystrokes: *Keyboard*
Go to DOS
Change to the directory that contains the WordPerfect program files
graphcnv
Enter

drive:\path\filename.ext (for input file)
Enter
drive:\path\filename.wpg (for output file)
Enter
Any key

Example:

```
WordPerfect Graphics Conversion Utility
Version 1.1, (C)Copyright 1989, WordPerfect Corp., Orem UT

For HELP, type "graphcnv /h" at the DOS prompt
Press F1 to cancel

Enter name of file to convert: d:\pzp\hg\fig2-1.pzi          Input file
Enter name of output file: D:\WP51\files\FIG2-1.WPG

Converting:                                                  Output file

D:\PZP\HG\FIG2-1.PZI (.PLT) to D:\WP51\FILES\FIG2-1.WPG (.WPG)
```

Whenever you use the Graphics Figure Box, Table Box, Text Box, or User Box option to import a graphics file that was created in a supported format into your document, WordPerfect automatically converts the graphics file into the .WPG format. However, some formats cannot be converted this way, including AutoCAD's .PXF files or any other files in the .DXF format. To convert them, you can use the GRAPHCNV.EXE program. You can also use the Conversion program to convert several files at once or to use the start-up options in Table G.2. Also, if you are using the Graphic on Disk contents type to save space, you can save time printing or viewing the graphic by converting it beforehand.

Note: In order to run the Graphics Conversion program, you must have installed the Utilities when you installed WordPerfect. You cannot copy the Conversion program directly from the WordPerfect Program disk. If you did not install the Utilities, do so before you try to use the Conversion program.

Note: If your computer has insufficient memory to hold the Conversion program and WordPerfect, you must exit WordPerfect by pressing F7 (Exit) before you run the Conversion program.

Table G.2 *Graphics Conversion program start-up options.*

Syntax	Function
graphcnv drive:\path\infile.ext drive:\path\outfile.ext	Converts the files automatically.

graphcnv/b=#
# represents one of the following colors: 	
0=Black
1=Blue
2=Green
3=Cyan
4=Red
5=Magenta
6=Brown
7=White
	Sets background color for .WPG file. Default is white.

graphcnv/c=2	Converts color values to monochrome (black and white).
graphcnv/c=16	Converts color values to WordPerfect's 16-color palette.
graphcnv/c=256	Converts color values to WordPerfect's 256-color palette. Use only if your monitor can display 256 colors.
graphcnv/c=b	Converts color values to black. Do not use with bit-mapped images.
graphcnv/c=w	Converts color values to white.
graphcnv/g=16	Converts color values to WordPerfect's 16-shades-of-gray palette.
graphcnv/g=256	Converts color values to the 16 shades of gray in WordPerfect's 256-color palette. Use only if your monitor can display 256 colors.
graphcnv/h	Displays help for the Graphics Conversion program.
graphcnv/l	Sends status messages for each converted file to the printer.
graphcnv/l=filename	Sends status messages for each converted file to specified file, instead of to the printer.

continued

Table G.2 *(continued)*

Syntax	Function
graphcnv/o	Overrides `Replace Files?` warning that appears if a file of the same name as the one you are converting the image to exists. (Be careful with this switch.)

 ## Converting a Graphics File to .WPG Format

1. Go to DOS.

2. Change to the drive and directory that holds the GRAPHCNV.EXE file.

   The GRAPHCNV.EXE file is usually in the same directory as the WordPerfect program files.

3. Type `graphcnv` and press Enter.

   DOS loads the Graphics Conversion program and prompts you to enter the name of the file you want to convert.

4. Type the drive, path, and file name of the file(s) you want to convert and press Enter.

   You can use wild-card characters to convert several files at once. * stands for any group of characters. ? stands for a single character. The program displays a path and file name for the converted file.

5. If you don't want to use the suggested path and file name, type the drive, path, and file name of your choosing.

   To convert several files at once, omit the file name. The file names will be the same as the original names, except they will have the .WPG extension.

6. Press Enter.

   WordPerfect performs the conversion and displays the `->ok` message.

7. Press any key.

   This exits the Conversion program.

Note: During the conversion process, any of the following error messages may appear on screen:

Bad Format indicates that the file is in a format that the Conversion program cannot convert. You may have to use the graphics program in which the file was created to save the file in a format that's supported.

Bad Input File indicates that the Graphics Conversion program cannot access the file. You may have mistyped the path to the file, the file may not exist, or an error may have occurred during the conversion process. Try again. If you get the same message, try to export the file again using the graphics program you used to create it.

Disk Full indicates that there's not enough room on your disk to store the converted file. Some graphics files are huge; you may have to remove some files to make room.

End of File indicates that an error occurred during the conversion process. Try to export the file into a different supported format using the graphics program you used to create it.

File Not Found indicates the file does not exist or is not where you say it is. Try again or check the directory listing to make sure the file is there.

Graphics, Create

Function: Lets you import graphic figures into your documents or create equations inside a special equation screen.

Keystrokes: *Keyboard*   *Mouse*
Alt-F9 (Graphics)   **Graphics**
1 (Figure), **2** (Table   **Figure, Table Box, Text Box, User**
Box), **3** (Text **Box**), **4**   **Box, or Equation**
(**User Box**), or **6**   **Create**
(**Equation**)   Define box
1 (Create)   **Right mouse button**
Define box
F7 (Exit)

Codes: [Equ Box]
[Fig Box]
[Tbl Box]
[Text Box]
[Usr Box]

Example:

```
Definition: Figure
       1 - Filename          ROSE.PCX
       2 - Contents          Graphic
       3 - Caption           Figure 1 The PCPaintBrush Rose File...
       4 - Anchor Type       Paragraph
       5 - Vertical Position  0"
       6 - Horizontal Position Right
       7 - Size              4.78" (wide) x 3" high
       8 - Wrap Text Around Box Yes
       9 - Edit
Selection: 0
```

The WordPerfect Graphics feature lets you import graphic images, tables, spreadsheets, and equations into your document. You can also use the feature to type text in a box or retrieve a text file into a box. The process is simple: You select a graphics box type to hold the image and then select Create to define the box. To select a box, you simply choose one of the five types of boxes listed below. Generally, the boxes are used as described below, but it is not mandatory that you use them in this way. For example, you can create equations in a Figure Box or import a graphic image into a Text Box:

Figure Boxes for graphics files, diagrams, graphs, and charts.

Table Boxes for WordPerfect tables, statistical data, etc.

Text Boxes for quotes, margin notes, cautions, or other text that you want to set off or emphasize.

Equation Boxes for mathematical and scientific equations. Refer to *Equation Editor, Creating Equations.*

User Boxes for any special uses not covered in the other categories.

The five box types are maintained as separate lists by WordPerfect and have different default options for features such as border style, inside border space, and gray shading. For example, Figure Boxes have no inside border space by default, so if you type text inside a Figure Box, you'll have to use the Indent feature or change the margins to prevent the text from being printed against the borders. By contrast, Text Boxes have .167" of inside border space, so the text you type will be slightly indented. If you enter captions for your boxes, you can use the Mark Text: Generate option to automatically generate separate lists for each type of box. For example, if your document includes five Equation Boxes, the list will include their captions and page numbers.

After you select the box type, you must use the Create option to define it, unless you want to use the defaults. Defining a box consists of specifying the size of the box, the file you want to import, the contents of the box, how you want the box positioned on the page, and whether or not you want the text to wrap around the box. You can also type a caption for the box.

 Creating a Graphics Box

1. Press Alt-F9 (Graphics) or display the **Graphics** menu.

   A list of five box types appears.

2. Select the type of box that best suits the graphics image you want to import.

   A list of graphics box options appears: Create, Edit, New Number, and Options.

3. Select **Create (1)**.

   The Box Definition options appear. The remaining steps are optional, depending on what you are using the graphics box for.

4. To retrieve a graphics figure, select **1 (Filename)**, type the drive, path, and file name of the file you want to import, and press Enter, or press **F5 (List)**, highlight the graphic file name, and press **1 (Select)**.

   A message appears indicating that WordPerfect is loading the graphic; then the name of the file appears next to the option. The cursor moves back down to Selection:, and you can select another option.

5. Select **2 (Contents)** and select the type of file that will be imported into the box.

   Refer to the note following these steps.

6. Select **3 (Caption)** and enter a caption for the graphics box.

   This is optional. If you enter a caption, it will appear above or below the graphics box. If you include captions, you can generate a list of captions for the boxes using the Mark Text key.

7. Select **4 (Anchor Type)** and choose how you want to anchor the box in the text.

   Paragraph ensures that the graphics box moves with the paragraph the cursor was in when you created the box. *Page* anchors the box in a specified position on the page.

The cursor should be at the top of the page when you use this option.

Character type treats the box as a single character. Text leads into the left side of the box and out the right side on the same line.

8. Select **5** (Vertical Position) and select where you want to position the box vertically.

This setting varies depending on the anchor type you chose in step 7.

9. Select **6** (Horizontal Position) and select where you want to position the box horizontally.

This setting varies depending on the anchor type you chose in step 7. If you are using a Page Anchor type, you can change the horizontal position to Columns and align the graphics box at the left or right side of a column or center it between the columns, or select some other position.

10. Select **7** (Size), select the method of sizing, and enter a measurement.

To keep the original proportions of the image, it's best to enter a size for only one dimension (width or height) and let WordPerfect automatically calculate the size for the other dimension.

11. Select **8** (Wrap Text) and press Y to wrap the text around the box or press N, if you don't want the text to wrap.

If you select N, text may be printed over the graphic box, generally an undesirable effect. Change this option only to create superimposed graphics boxes.

12. Select **9** (Edit) if you want to edit the contents of the box.

If the box contains a graphic image, you can rotate, scale, or move the image within the box. If the box contains text, you can edit the text. If you selected Equation, use this screen to create the equation. Refer to *Graphics, Edit*.

13. Press F7 (Exit) or click the right mouse button.

This saves your choices and returns you to your document.

Note: If you are importing a graphics image and you select the Contents option as described above, you must use either the Graphic option or the Graphic on Disk option. The Graphic option tells WordPerfect to save the graphic along with this document, while the Graphic on Disk option does not. When you use Graphic on Disk, your file (containing the graphic box) will be smaller. However, the file with the graphic image must be in the default directory or graphic directory specified in the Setup: Location of Files menu. If it is not, you won't be able to print, edit, or see it in View Document. The Contents option also controls the type of editor you can use when you choose the Edit option from the Definition Figure menu. If you change it to Text or Equation, WordPerfect will ask if you want to delete the current contents of the box, since you cannot have a graphic file in one of these two types. If you want to include a graphic figure in a style, you must use the Graphic on Disk option.

Graphics, Edit (see also *Equation Editor, Creating Equations*)

Function: Lets you edit equations, imported graphics, and text that appears in a graphics box.

Keystrokes:

Keyboard	*Mouse*
Alt-F9 (Graphics)	Graphics
1 (Figure), 2 (Table Box), 3 (Text Box), 4 (User Box), or 6 (Equation)	Figure, Table Box, Text Box, User Box, or Equation
2 (Edit)	Edit
figure number, Enter	*figure number*, Enter
9 (Edit)	Edit
Enter changes	Enter changes
F7 (Exit)	Right mouse button

Example:

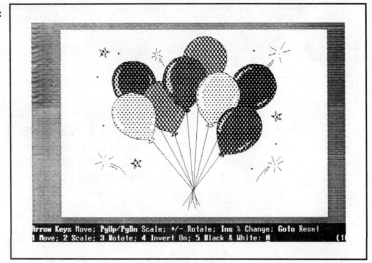

```
Arrow Keys Move; PgUp/PgDn Scale; +/- Rotate; Ins % Change; Goto Reset
1 Move; 2 Scale; 3 Rotate; 4 Invert On; 5 Black & White: 0                    (1
```

You can edit the contents of a graphics box at any time. If the box contains a graphic image, you can rotate, scale, or move the image within the box. If the box contains text, you can edit the text. If the box contains an equation, this option accesses the Equation Editor so you can enter an equation or modify an existing one. If the contents of the box is a graphics figure, choosing the Edit command accesses the Graphics Editor, which provides the following options:

Arrow Keys: Use the arrow keys to move the image horizontally and vertically in the window by the percent shown in the lower-right corner of the screen. To control the distance more precisely, you can use the Move option described below.

PgUp/PgDn (Scale): Use the PgUp or PgDn keys to expand or reduce the image by the percent shown in the lower-right corner of the screen. Width and height are changed by the same amount to retain original proportions. You can also use the Scale option, as described below, which provides more control.

+/- (Rotate): Use the + or - keys on the numeric keypad to rotate the image by the percent shown in the lower-right corner of the screen. For more precise control, use the Rotate option described below.

Ins (% Change): Use the Ins key to change the percentage in the lower-right corner of the screen to 1%, 5%, 10%, or 25%. This affects the rotation percent, the scale percent, and the move percent.

Goto (Reset) (Ctrl-Home): Cancels any changes you may have made to the image.

Move: Lets you enter a horizontal and vertical distance (in inches) to move the image from its starting point. Positive values move the image up and to the right. Negative values move it down and to the left.

Scale: Instead of using the PgUp and PgDn keys to scale an image by the percent shown on screen, you can use this option to enter your own percentage for the horizontal (x) and vertical (y). Be careful, however; if you enter a different percentage for horizontal and vertical scaling, you will distort the image. For example, if you enter 50 for the x value and leave the y value at 100, the image will be half as wide but will retain its original height.

Rotate: Use this option to enter a specific amount, in degrees, to rotate the image counterclockwise from its starting point. You can also use the +/– keys, but those keys offer only four percentages: 1%, 5%, 10%, and 25%. The image pivots around a center point. You can also choose to create a mirror image of the figure, so it is displayed in reverse.

Invert On: Inverts the colors for bit-mapped graphics. Black becomes white, and white becomes black. Colors are changed to their complementary colors.

Black & White: Lets you display and/or print a color image in black and white instead of using fill patterns or shading.

 ## Editing the Contents of a Graphics Box

1. Press Alt-F9 (Graphics) or display the Graphics menu.	A list of box types appears.
2. Select the type of box you want to edit.	You can then choose to create, edit, renumber, or change the box options.
3. Select Edit (2), type the number of the box you want to edit, and press Enter.	
4. Select 9 (Edit).	If you are editing a box that contains a graphic image, the Graphics Editor appears with the image inside.
5. Use the on-screen options, such as Move, Scale, or Rotate, to edit the graphic image.	
6. Press F7 (Exit) twice or click the right mouse button twice.	This returns you to the Edit screen.

Graphics, Lines (see also *Line Draw*)

Function: Lets you enhance a document with vertical and horizontal lines.

Keystrokes:

Keyboard	*Mouse*
Alt-F9 (Graphics)	Graphics
5 (Line)	Line
1 (Create Horizontal Line) or **2** (Create Vertical Line)	Create Horizontal or Create Vertical
Select option	Select option
Enter information	Enter information
F7 (Exit)	Right mouse button

Codes: [HLine:]
[VLine:]

Example:

```
                        Kathryn M. Appleton
                        3345 West 56th Place
                     Chicago, Illinois  60629
                          (312) 434-2670


        Career
        Objective:      To work in a progressive general acute care
                        setting as a staff physical therapist
                        responsible for direct patient care with
                        developing interest in pediatrics.


        Education:      The University of Illinois at Chicago
                        College of Associated Health Professions
                        Major: P.T. 1988-1990
                        Degree: Bachelor of Science June 1990
                        Honors: Dean's List Spring and Fall 1989,
                                Winter 1990

                        Moraine Valley Community College
                        Summer School 1988
                        GPA: 4.0/4.0
```

You can use horizontal and vertical lines to accent any document, to separate blocks of text or articles, to separate newspaper or parallel columns, or to act as a visual device that holds a page together. With WordPerfect's Graphics Line feature, you can specify the location, thickness, length, and gray shading of the line. WordPerfect inserts the specified line in your document, but the line does not appear on the Edit screen. To see the line, use the View Document feature.

Inserting a Line

1. Position the cursor where you want to insert the line.

2. Press Alt-F9 (Graphics) or select Line from the **Graphics** menu.

   A list of graphics options appears.

3. Select Create **Horizontal Line (1)** or Create **Vertical Line (2)**.

   The Line Definition screen appears, prompting you to enter various settings for the line, including position, width, and percent of gray shading.

4. If necessary, select **1** (Horizontal Position) and specify where you want the line positioned in relation to the left and right margins.

   You can left-justify, right-justify, or center a horizontal line; extend the line from margin to margin (the default); or start the line at a specific position. You can position a vertical line just left of the left margin (the default), just right of the right margin, between text columns, or at a specific position.

5. If necessary, select **2** (Vertical Position) and specify where you want the line positioned in relation to the top and bottom margins.

   The default setting is Baseline, so the line is positioned at the baseline of the line where the cursor was when you started creating the line. You can change this position.

6. If you did not choose full justification, select **3** (Length of Line) and enter a measurement for the line length.

   If you chose to extend the line from margin to margin earlier, you cannot set the length here.

7. Select **4** (Width of Line) and enter a measurement.

   This sets the line thickness.

8. If you want a line that is gray instead of black, select **5** (Gray Shading) and enter a percent of black setting.

   100% is black (the default), 50% is medium gray, and 10% is light gray. You can create a line that works like a shaded box by making it wide and decreasing the gray shading to 10%.

9.   Press F7 (Exit) or click the right   This inserts the line code into
     mouse button.   your document at the cursor
                                                 position.

 Tip: After creating a line, you can view it to see its exact
placement. Press Shift-F7 (Print) or select **Print** from the **File**
menu and select **6** (View Document). If necessary, you can
go back and edit the line. To do so, display the Graphics
menu, select **5** (Line), and select **3** (Edit Horizontal) or **4**
(Edit Vertical). WordPerfect searches backward until it finds
the first horizontal or vertical line code and then displays
the definition screen for that line. Enter the necessary
changes.

Graphics, New Numbers

Function: Renumbers subsequent graphics boxes from any point in
                the document.

Keystrokes: *Keyboard*   *Mouse*
                  Alt-F9 (Graphics)   **Graphics**
                  1 (Figure), **2** (Table   **Figure, Table Box, Text Box, User**
                  Box), **3** (Text Box), **4**   **Box, or Equation**
                  User Box), or **6**   **New Number**
                  (Equation)   *n* (where *n* is the number you
                  3 (New Number)   want to start with)
                  n (where *n* is the   Enter
                  number you want to
                  start with)
                  Enter

Codes: [New Equ Num]
             [New Fig Num]
             [New Tbl Num]
             [New Txt Num]
             [New Usr Num]

The New Number option lets you start a new numbering sequence for your
graphics boxes at any point in the document. The option inserts a [New
Num] code, which tells WordPerfect the new number you want to use for

the next Figure Box, Table Box, Text Box, User Box, or Equation Box. Each of these five box types is renumbered separately. From that point on, the box type you selected will be numbered consecutively, starting with the new number.

 Entering a New Number

1. Position the cursor where you want the new numbering to start.	Make sure the cursor is before any graphics box code that you want the renumbering to affect.
2. Press Alt-F9 (Graphics) or display the **G**raphics menu.	A list of box types appears.
3. Select the type of box that you want the renumbering to affect.	A menu appears that includes the New Number option for the type of graphic box you selected.
4. Select **N**ew Number (**3**).	WordPerfect prompts you to enter the new number.
5. Type the number and press Enter.	A [New Num:n] code is inserted at the cursor position. All graphics boxes of the type you selected will be renumbered when you move the cursor past them or rewrite the screen.

Graphics, Options

Function: Lets you change default settings, such as border style, caption style, and gray shading, for your graphics boxes.

Keystrokes:

Keyboard
Alt-F9 (Graphics)
1 (Figure), **2** (Table Box), **3** (Text Box), **4** (User Box), or **6** (Equation)
4 (Options)
Select option
Enter change

Mouse
Graphics
Figure, **T**able Box, Te**x**t Box, **U**ser Box, or **E**quation
Options
Select option
Enter change

Codes: [Equ Opt]
[Fig Opt]
[Tbl Opt]
[Txt Opt]
[Usr Opt]

Example:

```
Options: Figure
    1 - Border Style
            Left                               Single
            Right                              Single
            Top                                Single
            Bottom                             Single
    2 - Outside Border Space
            Left                               0.167"
            Right                              0.167"
            Top                                0.167"
            Bottom                             0.167"
    3 - Inside Border Space
            Left                               0"
            Right                              0"
            Top                                0"
            Bottom                             0"
    4 - First Level Numbering Method          Numbers
    5 - Second Level Numbering Method         Off
    6 - Caption Number Style                   [BOLD]Figure 1[bold]
    7 - Position of Caption                    Below box, Outside borders
    8 - Minimum Offset from Paragraph          0"
    9 - Gray Shading (% of black)              0%
Selection: 0
```

You can change the appearance of a graphics box and change the style of the caption through the Graphics Options menu. Keep in mind, however, that you're changing the options only for one particular type of box: Equation, Figure, Table, Text, or User box. This menu offers the following options:

Border Style lets you change the border style for each of the four borders. You can select no lines or single, dashed, double, dotted, thick, or extra-thick lines. You can also use it to create a drop-shadow for your box. To do this, set the border thickness to extra thick for the right and bottom borders and single thickness for the left and top borders.

Outside Border Space inserts the specified amount of space between the outside border and surrounding text.

Inside Border Space lets you insert blank space between the border and what's inside the box.

First Level Numbering Method lets you choose a numbering system for the first level of numbers. For example, if you're numbering figures Figure

A-1, Figure A-2, etc., your first level numbering would be letters and you would use option 5, Second Level Numbering Method, to designate numbers for the second level.

Second Level Numbering Method lets you choose a numbering system for the second level of numbers.

Caption Number Style allows you to set the style for your caption. For example, if you want your first caption to appear as **Figure A-1**, you would press F6 (Bold) and then type Figure 1-2. The 1 represents the first level numbering method; 2 represents the second level.

Position of Caption controls where the caption is printed in relation to the box. For a Figure, Table, Text, or User box, the caption can be above or below the box. Equation Boxes can have a caption above, below, or at the left or right side of the box.

Minimum Offset from Paragraph tells WordPerfect how close a graphics box can be moved to the top of a paragraph to keep the box on the same page as the paragraph containing the box code. The default for all five box types is 0", so the box can be even with the first line of the paragraph.

Gray Shading (% of Black) lets you shade your box. 0% (the default for Figure, Table, User, and Equation boxes) adds no shading. 100% makes the box completely black. Text Boxes use 10% shading by default.

 Changing Graphics Options

1. Position the cursor where you want the new options to take effect.

   Make sure the cursor is before any graphics box code that you want the changes to affect.

2. Press Alt-F9 (Graphics) or display the **Graphics** menu.

   A list of box types appears.

3. Select the type of box that you want the changes to affect.

   An option change affects only one type of box: Figure, Table, Text, User, or Equation.

4. Select 4 (**Options**).

   The Graphics Options menu appears for the selected box type.

5. Select an option and enter your change.

   After you finish changing an option, the cursor goes back down to Selection: and you can choose another option to change.

6. Press Enter when you're finished.   An option code is inserted at the cursor location, and the new options are in effect from that point forward.

Graphics Quality (see *Print Quality*)

Graphics, Screen Capture (GRAB.COM)

Function: Lets you save a graphic image displayed on your monitor to a file that can be imported into a WordPerfect document.

Keystrokes: *Keyboard*
Exit WordPerfect
Change to WP51 directory
grab
Enter
Start program and display graphic image
Alt-Shift-F9
Arrows and Shift-arrows (to size and position image)
Enter
d:\path\filename.wpg
Enter

Example:

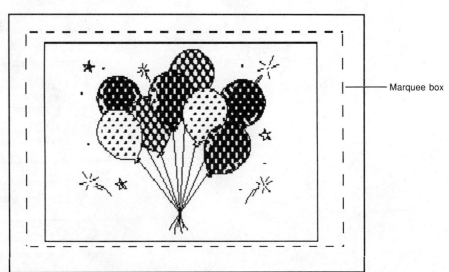

Marquee box

WordPerfect's Screen Capture program lets you save graphics images that are displayed on screen to files. You can then import the images you capture into graphics boxes in WordPerfect Documents. For example, since View Document is a graphic screen, you can use GRAB.COM to capture a View Document screen. You cannot, however, use the Screen Capture program to capture text screens, such as the WordPerfect Edit screen.

In order to run the Screen Capture program, you must have installed the Utilities when you installed WordPerfect. You cannot copy the GRAB.COM file directly from the original WordPerfect disk. If you did not install the Utilities, do so now. Before running the program, exit all other programs, including WordPerfect and the Library or Office Shell. (You'll be less likely to run into problems if you clear all memory-resident programs from memory.) Change to the directory that contains the GRAB.COM file. Type one of the start-up commands listed in Table G.3, and press Enter. Once the program is running, you can start another program to display the screen you want to capture.

Table G.3 *Screen Capture program start-up commands.*

Syntax	Function
`grab`	Loads the screen capture program into memory without start-up options.
`grab/c`*n* *n* is any number from 0 to 5.	Use if you are running Sidekick or other TSR programs to keep computer from locking up when you use GRAB. *n* represents the number of times GRAB.COM will attempt to get keyboard interrupt back from the other program. With Sidekick, use `grab/c0`.
`grab/d=`*pathname* *pathname* is the path to the directory where you want to store the files.	Lets you specify in which directory you want the files stored—for example, `grab/d=c:\wp51\capture`.
`grab/f=`*fileroot* *fileroot* is a 4-character base name for the file.	The first file you create using GRAB is GRAB.WPG, then GRAB1.WPG, then GRAB2.WPG, etc. This option lets you change the first four characters, GRAB, to some other name.

continued

Table G.3 *(continued)*

Syntax	Function
grab/i	Tells the program to ignore the "DOS busy" flag, allowing it to run under some applications that it might not otherwise run under.
grab/k	Retains size of the image box from the previous capture, letting you capture the same area on each subsequent screen.
grab/m	Captures color screens as monochrome bit-map files.
grab/p=2	Lets you capture page 2 when you're using a Hercules Graphics Adapter.
grab/s	Lets you use the space bar to toggle the function of the arrow keys from moving the box to sizing it.
grab/8	Use this option if you have an 8514A graphics card installed.

Capturing a Screen

1. Exit WordPerfect and go to the DOS prompt.

2. Change to the drive and directory that hold the GRAB.COM file.

   The GRAB.COM file is usually in the same directory as the WordPerfect program files.

3. Type one of the start-up commands listed in Table G.3 and press Enter.

   DOS loads the GRAB program.

4. Load your graphics program and display the graphics image you want to capture.

5. Press Alt-Shift-F9.	You should hear a two-toned chime, indicating that the GRAB program is ready to capture a screen. A marquee box appears, showing you what will be captured.
6. Use the arrow keys to position the marquee box on screen.	You can use the Ins key to toggle between fine and coarse increments when you are moving and sizing the box.
7. Use the Shift-arrow keys to change the size of the marquee box.	
8. Press Enter to capture the image to a file.	The GRAB program saves the screen to a file and sounds a two-toned chime when it's done.

 Note: If you hear a buzz instead of a two-toned chime after pressing Alt-Shift-F9, the graphics program you're using may not be compatible with the GRAB program, or there may be a problem with your hardware. Try clearing all memory-resident programs from memory and running only GRAB.COM. Then try to capture a View Document screen in WordPerfect. If you get the buzz, there's probably a problem with your hardware. If you don't get the buzz, try running only GRAB and the graphics program needed to generate the image you want to capture. If you get the buzz, the graphics program is probably incompatible with GRAB.

Graphics Screen Type

Function: Lets you select the graphics driver for your system if you need to override WordPerfect's automatic selection.

Keystrokes:

Keyboard	*Mouse*
Shift-F1 (Setup)	**File**
2 (Display)	Setup
2 (Graphics Screen Type)	**Display**
	Graphics Screen Type
Cursor to monitor or driver	Double-click selection
	Double-click selection
1 (Select)	Right mouse button
Cursor to resolution	
1 (Select)	
F7 (Exit)	

Example:

```
Setup: Display
        1 - Colors/Fonts/Attributes
        2 - Graphics Screen Type      Hercules 720x348 Mono
        3 - Text Screen Type          Auto Selected
        4 - Menu Options
        5 - View Document Options
        6 - Edit-Screen Options


Selection: 0
```

A graphics driver is a program that tells WordPerfect how to communicate with your monitor and display card. Whenever you attempt to display a graphics image using View Document, the Graphics Editor, or the Equation Editor, WordPerfect automatically selects the graphics driver for your system. You should not need to change WordPerfect's selection unless you want to change the resolution or the number of colors on an EGA or VGA monitor, or if you are using two monitors.

 Selecting a Graphics Driver

1. Press Shift-F1 (Setup) or select Setup from the **File** menu.

   The main Setup menu appears.

2. Select **Display** (2).

   The Setup: Display menu appears.

3. Select **2** (Graphics Screen Type).

   A list of graphics drivers and monitors appears.

4. Highlight the monitor and/or driver that's installed on your system and choose **1** (**Select**). You can choose **2** (**Auto-Select**) if you are unsure and you want WordPerfect to select for you.

Consult the documentation that came with your monitor and driver. If you select a monitor/driver yourself, another list appears, prompting you to select the resolution. Some monitors provide one option in this menu, while others, such as IBM EGA and IBM VGA, let you select from among several levels of resolution and a number of colors.

5. Select the resolution.

6. Press F7 (Exit) or click the right mouse button.

This saves the settings and returns you to the Edit screen.

 Note: The WordPerfect files that contain the information about graphics drivers end with the .VRS extension. The most common ones are in the STANDARD.VRS file. If your graphics driver or monitor does not appear on the list, make sure all your .VRS files are in the same directory as WP.EXE. If you have .VRS files in some other directory, press Shift-F1 (Setup) or select Setup from the File menu, select **2** (**Display**), **2** (**Graphics Screen Type**), and then select the **3** (**Other Disk**) option. Enter the path to your .VRS files. If your driver or monitor still is not listed, try running the Installation program for the Utilities and telling WordPerfect to install the Graphics Drivers. If you still have problems, contact WordPerfect Corporation.

Gray Shading (see *Graphics, Options*)

Hanging Indent (see also *Indent* and *Tab, Set*)

Function: Formats the first line of a paragraph to begin at the left margin, and indents all subsequent lines until the next hard return.

Keystrokes:

Keyboard	*Mouse*
F4 (→Indent)	Layout
Shift-Tab	Align
	Indent→
	Layout
	Align
	Margin Rel←

Codes: [→Indent]
[←Mar Rel]

Example:

> This is an example of a list created with hanging indents. Notice that the first line starts at the previous tab stop, and all subsequent lines are wrapped to the next tab stop.¶
> The next element begins here. Again, the first line is pushed left, and subsequent lines are indented.

The hanging indent format places the first line of a paragraph at the left margin and indents all subsequent lines in the paragraph one tab stop to the right. You can format an existing paragraph with a hanging indent or format as you are typing the paragraph.

Creating a Hanging Indent

1. Move the cursor to the left margin at the beginning of the paragraph.

2. Press F4 (→ Indent) or display the Layout menu and select Align and then Indent →. WordPerfect inserts an [→Indent] code and moves the cursor to the first tab stop.

3. Press Shift-Tab or display the Layout menu and select **Align** and then **Margin Rel ←**.

WordPerfect inserts the [←Mar Rel] code and moves the cursor to the left margin. If you are formatting an existing paragraph, this is your last step.

4. If you are formatting as you type, type the paragraph and then press Enter.

When you reach the right margin, the cursor wraps to the next line, and the next line of text will be indented one tab stop to the right of the first line. The remaining lines will be indented to the first tab stop, until you press Enter.

Hard Hyphen (see *Hyphenation*)

Hard Page (see *New Page*)

Hard Return (see *Return, Soft and Hard*)

Hard Return Display Character (see *Edit-Screen Options*)

Hard Space

Function: Keeps two or more words together as a unit, preventing the words from getting split by a soft return.

Keystrokes: *Keyboard*
Home
Space bar

Codes: [ ]

Example:

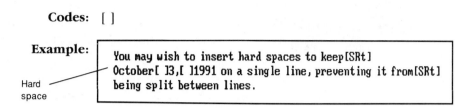

Hard
space

```
You may wish to insert hard spaces to keep[SRt]
October[ 13,[ ]1991 on a single line, preventing it from[SRt]
being split between lines.
```

As you type and the cursor reaches the right margin, WordPerfect automatically wraps the text as necessary, breaking lines at the spaces that separate the words. In some cases, however, you may want a phrase, such as a date, to remain on one line. You can keep the phrase on a single line by inserting *hard spaces,* rather than regular spaces, between the words. WordPerfect treats a hard space like a character instead of a space, treating two or more words as a single word.

 Inserting a Hard Space

1. Type the phrase as you normally would, but press Home before pressing the space bar between words.

The space looks the same on screen, but if you press Alt-F3 (Reveal Codes), you'll see the [ ] code instead of the space.

 Note: If the Automatic Hyphenation feature is on, WordPerfect may try to hyphenate the words separated by a hard space. You can press F1 (Cancel) to prevent hyphenation.

Hard Tab (see also *Tabs, Set*)

Function: Inserts a left, center, right, or decimal tab that will not be affected by any tab set changes that you may enter later.

Keystrokes: *Keyboard*
Home,Tab (Hard Left)
Home,Shift-F6 (Hard Center)
Home,Alt-F6 (Hard Right)
Ctrl-F6 (Hard Decimal)

Codes: [TAB]
          [CNTR TAB]
          [RGT TAB]
          [DEC TAB]

By default, WordPerfect's tab stops are all left tabs. The Hard Tab feature lets you create a center, right, or decimal tab on the fly, without having to set it up through the Tab Set option on the Format: Line menu. They are called hard tabs because the tab type will never change, even if you place the cursor above the hard tab position and change the type of tab at that position through the Tab Set option on the Format: Line menu. Following is a list of keystrokes and the codes they enter:

Keystroke	Code
Home,Tab	[TAB]
Home,Shift-F6 (Center)	[CNTR TAB]
Home,Alt-F6 (Flush Right)	[RGT TAB]
Ctrl-F6 (Tab Align)	[DEC TAB]

Headers and Footers

Function: Prints headings, which can include an automatic page number, at the top (header) or bottom (footer) of every page.

Keystrokes:

Keyboard	*Mouse*
Shift-F8 (Format)	Layout
2 (Page)	Page
3 (Header) or 4 (Footer)	Header or Footer
1 (A) or 2 (B)	A or B
1 (Discontinue), 2 (Every **Page**), 3 (Odd Pages), 4 (Even Pages), or 5 (Edit)	Discontinue, Every **Page**, Odd Pages, Even Pages, or Edit
Type text	Type text
F7 (Exit)	Right mouse button

Codes: [Header A]
          [Header B]
          [Footer A]
          [Footer B]

Example:

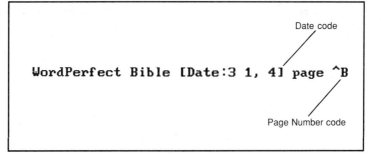

Date code

WordPerfect Bible [Date:3 1, 4] page ^B

Page Number code

Headers and footers can be set up to print on every page, or on all odd pages or all even pages of a document (for alternating headers or footers). A header is printed at the top of the document, and a footer is printed at the bottom. A blank line (.167") is left between the text and the header or footer. They are not printed in the space reserved for margins.

You can insert a page number by pressing Ctrl-B, which inserts the code ^B. This prints the correct page number on each page. You can insert the date by pressing Shift-F5 (Date/Outline) and selecting **1** (Date **T**ext) or **2** (Date **C**ode). If you use Date Code, the system date is printed. You can also use the same formatting features that you use in the body of your document: Center, Bold, Italic, Margin changes, Base Font, etc. You can suppress headers or footers on any page, such as on a page with a table or graphic, or on a title page. Refer to *Suppress*.

Tip: It's a good idea to create all headers and/or footers at the top of the first page of your document and then use Suppress to prevent them from being printed on selected pages. Otherwise, as you insert or delete text, the header or footer code may move away from the first line, and the header or won't be printed on that page.

 Creating a Header or Footer

1. Move the cursor to the top of the first page on which you want the header or footer to appear.	If the cursor isn't on the first line, the header or footer won't print until the following page.
2. Press Shift-F8 (Format) or display the **L**ayout menu.	A list of formatting options appears.

3. Select **Page (2)**.	The Format: Page menu appears.
4. Select **3 (Header)** or **4 (Footer)**.	The Header/Footer menu appears.
5. Select **1 (A)** or **2 (B)**.	If you are creating alternating headers or footers, such as for bound material, you may want Header A on all even pages and Header B on all odd pages.
6. Select **2 (Every Page)**, **3 (Odd Pages)**, or **4 (Even Pages)**.	This selection specifies on which pages the header or footer should appear. After you've made your choice, the Header or Footer Edit screen appears.
7. Type the text for your header or footer. It can include as many lines as you want.	The status line indicates that you are in the Header or Footer Edit screen. You can insert a Page Number code by pressing Ctrl-B, or a date by pressing Shift-F5 (Date/Outline) and selecting Date **Text** or Date **Code**.
8. Press F7 (Exit) or click the right mouse button.	The header or footer is saved, and the Format: Page menu reappears, listing the type of header or footer you just created next to the option.
9. Press F7 (Exit) or click the right mouse button.	You return to the Edit screen.

Editing a Header or Footer

1. Press Shift-F8 (Format) or display the **Layout** menu.	A list of formatting options appears.
2. Select **Page (2)**.	The Format: Page menu appears.
3. Select **3 (Header)** or **4 (Footer)**.	The Header or Footer menu appears, asking which header or footer you want to edit.
4. Select **1 (A)** or **2 (B)**.	

5. Select **5** (**Edit**).

WordPerfect searches the document for the header or footer you specified, and then places the cursor in the Header or Footer Edit screen.

6. Edit the header or footer.

7. Press F7 (Exit) twice or click the right mouse button twice.

This returns you to the Edit screen.

 ## Discontinuing a Header or Footer

1. Move the cursor to the top of the first page on which you want to discontinue the header or footer.

2. Press Shift-F8 (Format) or display the **Layout** menu.

A list of formatting options appears.

3. Select **Page** (**2**).

The Format: Page menu appears.

4. Select **3** (**Header**) or **4** (**Footer**).

The Header or Footer menu appears.

5. Select **1** (**A**) or **2** (**B**) for the header or footer you want to discontinue.

6. Select **1** (**Discontinue**).

From that page on, WordPerfect will discontinue the header or footer, so it won't be printed.

7. Press F7 (Exit) or click the right mouse button twice.

You return to the Edit screen.

 Note: To view the first 50 characters of your header or footer, press Alt-F3 or F11 (Reveal Codes) or select **Reveal Codes** from the **Edit** menu. To view your entire header or footer, you can display it in the Edit mode as explained earlier. To preview how the header or footer will look on a printed page, use View Document: Press Shift-F7 (Print) or display the **File** menu and select **Print**, select **6** (**View Document**), and select **1** (**100%**).

Help

Function: Provides information about WordPerfect's features, function keys, and cursor movement keys.

Keystrokes:

Keyboard	*Mouse*
F3 (Help)	**Help**
F3 (Help), *any character* (Index), or *function key*	**Help, Index, or Template**
	Double-click right mouse button
Enter or space bar	

Example:

```
Features [A]                                WordPerfect Key   Keystrokes

Absolute Tab Settings                       Format            Shft-F8,1,8,t,1
Acceleration Factor (Mouse)                 Setup             Shft-F1,1,5
Add Password                                Text In/Out       Ctrl-F5,2
Additional Printers                         Print             Shft-F7,s,2
Advance (To Position, Line, etc.)           Format            Shft-F8,4,1
Advanced Macro Commands (Macro Editor)      Macro Commands    Ctrl-PgUp
Advanced Merge Codes                        Merge Codes       Shft-F9,6
Align/Decimal Character                     Format            Shft-F8,4,3


Selection: 0                                        (Press ENTER to exit Help)
```

You can use WordPerfect's on-line help feature if you've forgotten how to use a feature or can't remember which keys to press to execute a command. There are many ways to use this feature. For example, you can press F3 (Help) followed by a letter to access an alphabetical list of features whose names start with that letter. You can then select a feature from the list. You can also press F3 (Help) and then press a function key or cursor key for information about how the key works.

 Note: You can only access WordPerfect's on-line help if you installed the Help files during installation. If you did not install the Help files, you must run the WordPerfect Installation program and answer Yes when asked if you want to install the Help files.

Accessing Context-Sensitive Help

1. If you get stuck while using one of WordPerfect's menus or features, press F3 (Help) while using it.

   WordPerfect presents a Help screen that offers information about the task you're trying to perform. Some Help screens, such as the one for the Main Format menu, display additional options leading to more information about those features.

2. Select any option you want to know more about.

3. Press Enter or the space bar to exit the Help screen.

   WordPerfect returns you to the point in your task where you asked for help.

 ## Getting Help from the Edit Screen

1. From the Edit screen, press F3 (Help).

   This displays the main Help menu, offering three choices: an alphabetical feature list, specific information about each function key, and a function key template.

2. To learn about a feature, type the first letter of the feature, such as L for Line Height.

   When you type a letter, a Help index appears with three columns. The first lists the features that begin with the letter you typed. The second shows the key's proper name. The last shows which keystrokes to press when you want to use the feature.

3. To get help concerning a particular function key, press the function key you want help with. You can do this from the main Help menu or any other help screen. If you are in the Edit screen, press F3 first.

   WordPerfect presents a Help screen that explains the function of the key you just pressed. Some of the screens include additional options leading to more information about these features.

4. To view a template for the function keys, press F3 (Help) again. If you are in the Edit screen, press F3 twice.

WordPerfect displays a function key template that duplicates the cardboard template. You can then press a function's keystroke to learn more about that function.

5. Press Enter or the space bar at any time to exit the Help menu.

Pressing F1 (Cancel), F7 (Exit), or Esc will only give you help about those particular keys.

 ## Using the Main Help Menu with the Mouse

1. From the Edit screen, select **Help** from the menu bar.

This displays the main Help menu, offering you three choices: an alphabetical features list, specific information about each function key, and a function key template.

2. To see the main Help menu, select **Help** from the **Help** menu.

Selecting **Help** from the Help menu performs the same function as pressing F3 (Help).

3. To learn about a particular feature, select **Index** from the **Help** menu, and then type the first letter of the feature, such as P for Print.

Selecting **Index** from the Help menu displays a list of WordPerfect's features that begin with "A". To see a list of features that begin with a different character, type that character.

4. To view a copy of the function key template, select **Template** from the **Help** menu.

WordPerfect displays a function key template that duplicates the cardboard template. You can then press a function's keystroke to learn more about that function.

5. Click the right mouse button twice at any time to exit the Help menu.

WordPerfect returns you to whatever you were doing before you asked for help.

Hidden Codes (see *Reveal Codes*)

Hide Document Comments (see *Comments*)

Home Key (see *Cursor Movement*)

Horizontal Lines (see *Graphics, Lines* and *Line Draw*)

Hyphenation (see also *Environment Setup* and *Hyphenation Zone*)

Function: Turns on WordPerfect's hyphenation feature, so WordPerfect will hyphenate words automatically or with your assistance.

Keystrokes:

Keyboard	*Mouse*
Shift-F8 (Format)	Layout
1 (Line)	Line
1 (Hyphenation)	Hyphenation
Y (Hyphenation On) or	Y (Hyphenation On) or N
N (Hyphenation Off)	(Hyphenation Off)
F7 (Exit)	Right mouse button

Codes: [Hyph On]
[Hyph Off]

Example:

> This is an example of text typed with WordPerfect's Automatic Hy- —→ Hyphens
> phenation setting on. Notice that at the end of the line, WordPer-
> fect has automatically hyphenated the words Hyphenation and Word-
> Perfect. The Hyphenation Zone settings have been changed to
> squeeze the hyphenation zone and increase the number of words that
> need to be hyphenated.

By default, WordPerfect does not hyphenate words, even if there is enough room for part of a word to fit on the line. Instead, if the entire word will exceed the right margin, it is wrapped to the next line. If you want to even out the length of your lines, you can turn on the Hyphenation feature and have WordPerfect hyphenate words for you. The advantage of using automatic hyphenation is that WordPerfect inserts a special type of hyphen, called a *soft hyphen*. If a word containing a soft hyphen moves away from the right margin after you insert or delete the text near it, the hyphen disappears. It reappears again if the word moves back to the right margin and must be split.

To select the method WordPerfect will use to hyphenate words, and when and if it will ask for your help in determining the correct hyphenation position, use the Setup: Environment menu. Through the Setup: Environment menu, you can instruct WordPerfect to hyphenate words automatically—without any input from you—or you can set it to ask for your assistance whenever it can't determine how to hyphenate a word, or you can set it to always ask for your confirmation of a hyphen. See *Environment Setup* for more information.

 ## Turning Hyphenation On or Off

1. Position the cursor where you want to turn Hyphenation on or off.

   By turning Hyphenation on and off, you can hyphenate words in only a section of your document, such as in an indented quote.

2. Press Shift-F8 (Format) or display the Layout menu.

   A list of formatting options appears.

3. Select Line (**1**).

   The Format: Line menu appears.

4. Select **1** (Hyphenation).

   The cursor moves up to the Hyphenation option.

5. Press Y to turn Hyphenation on or N to turn it off.

6. Press F7 (Exit) or click the right mouse button.

   WordPerfect inserts a Hyphenation On or Off code at the cursor location and returns you to your document.

As you move the cursor through the document, WordPerfect may ask your help in hyphenating words. Each time, a prompt appears asking you to position the hyphen and press Esc. It will be followed by the word that WordPerfect is trying to hyphenate, and show the suggested position for the hyphen. You then have three options:

1. Press Esc to accept the suggested hyphen.

2. Press F1 (Cancel) to prevent the word from being hyphenated.

3. Change the hyphen position by pressing Left Arrow or Right Arrow (although sometimes, WordPerfect won't let you press Right Arrow because the word would then exceed the right margin). When the hyphen is in the position you want, press Esc.

In addition to automatic or assisted hyphenation, you can insert several types of hyphens yourself:

The Hyphen: If you type a hyphen (-) to hyphenate a word, the hyphen remains in the word even if the word moves away from the right margin. For this reason, it is best to use soft hyphens. This type of hyphen is called the *hyphen character.*

Hard Hyphen: Press Home-hyphen (-) to insert a hyphen that should appear in a hyphenated word such as "full-length." The word will be treated as one word and won't be split at the right margin.

Soft Hyphen: This is the same type of hyphen that WordPerfect uses when you turn on hyphenation and it hyphenates words for you. You can insert a soft hyphen by pressing Ctrl-hyphen (-). If you edit the document, making it so that a hyphenated word no longer needs to be hyphenated, the Soft Hyphen code remains in the word but does not appear on screen or in the printed version.

Invisible Soft Return: Press Home,Enter to tell WordPerfect where to break a word or words without inserting a hyphen. This combination inserts a Soft Return code [ISRt]. For example, date/[ISRt]time moves the word "time" to the next line if it runs into the right margin, but does not place a hyphen between "date" and "time."

Deletable Soft Return: WordPerfect inserts the code [DSRt] when it must break a word that extends all the way from the left to right margins as in narrow columns. If you change the margins or hyphenate the word so that the code no longer appears at the end of a line or page, WordPerfect automatically removes the code.

Hyphenation Zone (see also *Hyphenation* and *Environment Setup*)

Function: Determines whether or not to hyphenate a word.

Keystrokes: *Keyboard*   *Mouse*
  Shift-F8 (Format)   Layout
  1 (Line)   Line

2 (Hyphenation Zone)	Hyphenation **Z**one
left setting	*left setting*
right setting	*right setting*
F7 (Exit)	Right mouse button

Example:

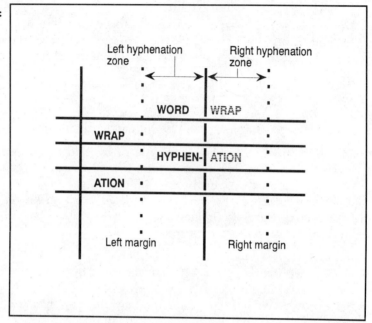

The hyphenation zone is an area that WordPerfect uses to determine whether a word should be hyphenated or moved to the next line when hyphenation is on. The zone consists of a left and a right boundary. If a word starts before the left boundary and extends past the right boundary, WordPerfect hyphenates the word. If a word starts at the left boundary and extends past the right one, it will be wrapped to the next line.

The boundaries are set according to a percent of the line length. To determine the hyphenation zone, WordPerfect uses the following formulas:

line length × left percent = left hyphenation zone
and
line length × right percent = right hyphenation zone

Say a line is 7 inches long and the hyphenation zone is 10% and 4%. The left hyphenation boundary is .7" (7" × .10) to the left of the right margin; the right boundary is .28" (7" × .04) to the right of the right margin. By increasing the boundary, you reduce the number of words that will need to be hyphenated. By decreasing it, you increase the number of words that WordPerfect will try to hyphenate.

Changing the Hyphenation Zone

1. Position the cursor where you want to change the hyphenation zone.

2. Press Shift-F8 (Format) or display the **Layout** menu.

   A list of formatting options appears.

3. Select **Line** (**1**).

   The Format: Line menu appears.

4. Select **2** (Hyphenation **Z**one).

   You can change either the left or right hyphenation zone, or both.

5. Enter a percentage for the left hyphenation zone setting, or press Enter to accept the default.

   The default is 10%.

6. Enter a percentage for the right hyphenation zone setting, or press Enter to accept the default.

   The default is 10%.

7. Press F7 (Exit) or click the right mouse button.

   This returns you to the Edit screen.

I–K

Import Spreadsheet (see *Spreadsheet*)

Inches (see *Units of Measure*)

Indent (see also *Hanging Indent*)

Function: Lets you indent a paragraph from the left margin or from both margins without changing the left or right margins.

Keystrokes:

Keyboard	*Mouse*
F4 (→Indent) or	Layout
Shift-F4 (→Indent←)	**Align**
	(Indent→) or (Indent→←)

Codes: [→Indent]
[→Indent←]

Example:

Left indent
Left and right indent
Hanging indent

> Following are examples of indented text:
>
> This text has a left indent. Only the left margin is indented. The rest of the text continues to the right margin.
>
> This text is indented from both the left and right margins. Notice that it does not reach as far right as the previous paragraph.
>
> This is a hanging indent. The first line reaches all the way to the left. Subsequent lines are indented. Refer to Hanging Indent.

Indents are useful for creating unnumbered lists, for quotations, and for setting off blocks of text from the rest of the document. A single [Indent] code indents an entire paragraph one tab stop position; you don't have to press the Tab key to indent subsequent lines. You can use these features while typing text or on an existing paragraph. Indenting ends with the next hard return.

Indenting Text as You Type

1. Position the cursor where you want to start typing the indented paragraph.

2. Press F4 (→Indent) to indent only the left side of the paragraph, or Shift-F4 (→Indent←) to indent both sides of the paragraph.

   →Indent indents one tab stop from the left; →Indent← indents one tab stop from both margins. You can press the key more than once to increase the indent to the second tab stop. You can also use the mouse to select the type of indent you want from the Layout/Align menu.

3. Type the text of the paragraph.

   The text wraps to the indented position, from the left margin or both margins, according to the [Indent] code you entered.

4. Press Enter.

   This ends the paragraph with a hard return and moves the cursor back to the left margin.

 Note: When you indent a paragraph, WordPerfect indents to the next tab stop. By default, this is 1/2 inch. You can change this distance by changing the tab settings. See also, *Tab, Set.*

 Indenting an Existing Paragraph

1. Position the cursor on the first character of the paragraph, at the left margin.

2. Press F4 (→Indent) to indent only the left side of the paragraph, or Shift-F4 (→Indent←) to indent both sides of the paragraph.

The entire paragraph is indented immediately. You can also use the mouse to select the type of indent you want from the Layout/Align menu.

Index, Concordance (see also *Index, Mark Text*; *Index, Define*; and *Generate*)

Function: Lets you create a separate file listing the words and phrases you want WordPerfect to use to generate an index.

Keystrokes:

Keyboard	*Mouse*
blank document screen	*blank document screen*
type *index entries*	type *index entries*
F10 (Save)	File
filename	Save
	filename

Example:

```
Trees[HRt]
[Index:Trees;Cypress]Cypress[HRt]
[Index:Trees;Elm]Elm[HRt]
[Index:Trees;Hickory]Hickory[HRt]
[Index:Trees;Oak]Oak[HRt]
[Index:Trees;Sycamore]Sycamore[HRt]
[Index:Trees;Walnut]Walnut[HRt]
Animals[HRt]
[Index:Animals;Beavers]Beavers[HRt]
[Index:Animals;Bison]Bison[HRt]
```

Heading   Subheading

You can create an index in two ways: either mark each occurrence of a word or phrase in your document, or type a *concordance* file that lists all the words and phrases you want indexed. The concordance file saves time; you don't have to search through a lengthy document to find each occurrence of a word or phrase that you want to include in the index. However, you do have to type all the words and phrases separately and save the concordance file before you can use it. Also, the file finds only exact matches; if you type a singular word in the concordance file, and you use the plural form throughout your document, the word won't be included when you generate the index. However, you can use the same concordance file over and over again to index any document that contains these words or phrases.

 Creating a Concordance File

1. Start with a blank WordPerfect screen.

2. Type a word or phrase you want indexed, and press Enter.

   You must press Enter after each entry, so that each word or phrase is on a separate line, in order to have the entries indexed correctly.

3. Repeat step 2 until the list is complete.

   If you alphabetize the list using the Sort feature, it will take less time to generate the index. Refer to *Sort and Select*.

4. Press F10 (Save) or select Save from the File menu.

   WordPerfect prompts you to enter a name for the file.

5. Type a name for the concordance file and press Enter.

   You may wish to use the extension .CON so you'll know this is a concordance file.

All the entries in your concordance file are now major headings; you have no subheadings. If you want to change some of the headings to subheadings, perform the following steps:

 Making Index Entries into Subheadings

1. Position the cursor at the entry you want to turn into a subheading.

2. Press Alt-F5 (Mark Text) or display the Mark menu.

   A list of Mark Text options appears.

3. Select Index (3).

   WordPerfect prompts you to enter a heading for the subheading you're creating.

4. Type the heading that's a level above the subheading you're creating and press Enter.

For example, if you're marking "Cypress" as a subheading of "Trees," you must type Trees and press Enter. WordPerfect then prompts you to enter a name for the subheading.

5. Press Enter to accept the displayed text.

WordPerfect inserts the code [Index:*heading;subheading*] to the left of the entry, making the entry a subheading.

6. Repeat steps 1-5 for each entry you want to make into a subheading.

7. Press F10 (Save) or select Save from the File menu.

WordPerfect prompts you to enter a name for the file.

8. Press Enter to save the file under its old name.

To generate an index using this concordance file, you must define the index in the document (see *Index, Define*) and then generate the index (see *Generate*).

Index, Define

Function: Lets you set the position and numbering style for your index.

Keystrokes:

Keyboard	*Mouse*
Alt-F5 (Mark Text)	**Mark**
5 (Define)	**Define**
3 (Define Index)	**Index**
concordance file name	*concordance file name*
Enter	Enter
numbering style	*numbering style*

Code: [Def Mark]

Example:

```
Index¶
¶
Animals¶
    Beavers . . . . . . . . . . . . . . . . . . . . . . . . . . . . .1¶
    Elephants . . . . . . . . . . . . . . . . . . . . . . . . . . .1¶
Trees¶
    Cypress . . . . . . . . . . . . . . . . . . . . . . . . . . . .1¶
    Sycamore. . . . . . . . . . . . . . . . . . . . . . . . . . . .1¶
    Walnut. . . . . . . . . . . . . . . . . . . . . . . . . . . . .1¶
```

Before you can generate an index for a specific document, you must tell WordPerfect where you want the index located in the document, and how you want it numbered. This inserts a [Def Mark] code at the cursor position, telling WordPerfect which of the five numbering styles to use and the name of the concordance file to use, if any. When you generate an index for a document in which you have marked individual words or phrases (as opposed to using a concordance file), WordPerfect searches the document from the beginning up to this code to find the terms you marked for indexing. WordPerfect does not search text that comes after this code, so unless you are only using a concordance file, be sure to put the code at the end of your document. If you're using a master document, place the code at the end of the master document.

Defining an Index

1. Position the cursor at the end of the document.

   If you are using a concordance file and have not marked entries in the document, you can position the cursor wherever you want WordPerfect to generate the index.

2. Press Ctrl-Enter if you want the index to start on a separate page.

   WordPerfect inserts a hard page break at the cursor position.

3. Type a heading for the index, if desired.

   For example, type Index. This step is optional.

4. Press Enter one or more times to insert space between the heading and the body of the index.

5. Press Alt-F5 (Mark Text) or display the **M**ark menu.

   The Mark Text menu appears.

6. Select **D**efine (**5**).

   The Mark Text Definition menu appears.

7. Select Index (3).

WordPerfect prompts you to enter the name of your concordance file.

8. If you're using a concordance file, type the file's name.

9. Press Enter.

WordPerfect prompts you to select a numbering style from five available options.

10. Select a numbering style from the list.

WordPerfect inserts the [Def Mark] code and returns you to your document.

After you define your index, you can generate it. Refer to *Generate*.

Index, Mark Text

Function: Lets you mark entries in a document that you want to include in your index.

Keystrokes:

Keyboard	*Mouse*
Alt-F5 (Mark Text)	**Mark**
3 (Index)	**Index**
heading, Enter	*heading*, Enter
subheading, Enter	*subheading*, Enter

Code: [Index:*heading;subheading*]

Index
code

Example:

```
Dutch [Index:Trees;Elms]Elms were one of the most popular trees in this area unt
il[SRt]
the early 1950s, when the dreaded Dutch elm disease struck.
```

You can create an index in either of two ways: type a *concordance* file that lists all the words and phrases you want indexed, or mark each occurrence of a word or phrase in your document. The concordance file saves time, but you have to create and save the file before you can use it to generate an index. You may find it easier to mark individual entries in your document.

Marking Existing Text for Indexing

1. Move the cursor to the first entry you want to include in the index.

   If the entry consists of more than one word, press Alt-F4 (Block) and highlight the entire phrase.

2. Press Alt-F5 (Mark Text) or display the **Mark** menu.

   A list of Mark Text options appears.

3. Select **Index (3)**.

   A prompt appears asking for the Index heading, and includes a word or phrase the cursor was highlighting. WordPerfect assumes you want to use this entry as a heading in your index. If you want it to appear as a subheading instead, type the word or phrase for the heading.

4. Press Enter to use the displayed text as a heading, or type the heading you want to use, and then press Enter.

   For example, if you're marking "Elms" as a subheading of "Trees," you must type Trees and press Enter. If you used the displayed text as a heading, WordPerfect displays a blank subheading prompt. If you did not use it as a heading, the text is displayed as the suggested subheading.

5. If text is displayed, press Enter to accept it as a subheading or press F1 (Cancel) if you don't want to include a subheading. If no text is displayed, enter a subheading or press Enter it you don't want a subheading.

   WordPerfect inserts the code [Index:*heading;subheading*] to the left of the entry.

6. Repeat steps 1-5 for each entry you want to include in the index.

After you mark all the entries in your document, you must define your index (see *Index, Define*); this tells WordPerfect where to put the index and how to number the entries. You can then generate the index (see *Generate*).

Initial Base Font (see *Fonts*)

Initial Codes (see also *Initial Settings*)

Function: Lets you set default formatting options for a single
document. These settings override the Initial Settings.

Keystrokes:

Keyboard	*Mouse*
Shift-F8 (Format)	Layout
3 (Document)	Document
2 (Initial Codes)	Initial Codes
Add formatting codes	Add formatting codes
F7 (Exit)	Right mouse button

Codes:

[Font]	[Box Num]
[Col Def]	[Box Opt]
[Col On]	[Hyph On/Off]
[Decml/Algn Char]	[HZone]
[New End Num]	[Just]
[End Opt]	[Kern]
[Ftn Num]	[Lang]
[Ftn Opt]	[Ln Height]
[Ln Num]	[Pg Num Style]
[Ln Spacing]	[Paper Sz/Typ]
[L/R Mar]	[Color]
[T/B Mar]	[Suppress]
[Math Def]	[Tab Set]
[Math On]	[Undrln]
[Pg Num]	[W/O On/Off]
[Pg Numbering]	[Wrd/Ltr Spacing]

Example:

```
Initial Codes:  Press Exit when done                    Ln 1" Pos 0.5"
[           ^        ^       ^        ^       ^       ^       ^         ^      ^       )
[L/R Mar:0.5",0.5"][W/O On][Center Pg][Pg Num Style:^B]
```

Whenever you create a document, WordPerfect uses certain default settings,
such as 1" margins and full justification. You can change any of these default
settings using the Initial Codes option on the Setup: Initial Settings menu
(refer to *Initial Settings*); these changes will then affect all new documents.
You can also change the format settings for an individual document by
entering *Document Initial Codes* for all the features you want to change.
These initial codes override the initial settings on the Setup: Initial Settings

screen, but only for the document on the Edit screen. They cannot be seen in the document's Reveal Codes screen. Codes you enter within the document, such as [Font] or [L/R Mar], override both the Setup Initial Codes and the Document Initial Codes.

Inserting Initial Codes

1. Press Shift-F8 (Format) or display the Layout menu.

A list of formatting options appears.

2. Select Document (3).

The Format: Document menu appears.

3. Select 2 (Initial Codes).

The Initial Codes screen appears. This screen resembles the Reveal Codes screen, except for the `Initial Codes` prompt above the tab ruler.

4. Select a feature the way you would normally change the formatting, and enter the necessary information and settings.

For instance, to change the left and right margins, press Shift-F8 (Format), select Line, Margins, and enter your changes. Press F7 (Exit). This inserts the appropriate formatting code into the Initial Codes screen. Repeat this step to insert all the codes you want to use.

5. Press F7 (Exit) or click the right mouse button to return to the Edit screen.

The new initial codes are now in effect.

Note: If you retrieve another document into the existing document, the initial codes in the existing document control the retrieved document. You may have to make some adjustments if you wish to retain the original formatting of the retrieved document.

Note: You should use Document Initial Codes when formatting a primary merge file for formatting changes like margins and paper size and type. Otherwise, when you merge it with a secondary file, each resulting document will include all the individual codes. If you are creating labels in a merge, it is mandatory that you place the paper size/type code in Document Initial Codes.

Initialize Printer (see also *Cartridges and Fonts*)

Function: Downloads selected soft fonts to printer.

Keystrokes:

Keyboard	*Mouse*
Shift-F7 (Print)	File
7 (Initialize Printer)	Print
Y (Yes)	Initialize Printer
	Yes

If you have a printer that uses soft fonts, and you have marked the fonts you want to use with an asterisk, you must initialize your printer before you can print a document in which you've used them. This process downloads those fonts to your printer, making the fonts available for the print job. You must initialize your printer after you turn on your printer but before you print your document. You must also initialize your printer whenever you select different soft fonts.

 Initializing Your Printer

1. Make sure the printer is turned on.

2. Press Shift-F7 (Print) or select **Print** from the **File** menu.

   The Print screen appears.

3. Select **7 (Initialize Printer)**.

   WordPerfect prompts you to confirm your request.

4. Press Y.

WordPerfect downloads the selected soft fonts to your printer.

5. Continue with your print job.

Initial Settings (see also *Initial Codes*)

Function: Lets you change default formatting options for all new documents.

Keystrokes:

Keyboard	*Mouse*
Shift-F1 (Setup)	**File**
4 (Initial Settings)	Setup
Select option	Initial Settings
Enter change	Select option
F7 (Exit)	Enter change
	Right mouse button

Example:

```
Setup: Initial Settings
      1 - Merge
      2 - Date Format              3 1, 4
                                   September 20, 1990

      3 - Equations
      4 - Format Retrieved Documents   No
             for Default Printer
      5 - Initial Codes
      6 - Repeat Value             8
      7 - Table of Authorities
      8 - Print Options



Selection: 0
```

The Initial Settings screen allows you to enter default settings for many of WordPerfect's features. These settings affect all subsequent documents you create, but do not affect previously created documents. You can change settings for the following features:

Merge: Determines the field and record delimiters for a DOS text file or a secondary merge file created with WordPerfect 4.0 or an earlier version. Select this option; then select **1** (Field Delimiters) or **2** (Record Delimiters). Type the characters that indicate where fields or records begin, press

Down Arrow, and type the characters that indicate where fields or records end. The Enter key inserts a Line Feed code. Ctrl-M inserts a Carriage Return code.

Date Format: Lets you change the date format that is used when you select Date Text or Date Code. Refer to *Date Format*.

Equations: Lets you change default printing and alignment options for equations. You can override the printing and alignment settings you change here in the Equation Editor itself. This option also lets you select a keyboard layout for the Equation Editor; select this option and then select **5** (**K**eyboard for Editing). Select a keyboard from the list and press F7 (Exit).

Format Retrieved Documents for Default Printer: If you set this option to Yes, whenever you retrieve a document that was formatted for a printer that is not the currently active printer, WordPerfect automatically reformats the document for the active printer, changing fonts if necessary. If you set this option to No, WordPerfect will try to format the document for the printer you used to create the document. If WordPerfect cannot find that printer, it formats the document for the currently active printer.

Initial Codes: Lets you change default formatting, such as margins, line spacing, and justification, for all new documents. Refer to *Initial Codes*.

Repeat Value: Determines the number of times a character or feature is repeated when you use the Repeat feature (Esc). Refer to *Repeat Value*.

Table of Authorities: Lets you specify default format settings for the Table of Authorities feature. Refer to *Table of Authorities*.

Print Options: Offers several options for changing the defaults for the appearance of printed documents. For example, you can select the graphics and text quality, choose a redlining method, and change the binding offset. You can override these settings for a single document by changing them on the Print screen, Shift-F7 (Print).

 Changing Initial Settings

1. Press Shift-F1 (Setup) or select Setup from the **F**ile menu.

   The main Setup menu appears.

2. Select **I**nitial Settings (**4**).

   The Setup: Initial Settings menu appears.

3. Select an option and enter your change.

When you select an option, the cursor moves up to that option. When you type Y or N or press Enter, the cursor moves back down to Selection: and you can choose another option.

4. Press F7 (Exit) or click the right mouse button.

The new settings are saved, and you are returned to the Edit screen.

Insert Key

Function: Toggles between Insert and Typeover modes.

Keystrokes: *Keyboard*
Ins

Normally, WordPerfect inserts text at the cursor position without deleting existing text. If you want to type over and replace existing text as you type, you must use the Ins key to switch to Typeover mode. If you press the Ins key once, Typeover appears in the lower-left corner of the screen. While this prompt appears, any characters you type literally type over and erase existing text, instead of pushing it to the right to make room. Press Ins again to return to the Insert mode; Typeover disappears.

Interrupt Print Job (see *Control Printer*)

Invisible Soft Return (see *Hyphenation*)

Italics (see *Appearance Attributes*)

Job List (see *Control Printer*)

Justification

Function: Aligns text against left and/or right margins, or centers it between margins.

Keystrokes:

Keyboard	*Mouse*
Shift-F8 (Format)	Layout
1 (Line)	Line
3 (Justification)	Justification
1 (Left), **2** (Center),	Left, Center, **Right**, or **Full**
3 (Right), or **4** (Full)	Right mouse button
F7 (Exit)	

Codes:
[Just:Left]
[Just:Right]
[Just:Center]
[Just:Full]

Example:

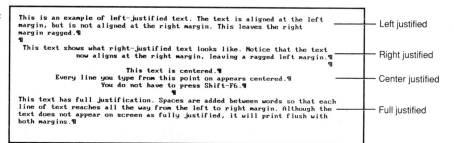

This is an example of left-justified text. The text is aligned at the left margin, but is not aligned at the right margin. This leaves the right margin ragged.¶ — Left justified

This text shows what right-justified text looks like. Notice that the text now aligns at the right margin, leaving a ragged left margin.¶ — Right justified

This text is centered.¶
Every line you type from this point on appears centered.¶
You do not have to press Shift-F6.¶ — Center justified

This text has full justification. Spaces are added between words so that each line of text reaches all the way from the left to right margin. Although the text does not appear on screen as fully justified, it will print flush with both margins.¶ — Full justified

The Justification feature inserts a code in your text that aligns all subsequent lines according to the selected justification: left, center, right, or full. You could, of course, press Shift-F6 to center a line of text or Alt-F6 to right-justify a line, but those features work only on individual lines. The benefit of the Justification feature is that it lets you justify as many lines as necessary. WordPerfect offers the following four justification options:

Left aligns the text flush against the left margin, leaving a ragged right margin. Text on the Edit screen appears ragged right, even though it may be full justified or left justified. You can use the View Document option on the Print menu to determine which method is in use.

Center aligns the text between the left and right margins.

Right pushes the text flush against the right margin, leaving a ragged left margin.

Full increases or reduces the space between words (during printing) to make the text flush with both the left and right margins. In WordPerfect 5.0 and earlier versions, this was called right justification.

 Justifying Text

1. Press Shift-F8 (Format) or display the Layout menu.	A list of formatting options appears.
2. Select Line (**1**).	The Format: Line menu appears.
3. Select **3** (Justification).	The Justification menu appears, offering four options.
4. Select **1** (Left), **2** (Center), **3** (Right), or **4** (Full).	Your selection appears next to Justification: on the Format: Line menu.
5. Press F7 (Exit) or click the right mouse button.	WordPerfect inserts the specified [Just] code at the cursor position.

From this point on, any text you type will be formatted according to the justification you selected. If you want to change the justification later in the document, you must repeat the steps to insert a new justification code.

Justification Limits

Function: Lets you specify the maximum percent a space between words can be expanded or compressed when Full Justification is in use.

Keystrokes:

Keyboard	*Mouse*
Shift-F8 (Format)	Layout
4 (Other)	Other
6 (Printer Functions)	Printer Functions
4 (Word Spacing Justification Limits)	Word Spacing Justification Limits
compression percent	*compression percent*
expansion percent	*expansion percent*
F7 (Exit)	Right mouse button

Code: [Just Lim]

When you use Full Justification, WordPerfect's default, WordPerfect expands or compresses the spaces between words to make each line of text flush with both margins. The Word Spacing Justification Limits option lets you change the limits for this automatic adjustment. If WordPerfect expands or compresses the spaces to the limit specified here and the line is still not flush with both margins, WordPerfect will then expand or compress the space between characters as needed.

 Setting Justification Limits

1. Position the cursor where you want to set the limits.

2. Press Shift-F8 (Format) or display the **L**ayout menu.

A list of formatting options appears.

3. Select **O**ther (4).

The Format: Other menu appears.

4. Select **6** (**P**rinter Functions).

A list of printer format settings appears.

5. Select **4** (**W**ord Spacing Justification Limits).

WordPerfect prompts you to enter compression and expansion percentages.

6. Type a compression percent and press Enter.

For example, type 50 to let WordPerfect compress the space between words up to half of the existing space.

7. Type an expansion percent and press Enter.

For example, type 150 to let WordPerfect expand the space between words up to 1 1/2 times the existing space.

8. Press F7 (Exit) or click the right mouse button.

WordPerfect inserts the [Just Lim] code at the cursor position.

Kerning

Function: Automatically decreases the space between pairs of letters. This feature is printer-dependent.

Keystrokes:

Keyboard	*Mouse*
Shift-F8 (Format)	Layout
4 (Other)	Other
6 (Printer Functions)	Printer Functions
1 (Kerning)	Kerning
Y (On) or N (Off)	Yes (On) or No (Off)
F7 (Exit)	Right mouse button

Code: [Kern:On]
[Kern:Off]

Example:

> UNKERNED: W ALLABY
> KERNED: WALLABY

Because of the way characters are shaped, certain character pairs may appear to have too much space between them when printed. For example, the *WA* or *To* combinations often have more space between them than *NO* or *PS*. The extra space may not look bad on screen, but on a printed page it stands out, especially when you are using a large point size, as in a heading. To correct for these loose character pairs, you can have WordPerfect *kern* the pairs. Kerning tightens all loose character pairs, giving the document a more professional look. However, kerning tables are defined in the printer resource file, and not all fonts include this feature. You can use the Printer program to define kerning tables.

 Kerning

1. Press Shift-F8 (Format) or display the **Layout** menu.

   A list of formatting options appears.

2. Select Other (4).

   The Format: Other menu appears.

3. Select 6 (**Printer Functions**).

   A list of printer formatting options appears.

4. Select 1 (**Kerning**).

   The cursor moves up to the Kerning option.

5. Press Y to turn kerning on or N to turn it off.

6. Press F7 (Exit) or click the right mouse button.

WordPerfect inserts a [Kern] code in your document, turning kerning on or off.

 Tip: If WordPerfect does not kern the loose character pairs to your liking, you can manually kern the pair by inserting an [Advance] code between the two characters. Refer to *Advance*.

 Tip: The KERN.TST file included with WordPerfect includes the most frequently kerned pairs of letters. You can retrieve this file and print it to see how letter pairs will be kerned. By changing the font before printing, you can test kerning for different fonts.

Keyboard Layout, Edit (see also *Keyboard Layout, Select* and *Keyboard Layout, Map*)

Function: Lets you edit an existing keyboard layout.

Keystrokes:

Keyboard	*Mouse*
Shift-F1 (Setup)	**File**
5 (Keyboard Layout)	Setup
Highlight keyboard layout	Keyboard Layout
	Highlight keyboard layout
7 (Edit)	**Edit**
Highlight key	Highlight key
Select option	Select option
Enter change	Enter change
F7 (Exit)	Right mouse button

Example:

```
Keyboard: Edit

  Name: ENHANCED

  Key              Action            Description

  Home             {KEY MACRO 1}     Home Home Home Left Arrow
  Num 5            {Home}            Home
  Shft-F11         {KEY MACRO 2}     Italics
  Shft-F12         {KEY MACRO 3}     Retrieve Block
  Ctrl-F11         {KEY MACRO 4}     Large
  Ctrl-F12         {KEY MACRO 5}     Move Block
  Alt-F11          {KEY MACRO 6}     Very Large
  Alt-F12          {KEY MACRO 7}     Copy Block
  Ctrl-Num 5       {Goto}            Go To
  Alt-Up           {KEY MACRO 10}    Move Up by Sentence
  Alt-Left         {KEY MACRO 8}     Move Left One Column
  Alt-Right        {KEY MACRO 9}     Move Right One Column
  Alt-Down         {KEY MACRO 11}    Move Down by Sentence

  1 Action; 2 Dscrptn; 3 Original; 4 Create; 5 Move; Macro: 6 Save; 7 Retrieve: 1
```

To edit the keyboard layout, you highlight the keyboard you want to edit and select Edit to display the Keyboard: Edit screen. At the bottom of the screen, a menu appears, offering the following options:

Action: Displays a macro editing screen for the key. You can use it to assign a different WordPerfect feature to this key or create a macro for it. To assign a feature, press Ctrl-V and then the function key. For example, you can assign Help by pressing Ctrl-V, then F3. Refer to *Macros, Macro Editor* for more information about how to use the Editor.

Dscrptn: Lets you change the description that appears in the third column to describe the function of a key in greater detail.

Original: Returns a key to its original function (the function that WordPerfect originally assigned to the key).

Create: Lets you assign a WordPerfect feature or option to a key that's not shown in the Keyboard: Edit screen. Select 4 (Create) and press the key to which you want to assign the feature or option, for example, Alt-B. Next, enter a description for the key's function. Press Enter and delete any codes that may appear. Then press the key that you would normally press to use the feature, for example F6 (Bold). (If you want to assign Cancel, Exit, Help, or any of the arrow keys to another key, you must press Ctrl-V before pressing the key.) Press F7 (Exit) when you finish.

Move: Lets you move a key assignment to another key. For example, if you want to move the key assignment for Alt-C to Alt-G, highlight Alt-C, select 5 (Move), and press Alt-G.

Save: Saves the highlighted key assignment as a macro. You can then use the Macro feature to execute the macro regardless of which keyboard layout you're using. To use Save, highlight the key, select **Save**, and then type up to eight characters for the macro name.

Retrieve: Lets you assign an existing macro to a key. To use Retrieve, select **Retrieve**, enter the key you want to assign the macro to, and then enter the macro name (up to eight characters).

 Editing a Keyboard Layout

1. Press Shift-F1 (Setup) or select Setup from the **File** menu.	A list of setup options appears.
2. Select **5** (Keyboard Layout).	The Setup: Keyboard Layout screen appears.
3. Highlight the name of the keyboard layout you want to edit.	You can use option **N** (Name Search) to move the cursor onto it.
4. Select **7** (Edit).	The Keyboard: Edit menu appears.
5. If the key you want to edit appears in the list, move the cursor to highlight it.	If the key is not displayed, its function is the same as on the original keyboard. In such a case, you must select **4** (Create) to modify the key.
6. Select one of the options listed at the bottom of the screen, and enter your changes.	
7. Press F7 (Exit) or click the right mouse button.	This saves the change and returns you to the Setup: Keyboard Layout screen. You can use this menu to make other changes or select the modified keyboard layout to begin using it.
8. Press F7 (Exit) or click the right mouse button.	This returns you to the Edit screen.

Keyboard Layout, Map (see also *Keyboard Layout, Select* and *Keyboard Layout, Edit*)

Function: Shows you the overall layout of your keyboard.

Keystrokes:

Keyboard	*Mouse*
Shift-F1 (Setup)	File
5 (Keyboard Layout)	Setup
Highlight keyboard layout	Keyboard Layout
	Highlight keyboard layout
8 (Map)	Map
Highlight key	Highlight key
Select option	Select option
Enter change	Enter change
F7 (Exit)	Right mouse button

Example:

```
Keyboard: Map
  Name: ENHANCED
  Alt  Key    ABCDEFGHIJKLMNOPQRSTUVWXYZ1234567890-=\`[];',./
       Action CCCCCCCCCCCCCCCCCCCCCCCCCCCCCCCCCCCCCCCCCC

  Ctrl Key    ABCDEFGHIJKLMNOPQRSTUVWXYZ[\]_              C = Command
       Action CCCCCCCCCCCCCCCCCCCCCCCCCCCCCCCC           M = Keyboard Macro
       Key    !"#$%&'()*+,-./0123456789:;<=>?@
       Action !"#$%&'()*+,-./0123456789:;<=>?@
       Key    ABCDEFGHIJKLMNOPQRSTUVWXYZ[\]^_`
       Action ABCDEFGHIJKLMNOPQRSTUVWXYZ[\]^_`
       Key    abcdefghijklmnopqrstuvwxyz{|}~
       Action abcdefghijklmnopqrstuvwxyz{|}~
  Key         Action        Description
  Alt-B       {Bold}

  1 Key; 2 Macro; 3 Description; 4 Original; 5 Compose; N Key Name Search: 1
```

The Keyboard: Map screen gives you a "big picture" view of your keyboard. This map shows the functions of most of the keys on your keyboard, including the Alt-letter and Ctrl-letter keys; characters and symbols such as !, ?, and ( ), and all numbers and upper- and lowercase letters. It does not display the function keys, cursor movement keys, or delete keys. You can change any of the key assignments displayed, just as you can with the Keyboard Layout Edit feature. You cannot, however, assign an existing macro to a key, assign a key's function to a macro, or assign features to function keys.

When you display the Keyboard: Map screen, you'll see the following options listed at the bottom of the screen:

Key: Lets you assign a feature that is already assigned to one key to another key or any letter, number, or symbol on the keyboard. For example, if you want to use Alt-B for Bold, move the cursor to Alt-B, select **1** (**Key**), and press F6 (Bold).

Macro: Displays a macro editing screen for the key, which you can use to assign a WordPerfect feature to the key or create a macro for it. Refer to *Macros, Macro Editor* for more information about how to use the editor.

Description: Lets you describe the function of a key in greater detail. The description will then appear on the Edit: Keyboard Layout screen, and under the `Description` heading in this screen when the cursor is highlighting the key.

Original: Returns a key to its original function, deleting the current assignment. You may be asked to confirm this command.

Compose: Lets you assign a character from one of WordPerfect's character sets to a key. To use it, move the cursor to the key you want to change and select **5** (**Compose**). In response to the `Key =` prompt, type the number of the WordPerfect character set you want to use, type a comma, and type the number of the WordPerfect character. Press Enter. (Refer to *Compose Key* and *Character Sets, WordPerfect's*).

Key Name Search: Lets you find a key quickly and move the cursor onto it for editing. Select this option; then press the key you want to look for. You can press any letter, number, or character, or Alt or Ctrl with any letter.

 Note: The Action row under each key shows the key's current assignment. If you see a letter, number, or character, it means that letter, number, or character is assigned to the key. If you see a bold M, a keyboard macro is assigned to the key. If you see a bold C, a feature or operation (not a macro) is assigned to the key. When the cursor is highlighting a key, its name, action (assignment), and description appear just above the menu line at the bottom of the screen. To move to another key, you can move the cursor up, down, left, or right using the four arrow keys.

Modifying the Keyboard Map

1. Press Shift-F1 (Setup) or select Setup from the **File** menu.

   The main Setup menu appears.

2. Select **5** (**Keyboard Layout**).

   The Setup: Keyboard Layout screen appears.

3. Highlight the name of the keyboard layout whose map you want to view.

   You can use option **N** (Name Search) to move the cursor onto the layout.

4. Select **8** (**Map**).

   The Keyboard: Map screen appears.

5. Highlight the key whose assignment you want to change.

6. Select one of the options listed at the bottom of the screen, and enter the required change.

   The change appears on the map.

7. Press F7 (Exit) or click the right mouse button.

   This returns you to the Setup: Keyboard Layout screen. There, you can make other changes or select the revised keyboard layout to begin using it, or press F7 (Exit) to return to the Edit screen without further action.

8. Press F7 (Exit) or click the right mouse button.

   This returns you to the Edit screen.

 Tip: If you change your mind about the modifications you've made, press F1 (Cancel) and press Y in response to the `Cancel Changes?` prompt.

Keyboard Layout, Select (see also *Keyboard Layout, Edit* and *Keyboard Layout, Map*)

Function: Lets you select a different keyboard layout.

Keystrokes:

Keyboard	*Mouse*
Shift-F1 (Setup)	**File**
5 (Keyboard Layout)	Setup
Highlight choice	**Keyboard** Layout
1 (Select)	Double-click on choice
F7 (Exit)	Right mouse button

Example:

```
Setup: Keyboard Layout

     ALTRNAT
     ENHANCED
     EQUATION
   * MACROS
     SHORTCUT



 1 Select; 2 Delete; 3 Rename; 4 Create; 5 Copy; 6 Original;
 7 Edit; 8 Map; N Name search; 1
```

By default, specific keys are assigned to execute certain WordPerfect functions. For example, you press F7 to exit, F1 to cancel, and F10 to save. If WordPerfect is the first word-processing program you've used, you should keep the existing assignments, so the keystrokes in this book and in the WordPerfect documentation will work as described. However, if you're comfortable with another word processing program, or if you want to assign frequently used macros to Ctrl-letter combinations, you can change the key assignments, effectively customizing your keyboard. (Refer to *Keyboard Layout, Edit* and *Keyboard Layout, Map* to determine how to change the key assignments.)

When you change your keyboard layout, WordPerfect saves the changes in a special file with the .WPK extension. You can then select the file from a list whenever you want to use your customized keyboard. WordPerfect has included several alternate keyboard layouts on disk. For example, the Altrnat keyboard assigns the Help function to F1, Escape to F3, and Cancel to Esc. If you have an enhanced keyboard, the Enhanced Keyboard Layout lets you press Alt-Up Arrow or Alt-Down Arrow to move by sentence, and Ctrl-Up Arrow and Ctrl-Down Arrow to move by paragraph. If you installed the Utility files during the installation process, you can choose a different keyboard layout, even if you have not yet created your own.

Selecting a Different Keyboard Layout

1. Press Shift-F1 (Setup) or select Setup from the File menu.

   The main Setup menu appears.

2. Select **Keyboard Layout (5)**.

   The Setup: Keyboard Layout screen appears. If you installed the Utility files, a list of alternate keyboard layouts appears.

3. Select the alternate keyboard layout you want to use or select 6 (Original) to use the original keyboard definition.

   You can select a layout by double-clicking the left mouse button on the layout or highlighting the layout and choosing 1 (Select). This returns you to the Setup menu.

4. Press F7 (Exit) or click the right mouse button.

   WordPerfect returns you to the Edit screen. The selected keyboard layout is now in effect.

When you display the Setup: Keyboard Layout screen, a list of options appears at the bottom of the screen. You have already seen that option **1** (Select) lets you choose a different layout, and option **6** (Original) lets you select the original layout. The following options are also available:

Delete: Lets you erase the highlighted keyboard layout file. Select the option and press Y.

Rename: Lets you change the name of a keyboard layout. You can enter up to eight characters. WordPerfect renames the file and adds the .WPK extension automatically.

Create: Lets you create a new keyboard layout. Select this option and enter a name, up to eight characters. This new layout initially is the same as the original layout. You can then select Edit to change any of the keys.

Copy: Allows you to copy an existing keyboard layout, so you can modify it instead of creating a new layout from scratch. To use it, highlight the keyboard you want to copy, select Copy, then enter a new name (up to eight characters). This becomes the keyboard and .WPK file name.

Edit: Displays the selected keyboard layout so you can edit any of the key assignments. (Refer to *Keyboard Layout, Edit*.)

Map: Displays the key assignments for each key. For example, if you assigned a macro to Alt-C, an M appears next to the letter C, indicating that a macro is assigned to that keystroke. You can also use this screen to edit key definitions. (Refer to *Keyboard Layout, Map.*)

Name Search: If you have a long list of keyboard layouts, this option lets you search for a layout by name and move the highlight cursor onto it more quickly. Select this option; then type the first letter of the keyboard layout.

 Tip: You can press Ctrl-6 while in any screen to return to the original keyboard definition for the current editing session.

Key Repeat Speed (see *Cursor Speed*)

L

Labels, Printing (see also *Paper Size and Type*)

Function: Lets you format and print on labels of any size.

Keystrokes:

Keyboard	*Mouse*
Shift-F8 (Format)	Layout
2 (Page)	Page
7 (Paper Size/Type)	Paper Size/Type
2 (Add) or 5 (Edit)	Add or Edit
4 (Labels)	Labels
Select option(s)	Select option(s)
Enter change(s)	Enter change(s)
8 (Labels), Y	Labels, Yes
Change settings	Change settings
F7 (Exit) twice	Right mouse button twice
1 (Select)	Select
F7 (Exit) twice	Right mouse button twice

Code: [Paper Sz/Typ: Labels]

Example:

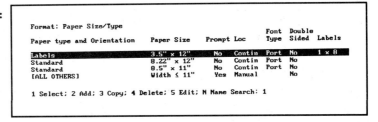

On most printers, WordPerfect can print on any size of paper, including labels of any size. To format a document such as an address list for printing on a sheet of labels, you select the specific label form from the Format: Paper Size/Type menu. However, if the labels you plan to use are not defined for your printer, they will not appear on this menu, so you must define them first. This is a one-time procedure that you use to set up a specific type of label for the currently selected printer, entering information such as the dimensions of the physical page, the number of rows and columns per page, the distance between columns, and the label margins. If the paper size (*physical page*) differs from the size of the individual labels, as on a sheet with three columns and ten rows of labels, each label is a *logical page*.

WordPerfect includes a Labels macro that you can use to define one or more commonly used label types, such as Avery 5160 and 5162, and 3M 7701 and 7712. Before trying to define labels yourself, run this macro to determine if your labels are included in this list. If they are, all you have to do is select them, and WordPerfect will automatically define them. The procedure is much easier than defining them yourself. If they are not listed, follow the steps in "Defining Labels Manually" to define them.

 Defining Labels Using WordPerfect's Label Macro

1. Make sure the currently selected printer is the one you want to define these labels for, since they can only be set up for one printer at a time.

   WordPerfect stores the label definitions in the printer's PRS file. To check on the printer, press Shift-F7 (Print) or select **Print** from the File menu. The currently selected printer appears next to the Select Printer option. You can use this option to change the printer, if necessary.

2. Start the macro by pressing Alt-F10 (Macro), or by displaying the **T**ools menu and selecting **M**acro, then **E**xecute.

   The Macro prompt appears, prompting you to enter a name for the macro.

3. Type labels and press Enter.

   WordPerfect runs the Labels macro and presents a list of common label types. If the labels you want to define are not listed, press Cancel (F1) or click both mouse buttons, and skip the rest of this section, since you'll have to define the labels yourself. If the macro does not start and you see an ERROR message indicating that the file was not found, WordPerfect cannot find the macro file, LABELS.WPM, in

	the current directory, or the one specified for your macros on the Setup: Location of Files menu. The Labels macro should have been installed with WordPerfect, if you copied the keyboard and macro files. If not, use the Install utility to do so now.
4. Move the cursor onto the labels that you want to define, and choose **1** (**Select**). If you want to define several, mark each one with an asterisk; then choose **1** (**Select**) and type Y.	If you selected several labels, a prompt appears asking if you want to set up the marked labels. If you selected only one, a menu appears prompting you to select a location. You can use continuous feed, specify a bin number, or use manual feed for your labels. If you are setting up several labels, after you type Y, this menu will appear for each label type.
5. Select the location for your labels: **1** (**Continuous**), **2** (**Bin Number**), or **3** (**Manual**).	If you select Bin Number, you will be asked to enter the bin number for the labels. If you select Manual, WordPerfect will ask if you want to be prompted to load the labels before printing. Next, the Format: Paper Size/Type menu appears, with a list of available paper sizes and types, including the label or labels you just defined.
6. If you want to format the current document using the labels, highlight the label definition and choose **1** (**Select**). If not, choose **2** (**Exit**).	WordPerfect returns you to the Edit screen. If you selected a label definition, WordPerfect inserts a Paper Size/Type code at the cursor position.

 ## Defining Labels Manually

1. Press Shift-F8 (Format), or display the **Layout** menu.	A list of formatting options appears.

2. Select **Page (2)**.	The Format: Page menu appears.
3. Select **7 (Paper Size/Type)**.	A list of defined paper sizes and types for this printer appears. If one of them closely resembles the labels you want to define, you can select Copy and then choose Edit to modify the copied labels to match the new specifications. Otherwise, use the Add option.
4. Select **2 (Add)**, or highlight existing labels and select **3 (Copy)**, then **5 (Edit)**.	If you selected Add, the Format: Paper Type menu appears. Otherwise, the Format: Edit Paper Definition screen appears, and you can skip to step 6.
5. Select **4 (Labels)**.	The Format: Edit Paper Definition screen appears.
6. Unless the labels are on an 8.5" x 11" backing, select **1 (Paper Size)**, and then select one of the paper sizes that represents the dimensions of the physical page. If your paper size is not listed, select **o (Other)** and enter the exact dimensions for Width and Height.	The physical page is the backing sheet for the labels. This is usually standard size paper, 8.5" x 11". If you use Other, the Width is either the width of the physical page or, if tractor-fed, the label itself. The Height is the physical length of the backing page or, if tractor-fed, the label itself. Unless tractor-fed labels are adjacent, include the space separating one label from the one below it in the measurement for Height.
7. Select **5 (Location)**, and specify how you will load these labels into your printer: as continuous forms, in a bin, or manually.	
8. Select **8 (Labels)**, and press Y (Yes).	The Format: Labels menu appears.
9. Select **1 (Label Size)** and enter the width and height for one label.	This specifies the width and height of the individual label. The specific dimensions are usually listed on the package that the labels came in. If they are in

fractions, type them that way (as in 7/8) and WordPerfect will convert them to decimal equivalents. If you selected Other in step 6, the dimensions should be defined already. If you are using tractor-fed, 1-across labels, you can skip this step and steps 10-13.

10. Select **2** (**N**umber of Labels) and enter the number of rows and columns.

For example, if there are two columns of labels across the page and six rows of labels down it, enter 2 for the columns and 6 for the rows. If you are defining tractor-fed labels (1-across), specify 1 column and 1 row. If you will be printing 1-across labels on a laser printer, the rows will correspond to the number of labels on the backing sheet that you feed into the printer (there is only one column).

11. Select **3** (Top Left **C**orner) and enter the distance from the top of the page to the top of the first label and the distance from the left corner of the page to the first label on the left.

Enter 0 if there is no space.

12. Select **4** (**D**istance Between Labels) and specify the distance between the columns and rows, if there is any.

If the labels are adjacent, without any space between them, enter 0 for both dimensions. If you defined the Paper Size as the width and height of one label in step 6, do not enter the space between rows in this option (or you'll duplicate it).

13. Select **5** (Label **M**argins) and specify the four margins for an individual label.

14. Press F7 (Exit), or click the right mouse button until you return to the Paper Size/Type menu.

The dimensions you just entered now appear on this menu.

15. Unless you want to use the labels in the current document, press F7 (Exit) twice, or click the right mouse button until you return to the Edit screen.

To format the current document with the Labels, highlight the definition and then choose **1** (**Select**).

 ## Selecting Labels to Format a Document

1. Place the cursor at the top of the first page in the document.

The Paper Size/Type code that WordPerfect inserts when you select Labels must be at the top of the document.

2. Press Shift-F8 (Format), or display the **Layout** menu.

3. Select **Page** (**2**).

The Format: Page menu appears.

4. Select **7** (Paper **Size/Type**).

The Format: Paper Size/Type menu appears.

5. Move the cursor onto the label type you want to use for this document, and choose **1** (Select).

The size and type of the labels you selected are displayed next to the option on the Format: Page menu.

6. Press F7 (Exit) or click the right mouse button.

WordPerfect inserts a [Paper Sz/Typ] code at the cursor position, and formats the document accordingly.

 Tip: If you are using labels where the physical page differs from the logical page, as on a backing sheet with two columns of labels across and six rows down, the Pg indicator on the status line will show each label to be on a separate page. However, in this case it refers to the logical page, not the physical page. If you use the Full Page option in View Document, you'll see that the labels are on the same physical page. Do not print labels using the Page option on the main Print menu, because WordPerfect will only print the label the cursor is on when you select the option. Instead, use the Full Document option to print your labels.

Landscape (see *Orientation, Portrait and Landscape*)

Language (see *Foreign Languages*)

Large Print (see *Size Attributes*)

Leaders (see *Dot Leaders*)

Leading Adjustment

Function: Lets you adjust the space between lines and paragraphs.

Keystrokes:

Keyboard	*Mouse*
Shift-F8 (Format)	Layout
4 (Other)	Other
6 (Printer Functions)	Printer Functions
6 (Leading Adjustment)	Leading Adjustment
Enter change	Enter change
F7 (Exit)	F7 (Exit)

Code: [Leading Adj]

Example:

```
Format: Printer Functions
        1 - Kerning                              No
        2 - Printer Command
        3 - Word Spacing                         Optimal
            Letter Spacing                       Optimal
        4 - Word Spacing Justification Limits
              Compressed to (0% - 100%)          60%
              Expanded to (100% - unlimited)     400%
        5 - Baseline Placement for Typesetters   No
              (First baseline at top margin)
        6 - Leading Adjustment
              Primary   - [SRt]                  0"
              Secondary - [HRt]                  1u

    Selection: 6
```

Leading Adjustment ──── (points to line "Primary - [SRt]")

If you are using a proportionally spaced font, two points of extra space (leading) are added to the font's height to create blank space between the lines. The amount of space between the baselines of two lines equals the point size of the font plus the two points of leading that WordPerfect adds. If you want to increase or decrease this measurement, use the Leading Adjustment option.

You can change the leading for lines within paragraphs or between paragraphs. The primary entry (for soft returns) lets you control the amount of space between lines. You will usually change this setting in small increments (2 or 3 points) to spread out your text. The secondary entry lets you control the amount of space between lines separated by hard returns, usually at the end of paragraphs. If you are single-spacing a document, you can use the Leading Adjustment option to add a little extra space between paragraphs.

 ## Changing Leading

1. Press Shift-F8 (Format) or display the **L**ayout menu.

   A list of formatting options appears.

2. Select **O**ther (4).

   The Format: Other menu appears.

3. Select **6** (**P**rinter Functions).

   The Format: Printer Functions menu appears.

4. Select **6** (**L**eading Adjustment).

   WordPerfect prompts you to enter a primary and secondary leading adjustment. The default is 0" for both. However, WordPerfect automatically includes 2 points of leading in the line height calculation for proportionally spaced fonts.

5. To change the space between lines within a paragraph, type a measurement and press Enter.

   For example, type 2p to insert two extra points between lines. To decrease the leading, enter a negative number. If your unit of measure is inches, WordPerfect converts the entry into inches. If you don't want to enter a primary leading adjustment, press Down Arrow.

6. To change the space between paragraphs, type a measurement and press Enter.

If you don't want to change the secondary adjustment, press Enter.

7. Press F7 (Exit) or click the right mouse button twice.

WordPerfect inserts the [Leading Adj] code at the cursor position.

 Note: Remember that you can use the Leading feature to *decrease,* as well as increase, leading. For example, you may wish to decrease the leading between a heading and the first paragraph of a section.

Left Justification (see *Justification*)

Left Margin Release (see *Margin Release*)

Left/Right Indent (see *Indent*)

Left/Right Margins (see *Margins, Left/Right*)

Line Draw

Function: Lets you draw lines, boxes, graphs, borders, and other illustrations using a variety of characters.

Keystrokes:

Keyboard	*Mouse*
Ctrl-F3 (Screen)	Tools
2 (Line Draw)	Line Draw
1 | or 2 | or 3 *	1 | or 2 | or 3 *
Arrow keys	Arrow keys
F7 (Exit)	F7 (Exit)

Example:

```
CAUTION!  Before you start to draw, make sure Left
Justification is on; otherwise, you may get some broken
lines.
```

You can use WordPerfect's Line Draw feature to draw horizontal or vertical lines, to box important text, construct organizational charts, and even create blocky schematics. WordPerfect uses the line-draw characters from its number 3 character set to construct these shapes.

Caution: Before you start drawing, make sure Left Justification is on and the font you are using is not a proportional one. If you draw with Full Justification on, you may get some broken lines.

 ### Drawing a Line

1. Press Ctrl-F3 (Screen) or display the **Tools** menu.

   A list of special tools appears.

2. Select **Line Draw (2)**.

   The Line Draw menu appears.

3. Select one of the characters displayed or select **4** (Change) and enter the character you want to use.

   To use the Other option, press 9, and then type any character on the keyboard, or enter a character from one of WordPerfect's character sets by pressing Ctrl-2 (Compose) and then typing the two numbers, such as 4, 0 for a bullet. The cursor is now in Line Draw mode. Pressing any arrow key will start drawing.

4. Use the arrow keys to move the cursor in the direction you want to draw the line.

   When you turn a corner, WordPerfect creates a corner, inserting a [HRt] code at that position. Arrows at the end of the line do not print, but you can press End to erase one.

5. If you need to move through the document without drawing a line, select **6** (**Move**).

When you're done moving the cursor, you can draw again by selecting the line-draw character you want to use.

6. If you need to erase a portion of the line, select **5** (**Erase**) and move the cursor over the section of the line you want to erase.

When you're done erasing, you can draw again by selecting the line-draw character you want to use.

7. Press F7 (**Exit**) when you're done.

The Line-Draw menu disappears from the bottom of your screen.

Note: For the Line Draw feature to work properly, your printer must support graphics. Also, if you choose to draw with a character from one of WordPerfect's character sets, make sure the character set supports graphics.

Tip: To insert text inside of a box drawn with Line Draw, press Ins so the Typeover prompt appears; then type your text. Don't press Enter, because each line already contains a [HRt] code. If you do, press Backspace right away to fix the mistake. To move down, press Down Arrow instead of Enter.

Line Format (see *Format Line*)

Line Height (see also *Leading Adjustment* and *Baseline Placement for Typesetters*)

Function: Lets you enter a fixed measurement for line height.

Keystrokes: *Keyboard*   *Mouse*
                 Shift-F8 (Format)   Layout
                 1 (Line)   Line
                 4 (Line Height)   Line Height
                 2 (Fixed)   Fixed
                 line height   *line height*
                 F7 (Exit)   Right mouse button

Code: [Ln Height]

By default, WordPerfect automatically calculates line height according to the font in use. If you use single-spacing, line height extends from the baseline of one line to the baseline of the next one. If you use two fonts on a line, line height will be measured according to the largest one. WordPerfect allows sufficient space for the characters and, in proportionally spaced fonts, additional space between lines of text called *leading*. This keeps lines of text from overlapping. However, some printing specifications may require an exact line height. In that case, you'll need to set the line height yourself, as follows:

 ## Setting Line Height

1. Press Shift-F8 (Format) or display the Layout menu.

    A list of formatting options appears.

2. Select Line (**1**).

    The Format: Line menu appears.

3. Select **4** (Line Height).

    The line height options appear: Fixed and Auto (the default).

4. Select **2** (Fixed).

    WordPerfect displays the current line height and prompts you to enter a different setting.

5. Type a measurement for line height and press Enter.

    For example, type .2. You can type it in points, such as 18p; WordPerfect will convert your entry into the unit of measure currently in use.

6. Press F7 (Exit) or click the right mouse button.

    WordPerfect inserts the [Ln Height] code at the cursor location and returns you to the Edit screen.

Line Numbering

Function: Tells WordPerfect to print numbers next to each line of text in a document.

Keystrokes:

Keyboard	*Mouse*
Shift-F8 (Format)	Layout
1 (Line)	Line
5 (Line Numbering), Y	Line **Numbering,** Yes
Select option	Select option
Enter change	Enter change
F7 (Exit)	Right mouse button

Code: [Ln Num:On]

Example:

```
        A central concern in Moby Dick is with the essential being of
     individuals and how people can perceive it. Melville casts aside
     both the Aristotelian notion of being, that reality exists only in
     individual beings and one can understand this reality only through
  5  categories, and the Platonic notion that reality exists only in
     ideals which the individual beings merely mirror. Like the skulls
     of the Right and Sperm whales hanging on opposite sides of the
     Pequod, these two philosophies slow the ship down and must be
     disposed of. They have expended their usefulness as tools of
 10  metaphysics.

        Metaphysics requires a more comprehensive view than that. It
     requires that you know the four causes of being--material, formal,
     essential, and final. You must know all the forces that govern a
 15  being, the forces that push and pull it, the purpose that the
     object fulfills, how it was intended to be used, how it is actually
     used. You must know yourself and all the forces that influence your
     own being and your being's Being. In other words, you must know
     everything. In Moby Dick, Melville calls not for an expansion of
 20  mind, however, but for subtlety of mind. You will know all you need
     to know if you come to know completely one sublime being:
```

Line numbers are often used in legal documents, literary pieces, and other manuscripts that require interpretation. The line numbers can then be used to quickly locate and reference the lines. Although the numbers do not appear on screen, they will appear in the printed document and can be seen in View Document. When you choose to number the lines, WordPerfect offers the following options:

Count Blank Lines: This option is set to Yes, meaning WordPerfect will count blank lines—lines that contain only a hard return. If you don't want WordPerfect to count the blank lines, change this option to No.

Number Every n Lines: Counts every line, but prints the count next to every *nth* line instead of every line.

Position of Number from Left Edge: Lets you enter a distance that you want the number printed from the left edge of the page. It refers to the physical edge of the page, not the left margin.

Starting Number: By default, WordPerfect starts numbering lines on each page with number 1. You can use this option to change the starting number to some other number.

Restart Number on Each Page: If you set this option to No, WordPerfect numbers lines consecutively throughout the document. If you leave the default of Yes, WordPerfect restarts numbering at the top of each page.

 ## Numbering Lines

1. Position the cursor where you want the line numbering to start.

   The cursor must be at the left edge of the line when you turn line numbering on, or the numbering won't start until the following line.

2. Press Shift-F8 (Format) or display the Layout menu.

   A list of formatting options appears.

3. Select **Line (1)**.

   The Format: Line menu appears.

4. Select **5** (Line Numbering).

   WordPerfect prompts you to confirm your selection.

5. Press Y.

   The Format: Line Numbering menu appears.

6. Select the option you want to change and enter your change.

7. Press F7 (Exit) or click the right mouse button.

   WordPerfect returns you to the Edit screen and inserts a [Ln Num:On] code. You can turn Line Numbering on and off throughout the document.

Line Spacing (see also *Leading Adjustment*)

Function: Sets the number of lines inserted between lines of text.

Keystrokes:
Keyboard	*Mouse*
Shift-F8 (Format)	Layout
1 (Line)	Line
6 (Line Spacing)	Line Spacing
Enter number	Enter number
F7 (Exit)	Right mouse button

Code: [Ln Spacing]

By default, WordPerfect single-spaces your text. You can change line spacing for a document or for a block of text by inserting a [Ln Spacing] code where you want the line spacing to change. At the end of the block, insert another Line Spacing code to change it back. If you want to change the line spacing for all documents you create from this point on, enter the code on the Initial Codes screen via the Setup menu (see *Initial Codes*).

 Changing Line Spacing

1. Press Shift-F8 (Format) or display the **Layout** menu.	A list of formatting options appears.
2. Select **Line** (**1**).	The Format: Line menu appears.
3. Select **6** (Line **S**pacing).	The cursor moves up to Line Spacing:.
4. Type the number of lines you want inserted between lines of text and press Enter.	For example, type 2 and press Enter to double-space the text. You can use the increments such as 1.5 or 1/2 if your printer is capable.
5. Press F7 (Exit) or click the right mouse button.	WordPerfect inserts the [Ln Spacing] code at the cursor location. The new spacing will affect all text from the cursor to the end of the document or until the next Line Spacing code.

Link (see *Spreadsheet*)

List Files (see also *Long Document Names*)

Function: Displays a list of files in any directory and provides file management options that help you organize your files and directories.

Keystrokes: *Keyboard*
F5 (List)
Enter

Mouse
File
List **F**iles
Enter

Example:

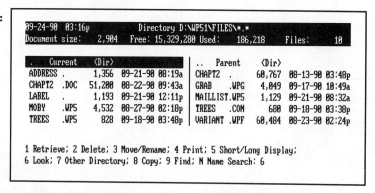

```
09-24-90  03:16p            Directory D:\WP51\FILES\*.*
Document size:    2,904  Free: 15,329,280 Used:     186,218     Files:        10

  .    Current   <Dir>            ..   Parent    <Dir>
  ADDRESS .       1,356 09-21-90 08:19a  CHAPT2  .      60,767 08-13-90 03:48p
  CHAPT2  .DOC   51,200 08-22-90 09:43a  GRAB    .WPG    4,049 09-17-90 10:49a
  LABEL   .       1,193 09-21-90 12:11p  MAILLIST.WP5    1,129 09-21-90 08:32a
  MOBY    .WP5    4,532 08-27-90 02:18p  TREES   .CON      680 09-18-90 03:38p
  TREES   .WP5      828 09-18-90 03:48p  VARIANT .WPF   60,484 08-23-90 02:24p

  1 Retrieve; 2 Delete; 3 Move/Rename; 4 Print; 5 Short/Long Display;
  6 Look; 7 Other Directory; 8 Copy; 9 Find; N Name Search: 6
```

The List Files screen displays a list of files in the current drive and directory. Using this list, you can perform the following operations:

Retrieve: Choose this option to retrieve the highlighted file for editing.

Delete: Deletes the highlighted file, the marked files, or directory (if empty) from disk. If you are deleting a directory, you must delete all the files in that directory or you'll receive an error message and won't be able to delete the directory. Be careful with this option.

Move/Rename: Lets you rename and/or move a file. This option is useful for moving several files to a different directory or disk.

Print: Lets you print a document or group of marked files without having to retrieve them. Refer to *Print File from the List Files Screen.*

Short/Long Display: Lets you change the display of the list of files from the default, short display, to a long display that includes additional information for each file, such as descriptive names and document types. To create the descriptive names, you can use Document Summary or change the Long Document Name option on the Setup: Document Management/Summary screen to Yes. You can also see alias names, if you created them for your directories.

Look: Lets you view the contents of a file without retrieving it. You can look at a file by highlighting its name and pressing Enter, but you cannot edit the file when it's displayed on the Look screen. (Refer to *Look.*)

Other Directory: Lets you change the default directory or create a new directory.

Copy: Copies a file under another name or to another disk or directory. Also copies a group of marked files to another disk or directory.

Find: Searches all displayed files for a word, phrase, or part of a file name, or for files created on a certain date or between a range of dates, and narrows the display to files that match your criteria. You can use wild-card characters in the search for file names. Use ? in place of a single character or * in place of a group of characters.

Name Search: Lets you move the cursor onto any file name or directory name by typing the first few characters of the name.

 Tip: You can change directories on the List Files screen by highlighting the directory's name and pressing Enter. You can move up one level in the directory tree by highlighting `Parent` and pressing Enter.

 ### Viewing a List of Files

1. Press F5 (List) or select List Files from the File menu.

   The path to the current drive and directory appears in the lower-left corner of your screen.

2. If you want to view the files in a different directory, type the path to that directory.

   When you begin typing, the default path disappears, and what you type appears in its place.

3. Press Enter.

   The List Files screen appears, displaying a list of files in the selected drive and directory.

4. Move the highlight to the file you want to work with, or type an asterisk (*) next to each file to work with a group of files.

   You can mark or unmark all files listed by pressing Alt-F5 (Mark Text) or Home,*.

5. Select an option from the menu at the bottom of the screen.

   WordPerfect will prompt you to enter additional information.

6. Answer the prompts.

   WordPerfect carries out the command.

7. Unless you selected **Retrieve**, exit the List Files screen by pressing F7 (Exit) or the space bar or by clicking the right mouse button.

WordPerfect returns you to the normal editing screen.

You can change drives and directories at any time on the List Files screen by pressing F5 (List) and entering the path to the directory whose contents you want to view. You can print the file list by pressing Shift-F7. If the short display is on screen, that display is printed. If the long display is shown, the long display is printed.

Lists, Define (see also *Lists, Mark Text* and *Generate*)

Function: Lets you set the position and numbering style for your list.

Keystrokes:

Keyboard	*Mouse*
Alt-F5 (Mark Text)	**Mark**
5 (Define)	**Define**
2 (Define List)	**List**
list number	*list number*
Enter	Enter
numbering style	*numbering style*

Code: [Def Mark:List]

Example:

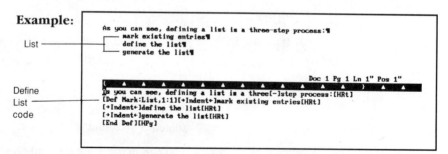

List

Define
List
code

WordPerfect can automatically generate a list of figures, tables, headings, or any other items in your document that you want to mark. To generate a list, you must mark each entry you want included in the list (see *Lists, Mark Text*), and then define it. This inserts a [Def Mark:List] code at the cursor position, telling WordPerfect which list you want to generate (lists 1-10) and what numbering style to use. The last step is to have WordPerfect generate the list. WordPerfect searches the document from the beginning up to this code to find the items you marked and includes them in the list. The items will be listed in the order they appear in the document.

Defining a List

1. Position the cursor where you want the list to appear but after all the marked items that you want to include in the list.

2. Press Ctrl-Enter if you want the list to start on a separate page.

   WordPerfect inserts a hard page break at the cursor position.

3. Type a heading for the list, if desired.

4. Press Enter one or more times to insert space between the heading and the list.

5. Press Alt-F5 (Mark Text) or display the **Mark** menu.

   The Mark Text menu appears.

6. Select **Define** (**5**).

   The Mark Text: Define menu appears.

7. Select **2** (Define List).

   WordPerfect prompts you to enter a number for the list. (You can generate up to 10 lists.) List 6 will automatically generate figure box captions; 7, table captions; 8, text box captions; 9, user-defined box captions; and 10, equation box captions.

8. Type a number for the list and press Enter.

   WordPerfect prompts you to select a numbering style from among five options.

9. Select a numbering style from the list.

   WordPerfect inserts the [Def Mark:List] code and returns you to the Edit screen.

After you define your list, you can generate it. Refer to *Generate*.

Lists, Mark Text (see also *Lists, Define* and *Generate*)

Function: Lets you mark entries in a document that you want to include in a list.

Keystrokes:

Keyboard	*Mouse*
Alt-F4 (Block)	Edit
Highlight text	Block
Alt-F5 (Mark Text)	Highlight text
2 (List)	Mark
list number, Enter	List
	list number, Enter

Codes: [Mark:List #]
          [End Mark:List #]

Example:

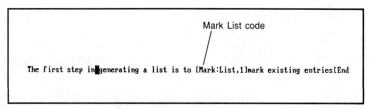

Mark List code

The first step in generating a list is to [Mark:List,1]mark existing entries[End

With WordPerfect's List feature, you can mark items such as headings, figures, or tables and generate a list from them. To do this, perform the following three-step process:

- Mark existing entries.
- Define the list.
- Generate the list.

The following steps lead you through the procedure for marking entries to include in the list. After marking the entries, you must define the list (see *Lists, Define*) and then generate the list (see *Generate*).

 Marking Existing Text for Lists

1.   Use Block feature to highlight the entry you want to include in the list.

After you've blocked the text, the List option will be available.

2. Press Alt-F5 (Mark Text) or display the **Mark** menu.	A list of Mark Text options appears.
3. Select List (**2**).	WordPerfect prompts you to enter the number of the list in which you want this entry to appear. You can have up to 10 lists in a document.
4. Type the number of the list in which you want the highlighted entry to appear.	If you want the text to appear in more than one list, you must mark the text separately for each list.
5. Press Enter.	WordPerfect inserts the code [Mark:List #] before the highlighted text and [End Mark:List #] to the right of the text.
6. Repeat steps 1-5 for each entry you want to include in the list.	

Location of Files

Function: Tells WordPerfect where certain types of files are located, such as backup files, macro files, and document files.

Keystrokes:

Keyboard	*Mouse*
Shift-F1 (Setup)	**File**
6 (Location of Files)	**Setup**
Select option	**Location of Files**
pathname	Select option
F7 (Exit)	*pathname*
	Right mouse button

Example:

```
Setup: Location of Files
      1 - Backup Files                      D:\WP51\BACKUP
      2 - Keyboard/Macro Files              D:\WP51\KEYMAC
      3 - Thesaurus/Spell/Hyphenation
                        Main                D:\WP51\DICTION
                        Supplementary       D:\WP51\DICTION
      4 - Printer Files                     D:\WP51\PRINTERS
      5 - Style Files
                Library Filename
      6 - Graphic Files                     D:\WP51\GRAPHICS
      7 - Documents                         D:\WP51\FILES
      8 - Spreadsheet Files                 E:\LOTUS

Selection: 0
```

The Location of Files feature lets you organize certain types of files into logical groups. You create the directories in which to store each group of files and use the Location of Files screen to specify the location of each group. Then whenever WordPerfect needs to access one of the files in a group, it knows where to search. You can also use this feature to specify a default directory for your documents. Using the Location of Files feature is a three-step process:

- If necessary, create the directories you want to use.

- Move each group of files to the proper directory.

- Use the Location of Files feature to tell WordPerfect where the files are located.

The Setup: Location of Files menu offers groupings for the various types of files, such as backup files, macro files, printer files, and style files. Table L.1 provides a list of sample directory names for each group, along with the file name extensions for the files included in each group. When you run the Installation program to install WordPerfect, most of the files were copied onto your hard disk, except backup files, your own macros and keyboards, and your document files. In fact, during this installation process, you can ask WordPerfect to create the directory for each file type automatically and copy all the appropriate files in each directory.

Table L.1 Groups of files.

Group	*Sample Directory Names*	*File Extensions*
Backup files	C:\WP51\BACKUP	Timed backup files (.BK1 and .BK2).
Keyboard and Macro files	C:\WP51\MACROS	Files ending in .WPM and .WPK or .SHM (for shell macros).
Thesaurus, Spelling, and Hyphenation files	C:\WP51\SPELL	Files ending in .THS, .LEX, and .HYC.
Printer files	C:\WP51\PRINTERS	Files ending in .PRS and .ALL.
Style files	C:\WP51\STYLES	Files ending in .STY.

Group	Sample Directory Names	File Extensions
Graphics files	C:\WP51\GRAPHICS	Files ending in .WPG.
Document files	Your choice	Any files you create.
Spreadsheet files	Your choice	Depends on spreadsheet you use.

Creating Directories

1. Press F5 (List) and then Enter, or select List Files from the File menu and press Enter.

   The List Files screen appears.

2. Select 7 (Other Directory).

   A New Directory = prompt appears, asking for the name and path of the directory you want to create.

3. Type the path and directory name for the new directory and press Enter.

   WordPerfect asks if you want to create the directory.

4. Press Y.

   WordPerfect creates the directory. If the new directory is one level below the current directory, its name will appear in the List Files screen.

Moving Files

1. Press F5 (List) or select List Files from the File menu.

   WordPerfect prompts you to enter a path to the directory whose files you want to move.

2. Type the path to the directory that contains the files you want to move, and press Enter twice.

   For example, if you installed all files to the C:\WP51 directory, type c:\wp51 and press Enter twice. A list of files for the selected directory appears.

3. Select **9** (**Find**), select **1** (**Name**), and then enter * .*ext* to find all files that have the specified extension.

For example, if you want to move all printer files, type * .prs and press Enter. Only those files with the specified extension appear on screen.

4. Press Alt-F5 (Mark Text).

An asterisk appears next to every file, indicating that all files have been selected.

5. Select **6** (**Move**) and press Y to confirm your command.

WordPerfect prompts you to enter the name of the directory or disk to which you want to move the files.

6. Enter the path to the directory to which you want to move the files.

For example, type c:\wp51\printers and press Enter. WordPerfect moves the selected files to the new directory.

7. Repeat the process for each group of files you want to move.

Now that you have moved groups of files to their new locations, you must tell where those files are located, or you won't be able to use them. For instance, if you moved the Speller files into a new directory, and now try to check your spelling, WordPerfect will greet you with an error message, telling you that it cannot locate the WP{WP}.LEX file (the Speller's dictionary). In order to prevent this from happening, use the Setup: Location of Files menu to tell WordPerfect where the files have been moved.

 ## Specifying the Locations of Files

1. Press Shift-F1 (Setup) or select Setup from the **File** menu.

The main Setup menu appears.

2. Select **L**ocation of Files (6).

The Setup: Location of Files menu appears.

3. Select the group of files that you just relocated, and enter the path and name of their directory.

For example, if you moved your printer files to the PRINTERS subdirectory of WP51, select **4** (**Printer Files**), type c:\wp51\printers, and press Enter. The path you typed appears in all uppercase characters, and the cursor returns to Selection:.

4. Repeat step 3 for each group of
   files you relocated.

5. Press F7 (Exit) or click the right   WordPerfect returns you to the
   mouse button.   Edit screen.

Locked Documents (see *Password Protection*)

Long Document Names (see also *List Files*)

Function: Lets you enter descriptive names for your files.

Keystrokes: *Keyboard*   *Mouse*

Keyboard	*Mouse*
Shift-F1 (Setup)	File
3 (Environment)	Setup
4 (Document	Environment
Management/Summary)	Document Management/Summary
3 (Long Document	Long Document Names, Yes
Names), Yes	Right mouse button
F7 (Exit)	

Example:

Long
document —
name

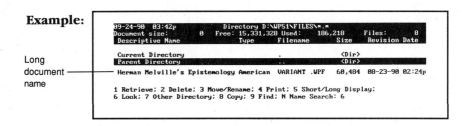

```
09-24-90  03:42p            Directory D:\WP51\FILES\*.*
Document size:      0   Free: 15,331,328 Used:     186,218    Files:      8
   Descriptive Name              Type    Filename     Size   Revision Date

   Current Directory                 .              <Dir>
   Parent Directory                  ..             <Dir>
 Herman Melville's Epistemology American  VARIANT  .WPF   60,484  08-23-90 02:24p

   1 Retrieve; 2 Delete; 3 Move/Rename; 4 Print; 5 Short/Long Display;
   6 Look; 7 Other Directory; 8 Copy; 9 Find; N Name Search: 6
```

Normally, when you save a document, WordPerfect prompts you to enter a
file name that follows the DOS rules: The name can consist of up to eight
characters and a three-character extension. If you haven't looked at a file
for some time, you may have trouble remembering what's in it because these
names offer little to jog your memory. To overcome the DOS name
restrictions, WordPerfect offers a naming system of its own, allowing you to
enter up to 68 characters (including spaces) for any file name. If you are
using this feature, WordPerfect will prompt you to enter a descriptive name
whenever you save any file. The name you enter will then appear on the
List Files screen when you use the Long Display method of viewing it.

Changing the Long Document Name Option

1. Press Shift-F1 (Setup) or select Setup from the File menu.

   The Setup menu appears.

2. Select Environment (3).

   The Setup: Environment menu appears.

3. Select 4 (Document Management/Summary).

   The Document Management/Summary menu appears.

4. Select 3 (Long Document Names).

   WordPerfect prompts you to turn the option on or off.

5. Press Y to turn the option on or N to turn it off.

   The cursor moves back down to Selection:.

6. Press F7 (Exit) or click the right mouse button.

   WordPerfect returns you to the Edit screen. If you selected Yes for Long Document Names, the next time you view the List Files screen, it will use the Long Display option.

Long Form (see *Table of Authorities, Mark Text*)

Look (see also *List Files*)

Function: Lets you view the contents of a file without leaving the List Files screen.

Keystrokes:

Keyboard	*Mouse*
F5 (List)	File
Enter	List Files
Highlight file	Enter
6 (Look) or Enter	Highlight file
	Look

Example:

```
File: D:\WP51\FILES\CHAPT2                    WP5.1       Revised: 08-13-90 03:48p
Chapter 2: Basic WordPerfect Skills

        In order to use WordPerfect effectively, there are some basic
procedures you must learn. After you learn how to type a document,
you'll need to know how to move the cursor around and edit it; how
to insert and delete text; and how to use WordPerfect's built-in
spelling checker to correct any spelling and typing errors you
might have made. Next, you'll need to print the document, and then
save it. After saving, may want to clear the screen to begin typing
another document. At the end of your work session, you'll need to
exit from WordPerfect so that you can either turn off the computer,
or use a different program. This chapter will guide you through all
of these operations. Since it's difficult to memorize them all the
first time you use them, you'll also learn how to use WordPerfect's
on-line help menus to refresh your memory. Are you ready?

Look: 1 Next Doc; 2 Prev Doc: 0
```

Whenever the List Files screen is displayed, you can view the contents of a file or its document summary without leaving the file list. Although you cannot edit the document in this mode, you can preview the contents or document summary without actually having to load the document into WordPerfect. If you're running WordPerfect through the Library Shell, you can also use this feature to append a block of text. Refer to *Append*.

 Looking at a Document

1. Press F5 (List) or select List Files from the **File** menu.

    The path to the current drive and directory appears in the lower-left corner of your screen.

2. If you want to view the files in a different directory, type the path to that directory.

    When you begin typing, the default path disappears, and what you type appears in its place.

3. Press Enter.

    The List Files screen appears, displaying a list of files in the selected drive and directory.

4. Move the cursor to highlight the file you want to view.

5. Select 6 (Look) or press Enter.

    The selected document or its document summary appears on screen. If the summary appears on screen, select **3** (Look at Text) to see the file's contents. You can now use the cursor movement keys—Up Arrow; Down Arrow; PgUp; PgDn; Home,Home,Up Arrow; or Home,Home,Down Arrow—to scroll through the file.

6. Select **1** (Next Document) to view the next document on the list or **2** (Previous Document) to see the previous one.

7. Press space bar or F7 (Exit), or click the right mouse button.

WordPerfect returns you to the List Files screen.

Lowercase Text (see *Capitalization, Converting Text*)

M

Macro, Execute (see also *Macro, Recording Keystrokes* and *Macros, Macro Editor*)

Function: Runs a macro.

Keystrokes:

Keyboard	*Mouse*
Alt-F10 (Macro)	Tools
macroname	Macro
Enter	Execute
OR	*macroname*
Alt-*letter*	Enter

How you run a macro depends on how you named it. If you assigned the macro to an Alt-*letter* combination, you can run that macro by pressing the Alt key and the letter key you assigned to the macro. If you did not use an Alt-*letter* combination, you must run the macro by pressing Alt-F10 (Macro) and entering its name. You can stop most macros at any time by pressing F1 (Cancel).

Running a Macro

1. Press Alt-F10 (Macro) or display the Tools menu and select Macro and then Execute.

   WordPerfect prompts you to enter the name of the macro.

2. Type the file name of the macro you want to run and press Enter.

   You don't need to type the file name extension (WPM). WordPerfect runs the macro.

Tip: If you forget the name of a macro, press F5 (List), type the path to the directory that holds your macro files, and press Enter. Select **9** (Find), then **1** (Name), and enter *.wpm to find all the macro files.

You can repeat a macro as many times as you like using the Esc key. To do this, press Esc and type the number of times you want the macro to repeat (don't press Enter). Press Alt-F10 (Macro) and enter the name of the macro, or press the Alt-*letter* combination that runs the macro. If WordPerfect cannot find the macro file, check the location of your macro files; refer to *Location of Files*.

Macro, Recording Keystrokes (see also *Macros, Macro Editor* and *Macro, Execute*)

Function: Lets you record keystrokes to "play back" later.

Keystrokes:

Keyboard	*Mouse*
Ctrl-F10 (Macro Define)	**Tools**
macroname.wpm	**Macro**
description	**Define**
Press keystrokes	*macroname.wpm*
Ctrl-F10 (Macro Define)	*description*
	Press keystrokes
	Tools
	Macro
	Define

As you perform tasks in WordPerfect, you may notice that you are repeating certain key combinations or typing standard text fairly often. Whenever you notice such a pattern developing, you should consider creating a macro to perform the task. A macro is simply a record of commands and/or text assigned to a special file. When you use the macro, WordPerfect replays the keystrokes exactly as you typed them when you defined the macro. Macros can include text, commands, such as formatting changes, and commands from the macro language.

You can create a macro in either of two ways. The first way is to define the macro and then have WordPerfect record your keystrokes as you perform the task in the usual way. This procedure is detailed below. The second way is to define the macro and then use the Macro Editor to insert a series of keystrokes and commands; this method is similar to writing a program, and is described in the section *Macros, Macro Editor*.

Recording Keystrokes

1. Press Ctrl-F10 (Macro Define), or display the **T**ools menu and select **Ma**cro and then **D**efine.

    WordPerfect prompts you to enter a file name for the macro.

2. Enter a name for the macro.

    You can enter a name in any one of three ways: enter a file name (up to eight characters), press Alt-*letter*, or press Enter. If you use an Alt-*letter* combination, you will be able to run the macro by holding down the Alt key and pressing the letter key of your choice. If you press Enter, you will be able to run the macro by pressing Alt-F10 and pressing Enter. (You can define only one macro in this way.)

3. Type a description for the macro (up to 39 characters) and press Enter. If you don't want to type a description, just press Enter.

    This is optional. If you type a description, it will appear when you use the Look option on the List Files menu, and it will appear in the Macro Editor.

4. Perform the task or tasks you want to record in the macro. You can also type any text you want recorded.

    Perform the task as you normally would. WordPerfect automatically records the keystrokes.

5. To complete the macro, press Ctrl-F10 (Macro Define), or display the **T**ools menu and select **Ma**cro and then **D**efine.

    The keystrokes are now saved to the designated file, and the `Macro Def` prompt disappears. See *Macro, Execute* to determine how to play back the macro.

If you want a macro to run another one as soon as the first one is finished, you can chain a second macro to the first. Whenever you want to run the two macros, you simply execute the first macro. After the first macro has finished, WordPerfect automatically starts running the second macro.

Chaining Macros When Creating the First Macro

1. Press Ctrl-F10 (Macro Define), or display the **Tools** menu and select **Macro** and then **Define**.

WordPerfect prompts you to enter a file name for the macro.

2. Enter a name for the macro.

You can enter a name in any one of three ways: enter a file name (up to eight characters), press Alt-*letter*, or press Enter. If you use an Alt-*letter* combination, you will be able to run the macro by holding down the Alt key and pressing the letter key of your choice. If you press Enter, you will be able to run the macro by pressing Alt-F10 and pressing Enter. (You can define only one macro in this way.)

3. Type a description for the macro (up to 39 characters), and press Enter. If you don't want to type a description, just press Enter.

This is optional. If you type a description, it will appear when you use the Look option on the List Files menu, and it will appear in the Macro Editor.

4. Perform the task or tasks you want to record in the macro. You can also type any text you want recorded.

Perform the task as you normally would. WordPerfect automatically records the keystrokes.

5. Press Alt-F10 (Macro), or display the **Tools** menu and select **Macro** and then **Execute**.

WordPerfect prompts you to enter the name of a macro you want to chain to this one.

6. Type the file name of the macro you want to chain to this one and press Enter.

WordPerfect places a {MACRO}macroname~ command in your macro that is visible in the Macro Editor.

7. To end the macro definition, press Ctrl-F10 (Macro Define), or display the **Tools** menu and select **Macro** and then **Define**.

The keystrokes are now saved to the designated file.

8. Create the second macro, if it does not already exist.

Macro Commands

Function: Lets you access a list of macro commands.

Keystrokes: *Keyboard*
Ctrl-PgUp (Macro Commands)

Example:

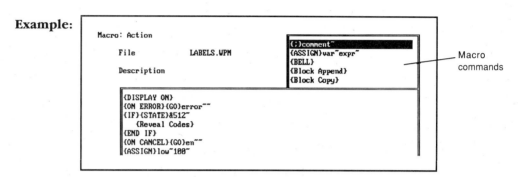

```
Macro: Action

    File              LABELS.WPM        {;}comment~
                                        {ASSIGN}var~expr~
    Description                         {BELL}                     ──── Macro
                                        {Block Append}                   commands
                                        {Block Copy}

    {DISPLAY ON}
    {ON ERROR}{GO}error~~
    {IF}{STATE}&512~
        {Reveal Codes}
    {END IF}
    {ON CANCEL}{GO}en~~
    {ASSIGN}low~100~
```

The function of the Ctrl-PgUp (Macro Commands) key varies depending on what you are in the process of doing. If you are using the Macro Editor, Ctrl-PgUp displays a list of available macro commands (refer to *Macros, Macro Editor*). If you are in the Edit screen, Ctrl-PgUp lets you assign a value to a variable. If you are marking a block of text, Ctrl-PgUp lets you assign the block to a variable. If you're in the process of creating a macro, Ctrl-PgUp lets you choose from the following four options:

Pause: This command tells the macro to pause and wait for user input. For example, when you are running a macro, at this point, you could enter text or perform a function or select an option from a menu. Your action may vary each time you perform the macro.

Display: This command displays the macro's keystrokes during execution. It shows all the menus and display changes that occur while the macro is running (although they may go by so rapidly you can barely see them). If you pause a macro to use a menu, you must use Display just before the pause.

Assign: Lets you assign values to variables.

Comment: This option lets you add comments in your macro to help you understand it if you ever edit the macro. These comments do not affect the macro's performance and can only be seen in the Macro Editor.

Macro Conversion Program

Function: Converts macros created with WordPerfect versions 4.x to
WordPerfect version 5.1.

Keystrokes: *Keyboard*
Exit WordPerfect
Activate directory containing MACROCNV.EXE
macrocnv path/filename
Enter

Example:

Conversion command

Conversion report

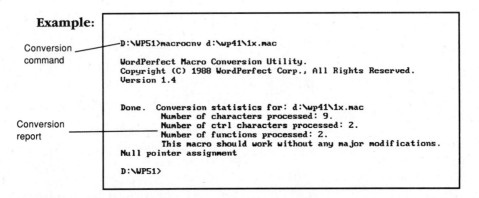

```
D:\WP51>macrocnv d:\wp41\1x.mac

WordPerfect Macro Conversion Utility.
Copyright (C) 1988 WordPerfect Corp., All Rights Reserved.
Version 1.4


Done.  Conversion statistics for: d:\wp41\1x.mac
          Number of characters processed: 9.
          Number of ctrl characters processed: 2.
          Number of functions processed: 2.
          This macro should work without any major modifications.
Null pointer assignment

D:\WP51>
```

WordPerfect's Macro Conversion program converts macros that were created in WordPerfect versions 4.x (4.1 and 4.2) to WordPerfect version 5.1. The Conversion program cannot convert all keystrokes from the earlier versions, such as function keys that have changed (Format, for example), so when it finds a keystroke that it cannot convert, it inserts a comment. After converting the macro, you can edit it using the Macro Editor. (See also, *Macros, Macro Editor*.)

In order to run the Macro Conversion program, you must have installed the Utilities when you installed WordPerfect. You cannot copy the MACROCNV.EXE directly from the original WordPerfect disk. If you did not install the Utilities, do so before trying to convert a macro. Next, activate the directory that contains the MACROCNV.EXE file. Type one of the conversion commands listed in Table M.1, and press Enter. For example, at the C:\WP51> prompt, type macrocnv c:\wp41*.mac. Converted macro files are stored in the same directory as the original macros; you must move the macros before or after converting them.

Table M.1 *Macro Conversion program commands.*

Syntax	Function
`macrocnv path\filename`	Converts the macro file to WordPerfect version 5.1.
`macrocnv path\*.ext`	Converts all macros with the specified extension (for example, .MAC) to WordPerfect version 5.1.
`macrocnv/h`	Displays help screen, providing information about the Conversion program.
`macrocnv/m path\filename`	Breaks a large macro file created in version 5.x into smaller parts, so that each part will fit in the Macro Editor. It then chains the parts together, so they'll run as a single macro. Don't use this for macros created in version 4.x or for macros that include subroutines or commands such as {IF}, {CASE}, and {WHILE}.
`macrocnv/o path\filename`	Converts the macro file to WordPerfect version 5.1, without asking permission to overwrite an existing macro file of the same name, if one exists.
`macrocnv/p path\filename >filename`	Converts the macro file to WordPerfect version 5.1 and prints a report to a disk file that represents the original macro and shows the results of the conversion, including keystrokes that could not be converted.
`macrocnv/p path\filename >prn`	Converts the macro file to WordPerfect version 5.1 and prints a report that represents the original macro, shows the results of the conversion, and notes keystrokes that could not be converted.

Note: If you convert large macro files that were created in versions 4.x, WordPerfect automatically breaks the file into parts and chains the parts together. You do not need to use and you should not use the /m switch.

Macros, Macro Editor (see also *Macro,*
Recording Keystrokes)

Function: Displays the Macro Editor, which lets you create a new macro or edit an existing macro.

Keystrokes:

Keyboard	*Mouse*
Home,Ctrl-F10 (Macro Define)	**Tools**
	Macro
macroname.wpm	**Define**
description	*macroname.wpm*
Create or edit macro	*description*
F7 (Exit)	**Edit**
	Create or edit macro
	Right mouse button

Example:

```
Macro: Action
     File          FOOTER.WPM
     Description    Creates Footer

 {DISPLAY OFF}
 {;}Creates·a·footer·with·file·name·at·left·margin,·page·number·at·
 right···Includes·pause·to·select·Base·Font.~

 {Home}{Home}{Home}{Up}        {;}Move·cursor·to·top·of·document~
 {Format}prap                  {;}Select·Footer·A,·Every·Page~
 {SYSTEM}Name~                 {;}Insert·file·name~
 {Flush Right}·{^B}            {;}Insert·page·number·code·at·right~

 {DISPLAY ON}                        {;}Turn·on·display~
 {Home}{Home}{Home}{Left}            {;}Move·cursor·to·left·edge~
 {Font}4{PAUSE}{Enter}{PAUSE}{Enter} {;}Select·font,·pause~
 {Exit}{Exit}                        {;}Exit·to·document

 Ctrl-PgUp for macro commands;  Press Exit when done
```

You can create a macro in either of two ways. The easiest way is to tell WordPerfect to record your keystrokes, and then perform the task as you normally would on the Edit screen. This method is described in the section *Macro, Recording Keystrokes*. The second way is to use the Macro Editor to insert a series of commands; this method is similar to writing a program. The macro commands you enter appear in all uppercase characters, between a set of curly braces {}. Keystroke commands and editing keys, such as Left Arrow and Del, appear within braces as well. Any text you type appears outside the braces. You can include the following information in your macro:

Macro Commands: Lets you insert commands, such as {BELL} to sound a beep, {PAUSE} to pause a macro, and {SPEED} to change the speed of macro execution. You must select these commands from the Macro Commands menu. Move the cursor where you want to insert the command, press Ctrl-PgUp to display the menu, highlight the command, and press Enter.

Keystroke Commands: You can insert commands for many of the function keys by simply pressing the desired key. For some keys, however, you must press Ctrl-V or Ctrl-F10 before pressing the key. These keys include the cursor keys, the Del and Backspace keys, Alt-*letter* combinations, the Tab key, variables, and the following four function keys: F1 (Cancel), F3 (Help), F7 (Exit), and Ctrl-F10 (Macro Define). Pressing Ctrl-V puts you in Command Insert mode for a single keystroke, so that the next keystroke becomes part of the macro. Ctrl-F10 puts you in this mode until you press Ctrl-F10 again, so all the keystrokes you press after pressing Ctrl-F10 become part of the macro until you press Ctrl-F10 again.

Text: Any text you type appears in the Macro Editor as you type it.

 Note: You cannot create a macro using the Macro Editor through the pull-down menus. You must press Home,Ctrl-F10. You can, however, use the pull-down menus to access the Macro Editor for editing an existing macro.

 ### Creating a Macro with the Macro Editor

1. Press Home,Ctrl-F10 (Macro Define).	WordPerfect prompts you to enter a file name for the macro.

2. Enter a name for the macro.

You can enter a name in any one of three ways: enter a file name (up to eight characters), press Alt-*letter*, or press Enter. If you use an Alt-*letter* combination, you will be able to run the macro by holding down the Alt key and pressing the letter key of your choice. If you press Enter, you will be able to run the macro by pressing Alt-F10 and pressing Enter. (You can define only one macro in this way.) If you type an existing name, WordPerfect assumes you want to edit the macro.

3. Type a description for the macro (up to 39 characters) and press Enter. If you don't want to type a description, just press Enter.

This is optional. If you type a description, it will appear when you use the Look option on the List Files menu, and it will appear in the Macro Editor. The Macro Editor appears.

4. Enter macro commands, keystroke commands, and text to create the macro.

The commands appear on screen. You can use the cursor movement keys, the Backspace key, and the Del key to edit the macro.

5. Press F7 (Exit) or click the right mouse button.

This ends the macro definition and saves the macro to the designated macro file or Alt-*letter* combination.

If you want to run another macro when the first one finishes, you can chain the second macro to the first. Whenever you want to run the two macros, you simply execute the first macro. When the first macro ends, WordPerfect automatically starts running the second macro. Regardless of where you insert the Chain command in the first macro, the second one won't start running until the first is finished.

Chaining Macros with the Macro Editor

1. Press Home,Ctrl-F10 (Macro Define), or display the Tools menu and select Macro and then Define.

2. Type the macro name, and press Enter until the Macro Editor appears. If you're using the pull-down menus to access the Macro Editor, select Edit when WordPerfect prompts that the file already exists.

   If you are editing an Alt-*letter* macro, press Enter only once. For a macro with a file name, press Enter twice. You should be in the Macro Editor.

3. Move the cursor to the end of the macro.

   It is best to place the Chain command at the end of the first macro, but it is not essential.

4. Press Ctrl-PgUp.

   The Macro Commands menu, a pop-up box of commands, appears.

5. Type ch to move the cursor to the {CHAIN}macroname~ command and press Enter.

   WordPerfect inserts the {CHAIN} code at the end of the macro file.

6. Type the file name of the macro you want to chain to this one, type ~ (tilde), and press Enter.

   For example, type labels~. The tilde is vital—without it, the chained macro probably won't be executed, unless it is the last entry in the Macro Editor.

7. Press F7 (Exit) or click the right mouse button to exit the Macro Editor and save the file.

   The keystrokes are now saved in the edited macro.

8. Create the second macro, if it does not already exist.

   If you try to use a macro that includes a Chain command before defining the second macro, you'll see an error message, indicating that the file cannot be found.

When you chain two macros, the first macro must be completed before WordPerfect will start running the second macro. If you want WordPerfect to start a second macro before the first one ends, then return to the first macro after the second one ends, you can *nest* one macro within another.

Nesting Macros with the Macro Editor

1. Press Home,Ctrl-F10 (Macro Define), or display the **Tools** menu and select **Macro** and then **Define**.

2. Type the macro name, and press Enter until the Macro Editor appears. If you're using the pull-down menus to access the Macro Editor, select **Edit** when WordPerfect prompts that the file already exists.

    If you are editing an Alt-*letter* macro, press Enter only once. For a macro with a file name, press Enter twice. You should be in the Macro Editor.

3. Move the cursor to the position where you want the nested macro to run.

4. Press Ctrl-PgUp.

    The Macro Commands menu appears.

5. Type n to move the cursor to the {NEST}macroname~ command and press Enter.

    WordPerfect inserts the {NEST} code at the cursor location.

6. Type the file name of the macro you want to nest within this one, type ~ (tilde), and press Enter.

    For example, type labels~. You must type the tilde, or the first macro will end at the Nest command.

7. Press F7 (Exit) or click the right mouse button to exit the Macro Editor and save the file.

    The keystrokes are now saved to the first macro file.

8. Create the second macro, if it does not already exist.

If you created chained or nested macros, you already have a basic idea of how to edit macros. Before you can edit a macro, the macro must be displayed in the Macro Editor. If you want to edit the text or commands in a macro, enter the Macro Editor using the rapid entry method. If you want to replace a macro or change its description, enter the Macro Editor with the standard entry method.

Editing Macros, Rapid Entry

1. Press Home,Ctrl-F10 (Macro Define), or display the **Tools** menu and select **Macro** and then **Define**

   WordPerfect prompts you to enter the name of the macro.

2. Enter the name of the macro or press the Alt-*letter* combination that runs the macro.

   WordPerfect displays the macro's description.

3. Edit the description, if desired, and press Enter.

   The Macro Editor appears with the selected macro displayed.

4. Edit the macro as desired.

   If you make a mistake, you can cancel all changes by pressing F1 (Cancel) and typing Y.

5. Press F7 (Exit) or click the right mouse button.

   WordPerfect saves the changes.

 Editing Macros, Standard Entry

1. Press Ctrl-F10 (Macro Define) or display the **Tools** menu and select **Macro** and then **Define**.

   WordPerfect prompts you to enter the name of the macro.

2. Enter the name of the macro or press the Alt-*letter* combination that runs the macro.

   WordPerfect displays a list of options. You can replace the selected macro, edit it, or change its description.

3. Select **Edit** (**2**).

   This places you in the Macro Editor, where the macro's keystrokes and commands appear for editing.

4. Edit the macro as desired.

   If you make a mistake, you can press F1 (Cancel) and type Y in response to the Cancel Changes prompt.

5. Press F7 (Exit) or click the right mouse button.

   WordPerfect saves the changes.

Mailing List (see *Labels, Printing*)

Margin Release (see also *Hanging Indent*)

Function: Moves cursor back to previous tab stop.

Keystrokes: *Keyboard*
Shift-Tab

Code: [←Mar Rel]

The margin release performs an action opposite to the Tab key: It moves the cursor left, to the previous tab stop. This is useful for creating hanging indents and for changing the level of a heading in an outline.

Margins, Left/Right (see also *Initial Codes* and *Initial Settings*)

Function: Lets you set the left and right margins.

Keystrokes:	*Keyboard*	*Mouse*
	Shift-F8 (Format)	Layout
	1 (Line)	Line
	7 (Margins)	Margins
	left margin	*left margin*
	Enter	Enter
	right margin	*right margin*
	Enter	Enter
	F7 (Exit)	Right mouse button

Code: [L/R Mar]

Example:

L/R
Margin
code

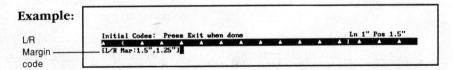

```
Initial Codes:  Press Exit when done                    Ln 1" Pos 1.5"
▲   {    ▲     ▲     ▲     ▲     ▲     ▲     ▲     ▲     ▲ ] ▲     ▲
[L/R Mar:1.5",1.25"]
```

You can set left and right margins in any of three ways, depending on how global you want the change to be. If you want the new margins to affect all documents you create from now on, change the margins in the Setup: Initial

Codes screen (see *Initial Settings*). If you want to change the default margins in the current document, change the margins on the Format: Initial Codes screen (see *Initial Codes*). If you want to change the margins within a document and insert a formatting code that affects all text from the cursor forward, position the cursor where you want the change to take effect, and then use the Format: Line menu to change the margins.

 ### Changing the Left/Right Margins Within a Document

1. Press Shift-F8 (Format) or display the Layout menu.	A list of formatting options appears.
2. Select Line (**1**).	The Format: Line menu appears.
3. Select **7** (**Margins**).	WordPerfect prompts you to enter settings for the left and right margins.
4. Type a setting for the left margin, and press Enter.	You can type the setting in points, inches, centimeters, or any unit of measure WordPerfect supports; it will automatically be converted to the unit in use. For instance, if you type 75p. and the unit of measure is inches, WordPerfect will convert it to 1.04". (*See Units of Measure.*) When you press Enter, the cursor moves down to the right margin setting.
5. Type a setting for the right margin, and press Enter.	
6. Press F7 (Exit) or click the right mouse button.	WordPerfect inserts the [L/R Mar] code at the cursor location. This change affects all text from the cursor position to the end of the document or until the next [L/R Mar] code.

Margins, Top/Bottom (see also *Baseline Placement for Typesetters*)

Function: Lets you set the top and bottom margins.

Keystrokes: *Keyboard*   *Mouse*
Shift-F8 (Format)   Layout
2 (Page)   Page
5 (Margins)   Margins
top margin   *top margin*
Enter   Enter
bottom margin   *bottom margin*
Enter   Enter
F7 (Exit)   Right mouse button

Code: [T/B Mar]

Example:

T/B
Margin ——
code

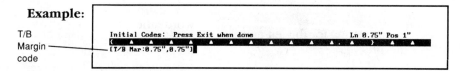

```
Initial Codes:  Press Exit when done                    Ln 0.75" Pos 1"
{   ▲    ▲    ▲    ▲    ▲    ▲    ▲    ▲    ▲  , ▲    }   ▲    ▲
[T/B Mar:0.75",0.75"]
```

You can set top and bottom margins in any of three ways, depending on how global you want the change to be. If you want the new margins to affect all documents you create from now on, change the margins in the Setup: Initial Codes screen (see *Initial Settings*). To change the default margins in the current document, change the margins on the Format: Initial Codes screen (see *Initial Codes*). If you want the change to affect the margins of specific pages within a document, position the cursor at the top of the page on which you want the change to take affect, and use the Margins option on the Format: Page menu to change them. The third method is the only one that inserts an embedded formatting code.

Changing the Top/Bottom Margins Within a Document

1. Press Shift-F8 (Format) or display the Layout menu.   A list of formatting options appears.

2. Select **Page (2)**.   The Format: Page menu appears.

3. Select **5** (Margins).

WordPerfect prompts you to enter settings for the top and bottom margins.

4. Type a setting for the top margin, and press Enter.

You can type the setting in points, inches, centimeters, or any unit of measure WordPerfect supports; it will automatically be converted to the unit in use. For instance, if you type 75p. and the unit of measure is inches, WordPerfect will convert it to 1.04". (*See Units of Measure*.) When you press Enter, the cursor moves down to the bottom margin setting.

5. Type a setting for the bottom margin, and press Enter.

6. Press F7 (Exit) or click the right mouse button.

WordPerfect inserts the [T/B Mar] code at the cursor location. This change affects this page, assuming the cursor is on the first line of the page, and all subsequent pages, or until the next [T/B Mar] code.

Mark Text (see *Index, Mark Text*; *Lists, Mark Text*; *Table of Authorities, Mark Text*; and *Table of Contents, Mark Text*)

Master Document

Function: Links several files together to create a master document, so you can manage a large project, such as a book or manual.

Keystrokes:

Keyboard	*Mouse*
Alt-F5 (Mark Text)	Mark
2 (Subdoc)	Subdocument
d:\path\filename.ext	*d:\path\filename.ext*
Enter	Enter

Codes: [Subdoc]
[Subdoc Start]
[Subdoc End]

Example:

Subdocument
comment
boxes

Subdoc: D:\PLANTS\TREES

Subdoc: D:\PLANTS\FLOWERS

Subdoc: D:\PLANTS\FRUITS

Subdoc: D:\PLANTS\VEGIES

You can use a master document whenever you want to treat several documents as a single document. For example, if you're writing a book, you will probably divide the book into chapters and store each chapter in a separate file. Although this makes each file more manageable, it introduces new problems. For example, you face the problems of numbering the pages consecutively throughout the book and generating an index for the entire book. But you can overcome these problems by creating a master document. The individual files containing the text are called subdocuments.

Creating a Master Document

1. Start with a blank WordPerfect editing screen.

2. Enter any formatting codes you wish to use to format this master document, such as a page numbering or footer code.

   Press Alt-F3 (Reveal Codes) if you want to see the codes you're adding.

3. Move the cursor to the place where you want one of the subdocuments to be inserted.

   You may want to press Ctrl-Enter to start a new page before the subdocument.

4. Press Alt-F5 (Mark Text) or display the **M**ark menu.

   A list of Mark Text options appears.

5. Select Subdocument (**2**).

   WordPerfect prompts you to enter the name of the subdocument you want to insert.

6. Enter the path and file name of the subdocument you want to insert.	WordPerfect inserts the [Subdoc] code and displays the subdocument link as a boxed comment on the editing screen.
7. Repeat steps 3-6 for all the documents you want the master document to link.	Make sure you link the documents in the order in which you want them to appear.
8. Press Shift-F10 (Save) or select **S**ave from the **F**ile menu.	WordPerfect prompts you to enter a name for the master document.
9. Enter a file name for the master document.	WordPerfect saves the master document to disk.

Now that you have all your subdocuments linked by way of the master document, you can generate cross-references, tables, lists, and indexes for all the subdocuments by placing the definition code in the master document. The following steps assume that you have marked in the subdocuments all the entries that you want included in your master document tables, lists, and index. Refer to *Cross-Reference*; *Index, Mark Text*; *Lists, Mark Text*; *Table of Authorities, Mark Text*; and *Table of Contents, Mark Text*.

Generating Lists, Tables, and Indexes

1. Move the cursor to the place in the master document where you want the generated item to appear.	For example, if you want to include an index, move the cursor to the end of the master document. You may want to press Ctrl-Enter so that the index starts on a separate page.
2. Enter a definition code for the item you want to generate.	For example, if you want to generate an index, use the Mark Text: Define menu to enter the [Def Mark:Index] code. Refer to the *Define* section for the item you want to generate. (For example, if you want to generate an index, refer to *Index, Define.)*
3. Repeat steps 1-2 for each item you want to generate.	

4. Generate the indexes, tables, and lists.	Refer to *Generate*. WordPerfect generates the material and inserts it at each [Def Mark] code.

When WordPerfect generates the lists, index, tables, and cross-references, it automatically expands the master document, pulling in all the subdocuments and using the material it needs, such as all text marked for a list. When it's finished, WordPerfect condenses the master document again, removing all the subdocuments, but leaving the generated material. During this process, WordPerfect asks if you want to update the subdocuments. Press N to delete any changes made to the subdocuments during the generation process or Y to save the changes before deleting the subdocuments from the master document.

After you have generated all the lists, indexes, and tables required for the master document, you may wish to print the entire collection of subdocuments as one document. Before you can do so, you must *expand* the master document. This pulls all the subdocuments into the master document and formats the subdocuments for the currently selected printer.

 ## Expanding the Master Document

1. Press Alt-F5 (Mark Text) or display the **Mark** menu.	The Mark Text menu appears.
2. Select **Generate** (6).	The Mark Text: Generate menu appears.
3. Select **3** (**Expand Master Document**).	Prompts appear on screen, telling you which subdocuments are currently being pulled into the master document.

After expanding the master document, you can make editing changes to the master document just as you can with any other document, or you can choose to print the document. When you're done working with the master document, you can condense it to remove the subdocuments. Since you can expand and condense the master document anytime, it's not necessary to leave it expanded, especially if it uses a large amount of disk space.

Condensing the Master Document

1. Press Alt-F5 (Mark Text) or display the **Mark** menu.	The Mark Text menu appears.
2. Select **G**enerate (6).	WordPerfect prompts you to select the item you wish to generate.
3. Select 4 (**C**ondense Master Document).	WordPerfect asks if you want to save changes to the subdocuments.
4. Press Y to save changes to the subdocuments or N to cancel changes.	If you press Y, WordPerfect presents you with three choices: you can replace the subdocument in question with the revised version, save the revised version under another name, or replace all subdocuments with their revised versions.
5. Select a save option.	WordPerfect condenses the master document; the document retains its [Subdoc] codes.

Math (see also *Table, Math*)

Function: Lets you enter and calculate equations in a document.

Keystrokes:	*Keyboard*	*Mouse*
	Alt-F7 (Columns/Table)	**Layout**
	3 (Math)	**Math**
	3 (Define)	**Define**
	Change settings	Change settings
	F7 (Exit)	Right mouse button
	1 (On)	**Layout**
	Enter data	**Math**
	Alt-F7 (Columns/Table)	**On**
	3 (Math)	Enter data
	4 (Calculate)	**Layout**
	Alt-F7 (Columns/Table)	**Math**

Keystrokes: *Keyboard*   *Mouse*
               3 (Math)   Calculate
               2 (Off)   Layout
                                     Math
                                     Off

Codes: [Math On]
          [Math Off]

Example:

```
           Retail Price    Sales Tax     Total Price¶
        ¶
        Ball    4.95         0.25↑          5.20↑¶
        ¶
        Bat    13.96         0.70↑         14.66!¶
        ¶
        Top     2.87         0.14↑          3.01!¶
        ¶
        Crib   69.95         3.50↑         73.45!¶
        ¶
```

The math feature lets you perform basic calculations within a document. You can add or subtract numbers, or calculate subtotals, totals, and grand totals down a column, or add, subtract, multiply, divide, or average numbers across a row. The process can be broken down into the following steps:

1. Set your tabs. Refer to *Tab, Set* to determine how to set the tabs. You can have up to 24 columns across the page, but make sure the columns are far enough apart to prevent the numbers you enter from reaching into other columns. The column between the left margin and the first tab stop is not considered a column for math; it can only be used for text entries.

2. If necessary, select a decimal/align character and thousands' separator. WordPerfect uses these characters to align your numbers in columns. By default, WordPerfect will use a decimal point (.) as the decimal character and a comma (,) as the thousands' separator. Refer to *Decimal/Align Character* and *Thousands' Separator* to determine how to change these characters.

3. Type any column heads you want to include before turning Math on, because tab stops will be converted to decimal tabs.

4. Unless you are adding or subtracting numbers down a column, define the columns. This process consists of specifying what kind of entry you will type in each column. See the steps under "Defining the Math Section" that follow. If you are adding or subtracting down a column, you can skip this step.

5. Turn on Math. See the steps under "Turning on Math" that follow.

6. Enter text, formulas, and math operators.

7. Calculate the results.

8. Turn Math off.

After you've set your tabs, selected a decimal/align character, and typed any column heads you wish to use, you're ready to define the math section. To do this, you will use the Math Definition screen to specify the type of entry for each column: calculation, text, numeric, or total, and to enter the calculation formulas in calculation columns. This screen lets you change the settings for 24 columns (A-X), excluding the "column" between the left margin and the first tab stop. Column A is at the first tab stop, column B is at the second, and so on. Use the arrow keys to move to the setting you want to change. You must specify the following settings for each column you use:

Type: This setting specifies the type of information you will enter in the column. You have four options:

(0) Calculation lets you enter a formula to calculate across columns. You can add (+), subtract (–), multiply (*), divide (/), or average (+/). You can use column letters as variables. For example, to figure 5% sales tax for each number you type in column B and insert the results in column C, enter B*.05 as the formula for column C. You can define up to four formulas in a math section (between a pair of Math On and Math Off codes).

(1) Text lets you enter text only. If you define a column as a text column and enter a number in the column, the number will be ignored during the calculation.

(2) Numeric lets you type numbers that can be included in your calculations, either down or across columns. This is the default setting, and explains why you don't have to define Math columns if you are only adding or subtracting *down* a column.

(3) Total lets you display the total of the column immediately to the left of the column. This sets the total off from the rest of the section.

Negative Numbers: This setting specifies how you want negative numbers displayed. By default, negative numbers are enclosed in parentheses, but you can change this to a negative sign (–).

Number of Digits to the Right: This setting specifies the number of digits you want to include to the right of the decimal place in numbers that will be calculated by your formulas. You can include up to four digits.

 ## Defining the Math Section

This procedure is not necessary if you are adding or subtracting down a column.

1. Press Alt-F7 (Columns/Table) or display the **Layout** menu.

A list of formatting options appears.

2. Select **Math (3)**.

The Math menu appears.

3. Select **Define (3)**.

The Math Definition screen appears, prompting you to specify the contents of each column.

4. Move the cursor to the setting you wish to change.

Start with the settings in column A and proceed to the right.

5. Enter the new setting.

The new setting appears at the cursor position.

6. Repeat steps 4-5 until all the settings appear as desired.

7. Press F7 (Exit) or click the right mouse button.

The Math menu reappears. At this point, you can turn Math on or press Enter to return to the Edit screen.

8. Press Enter to return to the edit screen, or select **On (1)** to turn Math on.

WordPerfect returns you to the Edit screen and inserts the [Math Def] code at the cursor position.

 ## Turning Math On

1. Position the cursor after the [Math Def] code.

2. Press Alt-F7 (Columns/Table) or display the **Layout** menu.

A list of formatting options appears.

3. Select **Math (3)**.	The Math menu appears.
4. Select **On (1)**.	WordPerfect inserts the [Math On] code at the cursor position, and a Math prompt appears at the bottom of the screen.

Now that your math section is defined and Math is on, you can type the numbers that you want to calculate in your numeric columns and labels and other text in your text columns. You don't have to enter anything in the Calculation or Total columns, because the Math feature will perform the calculations and insert the results in those columns later. However, you must tab over to these columns so that an exclamation point (!) appears. If you don't, WordPerfect won't be able to display the results of the formulas when you use the Calculate option.

In addition, you can type any of the following math operators at the bottoms of Numeric and Total columns to generate subtotals and totals:

+   Adds the numbers above in a column to determine a subtotal.

t   The extra subtotal character, which tells WordPerfect this number is to be treated like a subtotal and included in the next total calculation.

=   Add two or more subtotals to determine a total.

T   Extra total character, which tells WordPerfect this number is to be treated like a total and included in the next grand total calculation.

*   Adds two or more totals to determine a grand total.

N   Negative, used to subtract the number or place parentheses around it.

When you're done setting up the math section and entering the numbers, you are ready to generate the results and turn the Math feature off. If you change any of the values in a given math section, you can regenerate the results to update the results of your calculations.

 ## Calculating the Results of Your Math Formulas

1. Move the cursor inside the math section you want to calculate.	Math appears in the lower-left corner of the screen.
2. Press Alt-F7 (Columns/Table) or display the Layout menu.	A list of formatting options appears.

3. Select **Math** (**3**).

The Math menu appears.

4. Select **Calculate** (**4**).

WordPerfect performs the calculations. In the Math columns, each exclamation point (!) is replaced with a calculated value. If you change any numbers included in the calculations, repeat the steps to recalculate the formulas.

The following section is necessary only if you want to type text after the math section or if you want to define and use another Math section.

 Turning Math Off

1. Position the cursor after all entries in the math section.

2. Press Alt-F7 (Columns/Table) or display the **Layout** menu.

A list of formatting options appears.

3. Select **Math** (**3**).

The Math menu appears.

4. Select **Off** (**2**).

WordPerfect inserts the [Math Off] code at the cursor position and Math disappears from the bottom of the screen. The tab stops now function as they did before you turned Math on.

Menu Bar (see *Pull-Down Menus*)

Menu Options, Setup

Function: Lets you customize the way WordPerfect displays menu options.

Keystrokes: *Keyboard* *Mouse*
Shift-F1 (Setup) File
2 (**Display**) Setup
4 (**Menu Options**) Display
Select option Menu Options
Enter change Select option
F7 (Exit) Enter change
 Right mouse button

Example:

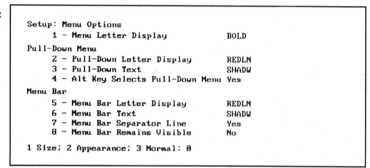

```
Setup: Menu Options
        1 - Menu Letter Display           BOLD
Pull-Down Menu
        2 - Pull-Down Letter Display      REDLN
        3 - Pull-Down Text                SHADW
        4 - Alt Key Selects Pull-Down Menu Yes
Menu Bar
        5 - Menu Bar Letter Display       REDLN
        6 - Menu Bar Text                 SHADW
        7 - Menu Bar Separator Line       Yes
        8 - Menu Bar Remains Visible      No

1 Size; 2 Appearance; 3 Normal: 0
```

The Setup: Menu Options menu gives you control over how the WordPerfect menus and menu options are displayed. You can customize how the following items are displayed:

Menu Letter Display: Each item on a menu has a mnemonic character you can press to select the item, such as P for Page on the main Print menu. You can use this option to change the way that character is displayed.

Pull-Down Letter Display: Each option on a pull-down menu has a mnemonic character you can press to select the option, such as S for Save on the pull-down File menu. This setting controls the appearance of that character.

Pull-Down Text: This controls the appearance of the options on each pull-down menu, excluding the letter that activates that option.

Alt Key Selects Pull-Down Menu: If you don't have a mouse, you have to press Alt-= to activate the pull-down menu bar. You can use this option to have the Alt key alone activate the menu bar.

Menu Bar Letter Display: Each option in the menu bar at the top of the screen has a mnemonic character you can press to pull down that menu. You can use this option to change the way that character is displayed on screen.

Menu Bar Text: This controls the appearance of the options listed in the pull-down menu bar, except for the letter that activates each option.

Menu Bar Separator Line: You can change this option to Yes to have WordPerfect display a double line between the pull-down menu and the editing screen, to separate the menu from your document.

Menu Bar Remains Visible: If you set this option to Yes, the menu bar will always appear at the top of the screen, but does not remain active. To activate the menu bar, you must press Alt-= or the Alt key (if you set that option to Yes) or click the right mouse button.

 Setting Up the Menu Options

1. Shift-F1 (Setup) or select Setup from the File menu.	The Setup menu appears.
2. Select Display (2).	The Setup: Display screen appears.
3. Select 4 (Menu Options).	The Setup: Menu Options screen appears.
4. Select an option and enter your change.	
5. Press F7 (Exit) or click the right mouse button.	WordPerfect saves your changes in the WP{WP}.SET file and returns you to the Edit screen. The changes you selected are now in effect.

Menus (see *Pull-Down Menus*)

Merge (see also *Merge Commands*; *Labels, Printing*; and *Sort and Select*)

Function: Merges a primary document with a secondary document. You can use Merge to create phone lists, form letters, contracts, mailing lists, and so on.

WordPerfect's Merge feature lets you combine information from two or more source files to create a document or series of documents. For example, you can combine a letter with a list of names and addresses to generate a series of letters, each having a different name and address. Then, you can use Merge to create labels or envelopes for mailing the letters.

To use Merge, you must create a primary and secondary file. The secondary file contains a list of all names, addresses, phone numbers, or any other information you commonly use; this is similar to a Rolodex or any other such data base. It also includes special codes to separate each piece of information and each set of data (record). The primary file contains a template for whatever document you wish to create, such as a form letter, memo, mailing label, or phone list. This template can include text and must include codes that tell WordPerfect where to insert information from the secondary file. When you merge the two files, WordPerfect inserts information from the secondary file into the appropriate places in the primary file, creating a new document or a series of new documents.

Your secondary file, containing the actual data, might appear as follows:

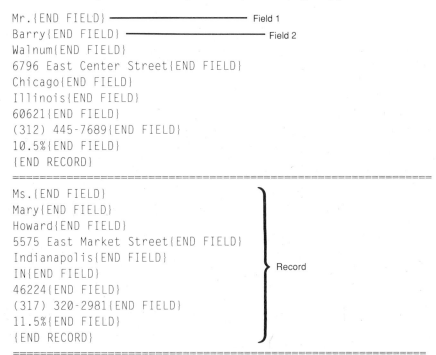

```
Mr.{END FIELD} ─────────────────── Field 1
Barry{END FIELD} ─────────────────── Field 2
Walnum{END FIELD}
6796 East Center Street{END FIELD}
Chicago{END FIELD}
Illinois{END FIELD}
60621{END FIELD}
(312) 445-7689{END FIELD}
10.5%{END FIELD}
{END RECORD}
==============================================================

Ms.{END FIELD}
Mary{END FIELD}
Howard{END FIELD}
5575 East Market Street{END FIELD}
Indianapolis{END FIELD}
IN{END FIELD}
46224{END FIELD}                                    } Record
(317) 320-2981{END FIELD}
11.5%{END FIELD}
{END RECORD}
==============================================================
```

Each distinct piece of information in the file is called a *field,* and the collection of all fields for one set (such as information for one person) is called a *record.* Each {END FIELD} code represents a field number and shows where the field ends. Individual fields can contain several lines.

Everything before the first {END FIELD} code up to the previous {END RECORD} code or the top of the document is Field 1, while everything between the first {END FIELD} code and the second one is Field 2. When you set up your primary document, you will be using these field numbers to tell WordPerfect which fields contain the appropriate pieces of information. If the information is in the wrong field in any record, WordPerfect will retrieve the wrong information, so it is essential that you keep the data in the fields in the same order for each listing. Make sure the {END RECORD} code is on a line of its own.

The primary file should resemble a template of how you want the information printed. An example is shown here:

```
{FIELD}1~ {FIELD}2~ {FIELD}3~
{FIELD}4~
{FIELD}5~, {FIELD}6~ {FIELD}7~

Dear {FIELD}2~,

As of Friday, January 12, home mortgage rates have fallen
to 8.25%. You are now paying {FIELD}9~! Don't you think it's
time to refinance your mortgage with a company that cares?

Sincerely,



Bill Grotto

Infield Mortgage Company
```

This primary file can be merged with the information from the secondary file to create the following letters:

```
Mr. Barry Walnum
6796 East Center Street
Chicago, Illinois  60621

Dear Barry,

As of Friday, January 12, home mortgage rates have fallen
to 8.25%. You are now paying 10.5%! Don't you think it's
time to refinance your mortgage with a company that cares?

Sincerely,



Bill Grotto

Infield Mortgage Company
```

and

```
Ms. Mary Howard
5575 East Market Street
Indianapolis, IN  46224

Dear Mary,

As of Friday, January 12, home mortgage rates have fallen
to 8.25%. You are now paying 11.5%! Don't you think it's
time to refinance your mortgage with a company that cares?

Sincerely,



Bill Grotto

Infield Mortgage Company
```

 ### Creating a Secondary File

1. **Start with a blank WordPerfect Edit screen.**

2. Type the data for the first field, and press F9 (End Field).

For example, type Ms. and press F9. When you press F9, WordPerfect inserts an {END FIELD} code and a hard return and moves the cursor to the next line.

3. Type the data for the second field, and press F9 (End Field).

For example, type Mary and press F9. It's a good idea to press F9 and create a separate field for each piece of information that you may wish to pull out as a separate entity later. For example, you may want to use "Mary" as a greeting in a letter, as in "Dear Mary,".

4. Continue typing data for the remaining fields and pressing F9 after each field.

5. When you've entered all the information for one record, press Shift-F9 (Merge) or select Merge Codes from the Tools menu.

A list of merge commands appears.

6. Select the End Record (2).

WordPerfect inserts the {END RECORD} code and a hard page break at the end of the block of information you just entered. The cursor moves to the next line.

7. Continue entering information for each record you want to include in your data file.

Enter data for each field in the same order for each record. For example, if you enter a phone number as field 8 in the first record, you must enter a phone number as field 8 for all the other records. If a piece of information that belongs in a field is missing, press F9 to insert an {END FIELD} code for the missing information, and leave the field blank.

8. Press F10 (Save) or select **Save** from the **File** menu and enter a name for the file.

For example, name the file DATA1.SF. The extension .SF identifies the file as a secondary file. Although optional, the SF is useful.

If you want to use more descriptive names for your fields rather than the cryptic numbering system, you can include a {Mrg:FIELD NAMES} command at the beginning of your secondary file:

 ## Naming Your Fields

1. Move the cursor to the beginning of your secondary file.

2. Press Shift-F9 (Merge) or select **Merge** Codes from the **Tools** menu.

A list of merge options appears.

3. Select **More (6)**.

The Merge Commands menu pops up in a box in the upper-right portion of your screen.

4. Type f, then press Down Arrow to highlight the {FIELD NAMES} command, and then press Enter.

WordPerfect prompts you to type a name for each field.

5. Type the names for your fields in the order in which the fields are listed in this file. Press Enter after typing each name.

For example, if *Mr.* or *Ms.* is in the first field, you might type Title as its name first.

6. After you've typed the name for the last field, press Enter in response to the Enter Field prompt

WordPerfect inserts a {FIELD NAMES} command, followed by the names you typed for each field and a hard page break. If you enter any more records in the secondary file, or move the cursor through it, a prompt will appear in the lower-left corner of the screen, telling you the name of the field you are entering data into.

7. Press F10 (Save) or select **Save**
   from the **File** menu and press
   Enter, and then press Y to replace
   the file.

Now that you have a secondary file that contains all the information
you need, you must create a primary file that can pull out and organize that
information.

 ## Creating a Primary File

1. Clear the screen and create a new
   document, leaving out any
   information that may vary.

   For example, you can create a
   form letter, omitting the inside
   address and greeting.

2. Move the cursor to the place
   where you want to insert a field
   from your secondary document.

   For example, if you created a
   letter omitting the inside address,
   move the cursor to the place
   where you want the inside
   address to appear.

3. Press Shift-F9 (Merge Codes) and
   select **1** (Field), or display the
   Tools menu and select **Merge
   Codes** and then **Field**.

   WordPerfect prompts you to
   enter the name or number of the
   field that contains the information
   you want to insert.

4. Enter the number or name of the
   field you inserted at this position.

   For example, if you want *Mr.* or
   Ms. to appear here and that
   information is in the first field in
   your address file, type **1**.
   WordPerfect inserts a {FIELD}n
   code, where *n* is the field
   number. If you named your
   fields, type the name, and it will
   appear instead of the number.

5. Repeat steps 2-4 until all the fields
   you want to include appear in the
   positions where you want them
   printed.

   You must include any spaces and
   punctuation required between
   field codes, such as a comma and
   a space between city and state.

6. Press F10 (Save) or select **Save**
   from the **File** menu and enter a
   name for the file.

   For example, name the file
   MORT.PF. Although optional, the
   PF is useful for identifying this as
   a primary file.

Now that you have created and saved both a primary file and a secondary file, you can merge the two files to generate a document or a series of customized documents. If you want to generate documents for a selected group of items in your data file, such as customers in a certain state, refer to *Sort and Select*.

Merging Your Primary and Secondary Files

1. Start with a blank WordPerfect screen.	
2. Press Ctrl-F9 (Merge/Sort) or display the **Tools** menu.	A list of merge/sort options appears.
3. Select **Merge (1)**.	WordPerfect prompts you to enter the name of the primary file.
4. Type the name of the primary file and press Enter.	For example, type `mort.pf` and press Enter. WordPerfect prompts you to enter the name of the secondary file.
5. Type the name of the secondary file and press Enter.	For example, type `data1.sf` and press Enter. WordPerfect then merges the two files. The merged documents appear on screen with the cursor at the end of the last document.

Now that you've generated the document(s), you can format the document(s) for the printer and use the Print menu to print them out.

 Tip: If you don't want to format your documents each time you generate them, insert formatting codes as Document Initial Codes in the primary file. That way, whenever you generate document(s) using that file, the formatting codes will automatically be included in each generated document. To insert formatting codes as initial codes, press Shift-F8 (Format) or display the Layout menu, select **Document (3)**, select **2** (Initial Codes), and then set your formatting options as you normally would.

Merge, Convert Old Codes

Function: Converts merge commands used in WordPerfect versions 4.x to version 5.1.

Keystrokes: *Keyboard*
Ctrl-F9 (Merge/Sort)
3 (Convert Old Merge Codes)
F10 (Save)

The Merge Codes Conversion feature lets you convert WordPerfect versions 4.x and 5.0 merge commands into version 5.1 merge commands. Although the version 5.0 merge commands function in 5.1, you may want to convert them for consistency's sake. However, primary files created in version 4.2 or earlier versions must be converted, or they won't work in version 5.1.

 Converting Merge Commands

1. Retrieve the file that contains the old merge commands.

2. Press Ctrl-F9 (Merge/Sort).   A list of merge commands appears.

3. Select 3 (Convert Old Merge Codes).   WordPerfect performs the conversion.

4. Press F10 (Save) or select Save from the File menu and enter a name for the file or press Enter and type Y to use the same name.

Merge Commands (see also *Merge*)

Function: Lets you insert merge commands into your primary and secondary documents.

Keystrokes: *Keyboard*   *Mouse*
                          Shift-F9 (Merge Codes)   Tools
                          6 (More)   Merge Codes
                          Highlight code   More
                          Enter   Double-click code
                          Answer prompts   Answer prompts

Example:

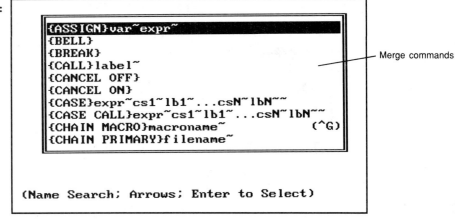

          — Merge commands

In addition to the merge commands such as {FIELD} and {END RECORD} that you must use in primary and secondary documents, WordPerfect offers several commands that can increase your merge power. You can use these commands to link a merge document with another file, combine Merge with macros, create "if...then..." statements, display messages, and much more. To use any of these commands, perform the following steps:

 Inserting Merge Commands

1. Press Shift-F9 (Merge Codes) or display the **Tools** menu and select **Merge Codes.**

   A list of merge options appears. The commonly used merge commands are listed, such as {FIELD}, {END RECORD}, and {NEXT RECORD}.

2. If the merge command you want to insert appears, select it. If it does not appear, select **More** (6).

   If you selected a merge command, that command is inserted. If you selected **More,** the Merge Commands menu appears in a box.

3. Select the merge command you want to insert from the Merge Commands menu.

You can highlight the command and press Enter or double-click on the command with your mouse. Some commands will prompt you to enter more information, such as a file name.

4. Answer any prompts that appear on screen.

If you want to see the merge commands you insert, the Merge Commands Display must be on, which it is by default. This display is helpful when you are using the Merge feature, but you may want to turn it off to see how the text will look without the merge commands.

 ### Turning the Merge Commands Display On/Off

1. Press Shift-F1 (Setup) or select Setup from the **File** menu.

A list of setup options appears.

2. Select **Display** (2).

The Setup: Display menu appears.

3. Select 6 (Edit-Screen Options).

The Setup: Edit Screen Options menu appears.

4. Select **5** (Merge Codes Display).

The cursor moves up to the option.

5. Press Y to turn on the Merge Commands Display or N to turn it off.

6. Press F7 (Exit) or click the right mouse button.

WordPerfect returns you to the Edit screen. The merge commands are still visible in the Reveal Codes screen.

Mouse Setup

Function: Lets you configure the mouse.

Keystrokes: *Keyboard*   *Mouse*
Shift-F1 (Setup)   File
1 (Mouse)   Setup
Select option   Mouse
Enter change   Select option
F7 (Exit)   Enter change
      Right mouse button

Example:

```
Setup: Mouse
     1 - Type                                    Mouse Driver (MOUSE.COM)
     2 - Port
     3 - Double Click Interval (1 = .01 sec) 70
     4 - Submenu Delay Time (1 = .01 sec)    15
     5 - Acceleration Factor                 24
     6 - Left-Handed Mouse                   No
     7 - Assisted Mouse Pointer Movement     No


   Selection: 0
```

Before you can set up your mouse in WordPerfect, you must install the mouse following the installation instructions that came with your mouse. Once the mouse is installed, you must display the Setup: Mouse menu to tell WordPerfect what kind of mouse you're using and where it is connected. This menu also lets you customize the mouse for your own use:

Type: This entry specifies the file name of the mouse driver you're using.

Port: Specifies the number of the serial port that your mouse is connected to. Refer to the documentation that came with your computer and mouse to determine which port to use. If your mouse is a bus mouse, you do not need to specify this.

Double Click Interval: Clicking your mouse button twice in quick succession is called double-clicking and performs a different action than if you press the button only once. It is like pressing the button once and then pressing Enter. The double click interval determines how fast you must press the button twice for WordPerfect to recognize it as a double-click rather than two single clicks. The setting is in hundredths of a second; for example, a setting of 50 is .50 seconds—a half second.

Submenu Delay Time: If you point to a pull-down menu item that has a submenu, and then hold down your mouse button, you can drag the cursor through a series of submenus instead of clicking on each item. This setting determines how long the cursor must remain on an option before WordPerfect displays that option's submenu.

Acceleration Factor: If your mouse moves the cursor too slow or fast, you can change this setting to increase or decrease its speed. The lower the setting, the slower the cursor will be to respond to your mouse movements.

Left-Handed Mouse: If you set this option to Yes, the functions of the mouse button are reversed. The left button will perform the functions of the right button and vice versa.

Assisted Mouse Pointer Movement: If this option is set to No, the mouse pointer remains in its current position when you activate the menu bar or a menu. If you set this option to Yes, the mouse pointer automatically moves to the menu or menu bar when you activate the bar or menu.

 ## Setting Up Your Mouse

1. Press Shift-F1 (Setup) or select Setup from the **File** menu.

   The main Setup menu appears.

2. Select **Mouse (1)**.

   The Setup: Mouse menu appears.

3. Select an option, and enter your change.

   When you select an option, the cursor moves up to that option. After you change it, you can select another option or exit to the Edit screen.

4. Press F7 (Exit) or click the right mouse button.

   WordPerfect saves the changes and returns you to your document.

Move Block (see also *Block* and *Move Sentence, Paragraph, or Page*)

Function: Moves a block from its original location to the location you specify.

Keystrokes:

Keyboard	*Mouse*
Alt-F4 (Block)	**Edit**
Ctrl-F4 (Move)	**Block**
1 (Block), **2** (Tabular Column), or **3** (Rectangle)	**Edit**
	Move
	Cursor to new location
1 (Move)	Double-click left mouse button
Cursor to new location	OR

Enter	**E**dit
	Block
	Edit
	Select
	Tabular **C**olumn or **R**ectangle
	Move
	Cursor to new location
	Double-click left mouse button

The Move Block feature lets you move various types of blocks. Your choice of how to treat the block depends on the layout of the block:

Block: Select this option when you want to move a regular block of text.

Rectangle: This option lets you move text within the perimeter of a rectangle without disturbing the text inside the rectangle. Within the rectangle, each line must end in a hard return. This option is useful for moving columns in DOS (ASCII) text files.

Tabular Columns: If you need to rearrange columns of text formatted with tabs or indents, select this option. The tab and indent codes are included in the block.

 Moving a Regular Block of Text

1. Move the cursor to the beginning or end of the block you want to mark.

   This position will become your pivot point, letting you *stretch* the highlight up, down, left, or right of this position.

2. Press Alt-F4 (Block) or select **Block** from the **Edit** menu.

   A Block on prompt starts flashing in the lower-left corner of your screen.

3. Move the cursor to the opposite end of the block you want to mark.

   As you move the cursor, the block highlighting stretches with it.

4. Press Ctrl-F4 (Move), select **1** (**Block**) and then **1** (**Move**), or select **Move** (Cut) from the **Edit** menu.

   The block disappears, and a prompt appears on screen telling you to position the cursor where you want to insert the block and press Enter.

5. Position the cursor where you want to insert the block.

6. Press Enter or double-click the left mouse button.

WordPerfect inserts the cut block at the cursor location.

 Tip: If you have an enhanced keyboard with an enhanced BIOS, you can skip step 4 by pressing Ctrl-Del. When the `Move Cursor, Press Enter` prompt appears, move the cursor to the new position and press Enter.

 ## Moving a Rectangular Block

1. Move the cursor to either the upper-right or the lower-left corner of the rectangle.

This position will become your pivot point, letting you *stretch* the highlight to the opposite corner of the block.

2. Press Alt-F4 (Block) or select **Block** from the **Edit** menu.

A `Block on` prompt starts flashing in the lower-left corner of your screen.

3. Move the cursor to the corner diagonally opposite the corner where you started.

As you move the cursor, the block highlighting stretches with it.

4. Press Ctrl-F4 (Move) and select **3** (Rectangle), or display the **Edit** menu and choose **Select** and then **Rectangle**.

The highlight changes, highlighting only the rectangular block defined by the starting and ending positions of the cursor. A menu line appears, offering several block options.

5. Select **1** (Move).

The block disappears, and a prompt appears on screen telling you to position the cursor where you want to insert the block and press Enter.

6. Position the cursor where you want to insert the block.

7. Press Enter or double-click the left mouse button.

WordPerfect inserts the cut block at the cursor location.

Moving a Tabular Column

1. Place the cursor on the first character at the top of the first column you want to move, after the tab or indent code.

   This position will become your pivot point, letting you *stretch* the highlight to the opposite corner of the column.

2. Press Alt-F4 (Block) or select **Block** from the **Edit** menu.

   A Block on prompt starts flashing in the lower-left corner of your screen.

3. Move the cursor onto any character in the last line of the last column you want to move.

   As you move the cursor, the block highlighting stretches with it.

4. Press Ctrl-F4 (Move) and select **2** (Tabular Column), or display the **Edit** menu and choose Select and then Tabular Column.

   The highlight changes, highlighting only the columns defined by the starting and ending positions of the cursor. A menu line appears, offering several block options.

5. Select **1** (**Move**).

   The column(s) disappears, and a prompt appears on screen telling you to position the cursor where you want to insert the column and press Enter.

6. Position the cursor where you want to insert the column.

7. Press Enter or double-click the left mouse button.

 Tip: You can use the mouse to highlight a block of text without using the pull-down menus. Move the mouse cursor to the beginning of the block you want to highlight, hold down the left mouse button, and drag the cursor to the end of the block. When you release the left mouse button, the block is highlighted.

Move Cursor (see *Cursor Movement*)

Move File

Function: Moves a file from one disk or directory to another.

Keystrokes:	*Keyboard*	*Mouse*
	F5 (List)	**File**
	Enter	**List Files**
	Highlight file name	Double-click left mouse button on
	3 (Move/Rename)	file name
	d:\path\filename.ext	**Move/Rename**
	Enter	*d:\path\filename.ext*
	F7 (Exit)	Enter
		Right mouse button

With WordPerfect, you can easily move a file or group of files from one directory or disk to another using the List Files menu. Just select the file you want to move, select the Move option, and type the new path and file name.

 Moving a File

1. Press F5 (List) or display the **File** menu and select List Files.

   The path to the current drive and directory appears in the lower-left corner of your screen.

2. If the file you want to move is in a different directory, type the path to that directory.

   When you begin typing, the default path disappears, and what you type appears in its place.

3. Press Enter.

   The List Files screen appears, displaying a list of files in the selected drive and directory.

4. Move the cursor to the file you want to move or type an asterisk (*) next to each file to move a group of files.

   You can mark or unmark all files listed by pressing Alt-F5 (Mark Text) or Home,*. You can also use **9** (Find), **1** (Name) to display a selected group of files.

5. Select **3** (**Move/Rename**).

WordPerfect displays a `New Name` prompt, asking you to enter the path to the target directory.

6. Type a complete path to the target directory. To move the file(s) to another disk, just type the drive designator, such as `a:`, and press Enter.

For example, type `c:\wp51\files`. You can also rename the file as you move it, by entering a different file name at the end of the path statement.

7. Press Enter.

WordPerfect moves the file to the drive or directory you specified.

8. Press space bar or F7 (Exit) or click the right mouse button.

WordPerfect returns you to the normal editing screen.

Move Rectangle (see *Move Block*)

Move Sentence, Paragraph, or Page

Function: Highlights a sentence, paragraph, or page and lets you move, copy, or delete it.

Keystrokes:

Keyboard	*Mouse*
Ctrl-F4 (Move)	**Edit**
1 (**Sentence**),	**Select**
2 (**Paragraph**), or	**Sentence**, **Paragraph**, or **Page**
3 (**Page**)	**Move**
1 (**Move**)	Cursor to new location
Cursor to new location	Double-click left mouse button
Enter	

Example:

A central concern in Moby Dick is with the essential being of individuals and how people can perceive it. Melville casts aside both the Aristotelian notion of being, that reality exists only in individual beings and one can understand this reality only through categories, and the Platonic notion that reality exists only in ideals which the individual beings merely mirror. Like the skulls of the Right and Sperm whales hanging on opposite sides of the Pequod, these two philosophies slow the ship down and must be disposed of. They have expended their usefulness as tools of metaphysics.¶

Marked block

Block options — 1 Move; 2 Copy; 3 Delete; 4 Append: 0

If you press Ctrl-F4 (Move) without selecting **B**lock first, WordPerfect can block logical units of text—sentences, paragraphs, and pages—and provide a Move option that you can use to move the text to any location in your document.

 ### Moving a Sentence, Paragraph, or Page

1. Position the cursor anywhere in the sentence, paragraph, or page you want to move.

2. Press Ctrl-F4 (Move) or display the **E**dit menu and choose **S**elect.

   WordPerfect prompts you to select the block of text you want to move: sentence, paragraph, or page.

3. Select Sentence (**1**), Paragraph (**2**), or Page (**3**).

   A list of block options appears: Move, Copy, Delete, or Append.

4. Select **1** (Move).

   The highlighted text disappears, and a prompt appears on screen telling you to position the cursor and press Enter.

5. Position the cursor where you want to insert the block.

6. Press Enter or double-click the left mouse button.

   WordPerfect inserts the marked block at the cursor location.

Move Tabular Column (see *Move Block*)

Multiple Copies (see *Print Multiple Copies*)

Name Search

Function: Moves the cursor onto a specified item in a menu featuring a list of items, such as file names, keyboard names, printer names, and font names.

Keystrokes:

Keyboard
N (Name Search)
search characters
Enter

Mouse
Name Search
search characters
Enter

Example:

```
Base Font

  * Roman 10cpi
    Roman 10cpi Italic
    Roman 12cpi
    Roman 12cpi Italic
    Roman 20cpi
    Roman 20cpi Italic
    Roman PS
    Roman PS Condensed
    Roman PS Condensed Italic
    Roman PS Dbl-Wide
    Roman PS Dbl-Wide Italic

  Roman PS                          (Name Search; Enter or arrows to Exit)
```

The Name Search feature works inside menus that include a list, such as a list of files, printers, fonts, graphic screen types, keyboard layouts, and styles, to move the cursor onto the specific item you're looking for. The option is available in most screens with a list; check the bottom of the screen for N (Name Search). If you don't see the option, it still may be available, as in the Styles menu. Press N to find out if it is available, and activate it if it is.

 Searching for a Name

1. Select **N** (Name Search).

The Name Search prompt appears and reminds you to press Enter or an arrow key to exit Name Search.

2. Type the first character of the name or item you are searching for. If necessary, continue typing the next several characters in the name.

As you type, the cursor moves to the first item in the list that matches the characters you've already typed. For example, if you type t. the cursor moves to the first item that starts with T. As soon as the cursor is at the item you're looking for, you can stop typing; you need not type the entire name.

3. To exit Name Search with the cursor remaining on the highlighted item, press Enter.

> **Tip:** In the List Files menu, you can use Name Search to move the cursor onto a subdirectory name by typing N, then a backslash (\), then the first few characters of the directory name.

New Page (see also *Force Odd/Even Page*)

Function: Lets you create a page break before the position where WordPerfect would automatically end the page.

Keystrokes: *Keyboard*
Ctrl-Enter

Code: [HPg]

Example:

```
================================================================= ──── Page break
Index¶
¶
Animals¶
    Beavers . . . . . . . . . . . . . . . . . . . . . . . . . .1¶
    Elephants . . . . . . . . . . . . . . . . . . . . . . . .1¶
Trees¶
    Cypress . . . . . . . . . . . . . . . . . . . . . . . . .1¶
    Sycamore. . . . . . . . . . . . . . . . . . . . . . . . .1¶
    Walnut. . . . . . . . . . . . . . . . . . . . . . . . . .1¶
```

WordPerfect automatically divides a document into pages as you type it, inserting soft page breaks at the end of each page as determined by the top and bottom margins and paper size and type. Sometimes, however, you may need to force a page break. For example, if you are generating an index for a document, you should make sure the index starts on a separate page. To do so, you can enter a hard page break just before the Index Definition code.

 Entering a Hard Page Break

1. Move the cursor to the position where you want to begin the new page.

   Make sure the cursor is before any codes you want included on the new page.

2. Press Ctrl-Enter.

   A double line of dashes appears, showing where the page break will fall. The Page indicator on the status line changes.

 Note: You can erase a hard page break by positioning the cursor after the page break and pressing the Backspace key.

New Page Number (see also *Force Odd/Even Page*)

Function: Lets you start renumbering pages at any point in a document or change the type of numbers to uppercase or lowercase Roman numerals.

Keystrokes:

Keyboard	*Mouse*
Shift-F8 (Format)	Layout
2 (Page)	Page
6 (Page Numbering)	Page Numbering
1 (New Page Number)	New Page Number
new number	*new number*
F7 (Exit)	Right mouse button

Code: [Pg Num]

Example:

```
Format: Page Numbering

    1 - New Page Number        i

    2 - Page Number Style      ^B

    3 - Insert Page Number

    4 - Page Number Position No page numbering

Selection: 1
```

The New Page Number option lets you start a new numbering sequence for your pages at any point in the document. When you use this feature, WordPerfect enters a [Pg Num] code, specifying the new number and type of numbers you want to use: Arabic, lowercase Roman numerals, or uppercase Roman numerals. Pages from that point on will be numbered consecutively starting with the new number. However, unless you've created a new header or footer with a page number or selected the Page Number Position option to insert a page number, WordPerfect will not print page numbers in your document, regardless of what you enter for the New Page Number option.

Changing the type of numbers is especially useful in a master document. For example, if you have preliminary pages, such as a table of contents, you may wish to use lowercase Roman numerals (i, ii, iii, etc.) to set those pages apart from the main document. You have three options for the type: Arabic (1, 2, 3), uppercase Roman (I, II, III), and lowercase Roman.

 ## Changing Page Numbers

1. Move the cursor to the top of the page on which you want the new page numbers to start.

    The cursor should be on the first line of the page.

2. Press Shift-F8 (Format) or display the Layout menu.

    A list of formatting options appears.

3. Select **Page** (**2**).

    The Format: Page menu appears.

4. Select **6** (Page **N**umbering).

    The Format: Page Numbering menu appears.

5. Select **1** (New Page Number).

    WordPerfect prompts you to enter the number you want to use as the new page number.

6. Enter the new page number you want to use in the style in which you want the numbers to appear.

For example, if you want the renumbering to start with the first lowercase Roman numeral, enter **i**.

7. Press F7 (Exit) or click the right mouse button.

WordPerfect returns you to the Edit screen and inserts the [Pg Num] code with the new page number at the cursor location. The Page number indicator on the status line shows the new page number in Arabic. All pages that follow are renumbered. Page numbers do not appear on the Edit screen, except for the indicator on the status line.

Newspaper Columns (see *Column Definition*)

Number of Copies (see *Print Multiple Copies*)

Num Lock Key

Function: Toggles the numeric keypad between Numeric Entry mode and Cursor Movement mode.

Keystrokes: *Keyboard*
Num Lock

The Num Lock key is located on the numeric keypad. If you press the key once, the Num Lock light on your keypad goes on, if you have one, and Pos on the WordPerfect status line starts to blink on and off. You can now use the keypad to type numbers and symbols such as + or −. If you press the key again, the Num Lock light goes off, Pos stops blinking, and you can use keys such as the four arrow keys and PgUp and PgDn on the numeric keypad to move your cursor.

Odd/Even Page (see *Force Odd/Even Page*)

Orientation, Portrait and Landscape (see also *Paper Size and Type*)

Function: Lets you print parallel or perpendicular to the inserted edge of the page.

Keystrokes:

Keyboard	*Mouse*
Shift-F8 (Format)	Layout
2 (Page)	Page
7 (Paper Size/Type)	Paper Size/Type
2 (Add) or 5 (Edit)	Add or Edit
Select paper type	Select paper type
3 (Font Type)	Font Type
2 (Landscape)	Landscape
1 (Paper Size)	Paper Size
Select dimensions	Select dimensions
F7 (Exit)	F7 (Exit)
1 (Select)	Select
F7 (Exit)	Right mouse button

Code: [Paper Sz/Typ]

With *portrait* orientation, the default, WordPerfect prints text parallel to the short edge of the page, so the page is taller than it is wide. On a regular 8 1/2" wide by 11" long page, it prints across the width of the page. With *landscape* orientation, the text is printed sideways, parallel to the long edge of the page, making the page wider than it is tall, as on envelopes. For charts and wide tables, you may need to print with landscape orientation in order to fit all the material on a page.

The process you will use to select landscape orientation varies depending on whether or not your printer can rotate fonts. Most laser printers can rotate the fonts 90 degrees to print the text in landscape orientation. Most dot-matrix and daisywheel printers cannot rotate fonts, so you have to feed the paper into the printer long edge first in order to print text parallel to this edge. To switch to landscape, you must use the Paper Size and Type option to select a form that will print in landscape orientation. WordPerfect then enters a code in your document specifying the dimensions and orientation of the paper you will be using.

Setting Landscape Orientation for a Printer That Can Rotate Fonts (Laser Printers)

1. Move the cursor to the top of the page.

2. Press Shift-F8 (Format) or display the **L**ayout menu.

   A list of formatting options appears.

3. Select **Page** (**2**).

   The Format: Page menu appears.

4. Select **7** (Paper Size/Type).

   A list of paper sizes and types appears. If, under the heading Paper Type and Orientation, the form is listed with the word "Wide" or if the long edge is listed first, it uses a landscape orientation.

5. If a landscape paper type appears, you can highlight it and press 1 to select it, and then exit. If not, either select **2** (**Add**) to create a size, or highlight a size you want to edit and select **5** (**Edit**).

   If you select **Edit**, skip to step 7. If you select **Add**, a list of paper types appears.

6. Select a paper type or choose **o** (Other) and enter the type of paper you're using.

   The Format: Edit Paper Definition menu appears.

7. Select **3** (**Font Type**) and select **2** (**Landscape**).

8. Select **1** (Paper Size).

   A list of available paper sizes appears, including several in landscape orientation, such as Standard Landscape and Legal Landscape.

9. Select a landscape paper size from the list or select **o** (Other) and enter your own dimensions.

   If you choose to enter your own dimensions, remember that the page is now wider than it is tall, so the long measurement is first, as in 11" by 8 1/2". The Format: Edit Paper Definition menu appears.

10. Select any of the other options you wish to change and enter your change.

11. Press F7 (Exit), or click the right mouse button until you return to the Paper Size/Type menu.

The dimensions you just entered now appear on this menu.

12. Highlight the paper size and type that represents the paper and orientation you're using and choose **1** (Select).

13. Press F7 (Exit) or click the right mouse button to return to your document.

WordPerfect inserts a [Paper Sz/Typ] code at the cursor location.

 ## Setting Landscape Orientation for a Printer That Cannot Rotate Fonts

1. Move the cursor to the top of the page.

2. Press Shift-F8 (Format) or display the Layout menu.

A list of formatting options appears.

3. Select **Page** (**2**).

The Format: Page menu appears.

4. Select **7** (Paper Size/Type).

A list of paper sizes and types appears. If, under the heading `Paper Type and Orientation`, the form is listed with the word "Wide" or if the long edge is listed first, it uses a landscape orientation.

5. If a landscape paper type appears, you can highlight it and press 1 to select it, and then exit. If not, either select **2** (Add) to create a size or highlight a size you want to edit and select **5** (Edit).

If you select Edit, skip to step 7. If you select Add, a list of paper types appears.

6. Select a paper type or choose **o** (Other) and enter the type of paper you're using.

The Format: Edit Paper Definition menu appears.

7. If the font type is listed as landscape, select **3** (**Font Type**) and then **1** (**Portrait**).

Although your printer will print the text parallel to the long edge when you insert the paper lengthwise, it will not rotate the fonts, so you must keep the font type set to portrait.

8. Select **1** (**Paper Size**).

A list of available paper sizes appears.

9. Select a landscape paper size from the list or select **o** (**Other**) and enter your own dimensions.

If you choose to enter your own dimensions, remember that the page is now wider than it is tall, so you must type the long measurement first, as in 11" by 8 1/2". The Format: Edit Paper Definition menu appears.

10. Select any of the other options you wish to change and enter your change.

11. Press F7 (Exit), or click the right mouse button until you return to the Paper Size/Type menu.

The dimensions you just entered now appear on this menu.

12. Highlight the paper size and type that represents the paper and orientation you're using and choose **1** (**Select**).

13. Press F7 (Exit) or click the right mouse button to return to your document.

WordPerfect inserts a [Paper Sz/Typ] code at the cursor location. When you print the page, be sure to insert the paper into the printer lengthwise.

Original Backup (see *Backup Timed and Original*)

Orphan (see *Widow/Orphan Protection*)

Other Format (see *Format Other*)

Outlines

Function: Lets you create and manage outlines by automatically generating paragraph numbers that are updated as you insert or delete other paragraph numbers.

Keystrokes:
Keyboard	*Mouse*
Shift-F5 (Date/Outline)	Tools
4 (Outline)	Outline
1 (On)	On
Type text	Type text
Enter, Tab	Enter, Tab
Shift-F5 (Date/Outline)	Tools
4 (Outline)	Outline
2 (Off)	Off

Codes: [Par Num Def]
[Outline On]
[Outline Off]

Example:

Formats —————

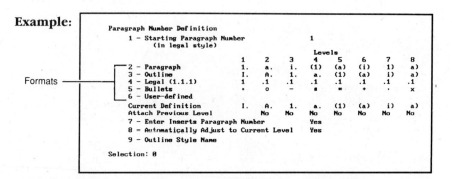

The Outline feature provides a convenient way for you to create detailed outlines within your documents. WordPerfect will update these documents automatically as you add or delete paragraph numbers. The process consists of the following four steps:

1. Define your outline. This consists of telling WordPerfect the style you want to use, which specifies how each level heading in the outline will be numbered: with Roman or Arabic numerals, uppercase or lowercase letters, bullets, and more. Each level is separated by a tab or indent. This step is optional.

2. Turn the Outline feature on.

3. Enter the text for your outline.

4. Turn the Outline feature off. This step is optional.

If you want to use WordPerfect's default style, Outline, you can skip the first step; simply turn on the Outline feature and start typing. The first-level paragraphs will be numbered with uppercase Roman numerals, the second-level with uppercase letters, the third-level with Arabic numbers, the fourth with lowercase letters, etc. However, if you want your outline headings numbered in some other way, you must use the Paragraph Number Definition menu to define the outline. You can also use this menu to change the following settings:

Starting Paragraph Number: Lets you select any starting number for your outline. You must enter Arabic numerals for this setting or leave it blank so WordPerfect will continue with the previous numbers in use before Outline was turned off in the document. This is useful if you want to interrupt an outline with a block of text, and you want the numbering to pick up where you left off instead of starting over again with I.

Formats: You can select any of four standard numbering schemes for your outline or select 6 (User-Defined) to create your own scheme. The currently selected numbering scheme is displayed on the Current Definition line. Next to each format, WordPerfect displays the first number that will be used for each level if you select that format.

Attach Previous Level: If you create your own numbering scheme, you can change the Attach setting for any level to Yes. This attaches the character used for the previous level to the character used for this level. For example, if you mark your first level A. and your second level 1. and change Attach Previous Level for your second level to Yes, the second level will be marked A.1, A.2, A.3, etc. Normally, this option is only set to Yes in the Legal style.

Enter Inserts Paragraph Number: When Outline is on and you press Enter, WordPerfect automatically enters a paragraph number, such as I or A. If you don't want WordPerfect to enter a number when you press Enter, select this option and type **N** (**No**). This lets you take advantage of outline options while using the Paragraph Numbering feature to enter paragraph numbers. Refer to *Paragraph Numbering*.

Automatically Adjust to Current Level: Whenever Outline is on and you press Enter to insert an automatic paragraph number, WordPerfect assumes you want that number to be at the same level as the previous one. For example, if the previous number was at level 2 and you are using the Outline style when you press Enter, the next number will be an uppercase letter such as B or C. To change it back to the first level, a

Roman numeral such as II, you would press Shift-Tab (Margin Release). If you set this option to No, WordPerfect will treat each entry as though it's a first-level entry, and you can change levels only by pressing Tab.

Outline Style Name: This option lets you create and use customized styles for your outline. Refer to *Outline Style*.

 Defining an Outline

1. Move the cursor before the position where you want the changes to take effect.

2. Press Shift-F5 (Date/Outline) or display the **T**ools menu.

3. Select **D**efine (6).   The Paragraph Number Definition screen appears.

4. Move the cursor to the setting you wish to change.

5. Enter the new setting.   The new setting appears in the menu.

6. Repeat steps 4-5 until you've made all the changes you want for this outline.

7. Press F7 (Exit) twice or click the right mouse button twice.   WordPerfect returns you to the Edit screen and inserts the [Par Num Def] code at the cursor position.

 Caution: If a [Par Num Def] code is entered in the middle of an outline, WordPerfect starts numbering over again, beginning with I, so be careful where the cursor is positioned when you use the Paragraph Number Definition menu. Even if you make no changes and only display the menu and press Enter, WordPerfect still inserts the code and begins numbering with I.

Turning Outline On

1. Position the cursor after the [Par Num Def] code.

2. Press Shift-F5 (Date/Outline) or display the **Tools** menu.

3. Select **Outline** (**4**).

   A list of outline options appears.

4. Select **On** (**1**).

   WordPerfect inserts the [Outline On] code at the cursor position and Outline appears at the bottom of the screen. Pressing Enter now inserts a paragraph number at level one.

Now that your outline is defined and the Outline feature is on, you can create your outline.

 Creating an Outline

1. Press Enter to create a first-level paragraph number.

   Assuming you turned Outline on, WordPerfect inserts a paragraph number for the head. If you are using the default Outline format, the paragraph number is I.

2. Press F4 (→Indent) or the space bar to insert space after the paragraph number, or press Enter to insert a blank line above it.

   You can't use the Tab key to insert space. Pressing Tab when Outline is on changes the level of the paragraph number.

3. Type text for the current outline entry.

4. Press Enter to create another paragraph number.

   The cursor moves to the next line and inserts a paragraph number at the first level.

5. Press Tab to change the paragraph number to the second level.

   For example, if you are using the Outline format. II becomes A. The next time you press Enter, WordPerfect will insert another paragraph number at level two, B. To move it back to level one, you can press Shift-Tab (Margin Release). The B will then become II.

6. Type the text for this outline entry, and then press Enter.

7. Repeat steps 4-6 until the outline is complete.

After you finish typing the outline, you can turn Outline off so that the Enter key reverts to its regular function, and you can type text in the usual way.

 ## Turning Outline Off

1. Position the cursor after the last outline entry.

2. Press Shift-F5 (Date/Outline) or display the **Tools** menu.

3. Select **Outline (4)**.

A list of outline options appears.

4. Select **Off (2)**.

WordPerfect inserts the [Outline Off] code at the cursor position, and Outline disappears from the bottom of the screen. Pressing Enter now inserts a [HRt] code instead of an automatic paragraph number.

The Outline feature also offers three options to help you edit your outlines. These options let you move, copy, or delete groups of outline entries called *families*. A family consists of the paragraph number and text on the line where the cursor is positioned, plus all subsequent paragraph numbers and text that are at a level below the level of the line the cursor is on when you select the option. To move, copy, or delete a family, perform the following steps:

 ## Moving, Copying, or Deleting a Family

1. Place the cursor anywhere in the first line you want to include in the family.

If the cursor is on a line with a level-one paragraph number, such as I, the family will include everything through the next level-one paragraph number. For example, it will include I, A, B, C, and all text following these numbers up to II.

2. Press Shift-F5 (Date/Outline) or display the **T**ools menu.

3. Select **O**utline (**4**).

A list of outline options appears.

4. Select **M**ove Family (**3**), **C**opy Family (**4**), or **D**elete Family (**5**).

If you choose **D**elete Family, WordPerfect asks you to confirm that you want to delete it. If you type Y, the family is erased. You can restore it anywhere by pressing F1 (Cancel) and selecting **1** (**R**estore). If you select the Move or Copy option, the family is highlighted, and a prompt appears asking you to press the arrow keys to move the family and press Enter when done. After you move or copy a family, the paragraph numbers will be updated as needed.

5. If you used Move or Copy, move the cursor to where you want to insert the family and press Enter.

The family is copied or moved to the cursor position.

Outline Style

Function: Lets you create and select styles for your outline paragraphs.

Keystrokes:

Keyboard	*Mouse*
Shift-F5 (Date/Outline)	**T**ools
6 (**D**efine)	**D**efine
9 (**O**utline Style **N**ame)	**O**utline Style **N**ame
1 (**S**elect)	**S**elect

Example:

```
Outline Styles: Edit
  Name:              Vision
  Description:       Plans for upcoming fiscal year.
  Level  Type        Enter
    1    Paired      HRt
    2    Open
    3    Open
    4    Open
    5    Open
    6    Open
    7    Open
    8    Open

  1 Name; 2 Description; 3 Type; 4 Enter; 5 Codes: 0
```

Although the Paragraph Number Definition screen offers several different numbering formats, you may want to use styles to further modify their appearance. The Outline Style feature lets you create and select your own outline styles. An outline style, unlike a regular style, actually contains a group of styles, one for each level of paragraph numbers (1-8).

 ## Creating an Outline Style

1. Press Shift-F5 (Date/Outline) or display the **T**ools menu.

2. Select **D**efine (6). | The Paragraph Number Definition screen appears.

3. Select 9 (Outline Style **N**ame). | The Outline Styles menu appears, displaying a list of available outline styles, if any have been defined. If not, NON appears under the Name column, and you'll have to create an outline style.

4. Select 2 (Create). | The Outline Styles: Edit menu appears, displaying a list of the eight paragraph levels.

5. Select 1 (Name) and enter a name for your outline style. | You can type up to 12 characters, including spaces.

6. Select 2 (Description) and enter a description to help you remember what this style does. This step is optional. | You can type up to 54 characters, including spaces.

7. Highlight the level for which you want to create a style.

8. Select **3** (**Type**) and select **1** (**Paired**) or **2** (**Open**).

Paired turns the style on and then off like underline and bold codes. Anything between the on/off codes conforms to the style. Open turns the style on; the style remains in effect until another code is inserted that changes the style.

9. If you changed the type to paired, select **4** (**Enter**) and select **1** (**HRt**), **2** (**Off**), or **3** (**Off/On**).

This option has no effect for open styles, so you won't be able to select it. For paired styles, it controls the function of the Enter key. HRt is the default, so the Enter key inserts a hard return as normal. Off changes the function of the Enter key to turn a style off, and Off/On makes it turn a style off, then on.

10. Select **5** (**Codes**) and enter the formatting codes you want to use for this style.

Choosing this option displays a screen similar to the Reveal Codes screen except that it includes a code representing the paragraph number level. Be sure to include a tab or indent if you want this level indented one tab stop from the previous one. Place the formatting codes to the left of the [Par Num] code, so they will affect both the number and the text. You can enter formatting codes in the usual manner. For example, press F6 for bold, or press Shift-F8 to access the Format menu.

11. Press F7 (**Exit**) or click the right mouse button to return to the Outline: Styles Edit screen.

12. Repeat steps 7-11 for all the levels you want to format.

You need not enter styles for every level. If you don't enter a style, WordPerfect will use its default style for the level.

13. Press Enter or F7 (Exit), or click the right mouse button to return to the Outline Styles menu.

The name and description of the style you just created appear in the list of available styles.

14. To select the style you just created and turn the Outline feature on, press Enter twice, select **Outline**, and then select **On**.

WordPerfect inserts a [Par Num Def] code at the cursor position, and the `Outline` prompt appears at the bottom of the screen.

15. If you are not ready to turn Outline on yet, but you want to insert the [Par Num Def] code at this point, press Enter three times to return to the Edit screen.

WordPerfect inserts the [Par Num Def] code at the cursor position. Whenever you want to turn Outline on and use the style you just created, press Shift-F5 or display the **Tools** menu, select **Outline**, and then select **On**.

16. To exit from the Outline Style menu without inserting a [Par Num Def] code, press F1 (Cancel) twice, and then press Enter.

To turn Outline on and use the style you just created, press Shift-F5 or display the **Tools** menu, select **Define**, select **Outline Style Name**, highlight the outline style and choose **Select**, press Enter, select **Outline**, and then select **On**.

17. To use one of the styles, just press Enter to insert a paragraph number.

WordPerfect automatically formats the first paragraph number level with the level-one style.

18. When you finish typing the text for the first level, press **Right Arrow** to move the cursor past the Style Off code, or press Alt-F8 (Style) and select **Off**, then press Enter to insert the next paragraph number and turn on its style. If you want it to be at level 2, press Tab.

Continue typing your outline in the usual way, except that you must press **Right Arrow** to turn off each style after you finish typing the text for that paragraph number.

Tip: If you already created a non-outline style using the Style feature, you can use that style for your outline without having to re-create it. Press Alt-F8 (Style), highlight the style you want to change to an outline style, and select 4 (Edit), 2 (Type), and 3 (Outline). You'll be prompted to enter the name of the outline style and the level you want this style to affect. Enter the information. This style now appears on the Outline Styles menu.

Outline Typestyle (see *Appearance Attributes*)

Overstrike (see also *Compose Key*)

Function: Lets you type one character over another to create a new character.

Keystrokes:

Keyboard	*Mouse*
Shift-F8 (Format)	Layout
4 (Other)	Other
5 (Overstrike)	Overstrike
1 (Create)	Create
characters	*characters*
Enter	Enter
F7 (Exit)	Right mouse button

Code: [Ovrstk]

Example:

Second character typed

Overstrike code

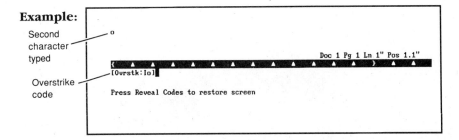

The most efficient way to type a character is to type the character directly from the keyboard, or use the Compose key to enter a character from one of WordPerfect's character sets. However, if the character does not appear on the keyboard or in one of the special character sets, you can use the Overstrike feature to type two or more characters in the same position. For example, you can combine I and o to create Ø. WordPerfect then inserts a code in your document, telling your printer to print one character on top of the other. Only the second character appears on your editing screen. To see both characters, press Alt-F3 (Reveal Codes).

Creating an Overstrike Character

1. Press Shift-F8 (Format) or display the **Layout** menu.

   A list of formatting options appears.

2. Select **Other** (4).

3. Select **5** (Overstrike).

4. Select **1** (Create).

   WordPerfect prompts you to type the characters you want to combine.

5. Type the first character you want to combine, and then type the second and any others.

   You can add appearance attributes to these characters by pressing F6 (Bold), F8 (Underline), or Ctrl-F8 (Font).

6. Press Enter.

   WordPerfect inserts the [Ovrstk] code at the cursor location. The last character of the combination you typed appears on screen. To see the combined characters, use View Document.

7. Press F7 (Exit) or click the right mouse button.

P

Page (see *Print Document on Screen*)

Page Break (see *New Page* and *Force Odd/Even Page*)

Page Format (see *Format Page*)

Page Length (see *Paper Size and Type*)

Page Number, Go To (see *Go To Key*)

Page Numbering (see also *Headers and Footers* and *New Page Number*)

Function:	Lets you turn on page numbering and select the type and location of numbers used for numbering pages.

Keystrokes:	*Keyboard*	*Mouse*
	Shift-F8 (Format)	Layout
	2 (Page)	Page
	6 (Page Numbering)	Page Numbering
	Select option	Select option
	Enter change	Enter change
	F7 (Exit)	Right mouse button

Codes:	[Pg Numbering]
	[Pg Num]
	[Pg Num Sty]

Example:

```
Format: Page Numbering

     1 - New Page Number        i

     2 - Page Number Style     Contents - ^B

     3 - Insert Page Number

     4 - Page Number Position Bottom Center


Selection: 0
```

The Page Numbering feature lets you turn on automatic page numbering and specify the type of number you want to use and where you want the number printed on each page. WordPerfect then automatically numbers your pages during printing. If you edit your document, WordPerfect renumbers the pages as necessary. To specify the numbering format, use the Format: Page Numbering menu. This menu offers the following options:

New Page Number lets you start page numbering with a number other than 1 and select the numbering style you want to use: Arabic (1, 2, 3); uppercase Roman (I, II, III); or lowercase Roman (i, ii, iii). Arabic is the default. This is useful if you keep chapters in separate files but want to continue the numbering scheme. Type the number you want to start with in the style in which you want it to appear, such as I for page I (Roman numerals).

Page Number Style lets you add up to 30 characters to format your page number entry. For example, you could enter Chapter 1, Page -^B and press Enter. You must Press Ctrl-B to insert the ^B page numbering code. If you just edit an existing style, you don't have to reenter the code.

Insert Page Number inserts the page number in the page number style as displayed next to option 2 (Page Number Style). However, this option inserts the page number only at the current cursor position, and it appears as text on the Edit screen. Also, if the Page Number code that this option inserts is moved, this option will print the page number wherever the code is moved, not where you originally inserted it. If you want the page number printed on every page, use the fourth option instead, Page Number Position.

Page Number Position displays various locations for the page number and lets you turn on automatic page numbering. Type the number that represents the place where you want the page numbers printed, such as 1 for top left, 2 for top center, or 6 for bottom center. If you use alternating pages, as in bound material, you can select options 4 or 8.

 Numbering Pages

1. Move the cursor to the top of the page where you want the page numbering to start.

2. Press Shift-F8 (Format) or display the **Layout** menu.

   A list of formatting options appears.

3. Select **Page (2)**.

   The Format: Page menu appears.

4. Select **6** (Page **Numbering**).

   The Format: Page Numbering menu appears.

5. Select the option you want to change and enter the change.

   WordPerfect will not print page numbers unless you use option 4 to select a position or option 3 to insert a number only at the cursor position.

6. Press F7 (Exit) or click the right mouse button.

   WordPerfect returns you to the Edit screen and inserts the code for the options you selected at the cursor position: [Pg Numbering], [Pg Num], or [Pg Num Sty].

 Tip: If you always use the same page numbering format for all your documents, insert the Page Numbering codes as initial codes via the Setup menu. Refer to *Initial Settings*.

Page Up and Page Down Keys (see *Cursor Movement*)

Paper Size and Type

Function: Lets you specify the size and type of paper on which you intend to print.

Keystrokes:

Keyboard	*Mouse*
Shift-F8 (Format)	Layout
2 (Page)	**Page**
7 (Paper Size/Type)	**Paper Size/Type**
2 (Add) or **5 (Edit)**	**Add** or **Edit**
Select option	Select option
Enter change	Enter change
F7 (Exit)	Right mouse button
1 (Select)	**Select**
F7 (Exit)	Right mouse button

Code: [Paper Sz/Typ]

Example:

```
Format: Edit Paper Definition
        Filename              EPLQ850.PRS
    1 - Paper Size            8.5" x 11"
    2 - Paper Type            Standard
    3 - Font Type             Portrait
    4 - Prompt to Load        No
    5 - Location              Continuous
    6 - Double Sided Printing No
    7 - Binding Edge          Left
    8 - Labels                No
    9 - Text Adjustment - Top 0"
                       Side   0"

Selection: 0
```

If you always print on standard paper (8 1/2" by 11"), you need not worry about selecting a paper size. If you intend to print on some other size or type of paper, however, you must specify the size and type so that WordPerfect can format your text to print correctly on each page. To select a size and type of paper, use the Format: Page menu's Paper Size/Type option. If the form isn't yet defined for your printer, it won't be listed, so you must create a definition for it, and then select it from a menu. To create a definition, use the Format: Edit Paper Definition screen. This screen offers the following options:

Paper Size: When you select this option, a list of commonly used paper sizes appears, such as Standard, Legal, Envelope, and Half Sheet. Select a size from the list or select **o** (Other) to enter specific dimensions. The first measurement you enter is for width, and the second is for height. Make sure you leave enough room for the 1" margins on all sides.

Paper Type: When you select this option, a list of paper types appears, including envelopes and labels. Select a type from the list or select **o** (Other) to specify a different type. This name will appear in the Format: Paper Size/Type menu, to help you identify it.

Font Type: This option lets you select portrait (the default orientation) or landscape orientation (to print sideways, as on an envelope). This option is printer-dependent. Refer to *Orientation, Portrait and Landscape*.

Prompt to Load: If you select this option and type Y, whenever you ask to print a document that uses this paper size and type, WordPerfect will prompt you to load the paper into your printer before it will begin printing. Your computer will beep, and a message will appear on the printer screen asking you to type g. Insert the paper into your printer, and type g to start printing.

Location: This option lets you specify how the paper is being fed into your printer. Choose **1** (**C**ontinuous) if you're using tractor-fed paper or if your printer has only one paper tray, **2** (**B**in Number) for bin-fed paper and enter the bin number you're using, or **3** (**M**anual) if you're feeding paper by hand.

Double Sided Printing: If your printer can print on both sides of a page (duplex printing), you can choose this option and press Y to print on both sides of the paper.

Binding Edge: This option lets you insert extra space in the inside margin (gutter) or top margin, so two-sided pages can be bound or inserted into a binder. When you select Left, text on odd-numbered (right-hand) pages is shifted to the right, and text on even-numbered (left-hand) pages is shifted to the left. If you select Top, the text will be moved up on even-numbered pages and down on odd-numbered pages. Refer to *Binding*.

Labels: If you are printing addresses on mailing labels, select this option and type Y. You will then see the Format: Labels menu, where you can specify the measurements for your labels. Refer to *Labels, Printing*.

Text Adjustment: If the text is not printing in the proper position on the page according to the margins specified, select this option to shift the text up, down, left, or right on the printed page.

Creating or Editing a Paper Definition

1. Press Shift-F8 (Format) or display the Layout menu.

   A list of formatting options appears.

2. Select **Page (2)**.

   The Format: Page menu appears.

3. Select **7** (Paper Size/Type).

   A list of paper sizes and types that have been defined for this printer appears.

4. Select **2** (Add) or highlight a size you want to edit and select **5** (Edit).

   If you select Edit, skip to step 6. If you select Add, a list of paper types appears.

5. Select a paper type, or choose **o** (Other) and enter the type of paper you're using.

   The Format: Edit Paper Definition menu appears.

6. Make any necessary changes to the options on this menu, such as Location, Binding Edge, and Font Type.

7. Press F7 (Exit), or click the right mouse button until you return to the Paper Size/Type menu.

   The dimensions you just entered now appear on this menu.

 Tip: It's easier to create a new paper definition by modifying an existing definition. Instead of selecting **Edit** or **Add** in step 4 above, highlight a definition that resembles the one you want to create, and select **3** (Copy). Next, select **5** (Edit) and modify the existing definition.

 ## Selecting a Paper Definition to Use in a Document

1. Move the cursor to the top of the document or page whose paper definition you wish to change.

2. Press Shift-F8 (Format) or display the Layout menu.

   A list of formatting options appears.

3. Select **Page** (**2**).	The Format: Page menu appears.
4. Select **7** (Paper Size/Type).	A list of defined paper sizes and types appears.
5. Highlight the paper size and type on which you intend to print, and choose **1** (Select) or press Enter.	WordPerfect returns you to the Format: Page menu. The paper size and type you selected will be listed next to the option.
6. Press F7 (Exit) or click the right mouse button.	WordPerfect returns you to your document and inserts the [Paper Sz/Typ] code at the cursor location.

WordPerfect uses the [ALL OTHERS] paper definition at the bottom of the Format: Paper Size/Type menu whenever it cannot find a paper definition to match a [Paper Sz/Typ] code in your document. You can edit this definition by highlighting it and selecting **5** (Edit), but your editing options are restricted.

Paragraph Numbering (see also *Outlines*)

Function: Lets you insert automatic paragraph numbers that WordPerfect updates as you insert or delete paragraph numbers or move them to another level.

Keystrokes: *Keyboard*   *Mouse*
Shift-F5 (Date/Outline)   Tools
5 (Para Num)   Paragraph Number
number   *number*
Enter   Enter

Codes: [Par Num Def]
[Par Num]
[Par Num: Auto]

Example:

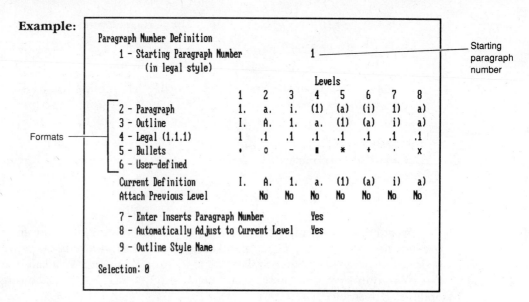

```
Paragraph Number Definition
    1 - Starting Paragraph Number              1 ─────────────────
           (in legal style)
                                        Levels
                            1    2    3    4    5    6    7    8
     ┌  2 - Paragraph       1.   a.   i.   (1)  (a)  (i)  1)   a)
     │  3 - Outline         I.   A.   1.   a.   (1)  (a)  i)   a)
     │  4 - Legal (1.1.1)   1    .1   .1   .1   .1   .1   .1   .1
     │  5 - Bullets         •    o    -    ■    *    +    ·    x
     └  6 - User-defined

        Current Definition  I.   A.   1.   a.   (1)  (a)  i)   a)
        Attach Previous Level    No   No   No   No   No   No   No

        7 - Enter Inserts Paragraph Number        Yes
        8 - Automatically Adjust to Current Level  Yes
        9 - Outline Style Name

     Selection: 0
```

Starting
paragraph
number

Formats

The Paragraph Numbering feature provides a convenient way for you to create bulleted or numbered lists or to number your paragraphs according to a hierarchical scheme. This feature is similar to the Outline feature, except that pressing Enter does not automatically insert a paragraph number. Instead, you select the Paragraph Number option each time you want one. Also, some of the Outline features are unavailable, such as Move, Copy, and Delete Family. To number your paragraphs, you must perform the following two steps:

1. Define your paragraph-numbering scheme. This consists of selecting a style that specifies how each paragraph level will be numbered: with Roman numerals, Arabic numbers, uppercase or lowercase letters, bullets, etc. Each level is separated by a tab or indent. If you want to use the default style, Outline, this step is unnecessary.

2. Select the Paragraph Numbering feature to number each paragraph. This consists of telling WordPerfect the level of the paragraph or letting WordPerfect insert one automatically, in which case the level corresponds to the tab stop position. WordPerfect numbers the paragraphs sequentially. For example, if you create two level-one paragraphs, WordPerfect numbers the first paragraph I and the second paragraph II.

If you want to select a numbering format other than the default, Outline, or if you want to change other features, use the Paragraph Number Definition menu to change any of the following settings:

Starting Paragraph Number: Lets you select any starting number for your paragraphs. You must enter Arabic numerals for this setting. This is useful if you interrupt a numbered section with an unnumbered block of text and want the numbering sequence to continue where you left off, instead of starting over at 1.

Formats: Lets you select any of four standard numbering schemes for your paragraphs or select User-Defined to create your own scheme. The currently selected numbering scheme is displayed on the Current Definition line. Next to each format, WordPerfect displays the first number that will be used for each level if you select that format. The default is Outline.

Attach Previous Level: If you create your own numbering scheme, you can change the Attach setting for any level to Yes. This attaches the character used for the previous level to the character used for this level. For example, if you mark your first level A. and your second level 1. and then change Attach Previous Level for your second level to Yes, the second level will be marked A.1, A.2, A.3, etc. The only format that uses this option is Legal.

Tip: You can create and use special styles (Outline styles) for your paragraph numbers. For more information, see *Outline Style*.

Defining Paragraph Numbers

1. Move the cursor before the position where you want the changes to take effect.

   If you already entered automatic paragraph numbers, you may want to move the cursor above them. Once you change something in the Paragraph Number Definition menu, numbering will start over with 1 unless you use the Starting Paragraph Number option to change the first number.

2. Press Shift-F5 (Date/Outline) or display the **Tools** menu.

3. Select **Define** (6).	The Paragraph Number Definition menu appears.
4. Select the setting you wish to change.	If you select 2-6, the numbering scheme appears in the menu.
5. Enter the new setting.	The new setting appears at the cursor position.
6. Repeat steps 4-5 until all the settings appear as desired.	
7. Press F7 (Exit) twice or click the right mouse button twice.	WordPerfect returns you to the Edit screen and inserts a [Par Num Def] code at the cursor position.

Whether or not you enter a [Par Num Def] code in your document, you can number paragraphs simply by selecting the Para Num option and indicating the level for the paragraph. WordPerfect does the rest, numbering the paragraphs sequentially and keeping the sequence accurate if you insert or delete other paragraph numbers.

 ## Entering Paragraph Numbers

1. Position the cursor at the beginning of the paragraph you want to number.	
2. Press Shift-F5 (Date/Outline) or display the **Tools** menu.	
3. Select **Paragraph Number** (5).	WordPerfect prompts you to type the level for this paragraph or press Enter for an automatic one.
4. Press Enter to select automatic numbering or type the level of the paragraph (any number from 1 to 8).	If you select automatic numbering, you can change the level of the paragraph later by moving the cursor to the paragraph number and pressing Tab or Shift-Tab, because automatic paragraph numbers are determined by the tab stop. If you type a level of your own, the level is fixed; Tab or Indent

has no effect on it. To change the level later, you have to delete the [Par Num] code and enter a new one.

Tip: To enter automatic paragraph numbers quickly, create a macro to perform the steps. If you use an Alt-*letter* macro, such as Alt-P, only two keystrokes are needed.

Parallel Columns (see *Columns, Side-by-Side*)

Password Protection

Function: Lets you prevent others from accessing your files.

Keystrokes:

Keyboard	*Mouse*
Ctrl-F5 (Text In/Out)	File
2 (Password)	Password
1 (Add/Change)	Add/Change
password	*password*
password	*password*
Save document	Save document

The Password feature lets you assign a password to your document to prevent other computer users from accessing your files without your permission. Unless you know the password, you won't be able to retrieve, print, or use the Look feature to view a password-protected file. However, you will be able to delete the file.

Locking Your Document

1. Start with your document displayed on screen.

2. Press Ctrl-F5 (Text In/Out) or display the File menu.

3. Select **2 (Password)** or Password.

4. Select **1** (Add/Change).	WordPerfect prompts you to enter a password.
5. Type the password (up to 24 characters), press Enter, and type the password a second time.	After you type the password, you will be prompted to re-enter it. The password does not appear on screen as you type it. WordPerfect forces you to enter the password twice to make sure you type it correctly.
6. Press F10 (Save) or select Save from the File menu.	WordPerfect prompts you to enter a name for the file. If the file was saved previously, its name appears on screen. If you press Enter, WordPerfect will ask whether you want to replace the old version with this version.
7. Press Y to replace the old version with this version, or type a file name and press Enter.	WordPerfect saves the file with the password. The next time you try to retrieve it, print it from disk, or view it using the Look option, WordPerfect will prompt you to enter the password.

 Tip: If you retrieve a password-protected file while another, unprotected document is on the Edit screen and then save the resulting file under the same name as the password-protected file, the file will no longer include password protection.

 ## Removing Password Protection

1. Retrieve the document to the Edit screen.	You must enter the password correctly, or WordPerfect won't let you retrieve it.
2. Press Ctrl-F5 (Text In/Out) or display the File menu.	

3. Select **2** (**Password**) or Password.	The Password menu appears, offering two options: **1** (**Add/Change**) and **2** (**Remove**).
4. Select **2** (**Remove**).	Although it appears as though nothing has happened, after you save the document, the password will be removed.
5. Press F10 (Save) or select Save from the File menu.	WordPerfect prompts you to enter a name for the file. If the file was saved previously, its name appears on screen. If you press Enter, WordPerfect will ask whether you want to replace the old version with this version.
6. Press Y to replace the old version with this version or type a file name and press Enter.	By replacing the previous version, which included password protection, with the on-screen version, which does not, you remove password protection from the file.

Path for Downloadable Fonts and Printer Files (see also *Location of Files* and *Printer Commands*)

Function: Tells WordPerfect where your downloadable font files (soft fonts) and printer command files are located.

Keystrokes:

Keyboard	*Mouse*
Shift-F7 (Print)	**File**
S (Select Printer)	**Print**
3 (Edit)	**Select Printer**
6 (Path for **Downloadable** Fonts and Printer Files)	**Edit**
pathname	**Path for Downloadable** Fonts and Printer Files
F7 (Exit)	*pathname*
	Right mouse button

Example:

```
Select Printer: Edit
        Filename                EPLQ850.PRS
     1 - Name                   Epson LQ-850
     2 - Port                   LPT1:
     3 - Sheet Feeder           None
     4 - Cartridges and Fonts
     5 - Initial Base Font      Roman 10cpi
     6 - Path for Downloadable  c:\wp51\printers ──────── Path
         Fonts and Printer
         Command Files

Selection: 6
```

If you use soft fonts or if you created a printer command file for your printer's special commands, you must tell WordPerfect where these files are located. If they are in the same directory listed for your printer files on the Setup: Location of Files menu, you don't need to use this option. However, if your soft font files and/or printer command file are in a different directory from your printer definition files, you must use this option to specify their location on the Select Printer: Edit screen.

Entering a Path for Downloadable Font Files

1. Press Shift-F7 (Print) or select **Print** from the **File** menu.

   The main Print menu appears.

2. Choose **S** (Select Printer).

   The Print: Select Printer menu appears, displaying a list of installed printers.

3. Highlight the printer you're using, and select **3** (Edit).

   The Select Printer: Edit screen appears.

4. Select **6** (Path for Downloadable Fonts and Printer Files).

   The cursor moves up to this option.

5. Enter the complete path of the directory where the soft fonts and/or printer command file for this printer is located.

6. Press F7 (Exit) or click the right mouse button.

Percent of Optimal Spacing (see *Word and Letter Spacing*)

Pica (see *Units of Measure*)

Portrait (see *Orientation, Portrait and Landscape*)

Preview Document (see *View Document*)

Primary File (see *Merge*)

Print Color

Function: Lets you print text in a different color, if your printer supports this feature.

Keystrokes:

Keyboard	*Mouse*
Ctrl-F8 (Font)	Font
5 (Print Color)	Print Color
Select color	Select color
F7 (Exit)	Right mouse button

Code: [Color]

Example:

```
Print Color
                                 Primary Color Mixture
                              Red      Green     Blue

         1 - Black            0%        0%        0%
         2 - White          100%      100%      100%
         3 - Red             67%        0%        0%
         4 - Green            0%       67%        0%
         5 - Blue             0%        0%       67%
         6 - Yellow          67%       67%        0%
         7 - Magenta         67%        0%       67%
         8 - Cyan             0%       67%       67%
         9 - Orange          67%       25%        0%
         A - Gray            50%       50%       50%
         N - Brown           67%       33%        0%
         O - Other
         Current Color       50%        0%       50%

     Selection: 0
```

If your printer has the capacity to print different colors, you can print entire documents or selected blocks of text in a different color. You can choose from the following 11 preset colors, or create your own colors by mixing percentages of the primary colors.

Black	Magenta
White	Cyan
Red	Orange
Green	Gray
Blue	Brown
Yellow	

 Printing in Color

1. Move the cursor to the beginning of the section you want to print in color.

2. Press Ctrl-F8 (Font) or display the Font menu.

   A list of font options appears.

3. Select Print Color (5).

   The Print Color menu appears, displaying a list of available colors.

4. Select a color or select a color and then modify it by selecting **o** (Other) and entering percentages for the primary colors.

5. Press F7 (Exit) or click the right mouse button.

WordPerfect inserts the [Color] code at the cursor location. If you have a color monitor, the color of the text on screen is no indication of how it will print, but View Document should portray the colors.

When you choose to print text in a color, WordPerfect inserts a [Color] code in your document. The text from that point on will print in the selected color. To return to the original color (for example, black), repeat the steps, choosing the original color. Black is the default selection.

Tip: If you have a PostScript printer, you can reverse out text; that is, you can create a graphics box to print white text on a black background. To do this, you must set the gray shading option on the Graphics Options menu to 100% (refer to *Graphics, Options*), and create a text box (refer to *Graphics, Create*). Next, select **9** (Edit) from the Definition Text Box menu, perform the steps listed above to select white as the font color, and type the text you want to appear white. Press F7 (Exit) to exit from the Edit menu and from the Definition Text Box.

Print Document on Disk (see also *Print Document on Screen* and *Print File from the List Files Screen*)

Function: Lets you print a document without retrieving it to the Edit screen.

Keystrokes:

Keyboard	*Mouse*
Shift-F7 (Print)	File
3 (Document on Disk)	Print
filename	Document on Disk
Enter	*filename*
	Enter

You can use the Document on Disk option to print a document summary, a complete document, or selected pages of a document without retrieving the file to the Edit screen. When you choose to print a document from disk, WordPerfect prompts you to enter the name of the document you want to print. After you enter the file name, WordPerfect asks if you want to print the entire document. At this point, you must type an entry to indicate what you want to print. The following list gives some examples:

Press	**To Print**
Enter	Entire document, no summary
s	Document summary only
s-	Document summary and entire document
3	Page 3 only
s,3,4	Document summary and pages 3 and 4
3,4	Pages 3 and 4 only
3-	Page 3 to the end of the document
3-18	Pages 3 through 18
-18	Beginning of document through page 18
o	All odd pages
e	All even pages

 Caution: If you have retrieved a file and made changes to it without saving the changes to disk, do not use this option to print it. If you do, the changes will not be in the printed version, since WordPerfect prints the file as it exists on disk.

Printing a Document from Disk

1. Press Shift-F7 (Print) or select **Print** from the File menu.

   The main Print menu appears.

2. Select **3** (Document on Disk).

   WordPerfect prompts you to enter the name of the file you want to print.

3. Enter the name of the file you want to print, including a path if the file is not in the default directory.

   The Page(s): (All) prompt appears, prompting you to select the pages you want to print. If you press Enter, the entire document will be printed.

4. Press Enter to print the entire document, or enter the page number(s) you want to print.

   WordPerfect starts printing the document.

Print Document on Screen

Function: Prints the document that's displayed on the Edit screen.

Keystrokes:
Keyboard	*Mouse*
Shift-F7 (Print)	**File**
1 (Full Document),	**Print**
2 (Page), or	**Full Document**, **Page**, or **Multiple**
5 (Multiple Pages)	**Pages**

The Print function lets you print an entire document or selected pages of a document displayed on the Edit screen. WordPerfect's main Print menu offers three options to print the text on the Edit screen: *Full Document*, *Page*, and *Multiple Pages*. Full Document prints the entire document. Page prints only the page on which the cursor is located. Multiple Pages lets you select one or more pages, a range of pages, the document summary, and other groupings for printing. Refer to the previous section, *Print Document on Disk*, for a list of examples.

Printing a Document on Screen

1. If you want to print a single page, start with the cursor on the page you want to print.

2. Press Shift-F7 (Print) or select Print from the File menu.

   The main Print menu appears.

3. Select **1** (**Full Document**), **2** (**Page**), or **5** (**Multiple Pages**).

   If you select Full Document or Page, WordPerfect starts printing. If you select Multiple Pages, the Page(s): prompt appears.

4. If the Page(s): prompt appears, enter the page or range of pages you want to print.

   WordPerfect starts printing the specified pages.

You can also print a selected block of text from the Edit screen. To do this, highlight the block using Alt-F4 (Block), and then press Shift-F7 (Print) or select Print from the File menu. WordPerfect asks if you want to print the block. Press Y to print the block.

Printer, Select

Function: Lets you select your printer from a list of installed printers.

Keystrokes:

Keyboard	*Mouse*
Shift-F7 (Print)	**File**
S (Select Printer)	**Print**
Highlight printer	**Select Printer**
1 (Select)	Double-click on selected printer
F7 (Exit)	Right mouse button

When you installed WordPerfect, the Installation program led you through the process of installing a printer and copied the necessary .ALL file from the Printer diskette to your printer directory. Next, it used the .ALL file to create an individual .PRS file for the printer you selected. Each .PRS file contains the specific information required by WordPerfect to communicate with a single printer. WordPerfect gets this information from the appropriate .ALL file, which contains information for a related group of printers, such as dot-matrix printers.

Whenever you want to print a document using a different printer, you must display the Select: Printer screen, which lists all the printers you installed. You can then highlight a printer and choose one of the following options:

Select: Choose this option to select the highlighted printer from a list of installed printers. Your documents are then formatted for this printer until you select a different printer. The specific printer information is saved with each document.

Additional Printers: If your printer is not listed on the Print: Select Printer screen, choose this option to view a list of additional printers. This list includes all printers found in the .ALL files you copied during installation. If your printer is still not listed, you must run the Installation program again so WordPerfect can copy the necessary .ALL file. Other options on this menu let you select a printer definition file (.PRS) to include on the Print: Select Printer screen, view a list of printer files in another directory, get help about a highlighted printer, view a list of .PRS files, or search for a printer in the list by name.

Edit: This option lets you edit the printer setup for the highlighted printer, to select fonts and cartridges, change the port, select an initial base font, specify the directory for soft fonts and printer command file, and more.

Copy: If you want to modify a printer setup without changing the original .PRS file, highlight the printer and select 4 (**Copy**). WordPerfect prompts you to enter a name for the copied printer file and suggests one that differs from the original. Type a name or press Enter to accept the suggested name. You can then edit the copy without affecting the original.

Delete: If your list of installed printers contains printer definitions no longer in use, you can use this option to delete their names from the list. Although the printer name is removed, this does not erase the .PRS file from disk. You can select the Additional Printers option and then use the List Printer Files option to select the printer(s) again.

Help: This option gives you more information about the highlighted file.

Update: If you receive a newer version of an .ALL file and you don't want to reinstall all your printer (.PRS) files, you can use this option to update the files with the new information. To use this option, first delete or rename the old .ALL file, and then run the Installation program to copy the new ones. Next, use this option to highlight the printer you want to update, and select 7 (**Update**). If you have modified a printer (.PRS) file or an .ALL file using the PTR.EXE program, or by installing soft fonts such as Bitstream, you should rename the old files instead of deleting them, since you may need to use them again.

Selecting a Printer

1. Press Shift-F7 (Print) or select Print from the File menu.

   The main Print menu appears.

2. Choose **S** (Select Printer).

   The Print: Select Printer screen appears, displaying a list of installed printers.

3. Highlight the printer you want to use, and choose **1** (Select) or choose one of the options from the bottom of the screen.

   If you select a printer, WordPerfect returns you to the Print menu. You can then proceed with your printing. If you selected an option from the bottom of the screen, go on to the next step.

4. Follow the on-screen prompts to complete the task.

5. Press F7 (Exit) or click the right mouse button to return to the Print menu.

Printer Commands

Function: Lets you insert printer commands into your document that are unique to your printer, or download a file of commands to the printer when the document is being printed.

Keystrokes: *Keyboard*
Shift-F8 (Format)
4 (Other)
6 (Printer Functions)
2 (Printer Command)
1 (Command) or
2 (Filename)
command or filename
F7 (Exit)

Mouse
Layout
Other
Printer Functions
Printer Command
Command or Filename
command or filename
Right mouse button

Code: [Ptr Cmnd]

If your printer has special features or functions that WordPerfect does not support, you can take advantage of those features and functions by entering printer command codes into the text. You can use this feature in either of two ways: Enter individual command codes, or create a printer command file using BASIC or a text editor. If you create a file, you must then enter a Printer Command code to tell WordPerfect to send that file to the printer when you print the document. (Refer to *Path for Downloadable Fonts and Printer Files*.)

 Entering Printer Command Codes

1. Move the cursor where you want to insert the printer command or printer command file.

2. Press Shift-F8 (Format) or display the **Layout** menu.

   A list of formatting options appears.

3. Select **Other** (4).

   The Format: Other menu appears.

4. Select **6** (**Printer Functions**) and then **2** (**Printer Command**).

   The Format: Printer Functions menu appears. When you select option 2, two choices appear: Command and Filename.

5. Select **1** (**Command**) or **2** (**Filename**).

   WordPerfect prompts you to enter a command or file name.

6. Enter the decimal equivalent of the printer command(s) you want to use, or enter the path and file name of your printer command file.

   To use a code between 32 and 126, simply type the code. If the code is less than 32 or greater than 126, enclose the code in angle brackets < >. WordPerfect inserts a [Ptr Cmnd] code at the cursor location, which includes the commands or file name. The printer command file must be in the directory specified on the Path for Downloadable Fonts and Printer Command Files option on the Select Printer: Edit menu.

Printer Control

Function: Lets you check and manage your print jobs.

Keystrokes: *Keyboard*   *Mouse*
Shift-F7 (Print)   **File**
4 (Control Printer)   **Print**
Select option   **Control Printer**
Enter change   Select option
F7 (Exit)   Enter change
                                          Right mouse button

Example:

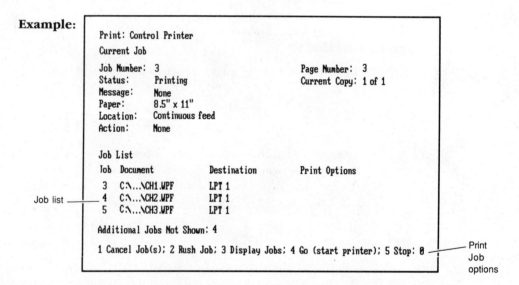

```
Print: Control Printer

Current Job

Job Number:  3                        Page Number:  3
Status:      Printing                 Current Copy: 1 of 1
Message:     None
Paper:       8.5" x 11"
Location:    Continuous feed
Action:      None


Job List

Job  Document              Destination      Print Options

  3  C:\...\CH1.WPF        LPT 1
  4  C:\...\CH2.WPF        LPT 1
  5  C:\...\CH3.WPF        LPT 1

Additional Jobs Not Shown: 4

1 Cancel Job(s); 2 Rush Job; 3 Display Jobs; 4 Go (start printer); 5 Stop: 0
```

Job list —

Print
Job
options

Whenever you select one of the print options to print a document, WordPerfect places the request into a *print job* list. If you choose to print several documents, WordPerfect handles each document as a separate print job, assigns a sequential number to it, and prints it in the order specified. You can check on the status of your print jobs and manage them using the following options on the Print: Control Printer screen:

Cancel Job(s) lets you cancel one or more print jobs. Enter the job number of the print job you want to cancel, or type *,Y to cancel all print jobs.

Rush Job lets you assign priority to a print job in the list. You can select any job and print it immediately or after the current print job is finished.

Display Jobs: If you have more than three print jobs that are waiting to be printed, this option displays a separate screen that includes the names of all the print jobs. Only three can fit on the Print: Control Printer screen (including the current job).

Go (start printer) resumes printing if WordPerfect interrupted printing for a manual feed form or print wheel or cartridge change or if you stopped the current print job by selecting **5** (Stop). Whenever you issue a print command and hear a beep or nothing happens, check this screen to see if a message such as `Press G to continue` appears in the Current Job information area.

Stop lets you interrupt the printing temporarily, but does not cancel the current print job. To resume printing, press G. To cancel printing, press C.

 ## Controlling Print Jobs

1. Press Shift-F7 (Print) or select **Print** from the **File** menu.

   The main Print menu appears.

2. Select **4** (Control Printer).

   The Print: Control Printer screen appears.

3. Check the status of your print jobs, or select one of the options at the bottom of the screen and enter your change, if necessary.

4. Press F7 (Exit) or click the right mouse button.

The current Job information is shown near the top of the screen, including Job Number, Status, Message, etc. The jobs waiting to be printed are displayed under Job List in the middle of the screen. If a number other than 0 appears next to `Additional Jobs Not Shown,` you can select option 3 to see them.

 Tip: WordPerfect remembers all print job requests, so if your printer does not start printing after you issue a print request, check the Print: Control Printer screen for information. Also, look for a loose printer cable, check the on-line button, and check to see if the printer is installed correctly and its name appears next to `Select Printer` on the main Print menu.

Printer Files Location (see *Location of Files*)

Print File from the List Files Screen

Function: Prints one or more files using the List Files Print option.

Keystrokes:

Keyboard	*Mouse*
F5 (List)	File
Enter	List Files
Highlight file or mark files	Enter
	Highlight file or mark files
4 (Print)	**Print**
Y, if printing a group of files	Y, if printing a group of files

Example:

```
11-06-90  12:27p              Directory D:\WP51\FILES\*.*
Document size:        0  Free: 19,120,128 Used:     278,967     Files:      22


    .   Current    <Dir>            ..    Parent     <Dir>
ADDRESS .         1,356  09-21-90 08:19a   CH7      .WP5   50,174  08-10-90 02:18p
CHAPT2  .        60,767  08-13-90 03:48p   CHAPT2   .DOC   51,200  08-22-90 09:43a
CONTRARY.WPG     10,159  10-15-90 09:13a   GRAB1    .WPG    9,263  10-15-90 09:26a
GRADES  .         2,087  10-08-90 03:03p   HPLASERI .CRS    1,170  10-12-90 04:24p
KATHY   .WP5      4,903  09-14-90 11:28a   L2       .WP5    2,224  08-16-90 04:34p
LABEL   .         1,193  09-21-90 12:11p   LEWIS    .WP5    5,206  10-12-90 03:19p
MAILLIST.WP5      1,129  09-21-90 08:32a   MATHCHAR .NUM    1,258  09-26-90 05:17p
MOBY    .WP4      2,782  10-10-90 02:25p   MOBY     .WP5    4,149  10-04-90 08:22a
MOBY2   .DOC      4,149  10-04-90 08:22a   PHONE    .WP5      770  10-12-90 03:19p
SCOTT   .WP5      2,665  10-12-90 03:19p   TREES    .CON      680  09-18-90 03:38p
TREES   .WP5      1,199  10-01-90 03:30p   VARIANT  .WPF   60,484  08-23-90 02:24p


Page(s): (All)
```

The List Files screen offers a convenient way of printing one or more files from disk. You select the file(s) you want to print from the list of files, and tell WordPerfect to start printing. WordPerfect does the rest automatically.

 Printing a Document from the List Files Screen

1. Press F5 (List) or select List Files from the File menu.

    A Dir prompt and the path to the current drive and directory appear in the lower-left corner of your screen.

2. If you want to print files in a different directory, type the path to that directory.

When you begin typing, the default path disappears, and what you type appears in its place.

3. Press Enter.

The List Files screen appears, displaying a list of files in the selected drive and directory.

4. Move the cursor to highlight the file you want to print, or highlight each file you want to print and type an asterisk (*).

You can mark or unmark all files listed by pressing Alt-F5 (Mark Text) or Home,*. The asterisks appear to the left of the file names.

5. Select 4 (**Print**).

If you are printing only the highlighted file, WordPerfect starts printing the file. If you marked one or more files, WordPerfect asks if you want to print the marked files.

6. If you selected several documents, type Y to confirm your selection.

WordPerfect prompts you to enter the page numbers or the range of pages you want to print.

7. Press Enter to print the entire document or type the page or range of pages you want to print.

Refer to *Print Document on Disk*. If you selected several files to print and you chose to print a range of pages, WordPerfect prints the same range of pages in each document.

Note: If a file you selected to print is formatted for a printer that differs from the currently selected printer, a message appears, warning you that the document is not formatted for the current printer. Press Y to print the document on the currently selected printer or N to cancel the printing. If you press Y, WordPerfect may have to substitute font changes and any other printer-specific formatting in the printed document. This will not affect the file itself. The alternative is to press N, retrieve the document, and print it from the Edit screen (refer to *Print Document on Screen*).

Printing, Stop (see *Printer Control*)

Print Job (see *Control Printer*)

Print Multiple Copies

Function: Prints two or more copies of the same document.

Keystrokes:

Keyboard	*Mouse*
Shift-F7 (Print)	**File**
N (Number of Copies)	**Print**
number	**Number of Copies**
U (Multiple Copies	*number*
Generated by)	**Multiple Copies Generated by**
1 (WordPerfect),	**WordPerfect, Printer, or Network**
2 (Printer) or	
3 (Network)	

Example:

```
Print
       1 - Full Document
       2 - Page
       3 - Document on Disk
       4 - Control Printer
       5 - Multiple Pages
       6 - View Document
       7 - Initialize Printer

Options
       S - Select Printer              Epson LQ-850
       B - Binding Offset              0"
       N - Number of Copies            1
       U - Multiple Copies Generated by  WordPerfect
       G - Graphics Quality            Medium
       T - Text Quality                High

Multiple Copies Generated by: 1 WordPerfect; 2 Printer: 1
```

The **Number of Copies** option on the Print menu lets you print several copies of a document or of selected pages. You can use the **Multiple Copies Generated By** option to select the source of the multiple copies: WordPerfect, your printer, or your network. If you select WordPerfect, the copies are collated as they print. If your printer is capable of generating copies, as are many laser printers, you can have your printer do it instead. Although the printer method prints the copies much more quickly, especially if they include graphics or use soft fonts, it does not collate them. If you're running WordPerfect from a network and your network supports this feature, you can have the network generate the copies.

 Printing Multiple Copies

1. Press Shift-F7 (Print) or select **Print** from the **File** menu.	The main Print menu appears.
2. Select **N** (Number of Copies), and enter the number of copies you want generated.	
3. Select **U** (Multiple Copies Generated by).	WordPerfect prompts you to select the source of the multiple copies.
4. Select **1** (WordPerfect), **2** (Printer), or **3** (Network).	
5. Select one of the print options to print the document as you normally would.	Refer to *Print Document on Disk* and *Print Document on Screen*.

Print Quality

Function: Sets the quality of print for text and graphics, or lets you print text only or graphics only.

Keystrokes:

Keyboard	*Mouse*
Shift-F7 (Print)	**File**
G (Graphics Quality)	**Print**
1 (Do Not Print),	**Graphics Quality**
2 (Draft), **3** (Medium),	**Do Not Print, Draft, Medium,** or
or **4** (High)	**High**
T (Text Quality)	**Text Quality**
1 (Do Not Print),	**Do Not Print, Draft, Medium,** or
2 (Draft), **3** (Medium),	**High**
or **4** (High)	**Right mouse button**
F7 (Exit)	

Example:

```
Print
     1 - Full Document
     2 - Page
     3 - Document on Disk
     4 - Control Printer
     5 - Multiple Pages
     6 - View Document
     7 - Initialize Printer
Options
     S - Select Printer              Epson LQ-850
     B - Binding Offset              0"
     N - Number of Copies            1
     U - Multiple Copies Generated by   WordPerfect
     G - Graphics Quality            Medium
     T - Text Quality                High


Graphics Quality: 1 Do Not Print; 2 Draft; 3 Medium; 4 High: 3
```

The Print Quality feature lets you set the quality of print for text, graphics, or both, or print text and graphics separately. However, as the print quality increases, speed of printing decreases, especially if you are using soft fonts on a laser printer. When printing a rough draft for proofreading, you may want to change the Text Quality to low, especially if you use a dot-matrix printer, to save unnecessary wear and tear.

Tip: To change Text Quality or Graphics Quality permanently, use the Setup menu. (See *Print Options* under *Initial Settings*.)

 Setting the Print Quality

1. Press Shift-F7 (Print) or select **Print** from the File menu.

   The main Print menu appears.

2. Select **G** (Graphics Quality) and select the quality setting for graphics.

   This setting controls the quality of your graphics boxes and any graphics characters you created.

3. Select **T** (**Text** Quality) and select a quality setting for text.

This setting controls the quality of the text you enter.

4. Unless you are ready to print your document, press F7 (Exit) or click the right mouse button.

WordPerfect saves the settings with the document, if you save the document again. The settings remain in effect until you change them or clear the screen. Then they change back to the default settings.

Most printers can print text and graphics on the same page. If your printer cannot, you can print text and graphics separately. On the first printing, set Graphics Quality to **1** (Do Not Print) and print the page. Reinsert the page in the printer. On the second printing, set Graphics Quality to one of the quality settings, set **Text** Quality to **1** (Do Not Print), and print the page again.

Tip: If you used Compose to insert special characters into your document from any of WordPerfect's character sets, WordPerfect can print them graphically, even if they are not contained in any of the printer's available fonts. This assumes that your printer can print graphics, as most laser or dot-matrix printers can. However, if you change Text Quality or Graphics Quality to Do Not Print, it will not work.

Print to Disk

Function: Lets you print a document to disk instead of to the printer, so the document can be printed on a computer that does not have WordPerfect.

Keystrokes:

Keyboard	*Mouse*
Shift-F7 (Print)	File
S (Select Printer)	Print
Highlight printer	Select Printer
3 (Edit)	Highlight printer
2 (Port)	Edit
o (Other)	Port
d:\path\filename	Other
F7 (Exit)	*d:\path\filename*
	Right mouse button

Example:

```
Select Printer: Edit
        Filename                EPLQ850.PRS
        1 - Name                Epson LQ-850
        2 - Port                C:\WP51\FILES\FILENAME.EXT ──
        3 - Sheet Feeder        None
        4 - Cartridges and Fonts
        5 - Initial Base Font   Roman 10cpi
        6 - Path for Downloadable
            Fonts and Printer
            Command Files


Selection: 0
```

Path to
print
file
to disk

If you want to be able to use the DOS PRINT command to print a document created in WordPerfect, you must either save the document as a DOS text file or print the document to disk. However, if you save the document as a DOS text file, all the formatting codes are stripped out, and when you print the document, the text appears without the formatting. If you want to retain your WordPerfect formatting, use this feature to print the document to disk.

 Printing a Document to Disk

1. Press Shift-F7 (Print) or select Print from the File menu.

    The main Print menu appears.

2. Choose **S** (Select Printer).

    A list of installed printers appears.

3. Highlight the printer that was used to format the document.

4. Select **3** (Edit).

    The Select Printer: Edit screen appears.

5. Select **2** (Port).

    A list of available ports appears. The LPT and COM options represent interfaces where the printer can be connected to the computer.

6. Select **o** (Other).

    The cursor moves up to the Port option.

7. Enter a complete path to the directory where you want to save the file followed by a file name.

    For example, type c:\wp51\files\filename.ext. If a prompt appears asking if you are using a network printer, type N.

8. Press F7 (Exit) twice, or click the right mouse button twice.

    This returns you to the main Print menu.

9. Print the document as you normally would, using one of the print options.

    Instead of sending the document to your printer, WordPerfect sends the document to a disk file.

 Caution: After you print the document to disk, follow the same steps to return to the Select Printer: Edit screen, and then select the printer you edited and change the port setting back to the original setting. Otherwise, every time you try to print a document using this printer, WordPerfect will print the document to disk, overwriting the document you just printed to disk, since the same file name will be used.

Protect Block (see *Block Protect*)

Pull-Down Menus (see also *Menu Options, Setup*)

Function: Lets you select WordPerfect features from pull-down menus, using either the mouse or the keyboard.

Keystrokes: *Keyboard*
Alt-=
OR
Alt (if you changed the
Alt Key Selects Pull-
Down Menu option on
the Setup menu)

Mouse
Right mouse button

Example:

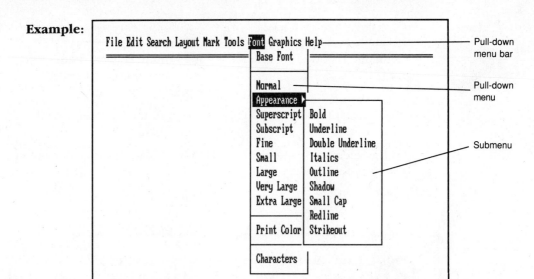

File Edit Search Layout Mark Tools Font Graphics Help — Pull-down menu bar

Base Font

Normal — Pull-down menu
Appearance ▶
Superscript | Bold
Subscript | Underline
Fine | Double Underline — Submenu
Small | Italics
Large | Outline
Very Large | Shadow
Extra Large | Small Cap
| Redline
Print Color | Strikeout

Characters

You can access WordPerfect's features in either of two ways. One way is to press the function key assigned to the feature. For example, you can press F6 for bold or Alt-F10 to run a macro. The other way is to select the feature from one of WordPerfect's pull-down menus, using the mouse or the keyboard.

To use the pull-down menus, you must activate the pull-down menu bar at the top of the screen. If you're using a mouse, click the right mouse button to activate the menu bar. If you don't have a mouse, press Alt-=. Either way, the menu bar appears, displaying nine pull-down menus. To use one, click on the menu you want to display with the left mouse button, or type the highlighted letter in the menu name. Use the same technique to select items that appear on the menu. You can also use the Right, Left, Up, and Down Arrow keys to move around in the pull-down menus, and press Enter to select an item.

 Using the Pull-Down Menus

1. Click the right mouse button or press Alt-=.

   The pull-down menu bar appears at the top of the screen. PgUp and PgDn or Home,Left Arrow and Home,Right Arrow move the cursor to the left or right end of the menu bar.

2. Click on the name of the menu you want to display with the left mouse button, or type the highlighted letter in the menu name, or use the arrow keys to move the cursor onto the menu name and press Enter.

This pulls the menu down from the menu bar, presenting a list of options. If an option appears in brackets, it is unavailable and another action, such as turning on Block mode, is required before you can select it.

3. Click on the option you want to use with the left mouse button, or type the highlighted letter in the item.

This may display another screen, a prompt, or another menu. If a triangle appears, it means another menu will pop out if you select the option. You can use Up Arrow and Down Arrow to move the cursor onto any item in the menu and press Enter to select it or type the highlighted letter.

4. Continue selecting items, answering prompts, and entering additional information until you've completed the task.

Tip: You can use an option on the Setup Menu options menu to change the way you select pull-down menus: Instead of pressing Alt-=, you can press the Alt key by itself to display the menu bar. To do this, press Shift-F1 (Setup) or select Setup from the File menu, select Display (2), then select 4 (Menu Options). Next, choose option 4 (Alt Key Selects Pull-Down Menu), and change the setting to Y.

Tip: To exit without selecting an item from one of the pull-down menus, press F7 (Exit), or move the mouse pointer into the Edit screen so that it is not pointing to a menu option, and click the left or right button.

Q-R

Quit WordPerfect (see *Exit*)

Rectangle, Move (see *Move Block*)

Redline (see *Appearance Attributes*)

Redline Method

Function: Lets you specify how you want redline text to be marked in the printed document.

Keystrokes:

Keyboard	*Mouse*
Shift-F8 (Format)	Layout
3 (Document)	Document
4 (Redline Method)	Redline Method
1 (Printer Dependent),	Printer Dependent, Left, or
2 (Left), or 3	Alternating
(Alternating)	Right mouse button
F7 (Exit)	

Example:

```
Format: Document
      1 - Display Pitch - Automatic Yes
                          Width    0.1"
      2 - Initial Codes
      3 - Initial Base Font      Roman 10cpi
      4 - Redline Method         Printer Dependent ──────── Redline
                                                            method
      5 - Summary


Redline Method: 1 Printer Dependent; 2 Left; 3 Alternating: 1 ──── Options
```

By default, redlined text is printed according to the method defined in your printer's definition file. If you prefer to use another method, you can use the Redline Method option, and select one of the following:

Printer Dependent, the default, prints the text according to the redline string in your printer file. On many laser printers, redline text appears with a shaded background. You can see what this mark will look like by retrieving the PRINTER.TST file and printing it from screen, or by typing any text using the Redline attribute, and then printing it.

Left marks the text with a vertical line (|) in the left margin. If you select this option, you can select a different character to use in place of the vertical line.

Alternating marks the text with a vertical line in the left margin on even-numbered pages and a vertical line in the right margin on odd-numbered pages. Again, you can use any other character in place of the vertical line.

 ### Selecting a Redline Method

1. Press Shift-F8 (Format) or display the Layout menu.	A list of formatting options appears.
2. Select **Document (3)**.	The Format: Document menu appears.
3. Select **4 (Redline Method)**.	A list of three redline methods appears.
4. Select **1 (Printer Dependent)**, **2 (Left)**, or **3 (Alternating)**.	If you select Left or Alternating, WordPerfect prompts you to enter a redline character. You can type any character on the keyboard or use Compose to enter one.
5. Enter a character of your choice, or press Enter to select the default character (|).	Your selection appears next to Redline Method.
6. Press F7 (Exit) or click the right mouse button.	WordPerfect returns you to the Edit screen.

This changes the redline method only for the document you are working on. To change it permanently, use the Setup: Print Options menu. Press Shift-F1 (Setup) or select Setup from the File menu. Select **4 (Initial Settings)**, **8 (Print Options)**, and **5 (Redline Method)**, and then select the method you want to use.

Redline/Strikeout Marks, Remove

Function: Removes redline codes and marks and erases all text marked for strikeout along with the strikeout codes.

Keystrokes:

Keyboard	*Mouse*
Alt-F5 (Mark Text)	**Mark**
6 (Generate)	**Generate**
1 (**R**emove Redline Markings and Strikeout Text from Document), Y	**R**emove Redline Markings and Strikeout Text from Document, Y

If you have used WordPerfect's Compare Screen and Disk Documents option to compare the on-screen version of a document with the disk version, WordPerfect marks text in the on-screen version with redline and strikeout, as follows: Text added to the screen version, which is not in the disk version, is redlined. Text that was in the disk version but which has been erased from the screen version is marked for strikeout.

When you finish comparing the two versions, you can use the Remove Redline Markings and Strikeout Text option to remove redline marks and strikeout text from the document on your Edit screen, so it will appear as it did before you used the Compare option. Also, if you have inserted redline and/or strikeout codes in your text yourself, independent of the Compare option, and are now ready to remove them and print the final copy, this option will erase all text marked for strikeout, and erase the redline marks.

 Removing Redline and Strikeout Codes

1. Press Alt-F5 (Mark Text), or display the **Mark** menu.

2. Select **Generate** (6). The Mark Text: Generate menu appears.

3. Select **1** (**R**emove Redline Markings and Strikeout Text from Document). WordPerfect asks if you want to delete redline markings and strikeout text.

4. Press Y to confirm or N to cancel. If you press Y, WordPerfect removes all redline and strikeout codes. You can now print a document free of redline marks and text marked for strikeout.

Referencing (see *Cross-Reference*)

Reformatting (see *Rewrite*)

Relative Tabs (see *Tab, Set*)

Rename File (see also *Move File*)

Function: Lets you change the name of a file.

Keystrokes:	*Keyboard*	*Mouse*
	F5 (List)	**File**
	Enter	**List Files**
	Highlight file	Double-click left mouse button
	3 (Move/Rename)	Select file
	newname.ext	Move/Rename
	Enter	*newname.ext*
		Enter

If you want to rename a file using DOS, you must enter the RENAME command along with the current name of the file and its new name. With WordPerfect, it's much easier: You highlight the file name in the List Files menu, select the Rename command, and type a new name for the file.

 Renaming a File

1. Press F5 (List) or select List Files from the **F**ile menu.

   The path to the current drive and directory appears in the lower-left corner of your screen.

2. If you want to rename a file in a different directory, type the path to that directory.

   When you begin typing, the default path disappears, and the characters you type appear in its place.

3. Press Enter or double-click the left mouse button on the path that's displayed.

The List Files screen appears, displaying a list of files in the selected drive and directory.

4. Highlight the name of the file you want to rename.

You can use **N** (Name Search) to highlight a specific file.

5. Select **3** (Move/Rename).

The New Name prompt appears, asking you to enter a new name for the file.

6. Type a new name for the file and press Enter. If you want to move the file at the same time, type the path to the directory where you want the file saved.

For example, to move and rename a file named LETTERII in the WP51 directory to a file named JONESII.LTR in the FILES subdirectory, you'd type c:\wp51\files\jonesii.ltr. If you move the file to another drive or directory, its name is erased from the list of the current directory.

7. Press F7 (Exit) or space bar, or click the right mouse button.

WordPerfect returns you to the Edit screen.

Repeat Value, Change

Function: Lets you change the repeat value for the Esc key.

Keystrokes: *Keyboard*
Esc
number
key to repeat
OR
Esc
number
Enter

Example:

```
Repeat Value = 8
```

If you press Esc when the screen is clear of any menu or prompt, the Repeat Value = 8 prompt appears. This indicates that the next key you press will be repeated eight times. For example, if you press Esc and then the

Del key, the next eight characters will be deleted. If you press Esc and then type a hyphen (-), WordPerfect will insert eight hyphens. You can change the repeat value (the number of times a keystroke will be repeated) for the next keystroke, for the rest of the editing session, or permanently.

Changing the Repeat Value for the Next Keystroke

1. Press Esc.

   The `Repeat Value = 8` prompt appears.

2. Type the number of times you want the next keystroke repeated.

   The number appears next to the `Repeat Value` prompt.

3. Press the key that you want repeated.

   The keystroke is repeated the specified number of times.

Changing the Repeat Value for the Current Editing Session

1. Press Esc.

   The `Repeat Value = 8` prompt appears.

2. Type the number of times you want your keystrokes repeated.

   The number appears next to the `Repeat Value` prompt.

3. Press Enter.

   The prompt disappears from the screen. The next time you press Esc, the prompt will reappear showing the number you just entered.

Changing the Repeat Value Permanently

1. Press Shift-F1 (Setup) or select Setup from the File menu.

   The main Setup menu appears.

2. Select Initial Settings (4).

   The Setup: Initial Settings menu appears.

3. Select 6 (Repeat Value).

   The cursor moves up to this option.

4. Enter the number of times you want your keystrokes repeated.

5. Press F7 (Exit) or click the right mouse button.

WordPerfect returns you to the Edit screen. From now on, or until you use Setup to change it again, whenever you press Esc, the number you just entered will appear as the repeat value.

Replace

Function: Replaces each occurrence of a specified word, phrase, or code with a different word, phrase, or code.

Keystrokes:

Keyboard	*Mouse*
Alt-F2 (Replace)	Search
Y (Confirm) or N (Replace All)	**R**eplace
Down Arrow or Up Arrow	Y (Confirm) or N (Replace All)
item to replace	Down Arrow or Up Arrow
F2 (→Search)	*item to replace*
replacement item	F2 (→Search)
F2 (→Search)	*replacement item*
	F2 (→Search)

Example:

```
<- Srch: [BOLD]dutch elm disease
```

The Replace option lets you search a document for all occurrences of a character, word, phrase, or formatting code, and replace it automatically with another or erase it altogether. There are two ways to use Replace: with or without Confirm. With Confirm means WordPerfect will stop each time it locates your search string and ask if you want to replace it here. Without Confirm, WordPerfect automatically replaces the search string everywhere, without stopping for your approval. If you're using the Replace feature for the first time, you should set Confirm to yes so that WordPerfect will ask for your confirmation before replacing each occurrence of an item.

The Search and Replace feature is case-sensitive. If you type the search string in all lowercase letters, WordPerfect will find both upper- and lowercase versions. If you type the first character of the search string in uppercase, WordPerfect will find only the occurrences that begin with an uppercase letter. If you type the replace string in lowercase letters, WordPerfect will replace the search string with the replace string but will uppercase the first character in the replace string whenever the first character in the search string is uppercase. If you uppercase the first letter of the replace string, the word is always replaced as capitalized.

Replacing Words, Codes, and Phrases

1. Move the cursor where you want the replace action to start.

   You will be able to replace items from this point forward or back.

2. Press Alt-F2 (Replace), or select Replace from the Search menu.

   The w/Confirm prompt appears, asking if you want it to pause at each occurrence of an item before performing the replacement.

3. Press Y to have WordPerfect request confirmation or N to replace all occurrences without asking.

   WordPerfect prompts you to type the text and/or enter the codes you want to replace. This is called the search string.

4. Press Up Arrow if you want WordPerfect to search and replace backward through the document.

   If you don't press Up Arrow, WordPerfect will search forward through the document, and the arrow will point to the right.

5. Type the text and/or enter the codes you want to replace.

   If you're entering codes, do not type the codes. Instead, enter the codes using the function keys. For example, press F6 for bold.

6. Press F2 (→Search).

   The Replace with prompt appears, asking you to enter the text and/or codes you want to use as replacements. Certain codes cannot be used, such as margins, line spacing, tab settings, and others that require measurements. Also, if you try to replace a code such as [BOLD] with a code such as [UND], Underline will be turned on and will remain on, starting at the position where the first [BOLD] code was found.

7. Type the text and/or enter the codes you want to use as replacements.

If you want to delete each occurrence of an item, skip this step. If you're entering codes, do not type the codes. Instead, enter the codes using the function keys.

8. Press F2 (→Search).

WordPerfect performs the replace operation. If you told WordPerfect to ask for confirmation, it stops on the first occurrence of the specified item and prompts you to type Y to confirm or N to move to the next occurrence without replacing this one. When the last occurrence has been found, WordPerfect stops, and the cursor remains there.

Tip: To replace every occurrence of an item with a bold or underline version, type the replacement string with a [BOLD] or [UND] code before and after it, such as [BOLD]Lesson 1[bold]. To insert the codes, just press F8 for Underline or F6 for Bold.

Tip: Replace will not locate and change a search string inside a header, footer, footnote, endnote, text box, or graphics box caption, unless you press Home before selecting Replace. This is called an extended Replace.

Restore (see *Undelete*)

Retrieve File (see also *List Files* and *Text In/Out*)

Function: Retrieves a copy of the selected file to the Edit screen.

Keystrokes: *Keyboard*   *Mouse*
Shift-F10 (Retrieve)   **File**
d:\pathname\filename   **Retrieve**
Enter   *d:\pathname\filename*
                      Enter

Example:

```
Document to be retrieved: c:\wp51\book\ch2.wpf
```

Before you can edit a previously saved document, you must retrieve a copy of the document from the file on disk to the Edit screen. You can retrieve a document in either of two ways. If you can't remember the name of the file or the directory it's in, you can select the file from a list of files (refer to *List Files*). However, if you know the location and name of the file, you can retrieve it much more quickly by using the Retrieve method described here:

Retrieving a File

1. Press Shift-F10 (Retrieve) or select **Retrieve** from the **File** menu.

   The Document to be retrieved prompt appears, asking you to enter the name of the file you want to retrieve.

2. Type the name of the file. If the file is not in the current directory, include a path name.

   For example, if the current directory is C:\WP51\FILES and you want to retrieve a file named CH2.WPF from the C:\WP51\BOOK directory, type c:\wp51\book\ch2.wpf. If you don't know which directory is the current one, press F5 (List), note the directory name, and press F1 (Cancel).

3. Press Enter.

   If the file exists, WordPerfect retrieves a copy of the file and displays it on screen. If WordPerfect cannot find the file, an error message appears, telling you the file was not found.

4. If an error message appears, try typing another name to retrieve the file, since you may have misspelled it or typed it incorrectly.

If the error message appears again, press F1 (Cancel), and then try using the List Files screen to retrieve it.

Retrieve Text

Function: Lets you retrieve text that WordPerfect has stored in a temporary buffer, after you used the Move or Copy option.

Keystrokes:

Keyboard	*Mouse*
Shift-F10 (Retrieve)	**File**
Enter	**Retrieve**
	Enter

When you use Block and Move or Move alone to highlight a block of text and move or copy it, WordPerfect stores the block in a temporary buffer. A prompt appears at the bottom of the screen telling you to move your cursor and press Enter to retrieve the block. After you move or copy the block or change your mind and press F1 (Cancel), the block remains in the temporary buffer. As long as you don't overwrite what's in that buffer by moving or copying another block, you can insert the block anywhere in your document, using the following methods:

 Retrieving a Block Using Retrieve

1. Move the cursor to the position where you want to insert the block.

2. Press Shift-F10 (Retrieve) or select **Retrieve** from the File menu.

WordPerfect asks the name of the document to be retrieved. If you leave it blank and press Enter, the last block you moved or copied will be retrieved.

3. Press Enter to retrieve the block or F1 to cancel the operation.

Retrieving a Block Using Move

1. Move the cursor to where you
   want to insert the block.

2. Press Ctrl-F4 (Move) or choose   The Retrieve menu appears.
   Paste from the **Edit** menu.

3. Select **Block (1)**.   WordPerfect inserts the block at
                                          the cursor location.

Return, Soft and Hard (see also *Edit-Screen Options* and *Leading Adjustment*)

Function: Ends each line of text you type with a soft return so that
               the lines are automatically wrapped. When you press Enter,
               WordPerfect inserts a hard return to end the paragraph.

Keystrokes: *Keyboard*
               Enter

Codes: [SRt]
               [HRt]
               [Dorm HRt]

Example:

```
ideals which the individual beings merely mirror. Like the skulls[SRt]
of the Right and Sperm whales hanging on opposite sides of the[SRt]
Pequod, these two philosophies slow the ship down and must be[SRt]
disposed of. They have expended their usefulness as tools of[SRt]
metaphysics.[HRt]
[HRt]
Metaphysics requires a more comprehensive view than that. It[SRt]
requires that you know the four causes of being[-][-]material, formal,[SRt]
essential, and final. You must know all the forces that govern a[SRt]
```

Soft return

Hard return

When the cursor reaches the right margin as you are typing, it automatically
wraps around to the next line. You do not have to press the Enter key at
the end of each line, as you do when using a typewriter. In fact, the only
time you should press Enter is when you want to end a paragraph or insert
a blank line. The type of return that WordPerfect automatically creates when
you allow it to wrap the cursor to the next line is called a *soft return*. When
you press Enter, you create a *hard return.*

WordPerfect places codes at the end of each line to indicate whether it ends in a soft return or a hard return: [SRt] and [HRt]. These codes can be seen in the Reveal Codes screen. If you let WordPerfect insert soft returns at the end of each line within a paragraph, you can later insert and delete text anywhere in the paragraph, and WordPerfect will automatically readjust the margins for you.

You can delete a hard return by placing the cursor at the end of the line and pressing Delete. However, you cannot delete a soft return, since the text would run into the right margin.

Tip: If a blank line is moved to the top of the following page as you insert or delete text, WordPerfect changes the Hard Return code into a Dormant Hard Return code [Dorm HRt]. This prevents it from appearing as a blank line at the top of the page. However, if the dormant hard return is moved back to the previous page, WordPerfect will convert it back to a regular [HRt] code, and it will appear as a blank line. This does not apply if you end a page with a Hard Page code.

Reveal Codes (see also *Edit-Screen Options*)

Function: Displays non-printing formatting codes.

Keystrokes: *Keyboard*   *Mouse*
Alt-F3 (Reveal Codes)   Edit
OR   Reveal Codes
F11 (Reveal Codes)

Example:

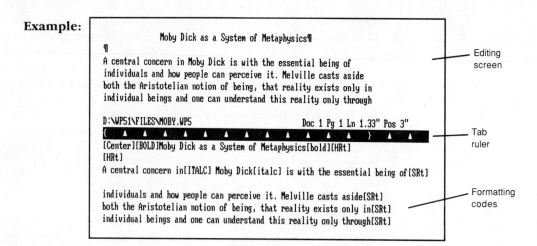

Moby Dick as a System of Metaphysics¶

¶

A central concern in Moby Dick is with the essential being of
individuals and how people can perceive it. Melville casts aside
both the Aristotelian notion of being, that reality exists only in
individual beings and one can understand this reality only through

Editing screen

D:\WP51\FILES\MOBY.WP5   Doc 1 Pg 1 Ln 1.33" Pos 3"

Tab ruler

[Center][BOLD]Moby Dick as a System of Metaphysics[bold][HRt]
[HRt]
A central concern in[ITALC] Moby Dick[italc] is with the essential being of[SRt]

individuals and how people can perceive it. Melville casts aside[SRt]
both the Aristotelian notion of being, that reality exists only in[SRt]
individual beings and one can understand this reality only through[SRt]

Formatting codes

Nearly all formatting changes that you make in WordPerfect insert hidden codes into your document, such as base font or font attributes, margin settings, headers and footers, and tab stop settings. To prevent clutter, these codes are not visible in the Edit screen, but you'll often need to know where they are located, especially if you are trying to remove a feature such as bold or underline. The codes can only be seen in a special area called the *Reveal Codes screen*.

To select the Reveal Codes option, either press Alt-F3 or F11 (Reveal Codes), or select **R**eveal Codes from the **E**dit menu. WordPerfect splits the screen in two horizontally. The top half is the regular Edit screen, and the lower half is the Reveal Codes screen. Between them is the tab ruler, a thick band with triangles and braces. The triangles represent the tab stop settings, pre-set for every half inch, and the braces represent the left and right margins. Since both margins are in the same position as a tab setting, they appear as braces.

The text in the top half of the screen is the same as in the lower half, except that you may see more lines in the lower half. The main difference is that in the lower half, WordPerfect displays both the text and the formatting codes affecting the text. The cursor is in the same position in both screens, but in the Reveal Codes screen it is represented by a rectangular block. When you move it onto a code, the cursor expands to highlight the entire code. You can erase a code and the formatting it represents by moving the cursor onto the code and then pressing the Delete key. If the cursor is to the right of a code, you can erase it by pressing the Backspace key. If you erase an open formatting code such as left/right margins or line spacing, you can use WordPerfect's Undelete feature to restore it. However, if you accidentally erase a paired formatting code such as [UND], you cannot get it back.

When Reveal Codes is on, you can do anything you can do when it's off: Move the cursor through the document, type, edit, and use any of WordPerfect's menus. You can even save a document and clear the Edit screen. While using it, watch for prompts and messages on the status line, just above the tab ruler. If you use a full-screen menu, such as one of the Format menus, it will take over the screen while you're using it, but Reveal Codes will still be on when you return.

Reveal Codes is a toggle, so you turn it off the same way you turned it on: press Alt-F3 or F11, or select **Reveal Codes** from the Edit menu.

 Tip: You can change the size of the Reveal Codes screen using the Setup: Edit Screen Options menu, as follows: Press Shift-F1 (Setup) or select Setup from the File menu, select **Display** (2), **6** (Edit-Screen Options), then **6** (Reveal Codes Window Size). Enter the number of lines that you want for the Reveal Codes window and then press F7 (Exit).

Reverse Search (see *Search*)

Rewrite (see also *Automatic Format and Rewrite*)

Function: Updates the document displayed on screen to show the effects of a formatting change.

Keystrokes: *Keyboard*
Ctrl-F3 (Screen)
3 (Rewrite)

Whenever you enter a formatting or editing change and it does not appear to be affecting all the text, you can reformat the document by moving the cursor down. Pressing keys such as Down Arrow, PgDn, Home, Home,Down Arrow rewrites the document as you move through it. However, they also move the cursor away from its original position. An alternative method is to use the Rewrite feature, which reformats the entire document at once without changing the cursor position.

Reformatting a Document

1. Press Ctrl-F3 (Screen). A list of screen options appears.

2. Select **3** (Rewrite) or press Enter. You return to the Edit screen, and WordPerfect rewrites the screen.

Right Justification (see *Justification*)

Ruler (see *Tab Ruler*)

Rush Print Job (see *Printer Control*)

S

Save File (see also *Exit, Fast Save, Password Protection*, and *Backup, Timed and Original*)

Function: Saves the file displayed on the Edit screen to disk and leaves it on screen so you can continue working on it.

Keystrokes:

Keyboard	*Mouse*
F10 (Save)	**File**
d:\path\filename.ext	**Save**
Enter	*d:\path\filename.ext*
	Enter

WordPerfect does not save files automatically. As you are typing, the text on the Edit screen is contained only in RAM, the computer's on-line memory. Once you turn the computer off, this memory is also shut off, so you must save your files to disk if you intend to use them again.

When you save a file, WordPerfect assumes that you want to save it in the current directory. To see what directory that is, press F5 (List). The `Dir` prompt appears in the lower left corner of the screen, followed by the path and directory name. To save the file to a different drive or directory, type the path to that drive or directory before typing the file name. For example, if the current directory were C:\WP51\FILES and you wanted to save a file named VARIANTS.WPF to the C:\WP51\DOCUMENT directory, you would type `c:\wp51\document\variants.wpf` when prompted to enter a file name.

When you save a file in this way, the file remains on screen. If you want to save the file and then clear the screen, you must use the F7 (Exit) key or select Exit from the File menu. (Refer to *Exit*.)

 Note: File names must follow DOS rules: a maximum of 11 characters, no spaces, and none of the following symbols:

$$* ? < > : ; = [ ] / \ " + ,$$

The first eight characters must be separated from the three-character extension by a period.

Saving a New File

1. Press F10 (Save) or select **Save** from the **File** menu.

   The `Dir` prompt appears, asking you to enter a name for the file.

2. Type a file name (up to eight characters), a period (.), and an extension (up to three characters).

   If you want to save the file to a different disk or directory, type the path to that disk or directory before typing the file name.

3. Press Enter.

   WordPerfect saves the file to the specified disk or directory using the name you entered.

 Saving an Existing File After Editing

1. Press F10 (Save), or select **Save** from the **File** menu.

   WordPerfect displays the `Document to be saved` prompt, followed by the name and path of the file, asking if you want to save it under its original name.

2. Press Enter to save the file under its original name, or type a new name for the file and then press Enter.

   If you press Enter, WordPerfect asks if you want to replace the original file with this file. If you type a new name and press Enter, WordPerfect will save the file, and you can skip the last two steps.

3. Press Y to replace the original file with the document on the Edit screen or N to enter a different name.

   If you press Y, the on-screen version is saved to disk and the disk version is erased. If you press N, WordPerfect prompts you to enter a new name for the file, still suggesting the original name. However, as soon as you type, it will disappear.

4. If you chose to save the file under a different name, enter a new name for the file.

   WordPerfect saves the file to disk.

Tip: WordPerfect's Long Document Names feature lets you create a second name for each file, containing up to 68 characters. You can see these names in the List Files menu when it is set to Long Display. Refer to *Long Document Names* for more information.

Save to Clipboard (see *Clipboard*)

Screen (Ctrl-F3)

Function: Lets you split the screen into two windows, rewrite the screen, and draw lines.

Keystrokes:

Keyboard	*Mouse*
Ctrl-F3 (Screen)	Edit, Window
Select option	OR
Enter changes	Tools, Line Draw
Enter	

Example:

```
1 Window; 2 Line Draw; 3 Rewrite: 3
```

The Screen feature provides the following three tools:

Window lets you divide the screen into two windows and edit a different document in each one. You can create or retrieve a different document in each one and switch back and forth between them, viewing them simultaneously. This is especially useful for cutting and pasting blocks between documents. (Refer to *Windows* and *Switch*.)

Line Draw gives you the ability to draw basic lines on screen. You can also use this feature to create lines, borders, and boxes. (Refer to *Line Draw*.)

Rewrite updates your Edit screen to show the effects of any formatting changes you have made. In versions after 3/3/90, this option lets you rewrite the List Files screen. (Refer to *Rewrite*.)

Screen Capture Program (see *Graphics, Screen Capture*)

Screen Down and Screen Up Keys (see *Cursor Movement*)

Search

Function: Searches forward or backward for a specified word, code, or phrase within a document.

Keystrokes: *Keyboard*   *Mouse*
F2 (→Search) or   Search
Shift-F2 (←Search)   Forward or Backward
search string   *search string*
F2 (→Search), Shift-F2   Double-click left mouse button
(←Search), or Esc

The Search feature moves the cursor to the first occurrence of the specified search string that you type. This string can contain words or codes, or both words and codes. Unless you specify otherwise, WordPerfect searches only the main text of a document to find the search string. If you want WordPerfect to search inside footnotes, endnotes, graphics box captions, headers, footers, and text boxes, press Home before selecting the Search feature or select Extended from the Search menu.

 Performing a Search

1. Move the cursor where you want to begin the search.

    You will be able to search forward or backward from this position.

2. If you want to perform an extended search, press Home or select Extended from the Search menu before selecting the Search feature.

3. Press F2 (→Search) for a forward search or Shift-F2 (←Search) for a backward search, or select **Forward** or **Backward** from the Search menu.

WordPerfect prompts you with an arrow and `Srch` prompt to enter a search string. If the arrow points right, WordPerfect will search forward. If the arrow points left, WordPerfect will search backward.

4. Press Up Arrow or Down Arrow if you want to change the direction of the search.

5. Type the text and/or enter the codes you want to search for.

If you're entering formatting codes, do not type the codes. You must enter the codes using their corresponding function keys. For example, you would press F6 for bold, or Shift-F8 (Format), **Line (1)**, and **7** (**Margins**) to change the left and right margin settings. You cannot use the pull-down menus.

6. Press F2 (→Search), Shift-F2 (←Search), or Esc, or double-click the left mouse button.

WordPerfect starts searching and stops on the first occurrence of the search string. If it is not found, a `Not Found` prompt appears, and the cursor remains in the same position. You can repeat the search to see if any more occurrences can be found by changing the search direction. If the cursor stops inside a header, footer, endnote, footnote, etc., press Home and the Search key to repeat the search.

7. Press F2 (→Search) twice or select **Next** or **Previous** from the Search menu.

WordPerfect continues searching for the same search string, unless you type a new one. It always retains the last search string used in the current edit session.

Tip: You can use the Search feature with the Block feature to quickly highlight a block of text. Press Alt-F4 (Block) or select **Block** from the **Edit** menu and then perform a search to stretch the highlight to the search string. All text between the cursor location and the search string is highlighted.

Search, List Files (see *Find* and *Name Search*)

Search and Replace (see *Replace*)

Secondary File (see *Merge*)

Select (see *Sort and Select*)

Select Printer (see *Printer, Select*)

Set Tabs (see *Tab, Set*)

Setup (see also *Display Setup*; *Environment Setup*; *Initial Settings*; *Keyboard Layout, Select*; *Location of Files*; and *Mouse Setup*)

Function: Lets you change the default settings to customize WordPerfect for your own use.

Keystrokes:

Keyboard	*Mouse*
Shift-F1 (Setup)	File
Select option	Setup
Enter change	Select option
F7 (Exit)	Enter change
	Right mouse button

Example:

```
Setup
        1 - Mouse
        2 - Display
        3 - Environment
        4 - Initial Settings
        5 - Keyboard Layout          EQUATION.WPK
        6 - Location of Files




     Selection: 0
```

The Setup menu lets you change many of WordPerfect's default settings. When you display the main Setup menu, a list of six options appears. Each leads to a more detailed Setup menu. The main Setup menu's options are:

Mouse: This option displays the Setup: Mouse menu. You can use it to install your mouse, configure it for left-handed use, change the speed of the mouse cursor, change the setting for the double-click interval or submenu display time, and have the mouse pointer move to the menu bar or a menu automatically whenever you display one. Refer to *Mouse Setup.*

Display: This option leads to the Setup: Display menu, where you can change screen colors, menu display options, Edit screen display options, View Document options, and more. Refer to *Display Setup.*

Environment: This option lets you change defaults that control the working environment. These include backup options, beep options, cursor speed, hyphenation, and units of measure. Refer to *Environment Setup.*

Initial Settings: This option lets you change initial settings for many of WordPerfect's features. You can change the date format, default formatting codes, merge-field and record delimiters, equation options, print options, and more. Formatting changes, such as Initial Codes that you enter here, affect all new documents. Refer to *Initial Settings.*

Keyboard Layout: This option lets you set up and select a customized keyboard layout. Refer to *Keyboard Layout, Select.*

Location of Files: If you decide to use separate directories for related files, such as backup files, document files, or style files, use this option to tell WordPerfect where those files are located. Refer to *Location of Files.*

 ### Changing the Setup Options

1. Press Shift-F1 (Setup) or select Setup from the **File** menu.

   The main Setup menu appears.

2. Select one of the options listed.

   This displays a detailed Setup menu for the selected option.

3. Select an option and enter your change.

4. Press F7 (Exit) or click the right mouse button.

   WordPerfect returns you to the Edit screen and saves any changes you made in the WP{WP}.SET file.

Shadow (see *Appearance Attributes*)

Sheet Feeders

Function: Lets you install a sheet feeder to feed paper to your printer.

Keystrokes:	*Keyboard*	*Mouse*
	Shift-F7 (Print)	**File**
	S (Select Printer)	**Print**
	Highlight printer	**Select Printer**
	3 (Edit)	Click left mouse button on printer
	3 (Sheet Feeder)	**Edit**
	Highlight sheet feeder	**Sheet Feeder**
	1 (Select)	Double-click left mouse button on
	F7 (Exit)	sheet feeder
		Right mouse button

Example:

```
Select Printer: Sheet Feeder

BDT LaserFeeder 890 (SF)
BDT MF 830 6 Bin (SF)
BDT MF 850 3 Bin (SF)
Build Your Own (SF)
HP LaserJet 2000 (SF)
HP LaserJet 500+ (SF)
HP LaserJet IID (SF)
HP LaserJet IIP (SF)
Ziyad PaperJet 400 (SF)



1 Select; 2 None; 3 Help; N Name search: 1
```

A sheet feeder has one or more paper bins that feed standard paper, envelopes, letterhead, and other types of paper to your printer. In order for WordPerfect to use your sheet feeder, you must use the Select Printer: Edit menu to install it by selecting the type of sheet feeder you're using from a list. This copies the sheet-feeder information into the printer's .PRS file. For individual documents, you must specify the bin number through the Paper Size/Type option on the Format: Document menu. For example, if you want to print addresses on envelopes, and your envelopes are in bin number 2, you must select a paper size and type, or create one, that uses that bin number. Refer to *Paper Size and Type*.

 Note: If you have a laser printer and the printer has only one paper tray, it usually is not considered a sheet feeder. When you select a paper size/type for such a printer, set the Feed option to Continuous Feed.

 ### Selecting a Sheet Feeder

1. Press Shift-F7 (Print) or select **Print** from the **File** menu.

   The main Print menu appears.

2. Choose **S** (Select Printer).

   The Print: Select Printer menu appears, presenting a list of installed printers.

3. Highlight the printer for which you want to select a sheet feeder.

4. Select **3** (Edit).

The Select Printer: Edit menu appears.

5. Select **3** (Sheet Feeder).

A list of sheet feeders appears, showing you the available sheet feeders for the selected printer.

6. Highlight the sheet feeder you intend to use and choose **1** (Select).

A Help screen appears, providing additional information about the sheet feeder and reminding you to select a bin number before printing. You can also choose the Build Your Own option, if your sheet feeder is not listed.

7. Press F7 (Exit), or click the right mouse button until you return to the Edit screen.

After installing the sheet feeder, be sure to change your Paper Size/Type definitions to include the bin number for each type of form, such as envelopes, letterhead, and labels. To do this, use the Edit option on the Format: Paper Size/Type menu for each form, changing the Location from Manual or Continuous to a Bin Number.

Shell (see also *Clipboard* and *Go to Shell*)

Function: A menu-driven user interface that lets you start all your software from a menu, and provides options to temporarily exit to DOS, transfer data between WordPerfect Corporation programs, and use several utilities supplied with the WordPerfect Office or Library.

Keystrokes: *Keyboard*
Activate drive and directory that contains WordPerfect Office or Library
shell

Example:

```
┌──────────────────────────────────────────────────────────────┐
│ WordPerfect Office              Thursday, November 8, 1990, 1:54pm │
│                                                                │
│   A - Appointment Calendar        D - DataPerfect              │
│   C - Calculator                  P - PlanPerfect              │
│   E - Edit Macros                 W - WordPerfect              │
│   F - File Manager                                             │
│   G - Go to Dos For One Command                                │
│   M - Mail                                                     │
│   N - NoteBook                                                 │
│   S - Scheduler                                                │
│   T - Program Editor                                           │
│                                                                │
│ D:\WP51\LIBRARY                                                │
│ 1 Go to DOS; 2 Clipboard; 3 Other Dir; 4 Setup; 5 Mem Map; 6 Log;    (F7 = Exit) │
└──────────────────────────────────────────────────────────────┘
```

WordPerfect's Shell is a menu-driven user interface that lets you run all your software from a single menu, including programs that are not supplied by WordPerfect Corporation, such as Lotus and dBASE. You can use the Shell to run WordPerfect; to temporarily exit to DOS; to use one of the Office's utility programs, such as the Calculator or MathPlan; to switch between two WordPerfect Corporation programs without exiting either one; and to move text and graphics from one compatible program to another, using the Clipboard.

Note: WordPerfect Office is not included with WordPerfect; the two programs are sold separately. However, the Shell part of the program is included with DrawPerfect. You can also purchase other compatible programs from WordPerfect Corporation, such as DrawPerfect and PlanPerfect.

 Starting Shell

1. Activate the drive where your WordPerfect Shell program files are located.

   For example, if your WordPerfect Shell files are on drive D, type d: at the DOS prompt and press Enter.

2. Change to the directory that contains the WordPerfect Shell program files.

   For example, if the files are in D:\SHELL, type cd\shell at the D:> prompt.

| 3. | Type shell and press Enter. | The WordPerfect Shell menu appears. |
| 4. | To start any of the programs in your list, type the letter that appears next to it. | Refer to *Clipboard* and *Go to Shell* for more information. |

Short Form (see *Table of Authorities*)

Size Attributes

Function: Lets you modify the size of the font currently in use. This feature is printer-dependent.

Keystrokes:

Keyboard	*Mouse*
Ctrl-F8 (Font)	Font
1 (Size)	Superscript, Subscript, Fine, Small,
1 (Superscript), **2**	Large, Vry Large, Ext Large
(Subscript), **3** (Fine),	
4 (Small), **5** (Large),	
6 (Vry Large), **7** (Ext	
Large)	

Codes: [SUPRSCPT] [suprscpt]
[SUBSCPT] [subscpt]
[FINE] [fine]
[SMALL] [small]
[LARGE] [large]
[VRY LARGE] [vry large]
[EXT LARGE] [ext large]

Whenever you type a document, WordPerfect formats it using the initial font for the printer, as specified on the Select Printer: Edit menu. Document Initial Font and Base Font change the actual font in use, while the size and appearance attributes provide variations of the initial or base font. For example, size attributes—such as large, small, and extra large—and appearance attributes—such as bold, italics, and underline—change these features for the current font.

The size attributes work like bold and underline in that you can turn them on and then type the text to be affected, or block an existing section of text and then select the feature. WordPerfect inserts two codes around the text: one that turns the attribute on and one that turns it off.

Note: The attributes are printer dependent, so your printer may not be able to change the font for each size attribute. You can check them or change them by using the Automatic Font Change option in the PTR program. Refer to *Automatic Font Change*s.

Selecting a Size Attribute Before Typing Text

1. Move the cursor where you want to type text with a different size attribute.

2. Press Ctrl-F8 (Font) and select **1** (**Size**), or display the **Font** menu.

   The Font menu appears. The size options include superscript, subscript, fine, small, large, very large, and extra large.

3. Select one of the size options.

   WordPerfect inserts a pair of hidden codes that turns the attribute on and off. The cursor is positioned between these codes, so all text typed between the codes will be formatted with the specified attribute.

4. Type the text as you normally would.

   The text may appear in another color or bolder on screen, but on most monitors, you won't be able to see the effect of the size attribute. Printing the text is the best way to see how it will look with the new attribute.

5. Press Right Arrow to move past the Attribute Off code.

   Text you type after the code will be normal.

Formatting an Existing Block of Text with a Size Attribute

1. Move the cursor to the beginning or end of the block you want to affect.

2. Press Alt-F4 (Block) or select **Block** from the **Edit** menu.

   This anchors the cursor, letting you stretch the highlight over the block.

3. Move the cursor to stretch the highlight over the text you want to change.

   You can use the cursor keys or the Search feature, or type the character or punctuation mark you want to stretch to.

4. Press Ctrl-F8 (Font) and select **1** (**Size**), or display the **Font** menu.

   The Font menu appears.

5. Select one of the size options.

   The highlighted text is now formatted with the size attribute. It may appear differently on screen, but you must print it to see the real effect.

Tip: To see how size attributes will print for a particular base font, retrieve the PRINTER.TST file, change the base font at the top of the document, and then print it. You can get a general idea of how the size attribute will appear in print by pressing Shift-F7 (Print) and selecting **6** (**View Document**).

Removing an Attribute

1. Press Alt-F3 or F11 (Reveal Codes), or select **Reveal Codes** from the **Edit** menu to display the Reveal Codes screen.

   Formatting codes, including the attribute codes, appear in the lower half of the screen, along with the text they affect.

2. Move the cursor to highlight the code for the attribute you want to remove, such as [FINE] or [LARGE].

3. Press Del.

   The highlighted code and the other member of its pair (the On or Off code) are deleted. The text will now be printed using the font or attribute that was in use before the size change.

Small Caps (see *Appearance Attributes*)

Small Print (see *Size Attributes*)

Soft Hyphen (see *Hyphenation*)

Soft Page (see *New Page*)

Soft Return (see *Return, Soft and Hard*)

Sort and Select

Function: Lets you restrict a list to specific items and/or sort those items alphabetically or numerically in ascending or descending order.

Keystrokes:

Keyboard	*Mouse*
Ctrl-F9 (Merge/Sort)	**Tools**
2 (Sort)	**Sort**
input filename, Enter (or just Enter, if data is on screen)	*input filename*, Enter (or just Enter, if data is on screen)
output filename, Enter (or just Enter, if you want output to go to Edit screen)	*output filename*, Enter (or just Enter, if you want output to go to Edit screen)
Enter sort and select criteria	Enter sort and select criteria
1 (Perform Action)	**Perform Action**

Example:

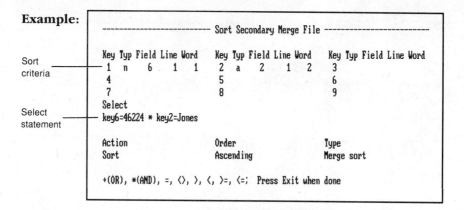

Sort criteria

Select statement

```
------------------------------ Sort Secondary Merge File ------------------------------

Key Typ Field Line Word   Key Typ Field Line Word   Key Typ Field Line Word
  1   n    6    1    1       2   a    2    1    2       3
  4                          5                          6
  7                          8                          9
Select
key6=46224 * key2=Jones


Action                    Order                     Type
Sort                      Ascending                 Merge sort

+(OR), *(AND), =, <>, >, <, >=, <=; Press Exit when done
```

To use WordPerfect's Sort and Select feature, perform the following steps:

1. Define an input file (the file you want to sort), and then define an output file (a file that will hold the results of the sort). If the file is already on the Edit screen and you want the results of the sort on the Edit screen, skip this step by pressing Enter for both. If you're sorting a block of text on the Edit screen, you can also skip this step. WordPerfect performs the sort and select operation and then replaces the highlighted block or the file on the Edit screen with the resulting block or document.

2. Select a type of sort. You can sort the records in a secondary merge document, sort individual lines in a list of entries, or sort paragraphs where one or more items exceed one line in length.

3. Define the sort criteria (called *keys*). Sort criteria is information that WordPerfect uses as the sort order. For example, you can sort a list of names alphabetically by last name, or sort a list of inventory items numerically by price, cost, or item number.

4. If you want to select only certain records, enter a select statement. WordPerfect uses the select statement to filter out some of the items from the list. For example, you can have WordPerfect select a group of records for people who live in a certain state or city.

When you're finished with these steps, the rest is easy. Tell WordPerfect to perform the action. WordPerfect then sends the altered list to the output file or to the Edit screen.

Defining Input and Output Files

1. Save the file before sorting or selecting.	This protects you in case the sort or select operation doesn't work as planned.
2. If you are sorting or selecting a block of text, highlight the block.	WordPerfect will take you directly to the Sort by Line menu, as soon as you select the Sort option in step 3.
3. Press Ctrl-F9 (Merge/Sort) and select **2** (**S**ort), or select **S**ort from the **T**ools menu.	If you highlighted a block, the Sort by Line menu appears; skip to step 6. If you are sorting or selecting an entire document, WordPerfect prompts you to enter the name of the file to be sorted or limited with select.
4. Press Enter to use the document on screen, or enter the path name and file name of the file you want to sort or select.	WordPerfect prompts you to enter a name for the output file that will contain the results of the sort or select action.
5. Press Enter to send the results of the action to the Edit screen, or enter a path name and file name for the file in which you want the results stored.	The Sort menu appears. Unless you've performed a previous sort of another type in the current edit session, you'll see the Sort Key Line screen.
6. Select **7** (**T**ype) if you need to change the type of sort.	WordPerfect prompts you to select a type of sort: Merge, Line, or Paragraph.
7. Select **1** (**M**erge), **2** (**L**ine), or **3** (**P**aragraph).	The Sort menu appears for the type you've selected.

After defining your input and output files, define your sort order using the Keys option. This option lets you set up nine "keys" to tell WordPerfect how to sort the entries. For each key, you select the type of sort (numeric or alphanumeric), the field, word, and (for paragraph and merge sorts) the line number you want to sort. For example, to sort a secondary merge file that contains the following entries by ZIP code first (the sixth field) and then by last name (word 2 in the second field):

```
Mr.{END FIELD}
Barry Walnum{END FIELD}
6796 East Center Street{END FIELD}
Chicago{END FIELD}
Illinois{END FIELD}
60621{END FIELD}
(312) 445-7689{END FIELD}
10.5%{END FIELD}
{END RECORD}
```
===
```
Ms.{END FIELD}
Mary Howard{END FIELD}
5575 East Market Street{END FIELD}
Indianapolis{END FIELD}
IN{END FIELD}
46224{END FIELD}
(317) 320-2981{END FIELD}
11.5%{END FIELD}
{END RECORD}
```
===

you would enter the following search criteria:

Key	Typ	Field	Line	Word
1	n	6	1	1
2	a	2	1	2

As a result, the records would first be sorted numerically by the entry in field 6 (the ZIP code) and then alphanumerically by the second word in field 2 (the last name). However, if one of the names included more than two words, such as Barry J. Walnum, you would have to enter −1 as the word, so WordPerfect would count from right to left. Since none of the fields contain more than one line, the Line option is not changed.

 Entering Sort Criteria

1. Select **3 (Keys).**

   The cursor moves up to the sort criteria for Key 1.

2. Type **a** or press Enter to sort alphanumerically (the default), or enter **n** to sort numerically.

   a or n appears under Type for Key 1, and the cursor moves to Field or to Line if you are using Paragraph Sort.

3. Enter the number of the field you want to use as the sort key under the `Field` heading.

   In a Line or Paragraph Sort, fields are defined by tab stops, with the first field at the left margin. In a merge sort, each field ends with an {END FIELD} code. When you press Enter, the cursor moves under the next heading.

4. If you are using a Merge or Paragraph Sort, enter the line number containing the data you want to use as the key.

   For example, if you are sorting by last name and the last name is in line 3 for each entry, enter 3.

5. Enter the number of the word containing the data you want to use as the key.

   To count from right to left, use a negative number. When you press Enter, the cursor moves to the next key. You can then enter search criteria for another search level.

6. Repeat steps 2-5 for each key you want to use in the sort.

7. Press F7 (Exit) or click the right mouse button.

If you have a long list of records or entries and you want to narrow the search to a specific set of entries, you can enter a select statement, telling WordPerfect which entries to select from the entire list. For example, if you use Key 2 to sort records according to last name, you can enter a sort statement in the form `key2=Jones` to select records only for people whose last name is Jones. WordPerfect will erase all other data from the resulting list, so make sure you save the list first. Table S.1 shows a list of select statements and what those statements will select.

Table S.1 *Select statements.*

Sample Statement	Selects
`key1=46224`	Records that have a ZIP code of 46224.
`key1=46224 + key2=Jones`	Records that have a ZIP code of 46224 *or* a last Name of Jones.
`key1=46224 * key2=Jones`	Records that have a ZIP code of 46224 *and* a last name of Jones.

continued

Table S.1 *(continued)*

Sample Statement	Selects
key2<>Jones	Records that do *not* have a last name of Jones.
key1>46224	Records that have a ZIP code *greater* than 46224.
key2<Jones	Records that have a last name preceding Jones in alphabetical order, such as Allen, Brown, and Jackson.
key2<=Jones	Records that have a last name of Jones or a last name preceding Jones in alphabetical order.
key1>=46224	Records that have a ZIP code greater than or equal to 46224.

 Entering a Select Statement

1. Choose **4** (Select) from the bottom of the Select menu.

   The cursor moves to the `Select Criteria` area.

2. Type a select statement.

   The key must already be defined, or you'll see an `Error` message when you try to exit.

3. Press **F7** (Exit) or click the right mouse button.

   The cursor moves down to the bottom of the screen so you can select your next option.

4. If you want to select only, without sorting, use the Action option to change the action to Select only.

Now that you have entered your sort and select criteria, you can have WordPerfect perform the sort.

 Performing Sort and Select

1. Select **1** (Perform Action).

   WordPerfect sorts and/or selects the records from the input file, according to your specifications, and writes the results to the output file or to the Edit screen.

Spacing (see *Line Spacing*)

Special Characters (see *Character Sets, WordPerfect's*)

Spell Checking

Function: Checks a word, page, block, or entire document for misspelled words, double words, words that include numbers, and capitalization errors.

Keystrokes:

Keyboard	*Mouse*
Ctrl-F2 (Spell)	**Tools**
1 (Word), **2** (Page), or	**Spell**
3 (Document)	**Word**, **Page**, or **Document**

Example:

WordPerfect's Spell Checker reveals mispelled words, typoes, double words words, cApitaliziation errors, and awkward charact3er-number combinations

Doc 1 Pg 1 Ln 1" Pos 4.6"

{ ▲ ▲ ▲ ▲ ▲ ▲ ▲ ▲ ▲ ▲ ▲ } ▲ ▲

A. misspelled   B. misspelt

Not Found: 1 Skip Once; 2 Skip; 3 Add; 4 Edit; 5 Look Up; 6 Ignore Numbers: 0

Word not found in Speller dictionary

Possible alternatives

Options

To spell check a word, page, or entire document, use the corresponding options on the main Speller menu, unless you block the text first, in which case spell checking will begin as soon as you select Spell. When you select one of these options and WordPerfect begins spell-checking your document, it will stop on the first word it cannot find in its dictionary. At the bottom of the screen a message appears, telling you why the Speller has paused on this word and providing a list of options for correcting the problem or ignoring it. For example, if WordPerfect comes across a word that cannot be found in the Speller dictionary, it displays the following message:

```
Not Found: 1 Skip Once; 2 Skip; 3 Add; 4 Edit; 5 Look Up;
6 Ignore Numbers: 0
```

If the correct spelling appears, you can select the letter next to it to insert the word in place of the incorrect version that appears in the text. However, if the word is not misspelled (for example, if it's a proper noun), you can choose to skip the word or add it to the Speller's Supplemental dictionary. The difference between the two skip options is that the first, Skip Once, only skips the word here; while the second, Skip, skips the word here and anywhere else in the document, page, or block.

If you choose **3** (Add), WordPerfect adds the word as it appears in your document to a supplementary dictionary. Use this for proper nouns, such as names. By default, WordPerfect uses a dictionary named WP{WP}US.SUP as its supplementary dictionary. If you want to create your own dictionary, Press Ctrl-F2 (Spell) or select Spell from the Tools menu. Select **4** (New Sup. Dictionary) and type the complete path name and file name of the dictionary you want to create. WordPerfect uses this dictionary as the supplementary dictionary until you exit WordPerfect or select a different supplementary dictionary.

 ## Performing a Spell Check

1. Retrieve the document you want to spell check.

2. If you want to check spelling in a block of text, highlight the block.

3. Press Ctrl-F2 (Spell), or select Spell from the **T**ools menu.

    If you blocked a section, WordPerfect begins spell checking, and you can skip to step 6. Otherwise, the Speller menu appears.

4. If you want to create or use a supplementary dictionary, select **4** (New Sup. Dictionary) and enter the path name and file name of the dictionary you want to create or use.

    If you don't choose a different supplementary dictionary, WordPerfect uses WP{WP}US.SUP by default.

5. Select **1** (Word), **2** (Page), or **3** (Document).

The Speller stops on the first unknown or otherwise problematic word and displays a message and menu at the bottom of the screen. It also displays possible corrections that are found in the dictionary. You can press the letter next to the correct spelling to substitute it in the document.

6. Select one of the options to correct the word, add it to the dictionary, edit it, or skip it. If you edit it, use the regular edit keys and then press F7 to return to the Speller.

The Speller continues until it finds another unknown word or reaches the end of the block or document.

7. Repeat step 6 until you reach the end of the document.

When a prompt appears displaying the word count and `Press Any Key to Continue`, the Speller has finished checking your text.

8. Press F7 (Exit) or click the right mouse button.

This returns you to the Edit screen if you spell checked a document or block. If you selected Word or Page, the main Speller menu appears again. You can then choose one of the other options, or press Enter to return to the Edit screen.

9. Press F10 (Save) or select **Save** from the **File** menu, and save the file in the usual way.

After correcting errors with the spell checker, you must save the document in order to retain the changes.

In addition to the options you can use to spell check your document, the Speller offers options to count the number of words in your document without spell checking and to look up the spelling of words you are unsure of. The Look Up option asks for a word pattern and lets you use wild-card characters in place of missing characters; type ? in place of a single character or * in place of a group of characters. For example, you can look up all words that begin with *thes* by typing `thes*`. To access either the Look Up or Word Count option, press Ctrl-F2 (Spell) or select **Spell** from the **Tools** menu.

Speller Utility

Function: Lets you edit the dictionary, compress dictionaries to optimize disk space, combine dictionaries, delete words from the dictionary, and convert dictionaries from WordPerfect 4.2 and 5.0 to WordPerfect 5.1.

Keystrokes: Exit WordPerfect
Activate drive and directory for SPELL.EXE
spell
Select option

Example:

```
┌─────────────────────────────────────────────────────────────────────┐
│ Spell -- WordPerfect Speller Utility          D:\WP51\DICTION\WP{WP}US.LEX │
│                                                                       │
│ 0 - Exit                                                              │
│ 1 - Change/Create Dictionary                                         │
│ 2 - Add Words to Dictionary                                          │
│ 3 - Delete Words from Dictionary                                     │
│ 4 - Optimize Dictionary                                              │
│ 5 - Display Common Word List                                         │
│ 6 - Check Location of a Word                                         │
│ 7 - Look Up                                                          │
│ 8 - Phonetic Look Up                                                 │
│ 9 - Convert 4.2 Dictionary to 5.1                                   │
│ A - Combine Other 5.0 or 5.1 Dictionary                             │
│ B - Compress/Expand Supplemental Dictionary                         │
│ C - Extract Added Words from Wordlist-based Dictionary              │
│                                                                       │
│ Selection:                                                            │
│                                                                       │
└─────────────────────────────────────────────────────────────────────┘
```

You can edit a dictionary in either of two ways. If you have added words to a supplemental dictionary, you can retrieve and edit it just as you would edit any other WordPerfect document, adding, deleting, or editing the words. However, if you want to edit WordPerfect's Speller dictionary or if you compressed one of your personal, supplementary dictionaries, you must use the Speller Utility to make changes such as adding or deleting words. You must also use the Speller Utility if you want to convert dictionaries you created in earlier versions of WordPerfect to the WordPerfect 5.1 format.

Note: Before you can use the Speller Utility, you must have installed it; you cannot directly copy the SPELL.EXE file from the installation disk to your WP51 directory. If you did not install this utility, start the installation program now, and perform that part of the installation.

Starting the Speller Utility

1. Exit WordPerfect.

2. Change to the drive and directory
   that contains the SPELL.EXE
   program.

3. Type `spell` at the DOS prompt   The WordPerfect Speller Utility
   and press Enter.   main menu appears on screen.

4. Select an option from the menu
   and perform the desired task.

5. Select **0** (**Exit**) when you're done.

Split Screen (see *Windows*)

Spreadsheet

Function: Lets you import or link a compatible spreadsheet file to a
WordPerfect document.

Keystrokes: *Keyboard*   *Mouse*

Keyboard	*Mouse*
Ctrl-F5 (Text In/Out)	File
5 (Spreadsheet)	Text **In**
1 (Import) or **2** (Create Link)	Spreadsheet
	Import or Create Link
1 (Filename)	Filename
d:\path\filename.ext, Enter	*d:\path\filename.ext*, Enter
2 (Range)	Range
range, Enter	*range*, Enter
3 (Type)	Type
1 (Table) or **2** (Text)	Table or Text
4 (Perform Import) or (Perform Link)	Perform Import or Perform Link

Codes: [Link]
[Link End]

Example:

```
Link:    F:\LOTUS\GRADES.WK1
```

Name¶	Quiz 1¶	Quiz 2¶	Quiz 3¶	Exam¶	Total¶
Appleton, J.¶	98%¶	99%¶	79%¶	97%¶	94.00¶
Binder, P.¶	67%¶	64%¶	89%¶	91%¶	80.40¶
Carmen, C.¶	85%¶	73%¶	90%¶	90%¶	85.60¶
Daltry, A.¶	79%¶	98%¶	86%¶	87%¶	87.40¶
Ferrel, L¶	83%¶	82%¶	84%¶	81%¶	82.20¶

```
Link End
```

```
                              Doc 1 Pg 1 Ln 1" Pos 1"
```

You can use WordPerfect's Spreadsheet feature to import a compatible spreadsheet or link a spreadsheet to a document. The difference between importing and linking is that importing treats the spreadsheet as a fixed element in WordPerfect; if you change the spreadsheet using your spreadsheet program, the changes do not appear on the spreadsheet you imported into WordPerfect. Linking, on the other hand, treats the spreadsheet as a dynamic element. If you modify the spreadsheet with your spreadsheet program, the changes are then reflected in your WordPerfect document when you update the link.

Before you import a spreadsheet file, you should be aware of some limitations. First, WordPerfect can import a limited number of columns: 20 text columns or 32 table columns. If you select a range of cells that exceeds those limits, WordPerfect will omit the additional cells. Second, if you choose to import a spreadsheet into an existing table, make sure your table has enough blank cells to hold the range of cells you want to import from the spreadsheet or WordPerfect will eliminate the ones that can't fit, and overwrite existing text in the table. Finally, if you are importing the spreadsheet into a graphics box, make sure the spreadsheet does not exceed one page; if it does, you'll get an error message.

Even if you select a range of cells within those limitations, there's no guarantee that the columns will fit across the page within the left and right margins. If they don't, try editing the spreadsheet itself, using your spreadsheet program. If the range is still too wide, try changing to a smaller font size or reducing the left and right margins before importing the spreadsheet. If your printer can print in landscape orientation, you may be able to rotate the fonts to print the spreadsheet sideways, parallel to the long edge of the page. Change these features as much as necessary before importing the spreadsheet; once the spreadsheet is in the document, changing it becomes more difficult.

> **Note:** Compatible spreadsheet files include those created in PlanPerfect (versions 3.0-5.0), Lotus 1-2-3 (versions 1.0-2.2 and version 3.0 in the .WK1 format), and Microsoft Excel (versions 2.x). WordPerfect 5.1's version dated 1/19/90 added support for Borland's Quattro and Quattro Pro spreadsheets. The 3/30/90 version added full support of Lotus version 3.0 (without translating to the WK1 format). If you try to import or link a file that's in an incompatible format, WordPerfect will display an error message telling you it is an incompatible file format.

Importing or Linking a Spreadsheet

1. Move the cursor where you want to import the spreadsheet.

   You can position the cursor in an existing table. WordPerfect will insert data from the spreadsheet into corresponding cells in the table, overwriting any existing data.

2. Press Ctrl-F5 (Text In/Out) or select Text **In** from the **File** menu.

   If you use the pull-down menu, WordPerfect prompts you to select the type of data you wish to import. If you use the Text In/Out key, a menu with five options appears.

3. Select **5** (**S**preadsheet) or Spreadsheet.

   A menu appears.

4. Select **1** (Import) or **2** (Create Link).

   The Spreadsheet: Import or Spreadsheet: Create Link menu appears.

5. Select **1** (Filename), and enter the path and file name of the spreadsheet you want to import.

   You can also use the Retrieve option on the List Files menu to select the file from a list. Refer to *List Files*.

6. Select **2** (**R**ange).

   WordPerfect prompts you to select the range of cells you want to import from the spreadsheet.

7. Enter the range of cells you want to import.

You can enter the range in one of the following formats: A1:F5, A1.F5, or A1..F5, or you can enter the name of the range (if the range is named in your spreadsheet). You can also press F5 to view a list of the ranges you may have defined when you created the spreadsheet, if there are any.

8. Select **3** (**Type**) and then **1** (**Table**) or **2** (**Text**).

The default is Table. Table imports the spreadsheet as a table, structuring the table with Cell and Row codes. You can then edit the spreadsheet as a table. Text treats the spreadsheet as text, using tabs to format the columns and placing each row on a separate line.

9. Select **4** (**Perform Import**) or (**Perform Link**).

If you are creating a link for a spreadsheet file that you haven't yet created with your spreadsheet program, you can press F7 (Exit) at this point. This inserts the Link codes, but does not import data. You can import the file later, after you create it.

If you choose to link a spreadsheet rather than import it, you must update your link whenever you want your WordPerfect document to include the most current version of the spreadsheet, as it appears in the spreadsheet program. To do this, you must access the Link Options menu, which offers the following options:

Update on Retrieve: If you want your links updated automatically when you retrieve the WordPerfect file, select this option and press Y for Yes. No is the default. If you change it to Yes, whenever you retrieve a file that has a spreadsheet link, data that has been changed in the spreadsheet file will replace the old data in the linked document, to update the WordPerfect document so it matches the spreadsheet file.

Show Link Codes: Whenever you create a link, two nonprinting codes appear on screen in a box that resembles a comment box, showing you where the link begins and where it ends, and showing the path and file name of the spreadsheet file being linked. By selecting this option and pressing N for No, you can keep the codes and boxes from being displayed. If you created the link in an existing WordPerfect table or column, these link comments will not be displayed, regardless of this setting.

Update all Links: To update a linked WordPerfect document to reflect the most current version of the spreadsheet file, select this option. When you do, data that has changed since you last imported or linked the original spreadsheet is replaced in the WordPerfect document with the updated information from the current version of the spreadsheet file.

 Setting the Link Options

1. Press Ctrl-F5 (Text In/Out) or select Text In from the File menu.

   If you used Ctrl-F5, the Text In/Out menu appears. If you used the pull-down menu, three Text In options appear.

2. Select **5** (Spreadsheet) or Spreadsheet.

   The Spreadsheet menu appears.

3. Select **4** (Link Options).

   The Link Options menu appears.

4. Select a link option and enter your setting.

5. Press F7 (Exit) or click the right mouse button.

   WordPerfect returns you to your document.

Start WordPerfect

Function: Starts WordPerfect.

Keystrokes: *Keyboard*
d: (where *d:* is the drive where your WordPerfect program files are stored)
Enter
cd\wp51 (where *wp51* is the directory that holds your WordPerfect 5.1 program files)
Enter
wp
Enter

You can start WordPerfect in either of two ways. If you have the WordPerfect Office installed and you want to run WordPerfect from the Shell menu, select the letter appearing next to the WordPerfect 5.1 option. If you don't have the Shell, you can start WordPerfect from the DOS prompt. Change to the drive and directory that holds your WordPerfect program files, such as WP51, and then enter the start-up command, `wp`.

When you start WordPerfect from the DOS prompt, you can use any of the start-up options listed in Table S.2 to change the way WordPerfect works. The start-up option consists of the start-up command, wp, plus a start-up switch. You can use more than one switch by separating the switches with forward slashes. For example, `wp/x/r` restores the default setup options and tells WordPerfect to use expanded memory.

Table S.2 *Start-up options.*

Start-up Option	Function
w p	Starts WordPerfect.
wp/cp=*code page number*	Tells WordPerfect which page code your BIOS uses to let you access the proper keyboard and ASCII character set for your system.
wp/d-*drive:\directory*	Establishes a path for the directory that holds your overflow files and temporary buffers.
wp *filename*	Automatically loads the specified file into WordPerfect.
wp/f2	Helps correct problems with extended text display (more than 25 lines and 80 columns) that the /ss switch cannot correct.
wp/m-*macroname*	Runs the specified macro at start-up.
wp/mono	Runs a computer that has a color adapter in monochrome mode, when the computer is set to emulate monochrome.

Table S.2 *Start-up options.*

Start-up Option	Function
wp/pf=path	(3/30/90 versions and later) Tells WordPerfect to redirect the temporary print queue files to this directory. Speeds up printing on networks and floppy disks.
wp/nb	Turns off the Original Backup feature if you have it set to On.
wp/nc	Turns off the Cursor Speed feature. This is useful if the Cursor Speed feature conflicts with other TSR (terminate and stay resident) programs, particularly those that prevent WordPerfect from starting.
wp/ne	Prevents access to expanded memory, if that memory is available.
wp/nf	Runs a "not fast" version of WordPerfect, when used with windowing programs. Helps prevent window from going blank, or text from printing over the window.
wp/nk	Turns off the enhanced keyboard. This is helpful if it conflicts with TSR programs or does not work on a compatible PC.
wp/ln	(3/30/90 versions and later) Tells WordPerfect to ask for your license number, so you can add or change it.
wp/no	Turns off the Keyboard Reset key (Ctrl-6), which normally can be used to return the keyboard to its original layout.

continued

Table S.2 *(continued)*

Start-up Option	Function
wp/ps=*path*	Tells WordPerfect to use the .SET (setup options) file on the specified path, useful on a network version.
wp/r	Tells WordPerfect to use expanded memory, if available, to speed up parts of the program. If used along with the /d switch, it will free up your disk drives if you're running WordPerfect from floppy disks, and you can remove the WordPerfect 2 diskette.
wp/ss=*rows,columns*	Lets you specify the screen size, if WordPerfect does not do it automatically.
wp/w=*workspace*	Limits the amount of conventional memory (cache) and/or expanded memory that WordPerfect uses. Minimum value is 53K. ∗ , ∗ lets WordPerfect use all conventional memory and all expanded memory.
wp/x	Restores the default values for all Setup options, if you've changed any.

Starting WordPerfect from a Hard Disk

1. At the DOS prompt, change to the drive where your WordPerfect program files are stored.

   For example, if your WordPerfect program files are on the D drive, type d: and press Enter.

2. Change to your WordPerfect 5.1 directory.

   For example, if your WordPerfect program files are in a directory called WP51, type cd\wp51 and press Enter.

3. Type one of the start-up commands listed above and press Enter.

To start WordPerfect without using an option, just type `wp` and press Enter. The WordPerfect Edit screen will appear.

Starting WordPerfect from a Floppy Disk

1. Turn on your computer and start DOS.

2. Insert the WordPerfect 1 diskette into drive A.

3. Insert a formatted disk into drive B. Use a blank disk or one you've used already to save Word-Perfect files.

The blank disk is needed to store the documents you create in WordPerfect.

4. At the DOS prompt, type `b:` and press Enter to activate drive B.

This will change the directory to drive B, so WordPerfect will automatically save and retrieve your files using the B drive.

5. At the `B>` prompt, type `a:` followed by one of the start-up options in Table S.2, or type `a:wp` to start WordPerfect without using an option. Press Enter.

DOS starts WordPerfect and prompts you to insert disk 2 into drive A.

6. Replace disk 1 in drive A with disk 2, and press Enter.

The WordPerfect Edit screen appears.

Status Line

Function: Displays important information regarding the document you're working on.

Example:

Name of current document — D:\WP51\FILES\GRADES   Doc 1 Pg 1 Ln 2.75" Pos 1" — Cursor position

The status line is in the lower-right corner of the WordPerfect Edit screen and displays information regarding the current position of your cursor. If you're working on two documents, the number next to `Doc` indicates which document screen you're working on, 1 or 2. The next two numbers indicate the page and line number where the cursor is located. The last number shows the position of the cursor relative to the left edge of the page. If you are using newspaper or parallel columns, the status line also shows the column number where the cursor is located. In tables, it displays the cell number. On the left side, WordPerfect displays the name of the document you're working on, if it has been saved or retrieved. You can choose to turn this display off, so the file name does not appear (refer to *Edit-Screen Options*).

The status line also displays important messages and warnings to keep you informed and to prevent you from making serious mistakes, such as overwriting a file or quitting WordPerfect without saving your changes.

Strikeout (see *Appearance Attributes*)

Style Library (see also *Location of Files* and *Styles*)

Function: Provides a default list of styles, which will always be available for use in any new document you create.

Keystrokes:
Keyboard	*Mouse*
Shift-F1 (Setup)	File
6 (Location of Files)	Setup
5 (Style Files/Library Filename)	Location of Files
	Style Files/Library Filename

Example:

```
Styles

    Name       Type      Description

    Bibliogrphy  Paired    Bibliography
    Doc Init     Paired    Initialize Document Style
    Document     Outline   Document Style
    Pleading     Open      Header for numbered pleading paper
    Right Par    Outline   Right-Aligned Paragraph Numbers
    Tech Init    Open      Initialize Technical Style
    Technical    Outline   Technical Document Style


  1 On; 2 Off; 3 Create; 4 Edit; 5 Delete; 6 Save; 7 Retrieve; 8 Update: 1
```

WordPerfect's Style feature lets you create styles to customize the formatting codes in your documents. Styles can include text and/or formatting codes and can be as complex as you like. Whenever you want to use a style, select it from a list of styles you created in the document. You can also create and use a file of frequently used styles that will automatically be available for use in new documents. This file is called a Style Library.

The Style Library (LIBRARY.STY) is a list of default styles, which you created and saved as a file. By using the Setup: Location of Files menu to name this file as your style library, you will always be able to use the styles. Whenever you access the main Style menu in a new document, they will appear automatically. They will also be available in a saved file as long as you did not save any other styles with the document. For more information about using styles, see *Styles*.

 ## Establishing a Style Library

1.	Press Shift-F1 (Setup) or select Setup from the **File** menu.	The main Setup menu appears.
2.	Select Location of Files (6).	The Setup: Location of Files menu appears.
3.	Select **5** (Style Files/Library Filename).	
4.	Type the path and directory name where your Style Library file is located and press Enter.	From now on, WordPerfect will automatically store any new files you created in this directory. The directory must already exist or you'll get an error message.
5.	Enter the name of the style file you want to use as the library.	The Style Library file must be contained in the directory specified in the previous step, or WordPerfect won't be able to locate your default styles when you display the main Styles menu.
6.	Press F7 (Exit) or click the right mouse button.	

To access a style in your style library, press Alt-F8 (Styles) or select **Styles** from the Layout menu. The styles will not be available if you retrieve a document that you already created and saved styles in.

Styles (see also *Style Library*)

Function: Lets you create and select styles to format documents.

Keystrokes:

Keyboard	*Mouse*
Alt-F8 (Style)	Layout
3 (Create)	Styles
Select option	Create
Enter change	Select option
F7 (Exit)	Enter change
Highlight style	Right mouse button
1 (On)	Click left mouse button on style
	On

Example:

```
Styles: Edit
      1 - Name           level-1 head
      2 - Type           Paired
      3 - Description     First-level head
      4 - Codes
      5 - Enter          Off


Selection: 0
```

The Styles feature lets you create styles (codes) for your text that can include text and/or WordPerfect formatting codes. These styles function as a set of your own custom formatting codes. For example, you can create a style for first-level headings that specifies a large font, bold type, baseline placement, and a hanging indent in case the heading wraps to a second line. Whenever you want to create a first-level heading, simply select the style you created from the Style menu. If you decide later that you want to change the type size of all first-level heads, all you have to do is change it inside the style you created, and WordPerfect will automatically change the type size for *all* first-level headings affected by that style.

 Creating a Style

1. Press Alt-F8 (Style) or select **Styles** from the **Layout** menu.

2. Select **3** (Create).   The Styles: Edit menu appears.

3. Select **1** (**Name**) and enter a name for your style.

You can type up to 12 characters, including spaces. If you don't type a number, WordPerfect will assign a number in sequential order.

4. Select **2** (**Type**) and select **1** (**Paired**), **2** (**Open**), or **3** (**Outline**).

Paired turns the style on and then off; anything between the On/Off codes conforms to the style. Open turns the style on; the style remains in effect until another code is inserted that changes the style. Outline lets you change a paired or open style to an outline style, so you can use it with WordPerfect's Outline feature. Refer to *Outline Style*.

5. Select **3** (**Description**) and enter a description to help you remember what this style does.

You can type up to 54 characters, including spaces.

6. Select **4** (**Codes**) and enter the formatting codes and any text you want to use for this style.

Choosing this option displays a screen similar to the Reveal Codes screen, except for the [Comment] code on this screen. You can enter formatting codes in the usual manner, but place them to the left of the [Comment] code. For example, press F6 for bold, or press Shift-F8 to access the Format menu and use any of its options.

7. Press F7 (**Exit**) to return to the Styles Edit menu.

8. Select **5** (**Enter**) and select **1** (**HRt**), **2** (**Off**), or **3** (**Off/On**).

This option has no effect for open styles and is unavailable when you change the style type to Open. For paired styles, it controls the function of the Enter key. HRt makes the Enter key function normally to insert a hard return. Off makes it turn a style off. Off/On makes it turn a style off then on.

9. Repeat steps 3-8 for all the styles you want to create.

10. Press Enter or click the right mouse button to return to the Styles menu.

The name and description of the style you just created appear in the list of available styles.

All the styles you created are saved to disk when you save the document they were created in. If you want to use these same styles for other documents without re-creating the styles each time, use the Save option on the File menu to save the styles in a separate style file.

Saving a Style File

1. Press Alt-F5 (Style) or select **Styles** from the Layout menu.

The Styles menu for the document you're working on appears.

2. Select 6 (**Save**) to save the styles whose names appear in the list to a separate file.

WordPerfect prompts you to enter a name for the style file. This file will contain only styles, not the text in the document.

3. Type a name for the style file, including a path to the directory where you keep your style files, and press Enter.

If you already specified a style directory using the Location of Files feature, you don't have to type a path, because WordPerfect will save it there automatically.

Selecting a Style for Use in a Document

1. Move the cursor where you want to start using the style. If the text has already been typed and you want to use a paired style, use the Block feature to highlight it.

Paired styles work just like bold and underline codes, surrounding selected text with On/Off codes.

2. Press Alt-F8 (Style) or select **Styles** from the Layout menu.

A Styles menu appears. If the styles differ from the ones you want to use, you can retrieve the Style file containing the ones you want or create new styles.

3. If the styles listed are not the styles you want to use, select **7** (**Retrieve**) and enter the path and file name of the style file you want to use.

4. Highlight the style you want to use and select **1** (**On**).

5. If you are using a paired style to format as you type, type everything you want to be affected by this style; then press Right Arrow to move the cursor past the Style Off code.

You can also select a style file from a list of files by pressing F5 (List) and Enter after selecting Retrieve. You may be asked to replace one or more styles if they have the same names as one already appearing in the list.

If you selected a paired code, a pair of codes is inserted at the cursor location to turn the style on and off. Anything you type between the two codes appears in the selected style. If you selected an open style, a single code is inserted to turn the style on.

Subdocuments (see *Master Document*)

Subject Search Text (see *Document Management/Summary*)

Subtraction (see *Math*)

Superscript and Subscript (see *Size Attributes*)

Supplementary Dictionary (see *Speller Utility*)

Suppress

Function: Lets you prevent page numbers, headers, and footers from being printed on a specific page without affecting the pages that follow.

Keystrokes:

Keyboard	*Mouse*
Shift-F8 (Format)	Layout
2 (Page)	Page
8 (Suppress)	Suppress
Select option(s)	Select option(s)
F7 (Exit)	Right mouse button

Code: [Suppress]

Example:

```
Format: Suppress (this page only)
    1 - Suppress All Page Numbering, Headers and Footers
    2 - Suppress Headers and Footers
    3 - Print Page Number at Bottom Center   No
    4 - Suppress Page Numbering              No
    5 - Suppress Header A                     No
    6 - Suppress Header B                     No
    7 - Suppress Footer A                     No
    8 - Suppress Footer B                     No

Selection: 0
```

The Suppress feature includes eight options for suppressing page numbers, headers, and footers, individually or in various combinations. For example, you can use the Suppress feature to keep a page number from printing on the first page of your document or to keep a page number, header, or footer from printing on a page where it might interfere with a table or with a graphic element. When you choose the Suppress option, WordPerfect displays the following list of items you can suppress:

Suppress All Page Numbering, Headers and Footers

Suppress Headers and Footers

Print Page Number at Bottom Center

Suppress Page Numbering

Suppress Header A

Suppress Header B

Suppress Footer A

Suppress Footer B

 ## Suppressing Page Numbering, Headers, and Footers

1. Move the cursor to the top of the page on which you want to use the Suppress option.

   The cursor must be at the top of the page, right after the [HPg] or [SPg] code, or the Suppress option will have no effect on this page.

2. Press Shift-F8 (Format) or display the Layout menu.

   A list of formatting options appears.

3. Select **Page** (2).

   The Format: Page menu appears.

4. Select **8** (**Suppress**).

   The Format: Suppress menu appears.

5. Select either of the first two options or select any of the last six options and type Y or N to set the options as desired.

   The last six options listed require you to type Y to suppress the option on or N to turn Suppression off.

6. Press F7 (Exit) or click the right mouse button.

   WordPerfect returns you to your document and inserts the [Suppress] code at the cursor location.

Switch (see also *Windows* and *Capitalization, Converting Text*)

Function: Moves the cursor from one document Edit screen to another, from one window to another, or lets you convert a blocked section of text to uppercase or lowercase.

Keystrokes: *Keyboard*   *Mouse*
                    Shift-F3 (Switch)   Edit
                                            Switch

WordPerfect lets you work in two different Edit screens: Doc 1 and Doc 2. By pressing Shift-F3 (Switch), or selecting Switch from the Edit menu, you can move from one Edit screen to another to work on two documents at once. You can then cut blocks of text from one document and paste them into another. The Doc message on the status line tells you which document you're working on.

Note: Make sure Block is not flashing in the lower left corner of your screen before you press Shift-F3. If it is, press Alt-F4 (Block) or F1 (Cancel). If you press Shift-F3 when a block of text is highlighted, WordPerfect assumes that you want to change the case for that block of text and provides a menu with two options: Uppercase and Lowercase.

   Switching Edit Screens

1. From the Doc 1 screen, press Shift-F3 (Switch), or select **Switch** from the Edit menu.

    A blank Edit screen appears with Doc 2 displayed in the lower-right corner.

2. Retrieve a document into the Doc 2 Edit screen.

    You can either press Shift-F10 (Retrieve) or F5 (List) to retrieve a document.

3. Press Shift-F3 (Switch) whenever you want to switch from one document to the other.

    Each time you switch, the number next to Doc changes to show which document you're working with.

4. To close the Doc 2 area, press F7 (Exit) and respond to the Save prompt.

    If you still have text in Doc 1, WordPerfect will ask if you want to exit Doc 2. If Doc 1 is clear, you'll be asked if you want to exit WordPerfect.

5. Answer the prompts to exit Doc 2 and/or to Exit WordPerfect.

T

Tab, Set

Function: Lets you change the types and positions of your tab stops.

Keystrokes:

Keyboard	*Mouse*
Shift-F8 (Format)	Layout
1 (Line)	Line
8 (Tab Set)	Tab Set
Enter changes	Enter changes
F7 (Exit) twice	Right mouse button twice

Code: [Tab Set]

Example:

```
                  Left   Center  Decimal    Right
.................L...C.........D........R.................
   ^     |    ^   |    ^   |    ^   |    ^   |    ^   |    ^
 -1"     0"      +1"     +2"     +3"     +4"     +5"     +6"
Delete EOL (clear tabs); Enter Number (set tab); Del (clear tab);
Type; Left; Center; Right; Decimal; .= Dot Leader; Press Exit when done.
```

By default, left tab stops are set every half inch, starting at position 0" (the left edge of the page). When you press the Tab key, WordPerfect inserts a left tab code at the cursor position and moves the cursor one half inch to the right. Since it is a left tab stop, text is inserted to the right, and the first character at the left is on the tab stop position. You can change these tab stops at any point in your document, using the Tab Set option on the Format: Line menu. This option displays a detailed tab ruler showing the location and type of each tab stop. The following options appear at the bottom of the screen:

Delete EOL (clear tabs): You can use the Delete EOL key, Ctrl-End, to clear all tab stop settings from the cursor position to the end of the tab ruler. To use it, move the cursor to the first tab stop you want to clear and press Ctrl-End. This tab stop setting and all the tab stop settings to the right of this one will be erased.

Enter Number (set tab): By typing a number and pressing Enter, you can set a tab stop at a specific position on the tab ruler. For example, if you're working in inches, enter 3 to set a tab stop 3" from the left margin. Since WordPerfect uses relative tabs, the actual position is relative to your left margin. If you use the default left margin of 1", the 3" tab stop will be at the 4" position. (If you are entering a number less than 1, type a fraction; if you try to enter a decimal figure, WordPerfect assumes you want a dot leader.) To set multiple tab stops, type the number for the first tab stop, a comma (,), and then the number that specifies the distance between tab stops. For example, type 0,2 to set a series of tab stops 2" apart starting at the left margin, since 0" means 0" from the left margin.

Del (clear tab): To delete a single tab stop, move the cursor to the tab stop you want to delete, and press Del.

Type: This option lets you specify whether you want the tab stops measured from the left margin (**R**elative) or from the left edge of the page (**A**bsolute). A relative tab is measured relative to the left margin, so entering a setting at 4" means 4" from the current left margin. Absolute sets the tab stop at a fixed position from the left edge of the page, so an absolute tab at 4" means the position will always be at 4", regardless of the left margin setting. If you choose **R**elative (the default setting), the actual tab stop positions change whenever you change margins. For instance, a tab stop 2" from the left margin changes from the 3" position to the 3.5" position if you changed the left margin to 1.5". This setting is especially useful for parallel columns.

Left, Center, Right, and Decimal: These four options let you insert new tab stops directly on the tab ruler, by typing L, C, R, or D, or change the type of existing tab stops, by typing over them with L, C, R, or D. Move the cursor to the place where you want to insert or change a tab stop, and type L, C, R, or D to set a tab stop of that type.

. = Dot Leader: This option lets you insert a row of dots between the previous tab stop and the tab stop you chose. To select this option, move the cursor to the tab stop you want the dot leader to precede, and type . to insert a dot leader. The tab stop appears in reverse video.

Exit: When you are finished setting your tab stops, press F7 (Exit) twice or click the right mouse button twice. WordPerfect returns you to the Edit screen and inserts a [Tab Set] code at the cursor location.

Table T.1 *Cursor movement on the Tab Set menu.*

Cursor Key	Moves Cursor
Left Arrow	Left one character
Right Arrow	Right one character
Up Arrow	Right one tab stop
Down Arrow	Left one tab stop
Home,Left Arrow	Left edge of screen
Home,Right Arrow	Right edge of screen
Home,Home,Left Arrow	Left end of tab ruler
Home,Home,Right Arrow or End	Right end of tab ruler

Tip: If you want certain tab settings to be in effect for every document you create, set your tabs as initial codes using the Setup: Initial Settings menu. Refer to *Initial Settings*.

Setting Tab Stops

1. Press Shift-F8 (Format) or display the Layout menu.

   A list of formatting options appears.

2. Select **Line (1)**.

   The Format: Line menu appears.

3. Select **8 (Tab Set)**.

   The Tab Set menu appears.

4. Set your tabs using the options described earlier.

   The changes appear as you enter them on the tab ruler.

5. Press F7 (Exit) twice or click the right mouse button twice.

   WordPerfect returns you to the Edit screen and inserts a [Tab Set] code at the cursor location. The new tabs take effect at this position.

The tab settings you just entered remain in effect until the end of the document, or until you change the settings again.

Note: Whenever you change the type of tab setting (left, right, center, or decimal) at a particular tab stop position, you change it for all tabs you may have already inserted into the document past the cursor position. For example, if you change a right tab setting to a left tab setting, all subsequent right tabs that you've already inserted *at that tab stop* become left tabs. If you don't want a particular tab to change in this way, insert it as a hard tab: Instead of pressing the regular Tab key, you press Home,Tab or Home,Shift-F6 (Center) or Home,Alt-F6 (Flush Right) or Ctrl-F6 (Tab Align). Refer to *Hard Tab*.

Tab Align (see also *Decimal/Align Character* and *Decimal Tabs*)

Function: Lets you align text vertically around a decimal/align character—a decimal point, unless you change it.

Keystrokes: *Keyboard*   *Mouse*
                  Ctrl-F6 (Tab Align)   Layout
                                                Align
                                                Tab Align

Code: [DEC TAB]

Alignment character

Example:

```
DATE:    December 11, 1991¶
  TO:    All Employees¶
FROM:    The Boss¶
  RE:    Company Christmas Party
```

You can use the Tab Align feature to align a tabular column of numbers, regardless of the number of digits they contain, or to align any text around an alignment character of your choice, such as a colon or even a blank space. For instance, you can align text along the colons in a memo, as shown in the example. If you choose to align text on a character other than a decimal point (.), you must change the decimal/align character before you use Tab Align (refer to *Decimal/Align Character*). Also, you may need to change the tab stop settings, because the Tab Align feature uses tab stops.

 Aligning Text

1. Press the Tab key to move the cursor to the tab stop preceding the one on which you want to align the text.

   If you changed the tab stop settings so that the first one is at the position where you will use Tab Align, you can skip this step.

2. Press Ctrl-F6 (Tab Align), or display the Layout menu and select **Align** and then **Tab Align**.

   The cursor moves to the next tab stop, and the `Align Char =` prompt appears at the bottom of the screen.

3. Type the text that should appear before the align character.

   This text is inserted to the left of the cursor. The cursor remains stationary.

4. Type the align character—a decimal point (.), unless you changed it.

   This character is positioned at the tab stop, and the `Align Char =` prompt disappears.

5. Type the text that should appear after the align character.

   This text is moved in the usual way, to the right of the cursor and tab stop position.

Tab Key (see also *Tab Ruler* and *Tab, Set*)

Function: Moves the cursor to the next tab stop position.

Keystrokes: *Keyboard*
Tab

Codes: [Tab]
[Ctr Tab]
[Rgt Tab]
[Dec Tab]

By default, pressing the Tab key inserts a [Tab] code at the cursor location and moves the cursor to the next tab stop position; anything you type after that is inserted to the right of the tab stop. Since the first (leftmost) character is at the tab stop, it is called a left tab. However, if you use the Tab Set option on the Format: Line menu to set center, right, or decimal tabs, WordPerfect inserts codes for those types of tabs and aligns the characters accordingly. If you use a center tab, text will be centered over the tab stop. If you use a right tab, text will be inserted to the left of the tab stop, so the last character is to the left of the tab stop position. Since the tab is just right of all text, it is called a right tab. If you use a decimal tab, it aligns the text around the decimal/align character, and the decimal point is at the tab stop. If you press Tab and then change your mind, you can move the cursor back to the previous tab stop position by pressing the Backspace key.

The function of the Tab key also differs depending on whether you press the key in Insert or Typeover mode. In Insert mode, the Tab key inserts a tab code as described earlier. In Typeover mode, the Tab key moves the cursor to the next tab stop without inserting a code. This is useful when you are editing text, to move the cursor rapidly between tab stop positions—every half inch by default.

Table Box (see *Graphics, Create*)

Table of Authorities, Define

Function: Lets you set the position and appearance for each section in a table of authorities.

Keystrokes:

Keyboard	*Mouse*
Alt-F5 (Mark Text)	Mark
5 (Define)	Define
4 (Define Table of Authorities)	Define Table of Authorities
Section number	*section number*
Select formatting options	Select formatting options
F7 (Exit)	Right mouse button

Code: [Def Mark:ToA]

Example:

```
                            TABLE OF AUTHORITIES¶
¶
Federal Regulations¶
¶
34 F.D.R 6113(a) . . . . . . . . . . . . . . . . . . . .1, 15, 63¶
¶
45 F.D.R 9002(e) . . . . . . . . . . . . . . . . . 12, 23, 45¶
¶
67 F.D.R 5674. . . . . . . . . . . . . . . . . . .7, 16, 32¶
¶
¶
Local Restrictions¶
1.101. . . . . . . . . . . . . . . . . . . . . . . . 45, 67¶
¶
21.72. . . . . . . . . . . . . . . . . . . . . . . . . 15¶
¶
67.8 . . . . . . . . . . . . . . . . . . . . . . . 34, 78¶
¶
```

After you mark the entries in your document that you want to cite in your table of authorities, you must tell WordPerfect where you want each section of the table located and how you want each section formatted. For example, you can have the page number printed at the right margin, with dot leaders between the citation and the page number; you can choose to use double-spacing between citations; and you can choose to eliminate any underlining codes that appear in the marked text.

Defining a Table of Authorities

1. Position the cursor at the end of the document or wherever you want this section to be placed after WordPerfect generates it.

2. Press Ctrl-Enter if you want the table to start on a separate page.

   WordPerfect inserts a hard page break at the cursor location, represented by a line of dashes.

3. Type a heading for the table.

   For example, type TABLE OF AUTHORITIES.

4. Press Enter one or more times to insert space between the heading and the body of the table.

5. Type a heading for the section you want to define.

   For example, type Federal Regulations.

6. Press Enter one or more times to insert space between the heading and the citations for this section.

7. Press Alt-F5 (Mark Text) or display the **M**ark menu. — The Mark Text menu appears.

8. Select **D**efine (**5**). — The Mark Text: Define menu appears.

9. Select Define Table of Authorities (**4**). — WordPerfect prompts you to enter the number of the section you want to define.

10. Enter the number of the section you want to define (1-16). — You don't have to define your sections in numerical order. The Definition for Table of Authorities menu appears with three formatting options.

11. If you want to change any of the defaults, select the formatting options you want to change for this section.

12. Press F7 (Exit) or click the right mouse button. — WordPerfect returns you to the Edit screen and inserts the [Def Mark:ToA] code at the cursor location. This code includes the section number.

13. Repeat steps 5-12 for each section of the table you want to define.

 Note: If your document contains more regular text after the table of authorities, you may want to insert a [Pg Num] code after the last section you define. Otherwise, page numbering may be incorrect from this point on. Refer to *New Page Number*. If you choose not to enter a New Page Number code, WordPerfect will display a warning message whenever you generate the table of authorities.

After you define your table of authorities sections and mark all the citations you want it to include, you can generate it. Refer to *Generate*.

Table of Authorities, Mark Text

Function: Lets you mark entries in a document that you want to include as citations in your table of authorities.

Keystrokes:

Keyboard	*Mouse*
Alt-F5 (Mark Text)	Mark
4 (ToA)	Table of Authorities
section number	Mark Full
Edit text	*section number*
F7 (Exit)	Edit text
short form name	Right mouse button
Enter	*short form name*
Home,Home,Up Arrow	Enter
Home,F2 (Extended	Home,Home,Up Arrow
Search)	Search
authority	Extended
F2 (→Search)	Forward
Alt-F5 (Mark Text)	*authority*
4 (ToA Short Form)	Search
Enter	Forward
	Mark
	Table of Authorities
	Mark Short
	Enter

Codes: [ToA:Full Form]
[ToA]

A table of authorities is a list of citations in a legal document. The citations include references to specific cases, statutes, regulations, and other legal documentation. To create a table of authorities, perform the following three steps:

- Mark the entries you want to cite in the document as described below.

- Define the table of authorities for each section of your table. Refer to *Table of Authorities, Define*.

- Generate the table of authorities. Refer to *Generate*.

When you mark entries to include in your table of authorities, you mark them using two methods. First, you mark a long entry. This entry is used to generate the citation as it will appear in your table of authorities. You can then mark all other occurrences of the entry in the document as short entries, an abbreviated version of the long form. You can mark text anywhere in the document, including in footnotes, endnotes, and graphics boxes.

Each long entry (citation) may be listed under a section heading to divide groups of citations by category. For example, you may have one group of citations that deals with federal regulations, and another group that deals with local restrictions. You can divide your citations into as many as 16 sections. When you mark an entry, WordPerfect prompts you to enter a section number for that entry.

 ## Marking Existing Text for a Table of Authorities

1. Move the cursor to an occurrence of the authority you want to mark as the long form for this citation.

   You can mark any occurrence of an authority as the long entry.

2. Press Alt-F4 (Block) and move the cursor to highlight all the text in the authority.

3. Press Alt-F5 (Mark Text) or display the Mark menu.

   A list of Mark Text options appears.

4. Select 4 (ToA), or select Table of Authorities and then Mark Full from the Mark menu.

   WordPerfect prompts you to enter a section number.

5. Enter a number for the section in which you want this entry to appear (1-16).

   WordPerfect displays the highlighted text in a special editing window.

6. If desired, edit the text to appear as you want it in your table.

   This should include the complete citation, up to 30 lines.

7. Press F7 (Exit) to accept the text.

   WordPerfect prompts you to enter a short form for the entry, which will make it easier to mark other occurrences of this authority in the document.

8. Press Enter to accept the suggested short form, or type the short form you want to use; then press Enter.

   You can use this short form to mark all other references to the authority, so make sure the entry is unique. WordPerfect inserts the [ToA:Full Form] code at the cursor location. Next, you can search for and mark other occurrences of this citation, using the short form.

9. Press Home,Home,Up Arrow.	The cursor moves to the beginning of the document.
10. Press Home,F2 (Extended Search), or select **Extended** from the **Search** menu and select **Forward**.	WordPerfect prompts you to enter a search string.
11. Type as much of the authority as needed to locate it.	
12. Press F2 (→Search).	WordPerfect finds the first occurrence of the search string and positions the cursor to the right of the string.
13. Press Alt-F5 (Mark Text) or display the **Mark** menu.	A list of Mark Text options appears.
14. Select **4** (ToA Short Form), or select Table of Authorities and then Mark **S**hort from the **Mark** menu.	WordPerfect displays the last short form name you entered earlier.
15. Press Enter to accept the suggested short form name, or type another.	WordPerfect inserts the [ToA] code at the cursor location.
16. Repeat steps 9-14 until you've marked all occurrences of an authority.	
17. Repeat steps 1-16 to mark other authorities to include in the table.	

After you mark all the entries in your document, you must define your table of authorities (see *Table of Authorities, Define*); this tells WordPerfect where to put the table and how to format it. You can then generate the table (see *Generate*).

Table of Contents, Define

Function: Lets you define a table of contents, specifying the number of levels, the position and numbering style for each level, and whether or not to display the last level in wrapped format.

Keystrokes:

Keyboard	Mouse
Keyboard	*Mouse*
Alt-F5 (Mark Text)	Mark
5 (Define)	Define
1 (Define Table of Contents)	Table of Contents
1 (Number of Levels)	Number of Levels
number of levels	*number of levels*
2 (Display Last Level in Wrapped Format)	Display Last Level in Wrapped Format
Y or N	Y or N
3 (Page Numbering)	Page Numbering
Select page numbering style for each level	Select page numbering style for each level
F7 (Exit)	Right mouse button

Code: [Def Mark:ToC]

Example:

```
Caring for Your Trees. . . . . . . . . . . . . . . . . . . .   21¶
    When You First Get Your Tree. . . . . . . . . . . .   21¶
    Choosing the Proper Location. . . . . . . . . . . .   22¶
        Sun or Shade?. . . . . . . . . . . . . . . . .   22¶
        Wet or Dry?. . . . . . . . . . . . . . . . . .   23¶
        Buildings and Power Lines. . . . . . . . . . .   24¶
    Planting Your Tree. . . . . . . . . . . . . . . . .   25¶
        Digging a Hole . . . . . . . . . . . . . . . .   25¶
        Preparing the Ground . . . . . . . . . . . . .   26¶
        Anchoring Your Tree. . . . . . . . . . . . . .   28¶
```

After you mark headings or other text in your document to include in a table of contents, use this option to tell WordPerfect where you want the table located, how many levels it will have, and how you want the page numbers formatted for each level. After you finish defining the table of contents, WordPerfect inserts a [Def Mark:ToC] code at the cursor location. When you generate the table, it will be inserted at this position, in the format you specified.

 ## Defining a Table of Contents

1. Move the cursor where you want the table of contents placed after WordPerfect generates it.   This is usually at the beginning of your document.

2. Press Ctrl-Enter if you want the rest of your document to start on a separate page from the table of contents.

WordPerfect inserts a hard page break at the cursor position.

3. Press Up Arrow if you are creating the table on the first page.

This moves the cursor to the page preceding the body of your document. If you want the body of your document to appear on a right-hand page, refer to *Force Odd/Even Page*.

4. Type a heading for the table of contents.

For example, type CONTENTS.

5. Press Enter one or more times to insert space between the heading and the table.

6. Press Alt-F5 (Mark Text) or display the **Mark** menu.

A list of Mark Text options appears.

7. Select **Define** (**5**).

The Mark Text: Define menu appears.

8. Select **1** (Define Table of Contents).

The Table of Contents Definition menu appears.

9. Select **1** (**Number of Levels**), and enter the number of levels you want to include in the table (1-5).

Each level is indented one tab stop position to the right of the previous level.

10. If you want to display the last level of your table in wrapped format, select **2** (**Display Last Level in Wrapped Format**) and press Y.

The default setting for this option is No. Typing Y changes it to Yes for this document.

11. Select **3** (**Page Numbering**) and select a numbering style from the list for each level.

You can have a different style for each level. You can have the page number follow the text immediately; have a parenthesized page number follow the text; have the page number flush right so it will appear at the right margin; have it flush right with dot leaders; or choose to have no page numbers. Flush Right with Dot Leaders is the default for all levels, and will be used unless you change it for one or more levels.

12. Press F7 (Exit) or click the right mouse button.

WordPerfect returns you to the Edit screen and inserts a [Def Mark] code at the cursor location. Once you use the Generate option on the Mark Text menu, the table will appear starting at the position of this code.

Note: If you place your table of contents at the beginning of the document, the table will insert one or more pages ahead of the other text, altering the page numbering for the rest of your document. If you want page numbering to begin with the first page of the document, use the New Page Number option on the Format: Page Numbering menu to start numbering on that page. Refer to *New Page Number*.

After you define your table of contents, you can generate it. Refer to *Generate*.

Table of Contents, Mark Text

Function: Lets you block and mark text, such as headings, that you want to include in a table of contents for the document.

Keystrokes:

Keyboard	*Mouse*
Alt-F4 (Block)	**Edit**
Alt-F5 (Mark Text)	**Block**
1 (ToC)	**Mark**
level of head	Table of Contents
Enter	*level of head*
	Enter

Codes: [Mark:ToC]
[End Mark:ToC]

WordPerfect lets you create a table of contents for any document, complete with page numbers, by marking existing headings and subheadings that you want to include in the table. The process is simple:

- Mark the headings or other text that you want to include in the table of contents, specifying the level for each entry (up to five levels), as described below. The first level will be at the left margin, and each subsequent level will be indented one tab stop.

- Define the table of contents. Refer to *Table of Contents, Define*.

- Generate the table of contents. Refer to *Generate*.

 ### Marking Existing Text for a Table of Contents

1. Move the cursor to the beginning or end of the text you want to mark.

2. Press Alt-F4 (Block), or select **Block** from the **Edit** menu and highlight the text you want to include in the table of contents.

3. Press Alt-F5 (Mark Text) or display the **Mark** menu. 　　The Mark Text menu appears.

4. Select **1** (ToC), or select Table of Contents from the **Mark** menu. 　　WordPerfect prompts you to enter the level for this entry.

5. Enter a number from 1-5. 　　WordPerfect inserts the code [Mark:ToC] (including the level number) to the left of the heading, and [End Mark:ToC] to the right of the heading.

6. Repeat steps 1-4 for each entry you want to include in the table of contents; then save the document to retain the codes.

Tables, Create

Function: Lets you create and work with rows and columns of tabular information.

Keystrokes:

Keyboard	*Mouse*
Alt-F7 (Columns/Table)	Layout
2 (Tables)	Tables
1 (Create)	Create
number of columns	*number of columns*
Enter	Enter
number of rows	*number of rows*
Enter	Enter

Codes: [Tbl Def]
[Row]
[Cell]
[Tbl Off]

Example:

Cell ⸺

Table
Edit
menu

```
Table Edit:  Press Exit when done        Cell A1 Doc 1 Pg 1 Ln 1.14" Pos 1.12"

Ctrl-Arrows Column Widths; Ins Insert; Del Delete; Move Move/Copy;
1 Size; 2 Format; 3 Lines; 4 Header; 5 Math; 6 Options; 7 Join; 8 Split; 0
```

WordPerfect's Table feature has a wide variety of applications. You can use it like a spreadsheet and perform basic mathematical operations, or create forms, such as invoices, or use it in place of the Parallel Columns feature, by removing all the lines.

A table consists of a series of rows and columns that intersect to form a matrix of boxes (called *cells*). The columns are assigned letters from left to right, A, B, C, D, etc., and the rows are assigned numbers from top to bottom, 1, 2, 3, 4, 5, etc. Each cell formed by the intersection of a row and column is assigned a letter-number combination that indicates the position of that cell in the matrix. For instance, the first cell in the upper-left corner is A1, the one below it is A2, and the one to the right of it is B1.

When you create a table, you specify the number of columns (up to 32) and the number of rows (up to 32,765) to include. WordPerfect automatically generates the empty table structure. You can then modify the structure or exit to the regular Edit screen and type your text or numbers in the table. You can even create a table from existing text that is formatted either in parallel columns or in tabular columns.

 ## Creating a Table

1. Position the cursor at the left margin on the line where you want the table to appear.

2. Press Alt-F7 (Columns/Table) or display the **L**ayout menu.

   A list of formatting options appears.

3. Select **Tables (2)**.

   The Tables menu appears.

4. Select **Create (1)**.

   WordPerfect prompts you to specify the number of columns.

5. Type the number of columns you want in your table (up to 32), and press Enter.

   WordPerfect prompts you to specify the number of rows.

6. Type the number of rows you want in your table (up to 32,765), and press Enter.

   The table structure appears, with the Table Edit menu at the bottom of the screen. This menu features options that you can use to change the structure and appearance of the table or of individual cells, columns, or rows. You cannot enter data while in this menu. To return to the regular Edit screen, where you can type and edit text in the table, press F7 (Exit).

When your table first appears on screen, you are automatically in Edit mode. The columns are all the same width, the rows are all the same height, and many other defaults for formatting and structure are in effect. You can modify the structure of your table while in the Table Edit menu, which you can toggle in and out of by pressing Alt-F7 (Columns/Table).

Column Widths: To widen or reduce a column, position the cursor in any cell in the column and press Ctrl-Right Arrow to widen or Ctrl-Left Arrow to reduce.

Insert: To insert one or more rows or columns into your table, move the cursor to the row or column where you want to insert them and press the Ins key. WordPerfect prompts you to select **1** (**R**ows) or **2** (**C**olumns). Select either option and then enter the number of columns or rows you want to insert. Rows will be inserted above the cursor, and columns will be inserted to the left of the cursor.

Delete: To delete a row or column of cells, move the cursor to the row or column you want to delete, and press the Del key. WordPerfect prompts you to select **1** (**R**ows) or **2** (**C**olumns). Select either option and then enter the number of rows or columns you want to delete. The specified number is deleted from the cursor position forward. You can press F1 (Cancel) to undelete them.

Move/Copy: To move, copy, or delete a row or column of cells, move the cursor to the row or column you want to move, copy, or delete and press Ctrl-F4 (Move). Select **2** (**R**ow) or **3** (**C**olumn); then select **1** (**M**ove), **2** (**C**opy), or **3** (**D**elete). If you selected Move or Copy, move the cursor where you want the row or column inserted, and press Enter.

Size: You can use this option to change the table size, by adding or deleting rows or columns from the end of the table. When you select this option, WordPerfect prompts you to select **1** (**R**ows) or **2** (**C**olumns). Select either option, and then enter the total number of rows or columns you want your table to have, just as you did when you first created the table. WordPerfect will display the current number, and you can type a larger number to add rows or columns, or a smaller number to delete them.

Format: This option lets you change formatting options for columns and cells, or for a block of cells. For example, you can select appearance attributes for the text that you type, center or right-align text in a cell, lock a cell to prevent its contents from being changed, specify numeric or text as the type of entry (for math), change column widths, and change row heights. Formatting options, such as bold, centering, and italics, that you use in the Table Edit menu will be overridden if you change them in the regular Edit screen. For example, if you use the Table Edit menu to select center justification for a cell, then exit to the Edit screen and use the Format: Line menu to select Left Justification for the cell, it will be left-justified, not centered.

Lines: By default, WordPerfect inserts a double line around the outside border of your table and separates cells with single lines. This option lets you specify the types of lines for the left, right, top, bottom, inside, outside, or all lines around a cell. It provides several types of lines, or lets you remove the lines altogether. You can also use it to shade one or more cells. To change lines for a group of cells or the entire table, use the Block feature to highlight them, and then select the Lines option.

Header: Lets you enter a header row (or rows) for your table. If the table exceeds one page in length, this row (or rows) will appear at the top of the table on each page.

Math: Lets you enter and calculate mathematical formulas in any cell. Refer to *Tables, Math*.

Options: Lets you change selected settings for all cells in the table. You can change the way WordPerfect displays the negative results of calculations; select a percentage of gray shading for cells formatted with this feature (using the Line option); change the alignment of the table in relation to the left and right margins; and specify the amount of blank space you want inserted between the cell borders.

Join: You can use this option to join a group of cells together to create one large cell. To use it, press Alt-F4 (Block), move the cursor to highlight the group of cells you want to join, and then select this option.

Split: This option lets you split an existing cell into a number of rows or columns. Move the cursor to the column or row you want to split and select this option. WordPerfect prompts you to choose **1** (**Rows**) or **2** (**Columns**). Select either option, and then enter the number of rows or columns you want this cell divided into.

 Tip: You can delete a table structure and leave the text, separated by tabs, by deleting the Table Definition code [Tbl Def]. To delete both the text and structure, block it all and then press Delete.

 ### Editing a Table's Structure

1. Place the cursor anywhere inside the table.

2. Press Alt-F7 (Columns/Table), or display the Layout menu and select **Tables** and then **Edit**.

   The Table Edit menu appears.

3. Move the cursor to the cell, column, or row you want to modify.

   If you want to modify a group of cells, press Alt-F4 and highlight the entire group.

4. Select an option and enter your change.

5. Repeat steps 3 and 4 to modify the table as desired.

6. Press F7 (Exit) or click the right mouse button.

This returns you to the Edit screen, with the cursor in the last cell it was on in the Table Edit menu.

After you create the structure of your table, you can exit to the Edit screen to type text in your table. Press Tab to move right to the next cell or Shift-Tab to move left to the previous cell. Type the text or numbers as you normally would. If text exceeds one line within a cell, it will automatically be wrapped to the next line, expanding the length of this cell and all cells in the row. You can also press Enter to insert blank lines and lengthen all cells in a row. If you have an enhanced keyboard, use Alt-Down Arrow to move down one cell, Alt-Up Arrow to move up one cell, Alt-Left Arrow to move left one cell, and Alt-Right Arrow to move right one cell. The Go To key (Ctrl-Home) also has cursor movement functions in tables as summarized in Table T.2.

Table T.2 *Using Go To in tables.*

Keystroke	Cursor Movement
Ctrl,Home,Up Arrow	First character in cell
Ctrl,Home,Down Arrow	First character in last line in cell
Ctrl,Home,Home,Up Arrow	First cell in column
Ctrl,Home,Home,Down Arrow	Last cell in column
Ctrl,Home,Home,Left Arrow OR Alt,Home,Left Arrow (enhanced keyboards)	First cell in row
Ctrl,Home,Home,Right Arrow OR Alt,Home,Right Arrow (enhanced keyboards)	Last cell in row
Ctrl,Home,Home,Home,Up Arrow OR Alt,Home,Home,Up Arrow (enhanced keyboards)	First cell in table
Ctrl,Home,Home,Home,Down Arrow OR Alt,Home,Home,Down Arrow (enhanced keyboards)	Last cell in table

Tip: You can simulate the effect of parallel columns by creating tables, typing text in the cells, and removing all lines inside and around the tables. Block the whole table, select **3** (Lines) on the Table Edit menu, select **7** (All), and then **1** (None). Tables are much easier to use than parallel columns, and you don't have to worry about the position of the Column On/Off codes and positioning the cursor correctly before pressing Ctrl-Enter. To convert columns into a table, block the columns, press Alt-F7 (Columns/ Table), select **2** (Tables) and then **1** (Create).

Tables, Math (see also *Math*)

Function: Lets you perform addition, subtraction, multiplication, and division using entries in a table.

Keystrokes: *Keyboard* *Mouse*
Alt-F7 (Columns/Table) **Layout**
5 (Math) **Tables**
1 (Calculate), **Edit**
2 (Formula), or **Math**
3 (Copy Formula) **Calculate, Formula, or Copy Formula**

Example:

Sales Staff¶	Foreign Sales¶	Domestic Sales¶	Total Sales¶	Returns¶	Net Sales¶
Peter¶	35,100¶	32,200¶	67,300.00¶	11,500¶	55,800.00¶
Paul¶	27,200¶	53,700¶	80,900.00¶	18,700¶	62,200.00¶
Mary¶	42,500¶	29,300¶	71,800.00¶	6,100¶	65,700.00¶

Table Edit: Press Exit when done   Cell F1 Doc 1 Pg 1 Ln 1.14" Pos 6.45"

Ctrl-Arrows Column Widths; Ins Insert; Del Delete; Move Move/Copy;
1 Size; 2 Format; 3 Lines; 4 Header; 5 Math; 6 Options; 7 Join; 8 Split: 0

You can perform mathematical operations in WordPerfect in either of two ways. You can use WordPerfect's Math feature, as described in the *Math* section. However, you may find it easier to use the Tables feature, since you don't have to set up and use tabular columns. This feature lets you use the table like a spreadsheet. You type numbers in cells, and then use the Table Edit menu to insert formulas in the cells where you want to perform calculations. WordPerfect automatically performs the mathematical operations and inserts the results in the specified cell. For example, if you type numbers in cell B2, C2, and D2, you can use the formula B2+C2+D2/3 to calculate the average of those three numbers in cell E2. As in WordPerfect's Math feature, you can use addition (+), subtraction (–), multiplication (*), and division (/) operators, and use parentheses in your formulas to change the order of the operations. You can also use the subtotals operator (+), totals operator (=), and the grand totals operator (*) to add numbers in a column.

 Creating a Math Table

1. Place the cursor anywhere inside the table and press Alt-F7 (Columns/Table), or display the Layout menu and select **Tables** and then **Edit**.

   The Edit Table menu appears.

2. Move the cursor to a cell where you want to insert a formula.

3. Select **5 (Math)**.

   The Math menu appears.

4. Select **2 (Formula)**.

   WordPerfect prompts you to enter a formula.

5. Type the formula you want WordPerfect to use to calculate the result for this cell, and press Enter. If you've already typed numbers in other cells and you reference those cells in the calculation, the results will appear as soon as you create the formula; otherwise, 0.00 will appear.

   You can use cell coordinates as variables and use fixed numbers, as in A1*100. You can omit row numbers if you are entering a formula that uses cell coordinates exclusively from one row. For example, if you are entering a formula in cell E14 that uses values in cells B14-D14, you may enter a formula in the form B+C+D. The formula will be displayed in the left side of the screen, just above the Table Edit menu, whenever you move the cursor into this cell.

Continue entering formulas in each cell where you want WordPerfect to calculate a result. If you want to use the same formula in several cells, you can save time by copying the formula instead of entering it in each cell.

 Copying Formulas

1. Move the cursor to the cell that contains the formula you want to copy.

2. Select **5** (**Math**).   The Math menu appears.

3. Select **3** (**Copy Formula**).   The Copy Formula menu appears, prompting you to copy one formula to a cell, down or to the right.

4. Select **1** (**Cell**), **2** (**Down**), or **3** (**Right**).   Cell lets you copy the formula to any other cell. Down lets you copy the formula to one or more cells below the current cell. **Right** lets you copy the formula to one or more cells to the right of the current cell.

5. If you selected Cell, move the cursor to the cell where you want to insert the Formula and press Enter. If you selected one of the other two options, enter the number of times you want the formula copied.   WordPerfect copies the formula to the specified cell(s).

Whenever you enter a formula in a cell, WordPerfect automatically performs the specified calculations and inserts the result, assuming the cells to be calculated in the formula contain numeric entries already. If they don't, or if you change any of the values used in the calculation, WordPerfect does not automatically update the formulas. Perform the following steps to have WordPerfect recalculate all formulas:

Recalculating Results

1. Place the cursor anywhere inside the table and press Alt-F7 (Columns/Table), or display the Layout menu and select **Tables** and then **Edit**.	The Edit Table menu appears.
2. Select **5** (Math).	The Math menu appears.
3. Select **1** (Calculate).	WordPerfect performs the calculations and updates the results on screen.

Tab Ruler

Function: Displays the position of each tab stop and the left and right margin settings.

Keystrokes:

Keyboard	*Mouse*
Alt-F3 (Reveal Codes)	**Edit**
OR	**Window**
Ctrl-F3 (Screen)	23, Enter
1 (Window)	
23, Enter	

Example:

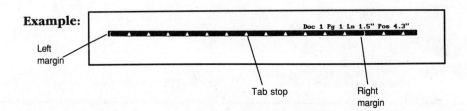

Left margin

Doc 1 Pg 1 Ln 1.5" Pos 4.3"

Tab stop   Right margin

On the normal Edit screen, WordPerfect does not display your tab settings. If you want to see the settings while you work, you have two options: You can either press Alt-F3 to display the Reveal Codes screen, which is split by the tab ruler, or perform the following steps to display the tab ruler permanently at the bottom of the Edit screen:

Display Tab Ruler

1. Press Ctrl-F3 (Screen) or display the Edit menu.

   The Screen options or Edit options appear.

2. Select **Window (1)**.

   WordPerfect prompts you to enter a size for the window. The default is 24 lines, which displays only one window.

3. Type 23 and press Enter, telling WordPerfect to make the top window 23 lines long. (If the pull-down menu bar is set up to always remain visible, enter 22 since one line is already being used to display the menu bar.)

   This leaves one line for the bottom window, so only the tab ruler fits there. The brackets on the tab ruler represent the left and right margins. If they appear as curly braces, they are in the same position as tab stop settings.

If you decide later to remove the tab ruler, repeat these steps and set the number of lines to 24 again.

 Note: The tab ruler shows only the position of the tab stops; it does not show the type of tab at each position. To see the types of tabs, you must display the Tab Set menu as described in the section *Tab, Set*.

Target (see *Cross-Reference*)

Text Box (see *Graphics, Create*)

Text In, Retrieve DOS Text

Function: Lets you retrieve files that are in DOS (ASCII) text format into WordPerfect.

Keystrokes: *Keyboard*   *Mouse*

Ctrl-F5 (Text In/Out)   **File**

1 (DOS Text)   **Text In**

2 (Retrieve CR/LF to   DOS Text (CR/LF to [**HRt**]) or

[**HRt**]) or **3** (Retrieve   DOS Text (CR/LF to [**SRt**])

CR/LF to [**SRt**])   *d:\path\filename.ext*

d:\path\filename.ext   Enter

Enter

The Text In feature provides two methods that let you retrieve DOS (ASCII) text files into WordPerfect. If you want the Carriage Return/Line Feed codes at the end of each line converted to Hard Return codes, use the first method (CR/LF to [HRt]). If you want soft returns at the end of each line within a paragraph, use the second option (CR/LF to [SRt]). In the latter method, WordPerfect will convert two or more Carriage Return/Line Feed codes in a row to a [HRt] code, not a [SRt] code, since paragraphs usually end in two of these codes.

In a DOS text file, each line of text ends with a carriage return and line feed code that moves the cursor to the next line. If you were to retrieve the file into WordPerfect in the usual way, using Retrieve or List Files, WordPerfect would convert all the Carriage Return/Line Feed codes to Hard Return codes. Inserting or deleting text within a paragraph would be more complex, since each line ends in [HRt].

By using the Text In feature to retrieve the DOS text file, you can choose whether you want the Carriage Return/Line Feed entries converted to hard returns or to soft returns if they fall within the hyphenation zone. If you choose to convert them into soft returns, WordPerfect inserts soft returns at the end of all lines except those that end in two or more Carriage Return/Line Feed codes, or those in which CR/LF codes are not in the hyphenation zone. This is helpful if you want to take advantage of word wrap. However, if you just want to edit a batch file or another DOS text file, such as AUTOEXEC.BAT or CONFIG.SYS, you should use the hard returns. (For more information about the hyphenation zone, refer to the *Hyphenation Zone* section.)

 Note: If you choose to convert the codes to hard returns, consider resetting your margins before retrieving to make them wider than the document you are retrieving. Otherwise, you may get hard returns in the middle of paragraphs.

Retrieving a DOS Text File

1. Press Ctrl-F5 (Text In/Out) and select **1** (DOS Text), or select Text In from the **File** menu.

    WordPerfect presents two options for importing a DOS text file and converting Carriage Return/Line Feed codes.

2. Select **2** (**R**etrieve CR/LF to [HRt]) or DOS Text (CR/LF to [HRt]) from the pull-down menu, or **3** (Retrieve CR/LF to [SRt]) or DOS Text (CR/LF to [SRt]) from the pull-down menu.

    CR/LF to [HRt] ends all lines in a hard return. CR/LF to [SRt] ends lines within paragraphs with soft returns (if the CR/LF falls in the hyphenation zone), and ends lines that have two or more CR/LF codes with a hard return. WordPerfect prompts you to enter the file name of the file you want to retrieve.

3. Type the complete path name and file name of the file you want to retrieve, and press Enter.

    WordPerfect retrieves the file into the Edit screen. If you edit it and later want to save it as a DOS text file again, to preserve the ASCII format, use the DOS Text Save option. Refer to *Text Out*.

 Tip: You can also retrieve a DOS text file in the List Files menu, by highlighting it and pressing Ctrl-F5. This method works like the CR/LF to [HRt] option, inserting a hard return at the end of each line.

Text Out (see also *WordPerfect File Conversion*)

Function: Lets you save files you created in WordPerfect 5.1 as DOS (ASCII) text files, WordPerfect 5.0 or 4.2 files, or in a generic word processing format.

Keystrokes: *Keyboard*   *Mouse*

Ctrl-F5 (Text In/Out)   **File**

and   **Text Out**

1 (DOS Text)   **DOS Text, Generic, WP5.0, or**

1 (Save)   **WP4.2**

d:\path\filename.ext   *d:\path\filename.ext*

Enter   Enter

OR

3 (Save As)

1 (Generic),

2 (WordPerfect 5.0), or

3 (WordPerfect 4.2)

d:\path\filename.ext

Enter

WordPerfect documents may be incompatible with other programs that you want to use to work on the documents. For example, you may want to use a grammar checker or provide a file to someone who uses a different word processor or an earlier version of WordPerfect. WordPerfect has provided three options that you can use to save a WordPerfect 5.1 file in a compatible format:

DOS Text File: This option converts tab, indent, center, and alignment codes to spaces; removes column formatting, headers, footers, endnotes, and footnotes; and converts codes for features such as Date and Outlines to ASCII text. In other words, most of the formatting codes are lost.

Generic: This option uses spaces for features such as center, indent, flush right, and soft returns. Tab codes are retained, and indent codes are changed to tabs. While most of the WordPerfect formatting codes are deleted, it will appear similar, because WordPerfect will try to maintain the effects of the formatting codes. Also, Soft Return codes will be converted to spaces, so you can use the file in another word processing program.

WordPerfect 4.2 or 5.0: This option converts files into WordPerfect 4.2 or 5.0, retaining as many formatting codes as possible. If version 4.2 or 5.0 has no equivalent formatting code for a code in the original document, an [Unknown] code is inserted. The Unknown codes are converted to their correct codes if you retrieve the document again.

 ### Saving a WordPerfect Document as a DOS Text File

1. Retrieve the WordPerfect document you want to convert.

2. Press Ctrl-F5 (Text In/Out), or select Text **Out** from the File menu.

3. Select **1** (DOS Text) and then **1** (**Save**), or select DOS **Text** on the pull-down menu.

   WordPerfect prompts you to enter a name for the converted file.

4. Type a file name for the converted file, and press Enter.

   If you want to save the converted file to a different directory or disk, type a path name before the file name. WordPerfect converts the file. It remains on the Edit screen after it is saved.

 ### Saving a WordPerfect Document in Another Format

1. Retrieve the WordPerfect document you want to convert.

2. Press Ctrl-F5 (Text In/Out) and select **3** (Save As), or select Text **Out** from the File menu.

3. Select **Generic** (**1**), **WordPerfect** 5.0 (**2**), or WordPerfect 4.2 (**3**).

   WordPerfect prompts you to enter a name for the converted file.

4. Enter a file name for the converted file.

   If you want to save the converted file to a different directory or disk, type a path name before the file name. WordPerfect converts the file. Since it remains on screen after it is saved, you can use F7 (Exit) to clear it out, but do not save it as a WordPerfect file.

Text Quality (see *Print Quality*)

Text Screen Type

Function: Lets you select a text driver for your type of display interface and monitor. The selected text driver is used to display text in the Edit screen and any non-graphics screen.

Keystrokes:

Keyboard	*Mouse*
Shift-F1 (Setup)	File
2 (Display)	Setup
3 (Text Screen Type)	Display
Cursor to selection	Text Screen Type
Enter	Double-click selection
Cursor to selection	Double-click selection
Enter	F7 (Exit)
F7 (Exit)	

Example:

```
Setup: Text Screen Driver

 ATI EGA Wonder
 Hercules Ramfont
 IBM EGA (& compatibles)
 IBM VGA (& compatibles)
 MDS Genius
 Paradise VGA Plus


 1 Select; 2 Auto-select; 3 Other Disk; N Name Search: 1
```

A text driver is a program that tells WordPerfect how to communicate with your monitor in text screens, such as the normal Edit screen. When you install WordPerfect, it automatically selects the text driver installed on your system, if it can. If text is not displayed correctly on your monitor, WordPerfect may be selecting the wrong driver, or you may have selected the wrong driver when you installed WordPerfect. Also, if you have a monitor card that can display font attributes, such as a Hercules Ram font interface, or that can display more rows and columns than the standard 80 columns and 25 rows, you can use this option to select the appropriate driver.

 ## Selecting a Text Driver

1. Press Shift-F1 (Setup), or select Setup from the **File** menu.　　The main Setup menu appears.

2. Select **Display** (**2**).

The Setup: Display menu appears.

3. Select **3** (**Text Screen Type**).

A list of text drivers and monitors appears.

4. Highlight the driver that corresponds to your system and choose **1** (**Select**), or, if none seems correct, choose **2** (**Auto-Select**).

To determine the correct driver, you may need to check the documentation that came with your monitor and interface card. If you choose Auto-Select, WordPerfect selects a driver for you. If you select a monitor/driver, another list appears, with options for that interface, such as the number of lines on the screen.

5. Highlight the option you want to use and choose **1** (**Select**).

6. Press F7 (Exit) twice or click the right mouse button twice.

This saves the settings and returns you to the Edit screen.

Note: The WordPerfect files that contain the information about text or graphics drivers end with the .VRS extension. If your text driver or monitor does not appear on the list, make sure all your .VRS files are in the same directory as WP.EXE. If you have .VRS files in a different directory, press Shift-F1 (Setup), select **2** (**Display**), **2** (**Graphics Screen Type**), and then select the **3** (**Other Disk**) option. Enter the path to your .VRS files. If your driver or monitor still is not listed, you may need to run the Install program to install additional .VRS files that are available or contact WordPerfect Corporation.

Thesaurus

Function: Lets you access a list of synonyms and antonyms for a selected word and substitute one into the document.

Keystrokes: *Keyboard*   *Mouse*
          Alt-F1 (Thesaurus)   Tools
          1 (Replace Word),   Thesaurus
          2 (View Document),   Replace Word, View Document,
          3 (Look Up Word), or   Look Up Word, or Clear Column
          4 (Clear Column)   Right mouse button
          F7 (Exit)

Example:

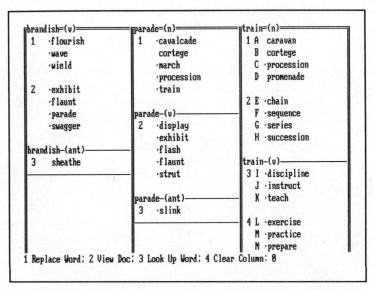

The Thesaurus provides a list of synonyms, words with similar meanings, and antonyms, words with opposite meanings, for thousands of commonly used words. You can look up a word by placing the cursor on it and then selecting Thesaurus, or by selecting Thesaurus and then typing the word. Either way, a list of synonyms and antonyms appears for the word. The list is broken down into *headwords*, *subgroups*, and *references*. The headwords are words you can look up in the Thesaurus. The words listed under the headwords are the synonyms and antonyms; these are called references. References are divided into groups of nouns (n), verbs (v), adjectives (a), and antonyms (ant). Within these groups are subgroups that are numbered 1, 2, 3, etc., which represent words that have essentially the same meaning. Words marked with a dot are other headwords that you can look up in the Thesaurus.

The Thesaurus displays up to three columns of words with a list of bold letters next to the active column. These letters make up what is called the *Reference menu*. You can use the letters to select a word to replace the one you are looking up without having to type the entire word. If there are any words in the second and third columns, you can move the letters from column to column by pressing the Left or Right Arrow keys. When a column is active, you can scroll up and down in it by pressing the Up or Down Arrow key. When the Thesaurus is displayed, you have the following options:

If a word is marked by a dot, you can type the letter next to the word to see a list of synonyms for that word. If the second column is clear, the synonyms will appear there. If not, they will appear in the third column. If all three columns contain words, typing the letter of a word with a dot next to it replaces the list in the last column.

Replace Word: To replace the word you were looking up with a word from the Thesaurus, use the arrow keys to move the bold letters (Reference menu) to the column that contains the word you want to use. Select **1** (Replace Word), and type the letter next to the word you want to use. WordPerfect will immediately substitute it for the word you were looking up in the document and exit the Thesaurus.

View Doc: This option lets you return to your document without leaving the Thesaurus. You can scroll through your document to see the context of the word you are looking up, and then press F7 (Exit) to return to the Thesaurus. You cannot type or edit while using this option. You can move the cursor onto another word and then press Alt-F1 to look up that word and clear the Thesaurus screen of the other headwords.

Look Up Word: This option lets you type a word to look up, which may be completely unrelated to the original word you were looking up.

Clear Column: To clear words from any column, use the arrow keys to move the bold letters to the column you want to delete, and select this option. If you use this option while the letters are in the first column, any words in the second column will be moved over to the first. If the second column is empty, all words will disappear, and you'll have to use the Lookup Word option to look up another word, or else press F7 (Exit) to exit the Thesaurus.

 Viewing a List of Synonyms

1. Move the cursor to the word you want to look up.

2. Press Alt-F1 (Thesaurus), or select **T**hesaurus from the **T**ools menu.

   A list of synonyms and antonyms for the highlighted word appears. If the word is not in the Thesaurus, a `Word Not Found` prompt appears, and you are prompted to type another word. The list may occupy only the first column or may extend into the second or even the third column. If you type the letter next to a headword and replace the column to the right, you can still view the original list by moving the cursor down through the column to the left. There may be more words in a column than can be shown on screen, so use Home,Home,Down Arrow to see if there are more.

3. Select one of the options described above.

If you use the Replace Word option, once the word is substituted into your document, the Thesaurus menu will disappear.

4. You can exit the Thesaurus at any time by pressing F7 (Exit) or clicking the right mouse button.

WordPerfect quits the Thesaurus and returns you to the Edit screen.

Thousands' Separator (see also *Decimal/Align Character*)

Function: Lets you choose the character WordPerfect uses to mark the thousands' place in a number with a value of 1,000 or greater.

Keystrokes:

Keyboard	*Mouse*
Shift-F8 (Format)	Layout
4 (Other)	Other
3 (Decimal/Align Character)	Decimal/Align Character
character	*character*

By default, WordPerfect uses a comma to mark the thousands' place in numbers that WordPerfect creates by calculating. For example, if you use the Math feature or Table Math to perform a calculation that results in a number over 1,000, such as 78654, WordPerfect automatically inserts a comma between the 8 and 6 (78,654). If you wish to use a different character, or a space, in place of the comma, you must enter the character you want to use on the Format: Other menu. This option has no effect on the characters you type.

 Changing the Thousands' Separator

1. Press Shift-F8 (Format) or display the Layout menu.	A list of formatting options appears.
2. Select Other (4).	The Format: Other menu appears.
3. Select 3 (Decimal/Align Character).	The cursor moves up to the decimal/align character.
4. Press Enter to keep the decimal/align character.	The cursor moves to the thousands' separator.
5. Enter the character you want to use for the thousands' separator.	
6. Press F7 (Exit) twice, or click the right mouse button twice.	This saves your selection and returns you to the Edit screen.

Time (see *Date and Time, Inserting*)

Timed Backup (see *Backup, Timed and Original*)

Top/Bottom Margins (see *Margins, Top/Bottom*)

Typeover (see *Insert Key*)

U–W

Undelete (see also *Delete Text*)

Function: Restores up to three separate deletions.

Keystrokes: *Keyboard*   *Mouse*
                   F1 (Cancel)   Edit
                   1 (Restore) or **2**   Undelete
                   (Previous Deletion)

Example:

```
Scott:
Enclosed are samples of custom floppy disk sleeves available from
the Ames Safety Envelope Co. Don't ask me where this joint is.
Thought you might find these helpful for the BBO Harvard Graphics
book. I also have some suggestions about handling the diskette
duplication:                                                    ──── Block to be
                                                                     restored
[o]  For the Mac Repair book, a company called CTEX did the
     diskette duplication. They offered the best price, they use
     quality materials, and they have a good reputation:



Undelete                  Undelete: 1 Restore; 2 Previous Deletion: 0
options
```

The Cancel key has two functions: If a menu or prompt is displayed, the Cancel key cancels it. If no menu or prompt appears, the Cancel key displays the most recently deleted text, codes, or blank space, and provides the option to restore it or to restore either of the two previous deletions.

    Whenever you delete using Delete, Backspace, Ctrl-Backspace, Ctrl-End, Ctrl-PgDn, Block Delete, or Block Backspace, WordPerfect stores the deletion in a specific buffer in RAM. If you delete a block that's too large to fit in RAM, the block is stored on disk, unless it's too large. Although this is unlikely, if it happens, you'll see a warning, and you can choose not to delete at that time.

    WordPerfect stores up to three deletions in the temporary buffer and lets you restore them one at a time. A deletion is defined as anything you erase, including codes and blank spaces, until you move the cursor or type text. For instance, pressing Delete 10 times is one deletion, as long as you don't move the cursor or type. Once you make more than three deletions in an edit session, the oldest deletion is removed from the buffer and replaced by the second oldest deletion. The Undelete feature lets you restore any or all of these three deletions at the cursor location. Codes that come in pairs, such as bold and italics, cannot be restored, but open codes, such as tab settings and margin changes, can.

Caution: You can use the Undelete feature to move text to another location in your document, but be careful that you restore it before you erase three more times, or you'll be unable to bring it back. Even pressing Delete to erase a blank space counts as one deletion, so it's easier than it sounds.

Restoring Text

1. Move the cursor where you want to restore the deletion.

The Undelete option restores deletions at the current cursor position. If you are restoring codes, turn on Reveal Codes to see them.

2. Make sure no prompt or menu appears on screen, and press F1 (Cancel) or select Undelete from the Edit menu.

The most recent deletion appears at the cursor location in reverse video. A prompt appears asking if you want to restore the deletion or view the previous deletion.

3. To view the previous deletions, select **2** (**Previous Deletion**) or use Up Arrow or Down Arrow.

The deletion appears in reverse video. If you don't see the deletion you want to restore, you've made three other deletions, and it is no longer available in the buffer.

4. If you see the deletion you want to bring back, select **1** (**Restore**).

The deletion is restored at the cursor position.

5. Repeat steps 1-4 to restore any of the other two deletions. To remove the Undelete prompt without restoring, press F1 (Cancel).

Tip: If Typeover is on and you erase text as you type over it, you can use Undelete to restore that text. This is useful when you thought you were in Insert mode and had intended to insert text, not type over it.

Underline

Function: Underscores text.

Keystrokes:

Keyboard	*Mouse*
F8 (Underline)	Font
OR	Appearance
Ctrl-F8 (Font)	Underline
2 (Appearance)	
1 (Underline)	

Codes: [UND]
[und]

The Underline feature underscores your text to add emphasis. You can add the underline attribute in either of two ways: by turning on Underline and typing your text, or by highlighting existing text with the Block feature and then selecting Underline. In either case, WordPerfect inserts two codes around the text—one that turns Underline on and one that turns it off.

 Typing Underlined Text

1. Position the cursor where you want to type the underlined text.

   If the Typeover prompt appears, press the Ins key so you will be in Insert mode.

2. Press F8 (Underline) or display the Font menu and select Appearance and then Underline.

   WordPerfect inserts the hidden [UND] and [und] codes and positions the cursor between them. Until you move the cursor past the second code, all text you type will be formatted in underline. The number next to the Pos indicator will be underlined.

3. Type the text you want to underline.

Text appears in a different color or underlined, depending on your monitor and interface. To see underline, you may have to use View Document or print the document.

4. Press Right Arrow or Down Arrow to move the cursor past the Underline Off code, or press F8 (Underline) again.

Text you type after the Underline Off code will not be underlined. The number next to Pos returns to normal, indicating Underline is off at this position.

 ## Underlining Existing Text

1. Move the cursor to the beginning of the text you want to underline.

2. Press Alt-F4 (Block) or select **B**lock from the Edit menu.

This anchors the cursor so you can stretch the highlight over your text.

3. Move the cursor to the end of the block you want to underline.

The entire block should be highlighted.

4. Press F8 (Underline), or display the Font menu and select **A**ppearance and then Underline.

This turns off Block mode, and WordPerfect inserts an [UND] code at the beginning of the block and an [und] code at the end of the block. The text is formatted with Underline.

 ## Removing Underline from a Section of Text

1. Press Alt-F3 (Reveal Codes).

This splits the screen. In the bottom half of the screen the underlined text appears surrounded by [UND] and [und] codes.

2. Move the cursor onto either the [UND] or [und] code, and press the Del key.

This erases both underline codes and removes underline formatting from all text between those codes.

Note: You can also remove underline by placing the cursor at the beginning of the underlined section, just to the right of the [UND] code, pressing Ctrl-F8 (Font), and choosing **3** (**Normal**). The cursor must be positioned properly, or this method will not work. If the cursor is on the [UND] code, it won't work.

 Note: If the underlined text does not appear different from other text on screen, refer to *Colors/Fonts/Attributes* to change the appearance of underlined text. Once you do, you won't have to use Reveal Codes to determine if Underline is on.

Underline Spaces and Tabs

Function: Lets you turn Underline on or off for spaces and tabs, so that when you use Underline, the blank spaces between words or tabs can appear with or without underline.

Keystrokes:

Keyboard	*Mouse*
Shift-F8 (Format)	Layout
4 (Other)	Other
7 (Underline)	Underline
Y or N (for spaces)	Y or N (for spaces)
Y or N (for tabs)	Y or N (for tabs)
F7 (Exit)	Right mouse button

Codes: [Undrln: Spaces]
[Undrln: Tabs]
[Undrln:]

Example:

<u>This is an example of text with underlined spaces.</u>¶
¶
<u>In</u> <u>this</u> <u>example,</u> spaces <u>are</u> <u>not</u> <u>underlined.</u>¶
¶

By default, when you add the underline or double-underline attribute to text, WordPerfect underlines the spaces between words, but does not underline the spaces between tabs. To change either of these default settings, perform the following steps:

Changing the Underline Spaces/Tabs Setting

1. Move the cursor where you want to change the Underline Spaces/Tabs setting.

2. Press Shift-F8 (Format) or display the Layout menu.

   A list of formatting options appears.

3. Select Other (4).

   The Format: Other menu appears.

4. Select 7 (Underline).

   The cursor moves to the Underline Spaces entry.

5. Press Y to underline spaces or N to prevent spaces from being underlined.

   The cursor moves down to the Underline Tabs entry.

6. Press Y to underline tabs or N to prevent tabs from being underlined.

   The cursor moves back down to Selection:.

7. Press F7 (Exit) or click the right mouse button.

   WordPerfect inserts a code at the cursor location and returns you to the Edit screen.

Units of Measure

Function: Lets you choose the unit of measure that will appear on the status line to show the cursor position and/or the one that appears when you change features such as margins, tabs, and line height.

Keystrokes:

Keyboard	*Mouse*
Shift-F1 (Setup)	File
3 (Environment)	Setup
8 (Units of Measure)	Environment
Select unit of measure	Units of Measure
F7 (Exit)	Select unit of measure
	Right mouse button

Example:

```
Setup: Units of Measure
      1 - Display and Entry of Numbers        "
            for Margins, Tabs, etc.
      2 - Status Line Display                 "

Legend:

      " = inches
      i = inches
      c = centimeters
      p = points
      w = 1200ths of an inch
      u = WordPerfect 4.2 Units (Lines/Columns)

Selection: 0
```

Whenever you change margins, tab settings, or other format features that use a measurement, WordPerfect displays the number you type, using inches as the default unit of measure. For example, if you enter 1 for a left margin setting and the unit of measure is inches, WordPerfect sets the margin at 1". WordPerfect also uses inches as its default unit of measure to show the current cursor position on the status line.

To specify a different unit of measure when changing a formatting option, you can enter your measurements followed by one of the characters shown in Table U.1. For example, to specify line height of 36 points, type 36p. WordPerfect automatically converts your entry into the current unit of measure (for example, .5" in this example). If you want to use another unit of measure, such as points, permanently, you can change the default using the Units of Measure option on the Setup: Environment menu.

Table U.1 *Units of measure.*

Selection	Unit of Measure
i or "	Inches (the default setting)
c	Centimeters
p	Points (1/72 of an inch)
w	1/1200 of an inch
u	WordPerfect 4.2 units, which measure vertically by lines and horizontally by columns.

Changing the Default Unit of Measure

1. Press Shift-F1 (Setup), or select Setup from the File menu.

A list of setup options appears.

2. Select Environment (3).

The Setup: Environment menu appears.

3. Select 8 (Units of Measure).

The Setup: Units of Measure menu appears.

4. Select 1 (Display and Entry of Numbers for Margins, Tabs, etc.).

This selection lets you change the unit of measure that will appear when you change formatting features that use a measurement.

5. Type one of the letters shown in Table U.1 for the unit of measure you want to use, and press Enter.

The cursor moves back down to Selection:.

6. Select 2 (Status Line Display).

This selection lets you change the unit of measure that will appear for the Ln and Pos indicators on the status line. For example, if you choose points, the status line will display the position of the cursor in points.

7. Type one of the letters shown in Table U.1 for the unit of measure you want to use for the Pos and Ln indicators on the status line.

8. Press F7 (Exit) or click the right mouse button.

WordPerfect returns you to the Edit screen. The new unit of measure is now in effect, and is saved in the WP{WP}.SET file.

Unlock Document (see *Password Protection*)

Uppercase Text (see *Capitalization, Converting Text*)

User Box (see *Graphics, Create*)

Variables (see *Macro Commands*)

Vertical Lines (see *Graphics, Lines* and *Line Draw*)

Very Large Print (see *Size Attributes*)

View Document

Function: Lets you preview how the document will look when printed and see features that cannot be displayed on the Edit screen, such as graphics.

Keystrokes:

Keyboard	*Mouse*
Shift-F7 (Print)	File
6 (View Document)	Print
1 (100%), **2** (200%), **3** (Full Page), or **4** (Facing Pages)	View Document
	100%, 200%, Full Page, or Facing Pages
F7 (Exit)	Right mouse button

Example:

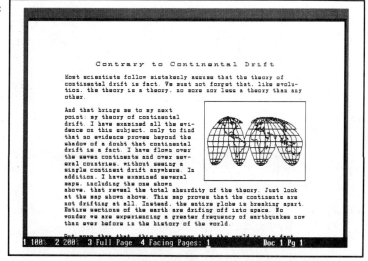

Many of WordPerfect's features cannot be displayed on the Edit screen, so the printed version will differ in most cases. Features such as graphics, font changes, page numbering, headers and footers, and footnotes and endnotes can only be seen in View Document. The View Document screen displays individual pages of your document, showing you the overall layout or enlarging it to 100% so you can read the text and view fonts. You can also choose to view the layout of two facing pages, such as pages 2 and 3. You cannot edit the document when it's displayed on the View screen, but you can scroll through it using the regular cursor movement keys.

 ## Viewing a Document

1. Move the cursor to the page you want to view.

2. Press Shift-F7 (Print) or select **Print** from the **File** menu.

   The main Print menu appears.

3. Select **6** (View Document).

   The View Document screen appears, showing you how the selected page will look when printed. If you see an error message, indicating the printer is not selected, you must go back to the main Print menu and use the Select Printer option to choose a printer. If you see a prompt indicating the graphics screen type is not installed, use the Setup: Display menu to install one. (Refer to *Display Setup*.)

4. Select **1** (100%), **2** (200%), **3** (Full Page), or **4** (Facing Pages) for different views of the current page(s).

   The page is displayed in the selected view. 100% shows it at actual size; 200% enlarges it to twice its size; Full Page shows the entire page; Facing Pages shows even pages on the left and odd pages on the right. Unless you have a page numbered 0, page 1 always appears alone on the right.

5. Press PgUp, PgDn, Screen Up, Screen Down, the arrow keys, Home,Home,Up Arrow, or Home,Home,Down Arrow to move through the document.

   You cannot edit text in View Document.

6. To return to the Edit screen, press F7 (Exit) or click the right mouse button. To return to the Print menu, press the space bar, or click both mouse buttons, or click the middle mouse button.

WordPerfect returns you to the normal Edit screen or to the Print menu.

If you have a graphics card and a color monitor, you can change the way text and graphics are displayed in the View Document screen through the Setup: View Document options. You can have bold text appear as it does in the Edit screen, in the bold color specified using the Colors/Fonts/Attributes feature; make color graphics appear in black and white; or make text appear in black with a white foreground.

 Changing the View Document Options

1. Press Shift-F1 (Setup) or select Setup from the File menu.

A list of setup options appears.

2. Select Display (2).

The Setup: Display menu appears.

3. Select 5 (View Document Options).

The Setup: View Document options menu appears.

4. Select the option you wish to change and press Y to turn the option on or N to turn it off.

5. Press F7 (Exit) or click the right mouse button.

WordPerfect returns you to the normal Edit screen.

Widow/Orphan Protection

Function: Prevents single lines of a paragraph from being isolated on the top or bottom of a page.

Keystrokes:

Keyboard	*Mouse*
Shift-F8 (Format)	Layout
1 (Line)	Line
9 (Widow/Orphan Protection), Y	Widow/Orphan Protection, Y
Protection), Y	Right mouse button
F7 (Exit)	

Code: [W/O On]
[W/O Off]

A widow is the last line of a paragraph that appears by itself at the top of a page because it couldn't fit with the rest of the paragraph on the previous page. An orphan is also a line that has been isolated from a paragraph, but this line appears alone at the end of a page, while the rest of the paragraph appears on the following page. In either case, such an isolated line is usually undesirable.

With WordPerfect's Widow/Orphan protection, you can prevent both of these situations. If you turn on Widow/Orphan protection, an orphan line will be moved to the next page, even if there is room for it on the current page, so it will appear with the rest of its paragraph. Since a widow line cannot be moved back to the previous page (unless you reduce the top or bottom margin), WordPerfect moves the previous line from its paragraph onto the page with the widow, so at least two lines from the paragraph appear together at the top of the page. If the paragraph contains only three lines, they will all be moved to join the widow.

 ### Turning Widow/Orphan Protection On

1. Move the cursor to the position in the document where you want to turn Widow/Orphan Protection on.

   Usually, you turn this feature on at the top of the document.

2. Press Shift-F8 (Format) or display the Layout menu.

   A list of formatting options appears.

3. Select Line (1).

   The Format: Line menu appears.

4. Select 9 (Widow/Orphan Protection) and press Y to turn it on.

5. Press F7 (Exit) or click the right mouse button.

   WordPerfect returns you to the Edit screen and inserts the [W/O On] code at the cursor location. This feature affects the current document only; to change it to Yes for all new documents, use the Initial Codes option on the Setup: Initial Settings menu. (Refer to *Initial Settings*.)

Windows (see also *Switch* and *Tab Ruler*)

Function: Lets you split your screen in two horizontally, so you can view and edit two documents at the same time.

Keystrokes:

Keyboard	*Mouse*
Ctrl-F3 (Screen)	**Edit**
1 (Window)	**Window**
Type number of lines or press Up Arrow or Down Arrow	Type number of lines or press Up Arrow or Down Arrow
Enter	Enter

Example:

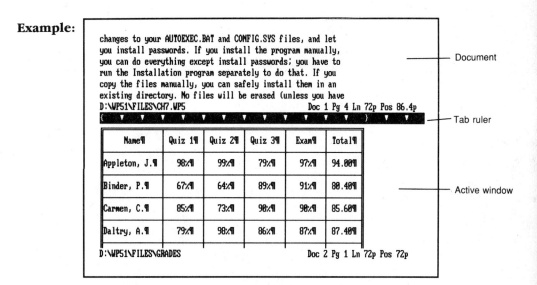

The Windows feature lets you open a second document editing screen and retrieve another document into it or type a new one. WordPerfect's Switch feature also lets you work with two documents at once, but when you switch from one document to another, the active document fills the entire screen. With the Windows feature, you can split your screen horizontally so both documents appear on screen at the same time. The tab ruler divides the two windows. The triangles in the tab ruler point to the active window, where the cursor is currently positioned. You can press Shift-F3 (Switch) to move the cursor from one window to the other. The Windows feature is especially useful for moving or copying blocks of text from one document and inserting them into the other, or when you want to work from an outline.

Splitting Windows

1. Make sure the Reveal Codes screen is not displayed, and press Ctrl-F3 (Screen) or display the Edit menu.

   If Reveal Codes is on, the Windows option has a different function. Instead of splitting the Edit screen in two, it lets you change the size of the Reveal Codes screen.

2. Select Window (**1**).

   WordPerfect prompts you to specify the number of lines you want in the current window.

3. Type the number of lines you want to appear in the current window, or press Up Arrow or Down Arrow to move the tab ruler to the line where you want to divide the screen into two windows.

   Type 11 to split the window in half, giving each window 11 lines of text.

4. Press Enter.

   WordPerfect splits the screen into two separate windows. Each has a separate status line, and you can edit a separate document in each window.

 Tip: To close a window, select the Windows option again, and then type 0 (zero) or use the arrow keys to move the tab ruler off the screen.

Word and Letter Spacing

Function: Gives you control over the spacing between adjacent words and letters.

Keystrokes:

Keyboard	*Mouse*
Shift-F8 (Format)	Layout
4 (Other)	Other
6 (**Printer Functions**)	**Printer Functions**
3 (Word Spacing/Letter Spacing)	Word Spacing/Letter Spacing
Select option for word spacing	Select option for word spacing
Enter change	Enter change
Select option for letter spacing	Select option for letter spacing
Enter change	Enter change
F7 (Exit)	Right mouse button

Code: [Wrd/Ltr Spacing]

Example:

```
Format: Printer Functions
     1 - Kerning                               No
     2 - Printer Command
     3 - Word Spacing                          Optimal              Word
         Letter Spacing                        Optimal              and
                                                                    letter
     4 - Word Spacing Justification Limits                          spacing
         Compressed to (0% - 100%)             60%
         Expanded to (100% - unlimited)        400%
     5 - Baseline Placement for Typesetters    No
         (First baseline at top margin)
     6 - Leading Adjustment
         Primary   - [SRt]                     0"
         Secondary - [HRt]                     0"

Word Spacing: 1 Normal; 2 Optimal; 3 Percent of Optimal; 4 Set Pitch: 2
```

By default, WordPerfect spaces your words and letters according to what the developers at WordPerfect Corporation thought was best for your printer. If you are using a proportionally spaced font, such as Times Roman, WordPerfect sets each space to one-third the point size of the font. If you are using a monospaced font, such as Courier, it uses a space that's equivalent to the pitch, the space allotted each character. If you print a document and find you don't like the spacing, you can change it using one of the following options:

Normal: This setting turns control of word and letter spacing over to your printer. Your printer spaces the words and letters according to the spacing set by the printer manufacturer.

Optimal: This is the default setting: WordPerfect Corporation's opinion of the spacing that looks best.

Percent of Optimal: This option lets you modify WordPerfect's Optimal setting. An entry over 100% increases the space between words and/or letters. An entry under 100% decreases the space. 100% is the same as the Optimal option.

Set Pitch: This option lets you specify a pitch, the number of characters per inch. When you enter a number, WordPerfect converts the entry to a Percent of Optimal setting that will print at this pitch for the font you selected.

 ## Changing Word and Letter Spacing

1. Move the cursor where you want to change the setting.

2. Press Shift-F8 (Format) or display the Layout menu.

   A list of formatting options appears.

3. Select **Other** (4).

   The Format: Other menu appears.

4. Select 6 (**Printer Functions**).

   The Format: Printer Functions menu appears.

5. Select 3 (Word Spacing/Letter Spacing).

   WordPerfect prompts you to select an option for word spacing: Normal, Optimal, Percent of Optimal, or Set Pitch.

6. Select one of the options described above, and enter requested information, if necessary.

   WordPerfect prompts you to select one of the options for letter spacing.

7. Select one of the options described above, and enter requested information, if necessary.

8. Press F7 (Exit) or click the right mouse button.

   WordPerfect returns you to the Edit screen and inserts the [Wrd/Ltr Spacing] code at the cursor location. This change affects the document from the cursor position forward or until you make another change to this feature.

Word Count

Function: Counts the total number of words in a document, without spell checking.

Keystrokes: *Keyboard*   *Mouse*
          Ctrl-F2 (Spell)   **Tools**
          6 (Count)   **Spell**
          any key   **Count**
          F7 (Exit)   **Right mouse button**

Example:

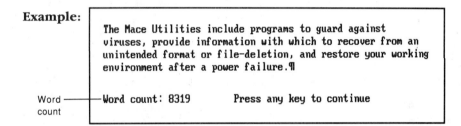

The Mace Utilities include programs to guard against
viruses, provide information with which to recover from an
unintended format or file-deletion, and restore your working
environment after a power failure.¶

Word ——— Word count: 8319   Press any key to continue
count

Writing projects often require you to submit a manuscript of a certain length, measured in words. For example, an advertising brochure may limit you to 750 words. Instead of estimating the word count yourself, you can have WordPerfect count the words for you. When you run the Speller to spell check a page, a highlighted block, or a document, WordPerfect automatically counts the words. If you want to count all the words without spell checking, use the Word Count option on the main Speller menu.

Tip: Although the Word Count feature is not available for counting words in a block of text, you can count them by spell checking the block. After the Speller finishes spell checking the block, it displays the word count.

Counting Words

1. Retrieve the document whose words you want to count.

2. Press Ctrl-F2 (Spell) or select **Sp**e**ll** from the **T**ools menu. — The main Speller menu appears.

3. Select **6** (**Count**). — The Speller counts the words and displays the final count at the bottom of the screen.

4. Press any key to return to the Speller menu.

5. Press F7 (Exit) or click the right mouse button. — This returns you to the normal Edit screen.

 Note: Words that contain hard hyphens, apostrophes, or only numbers (without letters) are not included in the word count.

WordPerfect File Conversion, 4.2 to 5.1

Function: Lets you create a conversion resource file that WordPerfect will use to convert files created in WordPerfect 4.2 into the WordPerfect 5.1 format, upon retrieval of the 4.2 document.

Keystrokes:

Keyboard	*Mouse*
Shift-F10 (Retrieve)	**File**
d:\path\standard.crs	**Retrieve**
Enter	*d:\path*\standard.crs
Alt-F3 (Reveal Codes)	Enter
Modify commands	**Edit**
F7 (Exit), Y	**Reveal Codes**
d:\path\printerfile.crs	Modify commands
Enter, N	**File**
	Exit, Y
	d:\path\printerfile.crs
	Enter, N

Example:

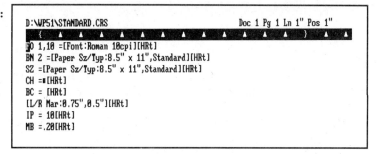

You can convert a file created in WordPerfect 4.2 into the WordPerfect 5.1 format by retrieving the WordPerfect 4.2 document into WordPerfect 5.1, but WordPerfect may not be able to convert all the codes. WordPerfect uses a file called STANDARD.CRS to convert most of the 4.2 formatting codes into 5.1 codes, but it doesn't convert 4.2 codes that have no equivalent in 5.1, such as bin numbers, font/pitch codes, and special characters. Instead, it places a comment box where the code was, indicating what it was in version 4.2, such as: This was Font/Pitch 1,10-On. To convert these codes correctly, you can create a customized .CRS (Conversion Resource) file by modifying the STANDARD.CRS file and saving it under another name. The same .CRS file is used to convert 4.2 documents to and from WordPerfect 5.1.

The .CRS file is a regular WordPerfect file that consists of several lines of 4.2 commands represented by letters and/or numbers and (for some) comments explaining what they did in version 4.2. Each 4.2 command is followed by an equal sign, where you can enter its 5.1 equivalent and a [HRt] code. You can also modify the .CRS file so that it inserts a set of initial formatting codes during the conversion process, useful if you changed default settings in 4.2 and want to retain them here.

To change most of the 4.2 command equivalents listed below, find the 4.2 to 5.1 conversion command (for example, BC), place the cursor after the equal sign, turn on Reveal Codes, and use the WordPerfect 5.1 feature as you normally would to enter the equivalent WordPerfect 5.1 code. For example, to include a margin setting as a beginning code, you would move the cursor after the equal sign next to BC, and then press Shift-F8 (Format), select **1** (Line), and **7** (Margins). Next, enter left and right margin settings and press F7 (Exit). WordPerfect inserts the [L/R Mar] code to the right of the equal sign. Since the codes are visible only in Reveal Codes, you should work with Reveal Codes on when modifying the .CRS file. After editing, make sure each line ends with a Hard Return code, [HRt].

Font On/Off Commands (FO #,# and FF #,#): STANDARD.CRS converts all WordPerfect 4.2 font/pitch codes to comments. To convert them to WordPerfect 5.1 base font codes or size/appearance attributes, you must replace the comment code to the right of the equals sign in the FO (Font On) code with a WordPerfect 5.1 code. If the 4.2 FO code is an open code (does not have a corresponding font-off code, such as italic font would), position the cursor after the equal sign in the FO code, select the 5.1 base font as you normally would, and then erase the [Comment] code and the entire line containing the FF (Font Off) code. If the 4.2 font code is the equivalent of a 5.1 paired code (such as [BOLD][bold]), you must enter the first member of the pair after the 4.2 FO and the second after the FF code. The easiest way to do this is to turn on Block and highlight everything from the equal sign following the FO code through the end of the FF command (after =), and then press the Font key and select the size or appearance attribute. Next, be sure to delete the bold [Comment] codes.

Bin Number Commands (BN#): The STANDARD.CRS file converts WordPerfect 4.2 bin number commands to comments. To convert them to equivalent WordPerfect 5.1 Paper Size/Type commands, you must replace the comment to the right of the equal sign with a [Paper Sz/Typ] code and erase the [Comment] code. Refer to *Paper Size and Type*.

Size Command (SZ): When converting a file from WordPerfect 4.2 to WordPerfect 5.1, WordPerfect assumes you are going to print the document on standard 8 1/2-by-11-inch paper and sets the margins, tabs, and columns accordingly. If you were printing the document on a different paper size in version 4.2 and want to retain it, you must delete the existing 5.1 code that follows the SZ= command and enter a new [Paper Sz/Typ] code, using the regular method on the Format: Page menu. Refer to *Paper Size and Type*. When the file is converted, this Paper Size/Type code will be at the top of the new document.

Extended Character Command (CH): If you used the WordPerfect 4.2 Printer program to change information in a WordPerfect 4.2 character table to display an ASCII character that was not displayable, you can use this command to specify the equivalent character in WordPerfect 5.1, so WordPerfect will convert it correctly. Move the cursor onto the equal sign following CH and type the 4.2 character's font number and character number, separated by a comma. Next, move the cursor to the right of the equal sign and use the Compose key (Ctrl-V) to select the equivalent character from the appropriate WordPerfect 5.1 character set. (Refer to *Compose Key*.)

Beginning Codes Command (BC): This command lets you insert formatting codes at the beginning of the converted document. For example, you can enter margin settings, tab settings, or a header or footer. This is how you can insert any formatting defaults you were using in 4.2 by starting 4.2 with the /s option. The codes you specify here are placed at the top of the converted documents or right after the Paper Size/Type code, if you used SZ.

Initial Pitch Command (IP): If your WordPerfect 4.2 document is set for a pitch other than the standard 10 pitch, use this option to specify that pitch, so WordPerfect can correctly convert settings such as margins, tabs, and indents, which were dependent on pitch. Move the cursor to the number representing the pitch (10), erase it, and then type the pitch you want WordPerfect to use.

Margin Bias Command (MB): Most laser printers have an unprintable region, an area on all four sides where you cannot print text. In WordPerfect 4.2, margin settings included the unprintable region. For example, on a laser printer, a 1" margin setting would actually be 1.2" if the unprintable region was .20". In 5.1, the unprintable region is not used; if you set a 1" margin, a 1" margin will be printed. If you reduced your margins in 4.2 to compensate for the unprintable region, you must add the correction back in during the conversion, or the new margins will differ. For example, if you subtracted .20" from all your margin settings in 4.2, enter .20 here.

 Modifying the STANDARD.CRS File

1. Press Shift-F10 (Retrieve) or select **R**etrieve from the **F**ile menu.

   WordPerfect prompts you to enter the name of the file you want to retrieve.

2. Type the drive and directory where your STANDARD.CRS file is located, followed by the file name, and press Enter.

   For example, type `c:\wp51\standard.crs` and press Enter. You can also use the F5 (List) feature to select the file from a list. If it's in the current directory, just type `standard.crs`.

3. Press Alt-F3 or F11 (Reveal Codes), or select **R**eveal Codes from the **E**dit menu, so you can see the codes as you edit them.

   The Reveal Codes screen appears.

4. Modify the conversion commands as explained above.

   Make sure each line ends in a [HRt] code, and that you've deleted the [Comment] codes from any FO, FF, or BN commands you've changed.

5. Press F7 (Exit) or select Exit from the File menu; then press Y.

WordPerfect asks if you want to save the file as STANDARD.CRS. If you use only one printer, you can use the same name. If not, use the printer file name, with the .CRS extension, as described in steps 6 and 7.

6. Type a path to the directory where you want to store the new .CRS file.

You must store the new .CRS file in the same directory where your printer files are stored, in your default directory, or in the same directory as WP.EXE. For example, type `c:\wp51\`.

7. Type the base name of your printer (.PRS) file followed by the .CRS extension and press Enter.

For example, if your printer file is called HPLASERII.PRS, type `hplaserii.crs` and press Enter. WordPerfect then asks if you want to exit WordPerfect.

8. Press N if you want to continue using WordPerfect, or Y to exit.

You can now retrieve any WordPerfect 4.2 document, and WordPerfect will use your new .CRS file to convert all codes as specified.

WordPerfect File Conversion, 5.1 to 4.2
(see also *Text Out*)

Function: Lets you create a conversion resource file that WordPerfect will use to convert files created in WordPerfect 5.1 into the WordPerfect 4.2 format.

Keystrokes:

Keyboard	*Mouse*
Shift-F10 (Retrieve)	File
d:\path\standard.crs	Retrieve
Enter	*d:\path*\standard.crs
Alt-F3 (Reveal Codes)	Enter
Modify commands	Edit
F7 (Exit), Y	Reveal Codes
d:\path\printerfile.crs	Modify commands
Enter, N	File
	Exit, Y
	d:\path\printerfile.crs
	Enter, N

Example:

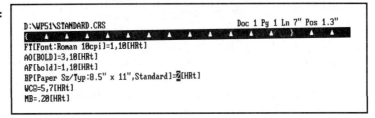

```
D:\WP51\STANDARD.CRS                                          Doc 1 Pg 1 Ln 7" Pos 1.3"
{   ▲   ▲   ▲   ▲   ▲   ▲   ▲   ▲   ▲   ▲   ▲ }  ▲   ▲
FT[Font:Roman 10cpi]=1,10[HRt]
AO[BOLD]=3,10[HRt]
AF[bold]=1,10[HRt]
BP[Paper Sz/Typ:8.5" x 11",Standard]=2[HRt]
WC@=5,7[HRt]
MB=.20[HRt]
```

You can convert a file created in WordPerfect 5.1 into the WordPerfect 4.2 format by saving the file as a WordPerfect 4.2 document using the Save as WordPerfect 4.2 option on the Text Out menu (refer to *Text Out*). When you do, WordPerfect uses a file called STANDARD.CRS to convert most of the 5.1 formatting codes into 4.2 codes. However, WordPerfect may not be able to convert all the codes correctly, such as fonts, attributes, and Paper Size/Type codes. To convert these codes to 4.2 equivalents, you can create a customized .CRS (Conversion Resource) file by modifying the STANDARD.CRS file and saving it under another name. (If you use only one printer, you can retain the name STANDARD.CRS.) WordPerfect uses the same .CRS file to convert 4.2 files into 5.1.

The .CRS file is a regular WordPerfect file that features a line for each 5.1 command that must be converted. The commands are represented by letters and/or numbers and (for some) comments explaining what the code does in version 5.1. Each 5.1 command is followed by an equal sign. To change an equivalent, you must enter the 5.1 code right before the equal sign and then enter the 4.2 equivalent after the equal sign. The following 5.1 commands can be converted into 4.2 equivalents:

Font Commands (FT): STANDARD.CRS converts WordPerfect 5.1 Base Font codes to WordPerfect 4.2 font/pitch codes. To convert them correctly, place the cursor to the immediate right of FT (you can use the Search feature to find FT). Select the WordPerfect 5.1 base font as you normally would, using the Base Font option on the Font menu or key. Next, move the cursor past the equal sign and enter the WordPerfect 4.2 font/pitch number, for example, 3,13. If the font is proportionally spaced, such as Times Roman, type an asterisk (*) after the pitch, as in 3,13*. You can enter as many FT commands as necessary, by typing FT and then using the procedure described above to enter the 5.1 codes and 4.2 equivalents. Make sure each line containing an FT command ends in a [HRt] code.

Attribute On/Off Commands (AO and AF): STANDARD.CRS converts WordPerfect 5.1 attribute codes, such as bold and italic, to WordPerfect 4.2 font/pitch codes. To convert them for specific 4.2 font/pitch codes, turn on Block after AO (Attribute On) and move the cursor to stretch the highlight from the immediate right of the AO command to the immediate right of the AF (Attribute Off) command. Next, select the 5.1 attribute as you normally would, using the Font key or menu, or Bold or Underline for those attributes. This inserts the on/off attribute codes, such as [BOLD][bold]; the On code belongs right after AO, and the Off code right after AF. Next, enter the equivalent 4.2 font/pitch commands after the equal signs; on the AO line, enter the 4.2 font/pitch command for this attribute. On the AF line, select the 4.2 font/pitch command you want to use after the attribute is turned off. When you're finished, your entry should resemble the following:

```
AO[UND]=5,2[HRt]
AF[und]=2,10[HRt]
```

Bin Paper Command (BP): The STANDARD.CRS file converts WordPerfect 5.1 Paper Size/Type codes into WordPerfect 4.2 bin number commands. To convert them correctly, delete the existing [Paper Sz/Typ] code to the right of BP, and insert a code for the paper size and type you want to convert from WordPerfect 5.1 to 4.2. Refer to *Paper Size and Type*. Next, move the cursor to the right of the equal sign and enter a WordPerfect 4.2 bin number. When you finish, the command will be similar to the following:

```
BP[Paper Sz/Typ:9.5"x4",Envelope]=2[HRt]
```

WordPerfect Character Command (WC): Converts WordPerfect 5.1 characters into WordPerfect 4.2 extended characters. Move the cursor to the right of WC and use the Compose key to select a WordPerfect 5.1 character (refer to *Compose Key*). Next, move the cursor to the right of the equal sign, press the space bar, and type the equivalent 4.2 character's font number and character number, separated by a comma.

Margin Bias Command (MB): Most laser printers have an unprintable region, an area on all four sides where you cannot print text. In WordPerfect 4.2, margin settings on most laser printers are measured from the unprintable region. For example, setting a 1" margin on a printer with a .20" unprintable region would actually create a 1.2" margin. In 5.1, the unprintable region is taken into account in the printer file, not in the margin setting, so a 1" margin is printed as a 1" margin. If you want your 5.1 margins to convert to equivalent 4.2 margins, you must add a correction for the unprintable region during the conversion. For example, if you have a .20" unprintable region, enter .20 after the equal sign. If you've already specified this figure for the WordPerfect 4.2 to 5.1 conversion, you don't need to change it again.

To change most of the command equivalents mentioned above, find the 5.1 Conversion command, such as WC, place the cursor before the equal sign, and use the WordPerfect 5.1 feature as you normally would to enter the formatting code you want to convert. Next, place the cursor after the equal sign and type the WordPerfect 4.2 equivalent for the feature. If you want to convert additional codes, such as eight 5.1 font codes, just start on a new line, type the command, such as `FT=`, and then follow the procedure described above to enter the 5.1 and 4.2 codes.

 ### Modifying the STANDARD.CRS File

1. Press Shift-F10 (Retrieve) or select **Retrieve** from the File menu.

   WordPerfect prompts you to enter the name of the file you want to retrieve.

2. Type the drive and directory where your STANDARD.CRS file is located, followed by the file name, and press Enter.

   For example, type `c:\wp51\standard.crs` and press Enter. You can also use the F5 (List) feature to select the file from a list. If it's in the current directory, just type `standard.crs`.

3. Press Alt-F3 or F11 (Reveal Codes), or select **Reveal Codes** from the Edit menu, so you can see the codes as you edit them.

   The Reveal Codes screen appears.

4. Modify the conversion commands as explained above.

   Be sure each line ends in a [HRt] code and that you've deleted the [Comment] codes.

5. Press F7 (Exit) or select Exit from the File menu, and then press Y.

   WordPerfect asks if you want to save the file as STANDARD.CRS. If you use only one printer, you can answer Yes and proceed to save it. If not, continue with steps 6 and 7.

6. Type a path to the directory where you want to store the new .CRS file, if it differs from the current directory.

   You must store the new .CRS file in the same directory where your printer files are stored, in your default directory, or in the same directory as WP.EXE. For example, type `c:\wp51\`.

7. Type the base name of your printer (.PRS) file followed by the .CRS extension and press Enter.

For example, if your printer file is called HPLASERII.PRS, type `hplaserii.crs` and press Enter. WordPerfect then asks if you want to exit WordPerfect.

8. Press N if you want to continue using WordPerfect, or press Y to exit.

WordPerfect Tutorial

Function: Leads you through on-screen lessons that teach you how to use many of WordPerfect 5.1's features.

Keystrokes:

Hard Disk
Exit WordPerfect
path=d:\wp51;d:\wp51
learn
tutor
Enter

Floppy Disk
Exit WordPerfect
path=a:\;b:
tutor
Enter

Example:

```
WordPerfect Beginning Lessons
_____

┌─────────────────────┐   ┌──────────────────────────────────┐
│ ▐Introduction▌       │   │        How to use the tutor      │
│ Lesson 1             │   │                                  │
│                      │   │ Start                            │
│ Lesson 2             │   │ Move the highlighted bar in the  │
│                      │   │ menu to any lesson and press the │
│ Lesson 3             │   │ Enter key (the █ and             │
│                      │   │ █ keys on the right side of the  │
│ Lesson 4             │   │ keyboard move the highlighted    │
│                      │   │ bar).                            │
│ Lesson 5             │   │                                  │
│                      │   │ Exit                             │
│ Lesson 6             │   │ Highlight EXIT at the bottom of  │
│                      │   │ the menu then press Enter ◄┘.     │
│ Advanced Lessons     │   │                                  │
│                      │   │ Lesson Summary and Estimated Time│
│ EXIT                 │   │ Highlight a lesson and press █.  │
│                      │   │                                  │
│                      │   │ Discontinue                      │
│                      │   │ Press █ anytime during a lesson  │
│                      │   │ to return to this menu.          │
└─────────────────────┘   └──────────────────────────────────┘
```

Note: Before you can run the On-Line Tutorial, you must have installed the Learning files in your WP51 directory or in the WP51\LEARN directory. If you did not install the Learning files, start the installation program now, and perform that part of the installation. If you did install them, WordPerfect placed them in a subdirectory called LEARN, unless you told it to use a different directory.

Starting the On-Line Tutorial from a Hard Disk

1. Exit any program you may be working in.

You must start the Tutorial from the DOS prompt.

2. Type `path` and press Enter.

DOS displays the path statement that's in your AUTOEXEC.BAT file, if there is one. This statement tells DOS where to search for executable files used to run a program, such as TUTOR.COM.

3. If the path statement includes the directories that contain the WP.EXE and WP.FIL files and the Learning files, such as TUTOR.COM, skip to step 5.

Your WP.EXE file should be in the C:\WP51 directory unless you chose to install the WordPerfect program files in another directory. Your learning files should be in C:\WP51\LEARN. If you asked WordPerfect to update your AUTOEXEC.BAT file during installation, these two directories should be in the path statement.

4. If the required directories are not in the path statement, type a new path statement to include those directories and press Enter.

For example, type `path=c:\wp51;c:\wp51\learn` and press Enter.

5. Type `tutor` to start the tutorial.

DOS loads the tutorial and prompts you to enter your name.

6. Enter your name, up to eight characters.

The Tutorial main menu appears, presenting a list of lessons from which to choose.

7. Highlight a lesson and press F3 (Help) for a brief description of the lesson.

A short explanation of the lesson's topics appears, including an estimated time for completing the lesson.

8. Highlight the lesson you want to run and press Enter to start it.

WordPerfect leads you step-by-step through the lesson with a series of on-screen prompts.

9. Press F3 (Help) at any time during the lesson to return to the Tutorial main menu.

10. Select another lesson, or highlight EXIT and press Enter to quit the Tutorial.

Starting the On-Line Tutorial from a Floppy Disk

1. Exit any program you may be working in.

You must start the Tutorial from the DOS prompt.

2. Insert the WordPerfect 1 disk into drive A and the WordPerfect Learning disk into drive B.

3. Type path=a:\;b:\ and press Enter.

This path statement tells DOS where to look for executable files, such as TUTOR.COM. Without the correct path command, WordPerfect cannot run the On-Line Tutorial.

4. Type tutor and press Enter to start the tutorial.

DOS starts to load the tutorial and then prompts you to load the WordPerfect 2 disk.

5. When prompted, replace the WordPerfect 1 disk in drive A with the WordPerfect 2 disk.

DOS loads the tutorial and prompts you to enter your name.

6. Enter your name, up to eight characters.

The Tutorial main menu appears, presenting a list of lessons from which to choose.

7. Highlight a lesson and press F3 (Help) for an explanation of the lesson.

A brief description of the lesson appears, including an estimated time for completing the lesson.

8. Highlight the lesson you want to run and press Enter to start it.

WordPerfect leads you step-by-step through the lesson with a series of on-screen prompts.

9. Press F3 (Help) at any time during the lesson to return to the Tutorial main menu.

10. Select another lesson or highlight EXIT and press Enter to quit the Tutorial.

4. Select **Yes**.

The main Installation menu appears, as shown in Figure A.1.

```
Installation

    1 - Basic        Perform a standard installation to E:\WP.

    2 - Custom       Perform a customized installation.  (User selected
                     directories.)

    3 - Network      Perform a customized installation onto a network.
                     (To be performed by the network supervisor.)

    4 - Printer      Install a new or updated Printer (.ALL) File.

    5 - Update       Install WordPerfect 5.1 Interim Release program file(s).
                     (Used for updating existing WordPerfect 5.1 software.)

    6 - Copy Disks   Install every file from an installation diskette to a
                     specified location.  (Useful for installing all the
                     Printer (.ALL) Files.)

    7 - Minimal      Install only the files for a standard configuration.


Selection: 4
```

Figure A.1 *WordPerfect's main Installation menu. (Your prompt will probably read C:\WP51, instead of E:\WP.)*

The first time you install WordPerfect, you can use either the **Basic** (1) or the **Custom** option (2) on this menu. Both these options let you install all the WordPerfect Program files, including printer files. If you are using a network, you should use the Network (3) option (although the procedure is not described in this appendix).

The **Printer** option (4) is useful if you have installed WordPerfect previously, and now want to add a new printer or update your existing printer definition file.

The Update option (5) is used for installing interim release files, updates that WordPerfect occasionally provides if you sign up for their update program, or have a problem with the version you are using.

You can use the Minimal option (7) to install only these files: the WordPerfect program, the Speller and Thesaurus, the Help file, your printer, and the .DRS file (which you need). It will also perform a check of your CONFIG.SYS and AUTOEXEC.BAT files (as described in the next section). Use the Minimal option if your computer has a limited amount of remaining disk space. Note that this option was added to the WordPerfect 5.1 program in the version that was released on 6/29/90; if you have an earlier version, it will not be available, and won't appear as an option.

The **Basic** option assumes that you want to put all of the WordPerfect Program files on drive C, in a directory named *\WP51*. (If WP51 has already been installed on your computer, it will probably name the drive and subdirectory containing WordPerfect 5.1, instead of suggesting C:\WP51.) The only exception is the group of learning files, which will be installed in C:\WP51\LEARN. If these directories (C:\WP51 and C:\WP51\LEARN) do not already exist, the Installation program will create them for you.

If you want to install WordPerfect on a different drive or subdirectory, use the Custom Installation option. Also, you may want to install files such as macros, styles, graphics, timed backup files, dictionaries, and printer definitions into their own subdirectories (of the main WordPerfect directory). If you would prefer to install the program this way, use the installation procedure described later in the section "Custom Installation."

How WordPerfect's Installation Program Works

The Installation program will ask you if you want to install groups of files, such as Utility files, Learning files, Help files, Speller files, Thesaurus files, Graphic Drivers, and the WordPerfect Program files. Many of these groups are optional. As you select groups, WordPerfect installs the corresponding program files. The instructions in this section (and prompts on the various installation screens) will indicate which files are optional and which are required.

If you choose to install a group of files such as the Utility files, WordPerfect will install all related files; you cannot be selective. However, after installation is complete and you start WordPerfect, you can erase any files you don't need or won't be using (such as graphic drivers for monitors you don't own). If you choose not to install a group of files, you can always run the INSTALL program another time to install the files. Appendix Q in the WordPerfect manual lists the files that belong to each installation group.

The instructions below vary slightly if you are using 3.5" diskettes (with 720K capacity). Since each diskette holds twice as much information as a 5.25" diskette (with 360K capacity), you won't be switching disks as frequently. Just follow the prompts on the installation screens, which will always tell you which disks to insert; since they are clearly labeled, you should have no problems distinguishing them.

You can cancel installation any time by pressing the Cancel key, F1. If you are several levels down in the installation menus, you may have to press F1 several times, until you return to the DOS prompt, A> or B>.

Basic Installation

Basic Installation installs the WordPerfect program on drive C, in a directory named *WP51*. This section assumes you are installing WordPerfect for the first time, and do not have another copy of WordPerfect on your hard disk. If you do have another copy and your AUTOEXEC.BAT file contains a PATH statement naming that

WordPerfect directory, the Installation program will detect this fact and try to install WordPerfect in the same directory as your earlier version. If this happens, you should not use Basic Installation unless you want it to erase the earlier version. Instead, use the Custom Installation procedure, described in a later section, "Custom Installation."

To use Basic Installation:

1. Select **Basic (1)** from the main Installation menu shown in Figure A.1. This prompt appears:

   ```
   Do you want to install the Utility Files? Yes (No)
   ```

   The files will be installed to C:\WP51\ The last two lines on the screen indicate that this group (the Utility files) includes the Conversion files, Speller Utility file, and the Installation program itself. The Conversion files let you convert text documents and graphics to and from other program formats. Other Utility files that will be installed if you select Yes are the CHARACTR.DOC file, which is discussed in Part Three, "Command Reference," under *Compose Key*; the CURSOR.COM program, which you can use to change the size and shape of the cursor (as detailed in "Command Reference"; and GRAB.COM, which you can use to create files from graphics screens (such as View Document).

   If you are low on disk space, you do not have to install these files; they are not necessary to run WordPerfect. However, if you do have the space, you should go ahead and select Yes to install them.

2. If you have enough disk capacity, select **Yes** to install the Utility files. Otherwise, select **No**.

   As the files are being copied to the hard disk, prompts appear indicating their names, such as

   ```
   Installing: CONVERT.EXE
   ```

   After a few moments you will see this prompt:

   ```
   Insert the Install/Learn/Utilities 2 master diskette
   into A:\
   ```

   Remove the Install/Learn/Utilities 1 disk from drive A, and replace it with the one labeled *Install/Learn/Utilities 2*.

   After the Utility files have all been installed, or if you selected No in step 2, this prompt will appear:

   ```
   Do you want to install the Learning Files? Yes (No)
   ```

3. If you will want to use the WordPerfect tutorial or Workbook lessons, select **Yes** to install the Learning files. Otherwise, select **No**.

After the Learning files are installed, or if you selected No in step 3, this prompt appears:

Do you want to install the Help File? Yes (No)

WordPerfect's on-line help is very useful, even if you are not a beginner. Chapter 2 describes the Help menus in more detail. If disk space is severely limited, you can forgo installing the Help file by selecting No.

4. If you have enough disk capacity, select **Yes** to install the Help file. If not, select **No**.

    After the Help file is installed (or if you selected No) this prompt appears:

    Do you want to install the Keyboard Files? Yes (No)

    The Keyboard files include several useful keyboard layouts that WordPerfect has designed for your use. See Part Three, "Command Reference," for more information about keyboard layout. Installation of these files is optional, although you'll need them for some of the Workbook lessons.

 Note: Some IBM-compatible computers cannot use Keyboard files and require that WordPerfect be started using the /nk start-up option that disables the keyboard remapping feature.

5. Select **Yes** if you want to install the Keyboard files, or **No** if you do not. After the Keyboard files are installed (or if you selected No), this prompt appears:

    Do you want to install the Style Library? Yes (No)

    The Style Library, *LIBRARY.STY*, is a file with several sample styles in it, including outline styles. For more information about styles, see Chapter 15. Installation of the Style Library is optional.

6. Select **Yes** if you want to install the Style Library, or **No** if you do not. After it is installed (or if you selected No), this prompt appears:

    Do you want to install the Printer Test File? Yes (No)

    You can use this file to test your printer's capabilities in WordPerfect. As the prompt indicates, it is recommended if you are a new user or are installing a new printer.

7. Select **Yes**.

    If a prompt appears asking you to insert the Install/Learn/Utilities 2 master diskette into drive A, remove the disk currently in drive A, insert the Install/Learn/Utilities 2 disk, and then press Enter.

After the Printer Test file is installed, this prompt appears:

```
Do you want to install the WordPerfect Program? Yes (No)
```

As the message below it indicates, the Program files are necessary to run WordPerfect. If this is the first time you are installing WordPerfect, you must select Yes to install them.

8. Select **Yes** to install the WordPerfect Program files. A prompt will appear, asking you to insert the Program 1 master diskette into A. Remove the disk from drive A and replace it with the Program 1 master diskette; then press Enter. When asked to insert the Program 2 master diskette, remove the Program 1 disk from drive A, insert the Program 2 disk, and press Enter.

   After the Program files are installed, you are asked:

```
Do you want to install the Speller?  Yes (No)
```

9. Select **Yes** to install the spell checker files, and the file needed for automatic hyphenation. You will be prompted to insert the Spell/Thesaurus 1 master diskette into A. Remove the Program 2 diskette, replace it with the Spell/Thesaurus 1 disk, and press Enter.

   After the Speller files are installed, this prompt appears:

```
Do you want to install the Thesaurus? Yes (No)
```

   The thesaurus provides on-line synonyms and antonyms, and is covered in Chapter 6.

10. Select **Yes** to install the Thesaurus. You will be prompted to insert the Spell/Thesaurus 2 disk into drive A. Remove the Spell/Thesaurus 1 disk from drive A, replace it with the Spell/Thesaurus 2 disk, and press Enter.

    After the Thesaurus file is installed, you are asked:

```
Do you want to install the PTR Program? Yes (No)
```

    This is a special program that runs separately from WordPerfect. If you are an advanced user, you may want to use it to create or modify a printer definition file (printer resource file), or to convert an existing WordPerfect 5.0 printer resource file for use with WordPerfect 5.1. However, it is not necessary for printer installation (since most printers are fully supported by WordPerfect).

11. Select **Yes** if you want to install the PTR program, or **No** if you do not.

    If you selected Yes, you will be prompted to insert the PTR Program/ Graphics 1 disk into drive A. Remove the Spell/Thesaurus 2 disk from drive A, replace it with the PTR Program/Graphics 1 disk, and press Enter.

This prompt appears next:

```
Do you want to install the Graphic Drivers? Yes (No)
```

If you have one of several special video interface cards for your monitor, such as Hercules InColor, Paradise VGA Plus, Video 7 VGA, ATI VIP VGA, or MDA Genius 1 or 2, you may need to install these graphic drivers. When you start WordPerfect, it will automatically detect the card in your computer and choose the correct graphic driver (also called a *video resource file,* or *VRS file*) for it.

You may also need one of the other files in this group, WP.DRS, to print special characters, such as the foreign language characters, typographic symbols like bullets, the section sign and the paragraph sign, and hundreds of others in the WordPerfect Character Sets. If your printer cannot print one of these characters, WordPerfect can usually force the printer to print them as graphical characters if you install this file (assuming your printer is capable of printing graphics, as are most laser printers and dot-matrix printers).

Unless your disk space is very limited, or you will not need to print these special characters, you should select Yes.

12. Select **Yes** to install the Graphic Drivers, or **No** if your disk space is limited.

    If you did not select Yes in step 11, you will be prompted to insert the PTR Program/Graphics 1 disk into drive A. Remove the Spell/Thesaurus 2 disk from drive A, replace it with the PTR Program/Graphics 1 disk, and press Enter.

    After a minute, you will be asked to insert the PTR Program/Graphics 2 disk into drive A. Remove the other disk, insert the PTR Program/Graphics 2 disk, and press Enter.

    After the files are installed, you will be asked:

    ```
    Do you want to install the Small .DRS File? Yes (No)
    ```

    This is a smaller version of WP.DRS that is useful if you are installing WordPerfect on two 720K or larger floppy disks. It is not necessary to install it if you selected Yes in step 12 to install the graphic drivers.

13. If you need to install the Small.DRS file, select **Yes**; otherwise, select **No**. Next, you are asked:

    ```
    Do you want to Install the Graphic Images? Yes (No)
    ```

The graphic images are 30 clip-art pictures that you can place in your WordPerfect documents, using options on the Graphics menu. They are shown in Appendix B of the WordPerfect manual. For more information about how to use them, see Chapter 14.

14. If you want to install the Graphic Images files, select **Yes**; otherwise, select **No**.

    The Installation program will then check the CONFIG.SYS file in your root directory to make sure it allows for 20 files, the number required to use WordPerfect. You should see a prompt like this at the top of the screen:

    ```
    Check C:\CONFIG.SYS file
    ```

    followed by information telling you how many files yours will allow, if you have one.

    CONFIG.SYS is a special file that the operating system (DOS) uses to configure your system each time you start your computer. Unless this file includes a statement that allows WordPerfect to open at least 20 files, you will not be able to run WordPerfect. The Installation program can increase the files in CONFIG.SYS to make it possible to run WordPerfect.

15. There are three possible prompts and responses:

    a) If your CONFIG.SYS file already includes a statement allowing at least 20 files to be opened, you will see this message:

    ```
    No changes are necessary
    ```

    and a prompt telling you to press any key to continue. If so, press Enter and continue to step 16.

    b) If WordPerfect finds that your CONFIG.SYS file allows fewer than 20 files to be open, you will be asked:

    ```
    Would you like to have it changed? Yes (No)
    ```

    Since this is necessary to run WordPerfect, select **Yes** to increase the number of files to 20; then press Enter and continue to step 16.

    c) If the program does not find a CONFIG.SYS file at all, you will be asked if you want to create it. Select **Yes** in response to this prompt, and the prompt that follows it (which asks if you want the *Files=20* command added to your CONFIG.SYS file). When prompted, press any key to continue (with step 16).

    The Installation program then checks the AUTOEXEC.BAT file in the root directory of your computer, and this prompt appears at the top of the screen:

`Check C:\AUTOEXEC.BAT file`

AUTOEXEC.BAT is a series of start-up commands, in DOS text file format, that DOS automatically runs when you start your computer. Although it is an optional file, most computers have been set up to use one. One of these commands is a PATH command, which tells DOS where to look for the special command files that you type to start a program such as WordPerfect. If you add the name of the WordPerfect directory to the PATH command inside this file, you can start WordPerfect from any directory or subdirectory.

16. Once again, there are three possible prompts and responses:

   a) If you have a PATH statement in your AUTOEXEC.BAT file and it does not include the name of your WordPerfect directory, you'll be asked if you want to add it (add the WordPerfect directory to the PATH statement). Advanced users may prefer to have WordPerfect start from a batch file and/or from a menu such as the WordPerfect Office Shell menu. Menus or batch files can make it easier to take advantage of WordPerfect's start-up options.

   If you want to add the WordPerfect directory to your PATH statement, select **Yes** in response to this prompt. The INSTALL program will then add the path and name of your WordPerfect directory (C:\WP51 if you are performing a basic installation) to the PATH statement in your AUTOEXEC.BAT file.

   b) If you have an AUTOEXEC.BAT file but it does not include a PATH statement, WordPerfect will offer to create the PATH command and add your WordPerfect directory name to the path. If so, select **Yes**.

   One caveat: The PATH statement will become the last statement in your AUTOEXEC.BAT file. If your AUTOEXEC.BAT file runs a menu or runs an interactive program before it reaches the PATH statement at the end of the file, your new PATH statement will be ineffective until the end of the batch file is allowed to run. If you are unsure, you can still select **Yes**; the worst that can happen is that you won't be able to start WordPerfect from any directory or subdirectory on your hard disk.

 Note: Manual alteration of the AUTOEXEC.BAT file is best left to users with an understanding of DOS commands and DOS text files (also called *ASCII files*).

c) If you don't have an AUTOEXEC.BAT file in the root directory of your hard disk, you will be asked if you want it created. Select **Yes** if you do, and then select **Yes** in response to the next prompt that appears. Otherwise, select **No**.

Next, WordPerfect will prompt you to insert the Printer master diskette, so you can install your printer. To continue, skip to the second paragraph of the "Printer Installation" section.

If you answered Yes to the prompt that appeared in step 15b or 15c, you'll have a few extra steps to perform before you can use the "Printer Installation" section of the INSTALL program. This happens because WordPerfect requires your CONFIG.SYS file to have a statement that allows WordPerfect to open at least 20 files. Because the new CONFIG.SYS file created in step 15b or 15c does not take effect until you restart the computer, the installation program will instruct you to do so (restart the computer) and run the INSTALL program again. The second time you run Install, choose the Custom Installation, and resume with the CHECK AUTOEXEC.BAT and CONFIG.SYS option; then choose menu item 4, Printer.

Printer Installation

Printer installation creates a printer resource file for each printer you install; each of these files ends in the extension *PRS*. These .PRS files, sometimes referred to as *printer drivers*, are automatically extracted (during WordPerfect installation) from a larger file that contains the information that WordPerfect needs to create drivers for a group of related printers. The larger files are called .ALL files because they end with the extension *ALL*.

The best time to install your printer is when you install WordPerfect. However, you can return to the INSTALL program anytime to perform this task, or if you want to install a different printer later. To return to the INSTALL program to install a printer, choose **Printer** (4) from the main Installation menu shown in Figure A.1 and then continue with the following steps:

This prompt will appear:

```
Insert the Printer master diskette into A:
```

A printer master diskette is either the Printer 1 disk or a Printer disk numbered 5 or greater.

1. Insert the Printer 1 master disk and press Enter.

   A list of printers appears. You can use Name Search to locate your printer name, if it is in this list.

2. Type N to use Name Search; then begin typing the name of the printer for which you are searching (they are listed alphabetically). Alternatively, you can use the PgDn and PgUp keys to find the screen that includes the

printer you want to install. When you find the screen that has a printer you wish to install, enter the number that appears next to the printer (left of the printer name).

 Note: If your printer is not on the list, phone WordPerfect Corporation to see if they have a printer definition file for your printer. Although WordPerfect supports hundreds of printers, the program only includes printer disks containing definitions for the most commonly used printers. If your printer is not among them, the company will send you the file, free of charge (or for a small shipping fee), if they have one for your printer.

The next prompt will ask if you want to select that printer. For example, if you selected the HP LaserJet II printer, you'll see:

```
Select printer HP LaserJet Series II Yes (No)
```

3. If the prompt names the printer you want to install, select **Yes**. (If you type N, you will return to the printer list, and can select a different printer.)

You will then be notified that an .ALL file is being copied to your hard disk. Files with an .ALL extension contain the definitions for many printers, including the one you selected. You may also be asked to insert another printer master disk into drive A, such as Printer 2 or Printer 3, if WordPerfect needs to install files from that disk. Follow the prompts on the screen.

The next prompt asks:

```
Do you want to install another printer? No (Yes)
```

4. If you do wish to install a second printer, select **Yes** and repeat the previous two steps to select your printer name from the list. You will be asked to reinsert the original Printer master diskette if you switched them in the previous step. If you don't want to install another printer, just select **No**.

Note that you can run the INSTALL program at any time to select additional printers to install.

5. You will then be asked to enter your customer registration number, so it can be displayed whenever you view the main Help menu. This is useful when you call WordPerfect's customer support line, or call to obtain a program update, since they will ask you for your registration number. If you have the number, type it and press Enter; otherwise, just press Enter.

WordPerfect will then create a printer resource file (a file that ends with
.PRS) for the printer(s) you have chosen. Chapter 13 provides more
information about this file.

6. When you see the `Press any key to exit` prompt, press Enter (or any
   key) to exit the Installation program. You should see a DOS prompt such
   as A> or B>.

If the INSTALL program changed your AUTOEXEC.BAT or CONFIG.SYS file,
restart your computer before starting WordPerfect, by pressing the CTRL, ALT, and
DEL keys simultaneously (or the Reset button, if you have one). Otherwise, you can
start the WordPerfect program immediately (Chapter 1 provides complete instructions for starting WordPerfect).

After you have installed and started WordPerfect, you can modify your printer
resource files as follows:

- You can add Paper Definitions—such as labels or envelopes—using the
  Paper Size/Type option on the Format: Page menu.

- You can edit the printer resource files to indicate which port your printer
  is connected to on the computer; which font cartridges or soft fonts you
  have purchased; and the name of the default font (Initial Base Font) you
  want to use. To make any of these changes, display the main Print menu,
  choose the Select Printer option, and then choose Edit.

See Chapter 13, "Printing and Fonts," for more details about these features.

Advanced users may want to further customize the printer resource files with
the printer program included with WordPerfect, PTR.EXE. For example, you can
use PTR.EXE to change features such as the size and appearance attributes for a
particular base font, as described in Part Three, "Command Reference," under
Automatic Font Changes.

 Tip: Installation of certain soft font programs, such as Bitstream
Fontware, automatically changes the printer resource file for your
printer.

Custom Installation

Custom Installation is useful if you want to create separate directories for graphics
files, keyboard and macro files, thesaurus and spell checking files, printer and PTR
program files, style files, tutorial files, and documents (files you create and save

while using WordPerfect). If you are installing WordPerfect on a drive other than C, or in a directory other than WP51, you must use the Custom Installation procedure.

For example, if you designate a graphics directory, the Installation program will copy all the graphics files (WPG files) to that directory, instead of to the main directory where WordPerfect is located (usually C:\WP51). The Installation program will even create the graphics directory, if it doesn't already exist. One advantage of installing graphics files in a separate directory is that when you are creating a graphic such as a Figure box and you press List (F5) to retrieve one of the graphics files into it, the resulting screen will display only the graphics files.

Custom Installation will place each type of file (speller, graphics, macros, etc.) into the directories you specify. After you start WordPerfect, you can use the Setup: Location of Files menu to view the list of directories and change them if you wish. If you were to do this after performing a basic installation, you would have to create the directories through the List Files menu, move all the appropriate files into the new directories, and then use the Setup: Location of Files menu to notify WordPerfect where you have placed them.

To use the Custom Installation program:

1. Start the Installation program, as described earlier in the section "Program Installation on a Hard Disk."

2. From the main Installation menu, shown in Figure A.1, select the second option, Custom. The Custom Installation menu will appear, as shown in Figure A.2.

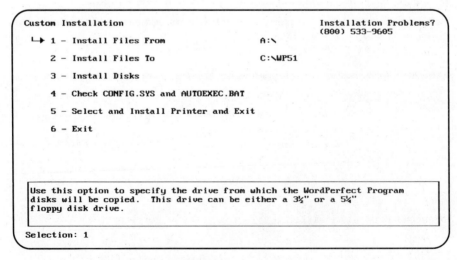

Figure A.2   The Custom Installation menu.

The first option (Install Files From) displays the name of the disk drive containing the original WordPerfect disks, from which you will be installing the program onto your hard disk.

3. If you need to change the name of the drive from which your WordPerfect files are being installed, press Enter to select the Install Files From option, and enter the correct drive letter. Otherwise, skip to the next step.

4. Type 2 to select the second option (Install Files To). Next, the Custom Install: Location of Files menu appears, as shown in Figure A.3.

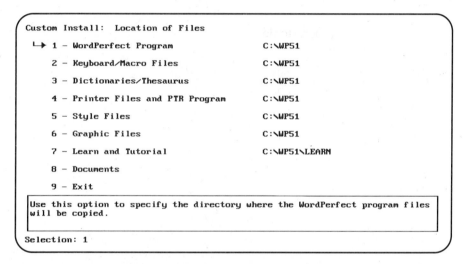

```
Custom Install:  Location of Files

 └─▶ 1 - WordPerfect Program                 C:\WP51

      2 - Keyboard/Macro Files               C:\WP51

      3 - Dictionaries/Thesaurus             C:\WP51

      4 - Printer Files and PTR Program      C:\WP51

      5 - Style Files                        C:\WP51

      6 - Graphic Files                      C:\WP51

      7 - Learn and Tutorial                 C:\WP51\LEARN

      8 - Documents

      9 - Exit
 ┌──────────────────────────────────────────────────────────────────┐
 │Use this option to specify the directory where the WordPerfect program files│
 │will be copied.                                                     │
 └──────────────────────────────────────────────────────────────────┘
Selection: 1
```

Figure A.3   *The Custom Install: Location of Files menu.*

5. To specify the drive and directory where you want the WordPerfect Program files installed, select the first option, **WordPerfect Program**.

6. Type the drive letter and path to the directory. For example, to install WordPerfect in a directory of drive D, whose name is WP, you would type:

   `D:\WP`

   and press Enter.

Note: If you have only a C drive on your hard disk, you must specify C as the drive, but you can always create your own directory name.

7. If the directory you specified in the previous step does not exist, a prompt will appear asking if you want it created. If so requested, select **Yes** to create the directory.

   All of the directory names in the right column of the menu will then change to match your WordPerfect directory name.

8. If you want to create separate directories for any of the other types of files (keyboard/macro files, graphic files, etc.), use options 2 through 8 to name them. When asked if you want to create them, select **Yes**.

9. When you are finished selecting directories, type 9 to exit from the Custom Install: Location of Files menu.

   You will then return to the Custom Installation menu, and the cursor will be on the third option, Install Disks.

10. Select the Install Disks option by pressing Enter.

    You will then be asked if you want to install various groups of files, and prompted to insert corresponding program diskettes, as described in the section "Basic Installation" (steps 2 through 14). The only difference is that WordPerfect will install your files in the customized directories you've just established.

11. When WordPerfect has finished installing your files, you will return to the Custom Installation menu. The cursor will be highlighting the fourth option (Check CONFIG.SYS and AUTOEXEC.BAT). This is an optional step, which is explained in the section "Basic Installation" (step 15).

12. Next, you can use the fifth option (Select and Install Printer and Exit) to install your printer(s), and then exit the INSTALL program. Once you select this option, printer installation is the same as described in the section "Printer Installation."

13. If you don't want to install a printer yet, use the last option, **Exit**, to return to the A> or B> DOS prompt. You can then start WordPerfect, following the instructions in Chapter 1.

New Printer Definitions

WordPerfect 5.1 supports hundreds of printers. Even if a printer definition for your printer is not shipped on the master distribution disks, a printer definition file may still be available if you contact WordPerfect Corporation. Also, existing printer definitions are periodically improved. If you receive a new printer definition file, you can use the INSTALL program to add or update a printer (.ALL) file.

To do this, choose the fourth option, Printer, from the main Installation menu and then follow the steps outlined in "Basic Installation" to install one or more printer definition files.

Update

WordPerfect releases periodic updates of 5.1 every few months. Usually these interim releases do not add new features, but simply fix minor problems in the program ("bugs"). If a new feature is added or you suspect a program bug, you may want to update your installation of WordPerfect.

1. Begin by determining what directories you are using for the different types of files (using the Setup: Location of Files menu, or List Files).

2. Once you know these, run INSTALL and choose the Update option (5) from the main Installation menu. You will be prompted for the name of the directory where your WordPerfect Program files are located, and the drive letter you are installing from.

3. The Install: Update menu will appear, as shown in Figure A.4. As you choose the different file types (such as Spell/Thesaurus, PTR Program/ Graphics, and Printer) and indicate where they should be installed, you will be prompted to insert the appropriate disks, and the INSTALL program will then update the files you've selected.

4. When you finish, select the Exit option (7) from the Install: Update menu.

```
Install:  Update

  ↳ 1 - Program                    Contains the WordPerfect Program.


    2 - Install/Learn/Utilities  Contains the Utility Files, Learning Files,
                                 Help File, Keyboard Files, and Style Library.

    3 - Spell/Thesaurus          Contains the Speller and Thesaurus.


    4 - PTR Program/Graphics     Contains the PTR Program, Graphic Drivers, and
                                 Graphic Images.

    5 - Printer                  Contains Printer (.ALL) Files.


    6 - Other


    7 - Exit


Selection: 1
```

Figure A.4   *The Install: Update menu.*

SETUP

Most WordPerfect features are preset, and these settings are referred to as their *defaults*. For example:

- The default left, right, top, and bottom margins are set to 1" each.

- The default for the Units of Measure—that is, the way measurements are displayed on the status line in the Edit screen and in menus such as the Format: Line menu—is the inch-mark symbol (").

- The default for the date format—that is, the format that WordPerfect uses to insert the current date into your document when you select the Date Text or Date Code option (either from the Date/Outline key or from the Tools pull-down menu)—is:

3 1, 4

where:

3 displays the month, spelled as a word

1 displays the day of the month, and is followed by a comma

4 displays the year, in four digits

as in January 26, 1991 (note that this default for the date format is for the United States version of WordPerfect).

With the Setup feature, you can change these, and numerous other defaults, so that WordPerfect will "remember" your settings and use them every time you start WordPerfect. The changes you make using the Setup menu (Shift-F1 or Setup on the pull-down File menu) are stored in a file named *WP{WP}.SET*.

The Setup Start-up Option

Sometimes it is desirable to create several different sets of defaults for WordPerfect, such as:

- In an office where several employees share a single computer, but use it at different times during the work day.

- Where a single user wants to maintain a separate set of default settings for each project or client, or for specific types of documents.

On a stand-alone computer, you can create different sets of defaults by placing the various WP{WP}.SET files in separate directories.

You can instruct WordPerfect to use a setup file that is located in a different directory by starting WordPerfect with the /ps=*path* option. For example, to start WordPerfect using a setup file located in this subdirectory:

```
C:\WP\SUSAN
```

(where SUSAN is a subdirectory of the WP directory on drive C) you would type the following command in DOS:

```
wp/ps=c:\wp\susan
```

and press Enter. If you were to start WordPerfect this way and make one or more changes in the Setup menu during the session, WordPerfect would change the default settings in the WP{WP}.SET file stored in the C:\WP\SUSAN subdirectory.

Reinstating WordPerfect's Original Defaults

You can return to WordPerfect's original defaults for a single session if you start WordPerfect by typing

```
WP/X
```

If you want to return permanently, just erase the WP{WP}.SET file, and then start WordPerfect again. WordPerfect will create a new SET file, with the original defaults.

Code Precedence Levels

The Setup: Initial Settings menu includes an Initial Codes option that you can use to permanently change formatting defaults such as margins, justification, tab positions (tab stops), and line spacing. The changes you make through this option will appear in any new documents you create after making the change. They will not affect previously saved documents.

The Format: Document menu also includes an Initial Codes option. The difference between this option and the one on the Setup: Initial Settings menu is that you can only use the one on the Format: Document menu to change formatting defaults for the document currently on your Edit screen.

The order of precedence for formatting codes is as follows:

- Formatting changes that you make using the Initial Codes option on the Format: Document menu override those you make using the Initial Codes option on the Setup: Initial Settings menu.

  For example, say you have used the Initial Codes option on the Setup: Initial Settings menu to permanently change Justification to Left. The next day, you type a new document, use the Initial Codes option on the Format: Document menu to select Full Justification, and then save it. The result: The Full setting is in effect for that document. However, after you clear that document from the Edit screen, Justification reverts to the default (Left), so any new documents you create will be formatted with Left Justification (unless you override it using one of the other two methods).

- Formatting changes you make that insert embedded codes, visible in the Reveal Codes screen of your document, override both Initial Codes options.

  For example, if you use the Format: Line menu to change the left and right margins, this will override any default left/right margins settings that you made using either Initial Codes option (the one on the Setup: Initial Settings menu or the one on the Format: Document menu).

For more information about the default formatting, see Chapter 3, "The Basics of Formatting."

The Setup Menu

To display the main Setup menu:

Keyboard: Press Setup (Shift-F1).

Mouse: Display the File menu and select Setup.

Once you have displayed the main Setup menu, using either the keyboard or mouse method, the rest of the steps are identical (and are listed in the chart at the end of this section).

The main Setup menu is divided into six categories:

1 - **Mouse**

2 - **Display**

3 - **Environment**

4 - **Initial Settings**

5 - **Keyboard Layout**

6 - **Location of Files**

The following chart lists each feature whose default settings you can change through the Setup menu. For each feature, it indicates which option (or options) you should select from the main Setup menu to change the feature. Note that the features are listed in alphabetical order.

Feature	Options
Alt Key Selects Pull-Down Menu	Display, Menu Options, Alt Key Selects Pull-Down Menu, **Y** or **N**
Alternate Keyboard	Environment, Alternate Keyboard, **Y** or **N**
Assisted Mouse Pointer Movement	Mouse, Assisted Mouse Pointer Movement, **Y** or **N**
Automatically Format and Rewrite Screen	Display, Edit-Screen Options, Automatically Format and Rewrite, **Y** or **N**
Beep on Error	Environment, Beep Options, Beep on Error
Beep on Hyphenation	Environment, Beep Options, Beep on Hyphenation
Beep on Search Failure	Environment, Beep Options, Beep on Search Failure
Binding Offset	Initial Settings, Print Options, Binding Offset, then number
Columns, Side-by-Side Columns Display	Display, Edit-Screen Options, Side-by-side Columns Display, **Y** or **N**
Comments Display	Display, Edit-Screen Options, Comments Display, **Y** or **N**

Feature	Options
Cursor Speed	Environment, Cursor Speed, then 1-6
Date Format	Initial Settings, Date Format, then format
Default Document Type	Environment, Document Management/Summary, Default Document Type, then document type
Document, default directory	Location of Files, Documents, then enter directory
Document Summary Created on Save/Exit	Environment, Document Management/Summary, Create Summary on Save/Exit, **Y** or **N**
Document Summary, Subject Search Text	Environment, Document Management/Summary, Subject Search Text, then text
Equations, Keyboard for Editing	Initial Settings, Equations, Keyboard for Editing, then select keyboard
Equations, Graphical Font Size	Initial Settings, Equations, Graphical Font Size, then **Default Font** or **Set Point Size**
Equations, Horizontal Alignment	Initial Settings, Equations, Horizontal Alignment, then **Left**, **Center**, or **Right**
Equations, Vertical Alignment	Initial Settings, Equations, Vertical Alignment, then **Top**, **Center**, or **Bottom**
Equations, Print as Graphics	Initial Settings, Equations, Print as Graphics, **Y** or **N**
Fast Save	Environment, Fast Save (unformatted), **Y** or **N**
Filename Displayed on Status Line	Display, Edit-Screen Options, Filename on Status Line, **Y** or **N**
Format Retrieved Documents for Default Printer	Initial Settings, Format Retrieved Documents for Default Printer, **Y** or **N**
Graphic files, default directory	Location of Files, Graphic Files, then enter directory
Graphics Quality	Initial Settings, Print Options, Graphics Quality, then **Do Not Print**, **Draft**, **Medium**, or **High**
Graphics Screen Type	Display, Graphics Screen Type, **Select**
Hard Return Display Character	Display, Edit-Screen Options, Hard Return Display Character, then compose character

Feature	Options
Hyphenation, External Dictionary Rules	Environment, Hyphenation, **External Dictionary/Rules**
Hyphenation, Internal Rules	Environment, Hyphenation, **Internal Rules**
Initial Codes	**Initial Settings, Initial Codes,** then choose the Setup Initial codes desired
Key, Create a definition for an individual key	**Keyboard Layout,** highlight keyboard, **Edit, Create,** press key(s), enter Description, and then enter new keystrokes
Key, Delete definition for an individual key and return key to its original function	**Keyboard Layout,** highlight keyboard, **Edit,** highlight individual key, **Original, Yes**
Key, Edit description (for individual key)	**Keyboard Layout,** highlight keyboard, **Edit,** highlight individual key, **Dscrptn**
Key, Edit definition (for individual key)	**Keyboard Layout,** highlight keyboard, **Edit,** highlight individual key, **Action,** edit or enter keystrokes
Key, Move key definition (for individual key) to another key	**Keyboard Layout,** highlight keyboard, **Edit,** highlight individual key, **Move,** press key(s) to which this definition will be moved
Key, Retrieve macro to redefine an individual key	**Keyboard Layout,** highlight keyboard, **Edit, Retrieve,** press key(s), enter macro name
Key, Save redefined key as a macro (for individual key)	**Keyboard Layout,** highlight keyboard, **Edit,** highlight individual key, **Save,** enter name of macro
Keyboard, Copy a keyboard definition	**Keyboard Layout,** highlight keyboard, **Copy,** then type name
Keyboard, Create definition	**Keyboard Layout, Create,** type keyboard name, then select **Edit** to define individual keys
Keyboard, Delete definition	**Keyboard Layout,** highlight keyboard, **Delete, Y** to confirm
Keyboard, Edit	**Keyboard Layout,** highlight keyboard, then **Edit**

Feature	Options
Keyboard, Look at map of current key assignments	Keyboard Layout, highlight keyboard, then Map
Keyboard/Macro Files, default directory	Location of Files, Keyboard/Macro Files, then enter directory
Keyboard Map, access key editor from	Keyboard Layout, highlight keyboard, Map, Macro
Keyboard Map, assign feature or operation to key	Keyboard Layout, highlight keyboard, Map, Key
Keyboard Map, Compose character, and assign to key	Keyboard Layout, highlight keyboard, Map, Compose
Keyboard Map, Edit Description of key	Keyboard Layout, highlight keyboard, Map, Description
Keyboard Map, Key Name Search	Keyboard Layout, highlight keyboard, Map, Key Name Search
Keyboard Map, Return individual key to Original unmapped value	Keyboard Layout, highlight keyboard, Map, highlight individual key, Original
Keyboard, Rename definition	Keyboard Layout, highlight keyboard, Rename, then type new name
Keyboard, Return to Original unmapped keyboard	Keyboard Layout, Original
Keyboard, Search for Keyboard by Name	Keyboard Layout, Name Search, then type name of keyboard
Keyboard, Select definition	Keyboard Layout, highlight keyboard, then Select
Long Document Names	Environment, Document Management/ Summary, Long Document Names, Y or N
Menu Bar Letter Display attribute	Display, Menu Options, Menu Bar Letter Display, then Size, Appearance, or Normal
Menu Bar Remains Visible	Display, Menu Options, Menu Bar Remains Visible, Y or N

Feature	Options
Menu Bar Separator Line	Display, Menu Options, Menu Bar Separator Line, Y or N
Menu Bar Text attribute	Display, Menu Options, Menu Bar Text, then Size or Appearance or Normal
Menu Letter Display attribute	Display, Menu Options, Menu Letter Display, then Size, Appearance, or Normal
Menu Options	Display, Menu Options
Merge Codes Display	Display, Edit-Screen Options, Merge Codes Display, Y or N
Merge Field Delimiters	Initial Settings, Merge, Field Delimiters, then delimiters
Merge Record Delimiters	Initial Settings, Merge, Record Delimiters, then delimiters
Minutes Between Timed Document Backups	Environment, Backup Options, Timed Document Backup, Y, press Enter and then type number of minutes
Mouse, Acceleration Factor	Mouse, Acceleration Factor, number
Mouse Double Click Interval	Mouse, Double Click Interval, number
Mouse, Left-Handed	Mouse, Left-Handed Mouse, Y or N
Mouse Port	Mouse, Port, then 1, 2, 3, or 4
Mouse Type	Mouse, Type, highlight a mouse type, Select
Multiple Copies Generated By WordPerfect or Printer	Initial Settings, Print Options, Number of Copies (then press Enter to skip Number of Copies), then Multiple Copies Generated By WordPerfect or Printer
Number of Copies	Initial Settings, Print Options, Number of Copies, enter the number, then press Enter to skip Multiple Copies Generated by WordPerfect or Printer
Printer files directory	Location of Files, Printer Files, then enter directory
Prompt for Hyphenation	Environment, Prompt for Hyphenation, then Never, When Required, or Always

Feature	Options
Pull-Down Letter Display attribute	**D**isplay, **M**enu Options, **P**ull-Down Letter Display, then **S**ize, **A**ppearance, or **N**ormal
Pull-Down Text attribute	**D**isplay, **M**enu Options, **P**ull-Down Text, then **S**ize, **A**ppearance, or **N**ormal
Redline Method	**I**nitial Settings, **P**rint Options, **R**edline Method, then **P**rinter Dependent, **L**eft or **A**lternating
Repeat Value	**I**nitial Settings, **R**epeat Value, then number
Reveal Codes Window Size	**D**isplay, **E**dit-Screen Options, **R**eveal Codes Window Size, then number of lines
Screen Colors	**D**isplay, **C**olors/Fonts/Attributes, **S**creen Colors
Screen Font	**D**isplay, **C**olors/Fonts/Attributes, choose font (Choices vary depending on graphics card and monitor)
Size Attribute Ratios	**I**nitial Settings, **P**rint Options, **S**ize Attribute Ratios, then enter a percentage for each size attribute
Spreadsheet Files, default directory	**L**ocation of Files, **S**preadsheet Files, then enter directory
Status Line Display, Units of Measure	**E**nvironment, **U**nits of Measure, **S**tatus Line Display, then ", **i**, **c**, **p**, **w**, or **u**
Style Files, directory and default style library filename	**L**ocation of Files, **S**tyle Files, then enter style directory and name of default style library file
Submenu Delay Time	**M**ouse, **S**ubmenu Delay Time, number
Table of Authorities, Underlining Allowed	**I**nitial Settings, **T**able of Authorities, **U**nderlining Allowed, **Y** or **N**
Table of Authorities, Blank Line between Authorities	**I**nitial Settings, **T**able of Authorities, **B**lank Line between Authorities, **Y** or **N**
Table of Authorities, Dot Leaders	**I**nitial Settings, **T**able of Authorities, **D**ot Leaders, **Y** or **N**
Text Quality	**I**nitial Settings, **P**rint Options, **T**ext Quality, then Do **N**ot Print, **D**raft, **M**edium or **H**igh
Text Screen Type	**D**isplay, **T**ext Screen Type, **S**elect

Feature	Options
Thesaurus/Spell/ Hyphenation File, directory	Location of Files, Thesaurus/Spell/Hyphenation, then enter directories for Main and Supplementary dictionaries
Timed Backup Files, directory	Location of Files, Backup Files, then enter directory
Timed Document Backup	Environment, Backup Options, Timed Document Backup, Y or N
Units of Measure, Display and Entry for Margins, Tabs, etc.	Environment, Units of Measure, Display and Entry of Numbers for Margins, Tabs, etc., then ", i, c, p, w, or u
View Document, Bold Displayed with Color	Display, View Document Options, Bold Displayed with Color, Y or N
View Document, Graphics in Black & White	Display, View Document Options, Graphics in Black & White, Y or N
View Document, Text in Black & White	Display, View Document Options, Text in Black & White, Y or N

Index

D

H

N

Feature	Keystrokes	Menu Selections
Fonts, Download to Printer	Shift-F7,i	File, Print, Initialize Printer
Footers	Shift-F8,p,f	Layout, Page, Footers
Footnote	Ctrl-F7,f	Layout, Footnote
Format Line/Page/Document/Other	Shift-F8	Layout
Generate Tables, Indexes, etc.	Alt-F5,g,g	Mark, Generate, Generate Tables, Indexed, Cross-References, etc.
Go To	Ctrl-Home	Search, Go To
Graphics Box Options	Alt-F9,(f t b or u),o	Graphics, (Figure, Table Box, Text Box, or User Box), Options
Graphics Quality	Shift-F7,g	File, Print, Graphics Quality
Hanging Indent	F4,Shift-Tab	Layout, Align, Indent, Layout, Align, Margin Release
Headers	Shift-F8,p,h	Layout, Page, Headers
Help	F3	Help, Help
Hyphen, Hard	Home	
Hyphen, Soft	Ctrl	
Hyphenation	Shift-F8,l,y	Layout, Line, Hyphenation
Indent Left and Right	Shift-F4	Layout, Align, Indent
Indent Left Only	F4	Layout, Align, Indent
Index (Define or Generate)	Alt-F5,d or g	Mark, Define or Generate
Index, Mark Text for (Block on)	Alt-F5,i	Mark, Index
Initial Codes (Default)	Shift-F1,i,c	File, Setup, Initial Settings, Initial Codes
Initial Codes, Document	Shift-F8,d,c	Layout, Document, Initial Codes
Italics	Ctrl-F8,a,i	Font, Appearance, Italics
Justification (Center, Full, Left, Right)	Shift-F8,l,j	Layout, Line, Justification
Keyboard Definitions/Layout	Shift-F1,k	File, Setup, Keyboard Layout
Labels	Shift-F8,p,s,e,a	Layout, Page, Paper Size and Type, Edit, Labels
Languages	Shift-F8,o,l	Layout, Other, Language
Line Draw	Ctrl-F3,l	Tools, Line Draw
Line, Graphics	Alt-F9,l	Graphics, Line
Line Height	Shift-F8,l,h	Layout, Line, Height
Line Numbering	Shift-F8,l,n	Layout, Line, Line Numbering
Line Spacing	Shift-F8,l,s	Layout, Line. Line Spacing
List Files	F5,Enter	File, List Files, Enter
Lists, Mark Text for (Block On)	Alt-F5,l	Mark, List
Location of Files	Shift-F1,l	File, Setup, Location of Files
Look at a File	F5,Enter,l	File, List Files, Enter, Look
Macro Commands (Macro Editor)	Ctrl-PgUp	Left mouse button
Macros, Define	Ctrl-F10	Tools, Macro, Define
Macros, Execute	Alt-F10	Tools, Macro, Execute
Margin Release	Shift-Tab	Layout, Align, Margin Rel
Margins—Left and Right	Shift-F8,l,m	Layout, Line, Margins
Margins—Top and Bottom	Shift-F8,p,m	Layout, Page, Margins
Math	Alt-F7,m	Layout, Math
Menu Bar	Alt-=	Right mouse button
Merge	Ctrl-F9,m	Tools, Merge
Merge Codes, More (Advanced)	Shift-F9,m	Tools, Merge Codes, More
Move Block (Block On)	Ctrl-Del	Edit, Move
Move/Rename File	F5,Enter,m	File, List Files, Enter, Move/Rename
Number of Copies	Shift-F7,n	File, Print, Number of Copies
Original Document Backup	Shift-F1,e,b,o	File, Setup, Environment, Backup Options, Original Document Backup
Outline	Shift-F5,o	Tools, Outline
Page Break, Hard	Ctrl-Enter	Layout, Align, Hard Page
Page Down	PgDn	
Page Number in Text	Shift-F8,p,n,i, or Ctrl-B	Layout, Page, Page Numbering, Insert Page Number
Page Number, New	Shift-F8,p,n,n	Layout, Page, Page Numbering, New Page Number
Page Number Style	Shift-F8,p,n,s	Layout, Page, Page Numbering, Page Number Style
Page Numbering	Shift-F8,p,n,p	Layout, Page, Page Numbering, Page Number Position
Page Up	PgUp	
Paper Size/Type	Shift-F8,p,s	Layout, Page, Paper Size and Type
Paragraph Numbering, Auto	Shift-F5,p	Tools, Paragraph Number
Password	Ctrl-F5,p	File, Password
Print (Cancel, Rush, Display, Stop)	Shift-F7,c, (c,r,d, or s)	File, Print, Control Printer, (Cancel, Rush, Display, Stop)